2000 Passport® to

World Band Radio

International Broadcasting Services, Ltd.

ISSN 0897-0157

OUR READER IS THE MOST IMPORTANT PERSON IN THE WORLD!

Editorial

Editor-in-Chief	Lawrence Magne
Editor	Tony Jones
Assistant Editor	Craig Tyson
Contributing Editors	Manosij Guha, George Heidelman, Toshimichi Ohtake, Chuck Rippel, Robert Sherwood, John Wagner, Dave Zantow, George Zeller
Consulting Editor	John Campbell
Founder Emeritus	Don Jensen
WorldScan® Contributors	Gabriel Iván Barrera (Argentina), James Conrad (U.S.), David Crystal (Israel), Alok Dasgupta (India), Graeme Dixon (New Zealand), Nicolás Eramo (Argentina), Manosij Guha (India), *Jembatan DX*/ Juichi Yamada (Japan), Anatoly Klepov (Russia), Marie Lamb (U.S.), *Número Uno*/Jerry Berg (U.S.), *Radio Nuevo Mundo* (Japan), *Relámpago DX*/Takayuki Inoue Nozaki (Japan), Nikolai Rudnev (Russia), Don Swampo (Uruguay), David Walcutt (U.S.)
WorldScan® Software	Richard Mayell
Laboratory	Sherwood Engineering Inc.
Artwork	Gahan Wilson, cover
Graphic Arts	Bad Cat Design; Mike Wright, layout
Printing	Master Litho

Administration

Publisher	Lawrence Magne
Associate Publisher	Jane Brinker
Offices	IBS North America, Box 300, Penn's Park PA 18943, USA; www.passband.com; Phone +1 (215) 598-9018; Fax +1 (215) 598 3794; mktg@passband.com
Advertising & Media Contact	Jock Elliott, Lightkeeper Communications, 29 Pickering Lane, Troy NY 12180, USA; Phone +1 (518) 271-1761; Fax +1 (518) 271 6131; media@passband.com

Bureaus

IBS Latin America	Tony Jones, Casilla 1844, Asunción, Paraguay; schedules@passband.com; Fax +1 (215) 598 3794
IBS Australia	Craig Tyson, Box 2145, Malaga WA 6062; Fax +61 (8) 9342 9158; addresses@passband.com
IBS Japan	Toshimichi Ohtake, 5-31-6 Tamanawa, Kamakura 247; Fax +81 (467) 43 2167; ibsjapan@passband.com

Library of Congress Cataloging-in-Publication Data

Passport to World Band Radio.
1. Radio Stations, Shortwave—Directories. I. Magne, Lawrence
TK9956.P27 1999 384.54'5 99-22739
ISBN 0-914941-49-6

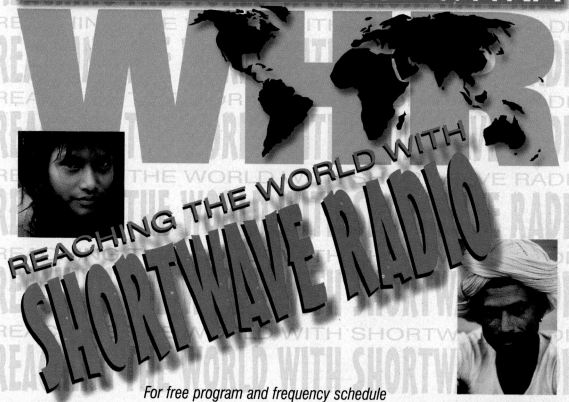

WORLD HARVEST RADIO

WHRI • KWHR • WHRA

For free program and frequency schedule
or to purchase airtime contact: **WORLD HARVEST RADIO**

61300 S. Ironwood Rd.
South Bend, IN 46614, U.S.A.
Phone (219) 291-8200
Fax (219) 291-9043
E-mail whr@lesea.com

(Schedules can also be downloaded from our web site)

All signals available on the Internet via at http:\\www.whr.org

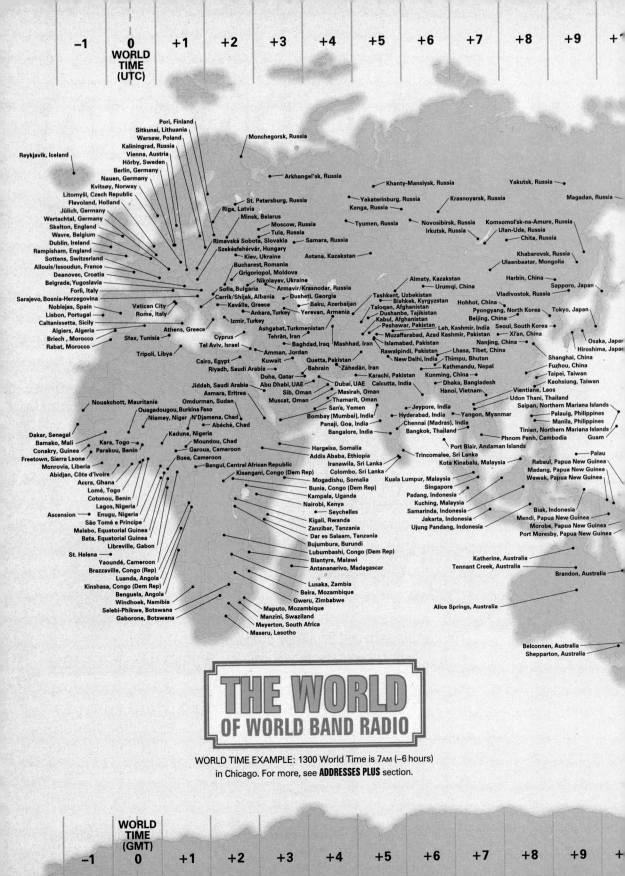

-1 0 WORLD TIME (UTC) +1 +2 +3 +4 +5 +6 +7 +8 +9 +1

Reykjavik, Iceland

Pori, Finland
Sitkunai, Lithuania
Warsaw, Poland
Kaliningrad, Russia
Vienna, Austria
Hörby, Sweden
Berlin, Germany
Nauen, Germany
Kvitsøy, Norway
Litomyšl, Czech Republic
Flevoland, Holland
Jülich, Germany
Wertachtal, Germany
Skelton, England
Wavre, Belgium
Dublin, Ireland
Rampisham, England
Sottens, Switzerland
Allouis/Issoudun, France
Deanovec, Croatia
Belgrade, Yugoslavia
Forlì, Italy
Sarajevo, Bosnia-Herzegovina
Noblejas, Spain
Lisbon, Portugal
Caltanissetta, Sicily
Algiers, Algeria
Briech , Morocco
Rabat, Morocco

Monchegorsk, Russia

Arkhangel'sk, Russia

Khanty-Mansiysk, Russia

Yakutsk, Russia

Magadan, Russia

St. Petersburg, Russia
Riga, Latvia
Minsk, Belarus
Moscow, Russia
Tula, Russia
Rimavská Sobota, Slovakia
Szekésfehérvár, Hungary
Kiev, Ukraine
Bucharest, Romania
Grigoriopol, Moldova
Nikolayev, Ukraine
Sofia, Bulgaria
Cerrik/Shijak, Albania
Kaválla, Greece

Yekaterinburg, Russia
Kenga, Russia
Tyumen, Russia
Samara, Russia

Krasnoyarsk, Russia

Novosibirsk, Russia
Irkutsk, Russia

Komsomol'sk-na-Amure, Russia
Ulan-Ude, Russia
Chita, Russia
Khabarovsk, Russia
Ulaanbaatar, Mongolia
Harbin, China

Astana, Kazakstan

Vatican City
Rome, Italy
Athens, Greece

Armavir/Krasnodar, Russia
Dusheti, Georgia
Baku, Azerbaijan
Ankara, Turkey
Yerevan, Armenia
Izmir, Turkey

Almaty, Kazakstan
Urumqi, China

Sapporo, Japan

Vladivostok, Russia

Tashkent, Uzbekistan
Bishkek, Kyrgyzstan
Taloqan, Afghanistan
Dushanbe, Tajikistan
Kabul, Afghanistan
Peshawar, Pakistan
Muzaffarabad, Azad Kashmir, Pakistan

Hohhot, China
Pyongyang, North Korea
Beijing, China

Hiroshima, Japan

Tokyo, Japan

Seoul, South Korea
Xi'an, China

Osaka, Japan

Cyprus
Tel Aviv, Israel
Tripoli, Libya

Ashgabat, Turkmenistan
Tehrān, Iran
Baghdad, Iraq
Amman, Jordan

Mashhad, Iran

Islamabad, Pakistan
Rawalpindi, Pakistan
New Delhi, India

Leh, Kashmir, India
Lhasa, Tibet, China
Thimpu, Bhutan
Kathmandu, Nepal

Nanjing, China
Shanghai, China
Fuzhou, China
Taipei, Taiwan
Kaohsiung, Taiwan

Cairo, Egypt
Riyadh, Saudi Arabia
Kuwait
Bahrain
Doha, Qatar
Abu Dhabi, UAE
Jiddah, Saudi Arabia

Quetta, Pakistan
Zāhedān, Iran
Karachi, Pakistan
Dubai, UAE
Masirah, Oman

Calcutta, India

Dhaka, Bangladesh
Hanoi, Vietnam

Kunming, China
Vientiane, Laos
Udon Thani, Thailand

Nouakchott, Mauritania
Ouagadougou, Burkina Faso
Niamey, Niger
N'Djamena, Chad
Omdurman, Sudan
Sib, Oman
Muscat, Oman
Thamarit, Oman
San'a, Yemen
Bombay (Mumbai), India
Abéché, Chad
Panaji, Goa, India
Bangalore, India

Jeypore, India
Hyderabad, India
Chennai (Madras), India
Bangkok, Thailand

Yangon, Myanmar

Saipan, Northern Mariana Islands
Palauig, Philippines
Manila, Philippines
Tinian, Northern Mariana Islands
Guam

Phnom Penh, Cambodia

Palau

Dakar, Senegal
Bamako, Mali
Conakry, Guinea
Freetown, Sierra Leone
Monrovia, Liberia
Abidjan, Côte d'Ivoire
Accra, Ghana
Lomé, Togo
Cotonou, Benin
Lagos, Nigeria
Enugu, Nigeria
Malabo, Equatorial Guinea
Bata, Equatorial Guinea
Libreville, Gabon

Kara, Togo
Parakou, Benin
Kaduna, Nigeria
Moundou, Chad
Garoua, Cameroon
Buea, Cameroon
Bangui, Central African Republic
Kisangani, Congo (Dem Rep)

Hargeisa, Somalia
Addis Ababa, Ethiopia
Bunia, Congo (Dem Rep)
Kampala, Uganda
Nairobi, Kenya
Seychelles
Kigali, Rwanda
Zanzibar, Tanzania
Dar es Salaam, Tanzania
Bujumbura, Burundi

Mogadishu, Somalia
Iranawila, Sri Lanka
Colombo, Sri Lanka

Trincomalee, Sri Lanka
Kota Kinabalu, Malaysia
Kuala Lumpur, Malaysia
Singapore
Padang, Indonesia
Kuching, Malaysia
Samarinda, Indonesia
Jakarta, Indonesia
Ujung Pandang, Indonesia

Port Blair, Andaman Islands

Rabaul, Papua New Guinea
Madang, Papua New Guinea
Wewak, Papua New Guinea
Biak, Indonesia
Mendi, Papua New Guinea
Morobe, Papua New Guinea
Port Moresby, Papua New Guinea

Ascension
São Tomé e Príncipe
St. Helena
Yaoundé, Cameroon
Brazzaville, Congo (Rep)
Luanda, Angola
Kinshasa, Congo (Dem Rep)
Benguela, Angola
Windhoek, Namibia
Selebi-Phikwe, Botswana
Gaborone, Botswana

Lubumbashi, Congo (Dem Rep)
Blantyre, Malawi
Antananarivo, Madagascar
Lusaka, Zambia
Beira, Mozambique
Gweru, Zimbabwe
Maputo, Mozambique
Manzini, Swaziland
Meyerton, South Africa
Maseru, Lesotho

Katherine, Australia
Tennant Creek, Australia

Brandon, Australia

Alice Springs, Australia

Belconnen, Australia
Shepparton, Australia

THE WORLD
OF WORLD BAND RADIO

WORLD TIME EXAMPLE: 1300 World Time is 7AM (–6 hours)
in Chicago. For more, see **ADDRESSES PLUS** section.

WORLD TIME (GMT)

-1 0 +1 +2 +3 +4 +5 +6 +7 +8 +9 +

+11 +12 −11 −10 −9 −8 −7 −6 −5 −4 −3 −2

Anchor Point, Alaska, USA

Palana, Russia

Petropavlovsk-Kamchatskiy, Russia

Calgary AB, Canada
Vancouver BC, Canada

Noblesville IN, USA
Toronto ON, Canada
Montréal PQ, Canada
Monticello ME, USA
Greenbush ME, USA
Sackville NB, Canada
St. John's NF, Canada
Halifax NS, Canada
Bethel PA, USA
Red Lion PA, USA
Upton KY, USA
Nashville TN, USA
McCaysville GA, USA
Greenville NC, USA
Newport NC, USA
Cypress Creek SC, USA
Macon GA, USA
Birmingham AL, USA
New Orleans LA, USA
Okeechobee FL, USA
Miami FL, USA
Havana, Cuba

Salt Lake City UT, USA
Boulder CO, USA
Delano CA, USA
Rancho Simi CA, USA
Dallas TX, USA
Mesquite NM, USA

Kekaha, Kauai Island, Hawai'i, USA

Naalehu, "Big Island," Hawai'i, USA

Hermosillo, Mexico

Linares, Mexico
Mérida, Mexico
México City, Mexico
Veracruz, Mexico
Puerto Cabezas, Nicaragua
Guatemala City, Guatemala
Tegucigalpa, Honduras
San José, Costa Rica
Santa Fé de Bogotá, Colombia
Villavicencio, Colombia
Florencia, Colombia
Quito, Ecuador
Tena, Ecuador
Loja, Ecuador
Iquitos, Peru
Cajamarca, Peru
Pucallpa, Peru
Guayaramerín, Bolivia
Cobija, Bolivia
Lima, Peru
Cusco, Peru
Arequipa, Peru
La Paz, Bolivia
Santa Cruz, Bolivia
Sucre, Bolivia
Asunción, Paraguay
Villarrica, Paraguay
Encarnación, Paraguay

Santo Domingo, Dominican Republic
Anguilla
Antigua
Bonaire, Netherlands Antilles
Caracas, Venezuela
Puerto Ayacucho, Venezuela
Georgetown, Guyana
Paramaribo, Surinam
Montsinéry, French Guiana
Cayenne, French Guiana

Belem, Brazil
Manaus, Brazil

Porto Velho, Brazil
Salvador, Brazil
Cuiabá, Brazil
Brasília, Brazil
Goiânia, Brazil

Belo Horizonte, Brazil
Río de Janeiro, Brazil
São Paulo, Brazil
Curitiba, Brazil
Foz do Iguaçu, Brazil
Florianópolis, Brazil
Porto Alegre, Brazil
Artigas, Uruguay
Montevideo, Uruguay
Buenos Aires, Argentina

Tarawa, Kiribati

Honiara, Solomon Islands

Port-Vila, Vanuatu

Tahiti, French Polynesia

Santiago, Chile
Malargüe, Argentina
Temuco, Chile

Coyhaique, Chile

Rangitaiki, New Zealand
Levin, New Zealand

Base Esperanza, Antarctica (−3)

+11 +12 −11 −10 −9 −8 −7 −6 −5 −4 −3 −2

The wait is over.
The millennium begins.
The legend continues.

Whether you're an experienced shortwave listener or a newcomer wanting to start out with the very best, the Satellit Millennium is the radio for you.

The unparalleled legacy of the Grundig Satellit series of shortwave receivers continues with the new Satellit 800 Millennium. In the history of shortwave receivers, no other manufacturer has maintained a continuously evolving series of high-end portable radios, decade after decade. The pinnacle of over three decades of evolution, the Satellit 800 Millennium embodies the dreams and wishes of serious shortwave listeners the world over.

The legend began in 1964 with the introduction of the Grundig Satellit 205/Transistor 5000, at that time, the most technologically advanced portable ever engineered for the non-military market. Incorporating the latest in solid state transistor technology, dual conversion

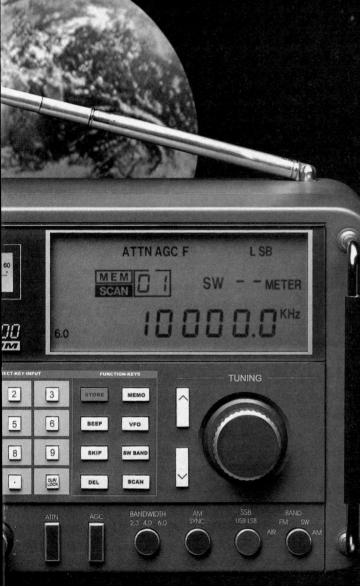

Tomorrow, the Universe

superheterodyne design and the first ever optional SSB module in a portable, this beginning of a legendary tradition led to generation after generation of Satellit series radios, all becoming coveted collector's items.

The Legend. The History. The Pride.
The Satellit 800 Millennium continues the tradition. Our goal was to create the dream. We listened to shortwave enthusiasts from every part of the globe who owned Grundig and other brands. We listened to what they wanted in a high-end shortwave portable: A big, easy to read, beautifully lit display. A large, traditional analog signal strength meter. A tuning knob they could really get a grip on. The option of push-button tuning and direct frequency entry. A tuner with absolutely no audible muting during tuning knob use. We listened. It's here. **The Dream. The Legend. The History. The Tradition.**

The Satellit 800 Millennium.

by GRUNDIG

Lextronix / Grundig, P.O. Box 2307, Menlo Park, CA 94026 Tel: 650-361-1611 Fax: 650-361-1724
Shortwave Hotlines: (US) 1-800-872-2228 (CN) 1-800-637-1648 • Web: www.grundigradio.net

GRUNDIG Tunes in the

The Grundig Satellit Legend continues. The Satellit 800 Millennium is your assurance of staying in touch with the world... Access radio programs the world over... fast-breaking news from the farthest corners of the globe... music from faraway countries.

CUTTING EDGE IN SPACE TECHNOLOGY

- You'll appreciate the smooth flowing design and functional control panel.
- Superbly appointed, fold away, easy grip handle for portability.
- Enter any station on the key pad, then tune up or down frequency or search specific meter bands.
- The tuner receives AM/FM and all shortwave frequencies from 100 to 30,000 KHz, FM from 87 to 108 MHz and VHF aircraft 118 to 137 MHz and locks onto broadcasts with digital accuracy...

World

- Receives FM stereo with the included high-quality headphones.
- Superior audio quality for which Grundig is known.
- A direct input digital key pad combined with manual tuning.
- 70 user-programmable memories.
- Upper and lower sideband capability (USB/LSB).
- A large 6" by 3 $\frac{1}{2}$" multifunction LCD.
- Last station memory.
- Synchronous detector for superior AM and shortwave reception.
- Multi voltage (110, 220 V) AC adapter.
- Dual clocks.
- Low battery indicator.

Whether you are cruising offshore, enjoying the cottage, or relaxing on an extended vacation in some distant land, the Satellit 800 Millennium is the most powerful and precise radio in the World. Search the globe, you can discover the hottest news first hand... listen to and witness the ongoing fascination with our evolving world today... tomorrow the universe.

by **GRUNDIG**

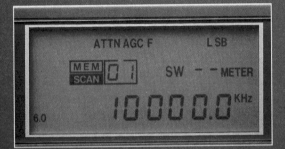

The LCD

Big! Bold! Brightly Illuminated 6" by 3¹/₂".
Liquid Crystal Display shows all important data:
Frequency, Meter band, Memory position, Time,
LSB/USB, Synchronous Detector and more.

SW, AM and Aircraft Band and 20 KHz in FM.
• For Fixed-step Tuning: Big, responsive Up/Down tuning buttons.
• For direct frequency entry: a responsive, intuitive numeric keypad.

The Signal Strength Meter

Elegant in its traditional Analog design, like the gauges in the world's finest sports cars. Large. Well Lit. Easy to read.

The Frequency Coverage

Longwave, AM and shortwave: continuous 100-30,000 KHz. FM: 87-108 MHz VHF Aircraft Band: 188-137 MHz.

The Tuning Controls

• For the traditionalist: a smooth, precise tuning knob, produces no audio muting during use. Ultra fine-tuning of 50Hz on LSB/USB, 100Hz in

THESE ARE THE SATELLIT 800 MILLENNIUM'S MAJOR FEATURES.
FOR A DETAILED SPECIFICATION SHEET, CONTACT GRUNDIG.

Digital Technology

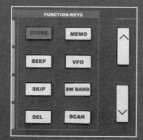

The Operational Controls
Knobs where you want them; Buttons where they make sense. The best combination of traditional and high-tech controls.

The Sound
Legendary Grundig Audio Fidelity with separate bass and treble controls, big sound from its powerful speaker and FM-stereo with the included high quality headphones.

The Technology
Today's latest engineering:
- Dual conversion superheterodyne circuitry.
- PLL synthesized tuner.

The Many Features
- 70 user-programmable memories.
- Two, 24 hour format clocks.
- Two ON/OFF sleep timers.
- Massive, built-in telescopic antenna.
- Connectors for external antennas – SW, AM, FM and VHF Aircraft Band.
- Line-out, headphone and external speaker jacks.

The Power Supply
A multi voltage (110, 220V) AC adapter is included. Also operates on 6 size D batteries. (not included)

Dimensions: 20.5" L x 9" H x 8" W

Weight: 14.50 lbs.

by GRUNDIG

Lextronix / Grundig, P.O. Box 2307, Menlo Park, CA 94026 Tel: 650-361-1611 Fax: 650-361-1724
Shortwave Hotlines: (US) 1-800-872-2228 (CN) 1-800-637-1648 • Web: www.grundigradio.net

Afghanistan: Jihad of the Airwaves

by Manosij Guha

Afghanistan is as vast as Texas, with a climate like Wyoming's and carbine culture to match. Landlocked, it shares smoldering borders with Iran, China, Pakistan and the former Soviet Union.

It is home to about 22 million—ten percent nomads, 90 percent farmers illiterate in any modern language. Four major tongues are spoken, but Dari, a form of Persian, and Pashto, used by Pushtuns, are the major and official languages. Regional dialects abound.

In the summer of 1994, the Taliban movement of religious Afghan students emerged in reaction to widespread lawlessness in the south. They seized the old royal capital of Kandahar, and by February were at the gates of Kabul.

The Taliban owes much of its success to military support from Pakistan and financial aid from Saudi Arabia, both Sunni Muslim countries. Though relationships with the Saudis have chilled recently—not least because of the Taliban government's refusal to hand over Osama bin Laden, the Saudi-born terrorist—private donations continue to pour in. Sporadic reports indicate that the United States has positioned a sizeable extraction force in Pakistan and the CIS to abduct bin Laden, besides readying its task force in the Arabian Sea to unleash another bout of Tomahawk Cruise missiles on Osama camps spotted around Jalālābād.

Osama bin Laden, believed hiding near Jalālābād, Afghanistan.

Also reliably reported is that about 3,500 "retired" Pakistani army officers are acting as military advisers to the Taliban. Pakistan has also turned a blind eye to the thousands of young Pakistanis who have been joining the movement.

So concerned are the Russians with the Talibanization of Tajikistan, fearing another Chechnya or Dagestan on their doorstep, that they have gone all out for their erstwhile foe, opening up their choicest arsenal at virtually no cost for Ahmad Shah Masood, the rebel leader who opposes the Taliban. A cable hoist operates across the mighty Amu Darya river, which forms a natural border between northern Afghanistan and Tajikistan, carrying T-62 tanks and YA-3 jeeps to bolster the Tajik leader's summer offensive. A ten-inch pipeline and truck convoys deliver precious diesel to the frontlines.

> Taliban forces were told there was gold and silver in the transmitter boxes, even inside the tubes.

King Pioneers Broadcasting

Despite Afghanistan being in the backwaters of development, broadcasting in this rugged country can be traced all the way back to 1925, when two 200 Watt mediumwave AM transmitters were purchased from Telefunken in Germany. They lay dormant because of technical difficulties, scarcity of receivers and absence of trained personnel.

A Few Good Men: Commander Masood insists that all his men at arms don proper battle fatigues so they can fight with dignity against their opponents, who don't wear uniforms. M. Guha

Anti-Taliban rebels operate clandestine Radio Takhar using a Russian RX-10 transmitter.

M. Guha

However, three years later one of the transmitters began operating on 833 kHz on a sustained basis from the King's palace in Kabul. The other transmitter, meant for the eastern city of Kandahar, never got fixed. When King Amanullah was deposed in 1929, Radio Kabul, as the station was called, ceased to exist, as its transmitter was damaged and studio facilities destroyed.

Thus, broadcasting in earnest as we know it today started only in 1931, when the new monarch, Mohammed Nader Shah, decided to purchase another mediumwave AM transmitter from Germany, this time a mighty 100 kW which was installed a year later. In 1940, a 20 kW transmitter on 660 kHz was added to the repertory.

World Band Starts in 1958

In 1953, Radio Kabul was renamed the Afghan Broadcasting System, although it identified as Radio Afghanistan. World band became regular only in 1958, when a German 10 kW shortwave transmitter was installed in Yakatut in the northern suburbs of the capital.

The following year saw the formal inauguration of the shortwave service when two more 25 kW transmitters were installed.

These were on for about 17 hours a day, belting out programs in Pashto, Dari, Hindi and French—the last two ostensibly for a foreign audience. In 1957, a 50 kW transmitter was added to relay the Kabul home service, which included a 20-minute program in English.

In 1966, German aid allowed the addition of two more 100 kW shortwave transmitters, one of which was installed at a new transmitter site at Pol-e-Charki in the outskirts of Kabul. In 1976, a further three 50 kW and two 10 kW mediumwave AM units were installed at the bustling transmitter field in Yakatut. Additionally, three 10 kW mobile mediumwave AM transmitters were procured, which after a technical snag were installed in 1978 in the provincial stations at Herat, Kandahar and Mazar-e-Sharif.

On July 17, 1973, King Mohammed Zahir Shah was overthrown in a coup, and the kingdom became a republic. The coup leader, General Sadar Mohammed Daud, chose to announce the change of government in a fiery speech broadcast over Radio Afghanistan. As newspapers and magazines were suspended, for the Afghan people Radio Afghanistan became their information lifeline.

Radio Afghanistan played an active role in persuading the population to live peacefully, airing news, commentaries and martial music. However, the rhetoric towards Pushtunistan became more intense, inviting a media war with Pakistan.

Eleven-Year Boost from Russian Aid

Broadcasting remained stagnant during the ensuing turmoil and instability, but it received a major boost during the Soviet occupation between 1979 and 1989. The transmitting capacity at Pol-e-Charki was bolstered by a pair of 100 kW shortwave and two 500 kW mediumwave AM transmitters to help prop up the new communist regime. 1980 saw Radio Afghanistan's external services also being relayed by powerful transmitters in the Soviet Union, a service which continued until the fall of Sovietism in 1990.

In subsequent years Radio Afghanistan's shortwave activity was limited to a 50 kW transmitter hovering around 7200 kHz, with a second transmitter operating intermittently on 4775 kHz. These broadcast about 14 hours a day, with an additional complement of two hours on Fridays, the Muslim day of rest. A 10 kW German shortwave transmitter was retrofitted for point-to-point communications, especially sending telegrams to Afghan embassies abroad and airing news dispatches by Bakhtar Agence, the official news agency.

In 1993, external services in Arabic, German, Russian and Urdu were initiated to strengthen foreign relations, adding to the existing services in French and Hindi. Subsequently, the radio network was expanded to establish provincial stations on mediumwave AM at Baghlan, Farah and Taloqan—that last station would play a significant role in times of strife.

Taliban Creates Voice of Shariah

When the Taliban militia overran the station in September 1996, the name was aptly changed to the Voice of Shariah. But

what transpired at one of the transmitter sites became among the most bizarre events in radio history.

When Taliban forces overran the Yakatut transmitter site, their Pakistani mentors told them there was gold and silver in the transmitter boxes, even inside the tubes. "They literally tore the transmitters apart with their bare hands, ravaging the station," laments Samshul Haq Aryanfar, then president of Afghan Radio, TV and Film. "When they didn't find anything, they set fire to the building."

For whatever reason, the newer transmitter site at Pol-e-Charki survived almost un-scathed. It consists of two 100 kW Russian and one 100 kW Siemens shortwave transmitters, besides two huge 500 kW mediumwave AM transmitters. The Russian transmitters are in serious disrepair, with spare parts and trained maintenance personnel a rarity since the Soviet pullout. But the sturdy 1966 Siemens continues to labor on, hovering around 7080 or 7200 kHz for a strenuous 17 hours a day, albeit at reduced power.

The limited external service of the Voice of Shariah is broadcast in the evening with a distorted signal. It airs programs in Urdu, Turkmen and Arabic, with a nightly 15-minute English stretch at 1700 hours World Time.

When the Taliban solidified its hold on power around Kabul in September 1996, a team of five dedicated men took it upon themselves to keep the official voice of

OUTLAWS IN UNIFORM

The only practical link with the outside world maintained by Afghan rebels is the Taloqan-Dushanbe air bridge. A dilapidated Kazak Mi-17 helicopter, still replete with Soviet markings, shuttles a fortunate few and visiting journalists between the Tajik capital and north Afghan towns controlled by rebel forces. Afghan pilots fly across undulating hills and high mountains without radio contact or radar, adding to the perils they face from unreliable machines and trigger-happy Russian soldiers.

Arriving Afghans are a constant source of amusement and money for corrupt Russian guards in charge of immigration and customs at the Dushanbe airport. When we arrived at dusk, what followed was an exercise in methodical exploita-tion of hapless people.

Afghan passengers were singled out and herded like cattle to the far corner of the tarmac. They were summarily told that they would be deported if they do not have a valid entry visa, which they could not possibly obtain in their strife-torn country. Then a $100 bribe per person was demanded, a king's ransom for today's Afghans.

All this took place while the Afghan pilot pleaded to take off, as he needed to get back to Taloqan before sundown. But the Russian guards would not hear of it. Instead, a small

Afghan pilot prepares for hazardous takeoff.   M. Guha

tanker was hauled next to the aircraft and the plane's fuel partially pumped out despite frantic cries from the pilot that he had barely enough fuel to get back. Then the resilient Afghans kneeled to say a few words in prayer while the resolute Afghan pilot took off in darkness towards Afghanistan, hoping to land safely on fumes and the mercy of Allah.

Afghanistan alive. First a mobile short-wave transmitter was moved by truck to Mazar-e-Sharif, where it broadcast from the premises of the existing station. When Mazar fell, the station moved to a make-shift base in the Panjshir valley, then to its current location in Taloqan.

The present facilities are actually those of the clandestine station of the Tajik opposition, Radio Free Tajikistan, which broadcast for a few years against the pro-Soviet regime in Dushanbe. With the signing of the peace accord in Kabul in 1994, the clandestine station ceased operations and the facilities fell vacant. They were used later by Radio Takhar, the official voice of the Afghan opposition. Radio Free Tajikistan was revived for six months in 1996, when the political climate in neighboring Tajikistan was inclement once again and there was a need for the Tajik opposition to make clandestine broadcasts back to their country.

When the Taliban took over Takhar province in August 1998, most employees fled. During the two month siege the radio station was

Frontline schools: Unlike in the fundamentalist Taliban-controlled areas, Afghan girls in northern Afghanistan attend school.   M. Guha

simply renamed Voice of Shariah of Takhar Province, in line with all other Taliban-controlled provincial radio stations.

Opposition Revives Radio Takhar

Anti-Taliban forces recaptured Radio Takhar on October 17, 1998. The next day Radio Takhar was heard with its hour-long

MAN WITH NO COUNTRY

Nikolai Sakharov is 38 and barely recognizable in his thick beard and regulation *salwar kameez*, but his hazel-blue eyes, gold-filled teeth and chaste Russian are a dead giveaway. He fled the Russian army but is no ordinary deserter. Nikolai Sakharov "went native." He is a turncoat, a man with no country.

He first came to Afghanistan as a private in the Soviet Army. When his commandant beat him over a minor accident with his APC, he fled, surrendering to Masoods' Afghan rebel forces. He was locked up for a year, then began fighting for the rebels where his experience with the Soviet Army was invaluable. He is now a top military adviser to Masood.

For the past eight years Sakharov has made Afghanistan his home, although he sometimes slips into his native Krasnodar for visits. He has converted to Islam, married a local girl, and goes by the new name of Islamuddin. He has been camera shy since a thoughtless journalist pictured him shooting at a Russian MiG, which he downed.

Nikolai Sakharov
M. Guha

Sakharov has been marked for death by Russia's security organization.

GRUNDIG Best in Technology

Yacht Boy 400 Professional Edition (YB 400PE)

The most powerful compact Radio AM/FM Shortwave Receiver.

"The Best compact shortwave portable we have tested" Lawrence Magne.-Editor in Chief, Passport to World Band Radio.

The Big Breakthrough! Power, performance, and design have reached new heights! The Grundig 400 Professional Edition with its sleek titanium look is packed with features like no other compact radio in the world.

Pinpoint Accuracy! The Grundig 400PE does it all: pulls in AM, FM, FM-Stereo, every shortwave band (even aviation and ship-to-shore)-all with lock-on digital precision.

Ultimate Features! Auto tuning! The Grundig 400PE has auto tuning on shortwave and stops at every signal and lets you listen. With the exceptional sensitivity of the 400PE, you can use the auto tune to catch even the weakest of signals.
Incredible timing features! The Grundig 400PE can send you to sleep listening to your favorite music.
You can set the alarm to wake up to music or the morning traffic report, then switch to BBC shortwave for the world news. The choice is yours!

Powerful Memory! Described as a smart radio with 40 memory positions, the Grundig 400PE remembers your favorites-even if you don't!

Never Before Value! Includes deluxe travel pouch, stereo earphones, owner's manual, external antenna and a 9 volt Grundig AC adapter. Uses 6 AA batteries (not included)

Style • Titanium look

Shortwave, AM and FM • Continuous shortwave from 1.6 - 30 MHz, covering all existing shortwave bands plus FM-stereo, AM and Longwave. • Single sideband (SSB) circuitry allows for reception of two-way communication such as amateur radio, military, commercial, air-to-ground, and ship-to-shore.

Memory Positions • 40 randomly programmable memory positions allow for quick access to favorite stations.

Multi-function Liquid Crystal Display • The LCD simultaneously displays the time, frequency, band, alarm and sleep timer.

Clock, Alarm and Timer • Two alarm modes: Beeper and radio.
• Dual clocks show time in 24 hour format.
• Sleep timer programmable in 15 minute increments.

Dimensions: 7.75" L x 4.5" H x 1.5" W

Weight: 1 lb. 5 oz.

Best in Value

Yacht Boy 300 Professional Edition (YB 300PE)

Power and Performance with the Affordable Yacht Boy 300 Professional.

Designed for the traveller, the titanium look digital radio provides incredible power and performance for an incredibly low price! Packed with features, this radio is an excellent value, accompanied with 3 AA batteries, AC adapter, earphones, supplementary Antenna and carrying case!

State of-the-art features include:
- Digital tuning with 24 user-programmable memory presets
- 13 SW Bands (2.30-7.30 MHz; 9.5-26.10 MHz)
- Illuminated multifunction LCD display screen
- AM/FM stereo via earphones
- Clock and 10 to 90 minute sleep timer
- Digital tuning display

- Direct frequency entry
- DX/ local selector
- Titanium look finish
- External antenna jack
- Dynamic micro speaker
- Earphone jack
- Telescopic antenna

Dimensions: 5.75" L x 3.5" H x 1.25" W

Weight: 9.92 oz

by **GRUNDIG**

Lextronix / Grundig, P.O. Box 2307, Menlo Park, CA 94026 Tel: 650-361-1611 Fax: 650-361-1724
Shortwave Hotlines: (US) 1-800-872-2228 (CN) 1-800-637-1648 • Web: www.grundigradio.net

evening broadcast at 1230 World Time on 7085 kHz, with a repeat the next morning.

Radio Takhar broadcasts from a small room in a military hutment upon a hill at the center of Taloqan, near the dried-up river of the same name. The transmitter is a modified Russian RX-10 renovated for broadcast use and housed in a small room towards the rear. Powered by a four-kilowatt Russian diesel generator, it has an effective rating of 1 kW and can operate in the frequency range 7000-7085 kHz.

All this hardware appears to have been vandalized from a Soviet military communications truck, which incongruously now acts as an outdoor van and also serves to relocate the transmitter quickly in the event of attack. Another disused Russian military communications tractor-trailer's transmitter, once used as a relay in Badakshan, has been vandalized for spare parts. There are also unconfirmed reports of a similar low-power shortwave repeater at Charikar, not far from the Kabul frontline.

The mainstay transmitter is often off because of technical snags or a lack of parts. Scarcity of diesel for the generator also forces the transmitter to operate at less than its normal output of 1 kW, making it a prize DX catch.

There is a cooped-up rudimentary studio consisting of a tape deck and a microphone, which injects directly into the transmitter without any equalization. It has distorted audio as the final output, but the signal steadies as the transmitter warms up. But the substandard audio quality listeners endure isn't just because of the transmitter and Spartan studio hardware. Even everyday audio cassettes are hard to come by, so they have to be used and reused until they sound warbled.

Radio Takhar presently broadcasts one hour each morning from 0130 to 0230 World Time around 7 MHz—it was on exactly 7000 kHz when I was there on assignment for PASSPORT. Programs consist of news and commentary in Dari and Pashto, as well as a segment in Uzbek, interwoven with muezzin calls to prayer and lively patriotic music.

Evening broadcasts of Radio Takhar at 1330-1430 World Time have been discontinued because of a lack of power. Instead,

BLOODSHED AS MASS ENTERTAINMENT

Since 1996, Kabul residents have turned to public executions, amputations and floggings as virtually their sole form of entertainment. These Romanesque spectacles are announced over the Voice of Shariah radio Thursday evenings, then carried out on Friday, the Muslim Sabbath.

About 20,000 people crowd into the football stadium to cheer as convicted murderers and rapists are shot dead by victims' relatives. Warmup acts include the flogging of young men who have been caught drinking whisky.

In the southern city of Kandahar the Taliban leader, Mullah Mohammed Omar, recently attended what the Voice of Shariah called, "a ceremony for the restoration of heavenly order." Three homosexual men were lined up next to a stone wall, which was then pushed over to bury them alive.

Qisas, the right of revenge, has become the norm throughout towns and cities in the two-thirds of Afghanistan under Taliban control. The condemned are executed employing the methods they themselves used. In one particularly gruesome case a killer had his throat slashed by one of his victim's relatives.

Long-barreled field gun, captured from Taliban by rebels, takes a break from shelling at the Pul-e-Bangi frontline. J. Barbee

there is a fleapower television station which started in May 1999. The staff consists of roughly 90 employees, including an engineer and two technicians working jointly for radio and television operations in morning and evening shifts.

Both Radio Takhar and Kabul's Voice of Shariah deliberately hover around 7080 kHz so that Afghan listeners can be tricked into listening to their station. Since Radio Takhar does not broadcast after dark, the station from Kabul sometimes identifies evenings as "Injá Takhar" in a bid to further confuse unsuspecting listeners.

On some days Kabul jams the morning broadcast. However, no officials in Kabul appear to be monitoring, as they have been jamming Radio Takhar on days when it was clearly off because of transmitter trouble.

Efforts are underway for Radio Takhar to procure an aging 50 kW shortwave transmitter from India, but the power supply and other difficulties need to be sorted out first, so it's a long shot. But even this is unlikely to be the last salvo in Afghanistan's media war. While military men battle it out along the fronts, the clash of information and disinformation will continue to crackle over the world band airwaves in this politically pivotal nation.

Manosij Guha, formerly news producer for German television, has been on exclusive assignment for PASSPORT *throughout the Central Asian region.*

REBEL LEADER AHMAD SHAH MASOOD

Rebel leader Ahmad Shah Masood, 53, has been hailed in a French documentary as one of the finest military commanders of the century. Speaking with PASSPORT in a rare one-on-one interview, he states, "It is not possible the problem is solved militarily alone. Pakistan has been isolated. The UAE and Saudi Arabia have stopped supplying money and weapons. Pakistan will not be able to go on much longer. So this year there will be maximum effort from both sides—it will be a year of reckoning."

In adjacent Tajikistan, Masood is a folk hero. Apart from being next of kin, he is credited with brokering the 1994 Tajik peace accord in Kabul.

Ahmad Shah Masood

GRUNDIG Tunes

SATELLIT 800 MILLENNIUM

The Satellit 800 Millennium. In the history of shortwave receivers, no other manufacturer has maintained a continuously evolving series of high-end portable radios, decade after decade.

Extensive frequency coverage.
- Long wave, AM-broadcast and Shortwave, 100-30,000 KHz, continuous.
- FM broadcast, 87-108 MHz.
- VHF aircraft band, 118-137 MHz.
- Multi-mode reception – AM, FM-stereo, Single Sideband USB/LSB and VHF aircraft band.

The right complement of high-tech features.
- Three built-in bandwidths, using electronically switched IF filters: 6.0, 4.0, 2.3 KHz.
- Synchronous detector for improved quality of AM and USB/LSB signals, minimizes the effects of fading distortion and adjacent frequency interference.
- Selectable AGC in fast and slow mode. Auto Backlight shutoff to conserve battery life. Low Battery Indicator.

Performance engineered for the best possible reception.
- High Dynamic Range, allowing for detection of weak signals in the presence of strong signals.

- Excellent sensitivity and selectivity.

Legendary Grundig audio.
- Outstanding audio quality, with separate bass and treble tone control - in the Grundig tradition.
- FM Stereo with headphones or external amplified stereo speakers.
- Includes high quality stereo headphones.
- Multiple audio outputs: line level output for recording, stereo headphone output.

Information displayed the way it should be.
- Large, illuminated, informational LCD display of operational parameters, measuring a massive 6" x 3½", easy to read.
- An elegant, calibrated, analog signal strength meter, in the finest tradition.
- Digital frequency display to 100 Hertz accuracy on AM, SW and VHF aircraft bands. 50 Hz when SSB used.

Traditional and high-tech tuning controls.
- A real tuning knob, like on traditional radios, but with ultra-precise digital tuning, with absolutely no audio muting when used.
- A modern, direct-frequency-entry keypad for instant frequency access, and pushbuttons for fixed-step tuning.

Plenty of user programmable memory.
- 70 programmable memories, completely immune to loss due to power interruptions.
- Memory scan feature.

Clocks and timers.
- Dual, 24 hour format clocks.
- Dual programmable timers.

Antenna capabilities that really make sense.
- Built in telescopic antenna for portable use on all bands.
- External antenna connections for the addition of auxiliary antennas, e.g. professionally engineered shortwave antennas; long-wire shortwave antennas; specialized AM broadcast band antennas for enthusiasts of AM DX'ing; FM broadcast band antennas; VHF air band antennas.

Power, dimensions, weight.
- Operation on six internal "D" cell batteries or the included Multi-voltage (110-220 V)AC wall transformer.
- Big dimensions and weight. A real radio. 20.5" L x 9.4" H x 8" W., 14.5 lb.

universal radio inc.

6830 Americana Pkwy.
Reynoldsburg, Ohio
43068-4113 U.S.A.

in the World

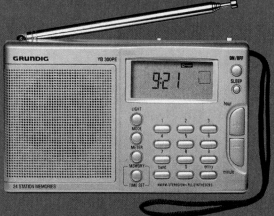

**The most powerful compact
Radio AM/FM Shortwave Receiver.**

Yacht Boy 400
Professional Edition

Powerful performance and sleek titanium look design
combined with sophisticated features make the YB 400 PE a
value! Covers shortwave, AM, FM-stereo and longwave: SW
1.6-30 MHz, AM 530-1710 KHz, FM 88-108 MHz, LW 150-353
KHz. SSB circuitry for reception of shortwave single sideband
two-way communications, e.g. ham radio, aeronautical and
marine. 2 clocks. 40 memories. Built-in antennas.
External SW antenna socket. Includes AC adapter, case,
earphones, supplementary SW antenna. Uses 6 AA batteries
(not included). Dimensions: 7.75" L x 4.5" H x 1.5" W.
Weight: 1 lb. 5 oz.

*German Look! German Sound!
German Quality! Power and Performance.*

Yacht Boy 300
Professional Edition

Listen to broadcasts from countries around the
globe on all 13 shortwave international broadcast
bands. Local AM and FM-stereo too. Fully digital
PLL. Direct frequency entry. Auto scan. Push-button
tuning. Clock. Sleep timer. 24 memories. Titanium
color. Easy-read LCD. Display light. External SW
antenna socket. Carrying strap. Includes AC adapter,
case, earphones, batteries, supplementary
SW antenna. Compact. One year warranty.
Dimensions: 5.75" L x 3.5" H x 1.25" W.
Weight: 12 oz.

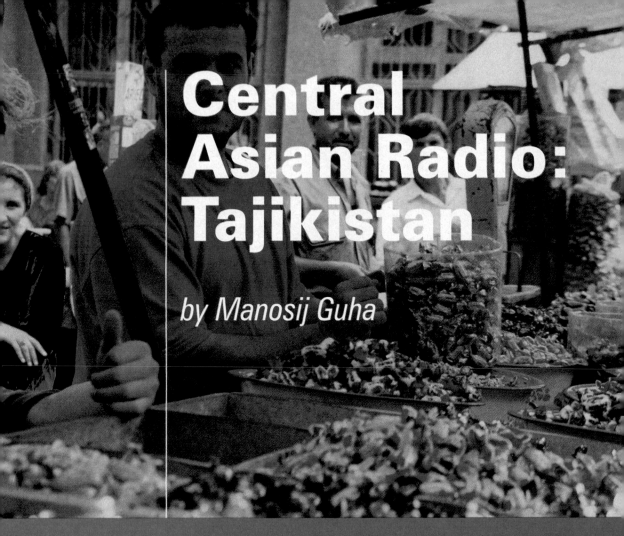

Central Asian Radio: Tajikistan

by Manosij Guha

Few outside Asia have ever heard of Tajikistan. Lost for decades in a remote mountainous backwater, it has risen from the carcass of the Soviet empire to reveal festering communal strife and a dismal human rights record.

The nation survives on a drip feed of loans and handouts from Moscow. It is a textbook case of a failed political system, a museum of social-ist relics with crumbling edifices that once bespoke of an egalitarian society. The people remain bitterly divided, thanks to Stalin's surgical scalpel that gave much of the re-public's territory and cultural heritage to neighboring Uzbekistan.

The country's six million inhabitants are mainly Sunni Muslim, although not militantly so, given that they were schooled on atheism for generations.

Although the harnessing of Islamic sentiment has been a stronger political force in Tajikistan than in other Central Asian republics, the rural, often semi-nomadic lifestyle preferred by most Tajiks is unsuited to any central religious authority.

Republic Divided into Two Camps

When the Soviet Union fell apart in 1991, Tajikistan declared independence and descended into a civil war that devastated agriculture and industry. Communist party veteran and Soviet ally Imomali Rakhmonov emerged as strongman president, but political opposition has been strident ever since, especially from an Islamic-democratic coalition. Meanwhile, Russian-dominated forces from the former Soviet Union continue to prop up the Rakhmonov regime, since Moscow views the Tajikistan border with Afghanistan as being of major strategic importance.

Russian military guards Tajik president against potential coup by his own soldiers. M. Guha

To consolidate its power, presidential forces embarked on an orgy of ethnic cleansing directed at anyone connected with the Islamists. Between 20,000 and 50,000 people were liquidated, and as recently as 1998 five more mass graves were discovered with some 2,600 bodies. There are still half a million refugees, including Tajik rebels who have fled to northern Afghanistan to live among the Tajik minority there.

A peace agreement was signed in June 1997 between President Rakhmonov and Islamic leader Sayed Abdullo Nuri of the United Tajik Opposition. The last of the rebels then returned home, yet tension remains high. Rakhmonov's control barely extends beyond the capital and main highways, and the country has become a patchwork of feudal fiefdoms controlled by maverick warlords.

A Tajik woman sells vegetables in Dushanbe's main market. Dushanbe means Monday, a name chosen because of the city's once-famous weekly market. M. Guha

Radio drama is aired live over Tajik Radio.
M. Guha

Tajikistan's support for anti-Taliban forces in Afghanistan could well inspire the Taliban to throw its weight behind one of the many anti-government armed groups. This, in turn, could provide the death blow for Rakhmonov's enfeebled regime.

Radio Inaugurated in Stalinabad

Tajik Radio was conceived in 1930, but the first transmitter wasn't installed until 1933—a 2.5 kW mediumwave AM unit in Dushanbe, then known as Stalinabad. A year before saw the establishment of the State Committee for Broadcasting of Tajikistan, which went on to regulate broadcasting in the Tajik SSR until the disintegration of the Soviet Union. It included just 13 journalists and broadcast only a few hours daily in Russian, Tajik and Uzbek.

Former rebels now work with government to clear landslides. Jeff Barbee

From 1941 to 1945, broadcasts were increased to seven and a half hours. After the war years, the station was expanded and new transmitters were installed in phases. Its World Service was started in 1948, in Dari towards Afghanistan and in Farsi towards Iran— these languages are not very different from Tajik.

In 1978, the committee was renamed the Television and Radio Broadcasting Committee of the Republic of Tajikistan, reflecting national political changes. By 1989, it was broadcasting a total of 34 program-hours. These shows were surprisingly popular, as indicated by some 25,000 letters received from listeners in the republic and abroad. There was little change even after the end of direct Soviet rule in 1991, except that the bulk of the programming was shifted to post-Soviet official propaganda, special programs for refugees and information on missing persons.

Afghan refugees haggle over watermelons and hidden narcotics. Afghanistan now produces 75 percent of the world's opium, which is taxed by the Taliban.

M. Guha

In 1993, external services in English and Arabic were introduced. It was only in 1994 that Tajik Radio took its present avatar under the newly created Ministry of Culture and Information. To strengthen the official rhetoric of the infant state, the new Sadoye Dushanbe (Voice of Dushanbe) service was added.

Three Radio Networks

The bright blue building of Tajik Radio can be easily mistaken for a theater hall. Its ornate floral alabaster and columns are a legacy of an earlier Soviet era, when the building was a hallowed center for recording music, drama and operas.

GREATEST FLOOD SINCE NOAH?

High in the Pamirs, Lake Sarez could unleash the largest flood the world has seen since Noah. Experts are afraid that the precarious lake, now contained by a natural dam, is in danger of rupturing.

Tajiks have long warned of potential catastrophe if Lake Sarez ever breaks its banks. It is a new and strange concoction, being formed only 90 years ago by an earthquake that created a natural dam of rocks and boulders. The fear is that another tremor could loosen the rocks, unleashing a monstrous torrent of water throughout much of Central Asia. The tsunami could reach as far as the Aral Sea, 600 miles (1000 km) distant, sweeping away thousands of villages and cities from the map.

Tajikistan's Lake Sarez.   Mercicor

It would almost certainly be the worst natural disaster in history.

IC-R75

IC-R8500 The expert's choice. 0.5 – 2000 MHz'; commercial grade; all mode; IF shift; noise blanker; audio peak filter (APF); 1000 memory channels; built-in CI-V command control and RS-232C port for PC remote control with ICOM software for Windows®.

IC-R8500
HF/VHF/UHF RECEIVER

The expert's choice combines the best of features and a handsome look

"If you want a receiver that is both a superior world band radio and a solid scanner, the new Icom IC-R8500 is the best choice."
— *Passport to World Band Radio, 1998*

IC-R75 Hear more of what's out there. Listen to more amateur, marine and shortwave broadcasts. The 'R75 covers from 0.03 – 60.0 MHz'– wider than most other HF receivers.

IC-R75
NEW HF RECEIVER

Cutting edge technology for today's serious DX'er, yet easy & affordable for a casual listener

IC-R8500

Pull out the weak signals. Outstanding features: triple conversion, automatic notch filter, the industry's only twin Pass Band Tuning (PBT) rig, ICOM's all new Synchronous AM detection (S-AM) technology, optional AF Digital Signal Processing (DSP) noise reduction, large front speaker, and two optional filter slots.

hear MORE of what you want to hear

IC-R10 Advanced HT performance & features. 0.5 - 1300 MHz'; all mode; alphanumeric backlit display; excellent audio; attenuator; 1000 memory channels; up to seven different scan types; beginners mode, band scope; includes AA Ni-Cds and charger, or use alkalines.

Both HTs are PC programmable*

IC-R2 Excellent audio, tiny package. 0.5 – 1300 MHz'; AM, FM, WFM; easy band switching; CTCSS decode; 400 memory channels; large speaker; priority watch; auto power off; includes 2 AA Ni-Cds & charger.

Computer not included.

IC-PCR1000 The original "World in a Little Black Box". 100% PC hardware external. 0.01 –1300 MHz' wide band reception, all modes. Listen to your favorite broadcasts while working in foreground applications. 9600 baud data connection point for third party software*, like weather fax. DSP optional. Use third party software or download full version ICOM software: www.icomamerica.com.

"The PCR1000 has something to intrigue and satisfy everyone. This is a fun product.
— *QST, 7/98*

Computer not included.

IC-PCR100 A little different look. 0.01 – 1300 MHz' reception on AM, FM and WFM. Great performance. Designed for Windows® 95 or 98. Download full version ICOM software: www.icomamerica.com.

ICOM®
www.icomamerica.com

*Cellular frequencies blocked: unblocked versions available only to FCC approved users. * Optional. ©1999 ICOM America, Inc. 2380 116th Ave NE, Bellevue, WA 98004 • 425-454-8155. The ICOM logo is a registered trademark of ICOM, Inc. Questions? Contact your authorized ICOM dealer, or contact ICOM America Tech Support through the HamNet forum on CompuServe® at 75540,525 (e-mail 75540.525@compuserve.com) All specifications subject to change without notice or obligation. CompuServe is a registered trademark of CompuServe, Inc. Windows is a registered trademark of Microsoft Corporation. R75/RCVRPASS799Y

Nasurllo Ramazonov reads news in English for Radio Tajikistan. He is only one at the station who speaks English. M. Guha

Tajik Radio has about 700 employees producing a combined output of 54 hours for the three services operating from studios in Dushanbe. First is the national service in Tajik, Russian and a small segment in

Uzbek, from 0030 to 2230 World Time on FM, mediumwave AM and world band. Second is the World Service—Radio Tajikistan—which produces an external service in Arabic, Dari, English and Farsi on mediumwave AM and world band.

Third is the official Sadoye Dushanbe between 0300 and 1100 World Time in Tajik and Russian on FM and mediumwave AM. This service contains countless eulogies to president Rakhmonov, reminiscent of Radio Peking in Mao's day or Radio Pyongyang during the reign of Kim Il Sung.

Throwback to Stalin Era

The onus of transmission has been transferred to a new communications organization that maintains all three transmitter sites. The oldest transmitting facility is smack in the middle of the capital, next to the venerable Gostinitsa Oktyabrskaya, or Hotel October. This facility has all the misplaced appeal of a Soviet-era factory, complete with posters of Lenin, hammers and sickles, and portly uniformed babushkas toiling over control panels.

The gloomy transmitter hall houses four 7 kW transmitters and one 40 kW Czech-

SECRET RADIO INSTALLATIONS

Transmitter sites are often out of bounds for those visiting stations within the former Soviet Union, but Tajik Radio initially wouldn't even allow us to step inside the studio or speak to its staff. After I gave them a copy of the 1999 PASSPORT, things warmed up, sort of: I was allowed to photograph the radio building . . . from the outside. But thanks to a series of long lunches and a new-found friend, I was finally allowed to take pictures in the studios.

I reckoned that if the radio station were so secretive, visiting a transmitter site would be out of the question, but we decided to give it a try anyhow. After rounds of insipid Russian beer and an equal number of miles on foot in the searing sun, our search ended. There, behind Dushanbe's Hotel Oktyabrskaya, something that looked like an antenna mast beckoned us.

We asked for the director, and were shown into a plush modern office. At the large desk was a man thumbing through a well-worn but familiar tome, the 1996 edition of PASSPORT. When I explained my mission and gave him a copy of the 1999 edition, he was ecstatic. From that point on, the frost vanished and we were able to complete our assignment.

The blue theatre building of Tajik Radio stands tall among the trees of Ulitsa Chapaeva in Dushanbe.

M. Guha

made Tesla which cover the Dushanbe area on 549 and 1323 kHz, along with one 7 kW unit that carries Moscow's Mayak service on 1503 kHz. In the adjacent hall are two vintage 20 kW Russian shortwave transmitters which fed the Vladivostok–Moscow link during the Soviet era. Giving them silent company is a mothballed 1 kW transmitter which once sent weather reports, and two 5 kW transmitters formerly used for wireless telegraphy. In the dense foliage outside are five decaying quad antennas and innumerable dipoles, some helical.

Two Substantial World Band Sites

World band operates from Yangi-yul, about 15 miles or 25 kilometers south of Dushanbe. This massive transmitter site is fortified like a military camp and guarded like a secret installation.

Russian soldiers who secure the entrance and perimeter have orders to shoot snoopers on sight, but we managed to see it anyway by flying over with a helicopter. It is clearly visible from the air as an oblong antenna farm with four tall masts supporting curtain and helical arrays.

The layout is about two miles or three kilometers wide, with transmitter halls between the masts. It reportedly houses a battery of eight Russian-built 100 kW shortwave transmitters, of which at least five are PKV-100 models. These carry the national and world services, including the external service of Tajik Radio. Four transmitters relay Golos Rossii (Voice of Russia) from Moscow in the evenings, and there is another 50 kW Russian shortwave transmitter whose operational status remains a mystery.

A 150 kW mediumwave AM transmitter airs the domestic service of Tajik Radio on 1143 kHz, along with the Voice of Russia in Dari. That same unit seconds as a relay of the Farsi, Uzbek and Kazak services of the BBC World Service on 1251 kHz, putting in a hefty signal around the underbelly of the former USSR. There is also a 150 kW longwave transmitter which carries the national program on 252 kHz.

Up north at Orzu, formerly Kolkhozabad, is a newer transmitter site nestled amidst Soviet-era collective farms. It was built in 1971 to relay programs from Moscow, a practice that continues to this day. There

**With authorities beyond earshot, a street musician
defies local fundamentalists by strumming a
Farsi tune in the Sufi tradition founded to counter
fundamentalist Islam.**   M. Guha

supplemented by two one-Megawatt mediumwave behemoths on 648 and 972 kHz which carry the Voice of Russia in Chinese, Dari, Hindi, Mongolian and Pashto.

A 150 kW unit pumps out the national program on 702 kHz mediumwave AM and relays Radio Rossiya from Moscow. Two more Megawatt gargantuas heave out signals for the national and world services on 648 and 972 kHz, while a relatively modest 40 kW unit rebroadcasts the Sadoye Dushanbe (Voice of Dushanbe) on 1161 kHz to the north of the country.

There are also two 4 kW FM transmitters each at Dushanbe, Kurgan-Tuybe and Khojand. These pretty much cover the entire country with the national and third programs of Tajik Radio.

Despite the trappings of independence, this beleaguered Central Asian republic retains its status as a Russian client state. This is reflected in the resources and authoritarian control lavished on Tajikistan's substantial radio system, which serves to bolster both the regime and its Russian allies.

are four mighty 500 kW PKV-500 shortwave transmitters which can be used in tandem to throw out a whopping 1,000 kW. This is

RUSSIAN ROULETTE

Even though Tajik rebel leader Ahmad Shah Masood was instrumental in driving Soviet troops from Afghanistan in 1989, the Russians now provide him with material and military aid (*see* Afghanistan: Jihad of the Airwaves, preceding this article).

Russian officials refuse to confirm openly that they are sending military aid to Afghan rebels. However, they admit that the airbase in southern Tajik city of Kulyab has become a "reserve airfield" for anti-Taliban forces, and that the town is used for rest and recreation by the Masood forces.

Russia's aid is designed to forestall a nightmare for Moscow and its Central Asian allies: the rout of Masood's anti-Taliban coalition, with the resulting mass exodus of refugees and fighters across what used to be the Soviet border. Tajiks, Uzbeks and Turkmen live on both sides of the Afghan frontier, so any refugees could meld easily with the local people. The refugees' political and religious views, formed during years of war in Afghanistan, could be deeply destabilizing for their host nations. And future refugees could use their host countries as a springboard to launch cross-border attacks, thereby inviting retaliation against Russian interests and adding to the turmoil in this volatile region.

You Don't Have
to
Really GO There
to
BE
THERE

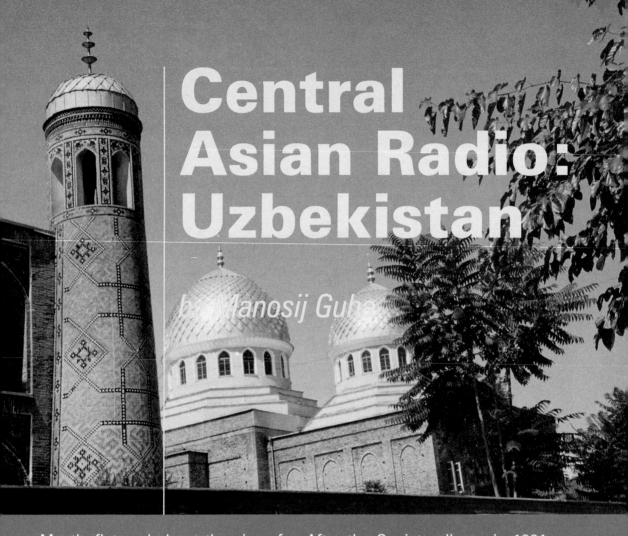

Central Asian Radio: Uzbekistan

by Manosij Guha

Mostly flat and about the size of Sweden, Uzbekistan encompasses some 23 million Sunni Muslims. Since the Bolsheviki took control after the October Revolution, the republic has changed shape and size many times. For rural Uzbeks, Soviet rule brought obligatory collectivization of their farms and a huge shift to cotton cultivation. For the intelligentsia it meant devastating purges.

After the Soviet collapse in 1991, Uzbekistan was declared independent. However, although the country's Communist Party changed its name the government remained pretty much as before. The party leader, Islam Karimov, was "elected" president—no opposition—and has held his grip on power ever since. His forces have hunted down Islamic militants (*see* sidebar, "Squabbling Neighbors"), but

Islamists are not the only group at odds with Karimov. He has also cracked down on student demonstrators and organized crime, effectively shutting down the Mafiya.

Central Asia's Largest Radio

Not far from the presidential palace is the nondescript Republican Radio and Recording House, also known as the Radio of Uzbekistan. Going by the generic name "Radio Tashkent," it is easily the largest operation of its type in Central Asia.

Uzbek radio commenced in Tashkent on February 11, 1927 with a program of five to ten minutes of news and press reports in Uzbek. In 1929, it was further integrated into the Soviet broadcast apparatus when it began large-scale relays of programs from Moscow.

It also set about producing its own programs as part of the State Radio Committee, in concert with other republics of the Soviet Union. By the time Uzbekistan started moving towards independence in 1990, its first radio channel was operating in Russian and Uzbek 24 hours a day, while the second channel relayed Moscow's Mayak service. After independence on September 1, 1991 the Mayak relays were drastically reduced and newscasts from Moscow were stopped.

Radio Tashkent currently has 1,500 employees, including 350 technicians. It operates four domestic channels for 76 program-hours a day in Russian, Uzbek, Tajik, Kazakh and two kinds of Tatar from 16 studios. There is also a low-profile fifth program which doesn't find mention in the official literature. It airs Radiostansiya Mayak in Russian from Moscow at 0100-0200, 1100-1500 and 1800-2000 World Time on frequencies otherwise used by the second channel.

Entrance to Uzbek Radio, where even news is prerecorded.   M. Guha

Radio Tashkent is easily the largest operation of its type in Central Asia.

An Uzbek woman butcher hawks beef entrails, used in a traditional goulash-like delicacy.   M. Guha

Unlike many other capitals of the former Soviet Union, Tashkent has reliable trolleys.   M. Guha

First is the Republican National channel, in Uzbek daily between 2359 and 2100 World Time. It operates on 162 kHz longwave, 1063 kHz mediumwave AM, 67.19 MHz FM in the old 65.9-73.1 MHz OIRT band, and 5995 kHz world band, plus a host of relay transmitters throughout the country.

Second is the Uzbek-language Radyo Mashal Kanala—Radio Torchlight Channel—at 0000-2300 World Time, with music and news on 667 kHz mediumwave AM and 4850 kHz world band. Also, 67.97 MHz FM for Tashkent, as well as over several regional outlets.

The third, Radyo Yoshlar Kanala, provides youth-oriented entertainment in Uzbek 20 hours a day at 0000-2000 World Time on 575 kHz mediumwave AM, plus 69.23 and 104 MHz FM.

Fourth is Radyo Dostilik Kanala—Radio Friendship Channel—which as the name suggests is a communications bridge among minority ethnic groups. This channel broadcasts at 0200-1100 World Time in Uzbek, Russian, Tajik, Tatar and Kazak on 756 kHz mediumwave AM and 66.41 MHz FM.

It also relays BBC World Service programs in Russian, formerly in Uzbek as well. In late 1998 the BBC was pulled from the Dostilik channel because it carried a series on Uzbek human rights. This prompted the BBC to hire a mediumwave AM facility in neighboring Tajikistan for its Uzbek programming. Since then, the BBC relay has resumed from Tashkent, but minus Uzbek programming.

External Service a Mixed Bag

The external service, on the third floor of the Radio of Uzbekistan building, started in 1947 with English and Uighur. There are five dedicated studios which use everything from antiquated Hungarian MechLabor reel decks to state-of-the-art editing suites provided by German aid.

JRC NRD-545

Legendary Quality. Digital Signal Processing. Awesome Performance.

With the introduction of the NRD-545, Japan Radio raises the standard by which high performance receivers are judged.

Starting with JRC's legendary quality of construction, the NRD-545 offers superb ergonomics, virtually infinite filter bandwidth selection, steep filter shape factors, a large color liquid crystal display, 1,000 memory channels, scan and sweep functions, and both double sideband and sideband selectable synchronous detection. With high sensitivity, wide dynamic range, computer control capability, a built-in RTTY demodulator, tracking notch filter, and sophisticated DSP noise control circuitry, the NRD-545 redefines what a high-performance receiver should be.

JRC *Japan Radio Co., Ltd.*

Japan Radio Company, Ltd., Seattle Branch Office —
1011 SW Klickitat Way, Building B, Suite 100, Seattle, WA 98134
Voice: 206-654-5644   Fax: 206-264-1168

Japan Radio Company, Ltd. — Akasaka Twin Tower (main), 17-22,
Akasaka 2-chome, Minato-ku, Tokyo 107, Japan   Fax: (03) 3584-8878

- LSB, USB, CW, RTTY, FM, AM, AMS, and ECSS (Exalted Carrier Selectable Sideband) modes.

- Continuously adjustable bandwidth from 10 Hz to 9.99 kHz in 10 Hz steps.

- Pass-band shift adjustable in 50 Hz steps up or down within a ±2.3 kHz range.

- Noise reduction signal processing adjustable in 256 steps.

- Tracking notch filter, adjustable within ±2.5 kHz in 10 Hz steps, follows in a ±10 kHz range even when the tuning dial is rotated.

- Continuously adjustable AGC between 0.04 sec and 5.1 sec in LSB, USB, CW, RTTY, and ECSS modes.

- 1,000 memory channels that store frequency, mode, bandwidth, AGC, ATT, and (for channels 0–19) timer on/off.

- Built-in RTTY demodulator reads ITU-T No. 2 codes for 170, 425, and 850 Hz shifts at 37 to 75 baud rates. Demodulated output can be displayed on a PC monitor through the built-in RS-232C interface.

- High sensitivity and wide dynamic range achieved through four junction-type FETs with low noise and superior cross modulation characteristics.

- Computer control capability.

- Optional wideband converter unit enables reception of 30 MHz to 2,000 MHz frequencies (less cellular) in all modes.

**Anchor records the
popular listener's mailbag
program.**   M. Guha

About 200-odd staff from various nationalities produce 16 hours daily in Uzbek and English, plus ten other languages. Programming is tightly controlled by the editor, with all news bulletins being prerecorded and meticulously screened beforehand. Most news and features are translated from regular Uzbek programs, anyway, so there's little room for originality.

Radio Tashkent can be a great verifier. There is a large Listeners' Mail Department which processes correspondence by the sackful, issuing colorful QSL cards and free goodies, as well as membership in the Salaam Aleikum Listeners' Club. The walls of the large room are proudly wallpapered with listeners' letters and cards. Still, the station has a ways to go—listeners in Australia, for example, complain that their correspondence usually goes unanswered.

Huge "Secret" Transmitter Site

On the outskirts of Tashkent is one of the republic's most closely guarded and not-so-well-kept secrets: Radio Tashkent's transmitter site, whose existence, in fine Orwellian fashion, is promptly denied. "Ask me all you want about our station or our programs. But about transmitters, it is another matter," says the visibly ruffled director, Fakhriddin Nizom, gesturing that his lips are sealed.

**The BBC's relay
was pulled from
the Dostilik
channel because
it carried a series
on Uzbek human
rights.**

In the post-Bolshevik period, when the then-Uzbek SSR was in favor with Soviet authorities, Tashkent was rewarded with one of the largest transmitting facilities in Central Asia—ostensibly to relay programs from Moscow. Today this huge "transmitting factory"

**Radio Tashkent still uses
vintage MechLabor reel
decks from Hungary.**
M. Guha

houses no less than nineteen 100 kW shortwave transmitters of Russian and East European origin. At least fourteen are KV-100 units which are sometimes run in tandem to double or triple the power. Five of these and a lone 50 kW shortwave transmitter carry Radio Tashkent's domestic services to local rural audiences, as well as to the sizeable Uzbek minority population living in the former Soviet Union.

This ex-Soviet powerhouse site has jumped onto the relay bandwagon, offering airtime in exchange for hard currency. At present it relays programs from the BBC in Bengali and Hindi, Radio Nederland Wereldomroep in English, and the religious IBRA Radio in Bengali—all beamed towards South Asia with powerhouse signals. Programs of old friend and benefactor Moscow have been eased out because of Russia's inability to cough up dollars.

News at Radio Tashkent is prerecorded for official scrutiny before airing. M. Guha

21ST CENTURY SILK ROAD

Last year Uzbekistan signed an agreement with a dozen foreign ministers to restore the ancient Silk Road to its former glory, this time as a three-lane motorway. For westernmost Iran and Turkey there is little to do, but for Uzbekistan the demands are enormous, as its road system is in need of a major overhaul. After all, much of the pathway that once linked Han-dynasty China with Roman Europe is in ruins after 500 years of abandonment.

One stretch will traverse the shifting deserts of Turkmenistan, where some of the world's highest temperatures have been recorded. Another, it is hoped, will run through Tajikistan, where the government actually governs only about half of the country, the rest being conceded to feuding armed groups.

In Kyrgyzstan, a part of the highway is already in operation—to ill effect. Rusting Soviet-era vehicles hauling raw opium in burlap sacks have replaced the camel caravans that carried tea and spices centuries ago. This is one of the most remote stretches of the Silk Road, the Pamir Highway, connecting Afghanistan's vast poppy fields with the narcotics bazaars of Central Asia.

In Kazakstan, the last section of the new Silk Road is nearing completion. It climbs high into the Tien Shan, or Celestial Mountains, after crossing the vast steppes. The only threat in the summer is from insect hordes, but in the winter the Siberian wind turns the region into a frozen tundra.

Once complete, the reincarnated turnpike will probably carry a stream of heavy trucks from Beijing to Istanbul, but with little of the romance of the old Silk Road followed by Marco Polo.

This Soviet-era building outshines most of Tashkent's recent architecture. M. Guha

Radio Tashkent's domestic services are also broadcast from the same facility over a 150 kW longwave transmitter on 162 kHz, a 50 kW mediumwave AM transmitter on 575 kHz, a 30 kW transmitter on 667 kHz, and a 5 kW unit on 1063 kHz. For Tashkent proper there are five FM transmitters on 66.41, 67.19, 67.97, 69.23 and 104 MHz emitting the four domestic channels of Radio Tashkent.

Beyond Tashkent there are stations in twelve *vellayats* or provincial capitals which have their own studios and prepare their own programs. These operate on FM and mediumwave AM, except Ferghana near the border with Kyrgyzstan—it uses a modest 5 kW world band transmitter. This DX catch operates with limited autonomy, airing two half-hour segments in the mornings and evenings in Tajik, Tatar, Uzbek and Russian on 4510 kHz. Extending the reach of these stations are about 50 repeater transmitters on FM.

Radio Tashkent may be long on programs, staff and facilities, but it is definitely short on programming appeal. Its monotonous humming of the official party line gives it low marks among listeners even as they appreciate the station's robust signals.

SQUABBLING NEIGHBORS

Accusation by Tajikistan that it has been bombed by planes from Uzbekistan is but the latest in a series of incidents heightening tensions among neighboring states. Adding to the intrigue is that Uzbek bombers were allowed to fly over the territory of another neighbor, Kyrgyzstan.

After urban guerilla bombings in Tashkent, the Uzbek capital, authorities launched a relentless hunt for opposition militants at home and abroad. This effort has been frustrated in part because an armed group of Uzbek Islamists is based in a mountain wilderness along the Tajik-Kyrgyz border.

But the squabbling goes both ways. The Tajik government now accuses the Uzbek government of having given active support to an armed force which has attacked Tajikistan's northern Khojand province, which in all but name has already become part of Uzbekistan.

All the worlds' listening!

No matter where you go, SANGEAN will keep you in touch. Whether you own the full-featured ATS-909, THE WORLD'S MOST ADVANCED SHORTWAVE RECEIVER or SANGEAN's ATS-818ACS Digital Receiver with programmable built-in cassette recorder or SANGEAN's ATS-404, the world's first full-featured, continuous coverage digital receiver under $100, you'll always receive the utmost in reliability and performance at a price just right for your budget.

SANGEAN PORTABLES.
GET AWAY FROM IT ALL AND STILL STAY IN TOUCH.

Central Asian Radio: Kyrgyzstan

by Manosij Guha

Kyrgyzstan looms larger than Austria and Hungary combined, with borders at Kazakstan to the north, China in the east, Tajikistan down south and Uzbekistan on the western edge. Fully 95 percent of this landlocked country is alligatored with high mountains mostly blanketed by permanent snow and glaciers.

Little known outside Central Asia, Kyrgyzstan is a breathtaking alpine outpost with only 4.5 million inhabitants, the majority occupying the lowlands. Most are Muslim, although Islam sits relatively lightly on the Kyrgyz people. The republic declared itself independent in August of 1991 and reelected former communist president Askar Akaev, who was unopposed.

Though widely used, the Kyrgyz language has not been imposed on non-speakers in Kyrgyzstan in the way Uzbek has in Uzbekistan. So the use of Russian persists, especially among Slavs who form a sizeable minority. Other significant minorities are Koreans and Dungans—Chinese Muslims—along with Volga Germans.

Broadcasting Followed Soviet Model

The history of Kyrgyzstan's radio broadcasting is similar to that of other Central Asian republics within the Soviet orbit. The first Kyrgyz station was started in the capital, Frunze—now Bishkek—in 1927, but it wasn't until 1931 that it managed to get a transmitter on the air, initially with programs in Russian and Kyrgyz.

A state radio broadcasting committee was established to manage it as an organ of the Communist Party, like other stations in the Soviet Union. By 1970, it was broadcasting 15 hours a day, whereupon the committee became the Kyrgyz Radio and TV Company, or simply Kyrgyz Radio.

Liberal Station

After independence the station was further expanded with a second channel. Reflecting widespread political reform, it became the most liberal of all stations of the former Soviet Union, both because of its programming and how the station was run.

Kyrgyz Radio is quartered in a Soviet-era building in the center of Bishkek, where eleven studios turn out 19 hours of programming daily for each of two channels. Five are used for live programming, such as newscasts and talk radio, while the others are dedicated to offline editing or music and drama recording. A majority of the

Bishkek is smartly cosmopolitan, right down to the dresses worn by young women. Their designer fare rivals chichi outfits from the catwalks of Paris and Milan.
M. Guha

Unlike most other capitals of the former Soviet Union, Bishkek is not caught in a Soviet time warp.

A Sufi mystic practices religious contemplation in Bishkek. M. Guha

Kyrgyzstan is a breathtaking alpine outpost half the size of the continental United States.

M. Guha

approximately 60 employees are young, giving a lively atmosphere to what could otherwise be a mausoleum.

The UNDP, BBC and Deutsche Welle have each donated one studio and have helped to train staff. These studios are spankingly modern, with digital tape decks and mixing consoles. Yet, those state-of-the-art facilities coexist alongside elder studios using East European hardware suitable for museum display.

Kyrgyz Radio broadcasts two networks, or channels, from 0000 until 1900 World Time. First is the national channel on world band 4010 kHz and 612 kHz mediumwave AM; the second channel provides youth-oriented entertainment on 4050 kHz and 1467 kHz. Most material is in Kyrgyz, but there are brief news segments in Russian, Dungan, Uighur and German aimed at ethnic minorities. There is

HISTORY INVENTED

Much Central Asian literature and history has traditionally been handed down from generation to generation in the form of songs, poems and stories by itinerant minstrels. This explains why seemingly every Kyrgyz seems to be a gifted singer, as is evident in the spontaneous singing matches at every social gathering.

Because the Kyrgyz people lacked an "official" history and heritage, Soviet scholars "gave" them Manas—a cycle of oral legends, 20 times longer than the *Odyssey*, about a hero-of-heroes also named Manas. This was part of a larger effort to create separate cultures for the various Central Asian peoples, and it has succeeded. In 1998, there were large celebrations throughout the republic to celebrate 1,000 years of the epic hero.

Kyrgyz farmer tills his land. Horses play a key role in nomadic life.
M. Guha

also a newscast in English for foreign residents and those fortunate enough to be tourists in this outsized Switzerland.

The transmitter site lies next to a highway about 19 miles or 30 kilometers north of Bishkek in the sleepy ethnic Russian village of Krasnyretcha—"Red River." In a secluded compound, antenna masts tower over green fields dotted with barracks housing transmitters.

Two 100 kW Russian-built Sneg-M and KV-50 shortwave transmitters were installed in the early sixties and seventies, respectively. Giving them company are one 150

A PEOPLE GERRYMANDERED

Until the Bolshevik Revolution, the clan, religion, land and way of life were the grouping factors for the diverse people of Central Asia. Islam and the Turkic culture formed a delicate unifying thread, but these were suppressed by Russian rulers who saw them as a threat to their overlordship.

In 1924, following the Russian policy of divide and rule, the Kazak, Kyrgyz, Tajik, Turkmen and Uzbek nations were invented to pit subject peoples against each other. Each was given a national heritage, along with a language and culture to nurture, with Islam being carefully sanitized out of existence. The boundaries of these nascent states were repeatedly redrawn, with numerous pockets of one republic's land being given to another in gerry-mandering power plays that were a hallmark of the Stalin era.

During and after World War II, one of Stalin's pet projects was a unique brand of social engineering. He evacuated war-threatened parts of the USSR of Koreans, Volga Germans, Ukrainians and Chechens whom he thought would side with the invading enemy, settling them in Central Asia where they form sizeable minorities to this day.

Central Asian republics which emerged independent after the end of the Soviet Union are now in a constant standoff with each other, thanks to this Machiavellian carving of borders, forced settlement and colonization.

kW longwave transmitter, one 500kW mediumwave AM giant, two 150 kW and two 30 kW mediumwave AM units, and at least one FM transmitter.

Ads and Relays Reduce Shortage

Alas, every year after independence has seen a steady reduction in funding for radio. As a result, Kyrgyz Radio has been unable to acquire new studio equipment or transmitters, expand its programming or hire new staff. Salaries have remained stagnant since the Soviet period, when pay was already at an all-time low.

A major source of revenue is from paid commercials—a new concept, as advertisements were previously free. Revenue from relays of foreign international broadcasters has been limited because of mediocre transmission facilities, but some activity takes place anyway: BBC World Service in Kyrgyz, Deutsche Welle in German, Radio Canada International in Russian and Ukrainian Radio in Ukrainian.

Policeman tames chaotic Bishkek traffic. M. Guha

But the largest foreign radio presence is Moscow's old nemesis, Radio Liberty, better known in these parts as Radio Svoboda— "Freedom." This station purchases and otherwise obtains airtime from a string of FM transmitters in every major urban center dotting the country. It pumps out about four hours daily in Russian and Kyrgyz, and leases a 30 kW mediumwave AM transmitter from Kyrgyz Radio on 1323 kHz that also relays Radio France Internationale.

Left over from earlier times are relays of Russian stations. Radio Odin can be heard for 17 hours daily on 198 kHz longwave over a 150 kW transmitter, and Radiostansiya Yunost is aired over 1278 kHz mediumwave AM via another 150 kW sender for 20 hours a day.

Most of the employees are young, giving a lively atmosphere to what could otherwise be a mausoleum.

Young technician helps enliven stodgy Kyrgyz Radio. M. Guha

When a Central Asian "Greyhound" breaks down, a horse cart is the only hope.   M. Guha

There are no state-run FM outlets, but in Bishkek there are a few private FM stations with Western-influenced programming almost round the clock. Beyond Bishkek, Kyrgyz Radio broadcasts on mediumwave AM from 13 regional centers; in provincial capitals like Osh and Jalal-Abad, they even have their own studios.

A detailed study for enhancement of broadcasting has recently been concluded by NHK, with Japanese assistance likely to

follow soon. Also on the cards is the introduction of a state-run FM service, as well as a relay agreement with Turkish Radio.

Though the station is currently lacking in facilities and resources, it can show its powerful brethren in the former Soviet Union a thing or two about radio journalism and production values. It underscores the dictum that more kilowatts and budget do not necessarily equate to better programming.

LAKE ISSYK-KUL'

Lake Issyk-Kul' is a huge dent filled with water, lying between the massive peaks of the Küngey Alatau and the Terskey Alatau ranges in Kyrgyzstan. Issyk-Kul' stands for warm lake, as its water never freezes and has a moderating effect on the region's climate. It sits fully 5,250 feet or 1,600 meters above sea level, and is a huge 105 miles by 43 miles (170 by 70 kilometers), making it the world's second-largest mountain lake after Lake Titicaca in South America.

Health spas lined the lakeshore in Soviet days, but spa tourism collapsed along with the "Evil Empire." The lake was also used by the Soviet Navy to test high-precision torpedoes far from prying Western eyes. This was one reason it was off limits to foreigners until recently, though the officially sanctioned opium poppy and cannabis plantations which once surrounded the lake may also have had something to do with it.

Today, the main reason tourists visit is to soak up the lakeside ambience, enjoy the thermal springs and remaining spas, and explore world-class hiking trails.

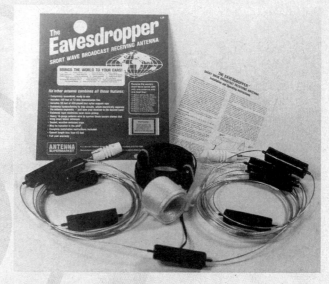

Central Asian Radio: Kazakstan

by Manosij Guha

Massive Kazakstan is the ninth-largest country in the world, roughly the size of Western Europe or half the mainland United States. It is bounded by Russia on the north and northwest; Turkmenistan, Uzbekistan and Kyrgyzstan on the south; China on the east; and the Caspian Sea on the southwest. The country is mostly dry and flat except for its alpine eastern and southeastern fringes which lie along the northern edge of the mighty Tian Shan range.

Seasons are extreme. Summer days sizzle, with desert temperatures topping 105 degrees (40 Celsius), but drop by more than half at night. Snowfall begins around November, blocking mountain passes until April or even May. Winters are bitterly cold, even in the desert.

This vast land has less than 17 million inhabitants, making it one of the world's most sparsely populated countries. Thanks to their fecundity, biological Kazaks now outnumber ethnic Russians.

Kazakstan contains massive deposits of iron, coal, oil, gas, lead, bismuth, cadmium and thallium—the last three are essential in electronics. Those and other minerals have drawn hefty, if shady, foreign investment interest to Kazakstan's otherwise unpromising plains.

Kazaks are Sunni Muslim, mostly moderates, so Islam is not a major political force. Hardly surprising, as Kazakstan is on the fringe of the Muslim world and their nomadic lifestyle is unsuited to any central religious authority. Kazak women are Central Asia's most self-confident and least restricted, despite the lingering custom of bride-stealing.

Russians Ruled from Nineteenth Century

The Kazaks were savagely and repeatedly pummeled by outside forces between 1690 and 1720, a period known as the "Great Disaster." This made them susceptible to Russian expansion in the 19th century, followed by Bolshevism, which quashed any hope of self-determination.

Meanwhile, Enver Pasha, charismatic hero of the 1908 Young Turk Revolution, had bent Lenin's ear and convinced the Soviet leader he could deliver him all of Central Asia and British India. In reality, Pasha was scheming to ditch Lenin and create a Pan-Turkic state for himself, with Central Asia as its core. The mighty Red Army and some astute Soviet concessions to Islam caused Pasha's support to wane and Moscow to prevail.

Soviet rule in Central Asia became a parade of woe: assimilation of the region's ethnic groups, conversion of the steppe into a giant cotton plantation, and the utilization of Kazakstan as a secret nuclear

In Almaty the custom of newlyweds paying homage to the departed lingers on. M. Guha

Kazak women are Central Asia's most self-confident and least restricted, despite the lingering custom of bride-stealing.

A typical wooden Kazak building is Almaty's 1903 Museum of Musical Instruments. M. Guha

This imposing structure is the new television station in Almaty. M. Guha

testing zone. The political, social, economic and ecological disasters resulting from these experiments meant all five republics had little to lose by declaring their sovereignty when glasnost and perestroika led to the disintegration of the USSR in 1991. Later that year, they joined with eleven other former Soviet republics to form the Commonwealth of Independent States (CIS).

Today, Kazakstan is grappling with the free market and an enthusiastic brand of deregulation which tends toward anarchy. President Nazarbayev, a former Communist, is pushing for a weakened parliament and constitutional changes which he hopes will help turn the nation into Central Asia's economic tiger. He has also relocated the capital from the peripheral Almaty to the more central Aqmola, unimaginatively renamed Astana, or "Capital."

Kazak Radio was established on May 4, 1930 in Almaty under the aegis of the Kazak Communist Party, which toed the line set by the Department of Propaganda and Ideology of the Soviet Central Committee in Moscow. Initially, it broadcast only in Kazak and Russian, with German

and Uighur added in 1958, then Korean and Tatar in 1984. By 1991, Kazak Radio was broadcasting 48 program-hours daily from Almaty, mainly in Kazak and Russian.

Domestic Programs Aired over World Band

The Kazak Radio building in Almaty looks all but deserted, with most of the staff and equipment having been carted off to Astana. As a result, broadcasting from Almaty is in a perpetual state of flux, with its production schedule being decided almost on a daily basis.

Since the shifting of the capital to Astana, Kazak Radio's studios in Almaty and Astana have produced 15 hours of programming apiece. These programs are relayed by each other's transmission facilities, as well as outlying world band and mediumwave AM transmitters.

The First Program of the Capital Radio Studio from Astana broadcasts at 0000-0100, 0600-0800 and 1700-1800 World Time. Roughly filling in the gaps is the Second Program of Almaty Radio Studio at

0100-0600 and 0030-1700. These are aired over 180 kHz and 243 kHz longwave, 1197 kHz mediumwave AM and 101.0 MHz FM from Almaty, plus 972 kHz from Astana. They are also rebroadcast by numerous FM and mediumwave AM outlets nationwide, as well as on the creatively chosen world band frequencies of 4545 and 12115 kHz (6255 and 17825 kHz are also used occasionally). From 0800 to 1230 World Time, when the rest of the republic's transmitters enjoy a technical break, a special program for Almaty is broadcast on 101.0 MHz.

Also emanating from the Almaty studios is the Third Program, called Avto Radio—Auto Radio—on 106.5 MHz FM. This motorists' channel is by far the city's most popular, being aired at 0000-1800 World Time.

The external service has all but ceased, as there is no longer a budget for it and all skilled staff have been transferred to studios in Astana. So the Kanal Evraziya, or Channel Eurasia, though aimed at domestic ethnic minorities, also masquerades as a sort of an external service. It is headed by Dr. Choi Yung Gun, whose response to a reporter's request for program schedules was that this information is secret and cannot be revealed. Fortunately, these lofty "secrets" appear routinely in the radio guide column of the local Kazakstanskaya Pravda newspaper.

The daily diet of recorded concert music, preceded and followed by news, is at 0443-0533 World Time in Azerbaijani, Tatar, Turkish, Korean, Uighur and German. All are produced by foreign language students at the local university, but the former English segment has been dropped because there is no one to do it. Not all languages are broadcast daily, but the schedule is arranged in such a manner that three different languages can be heard in any given day. This program is carried by mediumwave AM transmitters in Almaty and Astana, and was formerly also beamed to Europe via two 100 kW transmitters at Kiev in the Ukraine.

WEAVING BORDERS

Thanks to Stalin's penchant for drawing and re-drawing borders, the newly independent Central Asian countries face a mockery of their territorial integrity. Borders are not only porous but also difficult to administer, with Soviet-era roads, railways, communications links and gas pipelines weaving in and out.

For example, the only railway line between north and south Tajikistan passes through Uzbekistan, for which the Uzbeks make the Tajiks pay dearly, at times almost holding the impoverished country to ransom.

The border is most permeable between Kazakstan and Kyrgyzstan, where a small stream or little hill may be the only demarcation. Kyrgyz taxi drivers are in the habit of dashing just into Kazak territory to tank-up on gasoline, which is cheaper there, and border officials shrug. When we dutifully stopped at a new border post, we were waved on as the guards were too busy erecting a flagpole.

A new border post at the Kyrgyz-Kazak border.

M. Guha

Nursery Rhymes: Gaukhar Kassymzhanova conducts a very popular children's program over Kazak Radio. M. Guha

The old transmitter site with 1950s and 1960s hardware is purportedly at Chilik, about 70 kilometers from Almaty. Included are fourteen 100 kW shortwave transmitters, mostly Sneg-M from Eastern Europe. There is also one Russian-built PKV-200 shortwave transmitter of 200 kW, plus about five 50 kW and about seven other shortwave units of undetermined origin.

Shortwave is supplemented by two 150 kW and two 30 kW mediumwave AM transmitters, one 250 kW longwave units, a monster Megawatt longwave transmitter and two 1 kW FM senders.

Also in the Ashchysai region, near Almaty at Nikolayevka or Karaturk, is a newer transmitter site. Established in 1976, it has

ENVIRONMENTAL GULAG

Kazakstan has been ravaged by backyard Soviet projects which have poisoned, denuded and drained this Central Asian country's environment.

Kazak territory was set aside by the Soviet Union for massive wheat production in the 1960s, triggering a chain of ecological disasters. Water from the Syr-Darya and Amu-Darya rivers was diverted for irrigation, causing the Aral Sea, which they fed, to shrink dramatically. The fishing port of Aralsk was left high and dry and became a ghost town; the fish died out from rising salt levels; rains stopped; salt, sand and dust blew in storms for hundreds of miles around; birds and animals fled the river delta. Chemical residues from this grandiose agricultural undertaking have found their way into the rivers and Kazakstan's drinking water, while the Kazak steppe has become eroded, arid and salinized from over-cultivation.

Moscow also used the area west of Semey as a testing ground for nuclear weapons between 1949 and 1989. An undetermined number of locals have reportedly fallen ill and died prematurely from the resulting radiation, especially from nearby atmospheric detonations.

four Russian-built PKV-500 shortwave units of 500 kW and two ionosphere-pounding PKV-1000 Megawatt shortwave transmitters, as well as a lone 150 kW mediumwave AM unit.

Even with this lineup of horsepower there may be more. According to unconfirmed reports, there is a 20 kW shortwave transmitter at Astana, plus two more at Qaraghandy and Kaçiry.

Surplus Facilities Provide Leased Airtime

All this spare world band relay capacity has resulted in a bizarre free-for-all of international broadcasters and anti-establishment outfits to boom signals into South and Southeast Asia. In the mediumwave AM band, for example, there are relays of the Voice of America, Radio Liberty and Russia's Radiostantsiya Yunost.

Given the size of Kazakstan itself, and the fact that approximately 20 percent of ethnic Kazaks live outside the country, it is not inconceivable that Kazak Radio's world band operation may be restored to its former level once the move to Astana is completed. Stay tuned!

The majestic Zhenkov Cathedral in Almaty, built in 1904 entirely of wood and without nails.   M. Guha

THE CREEPING KILLER ISLAND

One of the Soviet Union's main biological weapons test sites in the Aral Sea region was bleak, uninhabited Vozrozhdeniya Island, shared by Kazakhstan and its southern neighbor Uzbekistan. As the Aral Sea has dried up and receded (see sidebar, "Environmental Gulag"), the dreaded island has spread closer to the mainland. This has prompted fears that, with no water barrier, virulent diseases may cross over.

The last of the scientists has departed, leaving behind little hard information about Frankenstein microorganisms which may remain active in the soil. Nevertheless, reports persist that the facility was used to develop a range of aerosol bomblets, as well as to test the impact of epidemic diseases on various animals.

The threat of biological contamination is believed to still be real. Several cases of flea-borne bubonic plague, one fatal, were reported in 1999 in the Kazak region around the Aral Sea, although scientists have not been able to establish a causal link to the abandoned test site.

GRUNDIG Gift Collection

A gift for the auto enthusiast

Maneuver the Porsche Design G2000A Digital Radio Alarm Clock

... to all points around the globe. Wake up to sports and talk radio on AM, soothing stereo (with earphones) on FM or fascinating shortwave from around the world... select from 13 International bands from 2.3 - 7.4 and 9.4 - 26.1 MHz. Punch in any station or lock your favorites into 20 memories... other features include digital clock and alarm with Quartz accuracy... earphones... butter-soft handcrafted leather case. Designed by F. A. Porsche, the G2000A is a pleasure to own and operate. Requires 3 AA batteries (not included).
Dimensions: 5.5" L x 3.5" H x 1.375" W
Weight: 11.52 oz.

A gift for the traveller

The Executive Traveller G4 Travel Organizer with World Band Radio

A sleek titanium-look pocket radio with a full complement of features from AM/FM-Stereo with earphones/SW with LED tuning indicator... 6 shortwave international broadcast bands and a telescopic antenna make listening easy. The soft high-quality leather organizer has compartments for credit cards, airline tickets, money, business cards and more. Comes with 2 AA batteries, earphones and detachable belt clip.

Dimensions: Organizer 4.25"L x 7.75"H x 1.5"W
Radio 2.75" L x 4.25" H x .75" W
Weight: Radio only 4.48 oz.
Organizer w/radio 11.52 oz.

A gift for the collector
50th Anniversary Edition
Classic 960

AM/FM Stereo Shortwave Radio Nostalgia... remember when a radio was a center piece... handcrafted wooden cabinet ...unforgettable European styling... legendary sound. Those days are back! With the solid-state 960, Grundig's Famous 1950s Classic is updated and improved... two 3" side speakers, left and right, and the 4" front speaker will fill your room with exquisite sound... and let you travel the globe without leaving home... receives shortwave continuously from 2.3-22.3 MHz... additional features include: stereo inputs for CD, tape, VCR, or TV sound.
Dimensions: 15.5" L x 11.25" H x 7" W
Weight: 9 lbs. 9.6 oz.

by **GRUNDIG**

Lextronix / Grundig, P.O. Box 2307, Menlo Park, CA 94026 Tel: 650-361-1611 Fax: 650-361-1724
Shortwave Hotlines: (US) 1-800-872-2228 (CN) 1-800-637-1648 • Web: www.grundigradio.net

Ten of the Best: 2000's Top Shows

PASSPORT's complete guide to world band shows is "What's On Tonight" (page 186). That *TV Guide*-type section takes you, hour-by-hour, through the whole enchilada of what's being aired in English. But for this section our worldwide team has pulled out ten of the very best programs from among those hundreds.

World Time is used throughout, with "winter" and "summer" refer-ring to seasons in the Northern Hemisphere.

"Omnibus"
BBC World Service

The BBC World Service is no longer the grand master of international broadcasting. The breadth and quality of entertainment that for decades made it the world's favorite international broadcaster have been replaced by a format geared more to news and current affairs than to full-scale entertainment.

Fortunately, a number of solid offerings remain from the old lineup, including the appropriately named "Omnibus." Each edition spotlights a single subject, which can be just about anything, from just about anywhere. It might be living with African elephants, the history of hamburger, a legacy of the Chicago Stockyards or revolutionary schooling in rural Pakistan. It is radio without borders.

Behind the program's success is a wealth of human interest. Sensitive subjects are treated with a deft touch, such as when the program covered the final 24 hours before an execution in the United States. On-site reporting from both inside and outside the prison, including the execution itself, was handled with a sensibility rarely found in broadcasting.

Helen Seeney, producer of "Inside Europe." DW

The first opportunity for listeners in *North America* is at 0430 Sunday (local Saturday evening in the U.S. and Canada) on 5975 and 6175 kHz, with a repeat at 1130 Tuesday on 5965, 6195 and 15220 kHz.

Europe gets two Tuesday slots: 1130 on 9410 (winter), 12095, 15565 and 17640 kHz; and seven hours later, at 1830, on 6195 (winter), 9410, 12095 and 15575 kHz.

In the *Middle East*, try 0430 Sunday and 1130 Tuesday on 11760 and 15575 kHz, and 1830 Tuesday on 12095 kHz.

Southern Africa gets two bites: 1930 Monday on 3255, 6190 and 15400 kHz; and 0830 Tuesday on 6190, 11940 and 15400 kHz.

In *East Asia*, the first airing is at 0620 Saturday on 15360, 17760 and 21660 kHz; with repeats at 0030 Monday on 15280 and 15360 kHz, and 1130 the same day on 9580, 9740, 11955 and 15280 kHz. Listeners in *Southeast Asia* can go for 0620 Saturday on 9740, 11955

Opposite: Stuart McLean hosts Canada's "Vinyl Cafe," a mix of storytelling and eclectic music.

Rajiv Sharma is host and producer of "Spectrum," Deutsche Welle's popular science show. DW

and 15360 kHz; 0030 Monday on 6195 and 15360 kHz; or 1130 Monday on 6195 and 9740 kHz.

Australasia has three slots: 0620 Saturday on 7145, 11955 and 15360 kHz; and 1830 Saturday and 0920 Monday on 9740 kHz.

"The Vinyl Cafe"
Canadian Broadcasting Corporation/ Radio Canada International

Program planners are a strange breed, often alienating their listeners with seemingly inexplicable changes.

In 1998, for example, the BBC World Service dropped the long-running and popular "Anything Goes" and "A Jolly Good Show." Anything Goes was a request program which fully lived up to its title, and when it disappeared, bewildered devotees were left wondering where they could find a suitable replacement. What they got, instead, was a mediocre hybrid, "Wright Around the World." Listeners howled, but their complaints fell on deaf ears. The decision stood.

Radio Canada International to the rescue. RCI's program lineup includes several popular shows from its parent organization, the Canadian Broadcasting Corporation. Among them is "The Vinyl Cafe," one of a kind on the international airwaves.

The Vinyl Cafe and its equally legendary owner, Dave, provide host Stuart McLean with all he needs for a 55-minute show which combines old-fashioned storytelling with an eclectic selection of music—some of it from way down memory lane.

Be warned—the music is, well, cosmopolitan: "Some Enchanted Evening," "Larry the Polar Bear" and Jack Teagarden's version of "I Gotta Right to Sing the Blues" all in one program. Or oink along with "Prom Night in Pigtown," followed by "Lullaby of Birdland" and Kid Ory's "Smokehouse Blues."

Still not sure? Then how about "The Egg Plant that Ate Chicago," "Tip-Toe Thru' the Tulips" and "Rule Britannia" sharing the same stage?

Since "The Vinyl Cafe" is intended primarily for North America, the rest of the world has to depend on the munificence of the ionosphere. Best bet is in summer, when the show is targeted farther afield and on more frequencies.

It is aired winters at 0305 Sunday (local Saturday evening in North America) and can be heard in the United States and Caribbean on 6155, 9755 and 9780 kHz; summers, it goes out one hour earlier and can be heard throughout the Americas on 9535, 9755, 11715, 13670 and 15305 kHz.

"Inside Europe"
Deutsche Welle

Perhaps it is because Europe has more countries broadcasting on world band than other continents, or maybe there are cultural factors. But whatever the reason, Europe is well ahead of the pack when it comes to informing the world what's happening on home soil.

Some of the best reporting from and about that continent originates with Deutsche Welle, whose flagship program, "NewsLink," concentrates on in-depth news and analysis. Supplementing this *tour de force* of European reporting is the weekly "Inside Europe," which explores topical issues from Iceland to the Urals.

The first five minutes are given over to a roundup of news from European capitals, with the rest of the half hour devoted to stories that are sometimes well off the beaten track. Sandwiched within the program is a regular "Inside Europe" quiz.

The first two items usually deal with important political developments, but then the focus is increasingly on topics of general interest, like bootlegging fuel into Britain, a home for homosexual senior citizens, or wine battles and tomato fights in Spain.

Deutsche Welle's "Inside Europe" staff: Helen Seeney (with script), Thorsten Karg, Gabriel von Radloff and Ellen Saenger. DW

For whatever reason, "Inside Europe" is transmitted only to Africa and North America. The first airing is for *North America* and the *Caribbean* at 0115 Sunday (Saturday evening local American date), winter on 6040, 6145, 9640, 9700 and 9790 kHz; and summer on 6040, 9640, 11810 and 13720 kHz.

A repeat broadcast is available three hours later, at 0415, for *Central*, *East* and *Southern Africa*, winter on 7280, 11785 and 11965 kHz; summer on 7225, 9565, 9765 and 13690 kHz. The final slot, for *West Africa* at 0615, is heard well beyond the intended target area, and can be found winter on 7225, 9565 and 11785 kHz; summer on 13790, 15185 and 17860 kHz. In the Middle East, try 21680 kHz.

"Russian Musical Highlights of the 20th Century"
Voice of Russia

Most international broadcasters have apparently decided to spare their listeners an onslaught of Y2K shows. One station, though, has decided to make the most of the opportunity. It is ending the old millennium and beginning the new one in style with two 100-part series covering events of the past century. It's solid stuff, what millennium shows should be but almost never are.

Not many broadcasters—world band or otherwise—have the resources to produce something that extensive, but the Voice of Russia, although woefully underfunded, has a vast collection of sound archives. "The 20th Century: Year After Year" is a noteworthy serial documentary, while "Russian Musical Highlights of the 20th Century" includes some of the greatest musical performances ever heard on radio.

No series trying to cover the events of an entire century can ever hope to be complete, and "Russian Musical Highlights" is no exception. Its primary focus is on the panorama of Russian music in the 20th century, and to that end it succeeds admirably. Programs emphasize classical music, but also include Russian ballads, jazz and other forms of musical expression. Some recordings are extremely rare and include electrifying performances from some of the greats of Russian music.

While it is the music that occupies center stage, the accompanying narrative is informative, occasionally anecdotal, and often surprising in some of the little-known facts it reveals. Although barely 20 minutes in length, each show is repeated several times a week, and the series is scheduled to continue throughout 2000.

If you are inspired by musical tradition and performance, this is "must" listening.

Winter in *North America*, try 0331 Wednesday (Tuesday evening local American date) and 0231 Friday on 7180, 9865, 9875 and 12020 kHz (5940 kHz should also be available at 0331). A third slot is available at 0531 Wednesday on 5920, 6065, 7125, 7180, 9850, 12000, 12020 and 13640 kHz. In summer, one hour earlier, there's 0231 Wednesday and 0131 Friday on 9665 and 15595 kHz; and 0431 Wednesday on 7125, 9665, 15595, 17630, 17660 and 17690 kHz.

First winter slot for *Europe* is at 1531 Tuesday on 6030 and 7440 kHz, with repeats at 2131 Wednesday on 5940, 5965, 7300, 7340 and 9890 kHz; and 1831 Thursday on 5940, 5965, 7340, 9480 and 9490 kHz. Summer slots are at 2031 Wednesday on 9720, 9775, 9820, 11675 and 15485 kHz; and 1731 Thursday on 9720, 9775, 9820, 11675 and 15545 kHz.

The *Middle East* and *Southern Africa* have nothing officially available to their parts of the world; best bet in winter is 1831 Thursday on 7305 kHz; one hour earlier in summer on 12065 kHz.

For *East* and *Southeast Asia* it's 1531 Tuesday, winter only, on 11500 kHz. Unfortunately, there's nothing available in summer.

Australasia is better served. In winter, tune in at 0631 Tuesday on 15460, 15470, 15525,

17570 and 21590 kHz; summer, it's an hour earlier on 17625 and 21790 kHz.

"Health Matters"
BBC World Service

There is no shortage of science shows on the international airwaves, and most include coverage of developments in medicine and medical research. Thing is, these tend to reflect the views of doctors and researchers.

The BBC's 25-minute "Health Matters" stands the concept on its head, looking at clinical medicine and health issues from the patient's perspective. It is often recorded *in situ* at hospitals, clinics and operating rooms—sometimes even at patients' bedsides.

As might be expected with such a broad sweep, the show covers not only conventional topics like nutrition, contraception, mental health and child care, but also alternative medicine, unconventional therapies and offbeat discoveries. It is here, for example, you'll discover that hepatitis B was found in an Egyptian mummy.

Listeners in *North America* have two opportunities to tune in: 1405 Monday on 9515, 9590 (winter), 11865 (summer), 15220 and 17840 kHz; and 0030 Tuesday

The "Russian Musical Highlights" team, including (standing, from left) Svetlana Afanasyeva, recording engineer; Emil Akopov, translator and editor; and Olga Fyodorova, author. Seated are Carl Watts and Svetlana Yekimenko, program hosts. VOR

Jane Hanson interviews José Carreras for "Health Matters." His cancer led to the formation of the Three Tenors, and he continues to raise funds for the José Carreras Leukemia Foundation.

A. Ward, BBC

(local Monday evening in the Americas) on 5975, 6175 and 9590 kHz.

Europe has three Monday slots: 0835 on 9410 (winter), 12095, 15565 and 17640 kHz; 1405 on 12095, 15565 and 17640 kHz; and 1905 on 3955 (winter), 6195, 9410 and (summer) 12095 kHz.

In the *Middle East* the timings are the same as for Europe, but on different channels: 0835 winter on 11760 or 15565 kHz, replaced summer by 17640 kHz; 1405 on 15575 kHz (12095 kHz may also be available in winter); and 1905 on 9410 and (summer) 12095 kHz.

For *Southern Africa* there are two options, both on Monday: 0805 on 6190, 11940 an 15400 kHz; and 1405 on 6190, 11940, 21470 and 21600 kHz.

In *East Asia*, Monday is again the day to listen: 0120 on 15280 and 15360 kHz; 0635 on 15360, 17760 and 21660 kHz; 1405 on 5990, 6195 and 9740 kHz; and 2130 on 5965, 6110, 6195 and 11945 kHz. For *Southeast Asia* (same slots), it's 0120 on 6195 and 15360 kHz; 0635 on 9740, 11955 and 15360 kHz; 1405 on 6195, 9740 and (summer) 15310 kHz; and 2130 on 3915, 6195 and 9740 kHz.

Australasia shares three of the timings for East and Southeast Asia: 0635 on 7145, 11955 and 15360 kHz; 1405 on 9740 kHz; and 2130 on 5975 and 9740 kHz.

"Global Village"
Canadian Broadcasting Corporation/ Radio Canada International

"Global Village" is radio's home of world music. Here you can find traditional folk music—very much alive despite efforts to reclassify it—along with ethnic music in its distinct manifestations and cross-cultural incarnations generally thought of as New Age.

Internationally known artists such as Taj Mahal, Gilberto Gil, Litto Nebbia and Ravi Shankar share the stage with lesser-known but equally proficient musicians like 90-year-old Cuban guitarist Compay Segundo, Indian popular singer Udit Naryan, the great Nubian 'ud and tar player Hamza El-Din, and the queen of black Peruvian music, Susana Baca.

For some really rare performances, lend an ear to the exotic sounds of Australian aborigine Keith Lapulung and the Wirrinyga Band, some exquisite Vietnamese melodies

Quality Communications Equipment Since 1942

COMMERCIAL RECEIVERS

The Watkins-Johnson HF-1000 is *the* ultimate receiver! Advanced D.S.P. technology, 58 bandwidths, 1 Hz display. Under $4000.

AMATEUR RADIO EQUIPMENT

iCOM ALINCO

STANDARD

KENWOOD
YAESU
JRC

Universal has been selling the finest new and used amateur radio equipment since 1942 and is an authorized sales *and* service center for all major lines.

WIDEBAND RECEIVERS & SCANNERS

AOR ALINCO SONY
uniden
Bearcat YAESU iCOM

Universal carries an extensive line of scanners and wideband receivers from all major manufacturers including AOR, Alinco, ICOM, Sony, Yaesu and Uniden-Bearcat. The models AOR AR8200 and Sony ICF-SC1PC are shown.

SPECIALTY RECEIVERS

Our latest catalog features an assortment of specialty receivers. We are pleased to offer the new line of self-powered Baygen AM/FM and AM/FM/SW FreePlay (shown) radios. Be prepared with the new Sony emergency radio. Grundig and Midland weather band radios are also available. Our affordable General Electric Super Radio III is a favorite for AM band DXing.

HUGE FREE CATALOG

The **Universal Communications Catalog** covers everything for the shortwave, amateur and scanner enthusiast. With prices, photos and informative descriptions. This 120 page catalog is **FREE** by bookrate or for $3 by Priority mail (5 IRCs airmail outside N. America). Rising postage costs prevent us from sending this catalog out automatically so request your copy today!

COMMUNICATIONS RECEIVERS

YAESU AOR KENWOOD
DRAKE
JRC
iCOM

Universal Radio carries an excellent selection of new and used communications receivers. JRC NRD-545 shown.

PORTABLE RECEIVERS

GRUNDIG
SONY
iCOM
SANGEAN

Universal offers over 40 portable receivers from $50 to over $500. Our **free** catalog fully describes all models.

BOOKS

Shortwave Receivers Past & Present *By F. Osterman*
This huge 473 page guide covers over 770 receivers from 98 manufacturers, made from 1942-1997. Entry information includes: receiver type, date sold, photograph, size & weight, features, reviews, specifications, new & used values, variants, value rating & availability. Become an instant receiver expert. $24.95 (+$2)

Passport To Worldband Radio *By L. Magne*
Graphic presentation of all shortwave broadcast stations. Equipment reviews, too. A *must have* book. $19.95 (+$2)

World Radio TV Handbook
All shortwave broadcast stations organized by country with schedules, addresses, power, etc. $24.95 (+$2)

Worldwide Aeronautical Frequency Dir. *By R. Evans*
The definitive guide to commercial and military, HF and VHF-UHF aero comms. including ACARS. $19.95 (+$2)

Guide to Utility Stations *By J. Klingenfuss*
Simply the best guide to non-broadcast stations. 11,600 frequencies CW, SSB, AM, RTTY & FAX. $39.95 (+$2)

Discover DXing! *By J. Zondlo*
An introduction to DXing AM, FM and TV. $5.95 (+$2)

Joe Carr's Receiving Antenna Handbook *By J. Carr*
Arguably the best book devoted to receiving antennas for longwave through shortwave. $19.95 (+$2)

☞ *Please add $2 per title for USA shipping, $4 for foreign.*

Universal Radio, Inc.
6830 Americana Pkwy.
Reynoldsburg, Ohio
43068-4113 U.S.A.

☎ **800 431-3939** Orders & Prices
☎ 614 866-4267 Information
→ 614 866-2339 FAX Line
📧 dx@universal-radio.com

www.DXing.com and
www.universal-radio.com

- Visa
- Mastercard
- Discover

- Prices and specs. are subject to change.
- Returns subject to a 15% restocking fee.
- Used equipment list available.

from the Khac Chi Ensemble, or evocative Yiddish tunes from the oddly named Flying Bulgar Klezmer Band.

But it's not all music. There are also reports and interviews from around the world, and this is where the show doesn't always live up to expectation. The talk can be intrusive, especially when the music is tantalizingly faded down. Overall, though, "Global Village" is an ear-opener like no other.

Alas, it is only aimed at listeners in the Americas, maybe because of the difficulty in fitting a 55-minute show into RCI's schedule for other parts of the world. "Global Village" is aired winters at 0005 Sunday (local Saturday evening in North America) and can be heard in the United States and Caribbean on 5960 and 9755 kHz; summers, it is available one hour earlier and can be heard throughout the Americas on 5960, 9755, 11895, 13670, 15305 and 17695 kHz.

"EuroQuest"
Radio Netherlands

This is not just another program from and about Europe. Rather, it is a selection of the best of Radio Netherlands' European reporting combined with reports from stringers scattered around the continent. It differs from Deutsche Welle's "Inside Europe" in that less airtime is given to political stories, but more to environmental issues, social trends, the arts, science and topics of general interest. Too, it has the unmistakable stamp of a lively, first-rate Radio Netherlands' production.

This is no sound-alike McProgram. Gun control in Switzerland, gypsies in France, lottery addiction in Italy, sumo wrestling in Holland, Russian mafiya in Poland, poetry in Iceland and pollution in Istanbul are just some of the offbeat topics.

The show is hosted by Jonathan Groubert, whose spell as host of the legendary "Happy Station" rankled some listeners.

However, he appears to have found his niche with "EuroQuest," to the delight of station and listeners alike.

All editions of the program are broadcast on Monday.

In *North America*, tune in at 2355 on 6165 and 9845 kHz. The timings for *Europe* are a little more complicated: winters, it's 1255 on 6045 and 9855 kHz; and summers, two hours earlier (1055) on 6045 and 9860 kHz.

In *Southern Africa*, expect a solid year-round signal at 1855 on 6020 kHz.

For *East* and *Southeast Asia* it's a 1055 slot, winters on 7260 and 12065 kHz; and summers on 12065 and 13710 kHz. *Australasia* has the same timing, but year round on 9820 kHz.

Not all editions start exactly at five minutes before the hour; sometimes the start is delayed for two or three minutes.

"Spectrum"
Deutsche Welle

"Spectrum" is Deutsche Welle's weekly half-hour peek into science and technology. Subjects like the diagnosis and treatment of terminal diseases are treated with sensitivity, while there is serious coverage of such esoterica as organophosphate toxins and bovine somatotropin. But when the topic is an analysis of Einstein's brain or the pros and cons of sunbathing, be prepared for fun, as well as some atrocious puns.

Host, editor and producer Rajiv Sharma feels that it's important for ordinary people to relate to developments that affect their lives. His program gives science and technology a lighter touch, presented in a way most people can relate to. As a result, it helps offset the dogmatic hostility toward science found in much of the world.

The only edition for *North America* is heard at 0315 Sunday (Saturday evening, locally),

Radio Netherlands'
"Euroquest" staff
displays its awards for
broadcasting excellence.
RNW

winter on 6045, 9535, 9640, 9700 and 11750 kHz; and summer on 9535, 9640, 11810, 13780 and 15105 kHz.

In *Southern Africa*, tune in at 1615 Saturday, winter on 9735, 11785, 15145, 17800 and 21780 kHz; and 7225, 9565, 9765 and 13690 kHz midyear.

"Spectrum" is not officially available for East and Southeast Asia, nor for Australasia. Fortunately, there is an edition for *South Asia* at 1615 Saturday which is also audible in other parts of Asia, as well as parts of Australasia. Winter, try 6170, 7225, 7305, 15380 and 17810 kHz; with 6170, 7225, 7305 and 17595 kHz the likely summer channels.

The only other opportunity is the 1915 Saturday airing for *West Africa*, which gets out far beyond the target area. Best winter bets are 7225, 9565 and 11785 kHz; summer, go for 11785, 11810, 13790, 15390 and 17810 kHz. At least one of these frequencies is usually audible in eastern North America.

> There is serious coverage of organophosphate toxins and bovine somatotropin, but be prepared for atrocious puns.

"Cadenza"
Radio New Zealand International

Peter Fry plays light classics in "Cadenza."
RNZI

Good radio shows are like wrestling matches. Some rely on star attractions to keep fans happy, while others stay popular by being consistently entertaining. Radio New Zealand International's "Cadenza" falls into the second group. There are few star performances in this weekday show of light classical music, but the program pleases time and again.

A harpsichord sonata fits snugly between a Verdi aria and a Ravel minuet; a Faustian song from Mephistopheles follows a rousing chorus from a Gilbert and Sullivan operetta; and a piano interlude by Chopin slows the pace after an Offenbach march. It's a musical balancing act performed with aplomb.

The VOA's "Talk to America" team doesn't shy away from controversy, which helps make the show a "must-hear" worldwide.   VOA

"Cadenza" can be heard Monday through Friday at 0006-0100 on 17675 kHz. There are also three weekly repeats, at 0606 Monday and Thursday and 0706 Wednesday on 9700 (or 17675) kHz. All times are one hour later midyear, when New Zealand, being in the Southern Hemisphere, is off daylight saving time.

"Talk to America"
Voice of America

The trouble with call-in shows is that too many things can go wrong. Guests don't respond well to questions, the questions aren't interesting, or the host has difficulty keeping the program lively when interest flags.

The VOA's "Talk to America" is not immune from these problems, but fares better than most. It is the most regular program of its kind on the international airwaves, and has earned a substantial following worldwide. Moreover, it is the best program on the CNN-without-pictures that the VOA has become.

Of special interest are pragmatic medical themes, such as eye disease and neo-natal mortality. More controversial have been programs like "Person of the Century—Adolf Hitler," "The Women of Afghanistan—Another View" and "Can Russia Survive?"

Keep a date with the VOA at 1710 Monday through Friday. There are no transmissions nominally available for lunchtime listeners in North America, since the VOA's charter prohibits it from broadcasting to a U.S. audience. Nevertheless, some of the higher frequencies beamed to other areas are audible within the U.S. and Canada.

"Talk to America" is heard in *Europe*, *North Africa* and the *Middle East* winters on 6040 and 9760 kHz, and summers on 9700, 9760 and 15255 kHz. For the rest of *Africa* there's 15410 (or 15240), 15445 and 17895 kHz year round.

East and *Southeast Asia* are served winters by 5990, 6110, 9670, 9795, 11955, 12005 and 15255 kHz; summers by 5990, 6110, 6160, 7125, 7150, 7170, 9550, 9645, 9770 and 11870 kHz. And last but not least, insomniacs in *Australasia* can hear the show winters on 9670 and 15255 kHz, and summers on 6045 and 15395 kHz.

———————————

Prepared by Don Swampo and the staff of PASSPORT TO WORLD BAND RADIO.

"The Best Results Throughout the Shortwave Spectrum."

— Larry Magne, Radio Database International White Paper

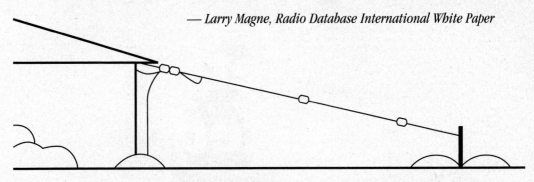

Get World-class, Multi-band Reception with
ALPHA DELTA DX-SWL SLOPER ANTENNA

Just $79.95 Plus Shipping from Your Alpha Delta Dealer!

- Fully assembled, ready to use, and built for long life. So strong, it can even be used to transmit—up to 2 kW! Stainless steel hardware.

- Superior multi-band performance on 13, 16, 19, 21, 25, 31, 41, 49, 60, 90, 120 meters, plus the AM broadcast band (.5–1.7 MHz). All in a single, compact antenna. Alpha Delta first!

- Efficient multi-band frequency selection by means of special RF choke-resonators—instead of lossy, narrow band traps.

- Coaxial feed system reduces electrical and computer noise pickup.

- Overall length just 60 feet. Requires only a single elevated support—easier to install than a dipole.

- 50-ohm feedpoint at apex of antenna for maximum DX reception. A UHF connector is provided on the mounting bracket for easy connection to your coax.

- A top overall rating in Radio Database International's hard-hitting White Paper, "RDI Evaluates the Popular Outdoor Antennas."

At your dealer, or add $5.00 for direct U.S. orders (exports quoted)

- Model DX-SWL, AM broadcast thru 13 meters, 60 ft. long $79.95
- Model DX-SWL-S, as above, but 90 thru 13 meters, only 40 ft. long $69.95

ALPHA DELTA COMMUNICATIONS, INC.

P.O. Box 620 • Manchester, KY 40962 • Toll-Free Order (888) 302-8777
Phone (606) 598-2029 • Fax (606) 598-4413 • www.alphadeltacom.com

Compleat
Idiot's Guide
to Getting
Started

Four "Must" Tips to Catch
the World

World band radio is information and entertainment, on the spot— your unfiltered connection to what's going on. But it's not as easy to receive as conventional radio, so here are three "must" tips to get started.

"Must" #1: **World Time and Day**

World band schedules use a single worldwide time, *World Time*. After

all, world band radio is global, with stations broadcasting around-the-clock from virtually every time zone.

Imagine the chaos if each station used its own local time for scheduling. In England, 9 PM is different from nine in the evening in Japan or Canada. How would anybody know when to tune in?

World Time, or Coordinated Universal Time (UTC), was formerly and in some circles is still known as Greenwich Mean Time (GMT) or, in the military, "Zulu." It is keyed to the Greenwich meridian in England and is announced in 24-hour format, like military time. So 2 PM, say, is 1400 ("fourteen hundred") hours.

There are four easy ways to find out World Time. First, near North America and the Pacific you can tune to one of the standard time stations, such as WWV in Colorado and WWVH in Hawaii in the United States, or CHU in Ottawa, Canada. WWV and WWVH are on 5000, 10000 and 15000 kHz, with WWV also on 2500 and 20000 kHz; CHU is on 3330, 7335 and 14670 kHz. There, you will hear time "pips" every second, followed just before the beginning of each minute by an announcement of the exact World Time. The ultimate in boring, but very handy when you need it.

> **Imagine the chaos if each station used its own local time for scheduling.**

Second, you can tune to one of the major international broadcasters, such as London's BBC World Service or Washington's Voice of America. Most announce World Time at the top of the hour.

Third, on the Internet you can access World Time at such sites as the U.S. Navy's tycho.usno.navy.mil/what.html site, or Canada's www.nrc.ca/inms/time/cesium.shtml site operated by the NRC.

Fourth, here are some quick calculations:

If you live on the East Coast of the United States, *add* five hours winter (four hours summer) to your local time to get World Time. So, if it is 8 PM EST (the 20th hour of the day) in New York, it is 0100 hours World Time.

On the U.S. West Coast, add eight hours winter (seven hours summer).

In Britain, it's easy—World Time is the same as local winter time. However, you'll have to subtract one hour from local summer time to get World Time.

PASSPORT'S FIVE-MINUTE START

No time? Here's how to get going now:

1. The night time is the right time, so wait until evening, when signals are strongest. If you live in a concrete-and-steel building, put your radio by a window or sit on the balcony.

2. Make sure your radio is plugged in or has fresh batteries. Extend the telescopic antenna fully and vertically. Set the DX/local switch (if there is one) to "DX," but otherwise leave the controls the way they came from the factory.

3. Turn on your radio. Set it to 5900 kHz and begin tuning slowly toward 6200 kHz; you can also try 9400-9900 kHz. You will now begin to encounter a number of stations from around the world. Adjust the volume to a level that is comfortable for you. *Voilà!* You are now initiated.

Other times? Read on, especially "Best Times and Frequencies for 2000."

Elsewhere in Western Europe, subtract one hour winter (two hours summer) from local time.

Live elsewhere? Flip through the next few pages until you come to "Setting Your World Time Clock."

Once you know the correct World Time, adjust your radio's World Time clock so you'll have the time handy whenever you want to listen. No World Time clock? Get one now unless you enjoy doing weird computations in your head (it's 6:00 PM here, so add five hours to make it 11:00 PM, which on a 24-hour clock converts to 23:00 World Time—but, whoops, forgot that it's summer so should have added four hours instead of five . . .), it'll be the best money you've ever spent.

Remember that at midnight a new *World Day* arrives. This can trip up even experienced listeners—sometimes radio stations, too. So if it is 9 PM EST Wednesday in New York, it is 0200 hours World Time *Thursday*. Don't forget to "wind your calendar"!

WORLD TIME CLOCKS

Because World Time uses 24-hour format, digital clocks are much less confusing to read than analog timepieces with hands. Some radios, such as the Sony ICF-2010 portable, include a World Time clock that is displayed at all times—these are best. Many other radios have World Time clocks, but you have to press a button to have the time replace the frequency in the display, while some radios have no 24-hour clock at all.

This clock from ZEIT boasts accuracy to within one second over a million-year period.

Basic Models

If your radio has no clock, a separate 24-hour clock is a virtual "must." Here are three value-priced choices, listed in order of cost, that work well and are easy to find. None displays seconds numerically, and all have slightly limited accuracy because they are not synchronized to an external time standard.

MFJ-107B, $9.95. Bare-bones, but this battery-powered LCD "Volksclock" is good enough for many. Seconds are not displayed numerically.

MFJ-118, $24.95, is similar to the '107B, but with large (1¼" or 32 mm) LCD time characters. Additionally, has an adjustable flip stand and a multilingual 100-year calendar. Seconds are not displayed numerically.

MFJ-114B/114BX, $54.95. If you want your World Time *VISIBLE* and need to see seconds numerically, this clock may be for you. MFJ's 114B uses tall (1¾ inches or 44 mm) bright-red LEDs instead of a limited-contrast LCD. Unlike the '107B and '118, the '114B plugs into the wall, using two "AA" batteries only for backup. The regular '114B model is for 120 VAC, whereas the "X" version is for 220/240 VAC.

Sophisticated Timepieces

For those who want only the very best, there are sophisticated 24-hour clocks ranging from under $100 to over $2,000. Nearly all display seconds numerically, and some synchronize the displayed time with one or another of the atomic clock standards.

A passing traveler plays his Grundig portable for PLA soldiers in Xinjiang, China. E.A. Hozour

"Must" #2: How to Find Stations

PASSPORT provides station schedules three ways: by country, time of day and frequency. By-country is best to hear a given station. "What's On Tonight," the time-of-day section, is like *TV Guide* and includes program descriptions from our listening panel. The by-frequency Blue Pages are ideal for when you're dialing around the bands.

World band frequencies are usually given in kilohertz (kHz), but a few stations use Megahertz (MHz). Forget all the technobabble—the main difference is three decimal places, so 6170 kHz is the same as 6.17 MHz, 6175 kHz identical to 6.175 MHz, and so on. All you need to know is that, either way, it refers to a certain spot on your radio's dial.

You're already used to hearing FM and mediumwave AM stations at the same spot on the dial, day and night, or Webcasts at the same URLs. But things are a lot different when you roam the international airwaves.

World band radio is like a global bazaar where a variety of merchants come and go at different times. Similarly, stations routinely enter and leave a given spot—

frequency—on the dial throughout the day and night. Where you once tuned in, say, a French station, hours later you might find a Russian or Chinese broadcaster roosting on that same spot.

Or on a nearby perch. If you suddenly hear interference from a station on an adjacent channel, it doesn't mean something is wrong with your radio; it probably means another station has begun broadcasting on a nearby frequency. There are more stations on the air than there is space for them, so sometimes they try to outshout each other.

Technology to the rescue! To cope with this, purchase a radio with superior adjacent-channel rejection, also known as selectivity, and give preference to radios with synchronous selectable sideband. PASSPORT REPORTS, a major section of this book, tells you which stand out.

One of the most pleasant things about world band radio is cruising up and down the airwaves. Daytime, you'll find most stations above 11500 kHz; night, below 16000 kHz. Tune slowly, savor the sound of foreign tongues sprinkled alongside English shows. Enjoy the music, weigh the opinions of other peoples, hear the events that shape their lives and yours.

BEST TIMES AND FREQUENCIES FOR 2000

With world band, if you dial around randomly you're just as likely to get dead air as a favorite program. For one thing, a number of world band segments are alive and kicking by day, while some spring to life at night. Others fare better at certain times of the year.

"Neighborhoods" Where to Tune

Official "neighborhoods," or segments, of the shortwave spectrum are set aside for world band radio by the International Telecommunication Union. However, the ITU countenances some broadcasting outside these parameters and enforcement is minimal, so the "real world" situation is actually more generous. This is what's shown below.

This guide is most accurate if you're listening from north of Africa or South America. Even then, what you'll actually hear will vary—depending upon such things as your location, where the station transmits from, the time of year and your radio (e.g., *see* Propagation in the glossary). Although world band is active 24 hours a day, signals are usually best from an hour or two before sunset until sometime after midnight. Too, try a couple of hours on either side of dawn.

Here, then, are the most attractive times and frequencies for world band listening, based on reception conditions forecast for the coming year. Unless otherwise indicated, frequency ranges are occupied mainly by international broadcasters, but also include some domestic stations or overseas relays of domestic stations. In the Americas, 3900-4000 kHz and 7100-7300 kHz are reserved for use by amateur radio ("hams"), even though world band transmissions from other parts of the world manage to be heard there. **Nighttime** refers to your local hours of darkness, plus dawn and dusk.

Possible Reception Nighttime

2 MHz (120 meters) **2300-2495 kHz** (overwhelmingly domestic stations)

Limited Reception Nighttime

3 MHz (90 meters) **3200-3400 kHz** (overwhelmingly domestic stations)

Good-to-Fair in Europe and Asia except Summer Nights; Elsewhere, Limited Reception Nighttime

4 MHz (75 meters) **3900-4050 kHz** (international and domestic stations, primarily not in or beamed to the Americas; 3900-3950 mainly Asian and Pacific transmitters; 3950-4000 also includes European and African transmitters)

Some Reception Nighttime; Regional Reception Daytime

5 MHz (60 meters) **4750-5100 kHz** (mostly domestic stations); eventually should expand to **4500-5400 kHz**.

Excellent Nighttime; Regional Reception Daytime

6 MHz (49 meters) **5730-6300 kHz**

If a station can't be found or fades out, there is probably nothing wrong with your radio. The atmosphere's sky-high *ionosphere* deflects world band signals earthward, Earth bounces them back up to the ionosphere, and so on like a dribbled basketball until they get to your radio. This is why world band radio is so unencumbered—its signals don't rely on cables or satellites or the Internet, just layers of ionized gases which have enveloped our planet for millions of years. World band is free from regulation, free from taxes, free from fees—and largely free from ads, as well.

But nature's ionosphere, like the weather, changes constantly, so world band stations have to adjust as best they can. The result is that broadcasters operate in different parts of the world band spectrum, depending upon the time of day and season of the year.

That same changeability can also work in your favor, especially if you like to eavesdrop on signals not intended for your part of the world. Sometimes stations from exotic locales—places you would not ordinarily hear—become surprise arrivals at your radio, thanks to the shifting characteristics of the ionosphere.

"Must" #3: The Right Radio

Choose carefully, but you shouldn't need a costly set. Avoid cheap radios—they suffer from one or more major defects. With one of the better-rated portables, usually around the price of a VCR, you'll be able to hear much more of what world band has to offer.

Two mighty useful tips: First, purchase a radio with digital frequency display. Its

Good Nighttime; Regional Reception Daytime

7 MHz (41 meters) **7100-7600 kHz (also 6890-6990 kHz)** (7100-7300 kHz, no American-based transmitters and few transmissions targeted to the Americas)

9 MHz (31 meters) **9250-9990 kHz**

Good Nighttime except Mid-Winter; Some Reception Daytime and Winter Nights; Good Asian and Pacific Reception Mornings in America

11 MHz (25 meters) **11500-12200 kHz**

Good Daytime; Good Summer Nighttime

13 MHz (22 meters) **13570-13870 kHz**

15 MHz (19 meters) **15030-15800 kHz**

Good Daytime; Variable, Limited Reception Summer Nighttime

17 MHz (16 meters) **17480-17900 kHz**

19 MHz (15 meters) **18900-19020 kHz**

21 MHz (13 meters) **21450-21850 kHz**

Some Reception Daytime

25 MHz (11 meters) **25670-26100 kHz**

World band signals bounce up and down like a dribbled basketball until they get to your radio.

Platinum Digital (G3D). Digital World Receiver with carrying case. It's an AM/FM/SW radio with Quartz controlled clock! Anyplace, anywhere, anytime – the digital G3D is designed for the person on the go. It's just packed with features that will make life on the road more enjoyable. News, weather, and sports – Grundig covers all the action. It's big on features, yet small enough to fit into a jacket or purse! Illuminated liquid crystal display indicates all operations... from 20-user programmable memories to the quartz-controlled alarm clock, with sleep timer 10 to 90 minutes.

Tuner (Wave ranges):
FM 87.5-108 MHz / MW (10 KHz steps)
520-1710KHz / MW 522-1620KHz /
SW1 2.30-7.40MHz / SW2 9.40-26.10MHz

Shortwave Bands:
120, 90, 75, 60, 49, 41, 31, 25, 22, 19, 16, 13, 11 meters

Batteries:	3 AA (not included)
Dimensions:	5.5" L x 3.5" H x 1.25" W
Weight:	11.52 oz.

Traveller II PE (TR2PE)
The world's best-selling travel radio. A compact radio with outstanding performance! This practical and stylish travel companion features AM, FM and five shortwave bands, plus a world clock for 24-time zones and simultaneous display of home and world time in a digital display. Titanium-look finish. Comes with 3 AA batteries, earphones, carrying pouch.

Tuner Frequency Ranges:
FM	88-108 MHz
AM	530-1600KHz
SW Bands	49, 41, 31, 25 and 19 meters
Output:	Micro Speaker or earphones
Batteries:	3 AA (included)
Dimensions:	5.5" L x 3.5" H x 1.25" W
Weight:	9.92 oz.

Companion

Mini World 100 PE (Mini). Grundig's smallest Pocket World Band Radio....Travel with the world in your pocket. Another exciting breakthrough in world band technology. A well built radio that fits in the palm of your hand. AM/FM-Stereo/SW radio with LED indicator, six shortwave broadcast bands, telescopic antenna, earphones and belt clip make listening easy. Comes with soft carrying case.

Tuner Frequency Ranges

FM	88-108MHz
AM	525-1625MHz
SW1	5.80-6.40MHz
SW2	6.90-7.50MHz
SW3	9.40-7.50MHz
SW4	11.65-12.15MHz
SW5	15.00-15.65MHz
SW6	17.50-18.14MHz

Output:	Micro Speaker or Earphones
Batteries:	2 AA (included)
Dimensions:	2.75" L x 4" H x .75" W
Weight:	4.48 oz.

Weather Band (G2). A radio you can count on to help you prepare for the day ahead. Always be prepared with the G2. Take this incredibly powerful AM/FM weather radio with you on all your outdoor activities. This weather resistant radio is your 24 hour hotline to AM, FM, and the national weather service reports and forecasts. Built-in speaker and telescopic antenna. Comes with earphones.

Frequency Range

AM	503-1710KHz
FM	87.5-108MHz
NOAA Weather Service	162.40
	162.475
	162.55

Out put:	Micro Speaker
Batteries:	3 AAA (not included)
Dimensions:	3" L x 5.25" H x 1" W
Weight:	6.0 oz.

by GRUNDIG

Lextronix / Grundig, P.O. Box 2307, Menlo Park, CA 94026 Tel: 650-361-1611 Fax: 650-361-1724
Shortwave Hotlines: (US) 1-800-872-2228 (CN) 1-800-637-1648 • Web: www.grundigradio.net

accuracy and related digital features will make tuning far easier than with out-moded slide-rule tuning. Second, ensure the radio covers at least 4750-21850 kHz with no tuning gaps. Otherwise, you may not be able to tune in some stations you'd otherwise be able to hear.

You won't need an exotic outside antenna unless you're using a tabletop model. All portables, and to some extent portatops, are designed to well work off the built-in telescopic antenna—or, better, with several yards or meters of insulated wire clipped on.

Does that mean you should avoid a tabletop or portatop model? Hardly, especially if you listen during the day, when signals are weaker, or to hard-to-

SETTING YOUR WORLD TIME CLOCK

PASSPORT's "Addresses PLUS" lets you arrive at the local time in another country by adding or subtracting from World Time. Use that section to determine the time within a country you are listening to.

This box, however, gives it from the other direction—that is, what to add or subtract from your local time to determine World Time at your location. Use this to set your World Time clock.

Where You Are	*To Determine World Time*
North America	
Newfoundland St. John's NF, St. Anthony NF	Add 3½ hours winter, 2½ hours summer
Atlantic St. John NB, Battle Harbour NF	Add 4 hours winter, 3 hours summer
Eastern New York, Atlanta, Toronto	Add 5 hours winter, 4 hours summer
Central Chicago, Nashville, Winnipeg	Add 6 hours winter, 5 hours summer
Mountain Denver, Salt Lake City, Calgary	Add 7 hours winter, 6 hours summer
Pacific San Francisco, Vancouver	Add 8 hours winter, 7 hours summer
Alaska Anchorage, Fairbanks	Add 9 hours winter, 8 hours summer
Hawaii Honolulu, Hilo	Add 10 hours year round
Europe	
United Kingdom, Ireland and Portugal London, Dublin, Lisbon	Same time as World Time winter, subtract 1 hour summer

hear stations. The best-rated tabletop, and even portatop, models have a better chance of bringing faint and difficult signals to life—especially when they're connected to a good external antenna. But if you just want to hear the major stations, you'll do fine with a moderately priced portable. PASSPORT REPORTS rates virtually all available models.

Radio in hand, read or at least glance over your owner's manual—yes, it *is* worth it.

You'll find that, despite a few unfamiliar controls, your new world band receiver isn't all that much different from radios you have used all your life. Experiment with those controls so you'll become comfortable with them. After all, you can't harm your radio by twiddling switches and knobs.

Prepared by Jock Elliott, Tony Jones and Lawrence Magne.

Continental Western Europe; parts of Central and Eastern Continental Europe Paris, Berlin, Stockholm, Prague, Rome, Madrid	Subtract 1 hour winter, 2 hours summer
Elsewhere in Continental Europe; Cyprus Belarus, Bulgaria, Cyprus, Estonia, Finland, Greece, Latvia, Lithuania, Moldova, Romania, Russia (Kaliningradskaya Oblast), Turkey and Ukraine	Subtract 2 hours winter, 3 hours summer

Mideast & Southern Africa

Egypt, Israel, Lebanon and Syria	Subtract 2 hours winter, 3 hours summer
South Africa, Zambia and Zimbabwe	Subtract 2 hours year round

East Asia & Australasia

China, including Taiwan	Subtract 8 hours year round
Japan	Subtract 9 hours year round
Australia: *Victoria, New South Wales, Tasmania*	Subtract 11 hours local summer, 10 local winter (midyear)
Australia: *South Australia*	Subtract 10½ hours local summer, 9½ hours local winter (midyear)
Australia: *Queensland*	Subtract 10 hours year round
Australia: *Northern Territory*	Subtract 9½ hours year round
Australia: *Western Australia*	Subtract 8 hours year round
New Zealand	Subtract 13 hours local summer, 12 hours local winter (midyear)

First Tries: Ten Easy Catches

Here are ten stations in English that are easy to hear nearly anywhere. All times are World Time, explained elsewhere in this PASSPORT.

EUROPE
France

Most international broadcasters are now used to budget cuts, but 1999 will be remembered at **Radio France Internationale** as the year of the financial guillotine. The omnipresent RFI found its transmissions slashed by roughly a third, with broadcasts to North America—already reduced in 1998—all but abandoned. Regular reception of English, small in comparison with French, is now only for the Eastern Hemisphere. Fortunately, RFI's English-language programs continue to be of high quality and are worth seeking out.

Europe: 1200-1300 on 15155 and 15195 kHz.

Middle East: 1400-1500 on 17560 kHz; plus 1600-1730 on 11615 or 15460 kHz (intended mainly for Africa).

South Asia: 1400-1500 on 11610 and 17680 kHz. The latter channel also serves *Southeast Asia* and should be audible in *Australia* (better to the west).

Africa: RFI's African broadcasts are an excellent source of news about that continent, and can often be heard well elsewhere. Audible at 1600-1700 on 11615, 11995, 12015, 15210 and 17605 (or 17850) kHz; and at 1700-1730 on 11615 (or 17605) and 15210 kHz. The 1200 transmission for Europe is also aired to West Africa on 15540 kHz, sometimes also heard in parts of *eastern North America*.

RFI's English-language programs about Africa are excellent.

Germany

The outcome of the 1998 German general election proved to be a disaster for **Deutsche Welle**, with the new government cutting the station's budget by an amount unprecedented among Western broadcasters. As we go to press, the station is fighting moves to eliminate the radio's English news section, which would be a serious blow both for Deutsche Welle and its listeners.

North and Central America: 0100-0145 winters on 6040, 6145, 9640, 9700 and 9790 kHz; summers on 6040, 9640, 11810 and 13720 kHz. The next edition is at 0300-0345: winters on 6045, 9535, 9640, 9700 and 11750 kHz; summers on 9535, 9640, 11810, 13780 and 15105 kHz. The third and final broadcast goes out at 0500-0545, winters on 6100, 6120, 9670 and 11795 kHz; and summers on 9670, 11795 and 11810 kHz. This last slot is best for western North America.

Europe: 2000-2045, winters on 9725 kHz and summers on 11970 kHz. Other English programming is also available at 0600-1330 and 1600-1900 on 6140 kHz.

Middle East: 0600-0645, winters on 21695 kHz; and summers on 21680 kHz.

Southern Africa: 0400-0445 winters (summer in the Southern Hemisphere) on 7280, 11785 and 11965 kHz; summers on 7225, 9565, 9765 and 13690 kHz. The second slot is at 0900-0945 on 9565 (summer), 11785 (winter), 15410, and (winter) 17860 kHz; and the third and final broadcast goes out at 1600-1645, winter on 9735, 11785, 15145 and 17800 kHz; and summer on 9735, 11810, 15135 and 21695 kHz.

East & Southeast Asia and the Pacific: 0900-0945 winters on 6160, 12055, 15255, 15490 and 17820 kHz; summers on 6160, 15470, 17560 and 21680 kHz. A second broadcast—to Australasia—airs at 2100-2145 on 9670 (winter), 9765, 11915 (summer) and (winter)

Deutsche Welle's "Inside Europe" producer Thorsten Karg. DW

A lush garden flourishes in the shadow of a transmitter site at Krasnoyarsk, Siberia. Arto Mujunen, IBB

15135 and 17560 kHz. An additional transmission for East and Southeast Asia is at 2300-2345, winters on 6010, 9690, 9815 and 13690 kHz; summers on 9715, 9815 and 11965 kHz.

Holland

Radio Nederland—or **Radio Netherlands**—is a favorite among listeners. A balanced format of news and entertainment combined with good production techniques places it at the forefront of world band stations.

North America: Solid reception throughout much of North America at 2330-0125 on 6165 and 9845 kHz. Listeners out west

should try 0430-0525 on 6165 and 9590 kHz.

Europe: 1130-1325 winters on 6045 and 9855 kHz, and 1030-1225 summers on 6045 and 9860 kHz.

Southern Africa: 1730-1925 on 6020 kHz.

East Asia: 0930-1125 winters on 7260 and 12065 kHz, and summers on 12065 and 13710 kHz.

Australia and the Pacific: 0930-1125 on 9820 kHz. Too, frequencies for East Asia, above, are well received in parts of the region.

Russia

After two years of having to endure cut after cut in its budget—when the very existence of the station was in doubt—the **Voice of Russia** seems to have finally ensured its survival, albeit at a cost. As part of the agreement for continued funding, the station has to reflect official government policy on domestic and international events. This was never more obvious than during the 1999 Kosovo crisis, when the Voice of Russia sounded like a throwback to the days of Radio Moscow and its infamous Cold War propaganda.

Now operating for 15 hours daily, the Voice of Russia continues to air a number of interesting and entertaining shows, some of which are longtime listener favorites. It is still widely heard in many areas despite budget limitations.

Eastern North America: 0200-0600 winter on 5940 (0300-0400), 7125 (0400-0600) and 7180 kHz; summer, one hour earlier, it's 9665 kHz at 0100-0500 and 7125 kHz at 0300-0500. During winter afternoons, try frequencies beamed to Europe—some make it to eastern North America.

Western North America: In winter, try the following: 0200-0400 on 9865, 9875, 12000

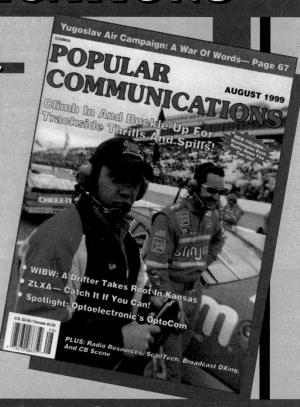

**BBC World Service's
Barbara Myers.**

John Turtle, BBC

and 12020 kHz; and 0400-0600 on 5920, 6065, 9850, 12000, 12020 and 13640 kHz. For summer, one hour earlier, it's 12050 and 15595 kHz at 0100-0300, and 12050, 15595, 17565, 17630, 17660 and 17690 kHz at 0300-0500.

Europe: Winter, at 1500-1600 on 6030 and 7440 kHz; 1800-2000, try 5920 (from 1900), 5940, 5965, 7310 (from 1900), 7340, 9480 and 9890 kHz; for 2000-2200, choose from 5940, 5965, 7300 (from 2100) and 9890 kHz. In summer, try 9730 and 15545 kHz at 1500-1600; then at 1700-1900 it's 7300 (from 1800), 9720, 9775, 9820, 11675 and 15545 kHz. For 1900-2100, pick from 9480 (till 2000), 9720, 9775, 9820, 11675, 12070 (till 2000), 15485 (from 2000) and (till 2000) 15545 kHz.

Middle East: 1600-1800 (1500-1700 in summer). Try 4730, 4940 and 4975 kHz during the first hour, especially to the east. Further winter possibilities are 7210 and 9775 kHz at 1600-1700, and 7305 and 9470 kHz during the next hour. In summer, look to 7325 and 12070 kHz at 1500-1600, and 12070 and 15490 kHz at 1600-1700.

Southern Africa: Officially, nothing is beamed this way, but try 7305 kHz at 1800-2000 winter and 12065 kHz at 1700-1900 summer. These channels are targeted at the Middle East and East Africa, but can make it farther south.

Southeast Asia: 1500-1600 winter on 9775, 9800 and 11500 kHz. In summer, try 0600-0800 on 17655 kHz, 1400-1500 on 12025 and 15550 kHz, 1500-1600 on 11500 kHz, and 1600-1700 on 15550 kHz. Some channels are intended for other regions, but are well heard in Southeast Asia.

SRI now broadcasts from transmitters outside the country.

Celebrating 10 years of BBC Radio Collection

Decades of peerless BBC entertainment is being diluted for more newscasting. BBC

Australasia: 0600-0800 winter on 15460, 15470, 15525, 17495 (from 0700), 17570 and 21790 kHz; and 0800-1000 on 9905, 15470, 15525, 17495 and (till 0900) 21790 kHz. Midyear, 0500-0900 on 15490 (except 0700-0800), 17495 (from 0700), 17625 and 21790 kHz.

Switzerland

Now mostly from transmitters located outside the country, **Swiss Radio International** continues to provide good reception in most parts of the world. Relays formerly via the People's Republic of China have been transferred to Singapore, and Deutsche Telekom's Jülich site has taken over from the long-used Schwarzenburg facility. Most of the Americas are well served by a powerful transmitter in French Guiana.

SRI continues to provide superior coverage of humanitarian and Third World issues, but the heavy news orientation of recent years has given way to a more balanced format of general programming. Fortunately, one thing remains unchanged—the broadcasts still have an unmistakable Swiss flavor.

North America: 0100-0130 and 0400-0500 on 9885 and 9905 kHz.

Europe: Winter at 0500-0530 and 0630-0700 on 9610 kHz; 1100-1130 and 1300-1330 on 9535 (or 9655) kHz; and 2000-2030 on 6165 kHz; summer, one hour earlier, 0400-0430 and 0530-0600 on 13635 kHz; 1000-1030 and 1200-1230 on 15315 kHz; 1900-1930 on 9885 kHz.

Southern Africa: 0730-0800 winter on 9885, 13635 and 15195 kHz; summer on 15545, 17685 and 21750 kHz; and 2000-2030 on (winter) 13790 and (summer), 13710 kHz.

East and Southeast Asia: 1100-1200 winter on 9540 and 21770 kHz; and summer on 13735 and 21770 kHz.

Australasia: 0830-0900 on 9885 and 13685 kHz.

Swiss Radio International is where to turn for humanitarian issues and developments in less prosperous countries.   Swissinfo

United Kingdom

Mediocre management and some inept program changes have left serious dents in the reputation of the **BBC World Service**. The station is still the undisputed world leader in news output, but gone are several entertainment shows enjoyed by millions worldwide. Worse, their "cool" replacements are mediocre.

The time devoted to news and current events continues to be excessive, especially to the Americas, but a number of the better feature and entertainment shows still make for superb listening.

North America: Winter mornings, easterners can tune in at 1000-1100 on 6195 kHz; 1100-1200 on 5965, 6195 and 15220 kHz (6195 and 15220 kHz carry alternative programs for the Caribbean at 1100-1130 on weekdays); 1200-1400 on 5965, 9515, 9590 (from 1300) and 15220 kHz; 1400-1615 on 9515, 9590 (till 1600) and 17840 kHz; and 1615-1700 on 17840 kHz (also available Saturdays on 9515 kHz). Summer is 1000-1100 on 5965 and 6195 kHz; 1100-1200 on 5965, 6195 and 15220 kHz; 1200-1400 on 9515 and 15220 kHz; and 1400-1700 on 9515 (till 1615,

BBC Broadcasting House, Portland Place, London.

Barry Boxall, BBC

Early evenings in eastern North America, go for 5975 kHz at 2100-2200. This slot contains the informative "Caribbean Report," aired at 2115-2130 Monday through Friday, also carried on 15390 and 17715 kHz.

Throughout the evening, most North Americans can listen in at 2200-0500 (0600 in winter) on 5975, 6175 and 9590 kHz (times vary on each channel). In or near the Caribbean you get a two-hour bonus on 6175 kHz at 0600-0800 (one hour earlier in summer).

Europe: A powerhouse 0300-2300 (one hour earlier in summer) on 3955, 6180, 6195, 9410, 12095, 15565, 15575 and 17640 kHz (times vary for each channel).

Middle East: 0300 (0200 in summer)-2100. Key frequencies (times vary according to whether it is winter or summer) are 9410, 11760, 11995 (summer), 12095 and 15575 kHz.

Southern Africa: 0300-2200 on, among others, 3255, 6005, 6190, 11765, 11835 (midyear), 11940, 15400, 21470 and 21660 kHz (times vary for each channel).

East and Southeast Asia: 0000-0300 on 6195 (till 0200), 15280 and 15360 kHz; 0300-0500 on 15280 (till 0530) 15360, 17760 and 21660 kHz; 0500-1030 on 6195 (from 0900), 9740, 11765 (from 0900), 11955, 15360, 17760 and 21660 kHz; 1030-1100 on 6195, 9740 and 11765 kHz; 1100-1300 on 6195, 9580, 9740, 11955 and 15280 kHz; 1300-1615 on 5990, 6195 and 9740 kHz; and 1615-1800 (to Southeast Asia) on 3915 and 7160 kHz. For mornings try 2100-2200 on 3915, 5965, 6110, 6195 and (summer) 11945 kHz; 2200-2300 on 5965, 6195, 7110 and 11955 kHz; and 2300-2400 on 5965, 6035, 6195, 7110, 9660 and 11955 kHz.

Australasia: 0500-0900 on 7145 (0600-0815), 11955 and 15360 kHz; 0900-1100 on 9740 (winter), 11765 (midyear) and (till 1030) 15360 kHz; 1100-1600 and 1800-

Sunday through Friday) and 17840 kHz. In or near the Caribbean tune in at 1000-1100 on 6195 kHz; 1100-1400 on 6195 and 15220 kHz; and 1400-1700 on 17840 kHz. These frequencies are used year round.

For winter in western North America, try 1200-1600 on 9515, 9590 (from 1300), 9740, 15220 and (from 1400) 17840 kHz; and 1600-1900 on 17840 kHz (9515 kHz is also available till 1615, extended to 1700 on Saturdays). In summer, it's 1200-1600 on 9515, 9740, 11865 (from 1300), 15220 and (from 1400) 17840 kHz; and 1600-1800 on 17840 kHz (extended to 2000 on Saturdays); 9515 kHz is also available till 1700 Saturday; 1615 on other days. Note that 9740 kHz carries programs for Asia and the Pacific, which are often different from those targeted at North America.

BRITAIN'S BEST SELLING RADIO MAGAZINES

ARE NOW AVAILABLE WORLDWIDE

TO SUBSCRIBE TO
PRACTICAL WIRELESS OR
SHORT WAVE MAGAZINE JUST
COMPLETE THE FORM BELOW AND
MAIL OR FAX IT THROUGH – OR
CALL US WITH YOUR CREDIT CARD
NUMBER AND WE'LL START YOUR
SUBSCRIPTION IMMEDIATELY.

Practical Wireless

Subscribe to *PW* now and you'll find out why we're
Britain's best selling amateur radio magazine.
We regularly feature:

★ News & reviews of the latest
   equipment
★ Antenna Workshop
★ Radio Scene
★ Radio Basics
★ Focal Point – the world of ATV
★ Valve & Vintage
★ Equipment construction

and much, much more. *PW*
has something for radio
enthusiasts everywhere.

Short Wave Magazine

For everyone, from the newcomer to the
experienced radio monitor, *SWM* is the listeners
magazine with articles and features
written specifically to help
the listener find out what to
buy and where and how to
listen. Regular features
include:

★ News & reviews of the latest
   equipment
★ Utility receiving & decoding
★ Broadcast Stations
★ Bandscan
★ Airband
★ Info in Orbit
★ Scanning

---

1 YEAR SUBSCRIPTION RATES

❏ **PRACTICAL WIRELESS**
❏ **£28.00** (UK)
❏ **£35.00** (Europe)
❏ **£38.00** (Rest of World)
❏ **$55** (USA)

❏ **SHORT WAVE MAGAZINE**
❏ **£33.00** (UK)
❏ **£40.00** (Europe)
❏ **£44.00** (Rest of World)
❏ **$65** (USA)

SPECIAL JOINT SUBSCRIPTION
(BOTH MAGAZINES – 1 YEAR)

❏ **£55.00** (UK)
❏ **£68.00** (Europe)

❏ **£74.00** (Rest of World)
❏ **$110** (USA)

(All credit card orders are charged in pounds sterling – all cheques
must be in US dollars or British pounds please.)

Name..

Address..

....

....

Post/Zip code ....

Telephone No ....
❏ I enclose cheque/PO (Payable to PW Publishing Ltd **£($)** ....
❏ Please charge to my Visa/Mastercard the amount of **£($)** ....

Card No..

Expiry Date ....

Please start my subscription with the ....issue

Signature ....

CREDIT CARD ORDERS
+44 (0) 1202 659930

FAX ORDERS
+44 (0) 1202 +659950

PW Publishing Ltd.,
Arrowsmith Court,
Station Approach,
Broadstone,
Dorset BH18 8PW, UK

E-MAIL
orders@pwpublishing.ltd.uk
WEB SITE
http://www.pwpublishing.ltd.uk

Buddhist monks listen to world band and sample portable television at the Potala, Lhasa, Tibet.

CRI

2000 on 9740 kHz; 2000-2200 on 5975 and 9740 kHz; and 2200-2400 on 11955 kHz. At 2200-2300, 9660 and 12080 kHz are also available for some parts of the region.

ASIA
China

With the new Kunming and Urümqi facilities now fully operational, and strategically placed overseas relays providing additional coverage, **China Radio International** has emerged as one of the major players on the international airwaves. Audio quality from some older transmitters continues to be substandard, but with newer equipment this is less of a problem.

Eastern North America: 0300-0400 on 9690 kHz; 0400-0500 on 9730 kHz; and 0500-0600 (0400-0500 in summer) on 9560 kHz. An experimental relay via Cuba inaugurated in the summer of '99 on 9570 kHz at 0100-0200 may continue into winter, possibly an hour later. Also, a former morning broadcast to eastern North America, dropped several years ago, may be resumed—try 9590 kHz at 1200-1300.

Western North America: As for the east coast 0300-0600, plus 1400-1600 (one hour earlier in summer) on 7405 (or 7265) kHz. Another experimental Cuban relay (see previous paragraph) was started to the western states on 5990 kHz at 2300-2400, and may be one hour later in winter.

Europe: 2000-2200 on 6950 (or 7170) and 9535 kHz. A relay via Moscow is heard winters at 2200-2300 on 7170 kHz, and summers one hour earlier on 9880 kHz.

Middle East: Nothing targeted here, but try the above 2000 transmission to Europe; also 1900-2100 on 9440 kHz for North Africa.

Southern Africa: 1600-1700 on 9565 kHz and 1700-1800 on 7405 and 9570 kHz. 2000-2100 and 2100-2130 are currently using experimental frequencies.

Asia: 1200-1300 on 9715 and 11980 kHz; 1300-1400 on 11980 and 15180 kHz; 1400-1500 on 11825 and 15110 kHz; and 1500-1600 on 7160 and 9785 kHz.

Australasia: 0900-1100 on 11730 and 15210 kHz; 1200-1300 on 7265, 11675 and 15110 kHz; and 1300-1400 on 11675 and 11900 kHz.

Japan

Although **Radio Japan** has recently added more music, it still maintains a strong commitment to news and current events, especially about Japan and the Pacific Rim.

Eastern North America: Best are 1100-1200 on 6120 kHz and 0000-0100 on 11705 kHz via a Canadian relay at Sackville, New Brunswick.

Western North America: 0500 on 6110, 9835 and 15230 kHz; 0600 on 9835 kHz; 1400-1600 on 9505 kHz; and 2100 on (winter) 13630 or (summer) 17825 kHz.

Europe: 0500 on 7230 kHz; 0600 on 5975 and 7230 kHz; 1700 on 7110 kHz; 2100 on 9725 kHz; and 0000 on 6155 and 6180 kHz.

Middle East: 0100 on 11870 kHz and 1400 on 11880 kHz.

Southern Africa: 1500 on 15355 kHz.

Asia: 0100 on 11860, 15325, 15570 and 15590 kHz; 0500 on 11715, 11760, 11840 and 15590 kHz; 0600 on 11740 and 11840 kHz; 1000-1200 on 9695 and 15590 kHz; 1400 on 11730 kHz; 1500 on 7200, 9750 and 11730 kHz; and 1700 on 6090 (winter) and 9825 kHz. Transmissions to Asia are also heard in other parts of the world.

Australasia: 0100 on 17685 kHz, 0300 on 21610 kHz, 0500-0700 on 11850 kHz, 1000 on 11850 kHz, and 2100 on 6035 and 11850 (or 21610) kHz.

NORTH AMERICA
Canada

With substantial budget cuts at RFI, Deutsche Welle and the BBC, **Radio Canada International** can afford a wry smile. After being threatened with imminent closure on more than one occasion, the station is now relatively secure—at least in the short-to-medium term.

RCI continues to rely heavily for programs on the domestic networks of its parent

Radio Canada International's English production staff, (from left) Marc Montgomery, Jim Craig, David Blair, Wojtek Gwiazda and regional reporters Lorn Curry, Frank Rackow, Lynn Desjardins, Robert Jaros and Philippe Murat. RCI

organization, the Canadian Broadcasting Corporation. Most of these shows used to be of interest mainly to Canadians abroad, but the balance has shifted towards programs with more universal appeal.

North America: Morning reception is better in eastern North America than farther west, but the evening broadcasts are usually audible throughout much of the continent. Winters, the first daytime slot is at 1300-1400 (weekdays till 1500) on 9640, 13650 and 17715 kHz. There are also three hours Sunday at 1400-1700 on those same frequencies. In summer it's one hour earlier on 9640, 13650, 17765 and 17820 kHz (except 1300-1600 Sunday, which is on 13650 and 17800 kHz). During winter, evening broadcasts air at 2300-0100 on 5960 and 9755 kHz (6040, 9535 and 11865 kHz are also available part of the time);

VOA News Now anchors Susan Clark and Ray Kouguell. VOA

0200-0300 on 6155, 9535, 9755, 9780 and 11865 kHz; and 0300-0330 (0400, weekends) on 6155, 9755 and 9780 kHz. Summer is 2200-2400 on 5960, 9755 and 13670 kHz; 0100-0200 on 5960, 9535, 9755, 11715, 13670 and 15305 kHz (only 5960 and 9755 kHz are available 0130-0200 weekday evenings); and 0200-0230 (0300, weekends) on 9535, 9755, 11715, 13670 and 15305 kHz. Summer evenings, there is an extra slot at 0500-0530 on 5995, 9755 and 11930 kHz.

The evening transmission for Africa is also audible in parts of North America; winters at 2100-2230 on 11945, 13690, 15150 and 17820 kHz; and summers one hour earlier on 13670, 15150 and 17820 kHz.

Europe: Winters at 1430-1500 on 9555 kHz; 2100-2200 on 5995, 7235, 9805, 11755 and 13650 kHz; and 2200-2230 on 5995, 7235 and 9805 kHz. Summer is one hour earlier: 1330-1400 on 11935 and 15325 kHz; and 2000-2130 on 5995 (till 2100), 7235, 11690, 13650, 15325, 15470 and (till 2100) 17870 kHz.

Europe, Middle East and Africa: 0600-0630 winter on 6090, 6150, 9670, 9780, 11710, 11905, 13690 and 15325 kHz. Summer is one hour earlier on 6145, 7295, 9595, 11710, 15330 and 15400 kHz.

Middle East: Winters, at 0400-0430 on 9505, 9535 and 9645 kHz; and 1430-1500 on 9555 kHz. Summers try 0400-0430 on 11835, 11975 and 15215 kHz; 1330-1400 on 11935 and 15325 kHz; 2000-2130 on 7235 (from 2100), 11690, 13650 and 15325 kHz.

Southern Africa: 2100-2230 winter (summer in Southern Hemisphere) on 13690, 15150 and (to 2200) 17820 kHz; and 2000-2130 summer on 13670, 15150 and 17820 kHz.

Asia: To East Asia at 1200-1230, winter on 6150 and 11730 kHz, and summer on 9660 and 15195 kHz; 1330-1400 on 6150 (summers on 11795) and 9535 kHz; to South Asia at 1630-1700 on 6140 and 7150 kHz; and to Southeast Asia at 2200-2230 on 11705 kHz.

United States

The **Voice of America** has ceased to be the VOA of old. Gone are nearly all music shows, and what few features remain have mostly been incorporated into a "rolling news" format which virtually no listeners appear to want.

Although a new director was appointed in 1999, there seems little hope that this mess will improve—at least, in the short term. But if you like this kind of programming, the VOA is audible just about everywhere.

North America: Best is at 0000-0200 Tuesday through Saturday (local weekday evenings in the Americas) on 5995, 6130, 7405, 9455, 9775 and 13740 kHz (plus 11695 kHz 0000-0100); and 1000-1100 daily on 6165, 7405 and 9590 kHz—this is when the VOA broadcasts to South America and the Caribbean. The African Service can also be heard in parts of North America; try at 1800-2200 (Saturday to 2130) on 15580 and (from 2000) 17725 kHz.

There's not much for *Europe*, but try 0400-0700 on 7170 kHz, 0500-0700 winter on 11825 kHz, 1500-1800 on 15205 kHz, 1700-2100 on 9760 kHz, and 2100-2200 on 6040 or 9760 kHz.

Middle East: 0500-0700 winter on 11825 and 15205 kHz, and 0400-0700 summer on 11965 and 15205 kHz; 1400-1500 (winter) on 15205 kHz; 1500-1800 on 9700 and 15205 kHz; 1700-1900 (winter) on 6040 kHz; and 1800-2200 on 9760 kHz.

Southern Africa: 0300-0500 on 6080, 7275 (midyear), 7340 (to 0330) and 9575 kHz; 0400-0600 (winter) on 9775 kHz; 0500-0700 on 6035 kHz; 1600-2200 (to 2130 Saturday) on 7415, 11920 (winter), 15410, 15445, 15580 and 17895 kHz (not all are available for the full broadcast).

East and Southeast Asia: 1100-1200 on 9760, 11720 and 15160 kHz; 1200-1330 on 9760, 11715 and 15160 kHz; 1330-1500 on 9760 and 15160 kHz; 2200-2400 on 15290, 15305, 17735 and 17820 kHz; and 0000-0100 on 15290, 17735 and 17820 kHz.

Australasia: 1000-1200 on 9645 (from 1100), 9770, 11720 and 15425 kHz; 1200-1330 on 11715 and 15425 kHz, 1330-1500 on 9645 (till 1400) and 15425 kHz; 1900-2000 on 9525, 11870 and 15180 kHz; 2100-2200 on 11870, 15185 and 17735 kHz; 2200-2400 on 15185, 15305 and 17735 kHz; and 0000-0100 on 15185 and 17735 kHz.

Katherine Cole and Judy Massa help keep good entertainment alive at the VOA. The station has shifted over to a "rolling news" format which shows little sign of listener acceptance. VOA

How to choose a World Band Radio

Some electronic goodies, like VCRs, are virtually commodities. With a little common sense you can pretty much get what you want without fuss or bother.

Not so world band receivers, which vary greatly from model to model. As usual, money talks—but even that's a fickle barometer. Some use old technology or misapply new technology, so they're unhandy or function poorly. But others perform nicely.

No Elbow Room

World band radio is a jungle: *1,100 channels*, with stations scrunched cheek-by-jowl. It's much more crowded than FM or mediumwave AM, and to make matters worse the international voyage can make signals weak and quavery. To cope, a

Like their parents, Chinese youngsters make considerable use of world band radio to learn English. E.A. Hozour

radio has to perform exceptional electronic gymnastics. Some succeed, others don't.

This is why PASSPORT REPORTS was created. We've tested hundreds of world band products—the good, the bad and the ugly. These evaluations include rigorous hands-on use by listeners, plus specialized lab tests we've developed over the years. These form the basis of PASSPORT REPORTS, and for some premium models there are Radio Database International White Papers®.

Five Things to Check for

Before you pore over which radio does what, here's a basic checklist:

What to spend? What do you want to hear? Just big stations, or soft voices from exotic lands? Decide, then choose a model that surpasses your needs by a good notch or so—this helps ensure against disappointment without wasting money. After all, you don't need a Ferrari to go to the mall, but you also don't want a motor scooter for the open road.

Research shows that once the novelty wears thin, most people give up on cheap radios. Low-cost radios sound terrible with most stations, and they're clumsy to tune.

> No AM/FM radio compares with the electronic sophistication of serious world band radios.

So if you're just starting out, consider models that sell for $75-200 in the United States or £50-130 in the United Kingdom with a rating of two-and-a-half stars or more. If you're looking for elite performance, shoot for a portable with three-and-a-half stars—at least $330 or £300—or look into one of the pricier portatop or tabletop models.

Keep in mind that, with precious few exceptions, portables don't do brilliantly with tough signals—those that are weak, or hemmed in by interference from other stations. If it's important to you to ferret out as much as possible, think four stars—perhaps five—in a portatop or tabletop. The rub is that these cost more.

Where are you located? Signals tend to be strongest in and around Europe, next-strongest in eastern North America. If you're in either place, you might get by with any of a number of reasonably rated models.

Elsewhere in the Americas, or in Hawaii or Australasia, choose with more care. You'll need a receiver that's unusually sensitive to weak signals—some sort of accessory antenna will help, too.

If you're in a high-rise building, where walls block signals, an ordinary portable radio may be insufficient. Try hedging your bet by buying on a refundable basis, and consider using a Sony AN-LP1 outboard antenna, which is designed especially for portables. Sometimes the best bet for "cliff dwellers" is a tabletop or portatop

FEATURES FOR SUPERIOR PERFORMANCE

A signal should not just be audible, but actually sound pleasant. Several features help bring this about—some keep out unwanted sounds, others enhance audio quality.

Multiple conversion (also called *double conversion*, *up conversion*, *dual conversion* or *two IFs*) is important to reject spurious "image" signals—unwanted growls, whistles, dih-dah sounds and the like. Few models under $100 or £70 have it; nearly all over $150 or £100 do. This borders on a "must" for all but casual listening.

Less vital, but useful, are two or more *bandwidths* for superior rejection of stations on adjacent channels. With multiple bandwidths one should measure between 4 kHz and 7 kHz (at –6 dB), another between 2 kHz and 3 kHz. Most portables come with only one bandwidth, which should measure between 4 kHz and 6 kHz.

A superb high-tech feature which has appeared in recent years is *synchronous selectable sideband* (synchronous detection with selectable sideband). It enhances adjacent-channel rejection while also reducing fading distortion. Some premium models incorporate this *and* multiple bandwidths—a killer combo for minimizing adjacent-channel interference.

Large speakers are an aural plus, as are *tone controls*—preferably continuously tunable with separate bass and treble adjustments. For world band reception, *single-sideband* (SSB) reception capability is irrelevant, but it is essential for utility or "ham" signals. On costlier models you'll get it whether you want it or not.

Heavy-hitting tabletop models and their portatop cousins are designed to flush out virtually the most stubborn signal, but they require experience to operate and are overkill for casual listening. Among these look for a tunable (manually or automatically) *notch filter* to zap howls; *passband offset*, also known as *passband tuning* and *IF shift*, for superior adjacent-channel rejection and audio contouring, especially in conjunction with synchronous selectable sideband; and multiple *AGC* decay rates (e.g., *AGC slow*, *AGC fast)*, ideally with selectable *AGC off*. At some electrically noisy locations a *noise blanker* is essential; some work much better than others.

> A signal should not just be audible, but actually sound pleasant.

Digital signal processing (DSP) is the latest high-tech attempt to enhance mediocre signal quality. Until recently it has been much smoke, little fire, but the technology is finally beginning to click. Watch for more DSP receivers in the years to come, but don't worship at their altar.

With portables and portatops an *AC adaptor* reduces operating costs and may improve weak-signal performance. With tabletop models an *inboard AC power supply* is preferable.

Looking ahead, *digital shortwave transmission* is more a question of how and when, not if. Provided it is compatible with existing analog receivers—*in-band, on-channel* (IBOC)—it should gradually replace traditional analog transmissions. This would result in improved reception quality and reduced transmission costs.

So far the push has been for non-compatible systems which require all-new receivers, not a promising approach. Either way, don't expect to hear world band broadcasts in digital mode anytime soon—they don't exist yet.

Esmail Hozour (center) leads Grundig's world band activities. Here, he inspects the Tecsun Radio manufacturing facility in Dongguang, China, south of Beijing. Lextronix

model fed by a short outboard antenna mounted at or just outside a window or balcony, out in the fresh air.

What features make sense? Divide up features into those which affect performance and those that do not (see sidebars), but don't rely on performance features alone. As PASSPORT REPORTS demonstrates, much more besides features goes into performance.

Where to buy? Whether you buy in a store, through the mail or on the Web

makes little difference. However, unlike TVs and ordinary radios, world band receivers don't test well except in the handful of world band specialty show-rooms with proper outdoor antennas. Even then, long-term satisfaction is hard to gauge from a spot test, so repeated visits are advisable.

Still, even if a radio can't pick up much world band in a store, you can get a good idea of its ergonomics, or "operating handiness." You can also get a thumbnail

PASSPORT STANDARDS: OUR THIRD DECADE

Our reviewers, and no one else, have written everything in PASSPORT REPORTS. These include our laboratory findings, all of which are done by an independent laboratory recognized as the world's leader. (For more on this, please see the Radio Database International White Paper, *How to Interpret Receiver Lab Tests and Measurements*.)

Our review process is completely separate from advertising. Our team members may not accept review fees from manufacturers, nor may they "permanently borrow" radios. International Broadcasting Services does not manufacture, sell or distribute world band radios, antennas or related hardware.

PASSPORT recognizes superior products regardless of when they first appear on the market. We don't bestow annual awards, but rather designate each exceptional model, regardless of its year of introduction, as *Passport's Choice*.

idea of fidelity by listening to mediumwave AM stations. But because mediumwave AM channels are 9 kHz or 10 kHz apart, what you hear may be deceptive, as world band uses 5 kHz spacing.

Are repairs important? Judging from reader feedback, quality and availability of repairs tends to correlate with price. At one extreme, some off-brand portables from China are essentially unserviceable, although most outlets will exchange a defective unit within the warranty. On the other hand, superb service is available for most tabletop and portatop models.

Better portables are almost always serviced or replaced within the warranty. If you can possibly swing it, insist upon a replacement.

Repairs to portables, even from the most respected of manufacturers, can be a nightmare.

After warranty expiration, nearly all factory-authorized service for portables tends to fall short, sometimes even making a radio perform worse instead of better. Swapping, if you can do it, is almost always better than a repair.

With tabletop and portatop models, factory-authorized service is usually available for years to come. Drake, Watkins-Johnson and AOR are legendary in this regard—although Drake recently cut back on its parts and service for models more than 15 years old. Of course, nothing quite equals service at the factory itself.

FEATURES FOR HANDY OPERATION

The most desirable operating feature for any world band radio is *digital frequency readout*—it's a virtual "must" to find stations quickly. A *24-hour clock* for World Time is another "must," being included on many receivers. Best is if it can be read while the frequency is being displayed, but if your favorite radio doesn't have a good clock, then standalone 24-hour clocks and watches are available.

Other important features: direct-access tuning via *keypad* and *presets* ("memories"); and any combination of a *tuning knob*, up/down *slewing controls* or *"signal-seek" scanning* to hunt around for stations. A few radios have handy *one-touch presets* buttons, like a car radio.

Presets are important because world band stations, unlike locals, don't stay on the same frequency throughout the day. Being able to store the various frequencies of a broadcaster makes it easy to tune it in at various hours. With sophisticated tabletop receivers, presets should be able to store not only frequency, but also such other parameters as bandwidth.

Useful but less important is an *on/off timer*—a couple of timer-controlled models even come with built-in cassette recorders. Also, look for an *illuminated display*; *numerically displayed seconds* on the 24-hour clock; and a good *signal-strength indicator*. Travelers prefer portables with power-lock switches that keep the radio from going on accidentally, but the lock on some Chinese portables doesn't prevent display illumination from coming on accidentally.

When ergonomics stand out, bad or good, this is mentioned in the individual receiver's evaluation in PASSPORT REPORTS. In general, though, receivers with comparable levels of performance that have many controls are easier to operate than like similar receivers with few controls. Yes, all those knobs and buttons can actually make operation less complicated.

But technology isn't standing still. If a PC can be operated by a mouse, world band receivers with excellent ergonomics and a minimum of controls can't be far off.

ACCESSORY ANTENNAS: WHO NEEDS THEM?

If you're wondering what accessory antenna you'll need, the answer for portables is usually simple: none, as they come with built-in telescopic antennas. Indeed, for evening use in Europe and eastern North America most portables will perform more poorly with sophisticated outboard antennas than with their built-in ones or a simpler external antenna.

"Volksantenna" for Portables

But if you listen during the day, or live in such places as the North American Midwest or West, your portable will probably benefit from more oomph. Best in the United States is also the cheapest: ten bucks or so for Radio Shack's 75-foot (23-meter or 25-yard) "SW Antenna Kit," which comes with insulators and other goodies, plus $2 for a claw or alligator clip. This sort of "inverted-L" antenna itself may be too long for your radio, but you can always shorten it. Experiment, but as a rough rule of thumb the less costly the portable, the shorter the antenna should be.

Many electronics and world band specialty firms sell parts and wire to make your own inverted-L antenna. An appendix in the Radio Database International White Paper® *Evaluation of Popular Outdoor Antennas* gives foolproof instructions for "rolling your own."

Basically, you attach the antenna to your radio using a claw clip clamped onto the radio's collapsed telescopic antenna—this is sometimes better than the set's external antenna input socket, which may have a desensitizing circuit. Then run the antenna out a window, as high as is safe and practical, to some tall point, like a tree. Unless you want to become Crispy the Cadaver, *keep your antenna clear of any hazardous wiring—the electrical service to your house, in particular—and respect heights.* If you live in an apartment, run it to your balcony, window or roof—away from the building as much as possible.

This "volksantenna" will help with most signals. But if it occasionally makes a station sound worse, just disconnect the claw clip and use your radio's extended telescopic antenna. Protect your radio's innards by disconnecting the antenna when you're not listening—especially when thunder, snow or sand storms are nearby.

Sony Antenna Helps Portables

For apartment dwellers and travelers the Sony AN-LP1 is one of those rare offerings: an active (amplified) antenna that actually improves reception with portables. It's no cure-all, but it definitely helps bring weaker stations out of the mud. ☞ Don't confuse this with the Sony AN-1 antenna, which is not as good.

The Sony ICF-SW07 portable comes with AN-LP2 antenna. The 'LP2 isn't sold separately and doesn't replace the AN-LP1, but rather works only with the 'SW07. Except for automated adjustment, it is identical to the AN-LP1.

Specialized Antennas for Tabletop Models

It's a different story with tabletop receivers. They require an external antenna, either passive or active. Although portatop models don't require an outboard antenna, they work better with one.

Most active antennas use short rods or wires, then amplify signals electronically. For apartment dwellers they can be a godsend—provided they work right. Some are awful, but certain models—notably, Britain's Datong AD 370—work relatively well with tabletop and portatop receivers, although not with portables.

If you have space outdoors, a passive outdoor wire antenna is much better, especially when it's designed for world band. Besides not needing problematic electronic circuits, a good passive antenna also tends to reduce interference from the likes of fluorescent lights and electric shavers—noises which amplified antennas boost, right along with the signal. As the cognoscenti put it, the "signal-to-noise ratio" tends to be better with passive antennas.

Among the best passive models—all less than $100 or £60—are those made by Antenna Supermarket ("Eavesdropper") and Alpha Delta Communications, both available direct or from world band vendors. Detailed test results and installation instructions for these and other models are in the same Radio Database International White Paper® mentioned above, *Evaluation of Popular Outdoor Antennas*.

Eavesdropper wire antennas not only come completely assembled, but are also usually equipped with built-in lightning protectors. For other antennas you can purchase a modestly priced Alpha Delta or DEO lightning protector. Or, if you have deep pockets, there's the Ten-Tec Model 100 protector, which automatically shuts out your antenna and power cord when lightning appears nearby. Still, with any outdoor antenna it is best to disconnect the lead-in and affix it to something like an outdoor ground rod if there is lightning nearby. Otherwise, sooner or later you may be facing a costly repair bill.

A surge protector on the radio's power cord is good insurance, too. These range from low-cost MOV units to innovative Zero Surge devices.

For apartment dwellers and travelers the Sony AN-LP1 active antenna works well with portables.

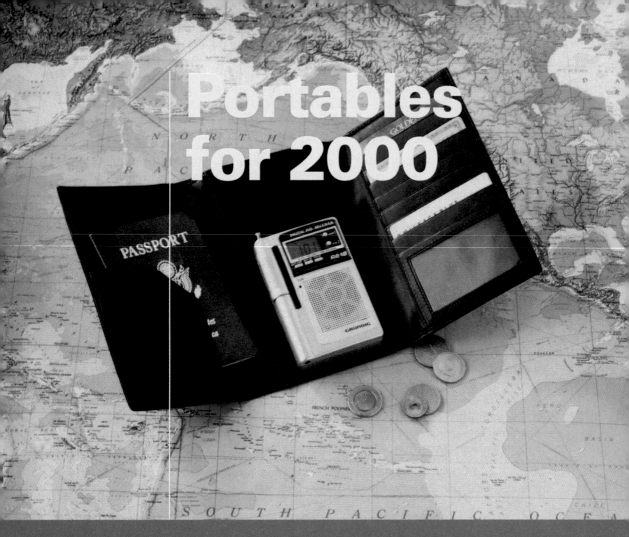

Portables for 2000

Want to hear just the major world band stations?

Look into a good portable. Unless you live in a high-rise the best portables will almost certainly meet your needs—notably during the evening prime-time hours, when signals are strongest. Especially in Europe and the Near East, and even east coast North America, signals tend to come in so well that virtu-ally any highly rated portable should be all you need.

Weak Signals?

Signals are weaker in places like central and western North America, Australasia, and the Caribbean or Pacific islands. There, you should focus on models PASSPORT has found to be unusually sensitive to weak signals. Even in Europe and eastern North America daytime signals tend to be weaker than at night. If you listen then—some programs are heard in North America only during the day—weak-signal performance should be a priority.

Longwave Useful for Some

The longwave band is still used for some domestic broadcasts in Europe, North Africa and Russia. If you live in or travel there, longwave coverage is a slight plus. Otherwise, forget it. Keep in mind that when a low-cost analog model is available with longwave, that band may be included at the expense of some world band coverage.

Sick Radio?

If you wind up purchasing a genuinely defective world band portable, insist upon an exchange, as manufacturers' repair facilities have an atrocious record. Many vendors and virtually all world band specialty outlets will be cooperative if a just-sold radio turns out to be defective or "DOA"; others even have 30-day or similar return policies.

Shelling Out

Only observed selling, or "street," prices (including VAT, where applicable) are cited in PASSPORT. These vary plus or minus, so take them as the general guide they are meant to be. Shortwave specialty outlets often have the best prices, but duty-free shopping is usually no bargain.

We try to stick to plain English, but some specialized terms have to be used. If you come across something that's not clear, check it out in this edition's glossary.

For the time being, Sony consumer electronic products cannot be purchased over the Web. This reportedly is a conscious corporate decision to examine the issue of e-commerce vis-à-vis the Sony organization and its established dealer network.

All Current Models Included

We've scoured the earth to evaluate nearly every digitally tuned portable that meets minimum standards of performance. Here, then, are the results of our hands-on and laboratory tests of current models.

What PASSPORT's Ratings Mean

Star ratings: ✪✪✪✪✪ is best, ✪ is a dog. We award stars solely for overall performance and meaningful features, plus to some extent ergonomics and build quality. Price, appearance, country of manufacture and the like are not taken into account. To facilitate comparison, the same rating system is used for portable and portatop models, reviewed elsewhere in this PASSPORT.

A rating of three or more stars should please most who listen to major stations regularly during the evening. However, for a throw-away on trips, a small portable with as little as one-and-a-half stars may suffice.

If you are listening from a weak-signal part of the world, such as central and western North America or Australasia, best are models that have weak-signal sensitivity among the listed advantages. Too, check out the portatop and tabletop sections of this PASSPORT REPORTS.

Passport's Choice. La crème de la crème. Our test team's personal picks of the litter—digitally tuned portables we would buy or have bought for our personal use.

✐: denotes a price-for-performance value. It may or may not be truly inexpensive, but it provides superior performance for the relatively reasonable amount of money spent.

How Portables Are Listed

Models are listed by size; and, within size, in order of world band listening suitability. Street, or typical selling, prices are given. Models designed for sale in Saudi Arabia do not receive single-sideband signals and may

MAKE YOUR PORTABLE "HEAR" BETTER

Regardless of which portable you own, you can give it at least some additional sensitivity on the cheap.

How cheap? Nothing, for starters.

Look for "sweet spots" to place your radio: near windows, appliances, telephones and the like. If your portable has an AC adaptor, try that, then batteries; usually the AC adaptor does better.

Outdoor Antenna Can Help

An outdoor antenna can help. With portable receivers, simplest is best. Run several meters or yards of insulated wire to a tree, then clip one end to your set's telescopic antenna with an alligator or claw clip. It's fast and cheap, yet effective.

Use it only when needed, disconnecting it during storms and when the radio is off. And don't touch the antenna during dry weather, as you may discharge static electricity from your body right into the radio.

Sophisticated outdoor wire antennas? These work well only with tabletop models, portatop models and field portables. These and even lesser outboard antennas can sometimes cause "overloading," usually at certain times of the night or day on frequency segments with lots of strong signals. You'll know this when you tune around and most of what you hear sounds like murmuring in a TV courtroom scene. Remedy: Disconnect the wire and just use the radio's telescopic antenna.

If you are in a weak-signal location, such as central or western North America, and want stronger signals from your portable, best is to erect an inverted-L (so-called "longwire") antenna. These are available at Radio Shack (278-758, $9.99) and other radio specialty outlets, or may be easily constructed from detailed instructions found in the RDI White Paper, *Popular Outdoor Antennas*.

Indoor Solutions

Antennas work best outdoors, away from inside electrical noises. But if your supplementary antenna has to be indoors, run it along the middle of a window with Velcro or tape. Another solution, in a reinforced-concrete building which absorbs radio signals, is to affix a long telescopic car antenna outdoors almost horizontally onto a windowsill or balcony rail.

Active Antennas

Amplified, or "active," antennas are small and handy, but often do more harm than good with portables—the aim is good signal-to-noise, not just raw gain which can overwhelm circuitry. Inexpensive electronic signal-booster devices also tend to fare poorly, although anecdotal evidence suggests that some do help in given listening situations. Purchase these on a money-back basis so you can experiment with little risk.

Sony has come up with a surprisingly good active antenna for portables, the AN-LP1, sold separately for $79.95. (The "LP" stands for "loop.") It connects to almost any world band portable through its external-antenna socket or by being clipped onto the telescopic antenna. A variety of adapters for this purpose comes with the 'LP1 when it is sold as a separate device.

The AN-LP1 can be used with nearly any portable. A variation, the AN-LP2, is the same thing but with automatic instead of manual bandswitching—it only comes bundled with the new ICF-SW07. As of now the 'LP2 cannot be used with any other radio, but as new Sony models appear presumably they will be designed to work with it.

Both versions use a small amplifier module powered by two "AA" cells, along with a separate loop antenna element that looks like the Jolly Green Giant's favorite tennis racket (see photo). The two parts are joined together by over a dozen feet—four meters—of cable which can be reeled into the amplifier module, like a tape measure. The amplifier, in turn, connects to the radio. For traveling, the "tennis racquet" part of the antenna folds up ingenuously so it can fit neatly into a briefcase.

The AN-LP1 and AN-LP2 both perform nicely, usually boosting signal strength enough to make a real difference with weaker signals. The 'LP1 version has a nine-position manual preselector which improves front-end selectivity and helps allow for suitable gain. The 'LP2 version accomplishes this automatically, but only in concert with the ICF-SW07 for which it was designed. When needed with low-quality portables, the 'LP1 can even do the opposite by allowing you to use a contiguous setting, like an upscale attenuator, to eliminate overloading from in-band powerhouse signals. Thanks to this sophisticated circuitry, antenna-induced overloading occurs only with the lowest quality of portables, and the antenna circuitry itself is thankfully free from cross-modulation and the like.

However, with some radios the antenna's powerful circuitry picks up traces of digital hash being emitted by the receiver itself—fundamentally the result of imperfect receiver shielding, but which wouldn't be a problem if the antenna's non-element components were fully shielded. Perhaps for this reason, the AN-LP1 is not supposed be used with the Sony ICF-SW77, although in practice the combination appears to work satisfactorily. With the top-rated Sony ICF-2010 only a bit of digital hash comes through.

Our tests show that the AN-LP1 provides varying degrees of improvement, depending upon the receiver. As a rough rule of thumb, smaller models benefit more than larger ones, but all show at least some audible improvement. As the ICF-SW07 portable was designed especially to work with the AN-LP2, it really helps with weak signals.

In all, Sony's AN-LP1 and AN-LP2 antennas do yeoman's service with world band radios in need of a modest improvement in weak-signal performance. For many portables, there's nothing better.

☞ Sony makes other models of active antennas (e.g., AN-1, AN-102) for portables. These are passable performers, but the AN-LP1 and AN-LP2 are much better.

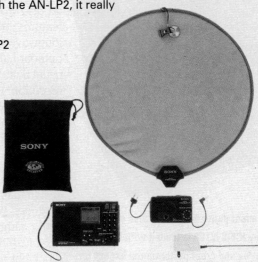

have reduced tuning ranges. Unless otherwise indicated, each digital model includes:

- Tuning by keypad, up/down slewing, presets and "signal-seek" scanning.
- Digital frequency readout.
- Coverage of the world band shortwave spectrum from at least 3200-26100 kHz.
- Coverage of the usual 87.5-108 MHz FM band.
- Coverage of the AM (mediumwave) band in selectable 9 and 10 kHz channel increments from about 530-1700 kHz.

POCKET PORTABLES

Handy for Travel, Poor for Home

Pocket portables weigh under a pound, or half-kilogram, and are somewhere between the size of an audio cassette box and one of the larger hand-held calculators. They operate off two to four ordinary small "AA" (UM-3 penlite) batteries. These diminutive models do one job well: provide news and entertainment when you're traveling.

The world's most petite portable is also one of the best. The Sony ICF-SW100 is loaded with high-tech features and great performance except for speaker audio.

Listening to tiny speakers can be tiring, so pocket portables aren't great for everyday listening. Too, none of the available digitally tuned pocket portables are as sensitive to weak signals as they could be, although some come close.

Don't forget to look over the large selection of compact models, just after the pocket portables reviewed in this section. Their bigger speakers mean they sound better, and they're still quite small.

✪✪✪
Sony ICF-SW100S

Price: $359.95 in the United States. CAN$599.00 as available in Canada. £209.95 in the United Kingdom.

Pro: Extremely small. Superior overall world band performance for size. Excellent synchronous detection with selectable sideband. Relatively good audio when earpieces (supplied) are used. FM stereo through earpieces. Exceptional number of helpful tuning features, including "page" storage with presets. Tunes in relatively precise 100 Hz increments. Worthy ergonomics for size and features. Illuminated display. Clock for many world cities, which can be made to work as a *de facto* World Time clock. Timer/snooze features. Travel power lock. Receives longwave and Japanese FM bands. Amplified outboard antenna (supplied), in addition to usual built-in antenna, enhances weak-signal reception. High-quality travel case for radio. *Except for North America:* Self-regulating AC adaptor, with American and European plugs, adjusts automatically to all local voltages worldwide.

Con: Tiny speaker, although an innovative design, has mediocre sound and limited loudness. Weak-signal sensitivity could be better, although outboard active antenna (supplied) helps. Expensive. No tuning knob. Clock not readable when station frequency displayed. As "London Time" is used by the clock for World Time, the summertime clock adjustment cannot be used if World Time is to be displayed accurately. Rejection of certain spurious signals ("images"), and 10 kHz "repeats" when synchronous selectable sideband off, could be better. In some urban locations, FM signals from 87.5 to 108 MHz can break through into world band segments with distorted sound, e.g. between 3200 and 3300 kHz. Synchronous selectable sideband tends to lose lock if batteries not fresh, or if NiCd cells are used. Batteries run down faster than usual when radio off. 0.1 kHz tuning resolution means that non-synchronous single-sideband reception can be mis-tuned by up to 50 Hz, so audio quality varies. Tuning of single sideband not helped by frequency readout only to nearest kilohertz. "Signal-seek" scanner sometimes stops 5 kHz before a strong "real" signal. No meaningful signal-strength indicator. Medium-wave AM reception only fair. Mediumwave AM channel spacing adjusts peculiarly. Flimsy battery cover. In early production samples, the cable connecting the two halves of the "clamshell" case tended to lose continuity with extended use because of a very tight radius and an unfinished edge; this was resolved with a design change in early 1996. *North America:* AC adaptor 120 Volts only.

Verdict: An engineering *tour de force*. Speaker and, to a lesser extent, weak-signal sensitivity keep it from being all it could have been. Yet, it still is the handiest pocket portable around, and one of the niftiest gift ideas in years.

✪✪✪
Sony ICF-SW100E

Price: £149.95 in the United Kingdom. AUS$649.00 in Australia.

Verdict: This version, not available in North America, nominally includes only a case, tape-reel-type passive antenna and earbuds. Otherwise, it is identical to the Sony ICF-SW100S, above.

Pocket portables are usually costly or pedestrian, but not the Sangean ATS 606. It is also available in the U.K. as the Roberts R617.

✪✪✪
Roberts R617, Sangean ATS 606A

Price: *R617:* £114.95 in the United Kingdom. *ATS 606A:* $139.95 in the United States. CAN$239.00 as available in Canada. £104.95 in the United Kingdom. AUS$249.00 in Australia.

Pro: Exceptional simplicity of operation for technology class. Speaker audio quality superior for size class, improves with (usually supplied) earpieces. Various helpful tuning features. Keypad has exceptional feel and tactile response. Longwave. World Time clock, displayed separately from frequency, and local clock. Alarm/snooze features. Travel power lock. Clear warning when batteries weak. Stereo FM via earpieces. Superior FM reception. Superior quality of construction.

Con: No tuning knob. World Time clock readable only when radio is switched off. Keypad not in telephone format. No meaningful signal-strength indicator. No carrying strap or handle. AC adaptor extra.

Verdict: A sensible choice, thanks to superior sound through speaker.

The new Platinum Digital G3D is Grundig's lowest-priced portable with digital tuning. Decent audio, too, but no keypad.

New for 2000
✪✪ ⏴

Grundig Platinum Digital G3D, Grundig Yacht Boy 320

Price: *Platinum Digital:* $79.95 in the United States. CAN$99.95 in Canada. *Yacht Boy 320:* £59.95 in the United Kingdom.

Pro: Price. Superior audio quality for pocket size. 24-hour clock with alarm and clock radio. Up/down slew tuning with "signal-seek" scanning. Illuminated LCD. Travel power lock (*see* Con). FM in stereo through earpieces, not included.

Con: Poor rejection of certain spurious signals ("images"). Doesn't cover 7400-9400 kHz world band range, although like other single-conversion sets it can be tricked into receiving the lower part of this range at reduced strength by tuning the 6505-6700 kHz "image" frequencies. Lacks keypad and tuning knob. Few presets (e.g., only five for 2300-7400 kHz range). Tunes world band only in coarse 5 kHz steps. Even-numbered frequencies displayed with final zero omitted; e.g., 5.73 rather than conventional 5.730 or 5730. Poor spurious-signal ("image") rejection. So-so adjacent-channel rejection (selectivity). Unhandy "SW1/SW2" switch to go between

2300-7400 kHz and 9400-26100 kHz ranges. World Time clock not displayed independent of frequency. Nigh-useless signal-strength and battery-dead indicators. LCD illumination not disabled when travel power lock activated. No carrying strap or handle. AC adaptor extra. No longwave.

Verdict: Warts and all, a decent offering at an attractive price, with audio quality superior to that of most pocket models.

New for 2000
✪½

Grundig G4 Executive Traveller

Price: $129.95 in the United States.

Pro: Great idea. Comes with and fits into luxurious black leather wallet with room for passport, money, spare batteries, earbuds and credit cards. Comes with batteries and earbuds. Sensitivity to world band signals at least average for pocket model. Clock with alarm (see Con).

Con: Analog radio with a digital frequency counter, so lacks tuning except by knob. Does not tune 90, 60, 22, 13 or 11 meter segments. Frequency counter omits last digit so, say, 9575 kHz appears as either 9.57 or 9.58 MHz. Clock in 12-hour format only. Poor image rejection. Mediocre audio quality. Telescopic antenna does not rotate or swivel. Medium-wave AM lacks weak-signal sensitivity. Pedestrian FM, with spurious signals.

Verdict: Innovative and stylish. A terrific idea that includes a five-star wallet, but the radio doesn't compare.

Evaluation of New Model: Normally when we refer to a pocket model, we mean something like a pack of cigarettes. But the new Grundig G4 Executive Traveller is something altogether different: a radio that fits into a jacket wallet like a thin book. And just to make sure you get the point, it comes with a first-rate leather wallet suitable for your passport, money and credit cards—as well as the radio, held in place by Velcro. Whether you wish to keep your cards next to a radio's speaker magnet is another matter, but you get the point: This is an innovative package for the globetrotter who has it all.

Unfortunately, after Grundig paid for the lovely wallet there wasn't much left for the radio, and it shows. Although it has digital frequency readout, the radio is actually analog with a digital frequency counter that doesn't show the last digit—6115 kHz appears as 6.11 or 6.12 MHz, for example. And since it's analog, the radio can be tuned only by knob. Tuning omits the 22, 13 and 11 meter segments, plus the tropical segments below 5.1 MHz. Oddly, the clock is in 12-hour format, which is unsuitable for World Time, although it does have an alarm.

Performance is passable, albeit with poor image rejection and mediocre audio quality. Sensitivity to weak signals is pretty good for a simple pocket model, and selectivity, although broad, is reasonable. FM and mediumwave AM are fair.

It's a great idea, poorly executed. Sony sells carloads of first-rate travel portables for hundreds of dollars each, so the market is there for a quality product, especially one as innovative as this. But as it stands, the G4 Executive Traveller is a limp offering.

Grundig's G4 Executive Traveller, a novel concept.

COMPACT PORTABLES
Good for Travel, Fair for Home

Compact portables are the most popular category because of their intersection of price, performance, size and speaker quality. They tip in at one to two pounds, under a kilogram, and are typically sized 8 × 5 × 1.5 inches, or 20 × 13 × 4 cm. Like pocket models, they feed off "AA" (UM-3 penlite) batteries—but, usually, more of them. They travel almost as well as pocket models, but sound better and usually receive better, too. They can also suffice as home sets.

TIPS FOR GLOBETROTTING

To avoid hassles with security officials:

- Use a pocket or compact model, nothing larger. Terrorists like big radios.
- Stow your radio in a carry-on bag, not in checked luggage or on your person.
- Take along fresh batteries so you can demonstrate that the radio actually works.
- If asked what the radio is for, say for personal use.
- If traveling in zones of war or civil unrest, or off the beaten path in much of Africa or parts of South America, take along a radio you can afford to lose and which fits inconspicuously in a pocket.
- If traveling to Bahrain, avoid taking a radio which has the word "receiver" on its cabinet. Security personnel may think you're a spy.

Theft? Radios, cameras, binoculars, laptop computers and the like are almost always stolen to be resold. The more worn the item looks—affixing scuffed stickers helps—the less likely it is to be confiscated by corrupt inspectors or stolen by thieves.

New for 2000

✪✪✪¼ *Passport's Choice*

Sony ICF-SW07

Price: $419.95 in the United States. £259.95 in the United Kingdom.

Pro: Non-audio performance best among travel portables. Has high-tech synchronous detection coupled to selectable sideband; this generally performs very well, reducing adjacent-channel interference and fading distortion on world band, longwave and mediumwave AM signals while adding slightly to weak-signal sensitivity. Unusually small and light for a compact-class model. Numerous tuning aids, including pushbutton access of frequencies for four stations stored on a replaceable ROM, keypad, two-speed up/down slewing, 20 presets (ten for world band) and "signal-seek, then resume" scanning. Clamshell design aids in handiness of operation, and is further helped by LCD readable from a wide variety of angles. Illuminated LCD. Case humpback angles keypad nicely. Comes with AN-LP2 outboard "tennis racquet" antenna, effective in enhancing weak-signal sensitivity on world band. Clock covers most world time zones, as well as World Time. Outstanding reception of weak and crowded FM stations, with limited urban FM overloading resolved by variable-level attenuator. FM stereo through earpieces or headphones. Receives longwave and Japanese FM bands. Above-average reception of mediumwave AM band. Travel power lock. Closing clamshell does not interfere with speaker. Low-battery indicator. Presets information is fully non-volatile, thus can't be erased when batteries changed. Two turn-on times for alarm/clock radio. Sixty-minute sleep delay function. Hinged battery cover can't be misplaced. Comes standard with AC adaptor and padded vinyl travel cover.

Con: Pedestrian audio quality, made worse by the lack of a second, wider, bandwidth and meaningful tone control. Lacks tuning knob. Display shows time and tuned frequency, but not both at the same time. 0.1 kHz tuning resolution means that non-synchronous single-sideband reception can be mis-tuned by up to 50 Hz, so audio quality varies. Tuning of single sideband not helped by frequency readout only to nearest kilohertz. No meaningful signal-strength indicator. LCD frequency/time numbers relatively small for size of display, with only average contrast. AN-LP2 accessory antenna has to be physically disconnected for proper mediumwave AM reception. 1621-1700 kHz portion of American AM band is treated as shortwave, although this does not harm reception quality. Low battery indicator misreads immediately after batteries installed; clears up when radio is turned on. Local time shown only in 24-hour format. UTC, or World Time, displays as "London" time even during the summer, when London is an hour off from World Time. DST button can be used to change UTC in error.

☞ A version without the AN-LP2 antenna and certain other accessories may eventually be offered for sale in Europe.

Verdict: For the Loved One Who Has Everything. Audio aside, it's the best travel model available and a killer eyeful. But if you can live without the laptop-wannabe layout, the Sony ICF-SW7600G is almost as good and has better audio for far less, even allowing for the value of the 'SW07's nifty accessories.

Evaluation of New Model: The snazzy new 'SW07 is a real bantamweight: only 10 ounces, or 0.3 kg including its two "AA" batteries. It measures $5^5/_{16}$ by $3^5/_8$ by $1^1/_4$ inches, or $135 \times 92 \times 32$ mm, with the top two-thirds of the case being covered by a clamshell containing the "information central" LCD; thankfully, the speaker remains uncovered when the top is closed. The radio comes standard with a worldwide AC adaptor and an AN-LP2 outboard active antenna (reviewed earlier in this chapter) that looks like the head of an oversized tennis racquet.

In order to help newbies and occasional users cope with the unique characteristics of shortwave broadcasting, the Sony ICF-SW07 is equipped with a replaceable ROM having world band frequency data for selected stations (replacement ROMs are $20 a pop). Dedicated keys scan through channels for four stations: BBC World Service, VOA, Deutsche Welle and any one of five other designated stations. There is also a fifth key you can program, bringing the total to five stations.

The radio's ROM scanner stops at the first occupied frequency, displaying the desired station's name. This ROM system stores only frequencies, not hours of transmission, so you may have to scan through several frequencies possibly occupied by other broadcasters before you uncover a usable frequency for the station you want.

There is also a worldwide 24-hour clock giving either local time or UTC, as you choose. Local time can be adjusted for DST, and using this does not cause UTC to misread. Alas, time is shared with the frequency display, so you can see one or the other but not both at the same time.

Local time corresponds to a time zone which you select, and in turn that zone determines whether the slew increment for mediumwave AM is to be 10 kHz (Americas) or 9 kHz (elsewhere). A niggling point is that the radio defines the mediumwave AM band as ending at 1620 kHz. As a result, from 1630-1700 kHz, the upper portion of the AM band in the Americas, coarse slewing changes from 9/10 kHz increments to 5 kHz increments and the display incorrectly reads "SW."

Selecting your time zone correctly is a requirement if the ROM feature is to work properly, as the only frequencies the radio will select for the four pre-programmed stations are those which are nominally beamed to your zone. That makes sense during the evening, when stations are targeted your way. At other times, though, you can receive off-beam transmissions from those stations either by normal tuning or by choosing another zone as your receiving location. Just remember to change the zone back when you're through.

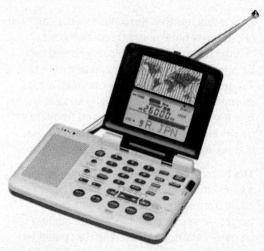

Computing has the Palm, world band has this Sony. The ICF-SW07 isn't cheap, but offers surprising performance except audio.

The 'SW07 tunes the Japanese and regular FM bands from 76-108 MHz, as well as the usual 150-29999 kHz range in one and five kilohertz increments above 1620 kHz. Single sideband is tuned in 0.1 kHz increments below 30 MHz, even though the frequency readout is only to the nearest kilohertz. There is no adjustment to tweak between 0.1 kHz increments, so while single sideband reception is okay it isn't as aurally clean as it could be.

Although there is no tuning knob, the keypad is alphanumeric, allowing four-character station identifiers to be entered in memory, and there are ten FM presets plus ten more for the 150-29999 kHz range. Additionally, there is "signal-seek" scanning of frequency segments, as well as the ROM scan. The frequency scan stops only at strong signals, even then sometimes halts one channel short of the intended signal.

The single bandwidth is very effective. When the synchronous selectable sideband feature is switched in, the result usually keeps most or all adjacent-frequency interference at bay. For nighttime listening there is timed illumination of the LCD, which is readable from a variety of angles but has only moderate contrast and character size.

A nice touch is that the battery cover can't fall off, and you have about three minutes to change batteries without losing stored time data (presets storage is completely non-volatile). Unfortunately, the one-step signal-strength indicator is of virtually no use, limiting the 'SW07 for DXing and frequency monitoring. It also makes listening less fun, like taking the tachometer off a car.

The telescopic antenna is robust. It swivels, rotates and includes an elevation base to allow for a wide variety of positioning angles—a useful characteristic for nulling co-channel FM interference. The rear panel has a humpback to tilt it upward slightly when laid down, and the clamshell top can be adjusted to nearly any angle for optimum viewing. The cabinet's aluminum finish appears to be imbedded in the plastic, and thus is unlikely to wear off.

The 'SW07 is an excellent overall performer by any measure except audio quality. FM reception is top-notch, with superb sensitivity to weak signals and an excellent capture radio to help kill co-channel interference by moving the antenna.

Mediumwave AM reception is above average, with good sensitivity and superior selectivity. This is aided by synchronous selectable

sideband, which also eliminates the awful selective-fading distortion that disrupts some "fringe" AM reception, especially around twilight. However, the accessory 'LP2 antenna has to be physically disconnected for proper mediumwave AM reception.

World band performance is very good, indeed, especially when the AN-LP2 outboard antenna is used—on the 'SW07 this antenna is audibly effective, giving this radio sensitivity to weak signals that is second to none among digital compact portables. Adjacent-channel rejection is nearly tops for a portable, although the sync doesn't hold lock quite so consistently as it does on the larger ICF-2010. Except on FM below 87 MHz, spurious signals are rare.

Audio quality is—politely put—mediocre, thanks to a tiny speaker and nigh-useless "news-music" tone switch. Yet, even with headphones the lack of a second, wider, bandwidth limits the fidelity potential with many stations.

The new Sony ICF-SW07 is neither the best buy in a compact portable, nor the smallest. Yet, aside from audio quality it is the ultimate performer among travel portables.

★★★¼ *ⓒ Passport's Choice*
Sony ICF-SW7600G, Sony ICF-SW7600GS

Price: *ICF-SW7600G:* $169.95 in the United States. CAN$299.95 in Canada. £124.95 in the United Kingdom. AUS$469.00 in Australia. ¥2,700 in China.

Pro: Exceptionally good value. Far and away the least-costly model available with high-tech synchronous detection coupled to selectable sideband; this generally performs very well, reducing adjacent-channel interfer-ence and fading distortion on world band, longwave and mediumwave AM signals while adding slightly to weak-signal sensitivity (*see* Con). Single bandwidth, especially when the synchronous-detection feature is used, exceptionally effective at adjacent-channel rejection. Superior quality of components and

Sony's ICF-7600G performs almost as well as the Sony ICF-SW07, but at half the price and with better audio quality.

assembly for price class. Numerous helpful tuning features, including keypad, two-speed up/down slewing, presets and "signal-seek, then resume" scanning. For those with limited hearing of high-frequency sounds, such as some men over the half-century mark, audio quality may be preferable to that of Grundig Yacht Boy 400PE. World Time clock, easy to set. Tape-reel-type outboard passive antenna accessory comes standard. Snooze/timer features. Illuminated display. Travel power lock. Superior reception of difficult mediumwave AM stations. Analog clarifier allows single-sideband signals to be tuned with uncommon precision, and thus superior audio quality, for a portable. FM stereo through earpieces or headphones. Receives longwave and Japanese FM bands. Weak-battery indicator. Comes standard with vinyl carrying case. *ICF-SW7600GS:* Comes with AN-LP1 active antenna system.

Con: Certain controls, notably for synchronous selectable sideband, located unhandily at the side of the cabinet. No tuning knob. Twenty presets, of which only ten function for world band stations. Clock not readable when radio is switched on. No meaningful signal-strength indicator. Tuning of single sideband not helped by frequency readout only to nearest kilohertz. No AC adaptor comes standard, and polarity difference disallows use of customary Sony adaptors. No earphones/earpieces come standard. *ICF-SW7600GS:* Not available in the United States or most other countries.

Verdict: The Sony '7600G excels in rejecting adjacent-channel interference and selective fading distortion, although audio quality is *ordinaire*. It is well constructed, and outstandingly priced for all it does so well.

✪✪✪¼ *Passport's Choice*
Grundig Yacht Boy 400PE

Price: $199.95 in the United States. CAN$249.95 in Canada. £159.95 in the United Kingdom. AUS$399.00 in Australia.

The Grundig Yacht Boy 400PE is a top seller, for good reason. It is simple to operate, with pleasant sound and two bandwidths. Free AC adaptor, too.

Pro: Unusually good value. Audio quality tops in size category for those with sharp hearing. Two bandwidths, both well-chosen. Ergonomically superior for advanced-technology radio. A number of helpful tuning features, including keypad, up/down slewing, 40 station presets, "signal seek" frequency scanning and scanning of station presets. Signal-strength indicator. World Time clock with second time zone, any one of which is shown at all times; however, clock displays seconds only when radio is off. Single-voltage AC adaptor comes standard. Illuminated display. Alarm/snooze features. Tunable BFO allows for superior aural resolution of single-sideband reception. Fishing-reel-type outboard passive antenna to supplement telescopic antenna. Generally superior FM performance. FM in stereo through headphones. Longwave.

Con: Circuit noise ("hiss") can be slightly intrusive with weak signals. No tuning knob. At some locations, there can be breakthrough of powerful AM or FM stations. Keypad not in telephone format. No LSB/USB switch. Aluminum finish has potential to wear off over time.

Verdict: An excellent choice, and a snap to operate. The Grundig Yacht Boy 400PE's audio quality is what sets this model apart, even though circuit noise with weak signals could be lower. (It helps if you clip on several yards or meters of strung-out doorbell wire to the built-in antenna).

Sony's classic ICF-SW55 performs well but lacks synchronous selectable sideband. It is still available in the United Kingdom.

✪✪✪
Sony ICF-SW55, Sony ICF-SW55E

Price: £229.95 in the United Kingdom.

Pro: Audio quality. Dual bandwidths. Logical controls. Innovative tuning, with alphabetic identifiers for groups ("pages") of stations. Weak-signal sensitivity a bit better than most. Comes with carrying case, reel-in antenna, AC adaptor, DC power cord and earbuds. Signal/battery strength indicator. Local and World Time clocks, one displayed separately from frequency. Snooze/alarm. Five-event (daily only) timer. Illuminated display. Longwave and Japanese FM.

Con: "Page" tuning system difficult for some. Spurious-signal rejection in higher segments not commensurate with price. Wide bandwidth rather broad. 0.1 kHz tuning and 1 kHz readout compromise single-sideband reception. Display illumination dim and uneven. Eats batteries.

Verdict: If you like the operating scheme and want a small portable with good audio, this model is a superior performer in its size class. But it lacks synchronous selectable sideband, a major plus found on newer Sony models.

✪✪✪
Radio Shack DX-398, Roberts R861, Sangean ATS 909

Price: *Radio Shack:* $249.99 ($199.99 during special sales) in the United States. *Roberts:* £179.95 in United Kingdom. *Sangean:* $259.95 in the United States. CAN$429.00 as available in Canada. £159.95 in the United Kingdom.

Pro: Exceptionally wide range of tuning facilities and hundreds of presets, including one which works with a single touch. Alphanumeric station descriptors. Two voice band-widths, well-chosen. Tunes single sideband in unusually precise 40 Hz increments, making this one of the best portables for listening to single-sideband signals. Superb multivoltage AC adaptor with North American and European plugs. Travel power lock. 24-hour clock shows at all times, and can display local time in various cities of the world (*see* Con). 1-10 digital signal-strength indicator. Clock radio function offers three "on" times for three discrete frequencies. Snooze feature. FM is sensitive to weak signals (see Con) and performs well overall, has RDS feature (*see* Con), and is in stereo through earpieces, included. Superior quality of construction.

Con: Tuning knob tends to mute stations during bandscanning; remediable by modification via at least one American dealer ($29.95 from C. Crane). Large for a compact. Signal-seek scanner tends to stop on few active shortwave signals. Although scanner can operate out-of-band, reverts to default (in-band) parameters after one pass. Two-second wait between when preset is keyed and station becomes audible. Under certain conditions, alphanumeric station descriptor may stay on full time. "Page" tuning system difficult for some to grasp. No carrying handle or strap. 24-hour clock set up to display home time, not World Time, although this is easily overcome by not using world-cities-time feature. Clock does not compensate for daylight (summer) time in each displayed city. FM can overload in high-signal-strength environments, causing false "repeat" signals to appear (*see* Pro). RDS, which can automatically display FM-station IDs and update clock, is of limited use, as on this model it requires a stronger signal than it should to activate (*see* Pro). Heterodyne interference, possibly related to the digital display, sometimes interferes with reception of strong mediumwave AM signals. Battery consumption above average. AC adaptor lacks UL approval.

Verdict: A pleasant offering for those seeking a wide range of operating features or superior tuning of single-sideband signals.

✪✪✪
Grundig Yacht Boy 500

Price: £79.95 in the United Kingdom. AUS$599.00 in Australia. Also available in the Middle East and Africa, but not the Americas.

Pro: Attractive layout. Audio-boost circuitry for superior volume. 40 presets. Alphanumeric names displayed by presets. RDS circuitry for FM. ROM with 90 preassigned channels for nine broadcasters. Two 24-hour clocks, one displays fulltime. Battery-low indicator. FM in stereo via headphones. Travel power lock. Three-increment signal-strength indicator. Elevation panel. Single-sideband reception via LSB/USB key. Illuminated display. Timer/snooze features. Comes with worldwide dual-voltage AC adaptor and two types of plugs. Audio quality pretty good. Longwave.

Con: Circuit noise relatively high. Lacks tuning knob. Telescopic antenna tends to get in the way of right-handed users. Volume slider fussy to adjust. Keypad not in telephone format. Chichi key design and layout increase likelihood of wrong key being pushed. Clocks show no leading zeroes. Elevation panel and AC adaptor socket flimsy. Factory-preassigned channels relatively complex for beginners to select. Excessive spurious "birdie" signals.

Verdict: Attractive design, good performance, with powerful audio and a number of interesting features. But better performance can be had in other models for the same price or less.

Sophisticated "page" tuning and good single-sideband reception are hallmarks of the popular Sangean ATS 909, also sold as the Radio Shack DX-398 and Roberts R861.

✪✪✪ ✐
Roberts R809, Sangean ATS-808A

Price: *Roberts:* £89.95 in the United Kingdom. *Sangean:* $139.95 in the United States. CAN$249.95 as available in Canada. £84.95 in the United Kingdom. AUS$299.00 in Australia.

Pro: A solid value. Relatively simple to operate for technology class. Dual bandwidths, unusual in this size radio (*see* Con).

Grundig's Yacht Boy 500 is more chichi than convenient, but performs well. Available worldwide outside the Americas.

If the Sony ICF-SW7600G or Grundig Yacht Boy 400PE are too much, look into the Sangean ATS-808A—nearly as good, but cheaper.

Various helpful tuning features. Weak-signal sensitivity a bit better than most. Keypad has exceptional feel and tactile response. Longwave. World Time clock, displayed separately from frequency, and local clock. Alarm/snooze features. Signal strength indicator. Travel power lock. Stereo FM via earpieces, included. Superior FM reception. Superior quality of construction.

Con: Fast tuning mutes receiver when tuning knob is turned quickly. Narrow bandwidth performance only fair. Spurious-signal ("image") rejection very slightly substandard for class. Pedestrian audio. Display not illuminated. Keypad not in telephone format. No carrying strap or handle. AC adaptor extra.

Under-$100 radios, like under-$500 PCs, have shortcomings. Sony's ICF-SW30 performs well, but is inconvenient to tune.

Verdict: With more presets, the revised version of this classic Sangean offering continues to be a good value, with relative simplicity of operation and good overall performance. However, mediocre for bandscanning.

✪✪½ ✪
Sony ICF-SW30

Price: $89.95 in the United States. CAN$179.95 as available in Canada. £69.95 in the United Kingdom. AUS$299.00 in Australia.

Pro: Excellent value. Superior reception quality, with excellent adjacent-channel rejection (selectivity) and spurious-signal rejection. Weak-signal sensitivity a bit better than most. World Time and local time clock. Audio, although lacking in bass, unusually intelligible. Alarm/snooze features. Travel power lock. FM stereo through headphones, not supplied. Battery-life indicator. Receives Japanese FM band.

Con: No keypad or tuning knob. Synthesizer chugging and poky slewing degrade bandscanning. Only seven world band station presets. Does not cover two minor world band segments (2 and 3 MHz), the new 19 MHz segment and a scattering of other world band channels. Clock not displayed independent of frequency. Radio suddenly goes dead when batteries get weak. No longwave. AC adaptor, much-needed, is extra.

Verdict: Simple to operate, but tuning convenience is pedestrian. Buy only if you listen to a limited number of stations.

New for 2000
✪✪½ ✪
Grundig Yacht Boy 300PE (Revised Version)

Price: $99.95 in the United States.

Pro: Unusually good value. Sensitive to weak world band signals. Good selectivity. Wide variety of helpful tuning features. World Time clock with alarm, clock radio and sleep delay (*see* Con). Illuminated LCD. AC adaptor. Travel power lock (*see* Con). Stereo FM via earbuds, supplied.

Con: Mediocre spurious-signal ("image") rejection. No tuning knob. Limited number of presets (e.g., only six for 2300-7800 kHz range). Tunes world band only in coarse 5 kHz steps. Even-numbered frequencies displayed with final zero omitted; e.g., 5.73 rather than conventional 5.730 or 5730. Keypad entry of even channels with all digits (e.g., 6190 as 6 - 1 - 9 - 0, Enter) result in radio being tuned five kilohertz higher (e.g., 6195); remedied by not entering trailing zero (e.g., 6 - 1 - 9, Enter). Mediocre spurious-signal ("image") rejection. Unhandy "SW1/SW2" switch to go between 2300-7800 kHz and 9100-26100 kHz ranges. World Time clock not displayed independent of frequency. Nigh-useless signal-strength indicator. LCD illumination not disabled when travel power lock activated. No longwave. Does not tune unimportant 7805-9095 kHz range.

Verdict: Improved in October 1999, the Grundig Yacht Boy 300PE is nicely priced for weak-signal parts of the world, such as central and western North America, the Pacific region and Australasia.

Evaluation of New Model: The just-revised version of the Yacht Boy 300PE covers short-wave 2.3-7.8 MHz (SW1) and 9.1-26.1 MHz (SW2) in 5 kHz increments; the original version, produced between May and September of 1999, covered only 2.3-7.3 and 9.5-26.1 MHz.

The 300PE is manufactured at a Grundig-controlled plant in China. It comes with all sorts of accessories, including an AC adaptor, batteries, outboard wire antenna, stereo earbuds, padded travel case, World Time clock with alarm, 10-90 minute sleep delay, elevation panel, travel power lock, illuminated dial and a telescopic antenna that swivels and rotates.

There is no tuning knob, but it has keypad tuning, presets, frequency scanning and a meter-band selector button. A technically obsolete "SW1/SW2" button (MW - SW1 - SW2 - FM) has to be pressed three times

The Grundig Yacht Boy 300PE was introduced in 1999, but within months a number of improvements had already been made.

before tuning from a frequency above 9100 kHz to one below 7800 kHz. Too, there are only six presets for SW1 and another six for SW2 (plus six for FM and six for AM). The original version muted annoyingly for over one second when the slew button was pressed to go to the next channel. The revised version improves upon this.

The LCD shows frequency in the peculiar XX.XX MHz format for even channels, XX.XX5 MHz format for odd. Too, if you key in an even channel in the customary kHz format (e.g., 9 - 7 - 6 - 0 kHz) the radio tunes one channel higher (*viz.*, 9.765 MHz). The LCD shows the frequency or the time, but not both at the same time, although you can toggle between the two.

As with virtually all under-$100 models the 300PE is single conversion, so powerful stations tend to "image" at lower strength 900 kHz down. In the original version selectivity, or adjacent-channel rejection, was slightly wide, but it has been tightened up in the revised version. The 300PE is commendably sensitive to weak world band signals, and distant reception is also superior on FM. Audio quality is okay but lacking in low-frequency ("bass") response.

The revised Yacht Boy 300PE is much improved over the original offering. It is especially well suited to such weak-signal parts of the world as central and western North America, Hawaii, Alaska, the Caribbean and Australasia.

✪✪½
Sony ICF-SW40

Price: $119.95 in the United States. £84.95 in the United Kingdom.

Pro: Relatively affordable. Technologically unintimidating, using advanced digital circuitry in a radio disguised as slide-rule, or analog, tuned. 24-hour clock. Double-conversion circuitry, unusual in price class, reduces likelihood of reception of spurious "image" signals. Two "on" timers and snooze facility. Travel power lock. Illuminated LCD. Covers Japanese FM band.

WHAT TO LOOK FOR

Tuning features. Digitally tuned models are so superior and cost-effective that they are virtual "musts." Most come with such handy tuning aids as direct-frequency access via keypad, presets (programmable channel memories), up-down tuning via tuning knob and/or slew keys, band/segment selection, and signal-seek or other scanning. In general, the more such features a radio has, the easier it is to tune—no small point, given that a hundred or more channels may be audible at any one time. However, there is the occasional model, identified in PASSPORT REPORTS under "Con," with features that can make tuning excessively complicated for some users.

Audio quality. Few portables have rich, full audio, but some are much better than others. If you listen regularly and have exacting ears or difficulty in hearing, focus on models with superior audio quality—and try to buy on a money-back or exchange basis.

Effective adjacent-channel rejection ("selectivity"). World band stations are packed together about twice as closely as ordinary mediumwave AM stations, so they tend to interfere with each other. Radios with superior selectivity are better at rejecting this. However, enhanced selectivity also means less high-end ("treble") audio response, so having more than one *bandwidth* allows you to choose between superior selectivity ("narrow bandwidth") when it is warranted, and more realistic audio ("wide bandwidth") when it is not.

Synchronous selectable sideband. Done correctly, this advanced feature further improves audio quality and selectivity by minimizing fading distortion. It also reduces adjacent-channel interference by selecting the "better half" of a signal.

Sensitivity to weak signals. Most models have enough sensitivity for hearing major stations if you're in such places as Europe, North Africa or the Near East. However, in locations like Australia or North America west of the east coast, received signals tend to be weak. There, sensitivity really counts.

Superior ergonomics. Some radios are easy to use because they don't have complicated features. But even models with complex features can be designed to operate relatively intuitively.

World Time clock. A World Time clock (24-hour format) is a "must." You can buy these separately, but many radios come with them built in. The best built-ins display World Time whether the radio is on or off.

AC adaptor. With portables an outboard AC adaptor is needed. An adaptor that comes with the radio is best, and one that's multivoltage is ideal if you travel abroad.

Con: Single bandwidth is relatively wide, reducing adjacent-channel rejection. No keypad. Lacks coverage of 1625-1705 kHz portion of North American mediumwave AM band. No single sideband or synchronous selectable sideband.

Verdict: If you're turned off by things digital and complex, Sony's ICF-SW40 will feel like an old friend in your hands. Otherwise, look elsewhere.

Sony's faux-analog ICF-SW40 aims to overcome digiphobia.

✪✪½
Roberts R881, Sangean ATS 404

Price: *Roberts:* £79.99 in the United Kingdom. *Sangean:* $99.95 in the United States. £59.95 in the United Kingdom.

Pro: Excellent value. Superior weak-signal sensitivity. Several handy tuning features. Stereo FM through earpieces (supplied). Two 24-hour clocks display seconds numerically. Alarm/snooze facilities. Travel power lock. Illuminated LCD. Battery indicator.

Con: Poor image rejection. No tuning knob. Overloading, controllable by shortening telescopic antenna on world band and collapsing it on mediumwave AM band. Picks up some internal digital hash. Tunes only in relatively coarse 5 kHz increments. No signal-strength indicator. Frequency and time cannot be displayed simultaneously. No single sideband or synchronous selectable sideband. Power lock does not disable LCD illumination. No single sideband. No longwave. No handle or carrying strap. AC adaptor extra.

Verdict: A welcome value-priced offering.

✪✪½ 🅒
Radio Shack DX-375

Price: Usually $99.99, but as low as $69.99 during special sales in the United States.

Pro: Excellent value at $100, rises to an outstanding value when on sale. Several handy tuning features. Weak-signal sensitivity a bit above average. Stereo FM through head-

phones, not supplied. Travel power lock. Timer. 30-day money-back trial period in the United States.

Con: Mediocre spurious-signal ("image") rejection. Unusually long pause of silence when tuning from channel to channel. Lacks tuning knob. Doesn't tune 6251-7099 kHz. Tunes only in relatively coarse 5 kHz increments. Antenna swivel sometimes needs tightening. AC adaptor plug easy to insert accidentally into headphone socket. Build quality, although adequate, appears to be slightly below average. Static discharges sometimes disable microprocessor (usually remediable if batteries are removed for a time, then replaced). No World Time clock. Signal-

Sangean's ATS 404 is inexpensive, but the Sangean ATS-808A is better and costs little more.

Radio Shack's DX-375 is especially tempting when on sale.

strength indicator only a single LED. No single sideband. AC adaptor extra. No longwave.

Verdict: A great buy when on sale for around $70.

✪✪
Grundig G2000A "Porsche Design"

Price: $149.95 in the United States, CAN$199.95 as available in Canada.

Pro: Arguably the most functionally attractive world band radio on the market, with generally superior ergonomics that include an effective and handy lambskin protective case. Superior adjacent-channel rejection—selectivity—for price and size class. Keypad (in proper tele-phone format), handy meter-

When the Porsche family isn't engineering cars, it designs products like the Grundig G2000A.

band carousel control, "signal-seek" scanning and up/down slew tuning. Twenty station presets, of which ten are for world band and the rest for FM and mediumwave AM stations. World Time clock. Timer/snooze/alarm. Illuminated display. Travel power lock. Microprocessor reset control.

Con: Sensitivity mediocre between 9400-26100 kHz, improving slightly between 2300-7400 kHz. Poor spurious-signal ("image") rejection. Does not tune such important world band ranges as 7405-7550 and 9350-9395 kHz. Tunes world band only in coarse 5 kHz steps and displays in nonstandard XX.XX MHz/XX.XX5 MHz format characteristic of low-cost Chinese radios. No tuning knob. Annoying one-second pause when tuning from one channel to the next. Old-technology SW1/SW2 switch complicates tuning. Protruding power button can get in the way of nearby slew-tuning and meter-carousel keys. Leather case makes it difficult to retrieve folded telescopic antenna. Magnetic catches weak on leather case. No carrying strap. No longwave. Signal-strength indicator nigh useless. Clock not displayed separately from frequency. AC adaptor extra.

Verdict: Five stars for design, two for performance.

✪✪
Grundig Traveller III

Price: $129.95 in the United States, CAN$149.95 as available in Canada.

Pro: Superior adjacent-channel rejection—selectivity—for price and size class. Keypad (in proper telephone format), handy meter-band carousel control, "signal-seek" scanning and up/down slew tuning. Twenty station presets, of which ten are for world band and the rest for FM and mediumwave AM stations. World Time clock. Timer/snooze/alarm. Travel power lock. Microprocessor reset control.

Con: Sensitivity mediocre between 9400-26100 kHz, improving slightly between 2300-

7400 kHz. Poor spurious-signal ("image") rejection. Does not tune such important world band ranges as 7405-7550 and 9350-9395 kHz. Tunes world band only in coarse 5 kHz steps and displays in nonstandard XX.XX MHz/XX.XX5 MHz format characteristic of cheap Chinese radios. No tuning knob. Annoying one-second pause when tuning from one channel to the next. Old-technology SW1/SW2 switch complicates tuning. No carrying strap. No longwave. Signal-strength indicator nigh useless. Clock not displayed separately from frequency. Display not illuminated. AC adaptor extra.

Verdict: Virtually identical to the Grundig G2000A, preceding, but cheaper and without the Porsche pizzazz and illuminated dial. Not the most appropriate choice for use in western North America and Australasia.

The Grundig Traveller III has the same electronics as the G2000A Porsche model, but it's cheaper and in a plain wrapper.

Verdict: Somewhat superior sensitivity to weak signals and excellent LCD notwithstanding, tortoise-slow tuning, missed frequencies and mediocre performance make this a model to avoid.

⊙⊙
Sangean ATS 303

Price: $64.95 in the United States.

Pro: LCD has large digits and excellent contrast at all viewing angles. Weak-signal sensitivity better than most. Five station preset buttons retrieve up to ten world band and ten AM/FM stations. Easy-to-set World Time clock. Timer/snooze/alarm. Travel power lock. Stereo FM via earpieces.

Con: Intolerably slow tuning by single-speed up/down slew buttons—no tuning knob or other remedy beyond presets and scanning. Mediocre spurious-signal ("image") rejection and adjacent-channel rejection (selectivity), plus some distorted spurious FM broadcast signals may intrude within the world band spectrum. Does not tune such important world band ranges as 7305-7600 and 9300-9495 kHz. Tunes world band only in coarse 5 kHz steps. Old-technology SW1/SW2 switch complicates tuning. No longwave. Signal-strength indicator nigh useless. No display illumination. Clock not displayed separately from frequency. No carrying strap or handle. AC adaptor extra.

⊙⊙
Bolong HS-490

Price: ¥360 in China.

Pro: Inexpensive for a model with digital frequency display, ten world band station presets, and ten station presets for medium-

Sangean's ATS 303 is a mundane performer with slow tuning.

If you're in China, the Bolong HS-490 is easy to find. Elsewhere, don't hold your breath.

wave AM and FM. World Time clock (*see* Con). Tape-reel-type outboard passive antenna accessory comes standard. AC adaptor. Illuminated display. Alarm/snooze features. FM stereo (*see* Con) via earbuds, included.

Con: Requires patience to get a station, as it tunes world band only via 10 station presets and multi-speed up/down slewing/scanning. Tunes world band only in coarse 5 kHz steps. Even-numbered frequencies displayed with final zero omitted; e.g., 5.75 rather than conventional 5.750 or 5750. Poor spurious-signal ("image") rejection. So-so adjacent-channel rejection (selectivity). World Time clock not displayed independent of frequency. Does not receive relatively unimportant 6200-7100 kHz portion of world band spectrum. Does not receive 1615-1705 kHz portion of expanded AM band in the Americas. No signal-strength indicator. No travel power lock. Mediumwave AM tuning increments not switchable, which may make for inexact tuning in some parts of the world other than where the radio was purchased. FM selectivity and capture ratio mediocre. FM stereo did not trigger on our unit.

Verdict: Made by a joint venture between Xin Hui Electronics and Shanghai Huaxin Electronic Instruments. No prize, but as good you'll find among the truly cheap, which probably accounts for its being the #1 seller among digital world band radios in China.

LAP PORTABLES
Good for Home, Fair for Travel

If you're looking for a home set, yet one that also can be taken out in the backyard and on the occasional trip, a lap portable is probably your best bet. These are large enough to perform well and can sound pretty good, yet are compact enough to tote in your suitcase now and then. Most take 3-4 "D" (UM-1) or "C" (UM-2) cells, plus they may also use a couple of "AA" (UM-3) cells for their microprocessors.

How large? Typically just under a foot wide—that's 30 cm—and weighing in around 3-4 pounds, or 1.3-1.8 kg. For air travel, that's okay if you are a dedicated listener, but a bit much otherwise. Too, larger sets with snazzy controls occasionally attract unwanted attention from suspicious customs and airport-security personnel in some parts of the world.

One model stands out for most listeners: the high-tech Sony ICF-2010, although some prefer Sony's more techy ICF-SW77. The Sangean ATS-818 is hardly in the same league, but at its current American pricing it is an outstanding buy.

★★★½ 📄 *Passport's Choice*
Sony ICF-2010

Price: $349.95 in the United States. CAN$599.00 in Canada. ¥4,500 in China. Not distributed at retail in much of the world, but available worldwide by mail order or email—but not, for now, the Web—from major U.S. and Canadian world band specialty firms.

Pro: High-tech synchronous detection with selectable sideband, thanks to a Sony proprietary chip with sideband phase canceling; on the '2010, this feature performs very well, indeed, reducing adjacent-channel interference and fading distortion on world band, longwave and mediumwave AM signals while adding slightly to weak-signal sensitivity. This is further aided by two bandwidths which offer superior tradeoff between audio fidelity and adjacent-channel rejection (selectivity). Use of 32 separate one-touch station preset buttons in rows and columns is ergonomically the best to be found on any model, portable or tabletop, at any price—simply pushing one button one time brings in your station, a major convenience. Numerous other helpful tuning features. Weak-signal world band sensitivity better than most. Tunes and displays in relatively precise 0.1 kHz increments (*see* Con). Separately displayed World Time clock. Alarm/snooze features, with four-event timer. Illuminated LCD. Travel power lock. Ten-LED digital signal-strength/battery-strength indicator better than most. Covers longwave and the Japanese FM band. FM very sensitive to weak signals, making it unusually appropriate for fringe reception in some areas (*see* Con). FM has superior capture ratio to minimize co-channel interference. Superior overall reception of fringe and distant mediumwave AM signals, although weak-signal sensitivity is only about average. Some

The Sony ICF-2010 is, by a skootch, the best genuine portable. Its 32 one-touch presets help make it one of the easiest to operate, as well.

passable reception of air band signals (most versions). AC adaptor.

Con: Audio quality only average, with simple three-level treble-cut tone control. Because there are so many controls and features, they may initially intimidate or confuse, although

CAN A VETERAN MODEL BE SUPERIOR?

Year after year we test new models, and year after year we continue to find the Sony ICF-2010 to be the best true portable available, irrespective of cost or size. Among fussy radio aficionados the '2010 continues to the portable of choice, yet this model first appeared 15 years back. How can it possibly pass muster today?

While PCs and many other electronic products have undergone profound technical advance in recent years, the high water point for world band technical innovation took place not in the nineties, but between the mid-1970s and mid-1980s, culminating in the introduction of the '2010 in 1985.

Too, the market for quality world band radios is far smaller than for many other consumer electronics products, limiting funding for R&D. But because Sony's synchronous detector chip was developed for another, potentially larger application, Sony's world band radios have benefitted from this technological windfall.

Finally, the '2010 was created before competition forced cost-cutting moves to become *de rigeur*. Its front panel is festooned with one-touch presets—the ultimate in tuning convenience, but too costly to pass muster in a new design. And because the '2010's R&D was written off years ago, in current dollars it sells for two thirds its introductory price.

Those who like the '2010 but are uncomfortable with the idea of something not of recent design, the closest substitute is the Sony ICF-SW77. It performs similarly, but uses a computer-type page tuning system in lieu of the '2010's one-touch buttons.

WORLD BAND ON THE ROAD

World band in the car isn't easy. Your everyday portable usually doesn't have enough audio oomph to overcome road and car noise, and the car's steel shell prevents most signals from getting to its antenna unless you stick it out a window.

As if that weren't enough, scanners are illegal in many localities. If you're stopped for something else and Officer McGruff sees your shortwave radio, he may think it's a scanner and confiscate it or worse.

Enter Becker, the German firm which provides bulletproof radios for Mercedes-Benz. Since 1996 it has been offering the Mexico 2340 world band car radio for roughly $460 in the United States and varying prices in Europe, the Middle East and Asia. It has the usual stereo features, including an inboard cassette drive and optional outboard CD changer.

However, Becker is no longer a family-owned German company, but part of the U.S. electronics organization Harmon-Kardon. Production of the Mexico was terminated in 1999, and existing inventory is expected to be exhausted by mid-2000. For the future Becker plans to limit shortwave coverage in its radios to 49 meters—the "European band"—perhaps one or two more segments.

Car shortwave radios have a tough row to hoe. They have to overcome electrical noise from ignitions, microprocessors and wiper motors. And although diesels generate no ignition noise, they are a poor substitute for a home environment.

There's not much you can do about electrical noise, but it's generally not serious enough to dampen listening to major world band stations. The Becker is sensitive enough for this and more, and you can improve weak-signal sensitivity by replacing your car's telescopic antenna with one that's longer, or one of the special antennas offered by C. Crane and some Becker dealers.

Ergonomics for Safe Driving

Car radio ergonomics are not a luxury, but an important safety issue. Fortunately, the Becker does well, albeit with a learning curve, weird keypad and no tuning knob. There are ten one-push buttons to call up presets—ten presets for world band, 30 for FM—as well as for direct-frequency entry. Better, its "signal-seek" frequency scanning works well.

There's only one bandwidth, an ergonomic virtue even if normally two bandwidths would be better. It is well chosen, being narrow enough to keep most interference at bay, yet wide enough to let through surprisingly pleasant audio.

Indeed, the Becker sounds magnificent for listening to world band programs, better than nearly any tabletop, portatop or portable model. FM and mediumwave AM also perform commendably, and FM comes with RDS for automatic identification of stations.

Limited Frequency Coverage

World band coverage is 5900-15700 kHz. Daytime, it misses the 17, 19, 21 and 26 MHz segments; evenings, you can't hear stations between 5730-5895 kHz, much less Latin American and other stations between 4750 and 5100 kHz. Too, mediumwave AM is only 531-1600 kHz, a hundred kilohertz below the upper limit in North America.

in practice this model tends to be quite straightforward to use. Station presets and clock/timer features immediately erase whenever microprocessor/memory batteries are replaced, and also sometimes when set is jostled (changing to a different brand of battery sometimes helps); this erasing also sometimes happens irregularly with no apparent cause on aging units. At 9.4 kHz, the wide bandwidth tends to be broad for world band reception; yet, narrower after-market replacement filters, notably the 4 kHz filter from Kiwa Electronics, reportedly cause sound to be too muffled for some ears, although others find the 6 kHz replacement filter to be worthwhile. "Signal-seek" scanning works poorly. Telescopic antenna swivel gets slack with heavy use, requiring periodic adjustment of tension screw. Synchronous selectable sideband alignment can drift slightly with temperature and battery voltage, causing synchronous selectable sideband reception to be more muffled in one sideband than the other, particularly with the narrow bandwidth. Synchronous selectable sideband won't hold lock fully once batteries begin to weaken (typically less than a "6" reading).

Synchronous selectable sideband does not switch off automatically during tuning. Frequency readout often off by 0.3-0.6 kHz in "lower" sync mode; depending upon sample and power source, off by as much as 0.3 kHz otherwise. Lacks up/down slewing. Keypad not in telephone format. LCD clearly readable only when radio viewed from below. Chugs slightly when tuned. 0.1 kHz tuning resolution means that non-synchronous single-sideband reception can be mis-tuned by up to 50 Hz, so audio quality varies. In high-signal-strength environments, FM band can overload, causing false "repeat" signals to appear (see Pro). FM band's capture ratio only fair. Air band insensitive to weak signals.

The ICF-2010's long carrying strap can be converted into a convenient handle either by 1) cutting it shorter, or 2) wrapping over the radio twice (same thing, but twice as strong).

For Americans seeking to have their ICF-2010 repaired, a helpful source at Sony of America suggests this as Sony's resident repair expert for this model: Steve Ulrich, Sony Service Center, 4300 W. 36½ Street, St. Louis Park MN 55416 USA.

Birdies, Images, Chugging and Pauses

There are spurious "images" from signals 900 kHz higher, as well as a few silent-carrier "birdies." There's chugging during bandscanning, and the radio has to stop to "think" for a second or two when coming onto a new frequency.

"World on Wheels" Works Well

The 2340 is not widely offered. Best bet for North Americans is to contact C. Crane at (800) 522-8863 or www.ccrane.com, Erie Aviation at (800) 395-8934 or hansb@erieaviation.com, or Becker's North American office at (888) 423-3537 or www.beckerautosound.com. Elsewhere, Becker headquarters is at Postfach 742260, D-76303 Karlsbad, Germany. Of course, if you own a Mercedes you can try out your local authorized M-B dealer.

Get it while you can!

Becker Mexico 2340 has superb sound.

NEW FOR 2000: GRUNDIG SATELLIT 800

The new and delightfully retro Grundig Satellit 800 is similar to the beloved Satellit 650 discontinued in 1992. Nearly two feet wide (54 cm) and weighing 15 pounds (7 kilos), this is the Jesse Ventura of world band portables. We tested a pre-production prototype, so our observations are provisional and we haven't rated this new receiver—tempted though we are by its considerable promise.

Grundig is North America's premiere marketer of world band products, but its R&D has never been the equal of such manufacturers as Sony. By the same token, the R.L. Drake Company has had legendary R&D for half a century, but has never been a leader in marketing. So an alliance between Grundig and Drake was quietly implemented in 1997, and this receiver is the first result.

Grundig on the Outside . . .

On the outside this is clearly a Grundig product, with the distinctive look, feel, and ergonomics of the erstwhile S-650. At under $500, street, it also reflects Grundig's tireless cost control—unlike the old S-650, it is made not in Europe but at a Grundig-controlled plant in China. Inside, the S-800's circuitry resembles Drake's SW8, the best-rated portatop in PASSPORT. It doesn't have the SW8's solid construction or all its performance, but it is surprisingly close.

The S-800 is laid out horizontally, like a boom box, rather than in the usual portable "book" format. This makes it ideal for desktops, and the long carrying handle helps in schlepping. It includes a sturdy 56 3/4 inch (144 cm) antenna, which rotates fully and has detents to secure it vertically or at an angle. There are also inputs for external antennas: a UHF connector for low-impedance designs such as dipoles, and push tabs for such high-impedance antennas as the inverted-L. Unlike other portables, the S-800's circuitry can handle the sorts of high-gain antennas designed for tabletop and portatop models.

The front panel has a huge illuminated LCD with large frequency numerals; the LCD reads with excellent contrast when viewed from above or head-on. There are two 24-hour clocks with a two-event (daily only) timer for automated listening, although there is no built-in cassette to record shows VCR-style. Only one clock displays at a time, and even that doesn't show unless the received frequency is not being displayed—just about the only dumb thing on this receiver.

Retro goodies include an analog signal-strength meter and separate bass and treble tone controls. Also welcome are the free large padded stereo headphones—they sound great for FM stereo and world band alike.

This ergonomic radio is a cinch to operate straight out of the box, except for presets and clock/timer adjustments. Those 70 tunable presets store frequency, mode, bandwidth, AGC decay, attenuator and synchronous detector, although there are no dedicated presets buttons such as on the Sony ICF-2010. The radio is also tuned by knob, slewing, presets scanning and meter band selection. Frequency readout is to the nearest 0.1 kHz, while tuning steps are 0.05 kHz for single sideband and 0.1 kHz for the AM mode.

. . . but Drake on the Inside

Drake's fingerprints are all over this radio. There are fully three voice bandwidths, nominally 6 kHz, 4 kHz and 2.3 kHz with nominal skirt selectivities of roughly 1:2. Bandwidths are

Verdict: With consumer electronic products and PCs, the best is often the newest or the most costly—but not with world band radios. Except for everyday audio quality and urban FM, the '2010 is our favorite and is the portable most preferred by experienced radio enthusiasts. It is among the best for rejection of one of world band's major bugaboos, adjacent-channel interference; yet, it is able to retain a relatively wide audio bandwidth for listening pleasure. Alone among sophisticated receivers, it allows dozens of stations to be brought up literally at the single touch of a button. Although it is costlier to manufacture than newer models—it is still made in Japan, notwithstanding rumors to the contrary—it sells at an affordable price because its development costs have been written off.

An *RDI WHITE PAPER* is available for this model.

---

selectable independent or dependent of mode (AM/SSB), as you prefer, via software command. Another sign of Drake's handiwork is that the S-800 is also the only portable around with selectable AGC decay times—fast and slow.

Coverage includes the 118-137 MHz air band. The receiver is powered by six "D" cells, as well as a multivoltage AC adaptor that Grundig promises will automatically detect incoming voltage anywhere in the world and adjust to it.

The S-800 also has synchronous selectable sideband and double sideband. Until now Sony was the only portable manufacturer to do this right, but they have company with the S-800. And no wonder, as Drake's recent sync circuits have been among the very best.

By and large the sync works very well. Its deep lock, coupled to three bandwidths, means this feature should go a long way towards reducing adjacent-channel interference and selective fading distortion. However, because on our test unit it introduced hiss when it was turned on, we found that faint DX was harder to copy with the sync on than off—the reverse of what it should be. Grundig states that this will be resolved before production.

Audio quality is delightful, superior to that of any other portable on today's market. Tone controls work well, although the treble circuit was scheduled to be altered before final production to eliminate hiss appearing at high-treble settings.

Except for front-end selectivity on longwave and image rejection, performance reflects its heritage as a portatop receiver. Indeed, we even found inadequate sensitivity with the telescopic antenna—precisely the same as with the Drake SW8. (Grundig tells us they are working to resolve this, too.)

The Grundig Satellit 800 is a field portable, suitable for use around the house, yard, and on trips by car or RV—not air trips. Its performance looks exceptionally promising, and its audio quality is delightful.

Grundig's new Satellit 800 portable, engineered by R.L. Drake.

WORLD BAND CASSETTE RECORDERS

What happens if your favorite show comes on at an inconvenient time? Why, tape it, of course, with a world band cassette recorder—just like on your VCR.

Two models are offered, and there's no question which is better: the Sony. Smaller, too, so it is less likely to raise eyebrows among airport security personnel. But its price difference over the Sangean—a nice, serviceable model—is considerable.

✪✪✪¼ *Passport's Choice*
Sony ICF-SW1000T, Sony ICF-SW1000TS

Price: *ICF-SW1000T:* $449.95 in the United States. CAN$779.00 as available in Canada. £369.95 in the United Kingdom.

Pro: Built-in recorder has two user-programmable on/off events. Relatively small, important for airport security. Synchronous selectable sideband reduces adjacent-channel interference and fading distortion on world band, longwave and mediumwave AM signals while adding slightly to weak-signal sensitivity (*see* Con). Single bandwidth, especially when the sync feature is used, exceptionally effective at adjacent-channel rejection. Numerous helpful tuning features, including keypad, two-speed up/down slewing, 32 presets and "signal-seek" scanning. Effectively demodulates single-sideband signals. World Time clock, easy to set. Snooze/timer features. Illuminated display. Travel power lock. Easy on batteries. Records on both sides of tape without having to flip cassette (provided FWD is set along with the "turning-around arrow"). FM stereo through earpieces (supplied). Receives longwave and Japanese FM bands. Tape-reel-type outboard passive antenna accessory included. Dead-battery indicator. Comes standard with lapel mic and vinyl carrying case. *ICF-SW1000TS:* Comes with AN-LP1 active antenna system.

Con: Costly. Incredibly at this price, only one bandwidth, and no AC adaptor comes standard. Synchronous selectable sideband tends to lose lock if batteries not fresh, or if NiCd cells are used. No tuning knob. Clock not readable when radio switched on except for ten-seconds when button is pushed. No meaningful signal-strength indicator. No recording-level indicator or tape counter. Lacks built-in mic and stereo mic facility. Reception is interrupted for two-to-three seconds when recording first commences. No pause control. Lacks flip-out elevation panel; uses less-handy plug-in elevation tab, instead. FM sometimes overloads. Telescopic antenna exits from the side, which limits tilting choices for FM. *ICF-SW1000TS:* Not available in the United States or most other countries.

Verdict: An innovative, neat little package—but not cheap.

✪✪½ ©
Roberts RC828, Sangean ATS-818ACS

Price: *Roberts:* £199.95 in the United Kingdom. *Sangean:* $224.95 in the United States. CAN$359.00 as available in Canada. £164.95 in the United Kingdom. AUS$399.95 in Australia.

Pro: Built-in cassette recorder. Price low relative to competition. Superior overall world band performance. Numerous tuning features, including 18 world band station presets. Two bandwidths for good fidelity/interference tradeoff. Superior spurious-signal ("image") rejection. Illuminated display. Signal-strength indicator. Two 24-hour clocks, one for World

✪✪✪½
Sony ICF-SW77, Sony ICF-SW77E

Price: $469.95 in the United States. £339.95 in the United Kingdom. AUS$1,249.00 in Australia. ¥8,000 in China.

Pro: A rich variety of tuning features, including innovative computer-type graphical interface found on few other world band models. Synchronous selectable sideband is exceptionally handy to operate; it significantly reduces fading distortion and adjacent-channel interference on world band, longwave and mediumwave AM signals; although the sync chip was changed recently, it performs virtually identically to the original. Two well-chosen bandwidths provide superior adjacent-channel rejection. Tunes in exacting 50 Hz increments; displays in 100 Hz increments,

For world band the Sony ICF-SW77 performs similarly to the ICF-2010, but with different tuning and 50 Hertz steps.

making this superior to the ICF-2010 for single-sideband reception. Two illuminated multi-function liquid crystal displays. Pre-set world band segments. Keypad tuning. Tuning "knob"

Time, with either displayed separately from frequency. Alarm/snooze/timer features. Travel power lock. Stereo through headphones. Longwave. Built-in condenser mic. Superior quality of construction, including tape deck. *Sangean:* Supplied with AC adaptor.

Con: Recorder has no multiple recording events, just one "on" time only (quits when tape runs out). Mutes when tuning knob turned quickly, making bandscanning difficult (C. Crane Company offers a modification to remedy this). Wide bandwidth a bit broad for world band reception. Unconfirmed reader reports suggest that the front end is unusually prone to malfunctioning from static discharge into the antenna, such as from fingertips during dry winter periods. Keypad not in telephone format. For single-sideband reception, relies on a touchy variable control instead of separate LSB/USB switch positions. Recorder has no level indicator and no counter. Fast-forward and rewind controls installed facing backwards.

Verdict: Great value, but only single-event.

Sony ICF-SW1000T is compact.

Sangean ATS-818CS costs less.

with two speeds. 162 station presets, including 96 frequencies stored by country or station name. "Signal-seek" scanning. Separately displayed World Time and local time clocks. Station name appears on LCD when station presets used. Signal-strength indicator. Flip-up chart for calculating time differences. VCR-type five-event timer controls radio and optional outboard recorder alike. Continuous bass and treble tone controls. Superior FM audio quality. Stereo FM through headphones. Receives longwave and Japanese FM. AC adaptor.

Con: Complex for many, but by no means all, to operate. Station presets can't be accessed simply, as they can on most models. Synthesizer chugging degrades the quality of tuning by knob. Dynamic range only fair. Synchronous selectable sideband subject to imperfect alignment, both from factory and from seeming drift after purchase, causing synchronous selectable sideband reception to be more muffled in one sideband than the other, particularly with the narrow bandwidth. Flimsy telescopic antenna. Display illumination does not stay on with AC power. On mediumwave AM band, relatively insensitive, sometimes with spurious sounds during single-sideband reception; this doesn't apply to world band reception, however. Mundane reception of difficult FM signals. Signal-strength indicator over-reads. Some readers report that painted

surfaces can wear off with use and become unsightly.

Verdict: The '77 has been all but the best performer since it was improved awhile back, and for single-sideband reception is as good as any. Ergonomics, however, are a mixed bag, so if you're interested try it out first.

✪✪½ ✐
Roberts R827, Sangean ATS-818

Price: *Roberts:* £139.95 in the United Kingdom. *Sangean:* $174.95 in the United States. CAN$289.00 as available in Canada. £119.95 in the United Kingdom.

Pro: Nicely priced in the United States. Superior overall world band performance. Numerous tuning features, including 18 world band station presets. Two bandwidths for good fidelity/interference tradeoff. Superior spurious-signal ("image") rejection. Illuminated display. Signal-strength indicator. Two 24-hour clocks, one for World Time, with either displayed separately from frequency. Alarm/snooze/timer features. Travel power lock. FM stereo through headphones. Longwave. Superior quality of construction. *Sangean:* AC adaptor.

Con: Mutes when tuning knob turned quickly, making bandscanning difficult (C. Crane offers a modification to remedy this). Wide bandwidth a bit broad for world band reception. Unconfirmed reader reports suggest that the front end is unusually prone to malfunctioning from static discharge into the antenna, such as from fingertips during dry winter periods. Keypad not in telephone format. For single-sideband reception, relies on a touchy variable control instead of separate LSB/USB switch positions. Does not come with tape-recorder jack.

Verdict: With a price in some places that's hard to resist, this is a decent, predictable radio—performance and features, alike—although unless modified it is mediocre for bandscanning.

Sangean's ATS-818 is also the Roberts R827, but no longer sold under Radio Shack's brand.

ANALOG PORTABLES

With digitally tuned portables now everyday, there's little reason to purchase an analog, or slide-rule-tuned, model. They lack every tuning aid except a knob, and their coarse indicators make it almost impossible to tell the frequency.

Yet, for the money—nearly all sell for under the equivalent of US$100 or £70—these models sometimes have better weak-signal sensitivity and battery consumption than some of their digital counterparts.

Pocket Analog Portables

✪✪ **Sony ICF-SW22.** Tiny, with superior spurious signal ("image") rejection, but tinny sound and limited world band frequency coverage.

✪½ **Grundig Yacht Boy 207, Grundig Yacht Boy 217, InterNational WR-689, Panasonic RF-B11, Roberts R101, Sangean MS-101, Sangean MS-103, Sangean MS-103L, Sangean SG-789A, Sangean SG-789L, Grundig Mini World 100, Sharper Image VA100, Tecsun R-808, Tecsun R-808A, Sony ICF-SW12.**

✪ **InterNational R-110**

Compact Analog Portables

✪½ **Amsonic AS-912, Cougar H-116, Cougar H-123, Elektro AC 100, Grundig Yacht Boy 205, InterNational AC 100, Kchibo KK-168, Kchibo KK-210B, MCE-7760, Pace, Roberts R622, Sangean SG 622, Sangean SG 789A, Sangean SG 789LA, SEG Precision World SED 110, Radio Shack DX-397, Sony ICF-SW11, Sony ICF-SW12, SoundTronic Multiband Receiver, TEC 235TR.**

✪ **Apex 2138, Cougar H-88, Cougar RC210, Garrard Shortwave Radio 217, Grundig Traveller II PE, InterNational MT-718, Opal OP-35, Panashiba FX-928, Precision World SED 901, Shiba Electronics FX-928, Silver InterNational MT-798, Windsor 2138.**

Analog Lap Portables

✪✪ ✐ **Sony ICF-SW600.** Superior audio and built-in AC power supply, although mediumwave AM has poor spurious-signal rejection. No longer available new within the United States.

✪ **Alconic Series 2959, Dick Smith D-2832, Electro Brand 2971, Electro Brand SW-2000, Rhapsody Multiband, Shimasu Multiband, Steepletone MBR-7, Steepletone MBR-8, Venturer Multiband.**

The PASSPORT portable-radio review team includes Lawrence Magne, Tony Jones and George Zeller, with laboratory measurements performed independently by Sherwood Engineering. Additional research by Craig Tyson.

Portatop Receivers for 2000

Sound Performers for Home, RV or Outdoors

Most of us buy a world band radio not for just one room, but for around the house—maybe outdoors, too. Yet, portables rarely sound as good as stationary tabletops, nor can most cut the mustard with really tough signals.

Solution: Combine the most desirable characteristics of portables and tabletops into one single rugged receiver—a portatop—which can be serviced, like tabletop models, for years to come.

Drawbacks? They're larger and costlier than most portables, require separate antennas for optimum performance and go through batteries with abandon. Also, only one, the American-made Drake SW8, receives FM broadcasts. If you can live with that, you'll find performance and fidelity that in many ways equals that of top-rated tabletop receivers.

What PASSPORT's Ratings Mean

Star ratings: ✪✪✪✪✪ is best. PASSPORT awards stars solely for overall performance and meaningful features, plus to some extent ergonomics and build quality. Price, appearance, country of manufacture and the like are not taken into account. With portatop models there is roughly equal emphasis on the ability to flush out tough, hard-to-hear signals, and program-listening quality with stronger broadcasts.

Passport's Choice. La crème de la crème. Our test team's personal picks of the litter—models we would buy or have bought for our personal use.

✪: A relative bargain.

Prices: Approximate selling, or "street," prices (including VAT, where applicable). Prices vary plus or minus, so take them as the general guide they are meant to be.

Unless otherwise stated, all portatop models have:

- Digital frequency synthesis and display.
- Full coverage of at least the 155-29999 kHz longwave, mediumwave AM and shortwave spectra—including all world band frequencies—but no coverage of the FM broadcast band (87.5-108 MHz). Models designed for sale in Saudi Arabia have reduced tuning ranges.
- A wide variety of helpful tuning features.
- Synchronous selectable sideband, using high-rejection discrete filters (not phasing) to reduce adjacent-channel interference and fading distortion.
- Proper demodulation of utility and "ham" shortwave signals, except for models designed to be sold in Saudi Arabia. These include single-sideband and CW (Morse code); also, with suitable

ancillary devices, radioteletype and radio fax.
- Meaningful signal-strength indication.
- Illuminated display.

✪✪✪✪½ 📖 *Passport's Choice*
Drake SW8

Price: $799.95 in the United States. CAN$1,299.00 in Canada. Also available in Germany.

Pro: Above-average audio quality with internal speaker or headphones. Synchronous selectable sideband reduces adjacent-channel interference and fading distortion with world band, longwave and mediumwave AM signals. Three bandwidths provide worthy adjacent-channel rejection. Continuous tone control. Numerous helpful tuning aids, including 70 presets. Helpful signal-strength indicator, digital. Single-sideband reception well above the portable norm. Weak-signal sensitivity excellent with external antenna (*see* Con). Superior blocking performance aids consistency of sensitivity. Two timers

The Drake SW8, improved since its introduction, is now tops in portatops. Alas, it is rarely sold outside North America.

NEW FOR 2000: PALSTAR R30/LOWE HF-350

The first radio to emerge from Ohio's Bramco Palstar Inc. is the R30, destined for sale not only in North America but also the European Community and Japan, as well.

We tested an engineering prototype. Production units will almost certainly perform differently, presumably better, so we can't yet assign this model a specific rating. While we did not test it in full portable regalia—battery pack, active antenna and handle—it is small enough to take along on car trips and even the occasional domestic flight. But the key to its success as a portable will be the performance of its AA30 active antenna, which was not available at the time we ran our tests.

Limited Features

At $549 the R30 is a low-cost receiver by portatop and tabletop standards. At this price everything can't be done, so the focus has been to do a few things well. As a result many aspects of performance are top-drawer, but features are scarce. Because of the receiver's size, operating controls are small to the point where some may avoid the radio altogether—only you can decide. Another ergonomic hiccup is that there is no tilt bail for a comfortable operating angle.

The R30 is a straightforward receiver, even by portatop standards—no passband shift, noise blanker, tunable notch filter or keypad. Also missing is synchronous selectable sideband, which Sony includes in $170 portables. As tuning increments are no finer than 100 Hz, so-called "ECSS" reception—tuning AM-mode signals as though they were single sideband—is suboptimal. Taken together, tuning increments and the lack of synchronous selectable sideband limit rejection of adjacent-channel interference and selective-fading distortion.

The manufacturer may eventually offer a mouse-type outboard pad, *à la* the Lowe HF-150. In the meantime, the R30's one hundred non-volatile station presets can't be quickly accessed, and hopping from one frequency to another—say, while bandscanning—is partially rescued only by the R30's creative multi-speed tuning knob.

Generally Superior Performance

The basic R30 comes with two voice bandwidths, 7.6 kHz—slightly broad—and 2.5 kHz, selectable independent of mode. The MuRata ceramic filters have shape factors of 1:1.4 (superb) and 1:1.6 (excellent), respectively. A third bandwidth of four-to-five kilohertz would help and is being considered for a possible later version.

Because of distribution agreements, the Lowe HF-350 incarnation will be offered in place of the Palstar R30 in Continental Europe and Japan. Both versions are identical, except that the '350's wide bandwidth reportedly will be around 4 kHz, surprisingly narrow for a "wide" except for DXing. Additionally, the R30—but not the '350—will be offered in a special $649 version having Collins mechanical bandwidth filters.

The AGC works well and has two user-selectable decay settings, but can't be switched off. This makes sense, as there is no RF gain control to act in lieu of an AGC. There are some spurious "birdies," usually on frequencies unlikely to be tuned by world band users, but experience indicates that these are more prevalent on prototypes than production units.

Image rejection measures 60 dB in our laboratory, and while this is a respectable figure it is not enough to keep all images at bay, as confirmed during hands-on listening.

Ultimate rejection measures a superb 90 dB, although in the prototype this measurement, although genuine (sort of, there were technical oddities), was not realized under real-world listening conditions. Presumably the production version will allow for unambiguous 90 dB rejection, and if so this will be world-class performance.

At 0.9 microvolts the AGC threshold is superb. Front-end selectivity is fair, while first IF rejection and phase noise measure good. The synthesizer does not always step properly, sometimes backing up—a minor nuisance which may not appear in production units. The front-panel emits slight RFI hash, undetectable much beyond six inches or 15 centimeters.

Dynamic range has traditionally been measured with test signals 20 kHz apart. However, for world band, where channel separation is 5 kHz, tests using signals 5 kHz apart are more telling of real-world listening results.

The R30's 20 kHz separation dynamic range is 84 dB, good, while the more important third-order intercept point is +9 dBm, excellent. This is the stuff of kilobuck supersets. Yet, at 5 kHz separation dynamic range plummets to a dismal 50 dB, third-order to –42 dBm—both poor. We typically find this anomaly with initial offerings from new manufacturers, who usually rely on general-purpose 20 kHz separation tests, and the R30 is no exception. However, we didn't encounter significant overloading.

Sensitivity measures between 0.9 and 1.25 microvolts within the shortwave spectrum, 1.4 microvolts in the mediumwave AM band, and 1.8 microvolts longwave—all fair. The more important noise-floor measurement is comparable, –111 to –117 dBm. Blocking at 117 dB is good, helping assure consistent sensitivity in the presence of nearby powerhouse signals. Since our tests were completed, the manufacturer has made semiconductor changes it claims improves sensitivity to 0.5 microvolts or better throughout the tuned radio spectrum.

Even without a tone control, audio quality is pleasant with a suitable outboard speaker, thanks in part to overall distortion that's never over one percent. However, occasional hum was audible, perhaps caused by the AC adaptor. With the inboard speaker above the 12 o'clock position, the hum became more intrusive and distortion rose. At the same time the normally accurate analog signal-strength indicator started displaying a lower reading and the LCD illumination dimmed, so this could be the result of an underpowered AC adaptor used for the prototype. If so, these issues should be cleared up before production.

The Palstar P30 shows real promise in certain critical areas of difficult-signal performance, but lacks a number of important features. Fortunately, improvements are in the works from this new American manufacturer, so what we've seen thus far may be but the beginning of an uphill curve.

The Palstar R30, with a narrower "wide" bandwidth, is sold as the Lowe HF-350. Both are manufactured by the new firm of Bramco Palstar Inc.

and 24-hour clocks (*see* Con). Display illuminated. FM—mono through speaker, stereo through headphones—performs well. Covers longwave down to 100 kHz and VHF aeronautical band. Superior factory service, although discontinued models are no longer supported for as long as they used to be. Optional carrying case. Fifteen-day money-back trial period if ordered from the factory or certain dealers.

Con: Audible circuit noise ("hiss") when used with built-in antenna; clipping a length of wire to the built-in antenna helps greatly. Lacks notch filter, adjustable noise blanker and passband tuning. Ergonomics only fair, including pushbuttons that rock on their centers. Key pushes must each be done within three seconds, lest receiver wind up being mis-tuned or placed into an unwanted operating mode. Wide band-width—nominally 6 kHz, actually 7.8 kHz—a bit broad. Outboard adaptor in lieu of inboard power supply. Telescopic antenna doesn't swivel fully for best FM reception. Unlike with a portable, no built-in ferrite rod antenna for directional longwave and mediumwave AM reception. Clocks don't display when frequency is shown. Carrying/elevation handle clunky

to adjust, with adjustment stops that can break if handle forced. Optional MS8 outboard speaker not equal to receiver's fidelity potential.

Verdict: The current version of the Drake SW8 is very nearly everything a top-notch portatop should be: performance only a skootch below that of the fanciest tabletop supersets, yet priced lower with portability and FM thrown in. A superior all-around receiver for use both indoors and out, but hiss with the built-in antenna is a drawback (a roll of insulated hookup wire creates an instant booster antenna).

📄 An *RDI WHITE PAPER* is available for this model.

★★★★ 📄
Lowe HF-150

Price, without keypad or other options: *HF-150:* £419.00 including VAT in the United Kingdom. *Keypad:* £39.95 in the United Kingdom.

Pro: Top-notch world band and mediumwave AM audio quality, provided a good external speaker or simple headphones are used. Synchronous selectable sideband reduces fading distortion with world band, longwave and mediumwave AM signals. Exceptionally rugged cast-aluminum housing. Mouse keypad, virtually foolproof and a *de rigeur* option. Sixty presets store frequency and mode. Tunes, but does not display, in exacting 8 Hz increments, unusually precise. Single-sideband reception well above the portable norm.

Con: Grossly inferior front-end selectivity can result in spurious signals if the radio is connected to a significant external antenna or used near mediumwave AM transmitters. Clumsy to use as a portable. Audio only okay through internal speaker. No tone control. Frequency displays no finer than 1 kHz resolution. Lacks lock

Superb audio quality is the hallmark of the Lowe HF-150. Apparently unavailable outside the United Kingdom, but there it offers good value for money.

indicator or similar aid (e.g., finer frequency-display resolution) for handy use of synchronous detector. No tunable notch filter, adjustable noise blanker, passband tuning or signal-strength indicator. Operation of some buttons may confuse initially. Tends to slide on table during operation. Lacks elevation feet or tilt bail. Erratic contact on outboard-speaker socket. Display not illuminated. AC power supply via a separate outboard adaptor, rather than inboard. Unlike with a portable, there is no built-in ferrite rod antenna for directional longwave and mediumwave AM reception.

☞ Lowe Electronics no longer makes the receivers which bear its name, although the new manufacturer's initial production difficulties now appear to have been resolved. In the meantime the HF-150's former international sales and service network has vanished.

Verdict: With so many unresolved shortcomings, the Lowe HF-150 has by now been surpassed by the current version of the Drake SW8. Still, in the U.K., where the SW8 is virtually unavailable, the HF-150 remains a tough little radio with superb fidelity.

📄 An *RDI WHITE PAPER* is available for this model.

_____

The PASSPORT *portatop review team includes Lawrence Magne, Tony Jones, Craig Tyson and George Zeller, with John Wagner. Laboratory measurements by Robert Sherwood.*

Tabletop Receivers for 2000

Tabletop receivers flush out tough game—faint stations, often swamped by competing signals. That's why they are prized by radio aficionados known as "DXers," a term meaning long distance.

But tabletop models aren't for everybody, and it shows. Even in prosperous North America tabletop unit sales are under five percent of the total, and elsewhere it's usually under one percent. If all you want to hear are non-DX signals—daytime stations, say—and your portable can't quite hack it, look instead to a portatop model or a better-rated portable. But if you're already using a portable with an outdoor antenna and it is being interfered with by electrical noise (from nearby motors, dimmers and such), you probably won't benefit from a tabletop. After all, its superior circuitry will boost the local noise right along with the distant signals.

Heavy Artillery

Tabletop supersets, like portatops, are the heavy artillery to call up where signals are weak—places like the North American Midwest and West, or Australia and New Zealand. Even elsewhere there can be a problem when world band signals have to follow paths over or near the geomagnetic North Pole. To check, place a string on a globe—a map won't do—between you and where signals come from. If the string passes near or above latitude 60° N, beware.

Daytime Signals Weaker

Since the end of the Cold War some stations have compressed their schedules, so some programs are now heard only during the day. Daytime signals tend to be weaker, especially when not beamed to your part of the world. However, thanks to the scattering properties of shortwave, you can still eavesdrop on many of these "off-beam" signals. But it's harder, and that's where a well-rated tabletop's longer reach comes in.

Cliff-Dwellers' Choice, but No FM

In high-rise buildings—especially urban—portables can disappoint. Reinforced buildings soak up signals, while local broadcast and cellular/PCS transmitters can interfere.

Here, your best bet for tough stations is a good tabletop or portatop model fed by a homebrew insulated-wire antenna along, or just outside, a window or balcony. Also, try an ordinary telescopic car antenna stuck perpendicularly out a window or balcony ledge. If your radio has a built-in preamplifier, all the better. With some portatop models, the built-in preamplifier

can be accessed by connecting the external antenna to the receiver's whip-antenna input.

You can also try amplified ("active") antennas that have reception elements and amplifiers in separate modules—avoid models where the antenna is affixed to the cabinet. Properly made active antennas are found at world band specialty outlets, but even these sometimes produce false signals—although Datong models have traditionally been superior in this regard. The quality of performance of active antennas is very location-specific, so try to purchase on a returnable basis.

Most tabletop receivers are pricier than portables. For that extra money you tend to get not only better performance, but also a better-made device. However, what you rarely find in a tabletop is reception of the everyday 87.5-108 MHz FM band.

Good Antenna Required

Tabletop receiver performance is greatly determined by antenna quality and placement. If you don't live in an apartment, go with a first-rate outdoor wire antenna, like those from Antenna Supermarket and Alpha Delta—usually under $100. A good world band antenna is the most cost-effective way to improve performance with a tabletop or portatop model. For performance findings and specifics for best installation, check with the Radio Database International White Paper, *Popular Outdoor Antennas*.

Complete Findings Now Available

Our unabridged laboratory and hands-on test results for each receiver are too exhaustive to reproduce here. However, they are available for selected models as PASSPORT's Radio Database International White Papers—details on availability are given elsewhere in this book.

Tips for Using this Section

Receivers are listed in order of suitability for listening to difficult-to-hear world band stations. Important secondary consideration is given to audio fidelity and ergonomics. We cite street—actual selling—prices, which are as of when we go to press. These vary, so take them as the general guide they are meant to be.

Unless otherwise stated, all tabletop models have:

- Digital frequency synthesis and display.
- Full coverage of at least the 155-29999 kHz longwave, mediumwave AM and shortwave spectra—including all world band frequencies—but no coverage of the FM broadcast band (87.5-108 MHz). Models designed for sale in Saudi Arabia have reduced tuning ranges.
- A wide variety of helpful tuning features.
- Synchronous selectable sideband, via high-rejection discrete filters (not phasing), which greatly reduces adjacent-channel interference and fading distortion.
- Proper demodulation of non-world-band shortwave signals, except for models designed to be sold in Saudi Arabia. These include single-sideband and CW (Morse code); also, with suitable ancillary devices, radioteletype and radio fax.
- Meaningful signal-strength indication.
- Illuminated display.

What PASSPORT's Rating Symbols Mean

Star ratings: ✪✪✪✪✪ is best. We award stars mainly for overall performance and meaningful features, plus to some extent ergonomics and construction quality. Price, appearance, country of manufacture and the like are not taken into account. With tabletop models there is a slightly greater emphasis on the ability to flush out tough, hard-to-hear signals, as this is one of the main reasons these sets are chosen.

Passport's Choice. La crème de la crème. Our test team's personal picks of the litter—models we would buy or have bought for our personal use.

✪: No, this doesn't mean cheap—none of these models is cheap. Rather, it denotes a model that costs appreciably less than usual for the satisfying level of performance provided.

✪✪✪✪✪ 📖 *Passport's Choice*
Watkins-Johnson HF-1000

Price: *HF-1000:* $3,799.00 in the United States. CAN$5,400 in Canada. £4,495.00 in the United Kingdom. No longer available in Australia. *Sherwood SE-3 MK III accessory:* $495.00 plus shipping worldwide.

Pro: Unsurpassed reception of weak world band DX signals. Exceptional reception of "utility" stations. Generally superior audio quality (*see* Con), especially when used with the Sherwood SE-3 fidelity-enhancing accessory and a worthy external speaker (*see* below). Unparalleled bandwidth flexibility, with no less than 58 outstandingly high-quality bandwidths. Digital signal processing (DSP). Tunes and displays in extremely precise 10 Hz increments. Extraordinary operational flexibility—virtually every receiver parameter is adjustable. One hundred station presets. Synchronous detection reduces distortion with world band, mediumwave AM and longwave signals (*see* Con). Built-in preamplifier. Tunable notch filter. Highly adjustable scanning of both frequency ranges and channel presets. Easy-to-read displays. Large tuning knob. Can be fully and effectively computer and remotely controlled. Passband tuning (*see* Con). Built-in test equipment (BITE) diagnostics. Built-in 455 kHz IF output makes for instant installation of Sherwood SE-3 accessory (*see* below). Superior factory service.

Con: Very expensive. Static and modulation splash sound harsher than with most other models, although this has been improved somewhat in the latest version of the receiver's operating software. Complex to operate to full advantage. Synchronous detection not sideband-selectable, so it does not aid in reduction of adjacent-channel interference. Requires coaxial antenna feed line to avoid receiver-generated digital noise emanating from audio output connector; however, thanks to a connector design change this problem is now less serious than it was with early production units (indeed, early production units also emanated digital noise from the headphone socket, but this was quickly resolved with a new, no-noise socket). Passband tuning operates only in CW mode. Jekyll-and-Hyde ergonomics: sometimes wonderful, sometimes awful. No traditional cabinet, and front-panel rack "ears" protrude. In principle, mediocre front-end selectivity; however, problems were not apparent during listening tests; and, if needed (say, if you live very close to a mediumwave AM station), a sub-octave preselector option can be added or installed at factory. Cumbersome operating manual.

☞ Within the Americas and many other parts of the world, the $599.95 optional sub-octave preselector offered by Watkins-Johnson is rarely necessary. However, within Europe and other strong-signal parts of the world, the preselector may improve spurious-signal rejection.

Improved Performance with Accessory: PASSPORT panelist George Zeller has been using his personal HF-1000 in combination with a Sherwood SE-3 outboard accessory for some time, now. He emphasizes that this receiver is noticeably better with the SE-3, and installation takes about one minute with no tools.

For starters, the receiver has only double-sideband synchronous detection, whereas the SE-3 allows it to have synchronous selectable sideband, a major improvement. Also, the receiver's passband tuning

Does more money buy a better receiver? Not always, but it does with the Watkins-Johnson HF-1000. It provides not only the ultimate in DX performance, but also ruggedness and high-quality construction.

operates only in the CW mode, while the SE-3 allows for passband tuning in all modes. Too, with the SE-3 no receiver-generated digital noise is present, as the receiver's audio output no longer needs to be used. Finally, with the SE-3 the receiver's audio quality improves noticeably.

Verdict: In its latest incarnation, the American-made HF-1000 is, by a hair, the ultimate machine for down-and-dirty DXing where money is no object. With a final solution to the digital hash problem—and the addition of a tone control, passband tuning and synchronous selectable sideband—the '1000 would have been even better, especially for program listening. Fortunately, the Sherwood SE-3 accessory remedies all these problems, and improves audio fidelity, to boot. For those who don't wish to go the SE-3 route, the outstanding Alpha-Delta "DX-Ultra" antenna eliminates nearly all the hash problem. Thus, the HF-1000 now is exceptionally well-suited to demanding aficionados with suitable financial wherewithal—provided they want a high degree of manual receiver control.

★★★★★ *Passport's Choice*
Drake R8B

Price: $1,199.00 in the United States. CAN$1,899.00 in Canada. £999.00 in the United Kingdom. Also available in Germany.

Pro: Superior all-round performance for listening to world band programs and hunting DX catches, as well as utility, amateur and mediumwave AM signals. Mellow, above-average audio quality, especially with suitable outboard speaker or headphones. Selectable-sideband synchronous detector excels at reducing distortion caused by fading, as well as at diminishing or eliminating adjacent-channel interference; also has synchronous double sideband. Five well-chosen bandwidths, four suitable for world band. Highly flexible operating controls, including a powerful tunable AF notch filter (tunes to 5,100 Hz AF and is now easier to adjust, but *see* Con) and an excellent passband offset control. Best ergonomics of any five-star model, plus LCD unusually easy to read. Tunes and displays in precise 10 Hz increments. Slow/fast/off AGC with superior performance characteristics. Exceptionally effective noise blanker. Helpful tuning features include 1,000 presets and sophisticated scanning functions; presets can be quickly accessed via tuning knob and slew buttons. Built-in preamplifier. Accepts two antennas, selectable via front panel. Two 24-hour clocks, with seconds displayed numerically and two-event timer (*see* Con). Helpful operating manual. Superior factory service, although older models aren't supported for as long as they used to be. Fifteen-day money-back trial period if ordered from the factory or certain dealers.

Con: Virtually requires a good outboard speaker for non-headphone listening, but optional Drake MS8 outboard speaker not equal to the receiver's audio potential; try a good amplified computer speaker or high-efficiency passive speaker instead. Neither clock shows when frequency displayed. Lightweight tuning knob lacks flywheel effect. No IF output. Otherwise-excellent tilt bail difficult to open. Notch filter does not tune below 500 Hz (AF).

Verdict: The American-made Drake R8B is the only receiver we have ever tested—portable, portatop or tabletop—that gets *everything* right, where something important isn't missing or sputtering. Still, a better (outboard) speaker is worth considering if you want to get the full benefit of the R8B's fidelity potential.

📄 An *RDI WHITE PAPER* is available for this model.

Revised for 2000
✪✪✪✪✪ *Passport's Choice*
AOR AR7030, AOR AR7030 "PLUS"

Price: *AR7030:* $1,149.95 in the United States. CAN$1,995.00 in Canada. £799.00 in the United Kingdom (£680.00 plus shipping for export). AUS$2,890.00 by special order in Australia. *AR7030 PLUS:* $1,299.95 in the United States. CAN$2,395.00 in Canada. £949.00 in the United Kingdom (£807.66 plus shipping for export). AUS$3,200.00 by special order in Australia.

Pro: In terms of sheer performance for program listening, as good a radio as we've ever tested. Except for sensitivity to weak signals (*see* Con), easily overcome, the same comment applies to DX reception. Exceptionally quiet circuitry. Superior audio quality. Synchronous selectable sideband performs quite well for reduced fading and easier rejection of interference. Synchronous detection circuit allows for either selectable-sideband or double-sideband reception. Best dynamic range of any

The Drake R8B is far and away the most popular tabletop receiver in North America. Tariff barriers reportedly make it harder to find elsewhere.

consumer-grade radio we've ever tested. Nearly all other lab measurements are top-drawer. Four voice bandwidths (2.3, 7.0, 8.2 and 10.3 kHz), with cascaded ceramic filters, come standard; up to six, either ceramic or mechanical, upon request (*see* Con). Superior audio quality, so well suited to listening to programs hour after hour. Advanced tuning and operating features aplenty, including passband tuning. Tunable AF notch and noise blanker now available, but as an option. Notch filter extremely effective, with little loss of audio fidelity. Built-in preamplifier (*see* Con). Automatically self-aligns and centers all bandwidth filters for optimum performance, then displays the actual measured bandwidth of each. Remote keypad (*see* Con). Accepts two antennas. IF output. Optional improved processor unit now has 400 memories, including 14-character alpha-numeric readout for station names. World Time clock, which displays seconds, calendar and timer/snooze features. Superior mediumwave AM performance. Superior factory service.

Con: Unusually hostile ergonomics, especially in PLUS version. Remote control unit, which has to be aimed carefully at either the front or the back of the receiver, is required to use certain features, such as direct frequency entry; not all panelists were enthusiastic about this arrangement, wishing that a mouse-type umbilical cable had been used instead. Although remote keypad can operate from across a room, the LCD characters are too small to be seen from such a distance. LCD omits certain important information, such as signal strength, when radio in various status modes. Sensitivity to weak signals good, as are related noise-floor measurements, but could be a bit better; a first-rate antenna overcomes this. Because of peculiar built-in preamplifier/attenuator design in which the two are linked, receiver noise rises slightly when preamplifier used in +10 dB position, or attenuator used in –10 dB setting;

The AOR AR7030 is an outstanding performer, but uses a menu-driven operating system that you'll probably either love or hate—nothing between.

however, PLUS version remedies this. When six bandwidths used (four standard ceramics, two optional mechanicals), ultimate rejection, although superb with widest three bandwidths, cannot be measured beyond –80/–85 dB on narrowest three bandwidths because of phase noise; still, ultimate rejection is excellent even with these three narrow bandwidths. Lacks, and would profit from, a bandwidth of around 4 or 5 kHz; a Collins mechanical bandwidth filter of 3.5 kHz (nominal at –3db, measures 4.17 kHz at –6 dB) is an option worth considering. Such Collins filters, in the two optional bandwidth slots, measure as having poorer shape factors (1:1.8 to 1:2) than the standard-slot MuRata ceramic filters (1:1.5 to 1:1.6). LCD emits some digital electrical noise, potentially a problem if an amplified (active) antenna is used with its pickup element (e.g. telescopic rod) placed near the receiver. Minor microphonics (audio feedback), typically when internal speaker is used, noted in laboratory; in actual listening, however, this is not noticeable. Uses outboard AC adapter instead of built-in power supply.

Verdict: This is definitely not your grandfather's shortwave receiver. AOR's sterling AR7030, designed and manufactured in England, is now an even better performer in its PLUS incarnation. Too, since mid-1999 the company, especially in the PLUS version, has addressed encoder-failure problems that sometimes showed up in earlier production. Yet, ergonomics, already peculiar and cumbersome in the "barefoot" version, is even more hostile in this advanced incarnation. These short-comings and slightly limited sensitivity to weak signals aside, the '7030 is the best DX choice available on the sweet side of a Watkins-Johnson HF-1000. This is a radio you'll really need to get your hands on for a few days before you'll know whether it's love or hate—or something in between.

☞ Features of the PLUS version can be incorporated into existing regular models by skilled electronic technicians. Contact the manufacturer or its agents for specifics.

Revision for 2000: Mechanical encoders on the '7030 have been subject to an above-average failure rate, possibly because of corrosion on contacts. Starting with serial number 102050, with production from late July of 1999, AOR has replaced the Bourns mechanical encoder with a metal-encased version from Alps as follows: AR7030 now uses Alps encoders; AR7030 PLUS now uses Alps mechanical and Bourns optical encoders. A conversion kit for earlier units out of warranty is available for £20 plus shipping, although it requires a degree of technical skill to install.

Revised for 2000, Retested for 2000
❋❋❋❋ 📋 *Passport's Choice*
Icom IC-R9000L, Icom IC-R9000, Icom IC-9000A

Price (receiver): $5,899.00 to authorized purchasers in the United States or for export. CAN$9,000.00 in Canada or for export. £4,080.00 in the United Kingdom. AUS$9,450.00 by special order in Australia.

Price (aftermarket options): *Three new filter bandwidths, installed by Sherwood:* $499.00. *Synchronous selectable sideband*

(Sherwood SE-3 with 9 MHz-to-455 kHz IF down converter): $720.00, installed.

Pro: Exceptional tough-signal performance, especially with faint DX signals that may be unreadable on other top-rated receivers. Flexible, above-average audio for a tabletop model when used with suitable outboard speaker; outstanding audio quality when used with Sherwood SE-3. Tunes and displays frequency in precise 10 Hz increments. Video display of radio spectrum occupancy, a rarely found feature. Sophis-ticated scanner/timer. Extraordinarily broad and high-quality coverage of radio spectrum, including portions forbidden to be listened to by the general public in the United States. Exceptional assortment of flexible operating controls and sockets. Good ergonomics. Superb reception of utility and ham signals. Superb reception of longwave DX, mediumwave DX, VHF/UHF scanner frequencies and FM broadcasts (monaural). Arguably the best available receiver for TV DX, using the built-in monochrome display. Two 24-hour clocks.

Con: In the United States, available only to Federal agencies, as it receives cellular frequencies; this ban is routinely circum-vented by purchasing from Canadian Icom dealers (service is available within the United States). Dreadfully expensive, especially with Sherwood aftermarket options, which are highly desirable. No synchronous selectable sideband (remedi-able with Sherwood SE-3). Power supply runs hot, although over the years this has not caused premature component failure. Two AM-mode bandwidths too broad for most world band applications (remediable with Sherwood aftermarket filter option). Both single-sideband bandwidths almost identical. Dynamic range merely adequate. Reliability, originally questionable, found to be above average in recent years. Front-panel controls of only average quality, although robust. Keypad frequency entry only in MHz, decimal and all.

☞ The five-star rating, above, applies only when it is equipped with aftermarket accessory filters and synchronous selectable sideband.

☞ The '9000A appears to be virtually identical to the regular 'R9000.

Verdict: The Icom IC-R9000/'R9000A/'R9000L, with changed AM-mode bandwidth filters—available from at least one world band specialty firm—is as good as it gets for DX reception of faint, tough signals throughout the radio spectrum. With the Sherwood SE-3 it is also top drawer for fastidious listening to world band programs. And it shines if you want a visual indication of spectrum occupancy and certain other characteristics of stations within a designated segment of the radio spectrum.

Revision for 2000: The "L" version, first made available in Japan in 1999, is scheduled to replace the current version in various world markets in the coming months. It is identical to the other versions except that the spectrum display uses an LCD instead of a CRT. According to unconfirmed reports, the changeover to an LCD is because the needed monochrome CRT is getting difficult to obtain.

📄 An *RDI WHITE PAPER* is available for this model.

✪✪✪✪¾
Kneisner + Doering KWZ 30

Price: *KWZ 30 receiver:* DM3,005 in Germany. *KWZ-TT remote keypad:* DM232 in Germany. Not available elsewhere.

Pro: Exceptional quality of construction. Exceptional audio quality with powerful amp (*see* Con). Superb skirt selectivity (*see* Con). Tunes and displays in ultra-precise 1 Hz increments. Precision four-level adjustment of AGC (decay, attack, hang and digital gain). Circuitry audibly very quiet. Large, easy-to-read illuminated LCD. Superior shielding. Innovative AM detector

Icom's IC-R9000L uses an LCD instead of a cathode-ray tube. Either way, it is unsurpassed among wideband receivers.

superior to ordinary detector, although inferior to synchronous detector, for reducing selective fading (*see* Con). DSP noise reduction sometimes aids in weak-signal comprehension. Wide range of tuning aids includes 250 presets. Superb wide (20 kHz separation) dynamic range (*see* Con). Superior reception of world band and utility DX signals. Signal-strength indicator, digital, the most accurate we have encountered—and arguably the most agreeable to read. Superior tuning knob. Automatic notch filter (*see* Con). Passband offset (*see* Con). Excellent if brief operating manual, also available in English.

Con: Available only from the manufacturer, and even then only when supplies on hand. Relatively few dedicated controls. Phase noise and effects of blocking limit measurement of ultimate rejection and skirt selectivity. Poor narrow (5 kHz separation) dynamic range. Slight artificiality to sound. Novel AM-mode detector keeps distortion low only when both sidebands are of equal strength, which is often not the case with world band and other skywave signals. No selectable sideband (except ordinary manual "ECSS"), as the unique AM-mode detector requires both sidebands to function. Runs off external AC adaptor rather than internal power supply. No World Time clock, timer or related facilities. Notch filter performance not all it could be, and no option for manual tuning of notch.

Probably the rarest nonprofessional receiver is the Kneisner + Doering KWZ 30, designed and manufactured in Germany. It is outstanding in many ways, yet long-contemplated improvements have yet to see the light of day.

Passband offset does not function in AM mode. No IF output.

☞ For over a year the manufacturer has been contemplating possible improvements to be incorporated in future production.

Verdict: In many ways the panzer-tough Kneisner + Doering receiver, made in Germany only in tiny quantities, is the best available. Yet, it falls short in certain respects, and there is no sign as yet of any long-contemplated improvements being implemented.

New for 2000
✪✪✪½
Japan Radio NRD-301A

Price: Under $8,000 in various countries—actual price varies considerably. Additional voice bandwidth filters roughly $150 each, installed.

Pro: Professional-quality construction with legendary durability that make the receiver unusually likely to survive round-the-clock use in punishing environments. Uncommonly easy to repair on the spot—aided by built-in test equipment (BITE), plug-in circuit boards and a spare-parts kit. Superior overall performance in nearly all respects. Superior ergonomics. Passband shift, operates in AM mode. Tunes in ultra-

precise 1 Hz increments. Three hundred presets, and VFO operates from presets' channels. Effective noise blanker. Adjustable AGC decay. Sophisticated scanning system. AF (audio) filter narrows high-and low-frequency audio response. Comes with spare parts for on-site repair. Operates from a wide range of AC voltages, using an easily adjusted inboard power supply and 24 VDC ship's power. Can be computer controlled. Room for additional bandwidths.

Con: Very expensive, but shop around—deals can be found. Lacks the operating flexibility of such professional supersets as the Watkins-Johnson HF-1000. Only two voice bandwidths (*see* Pro), although both perform nicely and are well chosen. No keypad tuning, a major omission. No synchronous selectable sideband (remediable by adding Sherwood SE-3 outboard accessory, which uses off-tuning to select sidebands). No tunable notch filter. Unusual audio, antenna and AC cord jacks. Signal-strength indicator not illuminated. Slight whine from LED display at high brightness after receiver has been on for over an hour. Slight AC "tingle" when touching cabinet, remediable by grounding the receiver or, for receive-only applications, by removing marine-oriented C1 and C2 capacitors from across the back of the AC socket. AC power transformer runs very hot and sometimes buzzes. Distribution limited to Japan Radio dealers, offices, and a few specialty organizations such as shipyards.

☞ The above star rating is for the receiver "as is" from the factory. With the addition of at least one more AM-mode voice filter and the Sherwood SE-3, the rating improves by a quarter star.

☞ Rack mounted, but a rugged optional cabinet is available for desktop use.

☞ A new professional-grade DSP receiver, the NRD-341, is to be introduced by Japan

Radio sometime in 2000. It is expected to sell for around ¥1.5 million, around $13-14 thousand. It is to have a specially designed IC with DSP after the second IF to generate a high-purity signal.

Verdict: Japan Radio's professional-grade NRD-301A receiver is exceptional. It is probably fit to be handed down from one generation to the next, what with its seemingly bulletproof construction, ease of repair and superior overall performance. Yet, because it is a professional receiver, as it comes from the factory it lacks certain features of use for everyday world band listening and DXing. And it is very, very costly.

Evaluation of New Model: The NRD-301A is made for heavy, pounding use and round-the-clock operation, mainly on the high seas. Its construction has much in common with U.S./NATO "mil-spec," which calls for precision components, oversize cooling and build quality designed for heavy use. These top-end components account in no small part for the receiver's steep price tag. Being a professional rig it is rack-mounted, with a rugged optional cabinet for desktop use. It operates off a wide range of AC voltages, as well as 24 VDC ship's power.

The NRD-301A self-diagnoses an internal failure using built-in test equipment, or BITE, which tests seven critical areas; any failure generates a numeric code to pinpoint the needed repair. To that end, the '301A comes with a "CARE package" of hardware to aid in repair and further diagnosis.

However, the receiver comes with no adaptor to allow antenna lead-in cables with BNC or other common types of connectors to be used. That's important— an adaptor is needed, as the receiver comes with an SO-239 antenna socket. When we tried three different over-the-counter PL259-to-BNC adaptors, the receiver's SO-239 threads turned out to be incompatible.

Japan Radio's bulletproof NRD-301A includes superb parts, self-diagnosis and a repair kit. It is the most dependable receiver tested.

There are two sensible recourses. You can snip off your antenna lead-in's BNC connector and use the lone M-P-5 antenna connector supplied with the radio—guard it with your life, you get only one! Or you can replace the receiver's SO-239 antenna socket with something else.

There is no adaptor supplied for the audio output jack, which also is nonstandard by consumer norms. Another offbeat socket is the line output, which uses a BK (break) connection and is 600 ohms, balanced. Socket issues aside, an external matching transformer is needed to interface with consumer equipment (e.g., tape recorders) having different impedances and unbalanced inputs.

The HRS-type AC power socket is durable, but as with so much else on this set is nonstandard for consumer products, so it may be difficult to replace except through JRC. More to the point, this set needs grounding—not so much to enhance antenna performance as to eliminate annoying but harmless AC "tingle." You can actually feel traces of juice on the cabinet when AC is being used; with 24 VDC ship's power, of course, this is not an issue.

Besides grounding, another solution is to remove the cause of the problem: C1 and C2 disc ceramic capacitors connected across the rear of the AC input socket, thence to the chassis. These are used for RF bypass when the receiver is being used with a transmitter, but for listening they serve no useful purpose. Snip 'em, and there goes the "tingle."

Rugged and Sensible

The '301A is one mighty tough hombre, designed for tireless service in the salty, slam-bang world of commercial shipping. For good reason, too—remember the *Titanic* if you want to see what can happen when emergency radio contact fails. So if you plan to spend the rest of your days on a deserted island or mountain redoubt, this is the one receiver to tuck along.

Still, it is not quite the "I survived Hiroshima" fortress that its NRD-93 predecessor was (an RDI White Paper is still available for the '93, while copies last). The '301A runs hot, which can work against long component life, and its tuning knob, although adjustable, lacks the '93's silky feel. However, the '301A is a better overall performer and can be computer controlled.

The '301A's disconcerting heat comes from the inboard AC power transformer, which also sometimes buzzes under load. This is in contrast to the rugged power transformer on the NRD-93, which ran relatively cool and silent.

The '301A's front panel is uncluttered and well organized, with dedicated controls for all functions. As a result, it is a snap to operate right out of the box. This makes it very much an offshoot of the NRD-93, except that some '301A controls are smaller and more tightly spaced. The easy-to-read LED frequency display is adjustable to four brightness levels. Settings for such functions as mode, bandwidth and AGC are also indicated by long-life LEDs, but the signal-strength meter is not illuminated.

This receiver tunes similarly to the long-discontinued R-390A, one of the most respected tube-type military receivers ever produced. A "MHz/Channel/Group" control changes frequency in 1 MHz increments.

Then the "Tuning" control more precisely tunes frequency in increments chosen by the user: 1 Hz, 10 Hz, 100 Hz, 1 kHz, 5 kHz, 9 kHz and 10 kHz. This is enhanced by two "quick feed" switches which tune in user-defined programmable steps. Fine frequency adjustment is further augmented by a Δ (delta) tune control which operates in 1 Hz increments. Once frequency, mode, bandwidth and AGC settings are selected, the combination can be stored in one of the 300 presets.

The receiver includes scan, sweep and run functions similar to those used in previous Japan Radio receivers. With scanning, various channel locations can be defined into groups and the receiver programmed to scan through a selected group. The scanning process can also be programmed to stop when a busy channel has caused the touchy squelch to close. The sweep function allows the receiver to step between two user-defined frequencies.

Other features include an effective noise blanker, as well as an AF (audio) filter to narrow both the high- and low-frequency audio response. Unlike consumer-grade Japan Radio receivers, the professional-grade '301A has no tunable notch filter, nor is there a keypad for direct frequency access—two features world band aficionados will sorely miss. Also missing is synchronous selectable sideband, an important listening advance found even on some $200 portables.

The receiver comes with five bandwidths: 6 kHz (measures 5.7 kHz), 3 kHz (measures 2.5 kHz), 1 kHz, 0.5 kHz (measures 0.57 kHz) and 0.3 kHz (1 kHz and 0.3 kHz are optional and were not tested by us). Of these, only the 5.7 kHz and 2.5 kHz bandwidths are available for use with AM-mode signals, the type emitted by world band stations. Equally, with single-sideband reception only those same two bandwidths may be used, plus the optional 1 kHz bandwidth.

The paucity of voice bandwidth choices is a real problem for the world band listener or DXer. The jump from 2.5 kHz to 5.7 kHz in the AM mode is excessive, especially considering that many other, less costly tabletop models have a much wider choice of voice bandwidths. The range of the passband shift control is varied by filter selection from plus or minus 0.12 kHz with the 0.3 kHz filter, to plus or minus 2.0 kHz with the 5.7 kHz filter.

Fortunately, the '301A accepts up to two additional bandwidth filters. Some JRC dealers will install additional Collins or other suitable filters, which are highly recommended if the '301A is going to be allowed to reach its potential with world band reception. Desirable extra bandwidths include one close to 4 kHz, another around 7.5 kHz.

Excellent Performance

So, how does the '301A perform? In a word, excellent. To begin with the passband shift control functions in the AM mode, and single-sideband performance is very good.

The '301A's AF filter is effective, although no substitute for a tunable IF notch filter. Although the AGC is far less user-controllable than some others—at least one more decay setting would have been appropriate—it provides smooth audio devoid of any "choppiness" in both AM and single-sideband operation, and this excellence is confirmed in the lab. "Fast" appears to be best for AM-mode signals, whereas "slow" is preferable for single sideband; however, overall distortion rises at 100 Hz AF when the "fast" setting is used.

Audio quality through the internal speaker is better than that of Japan Radio's various consumer-grade models, with low overall distortion—provided the receiver is properly tuned to the center of an AM-mode signal's frequency. (Even slight off-tuning of AM-mode signals raises distortion

The Japan Radio NRD-301A's AC power supply is not equal to that of the erstwhile NRD-93. This is probably deliberate, as most '301A receivers operate off 24 VDC ship's power.

considerably.) If you encounter audible audio distortion with world band or other AM-mode signals, try turning down the RF gain control, which is digital and thus operates in steps.

Even then, "bareback" audio is still no great shakes and there is no tone control. Additionally, with some undermodulated world band stations volume is inadequate even with the control turned up. The Sherwood SE-3 considerably improves audio quality, making the receiver sound very good throughout the bass, midrange and treble audio frequencies. Too, because the '301A is an unusually quiet receiver, there is virtually no noise for the SE-3 to magnify.

The two voice bandwidth filters measure up very well, with superb skirt selectivity and excellent ultimate rejection. Nonetheless, in A-B tests the '301A comes off as slightly less effective at adjacent-channel rejection than the Watkins-Johnson HF-1000, which has peerless selectivity and an almost limitless range of bandwidth choices.

Synchronous selectable sideband helps with selectivity, among other things. Indeed, the '301A lacks not only synchronous detection, but also an IF output. Fortunately, its 455 kHz IF is easily tapped (pin 14, connector 29 of the CAE-336A IF board) to accommodate a Sherwood SE-3 accessory, which provides the *ne plus ultra* in synchronous detection and audio quality, along with off-tuning to select sidebands.

The SE-3 bypasses the AF filter, which is no loss. However, it interferes with operation of the passband shift control; the SE-3 includes a similar facility, but it is less handy to use. Overall, for reducing interference and improving audio quality the SE-3 is two leaps forward, one step back.

Otherwise, the '301A performs with flying colors. Nearly every one of our lab measurements comes out as excellent or superb: sensitivity (0.14 &V), noise floor (–133 dBm), skirt selectivity (1:1.4), ultimate selectivity (75 dB), phase noise (124 dBc), image rejection (85 dB), first IF rejection (>95 dB), front-end selectivity (uses a tracking preselector!), stability (+/–10 Hz) and AGC threshold (1.5 &V). The '301A is even superior to the predecessor '93 with close-in dynamic range (75 dB *vs.* 63 dB at 5 kHz separation) and especially third-order intercept point (–19 dBm *vs.* –46 dBm at 5 kHz separation). Only longwave sensitivity (0.3 &V), longwave noise floor (–127 dBm) and blocking (122 dB) score average.

A minor oddity is a faint high-pitched whine from the radio itself, not the speaker, varying with the LED's brightness level. We never quite got to the bottom of this, but for those with sharp hearing it becomes audible only when the receiver is left on for at least an hour. Some NRD-93s do the same thing.

The Japan Radio NRD-301A is intended for commercial use, mainly maritime, with objectives that differ from those of a product aimed at landlubber radio enthusiasts. It is designed to provide long term,

bulletproof operation under heavy use in locations and environments that would make short work of a consumer-grade receiver. And should it act up you're likely to be able to fix it yourself, quickly and properly. But simply in terms of performance and flexibility of operation for shortwave listening or DXing, there are any number of other models available for much less money that do the job as well or better.

Retested for 2000
✪✪✪✪½
Japan Radio NRD-545

Price: $1,799.95 in the United States. £1,249.00 in the United Kingdom. AUS$3,890.00 by special order in Australia. ¥198,000 in Japan.

Pro: Fully 998 bandwidths provide unprecedented flexibility. Razor-sharp skirt selectivity, especially with voice bandwidths. Outstanding array of tuning aids, including 1,000 presets. Wide array of reception aids, including passband offset, tunable notch and synchronous selectable sideband having good lock. Highly adjustable AGC in all modes requiring BFO. Tunes in unusually precise 1 Hz increments; displays in 10 Hz increments. Superior ergonomics, among the best to be found. Some audio shaping. Virtually no spurious radiation of digital "hash." Superior reception of utility signals. Easily upgraded by changing software ROMs.

Con: Ultimate rejection only fair, although average ultimate rejection equivalent is 10-15 dB better; this unusual gap results from intermodulation (IMD) inside the digital signal processor. Audio quality is tough sledding in the unvarnished AM mode (the synchronous-AM detector helps clear things up). No AGC adjustment in AM mode or with synchronous selectable sideband, and lone AGC decay rate too fast. Dynamic range only fair. Synchronous selectable sideband sometimes slow to kick in. Notch filter tunes no higher than 2,500 Hz AF. Signal-strength indicator overreads at higher levels. Frequency display misreads by up to 30 Hz. No IF output, nor can one be retrofitted. World Time clock doesn't show when frequency displayed.

Verdict: In many ways Japan Radio's new NRD-545 is a remarkable performer, especially for utility and tropical-bands DXing. With its first-class ergonomics it is always a pleasure to operate, but more is needed to make this the ultimate receiver it could and should be.

Evaluation of newly tested units: We tested two new NRD-545s, finding no difference in performance from the most recent one tested for the 1999 PASSPORT. At the same time, the receiver's disappointing ultimate rejection (ultimate selectivity) grew puzzling, as with actual listening there were many instances where it behaved better than the lab numbers suggested. Obviously, something new was going on, which we ultimately resolved by analyzing the listening impact of processor limitations.

With digital-signal processing (DSP) circuitry there is the potential for intruding spurious noise or tones to prevent the usual measurement of ultimate rejection from being valid under all listening conditions. So we devised a new, separate measurement—average ultimate rejection equivalent, or ultimate rejection with those spurious tones allowed in. The difference is considerable: While the '545's pure ultimate rejection is only 45 dB, the average ultimate rejection equivalent is between 55 and 60 dB.

What this means is that the receiver's DSP filter leakage is not necessarily what is allowing in adjacent-or alternate-channel "monkey chatter" interference in any given instance. With the '545, there is a second potential culprit: intermodulation (IMD)

The NRD-545 is Japan Radio's first consumer-grade digital-signal processing (DSP) receiver. Its performance, already top-drawer in many respects, could have been more consistent and flexible with greater processing power.

inside the digital signal processor itself. These IMD products wind up smack atop the received signal. So while the end result sounds the same as filter leakage, the cause is different.

This new measurement will almost certainly have a brief useful life, as the technology to avoid this already exists—at a price. Before much longer, DSP IMD will be avoidable at a cost even the most tightfisted manufacturer will find acceptable, making the issue moot.

Nevertheless, the mystery has been solved. Now we know why the '545's ultimate rejection often seems satisfactory, yet at other times sounds woefully inadequate.

★★★★½
Japan Radio "NRD-345SE"

Price: $1,195.00 plus shipping worldwide.

Evaluation of Enhanced Model: Sherwood Engineering's Japan Radio "NRD-345SE" is the unofficial moniker for its version of the '345 sold by Sherwood with the Sherwood SE-3 fidelity-enhancing accessory and requisite IF output. The outboard SE-3 allows for first-rate synchronous selectable sideband and superior audio quality.

The least-costly way to obtain Japan Radio's legendary quality of construction is with the NRD-345. Its unofficial "SE" version has better audio quality than any standard JRC receiver.

It sounds very good, indeed—a major improvement in audio quality and interference rejection over the barefoot '345. The downside is that this version complicates operation, raises the price considerably, and does nothing to improve the '345's pedestrian dynamic range.

For other details, *see* Japan Radio NRD-345, farther on.

New for 2000
✪✪✪✪¼
Icom IC-R75, Icom IC-R75E

Price: *Receiver:* $799.95 in the United States. CAN$1,399.00 in Canada. £629.00 in the United Kingdom (usually includes UT-106 DSP Unit). AUS$1,675.00 in Australia. *UT-106 AF DSP Unit:* $139.95 in the United States. AUS$165.00 in Australia. Usually included with receiver in the United Kingdom. *Icom Replacement Bandwidth Filters:* $160-200 or equivalent worldwide. *Sherwood SE-3 Mark III (aftermarket):* $490.00 ($590.00 for deluxe version) including down converter and installation, plus shipping, in the United States. $460.00 ($560.00 for deluxe version) including down converter but not installation, plus shipping, outside the United States.

Pro: Dual passband tuning acts as variable bandwidth and a form of IF shift

(*see* Con). Reception of faint signals alongside powerful competing ones aided by excellent ultimate selectivity and good dynamic range. Outstanding rejection of spurious signals. Excellent reception of utility and ham signals, as well as world band signals painstakingly tuned via "ECSS" technique. Tunes and displays in precise 0.001 kHz increments. Two-level preamp allows excellent sensitivity to weak signals. Optional DSP unit helps improve intelligibility of some tough signals. Fairly good ergonomics. Adjustable AGC—fast, slow, off. Pretty good audio with suitable outboard speaker. Effective noise blanker. Two antenna inputs, switchable. Signal-strength indicator unusually linear above S-9, and can be set to hold a peak reading briefly. Audio out jack for recording or feeding low-power FM transmitter to hear world band around the house. Tunes to 60 MHz, including 6 meter VHF ham band.

Con: No synchronous selectable sideband without aftermarket SE-3 installed. Dual passband tuning usually has little impact on received world band signals and is inoperative when synchronous detection is in use. Double-sideband synchronous detector works so poorly as to be virtually useless. DSP unit, including automatic variable notch filter, comes at extra cost (except in U.K.) rather than being standard equipment. Automatic variable notch tends not to work with AM-mode signals not received via "ECSS" technique. Mediocre audio through internal speaker and no tone controls. Keypad requires frequencies to be entered in MHz format with decimal or trailing zeroes, a pointless inconvenience. Some knobs small. Weird knob adjusts RF gain to 12 o'clock position, then becomes a squelch control. Some distortion in AM mode, but only below 400 Hz AF. Uses outboard AC adaptor in lieu of internal power supply. Can read clock or frequency, but not both at the same time.

☞ The above star rating rises to ●●●¾ when the receiver is equipped with the Sherwood SE-3 aftermarket accessory. However, because the 'R75 uses two intermediate frequencies (IFs) for bandwidth filtering, the SE-3's offset has to be tweaked when going from a bandwidth having one IF to another with a different IF.

Verdict: The Icom IC-R75 is a first-rate receiver for unearthing tough utility and ham signals, as well as world band signals received via manual "ECSS" tuning. However, some features are absent or ineffective that should be alive and kicking in a newly designed receiver of this class. These can be largely overcome with the optional Icom DSP (usually standard equipment in the U.K.) and Sherwood SE-3, but this brings the price to over $1,400.

Evaluation of New Model: The Icom IC-R75 covers 30 kHz through 60 MHz, higher than most receivers. It tunes in increments as precise as 1 Hz, and the display reads out comparably. The receiver comes with typical tuning features, although the keypad requires that frequencies be entered in MHz—with either a decimal or trailing zeroes. It is nonstandard and less handy for shortwave than the usual decimal-free kHz.

There are typically three bandwidths for each mode. For world band the appropriate widths are 7.3 kHz and 2.3 kHz, both with excellent shape factors. High-quality replacement filters for other bandwidths are available from Icom. Although expensive, they are easy to install even if the clumsily written owner's manual is of little help.

Adding to bandwidth choice is the 'R75's innovative "twin passband tuning" feature. This not only allows the passband to be adjusted, rather like an IF shift, but also provides a form of variable bandwidth. It performs far better with narrow bandwidths than with most world band signals.

It is more complicated than several discrete bandwidths coupled to a standard IF shift. Also, depending upon a host of variables, the receiver's skirt selectivity has the potential of suffering when the twin passband tuning is used to shrink the bandwidth; replacement bandwidth filters help overcome this.

The usual potpourri of modes is received, plus there is synchronous detection. Alas, it is double-sideband (DSB) only, and the twin passband tuning can't be used to remedy this as it doesn't work when the sync is on. Even in DSB synchronous detection should be of some use, but on the 'R75 panelists couldn't hear any difference. As a practical matter it is useless.

DXers with older receivers have learned to accomplish much the same thing by manually tuning the receiver using so-called "ECSS" (exalted-carrier selectable sideband) tuning. They tune world band or other AM-mode signals with the receiver in the single-sideband mode, then adjust the receiver's tuned frequency as close as possible to the station's frequency. But ECSS is inconvenient, with at least some phase mismatch and occasional retuning required. With the R75, there is also a drop in volume, as well.

The aftermarket Sherwood SE-3 provides synchronous selectable sideband, and

Not tops for world band, yet Icom's new IC-R75 handles utility and amateur signals with aplomb.

works splendidly. But because the 'R75 uses two intermediate frequencies (IFs) for bandwidth filtering, the SE-3's offset has to be tweaked when going from a bandwidth having one IF to another with a different IF.

Generally Worthy Performance, Ergonomics

Audio quality through the radio's built-in speaker is only fair, but with a good outboard speaker it should satisfy most world band aficionados even though the radio has no tone controls. With the SE-3 audio quality improves even more, becoming excellent.

Automatic gain control (AGC) decay is adjustable to either fast or slow. For serious DXing with static present it may also be turned off, allowing the RF gain control to be used to adjust the sound level and distortion. Up to the 12 o'clock setting the RF gain knob functions as it should. However, if you turn it beyond that position the knob suddenly becomes reincarnated as a squelch control—a novel "two half moons" concept, indeed.

Separate high-and low-impedance antenna inputs are switchable from the front panel. The bar-type digital signal-strength indicator is commendably linear above S9; below that, it tends to overread. It can also be adjusted to hold a peak

reading briefly, which is convenient for technical station monitors.

Ergonomics are generally worthy, making this a fairly straightforward receiver to use. Although some knobs are disappointingly small, it has a panel full of discrete controls, making it much more intuitive to operate than, say, the menu-driven AOR AR7030.

By and large the display is well laid out and readable, with a wide variety of useful status indicators. The clock and frequency readout share the same display location, so you can read one or the other, but not both at the same time.

There is an audio-out jack to record or to feed a low-power FM transmitter (see sidebar) so you can hear your favorite world band station on any FM radio around the house or property.

The 'R75 performs commendably in our lab. Ultimate rejection and first IF rejection are both an excellent 80 dB, image rejection a superb >90 dB. Sensitivity to weak signals is excellent when the two-level preamplifier is used, and consistency of sensitivity is enhanced by good blocking performance.

However, phase noise is only fair, dynamic range average, and overall distortion in the AM mode not all it could be within the lower audio frequencies. Withal, in the lab the 'R75 shows no significant flaws and several strong points.

HEAR YOUR TABLETOP AROUND THE HOUSE

Whether you're using a tabletop receiver for world band or a desktop computer for Webcasts, you're stuck listening in one spot. Now, you can reach out with FM retransmission. Fleapower FM transmitters sold by C. Crane (www.ccrane.com) and Wal-Mart radiate around most living quarters and are a bargain at under $50.

Not enough power? If allowed within your jurisdiction, there's the quasi-professional LX-75S from Decade Transmitters (www.decade.ca)—$535 plus shipping worldwide. This stereo/mono unit has 200 kHz stepped tuning, modulation level, overmodulation warning, and adjustable 1-80 mW to cover anything from eight rooms in a house to eight hectares (20 acres) on a farm. It works well with the $30 AOR TW7030 antenna from Universal Radio and other dealers.

The receiver comes with an effective noise blanker, although it is not quite equal to the one on the Drake R8B. There is no tunable notch filter, although the $180 digital signal processing (DSP) feature, usually an optional extra, provides an automatic notch, along with digital audio processing to help make tough signals intelligible. Unfortunately, the notch tends not to work on many world band and other AM-mode signals unless they are tuned as single-sideband signals ("ECSS"). However, the DSP's noise reduction works pretty much as it should.

The new Icom IC-R75 excels in single-sideband and ECSS reception more than world band program listening, making it very well suited to serious DXing and utility chasing. In many parts of the world it is attractively priced relative to other available choices.

✪✪✪✪
Japan Radio NRD-345, Japan Radio NRD-345G

Price: $799.95 in the United States. £549.00 in the United Kingdom. AUS$1,600.00 by special order in Australia.

Pro: Superior construction quality by any yardstick, but especially for price. Excellent ergonomics, including superb tuning knob. Tunes in very precise 5 Hz increments with four manually selectable tuning speeds; displays to nearest 10 Hz. Superior weak-signal sensitivity and spurious-signal rejection. Two switchable antenna inputs, one low-impedance and the other high-impedance. Clock/timer functions. Tone control helps shape audio which, although lacking in treble, is already reasonably good and has minimal distortion. Slow/fast/off AGC (*see* Con). Memory scanning. Signal-strength indicator is analog. Double-fused for safety and protection. Worthy owner's manual.

Con: No tunable notch filter. Lacks passband tuning. Synchronous detector

not sideband-selectable and provides little improvement even in double-sideband. Mediocre dynamic range limits strong-signal handling. Uses AC adaptor instead of built-in power supply. World Time clock does not show when frequency displayed. AGC "off" virtually useless because of no RF gain control. Mediumwave AM performance suffers from reduced sensitivity and limited dynamic range.

Verdict: First rate ergonomics and construction quality, along with good performance, make the '345 an attractive value.

✪✪✪✪
Icom IC-R8500

Price: $1,869.00 in the United States. CAN$2,849.00 in Canada. £1,299.00 in the United Kingdom. AUS$2,730.00 in Australia.

Pro: Wide-spectrum multimode coverage from 0.1-2000 MHz includes longwave, mediumwave AM, shortwave and scanner frequencies all in one receiver. Physically very rugged, with professional-grade cast-aluminum chassis and impressive computer-type innards. Generally superior ergonomics, with generous-sized front panel having large and well-spaced controls, plus outstanding tuning knob with numerous tuning steps. 1,000 presets and 100 auto-write presets have handy naming function. Superb weak-signal sensitivity. Pleasant, low-distortion audio aided by audio peak filter. Passband tuning

"DC-to-daylight" receivers are a challenge to design, but the Icom IC-R8500 fares relatively well.

("IF shift"). Unusually readable LCD. Tunes and displays in precise 10 Hz increments. Three antenna connections. Clock-timer, combined with record output and recorder-activation jack, make for superior hands-off recording of favorite programs.

Con: No synchronous selectable sideband. Bandwidth choices for world band and other AM-mode signals leap from a very narrow 2.7 kHz to a broad 7.1 kHz with nothing between, where something is most needed; third bandwidth is 13.7 kHz, too wide for world band, and no provision is made for a fourth bandwidth filter. Only one single-sideband bandwidth. Unhandy carousel-style bandwidth selection with no permanent indication of which bandwidth is in use. Poor dynamic range, surprising at this price point. Passband tuning ("IF shift") does not work in the AM mode, used by world band and mediumwave AM-band stations. No tunable notch filter. Built-in speaker mediocre. Uses outboard AC adaptor instead of customary inboard power supply.

Versions Available: The Icom IC-R8500 is available in two similarly priced versions, "02" and "03." The "02" incarnation, sold to the public in the United States, is the same as the "03" version, but does not receive the *verboten* 824-849 and 869-894 MHz cellular bands. In the U.S., the "03" version is available legally only to government-approved organizations, although others reportedly have been bootlegging the "03" version by mail order from Canada. Outside the United States, the "03" version is usually the only one sold.

Sherwood SE-3: Also tested with Sherwood SE-3 non-factory accessory, which was outstanding at adding selectable synchronous sideband and provides passband tuning in the AM mode used, among other things, by world band stations. This and replacing the widest bandwidth with a 4 to 5 kHz bandwidth dramatically improve performance on shortwave, mediumwave AM and longwave.

Verdict: The large Icom IC-R8500 is really a scanner that happens to cover world band, rather than *vice versa*. As a standalone world band receiver, it makes little sense, but it is well worth considering if you want worthy scanner and shortwave performance all in one rig.

✪✪✪✪
AOR AR5000+3

Price: *AR5000+3 receiver:* $1,269.95 in the United States. CAN$3,695.00 in Canada. £1,574.00 in the United Kingdom. AUS$4,300.00 by special order in Australia. *Collins 6 kHz mechanical filter (recommended):* $149.95 in the United States. £69.95 in the United Kingdom.

Pro: Ultra-wide-spectrum multimode coverage from 0.1-2,600 MHz includes longwave, mediumwave AM, shortwave and scanner frequencies all in one receiver. Helpful tuning features include fully 2,000 presets. Narrow bandwidth filter and optional Collins wide filter both have superb skirt selectivity (standard wide filter's skirt selectivity unmeasurable because of limited ultimate rejection). Synchronous selectable and double sideband (*see* Con). Front-end selectivity, image rejection, IF rejection, weak-signal sensitivity, AGC threshold and frequency

AOR's AR5000+3, a wideband receiver that focuses on world band performance. Attractively priced, but its narrowband AR7030 cousin is still a better world band receiver.

stability all superior. Exceptionally precise frequency readout to nearest Hertz. Most accurate displayed frequency measurement of any receiver tested to date. Superb circuit shielding results in virtually zero radiated digital "hash." IF output (*see* Con). Automatic Frequency Control (AFC) works on AM-mode, as well as FM, signals. Owner's manual, important because of operating system, unusually helpful.

Con: Synchronous detector loses lock easily, especially if selectable sideband feature in use, greatly detracting from the utility of this high-tech feature. Substandard rejection of unwanted sideband with selectable synchronous sideband. Overall distortion rises when synchronous detector used. Ultimate rejection of "narrow" 2.7 kHz bandwidth filter only 60 dB. Ultimate rejection mediocre (50 dB) with standard 7.6 kHz "wide" bandwidth filter, improves to an uninspiring 60 dB when replaced by optional 6 kHz "wide" Collins mechanical filter. Installation of optional Collins filter requires expertise, patience and special equipment. Poor dynamic range. Cumbersome ergonomics. No passband offset. No tunable notch filter. Needs good external speaker for good audio quality. World Time clock does not show when frequency displayed. IF output frequency 10.7 MHz instead of standard 455 kHz.

Verdict: Unbeatable in some respects, inferior in others—it comes down to what use you will be putting the radio. The optional 6 kHz Collins filter is strongly recommended, but it should be installed by dealer at time of purchase.

Discontinued, still available
⭐⭐⭐⭐ 🅔
Yaesu FRG-100

Price: $599.95 in the United States. CAN$899.00 in Canada. £399.00 in the United Kingdom. AUS$999.00 in Australia. No longer available in Japan.

Going, going, gone! Yaesu no longer makes receivers, including this FRG-100. Yaesu's FRG-7 "Volksradio," introduced in 1976, helped fuel renewed growth in world band listening.

Pro: Excellent performance in many respects. Relatively low price. Covers 50 Hz to 30 MHz in the LSB, USB, AM and CW modes. Includes three bandwidths, a noise blanker, selectable AGC, two attenuators, the ability to select 16 pre-programmed world band segments, two clocks, on-off timers, 52 tunable station presets that store frequency and mode data, a variety of scanning schemes and an all-mode squelch. A communications-FM module, 500 Hz CW bandwidth and high-stability crystal are optional.

Con: No keypad for direct frequency entry (remediable, *see* ☞, below). No synchronous selectable sideband. Lacks features found in "top-gun" receivers: passband tuning, notch filter, adjustable RF gain. Simple controls and display, combined with complex functions, can make certain operations confusing. Dynamic range only fair. Uses AC adaptor instead of built-in power supply.

☞ An outboard accessory keypad is virtually a "must" for the FRG-100, and is a no-brainer to attach. Brodier E.E.I. (3 Place de la Fontaine, F-57420 Curvy, France) makes the best keypad, sold direct and for $59.95 through Universal Radio in the United States; also, Martin Lynch in England and Charly Hardt in Remscheid, Germany. Reasonably similar is the costlier QSYer—SWL Version, available from Stone

Mountain Engineering Company in Stone Mountain GA 30086 USA.

☞ In North America, the FRG-100 is sometimes thought of as having had two versions: the original "A" (American) version and, more recently, the "B", which incorporates one slight improvement. However, although the "A" designator was official, "B" is an informal suffix not actually indicated anywhere on the radio or its documentation.

Verdict: While sparse on features, in many respects the Yaesu FRG-100 succeeds in delivering worthy performance within its price class. Its lack of a keypad for direct frequency entry is now easily remediable (*see* ☞, above). According to the manufacturer, this model was discontinued in mid-1999. However, it continues to be available in various countries outside Japan, but supplies should be exhausted very soon.

🖹 An *RDI WHITE PAPER* is available for this model.

✪✪✪½
Drake SW2

Price: *Receiver:* $489.95 in the United States, but as low as $399.99 during special sales. CAN$799.00 in Canada. £499.00 in the United Kingdom. *Infrared remote control:* $49.00 in the United States. CAN$75.00 in Canada. £49.95 in the United Kingdom.

Pro: Synchronous selectable sideband performs unusually well for reduced fading and easier rejection of interference.

GOOD RADIO KIT, FADING MARKET

During the golden era of kits—the fifties and early sixties—most were from the Heath Company of Benton Harbor, Michigan. Electronic kits all but vanished after Heath dropped out, but radio kit building has been revived by Ten-Tec's 1254 world band radio.

It is in the best tradition of kit building, but the simple pleasure of constructing a radio seems to have lost its luster in today's hyper-cyber culture. From all indications, 1254 sales haven't lit any fires even though it is better than Heath's last world band kit.

The tabletop 1254 is actually smaller than some portables, and tunes 100 kilohertz through 30 Megahertz. Including shipping it sells for $204 to the continental United States, and US$210 to Hawai'i, Alaska and Canada. In the United Kingdom, dealers offer it for £189.95. Parts quality appears to be excellent, and assembly runs roughly 24 hours, 27 max.

Design Simplifies Assembly

The straightforward 1254 has precious little in the way of features to complicate assembly: no keypad, for example, and no signal-strength indicator. No synchronous selectable sideband or tilt bail, either, or LSB/USB settings for single-sideband—much less adjustable AGC or any of the other goodies found on pricey tabletop supersets. It is powered by a simple outboard AC adaptor, and won't accept inboard batteries.

Digitally synthesized tuning is in increments as small as 500 Hz for single sideband and 5 kHz for AM-mode reception, such as world band. Bright red LEDs read out to the nearest 2.5 kHz in the single-sideband mode, the nearest 5 kHz in the AM mode. There is also a fast-tuning rate for the knob, much needed for going from one part of the radio spectrum to another. For tweaking between synthesizer tuning increments, there is an analog clarifier. Rounding out the minimalist roster of features are 15 presets.

Several useful tuning features, including keypad, slewing and 100 presets. Superb dynamic range puts most other receivers to shame, regardless of price. This, combined with generally superior weak-signal sensitivity, make for generally good mediumwave DX performance. Pleasant audio with minimal distortion. Worthy ergonomics, including outstandingly easy-to-read frequency display with dimmer. Superior factory service.

Con: Only one (7 kHz) of two voice bandwidths usable in AM mode—the mode used *inter alia* for world band reception. Tunes in relatively coarse 50 Hz steps with some minor chugging. No notch filter, passband tuning, manually selectable AGC or noise blanker. No clock or timer. "Wall wart" AC adaptor instead of internal power supply. Optional remote control, which doesn't control volume, not worth

Drake's affordable SW2 offers much good performance, but its narrow bandwidth is not accessible in the AM mode.

the money for most, although its utility is aided by the receiver's bright LEDs, which can be read easily across a room.

Verdict: The American-made Drake SW2, where available, is a fine all-round performer and attractively priced. Nevertheless, although it has two voice band-widths—one narrow, one wide—only the "wide" is usable for world band listening in

---

Radios in this price class never soar with eagles, and the 1254 is no exception. The internal speaker is mediocre and phase noise is poor. Front-end selectivity is little better, as is evidenced by false signals within the longwave spectrum. Sensitivity on longwave and mediumwave AM is poor, and the set's digital circuitry radiates hash aplenty. AGC decay is somewhat fast for world band.

Decent Overall Performer

That having been said, the receiver is a decent overall performer. The lone bandwidth is 5.6 kHz, a good choice for AM-mode reception and with worthy ultimate rejection—70 dB. Also showing up well in PASSPORT's lab are image rejection, sensitivity to weak world band signals, blocking (related to sensitivity), AGC threshold and frequency stability. Dynamic range is fair, yet superior for its price class; first IF rejection is fair, too. Overall distortion averages out as good, and with an external speaker the audio is surprisingly pleasant.

Ten-Tec's sturdy little Model 1254 kit is definitely not a serious DX receiver, and is painfully slim on features. Rather, it is a different and fun project. And the manufacturer's track record for hand-holding means that even if you put "X" where "Y" belongs, in the end the radio will really work.

Ten-Tec's Model 1254 is a better performer than Heathkit's final world band radio kit.

the AM mode. For quality-fidelity listening to world band and mediumwave AM programs, this is often adequate because of the enhancement to adjacent-channel selectivity brought about by synchronous selectable sideband. But for world band listening or DXing when both sidebands are interfered with, the inaccessibility of the radio's second, narrower bandwidth is a significant drawback.

★★★ ✺
NASA HF-4, NASA HF-4E, Target HF3, Target HF3M, Target HF3S, Target HF3E

Price: *HF-4/HF-4E (not tested):* £199.00 in the United Kingdom. *HF3:* £159.95 in the United Kingdom. *HF3M:* £209.95 in the United Kingdom. *HF3S (not tested):* £159.95 in the United Kingdom. *HF3E (not tested):* £299.00 in the United Kingdom. *NASA AA-30 active antenna (not tested):* £59.95 in the United Kingdom.

Pro: *HF-4/HF-4E, HF3 and HF3M:* Low price. Superior rejection of spurious "image" signals. Third-order intercept point indicates superior strong-signal handling capability. Bandwidths have superb ultimate rejection. *HF-4/HF-4E, HF3M:* Equipped for weatherfax ("WEFAX") reception. *HF-4/HF-4E:* Two AM-mode bandwidths. Illuminated LCD. Configured to accept AA-30 active antenna.

Con: No keypad and variable-rate tuning knob is difficult to control. Broad skirt

The various versions of the Target HF3 and NASA HF-4 are attractively priced in the U.K., where they face no tariff. They are rarely offered elsewhere.

selectivity. Single-sideband bandwidth relatively broad. Volume control fussy to adjust. Synthesizer tunes in relatively coarse 1 kHz increments, supplemented by an analog fine-tuning "clarifier" control. Single sideband requires both tuning controls to be adjusted. No synchronous selectable sideband, notch filter or pass-band tuning. Frequency readout off by 2 kHz in single-sideband mode. Uses AC adaptor instead of built-in power supply. No clock, timer or snooze feature. *HF3 and HF3M:* Bandwidths not selectable independent of mode. Only AM-mode bandwidth for world band reception. LCD not illuminated. *HF3:* Only one preset. No elevation feet or tilt bail. When switched on, goes not to the last-tuned frequency and mode but rather to the frequency and mode in the lone preset. *HF3S and HF-4/HF-4E, HF3M:* Only ten presets.

☞ According to Target, the HF3S is identical to the HF3 but with ten presets, whereas the HF3E is comparable to the HF3M, but with a "quasi-synchronous" detector and illuminated LCD.

Verdict: Surprisingly good world band performance for the price, but frustrating to operate. If you would like to own the Target brand, go for the new "M" version; the new "E" version, not tested, appears to be relatively pricey for what is offered.

★★½ ✺
Radio Shack DX-394

Price: £149.95 in the United Kingdom. AUS$499.95 in Australia.

Pro: Low price in those parts of the world where the '394 is still sold. Advanced tuning features include 160 tunable presets (*see* Con). Tunes and displays in precise 10 Hz increments. Modest size, light weight and built-in telescopic antenna provide some portable capability. Bandwidths have superior shape factors and ultimate rejection. Two 24-hour clocks, one of which shows independent of frequency display. Five programmable timers. 30/60 minute snooze feature. Noise blanker.

Con: What appear to be four bandwidths turn out to be virtually one bandwidth, and it is too wide for optimum reception of many signals. Bandwidths, such as they are, not selectable independent of mode. No synchronous selectable sideband. Presets cumbersome to use. Poor dynamic range for a tabletop, a potential problem in Europe and other strong-signal parts of the world if an external antenna is used. Overall distortion, although acceptable, higher than desirable.

Verdict: Modest dimensions and equally modest performance, but a great U.K. price.

Radio Shack's DX-394 is no longer available in North America, but is still sold in the U.K. and Australia.

✪✪½ ✆
Drake SW1

Price: $249.95 in the United States, but $199.99 during special sales.

Pro: Exceptionally low price for such a high level of construction quality. Dynamic range, sensitivity to weak signals and certain other performance variables above average for price class. Pleasant audio. Large, bright digital display using LEDs much easier to read indoors than most. Easiest and simplest to use of any tabletop tested, with quality ergonomics. Superior factory service.

Con: Mediocre adjacent-channel rejection (selectivity) from the single bandwidth. No features—*nada*, not even a signal-strength indicator—except for tuning. No single sideband. No synchronous selectable sideband. Increments for tuning and frequency display are relatively coarse. Annoying chugging during bandscanning. Uses AC adaptor instead of built-in power supply. Currently available mainly from only one dealer, Universal Radio—an American firm which exports worldwide, although this may change.

Verdict: A great value as far as it goes, but where are the features? And why such mediocre selectivity and loud chugging? Still, in many respects, such as the display and quality of construction and service, Drake's American-made SW1 offers solid value at a rock-bottom price. Because of construction quality and service, no other model of world band radio of any type under $400 comes as close to being a "friend for life."

The PASSPORT tabletop-model review team consists of Tony Jones, Lawrence Magne, David Zantow and George Zeller; also, George Heidelman, Toshimichi Ohtake, Chuck Rippel, Craig Tyson and John Wagner. Laboratory measurements by J. Robert Sherwood.

Saved from the guillotine: Drake's SW1, scheduled to be dropped in late 1999, is back by popular demand.

WHERE TO FIND IT: INDEX TO DIGITAL RADIOS

PASSPORT TO WORLD BAND RADIO tests nearly every model on the market. This index lists all digitally tuned models reviewed, with those that are new, revised or retested for 2000 being in **bold**. Additionally, the following are evaluated:

- 59 analog portables, page 131
- Three emergency portables, page 180
- Sony AN-LP1 active antenna, page 104.

Comprehensive PASSPORT® Radio Database International White Papers® are available for the most popular premium receivers and antennas. Each RDI White Paper®—$6.95 in North America, $9.95 airmail elsewhere—contains virtually all our panel's findings and comments during hands-on testing, as well as laboratory measurements and what these mean to you. These unabridged reports are available from key world band dealers, or you can contact our 24-hour automated VISA/MC order channels (www.passband.com, autovoice +1 215/598-9018, fax +1 215/598 3794), or write us at PASSPORT RDI White Papers, Box 300, Penn's Park, PA 18943 USA.

🔖 *Radio Database International White Paper® available.*

PC Controlled Receivers for 2000

New Technology Succeeds

At the dawn of the Industrial Revolution, centralized steam and water energy was conveyed by belts and pulleys to various nearby machines. Only later, after the dawning of the electric motor, did each machine have its own power source.

World band receivers have evolved the opposite way. Traditionally they've been standalone devices.

But with PCs now commonplace, the power of computers are being mated to the capabilities of world band receivers to produce PC-controlled receivers. These not only allow manufacturers to save the cost of front panel controls, they also let the PC take care of tasks it can do efficiently: memory management, for example, or storage of schedule and frequency data.

All PC-controlled receivers are available in outboard versions, some also as plug-in cards. Internal mounting facilitates communication speed between the PC and the receiver while reducing clutter. However, with external mounting you don't have to disassemble the PC, and radio component failure is less likely to damage your PC and *vice versa*. Most important, there is greater isolation from computer noise. Accordingly, all units tested are outboard versions.

Some units appear to be sensitive to front-end damage from antenna static electricity, and any radio connected to a PC might transfer incoming static electricity to the computer, possibly damaging data or chips. Eavesdropper antennas come with built-in static discharge, but Alpha Delta and DEO make accessory dischargers for other antennas.

Coming up? Kachina (see sidebar) and Icom appear to have some interesting goodies in the works—possibly Ten-Tec, as well.

Tips for Using this Section

Models are listed in order of suitability for receiving difficult-to-hear world band stations, with secondary consideration given to audio fidelity and ergonomics. Street—actual selling—prices are cited, and are valid as of when we go to press. Most vary plus or minus, so take them as the general guide they are meant to be.

Unless otherwise stated, all PC-controlled models:

- Operate from Windows 95/98; also, NT4 and possibly Windows 2000, but with a higher likelihood of software glitches.
- Are controlled solely via PC, with no significant operating facilities on the receiver itself.
- Tune from at least 150 kHz through 30 MHz, but do not receive FM broadcasts.
- Have digital frequency synthesis and display.

- Incorporate a wide variety of helpful tuning features, but no genuine tuning knob.
- Include proper demodulation of non-world band shortwave signals. These include single-sideband (LSB/USB) and CW (Morse code); also, with suitable ancillary devices, radioteletype and radio fax.
- Show signal strength on-screen.

What PASSPORT's Rating Symbols Mean

Star ratings: ✪✪✪✪✪ is best. Stars are awarded mainly for overall performance and meaningful features, plus to some extent ergonomics and construction quality. Price, appearance, country of manufacture and the like are not taken into account.

Passport's Choice. La crème de la crème. Our test team's personal picks of the litter—models we would buy or have purchased for our personal use.

🄫: No, this doesn't mean cheap—none of these models is cheap. Rather, it denotes a model that costs appreciably less than usual for the satisfying level of performance provided.

New for 2000
✪✪✪✪ 🄫 *Passport's Choice*
Ten-Tec RX320

Price: *RX320:* $295 plus shipping worldwide. *Third-party control software:* Free-$99 worldwide.

Pro: Superior dynamic range for category and price class. Apparently superb bandwidth shape factors (*see* Con). In addition to the supplied factory control software, third-party software is available, often for free, and may improve operation. Up to 34 bandwidths with third-party software. Tunes in extremely precise 1 Hz increments (10 Hz with tested factory software); displays to the nearest Hertz, and frequency readout is easily user-aligned. Large, easy-to-read digital frequency display and faux-analog frequency bar. For PCs with sound cards, outstanding freedom from distortion aids in providing good audio quality with most but not all cards and speakers. Fairly good audio, but with limited treble, also available through radio for PCs without sound cards. Superb blocking performance helps maintain consistently good world band sensitivity. Passband offset (see Con). Spectrum display with wide variety of useful sweep widths (see Con). World time on-screen clock (see Con). Adjustable AGC decay. Thousands of memories (presets), with first-rate memory configuration, access and sorting—including by station name and frequency. Only PC-controlled model tested which returns to last tuned frequency when PC turned off. Superior owner's manual. Outstanding factory help and repair support.

Con: No synchronous selectable sideband. Some characteristic "DSP roughness" in the audio under certain reception conditions. Synthesizer phase noise measures only fair; among the consequences are that bandwidth shape factors cannot be measured exactly. Some tuning ergonomics only fair as compared with certain standalone receivers. No tunable notch filter. Passband offset doesn't function in AM mode. Signal-strength indicator,

ARE PC-CONTROLLED RECEIVERS FOR YOU?

If you're considering a PC-controlled receiver, make sure:

• You don't mind operating a radio tethered to a PC. If you're not certain and have a multimedia PC, try listening to Webcasts (http://www.broadcast.com/radio, http://realguide.real.com/stations, http://windowsmedia.microsoft.com/radio/radio/asp, http://www.wrn.org/listen.html).
• You don't mind substituting virtual control for hands-on knobs and buttons. Remember, among many other things you'll be giving up a real-life tuning knob.
• Your computer has Windows 95, 98 or NT4—perhaps Windows 2000—as well as a Pentium processor (the faster, the better).
• You have a spare COM port or can install one (or, if you spring for in inboard "radio," that you have a spare card slot).
• Electrical noise from your computer, peripherals and cables can be overcome (see below).
• You're not expecting five-star performance.

Computers and peripherals emit electrical noise which disrupts radio signals—particularly faint stations from afar. To check this out, take a portable with good batteries, extend its antenna, and tune to a very weak world band station while your PC and peripherals are turned off. Turn on your PC, monitor, speakers and modem, then place your radio near the computer. You will hear buzzing, which is electrical noise. Walk away from the PC until the buzzing is inaudible, then add at least a fourth to that distance. This is the closest to your computer that your antenna's receiving element should be placed.

If you're in a small apartment with an electrically noisy PC, you may find no suitable antenna location. If so, stick with a standalone receiver. But if you have land you can install a coaxial-fed trapped dipole antenna, like those made by Alpha Delta and Antenna Supermarket/Eavesdropper (see RDI White Paper on Popular Outdoor Antennas).

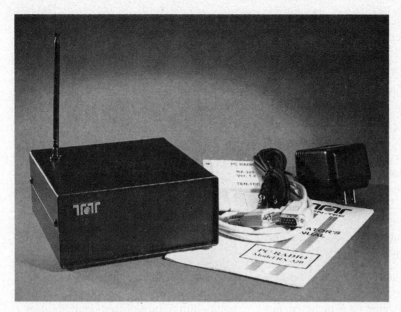

The Ten-Tec RX320 is king of the hill, but lacks synchronous selectable sideband. A separate antenna is needed for proper performance.

calibrated 0-80, too sensitive, reading 20 with no antenna connected and 30 with only band noise being received. Uses AC adaptor instead of built-in power supply. Spectrum display does not function with some third-party software. Spectrum display only a so-so performer and, in our lab tests (but not during actual listening), caused Windows to crash when unusually powerful signals were being swept. Use of high-pass and low-pass filtering results in marginal front-end selectivity; also, causes mediumwave AM reception below 1 MHz to suffer from reduced sensitivity and longwave sensitivity to be atrocious. Mediocre front-end selectivity also can allow powerful mediumwave AM stations to mix with received shortwave signals. No internal speaker on receiver module. World Time clock tied into computer's clock, which may not be accurate without periodic adjustment.

☞ Passport's four-star rating is for the RX320 with existing third-party control software (see sidebar). With current factory software the rating is lower, but this should improve as replacement

software is scheduled to appear from Ten-Tec by the time you read this, and again throughout 2000.

Verdict: No contest, the American-made Ten-Tec RX320 is the star of the PC show when it is coupled to solid control software. Were it to have better front-end selectivity, reduced synthesizer noise, passband offset in the AM mode, a variable notch filter and worthy synchronous selectable sideband, it might perform as well as standalone receivers costing far more. But even now, unless you live near a mediumwave AM station it runs circles around most models near its price class.

Evaluation of New Model: Here, at last, is a PC-controlled receiver that works almost like a tabletop model but is priced like a portable.

Ten-Tec's supplied control software installs quickly and flawlessly on Windows 98 machines, although on one of our Windows 95 PCs it refused to work and Windows 98 had to be used. Online software upgrades are available at www.tentec.com/Amateur.htm, as is the

"Programmer's Reference Manual" that helps you and others to write custom control software.

The RX320 and a PC are connected by a 9/9 serial cable that comes with the receiver. To use your PC's sound card and speaker system for listening to the RX320, a second radio-to-computer connection is needed but isn't provided. In practice, you'll probably prefer the audio quality through your PC's sound card and speakers (careful setting of the RX320's line level control helps minimize distortion) than through the receiver with an outboard speaker; the radio itself comes with no internal speaker.

The receiver is powered by an AC adaptor, rather than an inboard power supply. An 18-inch telescoping antenna is included, but it tends to pick up too much PC electrical noise, so an outdoor wire antenna should be used.

How It Works

When you click the RX320 icon, a likeness of the receiver front panel appears, with these controls:

- *World and local time:* displays multi-colored characters slaved to the internal clock of your computer, but PC clocks are notoriously inaccurate.
- *Station name display:* Stations in memory can display an alphanumeric "name tag."
- *Memory (presets):* In practice, thousands of memories are available—the exact number depends on your PC—and the memory menu is easily accessed.
- *Volume:* The cursor moves a volume slider up and down.
- *Time/UTC:* A menu shows where U.S. and Canadian time stations WWV, WWVH and CHU are heard. You can either exit this menu and keep the time station tuned in, or exit and return to the regular station to which you were listening.
- *Mode Selector:* AM, CW, LSB and USB.
- *Frequency Display:* Frequency can be entered in MHz or kHz, and there are up/down slewing controls on either side of the display. Right-hand controls change frequency by the value in the step control; left-hand controls work the same way, but change frequency by ten times the step amount. Frequency digits are large and easy to read, and are complemented by a splendid faux-analog frequency bar.
- *Tuning Steps:* The factory software offers tuning steps in programmable increments of 10 Hz, 100 Hz, 1 kHz, 5 kHz and 10 kHz.
- *IF Filters:* The factory software offers five DSP-based bandwidths of 8.5 kHz, 5.1 kHz, 2.5 kHz, 1.8 kHz and 500 Hz. You can choose whether you want the bandwidth to be selected dependent or independent of mode. The dependent configuration measures 8.5 kHz for AM, 2.8 kHz for single sideband and 2.1 kHz for CW.
- *Et cetera:* Other front panel features include a mode/bandwidth and frequency-step display, along with a dual "needle" 0-80 signal-strength indicator for real-time and peak readings. Alas, readings are excessive; even band noise can cause a reading of 30 or more, and with no antenna whatsoever we encountered readings of 20.

There is also a spectrum display, a feature until recently found only on costly professional receivers used for spectrum surveillance. The range of the displayed frequency range is excellent, running from a few kilohertz to about a fourth the width of an entire world band segment, such as 19 meters (15 MHz). Unfortunately, existing third-party software disables the spectrum display.

Early versions of the owner's manual indicated the spectrum display could not function while the receiver was tuned to a station. In fact, there are two ways this can be done, and the revised owner's manual will reflect this. Nevertheless, the display's sweep is slow, its resolution is not all it could be, and (as with the signal-strength indicator) the bottom 30 dB or so tends to show noise rather than signals.

The decay action of the AGC causes the display to trail off slowly after a strong signal is swept. In practice this is likely to be no more than an annoyance, but in the lab, where we were able to use the display to sweep powerful signals, the display tended to give a "divide by zero" error, causing Windows to crash. In practice, precious few users should run into this problem.

The Ten-Tec RX320 with factory software has no tunable notch control, noise blanker, synchronous selectable sideband or adjustable AGC decay. Synchronous selectable sideband might be offered sometime in 2000, but this depends on whether Ten-Tec has adequate research resources to pull this off. However, Ten-Tec is unequivocal that they will release new software very shortly and again throughout 2000.

The receiver can be tuned four ways. For direct keypad entry the frequency can be entered in kilohertz or Megahertz, but has to end with an "M" (Megahertz) or "K" (kilohertz). For the virtual tuning "knob," left clicking the mouse causes the frequency to increase, while right clicking tunes lower. Slewing controls also change frequency, and memories may be called up. Memories are sorted by station, frequency and country; a time sort would have also been desirable.

Performance

The RX320 performs well even against higher-priced portatop and tabletop models. Dynamic range is more than ample, so powerhouse stations on 31 and 49 meters at night rarely cause overloading. Like other DSP receivers the RX320

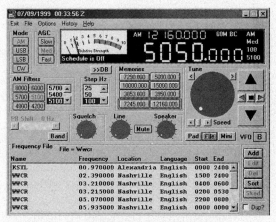

PC radios use virtual "control panels." There are several software packages which do this for the Ten-Tec RX320—free upgrades, too.

sometimes reacts strangely to fading, causing "rough edges" to the audio at times.

The AGC has an enhanced role to play in audio quality with DSP receivers. The RX320's factory settings for AGC decay are a bit slow, and the AGC threshold is such that there is slightly more variation in loudness than there could be. All in all, though, AGC performance is adequate.

Otherwise, the RX320's audio quality through a sound card and good speakers can be very pleasant—the lack of synchronous detection notwithstanding. In part this is thanks to the RX320's minimal overall distortion—between 0.1 and 1.0 percent. But if you don't wish to use your PC for audio or it doesn't have a sound card, the receiver has powerful built-in audio. Connect a good, efficient speaker to that and you're in business.

Unfortunately, we could not measure the –60 dB bandwidths to compute the shape factors for any bandwidths because of spurious responses and synthesizer noise—the synthesizer's phase noise is only fair. However, when we extrapolate from our –6 dB and –40 dB measurements, the shape factors appear to be nothing short of superb, especially at wider bandwidths. Ultimate rejection is a passable but uninspiring 60 dB, and spurious "birdie" signals appear infrequently.

Front-end selectivity is accomplished simply by high-pass and low-pass filters, and is marginally acceptable. However, the high-pass filter attenuates receiver sensitivity below 1 MHz, and at one test location a local mediumwave AM station "ghosted" into the shortwave spectrum, interfering with world band reception. With quality front-end selectivity neither of these things should happen.

Reliability originally was a problem, as during early production the front-end FET didn't have much in the way of protection from static electricity received through the antenna. However, since fall of 1998 a 2.2k resistor to ground has been added to reduce the odds of FET damage.

Noise floor, the best measure of weak-signal sensitivity, is good (–126 dBm) throughout the shortwave spectrum, fair (–111 dBm) on mediumwave AM below 1 MHz, and atrocious (–77 dBm) on longwave. Thanks to superb blocking performance—146 dB—the receiver's shortwave sensitivity tends to be uncommonly consistent. Of course, as always with PC-controlled receivers, a first-rate outdoor antenna is a "must" for hearing weaker stations.

Substandard dynamic range is a curse of many PC-controlled receivers, but not the RX320. Its dynamic range is fair, and the more telling third-order intercept point is actually quite good. This may seem like damnation by faint praise, but many costly standalone receivers measure comparably or worse. For a $295 rig to have this level of dynamic range is exceptional.

In hands-on use the RX320 is a capable DX machine. Manual "ECSS" tuning of AM-mode signals helps overcome the lack of synchronous selectable sideband, and

the bandwidth filtering is effective. As to recovered audio, during one fade-in period the RX320 got readable audio from Radio Ghana as early as the Drake R8B and only slightly behind the Japan Radio NRD-545—two pricey supersets. All began getting usable copy about 20 minutes later than the venerable military surplus R-390A/Sherwood SE-3 combo. The RX320 also works well for utility and ham monitoring—in the single-sideband modes it performs nicely, and CW filtering comes standard.

The RX320 is "king of the hill" among today's PC-operated world band receivers. All this for under $300 makes the Ten-Tec RX320 an excellent buy among shortwave receivers.

New for 2000
✪✪✪
Icom IC-PCR1000

Price: *IC-PCR1000:* $499.95 in the United States. CAN$799.00 in Canada. £299.95 in the United Kingdom. AUS$775.00 in Australia. *UT-106 DSP Unit:* $139.95 in the United States.

Pro: Wideband frequency coverage. Spectrum display with many useful sweep widths for shortwave, as well as good real-time performance. Tunes and displays in extremely precise 1 Hz increments. Comes with reasonably performing control software (*see* Con). Excellent sensitivity to weak signals. AGC, adjustable, performs well in AM and single-sideband modes. Nineteen banks of 50 memories each, with potential for virtually unlimited number of memories. Passband offset (*see* Con). Powerful audio with good weak-signal readability and little distortion (*see* Con).

Con: Poor dynamic range. Audio quality, not pleasant, made worse by presence of circuit hiss. No line output to feed PC sound card and speakers, so no alternative to

The Icom IC-PCR1000 is not the best for world band, but is attractively priced for a wideband receiver with spectrum display.

using receiver's audio. No synchronous selectable sideband. Only two AM-mode bandwidths—8.7 kHz (nominal 6 kHz) and 2.4 kHz (nominal 3 kHz)—both with uninspiring shape factors. Synthesizer phase noise, although not measurable, appears to be only fair; among the effects of this are that bandwidth shape factors cannot be exactly measured. Mediocre blocking slightly limits weak-signal sensitivity when frequency segment contains powerful signals. Closed-source programming means third-party software harder to make available for improved performance, although this is less of a drawback than if the receiver were truly DSP. Some tuning ergonomics only fair as compared with certain standalone receivers. Automatic tunable notch filter with DSP audio processing (UT-106, not tested) an extra-cost option. Lacks passband offset in AM mode used by virtually all world band stations. Uses AC adaptor instead of built-in power supply. Spectrum display mutes audio when single-sideband or CW signal being received. No clock. Mediocre inboard speaker, remediable by using outboard speaker. Sparse owner's manual.

☞ A similar but more rudimentary model, the IC-PCR100, is available worldwide at

roughly two-thirds the price of the IC-PCR1000. It has only one (broad) bandwidth.

Verdict: A mid-level shortwave performer between the top-rated Ten-Tec RX320 and bottom-drawer WinRadio 1500e. Of all the PC-controlled receivers tested, the Japanese-made Icom IC-PCR1000 is the most appropriate for wideband frequency coverage and first-rate shortwave spectrum display.

Evaluation of New Model: Unlike the Ten-Tec RX320, the Icom IC-PCR1000 is a conventional, non-DSP receiver with a limited number of bandwidth choices. A PC provides only the user interface and memory functions.

Also unlike the RX320, the 'PCR1000 has wideband frequency coverage. In the United States, the civilian version covers from 10 kHz-824 MHz, 849-869 MHz and 894-1300 MHz. Elsewhere and to approved U.S. Federal agencies, it covers 10 kHz through 1300 MHz with no gaps for the *verboten in Amerika* cellular bands.

A 9/9-pin serial cable is included to connect the receiver module to a PC. An AC adaptor is used in lieu of an inboard power supply, and there is a small internal

THIRD-PARTY CONTROL SOFTWARE

If you are into software design, you can "roll your own" control software for the RX320. But for everybody else there are readily available out-of-house packages, including:

- Turner package, free. Currently it does not use the mouse wheel as a tuning knob, but this should be added shortly. It does not allow the spectrum display to be used, although—who knows—this, too, may change. It is available at http://pages.prodigy.net/kf5oj/KF5OJ.htm.
- Privalov offering, also free. As of v1.1.106 it makes use of a mouse's center wheel as a tuning knob, but it does not allow the spectrum display to be used, although this could change. Available at www.mole3d.com/radio/rx.htm.
- ERGO, $99 from Universal Radio.

We chose Turner software v1.10b with firmware v1.06—at random and because it's free—to illustrate the features accessible only by third-party software. However, Ten-Tec has upgrades in the works that could cancel out the advantages of third-party software.

Key features of the Turner version we tested include:

- 34 bandwidths from 300 Hz to 8.5 kHz, independent of mode—ditto Privalov's package. This compares to five bandwidths with the original factory software.
- Six user-defined default bandwidths can be chosen to come up when a mode is selected or changed; yet, the other 28 bandwidths remain available at any time. Thus, you can have your cake and eat it, too—bandwidth automatically selected by mode, yet at the same time bandwidth user-selectable independent of mode.
- Tuning steps of 1 Hz, 5 Hz, 10 Hz, 25 Hz, 50 Hz, 100 Hz, 250 Hz, 500 Hz, 1 kHz, 2.5 kHz, 5 kHz, 9 kHz, 10 kHz, 25 kHz, 50 kHz and 100 kHz.
- Three selectable AGC decay rates (slow, medium and fast).
- Useful tuning features: frequency entry—either in kHz or MHz—from the numeric keypad, main keyboard keys, or by clicking on-screen display digits. You can also use the on-screen tuning knob, up/down slewing buttons or +/- keyboard keys to bandscan using your chosen step size. The current Turner software does not allow the mouse wheel to be used as a tuning knob, but this may change.
- Hands-off continuous tuning, or bandscanning.
- Passband offset for single-sideband, but not AM-mode, signals.
- A larger signal-strength indicator, which displays normal and average signal strength.
- Squelch with status and setting indicators.
- On-screen control of line and speaker controls.
- Memories (presets) with name/description, frequency, mode, bandwidth, AGC decay, tuning step, passband offset position and user notes.
- Data in the memories may be altered without exiting the main screen.
- All memories can be sorted alphabetically by station name, or numerically by ascending frequency.
- Any memory can be scheduled to come up at a designated time.
- Eight pushbutton memories for instant access to key stations.
- Frequencies displayed as kHz or MHz, with or without leading-zero suppression.
- However, the Turner software disables the spectrum display feature.

Bottom line, superior control software can turn a good radio into one that really stands out. Fortunately, Ten-Tec tells us it will be upgrading its own control software a number of times in the months to come.

speaker. There is no line output to feed the audio through the PC sound card and speakers, so the receiver's audio has to be used.

A sparse instruction manual is supplemented by useful on-screen help menus. We tested the receiver using Icom control software v1.3, with Windows 95/98—but it also nominally operates with Windows 3.1. Software upgrades are free from such regional sites as www.icomamerica.com/receivers/pcr1000download.html.

The 'PCR1000 worked fine when used alone with Windows 95, but when other applications were brought up Windows sometimes crashed on one of our test machines, necessitating cold rebooting. Icom's software is at least as worthy as Ten-Tec's current factory software for the RX320. However, Icom has made it harder to create third-party control software.

Startup is simple and straightforward. Clicking an icon brings up a likeness of four rack-mounted panels which can be shuffled about. Operation is sensible but excessively mouse-centric, with only direct frequency entry being possible by keyboard.

While the result may intimidate first time around, the overall screen graphics are nicely done with attention to detail. Yet, a few of the activation cubes are small and poorly marked, so a large-screen monitor helps. Also, fast access of a number of functions on the various screens can be difficult.

Overall, the software is complex with a long learning curve, but some aspects are inherently user-hostile and could have been more creatively designed.

Four Virtual Panels

• The first panel contains the virtual tuning "knob," keypad frequency entry, frequency display, and controls to access the standard 19 banks of 50 memories

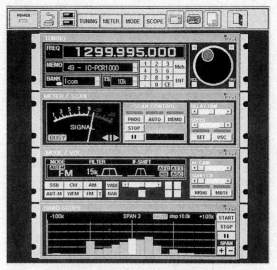

Icom's IC-PCR1000 provides four on-screen "rack-mounted modules."

each. Tuning steps are adjustable from 1 Hz to 10 MHz.

• The second panel includes the signal-strength indicator and controls for advanced scanning functions. Such variables as memory bank name, memory name, receive frequency, receive mode, bandwidth, attenuator and tuning step can be stored in each preset.

Scanning can be set to take place between any two frequencies. When a used channel is found, the 'PCR1000 can be configured to write that channel into a blank user-defined memory. This is a powerful tool to unearth intermittently used channels during unattended use.

• The third panel allows for selection among the LSB, USB, AM, CW, FM-wide and FM-narrow modes. Bandwidths are 2.4 kHz (nominal 3 kHz) and 8.7 kHz (nominal 6 kHz) in the AM, LSB, USB and CW modes; 8.7 kHz (nominal 6 kHz) and nominal 15 kHz in FM-narrow; as well as nominal 50 kHz and 230 kHz in FM-wide. For the AM mode, used by virtually all world band stations, a third bandwidth of 4-5 kHz would have been a huge improvement.

There is a passband offset control, but disappointingly it doesn't function in the AM mode used by virtually all world band stations. Also selectable are two AGC decay rates, a noise blanker, an attenuator, and (for FM) an AFC control.

The squelch level and volume control appear as virtual sliders. No notch control comes standard, although an automatic notch—only partially effective while AM-mode signals are being received—along with DSP audio processing is available at extra cost. There is no synchronous selectable sideband.

• The fourth panel contains the spectrum display. This versatile feature, once found only on a few costly professional receivers, allows you to make a visual check for signals on a specified frequency range in the AM, FM, LSB, USB or CW modes. Its "peek area" is somewhat limited for VHF/UHF, but is excellent for shortwave and mediumwave AM—a key plus for this model.

The display works well in real time, without the annoying "catch up" wait found with some other displays. It is a splendid example of how PC power can make a computer-controlled receiver into a better performer than a standalone model.

While receiving a signal in the AM or FM modes you can observe adjacent receive conditions, but when you're listening to signals in the LSB, USB and CW modes the audio is muted while the spectrum display is in use.

Shortwave Performance

For those into world band listening and VHF/UHF scanning, it is tempting to have a single receiver which does it all. Although advances in digital and analog circuits

allow for wideband receivers to be made cheaper and better than in years past, our experience continues to indicate that the best world band receivers cover no higher than the upper end of the HF spectrum (30 MHz) or perhaps into the lower reaches of the VHF spectrum. Alas, the performance of the wideband 'PCR1000 is another confirmation of this.

Many lab measurements of the 'PCR1000's performance are good or better. However, dynamic range (59 dB at 20 kHz separation; synthesizer birdies prevented measurement at 5 kHz separation) and the related third-order intercept point (–43 dB at 20 kHz separation) are poor. As a result, overloading routinely appears when an outdoor world band antenna is used.

The attenuator reduces the problem, but the normally excellent weak-signal sensitivity (noise floor –132 dB, sensitivity 0.16 μV) drops accordingly. Of course, the attenuator also increases circuit noise "hiss," especially with the 8.7 kHz bandwidth in the AM mode.

The 'PCR1000 does not include an audio line output, so the receiver can't be heard through a PC soundboard and speakers. Nevertheless, the 'PCR1000's built-in audio can be room filling, and there's little overall distortion. Yet, audio quality, complete with circuit hiss, is not pleasant for long-term program listening—although weak-signal intelligibility is superior. The small inboard speaker doesn't hack it, either—a good outboard speaker is needed.

For world band listening, many lab measurements come up nicely, the factory operating software performs well, and the spectrum display is a winner for shortwave and mediumwave AM. But the receiver is burdened by dynamic range limitations and only two AM-mode bandwidths—with pedestrian shape factors, at that.

Nevertheless, if you're looking for a "does it all" receiver with wideband frequency coverage, the 'PCR1000 does a better job for less money than many other offerings, including standalone models.

New for 2000
✪✪
WinRadio 1500e

Price: $549.95 in the United States. £365.00 in the United Kingdom. DM1,145.00 in Germany. AUS$899.95 in Australia. Exported worldwide for US$664.95 *(sic)* including DHL air shipping from the Australian factory.

Pro: Wideband frequency coverage. AM-mode bandwidth has superb shape factor and good ultimate rejection. Spectrum display with good real-time performance (*see* Con). Tunes in precise 10 Hz increments; display has 1 Hz resolution, but of course can show only tuned 10 Hz increments. Comes with reasonably performing control software (*see* Con). Excellent sensitivity to weak signals, generally best among PC-controlled receivers tested (*see* Con). Passband offset (*see* Con). World time on-screen clock (*see* Con). High quality of assembly and construction.

Con: Dreadful dynamic range, a crucial shortcoming for world band. Only one AM-mode bandwidth (6.5 kHz). Audio power limited. No decent line output to feed PC sound card and speakers, so receiver's audio has to be used. Microphonics from internal speaker, making outboard speaker *de rigeur*. No synchronous selectable sideband. AGC not adjustable. No tunable notch filter. Poor blocking limits weak-signal sensitivity when band contains powerful signals. Long learning curve due to complexity. Closed-source programming means third-party software hard to make available for improved performance. Some tuning ergonomics only fair as compared with certain standalone receivers. Lacks passband offset in AM mode used by

The WinRadio 1500e doesn't cut the mustard for world band. The higher-priced model 3100e fares slightly better, but at triple the price.

virtually all world band stations. Uses AC adaptor instead of built-in power supply. Spectrum display of limited utility because of numerous spurious signals. World Time clock tied into computer's clock, which may not be accurate. Comes with 9/25-pin cable and 25/9 adaptor, which doesn't fit onto some laptops, rather than usual 9/9 cable. Sparse owner's manual.

Verdict: Ill suited to world band applications.

Evaluation of New Model: There are multiple models of the WinRadio, among them the 1000i and 1500i that are inboard plug-in cards. The tested WinRadio is the outboard 1500e.

Like the Icom PCR1000 but unlike the Ten-Tec RX320, the 1500e has wideband frequency coverage. For example, in the United States the civilian version covers 150 kHz-824 MHz, 849-869 MHz and 894-1500 MHz. The version sold elsewhere and to approved U.S. Federal agencies covers 150 kHz through 1500 MHz with no cellular gaps.

The 1500e uses a small, rugged cast-aluminum cabinet with a two-inch (50 mm) inboard speaker. The PC and receiver are connected by a serial cable with a male DB-9 connector at one end and female

DB-25 at the other; a 25/9 adaptor is included for the nine-pin ports now used by recent computers. For some desktops and a number of laptops the adaptor is clunky—sometimes it won't even fit—so it's worth buying your own 9/9 cable.

An AC adaptor is used instead of an internal power supply. The 1500e, like all other PC-controlled receivers tested, lacks synchronous selectable sideband. It also has no notch control or switchable AGC. Most importantly, each mode has but one bandwidth—a fairly broad 6.5 kHz (measured) in the case of the AM mode used for world band. The cheaper Ten-Tec RX320 has no less than 34 bandwidths, and no receiver in this price range can be taken seriously if it doesn't have at least two or three well-chosen bandwidths available in the AM mode.

The owner's manual is oriented to installation of the internal, card-based version, not the outboard 1500e, which as we found can create hours of unnecessary confusion. The v2.54 software which came on a diskette with our receiver nominally operates with Windows 3.1 and Windows 95, but installation failed with Win95 on one PC because the internal COM-2 port was inactive.

We repeated the installation on a Win98 machine with a known, working COM-2 port, and only then discovered that the software needs no configuration when used with the 1500e—just click on the icon, and WinRadio springs to life. Later software, v3.12, downloaded perfectly onto a Win95 machine via www.winradio.com, so forget the diskette and go with the online download.

Clicking on the WinRadio icon causes a likeness of a receiver front panel to appear on the screen, with these functions:

- Sensitivity (attenuator), with two settings.
- World and local times and dates, slaved to the computer's clock, which may not be accurate. World and local clocks are displayed separately, a refreshing improvement over most other receivers.
- Station Name Display for stations in memory (presets) with alphanumeric labels.
- Memory controls, which display the memory number and memory menu.
- Volume and Squelch. Adjustable by inputting a number or clicking up/down arrows. Nice, but these controls, like some others, are too small.
- Mode Selector, which selects among AM, FM-narrow, FM-wide, CW, LSB and USB. As with some other indicators, these shift from black to gray, so are hard to discern.
- Frequency Display, which has splendidly large digits. Frequency can be entered in MHz, kHz or GHz. Although the display is to the nearest Hertz, the receiver tunes in no finer than 10 Hz increments—a peculiar arrangement—and the frequency readout on our unit misread by 200 Hz.
- Frequency Step Control for VHF/UHF/SHF scanning, including defining and displaying scanning steps. In practice, the scanner usually stops off channel, so you have to fine tune by hand.
- Passband offset, which unfortunately does not function in the AM mode used by virtually all world band stations.
- Miscellaneous controls, including a front panel on/off switch.

The WinRadio 1500e uses a tank-tough cabinet, but lacks a proper line audio port for audio cards.

Shortwave Performance

The lone AM-mode bandwidth, 6.5 kHz, has a superb shape factor—1:1.4. Too, shortwave sensitivity (–135 dBm noise floor, 0.11 µV sensitivity) and mediumwave AM sensitivity (–133 dBm, 0.14 µV) are excellent. However, these high marks for sensitivity are compromised by poor blocking performance (83 dB), which reduces sensitivity when powerful signals are present beyond the received frequency, but are within or near the received band.

Serious performance limitations made it impossible for us to obtain reliable measurement of image rejection, first-IF rejection and phase noise. In the single-sideband mode we were also unable to precisely measure ultimate rejection and some aspects of overall distortion.

From there, it's a toboggan ride downhill, especially with dynamic range. At 20 kHz signal spacing dynamic range is an astonishingly poor 55 dB, third-order intercept point –52 dBm. At the more realistic 5 kHz spacing these measure a pitiful 38 dB and –78 dBm, respectively. Although we couldn't ascertain the caliber of front-end selectivity on paper, in practice it appears to be inferior.

Not surprisingly, at various test locations in eastern, central and near-western North America we found the 1500e to be awash in overloading throughout the shortwave spectrum when outdoor wire antennas were used. To make matters worse, local mediumwave AM stations—even at low power and miles away—can bleed through in abundance to disrupt world band reception. To a lesser extent CB signals can ghost through, too, as was discovered by one panelist located near a major highway.

Changing sensitivity from DX to local makes little difference so long as a worthy outdoor antenna is in use. This problem appears to a limited extent even within the 162 MHz American weather band. There were also spurious responses at various exact MHz points in and below the lower portion of the shortwave spectrum, such as 1 MHz, 2 MHz and 3 MHz.

The 1500e comes with an excellent spectrum display for frequency monitoring and surveillance applications. It works fast, with little of the lag found in some other displays, so it is well suited for bandscanning. However, with so many spurious signals showing up on the display, it winds up serving little useful purpose except as visual confirmation of how poorly this receiver performs.

The receiver's data jack, seemingly meant to second as a line output for a PC sound card, is hissy, with inadequate gain and no level control. (The owner's manual doesn't properly explain its primary function, but in reality it is for VHF/UHF data decoding.) The speaker jack doesn't perform adequately as a line output, either. Thus, as a practical matter there is no acceptable way to run the 1500e's audio through a PC's sound card and speakers, so the receiver's audio amplifier has to be used.

The resulting audio quality is pleasant, although overall distortion in the AM mode varies from one percent at 3 kHz AF, to five percent at 1 kHz AF, to ten percent at 0.1 kHz AF. There are also microphonics with the internal speaker, so an outboard speaker is virtually a "must"—but it has to be very efficient, as the receiver has precious little in the way of audio power. Another oddity is that the speaker jack is stereo, even though the audio output is mono, so it doesn't work properly with the monaural jacks that come with most communications speakers. Best bet: Use an amplified outboard speaker custom fitted with a stereo plug.

Single sideband reception? The one bandwidth for single-sideband reception is unusually wide, ultimate rejection is limited and the AGC decay is too fast. Synthesizer chugging also makes manual bandscanning something of a chore, as you have to tune, stop, listen, resume tuning, and so on. And, of course, dynamic range problems are just as present as they are with AM-mode signals.

Seldom before have we come across a receiver with so much unrealized potential. There is much about the 1500e which is first class, so perhaps over time it will be improved.

New for 2000
Not Rated
WinRadio 3100e

Price: $1,895.95 in the United States. £995.00 in the United Kingdom. AUS$2,495 in Australia.

Verdict: A knowledgeable American importer, Grove Enterprises, tipped us off that the costlier WinRadio 3100e is very similar to the 1500e (see above), but with improved dynamic range. So we ran

COMING UP: KACHINA KC-105CRX

Given American dominance in the computer industry, it may come as a surprise to find that only one PC-controlled shortwave receiver—Ten-Tec's RX320—is an American product.

But that may be about to change. While Ten-Tec offers the lowest-priced model, the Cottonwood, Arizona firm of Kachina Communications hopes to release the top-priced KC-105CRX sometime in early 2000. Be prepared for sticker shock: $2,280 Stateside, if things go as planned—and that's without the computer!

The '105CRX is expected to be virtually identical to the existing KC-505 transceiver, but with such important enhancements as synchronous selectable sideband, FM demodulation, revised software and a more AM-mode-friendly bandwidth configuration (currently, there is only one bandwidth for the AM mode). So we put a KC-505 through our hurdles to at least get a taste of things to come.

Professional Performance

Right off, our laboratory figures show why this is no el cheapo offering. The third-order intercept point at 20 kHz signal separation points is a whopping +19 dBm (DR 94 dB), dropping only to +8 dBm (DR 87 dB) at 10 kHz separation points; phase noise prevented our making accurate measurements at 5 kHz separation points. Image rejection is greater than 80 dB, and first IF rejection comes in at an Olympian 100 dB. This is the stuff of professional supersets, and helps explain the steep price tag.

Although phase noise measures a decent –114 dBc, we found that in practice it manifests itself in strange ways, with IMD and noise being substantially inconsistent from the measurement high side to the low side. Among the consequences, we could not measure bandwidth below –40 dB and ultimate rejection below 55 dB.

Other measurements are virtually all good or better, but to get the most out of this rig you need to have the preamp on, which raises sensitivity from a modest 0.50 µV (noise floor –122 dBm, good) to a superb 0.16 µV (noise floor –132 dBm, excellent). The preamp also improves the AGC threshold from a poor 7 µV to an excellent 1.6 µV. Fortunately, the '105CRX has more than enough dynamic range to handle the preamp's 13 dB of gain. Superb blocking (137 dB) also means that powerful nearby signals are unlikely to desensitize this receiver one iota.

selected laboratory tests on the WinRadio 3100e to find out whether more money actually buys better performance.

Grove's claim is accurate. The 3100e's dynamic range, although still poor, is indeed better: The third-order intercept point at 20 kHz separation is –33 dBm (DR 62 dB) *vs.* –52 dBm (DR 55 dB) on the 1500e, and at 5 kHz separation it is –60 dBm (DR 44 dB) *vs.* –78 dBm (DR 38 dB) on the 1500e.

However, the piper must be paid, and not just in coin. The 3100e is also slightly less sensitive to weak signals, with a shortwave noise floor of only –126 dBm (sensitivity 0.3 µV) *vs.* –135 dBm (sensitivity 0.11 µV) on the 1500e. Nonetheless, the tradeoff is positive technically, even if not financially.

_____

The PASSPORT *PC radio review team consists of Chuck Rippel, Robert Sherwood and David Zantow, with Lawrence Magne.*

Average distortion is only two percent, overall. Although phase noise kept us from ascertaining skirt selectivity, it appears to be excellent (e.g., 2.9 kHz at –6 dB, 3.4 kHz at –40 dB, unmeasurable at –60 dB) except for the 6 kHz wide AM-mode bandwidth (6.2 kHz at –6 dB, 13.8 kHz at –40 dB, unmeasurable at –60 dB), with skirts that are only good or fair. The bar-type signal-strength indicator works well, although it is not quite so accurate as some others.

There is an automatic DSP variable notch filter, but in the transceiver it does not work in the AM or FM modes—an omission that presumably will be corrected in the receiver. Other "wish list" improvements include getting the passband offset and AGC decay to be selectable in the AM mode, more audio power, a virtual tuning knob/mouse-wheel tuning knob, and improved phase noise.

Actual operation is reminiscent of a computer-controlled version of the standalone tabletop AOR AR7030 *(see)*. This is hardly a ringing endorsement of Kachina's control software, as the AR7030's software is notoriously complex to operate, but Kachina says it will be improved before the receiver is released. More to the point, it uses open-source C++ programming, so anybody can go to www.kachina-az.com/software.htm to develop improved control software. Firmware upgrades are made via an $89 plug-in ROM board.

The Kachina KC-105CRX has enormous potential, mainly for commercial and governmental applications, assuming it emerges from the engineering womb with a number of enhancements. Then it will boil down to one question: Is it worth the money?

The forthcoming Kachina KC-105CRX receiver will target the high-end consumer and low-end professional markets.

Radios for Emergencies

Everything's cool.

For over a quarter century, now, some countries have been on a roll, with years of high-flying economic performance and social peace. So it's hardly surprising that, like stock market players who see only the upside, lots of us now think our environment is eternally beneficent.

But as baseball icon Dizzy Dean used to put it, we're due. Good times can last only so long before something comes along: war, economic failure, earthquake, tornado, hurricane, blizzard, contagion. Those who don't think like Dizzy may find themselves facing hard times with their knickers around their ankles.

For example, while the news media focus blissfully on how much air should be in air bags, American government officials solemnly report that the risk from "NBC" (nuclear, biological, chemical) attack from terrorists and rogue states is real and increasing—not to mention the growing threat from established powers such as China. Ditto, potential malfunctions in foreign weapons systems.

Perils can also work in concert to create even greater risk. For example, in the event of a major technological collapse or pandemic, hostile elements can spring into action before a shaken social structure can be repaired. Citizens thus face a choice: waiting to learn from precedent, or getting prepared now.

The Y2K issue, however overblown, has served as a canary in the mineshaft. It underscores our vast dependence on technology so complicated and intertwined that sooner or later there will be times when we will have to depend on our personal resources and those of our neighbors.

None of this calls for a closet full of canned soup and antelope jerky, but there are commonsense, low-cost steps you can take right now. Mormons, who came to know hard times early on, got it right by insisting that each family stock a year's essential provisions. Trim that down to a months' worth—along with perhaps a protective weapon, suitable clothing, emergency lighting, books and a smattering of civilized luxuries to keep a smile on your face—and you'll be prepared for just about any contingency.

> Those who don't think ahead may face hard times with their knickers around their ankles.

Information That's Always There

But what about communications? Knowing what's going on can literally save your life.

Sales of shortwave radios soared in San Francisco after the last shaker, for good reason: When push comes to shove, world band is

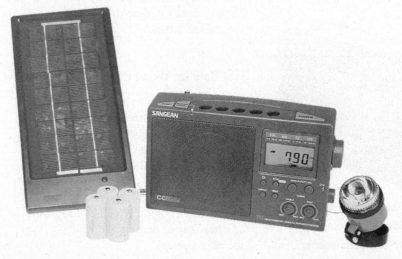

C. Crane's Special Edition radio runs off solar power that feeds rechargeable batteries. It also comes with a room-filling light.
C. Crane

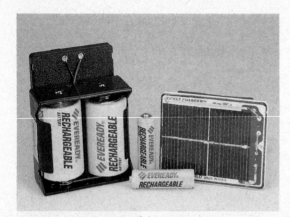

Solar battery systems allow portables and portatops to work in any emergency.

Edmund Scientific

Effective Battery Alternatives

What to do?

You already have a copy of PASSPORT and probably own a portable world band radio, as well. If so the answer may be disarmingly simple: Keep spare sets of batteries. Starting in 1999 the major alkaline battery manufacturers went to a "super" formula that does the trick nicely.

Alternatively, you can use a solar NiCd battery charger, available from such suppliers as Universal Radio, C. Crane, Sun-Mate, Real Goods, ICP Global Technologies and Edmund Scientific. Even more interesting is the forthcoming Freeplay Standalone Generator, due out sometime in 2000 for around the equivalent of $50. Using crank and solar power, this multivoltage power pack is being jointly designed by Freeplay and General Electric to handle all kinds of devices besides world band radios, including laptop computers, cellphones and two-way radios.

the *only real-time information medium that will always work.* Unlike local stations and the Internet, world band is reliable, long haul, multinational and nearly impossible to censor or jam. It is the ultimate vehicle for credible news in times of crisis.

Another plus is that all world band segments are within the shortwave spectrum, which harbors other types of radio activity, as well. This allows certain radios to eavesdrop on amateur ("ham") and point-to-point shortwave communications, which transmit beyond the range of VHF/UHF signals received by scanners.

How important can backup power be in a time of crisis? In 1999, terrorized Kosovars urgently needing to contact the outside world found their only means of interpersonal communication—cellular phones—failed because their batteries had given out. There was no local power to revive them, and they had no dynamos or solar chargers as backup.

The Info-Mate 837 uses solar power and a hand-cranked generator, but has atrocious performance. P. Bove

Best Bets for World Band and AM

If you don't already have a decent portable, here's what to consider when perusing PASSPORT REPORTS. First, concentrate on portables with digital tuning and station presets, which are the ones reviewed in detail. Also look for full coverage of shortwave and mediumwave AM from 530 kHz through roughly 30 MHz, along with the capability to demodulate single-sideband signals.

Portatops work, too, but these macho sets require mucho batteries. They are clumsy to carry around and receive best with at least some sort of external antenna.

Most of today's radios don't excel in the mediumwave AM band, which can be very useful at night when faraway stations roll in. Radios that are especially effective for long-haul reception in that band, as well as FM, include GE's $60 analog Superadio III and C. Crane's sophisticated new $160 CCRadio with digital tuning and presets. For $135 more, the CCRadio can be equipped with an outboard rechargeable solar power system that includes a room light suitable for reading.

Best for overall multiband performance is the Sony ICF-2010. It has top-rated world band reception, superior long-distance mediumwave AM reception and a degree of aircraft band reception. It also has decent FM DX reception, provided you're not near an FM transmitter. The '2010 is not widely available outside North America, but is commonly exported by American vendors.

Rechargeable Radios Lack Performance

What about world band radios made especially for emergencies?

The Info-Mate 837, under $100, is powered by NiCd cells which are recharged by built-in solar panels and a hand-cranked dynamo; these NiCd cells supposedly are good for five years. In addition to short-wave 4-24 MHz, the Info-Mate covers mediumwave AM 540-1700 kHz, FM, an air band, U.S. weather radio and audio for NTSC television channels 2-13 VHF.

Sounds almost ideal on paper, but in reality its performance is atrocious—poor sensitivity to weak signals, awful image rejection, poor selectivity, sticky tuning and the coarsest of "blind man's bluff" analog tuning. As if that weren't enough, it

MSNBC calls the CCRadio the world's best AM radio, and no wonder. It is an outstanding portable for pulling in mediumwave DX, includes a weather alarm and has digital frequency synthesis. C. Crane

takes fully five minutes of wearisome cranking to get an hour's worth of listening.

The $70 analog Luke DP-976 is similar but more compact, covering shortwave 6-17 MHz, so it misses only the 21 MHz and tropical world band segments. It covers FM, but mediumwave AM tunes no higher than 1610 kHz while the upper limit of the AM band in the Americas is 1700 kHz. Although it uses bandspreading to aid with shortwave tuning, its frequency accuracy is a coarse plus or minus 30 kHz.

Like the Info-Mate the Luke is powered by NiCd cells, which are charged by built-in

The solar-and-crank powered Luke DP-976 is a marginal performer, but slightly better than the similar Info-Mate 837. Universal Radio

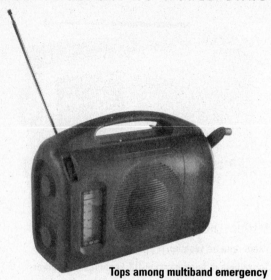

Tops among multiband emergency portables is the BayGen Freeplay FPR1-B. BayGen

solar cells, as well as by a dynamo that has to be cranked for a grueling ten minutes for an hour's listening. However, unlike the Info-Mate the Luke's cells are inside the sealed cabinet and thus not amenable to replacement. It also has a separate battery cavity for two regular "AA" batteries, but comes with no AC adaptor. Unfortunately, although it receives world band stations better than the dismal Info-Mate, the Luke is a marginal performer on all bands and does not demodulate single-sideband signals.

The GE Superadio III uses slide-rule analog tuning, but is a bargain for excellent reception of distant mediumwave AM stations. Superior FM, too. GE

Freeplay: No Cells, Always Works

The well-known BayGen "Freeplay" fares somewhat better. Larger than the Info-Mate and Luke, it comes in two world band versions: the FPR1-A covering 3-12 MHz, and the FPR1-B for 5.8-18 MHz; both also cover mediumwave AM 520-1700 kHz and the FM band. Unless you're listening from Africa or Latin America the "B" version is much better, especially now that we are in the years of sunspot maximum. It allows for reception both day and night, whereas the "A" version—designed for the specialized requirements of African listening—is limited except during the evening. Both versions are powered by an inboard dynamo driven by a hand-cranked spring—you get 30 minutes of listening for every 20 seconds of cranking. Boring and tiresome, yes, but acceptable.

The Freeplay has no batteries of any sort—remember, even NiCd cells have a rated life of only around five years. In principle, then, it should be able to spring to life after lengthy hibernation, provided the ambient humidity isn't so extreme as to cause deterioration. The downside of not using batteries is that the dynamo operates when the radio is on, making a slight mechanical sound while you're listening to your favorite program.

Neither of the Freeplay models, which sell for under the equivalent of $120, provides great world band reception, but they have relatively solid audio. Like the Info-Mate and Luke, the current Freeplay offerings lack digital tuning with station presets, so every time you change stations you have to scour around by ear to find what you want. Nor do they demodulate single-sideband signals so you can understand them. Nevertheless, the Freeplay's windup feature means that you never have to worry about dead batteries—regular or NiCd—so it passes muster as a backup radio in the event your "real" world band portable acts up or your batteries peter out.

Reports persist of fit-and-finish and other quality-control problems with the Freeplay. We can't confirm these, but common sense suggests you should purchase from a source that will replace the radio if it has a demonstrable defect.

The manufacturer plans to introduce a new world band portable around autumn of 2000—perhaps this will be a more inspiring performer. However, it is also likely to use batteries charged by dynamo, rather than using a spring-wound dynamo to power the radio directly. But as re-chargeable batteries don't last forever, some of the radio's appeal for emergencies would be lost.

Moral: If you want the ultimate in "anytime" emergency radio reliability, buy the current version of the Freeplay.

Outwitting Pursuers

What if you're in an "X-Files" situation, with powerful unfriendlies on your tail? Few ever are, but a variety of folks have occasion to find themselves on official or unofficial business on inhospitable turf. Survivors have revealed to us just how world band literally has saved their lives while they were on the run.

For this there is only one real choice, the $360 Sony ICF-SW100S or £150 ICF-SW100E. This tiny device is but the size of an audio cassette box, yet is almost as sophisticated as the best large portables. It comes in two versions—"S" and "E"—but either will do for listening on the lam. The new Sony ICF-SW07, although slightly larger, also fits into many pockets and performs even better by a skootch. If either of these is too pricey for your wallet, try the Sangean ATS 606A or Roberts R617. Go over the current PASSPORT for station frequencies you think you'll need, store them in the radio along with fresh batteries, and off you go.

The new Sony ICF-SW07 puts big-radio performance into a small, high-tech package. Excellent not only for world band, but also for distant FM and mediumwave AM. Sony

Bottom line is that for many of us the best options for everyday use are also usually tops for emergency use, provided you keep extra alkaline cells on hand. Given their long shelf life, you shouldn't have to toss out unused batteries, bringing your investment in emergency communications to virtually zero.

The Sony ICF-SW100 is only the size of an audio cassette box, but is highly rated. It is perfect if you risk being on the lam in hostile foreign territory. Sony

What's On Tonight?

PASSPORT's Hour-by-Hour Guide to Shows in English

World band offers it all, from un-paralleled news reporting to old-fashioned communist propaganda. Here are the main English-language programs, with these symbols for best bets:

■ Station with shows that are almost always superior

● A top-notch show

Key frequencies are given for North America, Western Europe, East Asia and Australasia, plus general coverage of the Mideast, Southern Africa and Southeast Asia. Information on secondary and seasonal channels, as well as channels for other parts of the world, are in "Worldwide Broadcasts in English" and the Blue Pages.

Times are given in World Time, days as World Day, both explained in PASSPORT's glossary and "Compleat

Idiot's Guide to Getting Started." Many stations announce World Time at the beginning of each broadcast or on the hour.

"Summer" and "winter"? These refer to seasons in the Northern Hemisphere. Many stations supplement their programs with news-letters, tourist brochures, magazines, books and other goodies—often free. See Addresses PLUS for how to obtain them.

To be as helpful as possible throughout the year, PASSPORT's schedules consist mainly of observed activity. When appropriate, this is supplemented by that which we have creatively opined will take place during the forthcoming year. This predictive material is original from us, but is inherently not so exact as real-time data.

Lenin's statue lords over Bishkek's central Ala-too Square, Kyrgyzstan.
M. Guha

0000-0559
North America—Evening Prime Time
Europe & Mideast—Early Morning
Australasia & East Asia—Midday and Afternoon

00:00

■**BBC World Service for the Americas.** Starts with 30 minutes of ●*The World Today*, which is followed by one or more features. Pick of the regular offerings, all at 0030, are Tuesday's ●*Health Matters* (Monday evening, local American date), Wednesday's ●*Discovery*, Thursday's environmental ●*One Planet*, and Saturday's ●*Science in*

Show times are given in World Time, days as World Day.

Torehan Rysbekovich Daniyarov, Director of Kazak Radio, with his copy of PASSPORT. M. Guha

Action. Continuous programming to North America and the Caribbean on 5975, 6175 and 9590 kHz.

■BBC World Service for East Asia. Similar to the service for the Americas, except for some of the features at 0030. Among the more interesting shows are ●*From Our Own Correspondent* (Sunday), ●*Omnibus* (Monday), *Sports International* (Wednesday), ●*Assignment* (Thursday), ●*Focus on Faith* (Friday) and Saturday's *People and Politics*. Audible in East Asia on 15280 and 15360 kHz; and in Southeast Asia on 6195 and 15360 kHz.

Radio Bulgaria. Winters only at this time. *News*, then Tuesday through Friday there's 15 minutes of current events in *Today*, replaced Saturday by *Weekly Spotlight*. The remainder of the broadcast is given over to features dealing with Bulgarian life and culture, and includes some lively Balkan folk music. Sixty minutes to eastern North America and Central America on 7375 and 9485 kHz. One hour earlier in summer.

Radio Exterior de España ("Spanish National Radio"). *News*, then Tuesday through Saturday (local weekday evenings in the Americas) it's *Panorama*, which features a recording of popular Spanish music, a commentary or a report, a review of the Spanish press, and weather. The remainder of the program is a mixture of literature, science, music and general programming. Tuesday (Monday evening in North America), there's *Sports Spotlight* and *Cultural Encounters*; Wednesday features *People of Today* and *Entertainment in Spain*; Thursday brings *As Others See Us* and, biweekly, *The Natural World* or *Science Desk*; Friday has *Economic Report* and *Cultural Clippings*; and Saturday offers *Window on Spain* and *Review of the Arts*. The final slot is given over to a language course, *Spanish by Radio*. On the remaining days, you can listen to Sunday's *Hall of Fame* and *Gallery of Spanish Voices*; and Monday's *Visitors' Book*, *Great Figures in Flamenco* and *Radio Club*. Sixty minutes to eastern North America; winter on 6055 or 9690 kHz, and summer on 15385 kHz.

Radio Canada International. Winters only at this time. Tuesday through Saturday (weekday evenings in North America), it's the final hour of the CBC domestic service news program ●*As It Happens*, which features International stories, Canadian news and general human interest features. A shortened Saturday edition is complemented by *C'est la Vie*. Sundays feature ●*Global Village* (world music), replaced Monday by another eclectic music show, ●*Roots and Wings*, both from the CBC's domestic output. Between these two shows, you can hear just about anything—from black Peruvian music to Mongolian horsehead fiddles. To North America on 5960 and 9755 kHz. A separate half-hour broadcast, ●*The World at Six*, can be heard Tuesday through Saturday on 6040, 9535 and 11865 kHz. All are heard one hour earlier in summer.

Radio Yugoslavia. Monday through Saturday (Sunday through Friday, local American evenings) and summers only at this time. *News* and information with a strong local flavor, and worth a listen if you are interested in the area. Thirty minutes to Eastern and Central North America on 9580 and 11870 kHz. One hour later in winter.

Radio Japan. *News*, then Tuesday through Saturday (weekday evenings local American date) it's *44 Minutes* (an in-depth look at current trends and events in Japan). This is replaced Sunday by *Asian Weekly*, and Monday by some lighter fare, *Hello from Tokyo*. One hour to eastern North America on 11705 kHz via the powerful relay facilities of Radio Canada International in

Sackville, New Brunswick. Also available to Europe on 6155 and 6180 kHz; and to Central Africa on 9665 kHz. A separate 15-minute news bulletin for Southeast Asia is aired on 11815 and 13650 kHz.

Radio Pyongyang, North Korea. Of curiosity value and to follow official thinking, this broadcasting dinosaur is almost totally removed from reality. Terms like "Great Leader" and "Beloved Comrade" seem destined for immortality, and choral adulation of the country's leader is as alive now as it was 20 or 30 years ago. An hour of old-style communist programming to Southeast Asia and the Americas on 11845, 13650 and 15230 kHz.

Radio Ukraine International. Summers only at this time. An hour's ample coverage of just about everything Ukrainian, including news, sports, politics and culture. Well worth a listen is ●*Music from Ukraine*, which fills most of the Monday (Sunday evening in the Americas) broadcast. Sixty minutes to Europe and eastern North America on 5905, 6020 and 9560 kHz. One hour later in winter. Budget and technical limitations have reduced audibility of Radio Ukraine International to only a fraction of what it used to be.

Radio Australia. Part of a 24-hour service to Asia and the Pacific, but which can also be heard at this time in parts of North America (better to the west). Begins with world *news*, then Tuesday through Friday there's *Asia Pacific*, replaced Saturday by *Feedback* (a listener-response program), Sunday by *Oz Sounds* and Monday by *Correspondents' Report*. On the half-hour, look for a bit of variety, depending on the day of the week. Monday's *Innovations* deals with the invented and innovative; Tuesday's cultural spot is *Arts Australia*; Wednesday, take a trip up country in *Rural Reporter*; Thursday, it's *Book Talk*; Friday spotlights the environment in *Earthbeat*; and weekends

there's Saturday's *Asia Pacific* and Sunday's *Correspondents' Report*. Targeted at Asia and the Pacific on 9660, 12080, 15240, 17715, 17750, 17795 and 21740 kHz. In North America (best during summer) try 17715, 17795 and 21740 kHz; and in East Asia go for 15240 and 17750 kHz. Best bet for Southeast Asia is 17750 kHz.

Radio Prague, Czech Republic. *News*, then Tuesday through Saturday (weekday evenings in the Americas), there's *Current Affairs*. These are followed by one or more features. Tuesday's offering is *Spotlight*; Wednesday, it's *Talking Point*; Thursday brings *History Czech*; Friday there's *Economic Report*; and Saturday features a listener-response program, *Between You and Us*. The Sunday slot is an excellent musical feature (strongly recommended), and Monday there's *A Letter from Prague*, *From the Weeklies* and *Readings from Czech Literature*. Thirty minutes to eastern North America, winter on 5930 and 7345 kHz, and summer on 11615 and 13580 kHz.

HCJB—Voice of the Andes, Ecuador. Tuesday through Saturday (weekday evenings in North America), you can hear *Insight for Living* and *Focus on the Family*. This is replaced weekends by Sunday's *Nite BriteKid's Club* and *Saludos Amigos,* and Monday's *Hour of Decision* and *Mountain Meditations*. To North America on 9745 and 12015 kHz.

Voice of America. The first 60 minutes of a two-hour broadcast to the Caribbean and Latin America which is aired Tuesday through Saturday (weekday evenings in the Americas). *News Now*, a rolling news format covering political, business and other developments. On 5995, 6130, 7405, 9455, 9775, 11695 and 13740 kHz. The final hour of a separate service to East and Southeast Asia and Australasia (see 2200) can be heard on 7215, 9770, 11760, 15185, 15290, 17735 and 17820 kHz.

GRUNDIG
Gives you the world

The Grundig Satellit 800 Millenium...
the wait is over!

SAT800 Millenium.

The Grundig Satellit 800 Millenium comes from a long line of overachievers like the Satellit 500, 600, 650 and the legendary Satellit 700.
The Satellit 800 is a perfect balance of form and function. Band coverage is complete: Shortwave from 100KHz to 30MHz, plus AM/FM and VHF aircraft band (118 to 137 MHz). The receiver has synchronous detector for superior reception, upper and lower sideband capability (LSB/USB),

AGC, built-in analog signal strength meter, and three-position switchable bandwidth. 70 user-programmable memory locations make your favourite stations a single touch away. Oversized multifunction LCD display gives you all the information you need, including frequency, band, mode, memory location and more. All this, and Grundig's world-renowned German engineering and legendary 'Grundig sound' make this the most exciting entry in shortwave radio in years. 201-8104*

GRUNDIG

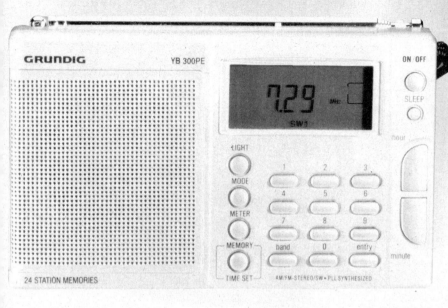

YB300PE shortwave radio.

Features PLL tuning and 24 station presets, titanium-look finish, dynamic micro speaker and external antenna connector. Includes travel cover, AC adapter, earphones, batteries and supplementary antenna. 2018103

99⁹⁹

Grundig YB400PE.

The incomparable YB400PE offers access to international bands on AM/FM/SW. With PLL tuner, 40-station memory, dual alarm clock, data monitor and upper and lower side band with BFO. Includes earphones, travel cover, AC adapter and supplementary antenna. 2018100

229⁹⁹

Available in Canada at:

 RadioShack®

You've got questions. We've got answers.

www.radioshack.ca

Available at RadioShack stores and participating dealers in Canada.

00:00–01:00

Traditionally decorated carriages ply the dusty roads of fuel-starved Afghanistan. M. Guha

Radio Thailand. *Newshour*. Not as dry as it used to be, but a little added vitality would help. Thirty minutes to eastern and southern parts of Africa (who listens at this hour?), winters on 9680 kHz and summers on 9690 kHz. An extra half hour is available for listeners in Asia on 9655 and 11905 kHz.

All India Radio. The final 45 minutes of a much larger block of programming targeted at Southeast Asia, and heard well beyond. On 7150, 9705, 9950 and 11620 kHz.

Radio Cairo, Egypt. The final half-hour of a 90-minute broadcast to eastern North America on 9900 kHz. See 2300 for specifics.

Radio New Zealand International. A friendly package of *news* and features sometimes replaced by live sports commentary. Part of a much longer broadcast for the South Pacific, but also heard in parts of North America (especially during summer) on 17675 kHz.

FEBC Radio International, Philippines. *Good Morning from Manila*, a potpourri of secular and religious programming targeted at South and Southeast Asia, but heard well beyond. The first 60 minutes of a two-hour broadcast on 15175 (or 15450) kHz.

WJCR, Upton, Kentucky. Twenty-four hours of gospel music targeted at North America on 7490 and (at this hour) 13595 kHz. Also heard elsewhere, mainly during darkness hours. For more religious broadcasting at this hour, try **WYFR-Family Radio** on 6085 kHz, and **KTBN** on (winters) 7510 or (summers) 15590 kHz. For something a little more controversial, tune to Dr. Gene Scott's University Network, via **WWCR** on 13845 kHz or **KAIJ** on 13815 kHz. Traditional Catholic programming can be heard via **WEWN** on 7425 kHz.

00:30

■**Radio Netherlands.** *News*, then Tuesday through Saturday (Monday through Friday evenings in North America) there's ●*Newsline* (current events). These are followed by a different feature each day, including the well-produced ●*Research File* (science, Tuesday); *Music 52-15* (eclectic,

Wednesday); the excellent award-winning ●*Documentary* (Thursday); *Media Network* (Friday); ●*A Good Life* (Saturday); and Sunday's *Europe Unzipped* and●*Weekend*. Monday's features are a listener-response program and *Sounds Interesting*. Fifty-five minutes to North America on 6165 and 9845 kHz.

Radio Austria International. Summers only at this time. ●*Report from Austria*, which includes a brief bulletin of *news*, followed by a series of current events and human interest stories. Ample coverage of national and regional issues, and an excellent source for news of Central Europe. Thirty minutes to eastern North America on 9655 kHz.

Radio Vilnius, Lithuania. A half hour that's heavily geared to *news* and background reports about events in Lithuania. Of broader appeal is *Mailbag*, aired every other Sunday (Saturday evenings local American date). For a little Lithuanian music, try the next evening, following the news. To eastern North America winters on 6155 kHz, and summers on 9855 kHz.

Voice of the Islamic Republic of Iran. One hour of *news*, commentary and features with a strong Islamic slant. Targeted at North and Central America. Try 6015, 6150, 6175, 7180, 9022 and 9670 kHz. Apart from 9022 kHz, channel usage tends to be variable.

Radio Thailand. *Newshour*. Thirty minutes to North America winters on 11905 kHz, and summers on 15395 kHz.

00:45

Radio Tirana, Albania. Summers only at this time. Approximately 15 minutes of *news* and commentary from this Balkan country. To North America on 6115 and 7160 kHz. One hour later in winter.

RAI International—Radio Roma, Italy. Actually starts at 0050. *News* and Italian music make up this 20-minute broadcast to North America on 6010, 9675 and 11800 kHz.

01:00

■**BBC World Service for the Americas.** Thirty minutes of ●*The World Today*, then it's a very mixed bag. Depending on the day of the week, you'll either get classical music, the arts show *Meridian,* or a mediocre soap opera called *Westway*. Definitely not the cream of the BBC's output. Continuous programming to North America and the Caribbean on 5975, 6175 and 9590 kHz.

■**BBC World Service for East Asia.** Monday through Friday, there's five minutes of *World News*, replaced weekends by a half hour of ●*The World Today*. Tuesday through Friday at 0105, look for ●*Insight* (current events). Weekdays, the final 15 minutes carry ●*Off the Shelf*, serialized readings from the best of world literature. The remaining airtime is taken up by a number of features, most of them highly informative. Take your pick from Monday's ●*The Farming World* (0105) and ●*Health Matters* (0120), Tuesday's ●*Discovery* (science), Wednesday's ●*One Planet* (the environment and development), and Friday's ●*Science in Action*. Weekends, try Sunday's *Global Business* on the half-hour. Continuous to East Asia on 15280 and 15360 kHz, and to Southeast Asia on 6195 and 15360 kHz.

Radio Canada International. Summers only. *News*, followed Tuesday through Saturday (weekday evenings local American date) by *Spectrum* (topics in the news), which in turn is replaced Sunday by *Venture Canada* (business and economics) and the interesting ●*Earth Watch*. On Monday (Sunday evening in North

America), *Arts in Canada* is followed by a listener-response program, *The Mailbag*. Sixty minutes to North America on 5960 and 9755 kHz. You can also try 9535, 11715, 13670 and 15305 kHz, but they are only available for the first 30 minutes, except at weekends. One hour later in winter.

■**Deutsche Welle,** Germany. *News*, followed Tuesday through Saturday (weekday evenings in the Americas) by the comprehensive ●*NewsLink*—commentary, interviews, background reports and analysis. This is followed by ●*Man and Environment* (ecology, Tuesday), ●*Insight* (analysis, Wednesday), *Living in Germany* (Thursday), *Spotlight on Sport* (Friday), or Saturday's *German by Radio*. Sunday fare is *Weekend Review* and ●*Inside Europe*, and next day there's *Religion and Society* (replaced by *Mailbag North America* on the last Monday of the month) and *Arts on the Air*. Forty-five minutes of very good reception in North America and the Caribbean, winter on 6040, 6145, 9640, 9700 and 9790 kHz; and summers on 6040, 9640, 11810 and 13720 kHz.

Radio Slovakia International. *Slovakia Today*, a 30-minute window on Slovak life and culture. Tuesday (Monday evening in the Americas), there's a variety of short features; Wednesday puts the spotlight on tourism and Slovak personalities; Thursday's slot is devoted to business and economy; and Friday is given over to a mix of politics, education and science. Saturday offerings include cultural features, *Slovak Kitchen* and the off-beat *Back Page News*; while Sunday brings the *"Best of"* series. Monday's fare is very much a mixed bag, and includes *Listeners' Tribune* and some enjoyable Slovak music. A friendly half hour to eastern North America and the Caribbean on 5930 kHz; to South America on 9440 kHz; and for African night owls on 7300 kHz.

Radio Budapest, Hungary. Summers only at this time. *News* and features, most of which are broadcast on a non-regular basis. Thirty minutes to North America on 9560 kHz. One hour later in winter.

Radio Prague, Czech Republic. Repeat of the 0000 broadcast; see there for specifics. Thirty minutes to North America, better to the East, on 6200 (winter), 7345 and (summer) 11615 kHz.

Swiss Radio International. *World Radio Switzerland*—a workmanlike compilation of news and analysis of world and Swiss events. Somewhat lighter fare on Sunday (Saturday evening in North America), when the biweekly *Capital Letters* (a listener-response program) alternates with *Name Game* (first Sunday) and *Sounds Good* (music and interviews, third Sunday). A half hour to North America and the Caribbean on 9885 and 9905 kHz.

Radio Exterior de España ("Spanish National Radio"). Repeat of the 0000 transmission. One hour to eastern North America; winter on 6055 or 9690 kHz, and summer on 15385 kHz.

Radio Japan. *News*, then Tuesday through Saturday there's *44 Minutes* (an in-depth look at current trends and events in Japan). This is replaced Sunday by *Weekend Break*, and Monday by *Hello from Tokyo*. One hour to East Asia on 15570 kHz; to South Asia on 15325 kHz; to Southeast Asia on 11860 and 15590 kHz; to Australasia on 17685 kHz; to South America on 17835 kHz; and to the Mideast on 6150 (winter), 9660 (summer) and 11870 kHz.

Radio For Peace International, Costa Rica. The first hour in English (the initial 60 minutes are in French or Spanish) of an eight-hour cyclical block of social-conscience and counterculture programming audible in Europe and the Americas on 6975 and (summers) 21460 kHz.

China Radio International. *News* and commentary, followed Tuesday through Saturday (Monday through Friday evenings in the Americas) by in-depth reporting and a review of the Chinese press. Next come feature programs like *Open Windows* and *Learn to Speak Chinese* (Tuesday); *Orient Arena* and *Opera House* (Wednesday); *Voices from Other Lands* (Thursday); *Focus* and *Cultural Spectrum* (Friday); and *Life in China* and *Global Review* (Saturday). Sunday's lineup includes *Asia-Pacific News*, *Report from Developing Countries*, *China Scrapbook* and ●*Music from China*; and Monday's offerings are *Cultural Information*, *People in the Know*, *On the Road* and *Letterbox*. This broadcast, via a Cuban relay, was inaugurated on an experimental basis during summer 1999, and may be one hour later in winter. Sixty minutes to North America on 9570 kHz.

Voice of Vietnam. A relay via the facilities of the Voice of Russia. Begins with *news*, then there's *Commentary* or *Weekly Review*, followed by short features and some pleasant Vietnamese music (especially at weekends). Thirty minutes to eastern North America; winters on 5940 kHz, and summers on 7250 kHz. Repeated at 0230 on the same channels.

Voice of Russia World Service. Summers only at this hour, and the start of a four-hour block of programming for North America. *News*, then Tuesday through Sunday (Monday through Saturday evenings in North America), there's *News and Views*, replaced Monday by *Sunday Panorama* and *Russia in Personalities*. The second half-hour contains some interesting fare, with just about everyone's favorite being Tuesday's ●*Folk Box*. For listeners who like classical music, don't miss Friday's ●*Music at Your Request* or

Yours for the Asking. Pick of the remaining fare is ●*Russia's Musical Highlights of the 20th Century* (Thursday), ●*Moscow Yesterday and Today* (Sunday and Monday), and Wednesday's *Jazz Show*. Where to tune? In eastern North America, try 9665 kHz; farther west, shoot for 12050 and 15595 kHz.

Radio Habana Cuba. The start of a two-hour cyclical broadcast to eastern North America, and made up of *news* and features such as *Latin America Newsline*, *DXers Unlimited*, *The Mailbag Show* and ●*The Jazz Place*, interspersed with some lively Cuban music (though not as much as there used to be). To eastern North America on 6000 and 9820 kHz. Also available on 9830 or 11705 kHz upper sideband (USB), though not all radios, unfortunately, can process such signals.

Radio Australia. *World News*, then a feature. Monday's offering—unusual, to say the least—is *Awaye*, a program dealing with indigenous affairs. This is replaced Tuesday by *Science Show* and Wednesday by *Natural Interest* (topical events). Thursday's presentation is *Background Briefing* (news analysis); Friday brings *Hindsight*; Saturday is given over to *Oz Sounds* and *Arts Australia*; and the Sunday slot belongs to *The Europeans*. Continuous programming to Asia and the Pacific on 9660, 12080, 15240, 15415, 17715, 17750, 17795 and 21740 kHz. In North America (best during summer), try 17715, 17795 and 21740 kHz. Best bets for East Asia are 15240, 15415 and 17750 kHz; in southeastern parts, shoot for 17750 kHz. Some channels carry a separate sports service on winter Saturdays.

Croatian Radio. Summers only at this time, and actually starts two or three minutes into a predominantly Croatian broadcast. Approximately 15 minutes of news from and about Croatia. To North

01:00–01:45

Young Afghan children blissfully sell cigarettes at a football game. M. Guha

America on 9925 kHz. One hour later in winter.

Radio Yugoslavia. Monday through Saturday (Sunday through Friday, local American evenings) and winters only at this time. *News* and short reports, dealing almost exclusively with local and regional topics. Professionally done, and worth a listen. Thirty minutes to eastern and central North America on 6195 and 7115 kHz. One hour earlier in summer.

HCJB—Voice of the Andes, Ecuador. Tuesday through Saturday (weekday evenings in North America) it's *Studio 9*, featuring nine minutes of world and Latin American *news*, followed by 20 minutes of in-depth reporting on Latin America. The second half hour is given over to one of a variety of 30-minute features—including *Adventures in Odyssey* (Tuesday), *El Mundo Futuro* (science, Wednesday), *Ham Radio Today* (Thursday), *Woman to Woman* (Friday), and the unique and enjoyable ●*Música del Ecuador* (Saturday). On

Sunday (Saturday evening in the Americas), the news is followed by *DX Partyline*, which in turn is replaced Monday by *Musical Mailbag*. Continuous programming to North America on 9745 and 12015 kHz.

Voice of America. The second and final hour of a two-hour broadcast to the Caribbean and Latin America which is aired Tuesday through Saturday (weekday evenings in the Americas). *News Now*, a rolling news format covering political, business and other developments. On the half-hour, a program in "Special" (slow-speed) English is carried on 7405, 9775 and 13740 kHz; with mainstream programming continuing on 5995, 6130 and 9455 kHz.

WRMI-Radio Miami International, Miami, Florida. Tuesday through Saturday only (local weekday evenings in the Americas). Part of a much longer multilingual transmission to the Caribbean. Thirty minutes of *Viva Miami!*—a potpourri of information, music and entertainment.

Also includes regular weather updates during the hurricane season (June-November). Heard in much of the Americas on 9955 kHz. Repeated one hour later during winter.

Radio Ukraine International. Winters only at this time; see 0000 for program details. Sixty minutes of informative programming targeted at eastern North America and European night owls. Radio Ukraine is now reduced to just three transmitters for its external service due to budget and technical constraints. Try 5905, 5940, 6020, 6080, 7420 and 9560 kHz. One hour earlier in summer.

Radio New Zealand International. A package of *news* and features sometimes replaced by live sports commentary. Part of a much longer broadcast for the South Pacific, but also heard in parts of North America (especially during summer) on 17675 kHz.

Radio Tashkent, Uzbekistan. *News* and features with a strong Uzbek flavor; some exotic music, too. A half hour to West and South Asia and the Mideast, occasionally heard in North America; winters on 5040, 5955, 5975, 7205 and 9540 kHz; summers on 7190, 9375, 9530 and 9715 kHz.

FEBC Radio International, Philippines. The final 30 minutes of *Good Morning from Manila* (see 0000 for specifics), followed by a half hour of religious fare. Targeted at South and Southeast Asia on 15175 (or 15450) kHz, but heard well beyond.

WJCR, Upton, Kentucky. Continues with country gospel music for North American listeners on 7490 and 13595 kHz. Also with religious programs to North America at this hour are **WYFR-Family Radio** on 6065 and 9505 kHz, **WWCR** on 13845 kHz and **KTBN** on 7510 kHz. For traditional Catholic programming, tune to **WEWN** on 7425 kHz.

01:30

Radio Austria International. Winters only at this time. ●*Report from Austria*, which includes a brief bulletin of *news* followed by a series of current events and human interest stories. Tends to spotlight national and regional issues, and is an excellent source of news about Central Europe. Thirty minutes to the Americas on 9655 (or 7325), 9495 (or 13730) and 9870 kHz. One hour later in summer.

Radio Sweden. Tuesday through Saturday, it's *news* and features in *Sixty Degrees North*, concentrating heavily on Scandinavian topics. Tuesday's accent is on sports; Wednesday has electronic media news; Thursday brings *Money Matters*; Friday features ecology or science and technology; and Saturday offers a review of the week's news. Sunday, there's *Spectrum* (arts) or *Sweden Today* (current events), while Monday's offering is *In Touch with Stockholm* (a listener-response program) or the musical *Sounds Nordic*. Thirty minutes to Asia and Australasia, winters on 7265 kHz and summers on 9435 and 11985 kHz.

Radio Tirana, Albania. Summers only at this time. Thirty minutes of Balkan news and music to North America on 6220 and 7160 kHz. One hour later during winter.

Voice of Greece. Preceded and followed by programming in Greek. Approximately 10 minutes of English *news*, then Greek music, a short feature about the country, and more music. Resumes programming in Greek at 0200. To North America on any three frequencies from 6260, 7450, 9420, 9935 and 11645 kHz.

01:45

Radio Tirana, Albania. Winters only at this time. Approximately 15 minutes of *news* and commentary from one of

Europe's smallest and least known countries. To North America on 6115 and 7160 kHz. One hour earlier in summer.

02:00

■BBC World Service for Europe, the Mideast and the Americas. Thirty minutes of ●*The World Today*, then Tuesday through Saturday (Monday through Friday evenings in the Americas) there's a quarter hour of ●*World Business Report* followed by ●*Insight* (current events). These are replaced Sunday by ●*World Business Review* and the long-running ●*Letter from America*, and Monday by *Global Business*. Continuous programming to North America and the Caribbean on 5975 and 6175 kHz; and available summers to Eastern Europe and the Mideast on 9410 kHz.

■BBC World Service for East Asia. Similar to the service for Europe and the Americas, but with different features on the half-hour. Take your pick from an interesting pack: ●*Everywoman* (Monday), ●*John Peel* (60 years young, Tuesday), *The Vintage Chart Show* (Wednesday) ●*Andy Kershaw's World of Music* (Friday), and Saturday's ●*Composer of the Month* (classical music). Continuous to East Asia on 15280 and 15360 kHz, and to Southeast Asia on 15360 kHz.

Radio Cairo, Egypt. Repeat of the 2300 broadcast, and the first hour of a 90-minute potpourri of *news* and features about Egypt and the Arab world. Fair reception, but often mediocre audio quality, to North America on 9475 kHz.

Radio Argentina al Exterior—R.A.E. Tuesday through Saturday only. *News* and short features dealing with multiple aspects of Argentinean life, and interspersed with samples of the country's various musical styles. Whether you tap your feet to the heavy beat of a tango, or listen to a chamamé or zamba from the provinces, there's some fine music to be enjoyed. Fifty-five minutes to North America on 11710 kHz. Sometimes preempted by live soccer commentary in Spanish.

Radio Budapest, Hungary. This time winters only; see 0100 for specifics. Thirty minutes to North America on 9835 kHz. One hour earlier in summer.

Radio Canada International. Starts off with *News*, then Tuesday through Saturday (weekday evenings local American date) it's the topical *Spectrum*. Winter Sundays, there's *Venture Canada* (business and economics) and the environmental ●*Earth Watch*, replaced Monday by *The Arts in Canada* and *The Mailbag*. Summer substitutes are Sunday's ●*Vinyl Café* (music and story-telling) and Monday's *Tapestry*. One hour winters to North America on 6155, 9535, 9755, 9780 and 11865 kHz. Summers, it's just 30 minutes Tuesday through Saturday, with a full hour on the remaining days. Choose from 9535, 9755, 11715, 13670 and 15305 kHz.

Radio Yugoslavia. Winters only at this time. *News* and reports with a strong local flavor. An informative half hour to western North America on 6100 and 7130 kHz.

■Deutsche Welle, Germany. *News*, followed Tuesday through Saturday by the excellent ●*NewsLink*—commentary, interviews, background reports and analysis. The final part of the broadcast consists of a feature. Take your pick from ●*Man and Environment* (ecology, Tuesday), ●*Insight* (analysis, Wednesday), *Living in Germany* (Thursday), *Spotlight on Sport* (Friday), or Saturday's *German by Radio*. Sunday's offerings are *Weekend Review* and *Mailbag*, replaced Monday by *Weekend Review* (second part) and ●*Marks and Markets*. Forty-five minutes nominally targeted at South Asia, but widely heard elsewhere. Winters on 7285, 9615, 9765, 11965 and 13690 kHz; and summers on 9615, 9690, 11945, 11965 and 13690 kHz.

Radio Bulgaria. Summers only at this time. Starts with 15 minutes of *news*, followed Tuesday through Friday by *Today* (current events), and Saturday by *Weekly Spotlight*, a summary of the major political events of the week. At other times, there are features dealing with multiple aspects of Bulgarian life and culture, including some lively Balkan folk music. To eastern North America and Central America on 9485 and 11720 kHz. One hour later in winter.

HCJB—Voice of the Andes, Ecuador. A mixed bag of religious and secular programming, depending on the day of the week. Tuesday (Monday evening in North America) is given over to *Simply Worship* and *Let My People Think*; Wednesday airs *The Book and the Spade*, *Words for Women* and *Unshackled*; and Thursday brings *Rock Solid*. On Friday, you can hear *Viewpoint* and *Radio Reading Room*; Saturday has *Inside HCJB* followed by *On Track* (contemporary Christian music); Sunday features *Rock Solid*; and Monday is devoted to *Sunday Nite*. Continuous to North America on 9745 and 12015 kHz.

Croatian Radio. Winters only at this time, and actually starts around 0203. Approximately 15 minutes of news from and about Croatia. To North America on 7280 or 9925 kHz. One hour earlier in summer.

Radio Taipei International, Taiwan. The broadcast opens with 15 minutes of *News*, and closes with a quarter-hour of *Let's Learn Chinese*, which has a series of segments for beginning, intermediate and advanced learners. In between, there are either one or two features. Take your pick from *Jade Bells and Bamboo Pipes* (Mon-

day), *People* and *Trends* (Tuesday), *Taiwan Today* and *Miss Mook's Big Countdown* (Wednesday), *Treasures of the Orient* and *Hot Spots* (Thursday), *Taipei Magazine* and *Life on the Outside* (Friday), *Kaleidoscope* and *Reflections* (Saturday) and *Food, Poetry and Others* followed by *Mailbag Time* on Sunday. Radio Taipei International is almost unrecognizable from its former incarnation as the "Voice of Free China"— the old stuffiness and formality have given way to a more lively presentation, and gone is much of the old propaganda against the Mainland. When you hear reports of Chinese delegations visiting Taiwan, and interviews with Taiwanese who live in Beijing, there's no doubting the magnitude of the changes. One hour to North and Central America on 5950, 9680 and 11740 kHz; and to Southeast Asia on 11825 and 15345 kHz.

Voice of Russia World Service. Winters, the start of a four-hour block of programming to North America; summers, it's the beginning of the second hour. *News*, features and music to suit all tastes. Winter fare includes *News and Views* (0211 Tuesday through Sunday), *Sunday Panorama* (same time Monday), and after 0230, ●*Folk Box* (Tuesday), ●*Music at Your Request* (Friday), ●*Russian Musical Highlights of the 20th Century* (Thursday), Russian jazz on Wednesday, ●*Moscow Yesterday and Today* (Saturday and Sunday) and *Timelines* (Monday). In summer, take your pick from *Moscow Mailbag* (0211 Sunday, Monday and Thursday), *Newmarket* (business, same time Wednesday and Saturday), and *Science and Engineering* (0211 Tuesday and Friday). After a news summary on the half-hour, try ●*Audio Book Club* (Saturday), ●*Songs from Russia* (Sunday), *This is Russia* (Monday), ●*Russian Musical Highlights of the 20th Century* (Wednesday), ●*Moscow Yesterday and Today* (Thursday), the multifaceted *Kaleidoscope* (Tuesday) or Friday's *Russian by Radio*. Note that these days are World Time; locally in North America it will be the previous evening. For eastern North America winter, try 7180 kHz; with 9665 kHz the best bet in summer. Listeners in western states should go for 9865, 9875, 12000 or 12020 kHz in winter; and 12050 and 15595 kHz in summer.

Radio Habana Cuba. The second half of a two-hour broadcast to eastern North America; see 0100 for program details. On 6000 and 9820 kHz. Also available on 9830 or 11705 kHz upper sideband (USB).

Radio Australia. Continuous programming to Asia and the Pacific, but well heard in parts of North America (especially to the west). Begins with *World News*, then Monday through Friday it's *The World Today* (comprehensive coverage of world events). At 0205 Saturday, look for some incisive scientific commentary in ●*Ockham's Razor*, which is then followed by *Health Report*. These are replaced Sunday by the more sedate *Fine Music Australia* and *Religion Report*. Targeted at Asia and the Pacific on 9660, 12080, 15240, 15415, 15510, 17715, 17750 and 21725 kHz. Best heard in North America (especially during summer) on 17715 kHz. For East and Southeast Asia, choose from 15240, 15415, 17750 and 21725 kHz. Some of these channels carry a separate sports service on summer (midyear) weekends and winter Saturdays.

YLE Radio Finland. Summers only at this time. Most days it's *Compass North* and a press review. Exceptions are Saturday's *Starting Finnish* (a language lesson), Sunday's *Capital Café* and Monday's *Nordic Update*. Thirty minutes to North America on 9780 and 11900 kHz.

Radio For Peace International, Costa Rica. The second hour in English of an eight-hour cyclical block of social-conscience and counterculture programming audible in Europe and the Americas on 6975 kHz.

Radio Korea International, South Korea. Opens with *news* and commentary, followed Tuesday through Thursday (Monday through Wednesday evenings in the Americas) by *Seoul Calling*. Weekly features include *Echoes of Korean Music* and *Shortwave Feedback* (Monday), *Tales from Korea's Past* (Tuesday), *Korean Cultural Trails* (Wednesday), *Pulse of Korea* (Thursday), *From Us to You* (a listener-response program) and *Let's Learn Korean* (Friday), *Let's Sing Together* and *Korea Through Foreigners' Eyes* (Saturday), and Sunday's *Discovering Korea, Korean Literary Corner* and *Weekly News*. Sixty minutes to the Americas on 11725, 11810 and 15575 kHz; and to East Asia on 7275 kHz.

Radio Romania International. *News*, commentary, press review and features on Romania. Regular spots include Wednesday's *Youth Club* (Tuesday evening, local American date), Thursday's *Romanian Musicians*, and Friday's *Listeners' Letterbox* and ●*Skylark* (Romanian folk music). Fifty-five minutes to North America on 5990, 6155, 9510, 9570 and 11940 kHz.

WJCR, Upton, Kentucky. Continues with country gospel music for North American listeners on 7490 kHz. Also with religious broadcasts to North America at this hour are **WYFR-Family Radio** on 6065 and 9505 kHz, **WWCR** on 5935 kHz, **KAIJ on** 5810 kHz, and **KTBN** on 7510 kHz. Traditional Catholic programming can be heard via **WEWN** on 7425 kHz.

02:30

Radio Austria International. Summers only at this time. ●*Report from Austria*, a popular compilation of news, current

GRUNDIG TUNES IN THE WORLD

50th Anniversary Edition Classic 960

Solid wood cabinet… solid-brass trimmed knobs and gold tone dial… the legendary sound and mystique of the original 1950s table top radio. The Classic 960 FM-stereo/AM shortwave radio is updated and improved. Two 3" side speakers, left and right, and the 4" front speaker fill the room with wondrous sound. Travel the world without leaving home… receives shortwave continuously from 2.3-22.3 MHz. Additional features of auxiliary inputs take the audio signal from CD, cassette player or TV and turns it into spacious, roomfilling Grundig sound. Dimensions: 15.5" L x 11.25" H x 7" W. Weight: 9 lbs. 9.6 oz.

LISTENING HAS NEVER BEEN MORE ENJOYABLE…

PORSCHE DESIGN G2000A RADIO ALARM CLOCK
Designed by F.A. Porsche. Wake up to talk radio on AM, soothing stereo (with earphones) on FM or fascinating shortwave from around the world, select from 13 International bands from 2.3-7.4 and 9.4-26.1 MHz. Punch in any station or lock your favorites into 20 memories, supple brown leather snap-on case. Weight: 11.52 oz.

EXECUTIVE TRAVELLER G4 RADIO
Wherever you go, the world goes with you! Nestled inside a luxurious leather travel organizer is the world's smallest AM, FM-stereo, six shortwave band radio with built-in digital quartz clock and travel alarm. The executive Traveler puts everything at your fingertips – passport, travel documents, credit cards, cash and more. Comes with 2 AA batteries and earphones. Radio dimensions: 2.75" L x 4.25" H x .75" W. Weight: 4.48 oz.

PLATINUM DIGITAL G3D
Big on features, the Platinum Digital radio is small enough to fit into a jacket or purse! PLL synthesizer FM/AM (SW1/SW2), FM-stereo with earphones, m-band scan function, 20 user programmable memories, illuminated LCD indicates all operations, auto search up/down, manual tuning up/down, quartz controlled dual alarm clock with sleep timer (10 to 90 minutes) and alarm by buzzer or radio. Uses 3 AA batteries. (not Included) Weighs only 11.52 oz.

TRAVELLER II PE
A proven compact portable with outstanding performance. Stylish titanium look finish combines with practical features for the traveler. AM/FM and five shortwave bands, world clock for 24 time zones and simultaneous display of home and world time in the digital display. Comes with 3 AA batteries, earphones and carrying pouch. Weighs 10.7 oz.

MINI WORLD BAND 100 PE
Smallest Pocket World Band Radio. Travel with the world in your pocket.Another exciting breakthrough in world band technology. A well built radio that fits in the palm of your hand. AM/FM stereo and six shortwave bands with LED indicator. Comes with earphones, belt clip and soft carrying pouch. Weighs 4 oz.

WEATHER BAND G2
Always be prepared with the G2. Take this incredibly powerful AM/FM weather radio with you on all your outdoor activities. This weather resistant radio is your 24 hour hotline to AM, FM, and the national weather service reports and forecasts. Built in speaker and telescopic antenna. Weighs 6 oz.

by GRUNDIG

universal radio inc.

6830 Americana Pkwy.
Reynoldsburg, Ohio
43068-4113 U.S.A.

Orders & Prices phone: 800 431-3939
Information phone: 614 866-4267
Fax: 614 866-2339
Web: dx@universal-radio.com
www.DXing.com
www.universal-radio.com

02:30–03:00

events and human interest stories. Good coverage of national and regional issues. Thirty minutes to the Americas on 9655, 9870 and 13730 kHz. One hour earlier in winter.

Radio Sweden. Tuesday through Saturday (weekday evenings in North America), it's *news* and features in *Sixty Degrees North*, with the accent heavily on Scandinavian topics. Tuesday's theme is sports; Wednesday has news of the electronic media; Thursday brings *Money Matters*; Friday features ecology or science and technology; and Saturday offers a review of the week's news. Sunday, there's *Spectrum* (arts) or *Sweden Today* (current events), while Monday's offering is *In Touch with Stockholm* (a listener-response program) or the musical *Sounds Nordic*. Thirty minutes to North America, winters on 7280 kHz and summers on 7135 or 9495 kHz.

Radyo Pilipinas, Philippines. Monday through Saturday, the broadcast opens with *Voice of Democracy* and closes with *World News*. These are separated by a daily feature: *Save the Earth* (Monday), *The Philippines Today* (Tuesday), *Changing World* (Wednesday), *Business Updates* (Thursday), *Brotherhood of Men* (Friday), and Saturday's *Listeners and Friends*. Sunday fare consists of *Asean Connection*, *Sports Focus* and *News Roundup*. Approximately one hour to South and East Asia on 17760, 17865 and 21580 kHz.

Radio Budapest, Hungary. Summers only at this time. *News* and features, a few of which are broadcast on a regular basis. Thirty minutes to North America on 9840 kHz. One hour later in winter.

Voice of Vietnam. Repeat of the 0100 broadcast; see there for specifics. A relay to eastern North America via the facilities of the Voice of Russia, winters on 5940 kHz, and summers on 7250 kHz.

Radio Tirana, Albania. Winters only at this time. The programs now have more variety than in the past, and still include some lively Albanian music. A half hour to North America on 6140 and 7160 kHz. One hour earlier in summer.

02:50

Vatican Radio. Concentrates heavily, but not exclusively, on issues affecting Catholics around the world. Twenty minutes to eastern North America, winters on 6095 and 7305 kHz, and summers on 7305 and 9605 kHz.

03:00

■**BBC World Service for the Americas.** Twenty minutes of ●*The World Today*, then ten minutes of ●*Sports Roundup*. Next comes a quarter-hour feature, with ●*Off the Shelf* (book readings) completing the hour. Pick of the features are Thursday's ●*From Our Own Correspondent* and Friday's ●*The Farming World*. Continuous programming to North America and the Caribbean on 5975 and 6175 kHz.

■**BBC World Service for Europe and the Mideast.** Winters and the first half hour in summer, the same programming as for the Americas. Summer weekdays at 0330, it's a continuation of the excellent news show, ●*The World Today*. This is replaced Saturday by ●*Weekend* and Sunday by ●*Agenda* (current events). Winters to Eastern Europe on 6195 and 9410 kHz, and summers to the entire continent on the same channels. To the Mideast on 9410 and 11760 kHz, although 9410 kHz may carry the service for Asia during winter.

■**BBC World Service for Africa.** Identical to the service for the Americas until 0330, then Monday through Friday it's

A Takhar vegetable seller counts his meager take after a long day of haggling. M. Guha

Network Africa, a fast-moving breakfast show. The Saturday substitute is ●*People and Politics*, replaced Sunday by *African Quiz* or *Postmark Africa*. If you are interested in what's happening in the continent, tune to 3255, 6005, 6190 and 11765 kHz.

■**BBC World Service for Asia**. Monday through Saturday, it's ●*The World Today* followed at 0320 by ●*Outlook* (not Saturday). These are replaced Sunday by five minutes of *World News* and a further 55 of *Wright Round the World*, a mediocre replacement for the popular *A Jolly Good Show*, dropped at the end of 1998. Best given a miss. Audible in East Asia on 15280, 15360 (till 0330), 17760 and 21660 kHz. For Southeast Asia there's only 15360 kHz until 0330.

Radio Canada International. Winters only at this time. Starts off with *News*, then Tuesday through Saturday (weekday evenings local American date) you can hear *Spectrum* (current events). Weekends, there's a full hour of programs from the domestic service of RCI's parent organiza-

tion, the Canadian Broadcasting Corporation. Sunday, expect some story-telling amidst a mélange of music in the thoroughly enjoyable ●*Vinyl Café*, while Monday's *Tapestry* is a more serious cultural offering. To eastern North America and the Caribbean on 6155, 9755 and 9780 kHz. One hour earlier in summer.

Croatian Radio. Summers only at this time, and actually starts two or three minutes into a predominantly Croatian broadcast. Approximately 15 minutes of news from and about Croatia. To North America on 9925 kHz. One hour later in winter.

Radio Taipei International, Taiwan. Similar to the 0200 transmission, but with the same programs broadcast one day later. To North and Central America on 5950 and 9680 kHz; to East Asia on 11745 kHz; and to Southeast Asia on 11825 and 15345 kHz.

China Radio International. *News* and commentary, followed Tuesday through Saturday (Monday through Friday evenings in the Americas) by in-depth reports and an overview of the Chinese press. These are followed by various feature programs, such as *Focus* and *Cultural Spectrum* (Friday); *Open Windows* and *Learn to Speak Chinese* (Tuesday); *Orient Arena* and *Opera House* (Wednesday); *Voices from Other Lands* (Thursday); and *Life in China* and *Global Review* (Saturday). Sunday's lineup includes *Asia-Pacific News*, *Report from Developing Countries*, *China Scrapbook* and ●*Music from China;* and Monday's replacements consist of *Cultural Information*, *People in the Know*, *On the Road* and *Listeners' Letterbox*. One hour to North America on 9690 kHz.

■**Deutsche Welle,** Germany. *News*, then Tuesday through Saturday (weekday evenings in North America) it's ●*NewsLink*—a comprehensive package of commentary, interviews, background reports and analysis. The remainder of the transmission is taken up by a feature: ●*Man and Environment* (Tuesday), ●*Insight* (Wednesday), *Living in Germany* (Thursday), *Spotlight on Sport* (Friday) and *German by Radio* on Saturday. The Sunday offerings are *Weekend Review* and ●*Spectrum* (science); while Monday brings *Religion and Society* and *Arts on the Air*. Forty-five minutes to North America and the Caribbean, winter on 6045, 9535, 9640, 9700 and 11750 kHz; and summer on 9535, 9640, 11810, 13780 and 15105 kHz.

Voice of America. Three and a half hours (four at weekends) of continuous programming aimed at an African audience. Monday through Friday, there's the informative and entertaining ●*Daybreak Africa*, with the remaining airtime taken up by *News Now*—a mixed bag of sports, science, business and other news and features. Although beamed to Africa, this service is widely heard elsewhere, including parts of the United States. Try 6035 (winter), 6080, 6115 (summer), 7105, 7275

(summer), 7290, 7415 (winter), 9575 (winter) and 9885 kHz.

Voice of Russia World Service. Continuous programming to North America at this hour. *News*, then winters it's a listener-response program, *Moscow Mailbag* (Monday, Thursday and Sunday), the business-oriented *Newmarket* (Wednesday and Saturday), or *Science and Engineering* (Tuesday and Friday). At 0331, there's ●*Audio Book Club* (Saturday), *Kaleidoscope* (Tuesday), *This is Russia* (Monday), ●*Moscow Yesterday and Today* (Thursday), *Russian by Radio* (Friday), ●*Songs from Russia* (Sunday), and ●*Russian Musical Highlights from the 20th Century* on Wednesday. Note that these days are World Time, so locally in North America it will be the previous evening. In summer, look for *News and Views* at 0311 Tuesday through Sunday, replaced Monday by *Sunday Panorama* and *Russia in Personalities*. After a brief news summary on the half-hour, you can choose from●*Christian Message from Moscow* (Sunday), ●*Audio Book Club* (Monday) or ●*The 20th Century: Year After Year* (Tuesday, Thursday and Saturday). The Wednesday and Friday slots are allocated to "alternative programs." These can be quality shows from the station's archives, mind-numbing religious paid programming, or anything in between. In eastern North America, choose from 5940 and 7180 kHz in winter, and go for 9665 kHz in summer. In western North America, the situation is a little better—for winter, try 9865, 9875, 12000 and 12020 kHz; in summer, take your pick from 12050, 15595, 17565, 17630, 17660 and 17690 kHz.

XERMX—Radio México Internacional. Summers only at this time. Tuesday through Saturday (weekday evenings in North America), there's a summary of the Spanish-language *Antena Radio*, replaced Sunday by *Universal Forum*. Monday's programming is in

Spanish. On the half-hour, look for 30 minutes of music. To North America on 9705 kHz. One hour later in winter.

Radio Australia. *World News*, then Monday through Friday it's *Australia Talks Back* (discussion of topical issues). Weekends, look for a novel experience in Saturday's *Book Reading*, which is followed by the out-of-town *Rural Reporter*. The Sunday offerings are *Feedback* (listener-response) and *Correspondents' Reports*. Continuous to Asia and the Pacific on 9660, 12080, 15240, 15415, 15510, 17715, 17750 and 21725 kHz. Also heard in western North America, best on 17715 kHz. In East and Southeast Asia, pick from 15240, 15415, 17750 and 21725 kHz. Some of these channels carry a separate sports service at weekends.

Radio Habana Cuba. Repeat of the 0100 broadcast. To eastern North America on 6000 and 9820 kHz, and also available on 9830 or 11705 kHz upper sideband (USB).

Radio Thailand. *Newshour*. Thirty minutes to western North America winters on 11890 kHz, and summers on 15395 kHz. Also available to Asia on 9655 and 11905 kHz.

HCJB—Voice of the Andes, Ecuador. Predominantly religious programming at this hour. Try *Radio Reading Room* at 0330 Monday and Friday (local Sunday and Thursday evenings in North America). Continuous to the United States and Canada on 9745 and 12015 kHz.

Radio Prague, Czech Republic. Repeat of the 0000 broadcast; see there for specifics. A half hour to North America, winter on 7345 and 9435 kHz, and summer on 7345 and 11615 kHz. This is by far the best opportunity for listeners in western parts.

Radio Cairo, Egypt. The final half-hour of a 90-minute broadcast to North America on 9475 kHz.

Radio Bulgaria. Winters only at this time; see 0200 for specifics. A distinctly Bulgarian potpourri of news, commentary, interviews and features, plus a fair amount of music. Sixty minutes to eastern North America and Central America on 7375 and 9485 kHz. One hour earlier in summer.

Radio Japan. *News*, then weekdays there's *Asian Top News*. This is followed by a half-hour feature. Take your pick from *Music Reflections* (Monday), *Let's Try Japanese* (Tuesday), *Music Journey Around Japan* (Wednesday), *My Japan Diary* (Thursday), and *Music Beat* (Friday). *Weekend Break* fills the Saturday slot, and *Hello from Tokyo* is aired Sunday. Sixty minutes to Australasia on 21610 kHz, and to Central America on 17825 kHz.

Radio New Zealand International. A friendly broadcasting package targeted at a regional audience. Part of a much longer transmission for the South Pacific, but also heard in parts of North America (especially during summer) on 17675 kHz. Often carries commentaries of local sporting events.

Voice of Turkey. Summers only at this time. *News*, followed by *Review of the Turkish Press* and features (some of them unusual) with a strong local flavor. Selections of Turkish popular and classical music complete the program. Fifty minutes to eastern North America on 9655 kHz, and to the Mideast on 7270 kHz. One hour later during winter.

WJCR, Upton, Kentucky. Continues with country gospel music for North American listeners on 7490 kHz. Also with religious programs to North America at this hour are **WYFR-Family Radio** on 6065 and 9505 kHz, **WWCR** on 5935 kHz, **KAIJ** on 5810 kHz and **KTBN** on 7510 kHz. For traditional Catholic fare, try **WEWN** on 7425 kHz.

03:00–04:00

Radio For Peace International, Costa Rica. Continues with a variety of counter-culture and social-conscience features. There is also a listener-response program at 0330 Wednesday (Tuesday evening in the Americas). Audible in Europe and the Americas on 6975 kHz.

03:30

United Arab Emirates Radio, Dubai. *News*, then a feature devoted to Arab and Islamic history or culture. Twenty minutes to North America on 12005, 13675 and 15400 kHz; heard best during the warm-weather months.

Radio Sweden. Repeat of the 0230 transmission; see there for program specifics. Thirty minutes to North America, winters on 7115 kHz and summers on 9475 or 11665 kHz.

Radio Prague, Czech Republic. *News*, then Tuesday through Saturday (weekday evenings in the Americas), there's *Current Affairs*. These are followed by one or more features. Tuesday's offering is *Spotlight*; Wednesday, it's *Talking Point*; Thursday brings *History Czech*; Friday there's *Economic Report*; and Saturday features a listener-response program, *Between You and Us*. The Sunday slot is an excellent musical feature (strongly recommended), and Monday there's *A Letter from Prague*, *From the Weeklies* and *Readings from Czech Literature*. A half hour to the Mideast and South Asia, winter on 9585 and 11600 kHz, and summer on 11600 and 15530 kHz.

Radio Budapest, Hungary. This time winters only; see 0230 for specifics. Thirty minutes to North America on 9835 kHz. One hour earlier in summer.

Voice of Greece. Actual start time subject to slight variation. Ten to fifteen minutes of English *news*, preceded by long periods of Greek music and programming. To North America on any three frequencies from 6260, 7448, 9420, 9935 and 11645 kHz.

04:00

■**BBC World Service for the Americas.** The first half hour consists of the news-oriented ●*The World Today*, and is followed by a feature. Best of the regular shows are Thursday's ●*Everywoman* (Wednesday evening in North America), Friday's ●*Focus on Faith*, Saturday's ●*People and Politics*, and Sunday's masterful documentary, ●*Omnibus*. A full hour of top-notch programming to North America on 5975 and 6175 kHz.

■**BBC World Service for Europe and the Mideast.** Except for 0430-0500 weekends, it's news and more in ●*The World Today*. Saturday at 0430 there's ●*People and Politics*, a look at the British political scene; and Sunday offers the excellent ●*Omnibus*. Continuous programming to Europe on 3955, 6195, 9410 and (summer) 12095 kHz, and audible in the Mideast on 9410, 11760 and 15575 kHz.

■**BBC World Service for Africa.** Thirty minutes of ●*The World Today*, followed Monday through Friday by *Network Africa*. Weekends at 0430, look for Saturday's *African Quiz* or *This Week and Africa*, and Sunday's *Art Beat*. Targeted at African listeners, but also heard elsewhere, on 3255, 6005, 6190, 7160, 11765 and 15420 kHz.

■**BBC World Service for Asia.** Starts with *World News* and ●*Sports Roundup*; then there's a 15-minute and a half-hour feature. Aficionados of classical music can choose from a variety of offerings: ●*The Greenfield Collection* (0430 Sunday), *Record News* (0415 Monday), ●*Performance* (0415 Friday), *Music Review* (0430 same day), and ●*Composer of the Month* (0430 Saturday).

Pick of the remaining shows are ●*The Farming World* (0415 Sunday), ●*Short Story* (0415 Wednesday), and ●*Letter From America* (same time Saturday). Continuous to East Asia on 15280, 17760 and 21660 kHz. Unfortunately, there's nothing for Southeast Asia at this hour.

Croatian Radio. Winters only at this time, and actually starts around 0403. Approximately 15 minutes of news from and about Croatia. To North America on 7285 or 9925 kHz. One hour earlier in summer.

Radio Habana Cuba. Continuous programming to eastern North America and the Caribbean on 6000, 6180 and 9820 kHz. Also available on 9830 or 11705 kHz upper sideband (USB).

Swiss Radio International. Repeat of the 0100 broadcast plus an additional 30 minutes of music and interviews in *Rendezvous with Switzerland*. A full hour year-round to North America and the Caribbean on 9885 and 9905 kHz, with the first half hour also available summer to southeastern Europe (one hour later in winter) on 9610 or 13635 kHz.

XERMX—Radio México Internacional. Tuesday through Saturday winters (weekday evenings in North America), there's a summary of the Spanish-language *Antena Radio*, replaced Sunday by *Universal Forum*. Monday's programming is in Spanish. The summer lineup consists of *Eternally Mexico* (Tuesday), *Mirror of Mexico* (Thursday), *The Sounds of Mexico* (Friday) and Saturday's *Mailbox*. Wednesday's broadcast is in French, and there are no programs on Sunday or Monday. On the half-hour, look for 30 minutes of music. To North America on 9705 kHz.

HCJB—Voice of the Andes, Ecuador. Tuesday through Saturday (weekday evenings in North America) it's *Studio 9*, featuring nine minutes of world and Latin American *news*, followed by 20 minutes of in-depth reporting on Latin America. The second half hour is given over to one of a variety of 30-minute features—including *Adventures in Odyssey* (Tuesday), *El Mundo Futuro* (science, Wednesday), *Ham Radio Today* (Thursday), *Woman to Woman* (Friday), and the unique and enjoyable ●*Música del Ecuador* (Saturday). On Sunday (Saturday evening in the Americas), the news is followed by *DX Partyline*, which in turn is replaced Monday by *Musical Mailbag*. Continuous programming to North America on 9745 and 12015 kHz.

Radio Australia. *World News*, then Monday through Friday it's *The World Today* (in-depth coverage of current events). The weekend fare is also news-oriented, with *Pacific Focus* followed by Saturday's *Asia Pacific* or Sunday's *Week's End*. Continuous to Asia and the Pacific on 9660, 12080, 15240, 15415, 15510, 17715, 17750 and 21725 kHz. Should also be audible in western North America (best during summer) on 17715 kHz. For East and Southeast Asia, choose from 15240, 15415, 17750 and 21725 kHz. Some channels carry separate sports programming at weekends.

■**Deutsche Welle, Germany.** *News*, followed Tuesday through Saturday by ●*NewsLink* and *Good Morning Africa* (replaced Saturday by *German by Radio*). The Sunday slots are *Weekend Review* and ●*Inside Europe*, replaced Monday by *Weekend Review* (second edition) and ●*Marks and Markets*. A 45-minute broadcast aimed primarily at eastern and southern Africa, but also heard in parts of the Mideast. Winters on 7280, 9565, 9765, 11785 and 11965 kHz; and summers on 7225, 9565, 9765 and 13690 kHz.

Radio Canada International. *News*, then Tuesday through Saturday it's the

04:00–05:00

topical *Spectrum*. This is replaced Sunday by *Venture Canada* (business and economics), and Monday by a listener-response program, *The Mailbag*. Thirty minutes to the Mideast, winters on 9505, 9535 and 9645 kHz; summers on 11835, 11975 and 15215 kHz.

Voice of America. Directed to Africa and the Mideast, but widely heard elsewhere. *News Now*—a mixed bag of sports, science, business and other news and features. Weekdays on the half-hour, the African service leaves the mainstream programming and carries its own ●*Daybreak Africa*. To North Africa year round on 7170 kHz, and to the Mideast summer on 11965 kHz. The African service is available on 6035 (winter), 6080, 7265 and 7275 (summer), 7415 (winter), 9575, 9775 (winter) and 9885 kHz. Some of these are only available until 0430. Reception of some of these channels is also possible in North America.

Radio Romania International. Similar to the 0200 transmission (see there for specifics). Fifty-five minutes to North America on 5990, 6155, 9510, 9570 and 11940 kHz.

Voice of Turkey. Winters only at this time. See 0300 for specifics. Fifty minutes to Europe and eastern North America on 7300 kHz, to the Mideast on 9685 kHz, and to Southeast Asia and Australasia on 17705 kHz. One hour earlier in summer.

WJCR, Upton, Kentucky. Continues with country gospel music for North American listeners on 7490 kHz. Also with religious programs to North America at this hour are **WYFR-Family Radio** on 6065 and 9505 kHz, **WWCR** on 5935 kHz, **KAIJ** on 5810 kHz and **KTBN** on 7510 kHz. Traditional Catholic programming is available via **WEWN** on 7425 kHz

Kol Israel. Summers only at this time. *News* for 15 minutes from Israel Radio's domestic network. To Europe and eastern

North America on 9435 and 11605 kHz, and to Australasia on 17535 kHz. One hour later in winter.

China Radio International. Repeat of the 0300 broadcast; one hour to North America on 9730 and (summers only) 9560 kHz.

Radio New Zealand International. Continues with regional programming for the South Pacific. Part of a much longer broadcast, which is also heard in parts of North America (especially during summer) on 17675 kHz. Sometimes carries commentaries of local sporting events.

Radio For Peace International, Costa Rica. Part of an eight-hour cyclical block of predominantly social-conscience and counterculture programming. Some of the offerings at this hour include a women's news-gathering service, *WINGS*, (0430 Friday); a listener-response program (same time Saturday); and *The Far Right Radio Review* (0400 Sunday). Audible in Europe and the Americas on 6975 kHz.

Voice of Russia World Service. Continues to North America at this hour. Tuesday through Sunday winters, it's *News and Views*, replaced Monday by *Sunday Panorama* and *Russia in Personalities*. During the second half hour, the Sunday slot is filled by ●*Christian Message from Moscow*, replaced Monday by ●*Audio Book Club*. On Tuesday, Thursday and Saturday, you can travel back into history with ●*The 20th Century: Year After Year*. The remaining days feature "alternative programs"— religious paid programming or a show from the Voice of Russia's archives or transcription department. The summer lineup has plenty of variety, and includes *Jazz Show* (0431 Monday), ●*Music at Your Request* or *Yours For the Asking* (same time Wednesday), the business-oriented *Newmarket* (0411 Thursday), *Science and Engineering* (same time Wednesday and

04:00–05:00

Chris Carzoli (left), Director, Broadcast Operations Department, Prague, discusses digital equipment with John Shattuck, U.S. Ambassador to the Czech Republic.
RFE/RL

Saturday), ●*Folk Box* (0431 Thursday), ●*Russian Musical Highlights of the 20th Century* (0431 Wednesday), *Moscow Mailbag* (0411 Tuesday and Friday) and Sunday's retrospective ●*Moscow Yesterday and Today* (0431 Sunday). In eastern North America, tune to 7125 and 7180 kHz in winter, and 7125 and 9665 kHz in summer. Best winter bets for the west coast are 5920, 6065, 9850, 12000, 12020 and 13640 kHz; in summer, try 12050, 15595, 17565, 17630, 17660 and 17690 kHz.

Radio Pyongyang, North Korea. One soporific hour of old-fashioned communist propaganda. To Southeast Asia on 15180, 15230 and 17765 kHz.

04:30

Radio Yugoslavia. Summers only at this time. *News* and short background reports heavily geared to local issues. Worth a listen if you are interested in the region. Thirty minutes to western North America on 9580 and 11870 kHz.

■**Radio Netherlands.** Repeat of the 0030 transmission (see there for specifics). Fifty-five minutes to western North America on 6165 and 9590 kHz.

Radio Austria International. Summers only at this time. ●*Report from Austria*, which includes a brief bulletin of *news*, followed by a series of current events and human interest stories. A popular source of news about Central Europe. Thirty minutes to Europe on 6155 and 13730 kHz. One hour later in winter.

05:00

■**BBC World Service for the Americas.** Thirty minutes of ●*The World Today*, then a feature. Pick of the week are Wednesday's ●*Andy Kershaw's World of Music* (Tuesday night in North America), Friday's ●*John Peel* (not for all tastes), and the first part of Sunday's ●*Play of the Week* (world theater). Audible in North America (better to the west) on 5975 and 6175 kHz.

05:00–05:00

■**BBC World Service for Europe and the Mideast.** Weekdays, a full hour of news in ●*The World Today*. Weekends, the second half hour is replaced by a Saturday feature and Sunday's *In Praise of God*. Continuous to Europe on 3955, 6195, 9410 and 12095 kHz, and to the Mideast on 11760 and 15575 kHz.

■**BBC World Service for Africa.** ●*The World Today*, then weekdays on the half-hour there's a continuation of *Network Africa*. Weekends, the final 30 minutes are devoted to Saturday's *Talkabout Africa* and Sunday's *Agenda* (current events). Continuous programming on 3255, 6005, 6190, 7160, 11765, 15420 and 17885 kHz.

■**BBC World Service for Asia and the Pacific.** Starts with 30 minutes of ●*The World Today*. Thereafter, it's a mixed bag of features. Best of the regular shows are ●*Andy Kershaw's World of Music* on Wednesday, and ●*Brain of Britain* (or a substitute quiz) on Saturday. Continuous to East Asia on 15280 (till 0530), 15360, 17760 and 21660 kHz; and to Southeast Asia on 9740, 11955 and 15360 kHz. In Australasia, choose from 11955 and 15360 kHz.

■**Deutsche Welle,** Germany. Repeat of the 45-minute 0100 transmission to North America, except that Sunday's ●*Inside Europe* is replaced by ●*Marks and Markets*; and Monday's *Arts on the Air* gives way to *Cool*. Winters on 6100, 6120, 9670 and 11795 kHz; and summers on 9670, 11795 and 11810 kHz. This slot is by far the best for western North America.

Radio Exterior de España ("Spanish National Radio"). *News*, then Tuesday through Saturday (local weekday evenings in the Americas) it's *Panorama*, which features a recording of popular Spanish music, a commentary or a report, a review of the Spanish press, and weather. The remainder of the program is a mixture of literature, science, music and general programming. Tuesday (Monday evening in North America), there's *Sports Spotlight* and *Cultural Encounters*; Wednesday features *People of Today* and *Entertainment in Spain*; Thursday brings *As Others See Us* and, biweekly, *The Natural World* or *Science Desk*; Friday has *Economic Report* and *Cultural Clippings*; and Saturday offers *Window on Spain* and *Review of the Arts*. The final slot is given over to a language course, *Spanish by Radio*. On the remaining days, you can listen to Sunday's *Hall of Fame* and *Gallery of Spanish Voices*; and Monday's *Visitors' Book*, *Great Figures in Flamenco* and *Radio Club*. Sixty minutes to eastern North America on 6055 kHz.

Radio Canada International. Summers only at this time. See 0600 for program details. To Europe, Africa and the Mideast on 6145, 7295, 9595, 11710, 15330 and 15400 kHz. One hour later during winter. Also available to western North America and Central America summers only (no corresponding winter transmission) on 5995, 9755 and 11830 kHz.

Vatican Radio. Summers only at this time. Twenty minutes of programming oriented to Catholics. To Europe on 5880 and 7250 kHz. Frequencies may vary slightly. One hour later in winter.

Croatian Radio. Summers only at this time, and actually starts two or three minutes into a predominantly Croatian broadcast. Approximately 15 minutes of news from and about Croatia. To Australasia on 9470 or 13820 kHz. One hour later in winter.

XERMX—Radio México Internacional. Winters only at this time. Starts with a feature: *Eternally Mexico* (Tuesday), *Mirror of Mexico* (Thursday), *The Sounds of Mexico* (Friday) and Saturday's *Mailbox*. Wednesday's broadcast is in French, and there are no programs on

05:00–05:00

This Kazak Radio broadcaster hosts a popular youth program.
M. Guha

Sunday or Monday. On the half-hour, there's 30 minutes of music. To North America on 9705 kHz.

Radio Japan. *News*, then Monday through Friday there's *44 Minutes* (an in-depth look at current trends and events in Japan). This is replaced Saturday by *Weekend Break* (discussion), and Sunday by *Hello from Tokyo*. One hour to Europe on 7230 kHz; to East Asia on 11715, 11760 and 11840 kHz; to Southeast Asia on 15590 kHz; to Australasia on 11850 kHz; to western North America on 6110, (winter) 9835 and (summer) 17825 kHz; and to Hawai'i and Central America on 15230 kHz. This last broadcast may differ slightly from the other transmissions.

China Radio International. This time winters only. Repeat of the 0300 broad-cast; one hour to North America on 9560 kHz.

HCJB—Voice of the Andes, Ecuador. Predominantly religious programming at this hour. For a general audience, try Saturday's *Inside HCJB* (Friday night in North America) or *Inspirational Classics* (0530 Thursday). Continuous programming to North America on 9745 and 12015 kHz.

Voice of America. Continues with the morning broadcast to Africa and the Mideast. *News Now*—a mixed bag of sports, science, business and other news and features. To North Africa on 7170 and (winters only) 5995 and 11805 kHz; to the Mideast on 11825 (winter) or (summer) 11965 kHz; and to the rest of Africa on 5970, 6035, 6080, 7195 (summer), 7295 (winter), 9630 (summer) and 12080 kHz. Some of these channels are audible in parts of North America.

Radio Habana Cuba. Repeat of the 0100 transmission. To western North America winter on 6000 (or 9505) kHz, and summer on 9820 kHz. Also available to Europe on 9830 or 11705 kHz upper sideband (USB).

Voice of Nigeria. Targeted mainly at West Africa, but also audible in parts of Europe and North America, especially during winter. Monday through Friday, opens with the lively *Wave Train* followed by *VON Scope*, a half hour of *news* and press comment. Pick of the weekend programs is ●*African Safari*, a musical journey around the African continent, which can be heard Saturdays at 0500. This is replaced Sunday by five minutes of *Reflections* and 25 minutes of music in *VON Link-Up*, with the second half-hour taken up by *News*. The first 60 minutes of a daily two-hour broadcast on 7255 and (when the transmitter is repaired) 15120 kHz.

Swiss Radio International. Winters only at this hour. *World Radio Switzerland*—news and analysis of Swiss and world events. Some lighter fare on Saturday, when the biweekly *Capital Letters* (a listener-response program) alternates with *Name Game* (first Saturday) and *Sounds Good* (music and interviews, third Saturday). Thirty minutes to Europe on 6165 kHz. One hour earlier in summer.

Radio New Zealand International. Continues with regional programming for the South Pacific. Part of a much longer broadcast, which is also heard in parts of North America (especially during summer) on 11690 or 11905 kHz.

Radio Australia. *World News*, then Monday through Friday there's *Pacific Beat* (background reporting on events in the Pacific)—look for a sports bulletin at 0530. Weekends, the news is followed by *Oz Sounds*; then, on the half-hour, it's either Saturday's *Sports Factor* or Sunday's *Media Report*. Continuous to Asia and the Pacific on 9660, 12080, 15240, 15510, 17715, 17750 and 21725 kHz. In North America (best during summer) try 17715 kHz. For East Asia, best options are 15240 and 21725 kHz. Some channels carry alternative sports programming at weekends.

Voice of Russia World Service. Winters, the *news* is followed by a wide variety of programs. These include *Jazz Show* (0531 Monday), ●*Music at Your Request* or *Yours For the Asking* (same time Tuesday), the business-oriented *Newmarket* (0511 Thursday), *Science and Engineering* (same time Wednesday and Saturday), ●*Folk Box* (0531 Thursday), *Moscow Mailbag* (0511 Tuesday and Friday), ●*Russian Musical Highlights of the 20th Century* (0531 Wednesday), and Sunday's retrospective ●*Moscow Yesterday and Today* (0531 Sunday). Tuesday through Saturday summers, there's *Focus on Asia and the Pacific*, replaced Sunday by *Science and Engineering* and Monday by *Moscow Mailbag*. On the half-hour, look for *This is Russia* (Monday and Friday), ●*Audio Book Club* (Sunday), ●*Russian Musical Highlights of the 20th Century* (Tuesday), ●*Moscow Yesterday and Today* (Thursday), ●*Christian Message from Moscow* (Saturday) and *Russian by Radio* on Wednesday. Winters only to eastern North America on 7125 and 7180 kHz, and to western parts on 5920, 6065, 9850, 12000, 12020 and 13640 kHz. Also available summers to Australasia on 15490, 17625 and 21790 kHz. If these channels are empty, dial around nearby—the Voice of Russia is not renowned for sticking to its frequencies, but it does tend to use the same world band segments.

Radio For Peace International, Costa Rica. Continues at this hour with a potpourri of United Nations, counterculture and other programs. These include *WINGS* (news for and of women, 0530 Wednesday) and *Vietnam Veterans Radio Network* (0530 Thursday). Audible in Europe and the Americas on 6975 kHz.

Kol Israel. Winters only at this time. *News* for 15 minutes from Israel Radio's domestic network. To Europe and eastern North America on 7465 and 9435 kHz, and to Australasia on 17545 kHz. One hour earlier in summer.

WJCR, Upton, Kentucky. Continues with country gospel music for North American

05:00–06:00

Modern shopping malls are fast replacing open-air markets throughout Almaty, Kazakstan.

M. Guha

listeners on 7490 kHz. Also with religious programs to North America at this hour are **WYFR-Family Radio** on 5985 kHz, **WWCR** on 5935 kHz, **KAIJ** on 5810 kHz and **KTBN** on 7510 kHz. For traditional Catholic programming (some of which may be in Spanish), tune to **WEWN** on 7425 kHz.

05:30

Radio Austria International. ●*Report from Austria*; see 0430 for more details. Thirty minutes year-round to North America on 6015 kHz; and winters only to Europe on 6155 and 13730 kHz, and to the Mideast on 15410 and 17870 kHz.

Swiss Radio International. Summers only at this time. Repeat of the 0400 broadcast; see 0500 for specifics. A half hour to southeastern Europe on 9610 or 13635 kHz. One hour later in winter.

United Arab Emirates Radio, Dubai. See 0330 for program details. To East Asia and Australasia on 15435, 17830 and 21700 kHz.

Radio Thailand. Thirty minutes of *news* and short features. To Europe on 15115 kHz. Also available to Asia on 9655 and 11905 kHz.

Radio Romania International. *News,* commentary, a press review, and one or more short features. Thirty minutes to southern Africa (and heard elsewhere) on 11810 (or 11740), 11940, 15250 (or 15270), 15340 (or 15365), 17745 (winter) and 17790 kHz.

0600-1159
Australasia & East Asia—Evening Prime Time
Western North America—Late Evening
Europe & Mideast—Morning and Midday

06:00

■**BBC World Service for the Americas.** Except for Sunday, starts with 15 minutes of *World News*. Tuesday through Saturday, this is followed by ●*Outlook*, a decades-old listeners' favorite, replaced Monday by a couple of features. Sunday, it's a continuation of ●*Play of the Week*, which can run to either 0630 or 0700. If it's the former, you also get 15 minutes of *Agenda* (current affairs) and an additional quarter-hour feature. Continuous to North America and the Caribbean (better to the west) on 6175 kHz.

■**BBC World Service for Europe and the Mideast.** Summers and winter weekends, identical to the service for the Americas, except Sunday, when you can hear 15 minutes of *World News* followed by ●*Letter from America* and *Agenda* (current events). Winter weekdays, it's the final hour of ●*The World Today*. Continuous to Europe on 3955 (winter), 6195, 9410, 12095 and 15565 kHz; and to the Mideast on 11760 and 15575 kHz.

■**BBC World Service for Africa.** Opens with 15 minutes of *World News*, then Monday through Friday it's ●*Sports Roundup* and the breakfast show *Network Africa*. Saturday on the half-hour there's *African Quiz* or *This Week and Africa*; Sunday, it's *Postmark Africa*. Continuous to most parts of the continent on 6005, 6190, 7160, 11765, 11940, 15400 and 15420 kHz.

■**BBC World Service for Asia and the Pacific.** Fifteen minutes of *World News*, then features—including some of the BBC's best. Of particular note are ●*Off the Shelf* (readings from world literature, 0620 Monday through Friday), ●*John Peel* (0615 Sunday), ●*Health Matters* (0635 Monday), ●*Discovery* (science, same time Tuesday), ●*One Planet* (the environment, 0635 Wednesday), *The Works* (technology, 0635 Thursday), ●*Science in Action* (same time Friday), and ●*Omnibus* (documentaries, 0620 Saturday). They don't come much better than these, and it's no fluke that most are long established listener favorites. Continuous to East Asia on 15360, 17760 and 21660 kHz; to Southeast Asia on 9740, 11955 and 15360 kHz; and to Australasia on 7145, 11955 and 15360 kHz.

■**Deutsche Welle, Germany.** Repeat of the 0400 broadcast. Forty-five minutes to the Mideast, winters on 21705 kHz, and summers on 21695 kHz. Also to West Africa (and sometimes heard well in Europe), winters on 7225, 9565 and 11785 kHz; and summers on 13790, 15185 and 17860 kHz. May also be available to East Asia on 17820 kHz.

■**Radio Habana Cuba.** Repeat of the 0200 transmission. To western North America winter on 6000 (or 9505) kHz, and summer on 9820 kHz. Also available to Europe on 9830 or 11705 kHz upper sideband (USB).

■**Radio Canada International.** Winters only at this hour. Monday through Friday, there's *First Edition* (current events). This is replaced weekends by a news bulletin followed by Saturday's environmental ●*Earthwatch* or Sunday's *Arts in Canada*. Thirty minutes to Europe, Africa and the

Mideast on 6090, 6150, 9670, 9780, 11710, 11905, 13690 and 15325 kHz. One hour earlier in summer.

Radio Japan. *News*, then weekdays there's *Asian Top News*. This is followed by a 30-minute feature: *Music Reflections* (Monday), *Let's Try Japanese* (Tuesday), *Music Journey Around Japan* (Wednesday), *My Japan Diary* (Thursday), and *Music Beat* (Friday). *Asian Weekly* fills the Saturday slot, and is replaced Sunday by *Hello from Tokyo*. One hour to Europe on 5975 and 7230 kHz; to East Asia on 11840 kHz; to Southeast Asia on 11740 kHz; to Australasia on 11850 kHz; and to western North America winter on 9835 kHz, and summer on 17825 kHz.

Croatian Radio. Winters only at this time, and actually starts around 0603. Approximately 15 minutes of news from and about Croatia. To Australasia on 11880 or 13820 kHz. One hour earlier in summer.

Voice of America. Final segment of the transmission to Africa and the Mideast. Monday through Friday, the mainstream African service carries just 30 minutes of ●*Daybreak Africa*, with other channels carrying a full hour of *News Now*—a mixed bag of sports, science, business and other news and features. Weekend programming is the same to all areas—60 minutes of *News Now*. To North Africa on 5995 (winter), 7170, 9680 (summer) and 11805 kHz; to the Mideast on 11825 (winter) or (summer) 11965 kHz; and to mainstream Africa on 5970, 6035, 6080, 7195 (summer), 7285 (winter), 9630 (summer), 11950 (winter), 11995 (summer), 12080 and (winter) 15600 kHz. Some of these channels are audible in North America.

Radio Australia. Ten minutes of *News* (five at weekends), then a couple of features. Weekdays, these are separated by a 10-minute sports bulletin on the half-

hour. Monday through Friday, the accent is heavily on music, and you get two bites at the same cherry. Each 20-minute show airing at 0610 is repeated at 0640 the following day (except for the Friday slot which is repeated on Monday). The lineup starts with Monday's *Australian Music Show*, then it's *At Your Request* (Tuesday), *Blacktracker* (Australian aboriginal music, Wednesday), *Australian Country Style* (Thursday), and Friday's *Music Deli*. Weekends bring Saturday's *Feedback* (a listener-response program) and *Arts Australia*, replaced Sunday by the sharp ●*Ockham's Razor* (science talk) and *Correspondents' Report*. Continuous to Asia and the Pacific on 9660, 12080, 15240, 15415, 15510, 17715, 17750 and 21725 kHz. Listeners in western North America should try 17715 kHz. For East and Southeast Asia, best bets are 15240, 15415 and 21725 kHz. Some channels carry an alternative sports program until 0700 on weekends (0800 midyear).

Voice of Nigeria. The second (and final) hour of a daily broadcast intended mainly for listeners in West Africa, but also heard in parts of Europe and North America (especially during winter). Features vary from day to day, but are predominantly concerned with Nigerian and West African affairs. There is a listener-response program at 0600 Friday and 0615 Sunday, and other slots include *Across the Ages* and *Nigeria and Politics* (Monday), *Southern Connection* and *Nigerian Scene* (Tuesday), *West African Scene* (0600 Thursday) and *Images of Nigeria* (0615 Friday). There is a weekday 25-minute program of *news* and commentary on the half-hour, replaced weekends by the more in-depth *Weekly Analysis*. To 0657 on 7255 and (when operating) 15120 kHz.

Radio New Zealand International. Continues with regional programming for the South Pacific. Part of a much longer

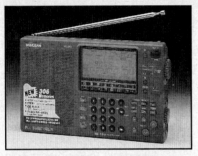

06:00–07:00

broadcast, which is also heard in parts of North America (especially during summer) on 11690 or 11905 kHz.

Voice of Russia World Service. *News*, then winters it's *Focus on Asia and the Pacific* (Tuesday through Saturday), *Science and Engineering* (Sunday), and *Moscow Mailbag* (Monday). On the half-hour, look for *This is Russia* (Monday and Friday), ●*Audio Book Club* (Sunday), ●*Russian Musical Highlights of the 20th Century* (Tuesday), ●*Moscow Yesterday and Today* (Thursday), ●*Christian Message from Moscow* (Saturday) and *Russian by Radio* on Wednesday. In summer, the news is followed by *Science and Engineering* (Monday and Friday), the business-oriented *Newmarket* (Wednesday and Saturday), and a listener-response program, *Moscow Mailbag*, on the remaining days. The lineup for the second half hour includes ●*Moscow Yesterday and Today* (Wednesday), ●*Audio Book Club* (Thursday), *Timelines* (Sunday), *Russian by Radio* (Monday); the eclectic *Kaleidoscope* (Tuesday and Friday) and *This is Russia* on Saturday. Continuous programming to Australasia (and also audible in Southeast Asia). In winter (local summer in Australasia), 15460, 15470, 15525, 17570 and 21790 kHz; midyear, go for 15490, 17625 and 21790 kHz. If there's nothing on these channels, dial around nearby—frequency usage tends to vary.

Radio For Peace International, Costa Rica. Continues with counterculture and social-conscience programs—try Monday's *The Far Right Radio Review*. Audible in Europe and the Americas on 6975 kHz.

Radio Pyongyang, North Korea. See 1100 for specifics. One hour to Southeast Asia on 15180 and 15230 kHz.

Vatican Radio. Winters only at this time. Twenty minutes with a heavy Catholic slant. To Europe on 4005 and 5882 kHz.

One hour earlier in summer. Frequencies may vary slightly.

WJCR, Upton, Kentucky. Continues with country gospel music to North America on 7490 kHz. Also with religious programs for North American listeners at this hour are **WYFR-Family Radio** on 5985 kHz, **WWCR** on 5935 kHz, **KAIJ** on 5810 kHz, **KTBN** on 7510 kHz, and **WHRI-World Harvest Radio** on 5760 and 7315 kHz. Traditional Catholic fare (some of it may be in Spanish) is available on 7425 kHz.

Voice of Malaysia. Actually starts at 0555 with opening announcements and program summary, followed by *News*. Then comes *This is the Voice of Malaysia*, a potpourri of news, interviews, reports and music. The hour is rounded off with *Personality Column*. Part of a 150-minute broadcast to Southeast Asia and Australia on 6175, 9750 and 15295 kHz.

HCJB—Voice of the Andes, Ecuador. Predominantly religious programming at this hour. A favorite with listeners is Monday's *Mountain Meditations* (Sunday night in North America). To North America on 9745 and 12015 kHz.

06:30

Radio Austria International. Winters only at this time. ●*Report from Austria* (see 0430). A half hour via the Canadian relay, aimed primarily at western North America on 6015 kHz.

Swiss Radio International. Winters only at this hour. Repeat of the 0500 broadcast; see there for specifics. A half hour to Europe on 6165 kHz. One hour earlier in summer.

YLE Radio Finland. Summers only at this time. Most days it's *Compass North* and a press review. Exceptions are Saturday's *Capital Café*; Sunday's world band curiosity, *Nuntii Latini* (news in Latin), heard at 0653; and Monday's *Nordic Update*. Thirty minutes to Asia and Australasia on 11945 and 17830 kHz.

Radio Romania International. Actually starts at 0631. A nine-minute news broadcast to Europe winters on 7105, 9510, 9570, 9665 and 11745 kHz; and summers on 9550, 9665 and 11810 kHz.

07:00

■**BBC World Service for the Americas, Europe and the Mideast.** Starts with five minutes of *World News*. This is followed Monday through Saturday by ten minutes of the latest business news in ●*World Business Report* or (Saturday) ●*World Business Review*. Weekdays at 0715, look for ●*Insight*, analysis of current events. Best of the remaining shows (on the half-hour) are Monday's ●*Everywoman* (also a good listen for everyman), Wednesday's *Sports International*, and Friday's ●*Focus on Faith* (a weekly look at the world's religions). Winters only to North America and the Caribbean (and better to the west) on 6175 kHz. Year round to Europe on 9410, 12095, 15565 and 17640 kHz; and to the Mideast on 11760, 15575 (weekends) and 17640 kHz.

■**BBC World Service for Asia and the Pacific.** Same as for Europe and the Americas for the first quarter hour. Then, Monday through Friday, there's ●*Insight* (current events). Pick of the remaining features include ●*Composer of the Month* (classical music, 0730 Monday), *Sports International* (same time Wednesday) and ●*Focus on Faith* (0730 Friday). Continuous to East Asia on 15360, 17760 and 21660 kHz; to Southeast Asia on 9740, 11955 and 15360 kHz; and to Australasia on 7145, 11955 and 15360 kHz.

Voice of Malaysia. First, there is a daily feature with a Malaysian theme (except for Thursday, when *Talk on Islam* is aired), then comes a half hour of *This is the Voice of Malaysia* (see 0600), followed by 15 minutes of *Beautiful Malaysia*. Not much doubt about where the broadcast originates! Continuous to Southeast Asia and Australia on 6175, 9750 and 15295 kHz.

Radio Prague, Czech Republic. Summers only at this time. See 0800 for specifics. Thirty minutes to Europe on 9880 and 11600 kHz. One hour later in winter.

Croatian Radio. Summers only at this time, and actually starts two or three minutes into a predominantly Croatian broadcast. Approximately 15 minutes of news from and about Croatia. To Australasia on 13820 kHz. One hour later in winter.

Radio Slovakia International. Summers only at this time. *Slovakia Today*, a 30-minute review of Slovak life and culture. Monday, there's a potpourri of short features; Tuesday spotlights tourism and Slovak personalities; Wednesday is devoted to business and economy; and Thursday brings a mix of politics, education and science. Friday offerings include cultural items, cooking recipes and the offbeat *Back Page News*; and Saturday has the "*Best of*" series. Sunday's show is a melange of this and that, and includes *Listeners' Tribune* and some enjoyable Slovak music. A friendly half hour to Australasia on 9440, 15460 and 17550 kHz.

Radio Australia. *World News*, then Monday through Friday it's *Pacific Beat*, news and features for listeners in the Pacific, with a 10-minute sports bulletin on the half-hour. Weekends, the news is followed by *Pacific Focus* and either Saturday's *Week's End* or Sunday's *Rural Reporter*. Continuous to Asia and the

07:00–07:30

**Red Army soldiers
practice martial arts in
the Forbidden City,
Beijing.** R. Crane

Pacific on 9660, 12080, 15240, 15415, 15510, 17715, 17750 and 21725 kHz. Listeners in western North America can try 17715 kHz (best during summer), while East Asia is served by 15240, 15415, 17750 and 21725 kHz. For Southeast Asia, take your pick from 15415 and 17750 kHz.

Radio For Peace International, Costa Rica. Continues with counterculture and social-conscience programming. Audible in Europe and the Americas on 6975 kHz.

Voice of Russia World Service. *News*, then a variety of features. The winter lineup includes *Science and Engineering* (Monday and Friday), the business-oriented *Newmarket* (Wednesday and Saturday), and a listener-response program, *Moscow Mailbag*, on the remaining days. During the second half hour, choose from ●*Moscow Yesterday and Today* (Wednesday), ●*Audio Book Club* (Thursday), *Russian by Radio* (Monday), the multifaceted *Kaleidoscope* (Tuesday and Friday), *Timelines* (Sunday) and *This is Russia* on Saturday. Summers, the news is followed by the informative ●*Update* on Tuesday, Thursday and Saturday. Other

offerings include *Science and Engineering* (Wednesday), *Moscow Mailbag* (Friday) and Monday's masterpiece, ●*Music and Musicians*. On the half-hour, there's some of the Voice of Russia's best—●*Audio Book Club* (Wednesday), ●*Moscow Yesterday and Today* (Friday), ●*Songs from Russia* (Sunday), ●*Folk Box* (Tuesday) and *This is Russia* on Thursday. Mondays, it's a continuation of ●*Music and Musicians*. Continuous programming to Australasia (also audible in Southeast Asia). In winter (local summer in Australasia), try 15460, 15470, 15525, 17495, 17570 and 21790 kHz; midyear, go for 17495, 17625 and 21790 kHz. If there's nothing on these channels, dial around nearby—frequency usage tends to be volatile.

WJCR, Upton, Kentucky. Continues with country gospel music for North American listeners on 7490 kHz. Also with religious programs to North America at this hour are **WWCR** on 5935 kHz., **KAIJ** on 5810 kHz, **KTBN** on 7510 kHz, and **WHRI-World Harvest Radio** on 5745 and 9495 kHz. For traditional Catholic programming, tune **WEWN** on 7425 kHz.

Radio Pyongyang, North Korea. See 1100 for specifics. Sixty minutes from the last of the old-time communist stations. To Southeast Asia on 15340 and 17765 kHz.

Radio New Zealand International. Continues with regional programming for the South Pacific. Part of a much longer broadcast, which is also heard in parts of North America (especially during summer) on 6100 or 9700 kHz.

Radio Taipei International, Taiwan. Repeat of the 0200 transmission. Best heard in southern and western parts of the United States on 5950 kHz.

HCJB—Voice of the Andes, Ecuador. Monday through Friday it's *Studio 9*, featuring nine minutes of world and Latin American *news*, followed by 20 minutes of in-depth reporting on Latin America. The

second half hour is given over to one of a variety of 30-minute features—including *Adventures in Odyssey* (Monday), *El Mundo Futuro* (science, Tuesday), *Ham Radio Today* (Wednesday), *Woman to Woman* (Thursday), and the unique and enjoyable ●*Música del Ecuador* (Friday). On Saturday, the news is followed by *DX Partyline*, which in turn is replaced Monday by *Musical Mailbag*. To Europe winter on 9775 kHz, and summer on 11730 kHz. A separate block of religious programming is broadcast to Australasia on 11755 kHz.

07:30

Swiss Radio International. *World Radio Switzerland*—news and analysis of Swiss and world events. Look for lighter fare on Saturday, when the biweekly

07:30–08:00

Capital Letters (a listener-response program) alternates with *Name Game* (first Saturday) and *Sounds Good* (music and interviews, third Saturday). A half hour to North and West Africa winters on 9885 and 11860 kHz, and summers on 15545 and 17685 kHz; also to southern Africa winters on 13635 kHz, and 21750 kHz midyear.

Radio Austria International. Summers only at this time. ●*Report from Austria*, which includes a short bulletin of *news* followed by a series of current events and human interest stories. Good coverage of national and regional issues. Thirty minutes to Europe on 6155 and 13730 kHz, and to the Mideast on 15410 and 17870 kHz. Winters, it's one hour later to Europe, and two hours earlier to the Mideast.

Radio Vlaanderen Internationaal, Belgium. Summers only at this time. *News*, then *Press Review* (except Sunday), followed Monday through Friday by *Belgium Today* (various topics) and features like *The Arts* (Monday and Thursday, *Tourism* (Monday), *Focus on Europe* (Tuesday), *Living in Belgium* and *Green Society* (Wednesday), *Around Town* (Thursday), and *Economics* and *International Report* (Friday). Weekend features consist of Saturday's *Music from Flanders* and Sunday's *P.O. Box 26* (a listener-response program) and *Radio World*. Twenty-five minutes to Europe on 7290 and 9940 kHz; and to Australasia on 9940 kHz. One hour later in winter.

07:45

KTWR-Trans World Radio, Guam. Actually starts at 0740. Ninety-five minutes of evangelical programming targeted at Southeast Asia on 15200 kHz.

Voice of Greece. Actual start time varies slightly. Ten minutes of English news from

and about Greece. Part of a longer broadcast of predominantly Greek programming. To Europe and Australasia on two or more channels from 7450, 9425 and 11645 kHz.

08:00

■**BBC World Service for Europe and the Mideast.** Starts with five minutes of *World News*, then it's a mixed bag of features. Select offerings include ●*Off the Shelf* (0820 Monday through Friday), ●*The Greenfield Collection* (classical music, 0805 Sunday), ●*From Our Own Correspondent* (0835 Tuesday and 0805 Thursday), ●*Performance* (classical music, 0805 Tuesday), ●*Discovery* (science, 0835 same day), ●*One Planet* (the environment, 0835 Wednesday), and ●*Science in Action* (0835 Friday). Continuous to Europe on 9410, 12095, 15565 and 17640 kHz; and to the Mideast on 15575 (weekends) and 17640 kHz.

■**BBC World Service for Asia and the Pacific.** Starts with *World News*. The next 55 minutes are a mixed bag of features, the best of which are undoubtedly ●*Outlook* (0820 Tuesday through Saturday) and ●*Short Story* (0805 Saturday). Aficionados of classical music should try ●*Performance* (0805 Tuesday). Continuous to East Asia on 15360, 17760 and 21660 kHz; to Southeast Asia on 9740, 11955 and 15360 kHz; and to Australasia on 11955 and 15360 kHz.

HCJB—Voice of the Andes, Ecuador. Continuous programming (mostly religious) to Europe and Australasia. To Europe winter on 9775 kHz, and summer on 11730 kHz ; and to Australasia year round on 11755 kHz.

Croatian Radio. Winters only at this time, and actually starts around 0803. Approximately 15 minutes of news from and about Croatia. To Australasia on 13820 kHz. One hour earlier in summer.

Voice of Malaysia. *News* and commentary, followed Monday through Friday by *Instrumentalia*, which is replaced weekends by *This is the Voice of Malaysia* (see 0600). The final 25 minutes of a much longer transmission targeted at Southeast Asia and Australia on 6175, 9750 and 15295 kHz.

Radio Prague, Czech Republic. Winters only at this time. *News*, then Monday through Friday there's *Current Affairs*, followed by one or more features. Monday's offering is *Spotlight*; Tuesday, it's *Talking Point*; Wednesday features *History Czech*; Thursday brings *Economic Report*; and Friday has *Between You and Us*, a listener-response show. The Saturday slot is filled by a highly recommended and enjoyable musical feature, replaced Sunday by *A Letter from Prague, From the Weeklies* and *Readings from Czech Literature*. Thirty minutes to Europe on 11600 and 15260 kHz. One hour earlier in summer.

Radio Australia. Part of a 24-hour service to Asia and the Pacific, but which can also be heard at this time throughout much of North America. Begins with a bulletin of *World News*, then Monday through Friday there's an in-depth look at current events in *PM*. Weekends, the news is followed by *Grandstand Wrap*, a roundup of the latest Australian sports action, which gives way to a feature on the half-hour. Saturday, it's *Asia Pacific*, replaced Sunday by *Innovations*. To Asia and the Pacific on 5995, 9580, 9710, 9770, 12080, 15415, 15510, 17750 and 21725 kHz. Audible in North America on 9580 kHz. Best bets for East and Southeast Asia are 9770, 15415, 17750 and 21725 kHz.

WJCR, Upton, Kentucky. Continues with country gospel music to North America on

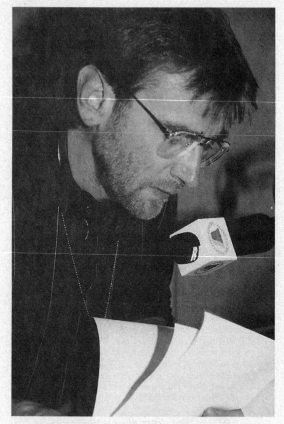

Ismet Hajdari covers current events in Albanian for the South Slavic Service of RFE/RL. RFE/RL

Monday's outstanding ●*Music and Musicians* (classical music). On the half-hour, there's some of the Voice of Russia's best—●*Audio Book Club* (Wednesday), ●*Moscow Yesterday and Today* (Friday), ●*Folk Box* (Tuesday), ●*Songs from Russia* (Sunday), *Kaleidoscope* (Saturday), and Thursday's *This is Russia*. In summer, ●*Update* is only available on Wednesday and Friday. It is replaced Monday by *Science and Engineering*, Tuesday by *Focus on Asia*, Thursday by *Newmarket* and Saturday by *Moscow Mailbag*. Sunday's offering is the 45-minute ●*Music and Musicians*—a jewel among classical music shows. Choice pickings from the second half hour include ●*Moscow Yesterday and Today* (Monday), ●*Folk Box* (Thursday) and Saturday's ●*Christian Message from Moscow*. Other slots include *This is Russia* (Wednesday) and Friday's *Jazz Show*. Continuous programming to Australasia (and also audible in Southeast Asia). In winter (local Oz summer), try 9905, 15470, 15525, 17495 and 21790 kHz; midyear, go for 15490, 17495, 17625 and 21790 kHz. If there's nothing on these channels, dial around nearby—Moscow's frequencies tend to change more than most.

KTWR-Trans World Radio, Guam. Continuation of evangelical programming to Southeast Asia on 15200 kHz, and the start of another ninety-minute block to Australasia on 15330 kHz.

Radio New Zealand International. Continues with regional programming for the South Pacific. Part of a much longer broadcast, which is also heard in parts of North America (especially during summer) on 6100 or 9700 kHz.

Radio Korea International, South Korea. Opens with *news* and commentary, followed Monday through Wednesday by *Seoul Calling*. Weekly features include *Echoes of Korean Music* and *Shortwave*

7490 kHz. Other U.S. religious broadcasters operating at this hour include **WWCR** on 5935 kHz, **KAIJ** on 5810 kHz, **KTBN** on 7510 kHz, and **WHRI-World Harvest Radio** on 5745 and 9495 kHz. Traditional Catholic programming can be heard via **WEWN** on 7425 kHz.

Radio Pyongyang, North Korea. See 1100 for specifics. One hour of mediocrity to Southeast Asia on 15180 and 15230 kHz.

Voice of Russia World Service. Winters, *News* is followed by ●*Update* on Tuesday, Thursday and Saturday. Other features include *Science and Engineering* (Wednesday), *Moscow Mailbag* (Friday) and

Feedback (Sunday), *Tales from Korea's Past* (Monday), *Korean Cultural Trails* (Tuesday), *Pulse of Korea* (Wednesday), *From Us to You* (a listener-response program) and *Let's Learn Korean* (Thursday), *Let's Sing Together* and *Korea Through Foreigners' Eyes* (Friday), and Saturday's *Discovering Korea, Korean Literary Corner* and *Weekly News Focus*. Sixty minutes to Europe on 13670 kHz, and to Australasia on 9570 kHz.

08:30

Radio Austria International. Winters only at this time. The comprehensive ●*Report from Austria*; see 0430 for more details. A half hour to Europe on 6155 and 13730 kHz, and to Australasia on 17870 kHz. Midyear, it's one hour earlier to Europe, and one hour later to Australasia.

Radio Slovakia International. Winters only at this time. *Slovakia Today*—30 minutes of *news*, reports and features, all with a distinct Slovak flavor. Tuesday, there's a potpourri of short features; Wednesday puts the accent on tourism and Slovak personalities; Wednesday has a historical feature; Thursday's slot is devoted to business and economy; and Friday brings a mix of politics, education and science. Saturday has a strong cultural content; Sunday features the *"Best of"* series; and Monday brings *Listeners' Tribune* and some enjoyable Slovak music. To Australasia on 11990, 17485 and 21705 kHz.

Swiss Radio International. *World Radio Switzerland*—news and background reports on world and Swiss events. Look for some lighter fare on Saturdays, when *Capital Letters* (a biweekly listener-response program) alternates with *Name Game* (first Saturday) and *Sounds Good* (third Saturday). To Australasia on 9885 and 13685 kHz.

Radio Vlaanderen Internationaal, Belgium. Winters only at this time. *News*, then *Press Review* (except Sunday), followed Monday through Friday by *Belgium Today* (various topics) and features like *The Arts* (Monday and Thursday, *Tourism* (Monday), *Focus on Europe* (Tuesday), *Living in Belgium* and *Green Society* (Wednesday), *Around Town* (Thursday), and *Economics* and *International Report*(Friday). Weekend features consist of Saturday's *Music from Flanders* and Sunday's *P.O. Box 26* (a listener-response program) and *Radio World*. Twenty-five minutes to Europe on 6130 and 13795 kHz; and to Australasia on 13795 kHz. One hour earlier in summer.

Voice of Armenia. Summer Sundays only. Mainly of interest to Armenians abroad. Thirty minutes of Armenian *news* and culture. To Europe on 15270 kHz. One hour later in winter.

09:00

■**BBC World Service for Europe and the Mideast.** Starts with five minutes of *World News* and ends with ten minutes of ●*Sports Roundup* (except Saturday). The rest is a mixed bag of features, two of which stand out: ●*Brain of Britain* (or its substitute) at 0920 Monday, and ●*Andy Kershaw's World of Music* at the same time Thursday. Also popular is *The Vintage Chart Show* at 0920 Friday. Continuous to Europe on 9410 (winter), 12095, 15565 and 17640 kHz; and to the Mideast on 11760, 15575 and 17640 kHz.

■**BBC World Service for Asia and the Pacific.** Starts and ends like the service for Europe, but the features are different. Monday through Friday at 0920-0950 there's a series of educational programs, and best of the weekend fare is ●*Letter from America* (0905 Saturday). To East Asia on 6065 (winter), 9580 (winter), 11945,

09:00–09:30

11955, 15360, 17760 and 21660 kHz; to Southeast Asia on 6195, 9740, 11765 and 15360 kHz; and to Australasia on 11765 and (winter) 15360 kHz.

■**Deutsche Welle,** Germany. *News*, followed Monday through Friday by ●*NewsLink*, and then a feature. Monday, it's *Development Forum* or *Women on the Move*; Tuesday has the interesting ●*Man and Environment*; Wednesday brings ●*Insight*; Thursday, there's *Living in Germany*; and Friday's slot is *Spotlight on Sport*. Weekend fare consists of Saturday's *Talking Point* and *African Kaleidoscope*; and Sunday's *Religion and Society* and *Cool*. Forty-five minutes to eastern and southern Africa, winter on 11785, 15410, 17800, 17860 and 21600 kHz; and midyear on 9565, 15210, 15410, 17800 and 21790 kHz. For a separate service to Asia and the Pacific, see the next item.

■**Deutsche Welle,** Germany. *News*, then Monday through Friday it's ●*NewsLink* and *Asia-Pacific Report*. These are replaced Saturday by *Talking Point* and ●*Marks and Markets*; and Sunday by *Religion and Society* and *Cool*. Forty-five minutes to East and Southeast Asia and Australasia, winter on 6160, 15105, 15470 and 17820 kHz; and summers on 6160, 12055, 17560 and 21680 kHz.

HCJB—Voice of the Andes, Ecuador. Monday through Friday it's *Studio 9*, featuring nine minutes of world and Latin American *news*, followed by 20 minutes of in-depth reporting on Latin America. The second half hour is given over to one of a variety of 30-minute features—including *Adventures in Odyssey* (Monday), *El Mundo Futuro* (science, Tuesday), *Ham Radio Today* (Wednesday), *Woman to Woman* (Thursday), and the unique ●*Música del Ecuador* (Friday). On Saturday, the news is followed by *DX Partyline*, which in turn is replaced Monday by *Musical Mailbag*. Continuous to Australasia on 11755 kHz.

China Radio International. *News* and commentary, followed Monday through Friday by in-depth reporting and an overview of the Chinese press. This is followed by features like *Focus* and *Cultural Spectrum* (Thursday); *Open Windows* and *Learn to Speak Chinese* (Monday); *Orient Arena* and *Opera House* (Tuesday); *Voices from Other Lands* (Wednesday); and *Life in China* and *Global Review* (Friday). Weekends, Saturday's lineup includes *Asia-Pacific News*, *Report from Developing Countries*, *China Scrapbook* and ●*Music from China*. These are replaced Sunday by *Cultural Information*, *People in the Know*, *On the Road* and *Listeners' Letterbox*. One hour to Australasia on 11730 (or 17755) and 15210 kHz.

Radio New Zealand International. Continuous programming for the islands of the South Pacific, where the broadcasts are targeted. Summers on 6100 kHz, and winters on 9700 kHz. Audible in much of North America.

Voice of Russia World Service. Winters only at this time. *News*, followed by ●*Update* on Wednesday and Friday. This is replaced Monday by *Science and Engineering*, Tuesday by *Focus on Asia*, Thursday by *Newmarket* and Saturday by *Moscow Mailbag*. Sunday's offering is the 45-minute ●*Music and Musicians*—not to be missed if you are an aficionado of classical music. Choice pickings from the second half hour include ●*Moscow Yesterday and Today* (Monday), ●*Folk Box* (Thursday) and Saturday's ●*Christian Message from Moscow*. Other slots include *This is Russia* (Wednesday) and Friday's *Jazz Show*. To Australasia (and also audible in Southeast Asia) on 9905, 15470, 15525 and 17495 kHz. If there's nothing on these channels, dial around nearby—frequency usage can be volatile.

Radio Prague, Czech Republic. Summers only at this time. *News*, then Monday through Friday there's *Current Affairs*, followed by one or more features. Monday, there's *Spotlight*; Tuesday, it's *Talking Point*; Wednesday features *History Czech*; Thursday brings *Economic Report*; and Friday has *Between You and Us*, a listener-response show. Saturday's offering is a highly recommended and thoroughly enjoyable musical feature, replaced Sunday by *A Letter from Prague*, *From the Weeklies* and *Readings from Czech Literature*. Thirty minutes to the Mideast and West Africa on 21745 kHz. One hour later in winter.

Radio Australia. *World News*, followed Monday through Friday by *Countrywide* and a five-minute sports bulletin at 0935. The final 20 minutes are devoted to a feature. Monday, it's *Australian Music Show*, replaced Tuesday by *At Your Request*, and Wednesday by *Blacktracker* (Australian aboriginal music). Thursday's *Australian Country Style* shows that country music is alive and well a long way from Nashville, while Friday's *Music Deli* spotlights music from a variety of cultures. These are replaced weekends by Saturday's *Science Show* and Sunday's *Hindsight* (a look at past events). Continuous to Asia and the Pacific on 6080, 9580, 9770, 11880 and 17750 kHz; and heard in North America on 9580 kHz. Listeners in East Asia can choose from 6080, 9770, 11880 and 17750 kHz; with the last two channels also audible in much of Southeast Asia.

KTWR-Trans World Radio, Guam. Final thirty minutes of evangelical programming to Australasia on 15330 kHz.

WJCR, Upton, Kentucky. Continues with country gospel music to North America on 7490 kHz. Other U.S. religious broadcasters operating at this hour include **WWCR** on 5935, **KAIJ** on 5810, **KTBN** on 7510 kHz, and **WHRI-World Harvest Radio** on 5745 and 9495 kHz. Traditional

Catholic programming is aired via **WEWN** on 7425 kHz.

09:30

Radio Austria International. ●*Report from Austria*, which consists of a short bulletin of *news* followed by a series of current events and human interest stories. Tends to focus on national and regional issues. To East Asia on 15455 kHz, and to Australasia on 17870 kHz. Daily in winter, but only Monday through Saturday in summer.

■**Radio Netherlands.** *News*, then Monday through Friday it's ●*Newsline* followed by a feature. Well worth a listen are ●*Research File* (science, Monday); ●*A Good Life* (Friday); ●*Weekend* (Saturday) and Wednesday's well produced ●*Documentary*. On the remaining days, you can hear *Music 52-15* (Tuesday) and *Media Network* (Thursday). The Sunday slots are filled by *Sincerely Yours* (a listener-response program) and *Sounds Interesting*. One hour to East and Southeast Asia on 7260 (winter), 12065 and (summer) 13710 kHz. Recommended listening.

Radio Vilnius, Lithuania. Summers only at this time; see 1030 for program specifics. Thirty minutes to western Europe on 9710 kHz. One hour later in winter.

FEBC Radio International, Philippines. Opens with *World News Update*, then it's mostly religious features. For something with a more general appeal, try Thursday's *Mailbag* or Sunday's *DX Dial* (a show for radio enthusiasts). The first half-hour of a 90-minute predominantly religious broadcast targeted at East and Southeast Asia on 11635 kHz.

Voice of Armenia. Winter Sundays only. Mainly of interest to Armenians abroad. Thirty minutes of Armenian *news* and culture. To Europe on 15270 kHz. One hour earlier in summer.

10:00

■**BBC World Service for the Americas, Europe and the Mideast.** Thirty minutes of ●*Newsdesk* followed by a quarter hour each of ●*Britain Today* and (Monday through Friday) ●*World Business Report.* The latter is replaced weekends by a Saturday feature and Sunday's *Record News* (classical music). To eastern North America and the Caribbean on 5965 (summer) and 6195 kHz; to Europe on 9410 (winter), 12095, 15565 and 17640 kHz; and to the Mideast on 11760, 15575 and 17640 kHz.

■**BBC World Service for Asia and the Pacific.** Virtually identical to the service for Europe and the Americas, except for the 1045 feature on weekends. ●*World Business Review* is aired Saturday, and *Science Extra* on Sunday. Continuous to East Asia on 9740 and (till 1030) 15360, 17760 and 21660 kHz; to Southeast Asia on 6195, 9740, 11765, and (till 1030) 15360 kHz; and to Australasia on 11765 kHz.

Radio Australia. *World News*, then weekdays it's *Asia Pacific* and a feature on the half-hour. Monday's slot is given over to *Innovations*, replaced Tuesday by *Arts Australia*, and Wednesday by *Rural Reporter*. Recommendations for a good read can be found in Thursday's *Book Talk*, with Friday spotlighting environmental topics in *Earthbeat*. The weekend lineup consists of Saturday's *Jazz Notes* and *Asia Pacific*, plus Sunday's *Oz Sounds* and *Correspondents' Report*. Continuous to Asia and the Pacific on 6080, 9580, 9770, 11880 and 17750 kHz; and well heard in North America on 9580 kHz. Listeners in East and Southeast Asia can choose from 6080 (East Asia only), 9770, 11880 and 17750 kHz.

Swiss Radio International. Summers only at this time. *World Radio Switzerland*—news and analysis of Swiss and world events. Look for something lighter on Saturdays, when the biweekly *Capital Letters* (a listener-response program) alternates with *Name Game* (first Saturday) and *Sounds Good* (third Saturday). Thirty minutes to southwestern Europe on 15315 kHz. One hour later in winter.

Radio Prague, Czech Republic. This time winters only. See 0900 for specifics. Thirty minutes to West Africa on 17485 kHz, and to the Mideast and beyond on 21745 kHz.

Radio Japan. *News*, then Monday through Friday there's *44 Minutes* (an in-depth look at current trends and events in Japan). This is replaced Saturday by *Weekend Break* (discussion), and Sunday by *Hello from Tokyo*. One hour to South Asia on 15590 kHz, to Southeast Asia on 9695 kHz, and to Australasia on 11850 kHz.

Voice of Vietnam. Begins with *news*, then there's *Commentary* or *Weekly Review*, followed by short features and some pleasant Vietnamese music (especially at weekends). Heard extensively on 9840 and 12020 (or 9730) kHz. Targeted to Asia at this hour.

Voice of America. The start of the VOA's daily broadcasts to the Caribbean. *News Now*—a mixed bag of sports, science, business and other news and features. On 6165, 7405 and 9590 kHz. For a separate service to Australasia, see the next item.

Voice of America. The ubiquitous *News Now*, but unlike the service to the Caribbean, this is part of a much longer broadcast. To Australasia on 5985, 11720, and 15425 kHz.

China Radio International. Repeat of the 0900 broadcast, but with news updates. One hour to Australasia on 11730 (or 17755) and 15210 kHz.

FEBC Radio International, Philippines. The final hour of a 90-minute mix of religious and secular programming for East and Southeast Asia. Monday through Friday, it's *Focus on the Family*, then a 15-minute religious feature, *Asian News Update* (on the half-hour) and *In Touch*. All weekend offerings are religious in nature. On 11635 kHz.

All India Radio. *News*, then a composite program of commentary, press review and features, interspersed with ample servings of enjoyable Indian music. To East Asia on 11585 and 17840 kHz; and to Australasia on 13700. 15050 and 17387 kHz.

WJCR, Upton, Kentucky. Continues with country gospel music to North America on 7490 kHz. Other U.S. religious broadcasters operating at this hour include **WWCR** on 5935 kHz, **KTBN** on 7510 kHz, **WYFR-Family Radio** on 5950 kHz, and **WHRI-World Harvest Radio** on 6040 and 9495 kHz. For traditional Catholic programming, try **WEWN** on 7425 kHz.

HCJB—Voice of the Andes, Ecuador. Sixty minutes of mostly religious programming to Australasia on 11755 kHz.

10:30

Radio Korea International, South Korea. Summers only at this time. Starts off with *News*, followed Monday through Wednesday by *Economic News Briefs*. The remainder of the 30-minute broadcast is taken up by a feature: *Shortwave Feedback* (Sunday), *Seoul Calling* (Monday and Tuesday), *Pulse of Korea* (Wednesday), *From Us to You* (Thursday), *Let's Sing Together* (Friday) and *Weekly News Focus* (Saturday). On 11715 kHz via their Canadian relay, so this is the best chance for North Americans to hear the station. One hour later in winter.

10:30–11:00

The traditional Osh bazaar in Bishkek, Kyrgyzstan, is stocked high with modern household goods.

M. Guha

Radio Prague, Czech Republic. This time summers only. Repeat of the 0700 broadcast; see 1130 for program specifics. A half hour to Europe on 9880 and 11615 kHz. One hour later during winter.

■**Radio Netherlands.** The second of two hours targeted at East and Southeast Asia. *News*, followed Monday through Friday by ●*Newsline*, then a feature. Quality shows include ●*EuroQuest* (Monday)●*A Good Life* (Tuesday), ●*Research File* (Thursday), ●*Roughly Speaking* (Saturday) and Friday's excellent ●*Documentary*. Other offerings include *Aural Tapestry* (Sunday), *Sounds Interesting* (Wednesday) and Sunday's *Wide Angle*. Fifty-five minutes to East and Southeast Asia (and also audible in parts of Australasia) on 7260 (winter), 12065 and (summer) 13710 kHz. A full hour summers to Western Europe on 6045 and 9860 kHz.

Radio Vlaanderen Internationaal, Belgium. Summers only at this time. *News*, then *Press Review* (except Sunday), followed Monday through Friday by *Belgium Today* (various topics) and features like *The Arts* (Monday and Thursday, *Tourism* (Monday), *Focus on Europe* (Tuesday), *Living in Belgium* and

Green Society (Wednesday), *Around Town* (Thursday), and *Economics* and *International Report*(Friday). Weekend features consist of Saturday's *Music from Flanders* and Sunday's *P.O. Box 26* (a listener-response program) and *Radio World*. Twenty-five minutes to Europe on 9925 and 15535 kHz.

Radio Vilnius, Lithuania. Winters only at this time. A half hour that's mostly *news* and background reports about events in Lithuania. Of broader appeal is *Mailbag*, aired every other Sunday. For a little Lithuanian music, try the second half of Monday's broadcast. To western Europe on 9710 kHz. One hour earlier in summer.

United Arab Emirates Radio, Dubai. *News*, then a feature dealing with one or more aspects of Arab life and culture. Weekends, there are replies to listeners' letters. To Europe and North Africa on 13675, 15370, 15395 and 21605 kHz.

11:00

■**BBC World Service for the Americas, Europe and the Mideast.** ●*Newsdesk*, followed on the half-hour by a variety of features, depending on the day of the week. Try *Pick of the World* (Monday), ●*Omnibus* (Tuesday), *Sports International* (Wednesday), ●*Focus on Faith* (Friday), and ●*People and Politics* (Saturday). Sunday's offering is the religious *In Praise of God.* Continuous programming to eastern North America and the Caribbean on 5965, 6195 and 15220 kHz. Weekdays, for the first half hour, 6195 and 15220 kHz carry alternative programming for the Caribbean (see next item). Also to Europe on 9410, 12095, 15565 and 17640 kHz; and to the Mideast on 11760, 15565 and 15575 kHz.

■BBC World Service for the Caribbean. A half-hour weekday broadcast consisting of *World News, Caribbean Report, Sport for the Caribbean* and *Caribbean Magazine.* On 6195 and 15220 kHz.

■BBC World Service for Asia and the Pacific. Starts with ●*Newsdesk*, and then there's a 30-minute feature. *Meridian* (the arts) is aired Wednesday and Thursday; Tuesday has *On Screen* (cinema); Friday, there's the classical *Music Review*; Sunday features ●*Everywoman*; and Monday's offering is ●*Omnibus.* Continuous to East Asia on 9580, 9740, 11955 and 15280 kHz; to Southeast Asia on 6195 and 9740 kHz; and to Australasia on 9740 kHz.

Voice of Asia, Taiwan. A broadcast divided into four 15-minute blocks, the first of which is *News.* This is followed by two quarter-hour features, except for Monday's *Floating Air* which occupies a full 30-minute slot. Tuesday's offerings are *People* and *Trends*; Wednesday brings *Taiwan Today* and *Miss Mook's Big Countdown*; Thursday's themes are *Treasures of the Orient* and *Hot Spots*; Friday features *Taipei Magazine* and *Life on the Outside*; Saturday, there's *Kaleidoscope* and *Amanda's Café*; and Sunday it's *Mailbag Time* and *Music Box.* Saturday's broadcast ends with *Reflections*; otherwise it's *English*

101 (Sunday and Wednesday) or *Let's Learn Chinese* on the remaining days. One hour to Southeast Asia on 7445 kHz. Some of these programs are also carried by Radio Taipei International.

■Deutsche Welle, Germany. *News*, then Monday through Friday it's ●*NewsLink* and *Africa Report.* These are replaced Saturday by *Talking Point* and *African Kaleidoscope*, and Sunday by *Religion and Society* and *Cool.* Forty-five minutes to Africa on 15370, 15410, 17680, (winter) 17800, (summer) 17860 and (winter) 21780 kHz. Best for southern Africa is 15370 and 21780 kHz in winter, and 15410 and 17680 kHz midyear.

Radio Australia. *World News*, then weekdays it's *Asia Pacific*, a sports bulletin on the half-hour, and *Countrywide* five minutes later. Weekends, the news is followed by Saturday's *Fine Music Australia* and *Book Reading*, or Sunday's *Jazz Notes* and *Week's End.* Continuous to East Asia and the Pacific on 6080, 9580 and 9770 kHz; and easily heard in much of North America on 9580 kHz.

Radio Bulgaria. Summers only at this time. *News*, then Monday through Thursday there's 15 minutes of current events in *Today.* This is replaced Friday by *Weekly Spotlight*, a summary of the week's major political events. The remainder of the broadcast is given over to features dealing with Bulgaria and its people, plus some lively folk music. Sixty minutes to Europe on 15175 and 17585 kHz. One hour later during winter.

HCJB—Voice of the Andes, Ecuador. First 60 minutes of more than five hours of religious programming to the Americas on 12005 and 15115 kHz.

Voice of America. A mixed bag of sports, science, business and other news and features. To East Asia on 6110 (or

11:00–11:30

6160), 9760, 11705 (winter) and 15160 kHz, and to Australasia on 5985 (or 9770), 9645, 11720 and 15425 kHz.

Radio Jordan. Summers only at this time. A 60-minute partial relay of the station's domestic broadcasts, beamed to Europe and eastern North America on 11690 kHz. One hour later in winter.

Radio Japan. *News*, then weekdays there's *Asian Top News*. This is followed by a 30-minute feature: *Music Reflections* (Monday), *Let's Try Japanese* (Tuesday), *Music Journey Around Japan* (Wednesday), *My Japan Diary* (Thursday), and *Music Beat* (Friday). *Asian Weekly* fills the Saturday slot, and is replaced Sunday by *Hello from Tokyo*. One hour to eastern North America on 6120 kHz; to South Asia on 15590 kHz; and to Southeast Asia on 9695 kHz.

Voice of Vietnam. Repeat of the 1000 broadcast. A half hour to Southeast Asia on 7285 kHz.

Radio Singapore International. A three-hour package for Southeast Asia, and widely heard beyond. Starts with nine minutes of *news* (five at weekends), then Monday through Friday there's *Business and Market Report*, replaced Saturday by *Asia Below the Headlines*, and Sunday by *The Film Programme*. These are followed on the quarter-hour by *Arts Arena* (Monday), *Profile* (Tuesday), and *Star Trax* (Wednesday). A self-denominated lifestyle magazine—*Living*—pairs up with *After-thought* on Thursday, and the eclectic and informative *Frontiers* fills the Friday slot. Weekends, look for *Regional Press Review* (1120 Saturday) and *Business World* (1115 Sunday). There's a daily 5-minute news bulletin on the half-hour, then one or more short features. Weekdays, take your pick from *Wired Up* (Internet, Monday), *Vox Box* (a radio soapbox, Tuesday), *Reflections* (musings, Wednesday), *The Film Programme* (Thursday), and *The Written*

Word (Friday). The hour is rounded off with the 15-minute *Newsline*. Saturday fare consists of *Eco-Watch*, *Comment* and *Business World*; Sunday, there's *Frontiers* and *Regional Press Review*. On 6015 and 6150 kHz.

CBC North-Québec, Canada. Summers only at this time; see 1200 for specifics. Intended for a domestic audience, but also heard in the northeastern United States on 9625 kHz.

Swiss Radio International. *World Radio Switzerland*—news and background reports on world and Swiss events. Some lighter fare on Saturday, when *Capital Letters* (a biweekly listener-response program) alternates with *Name Game* (first Saturday) and *Sounds Good* (music and interviews, third Saturday). On the half-hour, try something more relaxed, *Rendezvous with Switzerland*. To Europe (first 30 minutes and winters only) on 9535 kHz, and a full hour year round to East and Southeast Asia on (winter) 9540 and 17815 kHz, and (summer) 13735 and 21770 kHz.

Radio Pyongyang, North Korea. One of the last of the old-time communist stations, with quaint terms like "Great Leader" and "Unrivaled Great Man" being the order of the day. Starts with *"news,"* with much of the remainder of the broadcast devoted to revering the late Kim Il Sung. Abominably bad programs, but worth the occasional listen just to hear how awful they are. One hour to North America on 6575, 9975 and 11335 kHz.

WJCR, Upton, Kentucky. Continues with country gospel music to North America on 7490 kHz. Other U.S. religious broadcasters operating at this hour include **WWCR** on 5935 (or 15685) kHz, **KTBN** on 7510 kHz, **WYFR-Family Radio** on 5950 and 7355 (or 11830) kHz, and **WHRI-World**

11:00–11:30

The international HFCC Conference takes place semiannually to coordinate world band frequency usage. The Hotel Dom Pedro in Lisbon was the venue for the August 1999 gathering.

M. Prezelj

Harvest Radio on 6040 and 9495 kHz. Traditional Catholic programming can be found on **WEWN** on 7425 kHz.

11:30

Radio Korea International, South Korea. Winters only at this time. See 1030 for program details. A half hour on 9650 kHz via their Canadian relay, so a good chance for North Americans to hear the station. One hour earlier in summer.

■**Radio Netherlands.** *News*, then Monday through Friday it's ●*Newsline* followed by a feature. Pick of the pack are ●*Research File* (science, Monday); ●*A Good Life* (Friday); ●*Weekend* (Saturday) and Wednesday's award-winning ●*Documentary*. On the remaining days, you can hear *Music 52-15* (Tuesday) and *Media Network* (Thursday). Sunday fare consists of *Sincerely Yours* (a listener-response program)

and *Sounds Interesting*. One hour to western Europe, winters on 6045 and 9855 kHz, and summers on 6045 and 9860 kHz.

Radio Prague, Czech Republic. Winters only at this time. *News*, then Monday through Friday there's *Current Affairs*, followed by one or more features. Take your pick from *Spotlight* (Monday), *Talking Point* (Tuesday), *History Czech* (Wednesday), Thursday's *Economic Report* and Friday's *Between You and Us*, a listener-response show. Saturday's offering is a thoroughly enjoyable musical feature, replaced Sunday by *A Letter from Prague*, *From the Weeklies* and *Readings from Czech Literature*. Thirty minutes to Europe on 11640 kHz, and to East Africa and the Mideast on 21745 kHz.

Radio Sweden. Summers only at this time; see 1230 for program details. To North America on 15235 (or 15240) and 17870 kHz.

1200-1759
Western Australia & East Asia—Evening Prime Time
North America—Morning
Europe & Mideast—Afternoon and Early Evening

12:00

■**BBC World Service for the Americas, Europe and the Mideast.** Five minutes of *World News*, then Monday through Friday there's ●*Outlook*—a listeners' favorite for over three decades and still going strong. It is replaced Sunday by ●*From Our Own Correspondent* and ●*Letter From America*. The final 15 minutes are taken up by ●*Sports Roundup*. On Saturdays, the news is followed by the 55-minute *Wright Round the World*, an International request show of limited appeal. Continuous to North America and the Caribbean on 5965 (winter), 6195, 9515 and 15220 kHz. Weekdays, for the first 15 minutes, 6195 and 15220 kHz carry alternative programming for the Caribbean (see next item). In Europe, tune to 9410 (winter), 12095, 15565 or 17640 kHz; and in the Mideast, 11760 and 15575 kHz.

■**BBC World Service for the Caribbean.** A 15-minute weekday broadcast consisting of *World News*, ●*World Business Report* and *Caribbean Report*. On 6195 and 15220 kHz.

■**BBC World Service for Asia and the Pacific.** Almost identical to the service for Europe and the Americas, except that *Write On* (a listener response program) or *Waveguide* (a radio-related feature) replaces *Letter to America* at 1230 Sunday. Continuous to East Asia on 6195, 9580, 9740, 11955 and 15280 kHz; to Southeast Asia on 6195 and 9740 kHz; and to

Australasia on 9740 kHz. Also audible in western North America on 9740 kHz.

Radio Canada International. Summer only at this time. Monday through Friday, the *news* is followed by *Ontario Morning*. This is replaced Saturday by *The House* (current events), and Sunday by ●*Quirks and Quarks* (an irreverent look at science). To North America and the Caribbean on 9640, 13650, 17765 and 17820 kHz. One hour later in winter. For a separate year-round service to Asia, see the next item.

Radio Canada International. *News*, followed Monday through Friday by *Spectrum* (topical events). Saturday features the environmental *Earth Watch*, and *Arts in Canada* occupies the Sunday slot. Thirty minutes to East and Southeast Asia, winters on 6150 and 11730 kHz, and summers on 9660 and 15195 kHz.

Radio Tashkent, Uzbekistan. *News* and commentary, followed by features such as *Life in the Village* (Wednesday), a listeners' request program (Monday), and local music (Thursday). Heard better in Asia, Australasia and Europe than in North America. Thirty minutes winters on 5060, 5975, 6025 and 9715 kHz; and summers on 7285, 9715, 15295 and 17775 kHz.

■**Radio France Internationale.** The first 30 minutes are made up of *news* and correspondents' reports, with a review of the French press rounding off the half hour. The next 25 minutes are given over to a series of short features, including

Sunday's *Every Woman* and *Club 9516* (a listener-response program); Monday's *RFI Europe* and *Arts in France*, Tuesday's *Books* and *Drumbeat* (African culture); and Wednesday's *Power Policy* and *France Today*. On Thursday, look for *Bottom Line* (economics) and *Reach-Out* (humanitarian issues), replaced Friday by *Film Reel* and *Weekend*. Saturday's broadcast includes a French lesson. A fast-moving information-packed hour to Europe on 15155 and 15195 kHz. There's nothing scheduled for North America, but if you live near the east coast, try 15540 kHz, targeted at West Africa.

Radio Bulgaria. This time winters only; see 1100 for specifics. Sixty minutes to Europe on 15130 and 15290 kHz. One hour earlier in summer.

Radio Polonia, Poland. This time summers only. Fifty-five minutes of news,

commentary, features and music—all with a Polish accent. Monday through Friday, it's *News from Poland*—a potpourri of news, reports and interviews. This is followed by *Jazz, Folk, Rock and Pop from Poland* (Monday), *Request Concert* and *A Day in the Life of...* (Tuesday), classical music and the historical *Flashback* (Wednesday), a communications feature and *Letter from Poland* (Thursday), and a Friday feature followed by *Business Week*. The Saturday broadcast begins with a bulletin of *news*, then there's *Weekend Papers* (a press review), *What We Said* (a summary of the station's output during the previous week) and an arts magazine, *Focus*. Sundays, you can hear *Weekend Commentary*, *Panorama* (a window on day-to-day life in Poland) and *Postbag*, a listener-response program. To Europe on 6095, 7145, 7270, 9525 and 11815 kHz. This last frequency can be heard weekends

12:00–12:00

in the northeastern United States and southeastern Canada, when the broadcast is not subject to co-channel interference from the Radio Exterior de España relay in Costa Rica. One hour later in winter.

Radio Australia. *World News*, then Monday through Thursday it's *Late Night Live* (round-table discussion). On the remaining days you can listen to a relay of the domestic Radio National service. Continuous to the Pacific on 5995, 6020 and 9580 kHz; and well heard in much of North America on 5995 and 9580 kHz.

Radio Jordan. Winters only at this time. A 60-minute partial relay of the station's domestic broadcasts, beamed to Europe and eastern North America on 11690 kHz. One hour earlier in summer.

Swiss Radio International. Summers only at this time. Repeat of the 1000 broadcast; see there for specifics. Thirty minutes to southwestern Europe on 15315 kHz. One hour later in winter.

Radio Korea International, South Korea. Opens with *news* and commentary, followed Monday through Wednesday by *Seoul Calling*. Weekly features include *Echoes of Korean Music* and *Shortwave Feedback* (Sunday), *Tales from Korea's Past* (Monday), *Korean Cultural Trails* (Tuesday), *Pulse of Korea* (Wednesday), *From Us to You* (a listener-response program) and *Let's Learn Korean* (Thursday), *Let's Sing Together* and *Korea Through Foreigners' Eyes* (Friday), and Saturday's *Discovering Korea*, *Korean Literary Corner* and *Weekly News Focus*. Sixty minutes to East Asia on 7285 kHz.

CBC North-Québec, Canada. Part of an 18-hour multilingual broadcast for a domestic audience, but which is also heard in the northeastern United States. Weekend programming at this hour is in English, and features *news* followed by the enjoyably eclectic ●*Good Morning Québec* (Saturday) or *Fresh Air* (Sunday). Starts at this time winters, but summers it is already into the second hour. On 9625 kHz.

HCJB—Voice of the Andes, Ecuador. Continuous religious programming to the Americas on 12005 and 15115 kHz.

Voice of Mongolia. Most days, it's *news*, reports and short features, all with a local flavor. The programs provide an interesting insight into the life and culture of a nation largely unknown to the rest of the world. The entire Sunday broadcast is devoted to exotic Mongolian music. Thirty minutes to Australasia on 12015 or 12085 kHz.

Radio Singapore International. Continuous programming to Southeast Asia and beyond. Starts with five minutes of *news*, a weather report, and either the weekday *Front Page* (headlines from local and regional dailies) or instrumental music (Saturday and Sunday). Weekdays, the next 20 minutes are devoted to music. Take your pick from *E-Z Beat* (Monday and Tuesday), *Classic Gold* (Wednesday and Friday) and *Love Songs* on Thursday. There are two Saturday slots, *Star Trax* and *Currencies*, replaced Sunday by *Comment* and *Profile*. On the half-hour, it's either the weekday *Business and Market Report* or a five-minute news bulletin. The next 25 minutes are given over to features. Monday, it's *The Written Word* and *Business World*; Tuesday, there's *Living* and *Asia Below the Headlines*; and Wednesday's pairing is *Wired Up* and *Frontiers*. Thursday's offerings are *Vox Box* and *Arts Arena*; and Friday brings *Reflections* and *Profile*. Weekends are devoted to repeats of shows aired earlier in the week— Saturday's features are *Arts Arena* and *Wired Up*; and Sunday's lineup is *Living*, *Snapshots*, *Afterthought* and *Currencies*. On 6015 and 6150 kHz.

Radio Taipei International, Taiwan. The broadcast opens with 15 minutes of *News*, and closes with a quarter-hour of *Let's Learn Chinese*, which has a series of segments for beginning, intermediate and advanced learners. In between, you can take your pick from *Jade Bells and Bamboo Pipes* (Monday), *People* and *Trends* (Tuesday), *Taiwan Today* and *Miss Mook's Big Countdown* (Wednesday), *Treasures of the Orient* and *Hot Spots* (Thursday), *Taipei Magazine* and *Life on the Outside* (Friday), *Kaleidoscope* and *Reflections* (Saturday) and *Food, Poetry and Others* followed by *Mailbag Time* on Sunday. Formerly the "Voice of Free China," this station has gone through a metamorphosis few would have dared to predict. One hour to East Asia on 7130 kHz, and to Australasia on 9610 kHz.

Voice of America. A mixed bag of current events, sports, science, business and other news and features. To East Asia on 6110 (or 6160), 9760, 11715, 11705 (winter) and 15160 kHz; and to Australasia on 9645, 11715 and 15425 kHz.

China Radio International. *News* and commentary, followed Monday through Friday by in-depth reports and a review of the Chinese press. Next come features like *Open Windows* and *Learn to Speak Chinese* (Monday); *Orient Arena* and *Opera House* (Tuesday); *Voices from Other Lands* (Wednesday); *Focus* and *Cultural Spectrum* (Thursday); and *Life in China* and *Global Review* (Friday). On weekends, Saturday's lineup includes *Asia-Pacific News*, *Report from Developing Countries*, *China Scrapbook* and ●*Music from China*; and Sunday there's *Cultural Information*, *People in the Know*, *On the Road* and *Listeners' Letterbox*. One hour to Southeast Asia on 9715 and 11980 kHz; and to Australasia on 7265, 11675 and 15110 kHz. May also be available to eastern North America on 9590 kHz.

Radio Nacional do Brasil, Brazil. This service, considerably renovated during the

World band radio is a lifeline in much of Africa. Here, a Liberian listens to ELWA, which later was demolished by rebel forces.   SIM

first half of 1999, left the air around midyear when the parent organization, Radiobrás, was wound up by the government. It remains to be seen whether the successor to Radiobrás will reactivate the service at some future date. When last heard at this hour (to North America on 15445 kHz), the former 80-minute broadcast had been reduced to one hour, and consisted of a variety of short features mixed with exotic Brazilian music.

WJCR, Upton, Kentucky. Continues with country gospel music to North America on 7490 kHz. Other U.S. religious broadcasters operating at this hour include **WWCR** on 5935 (or 13845) and 15685 kHz, **KTBN**

12:00–13:00

on 7510 kHz, **WYFR-Family Radio** on 5950, 6015 (or 7355), 11830 and 11970 (or 17750) kHz, and **WHRI-World Harvest Radio** on 6040 and 9495 kHz. For traditional Catholic programming, tune **WEWN** on 7425 kHz.

12:15

Radio Cairo, Egypt. The start of a 75-minute package of news, religion, culture and entertainment, much of it devoted to Arab and Islamic themes. The initial quarter hour consists of virtually anything, from quizzes to Islamic religious talks, then there's *news* and commentary, which in turn give way to political and cultural items. To Asia on 17595 kHz.

12:30

Radio Austria International. Summers only at this time. ●*Report from Austria*, a compilation of national and regional news, current events and human interest stories. Thirty minutes to Europe on 6155 and 13730 kHz, with the latter frequency also available for eastern North America. One hour later in winter.

Radio Bangladesh. *News*, followed by Islamic and general interest features and pleasant Bengali music. Thirty minutes to Southeast Asia, also heard in Europe, on 7185 and 9550 kHz. Frequencies may vary slightly.

■**Radio Netherlands.** Winters only at this time. The second of two hours for European listeners. *News*, followed Monday through Friday by ●*Newsline*, then a feature. Highly recommended listening, with the best being ●*EuroQuest* (Monday) ●*A Good Life* (Tuesday), ●*Research File* (science, Thursday), ●*Roughly Speaking* (a youth program, Saturday) and Friday's ●*Documentary*. Other offerings include

Aural Tapestry (Sunday), *Sounds Interesting* (Wednesday) and Sunday's *Wide Angle*. On 6045 and 9855 kHz.

Radio Vlaanderen Internationaal, Belgium. Summers only at this time. *News*, then *Press Review* (except Sunday), followed Monday through Friday by *Belgium Today* (various topics) and features like *The Arts* (Monday and Thursday, *Tourism* (Monday), *Focus on Europe* (Tuesday), *Living in Belgium* and *Green Society* (Wednesday), *Around Town* (Thursday), and *Economics* and *International Report*(Friday). Weekend features consist of Saturday's *Music from Flanders* and Sunday's *P.O. Box 26* (a listener-response program) and *Radio World*. Twenty-five minutes to North America on 15545 kHz.

Radio Prague, Czech Republic. Winters only at this time. *News*, then Monday through Friday there's *Current Affairs*. These are followed by one or more features. Monday's offering is *Spotlight*; Tuesday, brings *Talking Point*; Wednesday features *History Czech*; Thursday has *Economic Report*; and Friday's slot is *Between You and Us*, a listener-response show. Come Saturday, make the most of a thoroughly enjoyable musical feature, which alternates between classical, folk and jazz. The Sunday lineup consists of *A Letter from Prague, From the Weeklies* and *Readings from Czech Literature*. Thirty minutes to Europe on 6055 kHz, and to Australasia on 21745 kHz.

YLE Radio Finland. Summer Sundays only at this hour. *Compass North* and *Capital Café*—Finnish news and general interest stories. Thirty minutes to North America on 11900 and 15400 kHz. One hour later in winter.

Voice of Vietnam. Repeat of the 1000 transmission. A half hour to Asia on 9840 and 12020 (or 9730) kHz. Frequencies may vary slightly.

Radio Thailand. Thirty minutes of *news* and short features. To Southeast Asia and Australasia, winters on 9810 kHz, and summers on 9885 kHz.

Voice of Turkey. This time summers only. Fifty minutes of *news*, features and Turkish music beamed to Europe on 15290 kHz. One hour later in winter.

Radio Sweden. Monday through Friday, it's *news* and features in *Sixty Degrees North*, concentrating heavily on Scandinavian topics. Monday's accent is on sports; Tuesday has electronic media news; Wednesday, there's *Money Matters*; Thursday features ecology or science and technology; and Friday offers a review of the week's news. Saturday's slot is filled by *Spectrum* (arts) or *Sweden Today*, and Sunday fare consists of *In Touch with Stockholm* (a listener-response program) or the musical *Sounds Nordic*. A half hour winters to North America on 11650 (or 13740) and 15240 kHz; and summers to Asia and Australasia on 13740 and 15240 kHz.

Radio Korea International, South Korea. Starts off with *news*, followed Monday through Wednesday by *Economic News Briefs*. The remainder of the broadcast is taken up by a feature: *Shortwave Feedback* (Sunday), *Seoul Calling* (Monday and Tuesday), *Pulse of Korea* (Wednesday), *From Us to You* (Thursday), *Let's Sing Together* (Friday) and *Weekly News Focus* (Saturday). Thirty minutes to East and Southeast Asia on 6055, 9570, 9640 and 13670 kHz.

Voice of Greece. Summers only at this time, and actually starts around 1235. Several minutes of English news surrounded by a lengthy period of Greek music and programming. To North America on 15175 and 15650 kHz. One hour later during winter.

13:00

■**BBC World Service for the Americas, Europe and the Mideast.** ●*Newshour*—the yardstick by which all other news broadcasts are measured. Sixty minutes to North America and the Caribbean on 5965 (winter), 6195, 9515, 9590 (winter), 11865 (summer) and 15220 kHz; to Europe on 9410 (winter), 12095, 15565 and 17640 kHz; and to the Mideast on 11760 and 15575 kHz.

■**BBC World Service for Asia and the Pacific.** Same as for Europe and the Americas. Broadcast worldwide at this hour, it's too good to miss. To East Asia on 5990, 6195 and 9740 kHz; to Southeast Asia on 6195 and 9740 kHz; and to Australasia on 9740 kHz. Also audible in western North America on 9740 kHz.

Radio Canada International. Monday through Friday winters, there's a *news* bulletin followed by *Ontario Morning*. This is replaced Saturday by *The House* (current events), and Sunday by a science show, ●*Quirks and Quarks*. In summer, it's the Canadian Broadcasting Corporation's *This Morning*, and weekdays only. Sixty minutes to North America and the Caribbean winter on 9640, 13650 and 17715 kHz; and Monday through Friday summer on 9640, 13650, 17765 and 17820 kHz. For an additional service, see the next item.

Radio Canada International. Summers only at this time; see 1400 for program details. Sunday only to North America and the Caribbean on 13650 and 17800 kHz.

Radio Pyongyang, North Korea. Repeat of the 1100 transmission. One hour to Europe on 9345 and 11740 kHz, to North America on 13760 and 15230 kHz, and to South and Southeast Asia on 9640 and 15230 kHz.

13:00–13:30

Swiss Radio International. Winters only at this time. *World Radio Switzerland*—a workmanlike compilation of news and background reports on world and Swiss events. Look for a change of rhythm on Saturdays, when *Capital Letters* (a biweekly listener-response program) alternates with *Name Game* (first Saturday) and *Sounds Good* (music and interviews, third Saturday). Thirty minutes to southwestern Europe on 9535 kHz, and one hour earlier in summer.

Radio Vlaanderen Internationaal, Belgium. Winters only at this time. *News,* then *Press Review* (except Sunday), followed Monday through Friday by *Belgium Today* (various topics) and features like *The Arts* (Monday and Thursday, *Tourism* (Monday), *Focus on Europe* (Tuesday), *Living in Belgium* and *Green Society* (Wednesday), *Around Town* (Thursday), and *Economics* and *International Report*(Friday). Weekend features consist of Saturday's *Music from Flanders* and Sunday's *P.O. Box 26* (a listener-response program) and *Radio World.* Twenty-five minutes to North America on 13680 kHz.

China Radio International. Repeat of the 1200 broadcast; see there for specifics. One hour to western North America summers on 7405 (or 7265) kHz. Also year-round to Southeast Asia on 11980 and 15180 kHz; and to Australasia on 11675 and 11900 kHz. Also available to eastern North America on 9570 kHz, via an experimental Cuban relay (may be one hour later in winter).

Radio Polonia, Poland. This time winters only. *News,* commentary, music and a variety of features. See 1200 for specifics. Fifty-five minutes to Europe on 6095, 7145, 7270, 9525 and 11815 kHz. Listeners in southeastern Canada and the northeastern United States can also try 11815 kHz. One hour earlier during summer.

Radio Prague, Czech Republic. Summers only at this time. *News,* then Monday through Friday there's *Current Affairs,* followed by one or more features. Monday, there's *Spotlight;* Tuesday, it's *Talking Point;* Wednesday has *History Czech;* Thursday brings *Economic Report;* and Friday's feature is *Between You and Us,* a listener-response show. Saturday's offering is a highly recommended and thoroughly enjoyable musical feature, replaced Sunday by *A Letter from Prague, From the Weeklies* and *Readings from Czech Literature.* Thirty minutes to Europe on 13580 kHz, and to South Asia on 17485 kHz.

Radio Cairo, Egypt. The final half-hour of the 1215 broadcast, consisting of listener participation programs, Arabic language lessons and a summary of the latest news. To Asia on 17595 kHz.

CBC North-Québec, Canada. Continues with multilingual programming for a domestic audience. *News,* then winter Saturdays it's the second hour of ●*Good Morning Québec,* replaced Sunday by *Fresh Air.* In summer, the news is followed by *The House* (Canadian politics, Saturday) or the highly professional ●*Sunday Morning.* Weekday programs are mainly in languages other than English. Audible in the northeastern United States on 9625 kHz.

Radio Romania International. First afternoon broadcast for European listeners. *News,* commentary, press review, and features about Romanian life and culture, interspersed with some lively Romanian folk music. Fifty-five minutes winters on 11940, 15390 and 17745 kHz; summers on 9690, 11940, 15365 and 17720 kHz.

Radio Australia. Monday through Friday, there's a quarter-hour of *news* followed by 45 minutes of World Music in ●*The Planet.* Weekends, after five minutes of *news,* look for a relay of the domestic ABC Radio National service. Continuous programming to the Pacific on 5995, 6020 and 9580 kHz; and easily audible in much of North America on the last two frequencies.

Radio Singapore International. The third and final hour of a daily broadcasting package to Southeast Asia and beyond. Starts with a five-minute bulletin of the latest *news*, then most days it's music: *Singapop* (local talent, Monday and Thursday); *Music and Memories* (nostalgia, Tuesday); *Spin the Globe* (world music, Wednesday and Saturday); and *Hot Trax* (new releases, Saturday). *Friends of the Airwaves*, a listener-participation show, occupies the Sunday slot. There's more news on the half-hour, then a short feature. Monday's offering is *Snapshots*, replaced Tuesday by *Afterthought*. Wednesday and Thursday feature *Eco-Watch*, with the Thursday edition repeated the following Wednesday. The rest of the lineup consists of *Comment* (Friday), *The Written Word* (Saturday) and Sunday's *Reflections*. Weekdays, these are followed by *Newsline*, replaced Saturday by *Regional Press Review*, and Sunday by *Vox Box*. The broadcast ends with yet another five-minute news update. On 6015 and 6150 kHz.

WJCR, Upton, Kentucky. Continues with country gospel music to North America on 7490 kHz. Other U.S. religious broadcasters operating at this hour include **WWCR** on 5935 (or 13845) and 15685 kHz, **KTBN** 7510 kHz, **WYFR-Family Radio** on 5950, 6015 (or 9705), 11830 and 11970 (or 17750) kHz, and **WHRI-World Harvest Radio** on 6040 and 15105 kHz. Traditional Catholic programming is available via **WEWN** on 7425 kHz.

HCJB—Voice of the Andes, Ecuador. A further 60 minutes of religious broadcasting to the Americas on 12005 and 15115 kHz.

FEBC Radio International, Philippines. The first 60 minutes of a three-hour

(mostly religious) package to South and Southeast Asia. Weekdays, starts with *Good Evening Asia*, which includes *News Insight* and a number of five-minute features (world band enthusiasts should look for Wednesday's *DX Dial*). Other offerings include *World News Update* (1330 Monday through Saturday) and *News from the Philippines* (1335 weekdays). Most of the remaining features are religious in nature. On 11995 kHz.

Voice of America. A mix of current events and sports, science, business and other news and features. To East Asia on 6110 (or 6160), 9760, 11705 (winter) and 15160 kHz; and to Australasia on 9645 and 15425 kHz. Both areas are also served by 11715 kHz until 1330.

13:30

United Arab Emirates Radio, Dubai. *News*, then a feature devoted to Arab and Islamic history and culture. Twenty minutes to Europe and North Africa (also audible in eastern North America) on 13630, 13675, 15395 and 21605 kHz.

Radio Austria International. Winters only at this time. ●*Report from Austria* (see 1230 for more details). Thirty minutes to Europe on 6155 and 13730 kHz, and to eastern North America on 13730 kHz. One hour earlier in summer.

Voice of Turkey. This time winters only. *News*, followed by *Review of the Turkish Press* and features (some of them unusual) with a strong local flavor. Selections of Turkish popular and classical music complete the program. Fifty minutes to Europe on 15290 kHz, and to the Mideast, Southeast Asia and Australasia on 9630 kHz. One hour earlier in summer.

Radio Yugoslavia. Winters only at this time. *News* and short background reports with a strong local flavor. Worth a listen if

13:30–14:00

The Vinyl Cafe, reviewed on page 62, is produced by the CBC's Stuart McLean. It is aired overseas via Radio Canada International. CBC

you are interested in the region. Thirty minutes to Australasia on 11835 kHz.

YLE Radio Finland. Winter Sundays only at this hour; see 1230 for program specifics. Thirty minutes to North America on 11735 and 15400 kHz. One hour earlier in summer.

Radio Canada International. *News*, followed Monday through Friday by *Spectrum* (topical events), Saturday by *Venture Canada*, and Sunday by a listener-response program, *The Mailbag*. To East Asia on 6150 (winter), 9535, and (summer) 11795 kHz. Also to Europe, the Mideast and Africa, summers only, on 11935 and 15325 kHz.

Radio Sweden. See 1230 for program details. Thirty minutes to North America summers on 15240 kHz, and winters to Asia and Australasia on 9705 and 13740 kHz.

Voice of Vietnam. Begins with *news*, then there's *Commentary* or *Weekly Review*, followed by short features and some pleasant Vietnamese music (especially at weekends). A half hour to East Asia on 9840 and 12020 (or 13740) kHz. Also audible in parts of North America, especially during summer.

Voice of Greece. Winters only at this time, and actually starts around 1335. Several minutes of English news, surrounded by lots of Greek music and programming. To North America on 9420 and 15650 kHz. One hour earlier during summer.

All India Radio. The first half-hour of a 90-minute package of exotic Indian music, regional and International *news*, commentary, and a variety of talks and features of general interest. To Southeast Asia and beyond on 9545, 11620 and 13710 kHz.

Radio Tashkent, Uzbekistan. *News* and commentary, then features. Look for an information and music program on Tuesdays, with more music on Sundays. Apart from Wednesday's *Business Club*, most other features are broadcast on a non-weekly basis. Heard in Asia, Australasia, Europe and occasionally in North America; winters on 5060, 5975, 6025 and 9715 kHz; and summers on 7285, 9715, 15295 and 17775 kHz.

13:45

Vatican Radio. Twenty minutes of religious and secular programming to Southeast Asia and Australasia on 9500, 11625 and 13765 (or 15585) kHz.

14:00

■BBC World Service for the Americas, Europe and the Mideast. *World News*, followed Monday through Friday by a 25-minute 'science' feature. Monday's offering is ●*Health Matters*; Tuesday, it's ●*Discovery*; Wednesday spotlights the environment in ●*One Planet*; Thursday's theme is technology, with *The Works*; and Friday's slot is occupied by ●*Science in Action*. Quality programming, by any standard. The second half hour is devoted mostly to the arts, with Tuesday's *On Screen* (film news from around the world) likely to have the widest appeal. Weekend programming consists of Saturday's *Sportsworld* and a Sunday feature—often a panel or call-in show. Continuous to North America and the Caribbean on 9515, 9590 (winter), 11865 (summer), 15220 and 17840 kHz; to Europe on 9410 (winter), 12095, 15565 and 17640 kHz; and to the Mideast on 15575 kHz.

■BBC World Service for Asia and the Pacific. Similar to the service for Europe and the Americas, but with different features during the second half-hour, Monday through Friday. Regular shows include ●*The Farming World* (Monday) and Friday's ●*Performance* (classical music). Look for the highly informative ●*World Business Report* at 1445. Continuous to East Asia on 5990, 6195 and 9740 kHz; to Southeast Asia on 6195, 9740 and 15310 kHz; and to Australasia on 9740 kHz. Also audible in western North America on 9740 kHz.

Radio Japan. *News*, then Monday through Friday there's *44 Minutes* (an in-depth look at current trends and events in Japan). This is replaced Saturday by *Weekend Break* (discussion), and Sunday by *Asian Weekly*. One hour to the Mideast on 11880 kHz; to western North America on 9505 kHz; and to South Asia on 11730 kHz.

■Radio France Internationale. *News*, press reviews and correspondents' reports, with emphasis on events in Asia and the Mideast. These are followed, on the half-hour, by two or more short features (see the 1200 broadcast for specifics, although there may be one or two minor alterations). An hour's interesting and well-produced programming to the Mideast and beyond on 17560 kHz; and to South and Southeast Asia winters on 11610 and 17680 kHz. Listeners in western parts of Australia should also get reasonable reception on 17680 kHz.

Voice of Russia World Service. Summers only at this time. Eleven minutes of *News*, followed Monday through Saturday by much of the same in *News and Views*. Making up the list is *Sunday Panorama* and *Russia in Personalities*. On the half-hour, the lineup includes some of the station's better entertainment features. Try ●*Folk Box* (Monday), ●*Music at Your Request* or *Yours For the Asking* (Tuesday and Thursday), and Friday's retrospective ●*Moscow Yesterday and Today*, all of which should please. For different tastes, there's *Jazz Show* (Wednesday), *Kaleidoscope* (Sunday) and Saturday's *Timelines*. Mainly to the Mideast and West Asia at this hour. Try 4730, 4940 and 4975 kHz, plus frequencies in the 11 and 15 MHZ world band segments.

Radio Australia. Begins some days with *World News*, and the rest of the time it's a relay of domestic ABC Radio National programming. Continuous to the Pacific on 5995 and 9580 kHz (both channels are also widely heard in North America, especially to the west). Additionally available to East and Southeast Asia from 1430 on 9500 and 11660 kHz (may also be heard in Europe).

Swiss Radio International. *World Radio Switzerland*—news and background analysis of Swiss and world events. Some

14:00–14:30

lighter fare on Saturday, when *Capital Letters* (a biweekly listener-response program) alternates with *Name Game* (first Saturday) and *Sounds Good* (music and interviews, third Saturday). After the half-hour, it's music and interviews in *Rendez-vous with Switzerland*. Sixty minutes to East and Southeast Asia on 9575 or 12010 kHz; and to West and South Asia winter on 15185 kHz, replaced summer by 17670 kHz.

Radio Prague, Czech Republic. Winters only at this time. *News*, then weekdays it's *Current Affairs*. These are followed by one or more features. Take your pick from *Spotlight* (Monday), *Talking Point* (Tuesday), *History Czech* (Wednesday), Thursday's *Economic Report* and Friday's *Between You and Us*, a listener-response show. Saturday's offering is a thoroughly enjoyable musical feature, replaced Sunday by *A Letter from Prague, From the Weeklies* and *Readings from Czech Literature*. A half hour to eastern North America and East Africa on 21745 kHz.

Voice of America. This time winters only. The first of several hours of continuous programming to the Mideast. *News*, current events and short features covering sports, science, business, entertainment and other topics. On 15205 kHz.

XERMX—Radio México Internacional. Summers only at this time. Monday through Friday, there's a summary of the Spanish-language *Antena Radio*, replaced Saturday by *The Sounds of Mexico*, and Sunday by *Mirror of Mexico*. On the half-hour, look for 30 minutes of musical programming. Best heard in western and southern parts of the United States on 5985 and 9705 kHz. One hour later in winter.

Kol Israel. Summers only at this time. A 30-minute relay from Israel Radio's domestic network. To Europe and eastern North America on 15650 and 17535 kHz. One hour later in winter.

China Radio International. *News* and commentary, followed Monday through Friday by in-depth reports and a review of the Chinese press. Next come features like *Open Windows* and *Learn to Speak Chinese* (Monday); *Orient Arena* and *Opera House* (Tuesday); *Voices from Other Lands* (Wednesday); *Focus* and *Cultural Spectrum* (Thursday); and *Life in China* and *Global Review* (Friday). On weekends, Saturday's lineup includes *Asia-Pacific News, Report from Developing Countries, China Scrapbook* and ●*Music from China*; and Sunday there's *Cultural Information, People in the Know, On the Road* and *Listeners' Letterbox*. One hour to western North America on 7405 (or 7265) kHz; to South Asia and beyond on two or more channels from 9700, 11750, 11825 and 15110 kHz; and to Africa on 13685 and 15125 kHz.

All India Radio. The final hour of a 90-minute package of regional and International *news*, commentary, features and exotic Subcontinental music. To Southeast Asia and beyond on 9545, 11620 and 13710 kHz.

Radio Canada International. *News* and the Canadian Broadcasting Corporation's popular Sunday edition of ●*This Morning*. A three-hour broadcast starting at 1400 winters, and 1300 summers. Sunday only to North America and the Caribbean on 9640 (winter), 13650, 17715 (winter) and (summer) 17800 kHz.

HCJB—Voice of the Andes, Ecuador. Another hour of religious fare to the Americas on 12005 and 15115 kHz.

CBC North-Québec, Canada. Continues with multilingual programming for a domestic audience. *News*, followed winter Saturdays by *The House* (Canadian politics). In summer, it's *The Great Eastern*, a magazine for Newfoundlanders. Sundays, there's the excellent ●*Sunday Morning*. Weekday programs are in languages other than English. Audible in the northeastern United States on 9625 kHz.

Radio Jordan. Summers only at this time. A partial relay of the station's domestic broadcasts, beamed to Europe on 11690 kHz. Continuous till 1630, and one hour later in winter.

Voice of America. *News* and reports on a variety of topics. To East Asia on 6110 (or 6160), 9760, 11705 (winter) and 15160 kHz; and to Australasia on 15425 kHz.

FEBC Radio International, Philippines. Continues with mostly religious programming for South and Southeast Asia. For some secular fare, try *World News Update* (1430 Monday through Saturday) and *DX Dial* (for radio enthusiast, 1440 Saturday). On 11995 kHz, and widely heard beyond the target areas.

Radio Thailand. Thirty minutes of *news* and short features for Southeast Asia and Australasia; winters on 9530 kHz, and summers on 9830 kHz.

WJCR, Upton, Kentucky. Continues with country gospel music to North America on 7490 kHz. Other U.S. religious broadcasters operating at this hour include **WWCR** on 13845 and 15685 kHz, **KTBN** on 7510 kHz, **WYFR-Family Radio** on 5950, 9705 (winter), 11830 and 17750 kHz, and **WHRI-World Harvest Radio** on 6040 and 15105 kHz. For traditional Catholic fare, try **WEWN** on 7425 kHz.

CFRX-CFRB, Toronto, Canada. Audible throughout much of the northeastern United States and southeastern Canada during the hours of daylight with a modest, but clear, signal on 6070 kHz. This pleasant, friendly station carries news, sports, weather and traffic reports—most of it intended for a local audience. Call in if you'd like at +1 (514) 790-0600—comments from outside Ontario are welcomed. Weekdays at this hour, you can hear *The Charles Adler Show*.

14:30

■**Radio Netherlands.** *News*, then Monday through Friday it's ●*Newsline* and a feature. Pick of an excellent pack are ●*Research File* (science, Monday); ●*A Good Life* (Friday); ●*Weekend* (Saturday) and Wednesday's award-winning ●*Documentary*. *Music 52-15* (Tuesday) and *Media Network* (Thursday) complete the lineup. Sunday fare consists of *Sincerely Yours* (a listener-response program) and *Sounds Interesting*. Aimed at South Asia, winters on 12070, 12090 and 15590 kHz; and summers on 9890, 12075 and 15585 kHz.

Radio Canada International. This time winters only. *News*, followed Monday through Friday by *Spectrum* (current events), Saturday by *Venture Canada* (business), and Sunday by *The Mailbag* (a listener-response program). Thirty minutes to Europe and the Mideast on 9555 kHz. One hour earlier in summer.

Voice of Mongolia. *News*, reports and short features, with Sunday featuring lots of exotic Mongolian music. Thirty minutes to South and Southeast Asia on 9720 and 12085 kHz. Frequencies may vary slightly.

Radio Romania International. Fifty-five minutes of *news*, commentary, features and some enjoyable Romanian folk music. Targeted at the Mideast and South Asia winters on 11740, 11810 and 15335 kHz; an summers on 11775 and 15335 kHz.

Radio Sweden. Winters only at this time. Repeat of the 1330 broadcast; see 1230 for program specifics. *News* and features (sometimes on controversial subjects not

14:30–15:00

George Otis, founder and head of High Adventure Ministries, reads from the Bible at a Voice of Hope studio. High Adventure

often discussed on radio), with the accent strongly on Scandinavia. Thirty minutes to North America on 11650 and 15240 kHz, and to Asia and Australasia on 11880 kHz.

15:00

■BBC World Service for the Americas, Europe and the Mideast. *News*, followed Monday through Thursday by 10 minutes of ●*Sports Roundup* (replaced Friday by *Football Extra*). The remainder is a thoroughly mixed bag of programs—some of them forgettable—depending on the day of the week. Try the following, all on the half-hour: ●*Composer of the Month* (classical music, Monday); ●*Everywoman* (Tuesday); *Jazzmattaz* (Wednesday); ●*The Greenfield Collection* (classical music, Thursday); and the inimitable●*John Peel* on Friday. Aficionados of classical music will not want to miss ●*Concert Hall* (or its substitute) at 1515 Sunday, while sports fans should tune to the second hour of Saturday's live extravaganza, *Sportsworld*.

Continuous to North America on 9515, 9590 (winter), 11865 (summer), 15220 and 17840 kHz; to Europe on 9410, 12095 and 15575 kHz; and to the Mideast on 12095 kHz.

■BBC World Service for South Asia. A Sunday opportunity to hear the best in world theater—●*Play of the Week*. On other days, this frequency carries mainstream programming for Asia and the Pacific. On 6195 kHz.

■BBC World Service for Asia and the Pacific. Monday through Friday, it's a half hour of ●*East Asia Today* followed by 15 minutes each of ●*Insight* (current events) and ●*Off the Shelf* (readings from world literature). Weekends, look for Saturday's *Sportsworld*, replaced Sunday by ●*From Our Own Correspondent* and *Global Business*. Be warned—the Sunday features are sometimes preempted by live sports. Continuous to East Asia on 5990, 6195 and 9740 kHz; to Southeast Asia on 6195, 9740 and 15310 kHz; and to Australasia on 9740 kHz. The ubiquitous 9740 kHz can also be heard in western North America.

China Radio International. See 1400 for program details. Sixty minutes to western North America winters on 7405 kHz, and one hour earlier during summer. Also available year-round to South Asia and beyond on 7160, 7215 and 9785 kHz; and to Africa on 13685 and 15125 kHz.

Radio Australia. Continuous programming to Asia and the Pacific. At this hour there's a relay of the domestic ABC Radio National service. To the Pacific on 5995 and 9580 kHz (also well heard in western North America). Additionally available to East and Southeast Asia on 9500 and 11660 kHz (may also be heard in Europe).

Radio Pyongyang, North Korea. See 1100 for program details. One hour to Europe, the Mideast and beyond on 9325, 9640, 9975 and 13785 kHz.

Voice of America. Continues with programming to the Mideast. A mixed bag of current events and sports, science, business and other news and features. Winters on 9575 and 15205 kHz, and summers on 9700 and 15205 kHz. Also heard in much of Europe.

Kol Israel. Winters only at this time. A 30-minute relay from Israel Radio's domestic network. To Europe and eastern North America on 9365 and 12080 kHz. One hour earlier in summer.

Radio Canada International. Continuation of the Sunday edition of the CBC domestic program ●*This Morning*. Sunday only to North America and the Caribbean on 9640 (winter), 13650, 17715 (winter) and (summer) 17800 kHz.

XERMX—Radio México Internacional. Winter weekdays, there's an English summary of the Spanish-language *Antena Radio*, replaced Saturday by *The Sounds of Mexico*, and Sunday by *Mirror of Mexico*. Summers, the lineup consists of *Universal Forum* (Monday and Friday), *Eternally Mexico* (Tuesday and Sunday) and *Mailbox* (Wednesday and Saturday). On Thursday, the English program is replaced by one in French. On the half-hour, look for 30 minutes of musical programming. Best heard in western and southern parts of the United States on 5985 and 9705 kHz.

Radio Japan. *News*, then Tuesday through Saturday there's *Asian Top News*. This is followed by a half-hour feature. Take your pick from *Music Reflections* (Tuesday), *Let's Try Japanese* (Wednesday), *Music Journey Around Japan* (Thursday), *My Japan Diary* (Friday), and *Music Beat* (Saturday). *Asian Weekly* fills the Sunday slot, and Monday's offering is *Hello from Tokyo*. One hour to western North America on 9505 kHz; to East Asia on 9750 kHz; to South Asia on 11730 kHz; and to Southeast Asia on 7200 kHz.

Voice of Russia World Service. Predominantly news-related fare for the first half-hour, then a mixed bag, depending on the day and season. At 1531 winter, look for ●*Folk Box* (Monday), *Jazz Show* (Wednesday), ●*Music at Your Request* or *Yours For the Asking* (Tuesday and Thursday), the multifaceted *Kaleidoscope* (Sunday) and Friday's retrospective ●*Moscow Yesterday and Today*. Summers at this time, look for some listener favorites. Take your pick from *This is Russia* (Monday), ●*Moscow Yesterday and Today* (Tuesday's journey into history), ●*Audio Book Club* (dramatized reading, Wednesday), ●*Folk Box* (Thursday), and ●*Songs from Russia* on Friday. Weekend fare is split between Saturday's *Kaleidoscope* and Sunday's *Russian by Radio*. Continuous to the Mideast and West Asia on 4730, 4940 and 4975 kHz, as well as frequencies in other world band segments. Winters, dial

15:00–16:00

around the 7 and 9 MHZ ranges; in summer, try 7325 and 12070 kHz.

FEBC Radio International, Philippines. The final 60 minutes of a three-hour (mostly religious) broadcast to South and Southeast Asia. For secular programming, try the five-minute *World News Update* at 1530 Monday through Saturday, and a listener-response feature at 1540 Saturday. On 11995 kHz, and often heard outside the target area.

WJCR, Upton, Kentucky. Continues with country gospel music to North America on 7490 and 13595 kHz. Other U.S. religious broadcasters operating at this hour include **WWCR** on 13845 and 15685 kHz, **KTBN** on 7510 (or 15590) kHz, and **WYFR-Family Radio** on 11830 and (winter) 15215 kHz. Traditional Catholic programming is available from **WEWN** on 7425 kHz.

Radio Jordan. A partial relay of the station's domestic broadcasts, beamed to Europe on 11690 kHz. Continuous till 1730, and one hour earlier in summer.

CFRX-CFRB, Toronto, Canada. See 1400. Monday through Friday, it's a continuation of *The Charles Adler Show*. Look for *News and Commentary* summers at 1550. Weekend fare consists of *The CFRB Gardening Show* (Saturday) replaced the following day by *CFRB Sunday*. On 6070 kHz.

15:30

■Radio Netherlands. The second of two hours aimed at South Asia, but heard well beyond. *News*, followed Monday through Friday by ●*Newsline*, then a feature. Choice selections include ●*EuroQuest* (Monday), ●*A Good Life* (Tuesday), ●*Research File* (science, Thursday), ●*Roughly Speaking* (an award-winning youth program, Saturday) and Friday's ●*Documentary* (winner of several presti-

gious awards). Other offerings include *Aural Tapestry* (Sunday), *Sounds Interesting* (Wednesday), *Europe Unzipped* (Saturday) and Sunday's *Wide Angle*. Winters on 12070, 12090 and 15590 kHz; and summers on 9890, 12075 and 15590 kHz.

Voice of the Islamic Republic of Iran. Sixty minutes of *news*, commentary and features, most of it reflecting the Islamic point of view. To South and Southeast Asia (and also heard elsewhere) on 9575 (winter), 11790 (winter), 11875 (summer), 15260 and 17750 kHz.

15:45

Radio Tirana, Albania. Summers only at this time. Approximately 15 minutes of *news* and commentary from and about Albania. To Europe on 11735 and 12085 kHz.

16:00

■BBC World Service for the Americas, Europe and the Mideast. Winter weekdays, the half-hour ●*Newsdesk* is followed by a 15-minute feature and ●*Sports Roundup*. Pick of the features are Wednesday's ●*Performance* (classical music) and Friday's ●*Short Story*. In summer, the hour starts with ●*Europe Today*, which is followed by 15 minutes of unmatched financial reporting in ●*World Business Report*. The final slot goes to ●*Insight* (analysis of current events). Weekends, a five-minute bulletin of *World News* is followed by *Sportsworld*. Continuous to North America on 9515 (till 1630 Sunday through Friday, and a full hour on Saturday) and 17840 kHz. Also to Europe on 9410, 12095 and 15575 kHz; and to the Mideast on 12095 kHz.

■BBC World Service for Asia and the Pacific. Fifteen minutes of *World News*, then weekdays it's a series of shows with the accent mostly on music. Popular choices are Tuesday's ●*John Peel*, Thursday's *The Vintage Chart Show*, and Friday's ●*Andy Kershaw's World of Music*. Weekends are given over to *Sportsworld*. The final hour to East Asia on 6195 kHz; and continuous to Southeast Asia on 3915, 6195, 7160 and 15310 kHz.

■**Radio France Internationale.** *News*, press reviews and correspondents' reports, with particular attention paid to events in Africa. These are followed by two or more short features (basically a repeat of the 1200 broadcast, except for weekends when there is more emphasis on African themes). A fast-moving hour to Africa on 11615, 11995, 12015, 15210 and 17605 or 17850 kHz.

United Arab Emirates Radio, Dubai. Starts with a feature on Arab history or culture, then music, and a bulletin of *news* at 1630. Answers listeners' letters at weekends. Forty minutes to Europe and North Africa (also heard in eastern North America) on 13630, 13675, 15395 and 21605 kHz.

■**Deutsche Welle,** Germany. *News*, then Monday through Friday it's ●*NewsLink* followed by *Africa Report*. Weekends, the Saturday news is followed by *Talking Point* and ●*Spectrum*, with *Religion and Society* and *Arts on the Air* filling the Sunday slots. Forty-five minutes aimed primarily at eastern, central and southern parts of Africa, but also audible outside the continent. Winter on 9735, 11785, 15145, 17800 and 21780 kHz; and summer on 9735, 11810, 15135 and 21695 kHz. For a separate service to South Asia and beyond, see the next entry.

■**Deutsche Welle,** Germany. Similar to the broadcast for Africa (see previous entry), except that *Asia-Pacific Report* replaces *Africa Report*, and *Cool* is aired in place of Sunday's *Arts on the Air*. Nomi-

nally to South Asia, but heard well beyond. Winter on 6170, 7225, 7305, 15380 and 17810 kHz; and summer on 6170, 7225, 7305 and 17595 kHz.

Radio Korea International, South Korea. Opens with *news* and commentary, followed Monday through Wednesday by *Seoul Calling*. Weekly features include *Echoes of Korean Music* and *Shortwave Feedback* (Sunday), *Tales from Korea's Past* (Monday), *Korean Cultural Trails* (Tuesday), *Pulse of Korea* (Wednesday), *From Us to You* (a listener-response program) and *Let's Learn Korean* (Thursday), *Let's Sing Together* and *Korea Through Foreigners' Eyes* (Friday), and Saturday's *Discovering Korea*, *Korean Literary Corner* and *Weekly News Focus*. One hour to East Asia on 5975 kHz, and to the Mideast and much of Africa on 9515 and 9870 kHz.

Radio Pakistan. Fifteen minutes of *news* from the Pakistan Broadcasting Corporation's domestic service. Intended for the Mideast and Africa, but heard well beyond on several channels. Try 9650, 11570, 15170, 15375, 15570 and 17720 kHz, some of which are seasonal.

Radio Prague, Czech Republic. Summers only at this time. *News*, then Monday through Friday there's *Current Affairs*. This is followed by *Spotlight* (Monday), *Talking Point* (Tuesday), *History Czech* (Wednesday), Thursday's *Economic Report*, and *Between You and Us* (a listener-response show) in the Friday slot. Weekend fare consists of a Saturday musical feature (well worth hearing), and Sunday's *A Letter from Prague*, *From the Weeklies* and *Readings from Czech Literature*. A half hour to Europe on 5930 kHz, and to East Africa on 21745 kHz. One hour later in winter.

Radio Algiers, Algeria. *News*, then western and Arab popular music, with an occasional feature thrown in. One hour of so-so reception in Europe, and sometimes heard in eastern North America. On 11715 and 15160 kHz.

Voice of Vietnam. *News*, followed by *Commentary* or *Weekly Review*, then some short features and pleasant Vietnamese music (especially at weekends). A half hour to Africa (and heard well beyond) on 9840 and 12020 (or 9730) kHz.

Radio Australia. Continuous to Asia and the Pacific. At this hour there's a relay of domestic ABC Radio National programs. Beamed to the Pacific on 5995 and 9580 kHz (also well heard in western North America). Additionally available to East and Southeast Asia on 9500 and 11660 kHz (may also be heard in Europe).

Radio Ethiopia. An hour-long broadcast divided into two parts by the 1630 *news* bulletin. Regular weekday features include *Kaleidoscope* and *Women's Forum* (Monday), *Press Review* and *Africa in Focus* (Tuesday), *Guest of the Week* and *Ethiopia Today* (Wednesday), *Ethiopian Music* and *Spotlight* (Thursday) and *Press Review* and *Introducing Ethiopia* on Friday. For weekend listening, try *Contact* and *Ethiopia This Week* (Saturday), or Sunday's *Listeners' Choice* and *Commentary*. Best heard in parts of Africa and the Mideast, but sometimes audible in Europe. On 7165, 9560 and 11800 kHz.

Radio Jordan. A partial relay of the station's domestic broadcasts, beamed to Europe on 11690 kHz. Continuous till 1730 (1630 during winter).

Voice of Russia World Service. *News*, then very much a mixed bag, depending on the day and season. Winter weekdays, there's *Focus on Asia and the Pacific*, with Saturday's *Newmarket* and Sunday's program preview making up the week. On the half-hour, choose from *This is Russia* (Monday), ●*Moscow Yesterday and Today* (Tuesday), ●*Audio Book Club* (dramatized

reading, Wednesday), the exotic and eclectic ●*Folk Box* (Thursday), and Friday's ●*Songs from Russia*. Weekend fare is split between Saturday's *Kaleidoscope* and Sunday's *Russian by Radio*. Summers, the news is followed by the business-oriented *Newmarket* (Monday and Thursday), *Science and Engineering* (Tuesday and Sunday), *Moscow Mailbag* (Wednesday and Friday), and Saturday's showpiece, ●*Music and Musicians*. On the half-hour, look for ●*The 20th Century: Year After Year* (Monday, Wednesday and Friday), and *Timelines* (Sunday). On Tuesday and Thursday you can hear "alternative programs"—religious paid programming or a show from the Voice of Russia's archives or transcription department. Continuous to the Mideast and West Asia on 4730, 4940 and 4975 kHz, as well as frequencies in other world band segments. Winter, dial around the 7 and 9 MHz ranges (try 7210 and 9775 kHz); in summer, 11 and 15 MHz should give better results (take a look at 12070 and 15490 kHz).

Radio Canada International. Winters only. Final hour of the Sunday edition of CBC's ●*This Morning*. Sunday only to North America and the Caribbean on 9640, 13650 and 17715 kHz.

XERMX—Radio México Internacional. Winters only at this time. Starts with a feature: *Universal Forum* (Monday and Friday), *Eternally Mexico* (Tuesday and Sunday) and *Mailbox* (Wednesday and Saturday). Thursdays, the English program is replaced by one in French. On the half-hour, there's 30 minutes of music. Best heard in western and southern parts of the United States on 5985 and 9705 kHz.

China Radio International. *News* and commentary, followed Monday through Friday by in-depth reporting and an overview of the Chinese press. This is followed by features like *Focus* and *Cultural Spectrum* (Thursday); *Open Windows* and *Learn to Speak Chinese* (Monday); *Orient Arena* and *Opera House* (Tuesday); *Voices from Other Lands* (Wednesday); and *Life in China* and *Global Review* (Friday). Weekends, Saturday's lineup includes *Asia-Pacific News, Report from Developing Countries, China Scrapbook* and ●*Music from China*. These are replaced Sunday by *Cultural Information, People in the Know, On the Road* and *Listeners' Letterbox*. One hour to eastern and southern Africa on 9565 and 9870 kHz.

Voice of America. Several hours of continuous programming aimed at an African audience. At this hour, there's a split between mainstream programming and news and features in "Special" (slow-speed) English. The former can be heard on 6035, 13710, 15225 and 15410 kHz, and the "Special" programs on 13600, 15445 and (summer) 17895 kHz. For a separate service to the Mideast, see the next item.

Voice of America. *News Now*—a mixed bag of news and reports on current events, sports, science, business and more. To the Mideast winters on 9575 and 15205 kHz, and summers on 9700 and 15205 kHz. Also heard in much of Europe.

WJCR, Upton, Kentucky. Continues with country gospel music to North America on 7490 and 13595 kHz. Other U.S. religious broadcasters operating at this hour include **WWCR** on 13845 and 15685 kHz, **KTBN** on 15590 kHz, and **WYFR-Family Radio** on 11705 (or 15215) and 11830 kHz. Traditional Catholic programming can be heard via **WEWN** on 7425 kHz.

CFRX-CFRB, Toronto, Canada. See 1400. Winter weekdays, it's the final part of *The Charles Adler Show*, with *The CFRB Gardening Show* and *CFRB Sunday* the weekend offerings. Summers, look for *The Motts*

Monday through Friday, and ●*The World at Noon* on weekends.

16:30

Radio Slovakia International. Summers only at this time; see 1730 for specifics. Thirty minutes of friendly programming to Western Europe on 5920, 6055 and 7345 kHz. One hour later in winter.

Radio Vlaanderen Internationaal, Belgium. Summers only at this time. Weekdays, there's *News, Press Review* and *Belgium Today*, followed by features like *Focus on Europe* (Monday), *Living in Belgium* and *Green Society* (Tuesday), *The Arts* (Wednesday and Friday), *Around Town* (Wednesday), *Economics* and *International Report* (Thursday), and *Tourism* (Friday). Weekend features include *Music from Flanders* (Saturday) and Sunday's *P.O. Box 26* (a listener-response program) and *Radio World*. Twenty-five minutes to Europe on 5910 and 7290 kHz. One hour later in winter.

Radio Canada International. *News,* then Monday through Friday it's *Spectrum* (current events). *Venture Canada* airs on Saturday, and *The Mailbag*, a listener-response program occupies Sunday's slot. A half hour to South Asia and beyond on 6140 and 7150 kHz.

Radio Austria International. Summers only at this time. See 1730 for more details. An informative half-hour of ●*Report from Austria*. Available to Europe on 6155 and 13730 kHz, to the Mideast on 11855 kHz, and to South and Southeast Asia on 13710 kHz. One hour later in winter.

Radio Cairo, Egypt. The first 30 minutes of a two-hour package of Arab music and features reflecting Egyptian life and culture,

16:30–17:00

Wind power generation fits in naturally with centuries-old architecture in Mallorca.   Stuart Pearce

with *news*, commentary, quizzes, mailbag shows, and answers to listeners' questions. To southern Africa on 15255 kHz.

17:00

■**BBC World Service for the Americas, Europe and the Mideast.** Winter weekdays, the hour starts with ●*Europe Today*, which is followed by 15 minutes of top-notch financial reporting in ●*World Business Report*. The final quarter-hour slot is filled by ●*Insight* (analysis of current events). In summer, the half-hour ●*Newsdesk* is followed by a 15-minute feature and ●*Sports Roundup*. Best of the features are ●*Performance* (classical music, Wednesday) and Friday's ●*Short Story*. Saturdays, ●*Newsdesk* is followed winters by *Sportsworld*, and summers by *Write On* (or *Waveguide*) and ●*Sports Roundup*. Sundays on the half-hour, look for ●*Letter From America* and yet another edition of ●*Sports Roundup*. Continuous to western North America on 17840 kHz; to Europe on 6195 (winter), 9410 and 12095 kHz; and to the Mideast on 9410, 11970 (or 11995) and 12095 kHz.

■**BBC World Service for Africa.** *World News*, *Focus on Africa*, and ●*Sports Roundup*. Part of a 20-hour daily service to the African continent on a variety of channels. At this hour, try 3255, 6190, 15400, 15420 and 17830 kHz. The last three channels are widely heard outside Africa, including parts of North America.

■**BBC World Service for Asia.** ●*Newsdesk*, then Monday through Friday there's ●*Off the Shelf* (readings from world literature). This is replaced Saturday by ●*Performance* (classical music), and Sunday by ●*Letter From America*. At 1745 you can catch up with the latest sports news in the daily ●*Sports Roundup*. The final hour of broadcasting to Southeast Asia on 3915 and 7160 kHz.

Radio Prague, Czech Republic. See 1600 for program specifics. A half hour of *news* and features beamed to Europe on 5930 kHz; also winters to West Africa on 17485 kHz, and summers to southern Africa on 21745 kHz.

Radio Australia. Continuous programming to Asia and the Pacific. At this hour there's a relay of the domestic ABC Radio

National service. Beamed to the Pacific on 5995, 9580 and 11880 kHz (and also heard in western North America). Additionally available to East and Southeast Asia on 9500 kHz (may also be heard in Europe).

Radio Polonia, Poland. This time summers only. Monday through Friday, it's *News from Poland*—a compendium of news, reports and interviews. This is followed by *Request Concert* and *A Day in the Life of...* (Monday), classical music and the historical *Flashback* (Tuesday), a communications feature and *Letter from Poland* (Wednesday), a feature and a talk or special report (Thursday), and Friday's *Focus* (the arts in Poland) followed by *Business Week*. The Saturday broadcast begins with a bulletin of *news*, then there's *Weekend Papers* (a press review), *Panorama* (a window on day-to-day life in Poland) and a listener-response program, *Postbag*. Sundays, you can hear *What We Said* (a summary of the station's output during the previous week) and *Jazz, Folk, Rock and Pop from Poland*. Fifty-five minutes to Europe on 6095, 7270 and 7285 kHz. One hour later during winter.

Radio Jordan. Winters only at this time. The last 30 minutes of a partial relay of the station's domestic broadcasts, beamed to Europe on 11690 kHz.

Voice of Russia World Service. *News*, then it's a mixed bag, depending on the day and season. Winters, the news is followed by the business-oriented *Newmarket* (Monday and Thursday), *Science and Engineering* (Tuesday and Sunday), *Moscow Mailbag* (Wednesday and Friday) and Saturday's 45-minute ●*Music and Musicians*. Tuesday and Thursday on the half-hour, you can hear "alternative programs"—religious paid programming or a show from the Voice of Russia's archives or transcription department. *Timelines* takes the Sunday slot, and ●*The 20th*

Century: Year After Year occupies the Monday, Wednesday and Friday berths. In summer, the news is followed by a series of features: *Moscow Mailbag* (Monday and Thursday), *Newmarket* (Tuesday and Friday), *Science and Engineering* (Wednesday and Saturday), and one of Moscow's musical jewels, ●*Music and Musicians*, on Sunday. On the half-hour, the lineup includes *Kaleidoscope* (Monday), ●*Moscow Yesterday and Today* (Wednesday), *Yours For the Asking* or●*Music at Your Request* (Tuesday), Friday's ●*Folk Box* and Saturday's ●*Songs from Russia*. Not to be missed is Thursday's ●*Russian Musical Highlights of the 20th Century*. To Europe summers on 9720, 9775, 9820, 11675 and 15545 kHz. Also to the Mideast winters—try 7305 and 9470 kHz. There's nothing officially for southern Africa, but 12065 kHz is worth a shot in summer.

Radio Japan. *News*, then Tuesday through Saturday there's in-depth reporting of Japanese events in *44 Minutes*. Sunday's offering is *Hello From Tokyo*, replaced Monday by *Weekend Break*. One hour to Europe on 7110 kHz; to southern Africa on 15355 kHz; and to Southeast Asia on 9825 kHz.

Radio Pyongyang, North Korea. Repeat of the 1100 transmission. One hour to Europe, the Mideast and beyond on 9325, 9640, 9975 and 13785 kHz.

China Radio International. Repeat of the 1600 transmission. One hour to eastern and southern parts of Africa on 7150 (winter), 7405, 9570, 9745 (winter) and (midyear) 11910 kHz.

Voice of America. Continuous programming to the Mideast and North Africa. *News*, then Monday through Friday it's the interactive *Talk to America*. Weekends, there's the ubiquitous *News Now*. Winters on 6040, 9760 and 15205 kHz; and summers on 9760, 15135 and 15255 kHz.

17:00–17:45

Also heard in much of Europe. For a separate service to Africa, see the next item.

Voice of America. Programs for Africa. Monday through Saturday, identical to the service for Europe and the Mideast (see previous item). Sunday on the half-hour, look for the entertaining ●*Music Time in Africa*. Audible well beyond where it is targeted. On 6035, 7415, 11920, 11975, 12040, 13710, 15410, 15445 and 17895 kHz, some of which are seasonal. For yet another service (to East Asia and the Pacific), see the next item.

Voice of America. Monday through Friday only. *News*, followed by the interactive *Talk to America*. Sixty minutes to Asia on 5990, 6045, 6110/6160, 7125, 7215, 9525, 9645, 9670, 9770, 11945, 12005 and 15255 kHz, some of which are seasonal. For Australasia, try 9525 and 15255 kHz in winter, and 7150 and 7170 kHz in summer.

■Radio France Internationale. An additional half-hour (see 1600) of predominantly African fare. To East Africa on any two frequencies from 11615, 15210 and 17605 kHz. Also audible in parts of the Mideast, and occasionally heard in eastern North America.

Radio Cairo, Egypt. See 1630 for specifics. Continues with a broadcast to southern Africa on 15255 kHz.

WJCR, Upton, Kentucky. Continues with country gospel music to North America on 7490 and 13595 kHz. Other U.S. religious broadcasters operating at this hour include **WWCR** on 13845 and 15685 kHz, **KTBN** on 15590 kHz, and **WHRI-World Harvest Radio** on 13760 and 15105 kHz.

CFRX-CFRB, Toronto, Canada. See 1400. Winter weekends at this time, there's ●*The World at Noon*; summers, it's *The Mike Stafford Show*. Monday through Friday, look for *The Motts*. On 6070 kHz.

17:30

■Radio Netherlands. Targeted at Africa, but heard well beyond. *News*, then Monday through Friday there's *Newsline* and a feature. Choice plums include ●*Research File* (Monday), ●*Documentary* (Wednesday), ●*A Good Life* (Friday), and Saturday's ●*Weekend*. For another interesting offering, try the eclectic *Music 52-15* aired each Tuesday. Other programs include Thursday's *Media Network* and Sunday's *Sincerely Yours* and *Sounds Interesting*. Monday through Friday there is also a *Press Review*. Sixty minutes on 6020 (best for southern Africa), 7120 (summer) and 11655 kHz.

Radio Austria International. Winters only at this time. ●*Report from Austria*, a half hour of news and human interest stories. Ample coverage of national and regional issues. To Europe on 6155 and 13730 kHz; to the Mideast on 9655 kHz; and to South and Southeast Asia on 13710 kHz. One hour earlier in summer

Radio Slovakia International. Winters only at this time. *Slovakia Today*, a 30-minute look at Slovak life and culture. Tuesday, there's a mixed bag of short features; Wednesday puts the accent on tourism and Slovak personalities; Thursday's slot is devoted to business and economy; and Friday brings a mix of politics, education and science. Saturday offerings include cultural items, *Slovak Kitchen* and the off-beat *Back Page News*; and Sunday brings the *"Best of"* series. Monday's show is more relaxed, and includes *Listeners' Tribune* and some enjoyable Slovak music. A friendly half hour to Western Europe on 5915, 6055 and 7345 kHz. One hour earlier in summer.

Radio Sweden. Summers only at this hour; see 1830 for program specifics. Thirty minutes of Scandinavian fare for

Tashkent's largest marketplace is alongside a dome softened by traditional architectural features. M. Guha

Europe, the Mideast and Africa on 6065 (Monday through Saturday), 13855 (Sunday) and 15735 kHz. One hour later during winter.

Radio Vlaanderen Internationaal, Belgium. Weekdays, there's *News*, *Press Review* and *Belgium Today*, followed by features like *Focus on Europe* (Monday), *Living in Belgium* and *Green Society* (Tuesday), *The Arts* (Wednesday and Friday), *Around Town* (Wednesday), *Economics* and *International Report* (Thursday), and *Tourism* (Friday). Weekend features include *Music from Flanders* (Saturday) and Sunday's *P.O. Box 26* (a listener-response program) and *Radio World*. Twenty-five minutes to Europe winters on 5910 and 9925 kHz; also to Africa summers on 17655 kHz; and year round to the Mideast on 11680 (winter) or (summer) 11810 kHz.

Radio Romania International. *News*, commentary, a press review, and one or more short features. Thirty minutes to Eastern and Southern Africa (also audible in parts of the Mideast). Winters on 9750, 11740 and 11940 kHz; and summers on 9550, 9750, 11830 and 11940 kHz.

Radio Almaty, Kazakhstan. Winters only at this time. Due to financial constraints, news and features have largely been replaced by recordings of exotic Kazakh music. If you like world music, this is definitely a station to try for. Heard in much of Asia on 9505 kHz. One hour earlier in summer.

17:45

All India Radio. The first 15 minutes of a two-hour broadcast to Europe and Africa, consisting of regional and International *news*, commentary, a variety of talks and features, press review and exotic Indian music. Continuous till 1945. To Europe on 7410, 9950 and 11620 kHz; and to Africa on 11935, 13780 and 15075 kHz. Easily audible in the Mideast, but dial around to find the best frequency for your location.

1800-2359
Europe & Mideast—Evening Prime Time
East Asia—Early Morning
Australasia—Morning
Eastern North America—Afternoon
Western North America—Midday

18:00

■**BBC World Service for the Americas, Europe and the Mideast.** Starts with 15 minutes of *World News*, then ●*Britain Today*. The second half hour is given over to features. Sunday, there's ●*Play of the Week* (world theater at its very best); Tuesday's offering is the top-notch ●*Omnibus*; Wednesday, has *Sports International*; and Friday spotlights religion in●*Focus on Faith*. The Saturday slot is given to a European co-production, ●*Weekend*. To North America winters on 17840 kHz; year round to Europe on 3955 (winter), 6195, 9410 and 12095 kHz; and to the Mideast on 9410, 11970 (or 11995) and 12095 kHz.

■**BBC World Service for Africa.** *World News*, then Monday through Friday it's ●*World Business Report* and *Focus on Africa*. Weekends, there's ●*Britain Today* followed by Saturday's ●*World Business Review* and a 15-minute feature or Sunday's *Global Business*. Continuous programming to the African continent (and heard well beyond) on 3255, 6005 (from 1830), 6190, 9630 (from 1830), 15400 and 17830 kHz. The last two channels are audible in parts of North America.

■**BBC World Service for the Pacific.** Identical to the service for Europe during the first half hour, but with different features some days at 1830. To Australasia on 9740 kHz.

Radio Kuwait. The start of a three-hour package of *news*, Islamic-oriented features and western popular music. Some interesting features, even if you don't particularly like the music. There is a full program summary at the beginning of each transmission, to enable you to pick and choose. To Europe and eastern North America on 11990 kHz.

Voice of Vietnam. Begins with *news*, then there's *Commentary* or *Weekly Review*, followed by short features and some pleasant Vietnamese music (especially at weekends). A half hour to Europe on 9840 and 12020 (or 9730) kHz.

Radio For Peace International, Costa Rica. Part of a continuous eight-hour cyclical block of predominantly social-conscience and counterculture programming. To Europe and North America on 15050 and 21460 kHz.

All India Radio. Continuation of the transmission to Europe, Africa and the Mideast (see 1745). *News* and commentary, followed by programming of a more general nature. To Europe on 7410, 9950 and 11620 kHz; and to Africa on 11935, 13780 and 15075 kHz. In the Mideast, choose the channel best suited to your location.

Radio Prague, Czech Republic. Winters only at this time. *News*, then Monday through Friday there's *Current Affairs*, followed by one or more features.

Monday's offering is *Spotlight*; Tuesday, it's *Talking Point*; Wednesday features *History Czech*; Thursday brings *Economic Report*; and Friday has *Between You and Us*, a listener-response show. The Saturday slot is taken by a thoroughly enjoyable musical feature, replaced Sunday by *A Letter from Prague*, *From the Weeklies* and *Readings from Czech Literature*. A half hour to Europe on 5930 kHz, and to Australasia on 7315 kHz.

Radio Australia. Friday and Saturday, you can hear a relay of the domestic ABC Radio National service. On the remaining days there's a ten-minute bulletin of world *news*, followed by regional news in *Asia Pacific*. Part of a continuous 24-hour service, and at this hour beamed to the Pacific on 6080, 7240, 9580, 9660 and 11880 kHz. Additionally available to East and Southeast Asia on 9500 kHz (may also be heard in Europe). In western North America, try 9580 and 11880 kHz.

Radio Nacional do Brasil, Brazil. This service, much improved during the first half of 1999, left the air around midyear when the parent organization, Radiobrás, was wound up by the government. It is not known if or when the successor to Radiobrás will reactivate the service. When last heard at this hour (to Europe on 15265 kHz), the former 80-minute broadcast had been reduced to one hour, and consisted of a potpourri of short features spiced with exotic Brazilian music.

Radio Polonia, Poland. This time winters only. See 1700 for program specifics. *News*, music and features, covering multiple aspects of Polish life and culture. Fifty-five minutes to Europe on 6095, 7270 and 7285 kHz. One hour earlier in summer.

World Service. Predominantly news-related fare during the initial half hour in summer, but the winter schedule offers a more varied diet. Winter, the news is followed by a series of features: *Moscow Mailbag* (Monday and Thursday), *Newmarket* (Tuesday and Friday), *Science and Engineering* (Wednesday and Saturday), and the outstanding ●*Music and Musicians* on Sunday. On the half-hour, the lineup includes *Kaleidoscope* (Monday), ●*Moscow Yesterday and Today* (Wednesday), *Yours For the Asking* or●*Music at Your Request* (Tuesday), ●*Russian Musical Highlights of the 20th Century* (Thursday), ●*Folk Box* (Friday) and Saturday's ●*Songs from Russia*. Summer weekdays, the first half hour consists of news followed by ●*Update*. At 1830 Tuesday and Thursday, there are "alternative programs"—regular shows, transcription programs or religious paid programming. The Saturday slot is filled by *This is Russia*, replaced Sunday by ●*Christian Message from Moscow* (an interesting insight into Russian Orthodoxy). On the remaining days, you can hear ●*The 20th Century: Year After Year*. Continuous to Europe and southern Africa. Winter, Europe is served by 5940, 5965 and 9890 kHz; best summer channels are likely to be 7300, 9720, 9775, 9820, 11675 and 15545 kHz. In southern Africa, try 7325 kHz in winter, 12065 kHz midyear. These channels are targeted at the Mideast and East Africa, but should make it farther south.

Voice of America. Continuous programming to the Mideast and North Africa. *News Now*—reports and features on a variety of topics. On 6040 (winter) and 9760 kHz. For a separate service to Africa, see the next item.

Voice of America. Monday through Friday, it's *News Now* and *Africa World Tonight*. Weekends, there's a full hour of the former. To Africa—but heard well beyond—on 7275, 11920, 11975, 12040, 13710, 15410, 15580 and 17895 kHz, some of which are seasonal.

18:00–19:00

Beer from Holland and other premium alcoholic beverages are widely available in Kyrgyzstan.

M. Guha

Radio Cairo, Egypt. See 1630 for specifics. The final 30 minutes of a two-hour broadcast to southern Africa on 15255 kHz.

Radio Omdurman, Sudan. A one-hour package of *news* and features (often from a pro-government viewpoint), plus a little ethnic Sudanese music. Better heard in Europe than in North America, but occasionally audible in the eastern United States. On 9200 kHz.

WJCR, Upton, Kentucky. Continues with country gospel music to North America on 7490 and 13595 kHz. Other U.S. religious broadcasters operating at this time include **WWCR** on 13845 and 15685 kHz, **KTBN** on 15590 kHz, and **WHRI-World Harvest Radio** on 13760 and 15105 kHz. For traditional Catholic programming, tune **WEWN** on 7425 kHz.

CFRX-CFRB, Toronto, Canada. Audible throughout much of the northeastern United States and southeastern Canada during the hours of daylight with a modest, but clear, signal on 6070 kHz. This pleasant, friendly station carries news, sports, weather and traffic reports—most of it

intended for a local audience. Winter weekdays at this hour, it's *The Motts*; summers, look for *The John Oakley Show*. Weekends feature *The Mike Stafford Show*.

18:15

Radio Bangladesh. *News,* followed by Islamic and general interest features; some nice Bengali music, too. Thirty minutes to Europe on 7190 and 9550 kHz, and irregularly on 15520 kHz. Frequencies may be slightly variable.

18:30

■**Radio Netherlands.** Part of a three-hour block of programming for Africa, but also well heard in parts of North America at this hour. *News,* followed Monday through Friday by *Newsline* and a feature. Some excellent shows, including ●*EuroQuest* (Monday), ●*A Good Life* (Tuesday), ●*Research File* (science, Thursday), ●*Roughly Speaking* (an award-winning youth program, Saturday) and Friday's ●*Documentary.* Other offerings include *Aural Tapestry* and *Wide Angle* (Sunday),

Sounds Interesting (Wednesday) and Saturday's *Europe Unzipped*. Sixty minutes on 6020, 7120 (summer), 9895, 11655, 13700 and 17605 kHz. The last frequency, via the relay in the Netherlands Antilles, is best for North American listeners. In southern Africa, tune to 6020 kHz.

Radio Slovakia International. Summers only at this time; see 1930 for specifics. Thirty minutes of *news* and features with a strong Slovak flavor. To Western Europe on 5920, 6055 and 7345 kHz. One hour later in winter.

Radio Vlaanderen Internationaal, Belgium. Winters only at this time. Weekdays, there's *News, Press Review* and *Belgium Today*, followed by features like *Focus on Europe* (Monday), *Living in Belgium* and *Green Society* (Tuesday), *The Arts* (Wednesday and Friday), *Around Town* (Wednesday), *Economics* and *International Report* (Thursday), and *Tourism* (Friday). Weekend features include *Music from Flanders* (Saturday) and Sunday's *P.O. Box 26* (a listener-response program) and *Radio World*. Twenty-five minutes to Africa (and heard well beyond) on 9925 and 13745 kHz. One hour earlier in summer.

Voice of Turkey. This time summers only. *News*, followed by *Review of the Turkish Press*, then features on Turkish history, culture and International relations, interspersed with enjoyable selections of the country's popular and classical music. Fifty minutes to Western Europe on 9445 and 11765 kHz. One hour later in winter.

Voice of Mongolia. *News*, reports and short features with the accent on local topics. Some exotic Mongolian music, too, especially on Sundays. Thirty minutes to Europe on 9720 and 12085 kHz. Frequencies may vary slightly.

Radio Sweden. Winters only at this time. Monday through Friday, it's *news* and

features in *Sixty Degrees North*, concentrating heavily on Scandinavian topics. Monday's accent is on sports; Tuesday spotlights electronic media news; Wednesday has *Money Matters*; Thursday features ecology or science and technology; and Friday offers a review of the week's news. Saturday's slot is filled by *Spectrum* (arts) or *Sweden Today*, and Sunday fare consists of *In Touch with Stockholm* (a listener-response program) or the musical *Sounds Nordic*. Thirty minutes to Europe, the Mideast and Africa on 6065 (not Sunday) and 9645 kHz. One hour earlier in summer.

Radio Yugoslavia. Summers only at this time. *News* and background reports with a strong local flavor. Thirty minutes to Europe on 6100 kHz, and to Southern Africa on 9720 kHz. One hour later during winter.

19:00

■**BBC World Service for Europe and the Mideast.** Starts with five minutes of *World News*, and ends weekdays with ●*Off the Shelf* (readings from world literature). The features in between include some of the BBC's best. Monday, there's ●*Health Matters* (1905) and ●*The Farming World* (1930); Tuesday at the same times, it's ●*Discovery* and *Science Extra*; Wednesday features ●*One Planet* (the environment) and ●*From Our Own Correspondent*; Thursday's first airing is *The Works* (technology); and Friday at the same time, you can hear ●*Science in Action*. Best of the Saturday fare is ●*From Our Own Correspondent* at 1905. Sunday brings continuation of ●*Play of the Week* and, if the play doesn't overrun, the popular ●*Andy Kershaw's World of Music*. Continuous to Europe on 3955 (winters), 6195, 9410 and 12095 kHz; and to the Mideast on 9410, 11970 (or 11995) and 12095 kHz. Some of these channels are also audible in eastern North America.

19:00–19:00

■**BBC World Service for Africa.** The first 30 minutes consist of a series of features aimed at the African continent, but are worth a listen even if you live farther afield. These are followed on the half-hour by features from the BBC's mainstream programming. The list includes *Fast Track* and ●*Omnibus* (Monday), *Art Beat* and *Pick of the World* (Tuesday), *Talkabout Africa* and *Sports International* (Wednesday), *Postmark Africa* (Thursday), *Fast Track* and ●*Focus on Faith* (Friday), ●*From Our Own Correspondent* (Saturday) and Sunday's *African Performance or African Perspective*. Continuous programming to the African continent (and heard well beyond) on 6005, 6190, 9630, 15400 and 17830 kHz. The last two channels are audible in parts of North America.

■**BBC World Service for the Pacific.** Starts with five minutes of *World News*, then weekdays there's the long-running and popular ●*Outlook* and a 15-minute feature. These are replaced Saturday by a request show, *Wright Round the World*, and Sunday by a talk program and *Record News* (classical music). To Australasia on 9740 kHz.

Radio Yugoslavia. Summers only at this time. *News* and short background reports heavily geared to local issues. Thirty minutes to Australasia on 7230 kHz.

Radio Australia. Begins with *World News*, then Sunday through Thursday it's *Pacific Beat* (in-depth reporting on the region). Friday's slots go to ●*Pacific Focus* and *Media Report*, replaced Saturday by the aptly named *Ockham's Razor* (science talk at its sharpest) and *The Sports Factor*. Continuous to Asia and the Pacific on 6080, 7240, 9500, 9580, 9660 and 11880 kHz. Listeners in western North America can try 9580 and 11880 kHz. Best bet for East and Southeast Asia is 9500 kHz (may also be audible in Europe).

Radio Kuwait. See 1800; continuous to Europe and eastern North America on 11990 kHz.

Kol Israel. Summers only at this time. ●*Israel News Magazine*. Thirty minutes of even-handed and comprehensive news reporting from and about Israel. To Europe and North America on 9435, 11605 and 15650 kHz; and to Africa and South America on 15640 kHz. One hour later in winter.

All India Radio. The final 45 minutes of a two-hour broadcast to Europe, Africa and the Mideast (see 1745). Starts off with *news*, then continues with a mixed bag of features and Indian music. To Europe on 7410, 9950 and 11620 kHz; and to Africa on 11935, 13780 and 15075 kHz. In the Mideast, choose the channel best suited to your location.

Radio Bulgaria. Summers only at this time. *News*, then Monday through Thursday there's 15 minutes of current events in *Today*, replaced Friday by *Weekly Spotlight*, a summary of the week's major political stories. The remainder of the broadcast is given over to features dealing with Bulgaria and Bulgarians, and includes some lively ethnic music. Sixty minutes to Europe on 9700 and 11720 kHz. One hour later during winter.

HCJB—Voice of the Andes, Ecuador. The first of three hours of religious and secular programming targeted at Europe. Monday through Friday it's *Studio 9*, featuring nine minutes of world and Latin American *news*, followed by 20 minutes of in-depth reporting on Latin America. The final portion is given over to one of a variety of 30-minute features—including *Adventures in Odyssey* (Monday), *El Mundo Futuro* (science, Tuesday), *Ham Radio Today* (Wednesday), *Woman to Woman* (Thursday) and Friday's exotic and enjoyable ●*Música del Ecuador*. On Saturday,

Afghan boys treat learning seriously in the only school in Taloqan, Afghanistan. M. Guha

the news is followed by *DX Partyline*, which in turn is replaced Sunday by *Musical Mailbag*. On 17660 kHz.

Radio Budapest, Hungary. Summers only at this time. *News* and features, only a few of which are broadcast on a regular basis. Thirty minutes to Europe on 6025 and 7170 kHz. One hour later in winter.

■**Deutsche Welle,** Germany. *News*, then Monday through Friday it's ●*NewsLink* followed by *Africa Report*. Weekends, the Saturday news is followed by *Talking Point* and ●*Spectrum* (science); Sunday, by *Religion and Society* and *Arts on the Air*. Forty-five minutes to Africa, but also well heard in parts of eastern North America. Winter, try 11765, 11785, 11810, 13610, 15135, 15390 and 17810 kHz; in summer, go for 9640, 11785, 11810, 13790, 15390 and 17810 kHz. Best winter options for North America are 11810 and 15135 kHz; and summer, 15390 kHz.

Radio Romania International. *News*, commentary, press review and features. Regular spots include *Youth Club* (Tuesday), *Romanian Musicians* (Wednesday), and Thursday's *Listeners' Letterbox* and ●*Skylark* (Romanian folk music). Fifty-five

minutes to Europe; winters on 6105, 7105, 7195 and 9510 kHz; and summers on 9550, 9690, 11810 and 11940 kHz. Also audible in eastern North America.

XERMX—Radio México Internacional. Summers only at this time. Monday through Friday, there's a summary of the Spanish-language *Antena Radio*, replaced Saturday by *Mirror of Mexico*, and Sunday by *Universal Forum*. On the half-hour, look for 30 minutes of musical programming. Best heard in western and southern parts of the United States on 5985 and 9705 kHz. One hour later in winter.

Voice of Russia World Service. *News*, followed winter weekdays by ●*Update* (news and reports from and about the CIS). Summer, this is replaced Tuesday through Sunday by *News and Views*, and Monday by *Sunday Panorama* and *Russia in Personalities*. Winter weekends at 1930, the Saturday slot is filled by *This is Russia*, replaced Sunday by ●*Christian Message from Moscow*. Tuesday and Thursday feature "alternative programs"—religious paid programming or a show from the Voice of Russia's archives or transcription

19:00–19:30

department. On the remaining days, listen to ●*The 20th Century: Year After Year*. The summer lineup includes ●*Moscow Yesterday and Today* (Monday), *This is Russia* (Tuesday and Sunday), *Kaleidoscope* (Wednesday), ●*Audio Book Club* (Thursday), *Russian by Radio* (Friday) and Saturday's ●*Christian Message from Moscow*. Winter, best channels for Europe are likely to be 5920, 5940, 5965, 7310, 7340, 9480 and 9890 kHz; for summer, try 9480, 9720, 9775, 9820, 11675, 12070 and 15545 kHz. In southern Africa, try the winter frequency of 7305 kHz.

China Radio International. Repeat of the 1600 transmission. One hour to North and West Africa on two or more channels from 6165, 9440, 9680 and 11840 kHz. Also audible in the Mideast.

Voice of Greece. Winters only at this time, and actually starts about three minutes into the broadcast, following some Greek announcements. Approximately ten minutes of *news* from and about Greece. To Europe on 9375 or 9380 kHz.

Radio Thailand. A 60-minute package of *news*, features and (if you're lucky) enjoyable Thai music. To Northern Europe winters on 7295 kHz, and summers on 7195 kHz. Also available to Asia on 9655 and 11905 kHz.

Radio For Peace International, Costa Rica. Continues with a variety of counterculture and social-conscience features. There is also a listener-response program at 1930 Tuesday. Audible in Europe and North America on 15050 and 21460 kHz.

Swiss Radio International. This time summers only. World and Swiss *news* and background reports, with some lighter and more general features on Saturdays. Thirty minutes to northern Europe on 9885 kHz. One hour later during winter.

Voice of Vietnam. Repeat of the 1800 transmission (see there for specifics). A half hour to Europe on 9840 and 12020 (or 9730) kHz.

Voice of America. Continuous programming to the Mideast and North Africa. *News Now*—news and reports on a wide variety of topics. On 9760 and (summer) 9770 kHz. Also heard in Europe. For a separate service to Africa, see the next item.

Voice of America. *News Now*, then Monday through Friday it's *World of Music*. Best of the weekend programs is ●*Music Time in Africa* at 1930 Sunday. Continuous to most of Africa on 6035, 7375, 7415, 11920, 11975, 12040, 15410, 15445 and 15580 kHz, some of which are seasonal. For yet another service, to Australasia, see the following item.

Voice of America. Sixty minutes of news and reports covering a variety of topics. One hour to Australasia on 9525, 11870 and 15180 kHz.

Radio Korea International, South Korea. Opens with *news* and commentary, followed Monday through Wednesday by *Seoul Calling*. Weekly features include *Echoes of Korean Music* and *Shortwave Feedback* (Sunday), *Tales from Korea's Past* (Monday), *Korean Cultural Trails* (Tuesday), *Pulse of Korea* (Wednesday), *From Us to You* (a listener-response program) and *Let's Learn Korean* (Thursday), *Let's Sing Together* and *Korea Through Foreigners' Eyes* (Friday), and Saturday's *Discovering Korea*, *Korean Literary Corner* and *Weekly News Focus*. Sixty minutes to East Asia on 5975 and 7275 kHz.

Radio Argentina al Exterior—R.A.E. Monday through Friday only. *News* and short features dealing with Argentinean life and culture, interspersed with fine examples of the country's various musical styles, from milongo to tango. Fifty-five minutes to Europe on 15345 kHz.

WJCR, Upton, Kentucky. Continues with country gospel music to North America on 7490 and 13595 kHz. Other U.S. religious broadcasters operating at this time include **WWCR** on 13845 and 15685 kHz, **KTBN** on 15590 kHz, and **WHRI-World Harvest Radio** on 13760 kHz. For traditional Catholic programming, try **WEWN** on 7425 kHz.

CFRX-CFRB, Toronto, Canada. See 1800. Weekdays at this time, you can hear *The John Oakley Show*; weekends, it's replaced by *The Mike Stafford Show*. On 6070 kHz.

19:15

Radio Tirana, Albania. Winters only at this time. Approximately 15 minutes of *news* and commentary from and about Albania. To Europe on 6025 and 7135 kHz.

19:30

Radio Polonia, Poland. Summers only at this time. Weekdays, it's *News from Poland*—news, reports and interviews on the latest events in the country. This is followed by classical music and the historical *Flashback* (Monday), *DX-Club* and *Letter from Poland* (Tuesday), a feature and a talk or special report (Wednesday), *Focus* (the arts in Poland) and *A Day in the Life of...* (Thursday), and *Postbag* (a listener-response program) followed by *Business Week* (Friday). The Saturday transmission begins with a bulletin of *news*, then there's *Weekend Papers* (a press review) and, later in the broadcast, *Jazz, Folk, Rock and Pop from Poland*. Sundays, you can hear *Panorama* (a window on day-to-day life in Poland) and *Request Concert*. Fifty-five minutes to Europe on 6035, 6095 and 7285 kHz. One hour later during winter.

Radio Slovakia International. Winters only at this time. *Slovakia Today*, a 30-minute review of Slovak life and culture. Monday, there's a potpourri of short features; Tuesday spotlights tourism and Slovak personalities; Wednesday is devoted to business and economy; and Thursday brings a mix of politics, education and science. Friday offerings include cultural items, cooking recipes and the off-beat *Back Page News*; and Saturday has the "*Best of*" series. Sunday's show is a melange of this and that, and includes *Listeners' Tribune* and some enjoyable Slovak music. A friendly half hour to Western Europe on 5915, 6055 and 7345 kHz. One hour earlier in summer.

Voice of Turkey. Winters only at this time. See 1830 for program details. Some unusual programming and friendly presentation make this station worth a listen. Fifty minutes to Europe on 5960 and 6175 kHz. One hour earlier in summer.

Voice of the Islamic Republic of Iran. Sixty minutes of *news*, commentary and features with a strong Islamic slant. Not the lightest of programming fare, but reflects a point of view not often heard in western countries. To Europe on 7260 and 9022 kHz.

Radio Yugoslavia. Winters only at this time; see 1830 for specifics. Thirty minutes to Europe on 6100 kHz, and to Southern Africa on 9720 kHz. One hour earlier in summer.

Radio Sweden. Summers only at this time, and a repeat of the 1730 broadcast. See 1830 for program details. Thirty minutes to Europe on 6065 kHz.

■**Radio Netherlands.** Repeat of the 1730 transmission; see there for specifics. Fifty-five minutes to Africa on 6020 (best for southern parts), 7120 (summer), 9895, 11655, 13700 and 17605 kHz. The last

19:30–20:00

frequency is heard well in many parts of North America.

RAI International—Radio Roma, Italy. Actually starts at 1935. Approximately 12 minutes of *news*, then some Italian music. Twenty minutes to western Europe winters on 6015 and 7225 kHz, and summers on 5970, 7145 and 9670 kHz.

19:50

Vatican Radio. Summers only at this time. Twenty minutes of programming oriented to Catholics. To Europe on 4005, 5880 and 7250 kHz. One hour later in winter.

20:00

■BBC World Service for Europe and the Mideast. ●*Newshour*, the standard for all in-depth news shows from International broadcasters. One hour to Europe on 3955, 6180, 6195, 9410 and 12095 kHz; and to the Mideast on 9410 and (summer) 12095 kHz. Some of these channels are also audible in eastern North America.

■BBC World Service for Africa. The incomparable ●*Newshour*. Continuous programming to the African continent (and heard well beyond) on 6005, 6190, 11835, 15400 and 17830 kHz. The last two channels are audible in parts of North America.

■BBC World Service for the Pacific. Identical to the service for Europe at this hour. To Australasia on 5975 and 9740 kHz.

■Deutsche Welle, Germany. *News*, then Monday through Friday there's the in-depth ●*NewsLink* followed by a feature. Monday, it's *German by Radio*; Tuesday has the ecological ●*Man and Environment*; Wednesday brings ●*Insight*; Thursday, try *Living in Germany*; and Friday's slot is

Spotlight on Sport. Weekend Review and ●*Weekend* (a European co-production) are aired Saturday, replaced Sunday by a second edition of *Weekend Review* and *Arts on the Air*. Forty-five minutes to Europe winters on 9725 kHz, and summers on 11970 kHz.

Radio Canada International. Summers only at this time. The first hour of a 90-minute broadcast to Europe and beyond. *News*, followed Monday through Friday by *Spectrum* (current events), which is replaced Saturday by *Venture Canada* (business) and ●*Earth Watch* (the environment). The Sunday slots are filled by *Arts in Canada* and *The Mailbag*, a listener-response show. To Europe, Africa and the Mideast on 5995, 11690, 13650, 13670, 15150, 15325, 15470, 17820 and 17870 kHz. Some of these channels are also audible in parts of North America. One hour later during winter.

Radio Damascus, Syria. Actually starts at 2005. *News*, a daily press review, and different features for each day of the week. These can be heard at approximately 2030 and 2045, and include *Arab Profile* and *Palestine Talk* (Monday), *Syria and the World* and *Listeners Overseas* (Tuesday), *Around the World* and *Selected Readings* (Wednesday), *From the World Press* and *Reflections* (Thursday), *Arab Newsweek* and *Cultural Magazine* (Friday), *Welcome to Syria* and *Arab Civilization* (Saturday), and *From Our Literature* and *Music from the Orient* (Sunday). Most of the transmission, however, is given over to Syrian and some western popular music. One hour to Europe, often audible in eastern North America, on 12085 and 13610 kHz.

Swiss Radio International. *World Radio Switzerland*—news and background reports on world and Swiss events. Some lighter fare on Saturdays, when the

Tajik village woman sells sugarplums at Dushanbe's Barakat market. M. Guha

biweekly *Capital Letters* (a listener-response program) alternates with *Name Game* (first Saturday) and *Sounds Good* (third Saturday). Thirty minutes to northern Europe winters on 6165 kHz (one hour earlier in summer), and year-round to Africa, winter on 9620, 9885, 11910 and 13700 kHz; summer on 13710, 13770, 15220 and 17580 kHz.

XERMX—Radio México Internacional. Winter weekdays, there's an English summary of the Spanish-language *Antena Radio*, replaced Saturday by *Mirror of Mexico*, and Sunday by *Universal Forum*. Summers, the lineup consists of Monday's *The Sounds of Mexico*, replaced Tuesday and Sunday by *Mailbox*, Thursday by *Eternally Mexico* and Friday by *Mirror of Mexico*. Wednesdays and Saturdays, the English program gives way to one in French. On the half-hour, look for 30

minutes of music. Best heard in western and southern parts of the United States on 5985 and 9705 kHz.

Radio Australia. Starts with *World News*, then Sunday through Thursday there's *Pacific Beat* (in-depth reporting). Friday fare consists of *Oz Sounds* and *Health Report*, and Saturday it's the first of four hours of *Australia All Over*. Continuous programming to the Pacific on 9580, 9660, 11880 and 12080 kHz; and to East and Southeast Asia on 9500 kHz (may also be audible in Europe). In western North America, try 9580 and 11880 kHz.

Voice of Russia World Service. *News*, then winter it's *News and Views* Monday through Saturday, with *Sunday Panorama* and *Russia in Personalities* the Sunday offerings. In summer, these are replaced by a variety of features. Take your pick

20:00–20:00

A Kyrgyz cattleman casually drives his herd along the Pamir highway.

M. Guha

from *Science and Engineering* (Monday and Thursday), *Newmarket* (Wednesday and Saturday), *Moscow Mailbag* (Tuesday and Friday), and the 45-minute ●*Music and Musicians*. Winters on the half-hour, the lineup includes ●*Moscow Yesterday and Today* (Monday), *This is Russia* (Tuesday and Sunday), *Kaleidoscope* (Wednesday), ●*Audio Book Club* (Thursday), *Russian by Radio* (Friday) and Saturday's ●*Christian Message from Moscow*. Best of the summer offerings at this time are Thursday's ●*Folk Box* and Wednesday's ●*Russian Musical Highlights of the 20th Century*. Other features include ●*Songs from Russia* (Monday), *Yours For the Asking* or ●*Music at Your Request* (Tuesday), Friday's *Jazz Show* and Saturday's *Russian by Radio*. Continuous to Europe winter on 5940, 5965 and 9890 kHz; best summer choices are 9720, 9775, 9820, 11675 and 15485 kHz. Some of these channels are audible in eastern North America.

Radio Kuwait. The final sixty minutes of a three-hour broadcast to Europe and eastern North America (see 1800). Regular features at this time include *Theater in Kuwait* (2000), *Saheeh Muslim* (2030) and *News in Brief* at 2057. On 11990 kHz.

Radio Bulgaria. This time winters only. *News*, then Monday through Thursday there's 15 minutes of current events in *Today*, replaced Friday by *Weekly Spotlight*, a summary of the week's major political stories. The remainder of the broadcast is given over to features dealing with Bulgaria and Bulgarians, and includes some lively ethnic music. To Europe, also audible in eastern North America, on 7530 and 9700 kHz. One hour earlier during summer.

Voice of Greece. Summers only at this time and actually starts about three minutes into the broadcast, after a little bit of Greek. Approximately ten minutes of *news* from and about Greece. To Europe on 7430 or 9420 kHz.

Radio Budapest, Hungary. Winters only at this time; see 1900 for specifics. Thirty minutes to Europe on 6125 and 7170 kHz. One hour earlier in summer.

Radio Algiers, Algeria. *News*, then western and Arab popular music, with an occasional feature thrown in. One hour of so-so reception in Europe, and sometimes heard in eastern North America. On 11715 and 15160 kHz. May be summer only at this time.

China Radio International. *News* and commentary, followed Monday through Friday by in-depth reporting and an overview of the Chinese press. Next come features like *Open Windows* and *Learn to Speak Chinese* (Monday); *Orient Arena* and *Opera House* (Tuesday); *Voices from Other Lands* (Wednesday); *Focus* and *Cultural Spectrum* (Thursday); and *Life in China* and *Global Review* (Friday). On weekends, Saturday's lineup includes *Asia-Pacific News*, *Report from Developing Countries*, *China Scrapbook* and ●*Music from China*; and Sunday there's *Cultural Information*, *People in the Know*, *On the Road* and *Listeners' Letterbox*. One hour to Europe on 7170 (or 6950) and 9535 kHz; to eastern and southern Africa on 11735 (or 11975) and 15500 kHz; and to North Africa (also audible in the Mideast) on 6165, 9440 and 9680 kHz. May also be available to Australasia on 11875 kHz.

Radio Nacional de Angola ("Angolan National Radio"). The first 30 minutes or so consist of a mix of music and short features, then there's *news* near the half-hour. The remainder of the broadcast is given over to some lively Angolan music. Sixty minutes to Southern Africa on 3354 and 7245 kHz.

Radio Pyongyang, North Korea. Repeat of the 1100 broadcast. To Europe, the Mideast and beyond on 6575, 9345, 9640 and 9975 kHz.

Kol Israel. Winters only at this time. Thirty minutes of *news* and in-depth reporting from and about Israel. To Europe and North America on 7465, 9365 and 9435 kHz; and to Australasia on 15640 kHz. One hour earlier in summer.

YLE Radio Finland. Summers only at this time; see 2100 for specifics. A half hour to Europe on 6135 kHz. One hour later in winter.

HCJB—Voice of the Andes, Ecuador. Continues with a three-hour block of religious and secular programming to Europe, with predominantly religious fare at this hour. On 17660 kHz.

Voice of America. Continuous programming to the Mideast and North Africa. *News*, reports and capsulated features covering everything from politics to entertainment. On 6095 (winter), 9760, and (summer) 9770 kHz. For African listeners there's the weekday *Africa World Tonight*, replaced weekends by *Nightline Africa*, on 6035, 7275, 7375, 7415, 11715, 11855, 15410, 15445, 15580, 17725 and 17755 kHz, some of which are seasonal. Both transmissions are heard well beyond their target areas, including parts of North America.

Radio For Peace International, Costa Rica. Part of an eight-hour cyclical block of predominantly social-conscience and counterculture programming. Some of the offerings at this hour include a women's news-gathering service, *WINGS*, (2030 Thursday) and a listener-response program (same time Friday). Audible in Europe and North America on 15050 and 21460 kHz.

WJCR, Upton, Kentucky. Continues with country gospel music to North America on 7490 and 13595 kHz. Other U.S. religious broadcasters which operate at this time include **WWCR** on 13845 and 15685 kHz, **KTBN** on 15590 kHz, and **WHRI-World Harvest Radio** on 13760 kHz. For traditional Catholic programming, tune **WEWN** on 7425 kHz.

Radio Prague, Czech Republic. Summers only at this time. *News*, then Monday through Friday there's *Current Affairs*. These are followed by one or more features. Monday has *Spotlight*; Tuesday, it's *Talking Point*; Wednesday's offering is *History Czech*; Thursday brings *Economic

20:00–21:00

Report; and Friday's presentation is a listener-response show, *Between You and Us*. Look for some excellent entertainment in Saturday's musical feature, which is replaced Sunday by *A Letter from Prague, From the Weeklies* and *Readings from Czech Literature*. Thirty minutes to Europe on 5930 kHz, and to Southeast Asia and Australasia on 11600 kHz.

CFRX-CFRB, Toronto, Canada. See 1800. Summer weekdays at this time, you can hear ●*The World Today*, three hours of news, interviews, sports and commentary. On 6070 kHz.

20:15

Voice of Armenia. Summers only at this time. Mainly of interest to Armenians abroad. Thirty minutes of Armenian *news* and culture. To Europe on 9965 kHz. Sometimes audible in eastern North America. One hour later in winter.

20:30

Radio Sweden. Daily in winter, but weekends only in summer. See 1830 for program details. Thirty minutes year round to Europe on 6065 kHz, and summers to Africa on 13830 kHz.

Voice of Vietnam. *News*, followed by *Commentary* or *Weekly Review*, then some short features and pleasant Vietnamese music (especially at weekends). A half hour to Europe on 9840 and 12020 (or 9730) kHz.

Radio Thailand. Fifteen minutes of *news* targeted at Europe. Winters on 9535 (or 11805) kHz, and summers on 9680 kHz. Also available to Asia on 9655 and 11905 kHz.

Voice of Turkey. This time summers only. *News*, followed by *Review of the*

Turkish Press and features (some of them unusual) with a strong local flavor. Selections of Turkish popular and classical music complete the program. Fifty minutes to Southeast Asia and Australasia on 7210 kHz. One hour later during winter.

Radio Tashkent, Uzbekistan. Thirty minutes of *news*, commentary and features, with some exotic Uzbek music. To Europe winters on 7105 and 9540 kHz, and summer on 9540 and 9545 kHz.

RAI International—Radio Roma, Italy. Actually starts at 2025. Twenty minutes of *news* and music targeted at the Mideast, winters on 7125, 9685 and 11840 kHz; and summers on 7120, 9710 and 11880 kHz.

20:45

All India Radio. The first 15 minutes of a much longer broadcast, consisting of a press review, Indian music, regional and International *news*, commentary, and a variety of talks and features of general interest. Continuous till 2230. To Western Europe on 7410, 9950 and 11620 kHz; and to Australasia on 7150, 9910, 11620 and 11715 kHz. Early risers in Southeast Asia can try the channels for Australasia.

Vatican Radio. Winters only at this time, and actually starts at 2050. Twenty minutes of predominantly Catholic fare. To Europe on 4015 and 5882 kHz. Frequencies may vary slightly. One hour earlier in summer.

21:00

■**BBC World Service for Europe and the Americas.** *World News*, then 10 minutes of specialized business and financial reporting—except Sunday, when *Write On*, a listener-response show is aired. These are followed at 2120 by ●*Britain Today* or (on 5975 kHz)

●*Caribbean Report*. On the half-hour, regular spots include the arts show *Meridian* (Monday, Tuesday, Thursday and Saturday); *On Screen* (film news from around the world, Wednesday), *Music Review* (classical music, Friday) and *Global Business* on Sunday. To eastern North America and the Caribbean on 5975 kHz. If you prefer *Britain Today* to the Caribbean alternative, try 12095 kHz, targeted at South America. For Europe, choose from 3955, 6180, 6195 and 9410 kHz.

■BBC World Service for Asia and the Pacific. Weekdays until 2130, as for Europe and the Americas. Then come a variety of interesting features: ●*Health Matters* (Monday); ●*Discovery* (science, Tuesday); ●*One Planet* (the environment, Wednesday); *The Works* (technology, Thursday); and ●*Science in Action* on Friday. Weekend replacements (Sunday and Monday mornings in Asia) are ●*Letter From America* (2105 Saturday), *In Praise of God* (2130 same day), and ●*The Farming World* and *Global Business* at the same times Sunday. To East Asia on 5965, 6110, 6195 and (summer) 11945 kHz; to Southeast Asia on 3915, 6195 and 9740 kHz; and to Australasia on 5975 and 9740 kHz.

Radio Exterior de España ("Spanish National Radio"). *News*, followed Monday through Friday by *Panorama* (Spanish popular music, commentary, press review and weather), then a couple of features: *Sports Spotlight* and *Cultural Encounters* (Monday); *People of Today* and *Entertainment in Spain* (Tuesday); *As Others See Us* and, biweekly, *The Natural World* or *Science Desk* (Wednesday); *Economic Report* and *Cultural Clippings* (Thursday); and *Window on Spain* and *Review of the Arts* (Friday). The broadcast ends with a language course, *Spanish by Radio*. On weekends, there's Saturday's *Hall of Fame*, *Distance Unknown* (for radio enthusiasts) and *Gallery of Spanish Voices*; replaced

Sunday by *Visitors' Book*, *Great Figures in Flamenco* and *Radio Club*. One hour to Europe on 6125 kHz, and to Africa on 11775 kHz.

Radio Ukraine International. Summers only at this time. *News*, commentary, reports and interviews, covering multiple aspects of Ukrainian life. Saturdays feature a listener-response program, and most of Sunday's broadcast is a showpiece for Ukrainian music. Sixty minutes to Europe on 5905, 6020 and 9560 kHz. One hour later in winter.

Radio Canada International. Winters, the first hour of a 90-minute broadcast; summers, the last half-hour of the same. Winters, there's *News*, followed Monday through Friday by *Spectrum* (current events), which is replaced Saturday by *Venture Canada* and ●*Earth Watch*, and Sunday by *Arts in Canada* and *The Mailbag*, a listener-response program. Summer weekdays, it's the CBC domestic service's ●*The World at Six*, with weekend fare consisting of Saturday's *The Great Eastern* and Sunday's *Madly Off in All Directions*, mainly of appeal to Canadians abroad. To Europe and Africa winters on 5995, 7235, 9770, 9805, 11755, 11945, 13650, 13690, 15150 and 17820 kHz; and summers on 5995, 7235, 11690, 13650, 13670, 15150, 15325, 15470 and 17820 kHz. Some of these are also audible in parts of North America.

Radio Prague, Czech Republic. Winters only at this time. See 2000 for program details. *News* and features dealing with Czech life and culture. A half hour to western Europe and eastern North America on 5930 and 7345 kHz.

Radio Bulgaria. This time summers only; see 1900 for specifics. *News*, features and some entertaining folk music. To Europe and eastern North America on 9700 and 11720 kHz. One hour later during winter.

21:00–21:00

China Radio International. Repeat of the 2000 transmission; see there for specifics. One hour to Europe on 7170 (or 6950) and 9535 kHz. May also be available to Australasia on 11875 kHz. kHz. A 30-minute shortened version is also available to eastern and southern Africa on 11735 (or 11975) and 15500 kHz.

Voice of Russia World Service. Winters only at this time. *News*, then *Science and Engineering* (Monday and Thursday), the business-oriented *Newmarket* (Wednesday and Saturday), *Moscow Mailbag* (Tuesday and Friday) or Sunday's sublime ●*Music and Musicians*. Best of the second half hour are Thursday's ●*Folk Box* and Wednesday's ●*Russian Musical Highlights of the 20th Century*. Other features include ●*Songs from Russia* (Monday), *Yours For the Asking* or ●*Music at Your Request* (Tuesday), Friday's *Jazz Show* and Saturday's *Russian by Radio*. The final hour for Europe on 5940, 5965, 7300 and 9890 kHz, and one hour earlier in summer. Some of these channels are audible in eastern North America.

Radio Budapest, Hungary. Summers only at this time. *News* and features, only some of which are broadcast on a regular basis. Thirty minutes to Europe on 6025 kHz. One hour later in winter.

Radio Japan. *News*, then Tuesday through Saturday there's *Asian Top News*. This is followed by a half-hour feature: *Music Reflections* (Tuesday), *Let's Try Japanese* (Wednesday), *Music Journey Around Japan* (Thursday), *My Japan Diary* (Friday), and *Music Beat* (Saturday). Sunday's show is *Hello From Tokyo*, and is replaced Monday by *Asian Weekly*. Sixty minutes to Europe on 9725 kHz; to Southeast Asia on 6035 kHz; to Australasia on 11850 kHz; and to western North America on (winter) 13630 or (summer) 17825 kHz.

Radio Australia. *World News*, then Sunday through Thursday it's current events in *AM* (replaced Friday by a listener-response program, *Feedback*). Next, on the half-hour, there's a daily feature. Take your pick from *Earthbeat* (environment, Sunday); *Innovations* (the invented and innovative, Monday and Friday); *Arts Australia* (culture, Tuesday) *Rural Reporter* (regional Australia, Wednesday); and *Book Talk* (new books, Thursday). The Saturday slot is filled by the second hour of *Australia All Over*. Continuous to the Pacific on 7240, 9660, 11880, 12080, 17715 and 21740 kHz; and to East and Southeast Asia (till 2130) on 9500 kHz. Listeners in western North America can try 11880 and 17715 kHz.

■**Deutsche Welle,** Germany. *News*, then weekdays (Tuesday through Saturday in the target areas) it's ●*NewsLink* followed by a feature. Monday, it's either *Development Forum* or *Women on the Move*; Tuesday, there's a look at ●*Man and Environment*; Wednesday's slot is ●*Insight*; Thursday, there's *Living in Germany*; and Friday's offering is *Spotlight on Sport*. Saturday's slots are *Weekend Review* (first edition) and *Mailbag*, replaced Sunday by *Weekend Review* (second edition) and *Arts on the Air*. Forty-five minutes to Southeast Asia and Australasia, winter on 9765, 15135 and 17560 kHz; and midyear on 9670, 9765 and 11915 kHz. An almost identical broadcast (except that Saturday's *Mailbag* is replaced by *African Kaleidoscope*) goes out simultaneously to West Africa, and is audible in much of eastern North America. Winters on 9615, 9690 and 15410 kHz; and summers on 9875, 11865 and 15135 kHz. In North America, try 15410 kHz in winter and 15135 kHz in summer.

Radio Yugoslavia. Summers only at this time. *News* and short background reports, mostly about local issues. An informative half hour to Europe on 6100 and 6185 kHz. One hour later in winter.

Radio Romania International. *News*, commentary and features (see 1900), interspersed with some thoroughly enjoyable Romanian folk music. One hour to Europe winters on 5955, 5990, 7105 and 7195 kHz; summers on 5990, 7105, 7195 and 9690 kHz. Also audible in eastern North America.

Radio Habana Cuba. A 60-minute package of *news* (predominantly about Cuba and Latin America), features about the island and its people, and some thoroughly enjoyable Cuban music. To Europe on (winter) 9550 kHz and (summer) 13750 kHz.

Radio Korea International, South Korea. Starts with *news*, followed Monday through Wednesday by *Economic News Briefs*. The remainder of the broadcast is taken up by a feature: *Shortwave Feedback* (Sunday), *Seoul Calling* (Monday and Tuesday), *Pulse of Korea* (Wednesday), *From Us to You* (Thursday), *Let's Sing Together* (Friday) and *Weekly News Focus* (Saturday). Thirty minutes to Europe summers on 3980 kHz, and one hour later in winter. Also at this time, a repeat of the 1900 one-hour broadcast to East Asia is beamed to Europe year round on 6480 and 15575 kHz.

Radio For Peace International, Costa Rica. Continues at this hour with a potpourri of United Nations, counterculture and other programs. These include *WINGS* (news for and of women, 2130 Tuesday) and *Vietnam Veterans Radio Network* (same time Wednesday). Audible in Europe and North America on 15050 and 21460 kHz.

YLE Radio Finland. Winters only at this time. Most days it's *Compass North* and a press review. Exceptions are Saturday's *Capital Café* and Sunday's world band curiosity, *Nuntii Latini* (news in Latin), heard at 2123. Thirty minutes to Europe on 6135 kHz. One hour earlier in summer.

Moscow resident Sergey Izyumov uses a Soviet military R-250/M2 to perform technical monitoring for RFE/RL. This massive vintage receiver uses 20 tubes.   S. Izyumov

HCJB—Voice of the Andes, Ecuador. The final sixty minutes of a three-hour block of predominantly religious programming to Europe on 15115 or 17660 kHz.

Voice of America. For Africa and Australasia, it's *News Now*—a series of reports and features covering a multitude of topics. Also available to the Mideast and North Africa on 6040, 9535 (summer) and 9760 kHz. In Africa, tune to 6035, 7375, 7415, 11715, 11975, 13710, 15410, 15445, 15580 and 17725 kHz (some of which are seasonal); and in Southeast Asia and the Pacific to 11870, 15185 and 17735 kHz.

XERMX—Radio México Internacional. Winters only at this time. Starts with a feature. Monday, it's *The Sounds of Mexico*, replaced Tuesday and

21:00–22:00

Sunday by *Mailbox*, Thursday by *Eternally Mexico* and Friday by *Mirror of Mexico*. Wednesdays and Saturdays, the English program gives way to one in French. On the half-hour, there's 30 minutes of music. Best heard in western and southern parts of the United States on 5985 and 9705 kHz.

All India Radio. Continues to Western Europe on 7410, 9950 and 11620 kHz; and to Australasia on 7150, 9910, 11620 and 11715 kHz. Look for some authentic Indian music from 2115 onwards. The European frequencies are audible in parts of eastern North America, while those for Australasia are also heard in Southeast Asia.

CFRX-CFRB, Toronto, Canada. If you live in the northeastern United States or southeastern Canada, try this pleasant little local station, usually audible for hundreds of miles/kilometers during daylight hours on 6070 kHz. Winter weekdays at this time, you can hear ●*The World Today* (summers, starts at 2000)—three hours of news, sport and interviews.

21:15

Radio Damascus, Syria. Actually starts at 2110. *News*, a daily press review, and a variety of features (depending on the day of the week) at approximately 2130 and 2145. These include *Arab Profile* and *Economic Affairs* (Sunday), *Camera and Masks* and *Selected Readings* (Monday), *Reflections* and *Back on the Stage* (Tuesday), *Listeners Overseas* and *Palestine Talking* (Wednesday), *From the World Press* and *Arab Women in Focus* (Thursday), *Arab Newsweek* and *From Our Literature* (Friday), and *Human Rights* and *Syria and the World* (Saturday). The transmission also contains Syrian and some western popular music. Sixty minutes to North America and Australasia on 12085 and 13610 (or 15095) kHz.

■**BBC World Service for the Caribbean.** *Caribbean Report*, although intended for listeners in the area, can also be clearly heard throughout much of eastern North America. This brief, 15-minute program provides comprehensive coverage of Caribbean economic and political affairs, both within and outside the region. Monday through Friday only, on 5975, 15390 and 17715 kHz.

Radio Cairo, Egypt. The start of a 90-minute broadcast devoted to Arab and Egyptian life and culture. The initial quarter-hour of general programming is followed by *news*, commentary and political items. This in turn is followed by a cultural program until 2215, when the station again reverts to more general fare. Beamed to Europe on 9900 kHz.

WJCR, Upton, Kentucky. Continuous gospel music to North America on 7490 and 13595 kHz. Other U.S. religious broadcasters operating at this hour include **WWCR** on 13845 and 15685 and kHz, **KTBN** on 15590 kHz, and **WHRI-World Harvest Radio** on 13760 kHz. Traditional Catholic programming is available from **WEWN** on 7425 kHz.

21:15

Voice of Armenia. Winters only at this time. Mainly of interest to Armenians abroad. Thirty minutes of Armenian *news* and culture. To Europe on 9965 kHz, and sometimes audible in eastern North America. One hour earlier in summer.

21:30

BBC World Service for the Falkland Islands. *Calling the Falklands* has been running for so long that it has almost ceased to be the broadcasting curiosity it used to be. This twice-weekly transmis-

21:00–22:00

"The New Soviet Men and Women," a heroic-style earthquake memorial to those who rebuilt Tashkent. M. Guha

sion for a small community in the South Atlantic consists of news and short features, often on unusual topics—like the tale of a wayward albatross that ended up in the North Atlantic. Audible for 15 minutes Tuesday and Friday on 11680 kHz, and easily heard in eastern North America.

Radio Austria International. Summers only at this time. Thirty minutes of news and human-interest stories in ●*Report from Austria*. A worthy source of national and regional news. To Europe on 6155 kHz; and to southern Africa on 13730 kHz. One hour later during winter.

Radio Prague, Czech Republic. Summers only at this time. See 2230 for program details. *News* and features dealing with Czech life and culture. A half hour to Australasia on 11600 kHz, and to West Africa on 15545 kHz.

Radio Budapest, Hungary. Summers only at this time. *News* and features, a few of which are broadcast on a regular basis. Thirty minutes to Europe on 3975 kHz. One hour later in winter.

Radio Tashkent, Uzbekistan. Thirty minutes of *news*, commentary and features, plus some exotic Uzbek music. To

Europe winters on 7105 and 9540 kHz, and summer on 9540 and 9545 kHz.

Radio Tirana, Albania. Summers only at this time. *News*, reports and some lively Albanian music. Thirty minutes to Europe on 6025 and 7165 kHz.

Voice of Turkey. This time winters only. *News*, followed by *Review of the Turkish Press* and features (some of them unusual) with a strong local flavor. Selections of Turkish popular and classical music complete the program. Fifty minutes to Southeast Asia and Australasia on 7200 kHz. One hour earlier in summer.

Radio Sweden. Daily in summer, but winter weekends only. Thirty minutes of predominantly Scandinavian fare (see 2230 for specifics). Year-round to Europe and the Mideast on 6065 kHz; and to Africa on 9655 (winter) or (summer) 9430 kHz.

22:00

■**BBC World Service for Europe and the Americas.** The first 30 minutes are split equally between *World News* and ●*Sports Roundup*, and are followed weekdays by a music feature on the half-hour—try ●*Andy Kershaw's World of Music* (Wednesday) or ●*John Peel* on Friday. At the same time Saturday, you can listen to the first part of ●*Play of the Week* (world theater); Sunday, it's ●*Brain of Britain* or a substitute quiz. Continuous programming to North America and the Caribbean on 5975, 6175 and 9590 kHz; and to Europe winters only on 3955 and 6195 kHz.

■BBC World Service for Asia and the Pacific. Sunday through Thursday (local Asian weekdays), it's a full hour of news fare in ●*The World Today*. Friday and Saturday, there's 30 minutes of the same, followed by ●*Everywoman* and *Meridian*, respectively. Continuous to East Asia on 5965, 6195 and 11955 kHz; to Southeast Asia on 6195, 7110, 9660 and 11955 kHz; and to Australasia on 9660, 11955 and 12080 kHz.

Radio Bulgaria. This time winters only. *News*, then Monday through Thursday there's 15 minutes of current events in *Today*, replaced Friday by *Weekly Spotlight*, a summary of the week's major political stories. The remainder of the broadcast is given over to features dealing with Bulgaria and Bulgarians, and includes some lively ethnic music. To Europe and eastern North America on 7530 and 9700 kHz. One hour earlier in summer.

Radio Cairo, Egypt. The second half of a 90-minute broadcast to Europe on 9900 kHz; see 2115 for program details.

China Radio International. Repeat of the 2000 transmission; see there for specifics. One hour to Europe, winter on 7170 kHz and summer on 9880 kHz.

Voice of America. The beginning of a three-hour block of programs to East and Southeast Asia and the Pacific. The ubiquitous *News Now*—news and reports on current events, sports, science, busi-

ness, entertainment and more. To East and Southeast Asia on 7215, 9705, 9770, 11760, 15185, 15290, 15305, 17735 and 17820 kHz; and to Australasia on 15185, 15305 and 17735 kHz. The first half hour is also available weekday evenings to Africa on 7340, 7375 and 7415 kHz.

Radio Australia. *News*, followed Sunday through Thursday by *AM* (current events). The hour is rounded off with a 20-minute music feature. The lineup starts with Sunday's sampling from different cultures, *Music Deli*, and ends with Thursday's *Australian Country Style*. In-between, choose from *Australian Music Show* (Monday); *At Your Request* (Tuesday); and *Blacktracker* (aboriginal music, Wednesday). Friday's features are *Jazz Notes* and a later-than-usual edition of *AM*; Saturday, it's the third hour of *Australia All Over*. Continuous programming to the Pacific on 17715, 17795 and 21725 kHz. Also audible in parts of western North America.

Radio Taipei International, Taiwan. *News*, then features. The last is *Let's Learn Chinese*, which has a series of segments for beginning, intermediate and advanced learners. Other features include *Jade Bells and Bamboo Pipes* (Monday), *People and Trends* (Tuesday), *Taiwan Today* and *Miss Mook's Big Countdown* (Wednesday), *Treasures of the Orient* and *Hot Spots* (Thursday), *Taipei Magazine* and *Life on the Outside* (Friday), *Kaleidoscope* and *Reflections* (Saturday) and *Food, Poetry and Others* followed by *Mailbag Time* on Sunday. Sixty minutes to western Europe, winters on 5810 and 9985 kHz, and summers on 15600 and 17750 kHz.

Radio Tirana, Albania. Winters only at this time. Thirty minutes of Balkan news and music. To Europe on 6025 and 7135 kHz.

Radio Habana Cuba. Sixty minutes of *news* (mainly about Cuba and Latin

America), features about the island and its inhabitants, and some thoroughly enjoyable Cuban music. To the Caribbean and southern United States on 6180 kHz, and to eastern North America and Europe on (winter) 9505 and (summer) 13720 kHz upper sideband (USB).

Radio Budapest, Hungary. Winters only at this time; see 2100 for specifics. Thirty minutes to Europe on 6025 kHz. One hour earlier in summer.

Voice of Turkey. Summers only at this time. *News*, followed by *Review of the Turkish Press* and features with a strong local flavor. Selections of Turkish popular and classical music complete the program. Fifty minutes to Europe on 7190 and 9655 kHz, and to eastern North America on 9655 kHz. One hour later during winter.

Radio Yugoslavia. Winters only at this time. Repeat of the 1930 broadcast. Thirty minutes to Europe on 6100 and 6185 kHz. One hour earlier in summer.

Radio Canada International. This time winters only. The final half-hour of a 90-minute broadcast. Monday through Friday, it's the CBC domestic service's ●*The World at Six*, with weekend fare consisting of Saturday's *The Great Eastern* and Sunday's *Madly Off in All Directions*, mainly of appeal to Canadians abroad. To Europe and Africa on 5995, 7235, 9770, 9805, 11755, 11945, 13650, 13690, 15150 and 17820 kHz. For a separate summer service, see the following item.

Radio Canada International. Summers only at this hour; and a relay of CBC domestic programming. Monday through Friday, there's ●*The World at Six*; Saturday and Sunday, *The World This Weekend*. On the half-hour, the weekday ●*As It Happens* is replaced Saturday by ●*The Mystery Project* and Sunday by *The Inside Track*. Sixty minutes to North America on 5960,

9755 and 13670 kHz. One hour later in winter. For a separate year-round service to Asia, see the next item.

Radio Canada International. Monday through Friday, it's ●*The World At Six*; Saturday and Sunday summer, *The World This Weekend*. Winter weekends, look for Saturday's *The Great Eastern* and Sunday's *Madly Off in All Directions*. Thirty minutes to Southeast Asia on 11705 kHz.

RAI International—Radio Roma, Italy. Approximately ten minutes of *news* followed by a quarter-hour feature (usually music). Twenty-five minutes to East Asia on 9675 and 11900 kHz.

Radio Korea International, South Korea. Winters only at this hour. Starts with *news*, followed Monday through Wednesday by *Economic News Briefs*. The remainder of the broadcast is taken up by a feature: *Shortwave Feedback* (Sunday), *Seoul Calling* (Monday and Tuesday), *Pulse of Korea* (Wednesday), *From Us to You* (Thursday), *Let's Sing Together* (Friday) and *Weekly News Focus* (Saturday). Thirty minutes to Europe on 3980 kHz, and one hour earlier in summer.

Radio Ukraine International. Winters only at this time. A potpourri of all things Ukrainian, with the Sunday broadcast often featuring some excellent music. Sixty minutes to Europe and beyond on 5905, 5940, 6020, 6080 and 7420 kHz. Often audible in eastern North America.

Radio For Peace International, Costa Rica. Continues with counterculture and social-conscience programs. Audible in Europe and North America on 15050 and 21460 kHz.

All India Radio. The final half-hour of a transmission to Western Europe and Australasia, consisting mainly of news-related fare. To Europe on 7410, 9950 and 11620 kHz; and to Australasia on 7150,

22:00–23:00

Other than one satellite phone for officials, this primitive telephone exchange is northern Afghanistan's only link with the outside world.

M. Guha

9910, 11620 and 11715 kHz. Frequencies for Europe are audible in parts of eastern North America, while those for Australasia are also heard in Southeast Asia.

WJCR, Upton, Kentucky. Continues with country gospel music to North America on 7490 and 13595 kHz. Other U.S. religious broadcasters heard at this hour include **WWCR** on 13845 kHz, **KAIJ** on 13815 kHz, **KTBN** on 15590 kHz, and **WHRI-World Harvest Radio** on 5745 (or 13760) kHz. For traditional Catholic programming, try **WEWN** on 7425 kHz.

CFRX-CFRB, Toronto, Canada. See 2100.

22:30

Radio Sweden. Winters only at this time. Monday through Friday, it's *news* and features in *Sixty Degrees North*, concentrating heavily on Scandinavian topics. Monday's accent is on sports; Tuesday brings the latest in electronic media news; Wednesday, there's *Money Matters*; Thursday features ecology or science and technology; and Friday offers a review of the week's news. Saturday's slot is filled by

Spectrum (arts) or *Sweden Today*, and Sunday fare consists of *In Touch with Stockholm* (a listener-response program) or the musical *Sounds Nordic*. Thirty minutes to Europe on 6065 kHz. One hour earlier in summer.

Radio Austria International. Winters only at this time. The informative and well-presented ●*Report from Austria*. Ample coverage of national and regional issues. Thirty minutes to Europe on 5945 and 6155 kHz, and to southern Africa on 13730 kHz. One hour earlier in summer.

Radio Budapest, Hungary. Winters only at this time; see 2100 for specifics. Thirty minutes to Europe on 3975 kHz. One hour earlier in summer.

Radio Prague, Czech Republic. *News,* then Monday through Friday there's *Current Affairs,* followed by one or more features. Early in the week, take your pick from Monday's *Spotlight,* Tuesday's *Talking Point,* and Wednesday's *History Czech.* The Thursday airing is *Economic Report,* and *Between You and Us* fills the Friday slot. Saturday's offering is a highly enjoyable musical feature, replaced Sunday by *A*

Letter from Prague, From the Weeklies and *Readings from Czech Literature.* A half hour to eastern North America, winter on 7345 and 9435 kHz, and summer on 11600 and 15545 kHz.

Voice of Greece. Actually starts around 2235. Fifteen minutes of English news from and about Greece. Part of a much longer, predominantly Greek, broadcast. To Australasia on 9425 kHz.

22:45

All India Radio. The first 15 minutes of a much longer broadcast, consisting of Indian music, regional and International *news*, commentary, and a variety of talks and features of general interest. Continuous till 0045. To Southeast Asia (and beyond) on 7150, 9705, 9950 and 11620 kHz.

Vatican Radio. Twenty minutes of religious and secular programming to East and Southeast Asia and Australasia on 6065, 7305, 9600 and 11830 kHz, some of them seasonal.

23:00

■BBC World Service for the Americas. Sunday through Friday, opens with *World News.* This is followed weekday evenings by the popular and long-running ●*Outlook.* The hour is rounded off with the 15-minute ●*Insight* (analysis of current events). These are replaced Sunday by *Wright Round the World* (an International request show), and Saturday there's a continuation of ●*Play of the Week.* Continuous to North America and the Caribbean on 5975, 6175 and 9590 kHz.

■BBC World Service for Asia and the Pacific. Sunday through Thursday (weekday mornings in Asia), it's the second hour of *The World Today,* a break-

fast news show for the region. On the remaining days, it's 30 minutes of the same, followed by a half-hour feature. Continuous to East Asia on 5965, 6035, 6195, 11945, 11955 and 15280 kHz; to Southeast Asia on 3915, 6195, 7110 and 11955 kHz; and to Australasia on 11955 kHz.

Voice of Turkey. Winters only at this hour. See 2200 for program details. Fifty minutes to Europe on 6135 and 9655 kHz, and to eastern North America on 9655 kHz. One hour earlier in summer.

■Deutsche Welle, Germany. Repeat of the 2100 broadcast to Southeast Asia and Australasia (see there for specifics). Forty-five minutes to South and Southeast Asia, winter on 6010, 9815 and 13690 kHz; and summer on 9715, 9815 and 11965 kHz.

Radio Australia. *World News,* followed Monday through Thursday by *Asia Pacific* (replaced Friday by *Book Reading,* and Sunday by *Correspondents' Reports*). On the half-hour, look for a feature. *Media Report* occupies the Sunday slot, and is replaced Monday by *The Sports Factor.* Then come Tuesday's *Health Report,* Wednesday's *Law Report,* Thursday's *Religion Report,* and Friday's *Week's End.* Not very original, but you know what you're getting. Saturday, there's the fourth and final hour of *Australia All Over.* Continuous to the Pacific on 9660, 12080, 17715, 17795 and 21740 kHz. Listeners in western North America should try the last three channels, especially in summer.

Radio Canada International. Summer weekdays, the final hour of ●*As It Happens* (a shorter edition on Fridays is complemented by *C'est la Vie*); winters, the first 30 minutes of the same, preceded by the up-to-the-minute *news* program ●*World at Six.* Summer weekends, look for ●*Global Village* (world music, Saturday) and ●*Roots and Wings* (eclectic music, Sunday). These are

23:00–23:30

Technician tunes the CCRadio with a calibrated AM loop antenna at the Sangean Electronics factory in China.

R. Crane

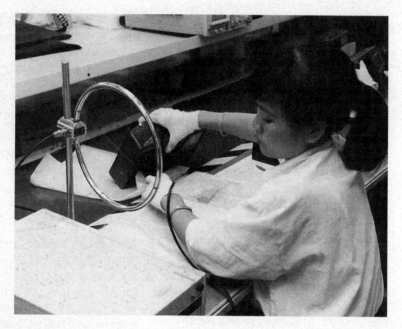

replaced winter by *The World This Weekend* (both days), ●*Mystery Project* (Saturday) and *The Inside Track* (Sunday). To eastern North America on 5960 and 9755 kHz, with 13670 kHz also available in summer. For the rest of North America and the Caribbean, try some additional weekend frequencies: 6040, 9535 and 11865 kHz in winter; and 11895, 15305 and 17695 kHz in summer.

China Radio International. *News* and commentary, followed Monday through Friday by in-depth reporting and an overview of the Chinese press. This is followed by features like *Focus* and *Cultural Spectrum* (Thursday); *Open Windows* and *Learn to Speak Chinese* (Monday); *Orient Arena* and *Opera House* (Tuesday); *Voices from Other Lands* (Wednesday); and *Life in China* and *Global Review* (Friday). Weekends, Saturday's lineup includes *Asia-Pacific News, Report from Developing Countries, China Scrapbook* and ●*Music from China*; and *Cultural Information, People in the Know, On the Road* and *Listeners' Letterbox* are aired on Sunday. Inaugurated during summer 1999,

this experimental broadcast via a Cuban relay may be one hour later in winter. Sixty minutes to the Caribbean and southern United States on 5990 kHz.

Radio Pyongyang, North Korea. Sixty minutes of old-time communist propaganda to the Americas on 11710 and 13650 kHz.

Radio For Peace International, Costa Rica. The final 60 minutes of a continuous eight-hour cyclical block of United Nations, counterculture, social-conscience and New Age programming. Audible in Europe and the Americas on 15050 and 21460 kHz.

Radio Cairo, Egypt. The first hour of a 90-minute potpourri of exotic Arab music and features reflecting Egyptian life and culture, with *news* and commentary about events in Egypt and the Arab world. There are also quizzes, mailbag shows, and answers to listeners' questions. Fair reception, but audio quality is often mediocre. To North America on 9900 kHz.

Radio Romania International. *News,* commentary and features, interspersed with some thoroughly enjoyable Romanian folk music. Fifty-five minutes to Northern Europe and eastern North America. Try 7135, 9570, 9625 and 11940 kHz.

WRMI-Radio Miami International, Miami, Florida. Part of a much longer multilingual transmission to the Caribbean. Summer weekdays at this time, you can hear 30 minutes of *Viva Miami!*—a potpourri of information, music and entertainment. Also includes regular weather updates during the hurricane season (June-November). Heard in much of the Americas on 9955 kHz. One hour later in winter.

Radio Bulgaria. Summers only at this time; see 1900 for specifics. A potpourri of *news* and features with a strong Bulgarian flavor. Sixty minutes to eastern North America on 9485 and 11720 kHz. One hour later during winter.

Voice of America. Continues with programs aimed at East Asia and the Pacific on the same frequencies as at 2200.

WJCR, Upton, Kentucky. Continuous country gospel music to North America on 7490 and 13595 kHz. Other U.S. religious broadcasters heard at this time include **WWCR** on 13845 kHz, **KAIJ** on 13815 kHz, **KTBN** on 15590 kHz, and **WHRI-World Harvest Radio** on 5745 kHz. For traditional Catholic programming, tune **WEWN** on 7425 kHz.

Technician adjusts audio levels on SLBC transmitters in Colombo, Sri Lanka. M. Guha

23:30

■**Radio Netherlands.** *News,* followed Monday through Friday by ●*Newsline,* then a feature program. Select offerings include ●*EuroQuest* (Monday), ●*A Good Life* (Tuesday), ●*Research File* (Thursday), ●*Roughly Speaking* (Saturday) and Friday's ●*Documentary.* The remaining lineup consists of *Aural Tapestry* and *Wide Angle* (Monday), *Sounds Interesting* (Wednesday) and Saturday's *Europe Unzipped.* One hour to North America on 6165 and 9845 kHz.

All India Radio. Continuous programming to Southeast Asia. A potpourri of *news,* commentary, features and exotic Indian music. On 7150, 9705, 9950 and 11620 kHz.

Voice of Vietnam. *News,* then it's *Commentary* or *Weekly Review.* These are followed by short features and some pleasant Vietnamese music (especially at weekends). A half hour to Asia (also heard in Europe) on 9840 and 12020 (or 9730) kHz.

Voice of Greece. Actually starts around 2335. Ten minutes of English news from and about Greece. Part of a much longer multilingual broadcast. To Central America (and well heard in eastern North America) on any two (sometimes three) frequencies from 9395, 9425, 9935, 11595 and 11640 kHz.

Prepared by Don Swampo and the staff of PASSPORT TO WORLD BAND RADIO.

Addresses 47
PLUS—2000

E-Mail and Postal Addresses . . .
PLUS World Wide Websites,
Phones and Faxes, Contact
Personnel, Bureaus, Future Plans,
Items for Sale, Free Gifts . . .
PLUS Summer and Winter Times
in Each Country!

Other parts of PASSPORT tell how stations' signals reach you, but this section is different: It spins the bottle the other way by showing how you can reach the stations. It also reveals other ways that stations can inform and entertain you.

"Applause" Replies

When radio was new, listeners sent in "applause" cards not only to let stations know about reception quality, but also how much their shows were—or weren't—being appreciated. By way of saying "thanks," stations would reply with a letter or attractive card verifying ("QSLing" in radio lingo) that the station the listener reported hearing was, in fact, theirs. While they were at it, some would also throw in a free souvenir—a station calendar, perhaps, or a pennant or sticker.

This is still being done today. You can see how by looking under Verification in the glossary farther back in this book, then making use of Addresses PLUS for contact specifics.

Electronic Bazaar

Stations sell items, too. Besides the obvious, such as world band radios, some peddle native recordings, books, magazines, station T-shirts, ties, tote bags, aprons, caps, watches, clocks, pens, knives, letter openers, lighters, refrigerator magnets, keyrings and other collectables.

Paying Postfolk

Most stations prefer to reply to listener correspondence—even e-mail—via the postal system. That way, they can send out printed schedules, verification cards and other "hands-on" souvenirs. Big stations usually do so for free, but smaller ones often want to be reimbursed for postage costs.

Most effective, especially for Latin American and Indonesian stations, is to enclose some unused (mint) stamps from the station's country. These are available from Plum's Airmail Postage, 12 Glenn Road, Flemington NJ 08822 USA, phone +1 (908) 788-1020, fax +1 (908) 782 2612. Too, you can try DX Stamp Service, 6137 Patriot Drive, Apt. 13, Ontario NY 14519-8606 USA, phone +1 (315) 524-8806; or DX-QSL Associates, 434 Blair Road NW, Vienna VA 22180 USA. One way to help ensure your return-postage stamps will be put to the intended use is to affix them onto a pre-addressed return airmail envelope. The result is a self-addressed stamped envelope, or SASE as it is referred to in this section.

You can also prompt reluctant stations by donating one or more U.S. dollars, preferably hidden from prying eyes by a piece of foil-covered carbon paper or the like. Registration helps, too, as cash tends to get stolen. Additionally, International Reply Coupons (IRCs), which recipients may exchange locally for air or surface stamps, are available at many post offices worldwide. Thing is, they're relatively costly, are not fully effective, and aren't accepted by postal authorities in some countries.

Villager hears a favorable weather report over Kyrgyz Radio 1. Climate forecasting is a life-and-death matter in this high-mountain country.
M. Guha

These fortunate children are able to attend a UNOPS-sponsored school in the sensitive Gharam valley in Tajikistan. M. Guha

Stamp Out Crime

Yes, even in 2000 mail theft is a problem in several countries. We identify these, and for each one offer proven ways to avoid theft. Remember that some postal employees are stamp collectors, and in certain countries they freely steal mail with unusual stamps. When in doubt, use everyday stamps or, even better, a postal meter. Another option is to use an aerogram.

¿Que Hora Es?

World Time, explained elsewhere in this book, is essential if you want to find out when your favorite station is on. But if you want to know what time it is in any given country, World Time and Addresses PLUS work together to give you the most accurate local times within each country.

How accurate? The United States' official expert on International local times tells us that her organization finds PASSPORT's local times to be the most accurate available from any source, anywhere.

So that you don't have to wrestle with seasonal changes in your own time, we give local times for each country in terms of hours' difference from World Time, which stays the same year-round. For example, if you look below under "Algeria," you'll see that country is World Time +1; that is, one hour ahead of World Time. So, if World Time is 1200, the local time in Algeria is 1300 (1:00 PM). On the other hand, México City is World Time -6; that is, six hours behind World Time. If World Time is 1200, in México City it's 6:00 AM. And so it goes for each country in this section. Times shown in parentheses are for the middle of the year—roughly April-October; specific dates of seasonal-time changeovers for individual countries can be obtained (U.S. callers only) by dialing toll-free 1 (800) 342-5624 during working hours.

Spotted Something New?

Has something changed since we went to press? A missing detail? Please let us know! Your update information, especially photocopies of material received from stations, is highly valued. Contact the IBS Editorial Office, Box 300, Penn's Park, PA 18943 USA, fax +1 (215) 598 3794, e-mail addresses@passband.com.

Muchas gracias to the kindly folks and helpful organizations mentioned at the end of this chapter for their tireless cooperation in the preparation of this section. Without you, none of this would have been possible.

Using PASSPORT's Addresses PLUS Section

Stations included: All stations known to reply, however erratically, or new stations which possibly may reply, to correspondence from listeners.

Leased-time programs: Private non-political organizations that lease air time, but which possess no world band transmitters of their own, are not necessarily listed. However, they may be reached via the stations over which they are heard.

Postal addresses. Communications addresses are given. These sometimes differ from the physical locations given in the Blue Pages.

E-mail addresses and URLs. Given in Internet format. Periods, commas and semicolons at the end of an address are normal sentence punctuation, *not* part of the address, and "http://" is used only when there is no "www."

Fax numbers. To help avoid confusion, fax numbers are given *without* hyphens, telephone numbers with hyphens, and are configured for International dialing once you add your country's International access code (011 in the United States and

Policeman scrutinizes a foreign visitor in the north Afghan "capital" of Taloqan.   M. Guha

Canada, 010 in the United Kingdom, and so on). For domestic dialing within countries outside the United States, Canada and the Caribbean, replace the country code (1-3 digits preceded by a "+") by a zero.

Giveaways. If you want freebies, say so politely in your correspondence. These are usually available until supplies run out.

Web simulcasting. World band stations which simulcast over the Web are indicated by 🖃.

Unless otherwise indicated, stations:

• Reply regularly within six months to most listeners' correspondence in English.

• Provide, upon request, free station schedules and verification ("QSL") postcards or letters (see "Verification" in the glossary for further information). We specify when other items are available for free or for purchase.

• Do not require compensation for postage costs incurred in replying to you. Where compensation is required, details are provided.

Local times. These are given in difference from World Time. For example, "World Time –5" means that if you subtract five hours from World Time, you'll get the local time in that country; so if it were 1100 World Time, it would be 0600 local time in that country. Times in (parentheses) are for the middle of the year—roughly April-October.

AFGHANISTAN World Time +4:30

NOTE: Postal service to this country is sometimes suspended.

ISLAMIC EMIRATE OF AFGHANISTAN (under Taliban control)

Radio Voice of Shari'ah, Afghan Radio TV, P.O. Box 544, Ansari Wat, Kabul, Afghanistan, via Pakistan (while direct postal service is unavailable)—under normal conditions, replace "Afghanistan, via Pakistan" with "Islamic Emirate of Afghanistan." Phone: +92 (91) 287-454. Fax: +92 (81) 447 300. External telephone links are currently suspended, except for a limited service provided by Pakistan Telecom. Contact: Abdul Rahman Nasseri, Department of Planning and Foreign Relations. Prefers correspondence in Dari, Farsi, Pashto or Urdu, but reception reports in English are sometimes verified when directed to Mr. Naseri. Given the erratic postal system that operates via Pakistan, replies may take several months.
NEW YORK OFFICE: Representative of the Islamic Emirate of Afghanistan to the United Nations, 55/16 Main Street, Flushing NY, USA. Phone: +1 (718) 359-0457; (Newsline) +1 (718) 762-8095. Fax: +1 (718) 661 2721. URL: www.taleban.com. Contact: Mowlawi Hakim Mujahed, United Nations Representative.

ISLAMIC REPUBLIC OF AFGHANISTAN (Northern Afghanistan, pro-Rabbani)

Takhar Radio, Operations Complex, Taloqan, Takhar Province, Northern Afghanistan, via Dushanbe, Tajikistan. Phone: +873 76201256 (c/o Abdul Ghani). Contact: (administration) Sayd Habib, Director; Habib Inayatullah, Deputy Director; (technical) Mohammed Taher Ramin, Engineer. Although there is no official verification policy, reception reports are welcomed. Correspondence in English, Dari or Farsi is best directed to Mr. Arayanfar at the embassy in Dushanbe (see, below), though listeners in North America may prefer sending their correspondence c/o the Afghan Mission to the United Nations.
TAJIKISTAN ADDRESS: Embassy of Afghanistan, ul. Pushkina, Dushanbe, Tajikistan. Phone: +7 (3772) 216-418 or +7 (3772) 216-072. Fax: +7 (3772) 216 394. Contact: Shamsul Haq Arayanfar, Cultural Attaché.
USA ADDRESS: Mission of Afghanistan to the United Nations, 360 Lexington Avenue, 11th Floor, New York NY 10010 USA. Phone: +1 (212) 972-1212/3. Fax: +1 (212) 972 1216. URL: (under construction) www.afghan-govt.com.

ALBANIA World Time +1 (+2 midyear)

Radio Tirana, External Service, Rruga Ismail Qemali Nr. 11, Tirana, Albania. Phone: (general) +355 (42) 23-239. Fax: (External Service) +355 (42) 23 650; (General Directorate) +355

(42) 26 203; (Technical Directorate) +355 (42) 23 650; or +355 (42) 27 745. E-mail: (Technical Directorate) 113566.3011@compuserve.com; or dcico@artv.tirana.al. URLs: (general) http://rtsh.sil.at; (RealAudio from Radio Tirana 1, domestic service) http://rtsh.sil.at/online.htm. Contact: Bardhyl Pollo, Director of External Services; Adriana Bislea, English Department; Marjeta Thoma; Pandi Skaka, Producer; or Diana Koci; (Technical Directorate) Irfan Mandija, Chief of Radio Broadcasting, Technical Directorate; Hector Karanxha; or Rifat Kryeziu, Director of Technical Directorate. May send free stickers & postcards. Replies from the station are again forthcoming, but it is advisable to include return postage ($1 should be enough).
Trans World Radio—see Monaco.

ALGERIA World Time +1 (+2 midyear)

Radio Algiers International—same details as "Radio Algérienne," below.
Radio Algérienne (ENRS)
NONTECHNICAL AND GENERAL TECHNICAL: 21 Boulevard des Martyrs, Algiers 16000, Algeria. Phone: (Direction Générale) +213 (2) 230-821; (Direction Commerciale) +213 (2) 590-700; (head of international relations) +213 (2) 594-266; (head of technical direction) +213 (2) 692-867. Fax: +213 (2) 605 814. E-mail: radioalg@ist.cerist.dz. URL: (includes RealAudio) www.algerian-radio.dz. Contact: (nontechnical) L. Zaghlami; Chaabane Lounakil, Head of International Arabic Section; Mrs. Zehira Yahi, Head of International Relations; or Relations Extérieures; (technical) M. Lakhdar Mahdi, Head of Technical Direction. Replies irregularly. French or Arabic preferred, but English accepted.
FREQUENCY MANAGEMENT OFFICE: Télédiffusion d'Algérie, Centre Nsdal, Bouzareah 1850, Algeria. Phone: +213 (2) 904-512; or 213 (2) 901-717. Fax: +213 (2) 901 499 or +213 (2) 901 522. Contact: Slimane Djematene; or Karim Zitouni. E-mail: tda@ist.cerist.dz.

ANGOLA World Time +1

Emissora Provincial de Benguela (if reactivated), C.P. 19, Benguela, Angola. Contact: Simão Martíns Cuto, Responsável Administrativo; Carlos A. A. Gregório, Diretor; or José Cabral Sande. $1 or return postage required. Replies irregularly.
Emissora Provincial de Bié (if reactivated), C.P. 33, Kuito, Bié, Angola. Contact: José Cordeiro Chimo, Diretor. Replies occasionally to correspondence in Portuguese.
Emissora Provincial de Moxico (if reactivated), C.P. 74, Luena, Angola. Contact: Paulo Cahilo, Diretor. $1 or return postage required. Replies to correspondence in Portuguese.
Other **Emissora Provincial** stations (if reactivated)—same address, etc., as Rádio Nacional, below.
Rádio Nacional de Angola, C.P. 1329, Luanda, Angola. Fax: +244 (2) 391 234. Contact: Bernardino Costa, Public Opinion Office; Sra. Luiza Fancony, Diretora de Programas; Lourdes de Almeida, Chefe de Secção; or César A.B. da Silva, Diretor Geral. Formerly replied occasionally to correspondence, preferably in Portuguese, but replies have been more difficult recently. $1, return postage or 2 IRCs most helpful.

ANTARCTICA World Time –3 Base Antártica Esperanza

Radio Nacional Arcángel San Gabriel—LRA36, Base Esperanza, 9411 Antártida Argentina, Argentina. Phone/Fax: +54 (2964) 421 519. E-mail: (do not include attachments!) esc38ant@

satlink.com. Contact: Tte. Cnel. Fernando García Pinasco, Jefe de Base Esperanza; or Francisco Cuba, Coordinación General. Return postage required. Replies to correspondence in Spanish, and sometimes to correspondence in English and French, depending upon who is at the station. If no reply, try sending your correspondence (but don't write the station's name on your envelope) and 2 IRCs via the helpful Gabriel Iván Barrera, Casilla 2868, 1000 Buenos Aires, Argentina.

ANGUILLA World Time –4

Caribbean Beacon, Box 690, Anguilla, British West Indies. Phone: +1 (809) 497-4340. Fax: +1 (809) 497 4311. Contact: Monsell Hazell, Chief Engineer. $2 or return postage helpful. Relays Dr. Gene Scott's University Network—*see* USA.

ANTIGUA World Time –4

BBC World Service—Caribbean Relay Station, P.O. Box 1203, St. John's, Antigua. Phone: +1 (809) 462-0994. Fax: +1 (809) 462 0436. Contact: (technical) G. Hoef, Manager; Roy Fleet; or R. Pratt, Company Engineer. Nontechnical correspondence should be sent to the BBC World Service in London (*see*).

Deutsche Welle—Relay Station Antigua—same address and contact as BBC World Service, above. Nontechnical correspondence should be sent to Deutsche Welle in Germany (*see*).

ARGENTINA World Time –3

"De Colección," Casilla 96, 1900 La Plata, Argentina. Phone: +54 (221) 4270-507; or +54 (221) 4216-607. Contact: Jorge Bourdet, Editor. Program from a medium wave station in the city of La Plata, aired local Sunday evenings to Antarctica in the SSB mode (try 15820 kHz, upper sideband); also heard via WRMI, USA and at least one Italian shortwave broadcaster. Include 2 IRCs when writing.

Radiodifusión Argentina al Exterior—RAE, C.C. 555 Correo Central, 1000 Buenos Aires, Argentina. Phone/Fax: +54 (11) 4325-6368. Fax: +54 (11) 4325 9433. E-mail: RNA@mecom.ar. Contact: (general) John Anthony Middleton, Head of the English Team; María Dolores López; or Sandro Cenci, Chief, Italian Section; (administration) Señorita Perla Damuri, Directora; (technical) Gabriel Iván Barrera, DX Editor; or Patricia Menéndez. Free paper pennant and tourist literature. Return postage or $1 appreciated.

Radio La Colifata—LT22, Casilla 17, 1640 – Martínez (B.A.), Argentina. E-mail: colifata@interactive.com.ar. Contact: Alfredo Olivera, Director General; or Norberto Pugliese, Producción onda corta. Verifies reception reports and replies to correspondence in Spanish. Return postage (2 IRCs) required. Normally transmits only on FM, from its location in the Dr. J. T. Borda Municipal Neuropsychiatric Hospital, but occasionally has special programs broadcast via stations like WRMI, USA. Programs are produced by residents of the hospital.

Radio Malargüe (if reactivated), Esq. Aldao 350, 5613 Malargüe, Argentina. Contact: Eduardo Vicente Lucero, Jefe Técnico; Nolasco H. Barrera, Interventor; or José Pandolfo, Departamento Administración. Free pennants. Return postage necessary. Prefers correspondence in Spanish.

Radio Nacional Buenos Aires, Maipú 555, 1006 Buenos Aires, Argentina. Phone: +54 (11) 4325-9100. Fax: (general) +54 (11) 4325 9433; (technical) +54 (11) 4325 5742. Contact:

Patricia Ivone Barral, Directora Nacional; Patricia Claudia Dinale de Jantus, Directora Administrativa; or María Eugenia Baya Casal, Directora Operativa. $1 helpful. Prefers correspondence in Spanish, and usually replies via RAE (*see,* above). If no reply, try sending your correspondence (but don't write the station's name on your envelope) and 1 IRC via the helpful Gabriel Iván Barrera, Casilla 2868, 1000 Buenos Aires, Argentina.

Radio Nacional Mendoza (if reactivated), Av. Emilio Civit 460, 5500 Mendoza, Argentina. Phone: (administrative) +54 (261) 438-1527. Phone/fax: (general) +54 (261)425-7931. Fax: +54 (261) 438 0596. Contact: (general/administrative) Lic. Jorge Horacio Parvanoff, Director; (technical) Juan Carlos Fernández, Jefe del Departamento Técnico. Free pamphlets and stickers. Replies to correspondence, preferably in Spanish, but English also accepted.

Radio Pasteur, Casilla 1852 Correo Central, 1000 Buenos Aires, Argentina. Phone/Fax: (Morales) +54 (11) 4503 6317. E-mail: radio-pasteur@iname.com or (Morales) morales.arg@ sicoar.com. Contact: Claudio Morales. A radio production carried out by students of a journalism workshop in Buenos Aires. Features sports, arts, culture and entertainment. Also looks at ecology and the environment, customs and traditions, plus social and human rights in Argentina. Letters and reception reports welcome. Return postage helpful.

Radio Rivadavia (when operating to Antarctica), Arenales 2467, 1124 Buenos Aires, Argentina. Fax: +54 (11) 4824 6927.

ARMENIA World Time +3 (+4 midyear)

Armenian Radio—*see* Voice of Armenia for details.

Radio Intercontinental, Vardanants 28, No. 34, Yerevan 70, Armenia. If a reply from the station is not forthcoming, try writing direct to the program you heard. Contact information for "Lutherische Stunde" and "Missionswerk Werner Heukelbach" are listed later in this section, under 'Germany'; and "Mitternachtsruf" and "Stimmes des Trostes" under 'Switzerland'.

Voice of Armenia, Radio Agency, Alek Manoukyan Street 5, 375025 Yerevan, Armenia. Phone: +374 (2) 558-010. Fax: +374 (2) 551 513. Contact: V. Voskanian, Deputy Editor-in-Chief; R. Abalian, Editor-in-Chief; Armenag Sansaryan, International Relations Bureau; Laura Baghdassarian, Deputy Manager, Radioagency; or Dr. Levon V. Ananikian, Director. Free postcards and stamps. Replies slowly.

ASCENSION World Time exactly

BBC World Service—Atlantic Relay Station, English Bay, Ascension (South Atlantic Ocean). Fax: +247 6117. Contact: (technical) Jeff Cant, Staff Manager; M.R. Watkins, A/Assistant Resident Engineer; or Mrs. Nicola Nicholls, Transmitter Engineer. Nontechnical correspondence should be sent to the BBC World Service in London (*see*).

Radio Japan, Radio Roma and Voice of America via BBC Ascension Relay Station—All correspondence should be directed to the regular addresses in Japan, Italy and USA (*see*).

AUSTRALIA World Time +11 (+10 midyear) Victoria (VIC), New South Wales (NSW), Australian Capital Territory (ACT) and Tasmania (TAS); +10:30 (+9:30 midyear) South Australia (SA); +10 Queensland (QLD); +9:30 Northern Territory (NT); +8 Western Australia (WA)

Arbana Islami reads the news in Albanian over the Southern Slavic Service of RFE/RL, which has gained importance since the Kosovo crisis. RFE/RL

Australian Broadcasting Corporation Northern Territory HF Service—ABC Radio 8DDD Darwin, Administrative Center for the Northern Territory Shortwave Service, ABC Box 9994, GPO Darwin NT 0820, Australia. Phone: +61 (8) 8943-3222; (engineering) +61 (8) 8943-3209. Fax: +61 (8) 8943 3235 or +61 (8) 8943 3208. Contact: (general) Tony Bowden, Branch Manager; (administration) Carole Askham, Administrative Officer; (technical) Peter Camilleri or Yvonne Corby. Free stickers & postcards. "Traveller's Guide to ABC Radio" for $1. T-shirts US$20. Three IRCs or return postage helpful.

Australian Defence Forces Radio (when active), Department of Defence, EMU (Electronic Media Unit) ANZAC Park West, APW 1-B-07, Reid, Canberra, ACT 2601, Australia. Phone: +61 (2) 6266-6669. Fax: +61 (2) 6266 6565. Contact: (general) Adam Iffland, Presenter; (technical) Hugh Mackenzie, Managing Presenter; or Brian Langshaw. SAE and 2 IRCs needed for a reply. Station broadcasts irregularly, and replies to verification inquiries only.

BBC World Service via Radio Australia—For verification direct from the Australian transmitters, contact John Westland, Director of English Programs at Radio Australia (see). Nontechnical correspondence should be sent to the BBC World Service in London (see).

CAAMA Radio—ABC, Central Australian Aboriginal Media Association, Bush Radio Service, P.O. Box 2924, Alice Springs NT 0871, Australia. Phone: +61 (8) 8952-9204. Fax: +61 (8) 8952 9214. Contact: Merridie Satoar, Department Manager; Mark Lillyman, News Director; Nova Mack, Receptionist; or Owen Cole, CAAMA General Manager; (administration) Graham Archer, Station Manager; (technical) Warren Huck, Technician. Free stickers. Two IRCs or return postage helpful.

⧉**Radio Australia—ABC**

STUDIOS AND MAIN OFFICES: GPO Box 428G, Melbourne VIC 3001, Australia. Phone: ("Openline" voice mail for listeners' messages and requests) +61 (3) 9626-1825; (switchboard) +61 (3) 9626-1800; (English programs) +61 (3) 9626-1922. Fax & Faxpoll: (general) +61 (3) 9626 1899; (engineering) +61 (3) 9626

1917. E-mail: (general) english@ra.abc.net.au; (Radio Australia transmissions & programs) raelp@radioaus.abc.net.au; (Pacific Services) rapac@radioaus.abc.net.au; (Internet and World Wide Web Coordinator) naughton.russell@a2.abc.net.au. URL: (includes RealAudio) www.abc.net.au/ra/ (RealAudio in English also at www.wrn.org/ondemand/australia.html). Contact: (general) John Westland, Head, English Language Programming; Roger Broadbent, Producer "Feedback"; Tony Hastings, Director of Programs; Caroline Bilney, Information Officer; or Jean-Gabriel Manguy, General Manager; (technical) Nigel Holmes, Transmission Manager, Transmission Management Unit. Free stickers and sometimes pennants and souvenirs available. On-air language courses available in Chinese, Indonesian, Khmer and Vietnamese. Course notes available at cost price. As from the 1st of July 1997, Radio Australia has been operating at a greatly reduced capacity. Budget cuts of more than 50% in 1997 and continuing over the next 3 years, will reduce this station's ability to broadcast successfully on shortwave. Despite this situation, Radio Australia will attempt to answer listener's letters even though this will largely depend on the availability of resources and a reply may no longer be possible in all cases. All reception reports received by Radio Australia will now be forwarded to the Australian Radio DX Club for assessment and checking. ARDXC will forward completed QSLs to Radio Australia for mailing. For further information, contact John Westland, Director of English Programs at Radio Australia (E-mail: westland.john@a2.abc.net.au); or John Wright, Secretary/Editor, ARDXC (E-mail: dxer@fl.net.au). Plans to add new aerials and re-locate 250 kW transmitters.

NEW YORK BUREAU, NONTECHNICAL: Room 2260, 630 Fifth Avenue, New York NY 10020 USA. Phone: (representative) +1 (212) 332-2540; or (correspondent) +1 (212) 332-2545. Fax: +1 (212) 332 2546. Contact: Maggie Jones, North American Representative.

LONDON BUREAU, NONTECHNICAL: 54 Portland Place, London W1N 4DY, United Kingdom. Phone: +44 (171) 631-4456. Fax: (administration) +44 (171) 323 0059, (news) +44 (171) 323 1125. Contact: Robert Bolton, Manager.

BANGKOK BUREAU, NONTECHNICAL: 209 Soi Hutayana off Soi Suanplu, South Sathorn Road, Bangkok 10120, Thailand. Fax: +66 (2) 287 2040. Contact: Nicholas Stuart.

Radio Rum Jungle—ABC (program studios), Top End Aboriginal Bush Broadcasting Association (TEEBA), Shop 29 Rapid Creek Shopping Centre, Millner NT 0810, Australia. Phone: (general) +61 (8) 8948-3023; (studio talkback) +61 (8) 8948-0100. Fax: +61 (8) 8948 3027. Contact: Mae-Mae Morrison, Announcer; Andrew Joshua, Chairman; or George Butler. Three IRCs or return postage helpful. May send free posters.

Radio VNG (official time station)
PRIMARY ADDRESS: National Standards Commission, P.O. Box 282, North Ryde, NSW 1670, Australia. Toll-free telephone number (Australia only) (1800) 251-942. Phone: +61 (2) 9888-3922. Fax: +61 (2) 9888 3033. E-mail: rbrittain@nsc.gov.au. Contact: Dr. Richard Brittain, Secretary, National Time Committee. Station offers a free 16-page booklet about VNG and free promotional material. Free stickers and postcards. One IRC or $1 helpful. May be forced to close down if sufficient funding is not found by June 30th 2002.
ALTERNATIVE ADDRESS: VNG Users Consortium, GPO Box 1090, Canberra, ACT 2601, Australia. Fax: +61 (2) 6249 9355. Contact: Dr. Marion Leiba, Honorary Secretary. Three IRCs appreciated.

AUSTRIA   World Time +1 (+2 midyear)

🖥Radio Austria International
MAIN OFFICE: Würzburggasse 30, A-1136 Vienna, Austria. Phone: (general) +43 (1) 87878-12130; (voice mail) +43 (1) 87878-13636; (technical) +43 (1) 87878-12629. Fax: (general) +43 (1) 87878 14404; (technical) +43 (1) 87878 12773. E-mail: (frequency schedules, reception reports) roi.service@orf.at; (intermedia/special programmes) roi@orf.at; (technical) hfbc@orf.at. URLs: (general) www.orf.at/roi/; (RealAudio news in German) www.wrn.org/ondemand/austria.html; (Live audio in RealAudio/NetShow/Streamworks) www.wrn.org/live.html—schedule information available at www.wrn.org/schedules.html. Contact: (general) Vera Bock, Listener's Service; "Postbox"/"Hörerbriefkasten" listeners' letters shows; Wolf Harranth, Editor, "Intermedia"; (administration) Prof. Paul Lendvai, Director; Dr. Edgar Sterbenz, Deputy Director; or Prof. Roland Machatschke, Managing Director; (English Department) David Ward; (German Department) Helmut Blechner; (French Department) Robert Denis; (Spanish Department) Jacobo Naar-Carbonell; (Internet Service) Marianne Veit or Oswald Klotz; (technical) Ing. Ernst Vranka, Frequency Manager; Ing. Klaus Hollndonner, Technical Director; or Listener's Service. Free stickers and program schedule twice a year, as well as quiz prizes. Mr. Harranth seeks collections of old verification cards and letters for the highly organized historical archives he is maintaining. Plans to add two 100kW shortwave transmitters
WASHINGTON NEWS BUREAU: 1206 Eaton Ct. NW, Washington DC 20007 USA. Phone: +1 (202) 822-9570. Contact: Eugen Freund.

AZERBAIJAN   World Time +3 (+4 midyear)

Azerbaijani Radio—*see* Radio Dada Gorgud for details.
Radio Dada Gorgud (Voice of Azerbaijan), Medhi Hüseyin küçäsi 1, 370011 Baku, Azerbaijan. Phone: +994 (12) 398-585. Fax: +994 (12) 395 452. Contact: Mrs. Tamam Bayatli-

Öner, Director; or Kamil Mamedov, Director of Division of International Relations. Free postcards, and occasionally, books. $1 or return postage helpful. Replies irregularly to correspondence in English.

BAHRAIN   World Time +3

Radio Bahrain (if reactivated), Broadcasting & Television, Ministry of Information, P.O. Box 702, Al Manãmah, Bahrain. Phone: (Arabic Service) +973 781-888; (English Service) +973 629-085. Fax: (Arabic Service) +973 681 544; (English Service) +973 780 911. URL: www.gna.gov.bh/brtc/radio.html. Contact: A. Suliman (for Director of Broadcasting). $1 or IRC required. Replies irregularly.

BANGLADESH   World Time +6

🖥Bangladesh Betar
NONTECHNICAL CORRESPONDENCE: External Services, Bangladesh Betar, Shahbagh Post Box No. 2204, Dhaka 1000, Bangladesh; (physical address) Betar Bhaban Sher-e-Bangla Nagar, Agargaon Road, Dhaka 1207, Bangladesh. Phone: (general) +880 (2) 865-294; (Rahman Khan) +880 (2) 863-949; (external services) +880 (2) 868-119. Fax: +880 (2) 862 021. URL: (RealAudio only—news and Bengali songs) www.banglaradio.com. Contact: Mrs. Dilruba Begum, Director, External Services; Ashfaque-ur Rahman Khan, Director – Programmes; or (technical) Muhammed Nazrul Islam, Station Engineer. For further technical contacts, *see* below.
TECHNICAL CORRESPONDENCE: National Broadcasting Authority, NBA Bhaban, 121 Kazi Nazrul Islam Avenue, Shahabagh, Dhaka 1000, Bangladesh. Phone: +880 (2) 500-143/7, +880 (2) 500-490, +880 (2) 500-810, +880 (2) 505-113 or +880 (2) 507-269; (Shakir) +880 (2) 818-734; (Das) +880 (2) 500-810. Fax: +880 (2) 817 850; (Shakir) +880 (2) 817 850. E-mail: dgradio@drik.bgd.toolnet.org. Contact: Syed Abdus Shakir, Chief Engineer; (reception reports) Manoranjan Das, Station Engineer, Dhaka; or Muhammed Romizuddin Bhuiya, Senior Engineer (Research Wing). Verifications not common from this office.

BARBADOS   World Time – 4

Caribbean Broadcasting Union, Wilkins Lodge, Two Mile Hill, St. Michael, Barbados, West Indies. Phone: +1 (246) 430-1000. Fax: +1 (246) 429 2171. E-mail: cbusat@caribsurf.com. URL: www.caribunion.com. Contact: Patrick Cozier, Secretary General; or Ainsley Sahai, Administrative Officer. Umbrella organization for English and Dutch speaking broadcasters in the Caribbean.

BELARUS   World Time +2 (+3 midyear)

Belarusian Radio—*see* Radio Belarus for details.
Grodno Radio—*see* Radio Belarus for details.
Mogilev Radio—*see* Radio Belarus for details.
Radio Belarus/Radio Minsk, vul. Chyrvonaya 4 [German Service: ul. Krasnaja 4], 220807 Minsk, Belarus. Phone: +375 (172) 395-831; +375 (172) 395-875. Fax: +375 (172) 366 643. URL: www.nestor.minsk.by/radiorod/indexen.htm. Contact: Irina Polozhentseva, English Program Editor; Jürgen Eberhardt, Editor, German Service. Free Belarus stamps.

BELGIUM   World Time +1 (+2 midyear)

⚅RTBF-International, B-1044 Brussels, Belgium. Phone: +32 (2) 737-4024. Fax: +32 (2) 737 3032. E-mail: relint.r@ rtbf.be. URLs: (RTBF-International) www.rtbf.be/ri/; ("La Première") www.rtbf.be/premiere/; (RealAudio) www.rtbf.be/jp/. Contact: Jean-Pol Hecq, Directeur des Relations Internationales (or "Head, International Service" if writing in English). Broadcasts are essentially a relay of news and information programs from the domestic channel "La Première" of RTBF (Radio-Télévision Belge de la Communauté Française) via facilities of Deutsche Telekom (see) in Jülich, Germany. Return postage not required. Accepts e-mail reports.

⚅Radio Vlaanderen Internationaal (RVI)

NONTECHNICAL AND GENERAL TECHNICAL: B-1043 Brussels, Belgium; (English Section) RVI Brussels Calling, B-1043 Brussels, Belgium. Phone: +32 (2) 741-5611, +32 (2) 741-3806/7 or +32 (2) 741-3802. Fax: (administration and Dutch Service) +32 (2) 732 6295; (other language services) +32 (2) 732 8336. BBS: +32 (3) 825-3613. E-mail: info@rvi.be. URLs: (text and RealAudio) www.rvi.be; (RealAudio in English, French, German and Dutch) www.wrn.org/ondemand/belgium.html. Contact: (general) Deanne Lehman, Producer, "Brussels 1043" letterbox program; Liz Sanderson, Head, English Service;

Maryse Jacob, Head, French Service; Martina Luxen, Head, German Service; or Wim Jansen, Station Manager; (general technical) Frans Vossen, Producer, "Radio World." Sells RVI T-shirts (large/extra large) for 400 Belgian francs. Remarks and reception reports can also be sent c/o the following diplomatic addresses:

NIGERIA EMBASSY: Embassy of Belgium, 1A, Bak Road, Ikoyi-Island, Lagos, Nigeria.

ARGENTINA EMBASSY: Embajada de Bélgica, Defensa 113 – 8º Piso, 1065 Buenos Aires, Argentina.

FREQUENCY MANAGEMENT OFFICE: BRTN, August Reyerslaan 52, B-1043 Brussels, Belgium. Phone: +32 (2) 741-5020. Fax: +32 (2) 741 5567. E-mail: (De Cuyper) hector.decuyper@vrt.be. Contact: Hector De Cuyper, Frequency Manager.

BENIN   World Time +1

Office de Radiodiffusion et Télévision du Benin, La Voix de la Révolution, B.P. 366, Cotonou, Bénin; this address is for Cotonou and Parakou stations, alike. Contact: (Cotonou) Damien Zinsou Ala Hassa; Emile Desire Ologoudou, Directeur Generale; or Leonce Goohouede; (technical) Anastase Adjoko, Chef de Service Technique; (Radio Parakou, general) J. de Matha, Le Chef de la Station, or (Radio Parakou, technical)

TIPS FOR EFFECTIVE CORRESPONDENCE

Write to be read. Be interesting and helpful from the recipient's point of view, yet friendly without being chummy. Comments on specific programs are almost always appreciated.

Incorporate language courtesies. Writing in the broadcaster's tongue is always a plus—this section of PASSPORT indicates when it is a requirement—but English is usually the next-best bet. In addition, when writing in any language to Spanish-speaking countries, remember that what gringos think of as the "last name" is actually written as the penultimate name. Thus, Juan Antonio Vargas García, which can also be written as Juan Antonio Vargas G., refers to Sr. Vargas; so your salutation should read, *Estimado Sr. Vargas.*

What's that "García" doing there, then? That's *mamita's* father's family name. Latinos more or less solved the problem of gender fairness in names long before the Anglos.

But, wait—what about Portuguese, used by all those lovely stations in Brazil? Same concept, but in reverse. *Mamá's* father's family name is penultimate, and the "real" last name is where English-speakers are used to it, at the end.

In Chinese, the "last" name comes first. However, when writing in English, Chinese names are sometimes reversed for the benefit of *weiguoren*—foreigners. Use your judgement. For example, "Li" is a common Chinese last name, so if you see "Li Dan," it's "Mr. Li." But if it's "Dan Li"—and certainly if it's been anglicized into "Dan Lee"—he's already one step ahead of you, and it's still "Mr. Li" (or Lee). Less widely known is that the same can also occur in Hungarian. For example, "Bartók Béla" for Béla Bartók.

If in doubt, fall back on the ever-safe "Dear Sir" or "Dear Madam," or use e-mail, where salutations are not expected. And be patient—replies by post usually take weeks, sometimes months. Slow responders, those that tend to take many months to reply, are cited in this section, as are erratic repliers.

Léon Donou, Le Chef des Services Techniques. Return postage, $1 or IRC required. Replies irregularly and slowly to correspondence in French.

BHUTAN World Time +7

Bhutan Broadcasting Service
STATION: Department of Information and Broadcasting, Ministry of Communications, P.O. Box 101, Thimphu, Bhutan. Phone: +975 223-070. Fax: +975 223 073. Contact: (general) Ashi Renchen Chhoden, News and Current Affairs; Narda Gautam; or Sonam Tshong, Executive Director; (technical) Sonam Tobgyal, Station Engineer; or Technical Head. Two IRCs, return postage or $1 required. Replies extremely irregularly; correspondence to the U.N. Mission (*see* following) may be more fruitful.
UNITED NATIONS MISSION: Permanent Mission of the Kingdom of Bhutan to the United Nations, Two United Nations Plaza, 27th Floor, New York NY 10017 USA. Fax: +1 (212) 826 2998. Contact: Mrs. Kunzang C. Namgyel, Third Secretary; Mrs. Sonam Yangchen, Attaché; Ms. Leki Wangmo, Second Secretary; Thinley Dorrji, Second Secretary; or Hari K. Chhetri, Second Secretary. Free newspapers and booklet on the history of Bhutan.

BOLIVIA World Time −4

NOTE ON STATION IDENTIFICATIONS: Many Bolivian stations listed as "Radio..." may also announce as "Radio Emisora..." or "Radiodifusora..."
Galaxia Radiodifusión—*see* Radio Galaxia, below.
Hitachi Radiodifusión—*see* Radio Hitachi, below.
Paititi Radiodifusión—*see* Radio Paititi, below.
Radio Abaroa, Calle Nicanor Gonzalo Salvatierra 249, Riberalta, Beni, Bolivia. Contact: René Arias Pacheco, Director. Return postage or $1 required. Replies occasionally to correspondence in Spanish.
Radio A.N.D.E.S., Casilla No. 16, Uyuni, Provincia Antonio Quijarro, Departamento de Potosí, Bolivia. Phone: +591 (69) 32-145. Owners: La Federación Unica de Trabajadores Campesinos del Altiplano Sud. Contact: Francisco Quisbert Salinas, Secretario Permanente del Consejo de Administración; Audo Ramos Colque; Rita Salvatierra Bautista; Erwin Freddy Mamani, Reportero, Radio Anos; or César Gerónimo Alí Flores, Reporteros. Spanish preferred. Return postage in the form of two U.S. dollars appreciated, as the station depends on donations for its existence.
Radio Animas, Chocaya, Animas, Potosí, Bolivia. Contact: Julio Acosta Campos, Director. Return postage or $1 required. Replies irregularly to correspondence in Spanish.
Radio Camargo—*see* Radio Emisoras Camargo, below.
Radio Carlos Palenque, Casilla de Correo 8704, La Paz, Bolivia. Phone: +591 (2) 354-418, +591 (2) 375-953, +595 (2) 324-394 or +595 (2) 361-176. Fax: +591 (2) 356 785. Contact: Rodolfo Beltrán Rosales, Jefe de Prensa de "El Metropolicial." Free postcards and pennants. $1 or return postage necessary.
Radio Centenario "La Nueva"
MAIN OFFICE: Casilla 818, Santa Cruz de la Sierra, Bolivia. Phone: +591 (3) 529-265. Fax: +591 (3) 524 747. E-mail: mision.eplabol@mail.sobbs-bo.com. Contact: Julio Acosta Campos, Director. May send a calendar. Free stickers. Return postage or $1 required. Audio cassettes of contemporary Christian music and Bolivian folk music $10, including postage; CDs of Christian folk music $15, including postage. Replies to correspondence in English and Spanish.

U.S. BRANCH OFFICE: LATCOM, 1218 Croton Avenue, New Castle PA 16101 USA. Phone: +1 (412) 652-0101. Fax: +1 (412) 652 4654. Contact: Hope Cummins.
Radio Eco
MAIN ADDRESS: Correo Central, Reyes, Ballivián, Beni, Bolivia. Contact: Gonzalo Espinoza Cortés, Director. Free station literature. $1 or return postage required. Replies to correspondence in Spanish.
ALTERNATIVE ADDRESS: Rolmán Medina Méndez, Correo Central, Reyes, Ballivián, Bolivia.
Radio Eco San Borja (San Borja la Radio), Correo Central, San Borja, Ballivián, Beni, Bolivia. Contact: Gonzalo Espinoza Cortés, Director. Free station poster promised to correspondents. Return postage appreciated. Replies slowly to correspondence in Spanish.
Radio El Mundo (when operating), Casilla 1984, Santa Cruz de la Sierra, Bolivia. Phone: +591 (3) 464-646. Fax: +591 (3) 465 057. Contact: Freddy Banegas Carrasco, Gerente; Lic. José Luis Vélez Ocampo C., Director; or Lic. Juan Pablo Sainz, Gerente General. Free stickers and pennants. $1 or return postage required. Replies irregularly to correspondence in Spanish.
Radio Emisora Dos de Febrero (if reactivated), Calle Vaca Diez 400, Rurrenabaque, Beni, Bolivia. Contact: John Arze von Boeck. Free pennant, which is especially attractive. Replies occasionally to correspondence in Spanish.
Radio Emisora Galaxia—*see* Radio Galaxia, below.
Radio Emisora Padilla—*see* Radio Padilla, below.
Radio Emisora San Ignacio, Calle Ballivián s/n, San Ignacio de Moxos, Beni, Bolivia. Contact: Carlos Salvatierra Rivero, Gerente y Director. $1 or return postage necessary.
Radio Emisora Villamontes—*see* Radio Villamontes, below.
Radio Emisoras Camargo, Casilla 09, Camargo, Provincia Nor-Cinti, Bolivia. Contact: Pablo García B., Gerente Propietario. Return postage or $1 required. Replies slowly to correspondence in Spanish.
Radio Emisoras Minería—*see* Radiodifusoras Minería.
Radio Estación Frontera—*see* Radio Frontera, below.
Radio Fides, Casilla 9143, La Paz, Bolivia. Fax: +591 (2) 379 030. E-mail: rafides@caoba.entelnet.bo (rafides@wara.bolnet.bo may also work). URL: www.fides2001.com. Contact: Pedro Eduardo Pérez Iribarne, Director; Felicia de Rojas, Secretaria; Roberto Carrasco Guzmán, Gerente de Ventas y RR HH; or Roxana Beltrán C. Replies occasionally to correspondence in Spanish.
Radio Frontera (when active), Casilla 179, Cobija, Pando, Bolivia. Contact: Lino Miahuchi von Ancken, CP9AR. Free pennants. $1 or return postage necessary. Replies to correspondence in Spanish.
Radio Galaxia (when operating), Calle Beni s/n casi esquina Udarico Rosales, Guayaramerín, Beni, Bolivia. Contact: Dorián Arias, Gerente; Héber Hitachi Banegas, Director; or Carlos Arteaga Tacaná, Director-Dueño. Return postage or $1 required. Replies to correspondence in Spanish.
Radio Grigotá (if reactivated), Casilla 203, Santa Cruz de la Sierra, Bolivia. Phone/fax: +591 (3) 326-443. Fax: +591 (3) 362 795. Contact: (general) Víctor Hugo Arteaga B., Director General; (technical) Tania Martins de Arteaga, Gerente Administrativo. Free stickers, pins, pennants, key rings and posters. $1 or return postage required. Replies occasionally to correspondence in English, French, Portuguese and Spanish. May replace old Philips transmitter.
Radio Hitachi (Hitachi Radiodifusión) (when operating), Calle Sucre 20, Guayaramerín, Beni, Bolivia. Contact: Héber

Hitachi Banegas, Director. Return postage of $1 required.

Radio Illimani, Casilla 1042, La Paz, Bolivia. Phone: +591 (2) 376-364. Fax: +591 (2) 359 275. E-mail: beucho@zuper.net. Contact: Rubén D. Choque, Director; or Lic. Manuel Liendo Rázuri, Gerente General. $1 required, and your letter should be registered and include a tourist brochure or postcard from where you live. Replies irregularly to friendly correspondence in Spanish.

Radio Integración (if reactivated), Casilla 7902, La Paz, Bolivia. Contact: Lic. Manuel Liendo Rázuri, Gerente General; Benjamín Juan Carlos Blanco Q., Director Ejecutivo; or Carmelo de la Cruz Huanca, Comunicador Social. Free pennants. Return postage required.

Radio Juan XXIII [Veintitrés], Avenida Santa Cruz al frente de la plaza principal, San Ignacio de Velasco, Santa Cruz, Bolivia. Phone: +591 (962) 2188. Contact: Fernando Manuel Picazo Torres, Director; or Pbro. Elías Cortezón, Director. Return postage or $1 required. Replies occasionally to correspondence in Spanish.

Radio La Cruz del Sur, Casilla 1759, La Paz, Bolivia. E-mail: cruzdel-sur@mail.zuper.net. Contact: Hazen Parent, General Director; or Dott Reyes Baltqzar Quispe; José Luis Chávez Zambrana, Director Gerente. Pennant $1 or return postage. Replies slowly to correspondence in Spanish.

Radio La Palabra, Parroquia de Santa Ana de Yacuma, Beni, Bolivia. Phone: +591 (848) 2117. Contact: Padre Yosu Arketa, Director. Return postage necessary. Replies to correspondence in Spanish.

Radio La Plata (when operating), Casilla 276, Sucre, Bolivia. Phone: +591 (64) 31-616. Fax: +591 (64) 41 400. Contact: Freddy Donoso Bleichner, Director Ejecutivo..

Radio Libertad (if reactivated), Casilla 5324, La Paz, Bolivia. Phone: +591 (2) 365-154. Fax: +591 (2) 363 069. Contact: (general) Oscar Violetta Barrios; (technical) Lic. Teresa Sanjinés Lora, Gerente General. Depending upon what's on hand, pamphlets, stickers, pins, pennants, purses, pencil sharpeners, key rings and calendars. If blank cassette and $2 is sent, they will be happy to dub recording of local music. Sells T-shirts for $10. Return postage or $1 required for reply. Upon request, they will record for listeners any type of Bolivian music they have on hand, and send it to that listener for the cost of the cassette and postage; or, if the listener sends a cassette, for the cost of postage. Replies fairly regularly to correspondence in English and Spanish.

Radio Loyola, Casilla 40, Sucre, Bolivia. Phone: +591 (64) 30-222. Fax: +591 (64) 42 555. URL: (experimental RealAudio) www.nch.bolnet.bo/loyola.ram. Contact: (general) Lic. José Weimar León G., Director; (technical) Tec. Norberto Rosales. Free stickers and pennants. Replies occasionally to correspondence in English, Italian and Spanish. Considering replacing 19-year old transmitter.

Radio Mauro Núñez, Centro de Estudios para el Desarrollo de Chuquisaca (CEDEC), Casilla 196, Sucre, Bolivia. Phone: +591 (64) 25-008. Fax: +591 (64) 32 628. Contact: Jorge A. Peñaranda Llanos; Ing. Raúl Ledezma, Director Residente "CEDEC"; José Peneranda; or Jesús Urioste. Replies to correspondence in Spanish.

Radio Minería—*see* Radiodifusoras Minería.

Radio Mosoj Chaski, Casilla 4493, Cochabamba, Bolivia. Phone: +591 (42) 220-641 or +591 (42) 220-644. Fax: +591 (42) 251 041. E-mail: chaski@bo.net. URL: http://tunari.socs.utsedu.au/rmc/. Contact: Eldon Porter, Gerente.

Radio Movima, Calle Baptista No. 24, Santa Ana de Yacuma, Beni, Bolivia. Contact: Rubén Serrano López, Director; Javier Roca Díaz, Director Gerente; or Mavis Serrano, Directora. Return postage or $1 required. Replies irregularly to correspondence in Spanish.

Radio Nacional de Huanuni, Casilla 681, Oruro, Bolivia. Contact: Rafael Linneo Morales, Director General; or Alfredo Murillo, Director. Return postage or $1 required. Replies irregularly to correspondence in Spanish.

Radio Norte, Calle Warnes 195, 2do piso del Cine Escorpio, Montero, Santa Cruz, Bolivia. Phone: +591 (92) 20-970. Fax: +591 (92) 21 062. Contact: Leonardo Arteaga Ríos, Director.

Radio Padilla, Padilla, Chuquisaca, Bolivia. Contact: Moisés Palma Salazar, Director. Return postage or $1 required. Replies to correspondence in Spanish.

Radio Paitití, Casilla 172, Guayaramerín, Beni, Bolivia. Contact: Armando Mollinedo Bacarreza, Director; Luis Carlos Santa Cruz Cuéllar, Director Gerente; or Ancir Vaca Cuéllar, Gerente-Propietario. Free pennants. Return postage or $3 required. Replies irregularly to correspondence in Spanish.

Radio Panamericana, Casilla 5263, La Paz, Bolivia (physical address: Av. 16 de Julio, Edif. 16 de Julio, Of. 902, El Prado, La Paz, Bolivia). Phone: +591 (2) 324-606, +591 (2) 325-239 or +591 (2) 358-945. Fax: +591 (2) 392 353. E-mail: pana@panamericana-bolivia.com. URL: www.panamericana-bolivia.com. Contact: Daniel Sánchez Rocha, Director. Replies irregularly, with correspondence in Spanish preferred. $1 or 2 IRCs helpful.

Radio Perla del Acre, Casilla 7, Cobija, Departamento de Pando, Bolivia. Return postage or $1 required. Replies irregularly to correspondence in Spanish.

Radio Pío XII [Doce], Siglo Veinte, Potosí, Bolivia. Phone: +591 (58) 20-250. Contact: Pbro. Roberto Durette, OMI, Director General; or René Paco, host of "Los Pikichakis" program (aired Saturdays at 2300-0100 World Time). Return postage necessary. As mail delivery to Siglo Veinte is erratic, latters may be sent instead to: Casilla 434, Oruro, Bolivia; to the attention of Abenor Alfaro Castillo, periodista de Radio Pío XX. Phone: +591 (52) 76-163).

Radio San Gabriel, Casilla 4792, La Paz, Bolivia. Phone: +591 (2) 355-371. Phone/fax: +591 (2) 321 174. Contact: Hno. José Canut Saurat, Director General; or Sra. Martha Portugal, Dpto. de Publicidad. $1 or return postage helpful. Free book on station, Aymara calendars and *La Voz del Pueblo Aymara* magazine. Replies fairly regularly to correspondence in Spanish. Station of the Hermanos de la Salle Catholic religious order.

Radio San Miguel, Casilla 102, Riberalta, Beni, Bolivia. Phone: +591 (852) 8268. Contact: Félix Alberto Rada Q., Director; or Gerin Pardo Molina, Director. Free stickers and pennants; has a different pennant each year. Return postage or $1 required. Replies irregularly to correspondence in Spanish. Feedback on program "Bolivia al Mundo" (aired 0200-0300 World Time) especially appreciated.

Radio Santa Ana, Calle Sucre No. 250, Santa Ana de Yacuma, Beni, Bolivia. Contact: Mario Roberto Suárez, Director; or Mariano Verdugo. Return postage or $1 required. Replies irregularly to correspondence in Spanish.

Radio Santa Cruz, Emisora del Instituto Radiofónico Fé y Alegría (IRFA), Casilla 672 (or 3213), Santa Cruz, Bolivia. Phone: +591 (3) 531-817. Fax: +591 (3) 532 257. E-mail: infacruz@roble.scz.entelnet.bo. Contact: Padre Francisco Flores, S.J., Director General; Srta. María Yolanda Marco E., Secretaria; Señora Mirian Suárez, Productor, "Protagonista Ud."; or Lic. Silvia Nava S. Free pamphlets, stickers and pennants. Return postage required. Replies to correspondence in English, French and Spanish.

Radio Sararenda, Casilla 7, Camiri, Santa Cruz, Bolivia. Phone: +595 (952) 2121. Contact: Freddy Lara Aguilar, Director; or Kathy Arenas, Administradora. Free stickers and photos of Camiri. Replies to correspondence in Spanish.

Radio Televisión Colonia (if reactivated), Correo Central, Yapacani, Santa Cruz de la Sierra, Bolivia. Phone/fax: +591 (933) 61-64. Fax: +591 (933) 60 00. Contact: (general) Yrey Fausto Montaño Ustárez, Gerente Propietario; (technical) Ing. Rene Zambrana. Replies to correspondence in English, French, Italian, Japanese, Portuguese and Spanish. Free pamphlets, stickers, pins, pennants and small handicrafts made by local artisans. Return postage required for reply.

Radio Villamontes, Avenida Méndez Arcos No. 156, Villamontes, Departamento de Tarija, Bolivia. Contact: Gerardo Rocabado Galarza, Director. $1 or return postage required.

Radiodifusoras Integración—*see* Radio Integración, below.

Radiodifusoras Minería, Casilla de Correo 247, Oruro, Bolivia. Phone: +591 (52) 77-736. Contact: Dr. José Carlos Gómez Espinoza, Gerente Propietario; or Srta. Costa Colque Flores, Responsable del programa "Minería Cultural." Free pennants. Replies to correspondence in Spanish.

Radiodifusoras Trópico, Casilla 60, Trinidad, Beni, Bolivia. Contact: Eduardo Avila Alberdi, Director. Replies slowly to correspondence in Spanish. Return postage required for reply.

BOSNIA-HERCEGOVINA   World Time +1 (+2 midyear)

Radio & Television of Bosnia-Hercegovina (if reactivated), Bulevar Mese Selimovica 4, BH-71000 Sarajevo, Bosnia-Hercegovina. Phone: +387 (71) 646-014, +387 (71) 462-886 or +387 (71) 455-124. Fax: +387 (71) 645 142, +387 (71) 464 061 or +387 (71) 455 104. Contact: Milenko Vockic, Director; Mr. N. Dizdarevic; or Rodzic Nerin.

BOTSWANA   World Time +2

Radio Botswana, Private Bag 0060, Gaborone, Botswana. Phone: +267 352-541 or +267 352-861. E-mail: (general) sec.makgekgenene@info.bw. Fax: +267 357 138. Contact: (general) Ted Makgekgenene, Director; or Monica Mphusu, Producer, "Maokaneng/Pleasure Mix"; (technical) Kingsley Reetsang, Principal Broadcasting Engineer. Free stickers, pennants and pins. Return postage, $1 or 2 IRCs required. Replies slowly and irregularly.

Voice of America/IBB—Botswana Relay Station
TRANSMITTER SITE: Voice of America, Botswana Relay Station, Moepeng Hill, Selebi-Phikwe, Botswana. Phone: +267 810-932. Fax: +267 810 252. Contact: Station Manager. This address for specialized technical correspondence only. All other correspondence should be directed to the regular VOA or IBB addresses (*see* USA).

BRAZIL   World Time –1 (–2 midyear) Atlantic Islands; –2 (–3 midyear) Eastern, including Brasília and Rio de Janeiro, plus the town of Barra do Garças; –3 (–4 midyear) Western; –5 Acre. Most, if not all, northern states keep midyear time year round.

NOTE: Postal authorities recommend that, because of the level of theft in the Brazilian postal system, correspondence to Brazil be sent only via registered mail.

Emissora Rural A Voz do São Francisco, C.P. 8, 56300-000 Petrolina PE, Brazil. Contact: Maria Letecia de Andrade Nunes. Return postage necessary. Replies to correspondence in Portuguese.

Rádio Alvorada (Londrina) (when operating), Rua Senador Souza Naves 9, 9 Andar, 86010-921 Londrina PR, Brazil. Contact: Padre José Guidoreni, Diretor; or Padre Manuel Joaquim. Pennants $1 or return postage. Replies to correspondence in Portuguese.

Rádio Alvorada (Parintins), Travessa Leopoldo Neves 503, 69150-000 Parintins AM, Brazil. Contact: Raimunda Ribeira da Motta, Diretora. Return postage required. Replies occasionally to correspondence in Portuguese.

Rádio Alvorada (Rio Branco), Avenida Ceará 2150—Altos de Gráfica Globo, 69900-470 Rio Branco AC, Brazil. Occasionally replies to correspondence in Portuguese.

Rádio Araguaia—FM sister-station to Rádio Anhanguera (*see* next entry) and often relayed via the latter's shortwave outlet. URLs: (general) www.opopular.com.br/araguaia/; (RealAudio) www2.opopular.com.br/radio.htm. Usually identifies as "Araguaia FM."

Rádio Anhanguera, BR-157 Km. 1103, Zona Rural, 77804-970 Araguaína TO, Brazil. Return postage required. Occasionally replies to correspondence in Portuguese. Often airs programming from sister-station Rádio Araguaia, 97.1 FM (*see* previous item).

A young Chinese boy snoozes while papa dutifully pushes him to their destination.
R. Crane

📻**Rádio Anhanguera**, C.P. 13, 74823-000 Goiânia GO, Brazil. URL: (RealAudio only) www2.opopular.com.br/radio.htm. Contact: Rossana F. da Silva; or Eng. Domingos Vicente Tinoco. Return postage required. Replies to correspondence in Portuguese. Although—like its namesake in Araguaína (see, above)—a member of the Sistema de Rádio da Organização Jaime Câmara, this station is also an affiliate of the CBN network and often identifies as "CBN Anhanguera," especially when airing news programming.

Rádio Aparecida, Avenida Getulio Vargas 185, 12570-000 Aparecida SP, Brazil; or C.P. 14547, 03698-970 Aparecida SP, Brazil. Phone: +55 (12) 565-1133. Fax: +55 (12) 565 1138. Contact: Padre C. Cabral; Savio Trevisan, Departamento Técnico; Cassiano Macedo, Producer, "Encontro DX"; Ana Cristina Carvalho, Secretária da Direção; Padre Cesar Moreira; or João Climaco, Diretor Geral. Return postage or $1 required. Replies occasionally to correspondence in Portuguese.

📻**Rádio Bandeirantes**, C.P. 372, Rua Radiantes 13, Morumbí, 01059-970 São Paulo SP, Brazil. Fax: +55 (11) 843 5391. E-mail: rbradio@uol.com.br. URL: (includes RealAudio) www.uol.com.br/bandeirantes/. Contact: Samir Razuk, Diretor Geral; Carlos Newton; or Salomão Esper, Superintendente. Free stickers, pennants and canceled Brazilian stamps. $1 or return postage required.

Rádio Baré, Avenida Santa Cruz Machado 170 A, 69010-070 Manaus AM, Brazil. Contact: Fernando A.B. Andrade, Diretor Programação e Produção. The Diretor is looking for radio catalogs.

Rádio Brasil, C.P. 625, 13000-000 Campinas, São Paulo SP, Brazil. Contact: Wilson Roberto Correa Viana, Gerente. Return postage required. Replies to correspondence in Portuguese.

Rádio Brasil Central, C.P. 330, 74001-970 Goiânia GO, Brazil. Contact: Ney Raymundo Fernández, Diretor Administrativo; Sergio Rubens da Silva; or Arizio Pedro Soárez, Diretor Gerente. Free stickers. $1 or return postage required. Replies to correspondence in Portuguese.

Rádio Brasil Tropical, C.P. 405, 78005-970 Cuiabá MT, Brazil (physical address: Rua Joaquim Murtinho 1456, 78020-830 Cuiabá MT, Brazil). Phone: +55 (65) 321-6882 or +55 (65) 321-6226. Fax: +55 (65) 624 3455. E-mail: rcultura@nutecnet.com.br. Contact: Klécius Antonio dos Santos, Diretor Comercial; or Roberto Ferreira, Gerente Comercial. Free stickers. $1 required. Replies to correspondence in Portuguese. Shortwave sister-station to Rádio Cultura de Cuiabá (see).

Rádio Caiari, C.P. 104, 78900-000 Porto Velho RO, Brazil. Contact: Carlos Alberto Diniz Martins, Diretor Geral. Free stickers. Return postage helpful. Replies irregularly to correspondence in Portuguese.

📻**Rádio Canção Nova**, C.P. 15, 12630-000 Cachoeira Paulista SP, Brazil; (physical address) Rua João Paulo II s/n, Alto da Bela Vista, 12630-000 Cachoeira Paulista SP, Brazil. Phone: +55 (12) 561-2400. Fax: +55 (12) 561 2074. E-mail: (general) radio@cancaonova.org.br; (Director) adriana@cancaonova.org.br. URL: (includes RealAudio) www.cancaonova.org.br. Contact: (general) Benedita Luiza Rodrigues; Ana Claudia de Santana; or Valera Guimarães Massafera, Secretária; (administration) Adriana Pereira, Diretora da Rádio. Free stickers, pennants and station brochure sometimes given upon request. May send magazines. $1 helpful.

Rádio Capixaba, C.P. 509, 29000-000 Vitória ES, Brazil. Contact: Jairo Gouvea Maia, Diretor; or Sofrage do Benil. Replies occasionally to correspondence in Portuguese.

📻**Rádio Clube de Ribeirao Preto** (when active), Ribeirao Preto SP, Brazil. Phone/fax: +55 (16) 610-3511. E-mail: scc@clube.com.br; clubeam@clube.com.br. URL: (includes RealAudio) www.clube.com.br.

Rádio Clube de Rondonópolis (when active), C.P. 190, 78700-000 Rondonópolis MT, Brazil. Contact: Canário Silva, Departamento Comercial; or Saúl Feliz, Gerente-Geral. Return postage helpful. Replies to correspondence in Portuguese.

Rádio Clube do Pará, C.P. 533, 66000-000 Belém PA,

Brazil. Contact: Edyr Paiva Proença, Diretor Geral; or José Almeida Lima de Sousa. Return postage required. Replies irregularly to correspondence in Portuguese.

Radio Clube Paranaense, Rua Rockefeller 1311, Prado Velho, 80230-130 Curitiba, Brazil. Phone: +55 (41) 332-4255 or +55 (41) 332-6644. Contact: Vicente Mickosz, Superintendente.

Rádio Clube Varginha, C.P. 102, 37000-000 Varginha MG, Brazil. Contact: Juraci Viana. Return postage necessary. Replies slowly to correspondence in Portuguese.

Rádio Coari—*see* Rádio Educação Rural-Coari.

Rádio Cultura Araraquara, Avenida Feijó 583 (Centro), 14801-140 Araraquara SP, Brazil. Phone: +55 (16) 232-3790. Fax: +55 (16) 232 3475. E-mail: cultura@techs.com.br. URL: www.techs.com.br/cultura/. Contact: Antonio Carlos Rodrigues dos Santos, Gerente Comercial. Return postage required. Replies slowly to correspondence in Portuguese.

Rádio Cultura de Campos, C.P. 79, 28100-970 Campos RJ, Brazil. $1 or return postage necessary. Replies to correspondence in Portuguese.

Rádio Cultura de Cuiabá—AM sister-station of Rádio Brasil Tropical (*see*) and whose programming is partly relayed by RBT. E-mail: rcultura@nutecnet.com.br. URL: www.solunet.com.br/rcultura/.

Rádio Cultura de Foz do Iguaçu (Onda Corta), C.P. 84, 85852-520 Foz do Iguaçu PR, Brazil. Phone: +55 (45) 574-3010. Contact: Pastor Francisco Pires dos Santos, Gerente-Geral; or Sandro Souza. Return postage necessary. Replies to correspondence in Portuguese. Observation: this station was observed during 1999 identifying as "Rádio Cultura Filadelfia" (*see*), and announcing a different address and phone number to that listed above. It is unknown if this reflects a change of ownership or whether the station is leasing its airtime to the Filadelfia evangelical organization.

Rádio Cultura do Pará, Avenida Almirante Barroso 735, 66090-000 Belém PA, Brazil. Phone: +55 (91) 228-1000. Fax: +55 (91) 226 3989. Contact: Ronald Pastor; or Augusto Proença. Return postage required. Replies irregularly to correspondence in Portuguese.

Rádio Cultura Filadelfia, Rua Antonio Barbosa 1353, C.P. 89, 85851-090 Foz do Iguaçu PR, Brazil. Phone: +55 (45) 523-2930. Also, *see* Rádio Cultura de Foz do Iguaçu (Onda Corta), above.

Rádio Cultura Ondas Tropicais, Rua Barcelos s/n Praça 14, 69020-060 Manaus AM, Brazil. Phone: +55 (92) 633-3857/2030. Fax: +55 (92) 633 3332. Contact: Luíz Fernando de Souza Ferreira; or Maria Jerusalem dos Santos, Chefe da Divisão de Rádio. Replies to correspondence in Portuguese. Return postage appreciated. Station is part of the FUNTEC, Fundação Televisão e Rádio Cultura do Amazonas network.

Rádio Cultura São Paulo, Rua Cenno Sbrighi 378, 05099-900 São Paulo SP, Brazil. Phone: +55 (11) 861-2140, +55 (11) 874-3080, +55 (11) 874-3086. Fax: +55 (11) 861 1914. E-mail: (general) radio@tvcultura.com.br; (Cultura AM, relayed on 9615 and 17815 kHz) radioam@tvcultura.com.br; (Cultura FM, relayed on 6170 kHz) radiofm@tvcultura.com.br; (technical) tecnica@tvcultura.com.br. URL: www.tvcultura.com.br. Contact: Thais de Almeida Dias, Chefe de Produção e Programação; Sra. Maria Luíza Amaral Kfouri, Chefe de Produção; or Valvenio Martins de Almeida, Coordenador de Produção. $1 or return postage required. Replies slowly to postal correspondence in Portuguese. May respond to English messages sent to the "radio" and "tecnica" e-mail addresses, above.

Rádio Difusora Acreana, Rua Benjamin Constant 161, 69908-520 Rio Branco AC, Brazil. Contact: Washington Aquino, Diretor Geral. Replies irregularly to correspondence in Portuguese.

Rádio Difusora Cáceres (when operating), C.P. 297, 78200-000 Cáceres MT, Brazil. Contact: Sra. Maridalva Amaral Vignardi. $1 or return postage required. Replies occasionally to correspondence in Portuguese.

Rádio Difusora de Aquidauana, C.P. 18, 79200-000 Aquidauana MS, Brazil. Phone: +55 (67) 241-3956 or +55 (67) 241-3957. Contact: Primaz Aldo Bertoni, Diretor; or João Stacey. Free tourist literature and used Brazilian stamps. $1 or return postage required. This station sometimes identifies during the program day as "Nova Difusora," but its sign-off announcement gives the official name as "Rádio Difusora, Aquidauana."

Rádio Difusora de Londrina, C.P. 1870, 86000-000 Londrina PR, Brazil. Contact: Walter Roberto Manganoti, Gerente. Free tourist brochure, which sometimes seconds as a verification. $1 or return postage helpful. Replies irregularly to correspondence in Portuguese.

Rádio Difusora de Roraima, Avenida Capitão Ene Garcez 830, 69304-000 Boa Vista RR, Brazil. Contact: Francisco G. França, Diretor Gerente; Galvão Soares, Diretor Geral; Benjamin Monteiro, Locutor; or Francisco Alves Vieira. Return postage required. Replies occasionally to correspondence in Portuguese.

Rádio Difusora do Amazonas, C.P. 311, 69000-000 Manaus AM, Brazil. Contact: J. Joaquim Marinho, Diretor. Joaquim Marinho is a keen stamp collector and especially interested in Duck Hunting Permit Stamps. Will reply to correspondence in Portuguese or English. $1 or return postage helpful.

Rádio Difusora do Maranhão (when active), C.P. 152, 65000-000 São Luís MA, Brazil. Contact: Alonso Augusto Duque, BA, Presidente; José de Arimatéa Araújo, Diretor; or Fernando Souza, Gerente. Free tourist literature. Return postage required. Replies occasionally to correspondence in Portuguese.

Rádio Difusora Jataí, C.P. 33 (or Rua de José Carvalhos Bastos 542), 75800-000 Jataí GO, Brazil. Contact: Zacarías Faleiros, Diretor Gerente.

Rádio Difusora Macapá (when active), C.P. 2929, 68900-000 Macapá AP, Brazil. Contact: Francisco de Paulo Silva Santos; Rui Lobato; or Eng. Arquit. Benedito Rostan Costa Martins, Diretor. $1 or return postage required. Replies irregularly to correspondence in Portuguese.

Rádio Difusora Poços de Caldas, C.P. 937, 37701-970 Poços de Caldas MG, Brazil; or (street address) Rua Rio Grande do Sul 631, 37701-001 Poços de Caldas MG, Brazil. Phone/fax: +55 (35) 722-1530. E-mail: difusora@pocos-net.com.br. URL: www.pocos-net.com.br/difusora/. Contact: Marco Aurelio C. Mendoça, Diretor; or Dr. Wanderley de Mello, Gerente. $1 or return postage required. Replies to correspondence in Portuguese.

Rádio Difusora "6 de Agosto," Rua Pio Nazário 31, 69930-000 Xapuri AC, Brazil. Contact: Francisco Evangelista de Abreu. Replies to correspondence in Portuguese.

Rádio Difusora Taubaté (when active), Rua Dr. Sousa Alves 960, 12020-030 Taubaté SP, Brazil. No contact details available at press time.

Rádio Educação Rural—Campo Grande, C.P. 261, 79002-233 Campo Grande MS, Brazil. Phone: +55 (67) 384-3164, +55 (67) 382-2238 or +55 (67) 384-3345. Contact: Ailton Guerra, Gerente-Geral; Angelo Venturelli, Diretor; or Diácono Tomás Schwamborn. $1 or return postage required. Replies to correspondence in Portuguese.

Rádio Educação Rural—Coari, Praça São Sebastião 228, 69460-000 Coari AM, Brazil. Contact: Lino Rodrigues Pessoa, Diretor Comercial; Joaquim Florencio Coelho, Diretor Administrador da Comunidade Salgueiro; or Elijane Martins Correa. $1 or return postage helpful. Replies irregularly to correspondence in Portuguese.

Rádio Educadora Cariri, C.P. 57, 63100-000 Crato CE, Brazil. Contact: Padre Gonçalo Farias Filho, Diretor Gerente. Return postage or $1 helpful. Replies irregularly to correspondence in Portuguese.

☞Rádio Educadora da Bahia, Centro de Rádio, Rua Pedro. Gama 413/E, Alto Sobradinho Federação, 40230-291 Salvador BA, Brazil. Phone: +55 (71) 339-1180. Fax: +55 (71) 339 1170. URL: (includes RealAudio) www.educadora.com.br. Contact: Elza Correa Ramos; or Walter Sequieros R. Tanure. $1 or return postage required. May send local music CD. Replies to correspondence in Portuguese.

Rádio Educadora de Bragança, Rua Barão do Rio Branco 1151, 68600-000 Bragança PA, Brazil. Contact: José Rosendo de S. Neto; Zelina Cardoso Gonçalves; or Adelino Borges, Aux. Escritório. $1 or return postage required. Replies to correspondence in Portuguese.

Rádio Educadora de Guajará Mirim, Praça Mario Correa No.90, 78957-000 Guajará Mirim RO, Brazil. Contact: Padre Isidoro José Moro. Return postage helpful. Replies to correspondence in Portuguese.

☞Rádio Gaúcha, Avenida Ipiranga 1075 2do andar, Azenha, 90169-900 Porto Alegre RS, Brazil. Phone: +55 (51) 223-6600. E-mail: (general) gaucha@rdgaucha.com.br; (technical) gilberto.kussler@rdgaucha.com.br. URL: (includes RealAudio) www.rdgaucha.com.br:8080/index2.htm. Contact: Marco Antônio Baggio, Gerente de Jornalismo/Programação; Armindo Antônio Ranzolin, Diretor Gerente; Gilberto Kussler, Gerente Técnico; Geraldo Canali. Replies occasionally to correspondence, preferably in Portuguese.

Rádio Gazeta, Avenida Paulista 900, 01310-940 São Paulo SP, Brazil. Fax: +55 (11) 285 4895. Contact: Shakespeare Ettinger, Superv. Geral de Operação; Bernardo Leite da Costa; José Roberto Mignone Cheibub, Gerente Geral; or Ing. Aníbal Horta Figueiredo. Free stickers. $1 or return postage necessary. Replies to correspondence in Portuguese. Currently leasing all its airtime to the "Deus é Amor" Pentecostal church, but has been observed in the past to sometimes carry its own programming on at least one of its three shortwave channels.

☞Rádio Globo, Rua do Russel 434-Glória, 22213-900 Rio de Janeiro RJ, Brazil. E-mail: (administration) gerenciaamrio@radioglobo.com.br URL: (includes Real Audio) www.radioglobo.com.br/globorio/. Contact: Marcos Libretti, Diretor Geral. Replies irregularly to correspondence in Portuguese. Return postage helpful.

☞Rádio Globo, Rua das Palmeiras 315, 01288-900 São Paulo SP, Brazil. URL: (includes RealAudio) www.radioglobo.com.br/globosp/. Contact: Ademar Dutra, Locutor, "Programa Ademar Dutra"; Guilherme Viterbo; or José Marques. Replies to correspondence, preferably in Portuguese.

☞Rádio Guaíba, Rua Caldas Junior 219, 90019-900 Porto Alegre RS, Brazil. Phone: +55 (51) 224-3755 or +55 (51) 224-4555. E-mail: guaiba@cpovo.net. URL: (includes RealAudio) www.cpovo.net/radio/. Return postage helpful.

☞ Rádio Guarani, Avenida Assis Chateaubriand 499, Floresta, 30150-101 Belo Horizonte MG, Brazil. URL: (includes RealAudio) www.guarani.com.br/index.html. Contact: Junara Belo, Setor de Comunicações. Replies slowly to correspondence in Portuguese. Return postage helpful.

Rádio Guarujá

STATION: C.P. 45, 88000-000 Florianópolis SC, Brazil. Contact: Mario Silva, Diretor; Joana Sempre Bom Braz, Assessora de Marketing e Comunicação; or Rosa Michels de Souza. Return postage required. Replies irregularly to correspondence in Portuguese.

NEW YORK OFFICE: 45 West 46 Street, 5th Floor, Manhattan, NY 10036 USA.

☞Rádio Inconfidência, C.P. 1027, 30650-540 Belo Horizonte MG, Brazil. Fax: +55 (31) 296 3070. E-mail: inconfidencia@plugway.com.br. URL: (includes RealAudio) www.plugway.com.br/inconfidencia/. Contact: Isaias Lansky, Diretor; Manuel Emilio de Lima Torres, Diretor Superintendente; Jairo Antolio Lima, Diretor Artístico; or Eugenio Silva. Free stickers and postcards. May send CD of Brazilian music. $1 or return postage helpful.

Rádio Integração (when active), Rua Alagoas 270, 69980-000 Cruzeiro do Sul AC, Brazil. Contact: Oscar Alves Bandeira, Gerente. Return postage helpful.

Rádio IPB AM, Rua Itajaí 473, Bairro Antonio Vendas, 79041-270 Campo Grande MS, Brazil. Contact: Iván Páez Barboza, Diretor Geral (hence, the station's name, "IPB"); Pastor Laercio Paula das Neves, Dirigente Estadual; Agenor Patrocinio S., Locutor; Pastor José Adão Hames; or Kelly Cristina Rodrigues da Silva, Secretária. Return postage required. Replies to correspondence in Portuguese. Most of the airtime is leased to the "Deus é Amor" Pentecostal church.

☞Rádio Itatiaia, Rua Itatiaia 117, 31210-170 Belo Horizonte MG, Brazil. Fax: +55 (31) 446 2900. E-mail: itatiaia@itatiaia.com.br. URL: (includes RealAudio) www.itatiaia.com.br. Contact: Lúcia Araújo Bessa, Assistente da Diretória; or Claudio Carneiro.

Rádio Jornal "A Crítica," C.P. 2250, 69061-970 Manaus AM, Brazil; or Av. Andre Araujo s/n, Aleixo, 69060-001 Manaus AM, Brazil. Contact: Sr. Cotrere, Gerente.

☞Rádio Liberal, C.P 498, 66017-970 Belém PA, Brazil; (physical address) Av. Nazaré 350. 66035-170 Belém PA, Brazil. Phone: +55 (91) 244-6000 or +55 (91) 241-1330. Fax: +55 (91) 224 5240. E-mail: radio@radioliberal.com.br. URL: (includes RealAudio from the station's FM outlet) www.radioliberal.com.br. Contact: Flavia Vasconcellos; Advaldo Castro, Diretor de Programação AM; João Carlos Silva Ribeiro, Coordenador de Programação AM.

Rádio Marajoara (if reactivated), Travessa Campos Sales 370, Centro, 66019-904 Belém PA, Brazil. Contact: Elizete Maria dos Santos Pamplona, Diretora Geral; or Sra. Neide Carvalho, Secretária da Diretoria Executiva. Return postage required. Replies irregularly to correspondence in Portuguese.

Rádio Marumby, C.P. 296, 88010-970 Florianópolis SC, Brazil; Rua Angelo Laporta 841, C. P. 62, 88020-600 Florianópolis SC, Brazil; or (missionary parent organization) Gideões Missionários da Última Hora—GMUH, Ministério Evangélico Mundial, Rua Joaquim Nunes 244, C.P. 4, 88340-000 Camboriú SC, Brazil. E-mail: (GMUH parent organization) gmuh@gmuh.com.br. URL: www.gmuh.com.br/Radio/Marumby.htm. Contact: Davi Campos, Diretor Artístico; Dr. Cesario Bernardino, Presidente, GMUH; Pb. Claudiney Nunes, Coordenador Rádio e Jornalismo; or Jair Albano, Diretor. $1 or return postage required. Free diploma and stickers. Replies to correspondence in Portuguese.

Rádio Marumby, Curitiba—*see* Rádio Novas de Paz, Curitiba, below.

Rádio Meteorologia Paulista, C.P. 91, 14940-970 Ibitinga, São Paulo SP, Brazil. Contact: Roque de Rosa, Diretora.

Replies to correspondence in Portuguese. $1 or return postage required.

Rádio Missões da Amazônia, Travessa Ruy Barbosa 142, 68250-000 Obidos PA, Brazil. Contact: Max Hamoy; Edérgio de Moras Pinto; or Maristela Hamoy. Return postage required. Replies occasionally to correspondence in Portuguese.

Rádio Mundial, Rua da Consolação 2608, 1° Andar, CJ. 11, 01416-000 Consolação, São Paulo SP, Brazil. Fax: +55 (11) 258 5838 or +55 (11) 258 0152. E-mail: webmaster@ radiomundial.com.br. URL: (includes RealAudio) www.radiomundial.com.br. Contact: (nontechnical) Luci Rothschild de Abreu, Diretora Presidente.

Rádio Nacional da Amazônia, Radiobrás, SCRN 702/3 Bloco B Lote 16/18, Ed. Radiobrás, 70323-900 Brasília DF, Brazil. Fax: +55 (61) 321 7602. URLs: (general) www.radiobras.gov.br/institucional/radioamz.htm; (NetShow audio) www.radiobras.gov.br/radios/radios.htm. Contact: (general) Luíz Otavio de Castro Souza, Diretor; Fernando Gómez da Camara, Gerente de Escritório; or Januario Procopio Toledo, Diretor. Free stickers, but no verifications.

Rádio Nacional do Brasil—Radiobrás, External Service, C.P. 08840, 70912-790, Brasília DF, Brazil. Phone: +55 (61) 321-3949. Fax: +55 (61) 321 7602. E-mail: radiobras@ radiobras.gov.br. URL: www.radiobras.gov.br/institucional/ranacbr.htm. Contact: Otavio Bonfim, Gerente do Serviço Internacional; Michael Brown, Announcer; or Gabriela Barga. Free stickers. Correspondence welcomed in English and other languages. Unlike Radiobrás' domestic service (preceding entry), Radiobrás' External Service verifies regularly.

Rádio Nacional São Gabriel da Cachoeira, Avenida Alvaro Maia 850, 69750-000 São Gabriel da Cachoeira AM, Brazil. Contact: Luíz dos Santos França, Gerente; or Valdir de Souza Marques. Return postage necessary. Replies to correspondence in Portuguese.

Rádio Novas de Paz, Avenida Paraná 1896, 82510-000 Curitiba PR, Brazil; or C.P. 22, 80000-000 Curitiba PR, Brazil. Phone: +55 (41) 257-4109. Contact: João Falavinha Ienzen, Gerente. $1 or return postage required. Replies irregularly to correspondence in Portuguese.

Rádio Nova Visão
STUDIOS: Rua do Manifesto 1373, 04209-001 São Paulo SP, Brazil. Contact: José Eduardo Dias, Diretor Executivo; Rev. Iván Nunes; Cesino Bernardino, Presidente GMUH; Claudiney Nunes, Gerente Geral; Nildair Santos, Coordenador; or Marlene P. Nunes, Secretária. Return postage required. Replies to correspondence in Portuguese. Free stickers. Relays Rádio Trans Mundial fulltime.
TRANSMITTER: C.P. 551, 97000-000 Santa Maria RS, Brazil; or C.P. 6084, 90000-000 Porto Alegre RS, Brazil. Reportedly issues full-data verifications for reports in Portuguese or German, upon request, from this location. If no luck, try contacting, in English or Dutch, Tom van Ewijck, via e-mail at egiaroll@mail.iss.lcca.usp.br.

Rádio Oito de Setembro, C.P. 8, 13690-000 Descalvado SP, Brazil. Contact: Adonias Gomes. Replies to corrrespondence in Portuguese.

Rádio Pioneira de Teresina, Rua 24 de Janeiro 150 sul/centro, 64001-230 Teresina PI, Brazil. Contact: Luíz Eduardo Bastos; or Padre Tony Batista, Diretor. $1 or return postage required. Replies slowly to correspondence in Portuguese.

Rádio Poti (if reactivated), C.P. 145, 59001-970 Natal RN, Brazil. Contact: Cid Lobo. Return postage helpful. Replies slowly to correspondence in Portuguese.

Rádio Progresso (when operating), Estrada do Belmont s/n, B° Nacional, 78903-400 Porto Velho RO, Brazil. Return postage required. Replies occasionally to correspondence in Portuguese.

Rádio Record
STATION: C.P. 7920, 04084-002 São Paulo SP, Brazil. E-mail: (nontechnical) programacao@rederecord.com.br. URL: www.rederecord.com.br/radio/index.htm. Contact: Mário Luíz Catto, Diretor Geral. Free stickers. Return postage or $1 required. Replies occasionally to correspondence in Portuguese.
NEW YORK OFFICE: 630 Fifth Avenue, Room 2607, New York NY 10111 USA.

Rádio Relógio, Rua Paramopama 131, Ribeira, Ilha do Governador, 21930-110 Rio de Janeiro RJ, Brazil. Phone: +55 (21) 467-0201 or +55 (21) 467-4656. E-mail: relogio@ radiorelogio.com.br. URL: www.radiorelogio.com.br. Replies occasionally to correspondence in Portuguese.

Rádio Ribeirão Preto (when active), C.P. 1252, 14025-000 Ribeirão Preto SP, Brazil (physical address: Av. 9 de Julho 600, 14025-000 Ribeirão Preto SP, Brazil). Phone/fax: +55 (16) 610-3511. E-mail: scc@clube.com.br. URL: (includes RealAudio) www.clube.com.br. Contact: Lucinda de Oliveira, Secretária; Luis Schiavone Junior; or Paulo Henríque Rocha da Silva. Replies to correspondence in Portuguese.

Rádio Rio Mar, Rua José Clemente 500, 69010-070 Manaus AM, Brazil. Replies to correspondence in Portuguese. $1 or return postage necessary.

Rádio Rural Santarém, Rua Floriano Peixoto 632, 68005-060 Santarém PA, Brazil. Contact: João Elias B. Bentes, Gerente Geral; or Edsergio de Moraes Pinto. Replies slowly to correspondence in Portuguese. Free stickers. Return postage or $1 required.

Rádio Senado. E-mail: radio@senado.gov.br. URL: (includes RealAudio) www.senado.gov.br/web/comunica/copres/frmRadio.cfm.

Rádio Timbira (if reactivated), Rua do Correio s/n, Bairro de Fátima, 65030-340 São Luís MA, Brazil. Contact: Sandoval Pimentel Silva, Diretor Geral. Free picture postcards. $1 helpful. Replies occasionally to correspondence in Portuguese; persist.

Rádio Trans Mundial, Caixa Postal 18300 (Aeroporto), 04699-970 São Paulo SP, Brazil. Phone: +55 (11) 533-3533. Fax: +55 (11) 533 5271. E-mail: transmun@uol.com.br; or transmun@sp.dglnet.com.br. URL: www.transmundial.com.br. Contact: José Eduardo Dias, Diretor. Sells religious books and cassettes of religious music (from choral to bossa nova). Prices, in local currency, can be found at the website (click on "catálogo"). Program provider for Rádio Nova Visão—see, above.

Rádio Tropical (if reactivated), C.P. 23, 78600-000 Barra do Garças MT, Brazil. Contact: Alacir Viera Cándido, Diretor e Presidente; or Walter Francisco Dorados, Diretor Artístico. $1 or return postage required. Replies slowly and rarely to correspondence in Portuguese.

Rádio Tupi, Avenida Nadir Dias Figueiredo 1329, 02110-901 São Paulo SP, Brazil. Contact: Alfredo Raymundo Filho, Diretor Geral; Montival da Silva Santos; or Elia Soares. Free stickers. Return postage required. Replies occasionally to correspondence in Portuguese.

Rádio Universo/Rádio Tupi, C.P. 7133, 80000-000 Curitiba PR, Brazil. Contact: Luíz Andreu Rúbio, Diretor. Replies occasionally to correspondence in Portuguese. Rádio Universo's program time is rented by the "Deus é Amor" Pentecostal church, and is from the Rádio Tupi network. Identifies on the air as "Radio Tupi, Sistema Universo de Comunicação" or, more often, just as "Radio Tupi."

Rádio Verdes Florestas, C.P. 53, 69981-970 Cruzeiro do Sul AC, Brazil. Contact: Marlene Valente de Andrade. Return postage required. Replies occasionally to correspondence in Portuguese.

Rádio Voz do Coração Imaculado, C.P. 354, 75001-970 Anápolis GO, Brazil. A new station which appeared in 1999, broadcasting via the transmitter formerly used by Rádio Carajá.

▣**Sistema LBV Mundial**, Legião da Boa Vontade, Rua Sérgio Tomás 740, Bom Retiro, 01131-010 São Paulo SP, Brazil. Phone: +55 (11) 250-4513. Fax: +55 (11) 250 4639. URL: (includes RealAudio) www.lbv.org/radio/index.html. Contact: André Tiago, Diretor; or Sandra Albuquerque, Asessoria de Relações Internacionais. Replies slowly to correspondence in all main languages.
NEW YORK OFFICE: 383 5th Avenue, 2nd Floor, New York NY 10016 USA. Phone: +1 (212) 481-1004. Fax: +1 (212) 481 1005. E-mail: lgw2000@aol.com.

▣**Voz de Libertação**. Ubiquitous programming originating from the "Deus é Amor" Pentecostal church's Rádio Universo (1300 kHz) in São Bernardo do Campo, São Paulo, and heard over several shortwave stations, including Rádio Universo, Curitiba (*see*) and Rádio Gazeta, São Paulo (*see*). A RealAudio feed is available at the "Deus é Amor" website, www.ipda.org.br.

Voz do Coração Imaculado—*see* Rádio Voz do Coração Imaculado.

BULGARIA   World Time +2 (+3 midyear)

Bulgarian National Radio, 4 Dragan Tsankov Blvd., 1040 Sofia, Bulgaria. Phone: +359 (2) 652-871. Fax: (weekdays) +359 (2) 657 230. URL: www.bgradio.bg. Contact: Borislav Djamdjiev, Director; Iassen Indjev, Executive Director; or Martin Minkov, Editor-in-Chief.

Radio Bulgaria
NONTECHNICAL AND TECHNICAL: P.O. Box 900, BG-1000, Sofia, Bulgaria. Phone: (general) +359 (2) 661-954 or +359 (2) 854-633; (Managing Director) +359 (2) 854-604. Fax: (general, usually weekdays only) +359 (2) 871 060, +359 (2) 871 061 or +359 (2) 650 560; (Managing Director) +359 (2) 946 1576; or +359 (2) 988 5103; (Frequency Manager) +359 (2) 963 4464. E-mail: rcorresp1@fon15.bnr.acad.bg; or rbul1@nationalradio.bg. Contact: (general) Mrs. Iva Delcheva, English Section; Kristina Mihailova, In Charge of Listeners' Letters, English Section; Christina Pechevska, Listeners' Letters, English Section; Svilen Stoicheff, Head of English Section; (administration and technical) Anguel H. Nedyalkov, Managing Director; (technical) Atanas Tzenov, Director. Replies regularly, but sometimes slowly. Return postage helpful, as the station is financially overstretched due to the economic situation in the country. For concerns about frequency usage, contact BTC, below, with copies to Messrs. Nedyalkov and Tzenov of Radio Bulgaria.
FREQUENCY MANAGEMENT AND TRANSMISSION OPERATIONS: Bulgarian Telecommunications Company (BTC), Ltd., 8 Totleben Blvd., 1606 Sofia, Bulgaria. Phone: +359 (2) 88-00-75. Fax: +359 (2) 87 58 85 or +359 (2) 80 25 80. Contact: Roumen Petkov, Frequency Manager; or Mrs. Margarita Krasteva, Radio Regulatory Department.

Radio Horizont—a service of Bulgarian National Radio (*see*, above).

Radio Varna, 22 blv. Primorski, 9000 Varna, Bulgaria. Replies irregularly. Return postage required.

BURKINA FASO   World Time exactly

Radiodiffusion-Télévision Burkina, B.P. 7029, Ouagadougou, Burkina Faso. Phone: +226 310-441. Contact: (general) Raphael L. Onadia or M. Pierre Tassembedo; (technical) Marcel Teho, Head of Transmitting Centre. Replies irregularly to correspondence in French. IRC or return postage helpful.

BURMA—*see* MYANMAR.

BURUNDI   World Time +2

La Voix de la Révolution, B.P. 1900, Bujumbura, Burundi. Phone: +257 22-37-42. Fax: +257 22 65 47 or +257 22 66 13. Contact: (general) Grégoire Barampumba, Head of News Section; or Frederic Havugiyaremye, Journaliste; (administration) Gérard Mfuranzima, Le Directeur de la Radio; or Didace Baranderetse, Directeur Général de la Radio; (technical) Abraham Makuza, Le Directeur Technique. $1 required.

CAMBODIA   World Time +7

National Radio of Cambodia
STATION ADDRESS: 106 Preah Kossamak Street, Monivong Boulevard, Phnom Penh, Cambodia. Phone: +855 (23) 423-369 or +855 (23) 422-869. Fax: + 855 (23) 427 319. Contact: (general) Miss Hem Bory, English Announcer; Kem Yan, Chief of External Relations; or Touch Chhatha, Producer, Art Department; (administration) In Chhay, Chief of Overseas Service; Som Sarun, Chief of Home Service; Van Sunheng, Deputy Director General, Cambodian National Radio and Television; or Ieng Muli, Minister of Information; (technical) Oum Phin, Chief of Technical Department. Free program schedule. Replies irregularly and slowly. Do not include stamps, currency, IRCs or dutiable items in envelope. Registered letters stand a much better chance of getting through.

CAMEROON   World Time +1

NOTE: Any CRTV outlet is likely to be verified by contacting via registered mail, in English or French with $2 enclosed, James Achanyi-Fontem, Head of Programming, CRTV, B.P. 986, Douala, Cameroon.

Cameroon Radio Television Corporation (CRTV)— Bafoussam (when active), B.P. 970, Bafoussam (Ouest), Cameroon. Contact: (general) Boten Celestin; (technical) Ndam Seidou, Chef Service Technique. IRC or return postage required. Replies irregularly in French to correspondence in English or French.

Cameroon Radio Television Corporation (CRTV)— Bertoua (when active), B.P. 230, Bertoua (Eastern), Cameroon. Rarely replies to correspondence, preferably in French. $1 required.

Cameroon Radio Television Corporation (CRTV)— Buea, P.M.B., Buea (Sud-Ouest), Cameroon. Contact: Ononino Oli Isidore, Chef Service Technique. Three IRCs, $1 or return postage required.

Cameroon Radio Television Corporation (CRTV)— Douala (when active), B.P. 986, Douala (Littoral), Cameroon. Contact: (technical) Emmanual Ekite, Technicien. Free pennants. Three IRCs or $1 required.

Cameroon Radio Television Corporation (CRTV)—Garoua, B.P. 103, Garoua (Nord/Adamawa), Cameroon. Contact: Kadeche Manguele. Free cloth pennants. Three IRCs or return postage required. Replies irregularly and slowly to correspondence in French.

Cameroon Radio Television Corporation (CRTV)—Yaoundé, B.P. 1634, Yaoundé (Centre-Sud), Cameroon. Phone: +237 214-035, +237 208-037. Fax: +237 204 340. Contact: (technical or nontechnical) Prof. Gervais Mendo Ze, Directeur-Général; (technical) Eyebe Tanga, Directeur Technique. $1 required. Replies slowly (sometimes extremely slowly) to correspondence in French.

CANADA   World Time –3:30 (–2:30 midyear)

Newfoundland; –4 (–3 midyear) Atlantic; –5 (–4 midyear) Eastern, including Quebec and Ontario; –6 (–5 midyear) Central; except Saskatchewan; –6 Saskatchewan; –7 (–6 midyear) Mountain; –8 (–7 midyear) Pacific, including Yukon

BBC World Service via RCI/CBC—For verification direct from RCI's CBC shortwave transmitters, contact Radio Canada International (*see* below). Nontechnical correspondence should be sent to the BBC World Service in London (*see*).

Canadian Broadcasting Corporation (CBC)—English Programs, P.O. Box 500, Station A, Toronto, Ontario, M5W 1E6, Canada. Phone: (Audience Relations) +1 (416) 205-3700. E-mail: cbcinput@toronto.cbc.ca. URL: (includes RealAudio) www.radio.cbc.ca. CBC prepares some of the programs heard over Radio Canada International (*see*).

LONDON NEWS BUREAU: CBC, 43-51 Great Titchfield Street, London W1P 8DD, England. Phone: +44 (171) 412-9200. Fax: +44 (171) 631 3095.

PARIS NEWS BUREAU: CBC, 17 avenue Matignon, F-75008 Paris, France. Phone: +33 (1) 4421-1515. Fax: +33 (1) 4421 1514.

WASHINGTON NEWS BUREAU: CBC, National Press Building, Suite 500, 529 14th Street NW, Washington DC 20045 USA. Phone: +1 (202) 383-2900. Contact: Jean-Louis Arcand, David Hall or Susan Murray.

Canadian Broadcasting Corporation (CBC)—French Programs, Société Radio-Canada, C.P. 6000, succ. centre-ville, Montréal, Québec, H3C 3A8, Canada. Phone: (Audience Relations) +1 (514) 597-6000. E-mail (comments on programs): auditoire@montreal.radio-canada.ca. Welcomes correspondence sent to this address but may not reply due to shortage of staff. URL: (includes RealAudio) www.radio-canada.ca. CBC prepares some of the programs heard over Radio Canada International (*see*).

CBC Northern Quebec Shortwave Service—*see* Radio Canada International, below.

CFRX-CFRB

MAIN ADDRESS: 2 St. Clair Avenue West, Toronto, Ontario, M4V 1L6, Canada. Phone:(main switchboard) +1 (416) 924-5711; (access line) +1 (416) 872-CFRB; (news centre) +1 (416) 924-6717; (talk shows) +1 (416) 872-1010. Fax: +1 (416) 323 6830. E-mail: CFRBcomments@cfrb.com. URL: www.cfrb.com. Contact: (nontechnical) Bob Macowycz, Operations Manager; or Gary Slaight, President; (technical) Ian Sharp. Reception reports should be sent to verification address, below.

VERIFICATION ADDRESS: Ontario DX Association, P.O. Box 161, Station 'A', Willowdale, Ontario, M2N 5S8, Canada. Phone: +1 (416) 293-8919. Fax: +1 (416) 293 6603. E-mail: 70400.2660@compuserve.com. URL: www.durhamradio.ca/odxa. Contact: Steve Canney. Free CFRB/CFRX information

sheet and ODXA brochure enclosed with verification. Reception reports are processed quickly if sent to this address, rather than to the station itself.

CFVP-CKMX, AM 1060, Standard Broadcasting, P.O. Box 2750, Station 'M', Calgary, Alberta, T2P 4P8, Canada. Phone: (general) +1 (403) 240-5800; (news) +1 (403) 240-5844; (technical) +1 (403) 240-5867. Fax: (general and technical) +1 (403) 240 5801; (news) +1 (403) 246 7099. Contact: (general) Gary Russell, General Manager; or Beverley Van Tighem, Exec. Ass't.; (technical) Ken Pasolli, Technical Director.

CHNX-CHNS, P.O. Box 400, Halifax, Nova Scotia, B3J 2R2, Canada. Phone: +1 (902) 422-1651. Fax: +1 (902) 422 5330. E-mail: (station) chns@ns.sympatico.ca; (Harvey) Wharvey@Fundyweb.com. Contact: Garry Barker, General Manager; (programs) Troy Michaels, Operations Manager; (technical) Wayne Harvey, Chief Engineer. Program schedules, stickers and small souvenirs sometimes available. Return postage or $1 helpful. Replies irregularly.

CHU, Time and Frequency Standards, Bldg. M-36, National Research Council, Ottawa, Ontario, K1A 0R6, Canada. Phone: (general) +1 (613) 993-5186; (administration) +1 (613) 993-1003 or +1 (613) 993-2704. Fax: +1 (613) 993 1394. E-mail: time@nrc.ca. URL: www.cisti.nrc.ca/inms/time/ctse.html. Contact: Dr. Rob Douglas; Dr. Jean-Simon Boulanger, Group Leader; or Ray Pelletier, Technical Officer. Official standard frequency and World Time station for Canada on 3330, 7335 and 14670 kHz. Brochure available upon request.Those with a personal computer, Bell 103 compatible modem and appropriate software can get the exact time, from CHU's cesium clock, via the telephone; details available upon request, or direct from the website.

CKZN-CBN, CBC, P.O. Box 12010, Station 'A', St. John's, Newfoundland, A1B 3T8, Canada. Phone: +1 (709) 576-5155. Fax: +1 (709) 576 5099. URL: (includes experimental RealAudio) www.radio.cbc.ca/regional/nfld/. Contact: (general) Heather Elliott, Communications Officer; (technical) Shawn R. Williams, Manager, Transmission & Distribution; or Jerry Brett, Transmitter Department. Free CBC sticker and verification card with the history of Newfoundland included. Don't enclose money, stamps or IRCs with correspondence, as they will only have to be returned.

CKZU-CBU, CBC, P.O. Box 4600, Vancouver, British Columbia, V6B 4A2, Canada. Toll-free telephone (U.S & Canada only) 1-800-961-6161. Phone: (general) +1 (604) 662-6000; (engineering) +1 (604) 662-6064. Fax: (general) +1 (604) 662 6350; (engineering) +1 (604) 662 6350. URLs: www.vancouver.cbc.ca/; www.radio.cbc.ca/regional/BC/. Contact: (general) Public Relations; (technical) Dave Newbury, Transmission Engineer.

Radio Canada International

NOTE: (CBC Northern Quebec Service) The following RCI address, fax and e-mail information for the Main Office and Transmission Office is also valid for the CBC Northern Quebec Shortwave Service, provided you make your communication to the attention of the particular service you seek to contact.

MAIN OFFICE: P.O. Box 6000, Montréal, Quebec, H3C 3A8, Canada. Phone: (general) +1 (514) 597-7500; (Audience Relations, Ms. Maggie Akerblom) +1 (514) 597-7555; (English and French programming) +1 (514) 597-7551; (Russian programming) +1 (514) 597-6866; (CBC's "As It Happens" Talkback Machine) +1 (416) 205-3331; or (Communications, Marketing & Research) +1 (514) 597-7659. Fax: (RCI) +1 (514) 284 0891 or +1 (514) 284 9550; (English and French Programming) +1 (514) 597 7617; or (Communications, Marketing & Research) +1 (514) 597 6607. E-mail: (general)

China National Radio hosts Grundig executives in Beijing. From left, Wang Chunjun, "Rocky" Leung, Liang Wei, Grundig's Dan Johnson and Esmail Hozour, Wang Yanchun, Sun Uing Nian, Soon Ying, Yan Hui and Li Xiao Lei.

E.A. Hozour

rci@montreal.radio-canada.ca; (Audience Relations) rci@cam.org. URL: (includes RealAudio) www.rcinet.ca. Contact: (general) Maggy Akerblom, Director of Audience Relations; Stéphane Parent, "Le courrier des auditeurs"; or Mark Montgomery, Producer/Host, the "Mailbag"; (Communications, Marketing & Research) Héléne Robillard-Frayne, Director; (administration) Robert O'Reilly, Executive Director; (technical—verifications) Bill Westenhaver, CIDX. Free stickers and other small station souvenirs. 50th Anniversary T-shirts, sweatshirts, watches, lapel pins and tote bags available for sale; write to the above address for a free illustrated flyer giving prices and ordering information.

TRANMISSION OFFICE: 1055 boulevard René Lévesque East, Montréal, Québec, H2L 4S5, Canada. Phone: +1 (514) 597-7616/17/18/19/20. Fax: +1 (514) 284 2052. E-mail: (Théorêt) gtheoret@montreal.radio-canada.ca; (Bouliane) jbouliane@montreal.radio-canada.ca. Contact: (general) Gérald Théorêt, Manager, Frequency Management; or Ms. Nicole Vincent, Frequency Management; (administration) Jacques Bouliane, Co-ordinator Plant Engineering. This office only for informing about transmitter-related problems (interference, modulation quality, etc.), especially by fax. Verifications not given out at this office; requests for verification should be sent to the main office, above.

TRANSMITTER SITE: CBC, P.O. Box 6131, Sackville New Brunswick, E4L 1G6, Canada. Phone: +1 (506) 536-2690/1. Fax: +1 (506) 536 2342. Contact: Raymond Bristol, Plant Manager Transmitting Stations. All correspondence not concerned with transmitting equipment should be directed to the appropriate address in Montréal, above. Free tours given during normal working hours.

RCI MONITORING STATION: P.O. Box 322, Station C, Ottawa, Ontario, K1Y 1E4, Canada. Phone: +1 (613) 831-2801. Fax: +1 (613) 831 0343. Contact: Derek Williams, Manager Monitoring Station.

Radio Monte-Carlo Middle East (via Radio Canada International)—see Cyprus.

Shortwave Classroom, G.L. Comba Public School, P.O. Box 580, Almonte, Ontario, K0A 1A0, Canada. Phone: +1 (613) 256-2735. Fax: +1 (613) 256 3107. E-mail: 713861@ican.net. Contact: Neil Carleton, Organizer. The Shortwave Classroom newsletter, three times per year, for "$10 and an accompanying feature to share with teachers in the newsletter." Ongoing nonprofit volunteer project of teachers and others to use

shortwave listening in the classroom to teach about global perspectives, media studies, world geography, languages, social studies and other subjects. Interested teachers and parents worldwide are invited to make contact.

CENTRAL AFRICAN REPUBLIC   World Time +1

Radio Centrafrique, Radiodiffusion-Télévision Centrafricaine, B.P. 940, Bangui, Central African Republic. Contact: (technical) Jacques Mbilo, Le Directeur des Services Techniques; or Michèl Bata, Services Techniques. Replies on rare occasions to correspondence in French; return postage required.

Radio MINURCA, B.P. 2732, Bangui, Central African Republic. Phone: +236 612-043, X-6181. Fax: +236 612 108. E-mail: (general) radmin@intnet.cf; (Director) smith2.unep@un.org. Contact: David Smith, Director. Operated by the United Nations Mission in the Central African Republic, and was initially established to provide information to the public during the runup to legislative elections in 1999.

CHAD   World Time +1

Radiodiffusion Nationale Tchadienne—N'djamena, B.P. 892, N'Djamena, Chad. Contact: Djimadoum Ngoka Kilamian; or Ousmane Mahamat. Two IRCs or return postage required. Replies slowly to correspondence in French.

Radiodiffusion Nationale Tchadienne—Radio Moundou (when operating), B.P. 122, Moundou, Logone, Chad. Contact: Dingantoudji N'Gana Esaie.

CHILE   World Time –3 (–4 midyear)

Radio Esperanza

OFFICE: Casilla 830, Temuco, Chile. Phone/fax: +56 (45) 240-161. Contact: (general) Juanita Cárcamo, Departamento de Programación; Eleazar Jara, Dpto. de Programación; Ramón P. Woerner K., Publicidad; or Alberto Higueras Martínez, Locutor; (verifications) Rodolfo Campos, Director; Juanita Carmaco M., Dpto. de Programación; (technical) Juan Luis Puentes, Dpto. Técnico. Free pennants, stickers, bookmarks and tourist information. Two IRCs, $1 or 2 U.S. stamps appreciated. Replies, usually quite slowly, to correspondence in Spanish or English.

STUDIO: Calle Luis Durand 03057, Temuco, Chile. Phone/fax: +56 (45) 240-161.

Radio Santa María, Apartado 1, Coyhaique, Chile. Phone: +56 (67) 23-23-98, +56 (67) 23-20-25 or +56 (67) 23-18-17. Fax: +56 (67) 23 13 06. Contact: Pedro Andrade Vera, Coordinador. $1 or return postage required. May send free tourist cards. Replies to correspondence in Spanish and Italian.

Radio Triunfal Evangélica, Calle Las Araucarias 2757, Villa Monseñor Larrain, Talagante, Chile. Phone: +56 (1) 815-4765. Contact: Fernando González Segura, Obispo de la Misión Pentecostal Fundamentalista. Two IRCs required. Replies to correspondence in Spanish.

Radio Voz Cristiana, Casilla 490-3, Santiago, Chile. Phone: (engineering) +56 (2) 855-7046. Fax: +56 (2) 855 7053. E-mail: (engineering) vozing@interaccess.cl; or aflynn@interaccess.cl; (administration) vozcrist@interaccess.cl. URL: www.christianvision.org/christian-vision/chile.htm. Contact: (technical) Andrew Flynn, Chief Engineer. Free program & frequency schedules. Sometimes sends small souvenirs. All QSL requests should be sent to the Miami Address. May extend broadcasting targets beyond Latin America.

INTERNATIONAL OFFICE: Christian Vision, Ryder Street, West Bromwich, West Midlands B70 0EJ, United Kingdom. Contact: Terry Bennett, Regional Manager for the Americas.

MIAMI ADDRESS: P.O. Box 2889, Miami FL 33144 USA. Phone: +1 (305) 231-7704. Fax: +1 (305) 231 7447. E-mail: cv-usa@msn.com. Contact: (nontechnical) Mark Gallado.

CHINA
World Time +8; still nominally +6 ("Urümqi Time") in the Xinjiang Uighur Autonomous Region, but in practice +8 is observed there, as well.

NOTE: China Radio International, the Central People's Broadcasting Station and certain regional outlets reply regularly to listeners' letters in a variety of languages. If a Chinese regional station does not respond to your correspondence within four months—and many will not, unless your letter is in Chinese or the regional dialect—try writing them c/o China Radio International.

Central People's Broadcasting Station (CPBS)— China National Radio, Zhongyang Renmin Guangbo Diantai, P.O. Box 4501, Beijing 100866, China. Phone: +86 (10) 6851-2435 or +86 (10) 6851-5522. Fax: +86 (10) 6851 6630. E-mail: cnr@shcei.com.cn. URL: (includes RealAudio) http://cnr.net.cn/. Contact: Wang Changquan, Audience Department, China National Radio. Tape recordings of music and news $5 plus postage. CPBS T-shirts $10 plus postage; also sells ties and other items with CPBS logo. No credit cards. Free stickers, pennants and other small souvenirs. Return postage helpful. Responds regularly to correspondence in English and Standard Chinese (Mandarin). Although in recent years this station has officially been called "China National Radio" in English-language documents, all on-air identifications in Standard Chinese continue to be "Zhongyang Renmin Guangbo Diantai" (Central People's Broadcasting Station). CPBS-1 also airs Chinese-language programs co-produced by CPBS and Radio Canada International.

China Huayi Broadcasting Company, P.O. Box 251, Fuzhou, Fujian 350001, China. Contact: Lin Hai Chun, Announcer; or Wu Gehong. Replies to correspondence in English and Chinese.

China National Radio—see Central People's Broadcasting Station (CPBS), above.

China Radio International

MAIN OFFICE, NON-CHINESE LANGUAGES SERVICE: 16A Shijingshan Street, Beijing 100040, China. Phone: (Director's office) +86 (10) 6889-1676; (Audience Relations.) +86 (10) 6889-1617 or +86 (10) 6889-1652; (English newsroom) +86 (10) 6889-1619; (current affairs) +86 (10) 6889-1588; (Technical Director) +86 (10) 6609-2577. Fax: (Director's office) +86 (10) 6889 1582; (English Service) +86 (10) 6889 1378 or +86 (10) 6889 1379; (Audience Relations) +86 (10) 6851 3175; or (administration) +86 (10) 6851 3174. E-mail: (English Service) crieng@cri.com.cn; (Chinese Service) chn@cri.com.cn; (German Service) ger@box.cri.com.cn; (Spanish Service) servispa@box.cri.com.cn; ("Voices from Other Lands" program) voices@box.cri.com.cn. URLs: (official, including RealAudio) www.cri.com.cn/; (unofficial, but regularly updated) http://pw2.netcom.com/~jleq/cril.htm. Contact: Ms. Qi Guilin, Director of Audience Relations, English Service; Shang Chunyan, "Listener's Letterbox"; Xu Ming, Editor; or Xia Jixuan, Director of English Service; (technical) Wang Guoqing, Technical Director; (administration) Zhang Zhenhua, Director General, China Radio International; Wang Guoqing, Cong Yingmin and Wong Rufeng, Deputy Directors, China Radio International. Free bi-monthly *Messenger* newsletter for loyal listeners, pennants, stickers, desk calendars, pins and handmade papercuts. Sometimes, China Radio International holds contests and quizzes, with the overall winner getting a free trip to China. T-shirts for $8. Two-volume, 820-page set of *Day-to-Day Chinese* language-lesson books $15, including postage worldwide; a 155-page book, *Learn to Speak Chinese: Sentence by Sentence*, plus two cassettes for $15. Two chinese music tapes for $15. Various other books (on arts, medicine, Chinese idioms etc.) in English available from Audience Relations Department, English Service, China Radio International, 100040 Beijing, China. Payment by postal money order to Mr. Li Yi. Every year, the Audience Relations Department will renew the mailing list of the *Messenger* newsletter. CRI is also relayed via shortwave transmitters in Brazil, Canada, France, French Guiana, Mali, Russia and Spain.

FREQUENCY PLANNING DIVISION: Radio & Television of People's Republic of China, 2 Fuxingmenwai Street, Beijing 100866, China. Phone: (Wang Xiulan) +86 (10) 6609-2080 or +86 (10) 6609-2627; (Yang Minmin) +86 (10) 6609-2070. Fax: +86 (10) 6801 6436. E-mail: kejisi@public.fhnet.cn.net. Contact: Ms. Wang Xiulan or Mr. Yang Minmin.

MAIN OFFICE, CHINESE LANGUAGES SERVICE: China Radio International, Beijing 100040, China. Prefers correspondence in Chinese (Mandarin), Cantonese, Hakka, Chaozhou or Amoy.

ARLINGTON NEWS BUREAU: 2000 South Eads Street APT#712, Arlington VA 22202 USA. Phone: +1 (703) 521-8689. Contact: Mr. Zhenbang Dong.

CHINA (HONG KONG) NEWS BUREAU: 387 Queen's Road East, Room 1503, Hong Kong, China. Phone: +852 2834-0384. Contact: Ms. Zhang Jiaping.

JERUSALEM NEWS BUREAU: Flat 16, Hagdud, Ha'ivri 12, Jerusalem 92345, Israel. Phone: +972 (2) 566-6084. Contact: Mr. H. Yi.

LONDON NEWS BUREAU: 13B Clifton Gardens, Golders Green, London NW11 7ER, United Kingdom. Phone: +44 (181) 458-6943. Contact: Ms. Xu Huazhen

NEW YORK NEWS BUREAU: 630 First Avenue #35K, New York NY 10016 USA. Fax: +1 (212) 889 2076. Contact: Mr. Qian Yurun.

SYDNEY NEWS BUREAU: Unit 53, Block A15 Herbert Street, St. Leonards NSW 2065, Australia. Phone: +61 (2) 9436-1493. Contact: Mr. Shi Chungyong.

SAN FRANCISCO OFFICE, SCHEDULES: 2654 17th Avenue, San Francisco CA 94116 USA. Phone: +1 (415) 564-9968. E-mail: GPoppin@aol.com. Contact: George Poppin. This address, a volunteer office, only provides CRI schedules to listeners. All other correspondence should be sent directly to the main office in Beijing.

Fujian People's Broadcasting Station, 2 Gutian Lu, Fuzhou, Fujian 350001, China. $1 helpful. Replies occasionally and usually slowly.

Gansu People's Broadcasting Station, 226 Donggang Xilu, Lanzhou 730000, China. Phone: +86 (931) 841-1054. Fax: +86 (931) 882 5834. Contact: Li Mei. IRC helpful.

Guangxi People's Broadcasting Station, 12 Min Zu Avenue, Nanning, Guangxi 530022, China. Contact: Song Yue, Staffer; Yuan Ri Qin; or Li Hai Li, Staffer. Free stickers and handmade papercuts. IRC helpful. Replies irregularly.

Guizhou People's Broadcasting Station, 259 Qingyun Lu, Guiyang, Guizhou 550002, China.

Heilongjiang People's Broadcasting Station, 181 Zhongshan Lu, Harbin, Heilongjiang 150001, China. Phone: +86 (451) 262-7454. Fax: +86 (451) 289 3539. $1 or return postage helpful.

Honghe People's Broadcasting Station, 32 Jianshe Donglu, Gejiu, Yunnan 661400, China. Contact: Shen De-chun, Head of Station; or Mrs. Cheng Lin, Editor-in-Chief. Free travel brochures.

Hubei People's Broadcasting Station, 563 Jiefang Dadao, Wuhan, Hubei 430022, China.

Hunan People's Broadcasting Station, 27 Yuhua Lu, Changsha, Hunan 410007, China.

Jiangxi People's Broadcasting Station, 111 Hongdu Zhong Dadao, Nanchang, Jiangxi 330046, China. E-mail: gfzq@public.nc.jx.cn. Contact: Tang Ji Sheng, Editor, Chief Editor's Office. Free gold/red pins. Replies irregularly. Mr. Tang enjoys music, literature and stamps, so enclosing a small memento along these lines should help assure a speedy reply.

Nei Menggu (Inner Mongolia) People's Broadcasting Station, 19 Xinhua Darjie, Hohhot, Nei Menggu 010058, China. Contact: Zhang Xiang-Quen, Secretary; or Liang Yan. Replies irregularly.

Qinghai People's Broadcasting Station, 96 Kunlun Lu, Xining, Qinghai 810001, China. Contact: Liqing Fangfang; or Ghou Guo Liang, Director, Technical Department. $1 helpful.

Sichuan People's Broadcasting Station, 119-1 Hongxing Zhonglu, Chengdu, Sichuan 610017, China. Replies occasionally.

Voice of Jinling (Jinling zhi Sheng), P.O. Box 268, Nanjing, Jiangsu 210002, China. Fax: +86 (25) 413 235. Contact: Strong Lee, Producer/Host, "Window of Taiwan." Free stickers and calendars, plus Chinese-language color station brochure and information on the Nanjing Technology Import & Export Corporation. Replies to correspondence in Chinese and to simple correspondence in English. $1, IRC or 1 yuan Chinese stamp required for return postage.

Voice of Pujiang (Pujiang zhi Sheng), P.O. Box 3064, Shanghai 200002, China. Phone: +86 (21) 6208-2797. Fax: +86 (21) 6208 2850. Contact: Jiang Bimiao, Editor & Reporter.

Voice of the Strait (Haixia zhi Sheng), People's Liberation Army Broadcasting Centre, P.O. Box 187, Fuzhou, Fujian 350012, China. Replies irregularly.

Wenzhou People's Broadcasting Station, 19 Xianxue Qianlu, Wenzhou, Zhejiang 325000, China.

Xilingol People's Broadcasting Station, Xilin Dajie, Xilinhot, Nei Menggu 026000, China.

Xinjiang People's Broadcasting Station, 84 Tuanjie Lu, Urümqi, Xinjiang 830044, China. Contact: Zhao Ji-shu. Free tourist booklet, postcards and used Chinese stamps. Replies to correspondence in Chinese and to simple correspondence in English.

Xizang People's Broadcasting Station, 180 Beijing Zhonglu, Lhasa, Xizang 850000, China. Contact: Lobsang Chonphel, Announcer. Free stickers and brochures. Enclosing an English-language magazine may help with a reply.

Yunnan People's Broadcasting Station, 73 Renmin Xilu, Central Building of Broadcasting & TV, Kunming, 650031 Yunnan, China. Contact: Sheng Hongpeng or F.K. Fan. Free Chinese-language brochure on Yunnan Province, but no QSL cards. $1 or return postage helpful. Replies occasionally.

Zhejiang People's Broadcasting Station, 11 Wulin Xiang, Moganshan Lu, Hangzhou, Zhejiang 310005, China.

CHINA (TAIWAN)   World Time +8

⚑**Central Broadcasting System (CBS)**, 55 Pei'an Road, Tachih, Taipei 104, Taiwan, Republic of China. Phone: +886 (2) 2591-8161. Fax: +886 (2) 2585 0741. E-mail: cbs@cbs.org.tw. URLs: www.cbs.org.tw; www.cbs-taipei.org; (RealAudio) www.cbs.org.tw/cbsns.html. Contact: Lee Ming, Deputy Director. Free stickers.

⚑**Radio Taipei International**, P.O. Box 24-38, Taipei 106, Taiwan, Republic of China. Phone: +886 (2) 2591-8161. Fax: +886 (2) 2598 2254. E-mail: (nontechnical) prog@cbs.org.tw. URLs: (broadcast schedules) www.cbs.org.tw/engb.html; (RealAudio) www.cbs.org.tw/indexenglish.html; (RealAudio program schedule) www.cbs.org.tw/program/Program.htm. Contact: (general) Daniel Dong, Chief, Listeners' Service Section; Paula Chao, Producer, "Mailbag Time";Yea-Wen Wang; or Phillip Wong, "Perspectives"; (administration) John C.T. Feng, Director; or Dong Yu-Ching, Deputy Director; (technical) Wen-Bin Tsai, Engineer, Engineering Department; Tai-Lau Ying, Engineering Department; Tien-Shen Kao; or Huang Shuh-shyun, Director, Engineering Department. Free stickers, caps, shopping bags, annual diary, "Let's Learn Chinese" language-learning course materials, booklets and other publications, and Taiwanese stamps. T-shirts $5. The station's programs are relayed to the Americas via WYFR's transmitters in Okeechobee, Florida, USA (*see*).

OSAKA NEWS BUREAU: C.P.O. Box 180, Osaka Central Post Office, Osaka 530-091, Japan.

TOKYO NEWS BUREAU: P.O Box 21, Azubu Post Office, Tokyo 106, Japan.

SAN FRANCISCO NEWS BUREAU: P.O. Box 192793, San Francisco CA 94119-2793 USA.

⚑**Voice of Asia**, P.O. Box 24-777, Taipei, Taiwan, Republic of China. Phone: +886 (2) 2771-0151, X-2431. Fax: +886 (2) 2751 9277. URLs: same as for Radio Taipei International, above. Contact: (general) Vivian Pu, Co-Producer, with Isaac Guo of "Letterbox"; or Ms. Chao Mei-Yi, Deputy Chief; (technical) Engineering Department. Free shopping bags, inflatable globes, coasters, calendars, stickers and booklets. T-shirts $5.

CLANDESTINE

Clandestine broadcasts are often subject to abrupt change or termination. Being operated by anti-establishment political and/or military organizations, these groups tend to be suspi-

The Central State Museum in Almaty is a modern example of Kazak architectural vernacular.
M. Guha

cious of outsiders' motives. Thus, they are more likely to reply to contacts from those who communicate in the station's native tongue, and who are perceived to be at least somewhat favorably disposed to their cause. Most will provide, upon request, printed matter on their cause, though not necessarily in English.

For more detailed information on clandestine stations, refer to the annual publication, *Clandestine Stations List*, about $10 or 10 IRCs postpaid by air, published by the Danish Shortwave Clubs International, Tavleager 31, DK-2670 Greve, Denmark; phone (Denmark) +45 4290-2900; fax (via Germany) +49 6371 71790; e-mail 100413.2375@compuserve.com; its expert editor, Finn Krone of Denmark, may be reached at (e-mail) Krone@dk-online.dk. For CIA media contact information, *see* USA. Also available on the Internet, *The Clandestine Radio Intel Webpage,* specializing in background information on these stations and organized by region and target country. The page can be accessed via: www.qsl.net/yb0rmi/cland.htm. Another informative webpage specializing in Clandestine Radio information and containing a biweekly report on the latest news and developments affecting the study of clandestine radio is *Clandestine Radio Watch* and it can be found at: www.geocities.com/capecanaveral/2594/geocla.htm.

"Democratic Voice of Burma" ("Democratic Myanmar a-Than")
STATION: DVB Radio, P.O. Box 6720, St. Olavs Plass, N-0130 Oslo, Norway. Phone: +47 (22) 20-0021. Phone/fax: +47 (22) 36-2525. E-mail: euburma@online.no; dvbburma@online.no. URL: (includes RealAudio) www.communique.no/dvb/. Contact: (general) Dr. Anng Kin, Listener Liaison; Aye Chan Naing, Daily Editor; or Thida, host for "Songs Request Program"; (administration) Harn Yawnghwe, Director; or Daw Khin Pyone, Manager; (technical) Saw Neslon Ku, Studio Technician; or Technical Dept. Free stickers and booklets to be offered in the near future. Norwegian kroner requested for a reply, but

presumably Norwegian mint stamps would also suffice. Programs produced by Burmese democratic movements, as well as professional and independent radio journalists, to provide informational and educational services for the democracy movement inside and outside Burma. Opposes the current Myanmar government. Transmits via the facilities of Radio Norway International, among others.
AFFINITY GROUPS URLs:
BURMA NET. E-mail: (BurmaNet News editor, Free Burma Coalition, USA) strider@igc.apc.org; (Web coordinator, Free Burma Coalition, USA) freeburma@pobox.com. URL: (BurmaNet News, USA) http://sunsite.unc.edu/freeburma/listservers.html.
FREE BURMA COALITION. E-mail: justfree@ix.netcom.com. URL: http://danenet.wicip.org/fbc/.
"National Radio of the Democratic Saharan Arab Republic"—*see* "Radio Nacional de la República Arabe Saharaui Democrática."
"Radio Free Iraq"—*see* USA.
"Radio Free Somalia," 2 Griffith Avenue, Roseville NSW 2069, Australia. Phone/fax: +61 (2) 9417-1066. Contact: Sam Voron, Australian Director. $5, AUS$5 or 5 IRCs required. Station is operated from Gaalkacyo in the Mudug region of northeastern Somalia by the Somali International Amateur Radio Club. Seeks volunteers and donations of radio equipment and airline tickets.
"Radio Independence Bougainville," 2 Griffith Avenue, Roseville NSW 2069, Australia. Phone/fax: +61 (2) 9417-1066. Contact: Sam Voron, Australian Director. $5, AUS$5 or 5 IRCs required. Station is operated from Panguna, Central Bougainville by the pro independence forces of the Meekamui Defence Force led by Fransis Ona. Anti-Papua New Guinea Government.
"Radio Iran of Tomorrow." E-mail: riot_studio@hotmail.com. URL: (includes RealAudio) www.ri-ot.com. Contact: A. Khatarmi.

"Radio Kudirat," P.O. Box 9663, London SE1 3ZD, United Kingdom. Fax: (London) +44 (171) 403 6985; (Boston) +1 (617) 364 7362. E-mail: rkn@postlin.demon.co.uk; (contributions to Radio Kudirat) radio@udfn.com. URL: www.udfn.com/uradio.htm. Station set up to disseminate information concerning democracy, human rights and the environment in Nigeria. Requests broadcast material and funds to maintain a regular broadcasting schedule. Welcomes scripts, and recordings from listeners and supporters. Transmits via the South African facilities of Sentech. Has applied for a broadcasting license from the Nigerian government; if granted, the station will probably terminate its broadcasts on shortwave.

"Radio Kurdistan," ("Aira ezgay kurdistana, dangi hizbi socialisti democrati kurdistan"). E-mail: kurdish6065@aol.com. Station is run by the Kurdistan Socialist Democratic Party, a member of the Democratic Alliance of Kurdistan which is a made up of five parties under the leadership of the Patriotic Union of Kurdistan (PUK).

"Radio Nacional de la República Arabe Saharaui Democrática" (when operating), Directeur d'Information, Frente Polisario, B.P. 10, El-Mouradia, 16000 Algiers, Algeria; or c/o Ambassade de la République Arabe Saharaui Démocratique, 1 Av. Franklin Roosevelt, 16000 Algiers, Algeria. Phone (Algeria): +213 (2) 747-907. Fax, when operating (Algeria): +213 (2) 747 984. URL: (includes a RealAudio recording made in the station's studios) http://web.jet.es/rasd/amateur4.htm. Contact: Mohamed Lamin Abdesalem; Mahafud Zein; or Sneiba Lehbib. Two IRCs helpful. Pro-Polisario Front, and supported by the Algerian government.

"Radio Paru Paru," 2 Griffith Avenue, Roseville NSW 2069, Australia. Phone/fax: +61 (2) 9417-1066. Contact: Sam Voron, Australian Director. $5, AUS$5 or 5 IRCs required. Station is operated from Paru Paru, Central Bougainville by the pro independence faction of the Bougainville Revolutionary Army. Favors negotiation with the Papua New Guinea government and has signed a cease fire agreement.

"Radio Voice of Freedom & Renewal," ("Idha'at sawt al-hurriyah wa al-tajdid, sawt quwwat al-tahaluf al-sudaniyyah, sawt al-intifadah al-sha'biyyah al-musallahah"). URL: (Sudan Alliance Forces) www.safsudan.com. The Sudan Alliance Forces are an opposition guerrilla army of ex-government northern soldiers, affiliated to the Asmara, Eritrea-based National Democratic Alliance (NDA). Opposes the current Sudanese government. Also identifies as "Voice of the Sudan Alliance Forces" and "Voice of the Popular Armed Uprising."

"Radio Voice of the Mojahed"—see "Voice of the Mojahed," below.

"Radio Voice of United and Free Ethiopia" ("Yih ye andit netsa Ethiopia dimtse radio agelgilot new") (if reactivated), Ethiopian National Congress, P.O. Box 547, Swarthmore, PA 19081 USA. Fax: +1 (610) 543 3467. Also known as "Voice of One Free Ethiopia." Opposes Ethiopian government and believed to transmit from a site in Central Asia. Operated by the United Front of Ethiopians formed by the Ethiopian National Congress.

"Radio Rainbow" ("Kestedamena rediyo ye selamena yewendimamach dimtse"), c/o RAPEHGA, P.O. Box 140104, D-53056 Bonn, Germany. Contact: T. Assefa. Supposedly operated by an Ethiopian opposition group called Research and Action Group for Peace in Ethiopia and the Horn of Africa. Broadcasts via hired shortwave transmitters in Germany.

"Republic of Iraq Radio, Voice of the Iraqi People" ("Idha'at al-Jamahiriya al-Iraqiya, Saut al-Sha'b al-Iraqi"), Broadcasting Service of the Kingdom of Saudi Arabia, P.O. Box 61718, Riyadh 11575, Saudi Arabia. Phone: +966 (1) 442-5170. Fax: +966 (1) 402 8177. Contact: Suliman A. Al-Samnan, Director of Frequency Management. Anti-Saddam Hussein "black" clandestine supported by CIA, British intelligence, the Gulf Cooperation Council and Saudi Arabia. The name of this station has changed periodically since its inception during the Gulf crisis. Via transmitters in Saudi Arabia.

SPONSORING ORGANIZATION: Iraqi National Congress, 9 Pall Mall Deposit, 124-128 Barlby Road, London W10 6BL, United Kingdom. Phone: +44 (181) 964-8993; (office in Arbil, Iraq) +873 (682) 346-239. Fax: +44 (181) 960 4001; (office in Arbil, Iraq) +873 (682) 346 240. E-mail: pressoffice@inc.org.uk. URL: www.inc.org.uk.

"Voice of China" ("Zhongguo zhi Yin"), P.O. Box 273538, Concord CA 94527 USA; or (sponsoring organization) Foundation for China in the 21st Century, P.O. Box 11696, Berkeley CA 94701 USA. Contact: Bang Tai Xu, Director. Mainly "overseas Chinese students" interested in the democratization of China. Financial support from the Foundation for China in the 21st Century. Has "picked up the mission" of the earlier Voice of June 4th, but has no organizational relationship with it. Transmits via facilities of the Central Broadcasting System, Taiwan (see).

"Voice of Democratic Eritrea" ("Sawt Eritrea al-Dimuqratiya-Sawtu Jabhat al-Tahrir al-Eritrea") (when active), ELF-RC, P.O. Box 200434, D-53134 Bonn, Germany. Phone: +49 (0) 228-35618. Contact: Seyoum O. Michael, Member of Executive Committee, ELF-RC. Station of the Eritrean Liberation Front-Revolutionary Council, hostile to the government of Eritrea. Transmitter located in Sudan.

"Voice of Freedom and Renewal"—see "Radio Voice of Liberty & Renewal," above.

"Voice of Iranian Kordestan," KDPI, c/o AFK, Boite Postale 102, F-75623 Paris Cedex, France. Anti-Iranian government.

"Voice of Iraqi Kurdistan" ("Aira dangi Kurdestana Iraqa") (when active). Sponsored by the Kurdistan Democratic Party-Iraq (KDP), led by Masoud Barzani, and the National Democratic Iraqi Front. Broadcasts from its own transmitting facilities, reportedly located in the Kurdish section of Iraq. To contact the station or to obtain verification of reception reports, try going via one of the following KDP offices:

KURDISTAN-SALAHEDDIN CENTRAL MEDIA AND CULTURE OFFICE: Phone: +873 (761) 610-320. Fax: +873 (761) 610 321. E-mail: kdppress@aol.com.

KDP LONDON OFFICE: KDP International Relations Committee-London, P.O. Box 7725, London SW1V 3ZD, United Kingdom. Phone: +44 (171) 931-7764. Fax: +44 (171) 931 7765. E-mail: KdpEurope@aol.com; 106615.1017@compuserve.com.

KDP MADRID OFFICE: PDK Comité de Relaciones Internacionales-España, Avenida Papa Negro, 20-1º-105ª, E-28043 Madrid, Spain. Phone: +34 (91) 759-9475. Fax: +34 (91) 300 1638. E-mail: pdk@futurnet.es. URL: http://usuarios.futurnet.es/p/pdk/.

KDP WASHINGTON OFFICE: KDP International Relations Committee – Washington, 1015 18th Street, NW, Suite 704, Washington DC 20036 USA. Phone: +1 (202) 331-9505. Fax: +1 (202) 331 9506. E-mail: Kdpusa@aol.com. Contact: Namat Sharif, Kurdistan Democratic Party.

KDP-CANADA OFFICE: Phone: +1 (905) 387-3759. Fax: +1 (905) 387 3756. E-mail: kdpcanada@hotmail.com. URL: www.geocities.com/Paris/Gallery/3209/.

KDP-DENMARK OFFICE: Postbox 437, DK-3000 Helsingor,

Denmark; or Postbox 551, DK-2620 Albertslund, Denmark. Phone/Fax: +45 5577 9761. E-mail: kdpDenmark@ hotmail.com. URL: http://members.tripod.com/kdpDenmark/. *KDP-SWEDEN OFFICE:* Box 2017, SE-14502 Norsborg, Sweden. Phone: +46 (8) 361-446. Fax: +46 (8) 367 844. E-mail: taha_barwary@hotmail.com; party@kdp.pp.se. URL: www.kdp.pp.se. Contact: Alex Atroushi, who will verify e-mail reports sent to the "party" address.

"Voice of Kashmir Freedom" ("Sada-i Hurriyat-i Kashmir"), P.O. Box 102, Muzaffarabad, Azad Kashmir, via Pakistan. Favors Azad Kashmiri independence from India; pro-Moslem, sponsored by the Kashmiri Mojahedin organization. From transmission facilities believed to be in Pakistan.

"Voice of National Salvation" ("Gugugui Sori Pangsong"), Grenier Osawa 107, 40 Nando-cho, Shinjuku-ku, Tokyo, Japan. Phone: + 81 (3) 5261-0331. Fax: +81 (3) 5261 0332. E-mail: (National Salvation Front) kuguk@alles.or.jp. URL: (National Salvation Front parent organization) www.alles.or.jp/~kuguk/. Pro-North Korea, pro-Korean unification; supported by North Korean government. On the air since 1967, but not always under the same name. Via North Korean transmitters located in Pyongyang, Haeju and Wongsan.

"Voice of One Free Ethiopia"—see Radio Voice of United And Free Ethiopia, above.

"Voice of Oromo Liberation" ("Kun Segalee Bilisumma Oromooti"), Postfach 510610, D-13366 Berlin, Germany; SBO, Prinzenallee 81, D-13357 Berlin, Germany; or SBO, P.O. Box 73247, Washington DC 20056 USA. Phone: (Germany) +49 (30) 494-1036. Fax: (Germany) +49 (30) 494 3372. Contact: Taye Teferah, European Coordinator. Station of the Oromo Liberation Front of Ethiopia, an Oromo nationalist organization transmitting via facilities in Germany. Occasionally replies to correspondence in English or German. Return postage required.

"Voice of Palestine, Voice of the Palestinian Islamic Revolution" ("Saut al-Filistin, Saut al-Thowrah al-Islamiyah al-Filistiniyah")—for many years considered a clandestine station, but is now officially listed as part of the Arabic schedule of the Voice of the Islamic Republic of Iran, over whose transmitters the broadcasts are aired. *See* "Iran" for potential contact information. Supports the Islamic Resistance Movement, Hamas, which is anti-Arafat and anti-Israel.

"Voice of Peace and Brotherhood,"—see "Radio Rainbow," above.

"Voice of Rebellious Iraq" ("Sawt al-Iraq al-Tha'ir"), P.O. Box 11365/738, Tehran, Iran; P.O. Box 37155/146, Qom, Iran; or P.O. Box 36802, Damascus, Syria. Anti-Iraqi regime, supported by the Shi'ite-oriented Supreme Assembly of the Islamic Revolution of Iraq, led by Mohammed Baqir al-Hakim. Supported by the Iranian government and transmitted from Iranian soil. Hostile to the Iraqi government. *SPONSORING ORGANIZATION:* Supreme Council for Islamic Revolution in Iraq (SCIRI), 27a Old Gloucester St, London WC1N 3XX, United Kingdom. Phone: +44 (171) 371-6815. Fax: +44 (171) 371 2886. E-mail: 101642.1150@compuserve.com. URL: http://ourworld.compuserve.com/homepages/sciri/.

"Voice of Southern Azerbaijan" ("Bura Janubi Azerbaijan Sasi") (if reactivated), Vosa Ltd., Postfach 108, A-1193 Vienna, Austria. Phone: (Holland) +31 (70) 319-2189. This Azeri-language station is operated by the National and Independent Front of Southern Azerbaijan, which is opposed to Iranian and Armenian influence in Azerbaijan. Transmits via facilities in Israel.

"Voice of Sudan," NDA, 16 Camaret Court, Lorne Gardens, London W11 4XX, United Kingdom. Phone: (Asmara studio) +291 (1) 184-027. E-mail: sudanvoice@umma.org. URL: www.umma.org/nda/sudanvoice.html. Contact: Abdullahi Elmahdi, Secretary General, National Democratic Alliance. Broadcasts on behalf of the National Democratic Alliance (*see*, below), which is opposed to the present Sudanese government. Studios and transmitters located in Asmara, Eritrea. *NATIONAL DEMOCRATIC ALLIANCE (NDA):* (Headquarters) Asmara, Eritrea. Phone: +291 (1) 127-641. Fax: +291 (1) 127 632. E-mail: nda@umma.org. (U.K. Office) Phone: +44 (1344) 874-123. Fax: +44 (1344) 628 077. E-mail: aelmahdi@ cygnet.co.uk. (Egypt Office) Phone: +20 (2) 591-9408. Fax: +20 (2) 593 2908 or +20 (2) 271 5979.

"Voice of the Communist Party of Iran" ("Seda-ye Hezb-e Komunist-e Iran"), B.M. Box 2123, London WC1N 3XX, United Kingdom; or O.I.S., Box 50050, SE-104 05 Stockholm, Sweden. E-mail: wpi@wpiran.org. URL: www.wpiran.org. Sponsored by the Communist Party of Iran (KOMALA, formerly Tudeh).

"Voice of the Iranian Revolution" ("Aira Dangi Shurashi Irana")—*see* "Voice of the Communist Party of Iran," above, for details.

"Voice of the Islamic Revolution in Iraq"—*see* "Voice of Rebellious Iraq," above, for contact information. Affiliated with the Shi'ite-oriented Supreme Assembly for Islamic Revolution in Iraq, led by Mohammed Baqir al-Hakim.

The headquarters of Adventist World Radio's Spanish language network in Alajuela, Costa Rica.   AWR

📻**"Voice of the Mojahed"** ("Seda-ye Mojahed ast")
PARIS BUREAU: Mojahedines de Peuple d'Iran, 17 rue des Gords, F-95430 Auvers-sur-Oise, France; or Mojahed, c/o CCI, 147 rue St. Martin, F-75003 Paris, France. Fax: +33 (1) 4271-5627. E-mail: (People's Mojahedin Organization of Iran parent organization) Mojahed@mojahedin.org. URLs: (RealAudio) www.iran.mojahedin.org/Pages/seda/; (People's Mojahedin Organization of Iran parent organization) www.iran.mojahedin.org. Contact: Majid Taleghani. Station replies very irregularly and slowly. Pre-prepared verification cards and SASE helpful, with correspondence in French or Persian almost certainly preferable. Sponsored by the People's Mojahedin Organization of Iran (OMPI) and the National Liberation Army of Iran.
OTHER BUREAUS: Voice of the Mojahed, c/o Heibatollahi, Postfach 502107, 50981 Köln, Germany; M.I.S.S., B.M. Box 9720, London WC1N 3XX, United Kingdom; P.O. Box 951, London NW11 9EL, United Kingdom; or P.O. Box 3133, Baghdad, Iraq (Contact: B. Moradi, Public Relations).
"Voice of the Kurdistan People" ("Aira dangi kurdistana"). E-mail: said@aha.ru or webmaster@puk.org. URLs: www.aha.ru/~said/dang.htm; (PUK) www.puk.org. Official radio station of the Patriotic Union of Kurdistan (PUK) led by Jalal Talabani. Originally called "Voice of the Iraqi Revolution."
"Voice of the Popular Armed Uprising,"—*see* "Radio Voice of Liberty & Renewal," above.
"Voice of the Sudan Alliance Forces,"—*see* "Radio Voice of Liberty & Renewal," above.
"Voice of the Worker"—same contact details as "Voice of the Communist Party of Iran" (*see*, above).
"Voice of the Worker Communist Party of Iraq" ("Aira dangi kizb-e cummunist-e kargar-e iraqa"), WCPI Radio, Zargata, Sulaimania, Iraq. E-mail: radio@wpiraq.org. URL: (WCPI parent organization) www.wpiraq.org.
WCPI CANADIAN OFFICE: P.O. Box 491, Donmins Postal Station, North York, Ontario M3C 2T4, Canada.

WCPI GERMAN OFFICE: A.K.P.I., Postfach 160244, D-10336 Berlin, Germany.
WCPI UNITED KINGDOM OFFICE: P.O. Box 7926, London SE1 2ZG United Kingdom.
📻**"Voice of Tibet,"** Welhavensgate 1, N-0166 Oslo, Norway. Phone: (administration) +47 2211-4980; (studio) +47 2211-1209. Fax: +47 2211 5474. E-mail: mail@vot.org; or voti@online.no. URLs: (includes RealAudio) www.vot.org; (text only) www.voti.com. Contact: Øystein Alme, Project Manager; or Chophel Norbu, Journalist. Joint venture of the Norwegian Human Rights House, Norwegian Tibet Committee and World-View International. Programs, which are produced in Oslo, Norway, and elsewhere, focus on Tibetan culture, education, human rights and news from Tibet. Opposed to Chinese control of Tibet. Those seeking a verification for this program should enclose a prepared card or letter. Return postage helpful. Broadcasts via transmitters in Central Asia.
"Voz de la Resistencia," E-mail: (FARC parent organization) farc-ep@comision.internal.org; or elbarcino@laneta.apc.org. URL: (FARC parent organization) http://burn.ucsd.edu/%7Efarc-ep/. Program of the Fuerzas Armadas Revolucionarias de Colombia.

COLOMBIA   World Time –5

NOTE: Colombia, the country, is always spelled with two o's. It should never be written as "Columbia."
Armonías del Caquetá, Apartado Aéreo 71, Florencia, Caquetá, Colombia. Phone: +57 (88) 352-080. Contact: Padre Alvaro Serna Alzate, Director. Replies occasionally and slowly to correspondence in Spanish. Return postage required.
Caracol Arauca—see La Voz del Cinaruco.
📻**Caracol Colombia**
MAIN OFFICE: Apartado Aéreo 9291, Santafé de Bogotá, D.C., Colombia. Phone: +57 (1) 337-8866. Fax: +57 (1) 337 7126. URL: (includes RealAudio) www.caracol.com.co/webasp2/

homeneo.asp. Contact: Hernán Peláez Restrepo, Jefe Cadena Básica; Efraín Jiménez, Director de Operaciones; or Oscar López M., Director Musical. Free stickers. Replies to correspondence in Spanish and English.
MIAMI OFFICE: 2100 Coral Way, Miami FL 33145 USA. Phone: +1 (305) 285-2477 or +1 (305) 285-1260. Fax: +1 (305) 858 5907.
Caracol Florencia (when active), Apartado Aéreo 465, Florencia, Caquetá, Colombia. Phone: +57 (88) 352-199. Contact: Guillermo Rodríguez Herrera, Gerente; or Vicente Delgado, Operador. Replies occasionally to correspondence in Spanish.
Caracol Villavicencio—*see* La Voz de los Centauros.
Colmundo Bogotá, Diagonal 58 No. 26-29, Santafé de Bogotá, Colombia; or Apartado Aéreo 36750, Santafé de Bogotá, Colombia. Fax: +57 (1) 217 9358. Contact: María Teresa Gutiérrez, Directora Gerente; Marcela Aristizábal, Presidente; Jorge Eliecer Hernández, Gerente Nacional de Programación; Carlos Arturo Echeverry, Chief Engineer; or Néstor Chamorro, Presidente de la Red Colmundo. E-mail: colradio@latino.net.co.Actively seeks reception reports from abroad, preferably in Spanish. Free stickers and program schedule.
Ecos del Atrato, Apartado Aéreo 196, Quibdó, Chocó, Colombia. Phone: +57 (49) 711-450. Contact: Absalón Palacios Agualimpia, Administrador. Free pennants. Replies to correspondence in Spanish.
Ecos del Orinoco (when active), Gobernación del Vichada, Puerto Carreño, Vichada, Colombia.
La Voz de la Selva—*see* Caracol Florencia.
La Voz de los Centauros (Caracol Villavicencio), Cra. 31 No. 37-71 Of. 1001, Villavicencio, Meta, Colombia. Phone: +57 (986) 214-995. Fax: +57 (986) 623 954. Contact: Carlos Torres Leyva, Gerencia; or Olga Arenas, Administradora. Replies to correspondence in Spanish.
La Voz del Cinaruco (if reactivated), Calle 19 No. 19-62, Arauca, Colombia. Contact: Efrahim Valera, Director. Pennants for return postage. Replies rarely to correspondence in Spanish; return postage required.
La Voz del Guaviare, Carrera 22 con Calle 9, San José del Guaviare, Colombia. Phone: +57 (986) 840-153/4. Fax: +57 (986) 840 102. Contact: Luis Fernando Román Robayo, Director General. Replies slowly to correspondence in Spanish.
La Voz del Llano, Calle 41B No. 30-11, Barrio La Grama, Villavicencio, Meta, Colombia. Phone: +57 (986) 624-102. Fax: +57 (986) 625 045. Contact: Manuel Buenaventura, Director; or Edgar Valenzuela Romero. Replies occasionally to correspondence in Spanish. $1 or return postage necessary.
La Voz del Río Arauca
STATION: Carrera 20 No. 19-09, Arauca, Colombia. Phone: +57 (818) 52-910. Contact: Jorge Flórez Rojas, Gerente; Luis Alfonso Riaño, Locutor; or Mario Falla, Periodista. $1 or return postage required. Replies occasionally to correspondence in Spanish; persist.
BOGOTÁ OFFICE: Cra. 10 No. 14-56, Of. 309/310, Santafé de Bogotá, D.C., Colombia.
La Voz del Yopal (when active), Calle 9 No. 22-63, Yopal, Casanare, Colombia. Phone: +57 (87) 558-382. Fax: +57 (87) 557 054. Contact: Pedro Antonio Socha Pérez, Gerente; or Marta Cecilia Socha Pérez, Subgerente. Return postage necessary. Replies to correspondence in Spanish.
Ondas del Meta (when active), Calle 41B No. 30-11, Barrio La Grama, Villavicencio, Meta, Colombia. Phone: +57 (986) 626-783. Fax: +57 (986) 625 045. Contact: Yolanda Plazas Agredo, Administradora. Free tourist literature. Return

postage required. Replies irregularly and slowly to correspondence in Spanish. Plans to reactivate from a new antenna site.
Ondas del Orteguaza, Calle 16, No. 12-48, piso 2, Florencia, Caquetá, Colombia. Phone: +57 (88) 352-558. Contact: Sandra Liliana Vásquez, Secretaria; Señora Elisa Viuda de Santos; or Henry Valencia Vásquez. Free stickers. IRC, return postage or $1 required. Replies occasionally to correspondence in Spanish.
Radio Auténtica, Calle 38 No. 32-41, piso 7, Edif. Santander, Villavicencio, Meta, Colombia. Phone: +57 (986) 626-780. Phone/fax: +57 (986) 624 507. Contact: (general) Pedro Rojas Velásquez; or Carlos Alberto Pimienta, Gerente; (technical) Sra. Alba Nelly González de Rojas, Administradora. Sells religious audio cassettes for 3,000 pesos. Return postage required. Replies slowly to correspondence in Spanish.
Radiodifusora Nacional de Colombia
MAIN ADDRESS: Edificio Inravisión, CAN, Av. Eldorado, Santafé de Bogotá, D.C., Colombia. Phone: +57 (1) 222-0415. Fax: +57 (1) 222 0409 or +57 (1) 222 8000. Contact: Rubén Darío Acero, Jefe Sistemas AM y Onda Corta; or Dra. Athala Morris, Directora. Free lapel badges, membership in Listeners' Club and monthly program booklet.
CANAL INTERNACIONAL: Apartado Aéreo 93994, Santafé de Bogotá, D.C., Colombia. Contact: Jesús Valencia Sánchez.
☞RCN (Radio Cadena Nacional)
MAIN OFFICE: Apartado Aéreo 4984, Santafé de Bogotá, D.C., Colombia. Phone: +57 (1) 314-7070. Fax: +57 (1) 285 0121 or +57 (1) 288 6130. E-mail: rcn@impsat.net.co. URL: (RealAudio, news & correspondence) www.rcn.com.co. Contact: Antonio Pardo García, Gerente de Producción y Programación. Will verify all correct reports for stations in the RCN network. Spanish preferred and return postage necessary.
Radio Melodía (Cadena Melodía) (when active), Apartado Aéreo 58721, Santafé de Bogotá, D.C., Colombia; or Apartado Aéreo 19823, Santafé de Bogotá, D.C., Colombia. Phone: +57 (1) 217-0423, +57 (1) 217-0720, +57 (1) 217-1334 or +57 (1) 217-1452. Fax: +57 (1) 248 8772. Contact: Gerardo Páez Mejía, Vicepresidente; Elvira Mejía de Pérez, Gerente General; or Gracilla Rodríguez, Asistente Gerencia. Stickers and pennants. $1 or return postage.
Radio Mira, Apartado Aéreo 165, Tumaco, Nariño, Colombia. Phone: +57 (27) 272-452. Contact: Padre Jairo Arturo Ochoa Zea. Return postage required.
Radio Super (Ibagué) (when active), Parque Murillo Toro 3-31, P. 3, Ibagué, Tolima, Colombia. Phone: +57 (982) 611-652 or +57 (982) 637-004. Fax: +57 (82) 611 471. Contact: Fidelina Caycedo Hernández; or Germán Acosta Ramos, Locutor Control. Free stickers. Return postage or $1 helpful. Replies irregularly to correspondence in Spanish.

CONGO (DEMOCRATIC REPUBLIC) (formerly
Zaïre)   World Time +1 Western, including Kinshasa; +2 Eastern

Radio Bukavu (when active), B.P. 475, Bukavu, Democratic Republic of the Congo. Contact: Jacques Nyembo-Kibeya; Kalume Kavue Katumbi; or Baruti Lusongela, Directeur. $1 or return postage required. Replies slowly. Correspondence in French preferred.
Radio CANDIP Bunia (formerly La Voix du Peuple, and prior to that, Radio CANDIP), B.P. 373, Bunia, Democratic Republic of Congo. Letters should preferably be sent via registered mail. $1 or return postage required. Correspondence in French preferred.

Croatian Radio staffers Ivica Koščec, Dane Pavlić and Ivo Pavličić inspect the Deanovec station's antenna field.   M. Prezelj

Radio Kisangani (when active), B.P. 1745, Kisangani, Democratic Republic of the Congo. Contact: (general) Lumeto lue Lumeto, Directeur Regional; or Lumbutu Kalome, Directeur Inspecteur; (technical) Lukusa Kowumayi Branly, Technicien. $1 or 2 IRCs required. Correspondence in French preferred. Mail to this station may be interfered with by certain staff members. Try sending letters to Lumbutu Kalome at his private address: 10ᵉ Avenue 34, Zone de la Tshopo, Kisangani, Democratic Republic of the Congo. Registering letters may also help. Replies to North American listeners sometimes are mailed via the Oakland, California, post office.

Radio Lubumbashi (when active), B.P. 7296, Lubumbashi, Democratic Republic of the Congo. Contact: Senga Lokavu, Chef du Service de l'Audiovisuel; Bébé Beshelemu, Directeur; or Mulenga Kanso, Chef du Service Logistique. Letters should be sent via registered mail. $1 or 3 IRCs helpful. Correspondence in French preferred.

Radio-Télévision Nationale Congolaise, B.P. 3171, Kinshasa-Gombe, Democratic Republic of the Congo. Contact: Faustin Mbula, Ingenieur Technicien. Letters should be sent via registered mail. $1 or 3 IRCs helpful. Correspondence in French preferred

CONGO (REPUBLIC)   World Time +1

Radiodiffusion Nationale Congolaise (also announces as "Radio Liberté," "Radio Nationale" or "Radio Congo"), Radiodiffusion-Télévision Congolaise, B.P. 2241, Brazzaville, Congo. Contact: (general) Antoine Ngongo, Rédacteur en chef; (administration) Gilbert-David Mutakala, Directeur; or Zaou Mouanda. $1 required. Replies irregularly to letters in French sent via registered mail.

COSTA RICA   World Time –6

Adventist World Radio, the Voice of Hope, AWR, The Americas, Apartado 1177, 4050 Alajuela, Costa Rica. Phone: +506 483-0550/551. Fax +506 483 0555. E-mail: rmadvent@racsa.sol.cr. Contact: (general) Victor Shepherd, General Manager; (technical) Karl Thompson, Chief Engineer. Free stickers, calendars, Costa Rican stamps and religious printed matter. Return postage (3 IRCs or 1$) appreciated. Also, *see* AWR listings under Guam, Guatemala, Italy, Kenya and USA.

Faro del Caribe Internacional y Misionera—TIFC

MAIN OFFICE: Apartado 2710, 1000 San José, Costa Rica. Phone: +506 (226) 2573 or +506 (226) 2618. Fax: +506 (227) 1725. E-mail: al@casa-pres.go.cr. Contact: Carlos A. Rozotto Piedrasanta, Director Administrativo; or Mauricio Ramires; (technical) Minor Enrique, Station Engineer.Free stickers, pennants, books and bibles. $1 or IRCs helpful.

U.S. OFFICE, NONTECHNICAL: Misión Latinoamericana, P.O. Box 620485, Orlando FL 32862 USA.

Radio 88 Estéreo (when operating), Apartado 827-8000, Péréz Zeledón, Costa Rica. Phone: +506 257-8585, +506 771-6094 or (phone/fax) +506 771-6093. Fax: +506 771 5539. Contact: Juan Vega, Director.

Radio Casino, Apartado 287, 7301 Puerto Limón, Costa Rica. Phone: +506 758-0029. Fax: +506 758 3029. Contact: Edwin Zamora, Departamento de Notícias; or Luis Grau Villalobos, Gerente; (technical) Ing. Jorge Pardo, Director Técnico; or Geraldo Moya, Técnico.

Radio Exterior de España—Cariari Relay Station, Cariari de Pococí, Costa Rica. Phone: +506 767-7308, +506 767-7311. Fax: +506 225 2938.

🔊Radio For Peace International (RFPI)

MAIN OFFICE: Apartado 88, Santa Ana, Costa Rica. Phone: +506 249-1821. Fax: +506 249 1095. E-mail: info@rfpi.org; rfpicr@sol.racsa.co.cr. URL: (includes RealAudio) www.rfpi.org. Contact: (general) Debra Latham, General Manager of RFPI, Editor of *VISTA* and co-host of "RFPI Mailbag"; (programming) Joe Bernard, English Program Coordinator; Willie Barrantes, Director, Spanish Department; or Ms. Sabine Kapuschinski, Host of German program; (nontechnical or technical) James Latham, Station Manager. Replies sometimes slow in coming because of the mail. Quarterly *VISTA* newsletter, which includes schedules and program information, $40 annual membership ($50 family/ organization) in "Friends of Radio for Peace International"; station commemorative T-shirts and rainforest T-shirts $20; thermo mugs $10 (VISA/MC). Actively solicits listener contributions. Free online verification of e-mail reports, but $1 or 3 IRCs required for verification by QSL card. Limited number of places available for volunteer broadcasting and journalism interns; those interested should send résumé. RFPI was created by United Nations Resolution 35/55 on December 5, 1980.

U.S. OFFICE, NONTECHNICAL: P.O. Box 20728, Portland OR 97294 USA. Phone: +1 (503) 252-3639. Fax: +1 (503) 255 5216. Contact: Dr. Richard Schneider, Chancellor CEO, University of Global Education (formerly World Peace University). Newsletter, T-shirts and so forth, as above. University of the Air courses (such as "Earth Mother Speaks" and "History of the U.N.") $25 each, or on audio cassette $75 each (VISA/MC).

Radio Reloj, Sistema Radiofónico H.B., Apartado 341, 1000 San José, Costa Rica. Contact: Roger Barahona, Gerente; or Francisco Barahona Gómez. Can be very slow in replying. $1 required.

Radio Universidad de Costa Rica, San Pedro de Montes de Oca, 1000 San José, Costa Rica. Phone: +506 225-3936. Contact: Marco González Muñoz; Henry Jones, Locutor de Planta; or Nora Garita B., Directora. Marco González is a radio amateur, call-sign TI3AGM. Free postcards, station brochure and stickers. Replies slowly to correspondence in Spanish or English. $1 or return postage required.

CÔTE D'IVOIRE   World Time exactly

Radiodiffusion Télévision Ivoirienne (when active), B.P. 191, Abidjan 1, Côte d'Ivoire. Phone: +225 324-800. Correspondence in French preferred, but English accepted.

CROATIA   World Time +1 (+2 midyear)

🔊Croatian Radio (Hrvatska Radio-Televizija)
MAIN OFFICE: Hrvatska Radio-Televizija (HRT), Prisavlje 3, HR-1000 Zagreb, Croatia. Phone: (operator) +385 (1) 616-3366; (technical) +385 (1) 616-3355; or +385 (1) 616-3428. Fax: (general) +385 (1) 616 3308; (technical) +385 (1) 616 3347. E-mail: (Editor-in-Chief) i.lucev@hrt.hr; (technical) z.klasan@hrt.hr. URLs: (general) www.hrt.hr/; (program guide) www.hrt.hr/hr/program/; (RealAudio) www.hrt.hr/hr/audio/. Contact: (general) Ivanka Lucev; (technical) Zelimir Klasan. This station of HRT, is the domestic (first) national radio programme, transmitted via HRT Deanovec shortwave station, for listeners in Europe & the Mediterranean.
WASHINGTON NEWS BUREAU: Croatian-American Association, 2020 Pennsylvania Avenue NW., Suite 287, Washington DC 20006 USA. Phone: +1 (202) 429-5543. Fax: +1 (202) 429 5545. E-mail: 73150.3552@compuserve.com. URL: www.hrnet.org/CAA/. Contact: Frank Brozovich, President.
Radio Croatia (Radio Hrvatska), Hrvatski Info Centar/Radio Hrvatska, Trg Stjepana Radica 3, HR-1000 Zagreb, Croatia. Phone: (A. Beljo) +385 (1) 611-1553; or (M. Risek) +385 (1) 611-0729. Fax: (general) +385 (1) 455 0700; +385 (1) 611 1522; or (Phone/fax, technical M. Prezelj) +49 (69) 636 210. E-mail: (general) radio.hrvatska@hic.hr; (M. Risek) marica@hic.hr; or (E. Candrlic) eliana.candrlic@hic.hr; (technical) (M. Prezelj) prezelj@t-online.de. URL: www.hic.hr. Contact: (general) Ante Beljo, HIC Managing Director; Marica Risek, Head of Electronic Media; or Eliana Candrlic, Editor-in-Chief; (technical) Milan Prezelj. Sells books on Croatian heritage from website at: www.hic.hr/books/. All technical correspondence should be sent to: Milan Prezelj, Fr.-Lenbach-Str.10, D-60596 Frankfurt, Germany. This station is operated by the Hrvatski Informativni Centar (HIC) in Zagreb and is the shortwave foreign service, mainly for Croatian expatriates, transmitted via Deutsche Telekom's Jülich station.

CUBA   World Time –5 (–4 midyear)

Radio Habana Cuba, P.O. Box 6240, Habana, Cuba 10600. Phone: (general) +53 (7) 784-954 or +53 (7) 334-272; (English and Spanish Departments) +53 (7) 791-053; (French Department) +53 (7) 785-444; (Coro) +53 (7) 814-243 or (home) +53 (7) 301-794. Fax: (general) +53 (7) 783 518; (English and Span-

ish Departments) +53 (7) 795 007; (French Department) +53 (7) 705 810. E-mail: (general) cartas@radiohc.org; radiohc@mail.infocom.etecsa.cu; (engineering, technical, and "Dxers Unlimited") arnie@radiohc.org. URL: www.radiohc.org. Contact: (general) Lourdes López, Head of Correspondence Dept.; Jorge Miyares, English Service; or Mike La Guardia, Senior Editor; (administration) Ms. Milagro Hernández Cuba, General Director; (technical) Arnaldo Coro Antich, ("Arnie Coro"), Producer, "DXers Unlimited"; or Luis Pruna Amer, Director Técnico. Free wallet and wall calendars, pennants, stickers, keychains and pins. DX Listeners' Club. Free sample *Granma International* newspaper. Contests with various prizes, including trips to Cuba.

Radio Rebelde, Departamento de Relaciones Públicas, Apartado 6277, Habana 10600, Cuba; or (street address) Calle 23 No. 258 entre L y M, El Vedado, Habana, Cuba 10600. For technical correspondence (including reception reports), substitute "Servicio de Onda Corta" in place of "Departamento de Relaciones Públicas." Reception reports can also be e-mailed to Radio Habana Cuba's Arnie Coro (arnie@radiohc.org) for forwarding to Radio Rebelde. Phone: +53 (7) 334-269. Fax: +53 (7) 323 514. E-mail: (nontechnical) rebelde@ceniai.inf.cu. URLs: www2.cuba.cu/RRebelde/; www.ceniai.inf.cu/RRebelde/; www.ceniai.inf.cu/noticias/rebelde/. Contact: Daimelis Monzón; Noemí Cairo Marín; Iberlise González Padua; or Marisel Ramos Soca (all from "Relaciones Públicas"); or Jorge Luis Más Zabala, Director, Relaciones Públicas. Replies slowly, with correspondence in Spanish preferred.

Official representatives gather at the exclusive High Frequency Coordination Committee Conference in Lisbon, Portugal. M. Prezelj

CYPRUS   World Time +2 (+3 midyear)

📻Bayrak Radio—BRT International (when operating), BRTK Campus, Dr. Fazil Küçük Boulevard, P.O. Box 417, Lefkosa – T.R.N.C., via Mersin 10, Turkey. Phone: (general) +90 (392) 225-5555; (public relations office) +90 (392) 228-0577. Fax: (general) +90 (392) 225 2918; (news dept.) +90 (392) 225 4991. E-mail: (general) brt@cc.emu.edu.tr; (technical, including reception reports) tosun@cc.emu.edu.tr. URL: (includes RealAudio) www.emu.edu.tr/~brt/. Contact: Mustafa Tosun, Head of Transmission Department.

BBC World Service—East Mediterranean Relay Station, P.O. Box 209, Limassol, Cyprus. Contact: Steve Welch. This address for technical matters only. Reception reports and nontechnical correspondence should be sent to the BBC World Service in London (see).

📻Cyprus Broadcasting Corporation, Broadcasting House, P.O. Box 4824, 1397 Nicosia, Cyprus; or (physical address) RIK Street, Athalassa, Nicosia, Cyprus. Phone: +357 (2) 422-231. Fax: +357 (2) 314 050 or +357 (2) 335 010. E-mail: rik@cybc.com.cy. URL: (includes RealAudio) www.cybc.com.cy/. Contact: (general) Pavlos Soteriades, Director General; or Evangella Gregoriou, Head of Public and International Relations; (technical) Andreas Michaelides, Director of Technical Services. Free stickers. Replies occasionally, sometimes slowly. IRC or $1 helpful.

Radio Monte-Carlo Middle East, P.O. Box 2026, Nicosia, Cyprus. Contact: M. Pavlides, Chef de Station. This address for listeners to the RMC Arabic Service, which prepares its world band programs in Cyprus, but transmits them via facilities of Radio Canada International in Canada. For details of Radio Monte-Carlo's headquarters and other branch offices, see Monaco.

CZECH REPUBLIC   World Time +1 (+2 midyear)

📻Radio Prague, Czech Radio, Vinohradská 12, 12099 Prague 2, Czech Republic. Phone: (general) +420 (2) 2409-4608; (Czech Department) +420 (2) 2422-2236; (English Department) +420 (2) 2422-2211; (Internet) +420 (2) 2421 5456. Phone/fax: (Oldrich Cip, technical) +420 (2) 2271-5005. Fax: (nontechni-

cal and technical) +420 (2) 2421 8239 or +420 (2) 2422 2236; (English Department) +420 (2) 2421 8349. E-mail: (general) cr@radio.cz; (Director) Miroslav.Krupicka@radio.cz; (English Department) english@radio.cz; (Program Director) David.Vaughan@radio.cz; (free news texts) robot@radio.cz, writing "Subscribe English" (or other desired language) within the subject line; (technical, chief engineer) cip@radio.cz. URLs: (text and RealAudio in English, German, Spanish and French) www.radio.cz; www.prague.org; (text) ftp://ftp.radio.cz; gopher://gopher.radio.cz. Contact: (general) Markéta Atanasová; David Vaughan, Program Director; Libor Kubik, Head of English Section; (administration) Miroslav Krupiška, Director; (technical, all programs) Oldrich Čip, Chief Engineer. Free stickers, key chains, and calendars. Samples of *Welcome to the Czech Republic* and *Czech Life* available upon request from Orbis, Vinohradská 46, 120 41 Prague, Czech Republic. **RFE-RL**—*see* USA.

DENMARK   World Time +1 (+2 midyear)

📻Radio Danmark
MAIN OFFICE: Rosenørns Allé 22, DK-1999 Frederiksberg C, Denmark. Phone: (office, including voice mail, voice schedules in Danish and schedule by return fax) +45 3520-5784; or (technical) +45 3520-6722. Fax: + 45 3520 5781. E-mail: (schedule and program matters) rdk@dr.dk; (technical matters and reception reports) ehk@dr.dk. URL: (includes RealAudio) www.dr.dk/rdk/. Contact: (general) Kate Sand, Audience Communications; or Bjorn Schionning; (technical) Erik Køie, Technical Adviser; or Dan Helto, Head of Technical Section. Replies to correspondence in English or Danish. Will verify all correct reception reports; return postage ($1 or one IRC) appreciated. Uses transmitting facilities of Radio Norway International. All broadcasts are in Danish. "Tune In" letterbox program aired last Saturday/Sunday of the month, hourly 24 times from 16.37 UTC (summer; winter 17.37 UTC). *TRANSMISSION MANAGEMENT AUTHORITY:* Tele Danmark A/S-NPT, Telegade 2, DK-2630 Taastrup, Denmark. Phone: +45 4334-5746. Fax: +45 4371 1143. E-mail: ihl@tdk.dk. Contact: Ib H. Lavrsen, Senior Engineer.

NORWEGIAN OFFICE, TECHNICAL: Details of reception quality may also be sent to the Engineering Department of Radio Norway International (*see*), which operates the transmitters currently used by Radio Danmark.

DOMINICAN REPUBLIC World Time –4

Emisora Onda Musical (when active), Palo Hincado 204 Altos, Apartado Postal 860, Santo Domingo, Dominican Republic. Contact: Mario Báez Asunción, Director. Replies occasionally to correspondence in Spanish. $1 helpful.

La N-103/Radio Norte (when active), Apartado Postal 320, Santiago, Dominican Republic. Contact: José Darío Pérez Díaz, Director; Héctor Castillo, Gerente; or Antonio Pérez.

Radio Amanecer Internacional, Apartado Postal 4680, Santo Domingo, Dominican Republic. Phone: +1 (809) 688-5600, +1 (809) 688-5609, +1 (809) 688-8067. Fax: +1 (809) 227 1869. E-mail: amanecer@tricom.net. URL: www.tricom.net/amanecer/. Contact: (general) Señora Ramona C. de Subervi, Directora; (technical) Ing. Sócrates Domínguez. $1 or return postage required. Replies slowly to correspondence in Spanish.

Radio Barahona (when active), Apartado 201, Barahona, Dominican Republic; or Gustavo Mejía Ricart No. 293, Apto. 2-B, Ens. Quisqueya, Santo Domingo, Dominican Republic. Contact: (general) Rodolfo Z. Lama Jaar, Administrador; (technical) Ing. Roberto Lama Sajour, Administrador General. Free stickers. Letters should be sent via registered mail. $1 or return postage helpful. Replies to correspondence in Spanish.

Radio Cima, Apartado 804, Santo Domingo, Dominican Republic. Fax: +1 (809) 541 1088. Contact: Roberto Vargas, Director. Free pennants, postcards, coins and taped music. Roberto likes collecting stamps and coins.

Radio Cristal Internacional, Apartado Postal 894, Santo Domingo, Dominican Republic; or (street address) Calle Pepillo Salcedo No. 18, Altos, Santo Domingo, Dominican Republic. Phone: +1 (809) 565-1460 or +1 (809) 566-5411. Fax: +1 (809) 567 9107. Contact: (general) Fernando Hermón Gross, Director de Programas; or Margarita Reyes, Secretaria; (administration) Darío Badía, Director General; or Héctor Badía, Director de Administración. Seeks reception reports. Return postage of $2 appreciated.

Radio Quisqueya (if reactivated), Apartado Postal 363, Puerto Plata, Dominican Republic; or Apartado Postal 135-2, Santo Domingo, Dominican Republic. Contact: Lic. Gregory Castellanos Ruano, Director. Replies occasionally to correspondence in Spanish and English.

Radio Santiago (if reactivated), Apartado 282, Santiago, Dominican Republic.
Contact: Luis Felipe Moscos Finke, Gerente; Luis Felipe Moscos Cordero, Jefe Ingeniero; or Carlos Benoit, Announcer & Program Manager.

ECUADOR World Time –5 (–4 sometimes, in times of drought); –6 Galapagos

NOTE: According to HCJB's "DX Party Line," during periods of drought, such as caused by "El Niño," electricity rationing causes periods in which transmitters cannot operate because of inadequate hydroelectric power, as well as spikes which occasionally damage transmitters. Accordingly, many Ecuadorian stations tend to be irregular, or even entirely off the air, during drought conditions.

NOTE: According to veteran Dxer Harald Kuhl in Hard-Core-DX of Kotanet Communications Ltd., IRCs are exchangeable only in the cities of Quito and Guayaquil. Too, overseas airmail postage is very expensive now in Ecuador; so when in doubt, enclosing $2 for return postage is appropriate.

Ecos del Oriente (when active), Sucre y 12 de Febrero, Lago Agrio, Sucumbíos, Ecuador. Phone: +593 (6) 830-141. Contact: Elsa Irene Velástegui, Secretaria. Sometimes includes free 20 sucre note (Ecuadorian currency) with reply. $2 or return postage required. Replies, often slowly, to correspondence in Spanish.

Emisoras Jesús del Gran Poder (if reactivated), Casilla 17-01-133, Quito, Ecuador. Phone: +593 (2) 513-077. Contact: Mariela Villarreal; Padre Angel Falconí, Gerente; or Hno. Segundo Cuenca OFM.

Emisoras Luz y Vida, Casilla 11-01-222, Loja, Ecuador. Phone: +593 (7) 570-426. Contact: Hermana (Sister) Ana Maza Reyes, Directora; or Lic. Guida Carrión H., Directora de Programas. Return postage required. Replies irregularly to correspondence in Spanish.

Escuelas Radiofónicas Populares del Ecuador, Calles Juan de Velasco 2060 y Guayaquil, Casilla Postal 06-01-341, Riobamba, Ecuador. Phone: +593 (3) 961-608. Fax: +593 (3) 961 625. E-mail: admin@esrapoec.ecuanex.net.ec. URL: www.exploringecuador.com/erpe/. Contact: Juan Pérez Sarmiento, Director Ejecutivo; or María Ercilia López, Secretaria. Free pennants and key rings. "Chimborazo" cassette of Ecuadorian music for 10,000 sucres plus postage; T-shirts for 12,000 sucres plus postage; and caps with station logo for 8,000 sucres plus postage. Return postage helpful. Replies to correspondence in Spanish.

Estéreo Carrizal (when active), Avenida Estudiantil, Quinta Velásquez, Calceta, Ecuador. Phone: +593 (5) 685-5470. Contact: Ovidio Velásquez Alcundia, Gerente General. Free book of Spanish-language poetry by owner. Replies to correspondence in Spanish.

⧉HCJB World Radio, The Voice of the Andes
STATION: Casilla 17-17-691, Quito, Ecuador. Phone: (general) +593 (2) 266-808 (X-4441, 1300-2200 World Time Monday through Friday, for the English Dept.); (Frequency Management) +593 (2) 267-098 (X-5216). Fax: (general) +593 (2) 267 263. E-mail: (Frequency Management) irops@hcjb.org.ec or dweber@hcjb.org.ec; (language sections) format is language@hcjb.org.ec; so to reach, say, the Japanese Department, it would be japanese@hcjb.org.ec. URL: (includes RealAudio and online reception report form) www.hcjb.org. Contact: (general) English [or other language] Department; "Saludos Amigos"—letterbox program; (administration) Glen Volkhardt, Director of Broadcasting; John Beck, Station Manager; or Curt Cole, Director, English Language Service; (technical) Douglas Weber, Frequency Manager. Free religious brochures, calendars, stickers and pennants; free e-mail *The Andean Herald* newsletter. *Catch the Vision* book $8, postpaid. IRC or unused U.S. or Canadian stamps appreciated for airmail reply.
INTERNATIONAL HEADQUARTERS: HCJB World Radio, Inc., P.O. Box 39800, Colorado Springs CO 80949-9800 USA. Phone: +1 (719) 590-9800. Fax: +1 (719) 590 9801. E-mail: info@hcjb.org. Contact: Andrew Braio, Public Information; (administration) Richard D. Jacquin, Director, International Operations. Various items sold via U.S. address—catalog available. This address is not a mail drop, so listeners' correspondence, except those concerned with purchasing HCJB items, should be directed to the usual Quito address.
ENGINEERING CENTER: 2830 South 17th Street, Elkhart IN 46517 USA. Phone: +1 (219) 294-8201. Fax: +1 (219) 294 8391. E-mail: info@hcjbeng.org. URL: www.hcjbeng.org/. Contact:

Dave Pasechnik, Project Manager; or Bob Moore, Engineering. This address only for those professionally concerned with the design and manufacture of transmitter and antenna equipment. Listeners' correspondence should be directed to the usual Quito address.

REGIONAL OFFICES: Although HCJB has over 20 regional offices throughout the world, the station wishes that all listener correspondence be directed to the station in Quito, as the regional offices do not serve as mail drops for the station.

La Voz de los Caras (if reactivated), Casilla 608, Calle Montúfar 1012, Bahía de Caráquez, Manabí, Ecuador. Fax: +593 (4) 690 305. Contact: Ing. Marcelo A. Nevárez Faggioni, Director-General. Free 50th anniversary pennants, while they last. $2 or return postage required. Replies occasionally and slowly to correspondence in English and Spanish.

La Voz de Saquisilí—Radio Libertador, Calle 24 de Mayo, Saquisilí, Cotopaxi, Ecuador. Phone: +593 (3) 721-035. Contact: Arturo Mena Herrera, Gerente-Propietario, who may also be contacted via his son-in-law, Eddy Roger Velástegui Mena, who is studying in Quito (E-mail: eddyv@uio.uio.satnet.net). The shortwave ferequency was reactivated in August 1998, after four years of silence. Reception reports actively solicited, and will be confirmed with a special commemorative QSL card. Return postage, in the form of $2 or mint Ecuadorian stamps, appreciated; IRCs difficult to exchange. Spanish strongly preferred.

La Voz del Napo, Misión Josefina, Tena, Napo, Ecuador. Phone: +593 (6) 886-422. Contact: Ramiro Cabrera, Director. Free pennants and stickers. $2 or return postage required. Replies occasionally to correspondence in Spanish.

La Voz del Río Tarqui (when operating), Manuel Vega 653 y Presidente Córdova, Cuenca, Ecuador. Phone: +593 (7) 822-132. Contact: Sra. Alicia Pulla Célleri, Gerente. Replies irregularly to correspondence in Spanish. Has ties with station WKDM in New York.

La Voz del Upano
STATION: Vicariato Apostólico de Méndez, Misión Salesiana, 10 de Agosto s/n, Macas, Ecuador; or Casilla 602, Quito, Ecuador. Phone: +593 (7) 700-186. Contact: P. Domingo Barrueco C., Director. Free pennants and calendars. On one occasion, not necessarily to be repeated, sent tape of Ecuadorian folk music for $2. Otherwise, $2 required. Replies to correspondence in Spanish.
QUITO OFFICE: Procura Salesiana, Equinoccio 623 y Queseras del Medio, Quito, Ecuador. Phone: +593 (2) 551-012.

Radio Bahá'í, "La Emisora de la Familia," Casilla 10-02-1464, Otavalo, Imbabura, Ecuador. Phone: +593 (6) 920-245. Fax: +593 (6) 922 504. Contact: (general) William Rodríguez Barreiro, Coordinador; or Juan Antonio Reascos, Locutor; (technical) Ing. Tom Dopps. Free information about the Bahá'í faith, which teaches the unity of all the races, nations and religions, and that the Earth is one country and mankind its citizens. Free pennants. Return postage appreciated. Replies regularly to correspondence in English or Spanish. Enclosing a family photo may help getting a reply. Station is property of the Instituto Nacional de Enseñanza de la Fe Bahá'í (National Spiritual Assembly of the Bahá'ís of Ecuador). Although there are many Bahá'í radio stations around the world, Radio Bahá'í in Ecuador is the only one on shortwave.

Radio Buen Pastor—*see* Radio "El Buen Pastor."

Radio Católica Nacional del Ecuador (when active), Av. América 1830 y Mercadillo (Apartado 540A), Quito, Ecuador. Phone: +593 (2) 545-770. Contact: John Sigüenza, Director; or Sra. Yolanda de Suquitana, Secretaria; (technical) Sra.

Gloria Cardozo, Technical Director. Free stickers. Return postage required. Replies to correspondence in Spanish.

Radio Centro, Casilla 18-01-574, Ambato, Ecuador. Phone: +593 (3) 822-240 or +593 (3) 841-126. Fax: +593 (3) 829 824. Contact: Luis Alberto Gamboa Tello, Director Gerente; or Lic. María Elena de López. Free stickers. Return postage appreciated. Replies to correspondence in Spanish.

Radio Centinela del Sur (C.D.S. Internacional), Casilla 11-01-106, Loja, Ecuador; or (studios) Olmedo 11-56 y Mercadillo, Loja, Ecuador. Phone: +593 (7) 561-166 or +593 (7) 570-211. Fax: +593 (7) 562 270. Contact: (general) Marcos G. Coronel V., Director de Programas; or José A. Coronel V., Director del programa "Ovación"; (technical) José A. Coronel Illescas, Gerente General. Return postage required. Replies occasionally to correspondence in Spanish.

Radiodifusora Cultural Católica La Voz del Upano—*see* La Voz del Upano, above.

Radiodifusora Cultural, La Voz del Napo—*see* La Voz del Napo, above.

Radio "El Buen Pastor," Asociación Cristiana de Indígenas Saraguros (ACIS), Reino de Quito y Azuay, Correo Central, Saraguro, Loja, Ecuador. Phone: +593 (2) 00-146. Contact: (general) Dean Pablo Davis, Sub-director; Segundo Poma, Director; Mark Vogan, OMS Missionary; Mike Schrode, OMS Ecuador Field Director; Juana Guamán, Secretaria; or Zoila Vacacela, Secretaria; (technical) Miguel Kelly. $2 or return postage in the form of mint Ecuadorian stamps required, as IRCs are difficult to exchange in Ecuador. Station is keen to receive reception reports; may respond to English, but correspondence in Spanish preferred. $10 required for QSL card and pennant.

Radio Federación Shuar (Shuara Tuntuiri), Casilla 17-01-1422, Quito, Ecuador. Phone/fax: +593 (2) 504-264. Contact: Manuel Jesús Vinza Chacucuy, Director; Yurank Tsapak Rubén Gerardo, Director; or Prof. Albino M. Utitiaj P., Director de Medios. Return postage or $2 required. Replies irregularly to correspondence in Spanish.

Radio Interoceánica, Santa Rosa de Quijos, Cantón El Chaco, Provincia de Napo, Ecuador. Contact: Byron Medina, Gerente; or Ing. Olaf Hegmuir. $2 or return postage required, and donations appreciated (station owned by Swedish Covenant Church). Replies slowly to correspondence in Spanish or Swedish.

Radio Jesús del Gran Poder—*see* Emisoras Jesús del Gran Poder, above.

Radio La Voz del Río Tarqui—*see* La Voz del Rio Tarqui.

Radio Luciérnaga del Cóndor, Yansatza, Zamora-Chinchipe, Ecuador. Contact: Arturo Paladínez, Director, who is looking for donations to purchase an FM transmitter.

Radio Luz y Vida—*see* Emisoras Luz y Vida, above.

Radio Municipal (if activated on shortwave), Alcaldía Municipal de Quito, García Moreno 887 y Espejo, Quito, Ecuador. Contact: Miguel Arízaga Q., Director. Currently not on shortwave, but hopes to activate a 2 kW shortwave transmitter—its old mediumwave AM transmitter modified for world band—on 4750 kHz once the legalities are completed. If this station ever materializes, which is looking increasingly doubtful, it is expected to welcome correspondence from abroad, especially in Spanish.

Radio Nacional Espejo, Casilla 17-01-352, Quito, Ecuador. Phone: +593 (2) 21-366. E-mail: (Marco Caicedo) mcaicedo@hoy.net. Contact: Marco Caicedo, Gerente; Steve Caicedo; or Mercedes B. de Caicedo, Secretaria. Replies irregularly to correspondence in English and Spanish.

Radio Nacional Progreso, Casilla V, Loja, Ecuador. Contact: José A. Guamán Guajala, Director del programa "Círculo Dominical." Replies irregularly to correspondence in Spanish, particularly for feedback on "Círculo Dominical" program aired Sundays from 1100 to 1300. Return postage required.

Radio Oriental, Casilla 260, Tena, Napo, Ecuador. Phone: +593 (6) 886-033 or +593 (6) 886-388. Contact: Luis Enrique Espín Espinosa, Gerente General. $2 or return postage helpful. Reception reports welcome.

Radio Popular de Cuenca (when active), Av. Loja 2408, Cuenca, Ecuador. Phone: +593 (7) 810-131. Contact: Sra. Manena Escondón Vda. de Villavicencio, Directora y Propietaria. Return postage or $2 required. Replies very rarely to correspondence in Spanish.

Radio Quito, Casilla 17-21-1971, Quito, Ecuador. Phone/fax: +593 (2) 508-301. E-mail: radioquito@elcomercio.com. Contact: Xavier Almeida, Gerente General; or José Almeida, Subgerente. Free stickers. Return postage normally required, but occasionally verifies e-mail reports. Replies slowly, but regularly.

Sistema de Emisoras Progreso—*see* Radio Nacional Progreso, above.

EGYPT   World Time +2 (+3 midyear)

WARNING: MAIL THEFT. Feedback from PASSPORT readership indicates that money is sometimes stolen from envelopes sent to Radio Cairo.

🕪**Egyptian Radio**, P.O. Box 1186, 11511 Cairo, Egypt. E-mail: rtu@idsc.gov.eg. URL: (RealAudio) www.sis.gov.eg/realpg/html/adfront9.htm (if you encounter difficulty loading the page, try one of the mirror sites: www.uk.sis.gov.eg/; www.us.sis.gov.eg/). For additional details, *see* Radio Cairo, below.

Radio Cairo

NONTECHNICAL: P.O. Box 566, Cairo 11511, Egypt. Phone: +20 (2) 677-8945. Fax: +20 (2) 575 9553. Contact: Mrs. Amal Badr, Head of English Programme; Mrs. Sahar Kalil, Director of English Service to North America & Producer, "Questions and Answers"; or Mrs. Magda Hamman, Secretary. Free stickers, postcards, stamps, maps, papyrus souvenirs, calendars and *External Services of Radio Cairo* book. Free booklet and individually tutored Arabic-language lessons with loaned textbooks from Kamila Abdullah, Director General, Arabic by Radio, Radio Cairo, P.O. Box 325, Cairo, Egypt. Arabic-language religious, cultural and language-learning audio and video tapes from the Egyptian Radio and Television Union sold via Sono Cairo Audio-Video, P.O. Box 2017, Cairo, Egypt; when ordering video tapes, inquire to ensure they function on the television standard (NTSC, PAL or SECAM) in your country. Once replied regularly, if slowly, but recently replies have been increasingly scarce. Comments welcomed about audio quality—*see TECHNICAL*, below. Avoid enclosing money (*see WARNING*, above). A new 500 kW shortwave transmitter is to be brought into service in the near future to improve reception.

TECHNICAL: Broadcast Engineering Department, 24th Floor—TV Building (Maspiro), Egyptian Radio and Television Union, P.O. Box 1186, 11151 Cairo, Egypt. Phone: +20 (2) 575-7155. Phone/fax: (propagation and monitoring office, set to automatically receive faxes outside normal working hours; otherwise, be prepared to request a switchover from voice to fax) +20 (2) 578-9491. Fax: +20 (2) 772 432; (ERTU projects) +20 (2) 766 909. E-mail: (Lawrence) niveenl@hotmail.com. Contact: Dr. Eng. Abdoh Fayoumi, Head of Propagation and Monitoring; or Niveen W. Lawrence, Director of Shortwave Department. Comments and suggestions on audio quality and level especially welcomed.

ENGLAND—*see* UNITED KINGDOM.

EQUATORIAL GUINEA   World Time +1

Radio Africa

TRANSMISSION OFFICE: Apartado 851, Malabo, Isla Bioko, Equatorial Guinea.

U.S. OFFICE FOR CORRESPONDENCE AND VERIFICATIONS: Pan American Broadcasting, 20410 Town Center Lane #200, Cupertino CA 95014 USA. Phone: +1 (408) 996-2033; (toll-free, within the United States) 1-800-726-2620. Fax: +1 (408) 252 6855. E-mail: pabcomain@aol.com. URL: www.radiopanam.com. Contact: (listener correspondence) Terry Kraemer; (general) Carmen Jung, Office & Sales Administrator; or James Manero. $1 in cash or unused U.S. stamps, or 2 IRCs, required for reply.

Radio East Africa—same details as "Radio Africa," above.

Radio Nacional de Guinea Ecuatorial—Bata (Radio Bata), Apartado 749, Bata, Río Muni, Equatorial Guinea. Phone: +240 (8) 2592. Fax: +240 (8) 2093. Contact: José Mba Obama, Director. If no response try sending your letter c/o Spanish Embassy, Bata, enclosing $1 for return postage. Spanish preferred.

Radio Nacional de Guinea Ecuatorial—Malabo (Radio Malabo), Apartado 195, Malabo, Isla Bioko, Equatorial Guinea. Phone: +240 (9) 2260. Fax: (general) +240 (9) 2097; (technical) +240 (9) 3122. Contact: (general) Román Manuel Mané-Abaga, Jefe de Programación; Ciprano Somon Suakin; or Manuel Sobede, Inspector de Servicios de Radio y TV; (technical) Hermenegildo Moliko Chele, Jefe Servicios Técnicos de Radio y Televisión. $1 or return postage required. Replies irregularly to correspondence in Spanish.

ERITREA   World Time +3

🕪**Voice of the Broad Masses of Eritrea** (Dimtsi Hafash), Ministry of Information, Radio Division, P.O. Box 872, Asmara, Eritrea; or Ministry of Information, Technical Branch, P.O. Box 243, Asmara, Eritrea. Phone: +291 (1) 119-100. Fax: +291 (1) 120 138. URL: (RealAudio) www.visafric.com/Dimtsi_hafash.htm. Contact: Ghebreab Ghebremedhin. Return postage or $1 helpful. Free information on history of the station and about Eritrea.

ETHIOPIA   World Time +3

Radio Ethiopia: (external service) P.O. Box 654; (domestic service) P.O. Box 1020—both in Addis Ababa, Ethiopia. Phone: (main office) +251 (1) 116-427 or +251 (1) 551-011; (engineering) +251 (1) 200-948. Fax: +251 (1) 552 263. E-mail: radioethiopia@angelfire.com. URL: www.angelfire.com/biz/radioethiopia/. Contact: (external service, general) Kahsai Tewoldemedhin, Program Director; Ms. Woinshet Woldeyes, Secretary, Audience Relations; Ms. Ellene Mocria, Head of Audience Relations; or Yohaness Ruphael, Producer, "Contact"; (administration) Kasa Miliko, Head of Station;

(technical) Terefe Ghebre Medhin or Zegeye Solomon. Free stickers. Very poor replier.

Radio Fana (Radio Torch), P.O. Box 30702, Addis Ababa, Ethiopia. Phone: +251 (1) 516-777. E-mail: radio-fana@telecom.net.et. Contact: Hameimat Tekle Haimanot, General Manager; Mesfin Alemayehu, Head, External Relations; or Girma Lema, Head, Planning and Research Department. Station is autonomous and receives its income from non-governmental educational sponsorship. Seeks help with obtaining vehicles, recording equipment and training materials.

Voice of Peace, Inter-Africa Group, P.O. Box 1631, Addis Ababa, Ethiopia. A humanitarian broadcast partially funded by UNICEF, seeking peace and reconciliation among warring factions in central and eastern Africa. Via Radio Ethiopia (see, above).

Voice of the Tigray Revolution, P.O. Box 450, Mek'ele, Tigray, Ethiopia. Contact: Fre Tesfamichael, Director. $1 helpful.

FINLAND   World Time +2 (+3 midyear)

YLE Radio Finland

MAIN OFFICE: Box 78, FIN-00024 Yleisradio, Finland. Phone: (general, 24-hour English speaking switchboard for both Radio Finland and Yleisradio Oy) +358 (9) 14801; (international information) +358 (9) 1480-3729; (administration) +358 (9) 1480-4320 or +358 (9) 1480-4316; (Technical Customer Service) +358 (9) 1480-3213. Fax: (general) +358 (9) 148 1169; (international information) +358 (9) 1480 3391; (Technical Affairs) +358 (9) 1480 3588. E-mail: rfinland@yle.fi; (Yleisradio Oy parent organization) fbc@yle.fi. To contact individuals, the format is firstname.lastname@yle.fi; so to reach, say, Pertti Seppä, it would be pertti.seppa@yle.fi. URLs: (includes RealAudio in Finnish, Swedish, English, German, French, Russian and Classic Latin) www.yle.fi/fbc/radiofin.html; (stored news audio in Finnish, Swedish, English, German, French and Russian) www.wrn.org/ondemand/finland.html; (online reception report form) www.yle.fi/sataradio/receptionreport.html. Contact—Radio Finland: (English) Eddy Hawkins; (Finnish & Swedish) Pertti Seppä; (German & French) Dr. Stefan Tschirpke; (Russian) Timo Uotila and Mrs. Eija Laitinen; (administration) Juhani Niinistö, Head of External Broadcasting. Contact—Yleisradio Oy parent organization: (general) Marja Salusjärvi, Head of International PR; (administration) Arne Wessberg, Managing Director; or Tapio Siikala, Director for Domestic & International Radio. Sometimes provides free stickers and small souvenirs, as well as tourist and other magazines. Replies to correspondence. Radio Finland will verify reception reports directly if sent to: Radio Finland, Attention: Raimo Mäkelä, PL 113, FIN-28101 Pori, Finland (E-mail: raimo.makela@pp.inet.fi). Also, see Transmission Facility, below. YLE Radio Finland external broadcasting is a part of YLE and not a separate administrative unit. Radio Finland itself is not a legal entity. NUNTII LATINI (Program in Latin): P.O. Box 99, FIN-00024 Yleisradio, Finland. Fax: +358 (9) 1480 3391. E-mail: nuntii.latini@yle.fi. URL: www.yle.fi/fbc/nuntii.html. Six years of Nuntii Latini now available in books I to III at US$30 each from: Bookstore Tiedekirja, Kirkkokatu 14, FIN-00170 Helsinki, Finland; fax: +358 (9) 635 017. VISA/MC/EURO.

FREQUENCY PLANNING: Bureau of Network Planning, Digita, P.O. Box 20, FIN-00024 Yleisradio, Finland. Phone: +358 (9) 1480-7287. Fax: +358 (9) 148 5260. E-mail: esko.huuhka@digita.fi. Contact: Esko Huuhka, Head of Network Planning.

DIGITA MEASURING STATION: Digita, FIN-05400 Jokela, Finland. Phone: +358 (9) 282-005/6. Fax: +358 (9) 417 2410. Contact: Urpo Kormano, Frequency Manager; or Kari Hautala, Monitoring Engineer.

TRANSMISSION FACILITY: Digita Shortwave Centre, Makholmantie 79, FIN-28660 Pori, Finland. URL: (Digita Oy) www.digita.fi. Contact: Ms. Marjatta Jokinen. Issues full-data verification cards for good reception reports, and provides free illustrated booklets about the transmitting station.

NORTH AMERICAN OFFICE—LISTENER & MEDIA LIAISON: P.O. Box 462, Windsor CT 06095 USA. Phone: +1 (860) 688-5540 or +1 (860) 688-5098. Phone/fax: (24-hour toll-free within U.S. and Canada for recorded schedule and voice mail) 1-800-221-9539. Fax: +1 (860) 688 0113. E-mail: yleus@aol.com. Contact: John Berky, YLE Finland Transcriptions. Free YLE North America newsletter. This office does not verify reception reports.

FRANCE   World Time +1

Radio France Internationale (RFI)

MAIN OFFICE: B.P. 9516, F-75016 Paris Cedex 16, France. Phone: (general) +33 (1) 42-30-22-22; (International Affairs and Program Placement) +33 (1) 44-30-89-31 or +33 (1) 44-30-89-49; (Service de la communication) +33 (1) 42-30-29-51; (Audience Relations) +33 (1) 44-30-89-69/70/71; (Media Relations) +33 (1) 42-30-29-85; (Développement et de la communication) +33 (1) 44-30-89-21; (Fréquence Monde) +33 (1) 42-30-10-86; (English Department) +33 (1) 42-30-30-62; (Spanish Department) +33 (1) 42-30-30-48. Fax: (general) +33 (1) 42 30 30 71; (International Affairs and Program Placement) +33 (1) 44 30 89 20; (Audience Relations) +33 (1) 44 30 89 99; (other nontechnical) +33 (1) 42 30 44 81; (English Department) +33 (1) 42 30 26 74; (Spanish Department) +33 (1) 42 30 46 69. URLs: (general) www.rfi.fr/; (RealAudio and StreamWorks in French, English, Spanish & Portuguese) www.francelink.com/radio_stations/rfi/. Contact: Simson Najovits, Chief, English Department; J.P. Charbonnier, Producer, "Lettres des Auditeurs"; Joël Amar, International Affairs/Program Placement Department; Arnaud Littardi, Directeur du développement et de la communication; Nicolas Levkov, Rédactions en Langues Etrangères; Daniel Franco, Rédaction en français; Mme. Anne Toulouse, Rédacteur en chef du Service Mondiale en français; Christine Berbudeau, Rédacteur en chef, Fréquence **Monde**; or Marc Verney, Attaché de Presse; (administration) Jean-Paul Cluzel, Président-Directeur Général; (technical) M. Raymond Pincon, Producer, "Le Courrier Technique." Free Fréquence **Monde** bi-monthly magazine in French upon request. Free souvenir keychains, pins, lighters, pencils, T-shirts and stickers have been received by some—especially when visiting the headquarters at 116 avenue du Président Kennedy, in the chichi 16th Arrondissement. Can provide supplementary materials for "Dites-moi tout" French-language course; write to the attention of Mme. Chantal de Grandpre, "Dites-moi tout." "Le Club des Auditeurs" French-language listener's club ("Club 9516" for English-language listeners); applicants must provide name, address and two passport-type photos, whereupon they will receive a membership card and the club bulletin. RFI exists primarily to defend and promote Francophone culture, but also provides meaningful information and cultural perspectives in non-French languages.

TRANSMISSION OFFICE, TECHNICAL: TéléDiffusion de France, Direction de la Production et des Méthodes, Shortwave service, 10 rue d'Oradour sur Glane, 75732 Paris Cedex 15, France. Phone: (Bochent) +33 (1) 5595-1369; or (Meunier) +33 (1) 5595-1161. Fax: +33 (1) 5595 2137. E-mail: 101317.2431@ compuserve.com; or danielbochent@compuserve.com. Contact: Daniel Bochent, Head of short wave service; Alain Meunier, Mme Annick Daronian or Mme Sylvie Greuillet (short wave service). This office is for informing about transmitter-related problems (interference, modulation quality), and also for reception reports and verifications.

UNITED STATES PROMOTIONAL, SCHOOL LIAISON, PROGRAM PLACEMENT AND CULTURAL EXCHANGE OFFICES:

NEW ORLEANS: Services Culturels, Suite 2105, Ambassade de France, 300 Poydras Street, New Orleans LA 70130 USA. Phone: +1 (504) 523-5394. Phone/fax: +1 (504) 529-7502. Contact: Adam-Anthony Steg, Attaché Audiovisuel. This office promotes RFI, especially to language teachers and others in the educational community within the southern United States, and arranges for bi-national cultural exchanges. It also sets up RFI feeds to local radio stations within the southern United States.

NEW YORK: Audiovisual Bureau, Radio France Internationale, 972 Fifth Avenue, New York NY 10021 USA. Phone: +1 (212) 439-1452. Fax: +1 (212) 439 1455. Contact: Gérard Blondel or Julien Vin. This office promotes RFI, especially to language teachers and others within the educational community outside the southern United States, and arranges for bi-national cultural exchanges. It also sets up RFI feeds to local radio stations within much of the United States.

NEW YORK NEWS BUREAU: 1290 Avenue of the Americas, New York NY 10019 USA. Phone: +1 (212) 581-1771. Fax: +1 (212) 541 4309. Contact: Ms. Auberi Edler, Reporter; or Bruno Albin, Reporter.

WASHINGTON NEWS BUREAU: 529 14th Street NW, Suite 1126, Washington DC 20045 USA. Phone: +1 (202) 879-6706. Contact: Pierre J. Cayrol.

SAN FRANCISCO OFFICE, SCHEDULES: 2654 17th Avenue, San Francisco CA 94116 USA. Phone: +1 (415) 564-9968. E-mail: GPoppin@aol.com. Contact: George Poppin. This address, a volunteer office, only provides RFI schedules to listeners. All other correspondence should be sent directly to the main office in Paris.

▣**Tamil-Oli Radio**, Radio Asia, 79 rue Rateau, F-93120 La Courneuve, France. Phone: +33 (1) 4311-2773. Fax: +33 (1) 4311 2772. E-mail: info@trt.net. URL: (includes RealAudio) www.trt.net. Broadcasts to Sri Lanka and southern India via a 50 kw transmitter in Madagascar.

LONDON ADDRESS: Tamil Radio & Television, 727 London Road, Thornton Heath, CR7 6AU, United Kingdom. Phone: +44 (20) 8689-7503. Fax: +44 (20) 8683 4445.

FRENCH GUIANA   World Time –3

Radio France Internationale/Swiss Radio International—Guyane Relay Station, TDF, Montsinéry, French Guiana. Contact: (technical) Chef des Services Techniques, RFI Guyane. All correspondence concerning non-technical matters should be sent directly to the main addresses (*see*) for Radio France International in France and Swiss Radio International in Berne. Can consider replies only to technical correspondence in French.

▣**RFO Guyane**, 43 bis, rue du Docteur-Gabriel-Devèze, BP 7013 – Cayenne Cedex, French Guiana. Phone: +595 299-900 or +594 299-907. Fax: +594 299 958. URL: (includes Quick-Time audio) www.rfo.fr/guyane/guyane.htm. Contact: (administration) George Chow-Toun, Directeur Régional; (editorial) Claude Joly, Rédacteur en Chef; (technical) Charles Diony, Directeur Technique. Free stickers. Replies occasionally and sometimes slowly; correspondence in French preferred, but English often okay.

FRENCH POLYNESIA   World Time –10 Tahiti

▣**RFO Polynésie Française** (also announces as "RFO-Radio Tahiti") (if reactivated), BP 60 125, Pamatai, 98 702 Faaa Cedex, Tahiti, French Polynesia. Phone: (general) +689 861-616 or +689 861-650; (Ruben) +689 861-610; (Bodin) +689 861-613. Fax: +689 861 651. E-mail: (general) rfopofr@mail.pf; (Bodin) jrbodin@mail.pf; (Ruben) ruben@mail.pf; (maintenance unit, technical) ditechm@rfo.pf. URL: (includes Quick-Time audio) www.rfo.fr/polynesie/homepoly.htm. Contact: (general) Claude Ruben, Directeur Régional; Jean-Raymond Bodin, Délégué de la Direction Régionale chargé du Patrimoine; (technical) Léon Siquin, Services Techniques. Free stickers, tourist brochures and broadcast-coverage map. Three IRCs, return postage, 5 francs or $1 helpful, but not mandatory. M. Siquin and his sons Xavier and Philippe, all friendly and fluent in English, collect pins from radio/TV stations, memorabilia from the Chicago Bulls basketball team and other souvenirs of American pop culture; these make more appropriate enclosures than the usual postage-reimbursement items.

GABON   World Time +1

Afrique Numéro Un, B.P. 1, Libreville, Gabon. Fax: +241 742 133. E-mail: africagc@club-internet.fr. URL: www.africa1.com/. Contact: (general) Gaston Didace Singangoye; or A. Letamba, Le Directeur des Programmes; (technical) Mme. Marguerite Bayimbi, Le Directeur [sic] Technique. Free calendars and bumper stickers. $1, 2 IRCs or return postage helpful. Replies very slowly.

RTV Gabonaise, B.P. 10150, Libreville, Gabon. Contact: André Ranaud-Renombo, Le Directeur Technique, Adjoint Radio. Free stickers. $1 required. Replies occasionally, but slowly, to correspondence in French.

GEORGIA   World Time +4

Georgian Radio, TV-Radio Tbilisi, ul. M. Kostava 68, Tbilisi 380071, Republic of Georgia. Phone: (domestic service) +995 (32) 368-362; (external service) +995 (32) 360-063. Fax: +995 (32) 955 137. Contact: (external service) Helena Apkhadze, Foreign Editor; Tamar Shengelia; Mrs. Natia Datuaschwili, Secretary; or Maya Chihradze; (domestic service) Lia Uumlaelsa, Manager; or V. Khundadze, Acting Director of Television and Radio Department. Replies erratically and slowly, in part due to financial difficulties. Return postage or $1 helpful.

Republic of Abkhazia Radio, Abkhaz State Radio & TV Co., Aidgylara Street 34, Sukhum 384900, Republic of Abkhazia; however, as of press time, according to the station there is a total embargo on mail to the Republic of Abkhazia. Phone: +995 (881) 24-867 or +995 (881) 25-321. Fax: +995 (881) 21 144. Contact: G. Amkuab, General Director; or Yury Kutarba, Deputy General Director. A 1992 uprising in northwestern Georgia drove the majority of ethnic Georgians from the region. This area remains virtually autonomous from Georgia.

GERMANY   World Time +1 (+2 midyear)

Adventist World Radio, the Voice of Hope

Stimme der Hoffnung, Am Elfengrund 66, D-64297 Darmstadt, Germany. Phone: +49 (6151) 954-465. Fax: +49 (6151) 954-470. E-mail: (general) webmaster@stimme-der-hoffnung.de; (reports on AWR broadcasts in German, especially when on new frequencies) dxer@stimme-der-hoffnung.de. Note: all postal correspondence concerning programs and reception should be sent to AWR's office in Forlì, Italy (see). URL: (includes online order form for cassettes, CDs and videos) www.stimme-der-hoffnung.de.
FREQUENCY MANAGEMENT OFFICE: Postfach 100252, D-64202 Darmstadt, Germany. Phone: +49 (6151) 953-151. Fax: +49 (6151) 953 152. E-mail: 102555.257@compuserve.com.

▣ Bayerischer Rundfunk, Rundfunkplatz 1, D-80300 München, Germany. Phone: +49 (89) 5900-01. Fax: +49 (89) 5900 2375. E-mail: info@br-online.de. URL: (includes RealAudio) www.br-online.de. Contact: Dr. Gualtiero Guidi; or Jutta Paue, Engineering Adviser. Free stickers and 250-page program schedule book.

▣ Deutsche Welle, Radio and TV International

MAIN OFFICE: Raderbergguertel 50, D-50968 Cologne, Germany. Phone: (general) +49 (221) 389-2001/2; (listeners' mail) +49 (221) 389-2500; (Program Distribution) +49 (221) 389-2731; (technical) +49 (221) 389-3221 or +49 (221) 389-3208;(Technical Advisory, Horst Scholz) +49 (221) 389-3201; (Frequency Manager, Peter Pischalka) +49 (221) 389-3228; (Public Relations) +49 (221) 2041. Fax: (general) +49 (221) 389 4155, +49 (221) 389 2080 or +49 (221) 389 3000; (listeners' mail) +49 (221) 389 2510; (English Service, general) +49 (221) 389 4599; (English Service, Current Affairs) +49 (221) 389 4554; (Public Relations) +49 (221) 389 2047; (Program Distribution) +49 (221) 389 2777; (Technical Advisory) +49 (221) 389 3200 or +49 (221) 389 3240. E-mail: (general) online@dwelle.de; (specific individuals or programs) format is firstname.lastname@ dw.gmd.de, so to reach, say, Harald Schuetz, it would be harald.schuetz@dw.gmd.de (if this fails, try the format firstname@dwelle.de); (Program Distribution) 100302.2003@ compuserve.com; (technical) (Pischalka) 100565.1010@ compuserve.com; (Scholz) 100536.2173@compuserve.com. URLs: (general) www.dwelle.de/; (German program, including RealAudio) www.dwelle.de/dpradio/ Welcome.html; (non-German languages, including RealAudio) www.dwelle.de/language.html. Contact: (general) Ursula Fleck-Jerwin, Audience Mail Department; Dr. Ralf Siepmann, Director of Public Relations; Michael Behrens, Head of English Service; or Dr. Burkhard Nowotny, Director of Media Department; Harald Schuetz; ("German by Radio" language course) Herrad Meese; (administration) Dieter Weirich, Director General; (technical—head of engineering) Peter Senger, Chief Engineer; (technical—Radio Frequency Department) Peter Pischalka; Frequency Manager; or Horst Scholz, Head of Transmission; (technical—Transmission Management/Technical Advisory Service) Mrs. Silke Bröker; or B. Klaumann, Transmission Management. Free pennants, stickers, key chains, pens, *Deutsch—warum nicht?* language-course book, *Germany—A European Country and its People* book. Free 40 page booklet *"Radio Worlds/Worlds of Radios"* featuring radio related articles and stories from different countries. Available from PR & Marketing. Local Deutsche Welle Listeners' Clubs in selected countries. Operates via world band transmitters in Germany, Antigua, Canada, Madagascar, Portugal, Russia, Rwanda and Sri Lanka. Deutsche Welle is sheduled to move from Cologne to Bonn in the near future.
ELECTRONIC TRANSMISSION OFFICE FOR PROGRAM PREVIEWS: Infomedia, 25 rue du Lac, L-8808 Arsdorf, Luxembourg. Phone: +352 649-270. Fax: +352 649 271. This office will electronically transmit Deutsche Welle program previews to you upon request; be sure to provide either a dedicated fax number or an e-mail address so they can reply to you.
BRUSSELS NEWS BUREAU: International Press Center, 1 Boulevard Charlemagne, B-1040 Brussels, Belgium.
U.S./CANADIAN LISTENER CONTACT OFFICE: 2800 South Shirlington Road, Suite 901, Arlington VA 22206-3601 USA. Phone: +1 (703) 931-6644.
RUSSIAN LISTENER CONTACT OFFICE: Nemezkaja Wolna, Abonentnyj jaschtschik 596, Glawpotschtamt, 190000 St. Petersburg, Russia.
TOKYO NEWS BUREAU: C.P.O. Box 132, Tokyo 100-91, Japan.
WASHINGTON NEWS BUREAU: P.O. Box 14163, Washington DC 20004 USA. Fax: +1 (202) 526 2255. Contact: Adnan Al-Katib, Correspondent.

Deutschlandfunk, Raderberggürtel 40, D-50968 Köln, Germany. Phone: +49 (221) 345-0. Fax: +49 (221) 345-4802. URL: www.dradio.de/dlf/themen/.

DeutschlandRadio-Berlin, Hans-Rosenthal-Platz, D-10825 Berlin Schönberg, Germany. Phone: +49 (30) 8503-0. Fax: +49 (30) 8503 6168. E-mail: dlrb@dlf.de; online@dlf.de. URL: www.dradio.de/dlrb/index.html. Contact: Dr. Karl-Heinz Stamm; or Ulrich Reuter. Correspondence in English accepted. Sometimes sends stickers, pens, magazines and other souvenirs.

▣ Evangeliums-Rundfunk—*see* Monaco (Trans World Radio).

Lutherische Stunde, Postfach 1162, D-27363 Sottrum, Germany; or (street address) Clüversborstel 14, D-27367 Sottrum, Germany. Religious program aired over Radio Intercontinental, Armenia.

Missionswerk Werner Heukelbach, D-51702 Bergneustadt 2, Germany. Contact: Manfred Paul. Religious program heard via the Voice of Russia and Radio Intercontinental, Armenia. Replies to correspondence in English and German.

Mitteldeutscher Rundfunk, Kantstrasse 71-73, Leipzig, Germany. Phone: +49 (341) 300-0. Fax: +49 (341) 300-5544. E-mail: (technical) technik@mdr.de; for nontechnical correspondence, use the online e-mail form at the station's website. URL: www.mdr.de. Relayed on shortwave during the night hours via the transmitter of Bayerischer Rundfunk.

Shortwave Radio Station Jülich—Deutsche Telekom AG

JÜLICH ADDRESS: Rundfunksendestelle Jülich, Merscher Höhe D-52428 Jülich, Germany. Phone: +49 (2461) 697-310; (Technical Engineer) +49 (2461) 697-330; (Technical Advisor & Sales Management) +49 (2461) 697-350. Fax: (all offices) +49 (2461) 697 372. E-mail: (Hirte) guenter.hirte@telekom.de; (Goslawski) roman.goslawski@telekom.de; (Brodowsky) walter.brodowsky@telekom.de; (Weyl) ralf.weyl@telekom.de. Contact: Günter Hirte, Head of Shortwave Radio Station Jülich; Roman Goslawski, Technical Engineer; (technical) Walter Brodowsky, Technical Advisor; or (nontechnical) Ralf Weyl, Sales Management. Reception reports accepted by mail or fax, and should be clearly marked to the attention of Walter Brodowsky.
KÖLN ADDRESS: Niederlassung 2 Köln, Service Centre Rundfunk, D-50482 Köln Germany. Phone: (Kraus) +49 (221) 575-4000; (Hufschlag) +49 (221) 575-4011. Fax: +49 (221) 575

4090. E-mail: info@dtag.de. URLs: www.dtag.de; www.telekom.de. Contact: Egon Kraus, Head of Broadcasting Service Centre; or Josef Hufschlag, Customer Advisor for High Frequency Broadcasting.

This organization operates transmitters on German soil used by Deutsche Welle, as well as those leased to various non-German world band stations.

Südwestrundfunk, Neckarstrasse 230, D-70190 Stuttgart, Germany. Phone +49 (711) 929-0. Fax: +49 (711) 929 2600. E-mail: (general) info@swr-online.de; (technical) technik@swr-online.de. URL: (includes RealAudio) www.swr-online.de.

SWR BADEN-BADEN: Hans-Bredow-Strasse, D-76530 Baden-Baden, Germany. Phone: +49 (7221) 929-0.

This station is the result of a merger between Süddeutscher Rundfunk and Südwestfunk. Based in Stuttgart, transmissions under the new banner commenced in September 1998.

Universelles Leben (Universal Life)

HEADQUARTERS: Postfach 5643, D-97006 Würzburg, Germany. Phone: +49 (931) 3903-264. Fax: (general) +49 (931) 3903 233 or +49 (931) 3903 195;(engineering) +49 (931) 3903 299. E-mail: info@universelles-leben.org. URL: (includes RealAudio) www.universelles-leben.org. Contact: Janet Wood, English Dept; "Living in the Spirit of God" listeners' letters program; or Johanna Limley. Free stickers, publications and occasional small souvenirs. Transmits "The Word, The Cosmic Wave" (Das Wort, die kosmische Welle) via the Voice of Russia, Deutsche Telekom, Jülich (Germany) and various other world band stations, as well as "Vida Universal" via Radio Miami Internacional and WHRI in the United States. Replies to correspondence in English, German or Spanish.

SALES OFFICE: Das WORT GmbH, Im Universelles Leben, Max-Braun-Str. 2, D-97828 Marktheidenfeld/Altfeld, Germany. Phone: +49 (9391) 504-135. Fax: +49 (9391) 504 133. E-mail: info@das-wort.com. URL: www.das-wort.com/. Sells books, audio cassettes and videos related to broadcast material.

NORTH AMERICAN BUREAU: The Inner Religion, P.O. Box 3549, Woodbridge CT 06525 USA. Phone: +1 (203) 281-7771. Fax: +1 (203) 230 2703.

GHANA   World Time exactly

WARNING—CONFIDENCE ARTISTS: Attempted correspondence with Radio Ghana may result in requests, perhaps resulting from mail theft, from skilled confidence artists for money, free electronic or other products, publications or immigration sponsorship. To help avoid this, correspondence to Radio Ghana should be sent via registered mail.

Ghana Broadcasting Corporation, Broadcasting House, P.O. Box 1633, Accra, Ghana. Phone: +233 (21) 221-161. Fax: +233 (21) 221 153 or +233 (21) 773 227. URL: (2000 UTC English news in RealAudio, only) www.ghanaclassifieds.com. Contact: (general) Mrs. Maud Blankson-Mills, Director of Corporate Affairs; (administration) Cris Tackie, Acting Director of Radio; (technical) K.D. Frimpong, Director of Engineering; or E. Heneath, Propagation Department. Replies are increasingly scarce. Registering your letter may help and enclose an IRC, return postage or $1.

GREECE   World Time +2 (+3 midyear)

Foni tis Helladas (Voice of Greece)

NONTECHNICAL: Hellenic Radio-Television, ERA-5, The Voice of Greece, 432 Mesogion Av., 153-42 Athens, Greece. Phone: + 30 (1) 606-6298, +30 (1) 606-6308 or +30 (1) 606-

Gerald Ondap, Chief Operator/Program Coordinator, prepares programs for Advetist World Radio's Guam station. AWR

6310. Fax: +30 (1) 606 6309. E-mail (program reports): fonel@hol.gr; era5@leon.nrcps.ariadne-t.grc. URLs: http://alpha.servicenet.ariadne-t.gr/Docs/Era5_1.html; www.greeknews.ariadne-t.gr/Docs/Era5_1.html; http://ert.ntua.gr/era5/index.htm; (RealAudio) http://ert.nua.gr/index.htm. Contact: Angeliki Barka, Head of Programmes. Free tourist literature.

TECHNICAL: Elliniki Radiophonia—ERA-5, General Technical Directorate, ERT/ERA Hellenic Radio Television SA, Mesogion 402, 15342 Athens, Greece. Phone: (Angelogiannis) +30 (1) 606-6255; (Vorgias) +30 (1) 606-6263; or +31 (1) 606-6264. Fax: +30 (1) 606 6243. E-mail: (Angelogiannis) dangelogiannis@ert.gr; or dangelogiannis@yahoo.com. Contact: (general) Ing. Dionysios Angelogiannis, Planning Engineer; or Sotiris Vorgias, Planning Engineer; (administration) Th. Kokossis, General Director; or Nicolas Yannakakis, Director. Technical reception reports may be sent via mail, fax or e-mail. Taped reports not accepted.

Radiophonikos Stathmos Makedonias—ERT-3, Angelaki 2, 546 21 Thessaloniki, Greece. Phone: +30 (31) 244-979. Fax: +30 (31) 236 370. E-mail: charter3@compulink.gr. Contact: (general) Mrs. Tatiana Tsioli, Program Director; or Lefty Kongalides, Head of International Relations; (technical) Dimitrios Keramidas, Engineer. Free booklets and other small souvenirs.

Voice of America/IBB—Kaválla Relay Station. Phone: +30 (5) 912-2855. Fax: +30 (5) 913 1310. These numbers for

Guayaquil, Ecuador. The Andes are home to a rich variety of low-power stations, some with exceptional indigenous music. HCJB

urgent technical matters only. Otherwise, does not welcome direct contact; *see* USA for acceptable VOA and IBB Washington addresses and related information.

GUAM   World Time +10

Adventist World Radio, the Voice of Hope—KSDA
AWR-Asia, P.O. Box 8990, Agat, Guam 96928 USA. Phone: +1 (671) 565-2000. Fax: +1 (671) 565 2983. E-mail: awrasia@ite.net. Contact: (general) Lolita Colegado, Listener Mail Services; (technical) Elvin Vence, Chief Engineer; Gary Benton, Assistant Engineer. Free stickers, bi-annual newsletter *AWR Current*, program schedule and religious printed matter. Also, *see* AWR listings under Costa Rica, Guatemala, Italy, Kenya and USA.

Trans World Radio—KTWR
MAIN OFFICE, NONTECHNICAL: P.O. Box CC, Agana, Guam 96910 USA. Phone: (main office) +1 (671) 477-9701; (engineering) +1 (671) 828-8637. Fax: (main office) +1 (671) 477 2838; (engineering) +1 (671) 828-8636. E-mail: (administration) estortro@twr.hafa.net.gu; (programming) wfrost@twr.hafa.net.gu; (technical) cwhite@twr.hafa.net.gu. URL: www.guam.net/home/twr/ktwrguam.htm. Contact: (general) Karen Zeck, Listener Correspondence; Byron Tyler, Producer, "Friends in Focus" listeners' questions program; Wayne T. Frost, Program Director & Producer, "Pacific DX Report"; Janette McSurk; or Mrs. Kathy Greggowski; (administration) Edward Stortro, Station Director; (programmes) Shelly Frost; (technical) Chuck White, Chief Engineer; or (Frequency Management) D. Gregson. Also, *see* USA. Free small publications.
"PACIFIC DX REPORT" PROGRAM: E-mail: (reports) bpadula@compuserve.com. URL: www.wp.com/edxp/. Program compiled by EDXP and aired via KTWR. Special EDXP QSLs. Reports to: Bob Padula, 404 Mont Albert Road, Surrey Hills, Victoria 3127, Australia. Return postage necessary. E-mail reports accepted and will be confirmed by return e-mail, to bpadula@compuserve.com.
FREQUENCY COORDINATION OFFICE: 1868 Halsey Drive, Asan, Guam 96922-1505 USA. Phone: +671 828-8637. Fax:

+1 (671) 828 8636. E-mail: ktwrfreq@twr.hafa.net.gu. Contact: George Zensen, Chief Engineer. This office will also verify e-mail reports with a QSL card.
AUSTRALIAN OFFICE: Trans World Radio ANZ, 2-6 Albert Street, Blackburn, Victoria 3130, Australia; or P.O. Box 390, Box Hill, Victoria 3128, Australia. Phone: +61 (3) 9878-5922. Fax: +61 (3) 9878 5944. E-mail: info@twradio.org. URLs: http://freehosting1.at.webjump.com/tw/twradio-webjump/; www.twradio.org. Contact: John Reeder, National Director.
CHINA (HONG KONG) OFFICE: TWR-CMI, P.O. Box 98697, Tsimshatsui Post Office, Kowloon, Hong Kong. Phone: +852 2780-8336. Fax: +852 2385 5045. E-mail: (general) info@twr.org.hk; (Ko) simon_ko@compuserve.com; (Lok) joycelok@compuserve.com. URL: www.twr.org.hk. Contact: Simon Ko, Acting Area Director; or Joyce Lok, Programming/Follow -up Director.
NEW DELHI OFFICE: P.O. Box 4310, New Delhi-110 019, India. Contact: N. Emil Jebasingh, Vishwa Vani; or S. Stanley.
SINGAPORE OFFICE: Trans World Radio Asia Pacific Office, 2A Martaban Road, Singapore 328627. Phone: +65 251-1887. Fax: +65 251 1846. E-mail: (Spieker) 76573.1147@compuserve.com; (Flaming) vflaming@mbox3.singnet.com.sg. Contact: Edmund Spieker, Acting Regional Director; or Vic Flaming, Regional Services Director.
TOKYO OFFICE: Pacific Broadcasting Association, C.P.O. Box 1000, Tokyo 100-91, Japan. Phone +81 (3) 3295-4921. Fax: +81 (3) 3233 2650. E-mail: pba@path.ne.jp. Contact: (administration) Nobuyoshi Nakagawa.

GUATEMALA   World Time –6

Adventist World Radio, the Voice of Hope—Unión Radio, Apartado de Correo 51-C, Guatemala City, Guatemala. Phone: +502 365-2509, +502 365-9067 or +502 365-9072. Fax:+502 365 9076. E-mail: mundi@guate.net. Contact: Rolando García P., General Manager. Free tourist and religious literature and Guatemalan stamps. Return postage (3 IRCs or $1) appreciated. Correspondence in Spanish preferred. Also, *see* AWR listings under Costa Rica, Guam, Italy, Kenya and USA.

La Voz de Atitlán—TGDS, Santiago Atitlán, Guatemala. Contact: Juan Ajtzip Alvarado, Director; José Miguel Pop Tziná, Director; or Esteban Ajtzip Tziná, Director Ejecutivo. Return postage required. Replies to correspondence in Spanish.

La Voz de Guatemala—TGW (when active), 18 Calle 6-70 2do piso, Zona 1, 01001 Guatemala City, Guatemala. Phone: +502 232-3321. Fax: +502 251 9873.

La Voz de Nahualá, Nahualá, Sololá, Guatemala. Contact: (technical) Juan Fidel Lepe Juárez, Técnico Auxiliar; or F. Manuel Esquipulas Carrillo Tzep. Return postage required. Correspondence in Spanish preferred.

Radio Buenas Nuevas, 13020 San Sebastián, Huehuetenango, Guatemala. Contact: Israel G. Rodas Mérida, Gerente. $1 or return postage helpful. Free religious and station information in Spanish. Sometimes includes a small pennant. Replies to correspondence in Spanish.

Radio Chortís, Centro Social, 20004 Jocotán, Chiquimula, Guatemala. Contact: Padre Juan María Boxus, Director. $1 or return postage required. Replies irregularly to correspondence in Spanish.

Radio Cultural—TGNA, Apartado de Correo 601, Guatemala City, Guatemala. Phone: +502 471-0807. Contact: Mariela Posadas, QSL Secretary; or Wayne Berger, Chief Engineer. Free religious printed matter. Return postage or $1 appreciated.

Radio Cultural Coatán, San Sebástian Coatán, Huehuetenango, Guatemala. Contact: Domingo Hernández, Director; or Virgilio José, Locutor.

Radio K'ekchi—TGVC, 3ra Calle 7-15, Zona 1, 16015 Fray Bartolomé de las Casas, Alta Verapaz, Guatemala; (Media Consultant) David Daniell, Asesor de Comunicaciones, Apartado Postal 25, Bulevares MX, 53140 Mexico. Phone: (station) +502 950-0299; (Daniell, phone/fax) +52 (5) 572-9633. Fax: +502 950 0398. E-mail: (Daniell) DPDaniell@aol.com. Contact: (general) Gilberto Sun Xicol, Gerente; Ancelmo Cuc Chub, Director; or Mateo Botzoc, Director de Programas; (technical) Larry Baysinger, Ingeniero Jefe. Free paper pennant. $1 or return postage required. Replies to correspondence in Spanish.

Radio Mam, Acu'Mam, Cabricán, Quetzaltenango, Guatemala. Contact: Porfirio Pérez, Director. Free stickers and pennants. $1 or return postage required. Replies irregularly to correspondence in Spanish. Donations permitting (the station is religious), they would like to get a new transmitter to replace the current unit, which is failing.

Radio Maya de Barillas—TGBA, 13026 Villa de Barillas, Huehuetenango, Guatemala. Contact: José Castañeda, Pastor Evangélico y Gerente. Free pennants and pins. Station is very interested in receiving reception reports. $1 or return postage required. Replies occasionally to correspondence in Spanish and Indian languages.

Radio Tezulutlán—TGTZ, Apartado de Correo 19, 16901 Cobán, Guatemala. Contact: Sergio W. Godoy, Director; or Hno. Antonio Jacobs, Director Ejecutivo. Pennant for donation to specific bank account. $1 or return postage required. Replies to correspondence in Spanish.

GUINEA   World Time exactly

Radiodiffusion-Télévision Guinéenne, B.P. 391, Conakry, Guinea. If no reply is forthcoming from this address, try sending your letter to: D.G.R./P.T.T., B.P. 33-22, Conakry, Guinea. Phone/fax: +224 451-408. Contact: (general) Yaoussou Diaby, Journaliste Sportif; Boubacar Yacine Diallo, Directeur Général/ORTG; or Seny Camara; (administration) Momo Toure, Chef Services Administratifs; or Alpha Sylla, Directeur, Sofoniya I Centre de Transmission; (technical, studio) Mbaye Gagne, Chef de Studio; (technical, overall) Direction des Services Techniques. Return postage or $1 required. Replies very irregularly to correspondence in French.

GUYANA   World Time –3

Voice of Guyana, Guyana Broadcasting Corporation, Broadcasting House, P.O. Box 10760, Georgetown, Guyana. Phone: +592 (2) 58734, +592 (2) 58083 or +592 (2) 62691. Fax: +592 (2) 58756, but persist as fax machine appears to be switched off much of the time. Contact: (general) Indira Anandjit, Personnel Assistant; or M. Phillips; (technical) Roy Marshall, Senior Technician; or Shiroxley Goodman, Chief Engineer. $1 or IRC helpful. Sending a spare sticker from another station helps assure a reply.

HOLLAND (THE NETHERLANDS)   World Time +1 (+2 midyear)

▣Radio Nederland Wereldomroep (Radio Netherlands)
MAIN OFFICE: P.O. Box 222, 1200 JG Hilversum, The Netherlands. Phone: (general) +31 (35) 672-4211; (English Language Service) +31 (35) 672-4242; (24-hour listener Answerline) +31 (35) 672-4222; (Programme Distribution & Frequency Planning Department) +31 (35) 672-4426. Fax: (general) +31 (35) 672 4207, but indicate destination department on fax cover sheet; (English Language Service) +31 (35) 672 4239; (Programme Distribution & Frequency Planning Department) +31 (35) 672 4429. E-mail: (English Language Service) letters@rnw.nl. ("Media Network") media@rnw.nl; (Web radio) pepijn.kalis@rnw.nl. URLs: (general) www.rnw.nl (online publications are listed in the section "Real Radio"); (RealAudio) www.rnw.nl/distrib/realaudio/. Contact: (management) Lodewijk Bouwens, Director General; Jonathan Marks, Director of Programmes; Jan Hoek, Director of Finance and Logistics; Diana Janssen, Head of Strategy and RN Interactive; Mike Shaw, Head of English Language Service; Ginger da Silva, Network Manager English; (listener correspondence) Helma Brugma, English Correspondence; or Veronica Wilson, Host of listener-contact programme: "Sincerely Yours" (include your telephone number or e-mail address). Full-data verification card for reception reports, following guidelines in the RNW folder, "Writing Useful Reception Reports," available free and on the Internet. Semiannual *On Target* newsletter also free upon request, as are stickers and booklets. Other language departments have their own newsletters. The Radio Netherlands Music Department produces concerts heard on many NPR stations in North America, as well as a line of CDs, mainly of classical, jazz, world music and the Euro Hit 40. Most of the productions are only for rebroadcasting on other stations, but recordings on the NM Classics label are for sale. More details are available at the RNW website. Visitors welcome, but must call in advance.
NORTH AMERICAN OPERATION: 316 Eisenhower Parkway, Livingston, NJ 07039 USA. Phone: toll-free in the USA 1-800-797-1670; or +1 (973) 533-6761. Fax: +1 (973) 533 6762. E-mail: lee.martin@rnw.nl. Contact: Lee Martin, Manager of Client Services. This bureau markets Radio Netherlands radio and television productions in English and Spanish for the North American market. These programs are available to stations on satellite and CD.

NEW DELHI OFFICE: (local correspondence only) P.O. Box 5257, Chanakya Puri Post Office, New Delhi, 110 021, India. Forwards mail from Indian listeners to Holland every three weeks.

HONDURAS World Time –6

La Voz de la Mosquitia (when operating)
STATION: Puerto Lempira, Dpto. Gracias a Dios, Honduras. Contact: Sammy Simpson, Director; or Larry Sexton. Free pennants.
U.S. OFFICE: Global Outreach, Box 1, Tupelo MS 38802 USA. Phone: +1 (601) 842-4615. Another U.S. contact is Larry Hooker, who occasionally visits the station, and who can be reached at +1 (334) 694-7976.

La Voz Evangélica—HRVC
MAIN OFFICE: Apartado Postal 3252, Tegucigalpa, M.D.C., Honduras. Phone: +504 234-3468/69/70. Fax: +504 233 3933. E-mail: hrvc@infanet.hn. Contact: (general) Srta. Orfa Esther Durón Mendoza, Secretaria; Tereso Ramos, Director de Programación; Alan Maradiaga; or Modesto Palma, Jefe, Depto. Tráfico; (technical) Carlos Paguada, Director del Dpto. Técnico; (administration) Venancio Mejía, Gerente; or Nelson Perdomo, Director. Free calendars. Three IRCs or $1 required. Replies to correspondence in English, Spanish, Portuguese and German.
REGIONAL OFFICE, SAN PEDRO SULA: Apartado 2336, San Pedro Sula, Honduras. Phone: +504 557-5030. Contact: Hernán Miranda, Director.
REGIONAL OFFICE, LA CEIBA: Apartado 164, La Ceiba, Honduras. Phone: +504 443-2390. Contact: José Banegas, Director.
Radio Costeña—relays Radio Ebenezer (1220 kHz medium wave), and all correspondence should be sent to the latter's address: Radio Ebenezer 1220 AM, Apartado 3466, San Pedro Sula, Honduras. E-mail: ebenezer@globalnet.hn. Contact: Germán Ponce.

Radio HRET
STATION: Primera Iglesia Bautista, Domicilio Conocido, Puerto Lempira, Gracias a Dios 33101, Honduras. Fax: +504 898 0018. Contact: Leonardo Alvarez López, Locutor y Operador; or Desiderio Williams, Locutor y Operador. Return postage necessary. Replies, sometimes slowly, to correspondence in Spanish.
NONTECHNICAL ENGLISH CORRESPONDENCE: David Daniell, Asesor de Comunicaciones, Apartado Postal 25, Bulevares, MX-53140, Mexico. E-mail: DPDaniell@aol.com. Replies to correspondence in English and Spanish.
TECHNICAL ENGLISH CORRESPONDENCE: Larry Baysinger, 8000 Casualwood Ct., Louisville KY 40291 USA. Replies to correspondence in English and Spanish, but calls not accepted.

Radio HRMI, La Voz de Misiones Internacionales
STATION: Apartado Postal 20583, Comayaguela, M.D.C., Honduras. Phone: +504 233-9029. Contact: Wayne Downs, Director. $1 or return postage helpful.
U.S. OFFICE: IMF World Missions, P.O. Box 6321, San Bernardino CA 92412, USA. Phone +1 (909) 370-4515. Fax: +1 (909) 370 4862. E-mail: JKPIMF@msn.com. Contact: Dr. James K. Planck, President; or Gustavo Roa, Coordinator.

Radio Litoral, Apartado Postal 878, La Ceiba, Provincia Atlántida, Honduras. Contact: José A. Mejía, Gerente-Propietario. Free postcards. 1$ or return postage required. Replies to correspondence in Spanish.

Radio Luz y Vida—HRPC, Apartado 303, San Pedro Sula, Honduras. Phone: +504 654-1221. Fax: +504 557 0394. Contact: C. Paul Easley, Director; Cristóbal "Chris" Fleck; or, to

have your letter read over the air, "English Friendship Program." Return postage or $1 appreciated.

HUNGARY World Time +1 (+2 midyear)

⌨Radio Budapest
STATION OFFICES: Bródy Sándor utca 5-7, H-1800 Budapest, Hungary. Phone: (general) +36 (1) 328-7339, +36 (1) 328-8328, +36 (1) 328-7357 +36 (1) 328-8588, +36 (1) 328-7710 or +36 (1) 328-7723; (voice mail, English) +36 (1) 328-8320; (voice mail, German) +36 (1) 328-7325; (administration) +36 (1) 328-7503 or +36 (1) 328-8415; (technical) +36 (1) 328-7226 or +36 (1) 328-8923. Fax: (general) +36 (1) 328 8517; (administration) +36 (1) 328 8838; (technical) +36 (1) 328 7105. E-mail: (Radio Budapest, English) ango11@kaf.radio.hu; (Radio Budapest, German) nemetl@kaf.radio.hu; (Hungarian Information Resources) avadasz@bluemoon.sma.com; (technical) (Füszlás) Fuszfasla@muszak.radio.hu. URLs: (general) www.kaf.radio.hu/index.html; (RealAudio in English, German, Hungarian and Russian) www.wrn.org/ondemand/hungary.html. Contact: (English Language Service) Ágnes Kevi, Correspondence; Charles Taylor Coutts, Producer, "Gatepost" (listeners' letters' program) & Head of English Language Service; Louis Horváth, DX Editor; or Sándor Laczkó, Editor; (administration) Antal Réger, Director, Foreign Broadcasting; Dr. Zsuzsa Mészáros, Vice-Director, Foreign Broadcasting; János Szirányi, President, Magyar Rádió; or János Simkó, Vice President, Magyar Rádió; (technical) László Füszfás, Deputy Technical Director, Magyar Rádió; Külföldi Adások Fõszerkesztõsége; or Lajos Horváth, Mu˝szaki Igazgatcˊsá; (Hungarian Information Resources) Andrew Vadasz. Free *Budapest International* periodical, stickers, pennants, stamps and printed tourist and other material. Also, for those whose comments or program proposals are used over the air, T-shirts, baseball-style caps and ballpoint pens. *RBSWC DX News* bulletin free to all Radio Budapest Shortwave Club members. Advertisements considered.
COMMUNICATION AUTHORITY: P.O. Box 75, H-1525 Budapest, Hungary. Phone: +36 (1) 457-7178. Fax: +36 (1) 457 7120 or 36 (1) 356 5520. E-mail: czuprak@hif.hu. Contact: Ernö Czuprák.
TRANSMISSION AUTHORITY: Ministry of Transport, Communications & Water Management, P.O. Box 87, H-1400 Budapest, Hungary. Phone: +36 (1) 461-3390. Fax: +36 (1) 461 3392. E-mail: horvathf@cms.khvm.hu. Contact: Ferenc Horváth, Frequency Manager, Radio Communications Engineering Services.

ICELAND World Time exactly

⌨Ríkisútvarpid, International Relations Department, Efstaleiti 1, IS-150 Reykjavík, Iceland. Phone: +354 515-3000. Fax: +354 515 3010. E-mail: isradio@ruv.is. URL: (includes RealAudio) www.ruv.is/utvarpid/. Contact: Dóra Ingvadóttir, Head of International Relations; or Markús Öern Antonsson, Director.

INDIA World Time +5:30

WARNING—MAIL THEFT: Several PASSPORT readers report that letters to India containing IRCs and other valuables have disappeared en route when not registered. Best is either to register your letter or to send correspondence in an unsealed envelope, and without enclosures.

⏪All India Radio

NOTE: The facility "New Broadcasting House" is being built to supplement the existing Broadcasting House on Parliament Street. It is to be used by the domestic and external services, alike, and is scheduled to be in full operation before 2001.

ADMINISTRATION: Directorate General of All India Radio, Akashvani Bhawan, 1 Sansad Marg, New Delhi-110 001, India. Phone: (general) +91 (11) 371-0006; (Engineer-in-Chief) +91 (11) 371-0058; (Frequency Management) +91 (11) 371-0145 or +91 (11) 371-4062; (Director General) +91 (11) 371-0300 or +91 (11) 371-4061. Fax: +91 (11) 371 1956. E-mail: faair@giasdl01.vsnl.net.in. Contact: (general) Dr. Om Prakash Kejariwal, Director General; (technical) H.M. Joshi, Engineer-in-Chief; or A.K. Bhatnagar, Director – Frequency Assignments; (programming) +91 (11) 371 5411, (voice mail, English) +91 (11) 376-1166, (Hindi) +91 (11) 376-1144.

AUDIENCE RESEARCH: Audience Research Unit, All India Radio, Press Trust of India Building, 2nd floor, Sansad Marg, New Delhi-110 001, India. Phone: +91 (11) 371-0033. Contact: S.K. Khatri, Director.

CENTRAL MONITORING SERVICES: Central Monitoring Services, All India Radio, Ayanagar, New Delhi-100 047, India. Phone: (Director) +91 (11) 680-1763 or +91 (11) 680-2955; (Control Room) +91 (11) 680-2362. Fax: +91 (11) 680 2679, +91 (11) 680 2362 or +91 (11) 680 2955. Contact: V.K. Arora, Director.

INTERNATIONAL MONITORING STATION—MAIN OFFICE: International Monitoring Station, All India Radio, Dr. K.S. Krishnan Road, Todapur, New Delhi-110 012, India. Phone: (general) +91 (11) 581-461;(administration) +91 (11) 680-2306; (Frequency Planning) +91 (11) 573-5936 (Chhabra) or +91 (11) 573-5937 (Malviya). Contact: D.P. Chhabra or R.K. Malviya, Assistant Research Engineers—Frequency Planning.

NEWS SERVICES DIVISION: News Services Division, Broadcasting House, 1 Sansad Marg, New Delhi-110 001, India. Phone: +91 (11) 371-0084 or +91 (11) 373-1510. Contact: D.C. Bhaumik, Director General—News.

RESEARCH & DEVELOPMENT: Office of the Chief Engineer R&D, All India Radio, 14-B Ring Road, Indraprastha Estate, New Delhi-110 002, India. Phone: (general) +91 (11) 331-1711, +91 (11) 331-1762, +91 (11) 331-3532 or +91 (11) 331-3574; (Chief Engineer) +91 (11) 331 8329. Fax: +91 (11) 331 8329 or +91 (11) 331 6674. E-mail: rdair@giasdl01.vsnl.net.in. URL: www.air.kode.net. Contact: K.M. Paul, Chief Engineer.

TRANSCRIPTION & PROGRAM EXCHANGE SERVICES: Akashvani Bhawan, 1 Sansad Marg, New Delhi-110 001, India. Phone: +91 (11) 371-7927. Contact: D.P. Jatav, Director; or A.V. Bhavan, Chief Engineer.

All India Radio—Aizawl, Radio Tila, Tuikhuahtlang, Aizawl-796 001, Mizoram, India. Phone: +91 (3652) 2415. Contact: (technical) D.K. Sharma, Station Engineer; or T.R. Rabha, Station Engineer.

All India Radio—Bangalore

HEADQUARTERS: see All India Radio—External Services Division. *AIR OFFICE NEAR TRANSMITTER:* P.O. Box 5096, Bangalore-560 001, Karnataka, India. Phone: +91 (80) 261-243. Contact: (technical) C. Iyengar, Supervising Engineer.

All India Radio—Bhopal, Akashvani Bhawan, Shamla Hills, Bhopal-462 002, Madhya Pradesh, India. Phone: +91 (755) 540-041. Contact: (technical) C. Lal, Station Engineer.

All India Radio—Calcutta, G.P.O. Box 696, Calcutta—700 001, West Bengal, India. Phone: +91 (33) 248-9131. Contact: (technical) R.N. Dam, Supervising Engineer.

All India Radio—Chennai

EXTERNAL SERVICES: see All India Radio—External Services Division.
DOMESTIC SERVICE: Kamrajar Salai, Mylapore, Chennai-600 004, Tamil Nadu, India. Phone: +91 (44) 845-975. Contact: (technical) S. Bhatia, Supervising Engineer.

All India Radio—Delhi—*see* All India Radio—New Delhi.

All India Radio—External Services Division

MAIN ADDRESS: Broadcasting House, 1 Sansad Marg, P.O. Box 500, New Delhi-110 001, India. Phone: (general) +91 (11) 371-5411; (Director) +91 (11) 371-0057. Contact: (general) P.P. Setia, Director of External Services; or S.C. Panda, Audience Relations Officer; (technical) S.A.S. Abidi, Assistant Director Engineering (F.A.). E-mail (Research Dept.): rdair@giasdl01.vsnl.net.in; (comments on programs) air@kode.net. URLs: (includes RealAudio in English and other languages) http://allindiaradio.com; http://air.kode.net; (unofficial, but contains updated schedule information) www.angelfire.com/in/alokdg/air.html. Free monthly *India Calling* magazine and stickers. Replies erratic. Except for stations listed below, correspondence to domestic stations is more likely to be responded to if it is sent via the External Services Division; request that your letter be forwarded to the appropriate domestic station.

VERIFICATION ADDRESS: Prasar Bharati Corporation of India, Akashvani Bhawan, Room 204, Sansad Marg, New Delhi-110 001, India; or P.O. Box 500, New Delhi-110 001, India. Fax: +91 (11) 372 5212 or +91 (11) 371 4697. E-mail: faair@giasdl01.vsnl.net.in. Contact: R.K. Bhatnagar, Director, Frequency Assignments.

All India Radio—Gangtok, Old MLA Hostel, Gangtok—737 101, Sikkim, India. Phone: +91 (359) 22636. Contact: (general) Y.P. Yolmo, Station Director; (technical) Deepak Kumar, Station Engineer.

All India Radio—Gorakhpur

NEPALESE EXTERNAL SERVICE: see All India Radio—External Services Division.
DOMESTIC SERVICE: Post Bag 26, Gorakhpur-273 001, Uttar Pradesh, India. Phone: +91 (551) 337-401. Contact: (technical) Dr. S.M. Pradhan, Supervising Engineer.

All India Radio—Guwahati, P.O. Box 28, Chandmari, Guwahati-781 003, Assam, India. Phone: +91 (361) 540-135. Contact: (technical) P.C. Sanghi, Superindent Engineer.

All India Radio—Hyderabad, Rocklands, Saifabad, Hyderabad-500 004, Andhra Pradesh, India. Phone: +91 (40) 234-904. Contact: (technical) N. Srinivasan, Supervising Engineer.

All India Radio—Imphal, Palau Road, Imphal-795 001, Manipur, India. Phone: +91 (385) 20-534. Contact: (technical) M. Jayaraman, Supervising Engineer.

All India Radio—Itanagar, Naharlagun, Itanagar-791 110, Arunachal Pradesh, India. Phone: +91 (3781) 4485. Contact: J.T. Jirdoh, Station Director; or Suresh Naik, Superintending Engineer. Verifications direct from station are difficult, as engineering is done by staff visiting from the Regional Engineering Headquarters at AIR—Guwahati (*see*); that address might be worth contacting if all else fails.

All India Radio—Jaipur, 5 Park House, Mirza Ismail Road, Jaipur-302 001, Rajasthan, India. Phone: +91 (141) 366-623. Contact: (technical) S.C. Sharma, Station Engineer.

All India Radio—Jammu—*see* Radio Kashmir—Jammu.

All India Radio—Jeypore, Jeypore-764 005, Orissa, India. Phone: +91 (685) 422-524. Contact: P. Subramanium, Assistant Station Engineer; or A.C. Subuddhi, Assistant Engineer.

All India Radio—Kohima, Kohima-797 001, Nagaland, India. Phone: +91 (3866) 2121. Contact: (technical) K.G. Talwar, Superintending Engineer; K.K Jose, Assistant Engineer; or K. Morang, Assistant Station Engineer. Return postage, $1 or IRC helpful.

All India Radio—Kurseong, Mehta Club Building, Kurseong-734 203, Darjeeling District, West Bengal, India. Phone: +91 (3554) 350. Contact: (general) George Kuruvilla, Assistant Director; (technical) A.S. Guin, Chief Engineer; or R.K. Shina, Station Engineer.

All India Radio—Leh—see Radio Kashmir—Leh.

All India Radio—Lucknow, 18 Vidhan Sabha Marg, Lucknow-226 001, Uttar Pradesh, India. Phone: +91 (522) 244-130. Contact: R.K. Singh, Supervising Engineer. This station now appears to be replying via the External Services Division, New Delhi.

All India Radio—Mumbai

EXTERNAL SERVICES: see All India Radio—External Services Division.

COMMERCIAL SERVICE (VIVIDH BHARATI): All India Radio, P.O. Box 11497, 101 M K Road, Mumbai-400 0020, Maharashtra, India. Phone: (general) +91 (22) 203-1341 or +91 (22) 203-594; (director) +91 (22) 203-7702. Fax: +91 (22) 287 6040. Contact: Vijayalakshmi Sinha, Director.

DOMESTIC SERVICE: P.O. Box 13034, Mumbai-400 020, Maharashtra, India. Phone: +91 (22) 202-9853. Contact: S. Sundaram, Supervising Engineer; or Lak Bhatnagar, Supervisor, Frequency Assignments. Return postage helpful.

All India Radio—New Delhi, P.O. Box 70, New Delhi-110 011, India. Phone: (general) +91 (11) 371-0113. Contact: (technical) G.C. Tyagi, Supervising Engineer. $1 helpful.

All India Radio—Panaji

HEADQUARTERS: see All India Radio—External Services Division, above.

AIR OFFICE NEAR TRANSMITTER: P.O. Box 220, Altinho, Panaji-403 001, Goa, India. Phone: +91 (832) 5563. Contact: (technical) V.K. Singhla, Station Engineer; or G.N. Shetti, Assistant Engineer.

All India Radio—Port Blair, Dilanipur, Port Blair-744 102, South Andaman, Andaman & Nicobar Islands, Union Territory, India. Phone: +91 (3192) 20-682. Contact: (technical) Yuvraj Bajaj, Station Engineer. Registering letter appears to be useful. Don't send any cash with your correspondence as it appears to be a violation of their foreign currency regulations.

All India Radio—Ranchi, 6 Ratu Road, Ranchi-834 001, Bihar, India. Phone: +91 (651) 302-358. Contact: (technical) H.N. Agarwal, Supervising Engineer.

All India Radio—Shillong, P.O. Box 14, Shillong-793 001, Meghalaya, India. Phone: +91 (364) 224-443 or +91 (364) 222-781. Contact: (general) C. Lalsaronga, Director NEIS; (technical) H.K. Agarwal, Supervising Engineer. Free booklet on station's history.

All India Radio—Simla, Choura Maidan, Simla-171 004, Himachal Pradesh, India. Phone: +91 (177) 4809. Contact: (technical) B.K. Upadhayay, Supervising Engineer; or P.K. Sood, Assistant Station Engineer. Return postage helpful.

All India Radio—Srinagar—see Radio Kashmir—Srinagar.

All India Radio—Thiruvananthapuram, P.O. Box 403, Bhakti Vilas, Vazuthacaud, Thiruvananthapuram-695 014, Kerala, India. Phone: +91 (471) 65-009. Contact: (technical) K.M. Georgekutty, Station Engineer.

Ministry of Information & Broadcasting, Main Secretariat, A-Wing, Shastri Bhawan, New Delhi-110 001, India. Phone: (general) +91 (11) 338-4340, +91 (11) 338-4782 or +91 (11) 379-338; (Information & Broadcasting Secretary) +91 (11) 338-2639. Fax: +91 (11) 338 3513, +91 (11) 338 7823, +91 (11) 338 4785, +91 (11) 338 7617 or +91 (11) 338 1043. Contact: (general) N.P. Nawani, Information & Broadcasting Secretary; (administration) C.M. Ibrahim, Minister for Information & Broadcasting.

Radio Kashmir—Jammu, Begum Haveli, Old Palace Road, Jammu-180 001, Jammu & Kashmir, India. Phone: +91 (191) 544-411. Fax: +91 (191) 546 658. Contact: (technical) S.K. Sharma, Station Engineer.

Radio Kashmir—Leh, Leh-194 101, Ladakh District, Jammu & Kashmir, India. Phone: +91 (1982) 2263. Contact: (technical) L.K. Gandotar, Station Engineer.

Radio Kashmir—Srinagar, Sherwani Road, Srinagar-190 001, Jammu & Kashmir, India. Phone: +91 (194) 71-460. Contact: L. Rehman, Station Director.

Radio Tila—see All India Radio—Aizawl.

Trans World Radio

STUDIO: P.O. Box 4407, L-15, Green Park, New Delhi-110 016, India. Phone: +91 (11) 685-2568, +91 (11) 685-5674 or +91 (11) 686-1319. Fax: +91 (11) 686 8049. E-mail: emiljeba@nda.vsnl.net.in. URL: www..gospelcom.net/twr/zsa.index.htm. Contact: N. Emil Jebasingh, Director. This office is used for program production and answering listeners' correspondence, and does not have its own transmission facilities.

ON-AIR ADDRESS: P.O. Box 5, Andhra Pradesh, India.

INDONESIA

World Time +7 Western: Waktu Indonesia Bagian Barat (Jawa, Sumatera); +8 Central: Waktu Indonesia Bagian Tengal (Bali, Kalimantan, Sulawesi, Nusa Tenggara); +9 Eastern: Waktu Indonesia Bagian Timur (Irian Jaya, Maluku).

NOTE: Except where otherwise indicated, Indonesian stations, especially those of the Radio Republik Indonesia (RRI) network, will reply to at least some correspondence in English. However, correspondence in Indonesian is more likely to ensure a reply.

Kang Guru II Radio English, Indonesia Australia Language Foundation, Kotak Pos 6756 JKSRB, Jakarta 12067, Indonesia. E-mail: kangguru@denpasar.wasantara.net.id. Contact: Walter Slamer, Kang Guru Project Manager. This program is aired over various RRI outlets, including Jakarta and Sorong. Continuation of this project, currently sponsored by Australia's AusAID, will depend upon whether adequate supplementary funding can be made available.

Radio Pemerintah Daerah Kabupaten TK II—RPDK Ende, Jalan Panglima Sudirman, Ende, Flores, Nusa Tenggara Timor, Indonesia. Contact: (technical) Thomas Keropong, YC9LHD. Return postage required.

Radio Pemerintah Daerah Kabupaten TK II—RPDK Manggarai, Ruteng, Flores, Nusa Tenggara Timur, Indonesia. Contact: Simon Saleh, B.A. Return postage required.

Radio Pemerintah Daerah Kabupaten Daerah TK II—RSPDKD Ngada, Jalan Soekarno-Hatta, Bjawa, Flores, Nusa Tenggara Tengah, Indonesia. Phone: +62 (384) 21-142. Contact: Drs. Petrus Tena, Kepala Studio.

Radio Republik Indonesia—RRI Ambon, Jalan Jenderal Akhmad Yani 1, Ambon, Maluku, Indonesia. Contact: Drs. H. Ali Amran or Pirla C. Noija, Kepala Seksi Siaran. A very poor replier to correspondence in recent years. Correspondence in Indonesian and return postage essential.

Radio Republik Indonesia—RRI Banda Aceh (when operating), Kotak Pos 112, Banda Aceh, Aceh, Indonesia. Contact: Parmono Prawira, Technical Director; or S.H. Rosa Kim. Return postage helpful.

Radio Republik Indonesia—RRI Bandar Lampung, Kotak Pos 24, Bandar Lampung 35213, Indonesia. Phone: +62 (721) 52-280. Fax: +62 (721) 62 767. Contact: M. Nasir Agun, Kepala Stasiun; Hi Hanafie Umar; Djarot Nursinggih, Tech. Transmission; Drs. Zulhaqqi Hafiz, Kepala Sub Seksi Periklanan; or Asmara Haidar Manaf. Return postage helpful. Replies in Indonesian to correspondence in English or Indonesian.

Radio Republik Indonesia—RRI Bandung (when operating), Stasiun Regional 1, Kotak Pos 1055, Bandung 40010, Jawa Barat, Indonesia. Contact: Drs. Idrus Alkaf, Kepala Stasiun; Mrs. Ati Kusmiati; or Eem Suhaemi, Kepala Seksi Siaran. Return postage or IRC helpful.

Radio Republik Indonesia—RRI Banjarmasin (when operating), Stasiun Nusantara 111, Kotak Pos 117, Banjarmasin 70234, Kalimantan Selatan, Indonesia. Contact: Jul Chaidir, Stasiun Kepala; or Harmyn Husein. Free stickers. Return postage or IRCs helpful.

Radio Republik Indonesia—RRI Bengkulu, Stasiun Regional 1, Kotak Pos 13 Kawat, Kotamadya Bengkulu, Indonesia. Contact: Drs. Drs. Jasran Abubakar, Kepala Stasiun. Free picture postcards, decals and tourist literature. Return postage or 2 IRCs helpful.

Radio Republik Indonesia—RRI Biak (when operating), Kotak Pos 505, Biak, Irian Jaya, Indonesia. Contact: D. Latuperissa, Head of Station.

Radio Republik Indonesia—RRI Bukittinggi (when operating), Stasiun Regional 1 Bukittinggi, Jalan Prof. Muhammad Yamin 199, Aurkuning, Bukittinggi 26131, Propinsi Sumatera Barat, Indonesia. Fax: +62 (752) 367 132. Contact: Mr. Effendi, Sekretaris; Zul Arifin Mukhtar, SH; or Samirwan Sarjana Hukum, Producer, "Phone in Program." Replies to correspondence in Indonesian or English. Return postage helpful.

Radio Republik Indonesia—RRI Denpasar (when operating), Kotak Pos 3031, Denpasar 80030, Bali, Indonesia. Contact: Drs. Utiek Ruktiningsih, Kepala Stasiun. Replies slowly to correspondence in Indonesian. Return postage or IRCs helpful.

Radio Republik Indonesia—RRI Dili (when operating), Stasiun Regional 1 Dili, Jalan Kaikoli, Kotak Pos 103, Dili 88000, Timor-Timur, Indonesia. Contact: Harry A. Silalahi, Kepala Stasiun; Arnoldus Klau; or Paul J. Amalo, BA. Return postage or $1 helpful. Replies occasionally to correspondence in Indonesian.

Radio Republik Indonesia—RRI Fak Fak, Jalan Kapten P. Tendean, Kotak Pos 54, Fak-Fak 98601, Irian Jaya, Indonesia. Contact: Bahrun Siregar, Kepala Stasiun; Aloys Ngotra, Kepala Seksi Siaran; or Richart Tan, Kepala Sub Seksi Siaran Kata. Station plans to upgrade its transmitting facilities with the help of the Japanese government. Return postage required. Replies occasionally.

Radio Republik Indonesia—RRI Gorontalo, Jalan Jenderal Sudirman, Gorontalo 96128, Sulawesi Utara, Indonesia. Contact: Drs. Muh. Assad, Kepala; or Saleh S. Thalib, Technical Manager. Return postage helpful. Replies occasionally, preferably to correspondence in Indonesian.

🔊**Radio Republik Indonesia—RRI Jakarta**
STATION: Stasiun Nasional Jakarta, Kotak Pos 356, Jakarta, Daerah Khusus Jakarta Raya, Indonesia. URL: (RealAudio via cyberstation Syahreza Radio) www.hway.net/syahreza/rri.htm. Contact: Drs.R. Baskara, Stasiun Kepala; or Drs. Syamsul Muin Harahap, Kepala Stasiun. Return postage helpful. Replies irregularly.

"DATELINE" ENGLISH PROGRAM: see Kang Guru II Radio English.
"U.N. CALLING ASIA" ENGLISH PROGRAM: Program via RRI Jakarta Programa Ibukota Satu, every Sunday. Contact address same as United Nations Radio *(see)*.

Radio Republik Indonesia—RRI Jambi
STATION: Jalan Jenderal A. Yani 5, Telanaipura, Jambi 36122, Propinsi Jambi, Indonesia. Contact: M. Yazid, Kepala Siaran; H. Asmuni Lubis, BA; or Buchari Muhammad, Kepala Stasiun. Return postage helpful.

Radio Republik Indonesia—RRI Jayapura, Kotak Pos 1077, Jayapura 99222, Irian Jaya, Indonesia. Contact: Harry Liborang, Direktorat Radio; or Dr. David Alex Siahainenia, Kepala. Return postage helpful.

Radio Republik Indonesia—RRI Kendari, Kotak Pos 7, Kendari 93111, Sulawesi Tenggara, Indonesia. Contact: H. Sjahbuddin, BA; Muniruddin Amin, Programmer; or Drs. Supandi. Return postage required. Replies slowly to correspondence in Indonesian.

Radio Republik Indonesia—RRI Kupang (Regional I), Jalan Tompello 8, Kupang, Timor, Indonesia. Contact: Drs. P.M. Tisera, Kepala Stasiun; Qustigap Bagang, Kepala Seksi Siaran; or Said Rasyid, Kepala Studio. Return postage helpful. Correspondence in Indonesian preferred. Replies occasionally.

Radio Republik Indonesia—RRI Madiun (when operating), Jalan Mayor Jenderal Panjaitan 10, Madiun, Jawa Timur, Indonesia. Fax: +62 (351) 4964. Contact: Imam Soeprapto, Kepala Seksi Siaran. Replies to correspondence in English or Indonesian. Return postage helpful.

Radio Republik Indonesia—RRI Malang (when operating), Kotak Pos 78, Malang 65112, Jawa Timur, Indonesia; or Jalan Candi Panggung No. 58, Mojolangu, Malang 65142, Indonesia. Contact: Drs.Tjutju Tjuar Na Adikorya, Kepala Stasiun; Ml. Mawahib, Kepala Seksi Siaran; or Dra Hartati Soekemi, Mengetahui. Return postage required. Free history and other booklets. Replies irregularly to correspondence in Indonesian.

Radio Republik Indonesia—RRI Manado, Kotak Pos 1110, Manado 95124 Propinsi Sulawesi Utara, Indonesia. Fax: +62 (431) 63 492. Contact: Costher H. Gulton, Kepala Stasiun. Free stickers and postcards. Return postage or $1 required. Replies occasionally to correspondence in Indonesian.

Radio Republik Indonesia—RRI Manokwari, Regional II, Jalan Merdeka 68, Manokwari, Irian Jaya, Indonesia. Contact: Nurdin Mokogintu. Return postage helpful.

Radio Republik Indonesia—RRI Mataram (when operating), Stasiun Regional I Mataram, Jalan Langko 83 Ampenan, Mataram 83114, Nusa Tenggara Barat, Indonesia. Phone: +62 (364) 33-713 or +62 (364) 21-355. Contact: Drs. Hamid Djasman, Kepala; or Bochri Rachman, Ketua Dewan Pimpinan Harian. Free stickers. Return postage required. With sufficient return postage or small token gift, sometimes sends tourist information and Batik print. Replies to correspondence in Indonesian.

Radio Republik Indonesia—RRI Medan, Jalan Letkol Martinus Lubis 5, Medan 20232, Sumatera, Indonesia. Phone: +62 (61) 324-222/441. Fax: +62 (61) 512 161. Contact: Kepala Stasiun, Ujamalul Abidin Ass; Drs. S. Parlin Tobing, SH, Produsennya, "Kontak Pendengar"; Drs. H. Suryanta Saleh; or Suprato. Free stickers. Return postage required. Replies to correspondence in Indonesian.

Radio Republik Indonesia—RRI Merauke, Stasiun Regional 1, Kotak Pos 11, Merauke, Irian Jaya, Indonesia. Contact: (general) Drs. Buang Akhir, Direktor; Achmad Ruskaya

B.A., Kepala Stasiun, Drs.Tuanakotta Semuel, Kepala Seksi Siaran; or John Manuputty, Kepala Subseksi Pemancar; (technical) Daf'an Kubangun, Kepala Seksi Tehnik. Return postage helpful.

Radio Republik Indonesia—RRI Nabire (when operating), Kotak Pos 110, Jalan Merdeka 74 Nabire 98801, Irian Jaya, Indonesia. Contact: Muchtar Yushaputra, Kepala Stasiun. Free stickers and occasional free picture postcards. Return postage or IRCs helpful.

Radio Republik Indonesia—RRI Padang, Kotak Pos 77, Padang 25121, Sumatera Barat, Indonesia. Phone: +61 (751) 28-363. Contact: H. Hutabarat, Kepala Stasiun; or Amir Hasan, Kepala Seksi Siaran. Return postage helpful.

Radio Republik Indonesia—RRI Palangkaraya, Jalan M. Husni Thamrin 1, Palangkaraya 73111, Kalimantan Tengah, Indonesia. Phone: +62 (514) 21-779. Fax: +62 (514) 21 778. Contact: Drs.Amiruddin; S. Polin; A.F. Herry Purwanto; Meyiwati SH; Supardal Djojosubrojo, Sarjana Hukum; Gumer Kamis; or Ricky D. Wader, Kepala Stasiun. Return postage helpful. Will respond to correspondence in Indonesian or English.

Radio Republik Indonesia—RRI Palembang, Jalan Radio 2, Km. 4, Palembang, Sumatera Selatan, Indonesia. Contact: Drs. H. Mursjid Noor, Kepala Stasiun; H.Ahmad Syukri Ahkab, Kepala Seksi Siaran; or H.Iskandar Suradilaga. Return postage helpful. Replies slowly and occasionally.

Radio Republik Indonesia—RRI Palu, Jalan R.A. Kartini 39, 94112 Palu, Sulawesi Tengah, Indonesia. Phone: +62 (451) 21-621. Contact: Akson Boole; Nyonyah Netty Ch. Soriton, Kepala Seksi Siaran; Gugun Santoso; Untung Santoso, Kepala Seksi Teknik; or M. Hasjim, Head of Programming. Return postage required. Replies slowly to correspondence in Indonesian.

Radio Republik Indonesia—RRI Pekanbaru, Kotak Pos 51, Pekanbaru, Riau, Indonesia. Phone: +62 (761) 22-081. Fax: +62 (761) 23 605. Contact: (general) Drs. Mukidi, Kepala Stasiun; Arisun Agus, Kepala Seksi Siaran; Drs. H. Syamsidi, Kepala Supag Tata Usaha; or Zainal Abbas. Return postage helpful.

Radio Republik Indonesia—RRI Pontianak, Kotak Pos 1005, Pontianak 78111, Kalimantan Barat, Indonesia. Contact: Ruddy Banding, Kepala Seksi Siaran; Achmad Ruskaya, BA; Drs. Effendi Afati, Producer, "Dalam Acara Kantong Surat"; Subagio, Kepala Sub Bagian Tata Usaha; Augustwus Campek; Rahayu Widati; Suryadharma, Kepala Sub Seksi Programa; or Muchlis Marzuki B.A. Return postage or $1 helpful. Replies some of the time to correspondence in Indonesian (preferred) or English.

Radio Republik Indonesia—RRI Samarinda, Kotak Pos 45, Samarinda, Kalimantan Timur 75001, Indonesia. Phone: +62 (541) 43-495. Fax: +62 (541) 41 693. Contact: Siti Thomah, Kepala Seksi Siaran; Tyranus Lenjau, English Announcer; S. Yati; Marthin Tapparan; or Sunendra, Kepala Stasiun. May send tourist brochures and maps. Return postage helpful. Replies to correspondence in Indonesian.

Radio Republik Indonesia—RRI Semarang (when operating), Kotak Pos 1073, Semarang Jateng, Jawa Tengah, Indonesia. Phone: +62 (24) 316 501. Contact: Djarwanto, SH; Drs. Sabeni, Doktorandus; Drs. Purwadi, Program Director; Dra. Endang Widiastuti, Kepala Sub Seksi Periklanan Jasa dan Hak Cipta; Bagus Giarto, Kepala Stasiun; or Mardanon, Kepala Teknik. Return postage helpful.

Radio Republik Indonesia—RRI Serui, Jalan Pattimura Kotak Pos 19, Serui 98211, Irian Jaya, Indonesia. Contact: Agus Raunsai, Kepala Stasiun; J. Lolouan, BA, Kepala Studio; Ketua Tim Pimpinan Harian, Kepala Seksi Siaran; Yance Yebi-Yebi; Natalis Edowai; Albertus Corputty; or Drs. Jasran Abubakar. Replies occasionally to correspondence in Indonesian. IRC or return postage helpful.

Radio Republik Indonesia—RRI Sibolga (when operating), Jalan Ade Irma Suryani, Nasution No. 5, Sibolga, Sumatera Utara, Indonesia. Contact: Mrs. Laiya, Mrs. S. Sitoupul or B.A. Tanjung. Return postage required. Replies occasionally to correspondence in Indonesian.

Radio Republik Indonesia—RRI Sorong
STATION: Kotak Pos 146, Sorong 98414, Irian Jaya, Indonesia. Phone: +62 (951) 21-003, +62 (951) 22-111, or +62 (951) 22-611. Contact: Drs. Sallomo Hamid; Tetty Rumbay S., Kasubsi Siaran Kata; Mrs. Tien Widarsanto, Resa Kasi Siaran; Ressa Molle; Mughpar Yushaputra, Kepala Stasiun; or Linda Rumbay. Return postage helpful. Replies to correspondence in English. *"DATELINE" ENGLISH PROGRAM: See* Kang Guru II Radio English.

Radio Republik Indonesia—RRI Sumenep (when operating), Jalan Urip Sumoharjo 26, Sumenep, Madura, Jawa Timur, Indonesia. Contact: Dian Irianto, Kepala Stasiun. Return postage helpful.

Radio Republik Indonesia—RRI Surabaya, Stasiun Regional 1, Kotak Pos 239, Surabaya 60271, Jawa Timur, Indonesia. Phone: +62 (31) 41-327. Fax: +62 (31) 42 351. Contact: Zainal Abbas, Kepala Stasiun; Usmany Johozua, Kepala Seksi Siaran; Drs. E. Agus Widjaja, MM, Kasi Siaran; or Ny Koen Tarjadi. Return postage or IRCs helpful.

Radio Republik Indonesia—RRI Surakarta (when operating), Kotak Pos 40, Surakarta 57133, Jawa Tengah, Indonesia. Contact: H. Tomo, B.A., Head of Broadcasting; or Titiek Sudartik, SH., Kepala. Return postage helpful.

Radio Republik Indonesia—RRI Tanjungpinang, Stasiun RRI Regional II Tanjungpinang, Kotak Pos 8, Tanjungpinang 29123, Riau, Indonesia. Contact: M. Yazid, Kepala Stasiun; Wan Suhardi, Produsennya, "Siaran Bahasa Melayu"; or Rosakim, Sarjana Hukum. Return postage helpful. Replies occasionally to correspondence in Indonesian or English.

Radio Republik Indonesia—RRI Ternate, Jalan Kedaton, Ternate (Ternate), Maluku, Indonesia. Contact: (general) Abd. Latief Kamarudin, Kepala Stasiun; (technical) Rusdy Bachmid, Head of Engineering; or Abubakar Alhadar. Return postage helpful.

Radio Republik Indonesia Tual (when operating), Tual, Kepulauan Kai, Maluku, Indonesia.

Radio Republik Indonesia—RRI Ujung Pandang, RRI Nusantara IV, Kotak Pos 103, Ujung Pandang, Sulawesi Selatan, Indonesia. Contact: H. Kamaruddin Alkaf Yasin, Head of Broadcasting Department; Beni Koesbani, Kepala Stasiun; L.A. Rachim Ganie; Ashan Muhammad, Kepala Bidang Teknik; or Drs. Bambang Pudjono. Return postage, $1 or IRCs helpful. Replies irregularly and sometimes slowly.

Radio Republik Indonesia—RRI Wamena, RRI Regional II, Kotak Pos 10, Wamena, Irian Jaya 99501, Indonesia. Contact: Yoswa Kumurawak, Penjab Subseksi Pemancar. Return postage helpful.

Radio Republik Indonesia—RRI Yogyakarta, Jalan Amat Jazuli 4, Kotak Pos 18, Yogyakarta 55224, Jawa Tengah, Indonesia. Fax: +62 (274) 2784. Contact: Phoenix Sudomo Sudaryo; Tris Mulyanti, Seksi Programa Siaran; Martono, ub. Kabid Penyelenggaraan Siaran; Mr. Kadis, Technical Department; or Drs. H. Hamdan Sjahbeni, Kepala Stasiun. IRC, return postage or $1 helpful. Replies occasionally to correspondence in Indonesian or English.

Radio Siaran Pemerintah Daerah TK II—RSPD Halmahera Tengah, Soasio, Jalan A. Malawat, Soasio, Maluku Tengah 97812, Indonesia. Contact: Drs. S. Chalid A. Latif, Kepala Badan Pengelola.

Radio Siaran Pemerintah Daerah TK II—RSPD Sumba Timur, Jalan Gajah Mada 10 Hambala, Waingapu, Nusa Tenggara Timur 87112, Indonesia. Contact: Simon Petrus, Penanggung Jawab Operasional. Replies slowly and rarely to correspondence in Indonesian.

Voice of Indonesia, Kotak Pos 1157, Jakarta 10001, Daerah Khusus Jakarta Raya, Indonesia. Phone: +62 (21) 720-3467, +62 (21) 355-381 or +62 (21) 349-091. Fax: +62 (21) 345 7132. Contact: Anastasia Yasmine, Head of Foreign Affairs Section. Free stickers and calendars. Very slow in replying.

IRAN   World Time +3:30 (+4:30 midyear)

🔊Voice of the Islamic Republic of Iran
MAIN OFFICE: IRIB External Services, P.O. Box 19395-6767, Tehran, Iran; or P.O. Box 19395-3333, Tehran, Iran. Phone: (IRIB Public Relations) +98 (21) 204-001/2/3 and +98 (21) 204-6894/5. Fax: (external services) +98 (21) 205 1635, +98 (21) 204 1097 or +98 (21) 291 095; (IRIB Public Relations) +98 (21) 205 3305/7; (IRIB Central Administration) +98 (21) 204 1051; (technical) +98 (21) 654 841. E-mail: (general) webmaster@irib.com; irib@dci.iran.com; (technical, Mohsen Amiri) rezairib@dci.iran.com; (Research Centre) iribrec@dci.iran.com. URL: (includes RealAudio) www.irib.com/. Contact: (general) Hamid Yasamin, Public Affairs; Ali Larijani, Head; or Hameed Barimani, Producer, "Listeners Special"; (administration) J. Ghanbari, Director General; or J. Sarafraz, Deputy Managing Director; (technical) M. Ebrahim Vassigh, Frequency Manageri. Free seven-volume set of books on Islam, magazines, calendars, book markers, tourist literature and postcards. Verifications require a minimum of two days' reception data, plus return postage. Station is currently asking their listeners to send in their telephone numbers so that they can call and talk to them directly. Upon request they will even broadcast your conversation on air. You can send your phone number to the postal address above or you can fax it to: +98 (21) 205 1635. If English Service doesn't reply, then try writing the French Service in French.
ENGINEERING ACTIVITIES, TEHRAN: IRIB, P.O. Box 15875-4344, Tehran, Iran. Phone: +98 (21) 2196-6127. Fax: +98 (21) 204 1051, +98 (21) 2196 6268 or +98 (21) 172 924. Contact: Mrs. Niloufar Parviz.
ENGINEERING ACTIVITIES, HESSARAK/KARAJ: IRIB, P.O. Box 155, Hessarak/Karaj, Iran. Phone: +98 (21) 204-0008, +98 (21) 216-2774/79, +98 (21) 872-7549, or +98 (21) 204-0008. Fax: +98 (21) 2617 4926 or +98 (21) 885 6863. E-mail: rezairib@dci.iran.com; (Mohsen Amiri) moazzami@irib.com; or (Majid Farahmandnia) farahmand@irib.com. Contact: Mohsen Amiri, Manager of Kamalabad Shortwave Center; M. Ebrahim Vasigh; or Majid Farahmandnia, Frequency Control & Design Bureau.
BONN BUREAU, NONTECHNICAL: Puetzsir. 34, 53129 Bonn, Postfach 150 140, D-53040 Bonn, Germany. Phone: +49 (228) 231-001. Fax: +49 (228) 231 002.
LONDON BUREAU, NONTECHNICAL: c/o WTN, IRIB, The Interchange Oval Road, Camden Lock, London NWI, United Kingdom. Phone: +44 (171) 284-3668. Fax: +44 (171) 284 3669.
PARIS BUREAU, NONTECHNICAL: 27 rue de Liège, escalier B, 1ᵉ étage, porte D, F-75008 Paris, France. Phone: +33 (1) 4293-1273. Fax: +33 (1) 4293 0513.

Mashhad Regional Radio, P.O. Box 555, Mashhad Center, Jomhoriye Eslame, Iran. Contact: J. Ghanbari, General Director.

IRAQ   World Time +3 (+4 midyear)

Radio Iraq International (Idha'at al-Iraq al-Duwaliyah)
MAIN OFFICE: P.O. Box 8145 CN.12222, Baghdad, Iraq; if no reply try, P.O. Box 8125, Baghdad, Iraq; or P.O. Box 7728, Baghdad, Iraq. Contact: M. el Wettar. All broadcasting facilities in Iraq are currently suffering from operational difficulties.
INDIA ADDRESS: P.O. Box 3044, New Delhi 110003, India.

IRELAND   World Time exactly (+1 midyear)

🔊Radio Telefis Eireann (Irish Overseas Broadcasting), P.O. Box 4950, Dublin 1, Ireland. Phone, offices: (general) +353 (1) 208-3111; (Broadcasting Development) +353 (1) 208-2350. Phone, concise news bulletins: (United States, special charges apply) +1 (900) 420-2411; (United Kingdom) +44 (891) 871-116; (Australia) +61 (3) 552-1140. Phone, concise sports bulletins: (United States, special charges apply) +1(900) 420-2412; (United Kingdom) +44 (891) 871-117; (Australia) +61 (3) 552-1141. Fax: (general) +353 (1) 208 3082; (Broadcasting Development) +353 (1) 208 3031. E-mail: (Boyd) boydw@rte.ie. URLs: (general, includes RealAudio) www.rte.ie/radio/; (RealAudio, some programs) www.wrn.org/ondemand/ireland.html. Contact: Wesley Boyd, Director of Broadcast Development; Julie Hayde; or Bernie Pope, Reception. IRC appreciated. Offers a variety of video tapes (mostly PAL, but a few "American Standard"), CDs and audio casettes for sale from RTE Commercial Enterprises Ltd, Box 1947, Donnybrook, Dublin 4, Ireland; (phone) +353 (1) 208-3453; (fax) +353 (1) 208 2620. A full list of what's on offer can be viewed at www.rte.ie/lib/store.html#music. Regular transmissions via Singapore and WWCR (USA)—*see* next item—and irregularly via other countries for sports or election coverage.
RTE Radio—a half-hour information bulletin from RTE's (*see*, above) domestic Radio 1, relayed on shortwave. Mailing address: Broadcasting Developments, RTE, Dublin 4, Ireland. Phone: +353 (1) 208-2350. Fax: +353 (1) 208 3031. E-mail: haydej@rte.ie. URL: www.rte.ie/radio/worldwide.html. Contact: Julie Hayde.

ISRAEL   World Time +2 (+3 midyear)

Bezeq, The Israel Telecommunication Corp Ltd, Engineering & Planning Division, Radio & T.V. Broadcasting Section, P.O. Box 62081, Tel-Aviv 61620, Israel. Phone: +972 (3) 626-4562 or +972 (3) 626-4500. Fax: +972 (3) 626 4558/59. E-mail: moshe_oren@bezeq.co.il. URL: www.bezeq.co.il. Contact: Moshe Oren, Frequency Manager. Bezeq is responsible for transmitting the programs of the Israel Broadcasting Authority (IBA), which *inter alia* parents Kol Israel. This address only for pointing out transmitter-related problems (interference, modulation quality, network mixups, etc.), especially by fax, of transmitters based in Israel. Verifications not given out at this office; requests for verification should be sent to English Department of Kol Israel (*see* below).

🔊Galei Zahal (Israel Defence Forces Radio), Zahal, Military Mail No. 01005, Israel. Phone: +972 (3) 512-6666. Fax: +972 (3) 512 6760. E-mail: ofer@glz.co.il. URL: (includes RealAudio) www.glz.co.il/~ofer/Hebrew/index.html. Israeli law allows the Galei Zahal, as well as the Israel Broadcasting

Toshimichi Ohtake is PASSPORT's **man in Japan. He first became involved with international broadcasting while still a young man in college.** IBS

Authority, to air broadcasts beamed to outside Israel. Occasionally heard on Kol Israel frequencies when the latter is affected by industrial action; also sporadically on out-of-band channels via unknown transmitters.

🕮Kol Israel (Israel Radio, the Voice of Israel)
STUDIOS: Israel Broadcasting Authority, P.O. Box 1082, Jerusalem 91010, Israel. Phone: (general) +972 (2) 302-222; (Engineering Dept.) +972 (2) 535-051; (administration) +972 (2) 248-715. Fax: (English Service) +972 (2) 530 2424; (Engineering Dept.) +972 (2) 388 821; (other) +972 (2) 248 392 or +972 (2) 302 327. E-mail: (general) ask@israel-info.gov.il; (correspondence relating to reception problems, only) engineering@israelradio.org. URLs: (schedule, RealAudio) www.israelradio.org; (IBA parent organization) www.iba.org.il; (Reshet Bet domestic Hebrew service, including RealAudio) http://bet.iba.org.il. Contact: Edmond Sehayeq, Head of Programming, Arabic, Persian & Yemenite broadcasts; Yishai Eldar, Senior Editor, English Service; or Sara Gabai, Head of English Service; (administration) Shmuel Ben-Zvi, Director; (technical, frequency management) Raphael Kochanowski, Director of Liaison & Coordination, Engineering Dept. Various political, religious, tourist, immigration and language publications. IRC required for reply.
SAN FRANCISCO OFFICE, SCHEDULES: 2654 17th Avenue, San Francisco CA 94116 USA. Phone: +1 (415) 564-9968. E-mail: GPoppin@aol.com. Contact: George Poppin. This address, a volunteer office, only provides Kol Israel schedules. All other correspondence should be sent directly to the main office in Jerusalem.

ITALY   World Time +1 (+2 midyear)

Adventist World Radio, the Voice of Hope, AWR Europe Region, P.O. Box 383, I-47100 Forlì, Italy. Phone: +39 (0543) 766-655. Fax: +39 (0543) 768 198. E-mail: awritaly@mbox.queen.it. Contact: Erika Gysin, Listener Mail Services. This office will verify reports for AWR broadcasts from Armenia, Italy, Russia and Slovakia. Free religious printed matter, bi-annual *AWR Current* newsletter, stickers, program schedules and other small souvenirs. Return postage, IRCs or $1 appreciated. Prepares "Radio Magazine," a DX program produced by Dario Villani. AWR has a license to operate the existing station at Forlì, as well as a new facility which is soon to be built near Argenta. Also, *see* AWR listings under Costa Rica, Guam, Guatemala, Kenya and USA.

🕮Italian Radio Relay Service, IRRS-Shortwave, Nexus-IBA, C.P. 10980, 20100 Milano, Italy; or alternatively, to expedite cassette deliveries only: NEXUS-IBA, Attn. Anna Boschetti, P.O. Box 11028, I-20110 Milano, Italy. Phone: +39 (02) 266-6971. Fax: +39 (02) 7063 8151. E-mail: (general) info@nexus.org; ("Hello There" program, broadcast on special occasions only) ht@nexus.org; (reception reports of test transmissions) reports@nexus.org; (International Public Access Radio, a joint venture of IRRS and WRMI, USA) IPAR@nexus.org; (Alfredo Cotroneo) alfredo@nexus.org; (Ron Norton) ron@nexus.org. URLs: (general) www.nexus.org; (RealAudio) www.nexus.org/IRN/index.html; (schedules) www.nexus.org/NEXUS-IBA/Schedules; (International Public Access Radio) www.nexus.org/IPAR; (Internet Services) www.nexus.org/NEXUS-IBA/Services/index-english.html. Contact: (general) Ms. Anna S. Boschetti, Verification Manager; Alfredo E. Cotroneo, President & Producer of "Hello There"; (technical) Ron Norton. Due to recent funding cuts, this station cannot assure a reply to all listener's mail. E-mail correspondence and reception reports by e-mail are answered promptly and at no charge. A number of booklets and sometimes stickers and small souvenirs are available for sale, but check their website for further details. Two IRCs or $1 helpful.

Radio Europa International, via Gerardi 6, 25124 Brescia, Italy. Contact: Mariarosa Zahella. Replies irregularly, but return postage helpful.

Radio Europe, P.O. Box 12, 20090 Limito di Pioltello, Milan, Italy. Phone: +39 (02) 3931-0347. Fax: +39 (02) 8645 0149. E-mail: 100135.54@compuserve.com. Contact: Dario Monferini, Foreign Relations Director; or Alex Bertini, General Manager. Pennants $5 and T-shirts $25. $30 for a lifetime membership to Radio Europe's Listeners' Club. Membership includes T-shirt, poster, stickers, flags, gadgets, and so forth, with a monthly drawing for prizes. Application forms available from station. Sells airtime for $20 per hour. Two IRCs or $1 return postage appreciated.

Radio Maria Network Europe, Spoleto relay, Via Turati 7, 22036 Erba, Italy. Fax: +39 (031) 611 288. URL: www.cta.it/aziende/r_maria/info.htm.

Radiorama Radio, C.P. 873, 34100 Trieste, Italy. Contact: Valerio G. Cavallo. Program over the Italian Radio Relay Service (*see*). Verifies directly.

🕮Radio Roma-RAI International (external services)
MAIN OFFICE: External/Foreign Service, Centro RAI, Saxa Rubra, 00188 Rome, Italy; or P.O. Box 320, Correspondence Sector, 00100 Rome, Italy. Phone: +39 (06) 33-17-2360. Fax: +39 (06) 33 17 18 95 or +39 (06) 322 6070. E-mail: raiinternational@rai.it. URL: www.raiinternational.rai.it/radio/radio.htm. Contact: (general) Rosaria Vassallo,

Correspondence Sector; or Augusto Milana, Editor-in-Chief, Shortwave Programs in Foreign Languages; Esther Casas, Servicio Español; (administration) Angela Buttiglione, Managing Director; or Gabriella Tambroni, Assistant Director. Free stickers, banners, calendars and *RAI Calling from Rome* magazine. Can provide supplementary materials, including on VHS and CD-ROM, for Italian-language video course, "Viva l' italiano," with an audio equivalent soon to be offered, as well. Is constructing "a new, more powerful and sophisticated shortwave transmitting center" in Tuscany; when this is activated, RAI International plans to expand news, cultural items and music in Italian and various other language services—including Spanish, Portuguese, Italian, plus new services in Chinese and Japanese. Responses can be very slow. Note: pictures of RAI's Shortwave Center at Prato Smeraldo can be found at www.mediasuk.org/rai/.

SHORTWAVE FREQUENCY MONITORING OFFICE: RAI Monitoring Station, Centro di Controllo, Via Mirabellino 1, 20052 Monza (MI), Italy. Phone: +39 (039) 388-389. Phone/fax (ask for fax): +39 (039) 386-222. E-mail: cqmonza@rai.it. Contact: Signora Giuseppina Moretti, Frequency Management; or Mario Ballabio.

ENGINEERING OFFICE, ROME: Via Teulada 66, 00195 Rome, Italy. Phone: +39 (06) 331-70721. Fax: +39 (06) 331 75142 or +39 (06) 372 3376. E-mail: isola@rai.it. Contact: Clara Isola.

ENGINEERING OFFICE, TURIN: Via Cernaia 33, 10121 Turin, Italy. Phone: +39 (011) 810-2293. Fax: +39 (011) 575 9610. E-mail: allamano@rai.it. Contact: Giuseppe Allamano.

NEW YORK OFFICE, NONTECHNICAL: 1350 Avenue of the Americas—21st floor, New York NY 10019 USA. Phone: +1 (212) 468-2500. Fax: +1 (212) 765 1956. Contact: Umberto Bonetti, Deputy Director of Radio Division. RAI caps, aprons and tote bags for sale at Boutique RAI, c/o the aforementioned New York address.

SAN FRANCISCO OFFICE, SCHEDULES: 2654 17th Avenue, San Francisco CA 94116 USA. Phone: +1 (415) 564-9968. E-mail: GPoppin@aol.com. Contact: George Poppin. This address, a volunteer office, only provides RAI schedules to listeners. All other correspondence should be sent directly to the main office in Rome.

Radio Speranza, Modena (when active), Largo San Giorgio 91, 41100 Modena, Italy. Phone/fax: +39 (059) 230-373. Contact: Padre Cordioli Luigi, Missionario Redentorista. Free Italian-language newsletter. Replies enthusiastically to correspondence in Italian. Return postage appreciated.

Radio Strike, Palermo, c/o R. Scaglione, P.O. Box 119, Succ. 34, 90144 Palermo, Italy.

RTV Italiana-RAI (domestic services)

CALTANISSETTA: Radio Uno, Via Cerda 19, 90139 Palermo, Sicily, Italy. Contact: Gestione Risorse, Transmission Quality Control. $1 required.

ROME: Centro RAI, Saxa Rubra, 00188 Rome, Italy. Fax: +39 (06) 322 6070. E-mail: grr@rai.it. URLs (experimental): (general) http:www.rai.it/; (RealAudio) www.rai.it/grr.

Tele Radio Stereo, Roma, Via Bitossi 18, 00136 Roma, Italy. Fax: + 39 (06) 353 48300.

IVORY COAST—*see* Côte d'Ivoire

JAPAN   World Time +9

NHK Fukuoka, 1-1-10 Ropponmatsu, Chuo-ku, Fukuoka-shi, Fukuoka 810-77, Japan.

NHK Osaka, 3-43 Bamba-cho, Chuo-ku, Osaka 540-01, Japan. Fax: +81 (6) 6941 0612. Contact: (technical) Technical Bureau. IRC or $1 helpful.

NHK Sapporo, 1-1-1 Ohdori Nishi, Chuo-ku, Sapporo 060-8703, Japan. Fax: +81 (11) 232 5951. Sometimes sends postcards, stickers or other small souvenirs.

NHK Tokyo/Shobu-Kuki, JOAK, 3047-1 Oaza-Sanga, Shoubu-cho, Minami Saitamagun, Saitama 346-01, Japan. Fax: +81 (3) 3481 4985 or +81 (480) 85 1508. IRC or $1 helpful. Replies occasionally. Letters should be sent via registered mail.

Radio Japan/NHK World (external service)

MAIN OFFICE: NHK World, Nippon Hoso Kyokai, Tokyo 150-8001, Japan. Phone: +81 (3) 3465-1111. Fax: (general) +81 (3) 3481 1350; ("Hello from Tokyo" and Production Center) +81 (3) 3465 0966. E-mail: (general) info@intl.nhk.or.jp; ("Hello from Tokyo" program) hello@intl.nhk.or.jp. URL: www.nhk.or.jp/rjnet/. Contact: (administration) Isao Kitamoto, Deputy Director General; Hisashi Okawa, Senior Director International Planning; (general) Yoshiki Fushimi; or K. Terasaka, Programming Division. Free *Radio Japan News* publication, sundry other small souvenirs and "Let's Learn/ Practice Japanese" language-course materials.

Radio Tampa/NSB

MAIN OFFICE: Nihon Shortwave Broadcasting, 9-15 Akasaka 1-chome, Minato-ku, Tokyo 107-8373, Japan. Fax: +81 (3) 3583 9062. E-mail: web@tampa.co.jp. URL: www.tampa.co.jp. Contact: H. Nagao, Public Relations; M. Teshima; Ms. Terumi Onoda; or H. Ono. Sending a reception report may help with a reply. Free stickers and Japanese stamps. $1 or 2 IRCs helpful.

NEW YORK NEWS BUREAU: 1325 Avenue of the Americas #2403, New York NY 10019 USA. Fax: +1 (212) 261 6449. Contact: Noboru Fukui, reporter.

JORDAN   World Time +2 (+3 midyear)

Radio Jordan, P.O. Box 909, Amman, Jordan; or P.O. Box 1041, Amman, Jordan. Phone: (general) +962 (6) 477-4111; (International Relations) +962 (6) 477-8578; (English Service) +962 (6) 475-7410 or +962 (6) 477-3111; (Arabic Service) +962 (6) 463-6454; (Saleh) +962 (6) 474-8048; (Al-Areeny) +962 (6) 475-7404. Fax: +962 (6) 478 8115. E-mail: (general) general@jrtv.gov.jo; (programs) rj@jrtv.gov.jo; (technical) eng@jrtv.gov.jo. URL: www.jrtv.com/radio.htm. Contact: (general) Jawad Zada, Director of English Service & Producer of

This deserted fairground in Bishkek's central park stands in mute testimony to better times. M. Guha

"Mailbag"; Mrs. Firyal Zamakhshari, Director of Arabic Programs; or Qasral Mushatta; (administrative) Hashem Khresat, Director of Radio; Mrs. Fatima Massri, Director of International Relations; or Muwaffaq al-Rahayifah, Director of Shortwave Services; (technical) Fawzi Saleh, Director of Engineering; or Yousef Al-Areeny, Director of Radio Engineering. Free stickers. Replies irregularly and slowly. Enclosing $1 helps.

KAZAKSTAN   World Time +6 (+7 midyear)

NOTE: Although "Kazakstan" is now considered to be the official spelling, "Kazakhstan" is still widely used both inside and outside the country. What happens eventually is anyone's guess, but for the time being, both versions are acceptable.

Kazak Radio, 175A Zheltoksan Street, 480013 Almaty, Kazakstan. Phone: (general) +7 (3272) 637-694, +7 (3272) 633-716 or +7 (3272) 631-207; (international service, when operational) +7 (3272) 627-733; (Director) +7 (3272) 628-639; (Kassymzhanova) +7 (3272) 636-895; (Abdelanov) +7 (3272) 636-895; (technical) +7 (3272) 634-878. Fax: + 7 (3272) 650 387. Note that the country and city codes are scheduled to be changed in the near future, and the current +7 (3272) should then become +997 (327). E-mail: kazradio@astel.kz (if the message comes back as undeliverable, try kazradio@asdc.kz). Contact: (administration) Torehan Rysbekovich Daniyarov, Director; or Dr. Choi Young Gun, Director International Service (when operating); (correspondence in English) Ms. Gaukhar Kassymzhanova, producer/announcer; (correspondence in French) Dias Abdelanov, producer/announcer; (technical) Aleksander Zaporogets, Technical Director. Part of the facilities and personnel were moved to the new capital—Astana—during 1999, and Kazak Radio's operations have been considerably interrupted as a result. The station welcomes correspondence in Russian or Kazakh. Letters in English and French are best sent to the contacts listed above. Replies to correspondence in German are erratic as there is only a part-time staff.

TRANSMISSION FACILITIES: Republican Enterprise of Post & Communications, Republic Ministry of Transport, Communication and Tourism, 86 Ablai Khan Batyr, Almaty, Kazakstan. Phone: +7 (3272) 627-366. Fax: +7 (3272) 627 527. E-mail: KAZPOST@mail.banknet.kz. Contact: Orazaly Santaevich Erhanov, Director General.

KENYA   World Time +3

Adventist World Radio, The Voice of Hope, AWR Africa Region, P.O. Box 42276, Nairobi, Kenya. Phone: +254 (2) 566-025. Fax: +254 (2) 568 433. E-mail: 74532.1575@compuserve.com. Contact: Samuel Misiani, AWR Africa Region Director. Free home Bible study guides, program schedule and other small items. Return postage (IRCs or 1$) appreciated. Also, *see* AWR listings under Costa Rica, Guam, Guatemala, Italy and USA.

Kenya Broadcasting Corporation, P.O. Box 30456, Harry Thuku Road, Nairobi, Kenya. Phone: +254 (2) 334-567. Fax: +254 (2) 220 675. URL: (RealAudio only) www.africaonline.co.ke/AfricaOnline/netradio.html. Contact: (general) Henry Makokha, Liaison Office; (administration) Simeon N. Anabwani, Managing Director; (technical) Nathan Lamu, Senior Principal Technical Officer; Augustine Kenyanjier Gochui; Lawrence Holnati, Engineering Division; or Daniel Githua, Assistant Manager Technical Services (Radio). IRC required. Replies irregularly.

MARALAL TRANSMITTING STATION: KBC, P.O. Box 38, Maralal, Kenya. Contact: Martin Ouma Ojwach, Engineer in Charge. Return postage helpful.

KIRIBATI   World Time +12

Radio Kiribati, P.O. Box 78, Bairiki, Tarawa, Republic of Kiribati. Phone: +686 21187. Fax: +686 21096. Contact: (general) Atiota Bauro, Programme Organiser; Mrs. Otiri Laboia; Batiri Bataua, News Editor; or Moia Tetoa, Producer, "Kaoti Ami Iango," a program devoted to listeners views; (administration)

Bill Reiher, Manager; (technical) Tooto Kabwebwenibeia, Broadcast Engineer; Martin Ouma Ojwach, Senior Superintendent of Electronics; or T. Fakaofo, Technical Staff. Cassettes of local songs available for purchase. $1 or return postage required for a reply (IRCs not accepted).

KOREA (DPR) World Time +9

Radio Pyongyang, External Service, Korean Central Broadcasting Station, Pyongyang, Democratic People's Republic of Korea (*not* "North Korea"). Phone and fax numbers valid only in those countries with direct telephone service to North Korea. Free book for German speakers to learn Korean, sundry other publications, pennants, calendars, newspapers, artistic prints and pins. Do not include dutiable items in your envelope. Replies are irregular, as mail from countries not having diplomatic relations with North Korea is sent via circuitous routes and apparently does not always arrive. Indeed, some PASSPORT readers continue to report that mail to Radio Pyongyang in North Korea results in their receiving anti-communist literature from *South* Korea, which indicates that mail interdiction has not ceased. One way around the problem is to add "VIA BEIJING, CHINA" to the address, but replies via this route tend to be slow in coming. Another gambit is to send your correspondence to an associate in a country—such as China, Ukraine or India—having reasonable relations with North Korea, and ask that it be forwarded. If you don't know anyone in these countries, try using the good offices of the following person: Willi Passman, Oberhausener Str. 100, D-45476, Mülheim, Germany. Send correspondence in a sealed envelope without any address on the back. That should be sent inside another envelope. Include 2 IRCs to cover the cost of forwarding.

Regional Korean Central Broadcasting Stations—Not known to reply, but a long-shot possibility is to try corresponding in Korean to: Korean Central Broadcasting Station, Ministry of Posts and Telecommunications, Chongsung-dong (Moranbong), Pyongyang, Democratic People's Republic of Korea. Fax: +850 (2) 812 301 (valid only in those countries with direct telephone service to North Korea). Contact: Chong Ha-chol, Chairman, Radio and Television Broadcasting Committee.

KOREA (REPUBLIC) World Time +9

☞**Korean Broadcasting System (KBS)**, 18 Yoido-dong, Youngdungpo-gu, Seoul, Republic of Korea 150-790. Phone: +82 (2) 781-2410. Fax: +82 (2) 761 2499. E-mail: webmaster@kbsnt.kbs.co.kr. URL: (includes RealAudio) www.kbs.co.kr/.

☞**Radio Korea International**
MAIN OFFICE: Overseas Service, Korean Broadcasting System, 18 Yoido-dong, Youngdungpo-gu, Seoul, Republic of Korea 150-790. Phone: (general) +82 (2) 781-3650 or +82 (2) 781-3660; (English Service) +82 (2) 781-3728/29/35; (Russian Service) +82 (2) 781-3714. Fax: +82 (2) 781 3788 or +82 (2) 781 3799 or (toll-free fax lines available for overseas listeners) (United States) 1-888-229-2312; (United Kingdom) 0800-89-5995; (Canada) 1-888-211-5865; (Australia) 1-800-142-644. E-mail: rki@kbsnt.kbs.co.kr. URL: (includes RealAudio) http://rki.kbs.co.kr/rki/. Contact: (general) Chae Hong-Pyo, Director of English Service; Robert Gutnikov, English Service; Ms. Han Hee-joo, Producer/Host, "Shortwave Feedback"; Jong Kyong-Tae, Producer, Russian Service; H.A. Staiger, Deputy Head of German Service; Ms. Lee Hae-Ok, Japanese Service;

or Ms. Kim Hae-Young, Producer, Japanese Service; (administration) Kim Sang-Soo, Executive Director; or Choi Jang-Hoon, Director. Free stickers, calendars, *Let's Learn Korean* book and a wide variety of other small souvenirs. *History of Korea* now available via Internet (*see* URL, above) and on CD-ROM (inquire).
WASHINGTON NEWS BUREAU: National Press Building, Suite 1076, 529 14th Street NW, Washington DC 20045 USA. Phone: +1 (202) 662-7345. Fax: +1 (202) 662 7347.

KUWAIT World Time +3

Ministry of Information, P.O. Box 193, 13002 Safat, Kuwait. Phone: +965 241-5301. Fax: +965 243 4511. URL: www.moinfo.gov.kw. Contact: Sheik Nasir Al-Sabah, Minister of Information.
☞**Radio Kuwait**, P.O. Box 397, 13004 Safat, Kuwait; (technical) Department of Frequency Management, P.O. Box 967, 13010 Safat, Kuwait. Phone: (general) +965 242-3774; (technical) +965 241-0301, +965 242-1422 or +965 243-6193. Fax: (general) +965 245 6660; (technical) +965 241 5498 or +965 241 5946. E-mail: (technical, including reception reports) kwtfreq@hotmail.com; (frequency matters) kwtfreq@ncc.moc.kw; (general) radiokuwait@radiokuwait.org. URLs: (technical) www.moinfo.gov.kw/ENG/FREQ/; (RealAudio) www.radiokuwait.org/. Contact: (general) Manager, External Service; (technical) Nasser M. Al-Saffar, Controller, Frequency Management; or Wessam Najaf. Sometimes gives away stickers, calendars, pens or key chains.

KYRGYZSTAN World Time +5 (+6 midyear)

Kyrgyz Radio, Kyrgyz TV and Radio Center, 59 Jash Gvardiya Boulevard, 720300 Bishkek, Kyrgyzstan. Phone: (general) +996 (312) 253-404 or +996 (312) 255-741; (Director) +996 (312) 255-700 or +996 (312) 255-709; (Assemov) +996 (312) 650-7341 or +996 (312) 255-703; (Atakanova) +996 (312) 251-927; (technical) +996 (312) 257-771. Fax: +996 (312) 257 952. Note that from a few countries, the dialing code is still the old +7 (3312). E-mail: trk@kyrnet.kg. Contact: (administration) Mrs. Baima J. Sutenova, Vice-Chairman – Kyrgyz Radio; or Eraly Ayilchiyev, Director; (general) Talant Assemov, Editor – Kyrgyz/Russian/German news; Gulnara Abdulaeva, Announcer – Kyrgyz/Russian/German news; Nargis Atakanova, Announcer – English news; (technical) Mirbek Uursabekov, Technical Director. Kyrgyz and Russian preferred, but correspondence in English and German can also be processed. For quick processing of reception reports, use e-mail in German to Talant Assemov. Reports are regularly verified and verifications are usually signed by Mrs. Sutenova.
TRANSMISSION FACILITIES: Ministry of Transport and Communications, 42 Issanova Street, 720000 Bishkek, Kyrgyzstan. Phone: +996 (312) 216-672. Fax: +996 (312) 213 667. Contact: Jantoro Satybaldiyev, Minister. The shortwave transmitting station is located at Krasny-Retcha (Red River), a military encampment in the Issk-Ata region, about 40 km south of Bishkek.

LAOS World Time +7

Lao National Radio, Luang Prabang (when active), Luang Prabang, Laos; or B.P. 310, Vientiane, Laos. Return postage required (IRCs not accepted). Replies slowly and very rarely.

Producer Elian Andramitantsoa records programs in Malagasy for broadcast on Adventist World Radio's Voice of Hope studio at Antananarivo, Madagascar. AWR

Best bet is to write in Laotian or French directly to Luang Prabang, where the transmitter is located.

Lao National Radio, Vientiane, Laotian National Radio and Television, B.P. 310, Vientiane, Laos. Phone: +856 (21) 212-429. Fax: +856 (21) 212 430. Contact: Khoun Sounantha, Manager-in-Charge; Bounthan Inthasai, Director General; Mrs. Vinachine, English/French Sections; Ms. Mativarn Simanithone, Deputy Head, English Section; or Miss Chanthery Vichitsavanh, Announcer, English Section who says, "It would be good if you send your letter unregistered, because I find it difficult to get all letters by myself at the post. Please use my name, and 'Lao National Radio, P.O. Box 310, Vientiane, Laos P.D.R.' It will go directly to me." Sometimes includes a program schedule and Laotian stamps when replying. The external service of this station tends to be erratic.

LEBANON   World Time +2 (+3 midyear)

High Adventure Radio (Voice of Hope), P.O. Box 3379, Limassol, Cyprus; or P.O. Box 77, Metulla, Israel. E-mail: voh@broadcast.net; radio98@hotmail.com. URL: www.intertvnet.net/~highorg/stations/middleeast/. Contact: Gary Hull, Station Manager; or Isaac Gronberg, Director. Free stickers. IRC requested.May send 214 page book *Voice of Hope* via USA headquarters *(see)*. Also, *see* KVOH—Voice of Hope/ High Adventure Ministries, USA.

📧**Voice of Charity**, Rue Fouad Chéhab, B.P. 850, Jounieh, Lebanon. Phone: +961 (9) 914-901 or +961 (9) 918-090. E-mail: radiocharity@opuslibani.org.lb. URL: (includes RealAudio) www.radiocharity.org.lb/. Contact: Frère Elie Nakhoul, Managing Director. Program aired via facilities of Vatican Radio from a station founded by the Order of the Lebanese Missionaries. Basically, a Lebanese Christian educational radio program.

📧**Voice of Lebanon** (when active), P.O. Box 165271, Al-Ashrafiyah, Beirut, Lebanon; or (street address) Radio Voice of Lebanon Bldg., Bachir Gémayel Avenue, Beirut, Lebanon. Phone: +961 (1) 201-380 or +961 (1) 323-458. Fax: +961 (1) 219 290. E-mail: vdl@cyberia.net.lb. URL: (includes RealAudio) www.vdl.com.lb. Contact: Sheik Simon El-Khazen, General Manager. $1 required. Replies occasionally to correspondence in French or Arabic. Operated by the Phalangist organization.

LESOTHO   World Time +2

Radio Lesotho, P.O. Box 552, Maseru 100, Lesotho. Phone: +266 323-561. Fax: +266 310 003. Contact: (general) Mamonyane Matsaba, Acting Programming Director; or Sekhonyana Motlohi, Producer, "What Do Listeners Say?"; (administration) Ms. Mpine Tente, Principal Secretary, Ministry of Information and Broadcasting; or Molahlehi Letlotlo, Director; (technical) Lebohang Monnapula, Chief Engineer; Basia Maraisane, Transmitter Engineer; or Motlatsi Monyane, Studio Engineer. Return postage necessary.

LIBERIA   World Time exactly

NOTE: Mail sent to Liberia may be returned as undeliverable.
ELBC (if reactivated), Liberian Broadcasting System, P.O. Box 10-594, 1000 Monrovia 10, Liberia. Phone: +231 224-984 or +231 222-758.

Radio Liberia International, Liberian Communications Network/KISS, P.O. Box 1103, 1000 Monrovia 10, Liberia. Phone: +231 226-963 or +231 227-593. Fax: (during working hours) +231 226 003. Contact: Issac P. Davis, Engineer-in-Charge/QSL Coordinator. $5 required for QSL card.

Radio Veritas, P.O. Box 3569, Monrovia, Liberia. Phone: +231 226-979. Contact: Steve Kenneh, Manager.

Star Radio (if granted a new license for shortwave operation), Sekou Toure Avenue, Mamba Point, Monrovia, Liberia. Phone: +231 226-820, +231 226-176 or +231 227-390. Fax: +231 227 360. E-mail: libe@atge.automail.com. URL: (Star Radio Daily News) www.hirondelle.org/. Contact: James Morlue, Station Manager. Star radio is staffed by Liberian journalists and managed by the Swiss NGO, Fondation Hirondelle, with financing from the U.S. Agency for International Developement through the International Foundation for Election Systems. Fondation Hirondelle can be contacted at: 3 Rue Traversière, CH 1018-Lausanne, Switzerland; (phone) +41 (21) 647-2805; (fax) +41 (21) 647 4469; (e-mail) info@hirondelle.org.

LIBYA   World Time +1 (+2 midyear)

Libyan Jamahiriyah Broadcasting (domestic service), Box 9333, Soug al Jama, Tripoli, Libya. Phone: +218 (21) 361-4508. Fax: +218 (21) 489 4240. Contact: Youssef Moujrab.

Voice of Africa/Voice of Libya, P.O. Box 4677, Tripoli, Libya. Phone: +218 (21) 444-0112, +218 (21) 444-9106 or +218 (21) 444-9872. Fax: +218 (21) 444 9875. This, the external service of Libyan Jamahiriyah Broadcasting, seems to be going through an identity crisis. It has been heard identifying as both "Voice of Africa" and "Voice of Libya" in its English and French programs, while in Arabic it uses the same identification as for the domestic service.

LITHUANIA   World Time +2 (+3 midyear)

Lietuvos Radijo ir Televizijos Centras (LRTC), Sausio 13-osios 10, LT-2044 Vilnius, Lithuania. Phone: +370 (2) 459-397. Fax: +370 (2) 451 738. E-mail: admin@lrtc.lt. URL: www.lrtc.lt. Contact: A. Vydmontas, Director General. This organization operates the transmitters used by Lithuanian Radio.

⬛Lithuanian Radio

STATION: Lietuvos Radijas, S. Konarskio 49, LT-2674 Vilnius MTP, Lithuania. Phone: (general) +370 (2) 333-182; (Grumadiene) +370 (2) 334-471; (Vilciauskas) +370 (2) 233-503. Fax: (general) +370 (2) 263 282; (Technical Director) +370 (2) 232 465. E-mail: format is initial.lastname@rtv.lrtv.ot.lt, so to contact, say, Juozas Algirdas Vilciauskas, it would be jvilciauskas@rtv.lrtv.ot.lt. URLs: (includes RealAudio) www.lrtv.lt/lt_lr.htm. Contact: (general) Mrs. Laima Grumadienë, Managing Director; Mrs. Kazimiera Mazgeliene, Programme Director; or Guoda Litvaitiene, International Relations; (technical) Juozas Algirdas Vilciauskas, Technical Director.

ADMINISTRATION: Lietuvos Nacionalinis Radijas ir Televizija (LNRT), Konarskio 49, LT-2674 Vilnius MTP, Lithuania. Phone: (general) +370 (2) 263-383; (Director General) +370 (2) 263-292. Fax: +370 (2) 263 282. E-mail: (Ilginis) ailginis@rtv.lrtv.ot.lt. URLs: www.lrtv.lt/lt_lrtv.htm. Contact: Arvydas Ilginis, Director General.

STATE RADIO FREQUENCY SERVICE: Algirdo str. 27, LT-2006 Vilnius, Lithuania. Phone: +370 (2) 261-511 or +370 (2) 261-177. Fax: +370 (2) 261 564. E-mail: (Medeisis) medeisis@radio.lt; (Norkunas) enorkuna@radio.lt. Contact: Arturas Medeisis, Head of Division of Strategic Planning; or Eugenijus Norkunas, Director.

Radio Baltic Waves (if activated). E-mail: (Pleikys) riplei@lrs.lt. Contact: Rimantas Pleikys, Project Coordinator. Scheduled to broadcast in Russian and Belarusian to audiences in Lithuania, Russia and Belarus, but has been subject to strong political opposition.

⬛Radio Vilnius, Lietuvos Radijas, Konarskio 49, LT-2674 Vilnius, Lithuania. Phone: +370 (90) 71297. Fax: +370 (2) 233 526. E-mail: ravil@rtv.lrtv.ot.lt. URL: (includes RealAudio) *see* Lithuanian Radio, above. Contact: Ms. Rasa Lukaite,

"Letterbox"; Audrius Braukyla, Editor-in-Chief; or Ilonia Rukiene, Head of English Department. Free stickers, pennants, Lithuanian stamps and other souvenirs. Transmissions to North America are via the facilities of Deutsche Telekom in Germany (*see*).

MADAGASCAR   World Time +3

Adventist World Radio, the Voice of Hope

ADMINISTRATION: B.P. 700, Antananarivo, Madagascar. Phone: +261 (2022) 404-65.

STUDIO: B.P. 460, Antananarivo, Madagascar.

TECHNICAL AND NON-TECHNICAL (e.g. comments on programs)—see USA and Italy. Reception reports are best sent to the Italian office.

Radio Madagasikara, B.P. 442, Antananarivo 101, Madagascar. Contact: Mlle. Rakotonirina Soa Herimanitia, Secrétaire de Direction, a young lady who collects stamps; Mamy Rafenomanantsoa, Directeur; or J.J. Rakotonirina, who has been known to request hi-fi catalogs. $1 required, and enclosing used stamps from various countries may help. Tape recordings accepted. Replies slowly and somewhat irregularly, usually to correspondence in French.

Radio Nederland Wereldomroep—Madagascar Relay, B.P. 404, Antananarivo, Madagascar. Contact: (technical) Rahamefy Eddy, Technische Dienst; or J.A. Ratobimiarana, Chief Engineer. Nontechnical correspondence should be sent to Radio Nederland Wereldomreop in Holland (*see*).

MALAWI   World Time +2

Malawi Broadcasting Corporation, P.O. Box 30133, Chichiri, Blantyre 3, Malawi. Phone: +265 671-222. Fax: +265 671 257 or +265 671 353. Contact: (general) Wilson Bankuku, Director General; J.O. Mndeke; or T.J. Sineta; (technical) Edwin K. Lungu, Controller of Transmitters; Phillip Chinseu, Engineering Consultant; or Joseph Chikagwa, Director of Engineering. Return postage or $1 helpful.

MALAYSIA   World Time +8

Asia-Pacific Broadcasting Union, P.O. Box 1164, Pejabat Pos Jalan Pantai Bahru, 59700 Kuala Lumpur, Malaysia; or (street address) 2nd Floor, Bangunan IPTAR, Angkasapuri, 50614 Kuala Lumpur, Malaysia. Phone: (general) +60 (3) 282-3592; (Programme Department)+60 (3) 282-2480; (Technical Department) +60 (3) 282-3108. Fax: +60 (3) 282 5292. E-mail: sg@abu.org.my; se2@abu.org.my; or tech@abu.org.my. URL: www.abu.org.my/. Contact: Hugh Leonard, Secretary-General; or Sharad Sadhu, Senior Engineer, Technical Department.

Radio Malaysia Kota Kinabalu, RTM, 88614 Kota Kinabalu, Sabah, Malaysia. Contact: Benedict Janil, Director of Broadcasting; Hasbullah Latiff; or Mrs. Angrick Saguman. Registering your letter may help. $1 or return postage required.

⬛Radio Malaysia, Kuala Lumpur

MAIN OFFICE: RTM, Angkasapuri, Bukit Putra, 50614 Kuala Lumpur, Peninsular Malaysia, Malaysia. Phone: +60 (3) 282-5333 or +60 (3) 282-4976. Fax: +60 (3) 282 4735, +60 (3) 282 5103 or +60 (3) 282 5859. E-mail: sabariah@rtm.net.my. URL: (general) www.asiaconnect.com.my/rtm-net/; (RealAudio, live) www.asiaconnect.com.my/rtm-net/live/; (RealAudio, archives) www.asiaconnect.com.my/rtm-net/online/

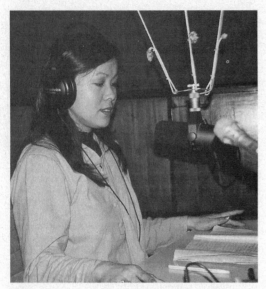

Radio Nepal news is heard throughout much of Asia and beyond. M. Guha

index.html. Contact: (general) Madzhi Johari, Director of Radio; (technical) Ms. Aminah Din, Deputy Director Engineering (Radio); Abdullah Bin Shahadan, Engineer, Transmission & Monitoring; or Ong Poh, Chief Engineer. May sell T-shirts and key chains. Return postage required.
TRANSMISSION OFFICE: Controller of Engineering, Department of Broadcasting (RTM), 43009 Kajang, Selangor Darul Ehsan, Malaysia. Phone: +60 (3) 836-1530. Fax: +60 (3) 836 1227. E-mail: rtmkjg@po.jaring.my. Contact: Jeffrey Looi.
Radio Malaysia Sarawak (Kuching), RTM, Broadcasting House, Jalan P. Ramlee, 93614 Kuching, Sarawak, Malaysia. Phone: +60 (82) 248-422. Fax: +60 (82) 241 914. Contact: (general) Yusof Ally, Director of Broadcasting; Mohd. Hulman Abdollah; or Human Resources Development; (technical, but also nontechnical) Colin A. Minoi, Technical Correspondence; (technical) Kho Kwang Khoon, Deputy Director of Engineering. Return postage helpful.
Radio Malaysia Sarawak (Miri), RTM, Miri, Sarawak, Malaysia. Contact: Clement Stia. $1 or return postage helpful.
Radio Malaysia Sarawak (Sibu), RTM, Jabatan Penyiaran, Bangunan Penyiaran, 96009 Sibu, Sarawak, Malaysia. Contact: Clement Stia, Divisional Controller, Broadcasting Department. $1 or return postage required. Replies irregularly and slowly.
Voice of Islam—Program of the Voice of Malaysia (*see*), below.
Voice of Malaysia, Suara Malaysia, Wisma Radio, P.O. Box 11272-KL, 50740 Angkasapuri, Kuala Lumpur, Malaysia. Phone: +60 (3) 282-5333. Fax: +60 (3) 282 5514. Contact: (general) Mrs. Mahani bte Ujang, Supervisor, English Service; Hajjah Wan Chuk Othman, English Service; (administration) Santokh Singh Gill, Director; or Mrs. Adilan bte Omar, Assistant Director; (technical) Lin Chew, Director of Engineering. Free calendars and stickers. Two IRCs or return postage helpful. Replies slowly and irregularly.

MALDIVES World Time +5

Voice of Maldives (when reactivated), Ministry of Information, Arts & Culture, Moonlight Higun, Malé 20-06, Republic of Maldives. Phone: (administration & secretaries) +960 321-642; (Director General) +960 322-577; (Director of Programs) +960 322-746; (Duty Officer) +960 322-841; (programme section) +960 322-842; (studio 1) +960 325-151; (studio 2) +960 323-416; (newsroom) +960 322-253, +960 324-506 or + 960 324-507; (office assistant/budget secretary) +960 320-508; (FM Studio) +960 314-217; (technical, office) +960 322-444 or +960 320-941; (residence) +960 323-211. Fax: +960 328 357 or +960 325 371. E-mail: informat@dhivehinet.net.mv. Contact: Maizan Ahmed Manik, Director General of Engineering. Long inactive on the world bands, this station is expected to resume shortwave broadcasts in the near future with a newly installed 10 kilowatt transmitter on the island of Mafushi.

MALI World Time exactly

Radiodiffusion Télévision Malienne, B.P. 171, Bamako, Mali. Phone: +223 22-47-27. Fax: +223 22 42 05. Contact: Karamoko Issiaka Daman, Directeur des Programmes; (administration) Abdoulaye Sidibe, Directeur General; (Technical) Nouhoum Traore. $1 or IRC helpful. Replies slowly and irregularly to correspondence in French. English is accepted.

MALTA World Time +1 (+2 midyear)

Voice of the Mediterranean (Radio Melita), St Francis Ravelin, Floriana, VLT 15, Malta; or P.O. Box 143, Valetta, CMR 01, Malta. Phone: +356 220-950, +356 240-421 or +356 248-080. Fax: +356 241 501. E-mail: vomradio@vom-malta.org.mt. URLs: (official, with RealAudio) www.vom-malta.org.mt; (unofficial) www.woden.com/~falcon/vom.html. Contact: (administration) Dr. Richard Vella Laurenti, Managing Director; (German Service and listener contact) Ingrid Huettmann; M. Delu. Letters and reception reports welcomed.

MAURITANIA World Time exactly

Office de Radiodiffusion-Télévision de Mauritanie, B.P. 200, Nouakchott, Mauritania. Phone: +222 (2) 52287. Fax: +222 (2) 51264. E-mail: rm@mauritania.mr. URL: www.mauritania.mr/Francais/Autres_sites_fr.htm (click on "Radio Mauritanie"). Contact: Madame Amir Feu; Lemrabott Boukhary; Madame Fatimetou Fall Dite Ami, Secretaire de Direction; or Mr. Hane Abou. Return postage or $1 required. Rarely replies.

MAURITIUS World Time +4

Mauritius Broadcasting Corporation (if reactivated), P.O. Box 48, Curepipe, Mauritius; (physical location) 1, Louis Pasteur Street, Forest Side, Mauritius. Phone: +230 675-5001. Fax: +230 675 7332. E-mail: (general) mbc@bow.intnet.mu; (engineering) mbceng@bow.intnet.mu. URL: www.mbc-tv.com. Contact: (general) Trilock Dwarka, Director General; or Mrs. Marie Michele Etienne, Officer in Charge of Programmes; (technical) Armoodalingum Pather, Managing Director, Engineering; or Ashok Kariman, Deputy Chief Engineer. Currently inactive on world band, but hopes to reactivate transmissions eventually on 4855 and 9710 kHz.

MEXICO
World Time –6 (–5 midyear) Central, including D.F.; –7 (–6 midyear) Mountain; –8 (–7 midyear) Pacific

Candela FM—XEQM (when operating), Apartado Postal 217, 97001-Mérida, YUC, Mexico. Phone: +52 (99) 236-155. Fax: +52 (99) 280 680. Contact: Lic. Bernardo Laris Rodríguez, Director General del Grupo RASA Mérida. Replies irregularly to correspondence in Spanish.

La Hora Exacta—XEQK (when operating), Real de Mayorazgo 83, Barrio de Xoco, 03330-México 13, D.F., Mexico. Phone: +52 (5) 628-1731, +52 (5) 628-1700 Ext. 1648 or 1659. Fax: +52 (5) 604-8292. URL: www.telecommex.com/imer/xeqk.html. Contact: Lic. Santiago Ibarra Ferrer, Gerente.

La Jarocha—XEFT (when operating), Apartado Postal 21, 91701-Veracruz, VER., Mexico. Phone: +52 (29) 322-250. Contact: C.P. Miguel Rodríguez Sáez, Sub-Director; or Lic. Juan de Dios Rodríguez Díaz, Director. Free tourist guide to Veracruz. Return postage, IRC or $1 probably helpful. Likely to reply to correspondence in Spanish.

Radio Educación—XEPPM, Apartado Postal 21-940, 04021-México 21, D.F., Mexico. Phone: (general) +52 (5) 559-6169. Fax: +52 (5) 575 6566. Contact: (general) Lic. Susana E. Mejía Vázquez, Jefe del Dept. de Audiencia y Evaluación; or María Teresa Moya Malfavón, Directora de Producción y Planeación; (administration) Luis Ernesto Pi Orozco, Director General; (technical) Ing. Gustavo Carreño López, Subdirector, Dpto. Técnico. Free stickers, calendars, station photo and a copy of a local publication, *Audio Tinta Boletín Informativo*. Return postage or $1 required. Replies, sometimes slowly, to correspondence in English, Spanish, Italian or French.

Radio Huayacocotla—XEJN
STATION ADDRESS: "Radio Huaya," Dom. Gutiérrez Najera s/n, Apartado Postal 13, 92600-Huayacocotla, VER, Mexico. Phone: +52 (775) 80067. Fax: +52 (775) 80118. E-mail: framos@uibero.uia.mx. URL: www.sjsocial.org/Radio/huarad.html. Contact: Martha Silvia Ortiz López, Coordinadora. Return postage or $1 helpful. Replies irregularly to correspondence in Spanish.

📻Radio México Internacional—XERMX, Instituto Méxicano de la Radio, Apartado Postal 21-300, 04021-México 21, D.F., Mexico. Phone: +52 (5) 604-7846 or +52 (5) 628-1720. Fax: +52 (5) 604 8292. E-mail: rmi@eudoramail.com. URLs: (with program samples in RealAudio) www.telecommex.com/imer/rmi/; or http://hello.to/rmi. Contact: Lic. Martín Rizo Gavira, Gerente; or Juan Josi Miroz, host "Mailbag Program." Free stickers, post cards and stamps. Sometimes free T-shirts and CDs. Welcomes correspondence, including inquiries about Mexico, in Spanish, English and French. $1 helpful. A bilingual reception report form can be downloaded and printed from the website.

Radio Mil—XEOI, NRM, Avda. Insurgentes Sur 1870, Col. Florida, 01030-México 20 D.F., Mexico; or Apartado Postal 21-1000, 04021-México 21, D.F., Mexico (this address for reception reports on the station's shortwave broadcasts). Phone: (station) +52 (5) 662-1000 or +52 (5) 662-1100; (Núcleo Radio Mil network) +52 (5) 662-6060, +52 (5) 663-0739 or +52 (5) 663 0590. Fax: (station) +52 (5) 662 0974; (Núcleo Radio Mil network) +52 (5) 662 0979. E-mail: info@nrm.com.mx. URL: www.nrm.com.mx/radiomil.html. Contact: Lic. Guillermo D. Salas Vargas, Vicepresidente Ejecutivo del Núcleo Radio Mil; Lic. Javier Trejo Garay, Gerente; or Zoila Quintanar Flores. Free stickers. $1 or return postage required.

Radio Transcontinental de América—XERTA, Apartado Postal 653, 06002 México 1, D.F., Mexico; or Torre "Latinoamericana" (Desp. 3706), 06007-México 1, D.F., Mexico. Phone: +52 (5) 510-9896. Fax: +52 (5) 510 3326. Contact: Roberto Najera Martínez, Presidente de Radio Transcontinental de América.

📻Radio Universidad Autónoma de México (UNAM)—XEYU, Adolfo Prieto 133, Colonia del Valle, 03100-México 12, D.F., Mexico. Phone: +52 (5) 523-2633. E-mail: radiounam@www.unam.mx. URL: (includes RealAudio) www.unam.mx/radiounam/. Contact: (general) Lic. Malena Mijares Fernández, Directora General de Radio UNAM; (technical) Ing. Gustavo Carreño, Departamento Técnico. Free tourist literature and stickers. $1 or return postage required. Replies irregularly to correspondence in Spanish.

MOLDOVA
World Time +2 (+3 midyear)

Radio Moldova International
GENERAL CORRESPONDENCE: If direct mail service is available from your location, try Maison de la Radio, Miorița str. 1, 277028 Chișinău, Moldova. Phone: +373 (2) 721-792, + (373) (2) 723-369, +373 (2) 723-379 or +373 (2) 723-385. Fax: +373 (2) 723 329 or +373 (2) 723 307. Contact: Constantin Marin, International Editor-in-Chief; Alexandru Dorogan, General Director of Radio Broadcasting; Constantin Rotaru, Director General; Daniel Lacky, Editor, English Service; Veleriu Vasilica, Head of English Department; Iurie Moraru, Director of Spanish Department; or Raisa Gonciar. Transmits via facilities of Radio România International. Free stickers and calendars.
RECEPTION REPORTS: RMI-Monitoring Action, P.O. Box 9972, 277070 Chișinău-70, Moldova.

MONACO
World Time +1 (+2 midyear)

Radio Monte-Carlo
MAIN OFFICE: 16 Boulevard Princesse Charlotte, MC-98080 Monaco Cedex, Monaco. Phone: +377 (93) 15-16-17. Fax: +377 (93) 15 16 30 or +377 (93) 15 94 48. E-mail: via URL. URL: www.twr.org/monte.htm. Contact: Jacques Louret; Bernard Poizat, Service Diffusion; or Caroline Wilson, Director of Communication. Free stickers. This station is on world band only with its Arabic Service.
MAIN PARIS OFFICE, NONTECHNICAL: 12 rue Magellan, F-75008 Paris, France. Phone: +33 (1) 40-69-88-00. Fax: +33 (1) 40 69 88 55 or +33 (1) 45 00 92 45.
PARIS OFFICE (ARABIC SERVICE): 78 Avenue Raymond Poincairé, F-75008 Paris, France. Phone: +33 (1) 45-01-53-30.
CYPRUS OFFICE (ARABIC SERVICE)—see Cyprus.

Trans World Radio
STATION: B.P. 349, MC-98007 Monte-Carlo, Monaco-Cedex. Phone: +377 (92) 16-56-00. Fax: +377 (92) 16 56 01. URL (transmission schedule): (Monte-Carlo) www.gospelcom.net/twr/t_europe.htm. Contact: (general) Mrs. Jeanne Olson; (administration) Richard Olson, Station Manager; (Technical) See VIENNA OFFICE, TECHNICAL below. Free paper pennant. IRC or $1 helpful. Also, see USA.
GERMAN OFFICE: Evangeliums-Rundfunk, Postfach 1444, D-35573 Wetzlar, Germany. Phone: +49 (6441) 957-0. Fax: +49 (6441) 957-120. E-mail: erf@erf.de; or siemens@arf.de. URL: (includes RealAudio) www.erf.de. Contact: Jürgen Werth, Direktor.
HOLLAND OFFICE, NONTECHNICAL: Postbus 176, NL-3780 BD Voorthuizen, Holland. Phone: +31 (0) 34-29-27-27. Fax: +31 (0) 34 29 67 27. Contact: Beate Kiebel, Manager Broadcast Department; or Felix Widmer.

Radio New Zealand staff Ian Johnston, Moera Fiti-Tuilaepa, Dmitri Edwards, Philippa Tolley, Greg Tatere, Adrian Sainsbury, Kevin Golding, Bruce Hill, Brian Strong, Florence de Ruiter, Walter Zweifel, Linden Clark and Myra Oh.
RNZI

VIENNA OFFICE, TECHNICAL: Postfach 141, A-1235 Vienna, Austria. Phone: +43 (1) 863-1233 or +43 (1) 863-1247. Fax: +43 (1) 863 1220. E-mail: (Menzel) 100615.1511@compuserve.com; (Schraut) eurofreq@twr.org; bschraut@twr.org; or 101513.2330@compuserve.com; (Dobos) kdobos@twr-europe.at. Contact: Helmut Menzel, Director of Engineering; Bernhard Schraut, Frequency Coordinator; or Kalman Dobos, Frequency Coordinator.
SWISS OFFICE: Evangelium in Radio und Fernsehen, Witzbergstrasse 23, CH-8330 Pfäffikon ZH, Switzerland. Phone: +41 (951) 0500. Fax: +41 (951) 0540. E-mail: erf@erf.ch. URL: www.erf.ch.

MONGOLIA World Time +8

Mongolian Radio (Postal and e-mail addresses same as Voice of Mongolia, *see* below). Phone: (administration) +976 (1) 323-520 or +976 (1) 328-978; (editorial) +976 (1) 329-766; (MRTV parent organization) +976 (1) 326-663. Fax: +976 (1) 327 234. E-mail: radiomongolia@magicnet.mn. URL: www.mol.mn/mrtv/MONGRAD.html. Contact: A. Buidakhmet, Director.
Voice of Mongolia, C.P.O. Box 365, Ulaanbaatar 13, Mongolia. Phone: +976 (1) 321-624 or (English Section) +976 (1) 327-900. Fax: +976 (1) 323 096 or (English Section) +976 (1) 327 234. E-mail: (general) radiomongolia@magicnet.mn; or (International Relations Office) mrtv@magicnet.mn. URL: www.mol.mn/mrtv/. Contact: (general) Mrs. Narantuya, Chief of Foreign Service; D. Batbayar, Mail Editor, English Department; N. Tuya, Head of English Department; Dr. Mark Ostrowski, Consultant, MRTV International Relations Department; or Ms. Tsegmid Burmaa, Japanese Department; (administration) Ch. Surenjav, Director; (technical) Ing. Ganhuu, Chief of Technical Department. Correpondence should be directed to the relevant language section and 2 IRCs or 1$ appreciated. Accepts taped reception reports, preferably containing five-minute excerpts of the broadcast(s) reported, but cassettes cannot be returned. Free pennants, postcards, newspapers and Mongolian stamps.

MOROCCO World Time exactly

☞Radio Medi Un
MAIN OFFICE: B.P. 2055, Tanger, Morocco (physical location: 3, rue Emsallah, 90000 Tanger, Morocco). Phone/fax: +212 (9) 936-363 or +212 (9) 935-755. E-mail: (general) medi1@medi1.com; (technical) technique@medi1.com. URLs: (with RealAudio) www.medi1.com; www.medi1.co.ma. Contact: J. Dryk, Responsable Haute Fréquence. Two IRCs helpful. Free stickers. Correspondence in French preferred.
PARIS BUREAU, NONTECHNICAL: 78 Avenue Raymond Poincaré, F-75016 Paris, France. Phone: +33 (1) 45-01-53-30. Correspondence in French preferred.
☞Radiodiffusion-Télévision Marocaine, 1 rue El Brihi, Rabat, Morocco. Phone: +212 (7) 766-881/83/85, +212 (7) 701-740; or +212 (7) 201-404. Fax: +212 (7) 722 047, or +212 (7) 703 208. E-mail: rtm@rtm.gov.ma. URLs: (general) www.rtm.gov.ma; (radio) www.rtm.gov.ma/Radiodiffusion/Radiodiffusion.htm; (RealAudio) www.maroc.net/rc/live.htm. Contact: (nontechnical and technical) Mrs. Naaman Khadija, Ingénieur d'Etat en Télécommunication; (technical) Tanone Mohammed Jamaledine, Technical Director; Hammouda Mohamed, Engineer; or N. Read. Correspondence welcomed in English, French, Arabic or Berber.
Voice of America/IBB—Morocco Relay Station, Briech. Phone: (office) +212 (9) 93-24-81; (transmitter) +212 (9) 93-22-00. Fax: +212 (9) 93 55 71. Contact: Station Manager. These numbers for urgent technical matters only. Otherwise, does not welcome direct correspondence; *see* USA for acceptable VOA and IBB Washington addresses and related information.

MOZAMBIQUE World Time +2

Rádio Maputo (when active)—*see* Radio Moçambique, below.
Rádio Moçambique, Rua da Rádio no. 2, Caixa Postal 2000, Maputo, Mozambique. Phone: +258 (1) 421-814, +258 (1) 429-826 or +258 (1) 429-836. Fax: +258 (1) 421 816. E-mail: (Iain

Christie) christie@christie.uem.mz. Contact: (general) João B. de Sousa, Administrador de Produção; Izidine Faquira, Diretor de Programas; Iain Patrick Christie, Director of External Service; Orlanda Mendes, Produtor, "Linha Direta"; (technical) Eduardo Rufino de Matos, Administrador Técnico; or Daniel Macabi, Diretor Técnico. Free medallions and pens. Cassettes featuring local music $15. Return postage, $1 or 2 IRCs required. Replies to correspondence in Portuguese or English.

MYANMAR (BURMA) World Time +6:30

Radio Myanmar
STATION: GPO Box 1432, Yangon-11181, Myanmar; or Pyay Road, Yangon-11041, Myanmar. Contact: Ko Ko Htway, Director of Radio.

NAMIBIA World Time +2 (+1 midyear)

Radio Namibia/Namibian Broadcasting Corporation, P.O. Box 321, Windhoek 9000, Namibia. Phone: (general) +264 (61) 291-3111; (studio, during "Chat Show" and "Openline") +264 (61) 236-381. Fax: (general) +264 (61) 217 760; (Duwe, technical) +264 (61) 231 881. E-mail: (Tyson) robin@imlt.org.na. URL: (National Radio) http://natradio.imlt.org.na. Contact: (nontechnical) Robin Tyson, Manager, National Radio; (technical) P. Schachtschneider, Manager, Transmitter Maintenance; Joe Duwe, Chief Technician. Free stickers.

NEPAL World Time +5:45

☞**Radio Nepal**, P.O. Box 634, Singha Durbar, Kathmandu, Nepal. Phone: (general) +977 (1) 223-910; (engineering) +977 (1) 225-467. Fax: +977 (1) 221 952. E-mail: rne@rne.wlink.com.np; radio@rne.wlink.com.np; (engineering) radio@engg.wlink.com.np. URLs: (include RealAudio in English and Nepali) www.catmando.com/news/radio-nepal/; www.catmando.com/radio-nepal/. Contact: (general) M.P. Acharya, Executive Director; M.P. Adhikari, Deputy Executive Director; Jayanti Rajbhandari, Director – Programming; or S.K. Pant, Producer, "Listener's Mail"; (technical) Ram Sharan Kharki, Director – Engineering. 3 IRCs necessary, but station urges that neither mint stamps nor cash be enclosed, as this invites theft by Nepalese postal employees.

NETHERLANDS—see Holland

NETHERLANDS ANTILLES World Time –4

Radio Nederland Wereldomroep—Bonaire Relay, P.O. Box 45, Kralendijk, Netherlands Antilles. Nontechnical correspondence should be sent to Radio Nederland Wereldomreop in Holland (see).

NEW ZEALAND World Time +13 (+12 midyear)

☞**Radio New Zealand International (Te Reo Irirangi O Aotearoa, O Te Moana-nui-a-kiwa)**, P.O. Box 123, Wellington, New Zealand. Phone: +64 (4) 474-1437. Fax: +64 (4) 474 1433 or +64 (4) 474 1886. E-mail: (general) info@rnzi.com; or rnzi@actrix.gen.nz; (technical, Adrian Sainsbury) adrian@actrix.gen.nz. URLs: (general) www.rnzi.com; (RealAudio) www.wrn.org/ondemand/

newzealand.html; www.audionet.co.nz/ranz.html. Contact: Florence de Ruiter, Listener Mail; Myra Oh, Producer, "Mailbox"; or Walter Zweifel, News Editor; (administration) Ms. Linden Clark, Manager; (technical) Adrian Sainsbury, Technical Manager. Free stickers, schedule/flyer about station, map of New Zealand and tourist literature available. English/Maori T-shirts for US$20; Sweatshirts $40; interesting variety of CDs, as well as music cassettes and spoken programs, in Domestic "Replay Radio" catalog (VISA/MC). Three IRCs for verification, one IRC for schedule/catalog. As of August 1998, Radio New Zealand International has been subject to reduced funding from the New Zealand Ministry of Foreign Affairs. This has resulted in staff and programming cuts.
Radio Reading Service—ZLXA, P.O. Box 360, Levin 5500, New Zealand. Phone: (general) +64 (6) 368-2229; (engineering) +64 (25) 985-360. Fax: +64 (6) 368 7290. E-mail: (general) nzrpd@xtra.co.nz; (Bell) ABell@radioreading.org; (Little) Alittle@radioreading.org; (Stokoe) BStokoe@radioreading.org. URL: www.radioreading.org. Contact: (general) Ash Bell, Manager/Station Director; (administration) Allen J. Little, Executive President; (technical, including reception reports) Brian Stokoe. Operated by volunteers 24 hours a day, seven days a week. Station is owned by the "New Zealand Radio for the Print Disabled Inc." Free brochure, postcards and stickers. $1, return postage or 3 IRCs appreciated.

NICARAGUA World Time –6

Radio Miskut, Barrio Pancasan, Puerto Cabezas, R.A.A.N., Nicaragua. Phone: +505 (282) 2443. Fax: +505 (267) 3032. Contact: Evaristo Mercado Pérez, Director de Operación y de Programas; or Abigail Zúñiga Fagoth. T-shirts $10, and *Resumen Mensual del Gobierno y Consejo Regional* and *Revista Informativa Detallada de las Gestiones y Logros* $10 per copy. Station has upgraded to a new shortwave transmitter and is currently improving its shortwave antenna. Replies slowly and irregularly to correspondence in English and Spanish. $2 helpful, as is registering your letter.

NIGER World Time +1

La Voix du Sahel, O.R.T.N., B.P. 361, Niamey, Niger. Fax: +227 72 35 48. Contact: (general) Adamou Oumarou; Issaka Mamadou; Zakari Saley; Souley Boubacou; or Mounkaïla Inazadan, Producer, "Inter-Jeunes Variétés"; (administration) Oumar Tiello, Directeur; (technical) Afo Sourou Victor. $1 helpful. Correspondence in French preferred. Correspondence by males with this station may result in requests for certain unusual types of magazines and photographs.

NIGERIA World Time +1

WARNING—MAIL THEFT: For the time being, correspondence from abroad to Nigerian addresses has a relatively high probability of being stolen.
WARNING—CONFIDENCE ARTISTS: For years, now, correspondence with Nigerian stations has sometimes resulted in letters from highly skilled "pen pal" confidence artists. These typically offer to send you large sums of money, if you will provide details of your bank account or similar information (after which they clean out your account). Other scams are disguised as tempting business proposals; or requests for money, free electronic or other products, publications or immigration sponsorship. Persons thus approached should

contact their country's diplomatic offices. For example, Americans should contact the Diplomatic Security Section of the Department of State [phone +1 (202) 647-4000], or an American embassy or consulate.

Radio Nigeria—Enugu, P.M.B. 1051, Enugu (Anambra), Nigeria. Contact: Louis Nnamuchi, Assistant Director Technical Services. Two IRCs, return postage or $1 required. Replies slowly.

Radio Nigeria—Ibadan, Broadcasting House, P.M.B. 5003, Ibadan, Oyo State, Nigeria. Fax: +234 (22) 413 930. Contact: V.A. Kalejaiye, Technical Services Department; Rev. Olukunle Ajani, Executive Director; Nike Adegoke, Executive Director; or Dare Folarin, Principal Public Affairs Officer. $1 or return postage required. Replies slowly.

Radio Nigeria—Kaduna, P.O. Box 250, Kaduna (Kaduna), Nigeria. Contact: Yusuf Garba, Ahmed Abdullahi, R.B. Jimoh, Assistant Director Technical Service; or Johnson D. Allen. May send sticker celebrating 30 years of broadcasting. $1 or return postage required. Replies slowly.

Radio Nigeria—Lagos, P.M.B. 12504, Ikoyi, Lagos, Nigeria. Contact: Willie Egbe, Assistant Director for Programmes; Babatunde Olalekan Raji, Monitoring Unit. Two IRCs or return postage helpful. Replies slowly and irregularly.

Voice of Nigeria, P.M.B. 40003 Falomo Post Office, Ikoyi, Lagos, Nigeria. Phone: +234 (1) 269-3078/3245/3075/. Fax: +234 (1) 269 1944. Contact: (general) Alhaji Lawal Yusuf Saulawa, Director of Programming; Mrs. Stella Bassey, Deputy Director Programmes; Alhaji Mohammed Okorejior, Acting Director News; or Livy Iwok, Editor; (administration) Alhaji Mallam Yaya Abubakar, Director General; Abubakar Jijiwa, Chairman; Frank Iloye, Station Manager; or Dr. Walter Ofonagoro, Minister of Information; (technical) J.O. Kurunmi, Deputy Director Engineering Services; O.I. Odumsi, Acting Director, Engineering; or G.C. Ugwa, Director Engineering. Replies from station tend to be erratic, but continue to generate unsolicited correspondence from supposed "pen pals" (*see* WARNING—CONFIDENCE ARTISTS, above); faxes, which are much less likely to be intercepted, may be more fruitful. Two IRCs or return postage helpful.

NORTHERN MARIANA ISLANDS World Time +10

Far East Broadcasting Company—Radio Station KFBS Saipan
MAIN OFFICE: FEBC, P.O. Box 209, Saipan, Mariana Islands MP 96950 USA. Phone: (main office) +1 (670) 322-3841. Fax: +1 (670) 322 3060. E-mail: febc@itecnmi.com. URL: www.febc.org. Contact: Chris Slabaugh, Field Director; Irene Gabbie, QSL Secretary; Mike Adams; or Robert Springer, Director. Replies sometimes take months. Also, *see* FEBC Radio International, USA.

NORWAY World Time +1 (+2 midyear)

☒Radio Norway International (Utenlandssendingen)
MAIN OFFICE, NONTECHNICAL: Utenlandssendingen, NRK, N-0340 Oslo, Norway. Phone: (general) + 47 (23) 048-441 or +47 (23) 048-444; (Norwegian-language 24-hour recording of schedule information +47 (23) 048-008 (Americas, Europe, Africa), +47 (23) 048-009 (elsewhere). Fax: (general) +47 (23) 047 134 or +47 (22) 605 719. E-mail: radionorway@nrk.no. URL: (includes RealAudio) www.nrk.no/radionyheter/radionorway/. Contact: (general) Kirsten Ruud Salomonsen,

Head of External Broadcasting; or Grethe Breie, Consultant; (technical) Gundel Krauss Dahl, Head of Radio Projects. Free stickers and flags.
WASHINGTON NEWS BUREAU: Norwegian Broadcasting, 2030 M Street NW, Suite 700, Washington DC 20036 USA. Phone: +1 (202) 785-1481 or +1 (202) 785-1460. Contact: Bjorn Hansen or Gunnar Myklebust.
SINGAPORE NEWS BUREAU: NRK, 325 River Valley Road #01-04, Singapore.
FREQUENCY MANAGEMENT OFFICE: Statens Teleforvaltning, Dept. TF/OMG, Revierstredet 2, P.O. Box 447 Sentrum, N-0104 Oslo, Norway. Phone: +47 (22) 824-889. Fax: +47 (22) 824 891.

OMAN World Time +4

BBC World Service—Eastern Relay Station, P.O. Box 6898 (or 3716), Ruwi Post Office, Muscat, Oman. Contact: Chris Dolman, Senior Transmitter Engineer; or Dave Plater, Senior Transmitter Engineer. Technical correspondence should be sent to "Senior Transmitter Engineer"; nontechnical goes to the BBC World Service in London (*see* United Kingdom).

☒Radio Sultanate of Oman, Ministry of Information, P.O. Box 600, Muscat, Post Code 113, Sultanate of Oman. Phone: +968 602-494 or +968 603-222. Fax: (general) +968 602 055 or +968 602 831; (technical) +968 604 629; or +968 607 239. E-mail: (technical) sjnornani@omantel.net.om; or abulukman@hotmail.com. URL: (RealAudio only) www.oman-tv.gov.om/. Contact: (Directorate General of Technical Affairs) Abdallah Bin Saif Al-Nabhani, Acting Chief Engineer; Rashid Haroon Al-Jabry, Head of Radio Maintenance; Salim Al-Nomani, Director of Frequency Management; or Ahmed Mohamed Al-Balushi, Head of Studio's Engineering. Replies regularly, and responses are from one to two weeks. $1, return postage or 3 IRCs helpful.

PAKISTAN World Time +5

Azad Kashmir Radio, Muzaffarabad, Azad Kashmir, Pakistan. Contact: (technical) M. Sajjad Ali Siddiqui, Director of Engineering; or Liaquatullah Khan, Engineering Manager. Registered mail helpful. Rarely replies to correspondence.

☒Pakistan Broadcasting Corporation—same address, fax and contact as "Radio Pakistan," below. E-mail: cnoradio@isb.comsats.net.pk. URL: (includes RealAudio) www.radio.gov.pk.

Radio Pakistan, P.O. Box 1393, Islamabad 44000, Pakistan. E-mail: same as for Pakistan Broadcasting Corporation, above. URL: www.radio.gov.pk/exter.html. Contact: (technical) Ahmed Nawaz, Senior Broadcast Engineer, Room No. 324, Frequency Management Cell; Syed Abrar Hussain, Controller of Frequency Management; Syed Asmat Ali Shah, Senior Broadcasting Engineer; or Nasirahmad Bajwa, Frequency Management. Free stickers, pennants and *Pakistan Calling* magazine. May also send pocket calendar. Very poor replier. Plans to replace two 50 kW transmitters with 500 kW units if and when funding is forthcoming.

PALAU World Time +9

KHBN—Voice of Hope, P.O. Box 66, Koror, Palau 96940, Pacific Islands. Phone: +680 488-2162. Fax: (main office) +680 488 2163; or (engineering) +680 544 1008. E-mail: (general) hamadmin@palaunet.com; or (engineering) khbntx@

palaunet.com. URL: www.intertvnet.net/~highorg/stations/asia_china/. Contact: (general) Regina Subris, Station Manager; (technical) Ernie Fontanilla, Engineer. Free stickers and publications. IRC requested. Also, *see* KVOH—Voice of Hope/High Adventure Ministries, USA.

PAPUA NEW GUINEA   World Time +10

NOTE: Stations are sometimes off the air due to financial or technical problems which can take weeks or months to resolve.

National Broadcasting Corporation of Papua New Guinea, P.O. Box 1359, Boroko, Papua New Guinea. Phone: + 675 325-5949. Fax: +675 325 0796 or +675 325 6296. Contact: (general) Renagi R. Lohia, CBE, Managing Director and C.E.O.; or Ephraim Tammy, Director, Radio Services; (technical) Bob Kabewa, Sr. Technical Officer; or F. Maredey, Chief Engineer. Two IRCs or return postage helpful. Replies irregularly.

Radio Bougainville, P.O. Box 35, Buka, North Solomons Province (NSP), Papua New Guinea. Contact: A.L. Rumina, Provincial Programme Manager; Ms. Christine Talei, Assistant Provincial Manager; or Aloysius Laukai, Senior Programme Officer. Replies irregularly.

Radio Central (when operating), P.O. Box 1359, Boroko, NCD, Papua New Guinea. Contact: Steven Gamini, Station Manager; or Amos Langit, Technician. $1, 2 IRCs or return postage helpful. Replies irregularly.

Radio Eastern Highlands (when operating), P.O. Box 311, Goroka, EHP, Papua New Guinea. Contact: Ignas Yanam, Technical Officer; or Kiri Nige, Engineering Division. $1 or return postage required. Replies irregularly.

Radio East New Britain (when operating), P.O. Box 393, Rabaul, ENBP, Papua New Guinea. Contact: Esekia Mael, Station Manager; or Oemas Kumaina, Provincial Program Manager. Return postage required. Replies slowly.

Radio East Sepik, P.O. Box 65, Wewak, E.S.P., Papua New Guinea. Contact: Elias Albert, Assistant Provincial Program Manager; or Luke Umbo, Station Manager.

Radio Enga, P.O. Box 300, Wabag, Enga Province, Papua New Guinea. Phone: +675 547-1213. Contact: (general) John Lyein Kur, Station Manager; or Robert Papuvo, (technical) Gabriel Paiao, Station Technician.

Radio Gulf (when operating), P.O. Box 36, Kerema, Gulf, Papua New Guinea. Contact: Robin Wainetta, Station Manager; or Timothy Akia, Provincial Program Manager.

Radio Madang, P.O. Box 2138, Madang, Papua New Guinea. Phone: +675 852-2415. Fax: +675 852 2360. Contact: (general) Damien Boaging, Senior Programme Officer; Geo Gedabing, Provincial Programme Manager; Peter Charlie Yannum, Assistant Provincial Programme Manager; or James Steve Valakvi, Senior Programme Officer; (technical) Lloyd Guvil, Technician.

Radio Manus, P.O. Box 505, Lorengau, Manus, Papua New Guinea. Phone: +675 470-9029. Fax: +675 470 9079. Contact: (technical and nontechnical) John P. Mandrakamu, Provincial Program Manager. Station is seeking the help of DXers and broadcasting professionals in obtaining a second hand, but still usable broadcasting quality CD player that could be donated to Radio Manus. Replies regularly. Return postage appreciated.

Radio Milne Bay(when operating), P.O. Box 111, Alotau, Milne Bay, Papua New Guinea. Contact: (general) Trevor Webumo, Assistant Manager; Simon Muraga, Station Manager; or Raka Petuely, Program Officer; (technical) Philip Maik, Technician. Return postage in the form of mint stamps helpful.

Radio Morobe, P.O. Box 1262, Lae, Morobe, Papua New Guinea. Fax: +675 472 6423. Contact: Ken L. Tropu, Assistant Program Manager; Peter W. Manua, Program Manager; Kekalem M. Meruk, Assistant Provincial Program Manager; or Aloysius R. Nase, Station Manager.

Radio New Ireland, P.O. Box 140, Kavieng, New Ireland, Papua New Guinea. Contact: Otto A. Malatana, Station Manager; or Ruben Bale, Provincial Program Manager. Return postage or $1 helpful.

Radio Northern (when operating), Voice of Oro, P.O. Box 137, Popondetta, Oro, Papua New Guinea. Contact: Roma Tererembo, Assistant Provincial Programme Manager; or Misael Pendaia, Station Manager. Return postage required.

Radio Sandaun, P.O. Box 37, Vanimo, Sandaun Province, Papua New Guinea. Contact: (nontechnical) Gabriel Deckwalen, Station Manager; Zacharias Nauot, Acting Assistant Manager; Elias Rathley, Provincial Programme Manager; Mrs. Maria Nauot, Secretary; (technical) Paia Ottawa, Technician. $1 helpful.

Radio Simbu, P.O. Box 228, Kundiawa, Chimbu, Papua New Guinea. Phone: +675 735-1038 or +675 735-1082. Fax: +675 735 1012. Contact: (general) Jack Wera, Manager; Tony Mill Waine, Provincial Programme Manager; Felix Tsiki; or Thomas Ghiyandiule, Producer, "Pasikam Long ol Pipel." Cassette recordings $5. Free two-Kina banknotes.

Radio Southern Highlands (when operating), P.O. Box 104, Mendi, SHP, Papua New Guinea. Contact: (general) Andrew Meles, Provincial Programme Manager; Miriam Piapo, Programme Officer; Benard Kagaro, Programme Officer; Lucy Aluy, Programme Officer; or Nicholas Sambu, Producer, "Questions & Answers"; (technical) Ronald Helori, Station Technician. $1 or return postage helpful; or donate a wall poster of a rock band, singer or American landscape.

Radio Western, P.O. Box 23, Daru, Western Province, Papua New Guinea. Contact: Robin Wainetti (Manager); (technical) Samson Tobel, Technician. $1 or return postage required. Replies irregularly.

Radio Western Highlands (when operating), P.O. Box 311, Mount Hagen, WHP, Papua New Guinea. Contact: (technical) Esau Okole, Technician. $1 or return postage helpful. Replies occasionally.

Radio West New Britain, P.O. Box 412, Kimbe, WNBP, Papua New Guinea. Fax: +675 983 5600. Contact: Valuka Lowa, Provincial Station Manager; Darius Gilime, Provincial Program Manager; Lemeck Kuam, Producer, "Questions and Answers"; or Esekial Mael. Return postage required.

PARAGUAY   World Time –3 (–4 midyear)

La Voz del Chaco Paraguayo, Filadelfia, Dpto. de Boquerón, Chaco, Paraguay. Contact: Erwin Wiens, Director; or Arnold Boschmann, Director de Programación. This station, currently only on mediumwave AM, hopes to add a world band transmitter within the 60-meter (5 MHz) band. Although the station is located above the Tropic of Capricorn, and therefore eligible to use the tropical bands, the telecommunications authorities in Asunción, south of the line, have never supported broadcasting on tropical band frequencies within Paraguay.

Radio Encarnación (when operating), Gral. Artigas casi Gral. B. Caballero, Encarnación, Paraguay. Phone: (general)

+595 (71) 4376 or +595 (71) 3345; (press) +595 (71) 4120. Fax: +595 (71) 4099. $1 or return postage helpful.

Radio Guairá (when operating), Alejo García y Presidente Franco, Villarrica, Paraguay. Phone: +595 (541) 2385 or +595 (541) 3411. Fax: +595 (541) 2130. Contact: (general) Lídice Rodríguez Vda. de Traversi, Propietaria; (technical) Enrique Traversi. Welcomes correspondence in Spanish. $1 or return postage helpful.

Radio Nacional del Paraguay, Blas Garay 241 entre Yegros e Iturbe, Asunción, Paraguay. Phone: +595 (21) 449-213. Fax: +595 (21) 332 750. Contact: Efraín Martínez Cuevas, Director. Free tourist brochure. $1 or return postage required. Replies, sometimes slowly, to correspondence in Spanish.

PERU   World Time –5 year-round in Loreto, Cusco and

Puno. Other departments sometimes move to World Time –4 for a few weeks of the year.

NOTE: Obtaining replies from Peruvian stations calls for creativity, tact, patience—and the proper use of Spanish, not form letters and the like. There are nearly 150 world band stations operating from Perú on any given day. While virtually all of these may be reached simply by using as the address the station's city, as given in the Blue Pages, the following are the only stations known to be replying—even if only occasionally—to correspondence from abroad.

Emisoras JSV—*see* Radio JSV.

Estación C, Casilla de Correo 210, Moyobamba, San Martín, Peru. Contact: Porfirio Centurión, Propietario.

Estación Tarapoto (if reactivated), Jirón Federico Sánchez 720, Tarapoto, Peru. Phone: +51 (94) 522-709. Contact: Luis Humberto Hidalgo Sánchez, Gerente General; or José Luna Paima, Announcer. Replies occasionally to correspondence in Spanish.

Estación Wari, Calle Nazareno 108, Ayacucho, Peru. Phone: +51 (64) 813-039. Contact: Walter Muñoz Ynga I., Gerente.

Estación X (Equis) (when operating), Plaza de Armas No. 106, Yurimaguas, Provincia de Alto Amazonas, Loreto, Peru. Contact: Franklin Coral Sousa, Director Propietario, who may also be contacted at his home address: Jirón Mariscal Castilla No. 104, Yurimaguas, Provincia de Alto Amazonas, Loreto, Peru.

Frecuencia Líder (Radio Bambamarca), Jirón Jorge Chávez 416, Bambamarca, Hualgayoc, Cajamarca, Peru. Phone: (office) +51 (74) 713-260; (studio) +51 (74) 713-249. Contact: (general) Valentín Peralta Díaz, Gerente; Irma Peralta Rojas; or Carlos Antonio Peralta Rojas; (technical) Oscar Lino Peralta Rojas. Free station photos. *La Historia de Bambamarca* book for 5 Soles; cassettes of Peruvian and Latin American folk music for 4 Soles each; T-shirts for 10 Soles each (sending US$1 per Sol should suffice and cover foreign postage costs, as well). Replies occasionally to correspondence in Spanish. Considering replacing their transmitter to improve reception.

Frecuencia San Ignacio, Jirón Villanueva Pinillos 330, San Ignacio, Cajamarca, Peru. Contact: Franklin R. Hoyos Cóndor, Director Gerente; or Ignacio Gómez Torres, Técnico de Sonido. Replies to correspondence in Spanish. $1 or return postage necessary.

Frecuencia VH—*see* Radio Frecuencia VH.

La Super Radio San Ignacio (when operating), Avenida Víctor Larco 104, a un costado del campo deportivo, San Ignacio, Distrito de Sinsicap, Provincia de Otuzco, La Libertad, Peru.

La Voz de Anta, Distrito de Anta, Provincia de Acobamba, Departamento de Huancavelica. Phone: +51 (64) 750-201.

La Voz de la Selva—*see* Radio La Voz de la Selva.

La Voz de San Juan—*see* Radio La Voz de San Juan.

La Voz del Campesino—*see* Radio La Voz del Campesino.

La Voz del Marañon—*see* Radio La Voz del Marañon.

Ondas del Suroriente—*see* Radio Ondas del Suroriente, below.

Radio Adventista Mundial—La Voz de la Esperanza, Jirón Dos de Mayo No. 218, Celendín, Cajamarca, Peru. Contact: Francisco Goicochea Ortiz, Director; or Lucas Solano Oyarce, Director de Ventas.

Radio Altura (Cerro de Pasco), Casilla de Correo 140, Cerro de Pasco, Pasco, Peru. Phone: +51 (64) 721-875, +51 (64) 722-398. Contact: Oswaldo de la Cruz Vásquez, Gerente General. Replies to correspondence in Spanish.

Radio Altura (Huarmaca), Antonio Raymondi 3ra Cuadra, Distrito de Huarmaca, Provincia de Huancabamba, Piura, Peru.

Radio Amauta del Perú, (when operating), Jirón Manuel Iglesias s/n, a pocos pasos de la Plazuela San Juan, San Pablo, Cajamarca, Nor Oriental del Marañón, Peru.

Radio América (if reactivated), Montero Rosas 1099, Santa Beatriz, Lima, Peru. Phone: +51 (1) 265-3841/2/3. Fax: +51 (1) 265 3844. Contact: Liliana Sugobono F., Directora; or Jorge Arriola Viván, Promociones y Marketing.

Radio Amistad, Manzana I-11, Lote 6, Calle 22, Urbanización Mariscal Cáceres, San Juan de Lurigancho, Lima, Peru. Phone: +51 (1) 392-3640. Contact: Manuel Mejía Barboza. Reception reports may also be e-mailed to Peruvian listener Alfredo Canote (alfca@mail.excite.com), who will forward them to the station.

Radio Ancash, Casilla de Correo 221, Huaraz, Peru. Phone: +51 (44) 721-381,+51 (44) 721-359, +51 (44) 721-487, +51 (44) 722-512. Fax: +51 (44) 722 992. Contact: Armando Moreno Romero, Gerente General. Replies to correspondence in Spanish.

Radio Andahuaylas, Jr. Ayacucho No. 248, Andahuaylas, Apurímac, Peru. Contact: Sr. Daniel Andréu C., Gerente. $1 required. Replies irregularly to correspondence in Spanish.

Radio Andina, Real 175, Huancayo, Junín, Peru. Phone: +51 (64) 231-123. Replies infrequently to correspondence in Spanish.

Radio Apurímac (when operating), Jirón Cusco 206 (or Ovalo El Olivo No. 23), Abancay, Apurímac, Peru. Contact: Antero Quispe Allca, Director General.

Radio Arcángel San Miguel—*see* Radio San Miguel Arcángel.

Radio Atlántida

STATION: Jirón Arica 441, Iquitos, Loreto, Peru. Phone: +51 (94) 234-452, +51 (94) 234-962. Contact: Pablo Rojas Bardales. LISTENER CORRESPONDENCE: Sra. Carmela López Paredes, Directora del prgrama "Trocha Turística," Jirón Arica 1083, Iquitos, Loreto, Peru. Free pennants and tourist information. $1 or return postage required. Replies to most correspondence in Spanish, the preferred language, and some correspondence in English. "Trocha Turística" is a bilingual (Spanish and English) tourist program aired weekdays 2300-2330.

Radio Ayabaca, Jirón Comercio 437, Ayabaca, Huancabamba, Peru. Phone: +51 (74) 471-076. Contact: José Heli Requejo Aldean, Gerente. Replies to correspondence in Spanish. Return postage helpful.

Radio Ayaviri (La Voz de Melgar) (when operating), Apartado 8, Ayaviri, Puno, Peru. Fax: +51 (54) 320 207, specify on fax "Anexo 127." Contact: (general) Sra. Corina Llaiqui

Ochoa, Administradora; (technical) José Aristo Solórzano Mendoza, Director. Free pennants. Sells audio cassettes of local folk music for $5 plus postage; also exchanges music cassettes. Correspondence accepted in English, but Spanish preferred.

Radio Bahía, Jirón Alfonso Ugarte 309, Chimbote, Ancash, Peru. Phone: +51 (44) 322-391. Contact: Margarita Rossel Soria, Administradora; or Miruna Cruz Rossel, Administradora.

Radio Bambamarca—*see* Frecuencia Líder, above.

Radio Bolívar. Provincia de Bolívar, Departamento de La Libertad, Peru. Contact: Julio Davila Echeverria, Gerente. May send free pennant. Return postage helpful.

Radio Cajamarca, Jirón La Mar 675, Cajamarca, Peru. Phone: +51 (44) 921-014. Contact: Porfirio Cruz Potosí.

Radio Chanchamayo, Jirón Tarma 551, La Merced, Junín, Peru.

Radio Chaski, Baptist Mid-Missions, Apartado 368, Cusco, Peru; or Alameda Pachacútec s/n B-5, Cusco, Peru. Phone: +51 (84) 225-052. Contact: Andrés Tuttle H., Gerente.

Radio Chincheros, Jirón Apurímac s/n, Chincheros, Departamento de Apurímac, Peru.

Radio Chota, Jirón Anaximandro Vega 690, Apartado Postal 3, Chota, Cajamarca, Peru. Phone: +51 (44) 771-240. Contact: Aladino Gavidia Huamán, Administrador. $1 or return postage required. Replies slowly to correspondence in Spanish.

Radio Comas Televisión, Avenida Estados Unidos 327, Urbanización Huaquillay, km 10 de la Avenida Túpac Amaru, Distrito de Comas, Lima, Peru. Phone: +51 (1) 525-0859. Fax: +51 (1) 525 0094. Contact: Edgar Saldaña R.; Juan Rafael Saldaña Reátegui (Relaciones Públicas) or Gamaniel Francisco Chahua, Productor-Programador General.

Radio Concordia (if reactived), Av. La Paz 512-A, Arequipa, Peru. If a reply is not forthcoming, try: Miguel Grau s/n Mz.2 Lt. 1, Arequipa, Peru. Phone: +51 (54) 446-053. Contact: Pedro Pablo Acosta Fernández. Free stickers. Return postage required.

Radio Continental (when operating), Av. Independencia 56, Arequipa, Peru. Phone: +51 (54) 213-253. Contact: J. Antonio Umbert D., Director General; or Leonor Núñez Melgar. Free stickers. Replies slowly to correspondence in Spanish.

⬛**Radio CORA**, Compañía Radiofónica Lima, S.A., Paseo de la República 144, Centro Cívico, Oficina 5, Lima 1, Peru. Phone: +51 (1) 433-5005, +51 (1) 433-1188, +51 (1) 433-0848. Fax: +51 (1) 433 6134. E-mail: cora@peru.itete.com.pe; cora@lima.business.com.pe. URL: (includes RealAudio) www.radiocora.com.pe/. Contact: (general) Juan Ramírez Lazo, Propietario y Director Gerente; Dra. Lylian Ramírez M., Directora de Prensa y Programación; Juan Ramírez Lazo, Director Gerente; or Srta. Angelina María Abie; (technical) Srta. Sylvia Ramírez M., Directora Técnica. Free station sticky-label pads, bumper stickers and may send large certificate suitable for framing. Audio cassettes with extracts from their programs $20 plus $2 postage; women's hair bands $2 plus $1 postage. Two IRCs or $1 required. Replies slowly to correspondence in English, Spanish, French, Italian and Portuguese.

Radio Cristal, Jirón Ucayali s/n, a un costado de la Carretera Marginal de la Selva, San Hilarión, Provincia de Picota, Región San Martín, Peru. Contact: Señora Marina Gaona, Gerente; or Lucho García Gaona.

Radio Cultural Amauta (Bambamarca) (when operating), Jirón Jaime de Martínez 645, Bambamarca, Cajamarca, Peru. Contact: Valentín Mejía Vásquez, Presidente de la Central Unica Provincial de Rondas Campesinas (also via his home address: Jirón Mariscal Sucre 644, Bambamarca, Cajamarca, Peru); Wilmer Vásquez Campos, Encargado Administración;

Mauricio Rodríguez R.; or Walter Hugo Bautista. Radio Cultural Amauta is a new name for the former Radio La Voz de San Antonio.

Radio Cultural Amauta (Huanta), Cahuide 278, Apartado Postal 24, Huanta, Ayacucho, Peru. Phone: +51 (64) 832-153. Contact: Vicente Saico Tinco.

Radio Cusco, Apartado 251, Cusco, Peru. Phone: (general)+51 (84) 225-851; (management) +51 (84) 232-457. Fax: +51 (84) 223 308. Contact: Sra. Juana Huamán Yépez, Administradora; or Raúl Siú Almonte, Gerente General; (technical) Benjamín Yábar Alvarez. Free pennants, postcards and key rings. Audio cassettes of Peruvian music $10 plus postage. $1 or return postage required. Replies irregularly to correspondence in English or Spanish. Station is looking for folk music recordings from around the world to use in their programs.

Radio del Pacífico, Apartado 4236, Lima 1, Peru. Phone: +51 (1) 433-3275. Fax: +51 (1) 433 3276. Contact: J. Petronio Allauca, Secretario, Departamento de Relaciones Públicas; or P.G. Ferreyra. $1 or return postage required. Replies occasionally to correspondence in Spanish.

Radio El Sol (Lima) (when active), Avenida Uruguay 355, 7°, Lima Peru. Phone: +51 (1) 330-0713, +51 (1) 424-6107. Rarely replies, and only to correspondence in Spanish.

Radio El Sol (Pucará), Avenida Jaén s/n, Distrito de Pucará, Jaén, Cajamarca, Peru.

Radio El Sol de los Andes, Jirón 2 de Mayo 257, Juliaca, Peru. Phone: +51 (54) 321-115. Fax: +51 (54) 322-981. Contact: Armando Alarcón Velarde.

Radio Estación Uno, Barrio Altos, Distrito de Pucará, Provincia Jaén, Nor Oriental del Marañón, Peru.

Radio Estudio 2000, Distrito Miguel Pardo Naranjos, Provincia de Rioja, Departamento de San Martín, Peru.

Radio Frecuencia VH ("La Voz de Celendín"; "RVC"), Jirón José Gálvez 1030, Celendín, Cajamarca, Peru. Contact: Fernando Vásquez Castro, Propietario.

Radio Frecuencia San Ignacio—*see* Frecuencia San Ignacio.

Radio Horizonte (Chachapoyas), Apartado 69 (or Jirón Amazonas 1177), Chachapoyas, Amazonas, Peru. Phone: +51 (74) 757-793. Fax: +51 (74) 757 004. Contact: Sra. Rocío García Rubio, Ing. Electrónico, Directora; Percy Chuquizuta Alvarado, Locutor; María Montaldo Echaiz, Locutora; Marcelo Mozambite Chavarry, Locutor; Ing. María Dolores Gutiérrez Atienza, Administradora; Juan Nancy Ruíz de Valdez, Secretaria; Yoel Toro Morales, Técnico de Transmisión; or María Soledad Sánchez Castro, Administradora. Replies to correspondence in English, French, German and Spanish. $1 required.

Radio Horizonte (Chiclayo), Jirón Incanato 387 Altos, Distrito José Leonardo Ortiz, Chiclayo, Lambayeque, Peru. Phone: +51 (74) 252-917. Contact: Enrique Becerra Rojas, Owner and General Manager. Return postage required.

Radio Hualgayoc, Jirón San Martín s/n, Hualgayoc, Cajamarca, Peru. Contact: Máximo Zamora Medina, Director Propietario.

Radio Huamachuco (if reactivated), Jirón Bolívar 937, Huamachuco, La Libertad, Peru. Contact: Manuel D. Gil Gil, Director Propietario.

Radio Huancabamba (when operating), Calle Unión 610-Barrio Chalaco, Huancabamba, Piura, Peru. Fax: +51 (74) 320 229, specifying "Radio Huancabamba" on fax. Contact: (general) Fredy Alberca, General Manager; (administration) Edwin Arrieta. Free picture postcards. Replies occasionally to correspondence in English, French, Italian, Portuguese and

**Studio for WTJC—
"Waiting 'Til Jesus
Comes"—which since
September 1999 has
been airing evangelical
programs to audiences
throughout North
America.**   D. Robinson

Spanish. Hopes to replace transmitter. Off the air since 1996 when manager César Colunche Bustamante moved to San Ignacio where he operated Radio Melodia (now off the air) and Radio San Ignacio (see).

Radio Huanta 2000, Jirón Gervacio Santillana 455, Huanta, Peru. Phone: +51 (64) 932-105. Fax: +51 (64) 832 105. Contact: Ronaldo Sapaico Maravi, Departamento Técnico; or Sra. Lucila Orellana de Paz, Administradora. Free photo of staff. Return postage or $1 appreciated. Replies to correspondence in Spanish.

Radio Huarmaca, Av. Grau 454 (detrás de Inversiones La Loretana), Distrito de Huarmaca, Provincia de Huancabamba, Región Grau, Peru. Contact: Simón Zavaleta Pérez. Return postage helpful.

Radio Ilucán, Jirón Lima 290, Cutervo, Región Nororiental del Marañón, Peru. Phone: +51 (44) 737-010, +51 (44) 737-231. Contact: José Gálvez Salazar, Gerente Administrativo. $1 required. Replies occasionally to correspondence in Spanish.

Radio Imagen, Casilla de Correo 42, Tarapoto, San Martín, Peru; Jirón San Martín 328, Tarapoto, San Martín, Peru; or Apartado 254, Tarapoto, San Martín, Peru. Phone: +51 (94) 522-696. Contact: Adith Chumbe Vásquez, Secretaria; or Jaime Ríos Tapullima, Gerente General. Replies irregularly to correspondence in Spanish. $1 or return postage helpful.

Radio Integración, Av. Seoane 200, Apartado Postal 57, Abancay, Departamento de Apurímac, Peru. Contact: Zenón Hernán Farfán Cruzado, Propietario.

Radio Internacional del Perú (when operating), Jirón Bolognesi 532, San Pablo, Cajamarca, Peru.

Radio Interoceánica (if reactivated), Provincia de Azángaro, Departamento de Puno, Peru.

Radio Jaén (La Voz de la Frontera), Calle Mariscal Castilla 439, Jaén, Cajamarca, Peru. Contact: Luis A. Vílchez Ochoa, Administrador.

Radio JSV, Jirón Aguilar 742-744, Huánuco, Peru. Phone: +51 (64) 512-930. Return postage required.

Radio Juliaca (La Decana), Ramón Castilla 949, Apartado Postal 67, Juliaca, San Román, Puno, Peru. Phone: +51 (54) 332-386. Fax: +51 (54) 321-372. Contact: Alberto Quintanilla Ch., Director.

Radio JVL, Jirón Túpac Amaru 105, Consuelo, Distrito de San Pablo, Provincia de Bellavista, Departamento de San Martín, Peru. Contact: John Wiley Villanueva Lara—a student of electronic engineering—who currently runs the station, and whose initials make up the station name. Replies to correspondence in Spanish. Return Postage required.

Radio La Hora, Av. Garcilaso 411, Cusco, Peru. Phone: +51 (84) 225-615, +51 (84) 231-371. Contact: Carlos Gamarra Moscoso, Director. Free stickers, pins, pennants and postcards of Cusco. Return postage required. Station Director is requesting reception reports. Replies occasionally to correspondence in Spanish. Hopes to increase transmitter power if and when the economic situation improves.

Radio La Inmaculada, Parroquia La Inmaculada Concepción, Frente de la Plaza de Armas, Santa Cruz, Provincia de Santa Cruz, Departamento de Cajamarca, Peru. Phone: +51 (74) 714-051. Contact: Reverendo Padre Angel Jorge Carrasco, Gerente; or Gabino González Vera, Locutor.

Radio Lajas, Jirón Rosendo Mendívil 589, Lajas, Chota, Cajamarca, Nor Oriental del Marañón, Peru. Contact: Alfonso Medina Burga, Gerente Propietario.

Radio La Merced, Junín 163, La Merced, Junín, Peru. Phone: +51 (64) 531-199. Occasionally replies to correspondence in Spanish.

Radio La Oroya, Calle Lima 190, Tercer Piso Of. 3, Apartado Postal 88, La Oroya, Provincia de Yauli, Departamento de Junín, Peru. Phone: +51 (64) 391-401. Fax: +51 (64) 391 440. E-mail: rlofigu@net.cosapidata.com.pe. URL: www.cosapidata.com.pe/empresa/rlofigu/rlofigu.htm. Contact: Jacinto Manuel Figueroa Yauri, Gerente-Propietario. Free pennants. $1 or return postage necessary. Replies to correspondence in Spanish.

Radio La Voz, Andahuaylas, Apurímac, Peru. Contact: Lucio Fuentes, Director Gerente.

Radio La Voz de Chiriaco, Jirón Ricardo Palma s/n, Chiriaco, Distrito de Imaza, Provincia de Bagua, Departamento de Amazonas, Peru. Contact: Hildebrando López Pintado, Director; Santos Castañeda Cubas, Director Gerente; or Fidel Huamuro Curinambe, Técnico de Mantenimiento. $1 or return postage helpful.

Radio La Voz de Cutervo (if reactivated), Jirón María Elena Medina 644-650, Cutervo, Cajamarca, Peru.

Radio La Voz de Huamanga (if reactivated), Calle El Nazareno, 2do Pasaje No. 161, Ayacucho, Peru. Phone: +51 (64) 812-366. Contact: Sra. Aguida A. Valverde Gonzales. Free pennants and postcards.

Radio La Voz de la Selva, Abtao 255, Casilla de Correo 207, Iquitos, Loreto, Peru. Phone: +51 (94) 265-244/5, +51 (94) 267-890. Fax: +51 (94) 239 360. Contact: Julia Jauregui Rengifo, Directora; Marcelino Esteban Benito, Director; Pedro Sandoval Guzmán, Announcer; or Mery Blas Rojas. Replies to correspondence in Spanish.

Radio La Voz de las Huarinjas, Barrio El Altillo, Huancabamba, Piura, Peru. Phone: +51 (74) 473-126. Contact: Alfonso García Silva, Gerente Director; or Bill Yeltsin, Administrador. Replies to correspondence in Spanish.

Radio La Voz de Oxapampa, Av. Mullenbruck 469, Oxapampa, Pasco, Peru. Contact: Pascual Villafranca Guzmán, Director Propietario.

Radio La Voz de San Juan, 28 de Julio 420, Lonya Grande, Provincia de Utcubamba, Región Nororiental del Marañón, Peru. Contact: Prof. Víctor Hugo Hidrovo; or Edilberto Ortiz Chávez, Locutor. Formerly known as Radio San Juan.

Radio La Voz de Santa Cruz (if reactivated), Av. Zarumilla 190, Santa Cruz, Cajamarca, Peru.

Radio La Voz del Campesino, Av. Piura 1015, Pampa Alegre, San Miguel de El Faique, Provincia de Huancabamba, Peru. Contact: Alberto Soto Santos, Director Propietario; Gonzalo Castillo Chanta, Locutor; or Araceli Bruno L. and Gloria Huamán Flórez, Locutoras.

Radio La Voz del Marañón (if reactivated), Jirón Bolognesi 130, Barrio La Alameda, Cajamarca, Nor Oriental del Marañón, Peru. Contact: Eduardo Díaz Coronado.

Radio Libertad de Junín, Cerro de Pasco 528, Apartado Postal 2, Junín, Peru. Phone: +51 (64) 344-026. Contact: Mauro Chaccha G., Director Gerente. Replies slowly to correspondence in Spanish. Return postage necessary.

Radio Líder, Portal Belén 115, 2do piso, Cusco, Peru. Contact: Mauro Calvo Acurio, Propietario.

Radio Lircay (when operating), Barrio Maravillas, Lircay, Provincia de Angaraes, Huancavelica, Peru.

Radio Los Andes (Huamachuco) (if reactivated), Pasaje Damián Nicolau 108-110, 2do piso, Huamachuco, La Libertad, Peru. Phone: +51 (44) 441-240.

Radio Los Andes (Huarmaca), Huarmaca, Provincia de Huancabamba, Región Grau, Peru. Contact: William Cerro Calderón.

Radio LTC (if reactivated), Jirón Unión 242, Juliaca, Puno, Peru. Phone: +51 (54) 322-452, +51 (54) 322-560. Fax: +51 (54) 322 570. Contact: Mario Leonidas Torres, Gerente Ejecutivo; Leoncio Z. Torres C. (whose initials make up the station name), Gerente General; or María Figueroa, Administradora.

Radio Luz y Sonido, Apartado 280, Huánuco, Peru; (physical address) Jirón Dos de Mayo 1286, Oficina 205, Huánuco, Peru. Phone: +51 (64) 512-394 or +51 (64) 518-500. Fax: +51 (64) 511 985. E-mail: luz.sonido@hys.com.pe. URL: www.hys.com.pe/page/luzysonido/. Contact: (technical) Jorge Benavides Moreno; (nontechnical) Pedro Martínez Tineo, Director Ejecutivo; Lic. Orlando Bravo Jesús; or Seydel Saavedra Cabrera, Operador/Locutor. Return postage or $2 required. Replies to correspondence in Spanish, Italian and Portuguese. Sells video cassettes of local folk dances and religious and tourist themes.

Radio Madre de Dios, D.A. Carrión 387, Apartado Postal 37, Puerto Maldonado, Madre de Dios, Peru. Phone: +51 (84) 571-050. Contact: Alcides Arguedas Márquez, Director del programa "Un Festival de Música Internacional," heard Mondays 0100 to 0200 World Time. Sr. Arguedas is interested in feedback for this letterbox program. Replies to correspondence in Spanish. $1 or return postage appreciated.

Radio Majestad, Calle Real 1033, Oficina 302, Huancayo, Junín, Peru.

Radio Marañón (if reactivated), Apartado 50, Jaén, Cajamarca, Peru. Phone: +51 (44) 731-579, +51 (44) 733-464. Phone/fax: +51 (74) 731-147. Contact: Padre Luis Távara Martín, S.J., Director. Return postage necessary. May send free pennant. Replies slowly to correspondence in Spanish.

Radio Marginal, San Martín 257, Tocache, San Martín, Peru. Phone: +51 (94) 551-031. Rarely replies.

Radio Máster, Jirón 20 de Abril 308, Moyobamba, Departamento de San Martín, Peru. Contact: Américo Vásquez Hurtado, Director

Radio Melodía, San Camilo 501, Arequipa, Peru. Phone: +51 (54) 232-071, +51 (54) 232-327, +51 (54) 285-152. Fax: +51 (54) 237 312. Contact: Hermogenes Delgado Torres, Director; or Señora Elba Alvarez de Delgado. Replies to correspondence in Spanish.

Radio Mi Frontera, Calle San Ignacio 520, Distrito de Chirinos, Provincia de San Ignacio, Región Nor Oriental del Marañón, Peru.

Radio Moderna, Jirón Arequipa 323, 2do piso, Celendín, Cajamarca, Peru.

Radio Mundial Adventista, Colegio Adventista de Titicaca, Casilla 4, Juliaca, Peru. Currently on mediumwave only, but is expected to add shortwave sometime in the future.

Radio Mundo, Calle Tecte 245, Cusco, Peru. Phone: + 51 (84) 232-076. Fax: +51 (84) 233 076. Contact: Valentín Olivera Puelles, Gerente. Free postcards and stickers. Return postage necessary. Replies slowly to correspondence in Spanish.

Radio Municipal de Cangallo (when active), Concejo Provincial de Cangallo, Plaza Principal No. 02, Cangallo, Ayacucho, Peru. Contact: Nivardo Barbarán Agüero, Encargado Relaciones Públicas.

Radio Nacional del Perú
ADMINISTRATIVE OFFICE: Avenida José Gálvez 1040 Santa Beatriz, Lima, Peru. Fax: +51 (14) 433 8952. Contact: Henry Aragón Ibarra, Director General; or Rafael Mego Carrascal, Jefatura de la Administración. Replies occasionally, by letter or listener-prepared verification card, to correspondence in Spanish. Return postage required.
STUDIO ADDRESS: Av. Petit Thouars 447, Lima, Peru.

Radio Naylamp, Avenida Andrés Avelino Cáceres 800, Lambayeque, Peru. Phone: +51 (74) 283-353. Contact: Dr. Juan José Grández Vargas, Director Gerente; or Delicia Coronel Muñoz, who is interested in receiving postcards and the like. Free stickers, pennants and calendars. Return postage necessary.

Radio Nor Andina, Jirón José Gálvez 602, Celendín, Cajamarca, Peru. Contact: Misael Alcántara Guevara, Gerente; or Víctor B. Vargas C., Departamento de Prensa. Free calendar. $1 required. Donations (registered mail best) sought for the Committee for Good Health for Children, headed by Sr. Alcántara, which is active in saving the lives of hungry youngsters in poverty-stricken Cajamarca Province. Replies irregularly to casual or technical correspondence in Spanish, but regularly to Children's Committee donors and helpful correspondence in Spanish.

Radio Nor Peruana, Emisora Municipal, Jirón Ortiz Arrieta 588, 1er. piso del Concejo Provincial de Chachapoyas,

Chachapoyas, Amazonas, Peru. Contact: Carlos Poema, Administrador; or Edgar Villegas, program host for "La Voz de Chachapoyas," (Sundays, 1100-1300).

Radio Nueva Sensación, Cadena Radial Nuevo Siglo, Panamericana Norte km. 361, Urbanización Ricardo Palma, Chiclayo, Peru.

Radio Onda Imperial, Calle Sacsayhuamán K-10, Urbanización Manuel Prado, Cusco, Peru. Phone: +51 (84) 232-521, +51 (84) 233-032.

Radio Ondas del Huallaga, Jirón Leoncio Prado 723, Apartado Postal 343, Huánuco, Peru. Phone: +51 (64) 511-525, +51 (64) 512-428. Contact: Flaviano Llanos Malpartida, Representante Legal. $1 or return postage required. Replies to correspondence in Spanish.

Radio Ondas del [Río] Marañón, Jirón Amazonas 315, Distrito de Aramango, Provincia de Bagua, Departamento de Amazonas, Región Nororiental del Marañón, Peru. Contact: Agustín Tongod, Director Propietario. "Rio"—river—is sometimes, but not always, used in on-air identification.

Radio Ondas del Río Mayo, Jirón Huallaga 348, Nueva Cajamarca, San Martín, Peru. Phone: +51 (94) 556-006. Contact: Edilberto Lucío Peralta Lozada, Gerente; or Víctor Huaras Rojas, Locutor. Free pennants. Return postage helpful. Replies slowly to correspondence in Spanish.

Radio Ondas del Suroriente, Jirón Ricardo Palma 510, Quillabamba, La Convención, Cusco, Peru.

Radio Oriente, Vicariato Apostólico, Calle Progreso 114, Yurimaguas, Loreto, Peru. Phone: +51 (94) 352-156. Phone/fax (ask to switch over to fax): +51 (94) 352-566. Contact: (general) Sra. Elisa Cancino Hidalgo; or Juan Antonio López-Manzanares M., Director; or (technical) Pedro Capo Moragues, Gerente Técnico. $1 or return postage required. Replies occasionally to correspondence in English, French, Spanish and Catalan.

Radio Origen, Acobamba, Departamento de Huancavelica, Peru.

Radio Paccha (if reactivated), Calle Mariscal Castilla 52, Paccha, Provincia de Chota, Departamento de Cajamarca, Peru.

Radio Panorama
STATION: Centro-poblado Recopampa, Distrito de Sorochuco, Provincia de Celendín, Departamento de Cajamarca, Región Autónoma del Marañón, Peru. Phone: +51 (44) 820-321. This is a public phone booth, so the person who answers may not necessarily work at the station! Contact: Segundo Ayala Brione, Propietario.
ADDRESS OF SISTER STATION, RADIO LA VOZ DE LOS ANDES: Plaza de Armas, Distrito de Sorochuco, Provincia de Celendín, Departamento de Cajamarca, Región Autónoma del Marañón, Peru.

Radio Paucartambo, Emisora Municipal
STATION ADDRESS: Paucartambo, Cusco, Peru.
STAFFER ADDRESS: Manuel H. Loaiza Canal, Correo Central, Paucartambo, Cusco, Peru. Return postage or $1 required.

Radio Perú ("Perú, la Radio")
STUDIO ADDRESS: Jirón Atahualpa 191, San Ignacio, Región Nororiental del Marañón, Peru.
ADMINISTRATION: Avenida San Ignacio 493, San Ignacio, Región Nororiental del Marañón, Peru. Contact: Oscar Vásquez Chacón, Director General; or Idelso Vásquez Chacón, Director Propietario. Sometimes relays the FM outlet, "Estudio 97."

Radio Power, Jirón 20 de Abril 467, Moyobamba, San Martín, Peru. Contact: Ricky Centurión Tapia, Propietario.

Radio Quillabamba, Apartado 76, Quillabamba, La Convención, Cusco, Peru. Phone: +51 (84) 281-002. Contact:

Padre Francisco Panera, Director. Replies very irregularly to correspondence in Spanish.

Radio Regional, Jirón Grau s/n frente al Colegio Nuestra Señora del Carmen, Celendín, Cajamarca, Peru.

Radio Reina de la Selva, Jirón Ayacucho 944, Plaza de Armas, Chachapoyas, Región Nor Oriental del Marañón, Peru. Phone: +51 (74) 757-203. Contact: José David Reina Noriega, Gerente General; or Jorge Oscar Reina Noriega, Director General. Replies irregularly to correspondence in Spanish. Return postage necessary.

Radio San Francisco Solano, Parroquia de Sóndor, Calle San Miguel No. 207, Distrito de Sóndor, Huancabamba, Piura, Peru. Contact: Reverendo Padre Manuel José Rosas Castillo, Vicario Parroquial. Station operated by the Franciscan Fathers. Replies to correspondence in Spanish. $1 helpful.

Radio San Ignacio, Jirón Victoria 277, San Ignacio, Región Nororiental del Marañón, Peru. Contact: César Colunche Bustamante, Director Propietario; or his son, Fredy Colunche, Director de Programación.

Radio San Juan, Distrito de Aramango, Provincia de Bagua, Departamento de Amazonas, Región Nororiental del Marañón, Peru.

Radio San Juan, 28 de Julio 420, Lonya Grande, Provincia de Utcubamba, Región Nororiental del Marañón, Peru. Contact: Prof. Víctor Hugo Díaz Hidrovo; or Edilberto Ortiz Chávez, Locutor.

Radio San Miguel, Av. Huayna Cápac 146, Huánchac, Cusco, Peru. Contact: Sra. Catalina Pérez de Alencastre, Gerente General; or Margarita Mercado. Replies to correspondence in Spanish.

Radio San Miguel Arcángel, Jirón Bolívar 356, a media cuadra de la Plaza de Armas, Provincia de San Miguel, Cajamarca, Peru.

Radio San Miguel de El Faique, Distrito de El Faique, Provincia de Huancabamba, Departamento de Piura, Peru.

Radio San Nicolás, Jirón Amazonas 114, Rodríguez de Mendoza, Peru. Contact: Juan José Grández Santillán, Gerente; or Violeta Grández Vargas, Administradora. Return postage necessary.

Radio Santa Rosa, Jirón Camaná 170, Casilla 4451, Lima 1, Peru. Phone: +51 (1) 427-7488. Fax: +51 (1) 426-9219. E-mail: santarosa@viaexpresa.com.pe. URL: www.viaexpresa.com.pe/santarosa/santarosa.htm. Contact: Padre Juan Sokolich Alvarado; or Lucy Palma Barreda. Free stickers and pennants. $1 or return postage necessary. 180-page book commemorating station's 35th anniversary $10. Replies to correspondence in Spanish.

Radio Santiago, Municipalidad Distrital de Río Santiago, Puerto Galilea, Provincia de Condorcanqui, Amazonas, Peru. Contact: Juan Tuchía Oscate, Alcalde Distrital; Sara Sánchez Cubas, Locutora Comercial; or Guillermo Gómez García, Director. Free pennants and postcards. Return postage necessary. Replies to correspondence in Spanish.

Radio Satélite, Jirón Cuervo No. 543, Provincia de Santa Cruz, Cajamarca, Peru. Phone: +51 (74) 714-074, +51 (74) 714-169. Contact: Sabino Llamo Chávez, Gerente. Free tourist brochure. $1 or return postage required. Replies to correspondence in Spanish.

Radio Selecciones, Chuquibamba, Provincia de Condesuyos, Arequipa, Peru.

Radio Sicuani, Jirón 2 de Mayo 206, Sicuani, Canchis, Cusco, Peru; or P.O. Box 45, Sicuani, Peru. Phone: +51 (84) 351-136. Contact: Mario Ochoa Vargas, Director.

Radio Soledad, Centro Minero de Retama, Distrito de Parcoy,

Provincia de Pataz, La Libertad, Peru. Contact: Vicente Valdivieso, Locutor. Return postage necessary.

Radio Sudamérica, Jirón Ramón Castilla 491, tercer nivel, Plaza de Armas, Cutervo, Cajamarca, Peru. Phone: +51 (74) 736-090 or +51 (74) 737-443. Contact: Jorge Luis Paredes Guerra, Administrador; or Amadeo Mario Muñoz Guivar, Propietario.

Radio Tacna, Aniceto Ibarra 436, Casilla de Correo 370, Tacna, Peru. Phone: +51 (54) 714-871. Fax: +51 (54) 723 745. E-mail: radiotac@principal.unjbg.edu.pe. URL: http://principal.unjbg.edu.pe/radio/radta.html. Contact: (nontechnical and technical) Ing. Alfonso Cáceres Contreras, Sub-Gerente/Jefe Técnico; (administration) Yolanda Vda. de Cáceres C., Directora Gerente. Free stickers and samples of *Correo* local newspaper. $1 or return postage helpful. Audio cassettes of Peruvian and other music $2 plus postage. Replies irregularly to correspondence in English and Spanish.

Radio Tawantinsuyo, Av. Sol 806, Cusco, Peru. Phone: +51 (84) 226-955, +51 (84) 228-411. Has a very attractive QSL card, but only replies occasionally to correspondence, which should be in Spanish.

Radio Tarma, Jirón Molino del Amo 167, Apartado Postal 167, Tarma, Peru. Phone/fax: +51 (64) 321 167 or +51 (64) 321 510. Contact: Mario Monteverde Pomareda, Gerente General. Sometimes sends 100 Inti banknote in return when $1 enclosed. Free stickers. $1 or return postage required. Replies irregularly to correspondence in Spanish.

Radio Tayacaja, Correo Central, Distrito de Pampas, Tayacaja, Huancavelica, Peru. Phone: +51 (64) 22-02-17, Anexo 238. Contact: (general) J. Jorge Flores Cárdenas (technical) Ing. Larry Guido Flores Lezama. Free stickers and pennants. Replies to correspondence in Spanish. Hopes to replace transmitter.

Radio Tingo María (when operating), Jirón Callao 115 (or Av. Raimondi No. 592), Casilla de Correo 25, Tingo María, Leoncio Prado, Departamento de Huánuco, Peru. Contact: Gina A. de la Cruz Ricalde, Administradora; or Ricardo Abad Vásquez, Gerente. Free brochures. $1 required. Replies slowly to correspondence in Spanish.

Radio Tropical, Casilla de Correo 31, Tarapoto, Peru. Phone: +51 (94) 522-083, +51 (94) 524-689. Fax: +51 (94) 522 155. Contact: Mery A. Rengifo Tenazoa, Secretaria; or Luis F. Mori Reátegui, Gerente. Free stickers, occasionally free pennants, and station history booklet. $1 or return postage required. Replies occasionally to correspondence in Spanish.

Radio Unión, Apartado 833, Lima 27, Peru. Phone: +51 (1) 440-2093. Fax: +51 (1) 440 7594. E-mail: runion@amauta.rcp.net.pe. Contact: Juan Zubiaga Santiváñez, Gerente; Natividad Albizuri Salinas, Secretaria; Carlos González Solimano; or Juan Carlos Sologuren, Dpto. de Administración, who collects stamps. Free satin pennants and stickers. IRC required, and enclosing used or new stamps from various countries is especially appreciated. Replies irregularly to correspondence and tape recordings, with Spanish preferred.

Radio Uno, Av. Balta 1480, 3er piso, frente al Mercado Modelo, Chiclayo, Peru. Phone: +51 (74) 224-967. Contact: Luz Angela Romero, Directora del noticiero "Encuentros"; Plutarco Chamba Febres, Director Propietario; Juan Vargas, Administrador; or Filomena Saldívar Alarcón, Pauta Comercial. Return postage required.

Radio Victoria, Reynel 320, Mirones Bajo, Lima 1, Peru. Phone: +51 (1) 336-5448. Fax: +51 (1) 427 1195. E-mail: soermi@mixmail.com. Contact: Marta Flores Ushinahua. This station is owned by the Brazilian-run Pentecostal Church "Dios Es Amor," with local headquarters at Av. Arica 248, Lima; phone: +51 (1) 330-8023. Their program "La Voz de la Liberación" is produced locally and aired over numerous Peruvian shortwave stations.

Radio Virgen del Carmen ("RVC"), Jirón Virrey Toledo 466, Huancavelica, Peru. Phone: +51 (64) 752-740. Contact: Rvdo. Samuel Morán Cárdenas, Gerente.

Radiodifusoras Huancabamba, Calle Unión 409, Huancabamba, Piura, Peru. Phone: +51 (74) 473-233. Contact: Federico Ibáñez M., Director.

Radiodifusoras Paratón, Jirón Alfonso Ugarte 1090, contiguo al Parque Leoncio Prado, Huarmaca, Huancabamba, Piura, Peru. Contact: Prof. Hernando Huancas Huancas, Gerente General; or Prof. Rómulo Chincay Huamán, Gerente Administrativo.

PHILIPPINES World Time +8

NOTE: Philippine stations sometimes send publications with lists of Philippine young ladies seeking "pen pal" courtships.

DZRM—Philippine Broadcasting Service (when operating), Bureau of Broadcasting Services, Media Center, Bohol Avenue, Quezon City, Philippines.

☞Far East Broadcasting Company—FEBC Radio International (External Service)
MAIN OFFICE: P.O. Box 1, Valenzuela, Metro Manila, Philippines 0560. Phone: +63 (2) 292-5603 or +63 (2) 292-9403. Fax: +63 (2) 292 9430 or +63 (2) 291 4982, but lacks funds to provide faxed replies. E-mail: febcomphil@febc.jmf.org.ph; or ieoffice@febc.org.ph; (English Department) english@febc.jmf.org.ph; (Peter McIntyre, Host "DX Dial") dx@febc.jmf.org.ph or pm@febc.jfm.org.ph; (Jane Colley) jane@febc.jmf.org.ph; (Roger Foyle) foyle@febc.jmf.org.ph; (Mrs. Fay Olympia) alvarez@febc.jmf.org.ph; (Christine Johnson) cjohnson@febc.jmf.org.ph; (Larry Podmore) lpodmore@febc.jmf.org.ph. URL: www.febc.org/. (For some really exotic musical clips, visit the station's RealAudio page: www.febc.org/music.html.) Contact: (general) Peter McIntyre, Manager, International Operations Division & Producer, "DX Dial"; Jane Colley, Head, Audience Relations; Roger P. Foyle, Audience Relations Counsellor & Acting DX Secretary; Ella McIntyre, Producer, "Mailbag" and "Let's Hear from You"; Fay Olympia, English Programme Supervisor; Ms. Madini Tluanga, Producer, "Good Morning from Manila"; Christine D. Johnson, Head, Overseas English Service; or David Miller, Chief News Editor, FEB-News Bureau; (administration) Carlos Peña, Managing Director; (engineering) Ing. Renato Valentin, Frequency Manager; Larry Podmore, IBG Chief Engineer; or Peter Hsu, International Frequency Manager. Free stickers, calendar cards and DX Club Registration. Three IRCs appreciated for airmail reply. Plans to add a new 100 kW shortwave transmitter.
NEW DELHI BUREAU, NONTECHNICAL: c/o FEBA, Box 6, New Delhi-110 001, India.

Far East Broadcasting Company (Domestic Service), Bgy. Bayanan Baco Radyo DZB2, c/o ONF Calapan, Orr. Mindoro, Philippines 5200. Contact: (general) Dangio Onday, Program Supervisor/OIC; (technical) Danilo Flores, Broadcast Technician.

Radyo Pilipinas, the Voice of Democracy, Philippine Broadcasting Service, 4th Floor, PIA Building, Visayas Avenue,

Tashkent's main thoroughfares are scarcely traveled during the lunch hour.
M. Guha

Quezon City 1100, Metro Manila, Philippines. Phone: (general) +63 (2) 924-2620; +63 (2) 920-3963; or +63 (2) 924-2548; (engineering) +63 (2) 924-2268. Fax: +63 (2) 924 2745. Contact: (nontechnical) Evelyn Salvador Agato, Officer-in-Charge; Mercy Lumba; Leo Romano, Producer, "Listeners and Friends"; or Richard G. Lorenzo, Production Coordinator; (technical) Danilo Alberto, Supervisor; or Mike Pangilinan, Engineer. Free postcards & stickers.

Radio Veritas Asia
STUDIOS AND ADMINISTRATIVE HEADQUARTERS: P.O. Box 2642, Quezon City, 1166 Philippines. Phone: +63 (2) 939-0011 to14, +63 (2) 939-4465, +63 (2) 939-7476 or +63 (2) 939-4692. Fax: (general) +63 (2) 938 1940; (Frequency and Monitoring) +63 (2) 939 7556. E-mail: (Program Dept.) veritas@ mnl.sequel.net; (technical) info@radio-veritas.org.ph; or fmrva@pworld.net.ph. URLs: www.radio-veritas.org.ph; www.pworld.net.ph/user/fmrva/. Contact: (administration) Ms. Erlinda G. So, Manager; (general) Ms. Cleofe R. Labindao, Audience Relations Supervisor; Mrs. Regie de Juan Galindez; or Msgr. Pietro Nguyen Van Tai, Program Director; (technical) Ing. Floremundo L. Kiguchi, Technical Director; Ing. Honorio L. Llavore, Assistant Technical Director; or Frequency and Monitoring Department. Free caps, T-shirts, stickers, pennants, rulers, pens, postcards and calendars. Return postage appreciated.
TRANSMITTER SITE: Radio Veritas Asia, Palauig, Zambales, Philippines. Contact: Fr. Hugo Delbaere, CICM, Technical Consultant.
BRUSSELS BUREAUS AND MAIL DROPS: Catholic Radio and Television Network, 32-34 Rue de l' Association, B-1000 Brussels, Belgium; or UNDA, 12 Rue de l'Orme, B-1040 Brussels, Belgium.
Voice of America/IBB—Poro and Tinang Relay Stations. Phone: +63 (2) 813-0470/1/2. Fax: +63 (2) 813 0469. Contact: Station Manager. These numbers for urgent technical matters only. Otherwise, does not welcome direct contact; see USA for acceptable VOA and IBB Washington addresses and related information.

PIRATE

Pirate radio stations are usually one-person operations airing home-brew entertainment and/or iconoclastic viewpoints. In order to avoid detection by the authorities, they tend to appear irregularly, with little concern for the niceties of conventional program scheduling. Most are found in Europe chiefly on weekends, and mainly during evenings in North America, often just above 6200 kHz, just below 7000 kHz and just above 7375 kHz. These sub rosa stations and their addresses are subject to unusually abrupt change or termination, sometimes as a result of forays by radio authorities.

Two worthy sources of current addresses and other information on American pirate radio activity are: The Pirate Radio Directory, by Andrew Yoder and George Zeller [Tiare Publications, P.O. Box 493, Lake Geneva WI 53147 USA, U.S. toll-free phone 1-800-420-0579; or for specific inquiries, contact author Zeller directly: (fax) +1 (216) 696 0770; (e-mail) George.Zeller@acclink.com], an excellent annual reference; and A*C*E, P.O. Box 12112, Norfolk VA 23541 USA (e-mail: pradio@erols.com; URL: www.frn.net/ace/), a club which publishes a periodical ($20/year U.S., US$21 Canada, $27 elsewhere) for serious pirate radio enthusiasts.

A show on a specialized form of American pirate activity— low-powered local (usually FM) stations—is "Micro-Power Radio in the U.S.," aired over Radio for Peace International, Costa Rica, some Mondays at 2130 and some Thursdays at 2200 World Time on 6200 or 7385 kHz, plus 15050 kHz. For further information, send an e-mail message to: sues@ricochet.net; or paul_w_griffin@bmug.org.

For Europirate DX news, try:
SRSNEWS, Swedish Report Service, Ostra Porten 29, SE-442 54 Ytterby, Sweden. E-mail: srs@ice.warp.slink.se. URL: www-pp.kdt.net/jonny/index.html.
Pirate Connection, P.O. Box 4580, SE-203 20 Malmoe, Sweden; or P.O. Box 7085, Kansas City, Missouri 64113, USA. Phone: (home, Sweden) +46 (40) 611-1775; (mobile, Sweden) +46 (70) 581-5047. E-mail: etoxspz@eto.ericsson.se, xtdspz@lmd.ericsson.se or spz@exallon.se. URL: www-pp.hogia.net/jonny/pc. Six issues annually for about $23. Related to SRSNEWS, above.
Pirate Chat, 21 Green Park, Bath, Avon, BA1 1HZ, United Kingdom.
FRS Goes DX, P.O. Box 2727, NL-6049 ZG Herten, Holland. E-mail: FRSH@pi.net; or peter.verbruggen@tip.nl. URL: http:// home.pi.net/~freak55/home.htm.
Free-DX, 3 Greenway, Harold Park, Romford, Essex, RM3 OHH, United Kingdom.
FRC-Finland, P.O. Box 82, FIN-40101 Jyvaskyla, Finland.
Pirate Express, Postfach 220342, Wuppertal, Germany.
For up-to-date listener discussions and other pirate-radio

information on the Internet, the usenet URLs are: alt.radio.pirate and rec.radio.pirate.

POLAND   World Time +1 (+2 midyear)

📻**Radio Maryja**, ul. Żwirki i Wigury 80, PL-87-100 Toruń, Poland. Phone: (general) +48 (56) 655-2361; (studio) +48 (56) 655-2333, +48 (56) 655-2366. Fax: +48 (56) 655 2362. E-mail: radio@radiomaryja.pl. URL: (includes RealAudio) www.radiomaryja.pl. Contact: Father Tadeusz Rydzk, Dyrektor; or Father Jacek Cydzik. Polish preferred, but also replies to correspondence in English. Transmits via the facilities of the Voice of Russia.

📻**Radio Polonia**

STATION: External Service, P.O. Box 46, PL-00-977 Warsaw, Poland. Phone: (general) +48 (22) 645-9305 or +48 (22) 444-123; (English Section) +48 (22) 645-9262; (German Section) +48 (22) 645-9333; (placement liaison) +48 (2) 645-9002. Fax: (general and administration) +48 (22) 645 5917 or +48 (22) 645 5919; (placement liaison) +48 (2) 645 5906. E-mail (general): piatka@radio.com.pl; (Polish Section) polonia@radio.com.pl; (English Section) english.section@radio.com.pl; (German Section) deutsche.redaktion@radio.com.pl. URLs: www.radio.com.pl/polonia/; (RealAudio in English and Polish) www.wrn.org/ondemand/poland.html. Contact: (general) Rafał Kiepuszewski, Head, English Section & Producer, "Postbag"; Peter Gentle, Presenter, "Postbag"; or Ann Flapan, Corresponding Secretary; (administration) Jerzy M. Nowakowski, Managing Director; Wanda Samborska, Managing Director; Bogumila Berdychowska, Deputy Managing Director; or Maciej Lętowski, Executive Manager. On-air Polish language course with free printed material. Free stickers, pens, key rings and possibly T-shirts depending on financial cutbacks. DX Listeners' Club.

TRANSMISSION AUTHORITY: PAR (National Radiocommunication Agency), ul. Kasprzaka 18/20, PL-01-211 Warsaw, Poland. Phone: +48 (22) 608-8140 or +48 (22) 608-8191. Fax: +48 (22) 608 8195. E-mail: (Grodzicka) f.grodzicka@par.gov.pl; (Trzos) l.trzos@par.gov.pl. Contact: Mrs. Filomena Grodzicka, Head of BC Section; Lukasz Trzos; Ms. Urszula Rzepa or Jan Kondej.

PORTUGAL   World Time exactly (+1 midyear); Azores World Time –1 (World Time midyear)

📻**RDP Internacional—Rádio Portugal**, Apartado 1011, 1001 Lisbon, Portugal. Phone: (engineering) +351 (1) 382-2000. Fax: (general) +351 (1) 387 1402; (engineering) +351 (1) 387 1381. E-mail: (general) rdpinternacional@rdp.pt; (Saraiva) isabelsaraiva@rdp.pt; or (Haupt) christianehaupt@rdp.pt; (engineering) (Abreu) teresaabreu@rdp.pt; or (Carvalho) paulacarvalho@rdp.pt. URL: (includes RealAudio) www.rdp.pt/internacional/. Contact: (administration) José Manuel Nunes, Chairman; Isabel Saraiva, Listener's Service Department; Christiane Haupt; or Jaime Marques Almeida, Director; (technical) Eng. Francisco Mascarenhas; or Rui de Jesús, Frequency Manager; (engineering) Mrs. Teresa Abreu; or Ms. Paula Carvalho. Free stickers, paper pennants and calendars. May send literature from the Portuguese National Tourist Office.

Rádio Renascença (when operating), Rua Ivens 14, 1294 Lisbon Codex, Portugal. Phone: +351 (1) 347-5270. Fax: +351 (1) 342 2658. E-mail: info@radiorenascenca.pt. URLs: www.radiorenascenca.pt; www.rr.pt. Contact: C. Pabil, Director-Manager.

Radio Trans Europe (transmission facilities), 6º esq., Rua Braamcamp 84, 1200 Lisbon, Portugal. Transmitter located at Sines.

Voice of Orthodoxy—*see* Belarus.

QATAR   World Time +3

Qatar Broadcasting Service, P.O. Box 3939, Doha, Qatar. Phone: (director) +974 86-48-05; (under secretary) +974 864-823; (engineering) +974 864-518; (main Arabic service audio feed) +974 895-895. Fax: +974 822 888 or +974 831 447. Contact: Jassim Mohamed Al-Qattan, Head of Public Relations. May send booklet on Qatar Broadcasting Service. Occasionally replies, and return postage helpful.

TECHNICAL OFFICE: Qatar Radio & Television Corporation, P.O. Box 1836, Doha, Qatar. Phone: +973 831-443. Fax: +974 831 447. Contact: Hassan Al-Mass or Issa Al-Hamadi.

ROMANIA   World Time +2 (+3 midyear)

📻**Radio România Actualitati**, Societatea Româna de Radiodifuziune, 60-62 Berthelot St., RO-70747 Bucharest, Romania. Phone: +40 (1) 615-9350. Fax: +40 (1) 223 2612. URL: (RealAudio only) www.ituner.com.

Radio România International

STATION: 60-62 Berthelot St., RO-70747 Bucharest, Romania; P.O. Box 111, RO-70756 Bucharest, Romania; or Romanian embassies worldwide. Phone: (general) +40 (1) 222-2556, +40 (1) 303-1172, +40 (1) 303-1488 or +40 (1) 312-3645; (English Department) +40 (1) 617-2856; (engineering) +40 (1) 303-1193. Fax: (general) +40 (1) 223 2613 [if no connection, try via the office of the Director General of Radio România, but mark fax "Pentru RRI"; that fax is +40 (1) 222 5641]; (Engineering Services) +40 (1) 312 1056/7 or +40 (1) 615 6992. E-mail: rri@radio.ror.ro; (Nisipeanu) emisie@radio.ror.ro. URL: http://indis.ici.ro/romania/news/rri.html. Contact: (communications in English or Romanian) Dan Balamat, "Listeners' Letterbox"; (radio enthusiasts' issues, English only) "DX Mailbox," English Department; (communications in French or Romanian) Doru Vasile Ionescu, Deputy General Director; (listeners' letters) Giorgiana Zachia; or Dan Dumitrescu; (technical) Ms. Sorin Floricu; Radu Ianculescu, Frequency Monitoring Engineer; or Marius Nisipeanu, Engineering Services. Free stickers, pennants, posters, pins and assorted other items. Can provide supplementary materials for "Romanian by Radio" course on audio cassettes. Listeners' Club. Annual contests. Replies slowly but regularly. Concerns about frequency management should be directed to the PTT (*see* below), with copies to the Romanian Autonomous Company (*see* farther below) and to a suitable official at RRI.

TRANSMISSION AND FREQUENCY MANAGEMENT, PTT: General Directorate of Regulations, Ministry of Communications, 14a Al. Libertatii, R-70060 Bucharest, Romania. Phone: +40 (1) 400-1312 or +40 (1) 400-177. Fax: +40 (1) 400 1230. Contact: Mrs. Elena Danila, Head of Frequency Management Department.

TRANSMISSION AND FREQUENCY MANAGEMENT, AUTONOMOUS COMPANY: Romanian Autonomous Company for Radio Communications, 14a Al. Libertatii, R-70060 Bucharest, Romania. Phone: +40 (1) 400-1072. Fax: +40 (1) 400 1228. Contact: Mr. Marian Ionita.

A proud Kyrgyz father holds up his son in Issk-Ata, Kyrgyzstan. M. Guha

RUSSIA (Times given for republics, oblasts and krays):

- World Time +2 (+3 midyear) Kaliningradskaya;
- World Time +3 (+4 midyear) Arkhangel'skaya (incl. Nenetskiy), Astrakhanskaya, Belgorodskaya, Bryanskaya, Ivanovskaya, Kaluzhskaya, Karelia, Kirovskaya, Komi, Kostromskaya, Kurskaya, Lipetskaya, Moscovskaya, Murmanskaya, Nizhegorodskaya, Novgorodskaya, Orlovskaya, Penzenskaya, Pskovskaya, Riazanskaya, Samarskaya, Sankt-Peterburgskaya, Smolenskaya, Tambovskaya, Tulskaya, Tverskaya, Vladimirskaya, Vologodskaya, Volgogradskaya, Voronezhskaya, Yaroslavskaya;
- World Time +4 (+5 midyear) Checheno-Ingushia, Chuvashia, Dagestan, Kabardino-Balkaria, Kalmykia, Krasnodarskiy, Mari-Yel, Mordovia, Severnaya Osetia, Stavropolskiy, Tatarstan, Udmurtia;
- World Time +5 (+6 midyear) Bashkortostan, Chelyabinskaya, Kurganskaya, Orenburgskaya, Permskaya, Yekaterinburgskaya, Tyumenskaya;
- World Time +6 (+7 midyear) Altayskiy, Omskaya;
- World Time +7 (+8 midyear) Kemerovskaya, Krasnoyarskiy (incl. Evenkiyskiy), Novosibirskaya, Tomskaya, Tuva;
- World Time +8 (+9 midyear) Buryatia, Irkutskaya;
- World Time +9 (+10 midyear) Amurskaya, Chitinskaya, Sakha (West);
- World Time +10 (+11 midyear) Khabarovskiy, Primorskiy, Sakha (Center), Yevreyskaya;
- World Time +11 (+12 midyear) Magadanskaya (exc. Chukotskiy, Sakha (East), Sakhalinskaya;
- World Time +12 (+13 midyear) Chukotskiy, Kamchatskaya, Koryakskiy;
- World Time +13 (+14 midyear) all points east of longtitude 172.30 E.

WARNING—MAIL THEFT: Airmail correspondence containing funds or IRCs from North America and Japan may not arrive safely even if sent by registered air mail, as such mail enters via Moscow Airport. However, funds sent from Europe, North America and Japan via surface mail enter via St. Petersburg, and thus stand a better chance of arriving safely. Airmail service is otherwise now almost on a par with that of other advanced countries.

VERIFICATION OF STATIONS USING TRANSMITTERS IN ST. PETERSBURG AND KALININGRAD: Transmissions of certain world band stations—such as the Voice of Russia, Mayak and China Radio International—when emanating from transmitters located in St. Petersburg and Kaliningrad, may be verified directly from: World Band Verification QSL Service, State Enterprise for Broadcasting and Radio Communications No. 2 (GPR-2), ul. Akademika Pavlova 13A, 197376 St. Petersburg, Russia. Fax: +7 (812) 234 2971 during working hours. Contact: Mikhail V. Sergeyev, Chief Engineer; or Mikhail Timofeyev, verifier. Free stickers. Two IRCs required for a reply, which upon request includes a copy of "Broadcast Schedule," which gives transmission details (excluding powers) for all transmissions emanating from three distinct transmitter locations: Kaliningrad-Bolshakovo, St. Petersburg and St. Petersburg-Popovka. This organization—which has 26 shortwave, three longwave, 15 mediumwave AM and nine FM transmitters—relays broadcasts for clients for the equivalent of about $0.70-1.00 per kW/hour.

Government Radio Agencies

C.I.S. FREQUENCY MANAGEMENT ENGINEERING OFFICE: The Main Centre for Control of Broadcasting Networks, 7 Nikolskaya Str., 103012 Moscow, Russia. Phone: +7 (095) 298-3302. Fax: +7 (095) 956 7546 or +7 (095) 921 1624. E-mail: (Titov) titov@mccbn.ru; or titov@nsl.ru. URL: www.mccbn.ru. Contact: (general) Mrs. Antonia Ostakhova, Mrs. Nina Bykova, or Ms. Margarita Ovetchkina; (administration) Anatoliy T. Titov, Chief Director. This office is responsible for the operation of radio broadcasting in the Russian Federation, as well as for frequency usage of transmitters throughout much of the C.I.S. Correspondence should be concerned only with significant technical observations or engineering suggestions concerning frequency management improvement—not regular requests for verifications. Correspondence in Russian preferred, but English accepted.

STATE ENTERPRISE FOR BROADCASTING AND RADIO COMMUNICATIONS NO. 2 (GPR-2)—see VERIFICATION OF STATIONS USING TRANSMITTERS IN ST. PETERSBURG AND KALININGRAD, above.

STATE RADIO COMPANY: AS Radioagency Co., Pyatnitskaya 25, 113326 Moscow, Russia. Phone: (Khlebnikov and Petrunicheva) +7 (095) 233-6474; (Komissarova) +7 (095) 233-6660; (Staviskaia) +7 (095) 233-7003. Fax: (Khlebnikov, Petrunicheva and Komissarova) +7 (095) 233 1342; (Staviskaia) +7 (095) 230 2828 or +7 (095) 233 7648. Contact: Valentin Khlebnikov, Mrs. Maris Petrunicheva, Mrs. Lyudmila Komissarova or Mrs. Rachel Staviskaia.

STATE TRANSMISSION AUTHORITY: Russian Ministry of Telecommunication, ul. Tverskaya 7, 103375 Moscow, Russia. Phone: +7 (095) 201-6568. Fax: +7 (095) 292 7086 or +7 (095) 292 7128. Contact: Anatoly C. Batiouchkine.

STATE TV AND RADIO COMPANY: Russian State TV & Radio Company, ul. Yamskogo 5, Polya 19/21, 125124 Moscow, Russia. Phone: +7 (095) 213-1054, +7 (095) 213-1054 or +7 (095) 250-0511. Fax: +7 (095) 250 0105. Contact: Ivan Sitilenlov.

Adygey Radio (Radio Maykop), ul. Zhukovskogo 24,

352700 Maykop, Republic of Adygeya, Russia. Contact: A.T. Kerashev, Chairman. English accepted but Russian preferred. Return postage helpful.

Amur Radio, GTRK Amur, per Svyatitelya Innokentiya 15, 675000 Blagoveschensk, Russia. Contact: V.I. Kal'chenko, Chief Engineer.

Arkhangel'sk Radio, GTRK "Pomorye", ul. Popova 2, 163000 Arkhangel'sk, Arkhangel'skaya Oblast, Russia; or U1PR, Valentin G. Kalasnikov, ul. Suvorov 2, kv. 16, Arkhangel'sk, Arkhangel'skaya Oblast, Russia. Replies irregularly to correspondence in Russian.

Bashkortostan Radio, ul. Gafuri 9/1, 450076 Ufa, Bashkortostan, Russia. Phone: +7 (3472) 220-943 or +7 (3472) 223-820. Fax: +7 (3472) 232 545. URL: http://info.ufanet.ru/radio/bashkort.htm. Replies irregularly to correspondence in Russian.

Buryat Radio, Dom Radio, ul. Erbanova 7, 670013 Ulan-Ude, Republic of Buryatia, Russia. Contact: Z.A. Telin; Mrs. M.V. Urbaeva, 1st Vice-Chairman; or L.S. Shikhanova.

Chita Radio (when active), ul. Kostushko-Grigorovicha 27, 672090 Chita, Chitinskaya Oblast, Russia. Contact: (technical) V.A. Klimov, Chief Engineer; V.A. Moorzin, Head of Broadcasting; or A.A. Anufriyev.

Evenkiyskaya Radio, ul. 50 let Oktyabrya 28, 663370 Tura, Evenkiyskiy Avt. Okrug, Russia. Contact: B. Yuryev, Engineer. Replies to correspondence in Russian.

Islamskaya Volna (Islamic Wave), Islamic Center of Moscow Region, Moscow Jami Mosque, Vypolzov per. 7, 129090 Moscow, Russia; or Pyatnitskaya ulitsa 25, 133326 Moscow, Russia. Phone: +7 (095) 233-6423/6, +7 (095) 233-6629 or +7 (095) 281-4904. Contact: Sheikh Ravil Gainutdin. Return postage necessary.

Kabardino-Balkar Radio (Radio Nalchik), ul. Nogmova 38, 360000 Nalchik, Republic of Kabardino-Balkariya, Russia. Contact: Kamal Makitov, Vice-Chairman. Replies to correspondence in Russian.

Kala Atouraya (Voice of Assyria) (when active), ul.Pyatnitskaya 25, 113326 Moscow. Contact: Marona Arsanis, Chief Editor; or Roland T. Bidjamov, Editor. Return postage helpful. Replies irregularly.

Kamchatka Radio, RTV Center, Dom Radio, ul. Sovietskaya 62-G, 683000 Petropavlovsk-Kamchatskiy, Kamchatskaya Oblast, Russia. Contact: A. Borodin, Chief OTK; or V.I. Aibabin. $1 required. Replies in Russian to correspondence in Russian or English.

Kamchatka Rybatskaya—a special program for fishermen off the western coast of North America; see "Kamchatka Radio," above, for contact details.

Khabarovsk Radio, RTV Center, ul. Lenina 71, 680013 Khabarovsk, Khabarovskiy Kray, Russia; or Dom Radio, pl. Slavy, 682632 Khabarovsk, Khabarovskiy Kray, Russia. Contact: (technical) V.N. Kononov, Glavnyy Inzhener.

Khanty-Mansiysk Radio, Dom Radio, ul. Mira 7, 626200 Khanty-Mansiysk, Khanty-Mansiyskiy Avt. Okrug, Tyumenskaya Oblast, Russia. Contact: (technical) Vladimir Sokolov, Engineer.

Koryak Radio, ul. Obukhova 4, 684620 Palana, Koryakskiy Khrebet, Russia.

Krasnoyarsk Radio, Krasnoyarskaya GTRK, "Tsentr Rossii", ul. Mechnikova 44A, 666001 Krasnoyarsk 28, Krasnoyarskiy Kray, Russia. Contact: Valeriy Korotchenko; or Anatoliy A. Potehin, RAØAKE. Free local information booklets in English/Russian. Replies in Russian to correspondence in English or Russian. Return postage helpful.

Magadan Radio, RTV Center, ul. Kommuny 8/12, 685013 Magadan, Magadanskaya Oblast, Russia. Contact: Viktor Loktionov or V.G. Kuznetsov. Return postage helpful. May reply to correspondence in Russian.

Mariy Radio, Mari Yel, ul. Osipenko 50, 424014 Yoshkar-Ola, Russia.

Mayak—see Radiostantsiya Mayak.

Murmansk Radio, Sopka Varnichnaya, 183042 Murmansk, Murmanskaya Oblast, Russia; or RTV Center, Sopka Varnichaya, 183042 Murmansk, Murmanskaya Oblast, Russia. E-mail: murmantv@com.mels.ru. Contact: D. Perederi (chairman).

Northern European Radio Relay Service (NERRS) (when inaugurated), World Band Verification QSL Service, The State Enterprise for Broadcasting and Radio Communications No. 2 (GPR-2), ul. Akademika Pavlova 13A, 197376 St. Petersburg, Russia. Fax: +7 (812) 234 2971. This planned operation hopes to air non-controversial commercial world band programs to Europe, but has so far failed to get a license.

Perm Radio, Permskaya Gosudarstvennaya Telekinoradiokompaniya, ul. Technicheskaya 21, 614600 Perm, Permskaya Oblast, Russia; or ul. Krupskoy 26, 614060 Perm, Permskaya Oblast, Russia. Contact: M. Levin, Senior Editor; or A. Losev, Acting Chief Editor.

Qala Atouraya—see Kala Atouraya.

Radio Maykop—see Adygey Radio, above.

Radio Nalchik—see Radio Kabardino-Balkar, above.

Radio Rossii (Russia's Radio), Room 121, ul. Yamskogo 5-A, Polya 19/21, 125124 Moscow, Russia. Phone: +7 (095) 213-1054, +7 (095) 250-0511 or +7 (095) 251-4050. Fax: +7 (095) 250 0105, +7 (095) 233 6449 or +7 (095) 214 4767. Contact: Sergei Yerofeyev, Director of International Operations [sic]; or Sergei Davidov, Director. Free English-language information sheet. For verification of reception from transmitters located in St. Petersburg and Kaliningrad, see NOTE, above, shortly after the country heading, "RUSSIA."

Radio Samorodinka, P.O. Box 898, Center, 101000 Moscow, Russia. Contact: Lev S. Shiskin, Editor. This station may be licensed as other than a regular broadcaster.

Radio Tatarstan, ul. Maksima Gor'kogo 15, 420015 Kazan, Tatarstan, Russia. Phone: (general) +7 (8432) 384-846; (editorial) +7 (8432) 367-493. Fax: +7 (8432) 361-283. Contact: Hania Hazipovna Galinova.

☞**Radiostantsiya Mayak** (when active), ul. Pyatnitskaya 25, 113326 Moscow, Russia. Phone: +7 (095) 950-2649. Fax: +7 (095) 959 4207. E-mail: inform@radiomayak.ru. URL: (includes RealAudio) www.radiomayak.ru/. Contact: (administration) Vladimir Povolyayev, Director. Correspondence in Russian preferred, but English increasingly accepted. For verification of reception from transmitters located in St. Petersburg and Kaliningrad, see NOTE, above, shortly after the country heading, "RUSSIA."

Radiostantsiya Tikhiy Okean (program of Primorsk Radio, also aired via Voice of Russia transmitters), RTV Center, ul. Uborevieha 20A, 690000 Vladivostok, Primorskiy Kray, Russia.

Sakha Radio, GTRK Respubliki Sakha, ul. Ordzhonikidze 48, 677007 Yakutsk, Republic of Sakha, Russia. Fax: +7 (095) 230 2919. Contact: (general) Alexandra Borisova; Lia Sharoborina, Advertising Editor; or Albina Danilova, Producer, "Your Letters"; (technical) Sergei Bobnev, Technical Director. Russian books $15; audio cassettes $10. Free station stickers and original Yakutian souvenirs. Replies to correspondence in English.

Sakhalin Radio, GTRK "Sakhalin", ul. Komsomolskaya 209, 693000 Yuzhno-Sakhalinsk, Sakhalinskaya Oblast, Russia. Phone/Fax: +7 (42242) 35286. E-mail: sakhtv@adm.sakhalin.ru. URL: www.snc.ru/Customers/gtrksakh/ (click on "ENGL" for english text). Contact: V. Belyaev, Chairman of Sakhalinsk RTV Committee.

Tyumen' Radio, RTV Center, ul. Permyakova 6, 625013 Tyumen', Tyumenskaya Oblast, Russia. Contact: (technical) V.D. Kizerov, Engineer, Technical Center. Sometimes replies to correspondence in Russian. Return postage helpful.

Voice of Russia, ul. Pyatnitskaya 25, Moscow 113326, Russia. Phone: (International Relations Department) +7 (095) 233-7801; (Deputy Editor-in-Chief) +7 (095) 950-6980 or +7 (095) 950-6586; (Programmes Directorate) +7 (095) 233-6793; (Commercial Dept.) +7 (095) 233-7934; (Audience Research) +7 (095) 233-6278; (Chairman's Secretariat) +7 (095) 233-6331; (News Directorate) +7 (095) 233-6513; (Technical Department) +7 (095) 950-6115. Fax: (Chairman's Secretariat) +7 (095) 230 2828; (Editor-in-Chief) +7 (095) 950 5693; (World Service) +7 (095) 233 7693; (Russian Service) +7 (095) 950 6116; (International Relations Department) +7 (095) 233 7648; (News Directorate) +7 (095) 233 7567; (technical) +7 (095) 233 1342. E-mail: (general) letters@vor.ru; (administrative) chairman@vor.ru. URLs: (general) www.vor.ru; (RealAudio in English, German, Russian and Spanish) www.wrn.org/ondemand/russia.html. Listeners with a computer equipped with a sound card can send a voice mail to the station via the Internet (detailed instructions are available at the Voice of Russia website). Contact: (English Service—listeners' questions to be answered over the air) Joe Adamov; (English Service—all other general correspondence) Ms. Olga Troshina, Mrs. Tanya Stukova; Elena Prolovskaya; or Elena Osipova, World Service, Letters Department; (general correspondence, all languages) Victor Kopytin, Director of International Relations Department; Vladimir Zhamkin, Editor-in-Chief; Yevgeny Nilov, Deputy Editor-in-Chief; Anatoly Morozov, Deputy Editor-in-Chief; (Japanese) Yelena Sopova, Japanese Department; (verifications, all services) Mrs. Eugenia Stepanova, c/o English Service; (Russian Service) Pavel Mikhailov, who also speaks English; (administration) Yuri Minayev, First Deputy Chairman, Voice of Russia; Armen Oganesyan, Chairman, World Service, Voice of Russia; (technical) Valentin Khleknikov, Frequency Coordinator; Leonid Maevski, Engineering Services; Rachel Staviskaya, Technical Department; or Maria Petrunicheva, Engineering Services. To get in touch with other language services, contact the International Relations Department. Because of budget restrictions, the Voice of Russia may sometimes be unable to answer correspondence except by e-mail. It is therefore advisable to include an e-mail address (if you have one) when writing to the station. For verification of reception from transmitters located in St. Petersburg and Kaliningrad, *see NOTE*, above, shortly after the country heading, "RUSSIA." For verification from transmitters in Khabarovsk, you can also write directly to the Voice of Russia, Dom Radio, Lenina 4, Khabarovsk 680020, Russia. For engineering correspondence concerning frequency management problems, besides "technical," preceding, *see NOTE* on C.I.S. Frequency Management towards the beginning of this "Russia" listing. Free stickers, booklets and sundry other souvenirs occasionally available upon request. Sells audio cassettes of Russian folk and classical music, as well as a Russian language-learning course. Although not officially a part of the Voice of Russia, an organization selling Russian art and handcrafts that sprung from contacts made with the Voice of Russia is "Cheiypouka," Box 266, Main St., Stonington ME 04681 USA; phone +1 (207) 367-5021.

Voice of Assyria—*see* Qala Atouraya, above.

RWANDA World Time +2

Deutsche Welle—Relay Station Kigali—Correspondence should be directed to the main offices in Cologne, Germany *(see)*.

Radio Rwanda, B.P. 404, Kigali, Rwanda. Fax: +250 (7) 6185. Contact: Marcel Singirankabo. $1 required. Rarely replies, with correspondence in French preferred.

ST. HELENA World Time exactly

Radio St. Helena (when operating once each year), Broadway House, Main Street, Jamestown, St. Helena, South Atlantic Ocean. Phone: +290 4669. Fax: +290 4542. E-mail: (Tony Leo) tony@sthelena.se; (Radio St. Helena Day Coordinator, Sweden) sthelena.coordinator@sthelena.se. URL: www.sthelena.se/radiosth.htm. Contact: (general) Tony Leo, Station Manager; (listeners' questions) Ralph Peters, Presenter, "Evening Shuttle." $1, required. Replies regularly but slowly; verifications can take several months or even a year. Radio St. Helena Day T-shirts (small/medium/large/XL/XXL) available for $25 airmail from: South Atlantic Travel & Trade, Box 6014, SE-600 06 Norrköping, Sweden. Is on the air on world band only once each year—"Radio St Helena Day"—usually late October on 11092.5 kHz in the upper-sideband (USB) mode.

SAO TOME E PRINCIPE World Time exactly

Voice of America/IBB—São Tomé Relay Station, P.O. Box 522, São Tomé, São Tomé e Príncipe. Phone: +23 912 22-800. Fax: +23 912 22 435. These numbers are for timely and significant technical matters only. Contact: Manuel Neves, Transmitter Plant Technician. Replies direct if $1 included with correspondence, otherwise all communications should be directed to the usual VOA or IBB addresses in Washington *(see* USA).

SAUDI ARABIA World Time +3

Broadcasting Service of The Kingdom of Saudi Arabia, P.O. Box 61718, Riyadh-11575, Saudi Arabia. Phone: (general) +966 (1) 404-2795; (administration) +966 (1) 442-5493; (technical) +966 (1) 442-5170. Fax: (general) +966 (1) 402 8177; (Frequency Management) +966 (1) 404 1692. Contact: (general) Mutlaq A. Albegami, European Service Manager; (technical) Suleiman Al-Smnan, Director of Frequency Management; Suleiman Al-Kalifa; or A. Shah, Department of Frequency Management. Free travel information and book on Saudi history.

SENEGAL World Time exactly

Radiodiffusion Télévision Sénégalaise (when active), B.P. 1765, Dakar, Senegal. Phone: +221 23-63-49. Fax: + 221 22 34 90. E-mail: rts@primature.sn. URL: (includes live NetShow audio) www.primature.sn/rts/. Contact: (technical) Joseph Nesseim, Directeur des Services Techniques; or Mme. Elisabeth Ndiaye. Free stickers and Senegalese stamps. Return postage, $1 or 2 IRCs required; as Mr. Nesseim collects

Staff at the Voice of Hope studio in Colombo, Sri Lanka, produce programs in Sinhalese for airing on Adventist World Radio.
AWR

stamps, unusual stamps may be even more appreciated. Replies to correspondence in French.

SEYCHELLES   World Time +4

BBC World Service—Indian Ocean Relay Station, P.O. Box 448, Victoria, Mahé, Seychelles; or Grand Anse, Mahé, Seychelles. Phone: +248 78-269. Fax: +248 78 500. Contact: (administration) Peter J. Loveday, Station Manager; (technical) Peter Lee, Resident Engineer; Nigel Bird, Resident Engineer; or Steve Welch, Assistant Resident Engineer. Nontechnical correspondence should be sent to the BBC World Service in London (see).

Far East Broadcasting Association—FEBA Radio
MAIN OFFICE: P.O. Box 234, Mahé, Seychelles, Indian Ocean. Phone: (main office) +248 282-2000 Fax: +248 242-146. E-mail: mmaillet@feba.org.sc. URL: www.feba.org.uk. Contact: (general) Hugh Barton, Seychelles Director; (technical) Richard Whittington, Schedule Engineer; or Andy Platts, Head of Engineering; (reception reports) N. Nugashe, QSL Secretary; or Doreen Dugathe. Free stickers, pennants and station information sheet. $1 or one IRC helpful. Also, *see* FEBC Radio International—USA and United Kingdom.
CANADA OFFICE: 6850 Antrim Avenue, Burnaby BC, V5J 4M4 Canada. Fax: +1 (604) 430 5272. E-mail: dpatter@axionet.com.
INDIA OFFICE: FEBA India, P.O. Box 2526, 7 Commissariat Road, Bangalore-560 025, India. Fax: +91 (80) 584 701. E-mail: 6186706@mcimail.com. Contact: Peter Muthl Raj.

SIERRA LEONE   World Time exactly

Sierra Leone Broadcasting Service, New England, Freetown, Sierra Leone. Phone: +232 (22) 240-123; +232 (22) 240-173; +232 (22) 240-497 or 232 (22) 241-919. Fax: +232 (22) 240 922. Contact: Cyril Juxon-Smith, Officer in Charge.

SINGAPORE   World Time +8

BBC World Service—Far Eastern Relay Station, 26 Olive Road, Singapore. Phone: + 65 260-1511. Fax: +65 253 8131. Contact: (technical) Far East Resident Engineer. Nontechnical correspondence should be sent to the BBC World Service in London (see).

☞**Radio Corporation of Singapore**, Farrer Road, P.O. Box 968, Singapore 912899; or (physical location) Caldecott Broadcast Centre, Caldecott Hill, Andrew Road, Singapore 299939. Phone: +65 251-8166, +65 251-8622 or +65 359-7340. Fax: +65 254 8062, +65 256 1995, +65 256 9533, +65 256 9556 or +65 256 9338. E-mail: (general) info@rcs.com.sg; (Engineering Dept.) engineering@rcs.com.sg. URLs: (general) www.rcs.com.sg; (RealAudio) http://rcslive.singnet.com.sg. Contact: (general) Lillian Tan, Public Relations Division; Lim Heng Tow, Manager, International & Community Relations; Tan Eng Lai, Promotion Executive; Hui Wong, Producer/Presenter; or Lucy Leong; (administration) Anthony Chia, Director General; (technical) Asaad Sameer Bagharib, V.P. Engineering; or Lee Wai Meng. Free regular and Post-It stickers, pens, umbrellas, mugs, towels, wallets and lapel pins. Do not include currency in envelope.

Radio Nederland via Singapore—For verification direct from the Singaporean transmitters, contact the BBC World Service—Far Eastern Relay Station (see, above). Nontechnical correspondence should be sent to Radio Nederland in Holland (see).

Radio Japan via Singapore—For verification direct from the Singaporean transmitters, contact the BBC World Service—Far Eastern Relay Station (see, above). Nontechnical correspondence should be sent to Radio Japan in Tokyo (see).

☞**Radio Singapore International**, Farrer Road, P.O. Box 5300, Singapore 912899, Singapore; or (physical address) Caldecott Broadcast Centre, Annex Building Level 1, Andrew Road, Singapore 299939. Phone: (general) + 65 359-7662; (programme listings) +65 353-5300; (publicity) +65 350-3708 or +65 256-0401. Fax: +65 259 1357 or +65 259 1380. E-mail: rsi@mediacity.com.sg; english@rsi.com.sg. URL: (includes RealAudio) www.rsi.com.sg/. Contact: (general) Anushia Kanagabasai, Producer, "You Asked For It"; Belinda Yeo, Producer, "Dateline RSI"; or Mrs. Sakuntala Gupta, Programme Manager, English Service; (administration) S. Chandra Mohan, Station Director; (technical) Selena Kaw, Office of the Administrative Executive; or Yong Wui Pin, Engineer. Free souvenir T-shirts and key chains to selected listeners. Do not include currency in envelope.

Tajik women take a break at the UNOPS collective in the Gharam valley of Tajikistan.
RRDPS/UNOPS, Dushanbe

SLOVAKIA World Time +1 (+2 midyear)

Radio Slovakia International, Mýtna 1, P.O. Box 55, 810 05 Bratislava 15, Slovakia. Phone: (Editor-in-Chief) +421 (7) 5727-3730; (English Service) +421 (7) 5727-3736 or +421 (7) 5727-2737. Fax: (English Service) +421 (7) 396-282. E-mail: (English Section) englishsection@slovakradio.sk; or (Helga Dingová) helga_dingova@slovakradio.sk; (French Section) maria_rovna@slovakradio.sk; (German Section) lydia_korecka@ slovakradio.sk; (Slovak Section) Jana_Raslavska@slovakradio.sk. URLs: (general) www.slovakradio.sk/rsi.html; (RealAudio in English) www.wrn.org/ondemand/slovakia.html. Contact: Helga Dingová, Director of English Broadcasting; (administration) PhDr. Karol Palkovič, Head of External Broadcasting; or Dr. Slavomira Kubickova, Head of International Relations; (technical) Edita Chocholatá, Frequency Manager; Jozef Krátky, Ing. May exchange stamps, recipes and coins. Free pennants, pocket calendars, T-shirts (occasionally) and other souvenirs and publications.

SOLOMON ISLANDS World Time +11

Solomon Islands Broadcasting Corporation, P.O. Box 654, Honiara, Solomon Islands. Phone: +677 20051. Fax: +677 23159. Contact: (general) Julian Maka'a, Producer, "Listeners From Far Away"; Cornelius Teasi; or Silas Hule; (administration) Johnson Honimae, General Manager; (technical) John Babera, Chief Engineer. IRC or $1 helpful. Problems with the domestic mail system may cause delays.

SOMALIA World Time +3

Radio Mogadishu—Currently, there are three stations operating under the rubric Radio Mogadishu. None is known to reply to listener correspondence.

SOMALILAND World Time +3

NOTE: "Somaliland," claimed as an independent nation, is diplomatically recognized only as part of Somalia.
Radio Hargeisa, P.O. Box 14, Hargeisa, Somaliland, Somalia. Contact: Sulayman Abdel-Rahman, announcer. Most likely to respond to correspondence in Somali or Arabic.

SOUTH AFRICA World Time +2

BBC World Service via South Africa—For verification direct from the South African transmitters, contact Sentech (*see* below). Nontechnical correspondence should be sent to the BBC World Service in London (*see*).
Channel Africa, P.O. Box 91313, Auckland Park 2006, South Africa. Phone: (executive editor) +27 (11) 714-2255; + 27 (11) 714-2551 or +27 (11) 714-3942; (technical) +27 (11) 714-3409. Fax: (executive editor) +27 (11) 482 3506; + 27 (11) 714 2546, +27 (11) 714 4956 or +27 (11) 714 6377; (technical) +27 (11) 714 5812. E-mail: (general) africancan@ channelafrica.org; (news desk) news.africa@channelafrica.org. URL: (RealAudio in English, French and Portuguese, plus text) www.channelafrica.org; (RealAudio in English) www.wrn.org/ ondemand/southafrica.html. Contact: (general) Tony Machilika, Head of English Service; Robert Michel, Head of Research and Strategic Planning; or Noeleen Vorster, Corporate Communications Manager; (technical) Mrs. H. Meyer, Supervisor Operations; or Lucienne Libotte, Technology Operations. T-shirts $11 and watches $25. Prices do not include shipping and handling. Free *Share* newsletter from the Department of Foreign Affairs, stickers and calendars. Reception reports are best directed to Sentech (*see* below), which operates the transmission facilities.
Radiosondergrense (Radio Without Boundaries), Posbus 91312, Auckland Park 2006, South Africa. Phone: (general) +27 (89) 110-2525; (live studio on-air line) +27 (89) 110-4553; (management) +27 (11) 714-2702; (administration) +27 (11) 714-4406. Fax: +27 (11) 714 6445. E-mail: (Shaikh) shaikhm@sabc.co.za. URL: www.sabc.co.za/radio/afrst/ 1index.htm. Contact: (general) Mohamed Shaikh, Manager; (administration) Sarel Myburgh. Reception reports are best directed to Sentech (*see* below), which operates the shortwave transmission facilities. A domestic service of the South African Broadcasting Corporation (*see* below), and formerly known as Afrikaans Stereo.
Sentech (Pty) Ltd, Shortwave Services, Private Bag X06, Honeydew 2040, South Africa. Phone: (shortwave) +27 (11) 475-1596 or (Otto) +27 (11) 471-4658; (general) +27 (11) 475-5600. Fax: +27 (11) 475 5112 or (Otto) +27 (11) 471 4605. E-mail: (general) comms@sentech.co.za; (Otto) ottok@sentech.co.za; (Smuts) smutsn@sentech.co.za. URL:

www.sentech.co.za. Contact: Mr. Neël Smuts, Managing Director; Rodgers Gamuti, Client Manager; or Kathy Otto. Sentech issues its own verification cards, and is the best place to send reception reports for world band stations broadcasting via South African facilities.

South African Broadcasting Corporation
ADMINISTRATION AND GENERAL TECHNICAL MATTERS: Private Bag X1, Auckland Park 2006, South Africa. Phone: (Head Office) +27 (11) 714-9111; (information) +27 (11) 714-9797; (technical) +27 (11) 714-3409. Fax: (general) +27 (11) 714 4086 or +27 (11) 714 5055; (technical) +27 (11) 714 3106 or +27 (11) 714 5812. URL: (includes RealAudio) www.sabc.co.za. Contact: (administration) Mrs. Charlotte Mampane, Chief Executive, Radio. Reception reports are best directed to Sentech (*see*, above), which operates the transmission facilities.
RADIO PROGRAMME SALES: Private Bag X1, Auckland Park 2006, South Africa. Phone: (general enquiries) +27 (11) 714-5681, +27 (11) 714-6039 or +27 (11) 714-4044; (actuality programs) +27 (11) 714-4709; (music) +27 (11) 714-4315. Fax: +27 (11) 714 3671. E-mail: botham@sabc.co.za; snymane@sabc.co.za; or corbinm@sabc.co.za. Offers a wide range of music, book readings, radio drama, comedy and other types of programs.

Trans World Radio Africa
NONTECHNICAL CORRESPONDENCE: Trans World Radio—South Africa, Private Bag 987, Pretoria 0001, South Africa. Phone: +27 (12) 807-0053. Fax: +27 (12) 807 1266. URL: www.gospelcom.net/twr/ttatlow/Welcome.htm.
TECHNICAL CORRESPONDENCE: Reception reports and other technical correspondence are best directed to Sentech (*see*, above) or to TWR's Swaziland office (*see*). Also, *see* USA.

SPAIN   World Time +1 (+2 midyear)

Radio Exterior de España (Spanish National Radio)
MAIN OFFICE: Apartado de Correos 156.202, E-28080 Madrid, Spain. Phone: (general) +34 (91) 346-1081/1083; (Audience Relations) +34 (91) 346-1149. Fax: +34 (91) 346 1815. E-mail: (Director) dir_ree.rne@rtve.es; (Spanish programming) audiencia_ree.rne@rtve.es; (foreign language programming, including English) lenguas_extranjeras.rne@rtve.es. URL: (includes RealAudio) www.rtve.es/rne/ree/. Contact: (nontechnical) Pilar Salvador M., Nuria Alonso Veiga, Head of Information Service; Alejo Garcia, Director; Ricardo H. Calvo, Webmaster; or Penelope Eades, Foreign Language Programmer; (technical) Relaciones con la Audiencia. Free stickers, calendars, pennants and tourist information. Reception reports can be sent to: Radio Exterior de España, Relaciones con la Audiencia, Sección DX, Apartado de Correos 156.202, E-28080 Madrid, Spain.
NOBLEJAS TRANSMITTER SITE: Centro Emisor de RNE en Onda Corta, Ctra. Dos Barrios s/n, E-45350 Noblejas-Toledo, Spain.
RUSSIAN OFFICE: P.O Box 88, 109044 Moscow, Russia.
Costa Rican Relay Facility—see Costa Rica.
TRANSCRIPTION SERVICE: Radio Nacional de España, Servicio de Transcripciones, Apartado 156.200, Casa de la Radio (Prado del Rey), E-28223 Madrid, Spain.
WASHINGTON NEWS BUREAU: National Press Building, 529 14th Street NW, Suite 1288, Washington DC 20045 USA. Phone: +1 (202) 783-0768. Contact: Luz María Rodríguez.
HF FREQUENCY PLANNING OFFICE: Prado del Rey. Pozuelo de Alarcom, E-28223 Madrid, Spain. Phone: +34 (91) 346-1276 or +34 (91) 346-1978. Fax: +34 (91) 346 1402. E-mail: (Huerta) plan_red.rne@rtve.es; or (Almarza) planif_red2.rne@rtve.es.

Contact: José M. Huerta, Frequency Manager; or Fernando Almarza.

SRI LANKA   World Time +6:00

Deutsche Welle—Relay Station Sri Lanka, 92/2 D.S. Senanayake Mawatha, Colombo 08, Sri Lanka. Phone: +94 (1) 699-449. Fax: +94 (1) 699 450. Contact: R. Groschkus, Resident Engineer. Nontechnical correspondence should be sent to Deutsche Welle in Germany (*see*).
Radio Japan/NHK, c/o SLBC, P.O. Box 574, Torrington Square, Colombo 7, Sri Lanka. This address for technical correspondence only. General nontechnical listener correspondence should be sent to the usual Radio Japan address in Japan. News-oriented correspondence may also be sent to the NHK Bangkok Bureau (*see* Radio Japan, Japan).
Sri Lanka Broadcasting Corporation (also announces as "Radio Sri Lanka" in the external service), P.O. Box 574, Independence (Torrington) Square, Colombo 7, Sri Lanka. Phone: (general) +94 (1) 697-491 or +94 (1) 697-493; (Director General) +94 (1) 696-140. Fax: (general) +94 (1) 697 150 or +94 (1) 698 576; (Director General) +94 (1) 695 488; (Sooryia, phone/fax) +94 (1) 696 1311. E-mail: slbc@sri.lanka.net; slbcweb@sri.lanka.net. URL: www.infolanka.com/people/sisira/slbc.html. Contact: (general) N. Jayhweera, Director – Audience Research; or Icumar Ratnayake, Controller, "Mailbag Program"; (SLBC administration) Eric Fernando, Director General; Newton Gunaratne, Deputy Director-General; (technical) H.M.N.R. Jayawardena, Engineer – Training & Frequency Management; Wimala Sooriya, Deputy Director – Engineering; or A.M.W. Gunaratne, Station Engineer, Ekala.
Voice of America/IBB—Iranawila Relay Station.
ADDRESS: International Broadcasting Bureau, Sri Lanka Transmission Station, c/o U.S. Embassy, 210 Galle Road, Colombo 3, Sri Lanka. This address for urgent technical matters only. All other correspondence should be directed to the regular VOA or IBB addresses in Washington (*see* USA).

SUDAN   World Time +2

Sudan National Radio Corporation, P.O. Box 572, Omdurman, Sudan. Phone: +249 (11) 553-151 or +249 (11) 552-100. Contact: (general) Mohammed Elfatih El Sumoal; (technical) Abbas Sidig, Director General, Engineering and Technical Affairs; Mohammed Elmahdi Khalil, Administrator, Engineering and Technical Affairs; Saleh Al-Hay; or Adil Didahammed, Engineering Department. Replies irregularly. Return postage necessary.

SURINAME   World Time –3

Radio Apintie, Postbus 595, Paramaribo, Suriname. Phone: +597 40-05-00. Fax: +597 40 06 84. Contact: Ch. E. Vervuurt, Director. Free pennant. Return postage or $1 required.

SWAZILAND   World Time +2

Swaziland Commercial Radio
NONTECHNICAL CORRESPONDENCE: P.O. Box 5569, Rivonia 2128, Transvaal, South Africa. Phone: +27 (11) 884-8400. Fax: +27 (11) 883 1982. Contact: Fernando Vaz-Osiori; Rob Vickers, Manager—Religion. IRC helpful. Replies irregularly.
TECHNICAL CORRESPONDENCE: P.O. Box 99, Amsterdam 2375, South Africa. Contact: Guy Doult, Chief Engineer.

SOUTH AFRICA BUREAU: P.O. Box 1586,Alberton 1450, Republic of South Africa. Phone: +27 (11) 434-4333. Fax: +27 (11) 434 4777.

Trans World Radio—Swaziland
MAIN OFFICE: P.O. Box 64, Manzini, Swaziland. Phone: +268 505-2781/2/3. Fax: +268 505 5333. E-mail: (James Burnett, Regional Engineer & Frequency Manager) jburnett.twr.org; (Chief Engineer) sstavrop@twr.org; (L. Stavropoulos, DX Secretary) lstavrop@twr.org; (Greg Shaw, Follow-up Department) gshaw@twr.org. URL (transmission schedule): www.icon.co.za/~ttatlow/schedule.htm. Contact: (general) Greg Shaw, Follow-up Department; G.J. Alary, Station Director; or Joseph Ndzinisa, Program Manager; (technical) Mrs. L. Stavropoulos, DX Secretary; Chief Engineer; or James Burnett, Regional Engineer. Free stickers, postcards and calendars. A free Bible Study course is available. May swap canceled stamps. $1, return postage or 3 IRCs required. Also, *see* USA.
AFRICA REGIONAL OFFICE: P.O. Box 4232,Kempton Park 1610, South Africa. Contact: Stephen Boakye-Yiadom, African Regional Director.
CÔTE D'IVOIRE OFFICE: B.P. 2131, Abidjan 06, Côte d'Ivoire.
KENYA OFFICE: P.O. Box 21514 Nairobi, Kenya.
MALAWI OFFICE: P. O. Box 52 Lilongwe, Malawi.
SOUTH AFRICA OFFICE: P.O. Box 36000, Menlo Park 0102, South Africa.
ZIMBABWE OFFICE: P.O. Box H-74, Hatfield, Harare, Zimbabwe.

SWEDEN   World Time +1 (+2 midyear)

IBRA Radio (program)
MAIN OFFICE: International Broadcasting Association, Box 396, SE-105 36 Stockholm, Sweden. Phone: +46 (8) 619-2540; Fax: +46 (8) 619 2539. E-mail: hq@ibra.se; or ibra@ibra.se. URLs: www.ibra.se/; www.ibra.org/. Contact: Mikael Stjernberg, Public Relations Manager. Free pennants and stickers. IBRA Radio is heard as a program over various world band stations, including the Voice of Hope (Lebanon) and Trans World Radio (Monaco); and also airs broadcasts via transmitters in Russia and the CIS.
CYPRUS OFFICE: P.O. Box 7420, 3315 Limassol, Cyprus. Contact: Rashad Saleem. Free schedules, calendars and stickers.

▣Radio Sweden
MAIN OFFICE: SE-105 10 Stockholm, Sweden. Phone: (general) +46 (8) 784-7200, +46 (8) 784-7207, +46 (8) 784-7288 or +46 (8) 784-5000; (listener voice mail) +46 (8) 784-7287; (technical department) +46 (8) 784-7286. Fax: (general) +46 (8) 667 6283; (polling to receive schedule) +46 8 660 2990. E-mail: (general) info@rs.sr.se; (schedule on demand) english@rs.sr.se; (Roxström) sarah.roxstrom@rs.sr.se; (Hagström) nidia.hagstrom@rs.sr.se; (Wood) george.wood@rs.sr.se; (Beckman, Technical Manager) rolf-b@stab.sr.se. URLs: (general) www.sr.se/rs/; (online reception report form) www.sr.se/rs/english/qsl.htm; (RealAudio multilingual archives) www.sr.se/rs/listen/; (RealAudio daily broadcast in English) www.sr.se/rs/english/sounds/ (replace "english" by "svenska" to hear the Swedish broadcasts). FTP versions of Radio Sweden's daily broadcasts (all languages) are available at www.sr.se/ftp/rs/. Contact: (general) Nidia Hagström, Host, "In Touch with Stockholm" [include your telephone number]; Sarah Roxström, Head, English Service; Greta Grandin, Program Assistant, English Service; George Wood, Producer, MediaScan; Olimpia Seldon, Assistant to the Director; or Charlotte Adler, Public Relations & Information; (administration) Finn Norgren, Director Gen-

eral; (technical) Rolf Erik Beckman, Head, Technical Department. T-shirts (two sizes) $12 or £8. Payment for T-shirts may be made by international money order, Swedish postal giro account No. 43 36 56-6 or internationally negotiable bank check.
NEW YORK NEWS BUREAU: Swedish Broadcasting, 825 Third Avenue, New York NY 10022 USA. Phone: +1 (212) 688-6872 or +1 (212) 643-8855. Fax: +1 (212) 594 6413. Contact: Elizabeth Johansson.
WASHINGTON NEWS BUREAU: Swedish Broadcasting, 2030 M Street NW, Suite 700, Washington DC 20036 USA. Phone: +1 (202) 785-1727. Contact: Folke Rydén, Lisa Carlsson or Steffan Ekendahl.
TRANSMISSION AUTHORITY: TERACOM, Svensk Rundradio AB, P.O. Box 17666, SE-118 92 Stockholm, Sweden. Phone: (general) +46 (8) 555-420-00; (Nilsson) +46 (8) 554-2066. Fax: (general) +46 (8) 555 420 01; (Nilsson) +46 (8) 554 2060. E-mail: (general) info@teracom.se; (Nilsson) magnus.nilsson@teracom.se. URL: www.teracom.se. Contact: (Frequency Planning Dept.—Head Office): Magnus Nilsson; (Engineering) H. Widenstedt, Chief Engineer. Free stickers; sometimes free T-shirts to those monitoring during special test transmissions. Seeks monitoring feedback for new frequency usages.

SWITZERLAND   World Time +1 (+2 midyear)

European Broadcasting Union, Case Postal 67, CH-1218 Grand-Saconnex, Geneva, Switzerland. Phone: +41 (22) 717-2111 or +41 (22) 717-2221. Fax: +41 (22) 798 5897 or +41 (22) 717 2481. E-mail: ebu@ebu.ch. URL: www.ebu.ch. Contact: Jean-Bernard Munch, Secretary-General; or Robin Levey, Strategic Information Service Database Manager. Umbrella organization for broadcasters in 49 European and Mediterranean countries.

International Telecommunication Union, Place des Nations, CH-1211 Geneva 20, Switzerland. Phone: (Fonteyne) +41 (22) 730-5983; or Pham) +41 (22) 730-6136. Fax: +41 (22) 730 5785. Contact: Jacques Fonteyne or Hai Pham. E-mail: (schedules & reference tables) Brmail@itu.int; (Fonteyne) jacques.fonteyne@itu.int; or (Pham) pham.hai@itu.int. URL: www.itu.ch. The ITU is the world's official regulatory body for all telecommunication activities, including world band radio. Offers a wide range of official multilingual telecommunication publications in print and/or digital formats.

Mitternachtsruf, Postfach 290, Eichholzstrasse 38, CH-8330 Pfaffikon, Switzerland. Contact: Jonathan Malgo or Paul Richter. Verifies reports with a QSL card. Free stickers and promotional material. Religious program aired over Radio Intercontinental, Armenia.
GERMAN OFFICE: Postfach 62, D-79807 Lottstetten, Germany.
U.S. OFFICE: P.O. Box 4389, W. Columbia, SC 29171 USA.

Stimmes des Trostes, Ebnat Kappel, Switzerland. Religious program aired via Radio Intercontinental, Armenia.

▣Swiss Radio International
MAIN OFFICE: Giacomettistrasse 1, CH-3000 Berne 15, Switzerland. Phone: (general) +41 (31) 350-9222; (English Department) +41 (31) 350-9790; (French Department) +41 (31) 350-9555; (German Department) +41 (31) 350-9535; (Italian Department) +41 (31) 350-9531); (Frequency Management) +41 (31) 350-9734. Fax: (general) +41 (31) 350 9569; (administration) +41 (31) 350 9744 or +41 (31) 350 9581; (Communication and Marketing) +41 (31) 350 9544; (Programme Department) +41 (31) 350 9569; (English Department) +41 (31) 350 9580; (French Department) +41 (31) 350 9664; (German

Department) +41 (31) 350 9562; (Italian Department) +41 (31) 350 9678; (Frequency Management) +41 (31) 350-9745. E-mail: (general) format is language@sri.ch (e.g. english@sri.ch, german@sri.ch); (marketing) marketing@swissinfo.org; (technical) technical@swissinfo.org; (Frequency Management): ulrich.wegmueller@sri.srg-ssr.ch. URLs: (including RealAudio in English) www.sri.ch; www.swissinfo.org. Contact: (general) Diana Zanotti, English Department; Marlies Schmutz, Listeners' Letters, German Programmes; Thérèse Schafter, Listeners' Letters, French Programmes; Esther Niedhammer, Listeners' Letters, Italian Programmes; Beatrice Lombard, Promotion; Giovanni D'Amico, Audience Officer; (administration) Ulrich Kündig, General Manager; Nicolas Lombard, Deputy General Manager; Walter Fankhauser, Head, Communication & Marketing Services; Rose-Marie Malinverni, Head, Editorial Co-ordination Unit; Ron Grünig, Head, English Programmes; James Jeanneret, Head, German Programmes; Philippe Zahne, Head, French Programmes; Fabio Mariani, Head, Italian Programmes; (technical) Paul Badertscher, Head, Engineering Services; Ulrich Wegmueller, Frequency Manager; or Bob Zanotti. Free station flyers, posters, stickers and pennants. Sells CDs of Swiss music, plus audio and video (PAL/NTSC) cassettes; also, Swiss watches and clocks, microphone lighters, letter openers, books, T-shirts, sweatshirts and Swiss Army knives. VISA/EURO/AX or cash, but no personal checks. For catalog, write to SRI Enterprises, c/o the above address, fax +41 (31) 350 9581, or e-mail shopping@sri.srg-ssr.ch.

WASHINGTON NEWS BUREAU: 2030 M Street NW, Washington DC 20554 USA. Phone: (general) +1 (202) 775-0894 or +1 (202) 429-9668; (French-language radio) +1 (202) 296-0277; (German-language radio) +1 (202) 7477. Fax: +1 (202) 833 2777. Contact: Christophe Erbeck, reporter.

SYRIA   World Time +2 (+3 midyear)

Radio Damascus, Syrian Radio & Television, Ommayad Square, Damascus, Syria. Phone: +963 (11) 221-7653. Fax: +963 (11) 222 2692. Contact: Mr. Afaf, Director General; Mr. Adnan Al-Massri; Adnan Salhab; Lisa Arslanian; or Mrs. Wafa Ghawi. Free stickers, paper pennants and *The Syria Times* newspaper. Replies can be highly erratic, but as of late have been more regular, if sometimes slow.

TAHITI—*see* FRENCH POLYNESIA.

TAJIKISTAN   World Time +5

Radio Tajikistan, Chapaev Street 31, 734025 Dushanbe, Tajikistan; or English Service, International Service, Radio Tajikistan, P.O. Box 108, 734025 Dushanbe, Tajikistan. Phone: (Director) +7 (3772) 210-877 or +7 (3772) 277-417; (English Department) +7 (3772) 277-417; (Ramazonov) +7 (3772) 277-667 or +7 (3772) 277-347. Fax: +7 (3772) 211 198. Note that the country and city codes are scheduled to be changed in the near future, so the current +7 (3772) should then become +992 (372). E-mail: treng@td.silk.org. Contact: (administration) Mansur Sultanov, Director – Tajik Radio; Nasrullo Ramazonov, Foreign Relations Department. Correspondence in Russian or Tajik preferred. There is no official policy for verification of listeners' reports, so try sending reception reports and correspondence in English to the attention of Mr. Ramazonov, who is currently the sole English speaker at the station. Caution should be exercised when contacting him

Pioneering 1936 tape recorder used at the BBC Empire Service, predecessor to today's World Service.   BBC

via e-mail, as it is his personal account and he is charged for both incoming and outgoing mail. In addition, all e-mail is routinely monitored and censored. Return postage of 5$ has been requested on at least one occasion, but enclosing currency notes is risky due to the high level of postal theft in the country. IRCs are not exchangeable, so including small souvenirs with your letter may help produce a reply.

TRANSMISSION FACILITIES: Television and Radiocommunications Ltd., ul. Internationalskaya 85, 734001 Dushanbe, Tajikistan. Phone: +7 (3772) 244-646. Fax: +7 (3772) 212 517. E-mail: nodir@uralnet.ru. Contact: Rakhmatillo Masharipovich Masharipov, Director General.

Tajik Radio, ul. Chapaeva 31, 734025 Dushanbe, Tajikistan. Contact information as for Radio Tajikistan, above.

TANZANIA   World Time +3

Radio Tanzania, Nyerere Road, P.O. Box 9191, Dar es Salaam, Tanzania. Phone: +255 (51) 860-760. Fax: +255 (51) 865 577. E-mail: radiotanzania@raha.com. Contact: (general) Abdul Ngarawa, Director of Broadcasting; Mrs. Edda Sanga, Controller of Programs; Ms. Penzi Nyamungumi, Head of English Service and International Relations Unit; or Ahmed Jongo, Producer, "Your Answer"; (technical) Taha Usi, Chief Engineer; or Emmanuel Mangula, Deputy Chief Engineer. Replies to correspondence in English.

Voice of Tanzania Zanzibar, Department of Broadcasting, Radio Tanzania Zanzibar, P.O. Box 2503, Zanzibar, Tanzania (if this address brings no reply, try P.O. Box 1178); (Muombwa, personal address) P.O. Box 2068, Zanzibar, Tanzania. Phone: +255 (54) 31-088. Fax: + 255 (54) 57 207. Contact: (general) Yusuf Omar Chunda, Director Department of Information and Broadcasting; Ndaro Nyamwolha; Ali Bakari Muombwa; Abdulrah'man M. Said; N. Nyamwochd, Director of Broadcasting; or Kassim S. Kassim; (technical) Nassor M. Suleiman, Maintenance Engineer. $1 return postage helpful.

During a lull in the fighting an Afghan farmer plows his field in fertile Kunduz province. M. Guha

THAILAND   World Time +7

BBC World Service—Asia Relay Station, P.O. Box 20, Muang Nakhon, Sawan 60000, Thailand. Contact: Jaruwan Meesaurtong, Personal Assistant.

Mukto Probaho

MAIN ADDRESS: P.O. Box 9406, Calcutta 700016, India. Contact: Sk Abdullah. Correspondence in English and reception reports welcomed. Members' Club. This daily Bengali-language Christian religious program/listener-response show, produced by a studio associated with IBRA Radio *(see* Sweden), is aired via transmission facilities of the Voice of Russia. Sometimes verifies via IBRA Radio in Sweden.
BANGKOK ADDRESS: GPO Box 1605, Bangkok 10501, Thailand.

Radio Thailand World Service, 236 Vibhavadi Rangsit Highway, Din Daeng, Huaykhwang, Bangkok 10400, Thailand. Phone: +66 (2) 277-1814, +66 (2) 274-9098. Phone/fax:+66 (2) 277-6139, +66 (2) 274-9099. E-mail: amporn@usa.net; or amporn@radiothailand.com. URL: www.radiothailand.com. Contact: Mrs. Amporn Samosorn, Chief of External Services; or Patra Lamjiack. Free pennants. Replies irregularly, especially to those who persist.

Voice of America/IBB—Relay Station Thailand, Udon Thani, Thailand. Phone: +66 (42) 271-490/1. Only matters of urgent importance should be directed to this site. All other matters should be referred to the regular VOA or IBB addresses in Washington *(see* USA).

TOGO   World Time exactly

Radio Lomé, B.P. 434, Lomé, Togo. Phone: + 228 212-492. Contact: (nontechnical) Batchoudi Malúlaba or Geraldo Isidine. Return postage, $1 or 2 IRCs helpful. French preferred but English accepted.

TUNISIA   World Time +1

📻**Radiodiffusion Télévision Tunisienne**, 71 Avenue de la Liberté, TN-1070 Tunis, Tunisia. Phone: +216 (1) 801-177. Fax: +216 (1) 781 927. E-mail: info@radiotunis.com. URL: (includes RealAudio) www.radiotunis.com/news.html. Contact: Mongai Caffai, Director General; Mohamed Abdelkafi,

Director; Kamel Cherif, Directeur; Masmoudi Mahmoud; Mr. Bechir Betteib; or Smaoui Sadok, Le Sous-Directeur Technique. Replies irregularly and slowly to correspondence in French or Arabic. $1 helpful. For reception reports try: Le Chef de Service du Controle de la Récepcion de l'Office National de la Télédiffusion, O.N.T, Cité Ennassim I, Bourjel, B.P. 399, TN-1080 Tunis, Tunisia. Phone: +216 (1) 801-177. Fax: +216 (1) 781 927. E-mail: ont.@ati.tn. Contact: Abdesselem Slim.

TURKEY   World Time +2 (+3 midyear)

Radyo Çinarli, Çinarli Anadolu Teknik ve Endüstri Meslek Lisesi Deneme Radyosu, Çinarli, TR-35.110 İzmir, Turkey. Phone: +90 (232) 486-6434; (technical) +90 (232) 461-7442. Fax: +90 (232) 435 1032. Contact: (general) Ahmet Ayaydin, School Manager; (technical) Göksel Uysal, Technical Manager. Station is run by the local technical institute. Free studio photos and, occasionally, other small souvenirs. Correspondence in English accepted.

Turkish Radio-Television Corporation, Voice of Turkey

MAIN OFFICE, NONTECHNICAL: TRT External Services Department, TRT Sitesi, Turan Günes Blv., Or-An Çankaya, 06450 Ankara, Turkey; or P.K. 333, Yenisehir, 06443 Ankara, Turkey. Phone: (general) +90 (312) 490-9800/9801; (English Service) +90 (312) 490-9842. Fax: +90 (312) 490 9835/45/46. E-mail: (general) infotsr@tsr.gov.tr; (Turkish broadcasts) turkceyayin@tsr.gov.tr; (English Service) englishservice@ tsr.gov.tr; same format applies for Arabic, French, German and Russian services, e.g. germanservice@tsr.gov.tr. URL: http://tsr.gov.tr/ (English: http://tsr.gov.tr/main_en.asp). Contact: (English & non-technical) Mr. Osman Erkan, Chief, English Service and Host of, "Letterbox"; or Ms. Reshide Morali, Announcer "DX Corner"; (other languages) Mr. Rafet Esit, Director, Foreign Languages Section; (administration) Mr. Danyal Gurdal, Head, External Services Department. Technical correspondence, such as on reception quality should be directed to: Ms. F. Elvan Boratav *see* next entry below. On-air language courses offered in Arabic and German, but no printed course material. Free stickers, pennants, women's embroidery artwork swatches and tourist literature.
MAIN OFFICE, TECHNICAL (FOR EMIRLER AND ÇAKIRLAR

TRANSMITTER SITES AND FOR FREQUENCY MANAGEMENT): TRT Teknik Yardimcilik, TRT Sitesi, Kat: 5/C, Oran, 06450 Ankara, Turkey. Phone: +90 (312) 490-1730/2. Fax: +90 (312) 490 1733. E-mail: utis@turnet.net.tr or utis2@trt.net.tr. Contact: Mr. Vural Tekeli, TRT Head of Engineering; F. Elvan Boratav, Chief Engineer, International Technical Relations Service; Ms. Sedef Somaltin; or Turgay Cakimci, Chief Engineer, International Technical Relations Service.

SAN FRANCISCO OFFICE, SCHEDULES: 2654 17th Avenue, San Francisco CA 94116 USA. Phone: +1 (415) 564-9968. E-mail: GPoppin@aol.com. Contact: George Poppin. This address, a volunteer office, only provides TRT schedules to listeners. All other correspondence should be sent directly to Ankara.

Türkiye Polis Radyosu (Turkish Police Radio), T.C. Içişleri Bakanliği, Emniyet Genel Müdürlüğü, Ankara, Turkey. Contact: Fatih Umutlu. Tourist literature for return postage. Replies irregularly.

Meteoroloji Sesi Radyosu (Voice of Meteorology), T.C. Tarim Bakanliği, Devlet Meteoroloji İşleri, Genel Müdürlüğü, P.K. 401, Ankara, Turkey. Phone: +90 (312) 359-7545, X-281. Fax: +90 (312) 314 1196. Contact: (nontechnical) Gühekin Takinalp; Recep Yilmaz, Head of Forecasting Department; or Abdullah Gölpinar; (technical) Mehmet Örmeci, Director General. Free tourist literature. Return postage helpful.

TURKMENISTAN World Time +5

Radio Turkmenistan, National TV & Radio Broadcasting Company, Mollanepes St. 3, 744000 Ashgabat, Turkmenistan. Phone: +993 (12) 251-515. Fax: +993 (12) 251 421. Contact: (administration) Yu M. Pashaev, Deputy Chairman of State Television and Radio Company; (technical) G. Khanmamedov; K. Karayev, Chief of Technical Department; or A.A Armanklichev, Deputy Chief, Technical Department. This country is currently under strict censorship and media people are closely watched. A lot of foreign mail addressed to a particular person may attract the attention of the security services. Best is not to address your mail to particular individuals but to the station itself.

UGANDA World Time +3

Radio Uganda
GENERAL OFFICE: P.O. Box 7142, Kampala, Uganda. Phone: +256 (41) 257-256. Fax: +256 (41) 256 888. Contact: (general) Charles Byekwaso, Controller of Programmes; or Mrs. Florence Sewanyana, Head of Public Relations. $1 or return postage required. Replies infrequently and slowly.
ENGINEERING DIVISION: P.O. Box 2038, Kampala, Uganda. Phone: +256 (41) 256-647. Contact: Leopold B. Lubega, Principal Broadcasting Engineer; or Rachel Nakibuuka, Secretary. Four IRCs or $2 required. Enclosing a self addressed envelope may also help to get a reply.

UKRAINE World Time +2 (+3 midyear)

WARNING-MAIL THEFT: For the time being, letters to Ukrainian stations, especially containing funds or IRCs, are more likely to arrive safely if sent by registered mail.

Government Transmission Authority: RRT/Concern of Broadcasting, Radiocommunication & Television, 10 Dorogajtshaya St., 254112 Kiev, Ukraine. Phone: +380 (44) 226-2262 or +380 (44) 444-6900. Fax: +380 (44) 440 8722. E-mail: ak@cbrt.freenet.kiev.ua. Contact: Mr. Mykola

Kyryliuk, Technical Exploitation & Management; Alexey Karpenko; Alexander Serdiuk; Nikolai P. Kiriliuk, Head of Operative Management Service; or Mrs. Liudmila Deretskaya, Interpreter.

Radio Ukraine International, Kreshchatik str., 26, 252001 Kiev, Ukraine. Phone: +380 (44) 228-2534, +380 (44) 229-1757 or (phone/fax) +380 (44) 228-7356. Fax: +380 (44) 229 4585; or +380 (44) 229 3477. E-mail: mo@ukrradio.ru.kiev.ua. Contact: (administration) Inna Chichinadze, Vice-Director of RUI; (technical) *see* Ukrainian Radio, below. Free stickers, calendars and Ukrainian stamps.

Ukrainian Radio, Kreshchatik str., 26, 252001 Kiev, Ukraine. Phone: +380 (44) 226-2253. Fax: (administration) +380 (44) 229 4226 or +380 (44) 229 4585. (technical) +380 (44) 220 6733. E-mail: mo@ukrradio.ru.kiev. Contact: (administration) Volodimyr Reznikov, President of National Radio Company of Ukraine; or Victor Nabrusko, First Vice-President of National Radio Company of Ukraine; (technical) Anatolii Ivanov, Frequency Coordination, Engineering Services.

UNITED ARAB EMIRATES World Time +4

UAE Radio from Abu Dhabi, Ministry of Information & Culture, P.O. Box 63, Abu Dhabi, United Arab Emirates. Phone: +971 (2) 451-000. Fax: (Ministry of Information & Culture) +971 (2) 452 504. Contact: (technical) Ibrahim Rashid, Director General, Technical Department; or Fauzi Saleh, Chief Engineer. Free stickers, postcards and stamps. Do not enclose money with correspondence.

FREQUENCY MANAGEMENT: Abu Dhabi Radio, P.O. Box 63, Abu Dhabi, United Arab Emirates. Phone: +971 (2) 436-849. Fax: +971 (2) 451 155 or +971 (2) 450 205. E-mail: waleed_alzaabi@ebc.co.ae. Contact: Mr. Samir Iskander, Senior Engineer; or Mr. Waleed Al-Zaabi, Chief Engineer.

UAE Radio in Dubai, P.O. Box 1695, Dubai, United Arab Emirates. Phone: +971 (4) 370-255. Fax: +971 (4) 374 111 +971 (4) 370 283 or +971 (4) 371 079. Contact: Ms. Khulud Halaby; or Sameer Aga, Producer, "Cassette Club Cinarabic"; (technical) K.F. Fenner, Chief Engineer—Radio; or Ahmed Al Muhaideb, Assistant Controller, Engineering. Free pennants. Replies irregularly.

UNITED KINGDOM World Time exactly (+1 midyear)

Adventist World Radio, the Voice of Hope, AWR Branch Administrative Office, Newbold College, Binfield, Bracknell, Berks. RG42 4AN, United Kingdom. Phone: +44 (1344) 401-401. Fax: +44 (1344) 401 419. E-mail: awrinfo@awr.org. Contact: Andrea Steele, Director, Public Relations and Listener Services. Also, *see* AWR listings under Costa Rica, Guam, Guatemala, Italy, Kenya and USA.

BBC Monitoring, Caversham Park, Reading RG4 8TZ, United Kingdom. Phone: (general) +44 (118) 947-2742; (Customer Service) +44 (118) 946-9338; (Foreign Media Unit—Broadcast Schedules/monitoring) +44 (118) 946-9261; (Marketing Department) +44 (118) 946-9204. Fax: (Customer Service) +44 (118) 946 1020; (Foreign Media Unit) +44 (118) 946 1993; (Marketing Department) +44 (118) 946 3828. E-mail: (Customer Service) csu@mon.bbc.co.uk; (Marketing Department) stephen_innes@mon.bbc.co.uk; (Foreign Media Unit/World Media) fmu@mon.bbc.co.uk; (Kenny) dave_kenny@mon.bbc.co.uk; (publications and real time services) marketing@mon.bbc.co.uk. URL: www.monitor.bbc.co.uk/Welcome.html. Contact: (administration) Andrew Hills, Director of Monitoring; (World Media) Chris McWhinnie, Editor "World Media"; (World Media Schedules) Dave Kenny, Sub Editor, "World Media"; (Publication Sales) Stephen Innes, Marketing. BBC Monitoring produces the weekly publication *World Media.* Available on yearly subscription, costing £390.00. Price excludes postage overseas. *World Media* is also available online through the Internet or via a direct dial-in bulletin board at an annual cost of £425.00. Broadcasting Schedules, issued weekly by e-mail at an annual cost of £99.00. VISA/ MC/AX. The Technical Operations Unit provides detailed observations of broadcasts on the long, medium and short wave bands. This unit provides tailored channel occupancy observations, reception reports, *Broadcast Schedules Database* (constantly updated on over 100 countries) and the *Broadcast Research Log* (a record of broadcasting developments compiled daily). BBC Monitoring works in conjunction with the Foreign Broadcast Information Service (*see* USA).

⬛BBC World Service

MAIN OFFICE, NONTECHNICAL: Bush House, Strand, London WC2B 4PH, United Kingdom. Phone: (general) +44 (171) 240-3456; (Press Office) +44 (171) 557-2947/1; (International Marketing) +44 (171) 557-1143. Fax: (general) +44 (171) 379 6841; (Audience Relations) +44 (171) 557 1258; ("Write On" listeners' letters program) +44 (171) 436 2800; (Audience & Market Research) +44 (171) 557 1254; (International Marketing) +44 (171) 557 1254. E-mail: (general listener correspondence) worldservice.letters@bbc.co.uk; ("Write On") writeon@ bbc.co.uk. URLs: (general, including RealAudio) www.bbc.co.uk/worldservice/; (entertainment and information) www.beeb.com. Contact: Patrick Condren, Presenter, of "Write On"; Alan Booth, International Marketing Manager; or Mark Byford, Chief Executive. Offers *BBC On Air* magazine (*see* below). Also, *see* Antigua, Ascension, Oman, Seychelles, Singapore and Thailand. The present facility at Masirah, Oman, is scheduled to be replaced in 2001 by a new site at Al-Ashkharah, also in Oman, which is to include four 300 kW shortwave transmitters.

SAN FRANCISCO OFFICE, SCHEDULES: 2654 17th Avenue, San Francisco CA 94116 USA. Phone: +1 (415) 564-9968. E-mail: GPoppin@aol.com. Contact: George Poppin. This address, a volunteer office, only provides BBC World Service schedules to listeners. All other correspondence should be sent directly to the main office in London.

TECHNICAL: See Merlin Communications International, below. BBC World Service—Publication and Product Sales

BBC ENGLISH magazine, Bush House, Strand, London WC2B 4PH, United Kingdom. Phone: (editorial office) +44 (171) 557-1110. Fax: +44 (171) 557 1316.

BBC WORLD SERVICE SHOP, Bush House Arcade, Strand, London WC2B 4PH, United Kingdom. Phone: +44 (171) 557-2576. Fax: +44 (171) 240 4811. Sells numerous audio/video (video PAL/VHS only) cassettes, publications (including PASSPORT TO WORLD BAND RADIO), portable world band radios, T-shirts, sweatshirts and other BBC souvenirs available from BBC World Service Shop.

BBC ON AIR monthly program guide, Room 227 NW, Bush House, Strand, London WC2B 4PH, United Kingdom. Phone: (editorial office) +44 (171) 557-2211; (Circulation Manager) +44 (171) 557-2855; (advertising) +44 (171) 557-2873; (subscription voice mail) +44 (171) 557-2211. Fax: +44 (171) 240 4899. E-mail: on.air.magazine@bbc.co.uk. Contact: (editorial) Kirsty Cockburn, Editor; (subscriptions) Rosemarie Reid, Circulation Manager; (advertising) Paul Cosgrove. Subscription $30 or £18 per year. VISA/MC/AX/Barclay/EURO/Access,

Postal Order, International Money Draft or cheque in pounds sterling.

Commonwealth Broadcasting Association, CBA Secretariat, 17 Fleet Street, London EC4Y 1AA, United Kingdom. Phone: +44 (171) 583-5550. Fax: +44 (171) 583 5549. E-mail: (general) cba@cba.org.uk; (Smith) elizabeth@cba.org.uk. URL: www.oneworld.org/cba/. Contact: Elizabeth Smith, Secretary-General; Colin Lloyd, Manager—Training & Development; or Hilary Clucas, Administrator. Publishes the annual *Commonwealth Broadcaster Directory* and the quarterly *Commonwealth Broadcaster* (online subscription form available).

Far East Broadcasting Association (FEBA), Ivy Arch Road, Worthing, West Sussex BN14 8BX, United Kingdom. Phone: +44 (1903) 237-281. Fax: +44 (1903) 205 294. E-mail: reception@febaradio.org.uk; or (Richard Whittington) dwhittington@feba.org.uk. URL: www.feba.org.uk. Contact: Tony Ford or Richard Whittington, Schedule Engineer. This office is the headquarters for FEBA worldwide.

High Adventure Radio (Voice of Hope), P.O. Box 109, Hereford HR4 9XR, United Kingdom. E-mail: mail@highadventure.net. URL: www.intertvnet.net/~highorg/ stations/europe/. Broadcasts via transmitters of Deutsche Telekom (*see*) in Jülich, Germany. Also, *see* KVOH—High Adventure Radio, USA.

IBC-Tamil, P.O. Box 1505, London SW8 2ZH, United Kingdom. Phone: +44 (171) 787-8000. Fax: +44 (171) 787 8010. E-mail: desk@ibc-tamil.com. URL: (includes RealAudio in English and Tamil) www.ibc-tamil.com. Contact: A.C. Tarcisius, Managing Director.

⬛London Radio Service (LRS), The Interchange, Oval Road, London NW1 7DZ, United Kingdom. Phone: +44 (171) 453-7500. Fax: +44 (171) 413 0072. E-mail: tayris@lrs.co.uk. URL: (includes RealAudio) www.lrs.co.uk. Contact: Tim Ayris, Marketing Officer. An award-winning producer and syndicator of news and feature programs in English, Arabic, Russian, Spanish and Portuguese, LRS is a service of Associated Press Television News on behalf of the Foreign and Commonwealth Office. Broadcasts on shortwave in English and Spanish via WWCR, USA (*see*).

Merlin Communications International Limited, 20 Lincoln's Inn Fields, London WC2A 3ES, United Kingdom. Phone: +44 (171) 969-0000. Fax: +44 (171) 396 6223; (Nicola Wallbridge) +44 (171) 396 6223. E-mail: marketing@ merlincommunications.com; (frequency-related matters) sfm@mercom.co.uk. URLs: www.merlincommunications.com; www.mercom.co.uk. Contact: Fiona Lowry, Chief Executive; Rory Maclachlan, Comercial Director; Richard Hurd, Business Development Manager, Transmission Sales; Ciaran Fitzgerald, Head of BBC Customer Services; Anver Anderson, Head of Satellite Sales; or Michelle Franks, Communications Assistant. Merlin has a ten year contract with the BBC World Service to provide a full range of complex programme transmission and distribution services from 11 strategic sites to over 100 countries worldwide. International customers include Radio Canada International, Voice of America, NHK, Radio Telefis Eireann, HCJB World Radio and Swiss Radio International.

Merlin Network One, 20 Lincoln's Inn Fields, London WC2A 3ES, United Kingdom. Phone: +44 (171) 396-6220. Fax: +44 (171) 396 6221. E-mail: mno@cix.co.uk. URLs: www.mno.co.uk; www.mno.net.

Sunrise Radio (when operating), Sunrise House, Sunrise Road, Southall, Middlesex UB2 4AU, United Kingdom. Phone: +44 (181) 574 6666. Fax: +44 (181) 813 9800. Contact: Somaira Sadeghi, Personal Assistant to Chief Executive.

Tamil Broadcasting Corporation—London ("TBC-London"). E-mail: kumartbc@tbc-london.com. URL: www.tbc-london.com. Plans to broadcast to Sri Lanka and southern India. No further information at press time.

🔊**World Radio Network Ltd**, Wyvil Court, 10 Wyvil Road, London SW8 2TY, United Kingdom. Phone: +44 (171) 896-9000. Fax: + 44 (171) 896 9007. E-mail: (general) online@wrn.org; wrn@cityscape.co.uk; (Cohen) jeffc@wrn.org. URL: www.wrn.org. Contact: Karl Miosga, Managing Director; Jeffrey Cohen, Director of Development; Tim Ashburner, Director of Technical Operations; or Simon Spanswick, Director of Corporate Affairs. Sells numerous items such as Polo T-shirts, baseball caps, pen knives and watches. Ask for WRN collection catalogue for further details. VISA/MC. Provides Web RealAudio, Streamworks and NetShow, plus program placement via satellite in various countries for nearly two dozen international broadcasters.

UNITED NATIONS World Time –5 (–4 midyear)

🔊**United Nations Radio**, S-850, United Nations, New York NY 10017 USA; or write to the station over which UN Radio was heard. Fax: +1 (212) 963 1307. E-mail: (general) unradio@un.org; (comments on programs) audiovisual@un.org. URLs: (general) www.un.org/av/radio; (RealAudio) www.wrn.org/ondemand/unitednations.html; www.internetbroadcast.com/unhome.htm. Contact: (general) Sylvester E. Rowe, Chief, Radio and Video Service; or Ayman El-Amir, Chief, Radio Section, Department of Public Information; (technical and nontechnical) Sandra Guy, Secretary. Free stamps and *UN Frequency* publication. Reception reports (including those sent by e-mail) are verified with a QSL card. *GENEVA OFFICE:* Room G209, Palais des Nations, CH-1211 Geneva 10, Switzerland. Phone: +41 (22) 917-4222. Fax: +41 (22) 917 0123.
PARIS OFFICE: UNESCO Radio, 7 Place de Fontenoy, F-75007 Paris, France. Fax: +33 (1) 45 67 30 72. Contact: Erin Faherty, Executive Radio Producer.

URUGUAY World Time –3

Emisora Ciudad de Montevideo, Canelones 2061, 11200 Montevideo, Uruguay. Phone: +598 (2) 402-0142. Fax: +598 (2) 402 0700. Contact: Aramazd Yizmeyian, Director General. Free stickers. Return postage helpful.
La Voz de Artigas (when active), Av. Lecueder 483, 55000 Artigas, Uruguay. Phone: +598 (772) 2447 or +598 (772) 3445. Fax: +598 (772) 4744. Contact: (general) Sra. Solange Murillo Ricciardi, Co-Propietario; or Luis Murillo; (technical) Roberto Murillo Ricciardi. Free stickers and pennants. Replies to correspondence in English, Spanish, French, Italian and Portuguese.
Radiodifusion Nacional—*see* S.O.D.R.E., below.
🔊**Radio Monte Carlo**, Av. 18 de Julio 1224 piso 1, 11100 Montevideo, Uruguay. Phone: +598 (2) 901-4433 or +598 (2) 908-3987. Fax: +598 (2) 901 7762. E-mail: cx20@netgate.com.uy. URL: (includes RealAudio) http://netgate.com.uy/cx20/. Contact: Ana Ferreira de Errázquin, Secretaria, Departamento de Prensa de la Cooperativa de Radioemisoras; Alexi Haysaniuk, Jefe Técnico; Déborah Ibarra, Secretaria; Emilia Sánchez Vega, Secretaria; or Ulises Graceras. Correspondence in Spanish preferred.
🔊**Radio Oriental**—Same mailing address as Radio Monte Carlo, above. Phone: +598 (2) 901-4433 or +598 (2) 900-5612. Fax: +598 (2) 901 7762. E-mail: cx12@netgate.com.uy. URL:

(includes RealAudio) http://netgate.com.uy/cx12/. Correspondence in Spanish preferred.
S.O.D.R.E.
PUBLICITY AND TECHNICAL: Radiodifusión Nacional, Casilla 1412, 11000 Montevideo, Uruguay. E-mail: radioact@chasque.apc.org. URL: www.chasque.apc.org/radioact/sodre.html. Contact: (publicity) Daniel Ayala González, Publicidad; (technical) Francisco Escobar, Dpto. Técnico. Reception reports may also be sent to the "Radioactividades" program (*see*, below).
OTHER: "Radioactividades," Casilla 7011, 11000 Montevideo, Uruguay. Fax: +598 (2) 575 4640. E-mail: radioact@chasque.apc.org. URL: www.chasque.apc.org/radioact/. Contact: Daniel Muñoz Faccioli.

USA World Time –4 Atlantic, including Puerto Rico and Virgin Islands; –5 (–4 midyear) Eastern, excluding Indiana; –5 Indiana, except northwest and southwest portions; –6 (–5 midyear) Central, including northwest and southwest Indiana; –7 (–6 midyear) Mountain, except Arizona; –7 Arizona; –8 (–7 midyear) Pacific; –9 (–8 midyear) Alaska, except Aleutian Islands; –10 (–9 midyear) Aleutian Islands; –10 Hawaii; –11 Samoa

🔊**Adventist World Radio, the Voice of Hope**
WORLD HEADQUARTERS: 12501 Old Columbia Pike, Silver Spring MD 20904-6600 USA. Phone: +1 (301) 680-6304. Fax: +1 (301) 680 6303. E-mail: 74617.1621@compuserve.com. URL: (includes RealAudio in English and Japanese and a printable reception report form) www.awr.org. Contact: (general) Don Jacobsen, President. Most correspondence and all reception reports are best sent to the station from which the transmission you heard actually emanated—*see* Costa Rica, Guam, Guatemala, Italy (also for transmissions from Armenia, Germany, Russia and Slovakia), rather than to the World Headquarters. Free religious printed matter, stickers, program schedules and other small souvenirs. IRC or $1 appreciated.
INTERNATIONAL RELATIONS: Box 29235, Indianapolis IN 46229 USA. Phone/fax: +1 (317) 891-8540. Contact: Dr. Adrian M. Peterson, International Relations. Provides publications with regular news releases and technical information. Sometimes issues special verification cards. QSL stamps and certificates also available from this address in return for reception reports.
DX PROGRAM: "Wavescan," prepared by Adrian Peterson (*see* preceding); aired on all AWR facilities.
LISTENER NEWSLETTER: Current, published bi-annually by AWR, is available through AWR stations in Costa Rica, Guam and Italy. Free, but IRCs are appreciated.
PUBLIC RELATIONS AND LISTENER SERVICES—*see* entry under "United Kingdom."
Also, *see* AWR listings under Costa Rica, Guam, Guatemala, Italy and Kenya.
BBC World Service via WYFR—Family Radio. For verification direct from WYFR's transmitters, contact WYFR—Family Radio (*see* below). Nontechnical correspondence should be sent to the BBC World Service in London (*see*).
Broadcasting Board of Governors (BBG), 330 Independence Avenue SW, Room 3360, Washington DC 20547 USA. Phone: +1 (202) 401-3736. Fax: +1 (202) 401 3376. Contact: (general) Kathleen Harrington, Public Relations; (administration) Mark Nathanson, Chairman. The BBG, created in 1994 and headed by nine members nominated by the President, is the overseeing agency for all official non-military United States international broadcasting operations, including the VOA, RFE-RL, Radio Martí and Radio Free Asia.

FEBC Radio International
INTERNATIONAL HEADQUARTERS: Far East Broadcasting Company, Inc., P.O. Box 1, La Mirada CA 90637 USA. Phone: +1 (310) 947-4651. Fax: +1 (310) 943 0160. E-mail: 3350911@mcimail.com; febc-usa@xc.org. URL: http://febc.org. Operates world band stations in the Northern Mariana Islands, the Philippines and the Seychelles. Does not verify reception reports from this address.
RUSSIA OFFICE: P.O. Box 2128, Khabarovsk 680020, Russia.
U.K. OFFICE: FEBA Radio, Ivy Arch Road, Worthing, West Sussex BN14 8BX, United Kingdom. Phone: +44 (903) 237-281. Fax: +44 (903) 205 294. E-mail: reception@feba.org.uk. URL: www.feba.org.uk.

Federal Communications Commission, 1919 M Street NW, Washington DC 20554 USA. Phone: +1 (202) 418-0200. Fax: +1 (202) 418 0232. E-mail: (general) fccinfo@fcc.gov; (Public Services Division) psd@fcc.gov; (specific individuals) format is initiallastname@fcc.gov, so to reach, say, Tom Polzin it would be tpolzin@fcc.gov. URLs: (general) www.fcc.gov/; (high frequency operating schedules) www.fcc.gov/ib/pnd/neg/hf_web/seasons.html; (FTP) ftp://ftp.fcc.gov/pub/. Contact: (consumer information) Martha Contee, Director, Public Services Division; (International Bureau, technical) Thomas E. Polzin.

⭐Fundamental Broadcasting Network, Grace Missionary Baptist Church, 520 Roberts Road, Newport NC 28570 USA. Phone: +1 (252) 223-6088; (toll-free, within the United States) 1-800-245-9685; (Robinson) +1 (252) 223-4600. URLs: (text) www.clis.com/fbn/; (RealAudio) www.worthwhile.com/fbn/. E-mail: fbn@bmd.clis.com. Alternative address: Morehead City NC 28557 USA. Phone: +1 (252) 240-1600. Fax: + (252) 726 2251. Contact: Pastor Clyde Eborn; (technical) David Robinson, Chief Engineer. Verifies reception reports if 1 IRC or (within USA) an SASE is included. Accepts e-mail reports. Plans to eventually broadcast in Chinese, French, Russian and Spanish in addition to English.

George Jacobs and Associates, Inc., 8701 Georgia Avenue, Suite 410, Silver Spring MD 20910 USA. Phone: +1 (301) 587-8800. Fax: +1 (301) 587 8801. E-mail: gja@gjainc.com; or gjacobs@clark.net. URL: www.gjainc.com/. Contact: (technical) Bob German or Mrs. Anne Case; (administration) George Jacobs, P.E. This firm provides frequency management and other engineering services for a variety of private U.S. and other world band stations, but does not correspond with the general public.

⭐Good News Hour, Good News World Radio, P.O. Box 895, Fort Worth TX 76101 USA. Phone: +1 (817) 226-6100 or +1 (817) 275-3334. E-mail: hope@goodnewsworld.org. URL: (includes RealAudio) www.goodnewsworld.org/content/broadcasts.htm. Contact: Robert Mawire, President. Welcomes reception reports both to postal and e-mail addresses. Free literature available. A program from Good News Ministries broadcast via the transmitters of Deutsche Telekom *(see)* in Jülich, Germany.

Herald Broadcasting Syndicate—Shortwave Broadcasts (all locations), Shortwave Broadcasts, P.O. Box 1524, Boston MA 02117-1524 USA. Phone: (general, toll-free within U.S.) 1-800-288-7090 or (general elsewhere) +1 (617) 450-2929 [with either number, extension 2060 to hear recorded frequency information, or 2929 for Shortwave Helpline and request printed schedules and information]. Fax: +1 (617) 450 2283. E-mail: (letters and reception reports) letterbox@csps.com; or (religious questions) sentinel@csps.com. URL: (*The Christian Science Monitor* newspaper) www.csmonitor.com; or

(information about the Christian Science Church in Boston) www.tfccs.com. Contact: Catherine Aitken-Smith, Director of International Broadcasting, Herald Broadcasting Syndicate (representative for station activity in Boston). Free schedules and information about Christian Science. *The Christian Science Monitor* newspaper and a full line of Christian Science books are available from: 1 Norway Street, Boston MA 02115 USA. *Science and Health with Key to the Scriptures* by Mary Baker Eddy is available in English $14.95 paperback ($16.95 in French, German, Portuguese or Spanish paperback; $24.95 in Czech or Russian hardcover) from Science and Health, P.O. Box 1875, Boston MA 02117 USA.

Herald Broadcasting Syndicate—WSHB Cypress Creek, 1030 Shortwave Lane, Pineland SC 29934 USA. Phone: (general) +1 (803) 625-5551; (station manager) +1 (803) 625-5555; (engineer) +1 (803) 625-5554. Fax: +1 (803) 625 5559. E-mail: (Station Manager) cee@csms.com, (Chief Engineer) damian@csms.com; (QSL coordinator) cindy@csms.com. URL: www.tfccs.com. Contact: (technical) Damian Centgraf, Chief Engineer; C. Ed Evans, Senior Station Manager; or Cindy Reihm, QSL Coordinator. Free station stickers when available. Visitors welcome from 9 to 4 Monday through Friday; for other times, contact transmitter site beforehand to make arrangements. This address is for technical feedback on South Carolina transmissions only; other inquiries should be directed to Shortwave Broadcasts, P.O. Box 1524, Boston MA 02117-1524 USA.

International Broadcasting Bureau (IBB)—Reports to the Broadcasting Board of Governors (*see*), and includes, among others, the Voice of America, RFE-RL, Radio Martí and Radio Free Asia. IBB Engineering (Office of Engineering and Technical Operations) provides broadcast services for these stations. Contact: (administration) Brian Conniff, Director; or Joseph O'Connell, Director of External Affairs; (technical) George Woodard, Director of Engineering. URL: www.ibb.gov/ibbpage.html.
FREQUENCY AND MONITORING OFFICE, TECHNICAL: USIA/IBB/EOF: Spectrum Management Division, International Broadcasting Bureau (IBB), Room 4611 Cohen Bldg., 330 Independence Avenue SW, Washington DC 20547 USA. Phone: +1 (202) 619-1669. Fax: +1 (202) 619 1680. E-mail: (scheduling) dferguson@ibb.gov; (monitoring) bw@his.com. URL: (general) http://monitor.ibb.gov; (e-mail reception report form) http://monitor.ibb.gov/now_you_try_it.html. Contact: Dan Ferguson (dferguson@ibb.gov); or Bill Whitacre (bw@his.com).

KAIJ
ADMINISTRATION OFFICE: Two-if-by-Sea Broadcasting Co., 22720 SE 410th St., Enumclaw WA 89022 USA. Phone/fax: (Mike Parker, California) +1 (818) 606-1254; (Washington State office, if and when operating) +1 (206) 825 4517. Contact: Mike Parker (mark envelope, "please forward"). Relays programs of Dr. Gene Scott's University Network (*see*). Replies occasionally.
STUDIO: Faith Center, 1615 S. Glendale Avenue, Glendale CA 91025 USA. Phone: +1 (818) 246-8121. Contact: Dr. Gene Scott, President.
TRANSMITTER: RR#3 Box 120, Frisco TX 75034 USA (physical location: Highway 380, 3.6 miles west of State Rt. 289, near Denton TX). Phone: +1 (214) 346-2758. Contact: Walt Green or Fred Bithell. Station encourages mail to be sent to the administration office, which seldom replies, or the studio (*see* above).

KJES—King Jesus Eternal Savior
STATION: The Lord's Ranch, 230 High Valley Road, Vado NM

88072 USA. Phone: +1 (505) 233-2090. Fax: +1 (505) 233 3019. E-mail: KJES@aol.com. Contact: Michael Reuter, Manager. $1 or return postage appreciated.
SPONSORING ORGANIZATION: Our Lady's Youth Center, P.O. Box 1422, El Paso TX 79948 USA. Phone: +1 (915) 533-9122.

KNLS—New Life Station
OPERATIONS CENTER: 605 Bradley Ct., Franklin TN 37067 USA (letters sent to the Alaska transmitter site are usually forwarded to Franklin). Phone: +1 (615) 371-8707 ext.140. Fax: +1 (615) 371 8791. E-mail: knls@aol.com. URL: www.knls.org. Contact: (general) Dale Ward, Executive Producer; L. Wesley Jones, Director of Follow-Up Teaching; or Steven Towell, Senior Producer, English Language Service; (technical and listener feedback) Mike Osborne, English Service Host and Webeditor; (technical) F.M. Perry, Frequency Coordinator. Free *Alaska Calling!* newsletter, pennants, stickers, English-language and Russian-language religious tapes and literature, and English-language learning course materials for Russian speakers. Free information about Alaska. Radio-related publications and bibles available; 2 IRCs appreciated for each book. Special, individually numbered, limited edition, verification cards issued for each new transmission period to the first 200 listeners providing confirmed reception reports. Swaps canceled stamps from different countries to help listeners round out their stamp collections. Accepts faxed reports. Return postage appreciated.
TRANSMITTER SITE: P.O. Box 473, Anchor Point AK 99556 USA. Phone: +1 (907) 235-8262. Fax: +1 (907) 235 2326. Contact: (technical) Kevin Chambers, Chief Engineer.

▣KTBN—Trinity Broadcasting Network
GENERAL CORRESPONDENCE: P.O. Box A, Santa Ana CA 92711 USA. Phone: +1 (714) 832-2950. Fax: +1 (714) 730 0661, +1 (714) 731 4196 or +1 (714) 665 2101. E-mail: tbntalk@tbn.org or comments@tbn.org. URLs: (Trinity Broadcasting Network, including RealAudio) www.tbn.org; (KTBN) www.tbn.org/ktbn.html. Contact: Dr. Paul F. Crouch, Managing Director; Jay Jones, Producer, "Music of Praise"; or Programming Department. Monthly TBN newsletter. Free booklets, stickers and small souvenirs sometimes available.
TECHNICAL CORRESPONDENCE: Engineering/QSL Department, 2442 Michelle Drive, Tustin CA 92780-7015 USA. Phone: +1 (714) 665-2145. Fax: +1 (714) 730 0661. E-mail: bmiller@tbn.org. Contact: Ginger Marvin, QSL Manager; or W. Ben Miller, Vice President of Engineering. Responds to reception reports. Write to : Trinity Broadcasting Network, Attention: Superpower KTBN Radio QSL Manager, Ginger Marvin, 2442 Michelle Drive, Tustin CA 92780 USA. Return postage (IRC or SASE) helpful.

KVOH—High Adventure Global Broadcasting Network
MAIN OFFICE: P.O. Box 100, Simi Valley CA 93062 USA. Phone: +1 (805) 520-9460; toll-free (within USA) 1-800-517-HOPE. Fax: +1 (805) 520 7823. E-mail: kvoh@highadventure.net. URL: www.highadventure.org. Contact: (listeners' correspondence) Pat Kowalick, "Listeners' Letterbox"; (nontechnical) Ralph McDevitt, Program Manager; (administration, High Adventure Ministries) George Otis, President and Chairman; (administration, KVOH) Paul Johnson, General Manager, KVOH; (technical) Paul Hunter, Director of Engineering. Free program schedules and *Voice of Hope* book. Sells books, audio and video cassettes, T-shirts and world band radios. Booklist available on request. VISA/MC. Also, *see* Lebanon, Palau and United Kingdom. Return postage (IRCs) required. Replies as time permits.
CORRESPONDENCE RELATING TO BROADCASTS TO SOUTH

ASIA: P.O. Box 100, Simi Valley, Los Angeles CA 93062 USA
WESTERN AUSTRALIA OFFICE, NONTECHNICAL: 79 Sycamore Drive, Duncraig WA 6023, Australia. Phone: +61 (9) 9345-1777. Fax: +61 (9) 9345 5407. Contact: Caron or Peter Hedgeland.
CANADA OFFICE, NONTECHNICAL: Box 425, Station 'E', Toronto, M6H 4E3 Canada. Phone/fax: +1 (900) 898-5447. Contact: Don McLaughlin, Director.
PALAU OFFICE, NONTECHNICAL: P.O. Box 66, Koror, Palau 96940, Pacific Islands. Phone: +680 488-2162. Fax: +680 488 2163. Contact: Rolland Lau.
SINGAPORE OFFICE, NONTECHNICAL: 265 B/C South Bridge Road, Singapore 058814, Singapore. Phone: + 65 221-2054. Fax: +65 221 2059. Contact: Cyril Seah.
U.K. OFFICE: P.O. Box 109, Hereford HR4 9XR, United Kingdom. Phone: +44 (1432) 359-099 or (mobile) +44 (0589) 078-444. Fax: +44 (1432) 263 408. E-mail: mail@highadventure.net. URL: www.highadventure.org/europe1.html. Contact: Peter Darg, Director. This office verifies reports of Voice of Hope ("European Beacon") broadcasts via Jülich, Germany.

▣KWHR-World Harvest Radio:
ADMINISTRATION OFFICE: see WHRI, USA, below.
TRANSMITTER: Although located 6½ miles southwest of Naalehu, 8 miles north of South Cape, and 2000 feet west of South Point (Ka La) Road (the antennas are easily visible from this road) on Big Island, Hawaii, the operators of this rural transmitter site maintain no post office box in or near Naalehu, and their telephone number is unlisted, Best bet is to contact them via their administration office (*see* WHRI, below), or to drive in unannounced (it's just off South Point Road) the next time you vacation on Big Island.

Leinwoll (Stanley)—Telecommunication Consultant, 305 E. 86th Street, Suite 21S-W, New York NY 10028 USA. Phone: +1 (212) 987-0456. Fax: +1 (212) 987 3532. E-mail:

Rural listeners in Xinjiang, China, tune in the world with their Tecsun radio.
E.A. Hozour

stanL00011@aol.com. Contact: Stanley Leinwoll, President. This firm provides frequency management and other engineering services for some private U.S. world band stations, but does not correspond with the general public.

National Association of Shortwave Broadcasters, P.O. Box 8700, Cary NC 27512 USA. Phone: +1 (919) 460-3750. Fax: +1 (919) 460 3702. E-mail: nasbmem@rocketmail.com. URL: www.shortwave.org. Contact: Glenn W. Sink, Secretary-Treasurer. Association of most private U.S. world band stations, as well as a group of other international broadcasters, equipment manufacturers and organizations related to shortwave broadcasting. Includes committees on various subjects, such as digital shortwave radio. Interfaces with the Federal Communications Commission's International Bureau and other broadcasting-related organizations to advance the interests of its members. Publishes *NASB Newsletter* for members and associate members; free sample upon request on letterhead of an appropriate organization. Annual one-day convention held near Washington DC's National Airport early each spring; non-members wishing to attend should contact the Secretary-Treasurer in advance; convention fee typically $50 per person.

⊠Overcomer Ministry ("Voice of the Last Day Prophet of God"), P.O. Box 691, Walterboro SC 29488 USA. Phone: (0900-1700 local time, Sunday through Friday) +1 (803) 538-3892. E-mail: brotherstair@overcomerministry.com. URLs (including RealAudio): www.overcomerministry.com; www.soundwaves2000.com/ocm99/default.htm. Contact: Brother R.G. Stair. Sample "Overcomer" newsletter and various pamphlets free upon request. Sells a Sangean shortwave radio for $50, plus other items of equipment and various publications at appropriate prices. Via Deutsche Telekom, Germany; and WINB, WRNO and WWCR, USA.

⊠Radio Free Asia, Suite 300, 2025 M Street NW, Washington DC 20036 USA. Phone: (general) +1 (202) 530-4900 or +1 (202) 457-6975; (programming) +1 (202) 530-4907; (president) +1 (202) 457-6948; (vice-president) +1 (202) 536 4402; (technical) +1 (202) 822-6234. Fax: +1 (202) 457 6996 or +1 (202) 530 7794/95. E-mail: (individuals) the format is lastnameinitial@rfa.org; so to reach, say, David Baden, it would

be badend@rfa.org; (language sections) the format is language@www.rfa.org; so to contact, say, the Cambodian section, address your message to khmer@www.rfa.org; (general) Webmaster@www.rfa.org. URL: (includes audio in Audio Active format) www.rfa.org. Contact: (administration) Richard Richter, President; Craig Perry, Vice President; Daniel Southerland, Executive Editor; (listener contact) Ms. Arin Basu, Secretary; (technical) David Baden, Director of Technical Operations. Free stickers. RFA, originally created in 1996 as the Asia Pacific Network, is funded as a private nonprofit U.S. corporation by a grant from the Broadcasting Board of Governors (*see*), a politically bipartisan body appointed by the President.

CHINA OFFICE: P.O. Box 28840, Hong Kong, China.

JAPAN OFFICE: P.O. Box 49, Central Post Office, Tokyo 100-91, Japan.

⊠Radio Free Europe-Radio Liberty/RFE-RL

PRAGUE HEADQUARTERS: Vinohradská 1, 110 00 Prague 1, Czech Republic. Phone: +420 (2) 2112-1111; (president) +420 (2) 2112-3000; (news & current affairs) +420 (2) 2112-6950; (public relations) +420 (2) 2112-3007; (engineering & technical operations) +420 (2) 2112-3700; (broadcast operations) +420 (2) 2112-3550. Fax: +420 (2) 2112 3013; (president) +420 (2) 2112 3002; (news & current affairs) +420 (2) 2112 3613; (public relations) +420 (2) 2112 2995; (engineering & technical operations) +420 (2) 2112 3702; (broadcast operations) +420 (2) 2112 3540. E-mail: the format is lastnameinitial@rferl.org; so to reach, say, David Walcutt, it would be walcuttd@rferl.org. URL: (general, including RealAudio) www.rferl.org/; (broadcast services) www.rferl.org/bd. Contact: Thomas A. Dine, President; Robert McMahon, Director of News & Current Affairs; Sonia Winter, Director of Public Affairs; Luke Springer, Acting Director of Engineering & Technical Services; or Christopher Carzoli, Director of Broadcast Operations.

WASHINGTON OFFICE: 1201 Connecticut Avenue NW, Washington DC 20036 USA. Phone: +1 (202) 457-6900; (news) +1 (202) 457-6950; (technical) +1 (202) 457-6963. Fax: +1 (202) 457 6992; (technical) +1 (202) 457 6913. E-mail and URL: *see* above. Contact: Jane Lester, Secretary of the Corporation; or

Paul Goble, Director of Communications; (news) Oleh Zwadiuk, Washington Bureau Chief; (technical) David Walcutt, Broadcast Operations Liaison. A private non-profit corporation funded by a grant from the Broadcasting Board of Governors, RFE/RL broadcasts in 21 languages (but not English) from transmission facilities now part of the International Broadcasting Bureau (IBB), *see*.

Radio Free Iraq—a service of Radio Free Europe-Radio Liberty (*see*, above). URL: (includes RealAudio) www.rferl.org.bd/iq/.

Radio Martí, Office of Cuba Broadcasting, 5325 N.W. 77th Avenue, Miami FL 33166 USA. Phone: +1 (305) 437-7000; or +1 (305) 994-1720. Fax: +1 (305) 597 4665. E-mail: ocb@usia.gov. URL: (includes RealAudio) www.ibb.gov/marti/index.html. Contact: (general) Herminio San Ramón, Director, Office of Cuba Broadcasting; Roberto Rodríguez-Tejera, Director, Radio Martí; Martha Yedra, Director of Programs; or William Valdez, Director, News; (technical) Michael Pallone, Director of Technical Operations.

Trans World Radio, International Headquarters, P.O. Box 8700, Cary NC 27512-8700 USA. Phone: +1 (919) 460-3700. Fax: +1 (919) 460 3702. E-mail: info2@twr.org. URL: www.gospelcom.net/twr/twr_index.htm. Contact: (general) Jon Vaught, Public Relations; Richard Greene, Director, Public Relations; Joe Fort, Director, Broadcaster Relations; or Bill Danick; (technical) Glenn W. Sink, Assistant Vice President, International Operations. Free "Towers to Eternity" publication for those living in the U.S. Technical correspondence should be sent to the office nearest the country where the transmitter is located—Guam, Monaco or Swaziland. For information on TWR offices in Asia and Australasia, refer to the entry under "Guam."
CANADIAN OFFICE: P.O. Box 444, Niagara Falls ON, L2E 6T8 Canada. URL: http://twrcan.ca.

University Network, P.O. Box 1, Los Angeles CA 90053 USA. Phone: (toll-free within U.S.) 1-800-338-3030; (elsewhere, call collect) +1 (818) 240-8151. E-mail: drgenescott@mail.drgenescott.org. URL: (includes VDO and RealAudio) www.drgenescott.org/. Contact: Dr. Gene Scott. Sells audio and video tapes and books relating to Dr. Scott's teaching. Free copies of *The Truth About* and *The University Cathedral Pulpit* publications. Transmits via KAIJ and WWCR (USA), Caribbean Beacon (Anguilla, West Indies) and the Voice of Russia.

USA Radio Network, 2290 Springlake #107, Dallas TX 75234 USA. E-mail: (general) newsroom@usaradio.com; (complaints/suggestions) tradup@usaradio.com; (technical) david@usaradio.com. URL: (includes RealAudio) www.usaradio.com/. Does not broadcast direct on shortwave, but some of its news and other programs are heard via KWHR, WHRA, WHRI and WWCR, USA.

Voice of America—All Transmitter Locations
MAIN OFFICE: 330 Independence Avenue SW, Washington DC 20547 USA. If contacting the VOA directly is impractical, write c/o the American Embassy or USIS Center in your country. Phone: (to hear VOA-English live) +1 (202) 619-1979; (Office of External Affairs) +1 (202) 619-2358 or +1 (202) 619-2039; (Audience Mail Division) +1 (202) 619-2770; (Africa Division) +1 (202) 619-1666 or +1 (202) 619-2879; ("Communications World") +1 (202) 619-3047; (Office of Research) +1 (202) 619-4965; (administration) +1 (202) 619-1088. Fax: (general information for listeners outside the United States) +1 (202) 376 1066; (Public Liaison for listeners within the United States) +1 (202) 619 1241; (Office of External Affairs) +1 (202) 205 0634 or +1 (202) 205 2875; (Africa Division) +1 (202) 619 1664; ("Communications World," Audience Mail Division and Office of Research) +1 (202) 619 0211; (administration) +1 (202) 619 0085; ("Communications World") +1 (202) 619 2543. E-mail: (general inquiries outside the United States) letters@voa.gov; (reception reports from outside the United States) qsl@voa.gov; (reception reports from within the United States) qsl-usa@voa.gov; ("Communications World") cw@voa.gov; (Office of Research) gmackenz@usia.gov; ("VOA News Now") newsnow@voa.gov; (VOA Special English) special@voa.gov. URLs: (including RealAudio) www.voa.gov; www.ibb.gov. Contact: Sanford J. Ungar, Director; Mrs. Betty Lacy Thompson, Chief, Audience Mail Division, B/K. G759A Cohen; Larry James, Director, English Programs Division; Leo Sarkisian, Africa Division; Kim Andrew Elliott, Producer, "Communications World"; or George Mackenzie, Audience Research Officer; (reception reports) Mrs. Irene Greene, QSL Desk, Audience Mail Division, Room G-759-C. Free stickers and calendars. Free "Music Time in Africa" calendar, to non-U.S. addresses only, from Mrs. Rita Rochelle, Africa Division, Room 1622. If you're an American and miffed because you can't receive these goodies from the VOA, don't blame the station—they're only following the law. The VOA occasionally hosts international broadcasting conventions, and as of 1996 has been accepting limited supplemental funding from the U.S. Agency for International Development (AID). Also, *see* Ascension, Botswana, Greece, Morocco, Philippines, São Tomé e Príncipe, Sri Lanka and Thailand.

Voice of America/IBB—Delano Relay Station, Rt. 1, Box 1350, Delano CA 93215 USA. Phone: +1 (805) 725-0150 or +1 (805) 861-4136. Fax: +1 (805) 725 6511. Contact: (technical) Brent Boyd, Manager. Nontechnical correspondence should be sent to the VOA address in Washington.

Voice of America/IBB—Greenville Relay Station, P.O. Box 1826, Greenville NC 27834 USA. Phone: +1 (919) 758-2171 or +1 (919) 752-7115. Fax: +1 (919) 752 5959. Contact: (technical) Bruce Hunter, Manager. Nontechnical correspondence should be sent to the VOA address in Washington.

WBCQ—"The Planet", 97 High Street, Kennebunk ME 04043 USA. E-mail: (Weiner, nontechnical) allanhw@cybertours.com; (Becker) Director@pcaudio.com. URL: http://theplanet.wbcq.net/. Contact: Allan H. Weiner; Elayne Star, Office Manager; or Scott Becker. Verifies reception reports if 1 IRC or (within USA) an SASE is included.

WEWN—EWTN Global Catholic Radio
TRANSMISSION FACILITY AND STATION MAILING ADDRESS: 1500 High Road, P.O. Box 176, Vandiver AL 35176 USA.
ENGINEERING AND MARKETING OFFICES: 5817 Old Leeds Rd., Irondale AL 35210 USA.
Phone: (general) +1 (205) 271-2900; (Station Manager) +1 (205) 271-2943; (Chief Engineer) +1 (205) 271-2959; (Marketing Manager) +1 (205) 271-2982; (Program Director, English) +1 (205) 271-2944; (Program Director, Spanish) +1 (205) 271-2900 ext. 2073; (Frequency Manager) +1 (205) 271-2900 ext. 2017. Fax: (general) +1 (205) 271 2926; (Marketing) +1 (205) 271 2925; (Engineering) +1 (205) 271 2953. E-mail: (general) wewn@ewtn.com. To contact individuals, the format is initiallastname@ewtn.com; so to reach, say, Thom Price, it would be tprice@ewtn.com. URLs: (EWTN parent organization) www.ewtn.com; (WEWN, including RealAudio) www.ewtn.com/wewn/. Contact: (general) Thom Price, Director of English Programming; or Doug Archer, Director of Spanish Programming; (marketing) Bernard Lockhart, Radio Marketing Manager; (administration) William Steltemeier, President; or Frank Leurck, Station Manager; (technical) Terry

Strolling along the periphery of central Dushanbe can be risky even by day. M. Guha

Borders, Vice President Engineering; Joseph A. Dentici, Frequency Manager; or Dennis Dempsey, Chief Engineer. Listener correspondence welcomed; responds to correspondence on-air and by mail. Free bumper stickers, program schedules and (sometimes) other booklets or publications. Sells numerous religious books, CDs, audio and video cassettes, T-shirts, sweatshirts and various other religious articles; list available upon request (VISA/MC). IRC or return postage appreciated for correspondence. Although a Catholic entity, WEWN is not an official station of the Vatican, which operates its own Vatican Radio (see). Rather, WEWN reflects the activities of Mother M. Angelica and the Eternal Word Foundation, Inc. Donations and bequests accepted by the Eternal Word Foundation.

WGTG—With Glory To God, Box 1131, Copperhill TN 37317-1131 USA. Phone/fax: +1 (706) 492-5944. URL: www.wgtg.com. Contact: (general) Roseanne Frantz, Program Director; (technical) Dave Frantz, Chief Engineer. WGTG is a family-run station partly supported by listener donations. Currently is not interested in reception reports, does not respond to listener mail, and the former e-mail address—wgtg@wgtg.com—appears to have been disconnected. Offers airtime at $50 per hour.

WHRA-World Harvest Radio:
ADMINISTRATION OFFICE: see WHRI, USA, below.
TRANSMITTER: Located in Greenbush, Maine, but all technical and other correspondence should be sent to WHRI (see next entry).

WHRI—World Harvest Radio, WHRI/WHRA/KWHR, LeSEA Broadcasting, P.O. Box 12, South Bend IN 46624 USA. Phone: +1 (219) 291-8200. Fax: (station) +1 (219) 291 9043. E-mail: whr@lesea.com; (Joe Brashier) jbrashier@lesea.com; (Joe Hill) jhill@lesea.com. URLs (including RealAudio): www.whr.org/; (LeSEA Broadcasting parent organization) www.lesea.com/. Contact: (listener contact) Loren Holycross; (general) Pete Sumrall, Vice President; or Joe Hill, Operations

Manager; (programming or sales) Joe Hill or Joe Brashier; (technical) Douglas Garlinger, Chief Engineer. World Harvest Radio T-shirts available from 61300 S. Ironwood Road, South Bend IN 46614 USA. Return postage appreciated.

WINB—World International Broadcasters, World International Broadcast Network, P.O. Box 88, Red Lion PA 17356 USA. Phone: (general) +1 (717) 244-5360; (administration) +1 (717) 246-1681; (studio) +1 (717) 244-3145. Fax: +1 (717) 246 0363. E-mail: info@winb.com. URL: www.winb.com. Contact: (general) Mrs. Sally Spyker, Correspondence Secretary; John Stockdale, Manager; Clyde H. Campbell, C.F.O.; or John H. Norris, Owner; (technical) Fred W. Wise, Technical Director. Return postage helpful outside United States. No giveaways or items for sale.

WJCR—Jesus Christ Radio, P.O. Box 91, Upton KY 42784 USA. Phone: +1 (502) 369-8614. E-mail: email@wjcr.com. URL: www.wjcr.com. Contact: (general) Pastor Don Powell, President; Gerri Powell; Trish Powell; or A.L. Burile; (technical) Louis Tate, Chief Engineer. Free religious printed matter. Return postage or $1 appreciated. Actively solicits listener contributions.

WMLK—Assemblies of Yahweh, P.O. Box C, Bethel PA 19507 USA. Toll free telephone (U.S only) 1-800-523 3827; (elsewhere) +1 (717) 933-4518 or +1 (717) 933-4880. E-mail: AOY@avana.net. URL: www.assembliesof yahweh.com/Log.htm. Contact: (general) Elder Jacob O. Meyer, Manager & Producer of "The Open Door to the Living World"; (technical) Gary McAvin, Engineer. Free *Yahweh* magazine, stickers and religious material. Bibles, audio and video (VHS) tapes and religious paperback books offered. Enclosing return postage ($1 or IRCs) helps speed things up.

WRMI—Radio Miami International, 8500 SW 8 Street, Suite 252, Miami FL 33144 USA. Phone: (general) +1 (305) 267-1728; (Chief Engineer) +1 (305) 827-2234. Fax: (general) +1 (305) 267 9253; (Chief Engineer) +1 (305) 819 8756. E-mail: wrmi@compuserve.com. URL: http://members.xoom.com/wrmi/. Contact: (technical and nontechnical) Jeff White, General Manager/Sales Manager; (technical) Indalecio "Kiko" Espinosa, Chief Engineer. Free station stickers and tourist brochures. Sells PASSPORT TO WORLD BAND RADIO $23-33 (Depending where in the world it is sent), T-shirts $15 (worldwide), baseball-style hats $10 (worldwide)—all postpaid by airmail. Sells "public access" airtime to nearly anyone to say virtually anything for $1 or more per minute. Radio Miami Internacional also acts as a broker for Cuban exile programs aired via U.S. stations WHRI and KWHR. Technical correspondence may be sent to either WRMI or the station over which the program was heard. Return postage appreciated.

WRNO, Box 100, New Orleans LA 70181 USA; or 4539 I-10 Service Road North, Metairie LA 70006 USA. Phone: +1 (504) 889-2424. Fax: +1 (504) 889 0602. URL: www.wrnoworldwide.com/. Contact: Paul Heingarten, Operations Manager. Single copy of program guide for 2 IRCs or an SASE. Stickers available for SASE. T-shirts available for $10. Sells World Band radios. Carries programs from various organizations; these may be contacted either directly or via WRNO. Correct reception reports verified for 2 IRCs or an SASE.

WSHB—*see* Herald Broadcasting Syndicate, above.

WTJC, Fundamental Broadcasting Network, 520 Roberts Road, Newport NC 28570 USA. Phone: +1 (252) 223-4600. Fax: +1 (252) 223 2201. E-mail: fbn@clis.com. URL: www.clis.com/fbn. Contact: Michael Ebron, General Manager; or David Robinson, FBN Missionary Engineer. Station is operated by

FBN, an educational non-commercial broadcasingt network. **WWBS**, P.O. Box 18174. Macon GA 31209 USA. Phone: +1 (912) 477-3433. E-mail: (general) wwbsradio@aol.com. Contact: Charles C. Josey; or Joanne Josey. Include return postage if you want your reception reports verified.

WWCR—World Wide Christian Radio, F.W. Robbert Broadcasting Co., 1300 WWCR Avenue, Nashville TN 37218 USA. Phone: (general) +1 (615) 255-1300. Fax: +1 (615) 255 1311. E-mail: (general) wwcr@aol.com; (head of operations) wwcrl@aol.com; ("Ask WWCR" program) askwwcr@aol.com. URL: www.wwcr.com. Contact: (general) Chuck Adair, Sales Representative; (administration) George McClintock, K4BTY, General Manager; Adam W. Lock, Sr., WA2JAL, Head of Operations; or Dawn Parton, Program Director; (technical) D. Reming, Chief Engineer. Free program guide, updated monthly. Free stickers and small souvenirs sometimes available. Return postage helpful. For items sold on the air, contact the producers of the programs, and *not* WWCR. Replies as time permits. Carries programs from various political organizations, which may be contacted directly.

WWV/WWVB (official time and frequency stations), Time and Frequency Division, NIST, 325 Broadway, Boulder CO 80303 USA. Phone: +1 (303) 497-3276. Fax: +1 (303) 497 6461. E-mail: nist.radio@boulder.nist.gov; (Wessels) wessels@boulder.nist.gov. URL: www.boulder.nist.gov/timefreq/wwv/. Contact: John Wessels. Along with branch sister station WWVH in Hawaii (*see* below), WWV and WWVB are the official time and frequency stations of the United States, operating over longwave (WWVB) on 60 kHz, and over shortwave (WWV) on 2500, 5000, 10000, 15000 and 20000 kHz.

WWVH (official time and frequency station), NIST—Hawaii, P.O. Box 417, Kekaha, Kauai HI 96752 USA. Phone: +1 (808) 335-4361; (live audio) +1 (808) 335-4363. Fax: +1 (808) 335 4747. Contact: (technical) Dean T. Okayama, Engineer-in-Charge. E-mail: None planned. Along with headquarters sister stations WWV and WWVB (*see* preceding), WWVH is the official time and frequency station of the United States, operating on 2500, 5000, 10000 and 15000 kHz.

📻**WYFR—Family Radio**
NONTECHNICAL: Family Stations, Inc., 290 Hegenberger Road, Oakland CA 94621 USA; or P.O. Box 2140 Oakland CA 94621-9985 USA. Phone: (toll-free, U.S. only) 1-800-543-1495; (elsewhere) +1 (510) 568-6200; (engineering) +1 (510) 568-6200 ext. 240. Fax: (main office) +1 (510) 568-6200; (engineering) +1 (510) 562 1023. E-mail: (general) famradio@familyradio.com; (shortwave department) shortwave@familyradio.com. URLs: (Family Radio Network, including RealAudio) www.familyradio.com; (WYFR) www.familyradio.com/shortwave/swlinks.html; (foreign-language broadcasts in RealAudio) www.familyradio.com/foreign.htm. Contact: (general) Harold Camping, General Manager; or Thomas Schaff, Shortwave Program Manager; (technical) Dan Elyea, Station Manager; or Shortwave Department. Free gospel tracts (33 languages), books, booklets, quarterly *Family Radio News* magazine and frequency schedule. 2 IRCs helpful.
BELARUS OFFICE: B.A International, Chapaeva Street #5, 220600 Minsk, Belarus.
INDIA OFFICE: Family Radio, c/o Rev. Alexander, Tekkali 532201 Andra Pradesh India.
TECHNICAL: WYFR—Family Radio, 10400 NW 240th Street, Okeechobee FL 34972 USA. Phone: +1 (941) 763-0281. Fax: +1 (941) 763 1034. Contact: Dan Elyea, Engineering Manager; or Edward F. Dearborn, Assistant Engineer Manager.

UZBEKISTAN   World Time +5

WARNING—MAIL THEFT: Due to increasing local mail theft, Radio Tashkent suggests that those wishing to correspond should try using one of the drop-mailing addresses listed below.

Radio Tashkent, 49 Khorazm Street, 700047 Tashkent, Uzbekistan. Phone: (Head of International Service) +998 (71) 133-8920; (Correspondence Section) +998 (71) 139-9657; (Shekhar) +998 (71) 139-0752 or +998 (71) 139-9521. Fax: +998 (71) 144 0021. E-mail: (Shekhar) alex@kirsh.silk.org. Contact: Sherzat Gulyamov, Head of International Service; Mrs. Alfia Ruzmatova, Head of Correspondence Section; Babur Turdiev, Head of English Service; Alok Shekhar, Announcer – Hindi Service. Correspondence is welcomed in English, German, Russian, Uzbek and nine other languages broadcast by Radio Tashkent. Reception reports are verified with colorful QSL cards. Free pennants, badges, wallet calendars and postcards. Books in English by Uzbek writers are apparently available for purchase. Station offers free membership to the "Salum Aleikum Listeners' Club" for regular listeners.
LONDON OFFICE: 72 Wigmore Street, London W18 9L, United Kingdom.
FRANKFURT OFFICE: Radio Taschkent, c/o Uzbekistan Airways, Merkurhaus, Raum 215, Hauptbahnhof 10, D-60329 Frankfurt, Germany.
BANGKOK OFFICE: 848-850 Ramapur Road, Bangkok 10050, Thailand.
TRANSMISSION FACILITIES: Pochta va Telekommunikasiyalar Agentligi, Aleksey Tolstoy küçä 1, 700000 Tashkent, Uzbekistan. Phone: +998 (71) 133-6645. Fax: +998 (71) 144 2603. Contact: Fatrullah Fazullahyev, Director General.
Uzbek Radio, Khorazm küçä 49, 700047 Tashkent, Uzbekistan. Phone: (general) +998 (71) 144-1210; (Director) +998 (71) 133-8920 or 998 (71) 139-9636; (technical) +998 (71) 136-2290. Fax: (general) +998 (71) 144 0021; (Director) +998 (71) 133 8920. E-mail: uzradio@online.ru. Contact: (administration) Fakhriddin N. Nizom, Director; (technical) Komoljon Rajapov, Chief Engineer.

VANUATU   World Time +12 (+11 midyear)

Radio Vanuatu, Information & Public Relations, Private Mail Bag 049, Port Vila, Vanuatu. Phone: +678 22999 or +678 23026. Fax: +678 22026. Contact: Jonas Cullwick, General Manager; Ambong Thompson, Head of Programmes; or Allan Kalfabun, Sales & Marketing Consultant, who is interested in exchanging letters and souvenirs from other countries; (technical) K.J. Page, Principal Engineer; Marianne Berukilkilu, Technical Manager; or Willie Daniel, Technician.

VATICAN CITY STATE   World Time +1 (+2 midyear)

📻**Radio Vaticana (Vatican Radio)**
MAIN AND PROMOTION OFFICES: 00120 Città del Vaticano, Vatican City State. Phone: (general) +39 (06) 6988-3551; (Director General) +39 (06) 6988-3945; (Programme Director) +39 (06) 6988-3996; (Publicity and Promotion Department) +39 (06) 6988-3045; (technical, general) +39 (06) 6988-4897; (frequency management) +39 (06) 6988-5258. Fax: (general) +39 (06) 6988 4565; (frequency management) +39 (06) 6988 5062. E-mail: sedoc@vatiradio.va; (Director General) dirigen@vatiradio.va; (frequency management) mc6790@mclink.it; (technical direction, general) sectec@vatiradio.va; (Programme Director)

dirpro@vatiradio.va; (Publicity and Promotion Department) promo@vatiradio.va; (English Section) englishpr@vatiradio.va, (French Section) magfra@vatiradio.va; (German Section) deutsch@vatiradio.va; (Japanese Section) japan@vatiradio.va. URLs: (general, including English, French and Italian news in RealAudio) www.vatican.va/news_services/radio/ vatrad_en.htm; (multilingual live broadcasts in RealAudio) www.vatican.va/news_services/radio/multimedia/ live_en.html; (RealAudio in English and other European languages, plus text) www.wrn.org/vatican-radio/. Contact: (general) Elisabetta Vitalini Sacconi, Promotion Office and schedules; Eileen O'Neill, Head of Program Development, English Service; Fr. Lech Rynkiewicz S.J., Head of Promotion Office; Fr. Federico Lombardi, S.J., Program Director; Solange de Maillardoz, Head of International Relations; Sean Patrick Lovett, Head of English Service; or Veronica Scarisbrick, Producer, "On the Air;" (administration) Fr. Pasquale Borgomeo, S.J., Director General; (technical) Umberto Tolaini, Frequency Manager, Direzione Tecnica; Sergio Salvatori, Assistant Frequency Manager, Direzione Tecnica; Fr. Eugenio Matis S.J., Technical Director; or Giovanni Serra, Frequency Management Department. Correspondence sought on religious and programming matters, rather than the technical minutiae of radio. Free station stickers and paper pennants. Music CDs $13; *Pope John Paul II: The Pope of the Rosary* double CD/cassette $19.98 plus shipping; "Sixty Years . . . a Single Day" PAL video on Vatican Radio for 15,000 lire, including postage, from the Promotion Office.
INDIA OFFICE: Loyola College, P.B. No 3301, Chennai-600 03, India. Fax: +91 (44) 825 7340. E-mail: (Tamil) tamil@vatiradio.va; (Hindi) hindi@vatiradio.va; (English) india@vatiradio.va.
REGIONAL OFFICE, INDIA: Pastoral Orientation Centre, P.B. No 2251, Palarivattom, India. Fax: +91 (484) 336 227. E-mail: (Malayalam) malayalam@vatiradio.va.
JAPAN OFFICE: 2-10-10 Shiomi, Koto-ku, Tokyo 135, Japan. Fax: +81 (3) 5632 4457.
POLAND OFFICE: Warszawskie Biuro Sekcji Polskiej Radia Watykanskiego, ul. Skwer Ks. Kard. S, Warsaw, Poland. Phone: +48 (22) 838-8796.

VENEZUELA   World Time –4

Ecos del Torbes, Apartado 152, San Cristóbal 5001-A, Táchira, Venezuela. Phone: +58 (76) 438-244 or (studio): +58 (76) 421-949. Contact: (general) Licenciada Dinorah González Zerpa, Gerente; (technical) Ing. Iván Escobar S., Jefe Técnico.
Observatorio Cagigal—YVTO, Apartado 6745, Armada 84-DHN, Caracas 103, Venezuela. Phone: +58 (2) 481—2761. E-mail: armdhn@ven.net. Contact: Jesús Alberto Escalona, Director Técnico; or Gregorio Pérez Moreno, Director. $1 or return postage helpful.
Radio Amazonas, Av. Simón Bolívar 4, Puerto Ayacucho 7101, Amazonas, Venezuela; or if no reply try Francisco José Ocaña at: Urb. 23 de Enero, Calle Nicolás Briceño, No. 18-266, Barinas 5201-A, Venezuela. Contact: Luis Jairo, Director; or Santiago Sangil Gonzales, Gerente. Francisco José Ocaña is a keen collector of U.S. radio station stickers. Sending a few stickers with your letter as well as enclosing $2 may help.
Radio Frontera (when active), Edificio Radio, San Antonio del Táchira, Táchira, Venezuela. Phone: +58 (76) 782-92. Fax: +58 (76) 785 08. Contact: Modesto Marchena, Gerente General. May reply to correspondence in Spanish. $1 or return postage suggested. If no reply, try sending your reports

to Venezuelan DXer Antonio J. Contín, Calle Los Lirios #1219, Urbanización Miraflores 4013, Cabimas, Estado Zulia, Venezuela. In return for this service he requests you send $2-3 and would like any spare Latin American pennants and stickers you might have.
Radio Mundial Los Andes (Radio Los Andes 1040) (if reactivated), Calle 44 No. 3-57, Mérida, Venezuela. Phone: +58 (74) 639-286. Contact: Celso Pacheco, Director. May reply to correspondence in Spanish. $1 or return postage suggested.
Radio Nacional de Venezuela (when operating), Final Calle Las Marías, El Pedregal de Chapellín, 1050 Caracas, Venezuela. If this fails, try: Director de la Onda Corta, Sr. Miguel Angel Cariel, Apartado Postal 3979, Caracas 1010-A, Venezuela. The transmitter site is actually located at Campo Carabobo near Valencia, some three hours drive from Caracas. Phone: +58 (2) 745-166. Contact: Miguel Angel Cariel, Director de la Onda Corta.
Radio Occidente, Carrera 4a. No. 6-46, Tovar 5143, Mérida, Venezuela.
☞Radio Rumbos (if reactivated)
MAIN ADDRESS: Apartado 2618, Caracas 1010A, Venezuela. Phone: +58 (43) 333-734, +58 (43) 335-179, +58 (43) 336-776 or +58 (43) 337-757. Fax: +58 (2) 335 164. E-mail: rumbos@tycom.com.ve. URL: (includes RealAudio) www.tycom.com.ve/rumbos/. Contact: (general) Andrés Felipe Serrano, Vice-Presidente; (technical) Ing. José Corrales; or Jaime L. Ferguson, Departamento Técnico. Free pamphlets, keychains and stickers. $1 or IRC required. Replies occasionally to correspondence in Spanish.
MIAMI ADDRESS: P.O. Box 020010, Miami FL 33102 USA.
Radio Táchira, Apartado 152, San Cristóbal 5001-A, Táchira, Venezuela. Phone: +58 (76) 430-009. Contact: Desirée González Zerpa, Directora; Sra. Albertina, Secretaria; or Eleázar Silva Malavé, Gerente.
Radio Valera, Av. 10 No. 9-31, Valera 3102, Trujillo, Venezuela. Phone: +58 (71) 53-744. Contact: Gladys Barroeta; or Mariela Leal. Replies to correspondence in Spanish. Return postage required. This station has been on the same world band frequency for almost 50 years, which is a record for Latin America. If no response try via Antonio J. Contín. *(see* Radio Frontera, above).

VIETNAM World Time +7

Bac Thai Broadcasting Service—contact via Voice of Vietnam—Overseas Service, below.
Lai Chau Broadcasting Service—contact via Voice of Vietnam—Overseas Service, below.
Lam Dong Broadcasting Service, Da Lat, Vietnam. Contact: Hoang Van Trung. Replies slowly to correspondence in Vietnamese, but French may also suffice.
Son La Broadcasting Service, Son La, Vietnam. Contact: Nguyen Hang, Director. Replies slowly to correspondence in Vietnamese, but French may also suffice.
Voice of Vietnam—Domestic Service (Đài Tiêng Nói Việt Nam, TNVN)—Addresses and contact numbers as for all sections of Voice of Vietnam—Overseas Service, below. Contact: Phan Quang, Director General.
☞Voice of Vietnam—Overseas Service
TRANSMISSION FACILITY (MAIN ADDRESS FOR NONTECHNICAL CORRESPONDENCE AND GENERAL VERIFICATIONS): 58 Quán Sú, Hànôi, Vietnam. Phone: +84 (4) 824-0044. Fax: +84 (4) 826 1122. E-mail: qhqt.vov@hn.vnn.vn. URL: (English text) www.vov.org.vn/docs1/english/; (RealAudio in Vietnamese) www.vov.org.vn. Contact: Dao Dinh Tuan, Director of

External Broadcasting; Tran Mai Hanh, Director General; or Ms. Hoang Minh Nguyet, Director of International Relations. Free paper pennant and, occasionally upon request, Vietnamese stamps. $1 helpful, but IRCs apparently of no use. Replies slowly. Try not to send stamps on correspondence to Vietnam. They're often cut off the envelopes and the station doesn't receive the letters. Machine-franked envelopes stand a better chance of getting through.

STUDIOS (NONTECHNICAL CORRESPONDENCE AND GENERAL VERIFICATIONS): 45 Ba Trieu Street, Hànôi, Vietnam. Phone: +84 (4) 825-7870. Fax: +84 (4) 826 6707. E-mail: btdn.vov@ hn.vnn.vn. Contact Dinh The Loc, Director.

TECHNICAL CORRESPONDENCE: Office of Radio Reception Quality, Central Department of Radio and Television Broadcast Engineering, Vietnam General Corporation of Posts and Telecommunications, Hànôi, Vietnam.

Yen Bai Broadcasting Station—contact via Voice of Vietnam, Overseas Service, above.

YEMEN   World Time +3

📻**Republic of Yemen Radio**, Ministry of Information, P.O. Box 2182 (or P.O. Box 2371), Sana'a, Yemen. Phone: +967 (1) 230-654. Fax: +967 (1) 230 761. URL: (RealAudio only) www.althawra.com. Contact: (general) English Service; (administration) Mohammed Dahwan, General Director of Sana'a Radio; (technical) Ali Al-Tashi, Technical Director; Mr. Adel Affara; or Abdulrahman Al-Haimi.

YUGOSLAVIA   World Time +1 (+2 midyear)

Radiotelevizija Srbije, Hilendarska 2/IV, 11000 Belgrade, Serbia, Yugoslavia. Phone: +381 (11) 322-1850 or +381 (11) 321-1119. Fax: +381 (11) 324 8808. E-mail: momcilo.simic@ itu.int or msimic@iname.com. Contact: Momcilo Simic.

📻**Radio Yugoslavia**, Hilendarska 2, P.O. Box 200, 11000 Belgrade, Serbia, Yugoslavia. Phone: +381 (11) 324-4455. Fax: +381 (11) 323 2014. E-mail: radioyu@bits.net. URL: (includes RealAudio in Serbian, English, French, German and Italian) www.radioyu.org (if it doesn't work, try http://62.229.99.175). Contact: (general) Nikola Ivanovic, Director; Aleksandar Georgiev; Aleksandar Popovic, Head of Public Relations; Pance Zafirovski, Head of Programs; or Slobodan Topović, Producer, "Post Office Box 200/Radio Hams' Corner"; (technical) B. Miletic, Operations Manager of HF Broadcasting; Technical Department; or Rodoljub Medan, Chief Engineer. Free pennants, stickers, pins and tourist information. $1 helpful.

ZAMBIA   World Time +2

Radio Christian Voice
STATION: Private Bag E606, Lusaka, Zambia. Phone: +260 (1) 274-251. Fax: +260 (1) 274 526. E-mail: cvoice@zamnet.zm. Contact: Andrew Flynn, Head of Transmission; Philip Haggar, Station Manager; Beatrice Phiri; or Lenganji Nanyangwe, Assistant to Station Manager. Free calendars and stickers pens, as available. Free religious books and items under selected circumstances. Sells T-shirts and sundry other items. $1 or 2 IRCs appreciated for reply. This station broadcasts Christian teachings and music, as well as news and programs on farming, sport, education, health, business and children's affairs. *U. K. OFFICE:* Christian Vision, Ryder Street, West Bromwich, West Midlands, B70 0EJ, United Kingdom. Phone:+44 (121)

Islamic elders act as schoolmasters at the local Taloqan school.   M. Guha

522-6087. Fax: +44 (121) 522 6083. E-mail: 100131.3711@ compuserve.com. URL: www.christianvision.org/.
MIAMI OFFICE: Christian Vision USA, 15485 Eagle Nest Lane, Suite 220, Miami Lakes, FL 33014 USA.

Radio Zambia, ZNBC Broadcasting House, P.O. Box 50015, Lusaka 10101, Zambia. Phone: (general) +260 (1) 254-989; (Public Relations) +260 (1) 254-989, X-216; (engineering) +260 (1) 250-380. Fax: +260 (1) 254 317 or +260 (1) 250 5424. E-mail: zambroad@zamnet.zm. Contact: (general) Keith M. Nalumango, Director of Programmes; or Lawson Chishimba, Public Relations Manager; (administration) Duncan H. Mbazima, Director7-General; (technical) Patrick Nkula, Director of Engineering. Free *Zamwaves* newsletter. Sometimes gives away stickers, postcards and small publications. $1 required, and postal correspondence should be sent via registered mail. Tours given of the station Tuesdays to Fridays between 9:00 AM and noon local time; inquire in advance. Used to reply slowly and irregularly, but seems to be better now.

ZIMBABWE   World Time +2

Zimbabwe Broadcasting Corporation, P.O. Box HG444, Highlands, Harare, Zimbabwe; or P.O. Box 2271, Harare, Zimbabwe. Phone: +263 (4) 498-610 or +263 (4) 498-630. Fax: (general) +263 (4) 498 613; (technical) +263 (4) 498 608. Contact: (general) Charles Warikandwa; or Luke Z. Chikani; (administration) Edward Moyo, Director General; or Thomas Mandigora, Director of Programmes; (technical) Sam Barrbis, I. Magoryo or Cloud Nyamundanda (engineers). $1 helpful.

CREDITS: Craig Tyson (Australia), Editor. Also, Tony Jones (Paraguay), Marie Lamb (USA) and Lawrence Magne (USA). Special thanks to Cumbre DX/*Hans Johnson (USA), David Crystal (Israel), Fotios Padazopulos (USA), Gabriel Iván Barrera (Argentina), Gary Neal (USA),George Poppin (USA), Graeme Dixon (New Zealand),* India Broadbase/*Manosij Guha (India),* Jembatan DX/*Juichi Yamada (Japan), Mike Swift (United Kingdom),* Número Uno *(USA),* Radio Nuevo Mundo/*Tetsuya Hirahara (Japan),* Relámpago DX/*Takayuki Inoue Nozaki (Japan/Latin America) and* RUS-DX/*Anatoly Klepov (Russia).*

Worldwide Broadcasts in English— 2000

Country-by-Country Guide to Best-Heard Stations

Dozens of countries reach out to us in English, and this section covers the times and frequencies where you're likely to hear them. If you want to know which shows are on hour-by-hour, check out the "What's On Tonight" section.

Some tips so you don't waste your time:

• **Best times and frequencies:** "Best Times and Frequencies," ear-

lier in this book, tells where each world band segment is found. It also gives helpful specifics as to when and where to tune.

In general, it is best to listen during the late afternoon and evening, when most programs are beamed your way; in your local winter, tune the world band segments within the 5730-10000 kHz range (5730-15800 kHz local summer). Around breakfast, you can also explore segments within the 5730-17900 kHz range for a smaller, but interesting, number of selections.

• **Strongest (and weakest) frequencies:** Frequencies shown in italics—say, *6175* kHz—tend to be the best, as they are from transmitters that may be located near you. Frequencies with no target zones are typically from transmitters designed for domestic coverage, so these are the least likely to be heard well unless you're in or near that country.

Programs Change Times Midyear

Some stations shift broadcast times by one hour midyear, typically April through October. These are indicated by ◄ (one hour earlier) and ► (one hour later). Stations may also extend their hours of transmission, or air special programs, for national holidays or sports events.

Eavesdropping on World Music

Broadcasts in other than English? Turn to the next section, "Voices from Home," or the Blue Pages. Keep in mind that stations for kinsfolk abroad sometimes carry delightful chunks of indigenous music. They make for exceptional listening, regardless of language.

Schedules Prepared for Entire Year

To be as helpful as possible throughout the year, PASSPORT includes not just observed activity and factual schedules, but also activity which we have creatively opined will take place. This predictive information is original from us, and although it's of real value when tuning the airwaves, it is inherently not so exact as real-time data.

Most frequencies are aired year round. Those that are only used seasonally are labeled **S** for summer (midyear, typically April through October), and **W** for winter.

Times and days of the week are in World Time, explained in "Setting Your World Time Clock" earlier in the book, as well as in the glossary.

> Stations have extended hours for holidays, special programs and sports events.

Those who write Radio Tashkent are offered free membership in the Salaam Aleikum Listener's Club. M. Guha

ALBANIA

RADIO TIRANA

0230-0245 &	
0330-0400 ▢	6115 (N America), 7160 (North Am)
2130-2200	🅂 7160 (W Europe)
2230-2300	🅆 7130 (W Europe)

ARGENTINA

RADIO ARGENTINA AL EXTERIOR-RAE

0200-0300	Tu-Sa 11710 (Americas)
1800-1900	M-F 15345 (Europe & N Africa)

ARMENIA

VOICE OF ARMENIA

0400-0430 ▢	Sa/Su 4810 (E Europe, Mideast & W Asia)
1000-1030 ▢	Su 4810 (E Europe, Mideast & W Asia), Su 15270 (Europe)
2115-2145 ▢	M-Sa 4810 (E Europe, Mideast & W Asia), M-Sa 9965 (Europe)

AUSTRALIA

ABC/CAAMA RADIO—(Australasia)

0000-0830	4835 & 4910
0830-2130	2310 & 2325
2130-2400	4835 & 4910

ABC/R RUM JUNGLE—(Australasia)

0830-2130	2485
2130-0830	5025

RADIO AUSTRALIA

0000-0200	17795 & 21740 (Pacific & W North Am)
0000-0500	17750 (E Asia & SE Asia)
0000-0800	9660 (Pacific), 15240 (Pacific & E Asia), 17715 (Pacific & W North Am)
0000-0900	12080 (S Pacific)
0100-0500	15415 (E Asia & SE Asia)
0200-0900	15510 (S Pacific), 21725 (Pacific & E Asia)
0600-0900	15415 (E Asia & SE Asia)
0600-1100	17750 (E Asia & SE Asia)
0800-0900	5995 & 9710 (Pacific)
0800-1200	9770 (Pacific & E Asia)
0800-2100	9580 (Pacific & N America)
0900-1100	11880 (E Asia & SE Asia)
0900-1200	6080 (Pacific & E Asia)
1200-1400	5995 (Pacific), 6020 (Pacific & W North Am)
1400-1800	5995 (Pacific & W North Am)
1430-1700	11660 (E Asia & SE Asia)
1430-2130	9500 (E Asia & SE Asia)
1700-2200	11880 (Pacific & W North Am)
1800-2000	6080 (Pacific & E Asia), 7240 (Pacific)
1800-2100	9660 (Pacific)
2000-2200	12080 (S Pacific)
2100-2200	7240 & 9660 (Pacific)
2100-2400	17715 & 21740 (Pacific & W North Am)
2200-2400	17795 (Pacific & W North Am)
2300-2400	9660 (Pacific), 12080 (S Pacific)

AUSTRIA

RADIO AUSTRIA INTERNATIONAL

0030-0100	🅆 7325 (E North Am)
0130-0200	🅆 7325 (E North Am), 🅆 9870 (S America)
0230-0300	🅂 9655 (E North Am), 🅂 9870 (C America)
0430-0500	🅂 6155 (Europe), 🅂 13730 (E Europe)
0530-0600	6015 (N America), 🅆 6155 (Europe), 🅆 13730 (E Europe), 🅆 15410 & 🅆 17870 (Mideast)
0630-0700	6015 (N America)
0730-0800	🅂 6155 (Europe), 🅂 13730 (E Europe), 🅂 15410 & 🅂 17870 (Mideast)
0830-0900	🅆 6155 (Europe), 🅆 13730 (N Europe), 🅆 17615 & 🅂 21650 (E Asia), 21765 (Australasia)
0930-1000	🅆 17615 (E Asia), 🅆 21765 (Australasia)
1230-1300	🅂 6155 (Europe), 🅂 13730 (W Europe & E North Am)
1330-1400	🅆 6155 (Europe), 13730 (W Europe & E North Am)
1630-1700	🅂 6155 (Europe), 🅂 13730 (S Europe & W Africa), 🅂 15240 (Mideast), 🅂 17560 (S Asia & SE Asia)
1730-1800	🅆 6155 (Europe), 🅆 9655 (Mideast), 🅆 13710 (S Asia & SE Asia), 🅆 13730 (S Europe & W Africa)
2130-2200	🅂 Sa-Th 5945 & 🅂 6155 (Europe), 🅂 Sa-Th 13730 (N Africa)
2230-2300	🅆 5945 & 🅆 6155 (Europe), 🅆 13730 (S Africa)

BANGLADESH

BANGLADESH BETAR

1230-1300	7185 & 9550 (SE Asia)
1530-1540	15520 (Mideast & Europe)
1700-1710	15520 (Mideast & Europe)
1745-1815 &	
1815-1900	7185, 9550 & 15520 (Irr) (Europe)

BELGIUM

RADIO VLAANDEREN INTERNATIONAAL

0400-0430	🅆 11750 & 🅂 15565 (W North Am)

Radio Austria International staff (from left) Lucien Giordani, Klaus Hollndonner, Jacobo Naar, Prof. Roland Machatschke, Oswald Klotz, David Ward and Michael Kerbler. ORF

0700-0730	**S** 9925 & **S** 15195 (Europe)
0800-0830	**W** 9925 (Europe)
1130-1200	**S** 5985 & **W** 9925 (Europe)
1830-1900 ◘	5910 (Europe), *13670* (Mideast)
2230-2300	**W** 13670 & **S** 15565 (N America)

CANADA

CANADIAN BROADCASTING CORP—(E North Am)

0000-0300 ◘	Su 9625
0200-0300 ◘	Tu-Sa 9625
0300-0310 &	
0330-0609 ◘	M 9625
0400-0609 ◘	Su 9625
0500-0609 ◘	Tu-Sa 9625
1200-1255 ◘	M-F 9625
1200-1505 ◘	Sa 9625
1200-1700 ◘	Su 9625
1600-1615 &	
1700-1805 ◘	Sa 9625
1800-2400 ◘	Su 9625
1945-2015,	
2200-2225 &	
2240-2330 ◘	M-F 9625

CFRX-CFRB—(E North Am)

24 Hr	6070

CFVP-CKMX—(W North Am)

24 Hr	6030

CHNX-CHNS—(E North Am)

24 Hr	6130

CKZN-CBN—(E North Am)

0950-0500 ◘	6160

CKZU-CBU—(W North Am)

24 Hr	6160

RADIO CANADA INTERNATIONAL

0000-0030	**W** Tu-Sa 6040 (C America), **W** Tu-Sa 9535 & **W** Tu-Sa 11865 (C America & S America)
0000-0100 ◘	9755 (E North Am & C America)
0000-0100	**W** 5960 (E North Am)
0100-0130	**S** 9535, **S** 11715 & **S** 13670 (C America & S America), **S** 15305 (E North Am & C America)
0100-0200	**S** 5960 (E North Am)
0130-0200	**S** Su/M 9535, **S** Su/M 11715 & **S** Su/M 13670 (C America & S America), **S** Su/M 15305 (E North Am & C America)
0200-0230	9535, **S** 11715 & **S** 13670 (C America & S America), **S** 15305 (E North Am & C America)
0200-0300 ◘	9755 (E North Am & C America)
0200-0300	**W** 11865 (C America & S America)
0200-0330	**W** 6155 (E North Am & C America), **W** 9780 (W North Am)
0230-0300	**S** Su/M 9535, **W** 9535, **S** Su/M 11715 & **S** Su/M 13670 (C America & S America), **S** Su/M 15305 (E North Am & C America)
0300-0330 ◘	9755 (E North Am & C America)
0330-0400 ◘	Su/M 9755 (E North Am & C America)
0330-0400	**W** Su/M 6155 (E North Am & C America), **W** Su/M 9780 (W North Am)
0400-0430	**W** *9505*, **W** *9535* & **W** *9645* (Mideast), **W** *11825* (C Africa & E Africa), **S** *11835*, **S** *11975* & **S** *15215* (Mideast)

0500-0530   🇸 5995 (W North Am), 🇸 *6145* (Europe), 🇸 *7295* (W Europe & N Africa), 🇸 *9595* (Europe), 🇸 9755 (W North Am), 🇸 11710 (Europe), 🇸 11830 (W North Am), 🇸 13755 (Africa), 🇸 *15330* (N Africa & Mideast), 🇸 *15400* (Africa)

0600-0630   🇼 6090 (Europe), 🇼 *6150* (Europe & Mideast), 🇼 9670 (N Africa & C Africa), 🇼 9780 (Europe & N Africa), 🇼 *11710* (Africa), 🇼 *11905* (Mideast & E Africa), 🇼 *13690* (Africa), 🇼 *15325* (N Africa & C Africa)

1200-1230   🇼 *6150* & 🇸 *9660* (E Asia), 🇼 *11730* & 🇸 *15195* (SE Asia)

1200-1300   🇸 17765 & 🇸 17820 (E North Am & C America)

1300-1400 ▭   9640 (E North Am), 13650 (E North Am & C America)

1300-1400   🇼 17715, 🇸 M-F 17765 & 🇸 M-F 17820 (E North Am & C America)

1300-1600   🇸 Su 17800 (E North Am & C America)

1330-1400   🇼 *6150*, *9535* & 🇸 *11795* (E Asia), 🇸 *11935* & 🇸 *15325* (Europe & Mideast)

1400-1500 ▭   M-F 9640 (E North Am), Su-F 13650 (E North Am & C America)

1400-1500   🇼 Su-F 17715 (E North Am & C America)

1400-1700   🇼 Su 9640 (E North Am)

1430-1500   🇼 *9555* (Europe & Mideast)

1500-1700 ▭   Su 13650 (E North Am & C America)

1500-1700   🇼 Su 17715 (E North Am & C America)

1630-1700   *6140* (S Asia), *6550* (E Asia), *7150* (S Asia)

2000-2100   🇸 13650 (Europe), 🇸 17820 (Africa)

2000-2130   🇸 *11690* (Europe), 🇸 13670 & 🇸 *15150* (Africa), 🇸 15325 (Europe), 🇸 15470 (W Europe)

2100-2130   🇸 *7235* (Europe & Mideast), 13650 (Europe), 17820 (Africa)

2100-2200 ▭   *5995* (Europe & N Africa)

2100-2200   🇼 11755 (W Europe)

2100-2230   🇼 *7235* (W Europe & N Africa), 🇼 9770 (N Africa & C Africa), 🇼 *9805* (W Europe & N Africa), 🇼 11945 (W Africa), 🇼 13690 & 🇼 15150 (Africa)

2130-2200   🇼 13650 (Europe), 🇼 17820 (Africa)

2200-2230   🇼 5995 (N Africa & C Africa), *11705* (SE Asia), 🇸 15305 (C America & S America), 🇸 17695 (E North Am & C America)

2200-2300   🇸 5960 (E North Am)

2200-2400   🇸 13670 (C America & S America)

2300-2330   🇼 6040 (C America), 🇼 9535, 🇼 11865, 🇸 11895 & 🇸 15305 (C America & S America), 🇸 17695 (E North Am & C America)

2300-2400 ▭   9755 (E North Am & C America)

2300-2400   5960 (E North Am)

2330-2400   🇼 Sa/Su 6040 (C America), 🇼 Sa/Su 9535, 🇼 Sa/Su 11865, 🇸 Sa/Su 11895 & 🇸 Sa/Su 15305 (C America & S America), 🇸 Sa/Su 17695 (E North Am & C America)

CHINA

CHINA RADIO INTERNATIONAL

0100-0200   *9570* (E North Am)

0300-0400   *9690* (N America & C America)

0400-0500   *9730* (W North Am)

0500-0600 ▭   *9560* (N America)

0900-1100   11730/17755 & 15210 (Australasia)

1200-1300   7265 (Australasia), 9590 (E North Am), 9715 (SE Asia), 15110 (Australasia)

1200-1400   11675 (Australasia), 11980 (SE Asia)

1300-1400   *9570* (E North Am), 11900 (Australasia), 15180 (SE Asia)

1400-1500   🇼 9700, 🇼 11750, 11825 & 15110 (S Asia)

1400-1600 ▭   7405/7265 (W North Am)

1400-1600   *13685* (E Africa), *15125* (W Africa & C Africa)

1500-1600   7160, 7215 & 9785 (S Asia)

1600-1700   9565 (S Africa), 9870 (E Africa)

1700-1800   5220 (E Asia), 🇼 7150 (E Africa), 7405 & 9570 (E Africa & S Africa), 🇼 9745 (N Africa), 🇸 11910 (E Africa)

1900-2000   🇸 11750 (N Africa & Mideast), 🇸 13650 (Mideast & W Asia)

1900-2100   🇼 6165 (Mideast & N Africa), 9440 & 9680 (N Africa), 🇼 11840 (Mideast & W Asia)

2000-2130   *11735/11975* & *15500* (E Africa & S Africa)

2000-2200   5220 (E Asia), 7170/6950 & 9535 (Europe), 11875 (Australasia)

2100-2130   🇸 15415 (Europe)

2200-2300   🇸 *9880* (Europe)

2300-2400   *5990* (C America)

CHINA (TAIWAN)

RADIO TAIPEI INTERNATIONAL

0200-0300   *5950* (E North Am), *11740* (C America)

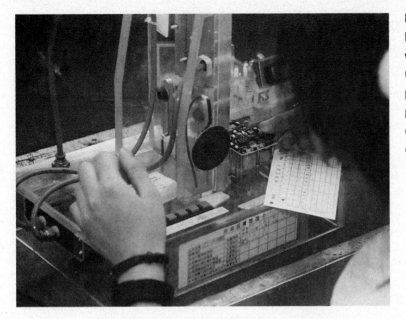

Family-owned Sangean Electronics manufactures world band radios in China and Taiwan. Here, a production inspector uses pneumatic jigs to check circuit board performance.

C. Crane

0200-0400	9680 (W North Am), 11825 & 15345 (SE Asia)
0300-0400	5950 (N America & C America), 11745 (E Asia)
0700-0800	5950 (W North Am & C America)
1200-1300	7130 (E Asia), 9610 (Australasia)
1800-1900	3925 (Europe)
2200-2300	W 5810, W 9355, S 11565 & S 15600 (Europe)

VOICE OF ASIA—(SE Asia)

| 1100-1200 | 7445 |

COSTA RICA

RADIO FOR PEACE INTERNATIONAL

0100-0200	21460 (N America & Europe)
0000-0600	6975 (N America)
1800-2130	15050 (N America), 21460 (N America & Europe)
2130-2230	Th-Tu 15050 (N America), Th-Tu 21460 (N America & Europe)
2230-2330	15050 (N America)
2230-2400	21460 (N America & Europe)

CROATIA

CROATIAN RADIO

0100-0115	S 9925 (W North Am)
0200-0215	W 7280/9925 (E North Am)
0300-0315	S 9925 (W North Am)
0400-0415	W 7285/9925 (W North Am)
0500-0515	S 13820/9470 (Australasia)
0600-0615	W 13820/11880 (Australasia)
0800-0815	◻ 13820 (Australasia)

CUBA

RADIO HABANA CUBA

0100-0500	6000 (E North Am), 9820 (N America)
0100-0700	11705/9830 USB (E North Am & Europe)
0500-0700	9550/6000 & 9820 (W North Am)
2030-2130	W 9620, S 13660 USB & S 13750 (Europe & E North Am)
2230-2330	9550 (C America)

CZECH REPUBLIC

RADIO PRAGUE

0000-0030	W 7345 (Americas), W 9465 (N America), S 11615 (Americas), S 13580 (N America & C America)
0100-0130	W 6200 (N America), S 7345 (N America & C America), W 7345 & S 11615 (Americas)
0300-0330	S 7345 (N America & C America), W 7345 (Americas), W 9435 & S 11615 (N America)
0330-0400	W 9585 (Mideast), S 11600 (Mideast & E Africa), W 11600 & S 15530 (Mideast & S Asia)
0700-0730	S 9880 (W Europe)
0800-0830 ◻	11600 (W Europe)
0800-0830	W 15260 (W Europe)
0900-0930	S 21745 (W Africa)
1000-1030 ◻	21745 (Mideast & S Asia)
1000-1030	W 17485 (W Africa)

Few transmitter sites are so meticulously maintained as Deutsche Telekom's Jülich facility, used by Deutsche Welle and other broadcasters.

Fotostudio Petersen

1030-1100	**S** 9880 & **S** 11615 (N Europe & W Europe)
1130-1200	**W** 11640 (N Europe & W Europe), **W** 21745 (E Africa & Mideast)
1230-1300	**W** 6055 (Europe), **W** 21745 (Australasia)
1300-1330	**S** 13580 (W Europe), **S** 17485 (S Asia)
1400-1430	**W** 21745 (E North Am & E Africa)
1600-1630	**S** 21745 (E Africa)
1700-1730 ▭	5930 (W Europe)
1700-1730	**W** 17485 (W Africa & C Africa), **S** 21745 (Africa)
1800-1830 ▭	5930 (W Europe)
1800-1830	**W** 7315 (S Asia & Australasia)
2000-2030	**S** 11600 (SE Asia & Australasia)
2100-2130 ▭	5930 (W Europe)
2100-2130	**W** 7345 (W Europe)
2130-2200	**S** 11600 (S Asia & Australasia), **S** 15545 (W Africa)
2230-2300	**W** 7345, **W** 9435, **S** 11600 & **S** 15545 (N America)

ECUADOR

HCJB-VOICE OF THE ANDES

0000-0400	9745 (E North Am)
0000-0700	12015 (N America)
0000-1630	21455 USB (Europe & Australasia)
0400-0700	9745 (W North Am)
0700-0900	**W** 9775 & **S** 11730 (Europe)
0700-1100	11755 (Australasia)
1100-1630	12005 (C America), 15115 (N America & S America)
1900-2100	17660 (Europe)
1900-2200	21455 USB (Europe & Australasia)
2100-2200	**W** 15115 & **S** 17660 (Europe)

EGYPT

RADIO CAIRO

0000-0030	9900 (E North Am)
0200-0330	9475 (N America)
1215-1330	17595 (S Asia)
1630-1830	15255 (C Africa & S Africa)
2030-2200	15375 (W Africa)
2115-2245	9900 (Europe)
2300-2400	9900 (E North Am)

ETHIOPIA

RADIO ETHIOPIA

1030-1100	M-F 5990, M-F 7110, M-F 9704
1600-1700	7165, 9560 & 11800 (E Africa)

FRANCE

RADIO FRANCE INTERNATIONALE

1200-1300	15155 & 15195 (E Europe), *15540* (W Africa)
1400-1500	*11610 & 17680*(S Asia), *17560* (Mideast)
1600-1700	*11995* (W Africa), *12015* & **S** 17850 (C Africa & S Africa)
1600-1730	**W** 11615, 15210 & **S** 17605 (E Africa)

GERMANY

DEUTSCHE WELLE

0100-0145	**S** *6040* (N America), **W** *6040*, **W** 6145 & **W** 9640 (N America & C America), *9700 & 9790* (N America), **S** *11810* & **S** *13720* (N America & C America)
0200-0245	**W** 7285, *9615*, **S** 9690, **W** 9765, **S** 11945, *11965* & *13690* (S Asia)

0300-0345	W 6045, *9535* & S *9640* (N America), W *9640* (N America & C America), W *9700*, W *11750* & S *11810* (N America), S *13780* (N America & C America), S *15105* (N America)
0400-0445	S *7225* & W *7280* (E Africa & S Africa), 9565 (S Africa), *9765* (Africa), W *11785* (E Africa), W *11965* (S Africa), S 13690 (E Africa & S Africa)
0500-0545	W 6100 & W *6120* (N America), 9670 (W North Am), *11795* (N America), S *11810* (N America & C America)
0600-0645	W *7225*, W 9565, W 11785, S *13790* & S 15185 (W Africa), *17820* (E Asia), S *17860* (W Africa), S *21680*, W *21695* & W *21705* (Mideast)
0600-1330	6140 (Europe)
0900-0945	*6160* (Australasia), S *9565* & W *11785* (Africa), S *12055* (E Asia), W *15105* (SE Asia & Australasia), S *15210* (E Africa), 15410 (S Africa), W *15470* (E Asia), S *17560* (SE Asia & Australasia), *17800* (W Africa), W *17820* (SE Asia & Australasia), W *17860* & W *21600* (E Africa), S *21680* (SE Asia & Australasia), S 21790 (Africa)
1100-1145	S *15370* (C Africa & W Africa), W *15370* & S *15410* (S Africa), W *15410* (W Africa), S *17680* (Africa), *17800* & S *17860* (W Africa), W *21780* (Africa)
1600-1645	*6170*, *7225* & *7305* (S Asia), *9735* (Africa), W *11785*, S *11810*, S *15135* & W *15145* (S Africa), W *15380* & S *17595* (S Asia), W *17800* (E Africa & S Africa), W *17810* (S Asia), S *21695* & W *21780* (E Africa & S Africa)
1900-1945	S *9640* & W *11765* (Africa), W *11785* (W Africa), S *11785* (Africa), *11810* (C Africa & W Africa), W *13610*, S *13790*, W *15135* & S *15390* (W Africa), W *15390* (E Africa), *17810* (Africa)
2000-2045	W *9725* & S *11970* (Europe)
2100-2145	W *9615* (W Africa), S *9670* (SE Asia & Australasia), W *9690* (Africa), *9765* (SE Asia & Australasia), W *9875* & S 11865 (W Africa), S *11915* (SE Asia & Australasia), S *15135* (W Africa & Americas), W *15135* (SE Asia & Australasia), W *15410* (W Africa & Americas), W *17560* (SE Asia & Australasia)
2300-2345	W *6010*, S *9715* & 9815 (S Asia & SE Asia), S *11965* & W *13690* (SE Asia)

GHANA

GHANA BROADCASTING CORPORATION

0530-0900	4915, 6130/3366
0900-1200	Sa/Su//Holidays 4915
0900-1700	6130
1200-1700	M-F 6130
1200-2400	4915
1700-2400	3366

GREECE

FONI TIS HELLADAS

0130-0200	W 7450, 9420 & S *12105* (N America)
0330-0345	W 7450, 9420 & S *12105* (N America)
0745-0755	7450, S *9425* & 11645 (Europe & Australasia)
1235-1245	S 15530 & 15630 (Europe & N America)
1335-1345	W 9420 & 15650 (Europe & N America)
1335-1350	*9590* (E North Am)
1840-1855	11645 & 15150 (Africa)
1900-1910	W 9375/9380 (Europe)
2000-2010	S 7430/9420 (Europe)
2235-2245	9425 (Australasia)
2335-2350	S 9395 (C America & S America), S 9425 (C America & Australasia), W 9425 (C America), 11595 & W 11640 (S America)

GUAM

KSDA-ADVENTIST WORLD RADIO

0130-0200	17645 (SE Asia)
1000-1100	W 11790/7455 (E Asia)
1030-1100	9530 (E Asia)
1230-1300	13720 (SE Asia)
1330-1400	9650 (E Asia)
1430-1500 &	
1530-1600	9385 (S Asia)
1600-1700	S 7395 & W 7400 (S Asia)
1730-1800	9355 (S Asia)
2130-2200	W 9495 & S 15310 (E Asia)
2300-2330	11775 (SE Asia)
2330-2400	F/Sa 11775 (SE Asia)

KTWR-TRANS WORLD RADIO

0740-0915	15200 (SE Asia)
0800-0930	15330 (Australasia)
0930-1100	9865 (E Asia)
1500-1630	15330/15105 (S Asia)

Nearly every public broadcasting building in Eastern Europe has some kind of sculpture near the entrance, and Radio Moldova is no exception. Arto Mujunen

GUYANA

VOICE OF GUYANA
24 Hr   5950/3290

HOLLAND

RADIO NETHERLANDS
0000-0125   *6165* (N America), *9845* (E North
                  Am)
0430-0525   *6165 & 9590* (W North Am)
0930-1125   **W** *7260 &* **S** *12065* (E Asia),
                  W *12065 &* **S** *13710* (SE Asia)
1030-1225   **S** *9860* (W Europe)
1130-1325 ▣   *6045* (W Europe)
1130-1325   **W** *9855* (W Europe)
1430-1625   **S** *9890,* **W** *12070,* **S** *12075,* **W** *12090
                  & 15590* (S Asia)
1730-2025   *6020* (S Africa), **S** *7120* (E Africa),
                  S *11655* (W Africa), **W** *11655* (E
                  Africa)
1830-2025   9895, 13700 & *17605* (W Africa)
2330-2400   *6165* (N America), *9845* (E North Am)

HUNGARY

RADIO BUDAPEST
0100-0130   **S** 9560 (N America)
0200-0230   **W** 9835 (N America)
0230-0300   **S** 9840 (N America)
0330-0400   **W** 9835 (N America)
2000-2030 ▣   6025 (Europe), 7170 (W Europe)
2200-2230 ▣   6025 (Europe)
2230-2300 ▣   3975 (Europe)

INDIA

ALL INDIA RADIO
0000-0045   7150 (Australasia), 7410 (E Asia),
                  9705 (SE Asia), 9950 (E Asia),
                  11620 (E Asia & SE Asia)
1000-1100   11585 (E Asia), 11735 (Australasia),
                  13700 & 15050 (E Asia &
                  Australasia), 17387 (Australasia),
                  17840 (E Asia)
1330-1500   9545, 11620 & 13710 (SE Asia)
1745-1945   7410 (W Europe), 9650 (N Africa &
                  W Africa), 9950 & 11620 (W
                  Europe), 11935 (E Africa), 13780 (N
                  Africa & W Africa), 15075 (E
                  Africa), 15200 (N Africa & W Africa)
2045-2230   7150 (Australasia), 7410 & 9650 (W
                  Europe), 9910 (Australasia), 9950
                  (W Europe), 11620 (W Europe &
                  Australasia), 11715 (Australasia)
2245-2400   7150 (Australasia), 7410 (E Asia),
                  9705 (SE Asia), 9950 (E Asia),
                  11620 (E Asia & SE Asia)

INDONESIA

VOICE OF INDONESIA
0100-0200   9525 (E Asia, SE Asia & Pacific),
                  11785 (Mideast & S Asia)
0800-0900   11785 (Australasia)
2000-2100   15150 (Europe)

IRAN

VOICE OF THE ISLAMIC REPUBLIC
0030-0130   **W** 6065 (E North Am & C America),
                  W 6135 (Europe & C America),
                  S 7260 (E North Am), 9022 (N
                  America), **W** 9670 (E North Am)
1100-1230   11930 (Mideast), 15260 (S Asia &
                  SE Asia)
1930-2030   7260 & 9022 (Europe)

IRELAND

RTE RADIO
0130-0200   *6155* (C America)
1000-1030   *11740* (Australasia)
1730-1800   **S** *17885* (Africa)

1830-1900	[W] *21630* (C Africa & S Africa)
1930-2000 ⇦	M-F *12160* (N America)
2000-2030 ⇦	Sa/Su *12160* (N America)

ISRAEL

KOL ISRAEL

0400-0415	[S] 15655/15650 (Europe & N America), [S] 17535 (Australasia)
0500-0515 ⇦	9435 (W Europe & E North Am)
0500-0515	[W] 11605 (W Europe & E North Am), [W] 17545 (Australasia)
1500-1530 ⇦	15650 (W Europe & E North Am), 17620 (Europe & N America)
1900-1930	[S] 17545 (C America)
2000-2030 ⇦	11605 (W Europe & E North Am), 15640 (S Africa), 15650 (W Europe & E North Am)
2000-2030	[W] 9435 (W Europe & E North Am)

ITALY

RADIO ROMA-RAI INTERNATIONAL

0050-0110	6010 (E North Am), 9675 (E North Am & C America), 11800 (N America & C America)
0425-0440	[S] 5975, [W] 6010 & 7270 (S Europe & N Africa)
1935-1955	[S] 5970, [W] 6015, [S] 7145 & [W] 7225 (N Europe), [S] 9760 (W Europe)
2025-2045	[S] 7120, [W] 7125, [W] 9685, [S] 9710, [W] 11840 & [S] 11880 (Mideast)
2200-2225	9675 & 11900 (E Asia)

JAPAN

RADIO JAPAN/NHK

0000-0015	11815 & 13650 (SE Asia)
0000-0100	*6155* (W Europe), *6180* (Europe), *9665* (C Africa), *11705* (E North Am)
0100-0200	[W] *6150* & [S] *9660* (Mideast), *11860* (SE Asia), 11870 (Mideast), 15325 (S Asia), 15570 (E Asia), 15590 (SE Asia), 17685 (Australasia), 17835 (S America)
0300-0400	[S] 17825 (C America), 21610 (Australasia)
0500-0600	*6110* (W North Am & C America), 11715 & 11760 (E Asia), 15230 (Pacific, C America & S America), 15590 (SE Asia)
0500-0700	*7230* (Europe), [W] 9835 (W North Am), 11840 (E Asia), 11850 (Australasia), [S] 17825 (W North Am)
0600-0700	*5975* (Europe), *11740* (SE Asia)
1000-1100	11850 (Australasia)
1000-1200	9695 (SE Asia), 15590 (S Asia)
1100-1200	*6120* (E North Am)
1400-1500	*11880* (Mideast)
1400-1600	9505 (W North Am), 11730 (S Asia)
1500-1600	7200 (SE Asia), 9750 (E Asia)
1700-1800	[W] 6090 (E Asia), 7110 (Europe), [S] 9825 (SE Asia), [W] *11880* (Mideast), *15355* (S Africa)
2100-2200	*6035* (SE Asia), 9725 (Europe), [W] 11850 (Australasia), [W] 13630 (W North Am), [S] 17825 (W North Am & C America)

JORDAN

RADIO JORDAN—(W Europe & E North Am)

1100-1730 ⇦	11690

KOREA (DPR)

RADIO PYONGYANG

0000-0100	11845 (SE Asia & C America), 13650 (N America & C America), 15230 (Americas)
0500-0600	3560 (E Asia), 11710 & 13790 (Europe)
1100-1200	3560 (E Asia), 9640 (SE Asia), 9975 & 11335 (SE Asia & C America), 13650 (N America & C America), 15230 (Americas)
1500-1600	3560 (E Asia), 9640 (Mideast & Africa), 9975 (Africa), 11735 (S Asia), 13650 (N America & C America)
1700-1800	13760 (N America)
1800-1900	4405 (E Asia), 6575 & 9335 (Europe), 11710 & 13760 (N America)
1900-2000	6520 & 9600 (Mideast & N Africa), 9975 (Africa)
2100-2200	4405 (E Asia), 6575 & 9335 (Europe), 11710 & 13760 (N America)
2300-2400	11335, 11710, 13760 & 15130 (N America)

KOREA (REPUBLIC)

RADIO KOREA INTERNATIONAL

0200-0300	7275 (E Asia), 11725 & 11810 (S America), 15575 (N America)
0800-0900	9570 (Australasia), 13670 (Europe)
1030-1100	[S] *11715* (E North Am)
1130-1200	[W] *9650* (E North Am)
1200-1300	7285 (E Asia)
1230-1300	6055 (E Asia), 9570 (SE Asia), 9640 (E Asia), 13670 (SE Asia)
1600-1700	5975 (E Asia), 9515 & 9870 (Mideast & Africa)
1900-2000	5975 & 7275 (E Asia)
2100-2130	[S] *3980* (Europe)
2100-2200	6480 & 15575 (Europe)
2200-2230	[W] *3980* (Europe)

KUWAIT
RADIO KUWAIT
0500-0800   15110 (S Asia & SE Asia)
1800-2100   11990 (Europe & E North Am)

LIBERIA
LIBERIAN COMMUNICATIONS NETWORK
0450-0800   6100/5100
0800-1800   6100
1800-2400   5100

LITHUANIA
RADIO VILNIUS
0030-0100   🆆 *6155* & 🆂 *9855* (E North Am)
1030-1100 ▭   9710 (W Europe)

MALAYSIA
RADIO MALAYSIA
24 Hr   7295
VOICE OF MALAYSIA
0500-0700 &
0700-0830   6175 & 9750 (SE Asia), 15295
              (Australasia)

MALTA
VOICE OF THE MEDITERRANEAN
1900-2000   🆂 Sa-Th *12060* (Europe & N Africa)
2000-2100   🆆 Sa-Th *7440* (Europe)

MEXICO
RADIO MEXICO INTERNATIONAL—(W North
Am & C America)
0400-0500 ▭   Tu-Su 9705
0500-0600 ▭   Tu/Th-Sa 9705
1500-1600 ▭   5985 & 9705
1600-1630 ▭   F-W 5985 & F-W 9705
1630-1700 &
2000-2100 ▭   5985 & 9705
2100-2130 ▭   Su-Tu/Th/F 5985 & Su-Tu/Th/F
              9705
2130-2200 ▭   5985 & 9705

MONACO
TRANS WORLD RADIO—(W Europe)
0745-0755 ▭   Sa/Su *9755*
0755-0920 ▭   *9755*
0920-0935 ▭   Sa/Su *9755*
0935-0950 ▭   Su *9755*

MONGOLIA
VOICE OF MONGOLIA
1200-1230   12015/12085 (Australasia)
1500-1530   11790 (S Asia), 12015/12085 (SE
              Asia)

NEPAL
RADIO NEPAL
0215-0225 &
1415-1425   5005, 7164/3230

NEW ZEALAND
RADIO NEW ZEALAND INTERNATIONAL—
(Pacific)
0000-0700   17675
0705-1015   9700
1106-1650   6100 (Irr)
1650-1850   6145 (Irr)
1950-2400   17675

NIGERIA
VOICE OF NIGERIA
0500-0700,
1000-1100,
1500-1700 &
1900-2100   7255 (Africa), 15120 (Europe &
              N America)

PAPUA NEW GUINEA
NBC
0000-0730   9675
0730-0900   9675/4890
0900-1200   4890
1200-1930   M-Sa 4890
1930-2200   M-Sa 9675/4890
2200-2400   9675

PHILIPPINES
FEBC RADIO INTERNATIONAL
0000-0200   15175/15450 (S Asia & SE Asia)
0930-1100   11635 (E Asia)
1300-1500   11995 (S Asia & SE Asia)
RADYO PILIPINAS—(Mideast)
0230-0330   🆆 11805, 🆂 11885, 15120 & 15270

POLAND
RADIO POLONIA
1300-1355 ▭   6095, 7270 & 9525 (W Europe),
              11820/11815 (W Europe & E North
              Am)
1300-1355   🆆 7145 (W Europe)
1800-1855 ▭   6095 & 7285 (W Europe)
1800-1855   🆆 6000 (W Europe)
2030-2125 ▭   6035, 6095 & 7285 (W Europe)

ROMANIA
RADIO ROMANIA INTERNATIONAL
0200-0300 &
0400-0500   5990, 6155, 9510, 9570 & 11940 (E
              North Am)

0530-0600	11940 (C Africa), [W] 15250 (C Africa & S Africa), [S] 15270 (E Asia), [S] 15340, [W] 15365, [W] 17720 & [W] 17745 (C Africa & S Africa), 17790 (S Africa)
0632-0641	[W] 7105, [S] 9550, 9665, [W] 11775 & [S] 11810 (Europe)
0645-0745	[S] 11740 (E Asia), [S] 11840 & 15250 (Australasia), [S] 15270 & [W] 15405 (E Asia), 17720 & [W] 17805 (Australasia)
1300-1400	[S] 9690 & 11940 (Europe), [S] 15365, [W] 15390 & [S] 17720 (W Europe)
1430-1530	[W] 11740 & [S] 11775 (S Asia), [W] 11810 (Mideast & S Asia), 15335 (S Asia)
1730-1800	[S] 9550, 9750 & [W] 11740 (S Africa), [S] 11830 & 11940 (C Africa & S Africa)
1900-2000	[W] 6105, [W] 7105, [W] 7195, [W] 9510, [S] 9550, [S] 9690, [S] 11810 & [S] 11940 (Europe)
2100-2200	[W] 5955, 5990, 7105, 7195, [W] 9510 & [S] 9690 (Europe)
2300-2400	7135 (Europe), 9570 (E North Am), 9625 (Europe), 11940 (E North Am)

RUSSIA

VOICE OF RUSSIA

0100-0500	[S] 9665 (E North Am), [S] 12050 & 15595 (W North Am)
0200-0400	[W] 9865 & 9875 (W North Am)
0200-0600	[W] 7180 (E North Am)
0300-0400	[W] 5940 (E North Am)
0300-0500	[S] 17565, 17630, 17660 & 17690 (W North Am)
0400-0600 [←]	7125 (E North Am)
0400-0600	[W] 6065 (W North Am)
0430-0600	[W] 5920 (W North Am)
0500-0900	[S] 15470 (E Asia & Australasia)
0600-0700	[S] 15490 (SE Asia & Australasia)
0600-0800	[W] 15470, 17570 & 21790 (Australasia)
0600-0900	[W] 17560 (SE Asia)
0800-1000	[W] 17860 (S Asia, SE Asia & Australasia)
1500-1600	[W] 6030 & [W] 7440 (Europe)
1500-1700 [←]	4730, 4940 & 4975 (W Asia & S Asia)
1500-1800	[W] 9470 (C Africa & S Africa)
1500-2000	[S] 11775 (N Africa & E Africa)
1600-1700	[W] 7210 (Mideast), [S] 11675 (N Europe), [S] 15490 (Mideast)
1700-1800	[W] 9560 (Mideast)
1700-1900	[W] 7305 (Mideast, E Africa & S Africa)
1700-2100	[S] 9765 & [S] 9775 (Europe)
1700-2300	[W] 9890 (N Europe)
1800-1900	[W] W/Th/Sa-M 5940 & [W] W/Th/Sa-M 5965 (N Europe)
1800-2100	[S] 11675 (N Europe)
1800-2200	[W] 7340 (Europe)
1900-2000	[W] 5920 (Europe), [S] Su/M/W/F 7300 (E Asia & SE Asia), [W] 7310 (Europe)
1900-2100	[W] 9470 (C Africa & S Africa), [S] 12070 (Europe & N Africa)
1900-2200	[W] 5940 & [W] 5965 (N Europe)
2000-2100	[S] 9470 (Europe), [S] 9710 (Europe & W Africa)
2100-2200	[W] 7300 (Europe)

SEYCHELLES
FEBA RADIO

0815-0900	F 15540 (S Asia)
1500-1600	11600 (W Asia & S Asia)
1630-1700	Su 11600 (W Asia & S Asia)

SINGAPORE
RADIO SINGAPORE INTERNATIONAL—(SE Asia)

1100-1400	6015 & 6150

RADIO CORPORATION OF SINGAPORE

1400-1600 & 2300-1100	6150

SLOVAKIA
RADIO SLOVAKIA INTERNATIONAL

0100-0130	5930 (E North Am & C America), 7300 (Africa), 9440 (S America)
0700-0730	[S] 9440, [S] 15460 & [S] 17550 (Australasia)
0830-0900	[W] 11990, [W] 17485 & [W] 21705 (Australasia)
1630-1700	[S] 5920 (W Europe)
1730-1800 [←]	6055 & 7345 (W Europe)
1730-1800	[W] 5915 (W Europe)
1830-1900	[S] 5920 (W Europe)
1930-2000 [←]	6055 & 7345 (W Europe)
1930-2000	[W] 5915 (W Europe)

SOLOMON ISLANDS
SOLOMON ISLANDS BROADCASTING CORP

0000-0030	M-F 5020, M-F 9545
0000-0230	Sa 5020, Sa 9545
0030-0230	Su 5020, Su 9545
0100-0800	M-F 5020, M-F 9545
0500-0800	Sa 5020, Su 5020, Sa 9545, Su 9545
0815-1130	Su 5020, Su 9545
0830-0900	M-F 5020, M-F 9545
0845-1100	Sa 9545
0845-1130	Sa 5020
0915-0930 & 0945-1130	M-F 5020, M-F 9545
1900-1930	Sa 5020

1900-2030	M-F 5020
1945-2400	Sa 5020
2000-2015 & 2030-2330	Su 5020
2045-2400	M-F 5020
2100-2330	Su 9545
2100-2400	M-F 9545, Sa 9545

SPAIN

RADIO EXTERIOR DE ESPAÑA

0000-0200	[W] 6055/9690 & [S] 15385 (N America & C America)
0500-0600	6055 (N America & C America)
2000-2100	M-F 9595 (W Africa), [S] M-F 15285 (Europe)
2100-2200	Sa/Su 9595 (Africa), [S] Sa/Su 15205 (Europe)

SRI LANKA

SRI LANKA BROADCASTING CORPORATION

0030-0430	6005, 9730 & 15425 (S Asia)
1030-1130	11835 (SE Asia & Australasia), 17850 (E Asia)
1230-1630	9730 & 15425 (S Asia)
1900-2000	Sa *6010* (Europe)

SUDAN

RADIO OMDURMAN—(Europe, Mideast & Africa)

1800-1900	9200

SWAZILAND

TRANS WORLD RADIO

0430-0500	3200 (S Africa)
0430-0605	[S] 6100 (S Africa)
0430-0700	4775 (S Africa)
0500-0600	[S] 3200 (S Africa)
0505-0735	9500 (E Africa)
0605-0735	6100 & [W] 9650 (S Africa)
0700-0735	[S] 4775 (S Africa)
0735-0805	[S] Sa/Su 4775 & Sa/Su 6100 (S Africa), Sa/Su 9500 (E Africa), [W] Sa/Su 9650 (S Africa)
1600-1830	9500 (E Africa)
1730-1745	M-Th 3200 (S Africa)
1745-2015	3200 (S Africa)

SWEDEN

RADIO SWEDEN

0130-0200	[W] 7265, [S] 9435 & [S] 11985 (E Asia & Australasia)
0230-0300 ←	7280 (N America)
0230-0300	[S] 9495/7135 (N America)
0330-0400	7115 & [S] 11665/9475 (N America)
1130-1200	[W] 13740 (Europe & N Africa), [S] 17870 (N America)
1230-1300 ←	15240/15235 (N America)
1230-1300	[W] 13740/11650 (N America), [S] 15240 (E Asia)
1330-1400 ←	13740 (SE Asia & Australasia)
1330-1400	[W] 9705 (E Asia), [S] 13740/17515 (S Asia)
1430-1500 ←	15240 (N America)
1430-1500	[W] 11880 (SE Asia & Australasia), [W] 13740/11650 (N America)
1730-1800	[S] Su 13855 (W Europe), [S] 15735 (Mideast)
1830-1900 ←	M-Sa 6065 (Europe & Mideast)
1830-1900	[W] 9645 (Europe & Mideast)
2030-2100 ←	6065 (Europe)
2030-2100	[S] Sa/Su 13830 (Europe & Africa)
2130-2200 ←	Sa/Su 6065 (Europe)
2130-2200	[S] 9430 (Europe & Africa), [W] Sa/Su 9655 (E Africa)
2230-2300 ←	6065 (Europe)
2230-2300	[W] 7325 (S Europe & W Africa)

SWITZERLAND

SWISS RADIO INTERNATIONAL

0100-0130	9885 & *9905* (N America & C America)
0400-0430	[S] *9610/13635* (E Europe)
0400-0500	9885 & *9905* (N America & C America)
0500-0530	[W] *9655* (E Europe)
0530-0600	[S] *9610/13635* (E Europe)
0630-0700	[W] *9655* (E Europe)
0730-0800	[W] *9885* (N Africa), [W] *11860* (N Africa & W Africa), [W] 13635 (S Africa), [S] *15545* (N Africa), [S] *17685* (N Africa & W Africa), [S] 21750 (S Africa)
0830-0900	*9885* & 13685 (Australasia)
1000-1030	[S] *15315* (W Europe)
1100-1130	[W] *9535* (W Europe)
1100-1200	[W] *9540* & [S] *13735* (E Asia), [W] 17815 & [S] 21770 (S Asia & SE Asia)
1200-1230	[S] *15315* (W Europe)
1300-1330	[W] *9535* (W Europe)
1400-1500 & 1600-1615	*9575/12010* (E Asia & SE Asia), [W] 15185 & [S] 17670 (W Asia & S Asia)
1900-1930	[S] *9885* (N Europe)
2000-2030	[W] *6165* (N Europe), [W] 9620 (E Africa), [W] *9885* (C Africa & S Africa), [W] *11910* (N Africa & W Africa), [W] *13700* & [S] *13710* (S Africa), [S] 13770 (E Africa), [S] *15220* (C Africa & S Africa), [S] *17580* (N Africa & W Africa)

SYRIA

RADIO DAMASCUS
2005-2105	12085 & 13610 (Europe)
2110-2210	12085 (N America), 13610 (Australasia)

TANZANIA

RADIO TANZANIA—(E Africa)
0330-0430 &	
0900-1030	5050
1030-1530	Sa/Su 5050
1530-1915	5050

THAILAND

RADIO THAILAND
0000-0030	🅦 9680 & 🆂 9690 (S Asia & E Africa)
0000-0100	9655 & 11905 (Asia)
0030-0100	🅦 13695 & 🆂 15395 (E North Am)
0300-0330	9655 & 11905 (Asia), 🆂 15395 & 🅦 15460 (W North Am)
0530-0600	9655 & 11905 (Asia), 🅦 15115 & 🆂 15445 (Europe)
1230-1300	9655 (Asia), 🅦 9810 & 🆂 9885 (SE Asia & Australasia), 11905 (Asia)
1400-1430	🅦 9530 & 🆂 9830 (SE Asia & Australasia)
1900-2000	🆂 7195 & 🅦 9535 (N Europe), 9655 & 11905 (Asia)
2030-2045	🅦 9535 (Europe), 9655 (Asia), 🆂 9680 (Europe), 11905 (Asia)

TURKEY

VOICE OF TURKEY
0300-0350	🆂 17705 (S Asia, SE Asia & Australasia)
0400-0450 ▱	9655 (Europe & E North Am), 9685 (Mideast & W Asia)
0400-0450	🅦 9560 (W Asia, S Asia & Australasia)
1330-1420 ▱	9445 (Europe), 9630 (W Asia & S Asia)
1830-1850	🆂 9535 (Europe)
1930-2020 ▱	9445 (Europe)
2300-2350 ▱	7280 (Europe), 9560 (W Asia, S Asia & Australasia), 9655 (Europe & E North Am)

UGANDA

RADIO UGANDA
0300-0545	3340, 4976, 5026
0600-1300	7110, 7196
1300-2100	3340, 4976, 5026

The BBC World Service's traditional headquarters, Bush House, is almost as well known in some countries as Buckingham Palace. BBC

UNITED ARAB EMIRATES

UAE RADIO IN DUBAI
0330-0350	12005, 13675 & 15400 (E North Am & C America)
0530-0550	15435 (Australasia), 17830 (E Asia), 21700 (Australasia)
1030-1050	13675 (Europe), 15370 (N Africa), 15395 & 21605 (Europe)
1330-1350 &	
1600-1640	13630 (N Africa), 13675, 15395 & 21605 (Europe)

UNITED KINGDOM

BBC WORLD SERVICE
0000-0030	*3915* (SE Asia), *11945* & 🅦 *17790* (E Asia)
0000-0200	*5965* (S Asia), *6195* (SE Asia), *9410* (S Asia), *9590* (C America & S America), *12095* (S America)
0000-0300	9915 (S America), *11955* (S Asia), *15280* (E Asia), *15310* (S Asia)
0000-0330	*5970* (S America), *6175* (N America), *15360* (SE Asia)
0000-0700	*5975* (N America & C America)
0030-0100	*17790* (E Asia)
0100-0200	🆂 *9605* (S Asia)
0200-0300	🆂 *6135* (E Africa), 🆂 6195 (N Europe), 🆂 9410 (Europe), 🅦 *9410* & *9605* (S Asia), 🅦 *9770* (E Africa)
0300-0330	🆂 9915 (S America), 🆂 *11850*, *17760* & 🅦 *21715* (E Asia)

Time	Listing
0300-0400	6005 (W Africa & S Africa), **S** Sa/Su 6050 (E Europe), **W** 7160 (W Africa & C Africa), 11730 & 12095 (E Africa)
0300-0430	**S** 9605 (S Asia)
0300-0500	**S** 11955 (S Asia)
0300-0530	17790 (S Asia), 21660 (E Asia)
0300-0600	3255 (S Africa)
0300-0730	6195 (Europe)
0300-0800	**S** 9600 (S Africa), 11760 (Mideast), **W** 11765 (S Africa)
0300-0815	15310 (S Asia)
0300-2200	6190 (S Africa), 9410 (Europe)
0330-0400	**S** 9610 & **W** 15420 (E Africa)
0330-0500	**W** 6175 (N America), **W** 9895 (C America & S America), **W** 11955 & **W** 17760 (E Asia)
0330-0530	15280 (E Asia)
0400-0500	**S** 12095 (Europe), **W** 12095 & **S** 17640 (E Africa)
0400-0600	3955 (Europe)
0400-0630	15420 (E Africa)
0400-0700	7160 (W Africa & C Africa)
0400-0730 ⬅	6180 (Europe)
0400-0730	6005 (W Africa), 15575 (Mideast & W Asia)
0430-0800 ⬅	6175 (C America)
0500-0630	17885 (E Africa)
0500-0700	17640 (E Africa)
0500-0900	11955 (Australasia)
0500-0915	15360 (SE Asia & Australasia), **W** 17760 (E Asia & SE Asia)
0500-1100	9740 (SE Asia)
0500-2000	12095 (Europe)
0530-1030	21660 (SE Asia)
0600-0700	**W** 3955 (Europe), **S** 11835 (W Africa)
0600-0800	17790 (S Asia)
0600-0810	7145 (Australasia)
0600-1500	15565 (Europe)
0600-1600	11940 (S Africa)
0630-0700	15420 & 17885 (E Africa)
0700-0730	11835 & 17830 (W Africa)
0700-0800	**W** 5975 (N America & C America)
0700-0900	Sa/Su 17885 (E Africa)
0700-1500	17640 (E Europe & C Asia)
0700-1800	15485 (W Europe & N Africa)
0715-1000	15400 (W Africa & S Africa)
0730-0745	**W** 9635 (W Europe)
0730-0800	**W** 6195 (Europe), **W** 11835 (W Africa)
0730-0900	Sa/Su 15575 (Mideast & W Asia)
0730-1000	17830 (W Africa & C Africa)
0815-0900	**W** 7325 (Europe), 15310 (S Asia)
0900-1000	6065, 9580, 11945 & 11955 (E Asia), 15190 (S America)
0900-1100	11765 (Australasia), 15310 & 17790 (S Asia)
0900-1400	11760 (Mideast), 17885 (E Africa)
0900-1500	15575 (Mideast & W Asia)
0900-1530	17705 (N Africa)
0900-1615	6195 (SE Asia)
0915-0930 ⬅	11680, 13745, 15325, 15340 & 17695 (E Europe)
0915-1000	15280 (E Asia)
0915-1030	**S** 15360 (SE Asia), **W** 15360 (Australasia), 17760 (E Asia & SE Asia)
1000-1100	**S** 5965 (E North Am), Sa/Su 15400 (W Africa), Sa/Su 17830 (W Africa & C Africa)
1000-1130	Sa/Su 15190 (S America)
1000-1400	6195 (C America & N America)
1100-1130	15400 (W Africa), 17790 (S America)
1100-1200	5965 (E North Am)
1100-1300	9580, 11955 & 15280 (E Asia), 17785 (S Asia)
1100-1400	15220 (Americas), 15310 (S Asia)
1100-1600	9740 (SE Asia & Australasia)
1100-1700	21660 (S Africa)
1100-2100	17830 (W Africa & C Africa)
1200-1400	**W** 5965 (E North Am)
1200-1615	9515 (N America)
1300-1400	**W** 17785 (S Asia)
1300-1415	15420 (E Africa)
1300-1600	**W** 9590 & **S** 11865 (W North Am)
1300-1615	5990 (E Asia)
1300-1700	11750 (S Asia)
1400-1415	11860, 17880 & 21490 (E Africa)
1400-1600	15220 (N America)
1400-1700	15310 (S Asia), 17840 (Americas), 21470 (E Africa)
1415-1430	Sa/Su 11860, Sa/Su 15420, Sa/Su 17880 & Sa/Su 21490 (E Africa)
1500-1530	11860, 15420 & 21490 (E Africa)
1500-1700	15400 (W Africa), 15575 (Europe & Mideast)
1500-1830	5975 (S Asia)
1530-1630	**S** 17705 (N Africa)
1600-1700	**S** 3255 & **W** 11940 (S Africa)
1600-1745	3915 & 7160 (SE Asia)
1600-1800	**W** 6195 (Europe), 9740 (S Asia)
1615-1700	**W** 6195 (SE Asia), **S** 9510 (S Asia), Sa 9515 (N America), 15420 (E Africa)
1630-1700	**S** 9750 (W Europe)
1700-1745	**S** 6005 & 9630 (E Africa)
1700-1830	**S** 6095 (Mideast & W Asia), 9510 (S Asia)
1700-1900	**S** 11860 (E Africa), 15400 (W Africa & S Africa), **W** 15420 (E Africa), **S** 15575 (Europe), **W** 17840 (W North Am)
1700-2200	3255 (S Africa), **W** 11980 (Mideast)
1700-2330	**W** 3955 (Europe)

Uzbek Radio performers rehearse at a senescent studio in the Radio of Uzbekistan building. Some studios are dated, but others have recently been modernized. M. Guha

1730-1745	*3390, 6070 & 9520* (S Africa), 🅂 W *11960 &* 🅂 W *15585* (S Europe)
1800-1830	🅂 *9740* (S Asia), 🅆 *9740* (Australasia)
1800-2000	🅂 *15485* (W Europe & N Africa)
1800-2100	*6180* (Europe)
1800-2230	6195 (Europe)
1830-2100	*9630* (E Africa)
1830-2200	*6005* (E Africa), *9740* (Australasia)
1900-2000	🅂 *5975* (Mideast & W Asia)
1900-2100	🅂 *11835 &* 🅆 *15400* (S Africa)
1900-2300	15400 (W Africa)
1930-2000	🅂 *11835* (W Africa)
2000-2200	*5975* (Australasia), 7325 (Europe)
2000-2300	11835 (W Africa)
2100-2200	*3915* (SE Asia), 🅆 *6110* (E Asia), *6180* (Europe), 🅂 *11945* (E Asia)
2100-2400	*5965* (E Asia), *5975* (N America & C America), *6195* (SE Asia), *12095* (S America)
2115-2130	M-F *15390* & M-F *17715* (C America)
2130-2145	Tu/F 11680 (Atlantic & S America)
2200-2300	9660 (SE Asia), *12080* (S Pacific)
2200-2400	*6175* (N America), *7110* (SE Asia), *9590* (N America), 9915 (S America), *11955* (SE Asia & Australasia)
2300-2400	*3915* (SE Asia), *6035, 11945,* 🅆 *15280 &* 🅆 *17790* (E Asia)

USA

HERALD BROADCASTING SYNDICATE

0000-0057	W/F-M 7535 (E North Am), M/W/F 9430 (C America & S America)
0100-0157	7535 (N America), M 9430 (C America & S America)
0200-0257	Su/M 5850 (W North Am), M/Th 7535 (W North Am & C America)
0300-0357	5850 (W North Am), M/W 7535 (E Africa)
0400-0457	M/W 9840 (C Africa & S Africa)
0500-0557	W 7535 (Europe)
0600-0657	Tu/F 7535 (W Europe)
0800-0857	Sa/Su 7535 (Europe), Sa-Th 9845 (Australasia)
0900-0957	Tu/Th 7535 (Europe)
0900-1000	*11725* (E Asia)
1000-1057	M/W/Th 6095 (E North Am), Su 7395 (S America)
1000-1100	*11840* (E Asia)
1100-1157	Tu/F-Su 6095 (E North Am), W/F 7395 (C America & S America)
1200-1257	M/W/Th 6095 (E North Am), Sa 9455 (C America & S America)
1200-1300	*11550* (S Asia)
1300-1357	Sa-Th 6095 (N America), Tu/F 9455 (W North Am & C America)
1600-1657	Sa 18915 (E Africa)
1700-1800	Tu/Th/Sa 18915 (C Africa)
1800-1857	🅆 Su 11550 & 🅂 Su 15665 (E Europe), Su/W 18915 (S Africa)
1900-1957	🅆 Su/Tu/Th 11550 & 🅂 Su/Tu/Th 15665 (E Europe)
2000-2057	🅆 W/Su 5850 & 🅂 Su/W 13770 (Europe)
2100-2157	🅆 Su 5850 (E North Am & Europe), 🅆 W/Sa-M 7510 & 🅂 Su 13770 (Europe), 🅂 W/Sa-M 15665 (W Europe)
2200-2257	Su/Th 7510 (Europe), 🅂 Su/Th 13770 (W Europe), 🅂 Su/W 13770 (S Europe & W Africa), 🅆 Su/W 13770 & 🅂 W/Su 15280 (S America)
2300-2357	Su/W 7510 (S Europe & W Africa), 🅆 Su/M 13770 & 🅂 Su/M 15280 (S America)

KAIJ—(N America)

0000-1400	5810
1400-2400	13815

KJES

0100-0230	7555 (W North Am)
1300-1400	11715 (N America)
1400-1500	11715 (W North Am)
1800-1900	15385 (Australasia)

KNLS-NEW LIFE STATION—(E Asia)

0800-0900	[W] 7365 & [S] 9615
1300-1400	7365

KTBN—(E North Am)

0000-0100	[W] 7510 & [S] 15590
0100-1500	7510
1500-1600	[W] 7510 & [S] 15590
1600-2400	15590

KVOH-VOICE OF HOPE—(C America)

0300-0600	9975

KWHR-WORLD HARVEST RADIO

0000-0100	M-Sa 17510 (E Asia)
0100-0400	17510 (E Asia)
0400-1000	17780 (E Asia)
0700-1600	11565 (Australasia)
1000-1030	Su-F 9930 (E Asia & SE Asia)
1030-1200,	
1300-1400 &	
1600-1800	9930 (E Asia & SE Asia)
1800-2000	[W] 9930 (E Asia & SE Asia), [S] 17510 (E Asia)
2000-2100	M-F 17510 (E Asia)
2330-2400	M-Sa 17510 (E Asia)

UNIVERSITY NETWORK—(S Asia)

0800-1200 ▭	17590
1130-1530	[S] 17795

VOA-VOICE OF AMERICA

0000-0100	7215, [S] 9770 & [W] 9890 (SE Asia), Tu-Sa 11695 (C America & S America), 11760 (SE Asia), 15185 (SE Asia & S Pacific), 15290 (E Asia), 17735 (E Asia & Australasia), 17820 (E Asia)
0000-0200	Tu-Sa 5995, Tu-Sa 6130, Tu-Sa 7405, Tu-Sa 9455, Tu-Sa 9775 & Tu-Sa 13740 (C America & S America)
0100-0300	7115, [W] 7200, [S] 9635, [W] 9740, [W] 9850, 11705, [S] 11725, [S] 11820, 15250, [W] 15300, 17740 & 17820 (S Asia)
0300-0330	M-F 4960 (W Africa & C Africa), 7340 (C Africa & E Africa)
0300-0400	[W] 6035 & [S] 6115 (E Africa & S Africa), 7105 (S Africa)
0300-0430	9885 (Africa)
0300-0500	6080 (S Africa), [S] 7275 (Africa), 7290 (C Africa & E Africa), [W] 7415 (Africa), 9575 (W Africa & S Africa)
0400-0500	[W] 6035 (W Africa & S Africa), [S] 7265 (S Africa & E Africa), [S] 15205 (Mideast & S Asia)
0400-0600	[W] 9775 (C Africa & E Africa)
0400-0700	7170 (N Africa), [S] 11965 (Mideast)
0500-0600	[W] 7295 (W Africa), [W] 9700 (N Africa & W Africa)
0500-0630	5970 (W Africa & C Africa), 6035 (W Africa & S Africa), 6080 & [S] 7195 (W Africa), [S] 9630 & 12080 (Africa)
0500-0700	[W] 11825 (Mideast), 15205 (Mideast & S Asia)
0600-0630	[W] 7285 (W Africa), 11950 (N Africa & E Africa), [S] 11995 (E Africa & S Africa), [W] 15600 (C Africa & E Africa)
0600-0700	[W] 5995 & [S] 9680 (N Africa), 11805 (N Africa & W Africa)
0630-0700	Sa/Su 5970 (W Africa & C Africa), Sa/Su 6035 (W Africa & S Africa), Sa/Su 6080, [S] Sa/Su 7195 & [W] Sa/Su 7285 (W Africa), [S] Sa/Su 9630 (Africa), Sa/Su 11950 (N Africa & E Africa), [S] Sa/Su 11995 (E Africa & S Africa), Sa/Su 12080 (Africa), [W] Sa/Su 15600 (C Africa & E Africa)
1000-1100	6165, 7405 & 9590 (C America)
1000-1200	[W] 5985 & [S] 9770 (Pacific & Australasia), 11720 (E Asia & Australasia)
1000-1500	15425 (SE Asia & Pacific)
1100-1300	[W] 6110 & [S] 6160 (SE Asia)
1100-1400	9645 (SE Asia & Australasia)
1100-1500	9760 (E Asia, S Asia & SE Asia), [W] 11705 & [S] 15160 (E Asia)
1200-1330	11715 (E Asia & Australasia)
1230-1300 ▭	11680 (E Europe)
1300-1800	[W] 6110 & [S] 6160 (S Asia & SE Asia)
1400-1800	7125, 7215 & 9645 (S Asia), [W] 15205 (Mideast & S Asia), [S] 15255 (Mideast), 15395 (S Asia)
1500-1600	[S] 9590 (S Asia & SE Asia), 9845 & 12040 (E Asia), 15460 (SE Asia)
1500-1700	[W] 9565 & [W] 9575 (Mideast & S Asia), 9760 (S Asia & SE Asia), [S] 15205 (Europe, N Africa & Mideast)
1500-1800	[S] 6110 (SE Asia), [S] 9700 (Mideast)
1600-1700	6035 (W Africa), 13600 (C Africa & E Africa), 13710 (Africa), 15225 (S Africa)
1600-1800	[W] 12040 & 15445 (E Africa), 17895 (Africa)
1600-2000	[W] 11920 (E Africa)

1600-2130	*15410* (Africa)
1700-1800	M-F *5990* & M-F *6045* (E Asia), [S] M-F *7150* (E Asia & S Pacific), [S] M-F *7170* (E Asia & Australasia), [W] M-F *9525* (E Asia, SE Asia & S Pacific), [S] M-F *9550* & [W] M-F *9670* (E Asia & SE Asia), [S] M-F *9770* (S Asia & E Asia), [W] M-F *9795* (S Asia & SE Asia), [W] M-F *12005* (SE Asia), [W] M-F *15255* (E Asia & Australasia)
1700-1900	[W] *6040* (N Africa & Mideast)
1700-2100	[S] *9760* (N Africa & Mideast), [W] *9760* (Mideast & S Asia)
1800-1830	[W] *6140* (S Asia)
1800-1900	[S] *7415* & [S] *17895* (Africa)
1800-2130	*6035* (W Africa), *11975* (C Africa), [W] *13710* (Africa), 15580 (W Africa)
1830-1900	[S] Sa/Su *7170*, [S] Sa/Su *7330*, [W] Sa/Su *9845*, [S] Sa/Su *9860* & [W] Sa/Su *15445* (E Africa)
1900-1930	Sa *4950* (W Africa & C Africa)
1900-2000	[W] *5965* (Mideast), *9525* & *11870* (Australasia), *15180* (Pacific)
1900-2100	[S] *9770* (N Africa & Mideast)
1900-2130	[S] *7375, 7415* & [S] *15445* (Africa)
1930-2030	*4950* (W Africa & C Africa)
2000-2030	*11855* (W Africa)
2000-2100	*17755* (W Africa & C Africa)
2000-2130	17725 (W Africa)
2000-2200	*6095* (Mideast)
2030-2100	Sa/Su *4950* (W Africa & C Africa)
2100-2200	*6040* (Mideast), [S] *9535* (N Africa & Mideast), [W] *9595* (Mideast), *9760* (E Europe & Mideast), *11870* (Australasia)
2100-2400	[S] *9705* (SE Asia), *15185* (SE Asia & S Pacific), *17735* (E Asia & Australasia)
2130-2200	Su-F *6035* (W Africa), [S] Su-F *7375* & Su-F *7415* (Africa), Su-F *11975* (C Africa), [W] Su-F *13710*, Su-F *15410* & [S] Su-F *15445* (Africa), Su-F 15580 & Su-F 17725 (W Africa)
2200-2230	M-F *6035* (W Africa), [S] M-F *7340*, [S] M-F *7375* & M-F *7415* (Africa), M-F *11975* (C Africa), [W] M-F *12080* & [W] M-F *13710* (Africa)
2200-2400	*7215* & [S] *9770* (SE Asia), [W] *9770* (SE Asia & Australasia), [W] *9890* & *11760* (SE Asia), *15290* (E Asia), *15305* (E Asia & Australasia), *17820* (E Asia)
2300-2400	[S] *7190* (E Asia)
2330-2400	[S] *6060* (SE Asia)

WBCQ-"THE PLANET"—(N America)

2100-1100	[◨]	7415

WEWN-ETERNAL WORD RADIO NETWORK

0000-0200	[S] 5825 (E North Am), [W] 5825 (N America & C America), [W] 9355 (Europe), [S] 13615 (W North Am & C America)
0200-1000	5825 (N America & C America)
1000-1100	[W] 7465 & [S] 15745 (Europe)
1000-1300	[W] 5825 & [S] 7425 (N America & C America)
1100-2100	15745 (Europe)
1300-1600	11875 (N America & C America)
1600-2200	11875 (E North Am)
1600-2400	13615 (W North Am & C America)
2100-2200	[W] 9975 & [S] 15745 (Europe)
2200-2400	9385 (E North Am), 9975 (Europe)

WGTG

0000-0300	6890 (W North Am)
0000-0600	5085 (W North Am & C America)
0300-0700	[W] 3270 (W North Am)
1000-2300	9400 (W North Am & C America)
1700-2400	[S] 12170 (W North Am)
2200-2400	6890 (W North Am)
2300-2400	5085 (W North Am & C America)

WHRA-WORLD HARVEST RADIO

0000-0500	7580 (Europe & Mideast)
0300-1000	[W] 7435 (Africa)
0500-1000	[S] 11565 (Africa)
1600-1800	17650 (Africa)
1800-1900	Su-F 17650 (Africa)
1900-2300	17650 (Africa)
2300-2400	7580 (Europe & Mideast)

WHRI-WORLD HARVEST RADIO

0000-1000	5745 (E North Am)
0045-0200	M 7315 (C America)
0200-0900	7315 (C America)
0900-1000	M-Sa 7315 (C America)
1000-1300	9495 (N America & C America)
1000-1600	6040 (E North Am)
1300-1700	15105 (C America)
1600-1715	13760 (E North Am & W Europe)
1700-1800	[S] 9495 (N America & C America), [W] 15105 (C America)
1715-1730	M-Sa 13760 (E North Am & W Europe)
1730-2000	13760 (E North Am & W Europe)
1800-2300	9495 (N America & C America)
2000-2145	[S] 5745 (E North Am), [W] 13760 (E North Am & W Europe)
2145-2400	5745 (E North Am)
2300-2400	M-Sa 9495 (N America & C America)

WINB-WORLD INTERNATIONAL BROADCASTERS—(C America & W North Am)

0000-0400	11950
1500-2100	13790/13800
2100-2400	13790

WJCR

24 Hr	7490 (E North Am), 13595 (W North Am)

WMLK—(Europe, Mideast & N America)

0400-0900 &	
1700-2200	Su-F 9465

WRMI-R MIAMI INTERNATIONAL—(N America & C America) Note: 7465 may replace 9955 at certain times.

0000-0100 ▣	Tu-Su 9955
0100-0115 ▣	Su-F 9955
0115-0145 ▣	M 9955
0145-0300 ▣	M-Sa 9955
0300-0400 ▣	Su 9955
0400-0430 ▣	Su/Tu/Sa 9955
0430-0445 ▣	Tu-Sa 9955
0445-0500 ▣	M-Su 9955
0500-1100 ▣	M-Sa 9955
1300-1400 ▣	Su 9955
1400-1445 ▣	Sa/Su 9955
1445-1500 ▣	9955
1500-1700 ▣	M-Sa 9955
1700-1715 ▣	M-F 9955
1715-1730 &	
1730-1900 ▣	Su-F 9955
1900-2000 ▣	9955
2000-2115 ▣	Su-F 9955
2115-2200 ▣	9955
2200-2230 &	
2230-2400 ▣	M-Sa 9955

WRNO WORLDWIDE—(E North Am)

0000-0300	▣ 7355
0400-0700 ▣	7395
1400-1500	▣ 7395
1500-1600	7395
1600-2300	7355/15420
2300-2400	▣ 7355

WTJC—(N America)

1200-1100	9370

WWCR

0000-0100	7435 (E North Am), 13845 (W North Am)
0000-0300	5070 (E North Am & Europe)
0000-0400	3215 (E North Am)
0100-1000	2390 (E North Am)
0100-1200	5935 (E North Am & Europe)
0200-0300	▣ M 5070 (E North Am & Europe)
0200-0400	Tu-Su 5070 (E North Am & Europe)
0300-0400	▣ M 5070 (E North Am & Europe)
0400-0900	3210 (E North Am)
0400-1100	5070 (E North Am & Europe)
0900-1000	▣ 3210 (E North Am)
0900-1100	▣ 7435 (E North Am)
1000-1100	▣ 15685 (E North Am & Europe)
1000-2200	9475 (E North Am)
1100-1200	▣ 5070 (E North Am & Europe)
1100-1300	7435 (E North Am)
1100-2100	15685 (E North Am & Europe)
1200-1400	▣ 5935 (E North Am & Europe), ▣ 13845 (W North Am)
1200-1500	▣ 12160 (E North Am & Europe)
1300-1500	▣ 7435 (E North Am)
1400-2400	13845 (W North Am)
1500-2300	12160 (E North Am & Europe)
2100-2200	▣ 15685 (E North Am & Europe)
2200-2300	▣ 9475 & ▣ 9475 (E North Am)
2200-2400	7435 (E North Am)
2215-2245 ▣	F-Tu 15685 (E North Am & Europe)
2245-2400 ▣	Sa/Su 15685 (E North Am & Europe)
2300-2400	5070 (E North Am & Europe), 9475 (E North Am)

WYFR-FAMILY RADIO

0000-0100	6085 (E North Am)
0000-0445	9505 (W North Am)
0100-0445	6065 (E North Am)
0400-0600	9985 (Europe)
0500-0600	▣ 11550 & ▣ 11580 (Europe)
0500-0700	5985 (W North Am)
0600-0745	7355 (Europe)
0700-0745	7520 (Europe)
0700-0800	▣ 9355 & ▣ 13695 (W Africa)
1000-1245	5950 (E North Am)
1100-1245	▣ 6015 & ▣ 7355 (W North Am)
1200-1300	▣ 11830 (W North Am)
1200-1345	▣ 11970 (C America)
1200-1700	▣ 17750 (C America)
1300-1400	13695 (E North Am)
1300-1500	▣ 11740 & ▣ 11970 (E North Am)
1300-1700	11830 (W North Am)
1400-1700	▣ 17760 (C America)
1600-1700	▣ 15600 (W North Am), 21525 (C Africa & S Africa)
1600-1800	▣ 17510 & ▣ 17555 (Europe)
1600-1845	15695 (Europe)
1604-1700	▣ 15215 (W North Am)
1845-2200	▣ 15695 (Europe)
1900-1945	▣ 17510 (Europe)
1900-2145	▣ 5760 (Europe)
2000-2045	▣ 17750 (Europe)
2000-2100	▣ 5810 (Europe)
2000-2200	▣ 7355 (Europe)
2000-2245	▣ 15565 & ▣ 17845 (W Africa), ▣ 21525 (C Africa & S Africa)
2100-2245	▣ 15215 (C Africa & S Africa)
2200-2345	11740 (W North Am)

UZBEKISTAN

RADIO TASHKENT

0100-0130	▣ 5040 & 5060 (C Asia), ▣ 5955 (S Asia), ▣ 5975 (Mideast & W Asia), ▣ 7105 (W Asia), ▣ 7190 (Mideast & W Asia), ▣ 7205 (Mideast), ▣ 9375 (W Asia), ▣ 9540 (Mideast & W Asia), ▣ 9715 (Mideast & S Asia)

1200-1230 &
1330-1400   W 5060 & W 5975 (S Asia), W 6025 & S 7285 (W Asia & S Asia), 9715 & S 15295 (S Asia), S 17775 (S Asia & SE Asia)

2030-2100 &
2130-2200   W 7105 (W Asia), 9540 (Mideast & W Asia), S 9545 (W Asia)

VATICAN STATE
VATICAN RADIO

0140-0200   5980, W 7335, S 9650 & S 11935 (S Asia)
0250-0310   W 6095 & 7305 (E North Am), S 9605 (E North Am & C America)
0310-0340   9660 (E Africa)
0320-0350   7360 (E Africa)
0500-0530   W 7360 (E Africa), 9660 (Africa), 11625 & S 13765 (E Africa)
0600-0620 ▭   4005 (Europe), 5880 (W Europe)
0630-0700   W 7360 & S 11625 (W Africa), W 11625 (Africa), S 13765 (W Africa), S 15570 (Africa)
0730-0745 ▭   M-Sa 4005 (Europe), M-Sa 5880 (W Europe), M-Sa 7250 & M-Sa 9645 (Europe), M-Sa 11740 (W Europe & N Africa), M-Sa 15210/15215 (Mideast)
1020-1030   M-Sa 17550 (Africa)
1120-1130 ▭   M-Sa 5880 & M-Sa 7250 (Europe), M-Sa 11740 (W Europe), M-Sa 15210 (Mideast)
1120-1130   W 17585 (Africa)
1345-1405   W 9500, 11625 & S 13765 (Australasia), 15585 (SE Asia)
1545-1600   W 9500, 11640 & S 15585 (S Asia)
1600-1630   W Sa 9500, Sa 11640 & Sa 15585 (S Asia)
1615-1630   S 7250 (N Europe), S 11810 (Mideast)
1715-1730 ▭   4005 & 5880 (Europe), 9645 (W Europe)
1715-1730   W 7250 (Mideast)
1730-1800   W 7305 (E Africa), 11625 (E Africa & S Africa), S 13765 (E Africa), S 15570 (Africa)
2000-2030   W 7355, 9645 & 9660 (Africa), 11625 & S 13765 (W Africa)
2050-2110 ▭   4005 (Europe), 5882/5885 (W Europe)
2245-2305   W 6065 (SE Asia), W 7310/7305 (E Asia), 9600 & 11830 (Australasia)

VIETNAM
VOICE OF VIETNAM

0100-0130 &
0230-0300   W 5940 & S 7250 (E North Am)

The Pope's image oversees the transmitter hall of Vatican Radio. Arto Mujunen

0330-0400   W 7260 & S 9830 (C America)
1000-1030   9840/15110 & 12020 (SE Asia)
1100-1130   7285 (SE Asia)
1230-1300   9840 & 12020 (SE Asia)
1330-1400   7145/9730 & 9840/9730 (Europe)
1600-1630   7145/9730 & 9840/13740 (Europe)
1800-1830   7145/9730, W 7440, 9840/13740 & S 12070 (Europe)
1900-1930 &
2030-2100   7145/9730 & 9840/13740 (Europe)
2330-2400   9840/13740 & 12020 (SE Asia)

YUGOSLAVIA
RADIO YUGOSLAVIA

0000-0030   S M-Sa 9580 & S M-Sa 11850 (E North Am)
0100-0130   W M-Sa 6195 & W M-Sa 7115 (E North Am)
0200-0230   W 6100 & W 7130 (W North Am)
0430-0500   S 9580 & S 11850 (W North Am)
1330-1400   W 11835 (Australasia)
1900-1930   S 7230 (Australasia)
1930-2000 ▭   6100 (W Europe), 9720 (S Africa)
2200-2230 ▭   6100 (Europe), 6185 (W Europe)

Voices from Home—2000

Country-by-Country Guide to Native Broadcasts

For some listeners, English offerings are merely icing on the cake. Their real interest is in eavesdropping on broadcasts for *nativos*—the home folks. These can be enjoyable regardless of language, especially when they offer traditional music from other cultures.

Some you'll hear, many you won't—depending on your location and receiving equipment. Keep in mind that native-language broadcasts are sometimes weaker than those in English, so you may need more patience and better hardware. PASSPORT REPORTS tests for which radios are best.

When to Tune

Some broadcasts come in best during the day within world band segments from 9300 to 21850 kHz.

However, signals from Latin America and Africa peak near or during darkness, especially from 4700 to 5100 kHz. See "Best Times and Frequencies" earlier in this book for solid guidance.

Times and days of the week are in World Time, explained in "Setting Your World Time Clock" earlier in the book, as well as in the glossary; for local times, see "Addresses PLUS." Midyear, some stations are an hour earlier (◧) or later (◨) because of daylight saving time, typically April through October. Stations may also extend their hours for holidays or sports events.

Frequencies in *italics* may be best, as they come from relay transmitters that might be near you. Frequencies with no target zones are typically from transmitters designed for domestic coverage, so these are the least likely to be heard well unless you're in or near that country.

"Good Morning, Japan" is a popular NHK offering.

NHK

Schedules Prepared for Entire Year

To be as helpful as possible throughout the year, PASSPORT includes not just observed activity and factual schedules, but also activity which we have creatively opined will take place. This predictive information is original from us, and although it's of real value when tuning the airwaves, it is inherently not so exact as real-time data.

Most frequencies are aired year round. Those used only seasonally are labeled ◘ for summer (midyear), and ◙ for winter.

> Stations from Latin America and Africa are best near or during darkness.

RFE/RL reporter interviews Kosovo Albanian students at UNMIK's headquarters.

RFE/RL

ALBANIA—Albanian

RADIO TIRANA

0000-0600	◨	6090 & 7270 (N America)
0400-0900	◨	6100 (Europe)
0800-1100	◨	7110 (Europe)
0900-1400	◨	9585/9760 (W Europe)
1000-1500	◨	7150 (Europe)
1500-1800	◨	5985 (S Europe), 7270 (Europe)
1800-2300	◨	6100 (Europe)
1900-2200	🅂	9575 (Europe)
2000-2300	◨	7295 (Europe)
2000-2300	🆆	9750 (Europe)

ARGENTINA—Spanish

RADIO ARGENTINA AL EXTERIOR-RAE

0000-0230	Tu-Sa 9690 (Irr) (S America)
1200-1400	M-F 11710 (S America)
2200-2400	M-F 9690 (S America), M-F 15345 (Europe & N Africa)

RADIO NACIONAL

0000-0400	Su/M 6060 (S America)
0100-0200	Tu-Sa 15345 (Americas)
0900-1100	M-F 15345 (Americas)
0900-1200	6060 (S America)
1200-2400	Sa/Su 6060 (S America)
1700-2400	M-F 6060 (Irr) & 11710 (Irr) (S America)
1800-2400	Sa/Su 15345 (Europe & N Africa)

ARMENIA—Armenian

VOICE OF ARMENIA

0300-0330 &		
0400-0430	◨	9965 (S America)
0815-0900	◨	Su 4810 (E Europe, Mideast & W Asia), Su 15270 (Europe)
1645-1715	◨	Sa/Su 4810 (E Europe, Mideast & W Asia)
1930-2015	◨	M-Sa 4810 (E Europe, Mideast & W Asia), M-Sa 9965 (Europe)

AUSTRIA—German

RADIO AUSTRIA INTERNATIONAL

0000-0030	🆆	7325 & 🅂 9655 (E North Am), 🅂 9870, 🆆 Tu-Su 9870, 🅂 13730 & 🆆 Tu-Su 13730/9495 (S America)
0100-0130	🆆	7325 (E North Am), 9870 & 13730/9495 (S America)
0100-0230	🅂	9655 (E North Am)
0130-0200	🅂	9870 & 🅂 13730 (S America)
0200-0230		9870 (C America), 13730/9495 (S America)
0200-0300	🆆	7325 (E North Am)
0230-0300	🆆	9870 (C America), 🆆 13730/9495 (S America)
0300-0330		9870 (C America), 13730/9495 (S America)
0400-0430		M-Sa 6155 (Europe), M-Sa 13730 (E Europe)
0430-0500	🆆	6155 (Europe), 🆆 13730 (E Europe)
0500-0530		6015 (N America), 🅂 6155 & 🆆 M-Sa 6155 (Europe), 🅂 13730 & 🆆 M-Sa 13730 (E Europe), 🅂 15410, 🆆 M-Sa 15410, 🅂 17870 & 🆆 M-Sa 17870 (Mideast)
0530-0600		🅂 6155 (Europe), 🅂 13730 (E Europe), 🅂 15410 & 🅂 17870 (Mideast)
0600-0630		6015 (N America), 🅂 M-Sa 6155 & 🆆 6155 (Europe), 🅂 M-Sa 13730 & 🆆 13730 (E Europe), 🅂 M-Sa 15410, 🆆 15410, 🅂 M-Sa 17870 & 🆆 17870 (Mideast)
0630-0700		🆆 6155 (Europe), 🆆 13730 (E Europe), 🆆 15410 & 🆆 17870 (Mideast)
0700-0730		6155 (Europe), 13730 (E Europe), 15410 & 17870 (Mideast)
0800-0830		6155 (Europe), 13730 (N Europe), 🆆 17615 & 🅂 21650 (E Asia), 21765 (Australasia)
0830-0900		🅂 6155 (Europe), 🅂 13730 (N Europe)
0900-0930		🆆 17615 (E Asia), 21765 (Australasia)
0900-1100		13730 (N Europe), 🅂 21650 (E Asia)
0900-1130		6155 (Europe)
0930-1000		🅂 21765 (Australasia)
1000-1100		🆆 17615 (E Asia), 21765 (Australasia)
1100-1130		13730 (W Europe & E North Am)
1130-1200		🆆 6155 (Europe), 🆆 13730 (W Europe & E North Am)
1200-1230 &		
1300-1330		6155 (Europe), 13730 (W Europe & E North Am)
1400-1430		🅂 M-Sa 6155 & 🆆 6155 (Europe), 🅂 M-Sa 13730 & 🆆 13730 (S Europe & W Africa)
1430-1500		🅂 6155 (Europe)
1430-1530		🅂 13730 (S Europe & W Africa)
1500-1530		🅂 6155 & 🆆 M-Sa 6155 (Europe), 🆆 M-Sa 13710 (S Asia & SE Asia), 🆆 M-Sa 13730 (S Europe & W Africa)
1500-1630		🅂 15240 (Mideast), 🅂 17560 (S Asia & SE Asia)
1500-1730		🆆 9655 (Mideast)
1530-1630		6155 (Europe), 13730 (S Europe & W Africa)
1530-1730		🆆 13710 (S Asia & SE Asia)
1630-1700		🆆 6155 (Europe), 🆆 13730 (S Europe & W Africa)
1700-1730		6155 (Europe), 13730 (S Europe & W Africa), 🅂 15240 (Mideast), 🅂 17560 (S Asia & SE Asia)

1800-1830   5945 & 6155 (Europe), [W] M-Sa
9655 & [W] M-Sa 13730 (Mideast)
1800-1900   [S] 15240 (Mideast)
1830-1900   [S] 5945 & [S] 6155 (Europe)
1900-2030   5945 & 6155 (Europe), 13730 (S
Africa)
2030-2100   [W] 5945 & [W] 6155 (Europe),
[W] 13730 (S Africa)
2100-2130   Sa-Th 5945 & 6155 (Europe), [S] Sa-
Th 13730 (N Africa), [W] 13730 (S
Africa)
2200-2230   M-Sa 5945, [S] M-Sa 6155 & [W] 6155
(Europe), [S] M-Sa 13730 (N Africa),
[W] 13730 (S Africa)
2300-2330   [W] 5945, [S] M-Sa 6155 & [W] 6155
(Europe), [S] M-Sa 9870 & [W] 9870 (S
America)

BANGLADESH—Bangla

BANGLADESH BETAR
1200-1530   15520 (Mideast & Europe)
1540-1700   15520 (Mideast & Europe)
1630-1730   7185 & 9550 (Mideast)
1710-1740   15520 (Mideast & Europe)
1915-2000   7185, 9550 & 15520 (Irr) (Europe)

BRAZIL—Portuguese

RADIO BANDEIRANTES
24 Hr   6090, 9645 & 11925
RADIO BRASIL CENTRAL
0600-0200 ➡   4985, 11815
RADIO CULTURA SAO PAULO
0000-0200 ➡   9615, 17815
0000-0400 ➡   6170
0700-2400 ➡   9615, 17815
0800-2400 ➡   6170
RADIO NACIONAL DA AMAZONIA
0900-2300 ➡   6175, 11780

CANADA—French

CANADIAN BROADCASTING CORP—(E North Am)
0100-0300 ➡   M 9625
0300-0400 ➡   Su 9625 & Tu-Sa 9625
1300-1310 &
1500-1555 ➡   M-F 9625
1700-1715 ➡   Su 9625
1900-1945 ➡   M-F 9625
1900-2310 ➡   Sa 9625
RADIO CANADA INTERNATIONAL
0000-0030   [S] Tu-Sa 9535, [S] Tu-Sa 11895 &
[S] Tu-Sa 13670 (C America &
S America), [S] Tu-Sa 15305 (E
North Am & C America)
0000-0100   [S] 5960 (E North Am)
0100-0130   [W] 9535 & [W] 11865 (C America &
S America)
0100-0200 ➡   9755 (E North Am & C America)
0130-0200   [W] Su/M 9535 & [W] Su/M 11865 (C
America & S America)
0230-0300   [S] Tu-Sa 9535, [S] Tu-Sa 11715 &
[S] Tu-Sa 13670 (C America & S
America), [S] Tu-Sa 15305 (E North
Am & C America)
0300-0330   [W] 6025, [W] 9505, [S] 9760 & [S] 11835
(Mideast)
0330-0400 ➡   Tu-Sa 9755 (E North Am &
C America)
0330-0400   [W] Tu-Sa 6155 (E North Am &
C America), [W] Tu-Sa 9780 (W North
Am)
0530-0600   [S] 5995 (W North Am), [S] 6145
(Europe), [S] 7295 (W Europe &
N Africa), [S] 9595 (Europe), [S] 9755
(W North Am), [S] 11710 (Europe),
[S] 11830 (W North Am), [S] 13755
(Africa), [S] 15330 (N Africa &
Mideast), [S] 15400 (Africa)
0630-0700   [W] 6090 (Europe), [W] 6150 (Europe &
Mideast), [W] 9670 (N Africa &
C Africa), [W] 9780 (Europe &
N Africa), [W] 11710 (Africa),
[W] 11905 (Mideast & E Africa),
[W] 13690 (Africa), [W] 15325 (N Africa
& C Africa)
1200-1300   [S] 15305 (E North Am & C America)
1230-1300   [W] 6150 & [S] 9660 (E Asia), [W] 11730
& [S] 15195 (SE Asia)
1300-1400 ➡   11855 (E North Am & C America)
1300-1400   [W] 15425 (C America)
1300-1600   [S] Su 15305 (E North Am &
C America)
1400-1500   [S] M-Sa 15305 (Europe), [S] 15325
(Europe & Mideast), [S] M-Sa 17895
(Africa)
1400-1700   [W] Su 17795 (E North Am &
C America)
1500-1600 ➡   11935 (Europe & Mideast)
1500-1600   [W] 9555 (Europe & Mideast), [W] M-
Sa 17820 (Africa)
1900-2000   [S] 7235 (W Europe), [S] 13650
(Europe), [S] 13670 & [S] 15150
(Africa), [S] 15325 (Europe), [S] 15470
(W Europe), [S] 17820 (Africa),
[S] 17870 (Europe & N Africa)
2000-2100 ➡   5995 (Europe & N Africa)
2000-2100   [W] 7235 (W Europe & N Africa),
[W] 9770 (N Africa & C Africa),
[W] 9805 (W Europe & N Africa),
[W] 11755 (W Europe), [W] 11945 (W
Africa), [W] 13650 (Europe), [W] 13690,
[W] 15150 & [W] 17820 (Africa)

This Kyrgyzstan woman's row of gold teeth buttresses the jest that fillings can pick up powerful radio signals. M. Guha

0030-0330	11720
0030-0600	9675, 15285, 15480, 15500, 15550
0055-0613	11680/11100, 11935, 15710
0100-0600	11960, 17550/17590, 17700
0130-0600	12080, 15540
0200-0600	9500, 11660, 11740, 15390, 17580, 17605
0230-0600	15570
0355-0603	15145/15880
0355-0604	11000
0600-0855	W-M 6030, W-M 7230, W-M 9645, W-M 9675, W-M 11630, W-M 11860, W-M 11960, W-M 12000, W-M 12030, W-M 12045, W-M 15390, W-M 15480, W-M 15550, W-M 17550/17590, W-M 17580, W-M 17605
0600-0955	Th/Sa-Tu 7200, Th/Sa-Tu 9500, Th/Sa-Tu 9625, Th/Sa-Tu 9810, Th/Sa-Tu 11610/11780, Th/Sa-Tu 11660, Th/Sa-Tu 11670, Th/Sa-Tu 11740, Th/Sa-Tu 11800, Th/Sa-Tu 12080, Th/Sa-Tu 15285, Th/Sa-Tu 15500, Th/Sa-Tu 15540, Th/Sa-Tu 15570, Th/Sa-Tu 17700
0603-0955	Th-Tu 15145/15880
0604-0955	W-M 11000
0855-0930	11960
0855-1000	9645, 15550
0855-1030	9675
0855-1100	17605
0855-1130	15390, 17550/17590
0855-1200	11630, 12045, 15480, 17580
0855-1230	11860
0855-1300	12000
0855-1400	12030
0855-1730	6030, 7230
0930-1300	[W] 6110, [S] 11960
0955-1030	15500
0955-1100	11000, 15570, 17700
0955-1130	11610/11780, 15285
0955-1200	9500, 9810, [S] 11660, 11740, 12080, 15540
0955-1300	15145/15880
0955-1400	9380, 11800
0955-1602	7200, 9625, [S] 11670
0955-2400	[W] 6015, [S] 11100, [S] 11935
1000-1200	[W] 6090
1000-1230	[W] 7345, [S] 15550
1000-1330	[W] 6055, [S] 9645
1000-1602	[W] 4850/6040
1000-1730	7210
1030-1602	[W] 5010, [S] 15500
1030-1730	[W] 5030/6195, [S] 9675
1100-1300	[W] 9775, [S] 15570, [S] 17605, [S] 17700
1100-1400	[W] 9830
1100-1730	5880, 5915/9800, 5955, 5975, 5980, 5990, 6125
1100-1804	[S] 11000

2130-2200	[S] *7235* (Europe & Mideast), [S] *11690* & [S] 13650 (Europe), [S] 13670 & [S] *15150* (Africa), [S] 15305 (C America & S America), [S] 15325 (Europe), [S] 17820 (Africa)
2230-2300 ⬌	9755 (E North Am & C America)
2230-2300	[W] 5960 (E North Am), [W] 5995 (N Africa & C Africa), [W] *7235* & [W] *9805* (W Europe & N Africa), *11705* (SE Asia), [W] 11945 (W Africa), [W] 13690 (Africa), [S] 15305 (C America & S America), [S] 17695 (E North Am & C America)

CHINA

CENTRAL PEOPLE'S BROADCASTING STATION
Chinese

0000-0030	[W] 5010, [W] 5030/6195, [W] 7290, [W] 7345, [S] 9675, [W] 9745, [S] 12080, [S] 15285, [S] 15480, [S] 15500, [S] 15550
0000-0100	5880, 5915, 5955, 5975, 5980, 5990, [W] 6110, 6125, [W] 9775, [W] 9845, [S] 11000, 11730, [S] 11960, [S] 17550/17590, [S] 17700
0000-0103	[W] 9710/9170, [S] 15145/15880
0000-0130	7210, 11630, 12000, 12045
0000-0200	[W] 6090, [W] 9830, [S] 11660, [W] 11925, [S] 15390, [S] 17580, [S] 17605
0000-0600	6030, 7200, 7230, 9625, 9645, 9810, 11610/11780, 11670, 11800, 11860, 12030
0030-0130	11710

1130-1300	[W] 9655
1130-1330	[W] 9845, [S] 17550/17590
1130-1400	[W] 9745, [S] 15285, [S] 15390
1130-1602	[W] 7140, [W] 11610/11780
1200-1330	[S] 15540
1200-1400	[W] 11925, [S] 17580
1200-1602	[W] 5163, 6090, [S] 9810
1200-1730	7290
1230-1730	[W] 5320/5965, 7345, [S] 11860
1300-1330	[W] 11730
1300-1602	9775
1300-1730	6110, 9655
1300-1804	9710/9170
1330-1602	11730
1330-1730	6055, 9845
1400-1602	[W] 3290, 9745, [S] 11800
1400-1730	[W] 7305, 7415/7180, 9830, 11925
1400-2300	[W] 5090, [W] 6070, [S] 9380
2000-2200	6055
2000-2230	7290
2000-2300	6110, 7345, 7415/7180, 9655, 9830, 9845, 11925, 11960
2000-2400	[W] 5030/6195, [W] 5320/5965, 5880, 5915, 5955, 5975, 5980, 5990, 6030, 6125, 7210, 7230, [S] 9675, 11630, [S] 11860, 12000, 12045
2055-2400	9710/9170
2100-2230	[W] 3290, [S] 11800
2100-2300	[W] 4850/6040, 6090, 9745, 9775, [S] 11670
2100-2330	5010, [W] 5163, [W] 7140, [S] 9810, [S] 11610/11780
2100-2400	7200, 9625, 11730
2200-2400	[W] 6055, [S] 9645, [S] 11000
2230-2400	[W] 7290, 11800, [S] 15480
2300-2400	[W] 6090, [W] 6110, [W] 7345, [W] 9380, [W] 9655, [W] 9745, [W] 9775, [W] 9830, [W] 9845, [S] 11660, 11670, [W] 11925, [S] 11960, 12030, [S] 15285, [S] 15390, [S] 15550, [S] 15710, [S] 17550/17590, [S] 17580, [S] 17700
2330-2400	[W] 5010, 9810, 11610/11780, [S] 12080, [S] 15500, [S] 17605

CHINA RADIO INTERNATIONAL
Chinese

0200-0300	*9570* (E North Am), *9690* (N America & C America), 15435 (S America)
0300-0400	*9720* (W North Am)
0900-1000	6165 (E Asia), 9690, 9945, 11700 & 15440 (Australasia)
0900-1100	6010 & 11685 (SE Asia), [W] 11875 (Australasia), 12015 & 17785 (SE Asia)
1200-1300	*9570* (E North Am)
1200-1400	9580 (Australasia), 9755, 11685, 15260 & 17785 (SE Asia)
1500-1600	7170 & [S] 8260 (E Asia), 11740 (SE Asia), 15300 (S Asia)

1730-1830	5250 (E Asia), [W] 7110 (Europe), [W] 7160 (Mideast), [W] 7255 (E Europe), 9645 (Africa), [S] 11825 (Europe), [S] 13650 (Mideast & W Asia), [S] 15165 (Europe)
2000-2100	[W] 7120 (Mideast), 7185 (Europe), [W] 7245 (Mideast), 7525 (E Europe), [W] 9685 & [S] 9710 (Mideast), 9730 (E Europe & W Asia), [S] 11650 (E Europe), [S] 11750 (N Africa & Mideast), [S] 13650 (Mideast & W Asia)
2230-2300	*15500* (E Africa)
2230-2330	6140, [W] 7130 & 7335 (SE Asia), [S] 8260 (E Asia), 9755, 11945, [S] 12065, 15100, [S] 15135, 15260, 15300 & 15400 (SE Asia)
2230-2400	*11975* (N Africa)
2300-2400	*7170* (W Africa & C Africa)

Cantonese

1000-1100	11915 (SE Asia), 15440 (Australasia)
1100-1200	11685, 11720 & 17785 (SE Asia)
1200-1300	[S] 15125 (SE Asia)
1700-1800	[W] 7220 (S Asia & E Africa), 7265 (E Africa & S Africa), 9675 (W Asia), 9690 (S Asia), 9770 & [S] 11675 (E Africa)
1900-2000	[W] 7255 (E Europe), 9730 (E Europe & W Asia)
2330-2400	6140, [W] 7130, 7335, 9755, 11945, [S] 12065, 15100, [S] 15135, 15260, 15300 & 15400 (SE Asia)

CHINA (TAIWAN)
CENTRAL BROADCASTING SYSTEM-CBS
Chinese

0000-0100	15125
0000-0200	9630 (E Asia)
0000-0500	6040 (E Asia)
0000-0600	9610 (E Asia)
0100-0500	9280 (E Asia)
0200-1000	11970 (E Asia)
0400-0600	7105/7108 (E Asia)
0400-0700	11775 (E Asia)
0400-0900	11725 (SE Asia)
0400-2000	6085 & 11840 (E Asia)
0700-1100	7285 (E Asia)
0700-2400	7105/7108 (E Asia)
0800-2400	3335 (E Asia)
0900-1100	6180 (E Asia)
0900-1130	9630 (E Asia)
0900-2400	6040 (E Asia)
1000-1600	11725 (SE Asia)
1100-1200	9610
1100-2400	6180 (E Asia)
1300-1500	9610
1400-1800	9630 (E Asia)

2200-2400	*5950* (E North Am), 9610 (E Asia), 15125, *15440* (W North Am & C America)

RADIO TAIPEI INTERNATIONAL
Amoy

0000-0100	*5950* (E North Am), 11550 (E Asia), *15440* (W North Am & C America)
0200-0300	11550 (SE Asia)
0200-0400	11915 (E Asia)
0300-0400	7130 (SE Asia)
0500-0600	11745 (SE Asia)
0800-0900	11745 (E Asia)
1000-1100	7130 (E Asia), 11550 (SE Asia), 11745 (E Asia), 15345 (SE Asia)
1300-1400	7130 & 11745 (E Asia), 11860 (SE Asia)

Chinese

0100-0200	◪ *11825, 15215* & ◧ *17845* (S America)
0400-0500	*5950* (N America & C America), 7130 (SE Asia), *9680* (W North Am), 11825, 15270 & 15345 (SE Asia)
0700-0800	7130 (SE Asia)
0900-1000	7445 (SE Asia), 9610 (Australasia), 11550 (SE Asia), 11745 (E Asia), 11915 (SE Asia)
1200-1300	11745 (E Asia), 15270 (SE Asia)
1900-2000	◪ *9355* (Europe), 9955 (Mideast & N Africa), ◧ *15600*, ◧ *17750* & ◪ *17760* (Europe)
2300-2400	*3975* (Europe)

Cantonese

0000-0200	9690 (E Asia)
0100-0200	*5950* (E North Am), *7520* (Europe), *15440* (W North Am & C America)
0300-0400	*11740* (C America)
0500-0600	*5950* (N America & C America), *9680* (W North Am), 11825 (SE Asia), 11915 (E Asia), 15270 & 15345 (SE Asia)
0800-0900	7445 (E Asia)
0900-1300 &	
0900-2400	9690 (E Asia)
1000-1100	9610 (Australasia), 11915 (SE Asia)
1000-1200	15270 (SE Asia)
1300-1400	9765 (SE Asia)

VOICE OF ASIA
Chinese

0500-0700	7285 (E Asia)
0700-1100	9280 (E Asia)
1300-1500	7445 (SE Asia)

COLOMBIA—Spanish
CARACOL COLOMBIA

24 Hr	5077

RADIODIFUSORA NACIONAL DE COLOMBIA

1100-1700	Su 4955
1700-0445	4955

CROATIA—Croatian
CROATIAN RADIO

0015-0200 ◪	*9925* (S America)
0115-0300	◧ *9925* (W North Am)
0215-0400	◪ *7280/9925* (E North Am)
0315-0500	◧ *9925* (W North Am)
0400-0500	◧ *7365* (Europe)
0400-0600	◧ *9830* (Europe)
0400-0900	◧ *5945* (Europe)
0415-0600	◪ *7285/9925* (W North Am)
0500-0900	◧ *13830* (Europe)
0500-1600	7365 (Europe)
0500-1730	◪ *6165* (Europe)
0515-0700	◧ *13820/9470* (Australasia)
0600-1700	9830 (Europe)
0615-0800	◪ *13820/11880* (Australasia)
0800-1730	◪ *7185* (Europe)
0815-1000 ◪	*13820* (Australasia)
0900-2000	13830 (Europe)
1430-1830	◪ *21475* (SE Asia & Australasia)
1500-1730	◧ *21475* (Mideast & S Asia)
1600-1800	◧ *7365* (Europe)
1700-1800	◧ *9830* (Europe)
2000-2100	◧ *13810* (Mideast & S Africa), ◪ *13830* (Europe)
2100-2200	◪ *11605/11645* (Mideast & S Africa)

CUBA—Spanish
RADIO HABANA CUBA

0000-0100	6000 (E North Am), 9820 (N America)
0000-0300	11970 (S America)
0000-0500	5965 (C America), 6070 (C America & W North Am), 9505 (S America), 11760 (Americas), 15230 (S America)
0200-0500	9550 (E North Am)
1100-1500	6000 & 11760 (C America)
1200-1400	15340 (S America)
1200-1500	6070 (C America & W North Am), 9550 (C America)
2100-2300	◪ *9820* (Europe & N Africa), 9830 USB (E North Am & Europe), 11760 & ◧ *13680* (Europe & N Africa)

RADIO REBELDE

24 Hr	5025
0300-0400	6120 (C America)
1100-1400	6140 & 9600 (C America)

CYPRUS
CYPRUS BROADCASTING CORP—(Europe)
Greek

2215-2245	F-Su 6180, F-Su 7205 & F-Su 9760

RADIO MONTE CARLO—(N America)
Arabic

0300-0320	◧ *6040*
0400-0420 ◪	*9755*
0400-0420	◪ *5960*

Although some foreign stations are jammed by Chinese authorities, they are often audible. The very fact that they are jammed adds to their credibility, enhancing listener interest.

E.A. Hozour

CZECH REPUBLIC—Czech

RADIO PRAGUE

0130-0200	ⓦ 6200 (N America), ⓢ 7345 (N America & C America), ⓦ 7345 & ⓢ 11615 (Americas)
0230-0300	ⓢ 7345 (N America & C America), ⓦ 7345 (Americas), ⓦ 9435 & ⓢ 11615 (N America)
0930-1000 ▣	11600 (W Europe), 21745 (Mideast & S Asia)
0930-1000	ⓦ 15260 (W Europe), ⓢ 21745 (W Africa)
1030-1100 ▣	21745 (Mideast & S Asia)
1030-1100	ⓦ 17485 (W Africa)
1200-1230	ⓦ 11640 (N Europe & W Europe), ⓦ 21745 (Australasia)
1330-1400 ▣	6055 (Europe), 7345 (W Europe)
1330-1400	ⓢ 13580 (W Europe), ⓢ 17485 (S Asia)
1430-1500	ⓦ 13580 (E North Am & E Africa)
1530-1600	ⓢ 21745 (E Africa)
1630-1700 ▣	5930 (Europe)
1630-1700	ⓦ 17485 (W Africa & C Africa)
1730-1800	ⓢ 21745 (Africa)
1830-1900 ▣	5930 (E Europe, Asia & Australasia)
1830-1900	ⓦ 7315 (S Asia & Australasia)
1930-2000	ⓢ 11600 (SE Asia & Australasia)
2030-2100 ▣	5930 (W Europe)
2030-2100	ⓦ 9430 (W Africa)
2100-2130	ⓢ 11600 (S Asia & Australasia), ⓢ 15545 (W Africa)
2330-2400	ⓦ 9435 (N America), ⓢ 11615 (Americas), ⓢ 17485 (S America)

DENMARK—Danish

RADIO DANMARK

0030-0055	ⓦ *7545* (SE Asia), ⓦ *7565* & ⓢ *11960* (E North Am & C America), ⓢ *13805* (N America), ⓢ *15735* (SE Asia & Australasia)
0130-0155	ⓦ *7465* (E North Am & C America), ⓦ *7545* (S Asia), ⓦ *9940* (N America), ⓢ *11960* (E North Am & C America), ⓢ *13800* (S Asia), ⓢ *13805* (N America)
0230-0255	ⓦ *7465* (E North Am & C America), ⓦ *7545* (S Asia), ⓦ *9940* (N America), ⓢ *13800* (Mideast & S Asia)
0330-0355	ⓦ *7465* (W North Am), ⓦ *7545* (Mideast), ⓦ *7565* (E Africa), ⓢ *9470* (E Europe & Mideast), ⓢ *11635* (W North Am), ⓢ *13800* (Mideast & E Africa)
0430-0455	ⓦ *7465* (N America), ⓦ *7480* (E Europe & E Africa), ⓦ *7545* (Mideast), ⓢ *9470* (E Europe & Mideast), ⓢ *11635* (W North Am), ⓢ *13800* (Mideast & E Africa)
0530-0555	ⓦ *5960* & ⓢ *7465* (W Europe), ⓦ *7480* (C Africa & S Africa), ⓦ *9590* (E Europe & W Asia), ⓢ *12055* (Mideast), ⓢ *13800* (Africa)
0630-0655	ⓦ *5960* (W Europe), ⓢ *7180* (Europe), ⓦ *7180* & ⓢ *9590* (W Europe), ⓦ *9590* (W Africa), ⓢ *15705* (W Africa & Australasia), ⓢ *18950* (Africa & Australasia)

0730-0755	◼ 7180 (Europe), ◼ 9590 (W Europe), ◼ 11650 (W Africa), ◼ 15705 (W Africa & Australasia)
0830-0855	◼ 15705 (Australasia), ◼ 18910 (S America & Australasia), ◼ 18950 (Mideast), ◼ 21760 (S Asia)
0930-0955	◼ 15230 (E Asia & Australasia), ◼ 15705 (Australasia), ◼ 18910 (S America & Australasia), ◼ 21755 (E Asia)
1030-1055	◼ 11605 & ◼ 13800 (W Europe), ◼ 21730 (S America), ◼ 21755 (W Africa & S America)
1130-1155	◼ 11605 & ◼ 13800 (W Europe), ◼ 15735 (E North Am & C America), ◼ 21730 (S America)
1230-1255	9590 (W Europe), ◼ 13800 (E Asia), ◼ 15735 (N America), ◼ 17535 (E Asia), ◼ 18910 & ◼ 18950 (E North Am & C America), ◼ 18950 & ◼ 21755 (SE Asia & Australasia)
1330-1355	9590 (W Europe), ◼ 13800 (E Asia), ◼ 15705 (N America, SE Asia & Australasia), ◼ 15735 (N America), ◼ 17535 (E Asia), ◼ 18950 (E North Am & C America), ◼ 21755 (SE Asia & Australasia)
1430-1455	◼ 17505 (W North Am), ◼ 18910 (N America), 18950 (S Asia)
1530-1555	◼ 13805 & ◼ 15705 (Mideast & S Asia), ◼ 15705 (Mideast), ◼ 15735 & ◼ 17505 (W North Am), ◼ 18950 (S Asia)
1630-1655	◼ 9985 (W Europe), ◼ 13800 (Mideast & S Asia), ◼ 13800 (E Europe & W Asia), ◼ 15705 (E Africa), ◼ 15735 (W North Am), ◼ 21730 (Mideast & E Africa)
1630-1700	◼ 18950 (E North Am & C America)
1730-1755	◼ 9985 (W Europe), 11895 (E Europe & W Asia), ◼ 15705 (E Africa), ◼ 15735 (Mideast), ◼ 17505 & ◼ 18950 (N America), ◼ 21730 (Mideast & E Africa)
1830-1855	◼ 5960 & ◼ 7485 (W Europe), ◼ 7485 (Europe), ◼ 9925 & ◼ 13800 (Australasia), ◼ 18950 (N America), ◼ 21730 (Africa)
1930-1955	7485 (W Europe), ◼ 11870 (Africa), ◼ 15705 (Australasia), ◼ 17500 (W North Am), ◼ 18950 (Africa)
2030-2055	◼ 7485 (W Europe), ◼ 7485 (Europe), ◼ 7560 (Australasia), ◼ 9590 (W Europe & W Africa), ◼ 9985 (Australasia), ◼ 15705 (W North Am)
2130-2155	◼ 9940 & ◼ 12045 (Australasia)
2230-2255	◼ 9410 (S America), ◼ 9940 (E Asia), ◼ 12050 (S America), ◼ 15735 (E Asia)
2330-2355	◼ 7565 (E North Am & C America), ◼ 9410 (S America), ◼ 9925 & ◼ 9935 (SE Asia & Australasia), ◼ 9940 (E Asia), ◼ 13805 (E North Am & C America), ◼ 15735 (E Asia)
2330-2400	◼ 12050 (S America)

ECUADOR—Spanish

HCJB-VOICE OF THE ANDES

0000-0100	15140 (N America & S America)
0000-0500	6050 (S America)
0100-0500	15140 (C America & W North Am)
0700-0730	◼ 9765 & ◼ 11875 (Europe)
0900-1100	◼ 9765 & ◼ 11960 (S America)
1100-1300	11960 (C America)
1100-1700	15140 (S America)
1100-2400	6050 (S America)
1300-1500	15295/17660 (C America & W North Am)
1630-1900	21455 USB (Europe & Australasia)
1700-1900	15140 (N America & S America)
1900-2100	15140 (C America & W North Am)
2100-2300	15140 (S America)
2130-2230	◼ 11960, 15550, ◼ 17795 & ◼ 21470 (Europe)
2300-2400	15140 (N America & S America), 21455 USB (Europe & Australasia)

EGYPT—Arabic

EGYPTIAN RADIO

0000-0030 ◼	9700 (N Africa), 11665 (C Africa & E Africa), 15285 (Mideast)
0150-0700 ◼	12050 (Europe & E North Am)
0200-2200 ◼	9755 (N Africa & Mideast)
0300-0600 ◼	9850 (N Africa & Mideast)
0300-2400 ◼	15285 (Mideast)
0350-0700 ◼	9620 & 9770 (N Africa)
0350-2400 ◼	9800 (Mideast)
0600-1400 ◼	11980 (N Africa & Mideast)
0700-1100 ◼	15115 (W Africa)
0700-1400 ◼	15475
0700-1500 ◼	11785 (N Africa)
0700-1530 ◼	12050 (Europe, E North Am & E Africa)
1100-2400 ◼	9850 (N Africa)
1245-1900 ◼	17670 (N Africa)
1530-2400 ◼	12050 (Europe & N America)
1800-2400 ◼	9700 (N Africa)
1900-2400 ◼	11665 (C Africa & E Africa)

RADIO CAIRO

0000-0045	15220 (C America & S America), 17770 (S America)
0030-0330	9900 (E North Am)
0330-0430	9900 (W North Am)
1015-1215	17745 (Mideast & S Asia)
1100-1130	17800 (C Africa & S Africa)
1245-1600	15220 (C Africa)

2000-2200	11990 (Australasia)
2345-2400	15220 (C America & S America), 17770 (S America)

FRANCE—French

RADIO FRANCE INTERNATIONALE

0000-0030	[S] *15440* (SE Asia)
0000-0100	[W] 5920 (C America), [W] 7120 (S Asia & SE Asia), 9800 (S America), [S] 9805 (S Asia & SE Asia), [S] 11670 (C America), [W] *12025* & [S] *15535* (SE Asia)
0000-0200	*9715* (S America)
0000-0300	9790 (C America)
0100-0200	[W] *11600* & [S] *15440* (S Asia)
0130-0200	5920 (C America & N America), 9800 & *11995* (S America)
0130-0500	*9800* (C America)
0200-0300	5920 (C America & N America), 9715 (S America)
0300-0400	[W] 3965 (Europe), 7315 & [S] *9805* (Mideast), [S] 11700 (E Africa)
0300-0500	[W] 5945 (E Africa & Mideast), [S] 9550 (Mideast), [S] 9805 (E Africa)
0300-0600	[W] 7280 & [S] 11685 (Mideast)
0300-0700	9790 (Africa)
0300-0800	7135 (Africa)
0330-0400	[S] 7280 (E Europe)
0330-0445	5990 (E Europe)
0330-0600	6045 (E Europe)
0400-0500	*5920* (C America & N America), [S] *6175* (S Africa), [W] *9845* (Mideast), 11700 (E Africa)
0400-0600	*4890* (C Africa), 5925 (N Africa), [W] 7315 (Mideast), [S] 9745 (E Europe), [S] 15155 (E Africa)
0400-0700	[W] 3965 (N Africa), 7280 (E Europe)
0500-0600	11700 (E Africa)
0500-0700 ▭	11995 (E Africa)
0500-0700	[W] 5945 (N Africa), [W] 9550 (Mideast), [S] 11975 (E Europe), [S] 15135 (E Africa), [S] 15605 (Mideast)
0500-1200	9805 (E Europe)
0600-0700	[W] 5925 (N Africa), [W] 6045 (E Europe), 7305 (Irr) (N Africa), [W] *9845* (W Africa), [W] 15155 (E Africa), [S] 15300 (C Africa & S Africa), [S] 17620 (E Africa)
0600-0800 ▭	17800 (E Africa)
0600-0800	[W] 11685 (Mideast), 11700 (Africa), [S] 11700 (N Africa), [S] 17650 (Mideast)
0600-0900 ▭	9790 (N Africa)
0700-0800	[W] 7280 (E Europe), [W] 7305 (N Africa), [W] 15135 (E Africa), [S] 15155 (E Europe), *15315* (W Africa), [S] 17850 (C Africa & S Africa)
0700-0900	11975 (E Europe)
0700-1100	15605 (Mideast & S Asia)
0700-1300	11670 (E Europe)
0700-1500	21620 (E Africa)
0700-1700	15300 & 17620 (Africa)
0800-0900	[W] 11700 (W Africa), [S] 15315 (N Africa & W Africa)
0800-1200	15155 & 15195 (E Europe)
0800-1300	17650 (Mideast & S Asia)
0800-1600	11845 (N Africa), 17850 (C Africa & S Africa)
0900-1100	[W] 21580 (C Africa & S Africa)
0900-1300	25820 (E Africa)
0900-1500	[W] 21685 (W Africa)
0900-1600	15315 (N Africa & W Africa)
1030-1100	[W] *9790* (C America), *11670* (S America), [S] *11670* (C America)
1030-1125	*5220* (E Asia)
1030-1130	[S] 17575 (C America & E North Am)
1030-1200	[W] *7140* (E Asia), *9830* & [S] *11710* (SE Asia), 15435 (S America)
1100-1200	6175 (W Europe & Atlantic), *11670* (C America & S America), [W] 11700 (E North Am), *11890* (SE Asia), *13640* (C America), [S] 15365 (E North Am), *17605* (S Africa)
1100-1500	21580 (C Africa & S Africa)
1130-1200	17575 (C America & E North Am)
1200-1400	*9790* (C Africa)
1230-1300	*13640* (C America), [S] *17560* (S America)
1230-1330	*15515* (C America)
1230-1400	*15435* (S America)
1300-1330	[W] 9805 & [W] 11670 (E Europe), *17860* (C America)
1300-1400	[S] 11615, [W] 15155 & 15195 (E Europe), *17560* (S America), 17650 (Mideast)
1330-1400	9805 & [W] 11670 (E Europe), M-Sa *15515* & M-Sa *17860* (C America)
1400-1500	[S] *6090* (SE Asia), 11615 (E Europe), [W] 15605 & [S] 17650 (Mideast)
1400-1600	[W] 9495, [S] 15155 & [S] 15195 (E Europe), [W] 15460 (E Africa)
1430-1500	[W] 9805 (E Europe)
1430-1600	[S] *15515* (C America), 17575 (S America), *17860* & [W] *21645* (C America), [S] *21765* (S America)
1500-1600	[W] 9605, [S] 11615 & [W] 11670 (E Europe), 12030 (S Asia & SE Asia), [S] 15605 (Mideast), [S] 21580 (C Africa & S Africa), [S] 21620 (E Africa)
1500-1700 ▭	17605 (E Africa)
1500-1700	[W] 9790 (N Africa)
1600-1700	9495 (E Europe)
1600-1800	[W] 7315 (E Europe), [S] 11705/11700 (N Africa)
1600-1900	[S] *21685* (W Africa)

Professor Simo S. Soininen operates an AOR AR7030 receiver at the Lahti Radio Museum in Finland.

S. Soininen

1600-2000	**S** 11995 (E Europe)
1700-1800	**W** 9495 (Irr) (E Europe), **W** 9790 (Irr) (N Africa), **S** 9805 & **S** 11670 (E Europe), **W** 11705 (E Africa)
1700-1900	**W** 11965 & 17620 (W Africa)
1700-2000	**W** 7160 (N Africa & W Africa)
1700-2200	15300 (Africa)
1730-1800	**W** 9485 (E Africa & Mideast), **W** 11615 & **S** 15210 (E Africa)
1730-1900	**S** 15460 (E Africa)
1800-1900	**W** 5900 (E Europe), **W** 9485 & 11995 (E Africa)
1800-2000	11705 (N Africa & E Africa)
1800-2100	**W** 7135 & **S** 9495 (E Europe), **S** 11615 (N Africa)
1800-2200	*7160* (C Africa), 9790 (Africa)
1900-2000	**W** 3965 (Europe), **W** 5995 & **S** 11670 (E Europe), 11965 (W Africa)
1900-2100	**W** 6175 (N Africa), **S** 11995 (E Africa)
1900-2200	9485 (E Africa), **S** 9605 (E Europe)
2000-2100	5915 (E Europe), **W** 7315 (E Africa & S Africa), **S** 11705 (N Africa & E Africa)
2000-2200	7160 (N Africa & W Africa), **S** 7350 (E Europe), **S** 11965 (W Africa)
2100-2200	**W** 3965 (N Africa), **S** 5900 & **W** 5915 (E·Europe), **W** 5945 (E Africa & Mideast), 6175 (N Africa), 7315 (E Africa & S Africa), **S** 9805 (E Europe)

2130-2200	**W** *15200, 17630* & **S** *21645* (C America), *21765* (S America)
2200-2300	**W** 5920 (C America), 9715 & 9800 (S America), **S** 11670 (C America)
2200-2400	9790 (C America)
2300-2400	**W** 7120 (S Asia & SE Asia), **W** *9570* (SE Asia), *9715* (S America), **S** 9805 (S Asia & SE Asia), **W** *9830* (E Asia), **S** *12005*, **W** *12025*, **S** *15440* & **S** *15535* (SE Asia)
2330-2400	**W** 5920 (C America), 9800 (S America), 11670 (C America), *11995* (S America), **W** *13640* (Irr), **S** *15200* & **S** *17620* (C America)

GABON—French

AFRIQUE NUMERO UN
0500-2300	9580 (C Africa)
0700-1600	17630 (W Africa)
1600-1900	15475 (W Africa & E North Am)

RTV GABONAISE
0500-0800	7270/4777
0800-1600	7270
1600-2300	4777

GERMANY—German

BAYERISCHER RUNDFUNK
24 Hr	6085

DEUTSCHE WELLE
0000-0150	*15410* (S America)
0000-0155	**S** *11785* (C America), **W** *11895* (W Africa & Americas), **W** *13750* & **S** *17860* (SE Asia)
0000-0200	6075 (Europe), 6100 (N America & C America), **S** 7130 (N Africa & S America), 9545 (S America), **W** 9545 (C America), **S** 9730 (S America), **W** 9730 (C America), **W** *11785* & **S** *13780* (S America), *15275* & **S** *15275* (C America), **W** *15370* (S Asia & SE Asia)
0000-0355	**W** *13780* (W Africa & Americas)
0000-0400	**W** 7130 (S Europe & S America)
0000-0600	3995 (Europe)
0200-0355	**S** 11795 (E Africa)
0200-0400	**S** 6100 (N America & C America), **W** 6100 (C America), **W** 6145 (N America & C America), **S** 9735 (N America), *15205* (S Asia)
0200-0555	**W** 9545 (E Africa)
0200-0600	6075 (Europe & N America)
0300-0500	**S** 9735 (E Europe & W Asia)
0400-0555	**S** 9735 (N America), **S** 13780 (Africa), **S** 15275 (E Africa & S Africa)

0400-0600	**S** 6100 & **W** 6145 (N America & C America), **W** *7235* (W Africa), *9640* (N America), **W** *9650* & **S** *9700* (S Africa), **W** 9735 (Mideast & Africa)
0500-0600	**S** 9735 (Australasia)
0600-0800	**W** 3995 (Europe), **S** *11985* & **W** *12000* (Australasia)
0600-0955	*9690* (Australasia), 11865 (E Europe & W Asia), **S** 21600 (Africa)
0600-1000	9735 & 11795 (Australasia), **S** 17845 & *21640* (SE Asia & Australasia), **W** 21780 (Africa)
0600-1800	6075 (Europe), 13780 (S Europe & Mideast)
0600-2000	9545 (S Europe)
0800-1355	**W** 25740 (S Asia & SE Asia)
0900-1155	*15135* (Africa)
1000-1355	**W** 17845 (E Europe, Mideast & W Asia), **S** *21640* (E Asia), **S** 21680 (E Europe & W Asia), **S** 21790 (S Asia & SE Asia), **W** *21790* (E Asia), **S** 21840 (Mideast)
1000-1400	**W** *9900*, **W** *12000*, **S** *13720*, **W** *13810* & **S** *15490* (E Asia), **S** 17560 (W Africa), **S** *17845* (SE Asia & Australasia)
1100-1330	**S** *12005* (Europe)
1200-1355	*15135* (S Africa)
1200-1400	**W** *6075* (N Africa), **W** *15490* & **W** 17650 (S Asia & SE Asia), *17730* (N America & C America), **S** *17730* & **W** *17765* (S America), **W** *17895* (Europe)
1330-1600	6140 (Europe)
1400-1555	**W** 15275 (S Europe & Mideast), **W** 21790 (S Asia)
1400-1600	17845 (S Asia)
1400-1700	**W** *15285* (N America & C America), *17730* (N America), *17765* (S America), **S** *17875* (N America)
1400-1755	**W** *9620* (S Asia), **W** *15135* (Mideast & E Africa), **S** 15275 (S Asia), **S** *21560* (Mideast)
1400-1800	**S** *9655* & *12055* (S Asia), **S** 17845 (Mideast)
1600-1755	**W** 11795, **W** 15275 & **S** 17845 (S Asia)
1600-1900	6140 (Europe)
1600-2000	**W** *9835* & **S** *15540* (Mideast)
1800-2000	**W** 3995 (Europe), **W** 9545 (E Africa & S Africa), **W** 11795 (Africa), **S** 13780 (S Europe & Mideast)
1800-2155	*9735* (S Africa), **S** *11765* & **W** *15275* (SE Asia & Australasia)
1800-2200	6075 (Europe & E Africa), **S** 7185 (Africa), **S** 15275 (W Africa & S America), *17860* (W Africa & Americas)
2000-2155	9545 (W Africa & S America)
2000-2200	11795 (Africa), *17810* (N America & S America)
2000-2400	3995 (Europe)
2200-2355	**W** *11840* & **S** *15250* (E Asia), **S** *17860* (C America), **W** *17860* (W Africa & Americas)
2200-2400	6075 (Europe), 6100 (N America & C America), 9545 (S America), **W** 9545 (C America), **W** 9715 (S Asia & SE Asia), **S** 9730 (S America), **W** 9730 & **S** *11785* (C America), **W** *11785* (S America), *11795* (E Asia), **S** 12035 & **S** *13690* (S Asia & SE Asia), **S** *13780* (S America), **W** *13780* (W Africa & Americas), *15275* & **S** *15275* (C America), **W** *15370* (S Asia & SE Asia), *15410* (S America)

DEUTSCHLANDFUNK—(Europe)

24 Hr	6190

DEUTSCHLANDRADIO—(Europe)

24 Hr	6005

SUDWESTRUNDFUNK—(Europe)

24 Hr	7265
0455-2305 **⊡**	6030

GREECE—Greek

FONI TIS HELLADAS

0000-0130 &	
0200-0350	**W** 7450, 9420 & 12105 (N America)
0400-0525	**W** 7450, 9425/9420, **W** 11645 & 15650 (Mideast)
0600-0745	7450, **S** 9425 & 11645 (Europe & Australasia)
0600-0800	*9775* (Australasia)
0900-0950	*9775* (Australasia), 15415/15630 (E Asia), 15650 (Australasia)
1000-1135	9425 & 9915 (Mideast)
1200-1230	**W** 9420 (Mideast), **W** 11645 & **W** 15650 (Africa)
1200-1235	**S** 15530 (Europe & N America)
1200-1335	*9590* (E North Am)
1245-1350	**S** 15530 (Europe & N America)
1300-1335 **⊡**	15650 (Europe & N America)
1300-1335	**W** 9420 (Europe & N America), 11645 (C Asia)
1345-1450 **⊡**	15650 (Europe & N America)
1345-1450	**W** 9420 (Europe & N America)
1400-1430	**S** 9420, 11645 & **S** 15630 (Mideast)
1500-1600	**W** 7450 (Europe), **S** 9375, 9420 & 11645 (E Europe)
1710-1725	**W** 7450, **S** 9375, 9425/9420 & **S** 11645 (E Europe)
1800-1840	11645 & 15150 (Africa)
1800-1900	**W** 7450, **W** 9395, **W** 9425 & **W** 11595 (Europe)

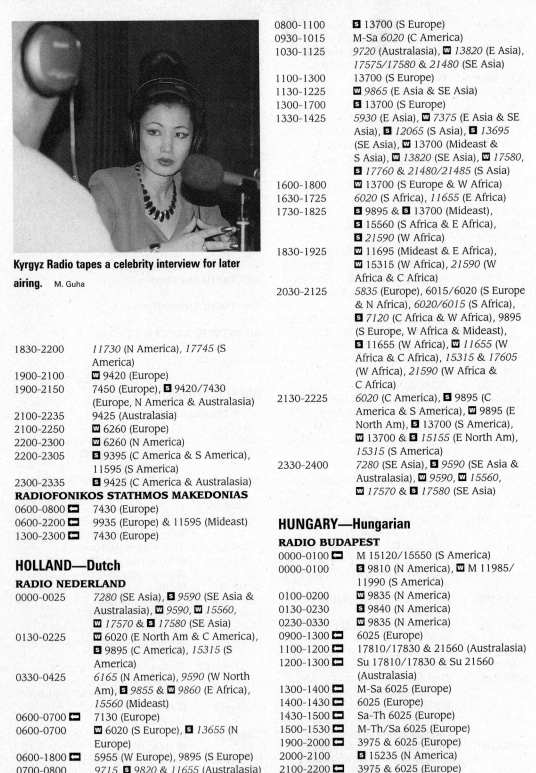

Kyrgyz Radio tapes a celebrity interview for later airing. M. Guha

1830-2200	*11730* (N America), *17745* (S America)
1900-2100	**W** *9420* (Europe)
1900-2150	7450 (Europe), **S** *9420/7430* (Europe, N America & Australasia)
2100-2235	9425 (Australasia)
2100-2250	**W** *6260* (Europe)
2200-2300	**W** *6260* (N America)
2200-2305	**S** *9395* (C America & S America), 11595 (S America)
2300-2335	**S** *9425* (C America & Australasia)

RADIOFONIKOS STATHMOS MAKEDONIAS

0600-0800 ▣	7430 (Europe)
0600-2200 ▣	9935 (Europe) & 11595 (Mideast)
1300-2300 ▣	7430 (Europe)

HOLLAND—Dutch

RADIO NEDERLAND

0000-0025	*7280* (SE Asia), **S** *9590* (SE Asia & Australasia), **W** *9590*, **W** *15560*, **W** *17570* & **S** *17580* (SE Asia)
0130-0225	**W** *6020* (E North Am & C America), **S** *9895* (C America), *15315* (S America)
0330-0425	*6165* (N America), *9590* (W North Am), **S** *9855* & **W** *9860* (E Africa), *15560* (Mideast)
0600-0700 ▣	7130 (Europe)
0600-0700	**W** *6020* (S Europe), **S** *13655* (N Europe)
0600-1800 ▣	5955 (W Europe), 9895 (S Europe)
0700-0800	*9715*, **S** *9820* & *11655* (Australasia)
0700-0900 ▣	11935 (S Europe)

0800-1100	**S** 13700 (S Europe)
0930-1015	M-Sa *6020* (C America)
1030-1125	*9720* (Australasia), **W** *13820* (E Asia), *17575/17580* & *21480* (SE Asia)
1100-1300	13700 (S Europe)
1130-1225	**W** *9865* (E Asia & SE Asia)
1300-1700	**S** 13700 (S Europe)
1330-1425	*5930* (E Asia), **W** *7375* (E Asia & SE Asia), **S** *12065* (S Asia), **S** *13695* (SE Asia), **W** 13700 (Mideast & S Asia), **W** *13820* (SE Asia), **W** *17580*, **S** *17760* & *21480/21485* (S Asia)
1600-1800	**W** 13700 (S Europe & W Africa)
1630-1725	*6020* (S Africa), *11655* (E Africa)
1730-1825	**S** 9895 & **S** 13700 (Mideast), **S** 15560 (S Africa & E Africa), **S** *21590* (W Africa)
1830-1925	**W** *11695* (Mideast & E Africa), **W** *15315* (W Africa), *21590* (W Africa & C Africa)
2030-2125	*5835* (Europe), 6015/6020 (S Europe & N Africa), *6020/6015* (S Africa), **S** *7120* (C Africa & W Africa), 9895 (S Europe, W Africa & Mideast), **S** 11655 (W Africa), **W** *11655* (W Africa & C Africa), 15315 & 17605 (W Africa), *21590* (W Africa & C Africa)
2130-2225	*6020* (C America), **S** 9895 (C America & S America), **W** 9895 (E North Am), **S** 13700 (S America), **W** 13700 & **S** *15155* (E North Am), *15315* (S America)
2330-2400	*7280* (SE Asia), **S** *9590* (SE Asia & Australasia), **W** *9590*, **W** *15560*, **W** *17570* & **S** *17580* (SE Asia)

HUNGARY—Hungarian

RADIO BUDAPEST

0000-0100 ▣	M 15120/15550 (S America)
0000-0100	**S** 9810 (N America), **W** M 11985/11990 (S America)
0100-0200	**W** 9835 (N America)
0130-0230	**S** 9840 (N America)
0230-0330	**W** 9835 (N America)
0900-1300 ▣	6025 (Europe)
1100-1200 ▣	17810/17830 & 21560 (Australasia)
1200-1300 ▣	Su 17810/17830 & Su 21560 (Australasia)
1300-1400 ▣	M-Sa 6025 (Europe)
1400-1430 ▣	6025 (Europe)
1430-1500 ▣	Sa-Th 6025 (Europe)
1500-1530 ▣	M-Th/Sa 6025 (Europe)
1900-2000 ▣	3975 & 6025 (Europe)
2000-2100	**S** 15235 (N America)
2100-2200 ▣	3975 & 6025 (Europe)
2100-2200	**W** 9840 (N America)

2200-2300	**S** 17565 (S America)
2300-2400	15120/15550 (S America)
2300-2400	**W** 11985/11990 & **S** Su 17565 (S America)

INDIA—Hindi
ALL INDIA RADIO

0315-0415	11855 & 13695 (Mideast & W Asia), 15075, 15180 & 17387 (E Africa)
0430-0530	15075 & 17387 (E Africa)
1615-1730	7410 (Mideast & W Asia), 9950 & 13720 (E Africa), 13770 (W Asia & Mideast), 15075 (E Africa)
1945-2045	7410, 9950 & 11620 (W Europe)
2300-2400	9910, 11740 & 13795 (SE Asia)

IRAN—Persian
VOICE OF THE ISLAMIC REPUBLIC

0000-1230	15084
0130-1330	15365 (W Asia & S Asia)
1300-2400	15084
1630-1730	7230 (Europe)
1830-2330	7130 (Europe)
2230-2330	6165

ISRAEL
KOL ISRAEL
Arabic

| 0400-2215 | 5915 (Mideast & N Africa), 9815 (Mideast), 12140 (Mideast & W Asia), 15480/15430 (Mideast) |

Hebrew

0000-0330	11585 (W Europe & E North Am)
0000-0400	**S** 15615 (Europe & N America)
0000-0600	**W** 7545 (W Europe & N America), **W** 9380 & **S** 15640 (W Europe & E North Am)
0330-0430	**W** 11585 (W Europe & E North Am)
0400-0600	**S** 15615 (W Europe & E North Am)
0430-0600	11590 (W Europe & E North Am)
0500-0600	**S** 17545 (Europe & N America)
0600-1900	15615 (W Europe & E North Am), 17545 (Europe & N America)
1600-1800	11590 (W Europe & E North Am)
1800-2400	11585 (W Europe & E North Am)
1900-1945	15650 (Europe & N America)
1900-2200	**W** 9380 (W Europe & E North Am)
1900-2400	**W** 7560 (W Europe & N America), **S** 15615 (W Europe & E North Am)
2100-2215	15640 (S America)
2100-2215	**W** 17535 (S America)
2200-2400	**W** 9380 (W Europe & E North Am)
2215-2400	**S** 15640 (W Europe & E North Am)

Yiddish

| 1700-1725 | 9435 & 11605 (Europe), 15640 (E Europe), 15650 (N Africa) |

1700-1725	**W** 17535 (Europe & N America)
1800-1825	9435 (Europe), 15640 (E Europe)
1800-1825	**W** 17535 (Europe & N America)

ITALY—Italian
RADIO ROMA-RAI INTERNATIONAL

0000-0050	6010 (E North Am), 9575 (S America), 9675 (E North Am & C America), 11755/11880 (S America), 11800 (N America & C America)
0130-0230	*6110* (S America), *11765* (C America)
0130-0305	6010 (E North Am), 9575 (S America), 9675 (N America & C America), 11755/11880 (S America), 11800 (E North Am & C America)
0415-0425	**S** 5975, **W** 6010 & 7270 (S Europe & N Africa)
0435-0510	**W** 9690, **W** 11840, 15250/15320 & **S** 17780 (E Africa)
1000-1100	*11925* (Australasia)
1320-1650	Su 21535 (S America), Su 21710 (C Africa & S Africa)
1400-1430	15250 & M-Sa 17780 (E North Am)
1500-1525	5990, 7290, **S** 9670 & **W** 9690 (S Europe & N Africa)
1555-1625	5990, 7290 & 9760 (W Europe)
1700-1800	7235 & 9670 (N Africa), 11840 (E Africa), **S** 11840 (N Africa), 15230 (Africa), *15320* (S Africa), 17870 (E Africa)
1830-1905	15250 & 17780 (E North Am)

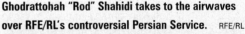

Ghodrattohah "Rod" Shahidi takes to the airwaves over RFE/RL's controversial Persian Service. RFE/RL

2230-2400	6010 (E North Am), 9575 (S America), 9675 (E North Am & C America), 11755/11880 (S America), 11800 (N America & C America)

RAI-RADIOTELEVISIONE ITALIANA

0000-0500 ⬜	6060 (Europe, Mideast & N Africa)
0500-2300 ⬜	6060 & 9515 (Europe, N Africa & Mideast)
0500-2300	7175 (Europe, Mideast & N Africa)
0530-1300 ⬜	6110 (E Europe)
0600-1000	7240 & 🅂 7240 (E Europe)
0600-1300	15240 & 21520 (E Africa)
1320-1650	Su 9855 (Europe), Su 17780 (E North Am), Su 21520 (E Africa)
2300-2400 ⬜	6060 (Europe, Mideast & N Africa)

JAPAN—Japanese

RADIO JAPAN/NHK

0100-0200	21670 (Pacific, C America & S America)
0200-0300	11860 (SE Asia), 15570 (E Asia), 21610 (Australasia)
0200-0400	5960 (E North Am), 11870 (Mideast), 13630 (W North Am), 15325 (S Asia), 17685 (Australasia), 17835 (S America)
0200-0500	11840 (E Asia), 15590 (SE Asia)
0300-0400	9515 (Mideast), 9660 (S America), 11890 (S Asia)
0700-0800	6145, 6165 & 11840 (E Asia)
0700-0900	17860 (SE Asia)
0700-1000	9685 (Pacific, C America & S America), 11740 (SE Asia), 11850 & 11920 (Australasia)
0800-1000	9530 (S America), 9835 (W North Am), 11710 (Europe), 12030 (C America), 🅆 15230 (Mideast), 15590 (S Asia), 17650 (C Africa & S Africa), 17895/15220 (W Africa), 🅂 21550 (Mideast)
0800-1500	9750 (E Asia)
0900-1500	11815 (SE Asia)
1300-1500	11705 (E North Am), 17695 (N Europe)
1500-1600	17885 (C Africa), 21600/15310 (S America)
1500-1700	9535 (W North Am & C America), 12045 (S Asia)
1600-1700	7110 (Europe), 9750 (E Asia), 11730 (S Asia), 15355 (S Africa)
1600-1800	7140 (Australasia), 9835 (Pacific)
1600-1900	6035 (E Asia), 7200 (SE Asia)
1700-1800	21630 (E Africa)
1700-1900	11880 (Mideast)
1900-2100	6165 (E Asia), 🅂 17810 (SE Asia)
1900-2200	🅆 7225 & 11665 (SE Asia)

1900-2400	11910 (E Asia)
2000-2100	6035 (Australasia)
2200-2300	6050, 6115 & 9725 (Europe), 11705 (E North Am), 11850 (Australasia), 11895 (C America), 🅆 13630 (W North Am), 15220 (S America), 🅂 17825 (W North Am & C America)
2200-2400	🅆 11665 (SE Asia)

RADIO TAMPA

0000-0800	3925, 9760
0000-1000	6115
0000-1300	3945
0000-1730	6055, 9595
0800-1500 & 2030-2300	3925
2030-2400	6055, 9595
2300-2400	3925, 3945, 6115, 9760

JORDAN—Arabic

RADIO JORDAN

0000-0205 ⬜	6105 (Irr) (Mideast)
0000-0208 ⬜	11935 (W Europe & E North Am), 15435 (S America)
0400-0600 ⬜	9630 (N Africa & E Africa)
0400-0810	11810 (Mideast, SE Asia & Australasia)
0400-0815 ⬜	15435 (W Europe)
0600-0900 ⬜	11835 (E Europe)
0815-0904 ⬜	Sa-Th 15435 (W Europe)
0830-1515	11810 (Mideast, SE Asia & Australasia)
1100-1300 ⬜	15355 (N Africa & C America)
1300-1625 ⬜	13630 (N Africa & E Africa)
1600-2155 ⬜	6105 (Mideast)
1633-2155 ⬜	13630/7155 (N Africa & E Africa)
1800-2155 ⬜	9830 (W Europe)
2155-2400 ⬜	6105 (Irr) (Mideast)
2200-2400 ⬜	11935 (W Europe & E North Am), 15435 (S America)

KOREA (DPR)—Korean

PYONGYANG BROADCASTING STATION—(E Asia)

0000-1800	6398
0000-1900	3320
0200-0630, 1500-2030 & 2100-2230	3250
2100-2400	3320 & 6398

RADIO PYONGYANG

0000-0925	6250 (E Asia)
0400-0600	4405 & 7200 (E Asia), 9345 (Asia)
0600-0650	3560 (E Asia), 11710, 13790 (Europe), 15180, 15340 & 17735 (SE Asia)

0800-0900	3560, 4405, 6125, 6575 & 7200 (E Asia), 9345 (Asia), 9975 (E Asia), 13790 (Asia)
1200-1300	4405, 6125 & 7200 (E Asia), 9345 (Asia)
1400-1450	3560 (E Asia), 9640 (SE Asia), 9975 & 11335 (SE Asia & C America), 13650 (N America & C America), 15230 (Americas)
1500-1900	6250 (E Asia)
1600-1650	3560 & 4405 (E Asia), 6520 (Mideast & N Africa), 6575 & 9335 (Europe), 9600 (Mideast & N Africa), 9640 (Mideast & Africa), 9975 (Africa), 11735 (S Asia), 13650 (N America & C America)
1700-1800	6520 (Mideast & N Africa)
2100-2400	6250 (E Asia)
2200-2250	4405 (E Asia), 6575 & 9335 (Europe), 11710 & 13760 (N America)

KOREA (REPUBLIC)—Korean

RADIO KOREA INTERNATIONAL

0000-0100	5975 (E Asia), 15575 (N America)
0100-0200	7275 (E Asia)
0300-0400	7275 (E Asia), 11725 & 11810 (S America), 15575 (N America)
0700-0800	7550 & *9535* (Europe)
0900-1000	7550 (S America)
0900-1100	5975 & 7275 (E Asia), 9570 (Australasia), 13670 (Europe)
1000-1100	6135 (E Asia)
1100-1130	*6145* (E North Am), 9640 (E Asia), *9650* (E North Am), 11725/9580 (S America)
1300-1400	9640 (E Asia), 13670 (SE Asia)
1700-1900	5975 (E Asia), 7550 & 15575 (Europe)
2100-2200	5975 & 7275 (E Asia), 9640 (SE Asia)
2300-2400	5975 (E Asia), 15575 (N America)

KUWAIT—Arabic

RADIO KUWAIT

0000-0530	11675 (W North Am)
0200-1305	6055 & 15495 (Mideast)
0400-0805	15505 (E Europe & W Asia)
0445-0500 &	
0800-0930	15110 (S Asia & SE Asia)
0815-1740	15505 (W Africa & C Africa)
0900-1505	17885 (E Asia)
0930-1605	13620 (Europe & E North Am)
1310-2130	9880 (Mideast)
1315-1730	15110 (S Asia & SE Asia)
1615-1800	11990 (Europe & E North Am)
1745-2300	15505 (Europe & E North Am)
1745-2400	15495 (W Africa & C Africa)
1800-2400	9855 (Europe & E North Am)

LIBYA—Arabic

RADIO JAMAHIRIYA

0000-0445	▣	11850/15435 (N Africa & Mideast), 15235/9700 (W Africa & S America), 15415 (Europe)
1115-1730	▣	11850/15435 (N Africa & Mideast)
1115-1800	▣	15415 (Europe)
1115-2400	▣	15235/9700 (W Africa & S America)
1800-2400	▣	11850/15435 (N Africa & Mideast)
1915-2400	▣	15415 (Europe)

LITHUANIA—Lithuanian

LITHUANIAN RADIO

1000-1030 &		
1130-1300	▣	9710 (W Europe)
1430-1445	▣	9555 (E Europe)
1445-1455	▣	M-F 9555 (E Europe)

RADIO VILNIUS

0000-0030		▣ *6155* & ⑤ *9855* (E North Am)
1100-1130	▣	9710 (W Europe)

MEXICO—Spanish

RADIO EDUCACION

0000-1200	▣	6185

RADIO MEXICO INTERNATIONAL—(W North Am & C America)

0000-0400	▣	9705
0400-0500	▣	M 9705
1300-1500,		
1900-2000 &		
2200-2400	▣	5985 & 9705

MOROCCO

RADIO MEDI UN—(Europe & N Africa)
French & Arabic

0500-0200	9575

RTV MAROCAINE
Arabic

0000-0500	11920 (N Africa & Mideast)
0900-2200	15345 (N Africa & Mideast)
1100-1500 &	
2200-2400	15335 (Europe)

NORWAY—Norwegian

RADIO NORWAY INTERNATIONAL

0000-0030	▣ 7545 (SE Asia), ▣ 7565 & ⑤ 11960 (E North Am & C America), ⑤ 13805 (N America), ⑤ 15735 (SE Asia & Australasia)
0100-0130	▣ 7465 (E North Am & C America), ▣ 7545 (S Asia), ▣ 9940 (N America), ⑤ 11960 (E North Am & C America), ⑤ 13800 (S Asia), ⑤ 13805 (N America)

**Somali producer Dalmar with Adventist World Radio
president Dan Jacobsen.**   AWR

0200-0230	ⓦ 7465 (E North Am & C America), ⓦ 7545 (S Asia), ⓦ 9940 (N America), ⓢ 13800 (Mideast & S Asia)
0300-0330	ⓦ 7465 (W North Am), ⓦ 7545 (Mideast), ⓦ 7565 (E Africa), ⓢ 9470 (E Europe & Mideast), ⓢ 11635 (W North Am), ⓢ 13800 (Mideast & E Africa)
0400-0430	ⓦ 7465 (W North Am), ⓦ 7480 (E Europe & E Africa), ⓦ 7545 (Mideast), ⓢ 9470 (E Europe & Mideast), ⓢ 11635 (W North Am), ⓢ 13800 (Mideast & E Africa)
0500-0530	ⓦ 5960 & ⓢ 7465 (W Europe), ⓦ 7480 (C Africa & S Africa), ⓦ 9590 (E Europe & W Asia), ⓢ 12055 (Mideast), ⓢ 13800 (Africa)
0600-0630	ⓦ 5960 (W Europe), ⓢ 7180 (Europe), ⓦ 7180 & ⓢ 9590 (W Europe), ⓦ 9590 (W Africa), ⓢ 15705 (W Africa & Australasia), ⓢ 18950 (Africa & Australasia)
0700-0730	7180 (Europe), 9590 (W Europe), ⓦ 11650 (W Africa), ⓢ 15705 (W Africa & Australasia)
0800-0830	ⓦ 15705 (Australasia), ⓢ 18910 (S America & Australasia), ⓢ 18950 (Mideast), ⓦ 21760 (S Asia)
0900-0930	ⓦ 15230 (E Asia & Australasia), ⓦ 15705 (Australasia), ⓢ 18910 (S America & Australasia), ⓢ 21755 (E Asia)
1000-1030	ⓢ 11605 & ⓦ 13800 (W Europe), ⓦ 21730 (S America), ⓢ 21755 (W Africa & S America)
1100-1130	ⓢ 11605 & ⓦ 13800 (W Europe), ⓢ 15735 (E North Am & C America), ⓦ 21730 (S America)
1200-1230	ⓦ 9590 (W Europe), ⓦ 13800 (E Asia), ⓢ 15735 (N America), ⓢ 17535 (E Asia), ⓦ 18910 & ⓢ 18950 (E North Am & C America), ⓦ 18950 & ⓢ 21755 (SE Asia & Australasia)
1300-1330	9590 (W Europe), ⓦ 13800 (E Asia), ⓦ 15705 (N America, SE Asia & Australasia), ⓦ 15735 (N America), ⓢ 17535 (E Asia), ⓢ 18950 (E North Am & C America), ⓢ 21755 (SE Asia & Australasia)
1400-1430	ⓢ 17505 (W North Am), ⓦ 18910 (N America), 18950 (S Asia)
1500-1530	ⓢ 13805 & ⓢ 15705 (Mideast & S Asia), ⓦ 15705 (Mideast), ⓦ 15735 & ⓢ 17505 (W North Am), ⓦ 18950 (S Asia)
1600-1630	ⓢ 9985 (W Europe), ⓢ 13800 (Mideast & S Asia), ⓦ 13800 (E Europe & W Asia), ⓦ 15705 (E Africa), ⓦ 15735 (W North Am), ⓢ 18950 (E North Am & C America), ⓢ 21730 (Mideast & E Africa)
1700-1730	ⓢ 9985 (W Europe), ⓦ 11895 (E Europe & W Asia), ⓦ 15705 (E Africa), ⓢ 15735 (Mideast), ⓢ 17505 & ⓦ 18950 (N America), ⓢ 21730 (Mideast & E Africa)
1800-1830	ⓦ 5960 & ⓢ 7485 (W Europe), ⓦ 7485 (Europe), ⓦ 9925 & ⓢ 13800 (Australasia), ⓦ 18950 (N America), ⓢ 21730 (Africa)
1900-1930	7485 (W Europe), ⓦ 11870 (Africa), ⓢ 15705 (Australasia), ⓢ 17500 (W North Am), ⓢ 18950 (Africa)
2000-2030	ⓢ 7485 (W Europe), ⓦ 7485 (Europe), ⓦ 9590 (W Europe & W Africa), ⓢ 9985 (Australasia), ⓦ 15705 (W North Am)
2100-2130	ⓦ 9940 & ⓢ 12045 (Australasia)
2200-2230	ⓦ 7560 (Australasia), ⓦ 9410 (S America), ⓦ 9940 (E Asia), ⓢ 12050 (S America), ⓢ 15735 (E Asia)

2300-2330	▥ 7565 (E North Am & C America), ▥ 9410 (S America), ▥ 9925 & ▤ 9935 (SE Asia & Australasia), ▥ 9940 (E Asia), ▤ 12050 (S America), ▤ 13805 (E North Am & C America), ▤ 15735 (E Asia)

OMAN—Arabic

RADIO OMAN

0000-0200	9735 (Mideast)
0000-0400	7230 (Mideast)
0200-0400	▥ 6085 (Mideast & W Asia), ▥ 7120 (E Africa)
0200-0500	▤ 9515 (Mideast), ▤ 15355 (E Africa)
0400-0600	▥ 7230 & ▥ 9730 (Mideast), ▥ 11890 (E Africa)
0500-0600	▤ 13640 (Mideast)
0500-0800	▤ 17590 (E Africa)
0600-0800	▥ 17730 (E Africa)
0600-1400	13640 (Mideast)
0800-1000	17630 (Mideast)
1000-1300	▥ 17630 (Mideast)
1100-1400	▥ 7230 (Mideast)
1300-1400	▥ 15140 (Mideast)
1400-1700	15140 (Mideast)
1400-1800	15375 (E Africa)
1400-2400	7230 (Mideast)
1700-1900	11805 (Mideast)
1800-2200	11890 (E Africa)
1900-2400	9735 (Mideast)

PARAGUAY—Spanish

RADIO NACIONAL DEL PARAGUAY

0700-1700 ▭	9735 (S America & E North Am)
1700-2000 ▭	9735 (Irr) (S America)
2000-0300 ▭	9735 (S America & E North Am)

POLAND—Polish

RADIO POLONIA

1130-1200 ▭	5995 & 7285 (Europe)
1200-1225 ▭	7270 (W Europe), 7285 (E Europe)
1630-1725 ▭	6000 (W Europe), 7285 (E Europe)
1630-1725	▥ 9690 (W Europe)
2100-2200	▤ 7270 (E Europe)
2200-2255 ▭	6035 (E Europe), 6095 (W Europe)

QATAR—Arabic

QATAR BROADCASTING SERVICE

0000-0245	7210 (Irr) & 9570 (Irr) (Mideast & N Africa)
0245-0704	▥ 7210 & ▤ 11785 (Mideast & N Africa)
0245-2125	9570 (Mideast & N Africa)
0704-1304	▥ 11820/15395 & ▤ 17880 (Mideast & N Africa)
1304-1704	11820/11655 (Europe)
1704-2125	▥ 7210 & ▤ 17895 (Europe)
2125-2400	7210 (Irr) & 9570 (Irr) (Mideast & N Africa)

ROMANIA—Romanian

RADIO ROMANIA INTERNATIONAL

0000-0100	5990, 9510 & 11940 (E North Am)
0100-0200	9570 (S America)
0600-0614	▥ 7105, ▤ 9550, 9665, ▥ 11775 & ▤ 11810 (Europe)
0715-0815	▤ Su 11740 & Su 15335 (W Asia), Su 15370 & Su 17790 (SE Asia)
0815-0915	▤ Su 11810 (C Africa), Su 15335 (S Africa), Su 15380 (C Africa), ▤ Su 17745 (S Africa), ▥ Su 17790 (W Africa)
0915-1015	Su 9570 (Europe), ▥ Su 9590 (W Europe), Su 9665, Su 11775 & Su 11810 (N Africa), ▤ Su 11970 (Europe & Atlantic)
1130-1200	▤ 11790 (Europe)
1300-1330	▤ 11775 (Europe), ▥ 15365 & ▥ 17790 (Australasia)
1630-1700	▥ 7105, ▤ 9510, ▥ 9665 & ▤ 11775 (Mideast)
1730-1800	▥ 5990, ▥ 6105, ▥ 7195 & ▤ 9510 (Europe)
2000-2030	▥ 7175 (Europe), ▤ 9625 (W Europe), ▥ 9690 (Europe), ▤ 11790 (W Europe)
2230-2300	▥ 9530 (W Europe), 9570 & ▤ 11830 (E North Am), ▥ 11830 (S America)
2300-2400	▤ 5990 (Australasia), ▥ 5990 (C America), 7105 & ▥ 9550 (Australasia), ▥ 11940 (S America)

RUSSIA—Russian

RADIO ROSSII

0000-0700	▥ 9700 (E Asia)
0000-1000	▤ 15475 (E Asia)
0000-1800 ▭	7220 (N Asia)
0100-0400	▤ 11980 (W Africa & S America)
0100-0500	▤ 6205 (E Europe), ▤ 7305 (W Asia & C Asia), ▤ 12020 (N Europe & E North Am)
0100-0600	▤ 9845 (E Europe)
0100-0800	▤ 12025 (W Asia & C Asia)
0200-0500 ▭	5910 (Arctic)
0200-0500	▥ 6115 (N Europe & E North Am), ▥ 6125 & ▥ 7365 (W Asia & C Asia), ▥ 7380 (W Africa & S America)
0200-0600	▥ 6110 (E Europe)
0200-0700	▥ 7335 (E Europe)
0430-0700	▤ 15455 (Europe & W Africa)

0430-1500   **S** 7440 (Arctic)
0520-0900   **W** 12065 (W Asia & C Asia)
0530-0800   **W** 9860 (N Europe & E North Am),
               W 12060 (Europe & W Africa)
0530-0830   **S** 13705 (N Europe & E North Am)
0530-0900   **S** 12065 (W Asia & C Asia)
0530-1200   **W** 11990 (W Asia & C Asia)
0530-1500   **W** 7250 (Arctic)
0630-0730   **S** 12045 (E Europe)
0630-1500 ▭ 9720 (Europe)
0730-1400   12045 (E Europe)
0730-1600   **W** 7440 (E Asia)
0730-1700   **S** 17660 (Europe & W Africa)
0820-1500   **S** 12015 (W Asia & C Asia)
0830-1500   **W** 17600 (Europe & W Africa)
0830-1700   **S** 13705 (N Europe & E North Am)
0920-1400   12005 (W Asia & C Asia)
0930-1300   **S** 11655 (W Asia)
1030-1500   **S** 9655 (E Asia)
1220-1600   **W** 7145 (W Asia & C Asia)
1230-2200   **W** 6125 (W Asia & C Asia)
1330-1700   **S** 7365 (W Asia & C Asia)
1330-2100   **S** 7355 (W Asia & C Asia)
1400-1700   **S** 12045 (E Europe)
1400-1800   **W** 12115 (E Europe)
1430-2000   **W** 7340 (E Europe)
1430-2100   **S** 5940 (E Europe)
1520-2100   **S** 9490 (N Europe)
1530-1900   **W** 12060 (Europe & W Africa)
1530-2100   **S** 5905 (Arctic)
1530-2200   **W** 5910 (Arctic), **W** 6060 (Europe)
1620-2200   **W** 5895 (N Europe & E Europe)
1700-1800   **S** 13705 (N Europe & E North Am)
1730-2000   **W** 7350 (N Europe & E North Am)
1730-2100   **S** 7445 (E Europe), **S** 11735
               (Europe & W Africa)
1830-2100   **S** 9845 (N Europe & E North Am)
1900-2200   **S** 9805 (E Asia)
1930-2200   **W** 6045 (W Europe & Atlantic)
2000-2300   **W** 7390 (E Asia)
2200-2400 ▭ 7220 (N Asia)
2230-2400   **S** 15475 (E Asia)
2330-2400   **W** 9700 (E Asia)

VOICE OF RUSSIA
0100-0300   **S** 12070 (S America), **S** 17565,
               S 17630, **S** 17660 & **S** 17690 (W
               North Am)
0200-0400 ▭ *7125* (E North Am)
0200-0400   **W** 7350 (S America), **W** 9580 (W
               North Am)
1200-1400   **S** 11675 (E Asia)
1300-1500   **W** 7170 (SE Asia), **W** 12015 (S Asia
               & SE Asia)
1500-1600   **S** 11975 & **S** 15490 (Mideast),
               S 17580 (Mideast & E Africa)
1600-1700   **W** 9560 (Mideast)
1700-2100   **S** 9810 (W Europe & Atlantic),
               S 12040 (Europe & Atlantic)

1800-1900   **W** 7310 (Europe)
1800-2000   **W** 9560 (Mideast), **S** 11980 (Europe)
1800-2200   9450 (Europe), **W** 9480 (S Europe &
               N Africa), **W** 9775 (Europe & W
               Africa)
1900-2000   **S** 15455 & **S** 15465 (Europe)
2000-2200   **W** 7185, **W** 7310 & **W** 7320 (Europe),
               W 7380 (S Europe)

SINGAPORE—Chinese

RADIO SINGAPORE INTERNATIONAL—(SE Asia)
1100-1400   6000 & 6120
RADIO CORPORATION OF SINGAPORE
1400-1600 &
2300-1100   6000

SLOVAKIA—Slovak

RADIO SLOVAKIA INTERNATIONAL
0130-0200   5930 (E North Am & C America),
               7300 (Africa), 9440 (S America)
0730-0800   **S** 9440, **S** 15460 & **S** 17550
               (Austra lasia)
0900-0930   **W** 11990, **W** 17485 & **W** 21705
               (Australasia)
1530-1630   **S** 5920 (W Europe)
1630-1730 ▭ 6055 & 7345 (W Europe)
1630-1730   **W** 5915 & **W** 5940 (W Europe)
1900-1930   **S** 5920 (W Europe)
2000-2030 ▭ 6055 & 7345 (W Europe)
2000-2030   **W** 5915 (W Europe)

SPAIN

RADIO EXTERIOR DE ESPAÑA
Galician, Catalan & Basque
1510-1555   M-F 9500 (W Europe), **W** M-F 12035
               & **S** M-F 15585 (Europe)
2230-2255   M-Sa 7275 (Europe), M-Sa *9765* (C
               America), M-Sa *11880* (C America
               & S America), M-Sa 15110/9630 (N
               America & C America), M-Sa *15170*
               (W North Am & C America)

Spanish
0000-0100   Su/M *9765* (C America), Su/M
               11815 (N America), Su/M *11880* (C
               America & S America), Su/M
               15170 (W North Am & C America)
0000-0200   11680/11945 (S America)
0000-0500   9540 (N America & C America),
               9620 & 15160/6125 (S America)
0100-0400   Tu-Sa *3210* & Tu-Sa *5970* (C
               America), Tu-Sa *5990* & Tu-Sa *6020*
               (W North Am & C America)
0200-0500   6055 (N America & C America)
0500-0700   9730 (Europe), **W** 11890/12015 &
               S 17665 (Mideast)
0500-0800   11920 (Europe)

0700-0900	17770 & 21610 (Australasia)
0700-1510	[W] 12035 & [S] 15585 (Europe)
0700-1600	[W] 9435 (W Europe)
0800-1700	21570 (S America)
0900-1200	Su 9520 (W Europe)
0900-1700	21610 (Mideast)
0900-1900	17755 (C Africa & S Africa)
1000-1200	9660 (E Asia)
1100-1300	M-F 15170 (W North Am & C America)
1100-1400	M-F 5970/6060 (C America), M-F 9630 (N America), M-F 11815 (C America)
1200-1400	5220 (E Asia), 11910 (SE Asia)
1200-1510	9500 (W Europe)
1200-1800	21700 (C America & S America)
1300-1400	15170 (W North Am & C America)
1400-1700	Sa/Su 15170 (W North Am & C America)
1400-1800	Sa/Su 9765 (C America), Sa/Su 15125 (C America & S America)
1510-1555	[W] Sa/Su 12035 & [S] Sa/Su 15585 (Europe)
1510-1600	Sa/Su 9500 (W Europe)
1555-1700	[W] 12035 & [S] 15585 (Europe)
1600-1700	Su 9500 (W Europe), M-Sa 15375 (W Africa & C Africa)
1700-1800	Sa/Su 17850 (W North Am & C America)
1700-1900	17715 (S America)
1700-2000	Sa/Su 9665 (C America)
1700-2230	7275 (Europe)
1800-2000	Sa/Su 21700 (C America & S America)
1800-2100	M-F 21700 (Irr) (C America & S America)
1800-2200	15125 (C America & S America), 17850 (W North Am & C America)
1800-2230	9765 (C America)
1900-2230	15110/9630 (N America & C America)
2000-2100	Sa 9665 (C America), Sa 21700 (C America & S America)
2200-2230	11880 (C America & S America), 15170 (W North Am & C America)
2200-2300	7270 (N Africa & W Africa)
2200-2400	[S] 17575 (Mideast)
2230-2255	Su 9765 (C America), Su 11880 (C America & S America), Su 15170 (W North Am & C America)
2230-2300	Su 7275 (Europe), Su 15110/9630 (N America & C America)
2255-2400	9765 (C America), 11880 (C America & S America), 15170 (W North Am & C America)
2300-2400	9540 (N America & C America), 9620, 11680/11945 & 15160/6125 (S America)

SWITZERLAND

SWISS RADIO INTERNATIONAL

French

0200-0230	9885 & 9905 (N America & C America)
0430-0500	[S] 9610/13635 (E Europe)
0500-0530	9885 (N America & C America)
0515-0530	[S] 9610/13635 (E Europe)
0530-0600	[W] 9655 (E Europe)
0600-0700	[W] 9885 (N Africa), [W] 11860 (N Africa & W Africa), [W] 13635 (S Africa), [S] 15545 (N Africa), [S] 17685 (N Africa & W Africa), [S] 21750 (S Africa)
0615-0630	[W] 9655 (E Europe)
1000-1030	9885 & 13685 (Australasia)
1100-1130	[S] 15315 (W Europe)
1200-1230	[W] 9535 (W Europe)
1230-1300	[W] 9540 & [S] 13735 (E Asia), [W] 17815 & [S] 21770 (S Asia & SE Asia)
1530-1600	9575/12010 (E Asia & SE Asia), [W] 15185 & [S] 17670 (W Asia & S Asia)
1800-1815	[W] 9620, [W] 13790 & [S] 15220 (Mideast), [W] 15555 (Mideast & E Africa), [S] 17640 (Mideast), [S] 21720 (Mideast & E Africa)
1830-1900	[S] 9885 (N Europe)
1930-2000	[W] 6165 (N Europe)
2100-2130	[W] 9620 (E Africa), [W] 9885 (C Africa & S Africa), [W] 13700 & [S] 13710 (S Africa), [S] 13770 (E Africa), [S] 15220 (C Africa & S Africa), [S] 17580 (N Africa & W Africa)
2200-2230	9885, [W] 11660 & [S] 11905 (S America)

German

0030-0100 & 0330-0400	9885 & 9905 (N America & C America)
0500-0515	[S] 9610/13635 (E Europe)
0600-0615	[W] 9655 (E Europe)
0800-0815	[W] 9885 (N Africa), [W] 11860 (N Africa & W Africa), [W] 13635 (S Africa), [S] 15545 (N Africa), [S] 17685 (N Africa & W Africa), [S] 21750 (S Africa)
0930-1000	9885 & 13685 (Australasia)
1030-1100	[S] 15315 (W Europe)
1130-1200	[W] 9535 (W Europe)
1200-1230	[W] 9540 & [S] 13735 (E Asia), [W] 17815 & [S] 21770 (S Asia & SE Asia)
1500-1530	9575/12010 (E Asia & SE Asia), [W] 15185 & [S] 17670 (W Asia & S Asia)
1730-1800	[S] 9885 (N Europe)
1830-1900	[W] 6165 (N Europe)

2030-2100 ▪ 9620 (E Africa), ▪ 9885 (C Africa & S Africa), ▪ 13700 & ▪ 13710 (S Africa), ▪ 13770 (E Africa), ▪ 15220 (C Africa & S Africa), ▪ 17580 (N Africa & W Africa)
2230-2300 9885, ▪ 11660 & ▪ 11905 (S America)

Italian
0300-0330 9885 & 9905 (N America & C America)
0530-0545 9885 (N America & C America)
0600-0630 ▪ 9610/13635 (E Europe)
0700-0730 ▪ 9655 (E Europe), ▪ 9885 (N Africa), ▪ 11860 (N Africa & W Africa), ▪ 13635 (S Africa), ▪ 15545 (N Africa), ▪ 17685 (N Africa & W Africa), ▪ 21750 (S Africa)
0900-0930 9885 & 13685 (Australasia)
1130-1200 ▪ 15315 (W Europe)
1230-1300 ▪ 9535 (W Europe)
1300-1330 ▪ 9540 & ▪ 13735 (E Asia), ▪ 17815 & ▪ 21770 (S Asia & SE Asia)
1630-1700 ▪ 9620, ▪ 13790 & ▪ 15220 (Mideast), ▪ 15555 (Mideast & E Africa), ▪ 17640 (Mideast), ▪ 21720 (Mideast & E Africa)
1800-1830 ▪ 9885 (N Europe)
1830-1900 ▪ 9620 (E Africa), ▪ 9885 (C Africa & S Africa), ▪ 11910 (N Africa & W Africa), ▪ 13770 (E Africa), ▪ 15220 (C Africa & S Africa), ▪ 17580 (N Africa & W Africa)
1900-1930 ▪ 6165 (N Europe)
2300-2330 9885, ▪ 11660 & ▪ 11905 (S America)

SYRIA—Arabic

RADIO DAMASCUS—(S America)
2215-2315 12085 & 13610
SYRIAN BROADCASTING SERVICE
0600-1600 ▪ 13610
0600-1700 ▪ 12085

THAILAND—Thai

RADIO THAILAND
0000-1700 4830, 6070, 7115
0100-0200 9655 & 11905 (Asia), ▪ 13695 & ▪ 15395 (E North Am)
0330-0430 9655 & 11905 (Asia), ▪ 15395 & ▪ 15460 (W North Am)
1330-1400 ▪ 7145 (E Asia), 9655 & 11905 (Asia), ▪ 11955 (E Asia)
1800-1900 9655 (Asia), ▪ 9690 & ▪ 11855 (Mideast), 11905 (Asia)
2045-2115 ▪ 9535 (Europe), 9655 (Asia), ▪ 9680 (Europe), 11905 (Asia)
2200-2400 4830, 6070, 7115

TURKEY—Turkish

VOICE OF TURKEY
0000-0400 ▪ 11725 (Europe & N America)
0000-0800 ▪ 9445 (Europe & E North Am), 9460 (Europe)
0000-0800 ▪ 11710 (Europe & E North Am)
0000-1000 ▪ 15385 (Europe)
24 Hr 11955 (Mideast)
0400-0700 ▪ 9505 (Europe, N America & C America)
0400-0900 ▪ 21715 (W Asia, S Asia & Australasia)
0500-1000 ▪ 11925 & 15145 (W Asia)
0500-1000 ▪ 9560 (W Asia, S Asia & Australasia)
0700-0900 ▪ 13670 (Europe)
0800-2200 ▪ 9460 (Europe & E North Am)
1000-1500 ▪ F 15625 (N Africa & E Africa)
1000-1700 ▪ 15350 (Europe)
1000-2300 ▪ 9560 (W Asia, S Asia & Australasia)
1100-1600 ▪ F 7150 (N Africa)
1300-1500 ▪ 13670 (Europe)
1600-2200 ▪ 7115 (N Africa & Mideast)
1600-2300 ▪ 5980 (Europe)
1700-2300 ▪ 7255 (Mideast & Africa)
1700-2400 ▪ 15385 (Europe)
2100-2400 ▪ 11725 (Europe & N America)
2200-2400 ▪ 9445 (Europe & E North Am), 9460 (Europe)
2200-2400 ▪ 11710 (Europe & E North Am)
2300-2350 ▪ 11810 (Europe & E North Am)

UNITED ARAB EMIRATES—Arabic

UAE RADIO FROM ABU DHABI
0200-0400 6180 (Mideast), ▪ 13605 & ▪ 17775 (E Asia)
0200-0600 21630 (Australasia)
0200-0700 21735 (E Asia)
0400-0600 11945 (Mideast)
0600-0800 ▪ 15265 (Europe)
0600-1000 ▪ 21630 (Europe)
0600-1200 ▪ 15380 (Mideast)
0600-1500 ▪ 17825 (Mideast)
0700-1600 ▪ 21630 & ▪ 21735 (N Africa)
0800-1600 ▪ 21735 (Europe)
0900-1100 17770 (E Asia)
1000-1800 ▪ 15265 (Europe)
1100-1300 ▪ 13605 & ▪ 17770 (E Asia)
1200-1900 ▪ 9605 (Mideast)
1300-1600 15315 (Australasia)
1500-1900 ▪ 15385 (Mideast)
1600-2000 ▪ 13755 (N Africa), ▪ 17760 (Mideast)
1800-2200 11710/11690 (Europe)
1900-2200 9605 (Mideast)
2000-2200 ▪ 13755 & ▪ 17760 (N Africa)

Interior of the Haghia Sophia Museum in Istanbul, Turkey. Voice of Turkey programs on Turkish culture are now heard worldwide.

Keshin Color/TRT

UAE RADIO IN DUBAI

0000-0200	11950 (Irr), 13675 (Irr) (E North Am & C America)
0230-0330	12005, 13675 & 15400 (E North Am & C America)
0400-0530	15435 (Australasia), 17830 (E Asia), 21700 (Australasia)
0600-1030	13675, 15395 & 21605 (Europe)
1050-1200	15370 (N Africa)
1050-1330	13675, 15395 & 21605 (Europe)
1200-1330	13630 (N Africa)
1350-1600	13630 (N Africa), 13675, 15395 & 21605 (Europe)
1640-1730	11950/21605 (Europe)
1640-2050	13630 (N Africa), 13675 & 15395 (Europe)
1730-2050	11950 (Europe)
2050-2400	11950 (Irr) & 13675 (Irr) (E North Am & C America)

VENEZUELA—Spanish

ECOS DEL TORBES

0900-1300	4980
1300-2400	9640
2000-0400	4980

RADIO NACIONAL—(C America)

0000-0100, 0300-0400, 1100-1200, 1400-1500, 1800-1900 & 2100-2200	9540 (Irr)

RADIO TACHIRA

0130-0400	4830 (Irr)

1000-1300 & 2000-0130	4830

RADIO VALERA

0300-0330	Tu-Su 4840
0330-0400	4840 (Irr)
1000-0300	4840

VIETNAM—Vietnamese

VOICE OF VIETNAM

0000-0100	15110/13740 (C Africa)
0000-1600	9875
0100-1000	12035
0130-0230	ⓦ *5940* & ⓢ *7250* (E North Am)
0400-0500	ⓦ *13665* & ⓢ *17595* (W North Am)
1700-1800	9840/13740 (Europe)
1830-1930	ⓦ *7440* & ⓢ *12070* (Europe)
1930-2030	ⓦ *7390* & ⓢ *12030* (Europe)
2300-2400	9875

YUGOSLAVIA—Serbian

RADIO YUGOSLAVIA

0000-0030	ⓢ Su 9580 & ⓢ Su 11850 (E North Am)
0030-0100	ⓦ 6195, ⓦ 7115, ⓢ 9580 & ⓢ 11850 (E North Am)
0100-0130	ⓦ Su 6195 & ⓦ Su 7115 (E North Am)
0130-0200	ⓦ 6195 & ⓦ 7115 (E North Am)
1400-1430	ⓦ 11835 (Australasia)
2030-2100 ◀	6100 (W Europe), 7230 (Australasia)
2100-2130 ◀	Sa 6100 (W Europe), Sa 7230 (Australasia)
2330-2400	ⓢ 9580 & ⓢ 11850 (E North Am)

Weird Words

PASSPORT's Ultimate Glossary of World Band Terms and Abbreviations

All sorts of terms and abbreviations are used in world band radio. Some are specialized and benefit from explanation; several are foreign words that need translation; and yet others are simply adaptations of everyday usage.

Here, then, is PASSPORT's A-Z guide to what's what in world band buzzwords—including what each one means. For a thorough writeup on nomenclature used in evaluating how well a world band radio performs, see the Radio Database International White Paper, *How to Interpret Receiver Specifications and Lab Tests*.

Active Antenna. An antenna that electronically amplifies signals. Active antennas are typically mounted indoors, but some models can also be mounted outdoors. Active antennas take up relatively little space, but their amplification circuits may introduce certain types of problems that can result in unwanted sounds being heard. *See* Passive Antenna.

Adjacent-Channel Rejection. *See* Selectivity.

AGC. *See* Automatic Gain Control.

Alt. Freq. Alternative frequency or channel. Frequency or channel that may be used in place of the regularly scheduled one.

Amateur Radio. *See* Hams.

AM Band. The local radio band, which currently runs from 520 to 1611 kHz (530–1705 kHz in the Western Hemisphere), within the Medium Frequency (MF) range of the radio spectrum. Outside North America, it is usually called the mediumwave (MW) band. However, in parts of Latin America it is sometimes called, by the general public and a few stations, *onda larga*—longwave—strictly speaking, a misnomer.

Amplified Antenna. *See* Active Antenna.

Analog Frequency Readout. Needle-and-dial or "slide-rule" tuning, greatly inferior to synthesized tuning for scanning the world band airwaves. *See* Synthesizer.

Audio Quality. At PASSPORT, audio quality refers to what in computer testing is called "benchmark" quality. This means, primarily, the freedom from distortion of a signal fed through a receiver's entire circuitry—*not* just the audio stage—from the antenna input through to the speaker terminals. A lesser characteristic of audio quality is the audio bandwidth needed for pleasant world band reception of music. Also, *see* Enhanced Fidelity.

Automatic Gain Control (AGC). Smooths out fluctuations in signal strength brought about by fading, a regular occurrence with world band signals.

AV. A Voz—Portuguese for "The Voice." In PASSPORT, this term is also used to represent "The Voice of."

Bandwidth. A key variable that determines selectivity (*see*), bandwidth is the amount of radio signal at –6 dB a radio's circuitry will let pass, and thus be heard. With world band channel spacing at 5 kHz, the best single bandwidths are usually in the vicinity of 3 to 6 kHz. Better radios offer two or more selectable bandwidths: at least one of 5 to 7 kHz or so for when a station is in the clear, and one or more others between 2 to 4 kHz for when a station is hemmed in by other signals next to it. Proper selectivity is a key determinant of the aural quality of what you hear, and some newer models of tabletop receivers have dozens of bandwidths.

Baud. Measurement of the speed by which radioteletype (*see*), radiofax (*see*) and other digital data are transmitted. Baud is properly written entirely in lower case, and thus is abbreviated as b (baud), kb (kilobaud) or Mb (Megabaud). Baud rate standards are usually set by the international CCITT regulatory body.

BC. Broadcasting, Broadcasting Company, Broadcasting Corporation.

Broadcast. A radio or television transmission meant for the general public. *Compare* Utility Stations, Hams.

BS. Broadcasting Station, Broadcasting Service.

Cd. Ciudad—Spanish for "City."

Channel. An everyday term to indicate where a station is supposed to be located on the dial. World band channels are spaced exactly 5 kHz apart. Stations operating outside this norm are "off-channel" (for these, PASSPORT provides resolution to better than 1 kHz to aid in station identification).

Chugging, Chuffing. The sound made by some synthesized tuning systems when the tuning knob is turned. Called "chugging" or "chuffing," as it is suggestive of the rhythmic "chug, chug" sound of a steam engine or "chugalug" gulping.

Cl. Club, Clube.

Cult. Cultura, Cultural.

Default. The setting at which a control of a digitally operated electronic device, including many world band radios, normally operates, and to which it will eventually return (e.g., when the radio is next switched on).

Digital Frequency Display, Digital Tuning. *See* Synthesizer.

Digital Signal Processing. Technique in which computer-type circuitry is used to enhance the readability or other characteristics of an analog audio signal. Used on certain world band supersets; also, available as an add-on accessory.

Dipole Antenna. *See* Passive Antenna.

Domestic Service. *See* DS.

DS. Domestic Service—Broadcasting intended primarily for audiences in the broadcaster's home country. However, some domestic programs are beamed on world band to expatriates and other kinfolk abroad, as well as interested foreigners. *Compare* ES.

DSP. *See* Digital Signal Processing.

DX, DXers, DXing. From an old telegraph term "to DX"; that is, to communicate over a great distance. Thus, DXers are those who specialize in finding distant or exotic stations that are considered to be rare catches. Few world band listeners are considered to be regular DXers, but many others seek out DX stations every now and then—usually by bandscanning, which is greatly facilitated by PASSPORT's Blue Pages.

Dynamic Range. The ability of a receiver to handle weak signals in the presence of strong competing signals within or near the same world band segment (*see* World Band Spectrum). Sets with inferior dynamic range sometimes "overload," especially with external antennas, causing a mishmash of false signals up and down—and even beyond—the segment being received.

Earliest Heard (or Latest Heard). See key at the bottom of each Blue Page. If the PASSPORT monitoring team cannot establish the definite sign-on (or sign-off) time of a station, the earliest (or latest) time that the station could be traced is indicated by a left-facing or right-facing "arrowhead flag." This means that the station almost certainly operates beyond the time shown by that "flag." It also means that, unless you live relatively close to the station, you're unlikely to be able to hear it beyond that "flagged" time.

EBS. Economic Broadcasting Station, a type of station found in China.

ECSS. Exalted-carrier selectable sideband, a term no longer in general use, yet sometimes mis-used when it does appear. Properly used, it refers to the manual tuning of a conventional AM-mode signal using the receiver's single-sideband circuitry to zero-beat the receiver's BFO with the transmitted signal's carrier. *See* Synchronous Detector.

Ed, Educ. Educational, Educação, Educadora.

Electrical Noise. *See* Noise.

Em. Emissora, Emisora, Emissor, Emetteur—in effect, "station" in various languages.

Enhanced Fidelity. Radios with good audio performance and certain types of high-tech circuitry can improve the fidelity of world band signals. Among the newer fidelity-enhancing techniques is synchronous detection (*see*), especially when coupled with selectable sideband. Another potential technological advance to improve fidelity is digital world band transmission, which is actively being researched and tested.

EP. Emissor Provincial—Portuguese for "Provincial Station."

ER. Emissor Regional—Portuguese for "Regional Station."

Ergonomics. How handy and comfortable—intuitive—a set is to operate, especially hour after hour.

ES. External Service—Broadcasting intended primarily for audiences abroad. *Compare* DS.

External Service. *See* ES.

F. Friday.

Fax. *See* Radiofax.

Feeder, Shortwave. A utility transmission from the broadcaster's home country to a relay site or placement facility some distance away. Although these specialized transmissions carry world band programming, they are not intended to be received by the general public. Many world band radios can process these quasi-broadcasts anyway. Feeders operate in lower sideband (LSB), upper sideband (USB) or independent sideband (termed ISL if heard on the lower side, ISU if heard on the upper side) modes. Nearly all shortwave feeders have now been replaced by satellite and Internet audio feeders. *See* Single Sideband, Utility Stations.

Frequency. The standard term to indicate where a station is located on the dial—regardless of whether it is "on-channel" or "off-channel" (*see* Channel). Measured in kilohertz (kHz) or Megahertz

Radio Croatia, Zagreb editorial team (standing, from left) Dinka Rimac, Darko Mažuranić, Daniela Nadj and (seated) Jasna Božičević.   M. Prezelj

(MHz), which differ only in the placement of a decimal; e.g., 5975 kHz is the same as 5.975 MHz. Either measurement is equally valid, but to minimize confusion PASSPORT and most stations designate frequencies only in kHz.

Frequency Synthesizer. *See* Synthesizer, Frequency.

Front-End Selectivity. The ability of the initial stage of receiving circuitry to admit only limited frequency ranges into succeeding stages of circuitry. Good front-end selectivity keeps signals from other, powerful bands or segments from being superimposed upon the frequency range you're tuning. For example, a receiver with good front-end selectivity will receive only shortwave signals within the range 3200-3400 kHz. However, a receiver with mediocre front-end selectivity might allow powerful local mediumwave AM stations from 520-1700 kHz to be heard "ghosting in" between 3200 and 3400 kHz, along with the desired shortwave signals. Obviously, mediumwave AM signals don't belong on shortwave. Receivers with inadequate front-end selectivity can benefit from the addition of a preselector (*see*).

GMT. Greenwich Mean Time—*See* World Time.

Hams. Government-licensed amateur radio hobbyists who *transmit* to each other by radio, often by single sideband (*see*), within special amateur bands. Many of these bands are within the shortwave spectrum (*see*). This is the same spectrum used by world band radio, but world band and ham radio, which laymen sometimes confuse with each other, are two very separate entities. The easiest way is to think of hams as making something like phone calls, whereas world band stations are like long-distance versions of ordinary FM or mediumwave AM stations.

Harmonic, Harmonic Radiation, Harmonic Signal. Usually, an unwanted weak spurious repeat of a signal in multiple(s) of the fundamental, or "real," frequency. Thus, the third harmonic of a mediumwave AM station on 1120 kHz might be heard faintly on 4480 kHz within the world band spectrum. Stations almost always try to minimize harmonic radiation, as it wastes energy and spectrum space. However, in rare cases stations have been known to amplify a harmonic signal so they can operate inexpensively on a second frequency. Also, *see* Subharmonic.

Hash. Electrical noise. *See* Noise.

High Fidelity. *See* Enhanced Fidelity.

IBS. International Broadcasting Services, Ltd., publishers of *PASSPORT TO WORLD BAND RADIO* and other international broadcasting publications.

Image. A common type of spurious signal found on low-cost radios where a strong signal appears at reduced strength, usually on a frequency 900 kHz or 910 kHz lower down. For example, the BBC on 5975 kHz might repeat on 5075 kHz, its "image frequency." *See* Spurious-Signal Rejection.

Independent Sideband. *See* Single Sideband.

Interference. Sounds from other signals, notably on the same ("co-channel") frequency or nearby channels, that are disturbing the one you are trying to hear. Worthy radios reduce interference by having good selectivity (*see*). Nearby television sets and cable television wiring may also generate a special type of radio interference called TVI, a "growl" usually heard every 15 kHz or so.

International Reply Coupon (IRC). Sold by many post offices worldwide, IRCs amount to official international "scrip" that may be exchanged for postage in most countries of the world. Because they amount to an international form of postage repayment, they are handy for listeners trying to encourage foreign stations to write them back. However, IRCs are very costly for the amount in stamps that is provided in return. Too, some countries are not forthcoming about "cashing in" IRCs. Specifics are provided in the Addresses PLUS section of this book.

International Telecommunication Union (ITU). The regulatory body, headquartered in Geneva, for all international telecommunications, including world band radio. Sometimes incorrectly referred to as the "International Telecommunications Union." In recent years, the ITU has become increasingly ineffective as a regulatory body for world band, with much of its former role having been taken up by groups of affiliated international broadcasters voluntarily coordinating their schedules a number of times each year.

Internet Radio. *See* Web radio.

Inverted-L Antenna. *See* Passive Antenna.

Ionosphere. *See* Propagation.

IRC. *See* International Reply Coupon.

Irr. Irregular operation or hours of operation; i.e., schedule tends to be unpredictable.

ISB. Independent sideband. *See* Single Sideband.

ISL. Independent sideband, lower. *See* Feeder.

ISU. Independent sideband, upper. *See* Feeder.

ITU. *See* International Telecommunication Union.

Jamming. Deliberate interference to a transmission with the intent of discouraging listening. Jamming is practiced much less now than it was during the Cold War.

Keypad. On a world band radio, like a computer, a keypad can be used to control many variables. However, unlike a computer, the keypad on most world band radios consists of ten numeric or multifunction keys, usually supplemented by two more keys, as on a telephone keypad. Keypads are used primarily so you can enter a station's frequency for reception, and the best keypads have real keys (not a membrane) in the standard telephone format of 3x4 with "zero" under the "8" key. Many keypads are also used for presets, but this means you have to remember code numbers for stations (e.g., BBC 5975 kHz is "07"); handier radios either have separate keys for presets, or use LCD-displayed "pages" to access presets.

kHz. Kilohertz, the most common unit for measuring where a station is on the world band dial. Formerly known as "kilocycles per second," or kc/s. 1,000 kilohertz equals one Megahertz.

Kilohertz. *See* kHz.

kW. Kilowatt(s), the most common unit of measurement for transmitter power (*see*).

LCD. Liquid-crystal display. LCDs, if properly designed, are fairly easily seen in bright light, but require illumination under darker conditions. LCDs, typically gray on gray, also tend to have mediocre contrast, and sometimes can be read from only a certain angle or angles, but they consume nearly no battery power.

LED. Light-emitting diode. LEDs are very easily read in the dark or in normal room light, but consume battery power and are hard to read in bright light.

Location. The physical location of a station's transmitter, which may be different from the studio location. Transmitter location is useful as a guide to reception quality. For example, if you're in eastern North America and wish to listen to the Voice of Russia, a transmitter located in St. Petersburg will almost certainly provide better reception than one located in Siberia.

Longwave Band. The 148.5–283.5 kHz portion of the low-frequency (LF) radio spectrum used in Europe, the Near East, North Africa, Russia and Mongolia for domestic broadcasting. As a practical matter, these longwave signals, which have nothing to do with world band or other shortwave signals, are not usually audible in other parts of the world.

Longwire Antenna. *See* Passive Antenna.

LSB. Lower Sideband. *See* Feeder, Single Sideband.

LV. La Voix, La Voz—French and Spanish for "The Voice." In PASSPORT, this term is also used to represent "The Voice of."

M. Monday.

Mediumwave Band, Mediumwave AM Band. *See* AM Band.

Megahertz. *See* MHz.

Memory, Memories. *See* Preset.

Meters. An outdated unit of measurement used for individual world band segments of the shortwave spectrum. The frequency range covered by a given meters designation—also known as "wavelength"—can be gleaned from the following formula: *frequency (kHz)* = 299,792 ÷ *meters*. Thus, 49 meters comes out to a frequency of 6118 kHz—well within the range of frequencies included in that segment (*see* World Band Spectrum). Inversely, meters can be derived from the following: *meters* = 299,792 ÷ *frequency (kHz)*.

MHz. Megahertz, a common unit to measure where a station is on the dial. Formerly known as "Megacycles per second," or Mc/s. One Megahertz equals 1,000 kilohertz.

Mode. Method of transmission of radio signals. World band radio broadcasts are almost always in the analog AM mode, the same mode used in the mediumwave AM band (*see*). The AM mode consists of three components: two "sidebands" and one "carrier." Each sideband contains the same programming as the other, and the carrier carries no programming, so a few stations have experimented with the single-sideband (SSB) mode. SSB contains only one sideband, either the lower sideband (LSB) or upper sideband (USB), and a reduced carrier. It requires special radio circuitry to be demodulated, or made intelligible, which is the main reason SSB has not succeeded, and is not expected to succeed, as a world band mode. There are yet other modes used on shortwave, but not for world band. These include CW (Morse-type code), radiofax, RTTY (radioteletype) and narrow-band FM used by utility and ham stations. Narrow-band FM is not used for music, and is different from usual FM. *See* Single Sideband, ISB, ISL, ISU, LSB and USB.

N. New, Nueva, Nuevo, Nouvelle, Nacional, National, Nationale. *Nac. Nacional*. Spanish and Portuguese for "National."

Nat, Natl, Nat'l. National, Nationale.

Noise. Static, buzzes, pops and the like caused by the earth's atmosphere (typically lightning), and to a lesser extent by galactic noise. Also, electrical noise emanates from such man-made sources as electric blankets, fish-tank heaters, heating pads, electrical and gasoline motors, light dimmers, flickering light bulbs, non-incandescent lights, computers and computer peripherals, office machines, electrical fences, and faulty electrical utility wiring and related components.

Other. Programs are in a language other than one of the world's primary languages.

Overloading. *See* Dynamic Range.

Passive Antenna. An antenna that is not electronically amplified. Typically, these are mounted outdoors, although the "tape-measure" type that comes as an accessory with some portables is usually strung indoors. For world band reception, virtually all outboard models for consumers are made from wire, rather than rod-type or tubular elements. The two most common designs are the inverted-L (so-called "longwire") and trapped dipole (either horizontal or sloper). These antennas are preferable to active antennas (*see*), and are reviewed in detail in the Radio Database International White Paper, PASSPORT *Evaluation of Popular Outdoor Antennas (Unamplified)*.

PBS. People's Broadcasting Station.

PLL (Phase-Locked Loop). With world band receivers, a PLL circuit means that the radio can be tuned digitally, often using a number of handy tuning techniques, such as a keypad and presets *(see)*.

Power. Transmitter power *before* amplification by the antenna, expressed in kilowatts (kW). The present range of world band powers is 0.01 to 1,000 kW.

Power Lock. *See* Travel Power Lock.

PR. People's Republic.

Preselector. A device—typically outboard, but sometimes inboard—that effectively limits the range of frequencies which can enter a receiver's circuitry or the circuitry of an active antenna *(see)*; that is, which improves front-end selectivity *(see)*. For example, a preselector may let in the range 15000-16000 kHz, thus helping ensure that your receiver or active antenna will encounter no problems within that range caused by signals from, say, 5800-6200 kHz or local mediumwave AM signals (520-1705 kHz). This range usually can be varied, manually or automatically, according to the frequency to which the receiver is being tuned. A preselector may be passive (unamplified) or active (amplified).

Preset. Allows you to select a station pre-stored in a radio's memory. The handiest presets require only one push of a button, as on a car radio.

Propagation. World band signals travel, like a basketball, up and down from the station to your radio. The "floor" below is the earth's surface, whereas the "player's hand" on high is the *ionosphere*, a gaseous layer that envelops the planet. While the earth's surface remains pretty much the same from day to day, the ionosphere—nature's own passive "satellite"—varies in how it propagates radio signals, depending on how much sunlight hits the "bounce points." Thus, some world band segments do well mainly by day, whereas others are best by night. During winter there's less sunlight, so the "night bands" become unusually active, whereas the "day bands" become correspondingly less useful (*see* World Band Spectrum). Day-to-day changes in the sun's weather also cause short-term changes in world band radio reception; this explains why some days you can hear rare signals.

Additionally, the 11-year sunspot cycle has a long-term effect on propagation. Currently, the sunspot cycle is at a vigorous phase. This means that the upper world band segments will remain unusually lively over the coming years.

PS. Provincial Station, Pangsong.

Pto. Puerto, Porto.

QSL. *See* Verification.

R. Radio, Radiodiffusion, Radiodifusora, Radiodifusão, Radiophonikos, Radiostantsiya, Radyo, Radyosu, and so forth.

Radiofax, Radio Facsimile. Like ordinary telefax (facsimile by telephone lines), but by radio.

Radioteletype (RTTY). Characters, but not illustrations, transmitted by radio. *See* Baud.

RDI. Radio Database International, a registered trademark of International Broadcasting Services, Ltd.

Receiver. Synonym for a radio, but sometimes—especially when called a "communications receiver"—implying a radio with superior tough-signal performance.

Reduced Carrier. *See* Single Sideband.

Reg. Regional.

Relay. A retransmission facility, often highlighted in "Worldwide Broadcasts in English" and "Voices from Home" in PASSPORT's WorldScan® section. Relay facilities are generally considered to be located outside the broadcaster's country. Being closer to the target audience, they usually provide superior reception. *See* Feeder.

Rep. Republic, République, República.

The Herald Broadcasting Syndicate continues to air Christian Science programs to the world, even though much of its former broadcasting operation has been sold. The Mother Church—First Church of Christ, Scientist—is a landmark in Boston, Massachusetts.

B. Grant

RN. *See* R and N.

RS. Radio Station, Radiostantsiya, Radiostudiya, Radiophonikos Stathmos.

RT, RTV. Radiodiffusion Télévision, Radio Télévision, and so forth.

RTTY. *See* Radioteletype.

S. As an icon ⬛: aired summer (midyear) only. As an ordinary letter: San, Santa, Santo, São, Saint, Sainte. Also, South.

Sa. Saturday.

Scan, Scanning. Circuitry within a radio that allows it to bandscan or memory-scan automatically.

Segments. *See* Shortwave Spectrum.

Selectivity. The ability of a radio to reject interference (*see*) from signals on adjacent channels. Thus, also known as adjacent-channel rejection, a key variable in radio quality. Also, *see* "Bandwidth" and "Synchronous Detector".

Sensitivity. The ability of a radio to receive weak signals; thus, also known as weak-signal sensitivity. Of special importance if you're listening during the day, or if you're located in such parts of the world as Western North America, Hawaii and Australasia, where signals tend to be relatively weak.

Shortwave Spectrum. The shortwave spectrum—also known as the High Frequency (HF) spectrum—is, strictly speaking, that portion of the radio spectrum from 3-30 MHz (3,000-30,000 kHz). However, common usage places it from 2.3-30 MHz (2,300-30,000 kHz). World band operates on shortwave within 14 discrete segments between 2.3-26.1 MHz, with the rest of the shortwave spectrum being occupied by hams (*see*) and utility stations (*see*). Also, *see* the detailed "Best Times and Frequencies" article elsewhere in this edition.

Sideband. *See* Mode.

Single Sideband, Independent Sideband. Spectrum- and power-conserving modes of transmission commonly used by util-ity stations and hams. Very few broadcasters use, or are expected ever to use, these modes. Many world band radios are already capable of demodulating single-sideband transmissions, and some can even process independent-sideband signals. Certain single-sideband transmissions operate with a minimum of carrier reduction, which allows them to be listened to, albeit with some distortion, on ordinary radios not equipped to demodulate single sideband. Properly designed synchronous detectors (*see*) may prevent such distortion. *See* Feeder, Mode.

Site. *See* Location.

Slew Controls. Elevator-button-type up and down controls to tune a radio. On many radios with synthesized tuning, slewing is used in lieu of tuning by knob. Better is when slew controls are complemented by a tuning knob, which is more versatile.

Sloper Antenna. *See* Passive Antenna.

SPR. Spurious (false) extra signal from a transmitter actually operating on another frequency. One such type is harmonic (*see*).

Spurious-Signal Rejection. The ability of a radio receiver not to produce false, or "ghost," signals that might otherwise interfere with the clarity of the station you're trying to hear. *See* Image.

St, Sta, Sto. Abbreviations for words that mean "Saint."

Static. *See* Noise.

Su. Sunday.

Subharmonic. A harmonic heard at 1.5 or 0.5 times the operating frequency. This anomaly is caused by the way signals are generated within vintage-model transmitters, and thus cannot take place with modern transmitters. For example, the subharmonic of a station on 3360 kHz might be heard faintly on 5040 or 1680 kHz. Also, *see* Harmonic.

Sunspot Cycle. *See* Propagation.

Synchronous Detector. World band radios are increasingly coming equipped with this high-tech circuit that greatly reduces fading distortion. Better synchronous detectors also allow for selectable sideband; that is, the ability to select the clearer of the two sidebands of a world band or other AM-mode signal. *See* Mode.

Synchronous Selectable Sideband. *See* Synchronous Detector.

Synthesizer, Frequency. Simple radios often use archaic needle-and-dial tuning that makes it difficult to find a desired channel or to tell which station you are hearing, except by ear. Other models utilize a digital frequency synthesizer to tune to signals without your having to hunt and peck. Among other things, such synthesizers allow for push-button tuning and presets, and display the exact frequency digitally—pluses that make tuning to the world considerably easier. Virtually a "must" feature.

Target. Where a transmission is beamed.

Th. Thursday.

Travel Power Lock. Control to disable the on/off switch to prevent a radio from switching on accidentally.

Transmitter Power. *See* Power.

Trapped Dipole Antenna. *See* Passive Antenna.

Tu. Tuesday.

Universal Day. *See* World Time.

Universal Time. *See* World Time.

URL. Universal Resource Locator; i.e., the Internet address for a given Webpage.

USB. Upper Sideband. *See* Feeder, Single Sideband.

UTC. *See* World Time.

Utility Stations. Most signals within the shortwave spectrum are not world band stations. Rather, they are utility stations—radio telephones, ships at sea, aircraft and the like—that transmit strange sounds (growls, gurgles, dih-dah sounds, etc.) point-to-point and are not intended to be heard by the general public. *Compare* Broadcast, Hams and Feeders.

v. Variable frequency; i.e., one that is unstable or drifting because of a transmitter malfunction or, less often, to avoid jamming or other interference.

Verification. A "QSL" card or letter from a station verifying that a listener indeed heard that particular station. In order to stand a chance of qualifying for a verification card or letter, you need to provide the station heard with, at a minimum, the following information in a three-number "SIO" code, in which "SIO 555" is best and "SIO 111" is worst:

- **S**ignal strength, with 5 being of excellent quality, comparable to that of a local mediumwave AM station, and 1 being inaudible or at least so weak as to be virtually unintelligible. 2 (faint, but somewhat intelligible), 3 (moderate strength) and 4 (good strength) represent the signal-strength levels usually encountered with world band stations.
- **I**nterference from other stations, with 5 indicating no interference whatsoever, and 1 indicating such extreme interference that the desired signal is virtually drowned out. 2 (heavy interference), 3 (moderate interference) and 4 (slight interference) represent the differing degrees of interference more typically encountered with world band signals. If possible, indicate the names of the interfering station(s) and the channel(s) they are on. Otherwise, at least describe what the interference sounds like.
- **O**verall quality of the signal, with 5 being best, 1 worst.
- In addition to providing SIO findings, you should indicate which programs you've heard, as well as comments on how you liked or disliked those programs. Refer to the "Addresses PLUS" section of this edition for information on where and to whom your report should be sent, and whether return postage should be included.
- Because of the time involved in listening, few stations wish to receive tape recordings of their transmissions.

Vo. Voice of.

W. As an icon 🅆: aired winter only. As a regular letter: Wednesday.

Wavelength. *See* Meters.

Weak-Signal Sensitivity. *See* Sensitivity.

Webcasting. *See* Web Radio.

Web Radio. Broadcasts aired to the public over the World Wide Web. These stations worldwide include existing FM, mediumwave AM and world band stations simulcasting over the Web ("Webcasting"), or Web-only "stations."

World Band Radio. Similar to regular mediumwave AM band and FM band radio, except that world band stations can be heard over enormous distances and thus often carry news, music and entertainment programs created especially for audiences abroad. Some world band stations have audiences of up to 120 million each day. Some 600 million people worldwide are believed to listen to world band radio.

World Band Spectrum. *See* "Best Times and Frequencies" elsewhere in this edition.

World Day. *See* World Time.

World Time. Also known as Coordinated Universal Time (UTC), Greenwich Mean Time (GMT) and Zulu time (Z). With nearly 170 countries on world band radio, if each announced its own local time you would need a calculator to figure it all out. To get around this, a single international time—World Time—is used. The difference between World Time and local time is detailed in the "Addresses PLUS" section of this edition, the "Compleat Idiot's Guide to Getting Started" and especially in the last page of this edition. It is also determined simply by listening to World Time announcements given on the hour by world band stations—or minute by minute by WWV and WWVH in the United States on such frequencies as 5000, 10000 and 15000 kHz, or CHU in Canada on 3330, 7335 and 14670 kHz. A 24-hour clock format is used, so "1800 World Time" means 6:00 PM World Time. If you're in, say, North America, Eastern Time is five hours behind World Time winters and four hours behind World Time summers, so 1800 World Time would be 1:00 PM EST or 2:00 PM EDT. The easiest solution is to use a 24-hour clock set to World Time. Many radios already have these built in, and World Time clocks are also available as accessories. World Time also applies to the days of the week. So if it's 9:00 PM (21:00) Wednesday in New York during the winter, it's 0200 *Thursday* World Time.

WS. World Service.

Printed in USA

Jock Elliott, Advertising Manager

IBS, Ltd.

29 Pickering Lane

Troy, NY 12180 USA

Voice: 518-271-1761

Fax: 518-271-6131

E-mail: media@passband.com

PASSPORT's Blue Pages— 2000

Channel-by-Channel Guide to World Band Schedules

If you scan the world band airwaves, you'll discover lots more stations than those aimed your way. That's because shortwave signals are capriciously scattered by the heavens, so you can often hear stations not targeted to your area.

PASSPORT's Blue Pages Help Identify Stations

But just dialing around can be frustrating if you don't have a "map"—PASSPORT's Blue Pages. Let's say that you've stumbled across something Asian-sounding on 7410 kHz at 2035 World Time. PASSPORT's Blue Pages show All India Radio in a distinctive tongue beamed to Western Europe, with a hefty 250 kW of power. These clues suggest this is probably what you're hearing, even if you're not in Europe. The Blue Pages also show that

English from India will commence on that same channel in about ten minutes.

Schedules for Entire Year

Times and days of the week are in World Time; for local times, see Addresses PLUS. Some stations are shown as one hour earlier (◄) or later (►) midyear—typically April through October. Stations may also extend their hours for holidays or sports events.

To be as helpful as possible throughout the year, PASSPORT's Blue Pages include not just observed activity and factual schedules, but also those which we have creatively opined will take place. This predictive information is original from us, and although it's of real value when tuning the airwaves, it is inherently not so exact as real-time data.

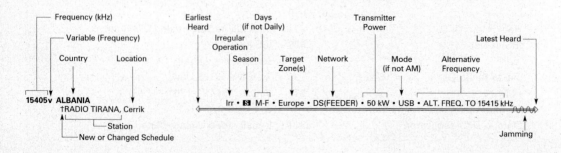

FREQUENCY　　COUNTRY, STATION, LOCATION　　　　　TARGET • NETWORK • POWER (kW)　　　World Time

0　1　2　3　4　5　6　7　8　9　10　11　12　13　14　15　16　17　18　19　20　21　22　23　24

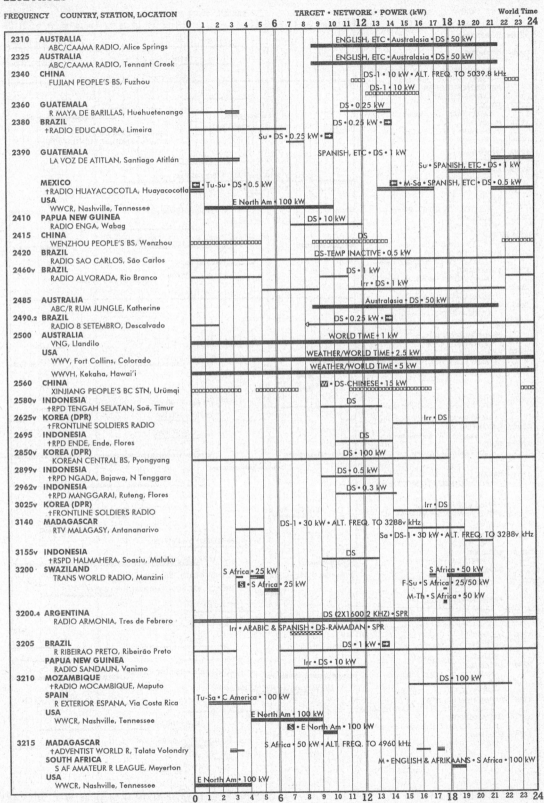

2310	**AUSTRALIA**	ENGLISH, ETC • Australasia • DS • 50 kW
	ABC/CAAMA RADIO, Alice Springs	
2325	**AUSTRALIA**	ENGLISH, ETC • Australasia • DS • 50 kW
	ABC/CAAMA RADIO, Tennant Creek	
2340	**CHINA**	DS-1 • 10 kW • ALT. FREQ. TO 5039.8 kHz
	FUJIAN PEOPLE'S BS, Fuzhou	DS-1 • 10 kW
2360	**GUATEMALA**	DS • 0.25 kW
	R MAYA DE BARILLAS, Huehuetenango	
2380	**BRAZIL**	DS • 0.25 kW • ▣
	†RADIO EDUCADORA, Limeira	Su • DS • 0.25 kW • ▣
2390	**GUATEMALA**	SPANISH, ETC • DS • 1 kW
	LA VOZ DE ATITLAN, Santiago Atitlán	Su • SPANISH, ETC • DS • 1 kW
	MEXICO	▣ • Tu-Su • DS • 0.5 kW ▣ • M-Sa • SPANISH, ETC • DS • 0.5 kW
	†RADIO HUAYACOCOTLA, Huayacocotla	
	USA	E North Am • 100 kW
	WWCR, Nashville, Tennessee	
2410	**PAPUA NEW GUINEA**	DS • 10 kW
	RADIO ENGA, Wabag	
2415	**CHINA**	DS
	WENZHOU PEOPLE'S BS, Wenzhou	
2420	**BRAZIL**	DS-TEMP INACTIVE • 0.5 kW
	RADIO SAO CARLOS, São Carlos	
2460v	**BRAZIL**	DS • 1 kW
	RADIO ALVORADA, Rio Branco	Irr • DS • 1 kW
2485	**AUSTRALIA**	Australasia • DS • 50 kW
	ABC/R RUM JUNGLE, Katherine	
2490.2	**BRAZIL**	DS • 0.25 kW • ▣
	RADIO 8 SETEMBRO, Descalvado	
2500	**AUSTRALIA**	WORLD TIME • 1 kW
	VNG, Llandilo	
	USA	WEATHER/WORLD TIME • 2.5 kW
	WWV, Fort Collins, Colorado	
	WWVH, Kekaha, Hawai'i	WEATHER/WORLD TIME • 5 kW
2560	**CHINA**	W • DS-CHINESE • 15 kW
	XINJIANG PEOPLE'S BC STN, Urümqi	
2580v	**INDONESIA**	DS
	†RPD TENGAH SELATAN, Soë, Timur	
2625v	**KOREA (DPR)**	Irr • DS
	†FRONTLINE SOLDIERS RADIO	
2695	**INDONESIA**	DS
	†RPD ENDE, Ende, Flores	
2850v	**KOREA (DPR)**	DS • 100 kW
	KOREAN CENTRAL BS, Pyongyang	
2899v	**INDONESIA**	DS • 0.5 kW
	†RPD NGADA, Bajawa, N Tenggara	
2962v	**INDONESIA**	DS • 0.3 kW
	†RPD MANGGARAI, Ruteng, Flores	
3025v	**KOREA (DPR)**	Irr • DS
	†FRONTLINE SOLDIERS RADIO	
3140	**MADAGASCAR**	DS-1 • 30 kW • ALT. FREQ. TO 3288v kHz
	RTV MALAGASY, Antananarivo	Sa • DS-1 • 30 kW • ALT. FREQ. TO 3288v kHz
3155v	**INDONESIA**	DS
	†RSPD HALMAHERA, Soasiu, Maluku	
3200	**SWAZILAND**	S Africa • 25 kW　　　　S Africa • 50 kW
	TRANS WORLD RADIO, Manzini	⑤ • S Africa • 25 kW　F-Su • S Africa • 25/50 kW
		M-Th • S Africa • 50 kW
3200.4	**ARGENTINA**	DS (2X1600 2 KHZ) • SPR
	RADIO ARMONIA, Tres de Febrero	Irr • ARABIC & SPANISH • DS-RAMADAN • SPR
3205	**BRAZIL**	DS • 1 kW • ▣
	R RIBEIRAO PRETO, Ribeirão Preto	
	PAPUA NEW GUINEA	Irr • DS • 10 kW
	RADIO SANDAUN, Vanimo	
3210	**MOZAMBIQUE**	DS • 100 kW
	†RADIO MOCAMBIQUE, Maputo	
	SPAIN	Tu-Sa • C America • 100 kW
	R EXTERIOR ESPANA, Via Costa Rica	
	USA	E North Am • 100 kW
	WWCR, Nashville, Tennessee	⑤ • E North Am • 100 kW
3215	**MADAGASCAR**	S Africa • 50 kW • ALT. FREQ. TO 4960 kHz
	†ADVENTIST WORLD R, Talata Volondry	
	SOUTH AFRICA	M • ENGLISH & AFRIKAANS • S Africa • 100 kW
	S AF AMATEUR R LEAGUE, Meyerton	
	USA	E North Am • 100 kW
	WWCR, Nashville, Tennessee	

0　1　2　3　4　5　6　7　8　9　10　11　12　13　14　15　16　17　18　19　20　21　22　23　24

ENGLISH ▬　ARABIC ▦　CHINESE □□□　FRENCH ▬　GERMAN ▬　RUSSIAN ═　SPANISH ▬　OTHER ▬

FREQUENCY   COUNTRY, STATION, LOCATION   TARGET • NETWORK • POWER (kW)   World Time

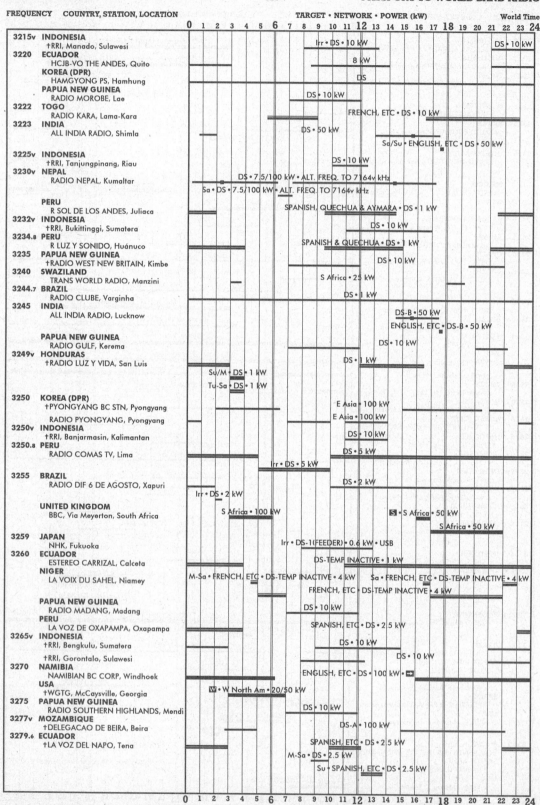

Frequency	Country, Station, Location	Target • Network • Power (kW)
3215v	**INDONESIA** †RRI, Manado, Sulawesi	Irr • DS • 10 kW / DS • 10 kW
3220	**ECUADOR** HCJB-VO THE ANDES, Quito	8 kW
	KOREA (DPR) HAMGYONG PS, Hamhung	DS
	PAPUA NEW GUINEA RADIO MOROBE, Lae	DS • 10 kW
3222	**TOGO** RADIO KARA, Lama-Kara	FRENCH, ETC • DS • 10 kW
3223	**INDIA** ALL INDIA RADIO, Shimla	DS • 50 kW / Sa/Su • ENGLISH, ETC • DS • 50 kW
3225v	**INDONESIA** †RRI, Tanjungpinang, Riau	DS • 10 kW
3230v	**NEPAL** RADIO NEPAL, Kumaltar	DS • 7.5/100 kW • ALT. FREQ. TO 7164v kHz / Sa • DS • 7.5/100 kW • ALT. FREQ. TO 7164v kHz
	PERU R SOL DE LOS ANDES, Juliaca	SPANISH, QUECHUA & AYMARA • DS • 1 kW
3232v	**INDONESIA** †RRI, Bukittinggi, Sumatera	DS • 10 kW
3234.8	**PERU** R LUZ Y SONIDO, Huánuco	SPANISH & QUECHUA • DS • 1 kW
3235	**PAPUA NEW GUINEA** †RADIO WEST NEW BRITAIN, Kimbe	DS • 10 kW
3240	**SWAZILAND** TRANS WORLD RADIO, Manzini	S Africa • 25 kW
3244.7	**BRAZIL** RADIO CLUBE, Varginha	DS • 1 kW
3245	**INDIA** ALL INDIA RADIO, Lucknow	DS-B • 50 kW / ENGLISH, ETC • DS-B • 50 kW
	PAPUA NEW GUINEA RADIO GULF, Kerema	DS • 10 kW
3249v	**HONDURAS** †RADIO LUZ Y VIDA, San Luis	DS • 1 kW / Su/M • DS • 1 kW / Tu-Sa • DS • 1 kW
3250	**KOREA (DPR)** †PYONGYANG BC STN, Pyongyang	E Asia • 100 kW
	RADIO PYONGYANG, Pyongyang	E Asia • 100 kW
3250v	**INDONESIA** †RRI, Banjarmasin, Kalimantan	DS • 10 kW
3250.8	**PERU** RADIO COMAS TV, Lima	DS • 5 kW / Irr • DS • 5 kW
3255	**BRAZIL** RADIO DIF 6 DE AGOSTO, Xapuri	DS • 2 kW / Irr • DS • 2 kW
	UNITED KINGDOM BBC, Via Meyerton, South Africa	S Africa • 100 kW / ⑤ • S Africa • 50 kW / S Africa • 50 kW
3259	**JAPAN** NHK, Fukuoka	Irr • DS-1(FEEDER) • 0.6 kW • USB
3260	**ECUADOR** ESTEREO CARRIZAL, Calceta	DS-TEMP INACTIVE • 1 kW
	NIGER LA VOIX DU SAHEL, Niamey	M-Sa • FRENCH, ETC • DS-TEMP INACTIVE • 4 kW / Sa • FRENCH, ETC • DS-TEMP INACTIVE • 4 kW / FRENCH, ETC • DS-TEMP INACTIVE • 4 kW
	PAPUA NEW GUINEA RADIO MADANG, Madang	DS • 10 kW
	PERU LA VOZ DE OXAPAMPA, Oxapampa	SPANISH, ETC • DS • 2.5 kW
3265v	**INDONESIA** †RRI, Bengkulu, Sumatera	DS • 10 kW
	†RRI, Gorontalo, Sulawesi	DS • 10 kW
3270	**NAMIBIA** NAMIBIAN BC CORP, Windhoek	ENGLISH, ETC • DS • 100 kW • ⇨
	USA †WGTG, McCaysville, Georgia	ⓌW • W North Am • 20/50 kW
3275	**PAPUA NEW GUINEA** RADIO SOUTHERN HIGHLANDS, Mendi	DS • 10 kW
3277v	**MOZAMBIQUE** †DELEGACAO DE BEIRA, Beira	DS-A • 100 kW
3279.6	**ECUADOR** †LA VOZ DEL NAPO, Tena	SPANISH, ETC • DS • 2.5 kW / M-Sa • DS • 2.5 kW / Su • SPANISH, ETC • DS • 2.5 kW

FREQUENCY   COUNTRY, STATION, LOCATION   TARGET · NETWORK · POWER (kW)   World Time

0 1 2 3 4 5 6 7 8 9 10 11 12 13 14 15 16 17 18 19 20 21 22 23 24

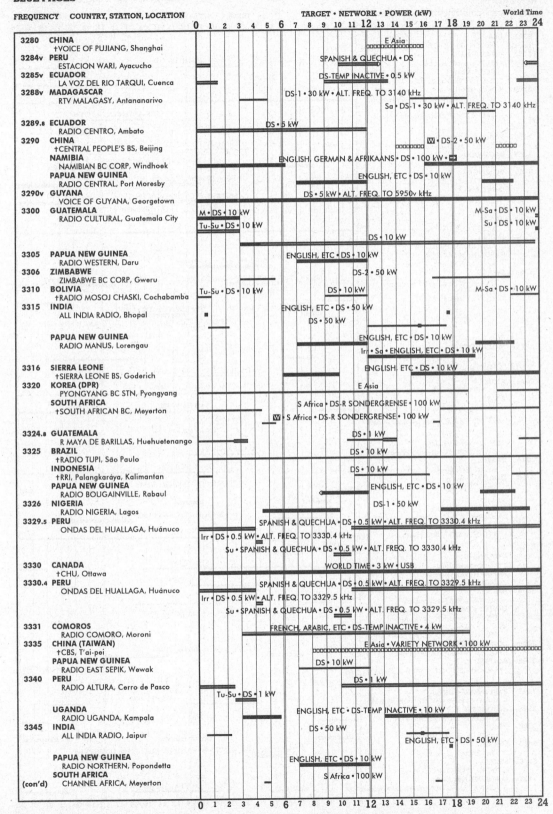

Frequency	Country, Station, Location	Target · Network · Power
3280	**CHINA** †VOICE OF PUJIANG, Shanghai	E Asia
3284v	**PERU** ESTACION WARI, Ayacucho	SPANISH & QUECHUA · DS
3285v	**ECUADOR** LA VOZ DEL RIO TARQUI, Cuenca	DS-TEMP INACTIVE · 0.5 kW
3288v	**MADAGASCAR** RTV MALAGASY, Antananarivo	DS-1 · 30 kW · ALT. FREQ. TO 3140 kHz / Sa · DS-1 · 30 kW · ALT. FREQ. TO 3140 kHz
3289.8	**ECUADOR** RADIO CENTRO, Ambato	DS · 5 kW
3290	**CHINA** †CENTRAL PEOPLE'S BS, Beijing	W · DS-2 · 50 kW
	NAMIBIA NAMIBIAN BC CORP, Windhoek	ENGLISH, GERMAN & AFRIKAANS · DS · 100 kW · ⟷
	PAPUA NEW GUINEA RADIO CENTRAL, Port Moresby	ENGLISH, ETC · DS · 10 kW
3290v	**GUYANA** VOICE OF GUYANA, Georgetown	DS · 5 kW · ALT. FREQ. TO 5950v kHz
3300	**GUATEMALA** RADIO CULTURAL, Guatemala City	M · DS · 10 kW / Tu-Su · DS · 10 kW / DS · 10 kW / M-Sa · DS · 10 kW / Su · DS · 10 kW
3305	**PAPUA NEW GUINEA** RADIO WESTERN, Daru	ENGLISH, ETC · DS · 10 kW
3306	**ZIMBABWE** ZIMBABWE BC CORP, Gweru	DS-2 · 50 kW
3310	**BOLIVIA** †RADIO MOSOJ CHASKI, Cochabamba	Tu-Su · DS · 10 kW / DS · 10 kW / M-Sa · DS · 10 kW
3315	**INDIA** ALL INDIA RADIO, Bhopal	ENGLISH, ETC · DS · 50 kW / DS · 50 kW
	PAPUA NEW GUINEA RADIO MANUS, Lorengau	ENGLISH, ETC · DS · 10 kW / Irr · Sa · ENGLISH, ETC · DS · 10 kW
3316	**SIERRA LEONE** †SIERRA LEONE BS, Goderich	ENGLISH, ETC · DS · 10 kW
3320	**KOREA (DPR)** PYONGYANG BC STN, Pyongyang	E Asia
	SOUTH AFRICA †SOUTH AFRICAN BC, Meyerton	S Africa · DS-R SONDERGRENSE · 100 kW / W · S Africa · DS-R SONDERGRENSE · 100 kW
3324.8	**GUATEMALA** R MAYA DE BARILLAS, Huehuetenango	DS · 1 kW
3325	**BRAZIL** †RADIO TUPI, São Paulo	DS · 10 kW
	INDONESIA †RRI, Palangkaráya, Kalimantan	DS · 10 kW
	PAPUA NEW GUINEA RADIO BOUGAINVILLE, Rabaul	ENGLISH, ETC · DS · 10 kW
3326	**NIGERIA** RADIO NIGERIA, Lagos	DS-1 · 50 kW
3329.5	**PERU** ONDAS DEL HUALLAGA, Huánuco	SPANISH & QUECHUA · DS · 0.5 kW · ALT. FREQ. TO 3330.4 kHz / Irr · DS · 0.5 kW · ALT. FREQ. TO 3330.4 kHz / Su · SPANISH & QUECHUA · DS · 0.5 kW · ALT. FREQ. TO 3330.4 kHz
3330	**CANADA** †CHU, Ottawa	WORLD TIME · 3 kW · USB
3330.4	**PERU** ONDAS DEL HUALLAGA, Huánuco	SPANISH & QUECHUA · DS · 0.5 kW · ALT. FREQ. TO 3329.5 kHz / Irr · DS · 0.5 kW · ALT. FREQ. TO 3329.5 kHz / Su · SPANISH & QUECHUA · DS · 0.5 kW · ALT. FREQ. TO 3329.5 kHz
3331	**COMOROS** RADIO COMORO, Moroni	FRENCH, ARABIC, ETC · DS-TEMP INACTIVE · 4 kW
3335	**CHINA (TAIWAN)** †CBS, T'ai-pei	E Asia · VARIETY NETWORK · 100 kW
	PAPUA NEW GUINEA RADIO EAST SEPIK, Wewak	DS · 10 kW
3340	**PERU** RADIO ALTURA, Cerro de Pasco	DS · 1 kW / Tu-Su · DS · 1 kW
	UGANDA RADIO UGANDA, Kampala	ENGLISH, ETC · DS-TEMP INACTIVE · 10 kW
3345	**INDIA** ALL INDIA RADIO, Jaipur	DS · 50 kW / ENGLISH, ETC · DS · 50 kW
	PAPUA NEW GUINEA RADIO NORTHERN, Popondetta	ENGLISH, ETC · DS · 10 kW
(con'd)	**SOUTH AFRICA** CHANNEL AFRICA, Meyerton	S Africa · 100 kW

0 1 2 3 4 5 6 7 8 9 10 11 12 13 14 15 16 17 18 19 20 21 22 23 24

ENGLISH ▬▬   ARABIC ≋≋≋   CHINESE □□□   FRENCH ═══   GERMAN ▬▬   RUSSIAN ══   SPANISH ▬▬   OTHER ▬▬

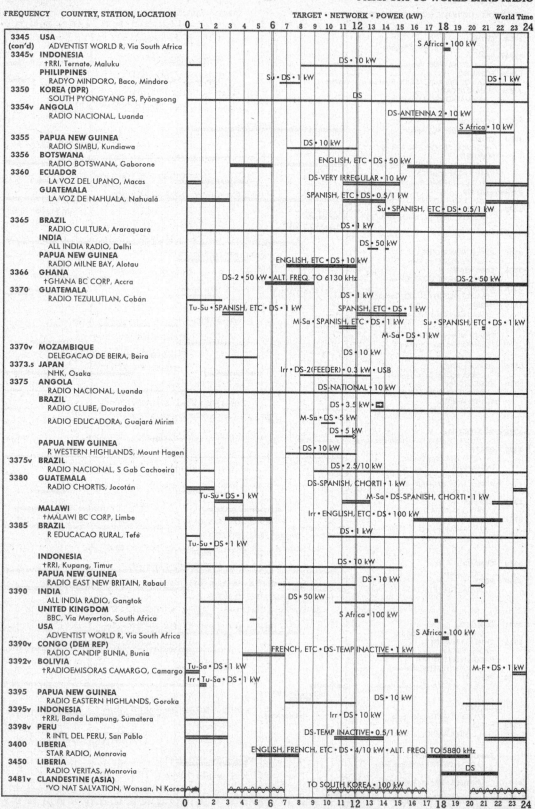

FREQUENCY	COUNTRY, STATION, LOCATION	TARGET • NETWORK • POWER (kW)	World Time

SEASONAL S OR W   **1-HR TIMESHIFT MIDYEAR ⬅ OR ➡**   **JAMMING / OR ∧**   **EARLIEST HEARD ◁**   **LATEST HEARD ▷**   **NEW FOR 2000 †**

FREQUENCY   COUNTRY, STATION, LOCATION   TARGET • NETWORK • POWER (kW)   World Time

0 1 2 3 4 5 6 7 8 9 10 11 12 13 14 15 16 17 18 19 20 21 22 23 24

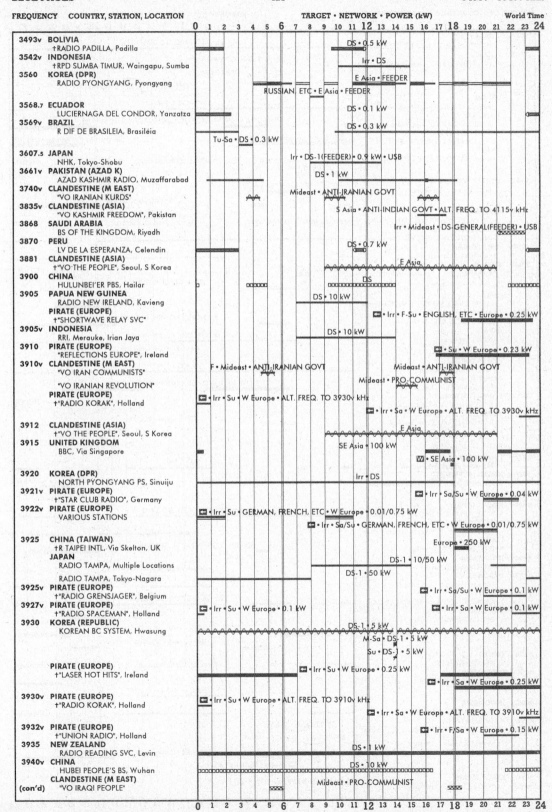

Frequency	Country, Station, Location	Target • Network • Power
3493v	**BOLIVIA** †RADIO PADILLA, Padilla	DS • 0.5 kW
3542v	**INDONESIA** †RPD SUMBA TIMUR, Waingapu, Sumba	Irr • DS
3560	**KOREA (DPR)** RADIO PYONGYANG, Pyongyang	E Asia • FEEDER / RUSSIAN, ETC • E Asia • FEEDER
3568.7	**ECUADOR** LUCIERNAGA DEL CONDOR, Yanzatza	DS • 0.1 kW
3569v	**BRAZIL** R DIF DE BRASILEIA, Brasiléia	DS • 0.3 kW / Tu-Sa • DS • 0.3 kW
3607.5	**JAPAN** NHK, Tokyo-Shobu	Irr • DS-1(FEEDER) 0.9 kW • USB
3661v	**PAKISTAN (AZAD K)** AZAD KASHMIR RADIO, Muzaffarabad	DS • 1 kW
3740v	**CLANDESTINE (M EAST)** "VO IRANIAN KURDS"	Mideast • ANTI-IRANIAN GOVT
3835v	**CLANDESTINE (ASIA)** "VO KASHMIR FREEDOM", Pakistan	S Asia • ANTI-INDIAN GOVT • ALT. FREQ. TO 4115v kHz
3868	**SAUDI ARABIA** BS OF THE KINGDOM, Riyadh	Irr • Mideast • DS-GENERAL(FEEDER) • USB
3870	**PERU** LV DE LA ESPERANZA, Celendin	DS • 0.7 kW
3881	**CLANDESTINE (ASIA)** †"VO THE PEOPLE", Seoul, S Korea	E Asia
3900	**CHINA** HULUNBEI'ER PBS, Hailar	DS
3905	**PAPUA NEW GUINEA** RADIO NEW IRELAND, Kavieng	DS • 10 kW
	PIRATE (EUROPE) †"SHORTWAVE RELAY SVC"	Irr • F-Su • ENGLISH, ETC • Europe • 0.25 kW
3905v	**INDONESIA** RRI, Merauke, Irian Jaya	DS • 10 kW
3910	**PIRATE (EUROPE)** "REFLECTIONS EUROPE", Ireland	Su • W Europe • 0.23 kW
3910v	**CLANDESTINE (M EAST)** "VO IRAN COMMUNISTS"	F • Mideast • ANTI-IRANIAN GOVT / Mideast • ANTI-IRANIAN GOVT
	"VO IRANIAN REVOLUTION"	Mideast • PRO-COMMUNIST
	PIRATE (EUROPE) †"RADIO KORAK", Holland	Irr • Su • W Europe • ALT. FREQ. TO 3930v kHz / Irr • Sa • W Europe • ALT. FREQ. TO 3930v kHz
3912	**CLANDESTINE (ASIA)** †"VO THE PEOPLE", Seoul, S Korea	E Asia
3915	**UNITED KINGDOM** BBC, Via Singapore	SE Asia • 100 kW / W • SE Asia • 100 kW
3920	**KOREA (DPR)** NORTH PYONGYANG PS, Sinuiju	Irr • DS
3921v	**PIRATE (EUROPE)** †"STAR CLUB RADIO", Germany	Irr • Sa/Su • W Europe • 0.04 kW
3922v	**PIRATE (EUROPE)** VARIOUS STATIONS	Irr • Su • GERMAN, FRENCH, ETC • W Europe • 0.01/0.75 kW / Irr • Sa/Su • GERMAN, FRENCH, ETC • W Europe • 0.01/0.75 kW
3925	**CHINA (TAIWAN)** †R TAIPEI INTL, Via Skelton, UK	Europe • 250 kW
	JAPAN RADIO TAMPA, Multiple Locations	DS-1 • 10/50 kW
	RADIO TAMPA, Tokyo-Nagara	DS-1 • 50 kW
3925v	**PIRATE (EUROPE)** †"RADIO GRENSJAGER", Belgium	Irr • Sa/Su • W Europe • 0.1 kW
3927v	**PIRATE (EUROPE)** †"RADIO SPACEMAN", Holland	Irr • Su • W Europe • 0.1 kW / Irr • Sa • W Europe • 0.1 kW
3930	**KOREA (REPUBLIC)** KOREAN BC SYSTEM, Hwasung	DS-1 • 5 kW / M-Sa • DS-1 • 5 kW / Su • DS-1 • 5 kW
	PIRATE (EUROPE) †"LASER HOT HITS", Ireland	Irr • Su • W Europe • 0.25 kW / Irr • Sa • W Europe • 0.25 kW
3930v	**PIRATE (EUROPE)** †"RADIO KORAK", Holland	Irr • Su • W Europe • ALT. FREQ. TO 3910v kHz / Irr • Sa • W Europe • ALT. FREQ. TO 3910v kHz
3932v	**PIRATE (EUROPE)** †"UNION RADIO", Holland	Irr • F/Sa • W Europe • 0.15 kW
3935	**NEW ZEALAND** RADIO READING SVC, Levin	DS • 1 kW
3940v	**CHINA** HUBEI PEOPLE'S BS, Wuhan	DS • 10 kW
(con'd)	**CLANDESTINE (M EAST)** "VO IRAQI PEOPLE"	Mideast • PRO-COMMUNIST

0 1 2 3 4 5 6 7 8 9 10 11 12 13 14 15 16 17 18 19 20 21 22 23 24

ENGLISH ▬   ARABIC ▨   CHINESE ▯▯▯   FRENCH ▬   GERMAN ▬   RUSSIAN ═   SPANISH ▬   OTHER ─

FREQUENCY   COUNTRY, STATION, LOCATION

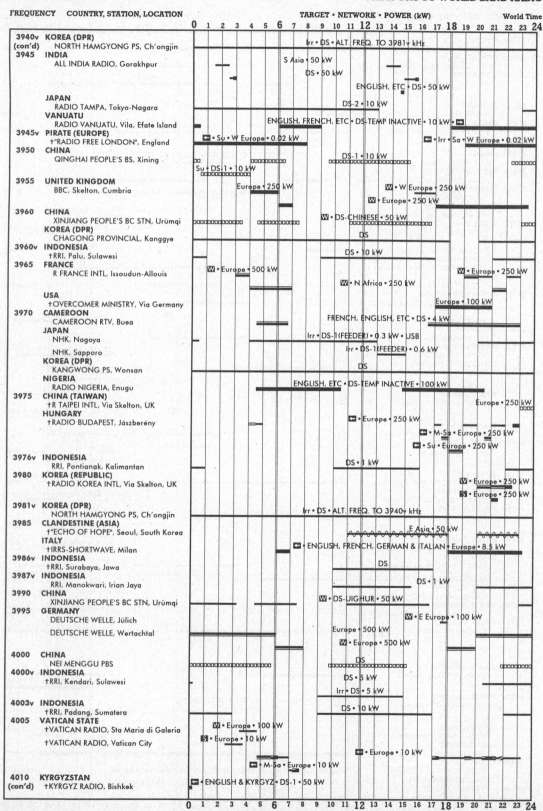

FREQUENCY   COUNTRY, STATION, LOCATION

TARGET • NETWORK • POWER (kW)   World Time

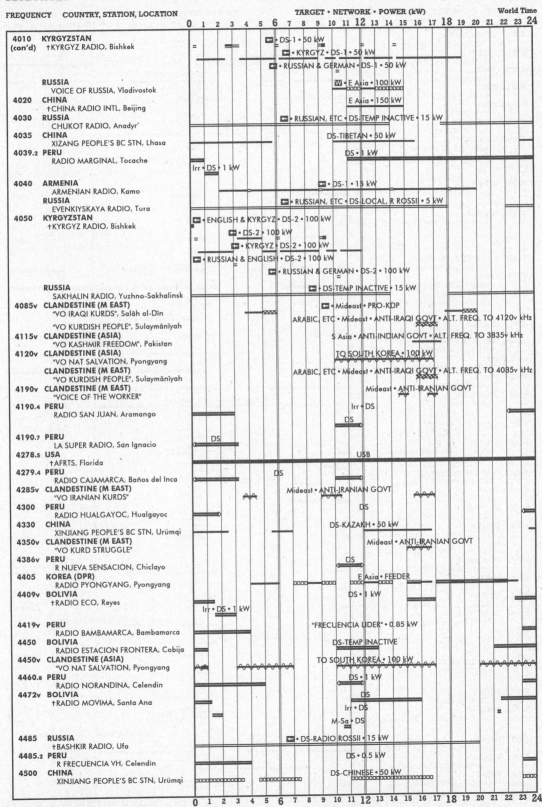

Frequency	Country, Station, Location	Notes
4010 (con'd)	**KYRGYZSTAN** †KYRGYZ RADIO, Bishkek	DS-1 • 50 kW / KYRGYZ • DS-1 • 50 kW / RUSSIAN & GERMAN • DS-1 • 50 kW
	RUSSIA VOICE OF RUSSIA, Vladivostok	E Asia • 100 kW
4020	**CHINA** †CHINA RADIO INTL, Beijing	E Asia • 150 kW
4030	**RUSSIA** CHUKOT RADIO, Anadyr'	RUSSIAN, ETC • DS-TEMP INACTIVE • 15 kW
4035	**CHINA** XIZANG PEOPLE'S BC STN, Lhasa	DS-TIBETAN • 50 kW
4039.2	**PERU** RADIO MARGINAL, Tocache	DS • 1 kW / Irr • DS • 1 kW
4040	**ARMENIA** ARMENIAN RADIO, Kamo	DS-1 • 15 kW
	RUSSIA EVENKIYSKAYA RADIO, Tura	RUSSIAN, ETC • DS-LOCAL, R ROSSII • 5 kW
4050	**KYRGYZSTAN** †KYRGYZ RADIO, Bishkek	ENGLISH & KYRGYZ • DS-2 • 100 kW / DS-2 • 100 kW / KYRGYZ • DS-2 • 100 kW / RUSSIAN & ENGLISH • DS-2 • 100 kW / RUSSIAN & GERMAN • DS-2 • 100 kW
	RUSSIA SAKHALIN RADIO, Yuzhno-Sakhalinsk	DS-TEMP INACTIVE • 15 kW
4085v	**CLANDESTINE (M EAST)** "VO IRAQI KURDS", Salāh al-Dīn	Mideast • PRO-KDP
	"VO KURDISH PEOPLE", Sulaymānīyah	ARABIC, ETC • Mideast • ANTI-IRAQI GOVT • ALT. FREQ. TO 4120v kHz
4115v	**CLANDESTINE (ASIA)** "VO KASHMIR FREEDOM", Pakistan	S Asia • ANTI-INDIAN GOVT • ALT. FREQ. TO 3B35v kHz
4120v	**CLANDESTINE (ASIA)** "VO NAT SALVATION, Pyongyang	TO SOUTH KOREA • 100 kW
	CLANDESTINE (M EAST) "VO KURDISH PEOPLE", Sulaymānīyah	ARABIC, ETC • Mideast • ANTI-IRAQI GOVT • ALT. FREQ. TO 4085v kHz
4190v	**CLANDESTINE (M EAST)** "VOICE OF THE WORKER"	Mideast • ANTI-IRANIAN GOVT
4190.4	**PERU** RADIO SAN JUAN, Aramango	Irr • DS / DS
4190.7	**PERU** LA SUPER RADIO, San Ignacio	DS
4278.5	**USA** †AFRTS, Florida	USB
4279.4	**PERU** RADIO CAJAMARCA, Baños del Inca	DS
4285v	**CLANDESTINE (M EAST)** "VO IRANIAN KURDS"	Mideast • ANTI-IRANIAN GOVT
4300	**PERU** RADIO HUALGAYOC, Hualgayoc	DS
4330	**CHINA** XINJIANG PEOPLE'S BC STN, Urümqi	DS-KAZAKH • 50 kW
4350v	**CLANDESTINE (M EAST)** "VO KURD STRUGGLE"	Mideast • ANTI-IRANIAN GOVT
4386v	**PERU** R NUEVA SENSACION, Chiclayo	DS
4405	**KOREA (DPR)** RADIO PYONGYANG, Pyongyang	E Asia • FEEDER
4409v	**BOLIVIA** †RADIO ECO, Reyes	DS • 1 kW / Irr • DS • 1 kW
4419v	**PERU** RADIO BAMBAMARCA, Bambamarca	"FRECUENCIA LIDER" • 0.85 kW
4450	**BOLIVIA** RADIO ESTACION FRONTERA, Cobija	DS-TEMP INACTIVE
4450v	**CLANDESTINE (ASIA)** "VO NAT SALVATION, Pyongyang	TO SOUTH KOREA • 100 kW
4460.8	**PERU** RADIO NORANDINA, Celendín	DS • 1 kW
4472v	**BOLIVIA** †RADIO MOVIMA, Santa Ana	DS / Irr • DS / M-Sa • DS
4485	**RUSSIA** †BASHKIR RADIO, Ufa	DS-RADIO ROSSII • 15 kW
4485.2	**PERU** R FRECUENCIA VH, Celendín	DS • 0.5 kW
4500	**CHINA** XINJIANG PEOPLE'S BC STN, Urümqi	DS-CHINESE • 50 kW

FREQUENCY   COUNTRY, STATION, LOCATION

TARGET • NETWORK • POWER (kW)   World Time

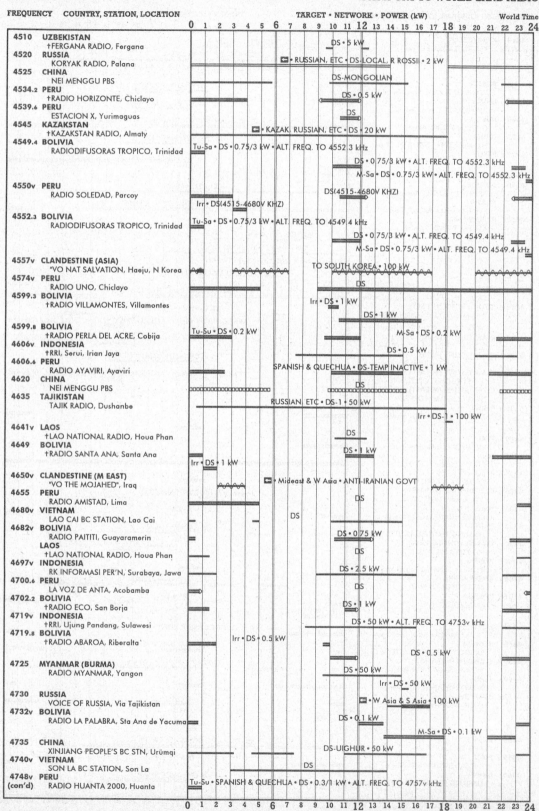

Freq	Country / Station	Notes
4510	**UZBEKISTAN** †FERGANA RADIO, Fergana	DS • 5 kW
4520	**RUSSIA** KORYAK RADIO, Palana	RUSSIAN, ETC • DS-LOCAL, R ROSSII • 2 kW
4525	**CHINA** NEI MENGGU PBS	DS-MONGOLIAN
4534.2	**PERU** †RADIO HORIZONTE, Chiclayo	DS • 0.5 kW
4539.6	**PERU** ESTACION X, Yurimaguas	DS
4545	**KAZAKHSTAN** †KAZAKSTAN RADIO, Almaty	KAZAK, RUSSIAN, ETC • DS • 20 kW
4549.4	**BOLIVIA** RADIODIFUSORAS TROPICO, Trinidad	Tu-Sa • DS • 0.75/3 kW • ALT. FREQ. TO 4552.3 kHz; DS • 0.75/3 kW • ALT. FREQ. TO 4552.3 kHz; M-Sa • DS • 0.75/3 kW • ALT. FREQ. TO 4552.3 kHz
4550v	**PERU** RADIO SOLEDAD, Parcoy	DS(4515-4680V KHZ); Irr • DS(4515-4680V KHZ)
4552.3	**BOLIVIA** RADIODIFUSORAS TROPICO, Trinidad	Tu-Sa • DS • 0.75/3 kW • ALT. FREQ. TO 4549.4 kHz; DS • 0.75/3 kW • ALT. FREQ. TO 4549.4 kHz; M-Sa • DS • 0.75/3 kW • ALT. FREQ. TO 4549.4 kHz
4557v	**CLANDESTINE (ASIA)** "VO NAT SALVATION, Haeju, N Korea	TO SOUTH KOREA • 100 kW
4574v	**PERU** RADIO UNO, Chiclayo	DS
4599.3	**BOLIVIA** †RADIO VILLAMONTES, Villamontes	Irr • DS • 1 kW; DS • 1 kW
4599.8	**BOLIVIA** †RADIO PERLA DEL ACRE, Cobija	Tu-Su • DS • 0.2 kW; M-Sa • DS • 0.2 kW
4606v	**INDONESIA** †RRI, Serui, Irian Jaya	DS • 0.5 kW
4606.6	**PERU** RADIO AYAVIRI, Ayaviri	SPANISH & QUECHUA • DS-TEMP INACTIVE • 1 kW
4620	**CHINA** NEI MENGGU PBS	DS
4635	**TAJIKISTAN** TAJIK RADIO, Dushanbe	RUSSIAN, ETC • DS-1 • 50 kW; Irr • DS-1 • 100 kW
4641v	**LAOS** †LAO NATIONAL RADIO, Houa Phan	DS
4649	**BOLIVIA** †RADIO SANTA ANA, Santa Ana	DS • 1 kW; Irr • DS • 1 kW
4650v	**CLANDESTINE (M EAST)** "VO THE MOJAHED", Iraq	Mideast & W Asia • ANTI-IRANIAN GOVT
4655	**PERU** RADIO AMISTAD, Lima	DS
4680v	**VIETNAM** LAO CAI BC STATION, Lao Cai	DS
4682v	**BOLIVIA** RADIO PAITITI, Guayaramerin	DS • 0.75 kW
	LAOS †LAO NATIONAL RADIO, Houa Phan	DS
4697v	**INDONESIA** RK INFORMASI PER'N, Surabaya, Jawa	DS • 2.5 kW
4700.6	**PERU** LA VOZ DE ANTA, Acobamba	DS
4702.2	**BOLIVIA** †RADIO ECO, San Borja	DS • 1 kW
4719v	**INDONESIA** †RRI, Ujung Pandang, Sulawesi	DS • 50 kW • ALT. FREQ. TO 4753v kHz
4719.8	**BOLIVIA** †RADIO ABAROA, Riberalta	Irr • DS • 0.5 kW; DS • 0.5 kW
4725	**MYANMAR (BURMA)** RADIO MYANMAR, Yangon	DS • 50 kW; Irr • DS • 50 kW
4730	**RUSSIA** VOICE OF RUSSIA, Via Tajikistan	W Asia & S Asia • 100 kW
4732v	**BOLIVIA** RADIO LA PALABRA, Sta Ana de Yacuma	DS • 0.1 kW; M-Sa • DS • 0.1 kW
4735	**CHINA** XINJIANG PEOPLE'S BC STN, Urümqi	DS-UIGHUR • 50 kW
4740v	**VIETNAM** SON LA BC STATION, Son La	DS
4748v (con'd)	**PERU** RADIO HUANTA 2000, Huanta	Tu-Su • SPANISH & QUECHUA • DS • 0.3/1 kW • ALT. FREQ. TO 4757v kHz

FREQUENCY	COUNTRY, STATION, LOCATION	TARGET • NETWORK • POWER (kW)	World Time

0 1 2 3 4 5 6 7 8 9 10 11 12 13 14 15 16 17 18 19 20 21 22 23 24

4748v PERU
(con'd) RADIO HUANTA 2000, Huanta — SPANISH & QUECHUA • DS • 0.3/1 kW • ALT. FREQ. TO 4757v kHz

4750 CHINA
HULUNBEI'ER PBS, Hailar — DS-MONGOLIAN
XIZANG PEOPLE'S BC STN, Lhasa — DS • 50 kW

PERU
R SAN FRANCISCO SOLANO, Sóndor — Tu-Sa • DS / Su • DS / M-F • DS

4753v INDONESIA
†RRI, Ujung Pandang, Sulawesi — DS • 50 kW • ALT. FREQ. TO 4719v kHz

4755.2 BRAZIL
R EDUCACAO RURAL, Campo Grande — DS • 10 kW / M-Sa • DS • 10 kW

4757v PERU
RADIO HUANTA 2000, Huanta — Tu-Su • SPANISH & QUECHUA • DS • 0.3/1 kW • ALT. FREQ. TO 4748v kHz / SPANISH & QUECHUA • DS • 0.3/1 kW • ALT. FREQ. TO 4748v kHz

4759 PERU
RADIO TINGO MARIA, Tingo Maria — Irr • DS • 1 kW

4759.8 CHINA
YUNNAN PEOPLE'S BS, Kunming — DS-1 • 50 kW / W-M • DS-1 • 50 kW

4760 INDIA
ALL INDIA RADIO, Port Blair — ENGLISH, ETC • DS • 20 kW / DS • 20 kW / Irr • DS • 20 kW

RADIO KASHMIR, Leh — S DS • 50 kW / ENGLISH, ETC • DS • 50 kW / DS • 50 kW / ENGLISH, ETC • DS • 10 kW / Irr • DS • 50 kW

SWAZILAND
TRANS WORLD RADIO, Manzini — S Africa • 25 kW / Sa • S Africa • 25 kW

4764v PERU
RADIO CHINCHEROS, Chincheros — SPANISH & QUECHUA • DS • 1 kW

4765 BRAZIL
RADIO INTEGRACAO, Cruzeiro do Sul — DS-TEMP INACTIVE • 10 kW / Tu-Su • DS-TEMP INACTIVE • 10 kW / DS • 10 kW

RADIO RURAL, Santarém — Tu-Su • DS • 10 kW / M-Sa • DS • 10 kW

4766v INDONESIA
†RRI, Medan, Sumatera — DS

4770 ECUADOR
CENTINELA DEL SUR, Loja — DS • 2 kW / Tu-Su • DS • 5 kW

NIGERIA
RADIO NIGERIA, Kaduna — ENGLISH, ETC • DS • 2 • 50 kW

4774v AFGHANISTAN
†VOICE OF SHARI'AH, Kabul — Sa-Th • DS • 100 kW / W Asia & Mideast • 100 kW / DS • 100 kW / F • DS • 100 kW

4775 BRAZIL
RADIO CONGONHAS, Congonhas — DS • 1 kW / M-Sa • DS • 1 kW

RADIO LIBERAL, Belém — DS • 5 kW

INDIA
ALL INDIA RADIO, Imphal — DS • 50 kW / ENGLISH, ETC • DS • 50 kW / Irr • DS • 50 kW

PERU
RADIO TARMA, Tarma — DS • 1 kW / Tu-Su • DS • 1 kW

SWAZILAND
TRANS WORLD RADIO, Manzini — S S Africa • 50 kW / S Africa • 50 kW / Sa/Su • S Africa • 50 kW

4777 GABON
RTV GABONAISE, Moyabi — DS • 250 kW • ALT. FREQ. TO 7270 kHz / DS • 250 kW

4777v INDONESIA
†RRI, Jakarta, Jawa — DS • 50 kW

4777.7 BOLIVIA
†RADIO ANDES, Uyuni — M-Sa • SPANISH & QUECHUA • DS • 1 kW / SPANISH & QUECHUA • DS • 1 kW

4779v GUATEMALA
†R CULTURAL COATAN, San Sebastián — SPANISH, ETC • DS • 1 kW

4779.8 ECUADOR
RADIO ORIENTAL, Tena — DS • 1 kW

4780 PERU
(con'd) RADIO BAHIA, Chimbote — DS

0 1 2 3 4 5 6 7 8 9 10 11 12 13 14 15 16 17 18 19 20 21 22 23 24

ENGLISH ▬▬   ARABIC ⌇⌇⌇   CHINESE ▢▢▢   FRENCH ▬▬   GERMAN ▬▬   RUSSIAN ═══   SPANISH ▬▬   OTHER ──

FREQUENCY   COUNTRY, STATION, LOCATION   TARGET • NETWORK • POWER (kW)   World Time

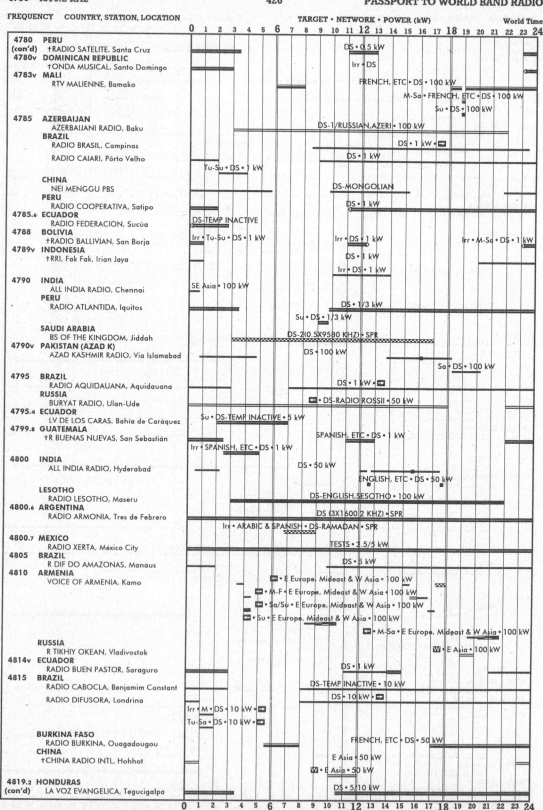

FREQUENCY	COUNTRY, STATION, LOCATION	TARGET • NETWORK • POWER (kW)
4780 (con'd)	PERU — †RADIO SATELITE, Santa Cruz	DS • 0.5 kW
4780v	DOMINICAN REPUBLIC — †ONDA MUSICAL, Santo Domingo	Irr • DS
4783v	MALI — RTV MALIENNE, Bamako	FRENCH, ETC • DS • 100 kW / M-Sa • FRENCH, ETC • DS • 100 kW / Su • DS • 100 kW
4785	AZERBAIJAN — AZERBAIJANI RADIO, Baku	DS-1/RUSSIAN, AZERI • 100 kW
	BRAZIL — RADIO BRASIL, Campinas	DS • 1 kW
	RADIO CAIARI, Pôrto Velho	DS • 1 kW
	CHINA — NEI MENGGU PBS	Tu-Su • DS • 1 kW / DS-MONGOLIAN
	PERU — RADIO COOPERATIVA, Satipo	DS • 1 kW
4785.6	ECUADOR — RADIO FEDERACION, Sucúa	DS-TEMP INACTIVE
4788	BOLIVIA — †RADIO BALLIVIAN, San Borja	Irr • Tu-Su • DS • 1 kW / Irr • DS • 1 kW / Irr • M-Sa • DS • 1 kW
4789v	INDONESIA — †RRI, Fak Fak, Irian Jaya	DS • 1 kW / Irr • DS • 1 kW
4790	INDIA — ALL INDIA RADIO, Chennai	SE Asia • 100 kW
	PERU — RADIO ATLANTIDA, Iquitos	DS • 1/3 kW / Su • DS • 1/3 kW
	SAUDI ARABIA — BS OF THE KINGDOM, Jiddah	DS-2(0.5X9580 KHZ) • SPR
4790v	PAKISTAN (AZAD K) — AZAD KASHMIR RADIO, Via Islamabad	DS • 100 kW / Sa • DS • 100 kW
4795	BRAZIL — RADIO AQUIDAUANA, Aquidauana	DS • 1 kW
	RUSSIA — BURYAT RADIO, Ulan-Ude	DS-RADIO ROSSII • 50 kW
4795.4	ECUADOR — LV DE LOS CARAS, Bahia de Caráquez	Su • DS-TEMP INACTIVE • 5 kW
4799.8	GUATEMALA — †R BUENAS NUEVAS, San Sebastián	SPANISH, ETC • DS • 1 kW / Irr • SPANISH, ETC • DS • 1 kW
4800	INDIA — ALL INDIA RADIO, Hyderabad	DS • 50 kW / ENGLISH, ETC • DS • 50 kW
	LESOTHO — RADIO LESOTHO, Maseru	DS-ENGLISH, SESOTHO • 100 kW
4800.6	ARGENTINA — RADIO ARMONIA, Tres de Febrero	DS (3X1600.2 KHZ) • SPR / Irr • ARABIC & SPANISH • DS-RAMADAN • SPR
4800.7	MEXICO — RADIO XERTA, México City	TESTS • 2.5/5 kW
4805	BRAZIL — R DIF DO AMAZONAS, Manaus	DS • 5 kW
4810	ARMENIA — VOICE OF ARMENIA, Kamo	E Europe, Mideast & W Asia • 100 kW / M-F • E Europe, Mideast & W Asia • 100 kW / Sa/Su • E Europe, Mideast & W Asia • 100 kW / Su • E Europe, Mideast & W Asia • 100 kW / M-Sa • E Europe, Mideast & W Asia • 100 kW / W • E Asia • 100 kW
	RUSSIA — R TIKHIY OKEAN, Vladivostok	
4814v	ECUADOR — RADIO BUEN PASTOR, Saraguro	DS • 1 kW
4815	BRAZIL — RADIO CABOCLA, Benjamim Constant	DS-TEMP INACTIVE • 10 kW
	RADIO DIFUSORA, Londrina	DS • 10 kW / Irr • M • DS • 10 kW / Tu-Sa • DS • 10 kW
	BURKINA FASO — RADIO BURKINA, Ouagadougou	FRENCH, ETC • DS • 50 kW
	CHINA — †CHINA RADIO INTL, Hohhot	E Asia • 50 kW / W • E Asia • 50 kW
4819.2 (con'd)	HONDURAS — LA VOZ EVANGELICA, Tegucigalpa	DS • 5/10 kW

FREQUENCY   COUNTRY, STATION, LOCATION   TARGET • NETWORK • POWER (kW)   World Time

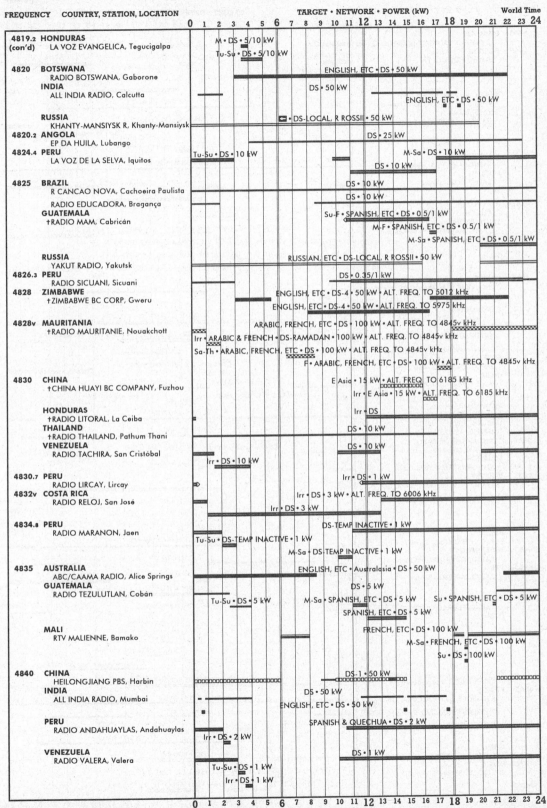

Frequency	Country / Station / Location	Schedule
4819.2 (con'd)	**HONDURAS** — LA VOZ EVANGELICA, Tegucigalpa	M • DS • 5/10 kW; Tu-Su • DS • 5/10 kW
4820	**BOTSWANA** — RADIO BOTSWANA, Gaborone	ENGLISH, ETC • DS • 50 kW
	INDIA — ALL INDIA RADIO, Calcutta	DS • 50 kW; ENGLISH, ETC • DS • 50 kW
	RUSSIA — KHANTY-MANSIYSK R, Khanty-Mansiysk	DS-LOCAL, R ROSSII • 50 kW
4820.2	**ANGOLA** — EP DA HUILA, Lubango	DS • 25 kW
4824.4	**PERU** — LA VOZ DE LA SELVA, Iquitos	Tu-Su • DS • 10 kW; M-Sa • DS • 10 kW; DS • 10 kW
4825	**BRAZIL** — R CANCAO NOVA, Cachoeira Paulista	DS • 10 kW
	RADIO EDUCADORA, Bragança	DS • 10 kW
	GUATEMALA — †RADIO MAM, Cabricán	Su-F • SPANISH, ETC • DS • 0.5/1 kW; M-F • SPANISH, ETC • DS • 0.5/1 kW; M-Sa • SPANISH, ETC • DS • 0.5/1 kW
	RUSSIA — YAKUT RADIO, Yakutsk	RUSSIAN, ETC • DS-LOCAL, R ROSSII • 50 kW
4826.3	**PERU** — RADIO SICUANI, Sicuani	DS • 0.35/1 kW
4828	**ZIMBABWE** — †ZIMBABWE BC CORP, Gweru	ENGLISH, ETC • DS-4 • 50 kW • ALT. FREQ. TO 5012 kHz; ENGLISH, ETC • DS-4 • 50 kW • ALT. FREQ. TO 5975 kHz
4828v	**MAURITANIA** — †RADIO MAURITANIE, Nouakchott	ARABIC, FRENCH, ETC • DS • 100 kW • ALT. FREQ. TO 4845v kHz; Irr • ARABIC & FRENCH • DS-RAMADAN • 100 kW • ALT. FREQ. TO 4845v kHz; Sa-Th • ARABIC, FRENCH, ETC • DS • 100 kW • ALT. FREQ. TO 4845v kHz; F • ARABIC, FRENCH, ETC • DS • 100 kW • ALT. FREQ. TO 4845v kHz
4830	**CHINA** — †CHINA HUAYI BC COMPANY, Fuzhou	E Asia • 15 kW • ALT. FREQ. TO 6185 kHz; Irr • E Asia • 15 kW • ALT. FREQ. TO 6185 kHz
	HONDURAS — †RADIO LITORAL, La Ceiba	Irr • DS
	THAILAND — †RADIO THAILAND, Pathum Thani	DS • 10 kW
	VENEZUELA — RADIO TACHIRA, San Cristóbal	DS • 10 kW; Irr • DS • 10 kW
4830.7	**PERU** — RADIO LIRCAY, Lircay	Irr • DS • 1 kW
4832v	**COSTA RICA** — RADIO RELOJ, San José	Irr • DS • 3 kW • ALT. FREQ. TO 6006 kHz; Irr • DS • 3 kW
4834.8	**PERU** — RADIO MARANON, Jaen	DS-TEMP INACTIVE • 1 kW; Tu-Su • DS-TEMP INACTIVE • 1 kW; M-Sa • DS-TEMP INACTIVE • 1 kW
4835	**AUSTRALIA** — ABC/CAAMA RADIO, Alice Springs	ENGLISH, ETC • Australasia • DS • 50 kW
	GUATEMALA — RADIO TEZULUTLAN, Cobán	DS • 5 kW; Tu-Su • DS • 5 kW; M-Sa • SPANISH, ETC • DS • 5 kW; Su • SPANISH, ETC • DS • 5 kW; SPANISH, ETC • DS • 5 kW
	MALI — RTV MALIENNE, Bamako	FRENCH, ETC • DS • 100 kW; M-Sa • FRENCH, ETC • DS • 100 kW; Su • DS • 100 kW
4840	**CHINA** — HEILONGJIANG PBS, Harbin	DS-1 • 50 kW
	INDIA — ALL INDIA RADIO, Mumbai	DS • 50 kW; ENGLISH, ETC • DS • 50 kW
	PERU — RADIO ANDAHUAYLAS, Andahuaylas	SPANISH & QUECHUA • DS • 2 kW; Irr • DS • 2 kW
	VENEZUELA — RADIO VALERA, Valera	DS • 1 kW; Tu-Su • DS • 1 kW; Irr • DS • 1 kW

ENGLISH ▬   ARABIC ▨   CHINESE ▫▫▫   FRENCH ▬   GERMAN ▬   RUSSIAN ═   SPANISH ▬   OTHER —

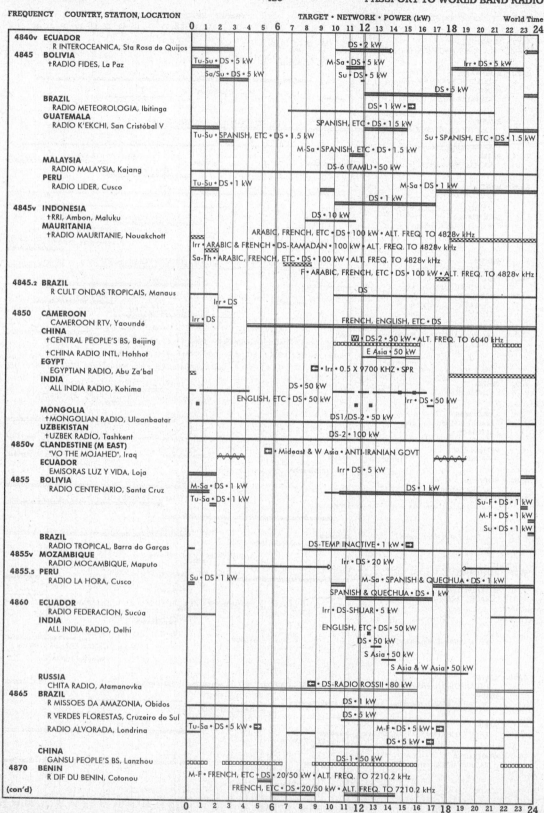

4840v ECUADOR
  R INTEROCEANICA, Sta Rosa de Quijos — DS • 2 kW
4845 BOLIVIA
  †RADIO FIDES, La Paz — Tu-Su • DS • 5 kW / M-Sa • DS • 5 kW / Irr • DS • 5 kW
  Sa/Su • DS • 5 kW / Su • DS • 5 kW
  DS • 5 kW
BRAZIL
  RADIO METEOROLOGIA, Ibitinga — DS • 1 kW •
GUATEMALA
  RADIO K'EKCHI, San Cristóbal V — SPANISH, ETC • DS • 1.5 kW
  Tu-Su • SPANISH, ETC • DS • 1.5 kW / Su • SPANISH, ETC • DS • 1.5 kW
  M-Sa • SPANISH, ETC • DS • 1.5 kW
MALAYSIA
  RADIO MALAYSIA, Kajang — DS-6 (TAMIL) • 50 kW
PERU
  RADIO LIDER, Cusco — Tu-Su • DS • 1 kW / M-Sa • DS • 1 kW
  DS • 1 kW

4845v INDONESIA
  †RRI, Ambon, Maluku — DS • 10 kW
MAURITANIA
  †RADIO MAURITANIE, Nouakchott — ARABIC, FRENCH, ETC • DS • 100 kW • ALT. FREQ. TO 4828v kHz
  Irr • ARABIC & FRENCH • DS-RAMADAN • 100 kW • ALT. FREQ. TO 4828v kHz
  Sa-Th • ARABIC, FRENCH, ETC • DS • 100 kW • ALT. FREQ. TO 4828v kHz
  F • ARABIC, FRENCH, ETC • DS • 100 kW • ALT. FREQ. TO 4828v kHz

4845.2 BRAZIL
  R CULT ONDAS TROPICAIS, Manaus — DS
  Irr • DS

4850 CAMEROON
  CAMEROON RTV, Yaoundé — Irr • DS / FRENCH, ENGLISH, ETC • DS
CHINA
  †CENTRAL PEOPLE'S BS, Beijing — W • DS-2 • 50 kW • ALT. FREQ. TO 6040 kHz
  †CHINA RADIO INTL, Hohhot — E Asia • 50 kW
EGYPT
  EGYPTIAN RADIO, Abu Za'bal — Irr • 0.5 X 9700 KHZ • SPR
INDIA
  ALL INDIA RADIO, Kohima — DS • 50 kW
  ENGLISH, ETC • DS • 50 kW / Irr • DS • 50 kW
MONGOLIA
  †MONGOLIAN RADIO, Ulaanbaatar — DS1/DS-2 • 50 kW
UZBEKISTAN
  †UZBEK RADIO, Tashkent — DS-2 • 100 kW
4850v CLANDESTINE (M EAST)
  "VO THE MOJAHED", Iraq — Mideast & W Asia • ANTI-IRANIAN GOVT
ECUADOR
  EMISORAS LUZ Y VIDA, Loja — Irr • DS • 5 kW
4855 BOLIVIA
  RADIO CENTENARIO, Santa Cruz — M-Sa • DS • 1 kW / DS • 1 kW
  Tu-Sa • DS • 1 kW
  Su-F • DS • 1 kW
  M-F • DS • 1 kW
  Su • DS • 1 kW
BRAZIL
  RADIO TROPICAL, Barra do Garças — DS-TEMP INACTIVE • 1 kW •
4855v MOZAMBIQUE
  RADIO MOCAMBIQUE, Maputo — Irr • DS • 20 kW
4855.5 PERU
  RADIO LA HORA, Cusco — Su • DS • 1 kW / M-Sa • SPANISH & QUECHUA • DS • 1 kW
  SPANISH & QUECHUA • DS • 1 kW

4860 ECUADOR
  RADIO FEDERACION, Sucúa — Irr • DS-SHUAR • 5 kW
INDIA
  ALL INDIA RADIO, Delhi — ENGLISH, ETC • DS • 50 kW
  DS • 50 kW
  S Asia • 50 kW
  S Asia & W Asia • 50 kW
RUSSIA
  CHITA RADIO, Atamanovka — DS-RADIO ROSSII • 80 kW
4865 BRAZIL
  R MISSOES DA AMAZONIA, Obidos — DS • 1 kW
  R VERDES FLORESTAS, Cruzeiro do Sul — DS • 5 kW
  RADIO ALVORADA, Londrina — Tu-Sa • DS • 5 kW • / M-F • DS • 5 kW •
  DS • 5 kW •
CHINA
  GANSU PEOPLE'S BS, Lanzhou — DS-1 • 50 kW
4870 BENIN
  R DIF DU BENIN, Cotonou — M-F • FRENCH, ETC • DS • 20/50 kW • ALT. FREQ. TO 7210.2 kHz
  FRENCH, ETC • DS • 20/50 kW • ALT. FREQ. TO 7210.2 kHz

(con'd)

SEASONAL ⒮ OR Ⓦ   1-HR TIMESHIFT MIDYEAR ⊡ OR ⊟   JAMMING / OR ∧   EARLIEST HEARD ◁   LATEST HEARD ▷   NEW FOR 2000 †

FREQUENCY   COUNTRY, STATION, LOCATION   TARGET • NETWORK • POWER (kW)   World Time

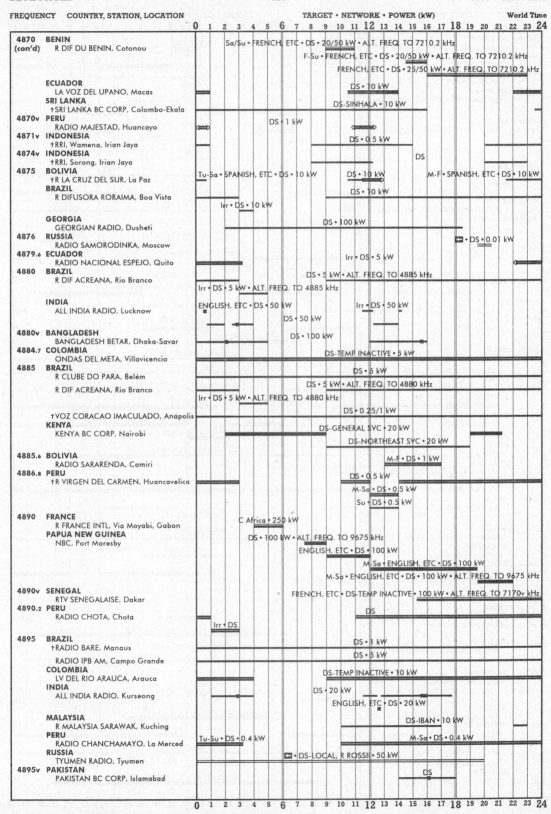

Frequency	Country, Station, Location	Programming
4870 (con'd)	BENIN R DIF DU BENIN, Cotonou	Sa/Su • FRENCH, ETC • DS • 20/50 kW • ALT. FREQ. TO 7210.2 kHz F-Su • FRENCH, ETC • DS • 20/50 kW • ALT. FREQ. TO 7210.2 kHz FRENCH, ETC • DS • 25/50 kW • ALT. FREQ. TO 7210.2 kHz
	ECUADOR LA VOZ DEL UPANO, Macas	DS • 10 kW
	SRI LANKA †SRI LANKA BC CORP, Colombo-Ekala	DS-SINHALA • 10 kW
4870v	PERU RADIO MAJESTAD, Huancayo	DS • 1 kW
4871v	INDONESIA †RRI, Wamena, Irian Jaya	DS • 0.5 kW
4874v	INDONESIA †RRI, Sorong, Irian Jaya	DS
4875	BOLIVIA †R LA CRUZ DEL SUR, La Paz	Tu-Sa • SPANISH, ETC • DS • 10 kW DS • 10 kW M-F • SPANISH, ETC • DS • 10 kW
	BRAZIL R DIFUSORA RORAIMA, Boa Vista	DS • 10 kW Irr • DS • 10 kW
	GEORGIA GEORGIAN RADIO, Dusheti	DS • 100 kW
4876	RUSSIA RADIO SAMORODINKA, Moscow	DS • 0.01 kW
4879.6	ECUADOR RADIO NACIONAL ESPEJO, Quito	Irr • DS • 5 kW
4880	BRAZIL R DIF ACREANA, Rio Branco	DS • 5 kW • ALT. FREQ. TO 4885 kHz Irr • DS • 5 kW • ALT. FREQ. TO 4885 kHz
	INDIA ALL INDIA RADIO, Lucknow	ENGLISH, ETC • DS • 50 kW Irr • DS • 50 kW DS • 50 kW
4880v	BANGLADESH BANGLADESH BETAR, Dhaka-Savar	DS • 100 kW
4884.7	COLOMBIA ONDAS DEL META, Villavicencio	DS-TEMP INACTIVE • 5 kW
4885	BRAZIL R CLUBE DO PARA, Belém	DS • 5 kW
	R DIF ACREANA, Rio Branco	DS • 5 kW • ALT. FREQ. TO 4880 kHz Irr • DS • 5 kW • ALT. FREQ. TO 4880 kHz
	†VOZ CORACAO IMACULADO, Anápolis	DS • 0.25/1 kW
	KENYA KENYA BC CORP, Nairobi	DS-GENERAL SVC • 20 kW DS-NORTHEAST SVC • 20 kW
4885.6	BOLIVIA RADIO SARARENDA, Camiri	M-F • DS • 1 kW
4886.8	PERU †R VIRGEN DEL CARMEN, Huancavelica	DS • 0.5 kW M-Sa • DS • 0.5 kW Su • DS • 0.5 kW
4890	FRANCE R FRANCE INTL, Via Moyabi, Gabon	C Africa • 250 kW
	PAPUA NEW GUINEA NBC, Port Moresby	DS • 100 kW • ALT. FREQ. TO 9675 kHz ENGLISH, ETC • DS • 100 kW M-Sa • ENGLISH, ETC • DS • 100 kW M-Sa • ENGLISH, ETC • DS • 100 kW • ALT. FREQ. TO 9675 kHz
4890v	SENEGAL RTV SENEGALAISE, Dakar	FRENCH, ETC • DS-TEMP INACTIVE • 100 kW • ALT. FREQ. TO 7170v kHz
4890.2	PERU RADIO CHOTA, Chota	DS Irr • DS
4895	BRAZIL †RADIO BARE, Manaus	DS • 1 kW
	RADIO IPB AM, Campo Grande	DS • 5 kW
	COLOMBIA LV DEL RIO ARAUCA, Arauca	DS-TEMP INACTIVE • 10 kW
	INDIA ALL INDIA RADIO, Kurseong	DS • 20 kW ENGLISH, ETC • DS • 20 kW
	MALAYSIA R MALAYSIA SARAWAK, Kuching	DS-IBAN • 10 kW
	PERU RADIO CHANCHAMAYO, La Merced	Tu-Su • DS • 0.4 kW M-Sa • DS • 0.4 kW
	RUSSIA TYUMEN RADIO, Tyumen	DS-LOCAL, R ROSSII • 50 kW
4895v	PAKISTAN PAKISTAN BC CORP, Islamabad	DS

ENGLISH ——   ARABIC ≈≈≈   CHINESE ☐☐☐   FRENCH ▬▬   GERMAN ▬▬   RUSSIAN ══   SPANISH ▬▬   OTHER ▬▬

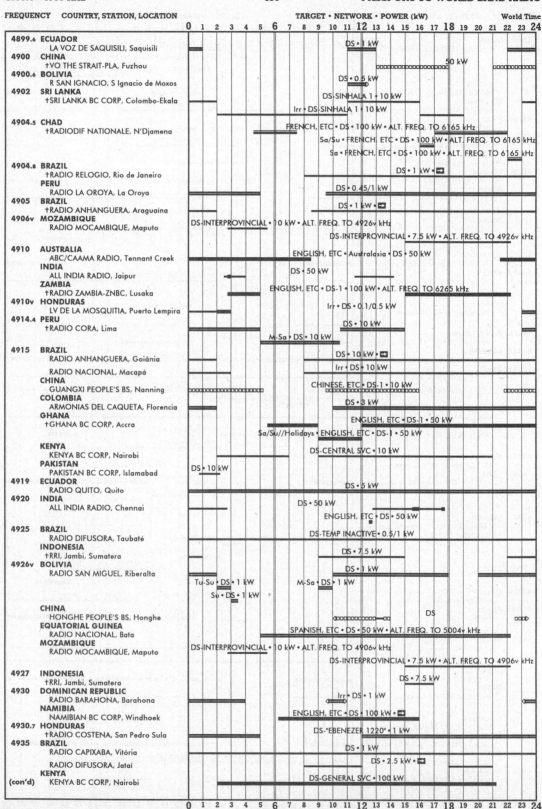

FREQUENCY   COUNTRY, STATION, LOCATION   TARGET • NETWORK • POWER (kW)   World Time

FREQUENCY	COUNTRY, STATION, LOCATION	TARGET • NETWORK • POWER (kW)
4899.6	**ECUADOR** LA VOZ DE SAQUISILI, Saquisilí	DS • 1 kW
4900	**CHINA** †VO THE STRAIT-PLA, Fuzhou	50 kW
4900.6	**BOLIVIA** R SAN IGNACIO, S Ignacio de Moxos	DS • 0.5 kW
4902	**SRI LANKA** †SRI LANKA BC CORP, Colombo-Ekala	DS-SINHALA 1 • 10 kW / Irr • DS-SINHALA 1 • 10 kW
4904.5	**CHAD** †RADIODIF NATIONALE, N'Djamena	FRENCH, ETC • DS • 100 kW • ALT. FREQ. TO 6165 kHz / Sa/Su • FRENCH, ETC • DS • 100 kW • ALT. FREQ. TO 6165 kHz / Sa • FRENCH, ETC • DS • 100 kW • ALT. FREQ. TO 6165 kHz
4904.8	**BRAZIL** †RADIO RELOGIO, Rio de Janeiro	DS • 1 kW • ⊡
	PERU RADIO LA OROYA, La Oroya	DS • 0.45/1 kW
4905	**BRAZIL** †RADIO ANHANGUERA, Araguaína	DS • 1 kW • ⊡
4906v	**MOZAMBIQUE** RADIO MOCAMBIQUE, Maputo	DS-INTERPROVINCIAL • 10 kW • ALT. FREQ. TO 4926v kHz / DS-INTERPROVINCIAL • 7.5 kW • ALT. FREQ. TO 4926v kHz
4910	**AUSTRALIA** ABC/CAAMA RADIO, Tennant Creek	ENGLISH, ETC • Australasia • DS • 50 kW
	INDIA ALL INDIA RADIO, Jaipur	DS • 50 kW
	ZAMBIA †RADIO ZAMBIA-ZNBC, Lusaka	ENGLISH, ETC • DS-1 • 100 kW • ALT. FREQ. TO 6265 kHz
4910v	**HONDURAS** LV DE LA MOSQUITIA, Puerto Lempira	Irr • DS • 0.1/0.5 kW
4914.4	**PERU** †RADIO CORA, Lima	DS • 10 kW / M-Sa • DS • 10 kW
4915	**BRAZIL** RADIO ANHANGUERA, Goiânia	DS • 10 kW • ⊡
	RADIO NACIONAL, Macapá	Irr • DS • 10 kW
	CHINA GUANGXI PEOPLE'S BS, Nanning	CHINESE, ETC • DS-1 • 10 kW
	COLOMBIA ARMONIAS DEL CAQUETA, Florencia	DS • 3 kW
	GHANA †GHANA BC CORP, Accra	ENGLISH, ETC • DS-1 • 50 kW / Sa/Su//Holidays • ENGLISH, ETC • DS-1 • 50 kW
	KENYA KENYA BC CORP, Nairobi	DS-CENTRAL SVC • 10 kW
	PAKISTAN PAKISTAN BC CORP, Islamabad	DS • 10 kW
4919	**ECUADOR** RADIO QUITO, Quito	DS • 5 kW
4920	**INDIA** ALL INDIA RADIO, Chennai	DS • 50 kW / ENGLISH, ETC • DS • 50 kW
4925	**BRAZIL** RADIO DIFUSORA, Taubaté	DS-TEMP INACTIVE • 0.5/1 kW
	INDONESIA †RRI, Jambi, Sumatera	DS • 7.5 kW
4926v	**BOLIVIA** RADIO SAN MIGUEL, Riberalta	DS • 1 kW / Tu-Su • DS • 1 kW / M-Sa • DS • 1 kW / Su • DS • 1 kW
	CHINA HONGHE PEOPLE'S BS, Honghe	DS
	EQUATORIAL GUINEA RADIO NACIONAL, Bata	SPANISH, ETC • DS • 50 kW • ALT. FREQ. TO 5004v kHz
	MOZAMBIQUE RADIO MOCAMBIQUE, Maputo	DS-INTERPROVINCIAL • 10 kW • ALT. FREQ. TO 4906v kHz / DS-INTERPROVINCIAL • 7.5 kW • ALT. FREQ. TO 4906v kHz
4927	**INDONESIA** †RRI, Jambi, Sumatera	DS • 7.5 kW
4930	**DOMINICAN REPUBLIC** RADIO BARAHONA, Barahona	Irr • DS • 1 kW
	NAMIBIA NAMIBIAN BC CORP, Windhoek	ENGLISH, ETC • DS • 100 kW • ⊡
4930.7	**HONDURAS** †RADIO COSTENA, San Pedro Sula	DS-"EBENEZER 1220" • 1 kW
4935	**BRAZIL** RADIO CAPIXABA, Vitória	DS • 1 kW
	RADIO DIFUSORA, Jataí	DS • 2.5 kW • ⊡
(con'd)	**KENYA** KENYA BC CORP, Nairobi	DS-GENERAL SVC • 100 kW

FREQUENCY   COUNTRY, STATION, LOCATION   TARGET • NETWORK • POWER (kW)   World Time

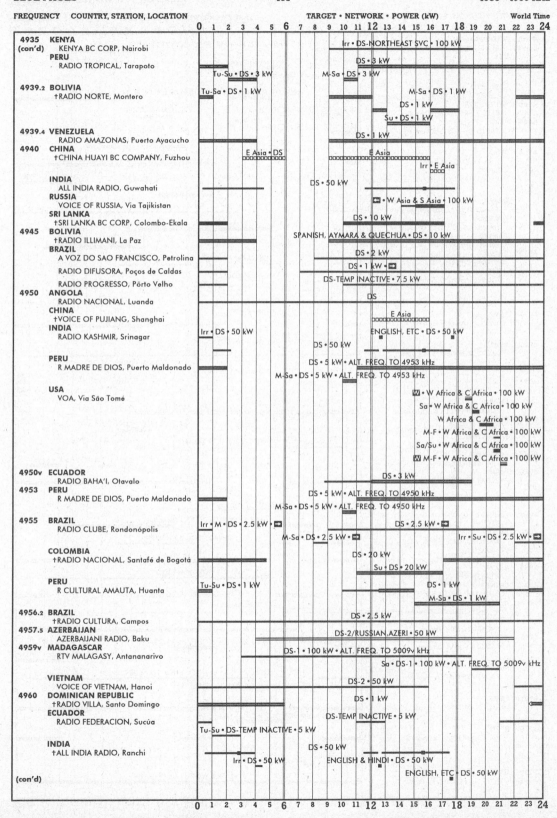

4935 KENYA
(con'd)   KENYA BC CORP, Nairobi — Irr • DS-NORTHEAST SVC • 100 kW
PERU
   RADIO TROPICAL, Tarapoto — DS • 3 kW / Tu-Su • DS • 3 kW / M-Sa • DS • 3 kW

4939.2 BOLIVIA
   †RADIO NORTE, Montero — Tu-Sa • DS • 1 kW / M-Sa • DS • 1 kW / DS • 1 kW / Su • DS • 1 kW

4939.4 VENEZUELA
   RADIO AMAZONAS, Puerto Ayacucho — DS • 1 kW
4940 CHINA
   †CHINA HUAYI BC COMPANY, Fuzhou — E Asia • DS / E Asia / Irr • E Asia

   INDIA
   ALL INDIA RADIO, Guwahati — DS • 50 kW
   RUSSIA
   VOICE OF RUSSIA, Via Tajikistan — W Asia & S Asia • 100 kW
   SRI LANKA
   †SRI LANKA BC CORP, Colombo-Ekala — DS • 10 kW
4945 BOLIVIA
   †RADIO ILLIMANI, La Paz — SPANISH, AYMARA & QUECHUA • DS • 10 kW
   BRAZIL
   A VOZ DO SAO FRANCISCO, Petrolina — DS • 2 kW
   RADIO DIFUSORA, Poços de Caldas — DS • 1 kW
   RADIO PROGRESSO, Pôrto Velho — DS-TEMP INACTIVE • 7.5 kW
4950 ANGOLA
   RADIO NACIONAL, Luanda — DS
   CHINA
   †VOICE OF PUJIANG, Shanghai — E Asia
   INDIA
   RADIO KASHMIR, Srinagar — Irr • DS • 50 kW / ENGLISH, ETC • DS • 50 kW / DS • 50 kW

   PERU
   R MADRE DE DIOS, Puerto Maldonado — DS • 5 kW • ALT. FREQ. TO 4953 kHz / M-Sa • DS • 5 kW • ALT. FREQ. TO 4953 kHz

   USA
   VOA, Via São Tomé — W • W Africa & C Africa • 100 kW / Sa • W Africa & C Africa • 100 kW / W Africa & C Africa • 100 kW / M-F • W Africa & C Africa • 100 kW / Sa/Su • W Africa & C Africa • 100 kW / W M-F • W Africa & C Africa • 100 kW

4950v ECUADOR
   RADIO BAHA'I, Otavalo — DS • 3 kW
4953 PERU
   R MADRE DE DIOS, Puerto Maldonado — DS • 5 kW • ALT. FREQ. TO 4950 kHz / M-Sa • DS • 5 kW • ALT. FREQ. TO 4950 kHz

4955 BRAZIL
   RADIO CLUBE, Rondonópolis — Irr • M • DS • 2.5 kW / DS • 2.5 kW / M-Sa • DS • 2.5 kW / Irr • Su • DS • 2.5 kW

   COLOMBIA
   †RADIO NACIONAL, Santafé de Bogotá — DS • 20 kW / Su • DS • 20 kW

   PERU
   R CULTURAL AMAUTA, Huanta — Tu-Su • DS • 1 kW / DS • 1 kW / M-Sa • DS • 1 kW

4956.2 BRAZIL
   †RADIO CULTURA, Campos — DS • 2.5 kW
4957.5 AZERBAIJAN
   AZERBAIJANI RADIO, Baku — DS-2/RUSSIAN, AZERI • 50 kW
4959v MADAGASCAR
   RTV MALAGASY, Antananarivo — DS-1 • 100 kW • ALT. FREQ. TO 5009v kHz / Sa • DS-1 • 100 kW • ALT. FREQ. TO 5009v kHz

   VIETNAM
   VOICE OF VIETNAM, Hanoi — DS-2 • 50 kW
4960 DOMINICAN REPUBLIC
   †RADIO VILLA, Santo Domingo — DS • 1 kW
   ECUADOR
   RADIO FEDERACION, Sucúa — DS-TEMP INACTIVE • 5 kW / Tu-Su • DS-TEMP INACTIVE • 5 kW

   INDIA
   †ALL INDIA RADIO, Ranchi — DS • 50 kW / Irr • DS • 50 kW / ENGLISH & HINDI • DS • 50 kW / ENGLISH, ETC • DS • 50 kW

(con'd)

ENGLISH ▬   ARABIC ≈≈≈   CHINESE □□□   FRENCH ▬▬   GERMAN ▬▬   RUSSIAN ══   SPANISH ▬▬   OTHER ▬

FREQUENCY   COUNTRY, STATION, LOCATION   TARGET • NETWORK • POWER (kW)   World Time

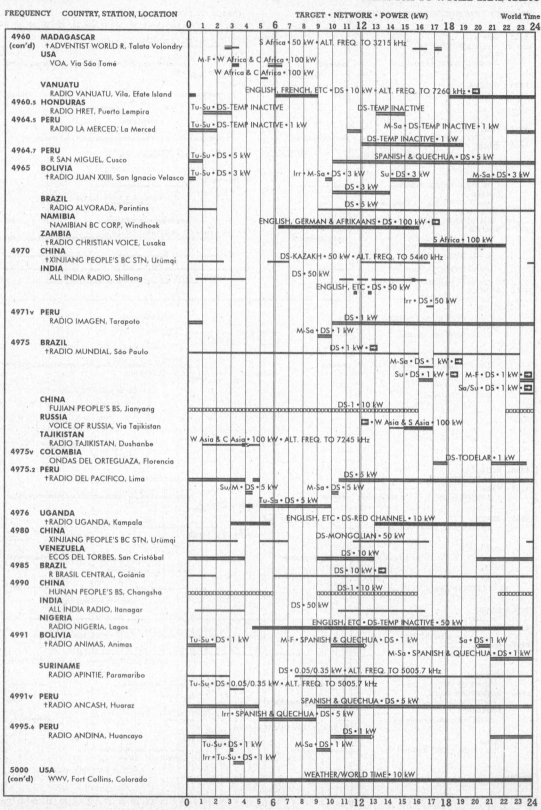

Frequency	Country / Station / Location	Notes
4960 (con'd)	MADAGASCAR — †ADVENTIST WORLD R, Talata Volondry	S Africa • 50 kW • ALT. FREQ. TO 3215 kHz
	USA — VOA, Via São Tomé	M-F • W Africa & C Africa • 100 kW / W Africa & C Africa • 100 kW
	VANUATU — RADIO VANUATU, Vila, Efate Island	ENGLISH, FRENCH, ETC • DS • 10 kW • ALT. FREQ. TO 7260 kHz •
4960.5	HONDURAS — RADIO HRET, Puerto Lempira	Tu-Su • DS-TEMP INACTIVE / DS-TEMP INACTIVE
4964.5	PERU — RADIO LA MERCED, La Merced	Tu-Su • DS-TEMP INACTIVE • 1 kW / M-Sa • DS-TEMP INACTIVE • 1 kW / DS-TEMP INACTIVE • 1 kW
4964.7	PERU — R SAN MIGUEL, Cusco	Tu-Su • DS • 5 kW / SPANISH & QUECHUA • DS • 5 kW
4965	BOLIVIA — †RADIO JUAN XXIII, San Ignacio Velasco	Tu-Su • DS • 3 kW / Irr • M-Sa • DS • 3 kW / Su • DS • 3 kW / M-Sa • DS • 3 kW / DS • 3 kW
	BRAZIL — RADIO ALVORADA, Parintins	DS • 5 kW
	NAMIBIA — NAMIBIAN BC CORP, Windhoek	ENGLISH, GERMAN & AFRIKAANS • DS • 100 kW •
	ZAMBIA — †RADIO CHRISTIAN VOICE, Lusaka	S Africa • 100 kW
4970	CHINA — †XINJIANG PEOPLE'S BC STN, Urümqi	DS-KAZAKH • 50 kW • ALT. FREQ. TO 5440 kHz
	INDIA — ALL INDIA RADIO, Shillong	DS • 50 kW / ENGLISH, ETC • DS • 50 kW / Irr • DS • 50 kW
4971v	PERU — RADIO IMAGEN, Tarapoto	DS • 1 kW / M-Sa • DS • 1 kW / DS • 1 kW •
4975	BRAZIL — †RADIO MUNDIAL, São Paulo	M-Sa • DS • 1 kW • / Su • DS • 1 kW • / M-F • DS • 1 kW • / Sa/Su • DS • 1 kW •
	CHINA — FUJIAN PEOPLE'S BS, Jianyang	DS-1 • 10 kW
	RUSSIA — VOICE OF RUSSIA, Via Tajikistan	• W Asia & S Asia • 100 kW
	TAJIKISTAN — RADIO TAJIKISTAN, Dushanbe	W Asia & C Asia • 100 kW • ALT. FREQ. TO 7245 kHz
4975v	COLOMBIA — ONDAS DEL ORTEGUAZA, Florencia	DS-TODELAR • 1 kW
4975.2	PERU — †RADIO DEL PACIFICO, Lima	DS • 5 kW / Su/M • DS • 5 kW / M-Sa • DS • 5 kW / Tu-Sa • DS • 5 kW
4976	UGANDA — †RADIO UGANDA, Kampala	ENGLISH, ETC • DS-RED CHANNEL • 10 kW
4980	CHINA — XINJIANG PEOPLE'S BC STN, Urümqi	DS-MONGOLIAN • 50 kW
	VENEZUELA — ECOS DEL TORBES, San Cristóbal	DS • 10 kW
4985	BRAZIL — R BRASIL CENTRAL, Goiânia	DS • 10 kW •
4990	CHINA — HUNAN PEOPLE'S BS, Changsha	DS-1 • 10 kW
	INDIA — ALL INDIA RADIO, Itanagar	DS • 50 kW
	NIGERIA — RADIO NIGERIA, Lagos	ENGLISH, ETC • DS-TEMP INACTIVE • 50 kW
4991	BOLIVIA — †RADIO ANIMAS, Animas	Tu-Su • DS • 1 kW / M-F • SPANISH & QUECHUA • DS • 1 kW / Sa • DS • 1 kW / M-Sa • SPANISH & QUECHUA • DS • 1 kW
	SURINAME — RADIO APINTIE, Paramaribo	DS • 0.05/0.35 kW • ALT. FREQ. TO 5005.7 kHz / Tu-Su • DS • 0.05/0.35 kW • ALT. FREQ. TO 5005.7 kHz
4991v	PERU — †RADIO ANCASH, Huaraz	SPANISH & QUECHUA • DS • 5 kW / Irr • SPANISH & QUECHUA • DS • 5 kW
4995.6	PERU — RADIO ANDINA, Huancayo	DS • 1 kW / Tu-Su • DS • 1 kW / M-Sa • DS • 1 kW / Irr • Tu-Su • DS • 1 kW
5000 (con'd)	USA — WWV, Fort Collins, Colorado	WEATHER/WORLD TIME • 10 kW

FREQUENCY   COUNTRY, STATION, LOCATION   TARGET • NETWORK • POWER (kW)   World Time

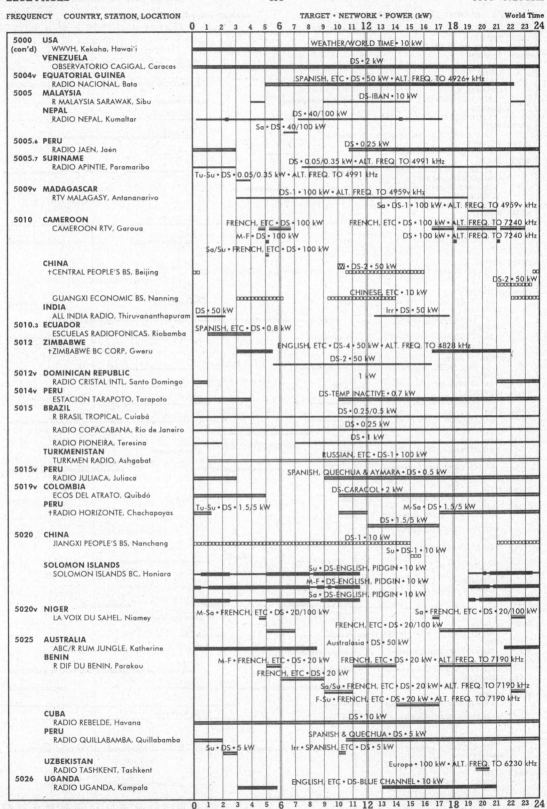

Freq	Country, Station, Location	Schedule
5000 (con'd)	**USA** WWVH, Kekaha, Hawai'i	WEATHER/WORLD TIME • 10 kW
	VENEZUELA OBSERVATORIO CAGIGAL, Caracas	DS • 2 kW
5004v	**EQUATORIAL GUINEA** RADIO NACIONAL, Bata	SPANISH, ETC • DS • 50 kW • ALT. FREQ. TO 4926v kHz
5005	**MALAYSIA** R MALAYSIA SARAWAK, Sibu	DS-IBAN • 10 kW
	NEPAL RADIO NEPAL, Kumaltar	DS • 40/100 kW / Sa • DS • 40/100 kW
5005.6	**PERU** RADIO JAEN, Jaén	DS • 0.25 kW
5005.7	**SURINAME** RADIO APINTIE, Paramaribo	DS • 0.05/0.35 kW • ALT. FREQ. TO 4991 kHz / Tu-Su • DS • 0.05/0.35 kW • ALT. FREQ. TO 4991 kHz
5009v	**MADAGASCAR** RTV MALAGASY, Antananarivo	DS-1 • 100 kW • ALT. FREQ. TO 4959v kHz / Sa • DS-1 • 100 kW • ALT. FREQ. TO 4959v kHz
5010	**CAMEROON** CAMEROON RTV, Garoua	FRENCH, ETC • DS • 100 kW / FRENCH, ETC • DS • 100 kW • ALT. FREQ. TO 7240 kHz / M-F • DS • 100 kW / DS • 100 kW • ALT. FREQ. TO 7240 kHz / Sa/Su • FRENCH, ETC • DS • 100 kW
	CHINA †CENTRAL PEOPLE'S BS, Beijing	W • DS-2 • 50 kW / DS-2 • 50 kW
	GUANGXI ECONOMIC BS, Nanning	CHINESE, ETC • 10 kW
	INDIA ALL INDIA RADIO, Thiruvananthapuram	DS • 50 kW / Irr • DS • 50 kW
5010.3	**ECUADOR** ESCUELAS RADIOFONICAS, Riobamba	SPANISH, ETC • DS • 0.8 kW
5012	**ZIMBABWE** †ZIMBABWE BC CORP, Gweru	ENGLISH, ETC • DS-4 • 50 kW • ALT. FREQ. TO 4828 kHz / DS-2 • 50 kW
5012v	**DOMINICAN REPUBLIC** RADIO CRISTAL INTL, Santo Domingo	1 kW
5014v	**PERU** ESTACION TARAPOTO, Tarapoto	DS-TEMP INACTIVE • 0.7 kW
5015	**BRAZIL** R BRASIL TROPICAL, Cuiabá	DS • 0.25/0.5 kW
	RADIO COPACABANA, Rio de Janeiro	DS • 0.25 kW
	RADIO PIONEIRA, Teresina	DS • 1 kW
	TURKMENISTAN TURKMEN RADIO, Ashgabat	RUSSIAN, ETC • DS-1 • 100 kW
5015v	**PERU** RADIO JULIACA, Juliaca	SPANISH, QUECHUA & AYMARA • DS • 0.5 kW
5019v	**COLOMBIA** ECOS DEL ATRATO, Quibdó	DS-CARACOL • 2 kW
	PERU †RADIO HORIZONTE, Chachapoyas	Tu-Su • DS • 1.5/5 kW / M-Sa • DS • 1.5/5 kW / DS • 1.5/5 kW
5020	**CHINA** JIANGXI PEOPLE'S BS, Nanchang	DS-1 • 10 kW / Su • DS-1 • 10 kW
	SOLOMON ISLANDS SOLOMON ISLANDS BC, Honiara	Su • DS-ENGLISH, PIDGIN • 10 kW / M-F • DS-ENGLISH, PIDGIN • 10 kW / Sa • DS-ENGLISH, PIDGIN • 10 kW
5020v	**NIGER** LA VOIX DU SAHEL, Niamey	M-Sa • FRENCH, ETC • DS • 20/100 kW / Sa • FRENCH, ETC • DS • 20/100 kW / FRENCH, ETC • DS • 20/100 kW
5025	**AUSTRALIA** ABC/R RUM JUNGLE, Katherine	Australasia • DS • 50 kW
	BENIN R DIF DU BENIN, Parakou	M-F • FRENCH, ETC • DS • 20 kW / FRENCH, ETC • DS • 20 kW • ALT. FREQ. TO 7190 kHz / FRENCH, ETC • DS • 20 kW / Sa/Su • FRENCH, ETC • DS • 20 kW • ALT. FREQ. TO 7190 kHz / F-Su • FRENCH, ETC • DS • 20 kW • ALT. FREQ. TO 7190 kHz
	CUBA RADIO REBELDE, Havana	DS • 10 kW
	PERU RADIO QUILLABAMBA, Quillabamba	SPANISH & QUECHUA • DS • 5 kW / Su • DS • 5 kW / Irr • SPANISH, ETC • DS • 5 kW
	UZBEKISTAN RADIO TASHKENT, Tashkent	Europe • 100 kW • ALT. FREQ. TO 6230 kHz
5026	**UGANDA** RADIO UGANDA, Kampala	ENGLISH, ETC • DS-BLUE CHANNEL • 10 kW

ENGLISH ▬▬   ARABIC ﹅﹅﹅   CHINESE □□□   FRENCH ══   GERMAN ▬▬   RUSSIAN ═══   SPANISH ▬▬   OTHER ──

FREQUENCY   COUNTRY, STATION, LOCATION   TARGET • NETWORK • POWER (kW)   World Time

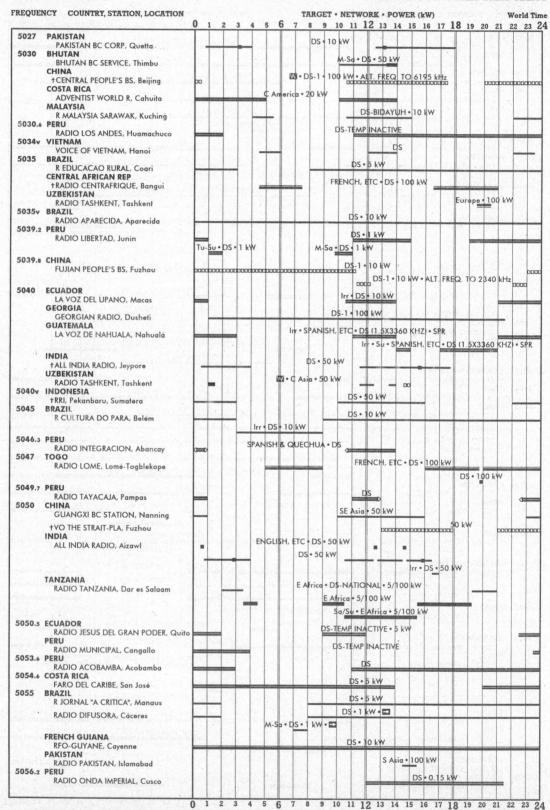

Frequency	Country, Station, Location	Target • Network • Power
5027	**PAKISTAN** PAKISTAN BC CORP, Quetta	DS • 10 kW
5030	**BHUTAN** BHUTAN BC SERVICE, Thimbu	M-Sa • DS • 50 kW
	CHINA †CENTRAL PEOPLE'S BS, Beijing	W • DS-1 • 100 kW • ALT. FREQ. TO 6195 kHz
	COSTA RICA ADVENTIST WORLD R, Cahuita	C America • 20 kW
	MALAYSIA R MALAYSIA SARAWAK, Kuching	DS-BIDAYUH • 10 kW
5030.6	**PERU** RADIO LOS ANDES, Huamachuco	DS-TEMP INACTIVE
5034v	**VIETNAM** VOICE OF VIETNAM, Hanoi	DS
5035	**BRAZIL** R EDUCACAO RURAL, Coari	DS • 5 kW
	CENTRAL AFRICAN REP †RADIO CENTRAFRIQUE, Bangui	FRENCH, ETC • DS • 100 kW
	UZBEKISTAN RADIO TASHKENT, Tashkent	Europe • 100 kW
5035v	**BRAZIL** RADIO APARECIDA, Aparecida	DS • 10 kW
5039.2	**PERU** RADIO LIBERTAD, Junin	DS • 1 kW / Tu-Su • DS • 1 kW / M-Sa • DS • 1 kW
5039.8	**CHINA** FUJIAN PEOPLE'S BS, Fuzhou	DS-1 • 10 kW / DS-1 • 10 kW • ALT. FREQ. TO 2340 kHz
5040	**ECUADOR** LA VOZ DEL UPANO, Macas	Irr • DS • 10 kW
	GEORGIA GEORGIAN RADIO, Dusheti	DS-1 • 100 kW
	GUATEMALA LA VOZ DE NAHUALA, Nahualá	Irr • SPANISH, ETC • DS (1.5X3360 KHZ) • SPR / Irr • Su • SPANISH, ETC • DS (1.5X3360 KHZ) • SPR
	INDIA †ALL INDIA RADIO, Jeypore	DS • 50 kW
	UZBEKISTAN RADIO TASHKENT, Tashkent	W • C Asia • 50 kW
5040v	**INDONESIA** †RRI, Pekanbaru, Sumatera	DS • 50 kW
5045	**BRAZIL** R CULTURA DO PARA, Belém	DS • 10 kW / Irr • DS • 10 kW
5046.3	**PERU** RADIO INTEGRACION, Abancay	SPANISH & QUECHUA • DS
5047	**TOGO** RADIO LOME, Lomé-Togblekope	FRENCH, ETC • DS • 100 kW / DS • 100 kW
5049.7	**PERU** RADIO TAYACAJA, Pampas	DS
5050	**CHINA** GUANGXI BC STATION, Nanning	SE Asia • 50 kW
	†VO THE STRAIT-PLA, Fuzhou	50 kW
	INDIA ALL INDIA RADIO, Aizawl	ENGLISH, ETC • DS • 50 kW / DS • 50 kW / Irr • DS • 50 kW
	TANZANIA RADIO TANZANIA, Dar es Salaam	E Africa • DS-NATIONAL • 5/100 kW / E Africa • 5/100 kW / Sa/Su • E Africa • 5/100 kW
5050.5	**ECUADOR** RADIO JESUS DEL GRAN PODER, Quito	DS-TEMP INACTIVE • 5 kW
	PERU RADIO MUNICIPAL, Cangallo	DS-TEMP INACTIVE
5053.6	**PERU** RADIO ACOBAMBA, Acobamba	DS
5054.6	**COSTA RICA** FARO DEL CARIBE, San José	DS • 5 kW
5055	**BRAZIL** R JORNAL "A CRITICA", Manaus	DS • 5 kW
	RADIO DIFUSORA, Cáceres	DS • 1 kW • ⊡ / M-Sa • DS • 1 kW • ⊡
	FRENCH GUIANA RFO-GUYANE, Cayenne	DS • 10 kW
	PAKISTAN RADIO PAKISTAN, Islamabad	S Asia • 100 kW
5056.2	**PERU** RADIO ONDA IMPERIAL, Cusco	DS • 0.15 kW

FREQUENCY   COUNTRY, STATION, LOCATION   TARGET • NETWORK • POWER (kW)   World Time

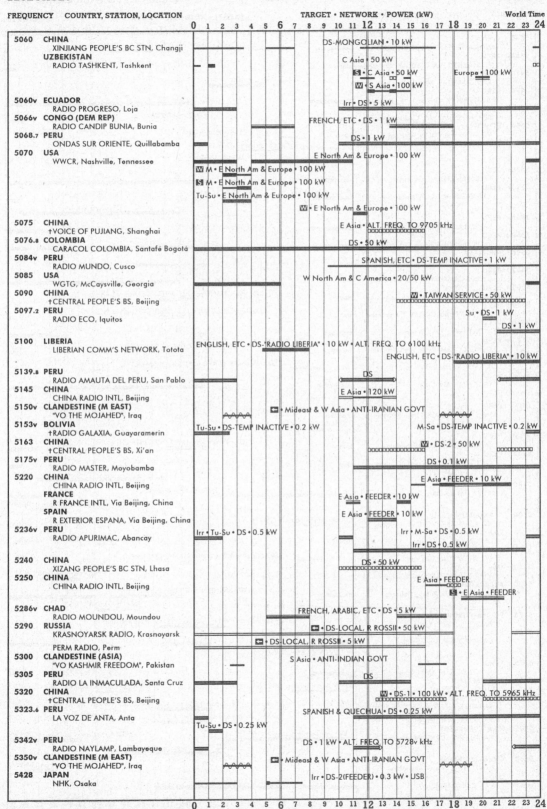

0 1 2 3 4 5 6 7 8 9 10 11 12 13 14 15 16 17 18 19 20 21 22 23 24

5060   CHINA
        XINJIANG PEOPLE'S BC STN, Changji   DS-MONGOLIAN • 10 kW
        UZBEKISTAN
        RADIO TASHKENT, Tashkent   C Asia • 50 kW
                                     S • C Asia • 50 kW   Europe • 100 kW
                                     W • S Asia • 100 kW
5060v   ECUADOR
        RADIO PROGRESO, Loja   Irr • DS • 5 kW
5066v   CONGO (DEM REP)
        RADIO CANDIP BUNIA, Bunia   FRENCH, ETC • DS • 1 kW
5068.7 PERU
        ONDAS SUR ORIENTE, Quillabamba   DS • 1 kW
5070   USA
        WWCR, Nashville, Tennessee   E North Am & Europe • 100 kW
                                     W M • E North Am & Europe • 100 kW
                                     S M • E North Am & Europe • 100 kW
                                     Tu-Su • E North Am & Europe • 100 kW
                                     W • E North Am & Europe • 100 kW
5075   CHINA
        †VOICE OF PUJIANG, Shanghai   E Asia • ALT. FREQ. TO 9705 kHz
5076.8 COLOMBIA
        CARACOL COLOMBIA, Santafé Bogotá   DS • 50 kW
5084v   PERU
        RADIO MUNDO, Cusco   SPANISH, ETC • DS-TEMP INACTIVE • 1 kW
5085   USA
        WGTG, McCaysville, Georgia   W North Am & C America • 20/50 kW
5090   CHINA
        †CENTRAL PEOPLE'S BS, Beijing   W • TAIWAN SERVICE • 50 kW
5097.2 PERU
        RADIO ECO, Iquitos   Su • DS • 1 kW
                              DS • 1 kW
5100   LIBERIA
        LIBERIAN COMM'S NETWORK, Totota   ENGLISH, ETC • DS-"RADIO LIBERIA" • 10 kW • ALT. FREQ. TO 6100 kHz
                                          ENGLISH, ETC • DS-"RADIO LIBERIA" • 10 kW
5139.8 PERU
        RADIO AMAUTA DEL PERU, San Pablo   DS
5145   CHINA
        CHINA RADIO INTL, Beijing   E Asia • 120 kW
5150v   CLANDESTINE (M EAST)
        "VO THE MOJAHED", Iraq   Mideast & W Asia • ANTI-IRANIAN GOVT
5153v   BOLIVIA
        †RADIO GALAXIA, Guayaramerin   Tu-Su • DS-TEMP INACTIVE • 0.2 kW   M-Sa • DS-TEMP INACTIVE • 0.2 kW
5163   CHINA
        †CENTRAL PEOPLE'S BS, Xi'an   W • DS-2 • 50 kW
5175v   PERU
        RADIO MASTER, Moyobamba   DS • 0.1 kW
5220   CHINA
        CHINA RADIO INTL, Beijing   E Asia • FEEDER • 10 kW
        FRANCE
        R FRANCE INTL, Via Beijing, China   E Asia • FEEDER • 10 kW
        SPAIN
        R EXTERIOR ESPANA, Via Beijing, China   E Asia • FEEDER • 10 kW
5236v   PERU
        RADIO APURIMAC, Abancay   Irr • Tu-Su • DS • 0.5 kW   Irr • M-Sa • DS • 0.5 kW
                                                              Irr • DS • 0.5 kW
5240   CHINA
        XIZANG PEOPLE'S BC STN, Lhasa   DS • 50 kW
5250   CHINA
        CHINA RADIO INTL, Beijing   E Asia • FEEDER
                                     S • E Asia • FEEDER
5286v   CHAD
        RADIO MOUNDOU, Moundou   FRENCH, ARABIC, ETC • DS • 5 kW
5290   RUSSIA
        KRASNOYARSK RADIO, Krasnoyarsk   • DS-LOCAL, R ROSSII • 50 kW
        PERM RADIO, Perm   • DS-LOCAL, R ROSSII • 5 kW
5300   CLANDESTINE (ASIA)
        "VO KASHMIR FREEDOM", Pakistan   S Asia • ANTI-INDIAN GOVT
5305   PERU
        RADIO LA INMACULADA, Santa Cruz   DS
5320   CHINA
        †CENTRAL PEOPLE'S BS, Beijing   W • DS-1 • 100 kW • ALT. FREQ. TO 5965 kHz
5323.6 PERU
        LA VOZ DE ANTA, Anta   SPANISH & QUECHUA • DS • 0.25 kW
                                Tu-Su • DS • 0.25 kW
5342v   PERU
        RADIO NAYLAMP, Lambayeque   DS • 1 kW • ALT. FREQ. TO 5728v kHz
5350v   CLANDESTINE (M EAST)
        "VO THE MOJAHED", Iraq   Mideast & W Asia • ANTI-IRANIAN GOVT
5428   JAPAN
        NHK, Osaka   Irr • DS-2(FEEDER) • 0.3 kW • USB

0 1 2 3 4 5 6 7 8 9 10 11 12 13 14 15 16 17 18 19 20 21 22 23 24

ENGLISH ▬   ARABIC ▨   CHINESE ▭   FRENCH ▬   GERMAN ▬   RUSSIAN =   SPANISH ▬   OTHER —

FREQUENCY   COUNTRY, STATION, LOCATION   TARGET • NETWORK • POWER (kW)   World Time

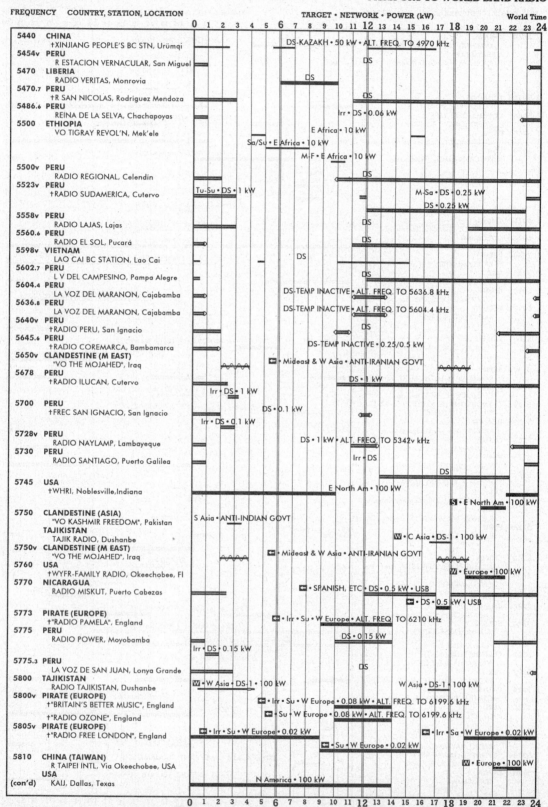

Frequency	Country / Station / Location	Notes
5440	**CHINA** †XINJIANG PEOPLE'S BC STN, Urümqi	DS-KAZAKH • 50 kW • ALT. FREQ. TO 4970 kHz
5454v	**PERU** R ESTACION VERNACULAR, San Miguel	DS
5470	**LIBERIA** RADIO VERITAS, Monrovia	DS
5470.7	**PERU** †R SAN NICOLAS, Rodriguez Mendoza	DS
5486.6	**PERU** REINA DE LA SELVA, Chachapoyas	Irr • DS • 0.06 kW
5500	**ETHIOPIA** VO TIGRAY REVOL'N, Mek'ele	E Africa • 10 kW / Sa/Su • E Africa • 10 kW / M-F • E Africa • 10 kW
5500v	**PERU** RADIO REGIONAL, Celendin	DS
5523v	**PERU** †RADIO SUDAMERICA, Cutervo	Tu-Su • DS • 1 kW / M-Sa • DS • 0.25 kW / DS • 0.25 kW
5558v	**PERU** RADIO LAJAS, Lajas	DS
5560.6	**PERU** RADIO EL SOL, Pucará	DS
5598v	**VIETNAM** LAO CAI BC STATION, Lao Cai	DS
5602.7	**PERU** L V DEL CAMPESINO, Pampa Alegre	
5604.4	**PERU** LA VOZ DEL MARANON, Cajabamba	DS-TEMP INACTIVE • ALT. FREQ. TO 5636.8 kHz
5636.8	**PERU** LA VOZ DEL MARANON, Cajabamba	DS-TEMP INACTIVE • ALT. FREQ. TO 5604.4 kHz
5640v	**PERU** †RADIO PERU, San Ignacio	DS
5645.6	**PERU** †RADIO COREMARCA, Bambamarca	DS-TEMP INACTIVE • 0.25/0.5 kW
5650v	**CLANDESTINE (M EAST)** "VO THE MOJAHED", Iraq	• Mideast & W Asia • ANTI-IRANIAN GOVT
5678	**PERU** †RADIO ILUCAN, Cutervo	DS • 1 kW / Irr • DS • 1 kW
5700	**PERU** †FREC SAN IGNACIO, San Ignacio	DS • 0.1 kW / Irr • DS • 0.1 kW
5728v	**PERU** RADIO NAYLAMP, Lambayeque	DS • 1 kW • ALT. FREQ. TO 5342v kHz
5730	**PERU** RADIO SANTIAGO, Puerto Galilea	Irr • DS / DS
5745	**USA** †WHRI, Noblesville, Indiana	E North Am • 100 kW / S • E North Am • 100 kW
5750	**CLANDESTINE (ASIA)** "VO KASHMIR FREEDOM", Pakistan	S Asia • ANTI-INDIAN GOVT
	TAJIKISTAN TAJIK RADIO, Dushanbe	W • C Asia • DS-1 • 100 kW
5750v	**CLANDESTINE (M EAST)** "VO THE MOJAHED", Iraq	• Mideast & W Asia • ANTI-IRANIAN GOVT
5760	**USA** †WYFR-FAMILY RADIO, Okeechobee, Fl	W • Europe • 100 kW
5770	**NICARAGUA** RADIO MISKUT, Puerto Cabezas	• SPANISH, ETC • DS • 0.5 kW • USB / • DS • 0.5 kW • USB
5773	**PIRATE (EUROPE)** †"RADIO PAMELA", England	• Irr • Su • W Europe • ALT. FREQ. TO 6210 kHz
5775	**PERU** RADIO POWER, Moyobamba	Irr • DS • 0.15 kW / DS • 0.15 kW
5775.3	**PERU** LA VOZ DE SAN JUAN, Lonya Grande	DS
5800	**TAJIKISTAN** RADIO TAJIKISTAN, Dushanbe	W • W Asia • DS-1 • 100 kW / W Asia • DS-1 • 100 kW
5800v	**PIRATE (EUROPE)** †"BRITAIN'S BETTER MUSIC", England	• Irr • Su • W Europe • 0.08 kW • ALT. FREQ. TO 6199.6 kHz
	†"RADIO OZONE", England	• Su • W Europe • 0.08 kW • ALT. FREQ. TO 6199.6 kHz
5805v	**PIRATE (EUROPE)** †"RADIO FREE LONDON", England	• Irr • Su • W Europe • 0.02 kW / • Irr • Sa • W Europe • 0.02 kW / • Su • W Europe • 0.02 kW
5810	**CHINA (TAIWAN)** R TAIPEI INTL, Via Okeechobee, USA	W • Europe • 100 kW
(con'd)	**USA** KAIJ, Dallas, Texas	N America • 100 kW

SEASONAL ⓈOR Ⓦ   1-HR TIMESHIFT MIDYEAR ⊡ OR ⊡   JAMMING / OR ∧   EARLIEST HEARD ◁   LATEST HEARD ▷   NEW FOR 2000 †

| FREQUENCY | COUNTRY, STATION, LOCATION | TARGET • NETWORK • POWER (kW) | World Time |

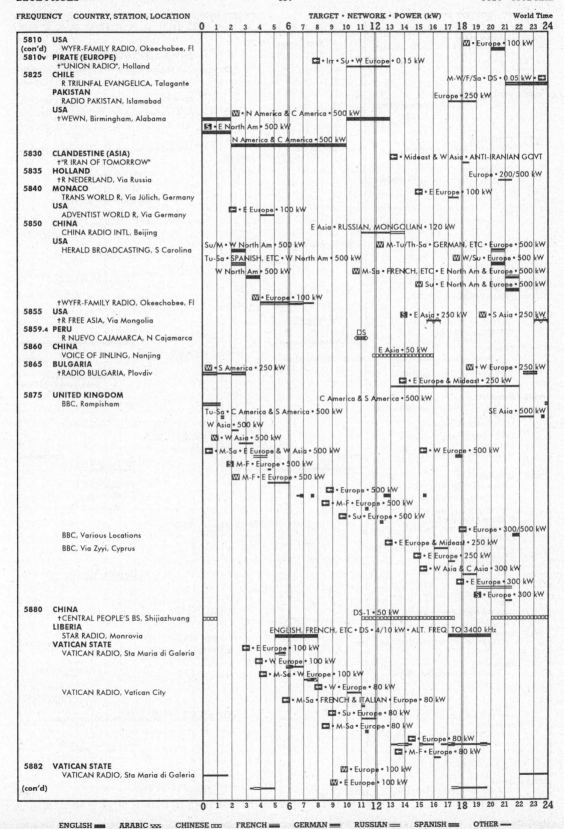

5810 **USA**
(con'd)   WYFR-FAMILY RADIO, Okeechobee, Fl   W • Europe • 100 kW
5810v **PIRATE (EUROPE)**
   †"UNION RADIO", Holland   • Irr • Su • W Europe • 0.15 kW
5825 **CHILE**
   R TRIUNFAL EVANGELICA, Talagante   M-W/F/Sa • DS • 0.05 kW •
   PAKISTAN
     RADIO PAKISTAN, Islamabad   Europe • 250 kW
   USA
     †WEWN, Birmingham, Alabama   W • N America & C America • 500 kW
     S • E North Am • 500 kW
     N America & C America • 500 kW

5830 **CLANDESTINE (ASIA)**
   †"R IRAN OF TOMORROW"   • Mideast & W Asia • ANTI-IRANIAN GOVT
5835 **HOLLAND**
   †R NEDERLAND, Via Russia   Europe • 200/500 kW
5840 **MONACO**
   TRANS WORLD R, Via Jülich, Germany   • E Europe • 100 kW
   USA
     ADVENTIST WORLD R, Via Germany   • E Europe • 100 kW
5850 **CHINA**
   CHINA RADIO INTL, Beijing   E Asia • RUSSIAN, MONGOLIAN • 120 kW
   USA
     HERALD BROADCASTING, S Carolina   Su/M • W North Am • 500 kW   M-Tu/Th-Sa • GERMAN, ETC • Europe • 500 kW
     Tu-Sa • SPANISH, ETC • W North Am • 500 kW   W/Su • Europe • 500 kW
     W North Am • 500 kW   M-Sa • FRENCH, ETC • E North Am & Europe • 500 kW
     Su • E North Am & Europe • 500 kW
     †WYFR-FAMILY RADIO, Okeechobee, Fl   W • Europe • 100 kW
5855 **USA**
   †R FREE ASIA, Via Mongolia   S • E Asia • 250 kW   W • S Asia • 250 kW
5859.4 **PERU**
   R NUEVO CAJAMARCA, N Cajamarca   DS
5860 **CHINA**
   VOICE OF JINLING, Nanjing   E Asia • 50 kW
5865 **BULGARIA**
   †RADIO BULGARIA, Plovdiv   W • S America • 250 kW   W • W Europe • 250 kW
     • E Europe & Mideast • 250 kW

5875 **UNITED KINGDOM**
   BBC, Rampisham   C America & S America • 500 kW
     Tu-Sa • C America & S America • 500 kW   SE Asia • 500 kW
     W Asia • 500 kW
     W • W Asia • 500 kW
     • M-Sa • E Europe & W Asia • 500 kW   • W Europe • 500 kW
     S • M-F • Europe • 500 kW
     W M-F • Europe • 500 kW
     • Europe • 500 kW
     • M-F • Europe • 500 kW
     • Su • Europe • 500 kW
   BBC, Various Locations   • Europe • 300/500 kW
   BBC, Via Zyyi, Cyprus   • E Europe & Mideast • 250 kW
     • E Europe • 250 kW
     • W Asia & C Asia • 300 kW
     • E Europe • 300 kW
     S • Europe • 300 kW

5880 **CHINA**
   †CENTRAL PEOPLE'S BS, Shijiazhuang   DS-1 • 50 kW
   LIBERIA
     STAR RADIO, Monrovia   ENGLISH, FRENCH, ETC • DS • 4/10 kW • ALT. FREQ. TO 3400 kHz
   VATICAN STATE
     VATICAN RADIO, Sta Maria di Galeria   • E Europe • 100 kW
     • W Europe • 100 kW
     • M-Sa • W Europe • 100 kW
     VATICAN RADIO, Vatican City   • W • Europe • 80 kW
     • M-Sa • FRENCH & ITALIAN • Europe • 80 kW
     • Su • Europe • 80 kW
     • M-Sa • Europe • 80 kW
     • Europe • 80 kW
     • M-F • Europe • 80 kW

5882 **VATICAN STATE**
   VATICAN RADIO, Sta Maria di Galeria   W • Europe • 100 kW
     W • E Europe • 100 kW
(con'd)

ENGLISH ▬▬   ARABIC ▨▨   CHINESE □□□   FRENCH ▬▬   GERMAN ▬▬   RUSSIAN ══   SPANISH ▬▬   OTHER ▬

FREQUENCY   COUNTRY, STATION, LOCATION   TARGET • NETWORK • POWER (kW)   World Time

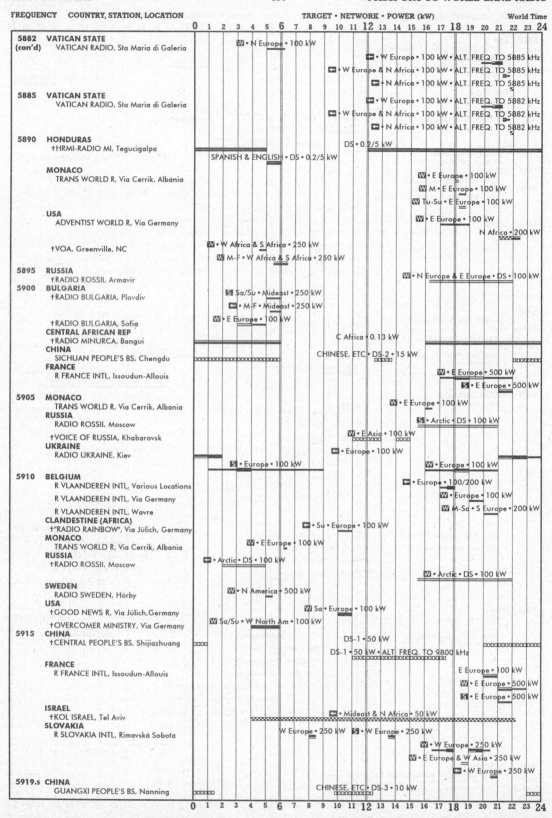

0 1 2 3 4 5 6 7 8 9 10 11 12 13 14 15 16 17 18 19 20 21 22 23 24

Frequency	Country, Station, Location	Target • Network • Power
5882 (con'd)	VATICAN STATE — VATICAN RADIO, Sta Maria di Galeria	W • N Europe • 100 kW
		W Europe • 100 kW • ALT. FREQ. TO 5885 kHz
		W Europe & N Africa • 100 kW • ALT. FREQ. TO 5885 kHz
		N Africa • 100 kW • ALT. FREQ. TO 5885 kHz
5885	VATICAN STATE — VATICAN RADIO, Sta Maria di Galeria	W Europe • 100 kW • ALT. FREQ. TO 5882 kHz
		W Europe & N Africa • 100 kW • ALT. FREQ. TO 5882 kHz
		N Africa • 100 kW • ALT. FREQ. TO 5882 kHz
5890	HONDURAS — †HRMI-RADIO MI, Tegucigalpa	DS • 0.2/5 kW
		SPANISH & ENGLISH • DS • 0.2/5 kW
	MONACO — TRANS WORLD R, Via Cerrik, Albania	W • E Europe • 100 kW
		W • M • E Europe • 100 kW
		W • Tu-Su • E Europe • 100 kW
	USA — ADVENTIST WORLD R, Via Germany	W • E Europe • 100 kW
		N Africa • 200 kW
	†VOA, Greenville, NC	W • W Africa & S Africa • 250 kW
		W • M-F • W Africa & S Africa • 250 kW
5895	RUSSIA — †RADIO ROSSII, Armavir	W • N Europe & E Europe • DS • 100 kW
5900	BULGARIA — †RADIO BULGARIA, Plovdiv	S • Sa/Su • Mideast • 250 kW
		M-F • Mideast • 250 kW
	†RADIO BULGARIA, Sofia	W • E Europe • 100 kW
	CENTRAL AFRICAN REP — †RADIO MINURCA, Bangui	C Africa • 0.13 kW
	CHINA — SICHUAN PEOPLE'S BS, Chengdu	CHINESE, ETC • DS-2 • 15 kW
	FRANCE — R FRANCE INTL, Issoudun-Allouis	W • E Europe • 500 kW
		S • E Europe • 500 kW
5905	MONACO — TRANS WORLD R, Via Cerrik, Albania	W • E Europe • 100 kW
	RUSSIA — RADIO ROSSII, Moscow	S • Arctic • DS • 100 kW
	†VOICE OF RUSSIA, Khabarovsk	W • E Asia • 100 kW
	UKRAINE — RADIO UKRAINE, Kiev	Europe • 100 kW
		S • Europe • 100 kW
		W • Europe • 100 kW
5910	BELGIUM — R VLAANDEREN INTL, Various Locations	Europe • 100/200 kW
	R VLAANDEREN INTL, Via Germany	W • Europe • 100 kW
	R VLAANDEREN INTL, Wavre	W • M-Sa • S Europe • 200 kW
	CLANDESTINE (AFRICA) — †"RADIO RAINBOW", Via Jülich, Germany	Su • Europe • 100 kW
	MONACO — TRANS WORLD R, Via Cerrik, Albania	W • E Europe • 100 kW
	RUSSIA — †RADIO ROSSII, Moscow	Arctic • DS • 100 kW
		W • Arctic • DS • 100 kW
	SWEDEN — RADIO SWEDEN, Hörby	W • N America • 500 kW
	USA — †GOOD NEWS R, Via Jülich, Germany	Sa • Europe • 100 kW
	†OVERCOMER MINISTRY, Via Germany	W Sa/Su • W North Am • 100 kW
5915	CHINA — †CENTRAL PEOPLE'S BS, Shijiazhuang	DS-1 • 50 kW
		DS-1 • 50 kW • ALT. FREQ. TO 9800 kHz
	FRANCE — R FRANCE INTL, Issoudun-Allouis	E Europe • 100 kW
		W • E Europe • 500 kW
		S • E Europe • 500 kW
	ISRAEL — †KOL ISRAEL, Tel Aviv	Mideast & N Africa • 50 kW
	SLOVAKIA — R SLOVAKIA INTL, Rimavská Sobota	W Europe • 250 kW S • W Europe • 250 kW
		W • W Europe • 250 kW
		W • E Europe & W Asia • 250 kW
		W Europe • 250 kW
5919.5	CHINA — GUANGXI PEOPLE'S BS, Nanning	CHINESE, ETC • DS-3 • 10 kW

0 1 2 3 4 5 6 7 8 9 10 11 12 13 14 15 16 17 18 19 20 21 22 23 24

FREQUENCY   COUNTRY, STATION, LOCATION   TARGET • NETWORK • POWER (kW)   World Time

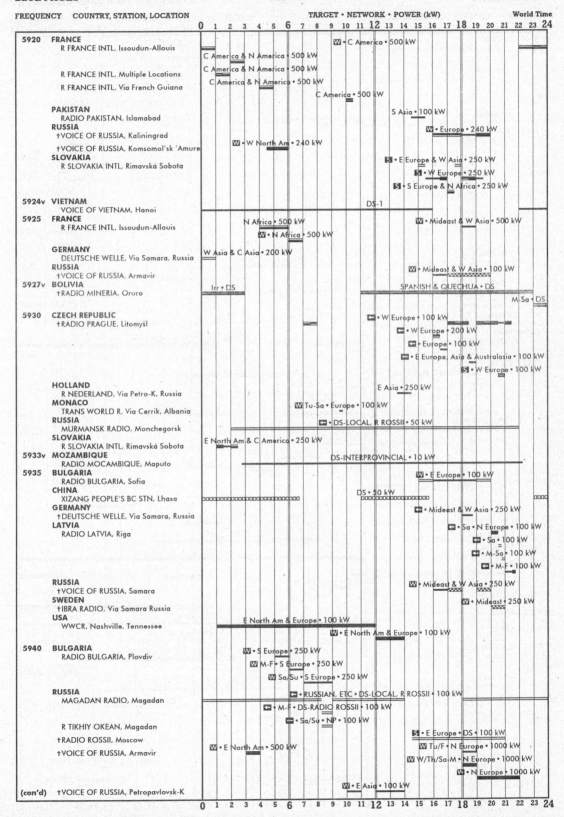

Freq	Country / Station / Location	Target • Network • Power
5920	**FRANCE** R FRANCE INTL, Issoudun-Allouis	W • C America • 500 kW; C America & N America • 500 kW
	R FRANCE INTL, Multiple Locations	C America & N America • 500 kW
	R FRANCE INTL, Via French Guiana	C America & N America • 500 kW; C America • 500 kW
	PAKISTAN RADIO PAKISTAN, Islamabad	S Asia • 100 kW
	RUSSIA †VOICE OF RUSSIA, Kaliningrad	W • Europe • 240 kW
	†VOICE OF RUSSIA, Komsomol'sk 'Amure	W • W North Am • 240 kW
	SLOVAKIA R SLOVAKIA INTL, Rimavská Sobota	S • E Europe & W Asia • 250 kW; S • W Europe • 250 kW; S • S Europe & N Africa • 250 kW
5924v	**VIETNAM** VOICE OF VIETNAM, Hanoi	DS-1
5925	**FRANCE** R FRANCE INTL, Issoudun-Allouis	N Africa • 500 kW; W • N Africa • 500 kW; W • Mideast & W Asia • 500 kW
	GERMANY DEUTSCHE WELLE, Via Samara, Russia	W Asia & C Asia • 200 kW
	RUSSIA †VOICE OF RUSSIA, Armavir	W • Mideast & W Asia • 100 kW
5927v	**BOLIVIA** †RADIO MINERIA, Oruro	Irr • DS; SPANISH & QUECHUA • DS; M-Sa • DS
5930	**CZECH REPUBLIC** †RADIO PRAGUE, Litomyšl	⊡ • W Europe • 100 kW; ⊡ • W Europe • 200 kW; ⊡ • Europe • 100 kW; ⊡ • E Europe, Asia & Australasia • 100 kW; S • W Europe • 100 kW
	HOLLAND R NEDERLAND, Via Petro-K, Russia	E Asia • 250 kW
	MONACO TRANS WORLD R, Via Cerrik, Albania	W Tu-Sa • Europe • 100 kW
	RUSSIA MURMANSK RADIO, Monchegorsk	⊡ • DS-LOCAL, R ROSSII • 50 kW
	SLOVAKIA R SLOVAKIA INTL, Rimavská Sobota	E North Am & C America • 250 kW
5933v	**MOZAMBIQUE** RADIO MOCAMBIQUE, Maputo	DS-INTERPROVINCIAL • 10 kW
5935	**BULGARIA** RADIO BULGARIA, Sofia	W • E Europe • 100 kW
	CHINA XIZANG PEOPLE'S BC STN, Lhasa	DS • 50 kW
	GERMANY †DEUTSCHE WELLE, Via Samara, Russia	⊡ • Mideast & W Asia • 250 kW
	LATVIA RADIO LATVIA, Riga	⊡ • Sa • N Europe • 100 kW; ⊡ • Sa • 100 kW; ⊡ • M-Sa • 100 kW; ⊡ • M-F • 100 kW
	RUSSIA †VOICE OF RUSSIA, Samara	W • Mideast & W Asia • 250 kW
	SWEDEN †IBRA RADIO, Via Samara Russia	W • Mideast • 250 kW
	USA WWCR, Nashville, Tennessee	E North Am & Europe • 100 kW; W • E North Am & Europe • 100 kW
5940	**BULGARIA** RADIO BULGARIA, Plovdiv	W • S Europe • 250 kW; W M-F • S Europe • 250 kW; W Sa/Su • S Europe • 250 kW
	RUSSIA MAGADAN RADIO, Magadan	⊡ • RUSSIAN, ETC • DS-LOCAL, R ROSSII • 100 kW; ⊡ • M-F • DS-RADIO ROSSII • 100 kW; ⊡ • Sa/Su • NP • 100 kW
	R TIKHIY OKEAN, Magadan	S • E Europe • DS • 100 kW
	†RADIO ROSSII, Moscow	W Tu/F • N Europe • 1000 kW
	†VOICE OF RUSSIA, Armavir	W • E North Am • 500 kW; W W/Th/Sa-M • N Europe • 1000 kW; W • N Europe • 1000 kW
(con'd)	†VOICE OF RUSSIA, Petropavlovsk-K	W • E Asia • 100 kW

ENGLISH ▬▬   ARABIC ⧚⧚⧚   CHINESE ☐☐☐   FRENCH ══   GERMAN ▬▬   RUSSIAN ═══   SPANISH ▬▬   OTHER ──

FREQUENCY   COUNTRY, STATION, LOCATION   TARGET • NETWORK • POWER (kW)   World Time

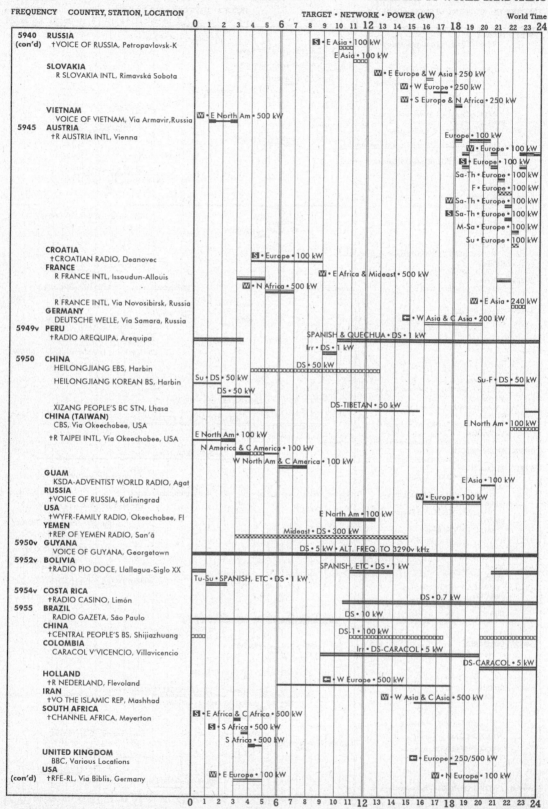

5940
(con'd)   **RUSSIA**
     †VOICE OF RUSSIA, Petropavlovsk-K   S • E Asia • 100 kW / E Asia • 100 kW

     SLOVAKIA
     R SLOVAKIA INTL, Rimavská Sobota   W • E Europe & W Asia • 250 kW / W • W Europe • 250 kW / W • S Europe & N Africa • 250 kW

     VIETNAM
     VOICE OF VIETNAM, Via Armavir, Russia   W • E North Am • 500 kW
5945   **AUSTRIA**
     †R AUSTRIA INTL, Vienna   Europe • 100 kW / W • Europe • 100 kW / S • Europe • 100 kW / Sa-Th • Europe • 100 kW / F • Europe • 100 kW / W Sa-Th • Europe • 100 kW / S Sa-Th • Europe • 100 kW / M-Sa • Europe • 100 kW / Su • Europe • 100 kW

     CROATIA
     †CROATIAN RADIO, Deanovec   S • Europe • 100 kW
     FRANCE
     R FRANCE INTL, Issoudun-Allouis   W • E Africa & Mideast • 500 kW / W • N Africa • 500 kW

     R FRANCE INTL, Via Novosibirsk, Russia   W • E Asia • 240 kW
     GERMANY
     DEUTSCHE WELLE, Via Samara, Russia   W Asia & C Asia • 200 kW
5949v   **PERU**
     †RADIO AREQUIPA, Arequipa   SPANISH & QUECHUA • DS • 1 kW

5950   **CHINA**   Irr • DS • 1 kW
     HEILONGJIANG EBS, Harbin   DS • 50 kW
     HEILONGJIANG KOREAN BS, Harbin   Su • DS • 50 kW / Su-F • DS • 50 kW / DS • 50 kW

     XIZANG PEOPLE'S BC STN, Lhasa   DS-TIBETAN • 50 kW
     CHINA (TAIWAN)
     CBS, Via Okeechobee, USA   E North Am • 100 kW
     †R TAIPEI INTL, Via Okeechobee, USA   E North Am • 100 kW / N America & C America • 100 kW / W North Am & C America • 100 kW

     GUAM
     KSDA-ADVENTIST WORLD RADIO, Agat   E Asia • 100 kW
     RUSSIA
     †VOICE OF RUSSIA, Kaliningrad   W • Europe • 100 kW
     USA
     †WYFR-FAMILY RADIO, Okeechobee, Fl   E North Am • 100 kW
     YEMEN
     †REP OF YEMEN RADIO, San'á   Mideast • DS • 300 kW
5950v   **GUYANA**
     VOICE OF GUYANA, Georgetown   DS • 5 kW • ALT. FREQ. TO 3290v kHz
5952v   **BOLIVIA**
     †RADIO PIO DOCE, Llallagua-Siglo XX   SPANISH, ETC • DS • 1 kW / Tu-Su • SPANISH, ETC • DS • 1 kW

5954v   **COSTA RICA**
     †RADIO CASINO, Limón   DS • 0.7 kW
5955   **BRAZIL**
     RADIO GAZETA, São Paulo   DS • 10 kW
     CHINA
     †CENTRAL PEOPLE'S BS, Shijiazhuang   DS • 1 • 100 kW
     COLOMBIA
     CARACOL V'VICENCIO, Villavicencio   Irr • DS-CARACOL • 5 kW / DS-CARACOL • 5 kW

     HOLLAND
     †R NEDERLAND, Flevoland   W Europe • 500 kW
     IRAN
     †VO THE ISLAMIC REP, Mashhad   W • W Asia & C Asia • 500 kW
     SOUTH AFRICA
     †CHANNEL AFRICA, Meyerton   S • E Africa & C Africa • 500 kW / S • S Africa • 500 kW / S Africa • 500 kW

     UNITED KINGDOM
     BBC, Various Locations   Europe • 250/500 kW
     USA
(con'd)   †RFE-RL, Via Biblis, Germany   W • E Europe • 100 kW / W • N Europe • 100 kW

FREQUENCY   COUNTRY, STATION, LOCATION   TARGET • NETWORK • POWER (kW)   World Time

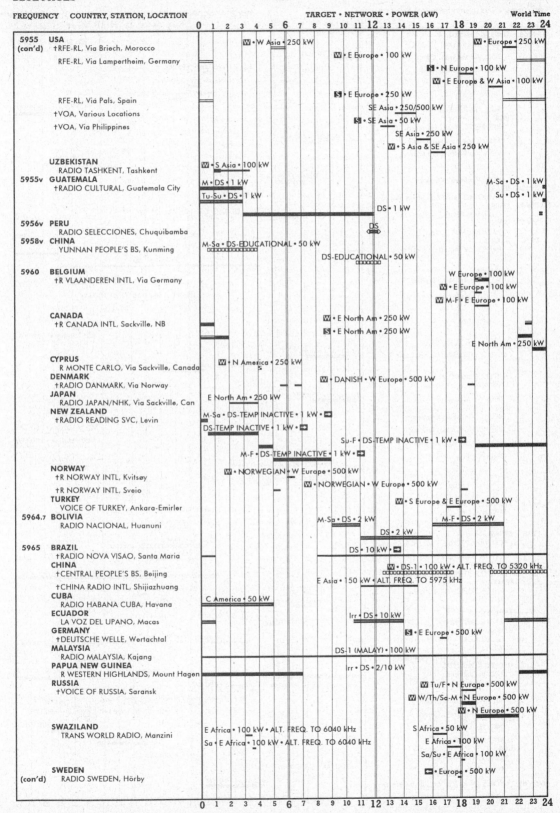

0 1 2 3 4 5 6 7 8 9 10 11 12 13 14 15 16 17 18 19 20 21 22 23 24

5955 USA
(con'd)   †RFE-RL, Via Briech, Morocco   W • W Asia • 250 kW   W • Europe • 250 kW
   RFE-RL, Via Lampertheim, Germany   W • E Europe • 100 kW   S • N Europe • 100 kW   W • E Europe & W Asia • 100 kW
   RFE-RL, Via Pals, Spain   S • E Europe • 250 kW
   †VOA, Various Locations   SE Asia • 250/500 kW
   †VOA, Via Philippines   S • SE Asia • 50 kW   SE Asia • 250 kW   W • S Asia & SE Asia • 250 kW

UZBEKISTAN
   RADIO TASHKENT, Tashkent   W • S Asia • 100 kW
5955v GUATEMALA
   †RADIO CULTURAL, Guatemala City   M • DS • 1 kW   M-Sa • DS • 1 kW
   Tu-Su • DS • 1 kW   Su • DS • 1 kW
   DS • 1 kW

5956v PERU
   RADIO SELECCIONES, Chuquibamba   DS
5958v CHINA
   YUNNAN PEOPLE'S BS, Kunming   M-Sa • DS-EDUCATIONAL • 50 kW   DS-EDUCATIONAL • 50 kW

5960 BELGIUM
   †R VLAANDEREN INTL, Via Germany   W Europe • 100 kW   W • E Europe • 100 kW   W M-F • E Europe • 100 kW

CANADA
   †R CANADA INTL, Sackville, NB   W • E North Am • 250 kW   S • E North Am • 250 kW   E North Am • 250 kW

CYPRUS
   R MONTE CARLO, Via Sackville, Canada   W • N America • 250 kW
DENMARK
   †RADIO DANMARK, Via Norway   W • DANISH • W Europe • 500 kW
JAPAN
   RADIO JAPAN/NHK, Via Sackville, Can   E North Am • 250 kW
NEW ZEALAND
   †RADIO READING SVC, Levin   M-Sa • DS-TEMP INACTIVE • 1 kW •
   DS-TEMP INACTIVE • 1 kW •
   Su-F • DS-TEMP INACTIVE • 1 kW •
   M-F • DS-TEMP INACTIVE • 1 kW •

NORWAY
   †R NORWAY INTL, Kvitsøy   W • NORWEGIAN • W Europe • 500 kW
   †R NORWAY INTL, Sveio   W • NORWEGIAN • W Europe • 500 kW
TURKEY
   VOICE OF TURKEY, Ankara-Emirler   W • S Europe & E Europe • 500 kW
5964.7 BOLIVIA
   RADIO NACIONAL, Huanuni   M-Sa • DS • 2 kW   M-F • DS • 2 kW   DS • 2 kW

5965 BRAZIL
   †RADIO NOVA VISAO, Santa Maria   DS • 10 kW •
CHINA
   †CENTRAL PEOPLE'S BS, Beijing   W • DS-1 • 100 kW • ALT. FREQ. TO 5320 kHz
   †CHINA RADIO INTL, Shijiazhuang   E Asia • 150 kW • ALT. FREQ. TO 5975 kHz
CUBA
   RADIO HABANA CUBA, Havana   C America • 50 kW
ECUADOR
   LA VOZ DEL UPANO, Macas   Irr • DS • 10 kW
GERMANY
   †DEUTSCHE WELLE, Wertachtal   S • E Europe • 500 kW
MALAYSIA
   RADIO MALAYSIA, Kajang   DS-1 (MALAY) • 100 kW
PAPUA NEW GUINEA
   R WESTERN HIGHLANDS, Mount Hagen   Irr • DS • 2/10 kW
RUSSIA
   †VOICE OF RUSSIA, Saransk   W Tu/F • N Europe • 500 kW   W/Th/Sa-M • N Europe • 500 kW   W • N Europe • 500 kW

SWAZILAND
   TRANS WORLD RADIO, Manzini   E Africa • 100 kW • ALT. FREQ. TO 6040 kHz   S Africa • 50 kW
   Sa • E Africa • 100 kW • ALT. FREQ. TO 6040 kHz   E Africa • 100 kW   Sa/Su • E Africa • 100 kW

SWEDEN
(con'd)   RADIO SWEDEN, Hörby   • Europe • 500 kW

0 1 2 3 4 5 6 7 8 9 10 11 12 13 14 15 16 17 18 19 20 21 22 23 24

ENGLISH ▬   ARABIC ≋   CHINESE ▯▯▯   FRENCH ═   GERMAN ▬   RUSSIAN ═   SPANISH ▬   OTHER ▬

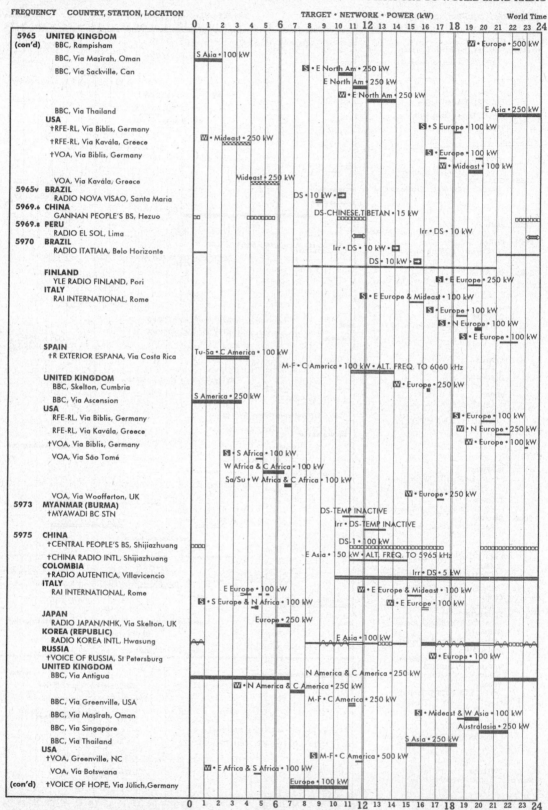

FREQUENCY   COUNTRY, STATION, LOCATION   TARGET • NETWORK • POWER (kW)   World Time

Frequency	Country, Station, Location	Target • Network • Power (kW)
5965 (con'd)	UNITED KINGDOM — BBC, Rampisham	W • Europe • 500 kW
	BBC, Rampisham	S Asia • 100 kW
	BBC, Via Maṣīrah, Oman	S • E North Am • 250 kW
	BBC, Via Sackville, Can	E North Am • 250 kW
		W • E North Am • 250 kW
	BBC, Via Thailand	E Asia • 250 kW
	USA — †RFE-RL, Via Biblis, Germany	S • S Europe • 100 kW
	†RFE-RL, Via Kavála, Greece	W • Mideast • 250 kW
	†VOA, Via Biblis, Germany	S • Europe • 100 kW
		W • Mideast • 100 kW
	VOA, Via Kavála, Greece	Mideast • 250 kW
5965v	BRAZIL — RADIO NOVA VISAO, Santa Maria	DS • 10 kW •
5969.6	CHINA — GANNAN PEOPLE'S BS, Hezuo	DS-CHINESE, TIBETAN • 15 kW
5969.8	PERU — RADIO EL SOL, Lima	Irr • DS • 10 kW
5970	BRAZIL — RADIO ITATIAIA, Belo Horizonte	Irr • DS • 10 kW •
		DS • 10 kW •
	FINLAND — YLE RADIO FINLAND, Pori	S • E Europe • 250 kW
	ITALY — RAI INTERNATIONAL, Rome	S • E Europe & Mideast • 100 kW
		S • Europe • 100 kW
		S • N Europe • 100 kW
		S • E Europe • 100 kW
	SPAIN — †R EXTERIOR ESPANA, Via Costa Rica	Tu-Sa • C America • 100 kW
		M-F • C America • 100 kW • ALT. FREQ. TO 6060 kHz
	UNITED KINGDOM — BBC, Skelton, Cumbria	W • Europe • 250 kW
	BBC, Via Ascension	S America • 250 kW
	USA — RFE-RL, Via Biblis, Germany	S • Europe • 100 kW
	RFE-RL, Via Kavála, Greece	W • N Europe • 250 kW
	†VOA, Via Biblis, Germany	W • Europe • 100 kW
	VOA, Via São Tomé	S • S Africa • 100 kW
		W Africa & C Africa • 100 kW
		Sa/Su • W Africa & C Africa • 100 kW
	VOA, Via Woofferton, UK	W • Europe • 250 kW
5973	MYANMAR (BURMA) — †MYAWADI BC STN	DS-TEMP INACTIVE
		Irr • DS-TEMP INACTIVE
5975	CHINA — †CENTRAL PEOPLE'S BS, Shijiazhuang	DS-1 • 100 kW
	†CHINA RADIO INTL, Shijiazhuang	E Asia • 150 kW • ALT. FREQ. TO 5965 kHz
	COLOMBIA — †RADIO AUTENTICA, Villavicencio	Irr • DS • 5 kW
	ITALY — RAI INTERNATIONAL, Rome	E Europe • 100 kW
		W • E Europe & Mideast • 100 kW
		S • S Europe & N Africa • 100 kW
		W • E Europe • 100 kW
	JAPAN — RADIO JAPAN/NHK, Via Skelton, UK	Europe • 250 kW
	KOREA (REPUBLIC) — RADIO KOREA INTL, Hwasung	E Asia • 100 kW
	RUSSIA — †VOICE OF RUSSIA, St Petersburg	W • Europe • 100 kW
	UNITED KINGDOM — BBC, Via Antigua	N America & C America • 250 kW
	BBC, Via Greenville, USA	W • N America & C America • 250 kW
	BBC, Via Maṣīrah, Oman	M-F • C America • 250 kW
	BBC, Via Singapore	S • Mideast & W Asia • 100 kW
	BBC, Via Thailand	Australasia • 250 kW
	USA — †VOA, Greenville, NC	S Asia • 250 kW
	VOA, Via Botswana	S M-F • C America • 500 kW
		W • E Africa & S Africa • 100 kW
(con'd)	†VOICE OF HOPE, Via Jülich, Germany	Europe • 100 kW

FREQUENCY	COUNTRY, STATION, LOCATION	TARGET • NETWORK • POWER (kW)	World Time

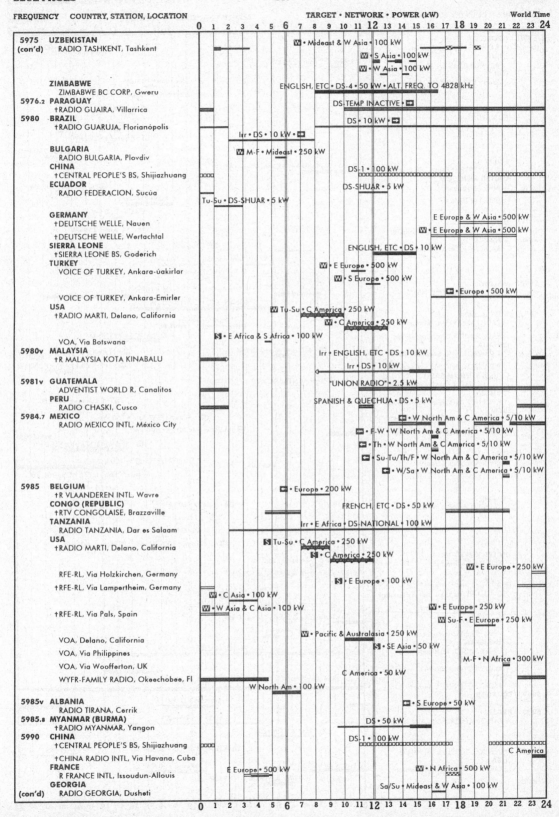

5975 **UZBEKISTAN**
(con'd)   RADIO TASHKENT, Tashkent
- W • Mideast & W Asia • 100 kW
- W • S Asia • 100 kW
- W • W Asia • 100 kW

ZIMBABWE
   ZIMBABWE BC CORP, Gweru — ENGLISH, ETC • DS-4 • 50 kW • ALT. FREQ. TO 4828 kHz

5976.2 **PARAGUAY**
   †RADIO GUAIRA, Villarrica — DS • TEMP INACTIVE •

5980 **BRAZIL**
   †RADIO GUARUJA, Florianópolis — DS • 10 kW •
     Irr • DS • 10 kW •

BULGARIA
   RADIO BULGARIA, Plovdiv — W • M-F • Mideast • 250 kW

CHINA
   †CENTRAL PEOPLE'S BS, Shijiazhuang — DS-1 • 100 kW

ECUADOR
   RADIO FEDERACION, Sucúa — DS-SHUAR • 5 kW
     Tu-Su • DS-SHUAR • 5 kW

GERMANY
   †DEUTSCHE WELLE, Nauen — E Europe & W Asia • 500 kW
   †DEUTSCHE WELLE, Wertachtal — W • E Europe & W Asia • 500 kW

SIERRA LEONE
   †SIERRA LEONE BS, Goderich — ENGLISH, ETC • DS • 10 kW

TURKEY
   VOICE OF TURKEY, Ankara-úakirlar
- W • E Europe • 500 kW
- W • S Europe • 500 kW
   VOICE OF TURKEY, Ankara-Emirler — • Europe • 500 kW

USA
   †RADIO MARTI, Delano, California
- W • Tu-Su • C America • 250 kW
- W • C America • 250 kW
   VOA, Via Botswana — S • E Africa & S Africa • 100 kW

5980v **MALAYSIA**
   †R MALAYSIA KOTA KINABALU
- Irr • ENGLISH, ETC • DS • 10 kW
- Irr • DS • 10 kW

5981v **GUATEMALA**
   ADVENTIST WORLD R, Canalitos — "UNION RADIO" • 2.5 kW

PERU
   RADIO CHASKI, Cusco — SPANISH & QUECHUA • DS • 5 kW

5984.7 **MEXICO**
   RADIO MEXICO INTL, México City
- • W North Am & C America • 5/10 kW
- • F-W • W North Am & C America • 5/10 kW
- • Th • W North Am & C America • 5/10 kW
- • Su-Tu/Th/F • W North Am & C America • 5/10 kW
- • W/Sa • W North Am & C America • 5/10 kW

5985 **BELGIUM**
   †R VLAANDEREN INTL, Wavre — • Europe • 200 kW

CONGO (REPUBLIC)
   †RTV CONGOLAISE, Brazzaville — FRENCH, ETC • DS • 50 kW

TANZANIA
   RADIO TANZANIA, Dar es Salaam — Irr • E Africa • DS-NATIONAL • 100 kW

USA
   †RADIO MARTI, Delano, California
- S • Tu-Su • C America • 250 kW
- S • C America • 250 kW
   RFE-RL, Via Holzkirchen, Germany — W • E Europe • 250 kW
   †RFE-RL, Via Lampertheim, Germany — S • E Europe • 100 kW
   †RFE-RL, Via Pals, Spain
- W • C Asia • 100 kW
- W • W Asia & C Asia • 100 kW
- W • E Europe • 250 kW
- W • Su-F • E Europe • 250 kW
   VOA, Delano, California — W • Pacific & Australasia • 250 kW
   VOA, Via Philippines — S • SE Asia • 50 kW
   VOA, Via Woofferton, UK — M-F • N Africa • 300 kW
   WYFR-FAMILY RADIO, Okeechobee, Fl
- C America • 50 kW
- W North Am • 100 kW

5985v **ALBANIA**
   RADIO TIRANA, Cerrik — • S Europe • 50 kW

5985.8 **MYANMAR (BURMA)**
   †RADIO MYANMAR, Yangon — DS • 50 kW

5990 **CHINA**
   †CENTRAL PEOPLE'S BS, Shijiazhuang — DS-1 • 100 kW
   †CHINA RADIO INTL, Via Havana, Cuba — C America

FRANCE
   R FRANCE INTL, Issoudun-Allouis
- E Europe • 500 kW
- W • N Africa • 500 kW

GEORGIA
(con'd)   RADIO GEORGIA, Dusheti — Sa/Su • Mideast & W Asia • 100 kW

ENGLISH ▬   ARABIC ▨   CHINESE ▭▭   FRENCH ▬   GERMAN ▬   RUSSIAN ═   SPANISH ▬   OTHER —

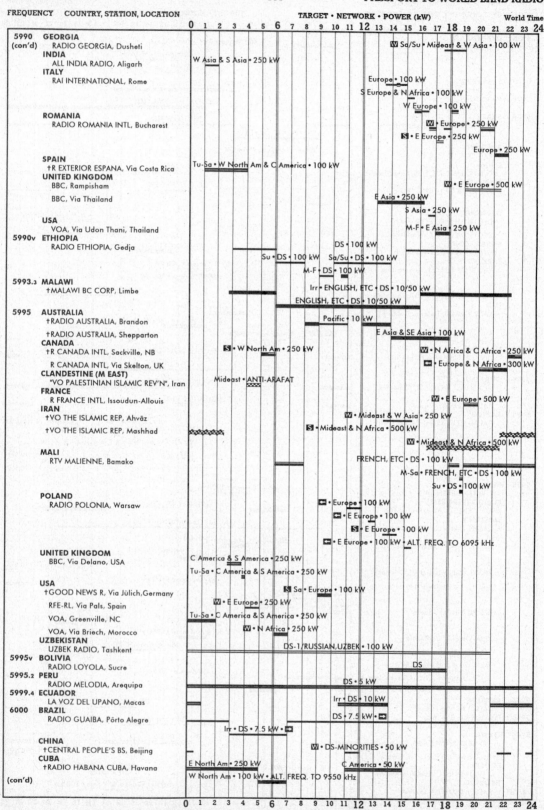

FREQUENCY   COUNTRY, STATION, LOCATION   TARGET • NETWORK • POWER (kW)   World Time

Frequency	Country, Station, Location	Target • Network • Power
5990 (con'd)	**GEORGIA** — RADIO GEORGIA, Dusheti	Sa/Su • Mideast & W Asia • 100 kW
	INDIA — ALL INDIA RADIO, Aligarh	W Asia & S Asia • 250 kW
	ITALY — RAI INTERNATIONAL, Rome	Europe • 100 kW; S Europe & N Africa • 100 kW; W Europe • 100 kW
	ROMANIA — RADIO ROMANIA INTL, Bucharest	W • Europe • 250 kW; S • E Europe • 250 kW; Europe • 250 kW
	SPAIN — †R EXTERIOR ESPANA, Via Costa Rica	Tu-Sa • W North Am & C America • 100 kW
	UNITED KINGDOM — BBC, Rampisham	W • E Europe • 500 kW
	BBC, Via Thailand	E Asia • 250 kW; S Asia • 250 kW
	USA — VOA, Via Udon Thani, Thailand	M-F • E Asia • 250 kW
5990v	**ETHIOPIA** — RADIO ETHIOPIA, Gedja	DS • 100 kW; Su • DS • 100 kW; Sa/Su • DS • 100 kW; M-F • DS • 100 kW
5993.3	**MALAWI** — †MALAWI BC CORP, Limbe	Irr • ENGLISH, ETC • DS • 10/50 kW; ENGLISH, ETC • DS • 10/50 kW
5995	**AUSTRALIA** — †RADIO AUSTRALIA, Brandon	Pacific • 10 kW
	†RADIO AUSTRALIA, Shepparton	E Asia & SE Asia • 100 kW
	CANADA — †R CANADA INTL, Sackville, NB	S • W North Am • 250 kW; W • N Africa & C Africa • 250 kW; Europe & N Africa • 300 kW
	R CANADA INTL, Via Skelton, UK	
	CLANDESTINE (M EAST) — "VO PALESTINIAN ISLAMIC REV'N", Iran	Mideast • ANTI-ARAFAT
	FRANCE — R FRANCE INTL, Issoudun-Allouis	W • E Europe • 500 kW
	IRAN — †VO THE ISLAMIC REP, Ahvāz	W • Mideast & W Asia • 250 kW
	†VO THE ISLAMIC REP, Mashhad	S • Mideast & N Africa • 500 kW; W • Mideast & N Africa • 500 kW
	MALI — RTV MALIENNE, Bamako	FRENCH, ETC • DS • 100 kW; M-Sa • FRENCH, ETC • DS • 100 kW; Su • DS • 100 kW
	POLAND — RADIO POLONIA, Warsaw	Europe • 100 kW; E Europe • 100 kW; S • E Europe • 100 kW; E Europe • 100 kW • ALT. FREQ. TO 6095 kHz
	UNITED KINGDOM — BBC, Via Delano, USA	C America & S America • 250 kW; Tu-Sa • C America & S America • 250 kW
	USA — †GOOD NEWS R, Via Jülich, Germany	Sa • Europe • 100 kW
	RFE-RL, Via Pals, Spain	W • E Europe • 250 kW
	VOA, Greenville, NC	Tu-Sa • C America & S America • 250 kW
	VOA, Via Briech, Morocco	W • N Africa • 250 kW
	UZBEKISTAN — UZBEK RADIO, Tashkent	DS-1/RUSSIAN, UZBEK • 100 kW
5995v	**BOLIVIA** — RADIO LOYOLA, Sucre	DS
5995.2	**PERU** — RADIO MELODIA, Arequipa	DS • 5 kW
5999.4	**ECUADOR** — LA VOZ DEL UPANO, Macas	Irr • DS • 10 kW
6000	**BRAZIL** — RADIO GUAIBA, Pôrto Alegre	DS • 7.5 kW; Irr • DS • 7.5 kW
	CHINA — †CENTRAL PEOPLE'S BS, Beijing	W • DS-MINORITIES • 50 kW
	CUBA — †RADIO HABANA CUBA, Havana	E North Am • 250 kW; C America • 50 kW; W North Am • 100 kW • ALT. FREQ. TO 9550 kHz
(con'd)		

FREQUENCY   COUNTRY, STATION, LOCATION   TARGET • NETWORK • POWER (kW)   World Time

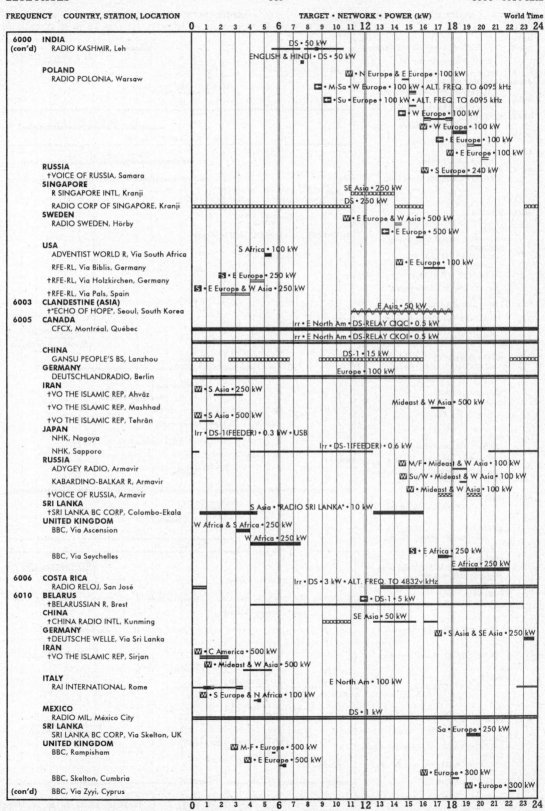

FREQUENCY	COUNTRY, STATION, LOCATION	TARGET • NETWORK • POWER (kW)
6000 (con'd)	**INDIA** — RADIO KASHMIR, Leh	DS • 50 kW / ENGLISH & HINDI • DS • 50 kW
	POLAND — RADIO POLONIA, Warsaw	W • N Europe & E Europe • 100 kW / M-Sa • W Europe • 100 kW • ALT. FREQ. TO 6095 kHz / Su • Europe • 100 kW • ALT. FREQ. TO 6095 kHz / W Europe • 100 kW / W • W Europe • 100 kW / E Europe • 100 kW / W • E Europe • 100 kW
	RUSSIA — †VOICE OF RUSSIA, Samara	W • S Europe • 240 kW
	SINGAPORE — R SINGAPORE INTL, Kranji	SE Asia • 250 kW
	RADIO CORP OF SINGAPORE, Kranji	DS • 250 kW
	SWEDEN — RADIO SWEDEN, Hörby	W • E Europe & W Asia • 500 kW / E Europe • 500 kW
	USA — ADVENTIST WORLD R, Via South Africa	S Africa • 100 kW
	RFE-RL, Via Biblis, Germany	W • E Europe • 100 kW
	†RFE-RL, Via Holzkirchen, Germany	S • E Europe • 250 kW
	†RFE-RL, Via Pals, Spain	S • E Europe & W Asia • 250 kW
6003	**CLANDESTINE (ASIA)** — †"ECHO OF HOPE", Seoul, South Korea	E Asia • 50 kW
6005	**CANADA** — CFCX, Montréal, Québec	Irr • E North Am • DS-RELAY CJQC • 0.5 kW / Irr • E North Am • DS-RELAY CKOI • 0.5 kW
	CHINA — GANSU PEOPLE'S BS, Lanzhou	DS-1 • 15 kW
	GERMANY — DEUTSCHLANDRADIO, Berlin	Europe • 100 kW
	IRAN — †VO THE ISLAMIC REP, Ahvāz	W • S Asia • 250 kW / Mideast & W Asia • 500 kW
	†VO THE ISLAMIC REP, Mashhad	
	†VO THE ISLAMIC REP, Tehrān	W • S Asia • 500 kW
	JAPAN — NHK, Nagoya	Irr • DS-1(FEEDER) • 0.3 kW • USB
	NHK, Sapporo	Irr • DS-1(FEEDER) • 0.6 kW
	RUSSIA — ADYGEY RADIO, Armavir	W • M/F • Mideast & W Asia • 100 kW
	KABARDINO-BALKAR R, Armavir	W • Su/W • Mideast & W Asia • 100 kW
	†VOICE OF RUSSIA, Armavir	W • Mideast & W Asia • 100 kW
	SRI LANKA — †SRI LANKA BC CORP, Colombo-Ekala	S Asia • "RADIO SRI LANKA" • 10 kW
	UNITED KINGDOM — BBC, Via Ascension	W Africa & S Africa • 250 kW / W Africa • 250 kW
	BBC, Via Seychelles	S • E Africa • 250 kW / E Africa • 250 kW
6006	**COSTA RICA** — RADIO RELOJ, San José	Irr • DS • 3 kW • ALT. FREQ. TO 4832v kHz
6010	**BELARUS** — †BELARUSSIAN R, Brest	DS-1 • 5 kW
	CHINA — †CHINA RADIO INTL, Kunming	SE Asia • 50 kW
	GERMANY — †DEUTSCHE WELLE, Via Sri Lanka	W • S Asia & SE Asia • 250 kW
	IRAN — †VO THE ISLAMIC REP, Sirjan	W • C America • 500 kW / W • Mideast & W Asia • 500 kW
	ITALY — RAI INTERNATIONAL, Rome	E North Am • 100 kW / W • S Europe & N Africa • 100 kW
	MEXICO — RADIO MIL, México City	DS • 1 kW
	SRI LANKA — SRI LANKA BC CORP, Via Skelton, UK	Sa • Europe • 250 kW
	UNITED KINGDOM — BBC, Rampisham	W • M-F • Europe • 500 kW / W • E Europe • 500 kW
	BBC, Skelton, Cumbria	W • Europe • 300 kW
(con'd)	BBC, Via Zyyi, Cyprus	W • Europe • 300 kW

ENGLISH ▬   ARABIC ≋   CHINESE ▫▫▫   FRENCH ═   GERMAN ▭   RUSSIAN =   SPANISH ▬   OTHER ─

FREQUENCY   COUNTRY, STATION, LOCATION   TARGET • NETWORK • POWER (kW)   World Time

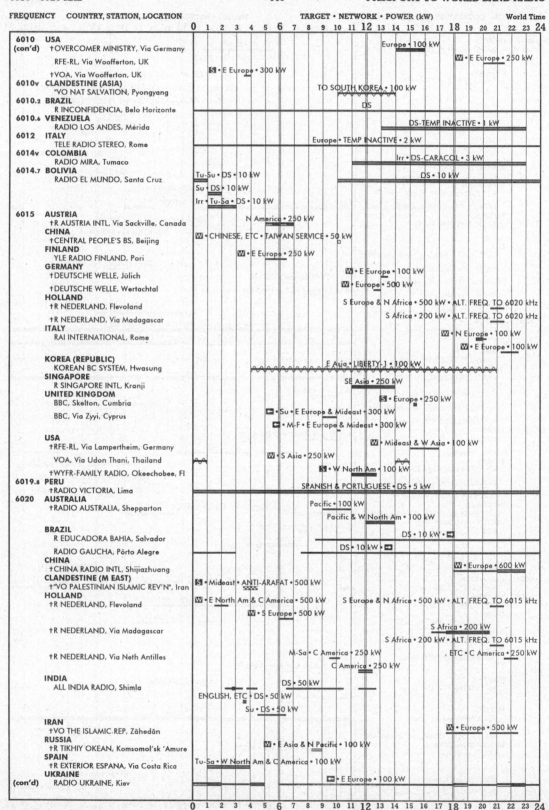

FREQUENCY	COUNTRY, STATION, LOCATION	TARGET • NETWORK • POWER (kW)
6010 (con'd)	USA	
	†OVERCOMER MINISTRY, Via Germany	Europe • 100 kW ; W • E Europe • 250 kW
	RFE-RL, Via Woofferton, UK	
	†VOA, Via Woofferton, UK	S • E Europe • 300 kW
6010v	CLANDESTINE (ASIA)	
	"VO NAT SALVATION, Pyongyang	TO SOUTH KOREA • 100 kW
6010.2	BRAZIL	
	R INCONFIDENCIA, Belo Horizonte	DS
6010.6	VENEZUELA	
	RADIO LOS ANDES, Mérida	DS-TEMP INACTIVE • 1 kW
6012	ITALY	
	TELE RADIO STEREO, Rome	Europe • TEMP INACTIVE • 2 kW
6014v	COLOMBIA	
	RADIO MIRA, Tumaco	Irr • DS-CARACOL • 3 kW
6014.7	BOLIVIA	
	RADIO EL MUNDO, Santa Cruz	Tu-Su • DS • 10 kW ; DS • 10 kW ; Su • DS • 10 kW ; Irr • Tu-Sa • DS • 10 kW
6015	AUSTRIA	
	†R AUSTRIA INTL, Via Sackville, Canada	N America • 250 kW
	CHINA	
	†CENTRAL PEOPLE'S BS, Beijing	W • CHINESE, ETC • TAIWAN SERVICE • 50 kW
	FINLAND	
	YLE RADIO FINLAND, Pori	W • E Europe • 250 kW
	GERMANY	
	†DEUTSCHE WELLE, Jülich	W • E Europe • 100 kW
	†DEUTSCHE WELLE, Wertachtal	W • Europe • 500 kW
	HOLLAND	
	†R NEDERLAND, Flevoland	S Europe & N Africa • 500 kW • ALT. FREQ. TO 6020 kHz
	†R NEDERLAND, Via Madagascar	S Africa • 200 kW • ALT. FREQ. TO 6020 kHz
	ITALY	
	RAI INTERNATIONAL, Rome	W • N Europe • 100 kW ; W • E Europe • 100 kW
	KOREA (REPUBLIC)	
	KOREAN BC SYSTEM, Hwasung	E Asia • LIBERTY-] • 100 kW
	SINGAPORE	
	R SINGAPORE INTL, Kranji	SE Asia • 250 kW
	UNITED KINGDOM	
	BBC, Skelton, Cumbria	S • Europe • 250 kW
	BBC, Via Zyyi, Cyprus	Su • E Europe & Mideast • 300 kW ; M-F • E Europe & Mideast • 300 kW
	USA	
	†RFE-RL, Via Lampertheim, Germany	W • Mideast & W Asia • 100 kW
	VOA, Via Udon Thani, Thailand	W • S Asia • 250 kW
	†WYFR-FAMILY RADIO, Okeechobee, Fl	S • W North Am • 100 kW
6019.8	PERU	
	†RADIO VICTORIA, Lima	SPANISH & PORTUGUESE • DS • 5 kW
6020	AUSTRALIA	
	†RADIO AUSTRALIA, Shepparton	Pacific • 100 kW ; Pacific & W North Am • 100 kW
	BRAZIL	
	R EDUCADORA BAHIA, Salvador	DS • 10 kW
	RADIO GAUCHA, Pôrto Alegre	DS • 10 kW
	CHINA	
	†CHINA RADIO INTL, Shijiazhuang	W • Europe • 600 kW
	CLANDESTINE (M EAST)	
	†"VO PALESTINIAN ISLAMIC REV'N", Iran	S • Mideast • ANTI-ARAFAT • 500 kW
	HOLLAND	
	†R NEDERLAND, Flevoland	W • E North Am & C America • 500 kW ; S Europe & N Africa • 500 kW • ALT. FREQ. TO 6015 kHz ; W • S Europe • 500 kW
	†R NEDERLAND, Via Madagascar	S Africa • 200 kW ; S Africa • 200 kW • ALT. FREQ. TO 6015 kHz
	†R NEDERLAND, Via Neth Antilles	M-Sa • C America • 250 kW ; , ETC • C America • 250 kW ; C America • 250 kW
	INDIA	
	ALL INDIA RADIO, Shimla	DS • 50 kW ; ENGLISH, ETC • DS • 50 kW ; Su • DS • 50 kW
	IRAN	
	†VO THE ISLAMIC REP, Zāhedān	W • Europe • 500 kW
	RUSSIA	
	†R TIKHIY OKEAN, Komsomol'sk 'Amure	W • E Asia & N Pacific • 100 kW
	SPAIN	
	†R EXTERIOR ESPANA, Via Costa Rica	Tu-Sa • W North Am & C America • 100 kW
	UKRAINE	
(con'd)	RADIO UKRAINE, Kiev	E Europe • 100 kW

FREQUENCY   COUNTRY, STATION, LOCATION   TARGET • NETWORK • POWER (kW)   World Time

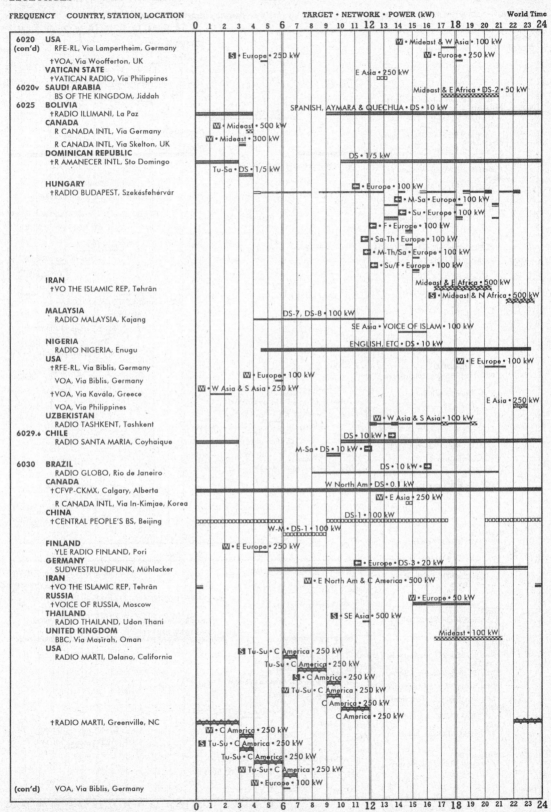

6020	USA	
(con'd)	RFE-RL, Via Lampertheim, Germany	W • Mideast & W Asia • 100 kW
	†VOA, Via Woofferton, UK	S • Europe • 250 kW W • Europe • 250 kW
	VATICAN STATE	
	†VATICAN RADIO, Via Philippines	E Asia • 250 kW
6020v	SAUDI ARABIA	
	BS OF THE KINGDOM, Jiddah	Mideast & E Africa • DS-2 • 50 kW
6025	BOLIVIA	
	†RADIO ILLIMANI, La Paz	SPANISH, AYMARA & QUECHUA • DS • 10 kW
	CANADA	
	R CANADA INTL, Via Germany	W • Mideast • 500 kW
	R CANADA INTL, Via Skelton, UK	W • Mideast • 300 kW
	DOMINICAN REPUBLIC	DS • 1/5 kW
	†R AMANECER INTL, Sto Domingo	Tu-Sa • DS • 1/5 kW
	HUNGARY	
	†RADIO BUDAPEST, Szekésfehérvár	• Europe • 100 kW
		• M-Sa • Europe • 100 kW
		• Su • Europe • 100 kW
		• F • Europe • 100 kW
		• Sa-Th • Europe • 100 kW
		• M-Th/Sa • Europe • 100 kW
		• Su/F • Europe • 100 kW
	IRAN	
	†VO THE ISLAMIC REP, Tehrān	Mideast & E Africa • 500 kW
		S • Mideast & N Africa • 500 kW
	MALAYSIA	
	RADIO MALAYSIA, Kajang	DS-7, DS-8 • 100 kW
		SE Asia • VOICE OF ISLAM • 100 kW
	NIGERIA	
	RADIO NIGERIA, Enugu	ENGLISH, ETC • DS • 10 kW
	USA	
	†RFE-RL, Via Biblis, Germany	W • E Europe • 100 kW
	VOA, Via Biblis, Germany	W • Europe • 100 kW
	†VOA, Via Kavála, Greece	W • W Asia & S Asia • 250 kW
	VOA, Via Philippines	E Asia • 250 kW
	UZBEKISTAN	
	RADIO TASHKENT, Tashkent	W • W Asia & S Asia • 100 kW
6029.6	CHILE	
	RADIO SANTA MARIA, Coyhaique	DS • 10 kW •
		M-Sa • DS • 10 kW •
6030	BRAZIL	
	RADIO GLOBO, Rio de Janeiro	DS • 10 kW •
	CANADA	
	†CFVP-CKMX, Calgary, Alberta	W North Am • DS • 0.1 kW
	R CANADA INTL, Via In-Kimjae, Korea	W • E Asia • 250 kW
	CHINA	DS-1 • 100 kW
	†CENTRAL PEOPLE'S BS, Beijing	W-M • DS-1 • 100 kW
	FINLAND	
	YLE RADIO FINLAND, Pori	W • E Europe • 250 kW
	GERMANY	
	SUDWESTRUNDFUNK, Mühlacker	• Europe • DS-3 • 20 kW
	IRAN	
	†VO THE ISLAMIC REP, Tehrān	W • E North Am & C America • 500 kW
	RUSSIA	
	†VOICE OF RUSSIA, Moscow	W • Europe • 50 kW
	THAILAND	
	RADIO THAILAND, Udon Thani	S • SE Asia • 500 kW
	UNITED KINGDOM	
	BBC, Via Maşīrah, Oman	Mideast • 100 kW
	USA	
	RADIO MARTI, Delano, California	S • Tu-Su • C America • 250 kW
		Tu-Su • C America • 250 kW
		S • C America • 250 kW
		W • Tu-Su • C America • 250 kW
		C America • 250 kW
	†RADIO MARTI, Greenville, NC	C America • 250 kW
		W • C America • 250 kW
		S • Tu-Su • C America • 250 kW
		Tu-Su • C America • 250 kW
		W • Tu-Su • C America • 250 kW
		W • Europe • 100 kW
(con'd)	VOA, Via Biblis, Germany	

ENGLISH ▬   ARABIC ⩾   CHINESE ▭▭   FRENCH ▬   GERMAN ▬   RUSSIAN ═   SPANISH ▬   OTHER ▬

FREQUENCY   COUNTRY, STATION, LOCATION   TARGET • NETWORK • POWER (kW)   World Time

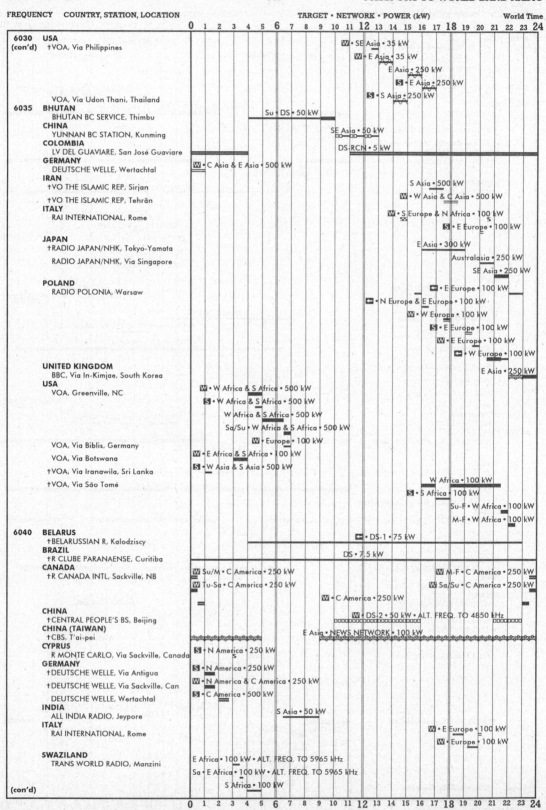

6030
(con'd)   **USA**
     †VOA, Via Philippines — W • SE Asia • 35 kW; W • E Asia • 35 kW; E Asia • 250 kW; S • E Asia • 250 kW; S • S Asia • 250 kW
     VOA, Via Udon Thani, Thailand

6035   **BHUTAN**
     BHUTAN BC SERVICE, Thimbu — Su • DS • 50 kW
   CHINA
     YUNNAN BC STATION, Kunming — SE Asia • 50 kW
   COLOMBIA
     LV DEL GUAVIARE, San José Guaviare — DS-RCN • 5 kW
   GERMANY
     DEUTSCHE WELLE, Wertachtal — W • C Asia & E Asia • 500 kW
   IRAN
     †VO THE ISLAMIC REP, Sirjan — S Asia • 500 kW
     †VO THE ISLAMIC REP, Tehrān — W • W Asia & C Asia • 500 kW
   ITALY
     RAI INTERNATIONAL, Rome — W • S Europe & N Africa • 100 kW; S • E Europe • 100 kW
   JAPAN
     †RADIO JAPAN/NHK, Tokyo-Yamata — E Asia • 300 kW
     RADIO JAPAN/NHK, Via Singapore — Australasia • 250 kW; SE Asia • 250 kW
   POLAND
     RADIO POLONIA, Warsaw — E Europe • 100 kW; N Europe & E Europe • 100 kW; W • W Europe • 100 kW; S • E Europe • 100 kW; W • E Europe • 100 kW; W Europe • 100 kW; E Asia • 250 kW
   UNITED KINGDOM
     BBC, Via In-Kimjae, South Korea
   USA
     VOA, Greenville, NC — W • W Africa & S Africa • 500 kW; S • W Africa & S Africa • 500 kW; W Africa & S Africa • 500 kW; Sa/Su • W Africa & S Africa • 500 kW; W • Europe • 100 kW
     VOA, Via Biblis, Germany
     VOA, Via Botswana — W • E Africa & S Africa • 100 kW
     †VOA, Via Iranawila, Sri Lanka — S • W Asia & S Asia • 500 kW
     †VOA, Via São Tomé — W Africa • 100 kW; S • S Africa • 100 kW; Su-F • W Africa • 100 kW; M-F • W Africa • 100 kW

6040   **BELARUS**
     †BELARUSSIAN R, Kalodziscy — DS-1 • 75 kW
   BRAZIL
     †R CLUBE PARANAENSE, Curitiba — DS • 7.5 kW
   CANADA
     †R CANADA INTL, Sackville, NB — W Su/M • C America • 250 kW; W Tu-Sa • C America • 250 kW; W • C America • 250 kW; W M-F • C America • 250 kW; W Sa/Su • C America • 250 kW
   CHINA
     †CENTRAL PEOPLE'S BS, Beijing — W • DS-2 • 50 kW • ALT. FREQ. TO 4850 kHz
   CHINA (TAIWAN)
     †CBS, T'ai-pei — E Asia • NEWS NETWORK • 100 kW
   CYPRUS
     R MONTE CARLO, Via Sackville, Canada — S • N America • 250 kW
   GERMANY
     †DEUTSCHE WELLE, Via Antigua — S • N America • 250 kW
     †DEUTSCHE WELLE, Via Sackville, Can — W • N America & C America • 250 kW
     DEUTSCHE WELLE, Wertachtal — S • C America • 500 kW
   INDIA
     ALL INDIA RADIO, Jeypore — S Asia • 50 kW
   ITALY
     RAI INTERNATIONAL, Rome — W • E Europe • 100 kW; W • Europe • 100 kW
   SWAZILAND
     TRANS WORLD RADIO, Manzini — E Africa • 100 kW • ALT. FREQ. TO 5965 kHz; Sa • E Africa • 100 kW • ALT. FREQ. TO 5965 kHz; S Africa • 100 kW

(con'd)

SEASONAL **S** OR **W**   1-HR TIMESHIFT MIDYEAR **⇦** OR **⇨**   JAMMING / OR ∧   EARLIEST HEARD ◁   LATEST HEARD ▷   NEW FOR 2000 †

FREQUENCY   COUNTRY, STATION, LOCATION   TARGET • NETWORK • POWER (kW)   World Time

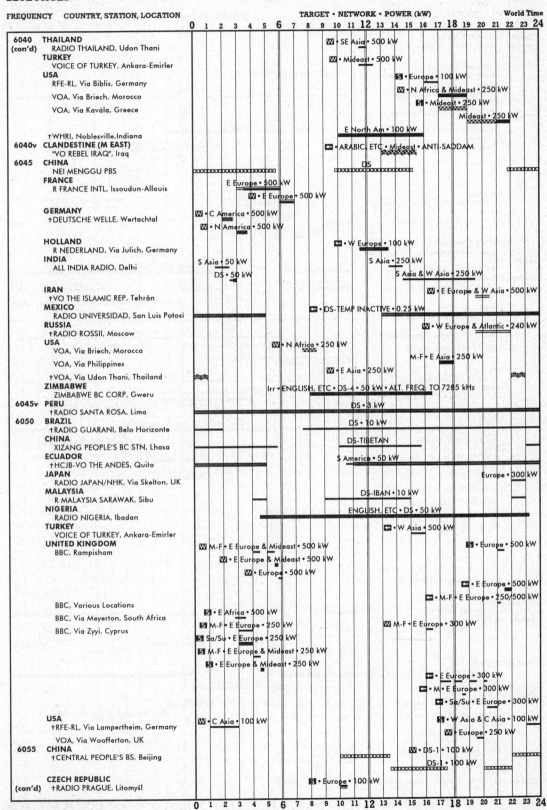

Freq	Country, Station, Location	Target • Network • Power
6040 (con'd)	**THAILAND** RADIO THAILAND, Udon Thani	W • SE Asia • 500 kW
	TURKEY VOICE OF TURKEY, Ankara-Emirler	W • Mideast • 500 kW
	USA RFE-RL, Via Biblis, Germany	S • Europe • 100 kW
	VOA, Via Briech, Morocco	W • N Africa & Mideast • 250 kW
	VOA, Via Kavála, Greece	S • Mideast • 250 kW / Mideast • 250 kW
	†WHRI, Noblesville, Indiana	E North Am • 100 kW
6040v	**CLANDESTINE (M EAST)** "VO REBEL IRAQ", Iraq	ARABIC, ETC • Mideast • ANTI-SADDAM
6045	**CHINA** NEI MENGGU PBS	DS
	FRANCE R FRANCE INTL, Issoudun-Allouis	E Europe • 500 kW / W • E Europe • 500 kW
	GERMANY †DEUTSCHE WELLE, Wertachtal	W • C America • 500 kW / W • N America • 500 kW
	HOLLAND R NEDERLAND, Via Julich, Germany	W Europe • 100 kW
	INDIA ALL INDIA RADIO, Delhi	S Asia • 50 kW / S Asia • 250 kW / DS • 50 kW / S Asia & W Asia • 250 kW
	IRAN †VO THE ISLAMIC REP, Tehrān	W • E Europe & W Asia • 500 kW
	MEXICO RADIO UNIVERSIDAD, San Luis Potosí	DS-TEMP INACTIVE • 0.25 kW
	RUSSIA †RADIO ROSSII, Moscow	W • W Europe & Atlantic • 240 kW
	USA VOA, Via Briech, Morocco	W • N Africa • 250 kW
	VOA, Via Philippines	M-F • E Asia • 250 kW
	†VOA, Via Udon Thani, Thailand	W • E Asia • 250 kW
	ZIMBABWE ZIMBABWE BC CORP, Gweru	Irr • ENGLISH, ETC • DS-4 • 50 kW • ALT. FREQ. TO 7285 kHz
6045v	**PERU** †RADIO SANTA ROSA, Lima	DS • 3 kW
6050	**BRAZIL** †RADIO GUARANI, Belo Horizonte	DS • 10 kW
	CHINA XIZANG PEOPLE'S BC STN, Lhasa	DS-TIBETAN
	ECUADOR †HCJB-VO THE ANDES, Quito	S America • 50 kW
	JAPAN RADIO JAPAN/NHK, Via Skelton, UK	Europe • 300 kW
	MALAYSIA R MALAYSIA SARAWAK, Sibu	DS-IBAN • 10 kW
	NIGERIA RADIO NIGERIA, Ibadan	ENGLISH, ETC • DS • 50 kW
	TURKEY VOICE OF TURKEY, Ankara-Emirler	W Asia • 500 kW
	UNITED KINGDOM BBC, Rampisham	W M-F • E Europe & Mideast • 500 kW / S • Europe • 500 kW / W • E Europe & Mideast • 500 kW / W • Europe • 500 kW / E Europe • 500 kW / M-F • E Europe • 250/500 kW
	BBC, Various Locations	S • E Africa • 500 kW
	BBC, Via Meyerton, South Africa	S M-F • E Europe • 250 kW / W M-F • E Europe • 300 kW
	BBC, Via Zyyi, Cyprus	S Sa/Su • E Europe • 250 kW / S M-F • E Europe & Mideast • 250 kW / S • E Europe & Mideast • 250 kW / E Europe • 300 kW / M • E Europe • 300 kW / Sa/Su • E Europe • 300 kW
	USA †RFE-RL, Via Lampertheim, Germany	W • C Asia • 100 kW / S • W Asia & C Asia • 100 kW
	VOA, Via Woofferton, UK	W • Europe • 250 kW
6055	**CHINA** †CENTRAL PEOPLE'S BS, Beijing	W • DS-1 • 100 kW / DS-1 • 100 kW
	CZECH REPUBLIC (con'd) †RADIO PRAGUE, Litomyšl	S • Europe • 100 kW

ENGLISH ▬   ARABIC ≋   CHINESE □□□   FRENCH ═   GERMAN ▬   RUSSIAN ═   SPANISH ▬   OTHER ▬

FREQUENCY   COUNTRY, STATION, LOCATION

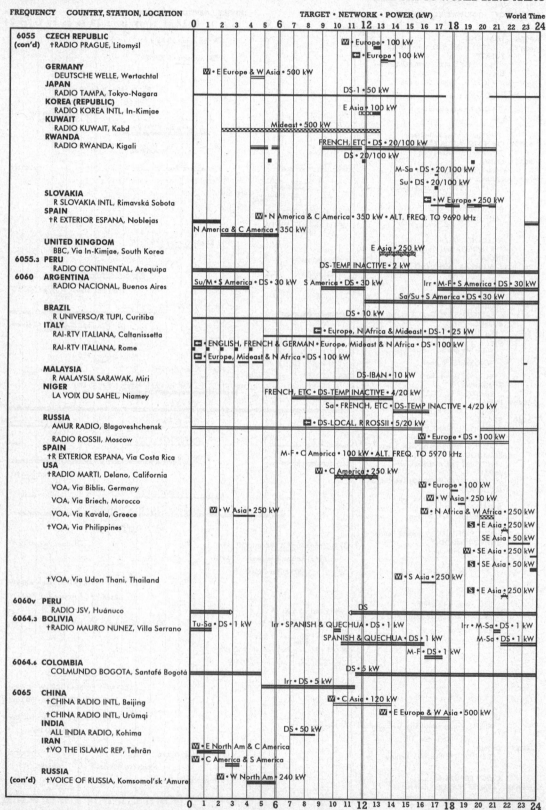

FREQUENCY   COUNTRY, STATION, LOCATION   TARGET • NETWORK • POWER (kW)   World Time

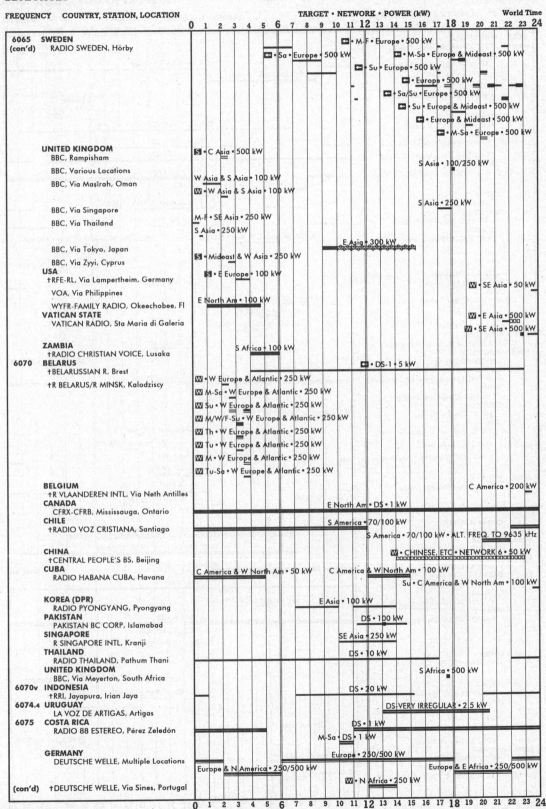

6065 (con'd) SWEDEN — RADIO SWEDEN, Hörby
- M-F • Europe • 500 kW
- Sa • Europe • 500 kW
- M-Sa • Europe & Mideast • 500 kW
- Su • Europe • 500 kW
- Europe • 500 kW
- Sa/Su • Europe • 500 kW
- Su • Europe & Mideast • 500 kW
- Europe & Mideast • 500 kW
- M-Sa • Europe • 500 kW

UNITED KINGDOM
- BBC, Rampisham — C Asia • 500 kW
- BBC, Various Locations — S Asia • 100/250 kW
- BBC, Via Maşīrah, Oman — W Asia & S Asia • 100 kW; W Asia & S Asia • 100 kW
- S Asia • 250 kW
- BBC, Via Singapore — M-F • SE Asia • 250 kW
- BBC, Via Thailand — S Asia • 250 kW
- BBC, Via Tokyo, Japan — E Asia • 300 kW
- BBC, Via Zyyi, Cyprus — Mideast & W Asia • 250 kW

USA
- †RFE-RL, Via Lampertheim, Germany — E Europe • 100 kW
- VOA, Via Philippines — SE Asia • 50 kW
- WYFR-FAMILY RADIO, Okeechobee, Fl — E North Am • 100 kW

VATICAN STATE
- VATICAN RADIO, Sta Maria di Galeria — E Asia • 500 kW; SE Asia • 500 kW

ZAMBIA
- †RADIO CHRISTIAN VOICE, Lusaka — S Africa • 100 kW

6070 BELARUS
- †BELARUSSIAN R, Brest — DS-1 • 5 kW
- †R BELARUS/R MINSK, Kalodziscy
  - W Europe & Atlantic • 250 kW
  - M-Sa • W Europe & Atlantic • 250 kW
  - Su • W Europe & Atlantic • 250 kW
  - M/W/F-Su • W Europe & Atlantic • 250 kW
  - Th • W Europe & Atlantic • 250 kW
  - Tu • W Europe & Atlantic • 250 kW
  - M • W Europe & Atlantic • 250 kW
  - Tu-Sa • W Europe & Atlantic • 250 kW

BELGIUM
- †R VLAANDEREN INTL, Via Neth Antilles — C America • 200 kW

CANADA
- CFRX-CFRB, Mississauga, Ontario — E North Am • DS • 1 kW

CHILE
- †RADIO VOZ CRISTIANA, Santiago — S America • 70/100 kW; S America • 70/100 kW • ALT. FREQ. TO 9635 kHz

CHINA
- †CENTRAL PEOPLE'S BS, Beijing — CHINESE, ETC • NETWORK 6 • 50 kW

CUBA
- RADIO HABANA CUBA, Havana
  - C America & W North Am • 50 kW
  - C America & W North Am • 100 kW
  - Su • C America & W North Am • 100 kW

KOREA (DPR)
- RADIO PYONGYANG, Pyongyang — E Asia • 100 kW

PAKISTAN
- PAKISTAN BC CORP, Islamabad — DS • 100 kW

SINGAPORE
- R SINGAPORE INTL, Kranji — SE Asia • 250 kW

THAILAND
- RADIO THAILAND, Pathum Thani — DS • 10 kW

UNITED KINGDOM
- BBC, Via Meyerton, South Africa — S Africa • 500 kW

6070v INDONESIA
- †RRI, Jayapura, Irian Jaya — DS • 20 kW

6074.4 URUGUAY
- LA VOZ DE ARTIGAS, Artigas — DS-VERY IRREGULAR • 2.5 kW

6075 COSTA RICA
- RADIO 88 ESTEREO, Pérez Zeledón — DS • 1 kW; M-Sa • DS • 1 kW

GERMANY
- DEUTSCHE WELLE, Multiple Locations
  - Europe • 250/500 kW
  - Europe & N America • 250/500 kW
  - Europe & E Africa • 250/500 kW
- (con'd) †DEUTSCHE WELLE, Via Sines, Portugal — N Africa • 250 kW

ENGLISH ▬   ARABIC ▩   CHINESE ▢▢▢   FRENCH ═   GERMAN ▬   RUSSIAN ═   SPANISH ▬   OTHER ▬

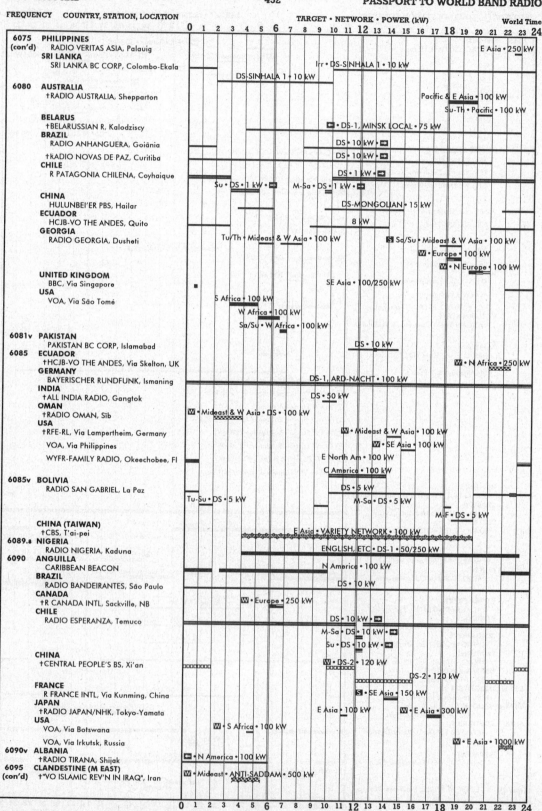

FREQUENCY	COUNTRY, STATION, LOCATION
6075	PHILIPPINES
(con'd)	RADIO VERITAS ASIA, Palauig
	SRI LANKA
	SRI LANKA BC CORP, Colombo-Ekala
6080	AUSTRALIA
	†RADIO AUSTRALIA, Shepparton
	BELARUS
	†BELARUSSIAN R, Kalodziscy
	BRAZIL
	RADIO ANHANGUERA, Goiânia
	†RADIO NOVAS DE PAZ, Curitiba
	CHILE
	R PATAGONIA CHILENA, Coyhaique
	CHINA
	HULUNBEI'ER PBS, Hailar
	ECUADOR
	HCJB-VO THE ANDES, Quito
	GEORGIA
	RADIO GEORGIA, Dusheti
	UNITED KINGDOM
	BBC, Via Singapore
	USA
	VOA, Via São Tomé
6081v	PAKISTAN
	PAKISTAN BC CORP, Islamabad
6085	ECUADOR
	†HCJB-VO THE ANDES, Via Skelton, UK
	GERMANY
	BAYERISCHER RUNDFUNK, Ismaning
	INDIA
	†ALL INDIA RADIO, Gangtok
	OMAN
	†RADIO OMAN, Sib
	USA
	†RFE-RL, Via Lampertheim, Germany
	VOA, Via Philippines
	WYFR-FAMILY RADIO, Okeechobee, Fl
6085v	BOLIVIA
	RADIO SAN GABRIEL, La Paz
	CHINA (TAIWAN)
	†CBS, T'ai-pei
6089.8	NIGERIA
	RADIO NIGERIA, Kaduna
6090	ANGUILLA
	CARIBBEAN BEACON
	BRAZIL
	RADIO BANDEIRANTES, São Paulo
	CANADA
	†R CANADA INTL, Sackville, NB
	CHILE
	RADIO ESPERANZA, Temuco
	CHINA
	†CENTRAL PEOPLE'S BS, Xi'an
	FRANCE
	R FRANCE INTL, Via Kunming, China
	JAPAN
	†RADIO JAPAN/NHK, Tokyo-Yamata
	USA
	VOA, Via Botswana
	VOA, Via Irkutsk, Russia
6090v	ALBANIA
	†RADIO TIRANA, Shijak
6095	CLANDESTINE (M EAST)
(con'd)	†"VO ISLAMIC REV'N IN IRAQ", Iran

TARGET • NETWORK • POWER (kW)   World Time

E Asia • 250 kW

Irr • DS-SINHALA 1 • 10 kW
DS-SINHALA 1 • 10 kW

Pacific & E Asia • 100 kW
Su-Th • Pacific • 100 kW

DS-1, MINSK LOCAL • 75 kW
DS • 10 kW
DS • 10 kW
DS • 1 kW
Su • DS • 1 kW   M-Sa • DS • 1 kW
DS-MONGOLIAN • 15 kW
8 kW
Tu/Th • Mideast & W Asia • 100 kW   Sa/Su • Mideast & W Asia • 100 kW
W • Europe • 100 kW
W • N Europe • 100 kW
SE Asia • 100/250 kW
S Africa • 100 kW
W Africa • 100 kW
Sa/Su • W Africa • 100 kW

DS • 10 kW
W • N Africa • 250 kW
DS-1, ARD-NACHT • 100 kW
DS • 50 kW
W • Mideast & W Asia • DS • 100 kW
W • Mideast & W Asia • 100 kW
W • SE Asia • 100 kW
E North Am • 100 kW
C America • 100 kW

DS • 5 kW
Tu-Su • DS • 5 kW   M-Sa • DS • 5 kW
M-F • DS • 5 kW
E Asia • VARIETY NETWORK • 100 kW
ENGLISH, ETC • DS-1 • 50/250 kW
N America • 100 kW
DS • 10 kW
W • Europe • 250 kW
DS • 10 kW
M-Sa • DS • 10 kW
Su • DS • 10 kW
W • DS-2 • 120 kW
DS-2 • 120 kW
S • SE Asia • 150 kW
E Asia • 100 kW   W • E Asia • 300 kW
W • S Africa • 100 kW
W • E Asia • 1000 kW
N America • 100 kW
W • Mideast • ANTI-SADDAM • 500 kW

SEASONAL Ⓢ OR Ⓦ   1-HR TIMESHIFT MIDYEAR ⊟ OR ⊞   JAMMING / OR ∧   EARLIEST HEARD ◁   LATEST HEARD ▷   NEW FOR 2000 †

| FREQUENCY | COUNTRY, STATION, LOCATION | TARGET • NETWORK • POWER (kW) | World Time |

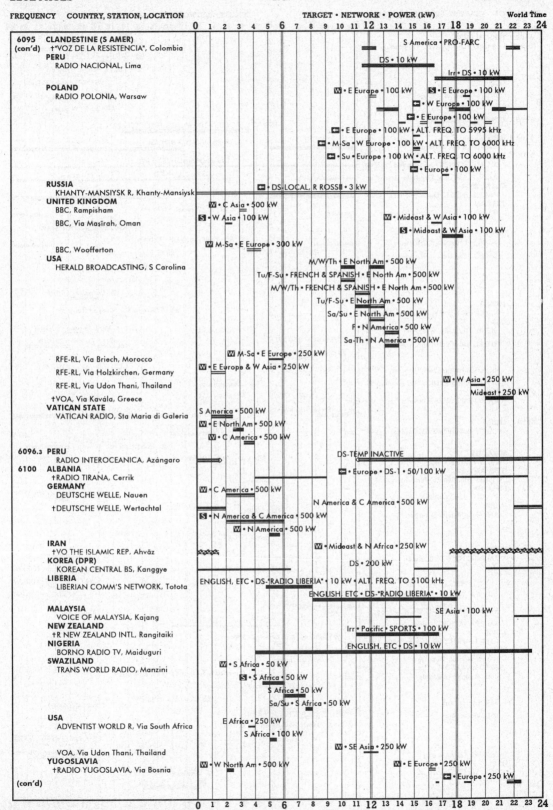

6095 (con'd)

CLANDESTINE (S AMER)
†"VOZ DE LA RESISTENCIA", Colombia — S America • PRO-FARC

PERU
RADIO NACIONAL, Lima — DS • 10 kW — Irr • DS • 10 kW

POLAND
RADIO POLONIA, Warsaw
- W • E Europe • 100 kW
- S • E Europe • 100 kW
- W Europe • 100 kW
- E Europe • 100 kW
- E Europe • 100 kW • ALT. FREQ. TO 5995 kHz
- M-Sa • W Europe • 100 kW • ALT. FREQ. TO 6000 kHz
- Su • Europe • 100 kW • ALT. FREQ. TO 6000 kHz
- Europe • 100 kW

RUSSIA
KHANTY-MANSIYSK R, Khanty-Mansiysk — DS-LOCAL, R ROSSII • 3 kW

UNITED KINGDOM
BBC, Rampisham — W • C Asia • 500 kW
BBC, Rampisham — S • W Asia • 100 kW — W • Mideast & W Asia • 100 kW
BBC, Via Maṣīrah, Oman — S • Mideast & W Asia • 100 kW
BBC, Woofferton — W M-Sa • E Europe • 300 kW

USA
HERALD BROADCASTING, S Carolina
- M/W/Th • E North Am • 500 kW
- Tu/F-Su • FRENCH & SPANISH • E North Am • 500 kW
- M/W/Th • FRENCH & SPANISH • E North Am • 500 kW
- Tu/F-Su • E North Am • 500 kW
- Sa/Su • E North Am • 500 kW
- F • N America • 500 kW
- Sa-Th • N America • 500 kW

RFE-RL, Via Briech, Morocco — W M-Sa • E Europe • 250 kW
RFE-RL, Via Holzkirchen, Germany — W • E Europe & W Asia • 250 kW
RFE-RL, Via Udon Thani, Thailand — W • W Asia • 250 kW
†VOA, Via Kavála, Greece — Mideast • 250 kW

VATICAN STATE
VATICAN RADIO, Sta Maria di Galeria
- S America • 500 kW
- W • E North Am • 500 kW
- W • C America • 500 kW

6096.3 **PERU**
RADIO INTEROCEANICA, Azángaro — DS-TEMP INACTIVE

6100 **ALBANIA**
†RADIO TIRANA, Cerrik — Europe • DS-1 • 50/100 kW

GERMANY
DEUTSCHE WELLE, Nauen — W • C America • 500 kW
†DEUTSCHE WELLE, Wertachtal
- N America & C America • 500 kW
- S • N America & C America • 500 kW
- W • N America • 500 kW

IRAN
†VO THE ISLAMIC REP, Ahvāz — W • Mideast & N Africa • 250 kW

KOREA (DPR)
KOREAN CENTRAL BS, Kanggye — DS • 200 kW

LIBERIA
LIBERIAN COMM'S NETWORK, Totota
- ENGLISH, ETC • DS-"RADIO LIBERIA" • 10 kW • ALT. FREQ. TO 5100 kHz
- ENGLISH, ETC • DS-"RADIO LIBERIA" • 10 kW

MALAYSIA
VOICE OF MALAYSIA, Kajang — SE Asia • 100 kW

NEW ZEALAND
†R NEW ZEALAND INTL, Rangitaiki — Irr • Pacific • SPORTS • 100 kW

NIGERIA
BORNO RADIO TV, Maiduguri — ENGLISH, ETC • DS • 10 kW

SWAZILAND
TRANS WORLD RADIO, Manzini
- W • S Africa • 50 kW
- S • S Africa • 50 kW
- S Africa • 50 kW
- Sa/Su • S Africa • 50 kW

USA
ADVENTIST WORLD R, Via South Africa
- E Africa • 250 kW
- S Africa • 100 kW
VOA, Via Udon Thani, Thailand — W • SE Asia • 250 kW

YUGOSLAVIA
†RADIO YUGOSLAVIA, Via Bosnia
- W • W North Am • 500 kW
- W • E Europe • 250 kW
- Europe • 250 kW

(con'd)

ENGLISH ▬▬   ARABIC ≋≋   CHINESE □□□   FRENCH ▬▬   GERMAN ▬▬   RUSSIAN ══   SPANISH ▬▬   OTHER ▬▬

FREQUENCY   COUNTRY, STATION, LOCATION   TARGET • NETWORK • POWER (kW)   World Time

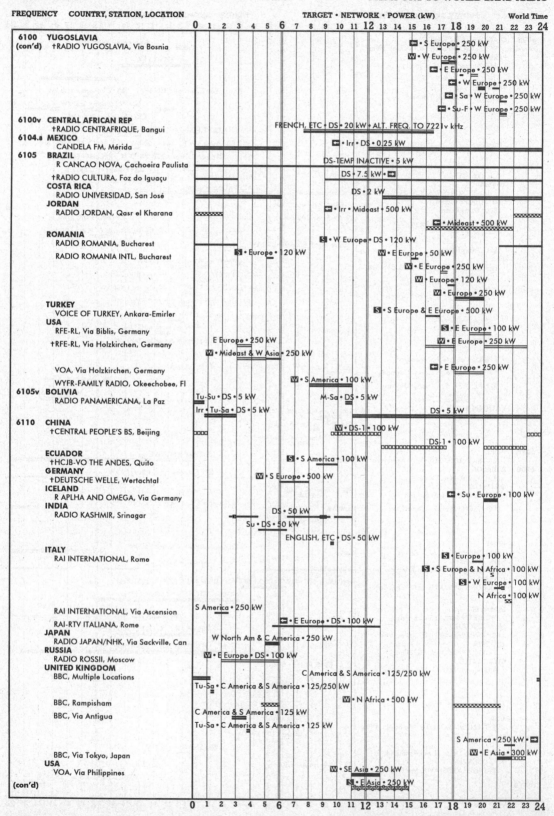

Frequency	Country, Station, Location	Target • Network • Power
6100 (con'd)	**YUGOSLAVIA** †RADIO YUGOSLAVIA, Via Bosnia	S Europe • 250 kW / W Europe • 250 kW / E Europe • 250 kW / W Europe • 250 kW / Sa • W Europe • 250 kW / Su-F • W Europe • 250 kW
6100v	**CENTRAL AFRICAN REP** †RADIO CENTRAFRIQUE, Bangui	FRENCH, ETC • DS • 20 kW • ALT. FREQ. TO 7221v kHz
6104.8	**MEXICO** CANDELA FM, Mérida	Irr • DS • 0.25 kW
6105	**BRAZIL** R CANCAO NOVA, Cachoeira Paulista	DS-TEMP INACTIVE • 5 kW
	†RADIO CULTURA, Foz do Iguaçu	DS • 7.5 kW
	COSTA RICA RADIO UNIVERSIDAD, San José	DS • 2 kW
	JORDAN RADIO JORDAN, Qasr el Kharana	Irr • Mideast • 500 kW / Mideast • 500 kW
	ROMANIA RADIO ROMANIA, Bucharest	W Europe • DS • 120 kW
	RADIO ROMANIA INTL, Bucharest	Europe • 120 kW / E Europe • 50 kW / E Europe • 250 kW / Europe • 120 kW / Europe • 250 kW
	TURKEY VOICE OF TURKEY, Ankara-Emirler	S Europe & E Europe • 500 kW
	USA RFE-RL, Via Biblis, Germany	E Europe • 100 kW
	†RFE-RL, Via Holzkirchen, Germany	E Europe • 250 kW / W • Mideast & W Asia • 250 kW / E Europe • 250 kW
	VOA, Via Holzkirchen, Germany	E Europe • 250 kW
	WYFR-FAMILY RADIO, Okeechobee, Fl	S America • 100 kW
6105v	**BOLIVIA** RADIO PANAMERICANA, La Paz	Tu-Su • DS • 5 kW / M-Sa • DS • 5 kW / Irr • Tu-Sa • DS • 5 kW / DS • 5 kW
6110	**CHINA** †CENTRAL PEOPLE'S BS, Beijing	DS-1 • 100 kW / DS-1 • 100 kW
	ECUADOR †HCJB-VO THE ANDES, Quito	S America • 100 kW
	GERMANY †DEUTSCHE WELLE, Wertachtal	S Europe • 500 kW
	ICELAND R APLHA AND OMEGA, Via Germany	Su • Europe • 100 kW
	INDIA RADIO KASHMIR, Srinagar	DS • 50 kW / Su • DS • 50 kW / ENGLISH, ETC • DS • 50 kW
	ITALY RAI INTERNATIONAL, Rome	Europe • 100 kW / S Europe & N Africa • 100 kW / W Europe • 100 kW / N Africa • 100 kW
	RAI INTERNATIONAL, Via Ascension	S America • 250 kW
	RAI-RTV ITALIANA, Rome	E Europe • DS • 100 kW
	JAPAN RADIO JAPAN/NHK, Via Sackville, Can	W North Am & C America • 250 kW
	RUSSIA RADIO ROSSII, Moscow	W • E Europe • DS • 100 kW
	UNITED KINGDOM BBC, Multiple Locations	C America & S America • 125/250 kW / Tu-Sa • C America & S America • 125/250 kW / N Africa • 500 kW
	BBC, Rampisham	C America & S America • 125 kW
	BBC, Via Antigua	Tu-Sa • C America & S America • 125 kW / S America • 250 kW
	BBC, Via Tokyo, Japan	E Asia • 300 kW
	USA VOA, Via Philippines	W • SE Asia • 250 kW / S • E Asia • 250 kW
(con'd)		

FREQUENCY   COUNTRY, STATION, LOCATION   TARGET • NETWORK • POWER (kW)   World Time

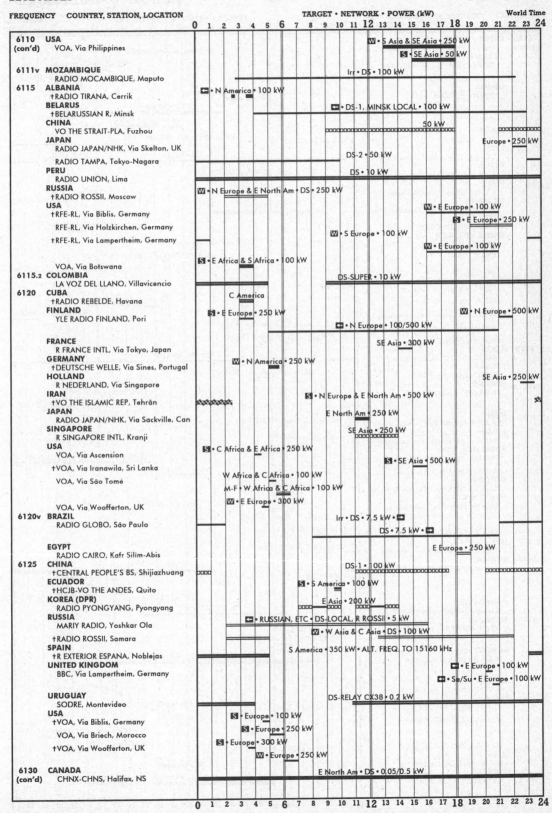

Frequency	Country, Station, Location	Target • Network • Power
6110 (con'd)	**USA** VOA, Via Philippines	W • S Asia & SE Asia • 250 kW; S • SE Asia • 50 kW
6111v	**MOZAMBIQUE** RADIO MOCAMBIQUE, Maputo	Irr • DS • 100 kW
6115	**ALBANIA** †RADIO TIRANA, Cerrik	N America • 100 kW
	BELARUS †BELARUSSIAN R, Minsk	DS-1, MINSK LOCAL • 100 kW
	CHINA VO THE STRAIT-PLA, Fuzhou	50 kW
	JAPAN RADIO JAPAN/NHK, Via Skelton, UK	Europe • 250 kW
	RADIO TAMPA, Tokyo-Nagara	DS-2 • 50 kW
	PERU RADIO UNION, Lima	DS • 10 kW
	RUSSIA †RADIO ROSSII, Moscow	N Europe & E North Am • DS • 250 kW
	USA †RFE-RL, Via Biblis, Germany	W • E Europe • 100 kW
	RFE-RL, Via Holzkirchen, Germany	S • E Europe • 250 kW
	†RFE-RL, Via Lampertheim, Germany	W • S Europe • 100 kW; W • E Europe • 100 kW
	VOA, Via Botswana	S • E Africa & S Africa • 100 kW
6115.2	**COLOMBIA** LA VOZ DEL LLANO, Villavicencio	DS-SUPER • 10 kW
6120	**CUBA** †RADIO REBELDE, Havana	C America
	FINLAND YLE RADIO FINLAND, Pori	S • E Europe • 250 kW; W • N Europe • 500 kW; N Europe • 100/500 kW
	FRANCE R FRANCE INTL, Via Tokyo, Japan	SE Asia • 300 kW
	GERMANY †DEUTSCHE WELLE, Via Sines, Portugal	W • N America • 250 kW
	HOLLAND R NEDERLAND, Via Singapore	SE Asia • 250 kW
	IRAN †VO THE ISLAMIC REP, Tehrān	S • N Europe & E North Am • 500 kW
	JAPAN RADIO JAPAN/NHK, Via Sackville, Can	E North Am • 250 kW
	SINGAPORE R SINGAPORE INTL, Kranji	SE Asia • 250 kW
	USA VOA, Via Ascension	S • C Africa & E Africa • 250 kW
	†VOA, Via Iranawila, Sri Lanka	S • SE Asia • 500 kW
	VOA, Via São Tomé	W Africa & C Africa • 100 kW; M-F • W Africa & C Africa • 100 kW
	VOA, Via Woofferton, UK	W • E Europe • 300 kW
6120v	**BRAZIL** RADIO GLOBO, São Paulo	Irr • DS • 7.5 kW; DS • 7.5 kW
	EGYPT RADIO CAIRO, Kafr Silim-Abis	E Europe • 250 kW
6125	**CHINA** †CENTRAL PEOPLE'S BS, Shijiazhuang	DS-1 • 100 kW
	ECUADOR †HCJB-VO THE ANDES, Quito	S • S America • 100 kW
	KOREA (DPR) RADIO PYONGYANG, Pyongyang	E Asia • 200 kW
	RUSSIA MARIY RADIO, Yoshkar Ola	RUSSIAN, ETC • DS-LOCAL, R ROSSII • 5 kW
	†RADIO ROSSII, Samara	W • W Asia & C Asia • DS • 100 kW
	SPAIN †R EXTERIOR ESPANA, Noblejas	S America • 350 kW • ALT. FREQ. TO 15160 kHz
	UNITED KINGDOM BBC, Via Lampertheim, Germany	E Europe • 100 kW; Sa/Su • E Europe • 100 kW
	URUGUAY SODRE, Montevideo	DS-RELAY CX38 • 0.2 kW
	USA †VOA, Via Biblis, Germany	S • Europe • 100 kW
	VOA, Via Briech, Morocco	S • Europe • 250 kW
	†VOA, Via Woofferton, UK	S • Europe • 300 kW; W • Europe • 250 kW
6130 (con'd)	**CANADA** CHNX-CHNS, Halifax, NS	E North Am • DS • 0.05/0.5 kW

ENGLISH ▬   ARABIC ▧   CHINESE □□□   FRENCH ═   GERMAN ▬   RUSSIAN ═   SPANISH ▭   OTHER ▬

FREQUENCY   COUNTRY, STATION, LOCATION   TARGET • NETWORK • POWER (kW)   World Time

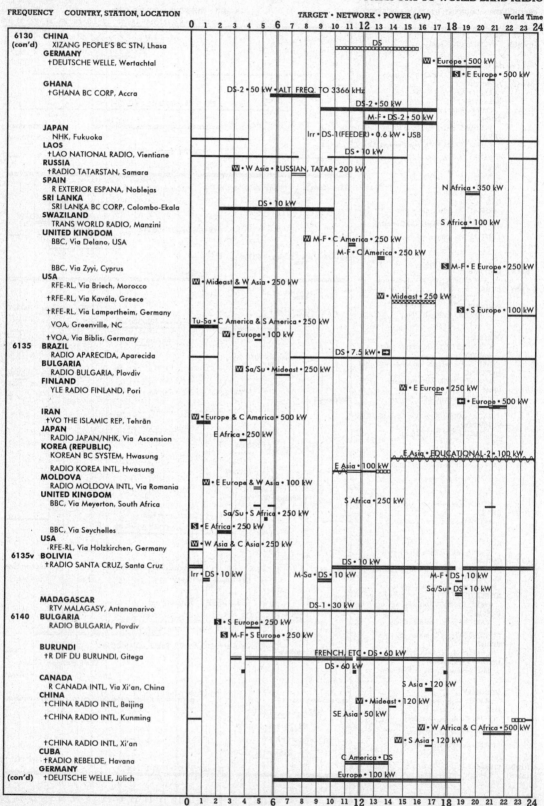

Frequency	Country, Station, Location	Target • Network • Power
6130 (con'd)	**CHINA** — XIZANG PEOPLE'S BC STN, Lhasa	DS
	GERMANY — †DEUTSCHE WELLE, Wertachtal	W • Europe • 500 kW / S • E Europe • 500 kW
	GHANA — †GHANA BC CORP, Accra	DS-2 • 50 kW • ALT. FREQ. TO 3366 kHz / DS-2 • 50 kW / M-F • DS-2 • 50 kW
	JAPAN — NHK, Fukuoka	Irr • DS-1 (FEEDER) • 0.6 kW • USB
	LAOS — †LAO NATIONAL RADIO, Vientiane	DS • 10 kW
	RUSSIA — †RADIO TATARSTAN, Samara	W • W Asia • RUSSIAN, TATAR • 200 kW
	SPAIN — R EXTERIOR ESPANA, Noblejas	N Africa • 350 kW
	SRI LANKA — SRI LANKA BC CORP, Colombo-Ekala	DS • 10 kW
	SWAZILAND — TRANS WORLD RADIO, Manzini	S Africa • 100 kW
	UNITED KINGDOM — BBC, Via Delano, USA	W • M-F • C America • 250 kW / M-F • C America • 250 kW
	BBC, Via Zyyi, Cyprus	S • M-F • E Europe • 250 kW
	USA — RFE-RL, Via Briech, Morocco	W • Mideast & W Asia • 250 kW
	†RFE-RL, Via Kavála, Greece	W • Mideast • 250 kW
	†RFE-RL, Via Lampertheim, Germany	S • S Europe • 100 kW
	VOA, Greenville, NC	Tu-Sa • C America & S America • 250 kW
	†VOA, Via Biblis, Germany	W • Europe • 100 kW
6135	**BRAZIL** — RADIO APARECIDA, Aparecida	DS • 7.5 kW • ➡
	BULGARIA — RADIO BULGARIA, Plovdiv	W • Sa/Su • Mideast • 250 kW
	FINLAND — YLE RADIO FINLAND, Pori	W • E Europe • 250 kW / ➡ • Europe • 500 kW
	IRAN — †VO THE ISLAMIC REP, Tehrān	W • Europe & C America • 500 kW
	JAPAN — RADIO JAPAN/NHK, Via Ascension	E Africa • 250 kW
	KOREA (REPUBLIC) — KOREAN BC SYSTEM, Hwasung	E Asia • EDUCATIONAL-2 • 100 kW
	RADIO KOREA INTL, Hwasung	E Asia • 100 kW
	MOLDOVA — RADIO MOLDOVA INTL, Via Romania	W • E Europe & W Asia • 100 kW
	UNITED KINGDOM — BBC, Via Meyerton, South Africa	S Africa • 250 kW / Sa/Su • S Africa • 250 kW
	BBC, Via Seychelles	S • E Africa • 250 kW
	USA — RFE-RL, Via Holzkirchen, Germany	W • W Asia & C Asia • 250 kW
6135v	**BOLIVIA** — †RADIO SANTA CRUZ, Santa Cruz	DS • 10 kW / Irr • DS • 10 kW / M-Sa • DS • 10 kW / M-F • DS • 10 kW / Sa/Su • DS • 10 kW
	MADAGASCAR — RTV MALAGASY, Antananarivo	DS-1 • 30 kW
6140	**BULGARIA** — RADIO BULGARIA, Plovdiv	S • S Europe • 250 kW / S • M-F • S Europe • 250 kW
	BURUNDI — †R DIF DU BURUNDI, Gitega	FRENCH, ETC • DS • 60 kW / DS • 60 kW
	CANADA — R CANADA INTL, Via Xi'an, China	S Asia • 120 kW
	CHINA — †CHINA RADIO INTL, Beijing	W • Mideast • 120 kW
	†CHINA RADIO INTL, Kunming	SE Asia • 50 kW
	†CHINA RADIO INTL, Xi'an	W • W Africa & C Africa • 500 kW / W • S Asia • 120 kW
	CUBA — †RADIO REBELDE, Havana	C America • DS
	GERMANY (con'd) — †DEUTSCHE WELLE, Jülich	Europe • 100 kW

FREQUENCY   COUNTRY, STATION, LOCATION   TARGET • NETWORK • POWER (kW)   World Time

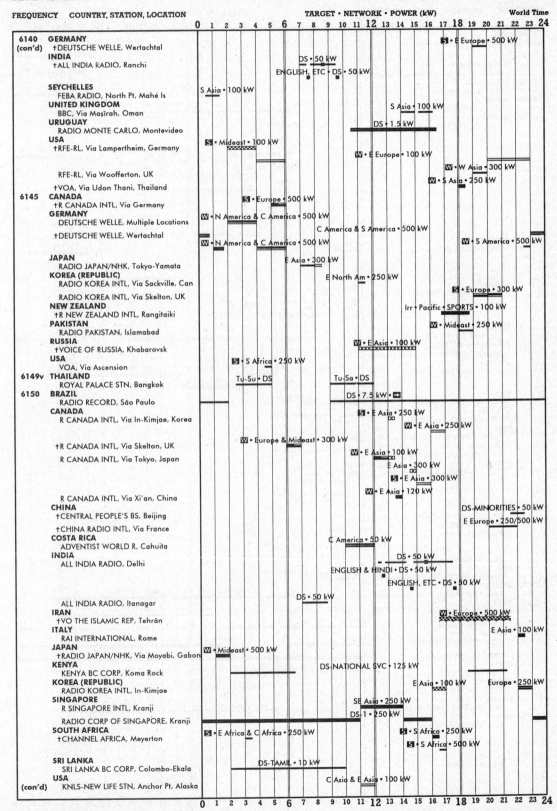

Frequency	Country, Station, Location	Target • Network • Power
6140 (con'd)	**GERMANY** †DEUTSCHE WELLE, Wertachtal	E Europe • 500 kW
	INDIA †ALL INDIA RADIO, Ranchi	DS • 50 kW / ENGLISH, ETC • DS • 50 kW
	SEYCHELLES FEBA RADIO, North Pt, Mahé Is	S Asia • 100 kW
	UNITED KINGDOM BBC, Via Maṣīrah, Oman	S Asia • 100 kW
	URUGUAY RADIO MONTE CARLO, Montevideo	DS • 1.5 kW
	USA †RFE-RL, Via Lampertheim, Germany	Mideast • 100 kW
	RFE-RL, Via Woofferton, UK	E Europe • 100 kW / W Asia • 300 kW
	†VOA, Via Udon Thani, Thailand	S Asia • 250 kW
6145	**CANADA** †R CANADA INTL, Via Germany	Europe • 500 kW
	GERMANY DEUTSCHE WELLE, Multiple Locations	N America & C America • 500 kW / C America & S America • 500 kW
	†DEUTSCHE WELLE, Wertachtal	N America & C America • 500 kW / S America • 500 kW
	JAPAN RADIO JAPAN/NHK, Tokyo-Yamata	E Asia • 300 kW
	KOREA (REPUBLIC) RADIO KOREA INTL, Via Sackville, Can	E North Am • 250 kW
	RADIO KOREA INTL, Via Skelton, UK	Europe • 300 kW
	NEW ZEALAND †R NEW ZEALAND INTL, Rangitaiki	Irr • Pacific • SPORTS • 100 kW
	PAKISTAN RADIO PAKISTAN, Islamabad	Mideast • 250 kW
	RUSSIA †VOICE OF RUSSIA, Khabarovsk	E Asia • 100 kW
	USA VOA, Via Ascension	S Africa • 250 kW
6149v	**THAILAND** ROYAL PALACE STN, Bangkok	Tu-Su • DS / Tu-Sa • DS
6150	**BRAZIL** RADIO RECORD, São Paulo	DS • 7.5 kW
	CANADA R CANADA INTL, Via In-Kimjae, Korea	E Asia • 250 kW / E Asia • 250 kW
	†R CANADA INTL, Via Skelton, UK	Europe & Mideast • 300 kW / E Asia • 100 kW
	R CANADA INTL, Via Tokyo, Japan	E Asia • 300 kW / E Asia • 300 kW / E Asia • 120 kW
	R CANADA INTL, Via Xi'an, China	
	CHINA †CENTRAL PEOPLE'S BS, Beijing	DS-MINORITIES • 50 kW
	†CHINA RADIO INTL, Via France	E Europe • 250/500 kW
	COSTA RICA ADVENTIST WORLD R, Cahuita	C America • 50 kW
	INDIA ALL INDIA RADIO, Delhi	DS • 50 kW / ENGLISH & HINDI • DS • 50 kW / ENGLISH, ETC • DS • 50 kW
	ALL INDIA RADIO, Itanagar	DS • 50 kW
	IRAN †VO THE ISLAMIC REP, Tehrān	Europe • 500 kW
	ITALY RAI INTERNATIONAL, Rome	E Asia • 100 kW
	JAPAN †RADIO JAPAN/NHK, Via Moyabi, Gabon	Mideast • 500 kW
	KENYA KENYA BC CORP, Koma Rock	DS-NATIONAL SVC • 125 kW
	KOREA (REPUBLIC) RADIO KOREA INTL, In-Kimjae	E Asia • 100 kW / Europe • 250 kW
	SINGAPORE R SINGAPORE INTL, Kranji	SE Asia • 250 kW
	RADIO CORP OF SINGAPORE, Kranji	DS-1 • 250 kW
	SOUTH AFRICA †CHANNEL AFRICA, Meyerton	E Africa & C Africa • 250 kW / S Africa • 250 kW / S Africa • 500 kW
	SRI LANKA SRI LANKA BC CORP, Colombo-Ekala	DS-TAMIL • 10 kW
	USA (con'd) KNLS-NEW LIFE STN, Anchor Pt, Alaska	C Asia & E Asia • 100 kW

ENGLISH ▬   ARABIC ▨   CHINESE ▫▫▫   FRENCH ═   GERMAN ▬   RUSSIAN ═   SPANISH ▬   OTHER ▬

FREQUENCY   COUNTRY, STATION, LOCATION   TARGET • NETWORK • POWER (kW)   World Time

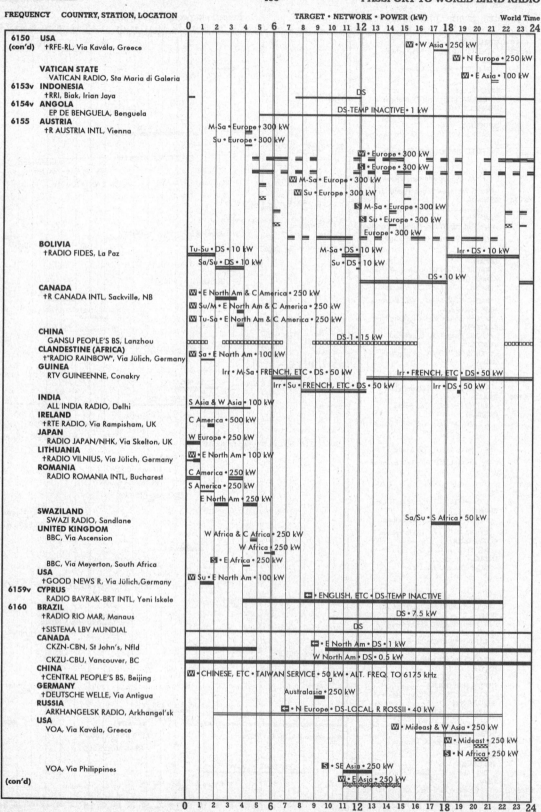

6150
(con'd)   **USA**
    †RFE-RL, Via Kavála, Greece — W • W Asia • 250 kW / W • N Europe • 250 kW / W • E Asia • 100 kW

    VATICAN STATE
      VATICAN RADIO, Sta Maria di Galeria
6153v   **INDONESIA**
    †RRI, Biak, Irian Jaya — DS
6154v   **ANGOLA**
      EP DE BENGUELA, Benguela — DS-TEMP INACTIVE • 1 kW
6155   **AUSTRIA**
    †R AUSTRIA INTL, Vienna
      M-Sa • Europe • 300 kW
      Su • Europe • 300 kW
      W • Europe • 300 kW
      S • Europe • 300 kW
      W M-Sa • Europe • 300 kW
      W Su • Europe • 300 kW
      S M-Sa • Europe • 300 kW
      S Su • Europe • 300 kW
      Europe • 300 kW

    BOLIVIA
    †RADIO FIDES, La Paz
      Tu-Su • DS • 10 kW / M-Sa • DS • 10 kW / Irr • DS • 10 kW
      Sa/Su • DS • 10 kW / Su • DS • 10 kW
      DS • 10 kW

    CANADA
    †R CANADA INTL, Sackville, NB
      W • E North Am & C America • 250 kW
      W Su/M • E North Am & C America • 250 kW
      W Tu-Sa • E North Am & C America • 250 kW

    CHINA
      GANSU PEOPLE'S BS, Lanzhou — DS-1 • 15 kW
    CLANDESTINE (AFRICA)
    †"RADIO RAINBOW", Via Jülich, Germany — W Sa • E North Am • 100 kW
    GUINEA
      RTV GUINEENNE, Conakry
      Irr • M-Sa • FRENCH, ETC • DS • 50 kW / Irr • FRENCH, ETC • DS • 50 kW
      Irr • Su • FRENCH, ETC • DS • 50 kW / Irr • DS • 50 kW

    INDIA
      ALL INDIA RADIO, Delhi — S Asia & W Asia • 100 kW
    IRELAND
    †RTE RADIO, Via Rampisham, UK — C America • 500 kW
    JAPAN
      RADIO JAPAN/NHK, Via Skelton, UK — W Europe • 250 kW
    LITHUANIA
    †RADIO VILNIUS, Via Jülich, Germany — W • E North Am • 100 kW
    ROMANIA
      RADIO ROMANIA INTL, Bucharest
      C America • 250 kW
      S America • 250 kW
      E North Am • 250 kW

    SWAZILAND
      SWAZI RADIO, Sandlane — Sa/Su • S Africa • 50 kW
    UNITED KINGDOM
      BBC, Via Ascension
      W Africa & C Africa • 250 kW
      W Africa • 250 kW
      BBC, Via Meyerton, South Africa — S • E Africa • 250 kW
    USA
    †GOOD NEWS R, Via Jülich, Germany — W Su • E North Am • 100 kW
6159v   **CYPRUS**
      RADIO BAYRAK-BRT INTL, Yeni Iskele — ENGLISH, ETC • DS-TEMP INACTIVE
6160   **BRAZIL**
    †RADIO RIO MAR, Manaus — DS • 7.5 kW
    †SISTEMA LBV MUNDIAL — DS
    CANADA
      CKZN-CBN, St John's, Nfld — E North Am • DS • 1 kW
      CKZU-CBU, Vancouver, BC — W North Am • DS • 0.5 kW
    CHINA
    †CENTRAL PEOPLE'S BS, Beijing — W • CHINESE, ETC • TAIWAN SERVICE • 50 kW • ALT. FREQ. TO 6175 kHz
    GERMANY
    †DEUTSCHE WELLE, Via Antigua — Australasia • 250 kW
    RUSSIA
      ARKHANGELSK RADIO, Arkhangel'sk — N Europe • DS-LOCAL R ROSSII • 40 kW
    USA
      VOA, Via Kavála, Greece
      W • Mideast & W Asia • 250 kW
      W • Mideast • 250 kW
      S • N Africa • 250 kW
      VOA, Via Philippines
      S • SE Asia • 250 kW
      W • E Asia • 250 kW

(con'd)

0 1 2 3 4 5 6 7 8 9 10 11 12 13 14 15 16 17 18 19 20 21 22 23 24

FREQUENCY   COUNTRY, STATION, LOCATION | TARGET • NETWORK • POWER (kW) | World Time

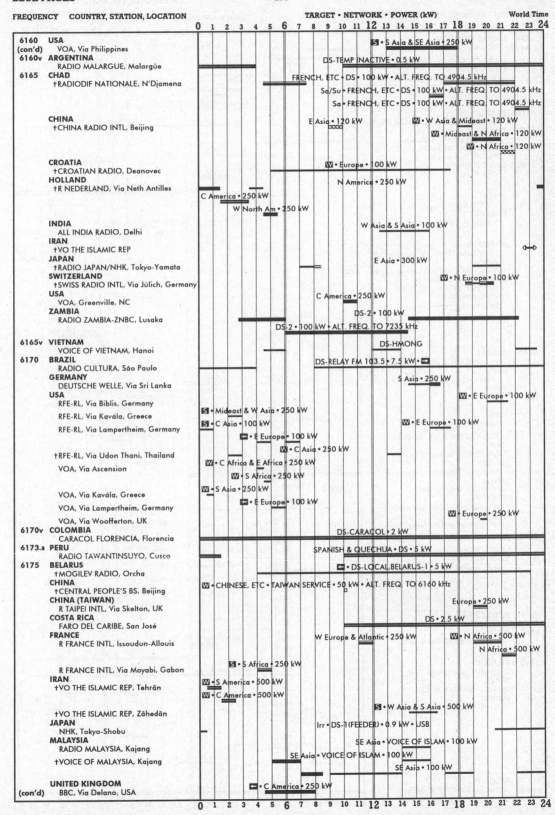

Freq	Country, Station, Location	Target • Network • Power
6160 (con'd)	USA VOA, Via Philippines	S • S Asia & SE Asia • 250 kW
6160v	ARGENTINA RADIO MALARGUE, Malargüe	DS-TEMP INACTIVE • 0.5 kW
6165	CHAD †RADIODIF NATIONALE, N'Djamena	FRENCH, ETC • DS • 100 kW • ALT. FREQ. TO 4904.5 kHz Sa/Su • FRENCH, ETC • DS • 100 kW • ALT. FREQ. TO 4904.5 kHz Sa • FRENCH, ETC • DS • 100 kW • ALT. FREQ. TO 4904.5 kHz
	CHINA †CHINA RADIO INTL, Beijing	E Asia • 120 kW W • W Asia & Mideast • 120 kW W • Mideast & N Africa • 120 kW W • N Africa • 120 kW
	CROATIA †CROATIAN RADIO, Deanovec	W • Europe • 100 kW
	HOLLAND †R NEDERLAND, Via Neth Antilles	N America • 250 kW C America • 250 kW W North Am • 250 kW
	INDIA ALL INDIA RADIO, Delhi	W Asia & S Asia • 100 kW
	IRAN †VO THE ISLAMIC REP	
	JAPAN †RADIO JAPAN/NHK, Tokyo-Yamata	E Asia • 300 kW
	SWITZERLAND †SWISS RADIO INTL, Via Jülich, Germany	W • N Europe • 100 kW
	USA VOA, Greenville, NC	C America • 250 kW
	ZAMBIA RADIO ZAMBIA-ZNBC, Lusaka	DS-2 • 100 kW DS-2 • 100 kW • ALT. FREQ. TO 7235 kHz
6165v	VIETNAM VOICE OF VIETNAM, Hanoi	DS-HMONG
6170	BRAZIL RADIO CULTURA, São Paulo	DS-RELAY FM 103.5 • 7.5 kW • →
	GERMANY DEUTSCHE WELLE, Via Sri Lanka	S Asia • 250 kW
	USA RFE-RL, Via Biblis, Germany	W • E Europe • 100 kW
	RFE-RL, Via Kavála, Greece	S • Mideast & W Asia • 250 kW W • E Europe • 100 kW
	RFE-RL, Via Lampertheim, Germany	S • C Asia • 100 kW □ • E Europe • 100 kW
	†RFE-RL, Via Udon Thani, Thailand	W • C Asia • 250 kW
	VOA, Via Ascension	W • C Africa & E Africa • 250 kW W • S Africa • 250 kW
	VOA, Via Kavála, Greece	W • S Asia • 250 kW
	VOA, Via Lampertheim, Germany	□ • E Europe • 100 kW
	VOA, Via Woofferton, UK	W • Europe • 250 kW
6170v	COLOMBIA CARACOL FLORENCIA, Florencia	DS-CARACOL • 2 kW
6173.8	PERU RADIO TAWANTINSUYO, Cusco	SPANISH & QUECHUA • DS • 5 kW
6175	BELARUS †MOGILEV RADIO, Orcha	□ • DS-LOCAL, BELARUS-1 • 5 kW
	CHINA †CENTRAL PEOPLE'S BS, Beijing	W • CHINESE, ETC • TAIWAN SERVICE • 50 kW • ALT. FREQ. TO 6160 kHz
	CHINA (TAIWAN) R TAIPEI INTL, Via Skelton, UK	Europe • 250 kW
	COSTA RICA FARO DEL CARIBE, San José	DS • 2.5 kW
	FRANCE R FRANCE INTL, Issoudun-Allouis	W Europe & Atlantic • 250 kW W • N Africa • 500 kW N Africa • 500 kW
	R FRANCE INTL, Via Moyabi, Gabon	S • S Africa • 250 kW
	IRAN †VO THE ISLAMIC REP, Tehrān	W • S America • 500 kW W • C America • 500 kW S • W Asia & S Asia • 500 kW
	†VO THE ISLAMIC REP, Zāhedān	
	JAPAN NHK, Tokyo-Shobu	Irr • DS-1 (FEEDER) • 0.9 kW • USB
	MALAYSIA RADIO MALAYSIA, Kajang	SE Asia • VOICE OF ISLAM • 100 kW
	†VOICE OF MALAYSIA, Kajang	SE Asia • VOICE OF ISLAM • 100 kW SE Asia • 100 kW
(con'd)	UNITED KINGDOM BBC, Via Delano, USA	□ • C America • 250 kW

ENGLISH ▬▬ **ARABIC** ﹌ **CHINESE** □□□ **FRENCH** ▬▬ **GERMAN** ▬▬ **RUSSIAN** ══ **SPANISH** ▬▬ **OTHER** —

FREQUENCY   COUNTRY, STATION, LOCATION   TARGET • NETWORK • POWER (kW)   World Time

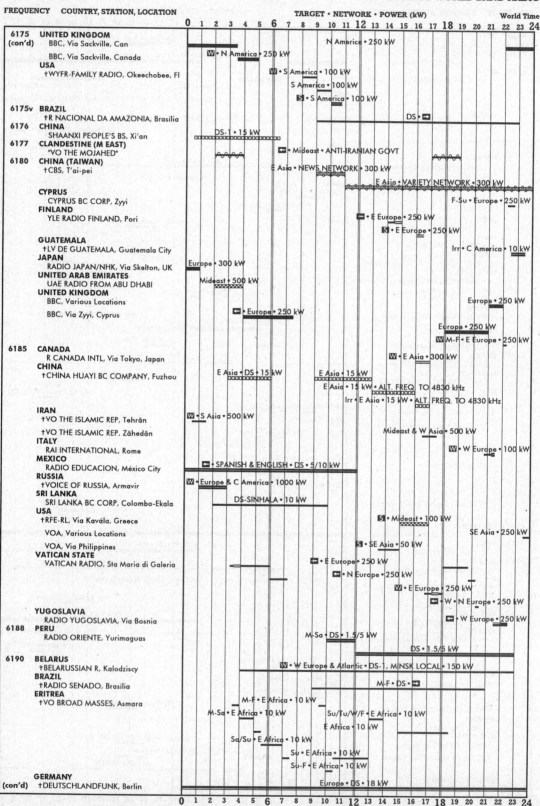

6175   **UNITED KINGDOM**
(con'd)   BBC, Via Sackville, Can — N America • 250 kW
     BBC, Via Sackville, Canada — W • N America • 250 kW
    USA
     †WYFR-FAMILY RADIO, Okeechobee, Fl — W • S America • 100 kW
     S America • 100 kW
     S • S America • 100 kW

6175v   **BRAZIL**
     †R NACIONAL DA AMAZONIA, Brasilia — DS
6176   **CHINA**
     SHAANXI PEOPLE'S BS, Xi'an — DS-1 • 15 kW
6177   **CLANDESTINE (M EAST)**
     "VO THE MOJAHED" — Mideast • ANTI-IRANIAN GOVT
6180   **CHINA (TAIWAN)**
     †CBS, T'ai-pei — E Asia • NEWS NETWORK • 300 kW
     E Asia • VARIETY NETWORK • 300 kW

    CYPRUS
     CYPRUS BC CORP, Zyyi — F-Su • Europe • 250 kW
    FINLAND
     YLE RADIO FINLAND, Pori — • E Europe • 250 kW
     S • E Europe • 250 kW

    GUATEMALA
     †LV DE GUATEMALA, Guatemala City — Irr • C America • 10 kW
    JAPAN
     RADIO JAPAN/NHK, Via Skelton, UK — Europe • 300 kW
    UNITED ARAB EMIRATES
     UAE RADIO FROM ABU DHABI — Mideast • 500 kW
    UNITED KINGDOM
     BBC, Various Locations — Europe • 250 kW
     BBC, Via Zyyi, Cyprus — • Europe • 250 kW
     Europe • 250 kW
     W • M-F • E Europe • 250 kW

6185   **CANADA**
     R CANADA INTL, Via Tokyo, Japan — W • E Asia • 300 kW
    CHINA
     †CHINA HUAYI BC COMPANY, Fuzhou — E Asia • DS • 15 kW
     E Asia • 15 kW
     E Asia • 15 kW • ALT. FREQ. TO 4830 kHz
     Irr • E Asia • 15 kW • ALT. FREQ. TO 4830 kHz

    IRAN
     †VO THE ISLAMIC REP, Tehrän — W • S Asia • 500 kW
     †VO THE ISLAMIC REP, Zähedän — Mideast & W Asia • 500 kW
    ITALY
     RAI INTERNATIONAL, Rome — W • W Europe • 100 kW
    MEXICO
     RADIO EDUCACION, México City — • SPANISH & ENGLISH • DS 5/10 kW
    RUSSIA
     †VOICE OF RUSSIA, Armavir — W • Europe & C America • 1000 kW
    SRI LANKA
     SRI LANKA BC CORP, Colombo-Ekala — DS-SINHALA • 10 kW
    USA
     †RFE-RL, Via Kavála, Greece — S • Mideast • 100 kW
     VOA, Various Locations — SE Asia • 250 kW
     VOA, Via Philippines — S • SE Asia • 50 kW
    VATICAN STATE
     VATICAN RADIO, Sta Maria di Galeria — • E Europe • 250 kW
     • N Europe • 250 kW
     W • E Europe • 250 kW
     • W • N Europe • 250 kW

    YUGOSLAVIA
     RADIO YUGOSLAVIA, Via Bosnia — • W Europe • 250 kW
6188   **PERU**
     RADIO ORIENTE, Yurimaguas — M-Sa • DS • 1.5/5 kW
     DS • 1.5/5 kW
6190   **BELARUS**
     †BELARUSSIAN R, Kalodziscy — W • W Europe & Atlantic • DS-1, MINSK LOCAL • 150 kW
    BRAZIL
     †RADIO SENADO, Brasilia — M-F • DS
    ERITREA
     †VO BROAD MASSES, Asmara — M-F • E Africa • 10 kW
     M-Sa • E Africa • 10 kW
     Su/Tu/W/F • E Africa • 10 kW
     E Africa • 10 kW
     Sa/Su • E Africa • 10 kW
     Su • E Africa • 10 kW
     Su-F • E Africa • 10 kW
    GERMANY
(con'd)   †DEUTSCHLANDFUNK, Berlin — Europe • DS • 18 kW

SEASONAL S OR W   1-HR TIMESHIFT MIDYEAR ▣ OR ▣   JAMMING / OR ∧   EARLIEST HEARD ◁   LATEST HEARD ▷   NEW FOR 2000 †

| FREQUENCY | COUNTRY, STATION, LOCATION | TARGET • NETWORK • POWER (kW) | World Time |

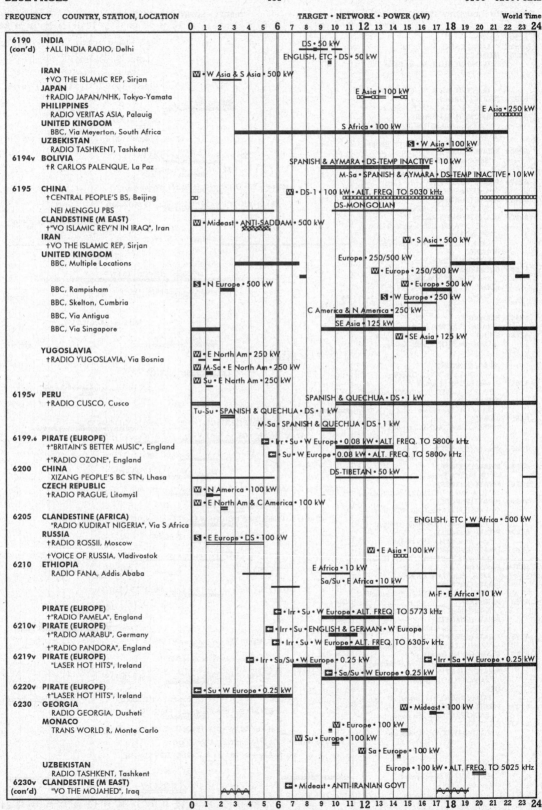

FREQUENCY	COUNTRY, STATION, LOCATION	TARGET • NETWORK • POWER (kW)
6190 (con'd)	INDIA †ALL INDIA RADIO, Delhi	DS • 50 kW; ENGLISH, ETC • DS • 50 kW
	IRAN †VO THE ISLAMIC REP, Sirjan	W • W Asia & S Asia • 500 kW
	JAPAN †RADIO JAPAN/NHK, Tokyo-Yamata	E Asia • 100 kW
	PHILIPPINES RADIO VERITAS ASIA, Palauig	E Asia • 250 kW
	UNITED KINGDOM BBC, Via Meyerton, South Africa	S Africa • 100 kW
	UZBEKISTAN RADIO TASHKENT, Tashkent	S • W Asia • 100 kW
6194v	BOLIVIA †R CARLOS PALENQUE, La Paz	SPANISH & AYMARA • DS-TEMP INACTIVE • 10 kW; M-Sa • SPANISH & AYMARA • DS-TEMP INACTIVE • 10 kW
6195	CHINA †CENTRAL PEOPLE'S BS, Beijing	W • DS-1 • 100 kW • ALT. FREQ. TO 5030 kHz
	NEI MENGGU PBS	DS-MONGOLIAN
	CLANDESTINE (M EAST) †"VO ISLAMIC REV'N IN IRAQ", Iran	W • Mideast • ANTI-SADDAM • 500 kW
	IRAN †VO THE ISLAMIC REP, Sirjan	W • S Asia • 500 kW
	UNITED KINGDOM BBC, Multiple Locations	Europe • 250/500 kW; W • Europe • 250/500 kW
	BBC, Rampisham	S • N Europe • 500 kW; W • Europe • 500 kW
	BBC, Skelton, Cumbria	S • W Europe • 250 kW
	BBC, Via Antigua	C America & N America • 250 kW
	BBC, Via Singapore	SE Asia • 125 kW; W • SE Asia • 125 kW
	YUGOSLAVIA †RADIO YUGOSLAVIA, Via Bosnia	W • E North Am • 250 kW; W M-Sa • E North Am • 250 kW; W Su • E North Am • 250 kW
6195v	PERU †RADIO CUSCO, Cusco	SPANISH & QUECHUA • DS • 1 kW; Tu-Su • SPANISH & QUECHUA • DS • 1 kW; M-Sa • SPANISH & QUECHUA • DS • 1 kW
6199.6	PIRATE (EUROPE) †"BRITAIN'S BETTER MUSIC", England	• Irr • Su • W Europe • 0.08 kW • ALT. FREQ. TO 5800v kHz
	†"RADIO OZONE", England	• Su • W Europe • 0.08 kW • ALT. FREQ. TO 5800v kHz
6200	CHINA XIZANG PEOPLE'S BC STN, Lhasa	DS-TIBETAN • 50 kW
	CZECH REPUBLIC †RADIO PRAGUE, Litomyšl	W • N America • 100 kW; W • E North Am & C America • 100 kW
6205	CLANDESTINE (AFRICA) "RADIO KUDIRAT NIGERIA", Via S Africa	ENGLISH, ETC • W Africa • 500 kW
	RUSSIA †RADIO ROSSII, Moscow	S • E Europe • DS • 100 kW
	†VOICE OF RUSSIA, Vladivostok	W • E Asia • 100 kW
6210	ETHIOPIA RADIO FANA, Addis Ababa	E Africa • 10 kW; Sa/Su • E Africa • 10 kW; M-F • E Africa • 10 kW
	PIRATE (EUROPE) †"RADIO PAMELA", England	• Irr • Su • W Europe • ALT. FREQ. TO 5773 kHz
6210v	PIRATE (EUROPE) †"RADIO MARABU", Germany	• Irr • Su • ENGLISH & GERMAN • W Europe
	†"RADIO PANDORA", England	• Irr • Su • W Europe • ALT. FREQ. TO 6305v kHz
6219v	PIRATE (EUROPE) "LASER HOT HITS", Ireland	• Irr • Sa/Su • W Europe • 0.25 kW; • Sa/Su • W Europe • 0.25 kW; • Irr • Sa • W Europe • 0.25 kW
6220v	PIRATE (EUROPE) †"LASER HOT HITS", Ireland	• Su • W Europe • 0.25 kW
6230	GEORGIA RADIO GEORGIA, Dusheti	W • Mideast • 100 kW
	MONACO TRANS WORLD R, Monte Carlo	W • Europe • 100 kW; W Su • Europe • 100 kW; W Sa • Europe • 100 kW
	UZBEKISTAN RADIO TASHKENT, Tashkent	Europe • 100 kW • ALT. FREQ. TO 5025 kHz
6230v (con'd)	CLANDESTINE (M EAST) "VO THE MOJAHED", Iraq	• Mideast • ANTI-IRANIAN GOVT

ENGLISH ▬   ARABIC ∽∽∽   CHINESE ▫▫▫   FRENCH ▬▬   GERMAN ▬▬   RUSSIAN ══   SPANISH ▬▬   OTHER ──

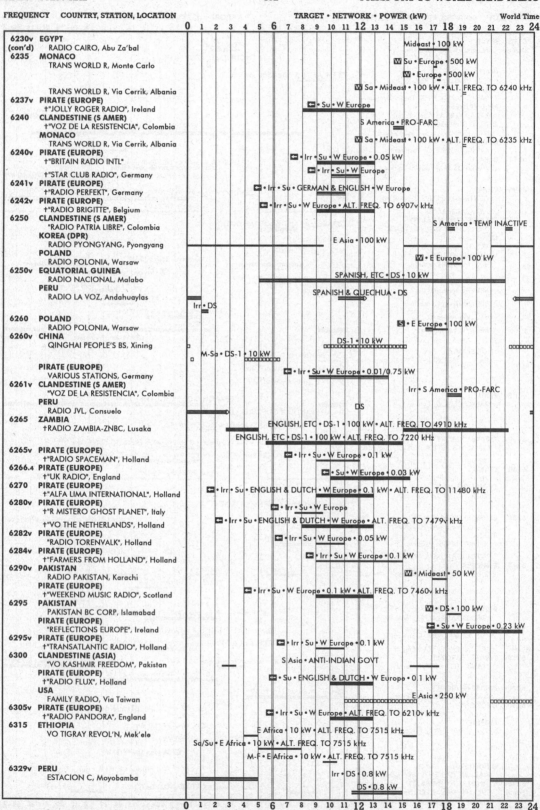

FREQUENCY   COUNTRY, STATION, LOCATION   TARGET • NETWORK • POWER (kW)   World Time

Frequency	Country, Station, Location
6230v (con'd)	EGYPT — RADIO CAIRO, Abu Za'bal
6235	MONACO — TRANS WORLD R, Monte Carlo
	TRANS WORLD R, Via Cerrik, Albania
6237v	PIRATE (EUROPE) — †"JOLLY ROGER RADIO", Ireland
6240	CLANDESTINE (S AMER) — †"VOZ DE LA RESISTENCIA", Colombia
	MONACO — TRANS WORLD R, Via Cerrik, Albania
6240v	PIRATE (EUROPE) — †"BRITAIN RADIO INTL"
	†"STAR CLUB RADIO", Germany
6241v	PIRATE (EUROPE) — †"RADIO PERFEKT", Germany
6242v	PIRATE (EUROPE) — †"RADIO BRIGITTE", Belgium
6250	CLANDESTINE (S AMER) — "RADIO PATRIA LIBRE", Colombia
	KOREA (DPR) — RADIO PYONGYANG, Pyongyang
	POLAND — RADIO POLONIA, Warsaw
6250v	EQUATORIAL GUINEA — RADIO NACIONAL, Malabo
	PERU — RADIO LA VOZ, Andahuaylas
6260	POLAND — RADIO POLONIA, Warsaw
6260v	CHINA — QINGHAI PEOPLE'S BS, Xining
	PIRATE (EUROPE) — VARIOUS STATIONS, Germany
6261v	CLANDESTINE (S AMER) — "VOZ DE LA RESISTENCIA", Colombia
	PERU — RADIO JVL, Consuelo
6265	ZAMBIA — †RADIO ZAMBIA-ZNBC, Lusaka
6265v	PIRATE (EUROPE) — †"RADIO SPACEMAN", Holland
6266.4	PIRATE (EUROPE) — †"UK RADIO", England
6270	PIRATE (EUROPE) — †"ALFA LIMA INTERNATIONAL", Holland
6280v	PIRATE (EUROPE) — †"R MISTERO GHOST PLANET", Italy
	†"VO THE NETHERLANDS", Holland
6282v	PIRATE (EUROPE) — "RADIO TORENVALK", Holland
6284v	PIRATE (EUROPE) — †"FARMERS FROM HOLLAND", Holland
6290v	PAKISTAN — RADIO PAKISTAN, Karachi
	PIRATE (EUROPE) — †"WEEKEND MUSIC RADIO", Scotland
6295	PAKISTAN — PAKISTAN BC CORP, Islamabad
	PIRATE (EUROPE) — "REFLECTIONS EUROPE", Ireland
6295v	PIRATE (EUROPE) — †"TRANSATLANTIC RADIO", Holland
6300	CLANDESTINE (ASIA) — "VO KASHMIR FREEDOM", Pakistan
	PIRATE (EUROPE) — †"RADIO FLUX", Holland
	USA — FAMILY RADIO, Via Taiwan
6305v	PIRATE (EUROPE) — †"RADIO PANDORA", England
6315	ETHIOPIA — VO TIGRAY REVOL'N, Mek'ele
6329v	PERU — ESTACION C, Moyobamba

FREQUENCY	COUNTRY, STATION, LOCATION	TARGET • NETWORK • POWER (kW)	World Time

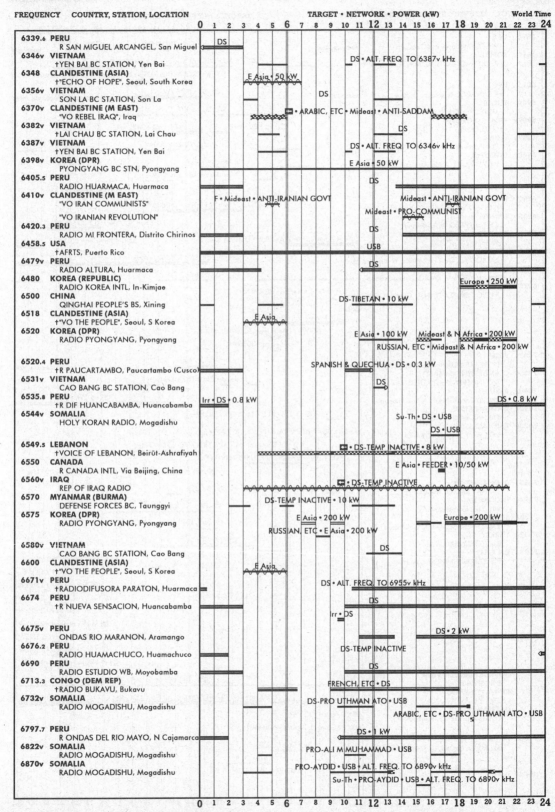

- **6339.6 PERU** — R SAN MIGUEL ARCANGEL, San Miguel — DS
- **6346v VIETNAM** — †YEN BAI BC STATION, Yen Bai — DS • ALT. FREQ. TO 6387v kHz
- **6348 CLANDESTINE (ASIA)** — †"ECHO OF HOPE", Seoul, South Korea — E Asia • 50 kW
- **6356v VIETNAM** — SON LA BC STATION, Son La — DS
- **6370v CLANDESTINE (M EAST)** — "VO REBEL IRAQ", Iraq — ARABIC, ETC • Mideast • ANTI-SADDAM
- **6382v VIETNAM** — †LAI CHAU BC STATION, Lai Chau — DS
- **6387v VIETNAM** — †YEN BAI BC STATION, Yen Bai — DS • ALT. FREQ. TO 6346v kHz
- **6398v KOREA (DPR)** — PYONGYANG BC STN, Pyongyang — E Asia • 50 kW
- **6405.5 PERU** — RADIO HUARMACA, Huarmaca — DS
- **6410v CLANDESTINE (M EAST)** — "VO IRAN COMMUNISTS" — F • Mideast • ANTI-IRANIAN GOVT / Mideast • ANTI-IRANIAN GOVT — "VO IRANIAN REVOLUTION" — Mideast • PRO-COMMUNIST
- **6420.3 PERU** — RADIO MI FRONTERA, Distrito Chirinos — DS
- **6458.5 USA** — †AFRTS, Puerto Rico — USB
- **6479v PERU** — RADIO ALTURA, Huarmaca — DS
- **6480 KOREA (REPUBLIC)** — RADIO KOREA INTL, In-Kimjae — Europe • 250 kW
- **6500 CHINA** — QINGHAI PEOPLE'S BS, Xining — DS-TIBETAN • 10 kW
- **6518 CLANDESTINE (ASIA)** — †"VO THE PEOPLE", Seoul, S Korea — E Asia
- **6520 KOREA (DPR)** — RADIO PYONGYANG, Pyongyang — E Asia • 100 kW / Mideast & N Africa • 200 kW / RUSSIAN, ETC • Mideast & N Africa • 200 kW
- **6520.4 PERU** — †R PAUCARTAMBO, Paucartambo (Cusco) — SPANISH & QUECHUA • DS • 0.3 kW
- **6531v VIETNAM** — CAO BANG BC STATION, Cao Bang — DS
- **6535.8 PERU** — †R DIF HUANCABAMBA, Huancabamba — Irr • DS • 0.8 kW / DS • 0.8 kW
- **6544v SOMALIA** — HOLY KORAN RADIO, Mogadishu — Su-Th • DS • USB / DS • USB
- **6549.5 LEBANON** — †VOICE OF LEBANON, Beirūt-Ashrafiyah — DS-TEMP INACTIVE • 8 kW
- **6550 CANADA** — R CANADA INTL, Via Beijing, China — E Asia • FEEDER • 10/50 kW
- **6560v IRAQ** — REP OF IRAQ RADIO — DS-TEMP INACTIVE
- **6570 MYANMAR (BURMA)** — DEFENSE FORCES BC, Taunggyi — DS-TEMP INACTIVE • 10 kW
- **6575 KOREA (DPR)** — RADIO PYONGYANG, Pyongyang — E Asia • 200 kW / Europe • 200 kW / RUSSIAN, ETC • E Asia • 200 kW
- **6580v VIETNAM** — CAO BANG BC STATION, Cao Bang — DS
- **6600 CLANDESTINE (ASIA)** — †"VO THE PEOPLE", Seoul, S Korea — E Asia
- **6671v PERU** — †RADIODIFUSORA PARATON, Huarmaca — DS • ALT. FREQ. TO 6955v kHz
- **6674 PERU** — †R NUEVA SENSACION, Huancabamba — DS / Irr • DS
- **6675v PERU** — ONDAS RIO MARANON, Aramango — DS • 2 kW
- **6676.2 PERU** — RADIO HUAMACHUCO, Huamachuco — DS-TEMP INACTIVE
- **6690 PERU** — RADIO ESTUDIO WB, Moyobamba — DS
- **6713.3 CONGO (DEM REP)** — †RADIO BUKAVU, Bukavu — FRENCH, ETC • DS
- **6732v SOMALIA** — RADIO MOGADISHU, Mogadishu — DS-PRO UTHMAN ATO • USB / ARABIC, ETC • DS-PRO UTHMAN ATO • USB
- **6797.7 PERU** — R ONDAS DEL RIO MAYO, N Cajamarca — DS • 1 kW
- **6822v SOMALIA** — RADIO MOGADISHU, Mogadishu — PRO-ALI M MUHAMMAD • USB
- **6870v SOMALIA** — RADIO MOGADISHU, Mogadishu — PRO-AYDID • USB • ALT. FREQ. TO 6890v kHz / Su-Th • PRO-AYDID • USB • ALT. FREQ. TO 6890v kHz

ENGLISH ▬▬   ARABIC ⩘⩘   CHINESE ▭▭▭   FRENCH ══   GERMAN ▬▬   RUSSIAN ══   SPANISH ▬▬   OTHER ▬

FREQUENCY   COUNTRY, STATION, LOCATION

TARGET • NETWORK • POWER (kW)   World Time

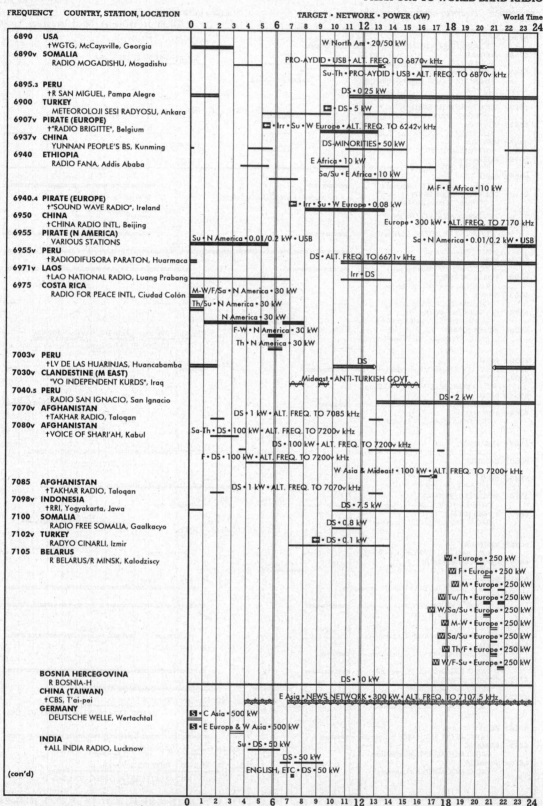

Frequency	Country, Station, Location	Details
6890	**USA** †WGTG, McCaysville, Georgia	W North Am • 20/50 kW
6890v	**SOMALIA** RADIO MOGADISHU, Mogadishu	PRO-AYDID • USB • ALT. FREQ. TO 6870v kHz / Su-Th • PRO-AYDID • USB • ALT. FREQ. TO 6870v kHz
6895.3	**PERU** †R SAN MIGUEL, Pampa Alegre	DS • 0.25 kW
6900	**TURKEY** METEOROLOJI SESI RADYOSU, Ankara	• DS • 5 kW
6907v	**PIRATE (EUROPE)** †"RADIO BRIGITTE", Belgium	• Irr • Su • W Europe • ALT. FREQ. TO 6242v kHz
6937v	**CHINA** YUNNAN PEOPLE'S BS, Kunming	DS-MINORITIES • 50 kW
6940	**ETHIOPIA** RADIO FANA, Addis Ababa	E Africa • 10 kW / Sa/Su • E Africa • 10 kW / M-F • E Africa • 10 kW
6940.4	**PIRATE (EUROPE)** †"SOUND WAVE RADIO", Ireland	• Irr • Su • W Europe • 0.08 kW
6950	**CHINA** †CHINA RADIO INTL, Beijing	Europe • 300 kW • ALT. FREQ. TO 7170 kHz
6955	**PIRATE (N AMERICA)** VARIOUS STATIONS	Su • N America • 0.01/0.2 kW • USB / Sa • N America • 0.01/0.2 kW • USB
6955v	**PERU** †RADIODIFUSORA PARATON, Huarmaca	DS • ALT. FREQ. TO 6671v kHz
6971v	**LAOS** †LAO NATIONAL RADIO, Luang Prabang	Irr • DS
6975	**COSTA RICA** RADIO FOR PEACE INTL, Ciudad Colón	M-W/F/Sa • N America • 30 kW / Th/Su • N America • 30 kW / N America • 30 kW / F-W • N America • 30 kW / Th • N America • 30 kW
7003v	**PERU** †LV DE LAS HUARINJAS, Huancabamba	DS
7030v	**CLANDESTINE (M EAST)** "VO INDEPENDENT KURDS", Iraq	Mideast • ANTI-TURKISH GOVT
7040.5	**PERU** RADIO SAN IGNACIO, San Ignacio	DS • 2 kW
7070v	**AFGHANISTAN** †TAKHAR RADIO, Taloqan	DS • 1 kW • ALT. FREQ. TO 7085 kHz
7080v	**AFGHANISTAN** †VOICE OF SHARI'AH, Kabul	Sa-Th • DS • 100 kW • ALT. FREQ. TO 7200v kHz / DS • 100 kW • ALT. FREQ. TO 7200v kHz / F • DS • 100 kW • ALT. FREQ. TO 7200v kHz / W Asia & Mideast • 100 kW • ALT. FREQ. TO 7200v kHz
7085	**AFGHANISTAN** †TAKHAR RADIO, Taloqan	DS • 1 kW • ALT. FREQ. TO 7070v kHz
7098v	**INDONESIA** †RRI, Yogyakarta, Jawa	DS • 7.5 kW
7100	**SOMALIA** RADIO FREE SOMALIA, Gaalkacyo	DS • 0.8 kW
7102v	**TURKEY** RADYO CINARLI, Izmir	• DS • 0.1 kW
7105	**BELARUS** R BELARUS/R MINSK, Kalodziscy	W • Europe • 250 kW / W F • Europe • 250 kW / W M • Europe • 250 kW / W Tu/Th • Europe • 250 kW / W/Sa/Su • Europe • 250 kW / W M-W • Europe • 250 kW / W Sa/Su • Europe • 250 kW / W Th/F • Europe • 250 kW / W/F-Su • Europe • 250 kW
	BOSNIA HERCEGOVINA R BOSNIA-H	DS • 10 kW
	CHINA (TAIWAN) †CBS, T'ai-pei	E Asia • NEWS NETWORK • 300 kW • ALT. FREQ. TO 7107.5 kHz
	GERMANY DEUTSCHE WELLE, Wertachtal	S • C Asia • 500 kW / S • E Europe & W Asia • 500 kW
	INDIA †ALL INDIA RADIO, Lucknow	Su • DS • 50 kW / DS • 50 kW / ENGLISH, ETC • DS • 50 kW

(con'd)

FREQUENCY   COUNTRY, STATION, LOCATION   TARGET • NETWORK • POWER (kW)   World Time

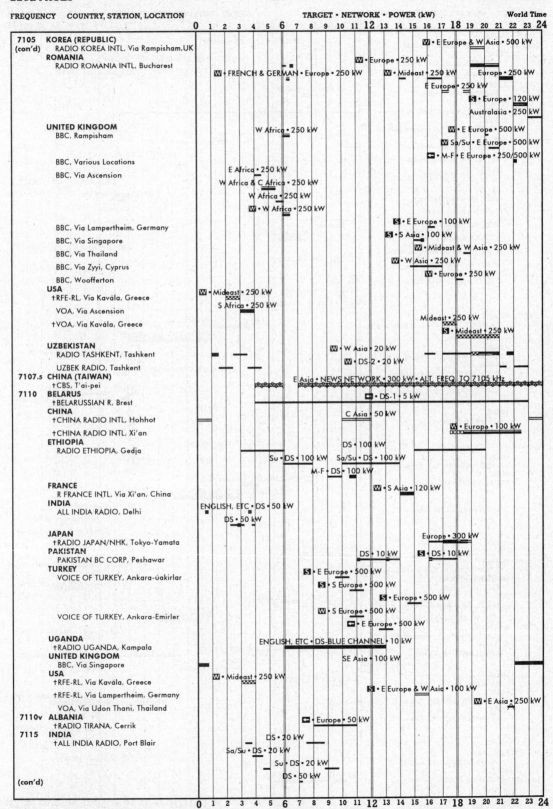

Frequency	Country, Station, Location	Target • Network • Power
7105 (con'd)	KOREA (REPUBLIC)	
	RADIO KOREA INTL, Via Rampisham, UK	W • E Europe & W Asia • 500 kW
	ROMANIA	
	RADIO ROMANIA INTL, Bucharest	W • Europe • 250 kW; W • FRENCH & GERMAN • Europe • 250 kW; W • Mideast • 250 kW; Europe • 250 kW; E Europe • 250 kW; S • Europe • 120 kW; Australasia • 250 kW
	UNITED KINGDOM	
	BBC, Rampisham	W Africa • 250 kW; W • E Europe • 500 kW; W • Sa/Su • E Europe • 500 kW; M-F • E Europe • 250/500 kW
	BBC, Various Locations	E Africa • 250 kW
	BBC, Via Ascension	W Africa & C Africa • 250 kW; W Africa • 250 kW; W • W Africa • 250 kW
	BBC, Via Lampertheim, Germany	S • E Europe • 100 kW
	BBC, Via Singapore	S • S Asia • 100 kW
	BBC, Via Thailand	W • Mideast & W Asia • 250 kW
	BBC, Via Zyyi, Cyprus	W • W Asia • 250 kW
	BBC, Woofferton	W • Europe • 250 kW
	USA	
	†RFE-RL, Via Kavála, Greece	W • Mideast • 250 kW
	VOA, Via Ascension	S Africa • 250 kW
	†VOA, Via Kavála, Greece	Mideast • 250 kW; S • Mideast • 250 kW
	UZBEKISTAN	
	RADIO TASHKENT, Tashkent	W • W Asia • 20 kW
	UZBEK RADIO, Tashkent	W • DS-2 • 20 kW
7107.5	CHINA (TAIWAN)	
	†CBS, T'ai-pei	E Asia • NEWS NETWORK • 300 kW • ALT FREQ TO 7105 kHz
7110	BELARUS	
	†BELARUSSIAN R, Brest	DS-1 • 5 kW
	CHINA	
	†CHINA RADIO INTL, Hohhot	C Asia • 50 kW
	†CHINA RADIO INTL, Xi'an	W • Europe • 100 kW
	ETHIOPIA	
	RADIO ETHIOPIA, Gedja	DS • 100 kW; Su • DS • 100 kW; Sa/Su • DS • 100 kW; M-F • DS • 100 kW
	FRANCE	
	R FRANCE INTL, Via Xi'an, China	W • S Asia • 120 kW
	INDIA	
	ALL INDIA RADIO, Delhi	ENGLISH, ETC • DS • 50 kW; DS • 50 kW
	JAPAN	
	†RADIO JAPAN/NHK, Tokyo-Yamata	Europe • 300 kW
	PAKISTAN	
	PAKISTAN BC CORP, Peshawar	DS • 10 kW; S • DS • 10 kW
	TURKEY	
	VOICE OF TURKEY, Ankara-úakirlar	S • E Europe • 500 kW; S • S Europe • 500 kW; S • Europe • 500 kW
	VOICE OF TURKEY, Ankara-Emirler	W • S Europe • 500 kW; S • E Europe • 500 kW
	UGANDA	
	†RADIO UGANDA, Kampala	ENGLISH, ETC • DS-BLUE CHANNEL • 10 kW
	UNITED KINGDOM	
	BBC, Via Singapore	SE Asia • 100 kW
	USA	
	†RFE-RL, Via Kavála, Greece	W • Mideast • 250 kW
	†RFE-RL, Via Lampertheim, Germany	S • E Europe & W Asia • 100 kW
	VOA, Via Udon Thani, Thailand	W • E Asia • 250 kW
7110v	ALBANIA	
	†RADIO TIRANA, Cerrik	Europe • 50 kW
7115	INDIA	
	†ALL INDIA RADIO, Port Blair	DS • 20 kW; Sa/Su • DS • 20 kW; Su • DS • 20 kW; DS • 50 kW
(con'd)		

ENGLISH ▬   ARABIC ⌇⌇⌇   CHINESE ▫▫▫   FRENCH ═   GERMAN ▬   RUSSIAN ═   SPANISH ▬   OTHER ▬

FREQUENCY   COUNTRY, STATION, LOCATION   TARGET • NETWORK • POWER (kW)   World Time

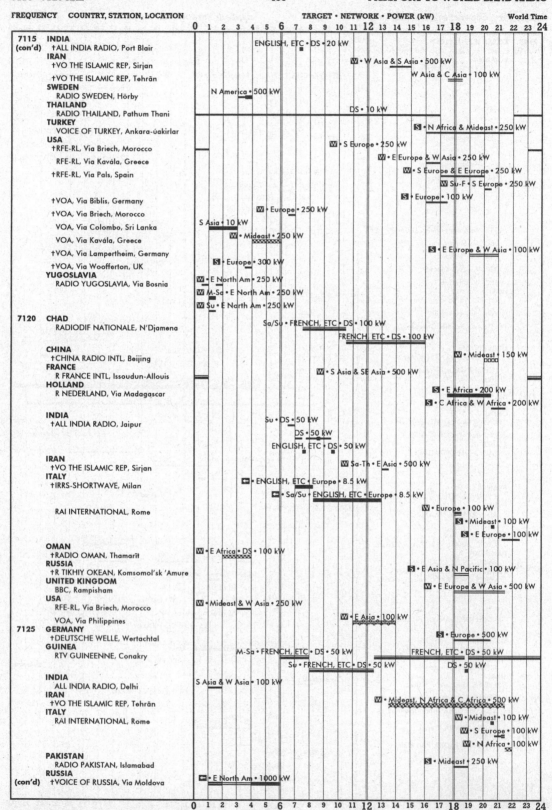

7115 **INDIA**	
(con'd) †ALL INDIA RADIO, Port Blair	ENGLISH, ETC • DS • 20 kW
IRAN	
†VO THE ISLAMIC REP, Sirjan	W • W Asia & S Asia • 500 kW
†VO THE ISLAMIC REP, Tehrān	W Asia & C Asia • 100 kW
SWEDEN	
RADIO SWEDEN, Hörby	N America • 500 kW
THAILAND	
RADIO THAILAND, Pathum Thani	DS • 10 kW
TURKEY	
VOICE OF TURKEY, Ankara-úakirlar	S • N Africa & Mideast • 250 kW
USA	
†RFE-RL, Via Briech, Morocco	W • S Europe • 250 kW
RFE-RL, Via Kavála, Greece	W • E Europe & W Asia • 250 kW
†RFE-RL, Via Pals, Spain	W • S Europe & E Europe • 250 kW
	W • Su-F • S Europe • 250 kW
†VOA, Via Biblis, Germany	S • Europe • 100 kW
†VOA, Via Briech, Morocco	W • Europe • 250 kW
VOA, Via Colombo, Sri Lanka	S Asia • 10 kW
VOA, Via Kavála, Greece	W • Mideast • 250 kW
†VOA, Via Lampertheim, Germany	S • E Europe & W Asia • 100 kW
†VOA, Via Woofferton, UK	S • Europe • 300 kW
YUGOSLAVIA	
RADIO YUGOSLAVIA, Via Bosnia	W • E North Am • 250 kW
	W • M-Sa • E North Am • 250 kW
	W • Su • E North Am • 250 kW
7120 **CHAD**	
RADIODIF NATIONALE, N'Djamena	Sa/Su • FRENCH, ETC • DS • 100 kW
	FRENCH, ETC • DS • 100 kW
CHINA	
†CHINA RADIO INTL, Beijing	W • Mideast • 150 kW
FRANCE	
R FRANCE INTL, Issoudun-Allouis	W • S Asia & SE Asia • 500 kW
HOLLAND	
R NEDERLAND, Via Madagascar	S • E Africa • 200 kW
	S • C Africa & W Africa • 200 kW
INDIA	
†ALL INDIA RADIO, Jaipur	Su • DS • 50 kW
	DS • 50 kW
	ENGLISH, ETC • DS • 50 kW
IRAN	
†VO THE ISLAMIC REP, Sirjan	W • Sa-Th • E Asia • 500 kW
ITALY	
†IRRS-SHORTWAVE, Milan	• ENGLISH, ETC • Europe • 8.5 kW
	• Sa/Su • ENGLISH, ETC • Europe • 8.5 kW
RAI INTERNATIONAL, Rome	W • Europe • 100 kW
	S • Mideast • 100 kW
	S • E Europe • 100 kW
OMAN	
†RADIO OMAN, Thamarīt	W • E Africa • DS • 100 kW
RUSSIA	
†R TIKHIY OKEAN, Komsomol'sk 'Amure	S • E Asia & N Pacific • 100 kW
UNITED KINGDOM	
BBC, Rampisham	W • E Europe & W Asia • 500 kW
USA	
RFE-RL, Via Briech, Morocco	W • Mideast & W Asia • 250 kW
VOA, Via Philippines	W • E Asia • 100 kW
7125 **GERMANY**	
†DEUTSCHE WELLE, Wertachtal	S • Europe • 500 kW
GUINEA	
RTV GUINEENNE, Conakry	M-Sa • FRENCH, ETC • DS • 50 kW
	FRENCH, ETC • DS • 50 kW
	Su • FRENCH, ETC • DS • 50 kW
	DS • 50 kW
INDIA	
ALL INDIA RADIO, Delhi	S Asia & W Asia • 100 kW
IRAN	
†VO THE ISLAMIC REP, Tehrān	W • Mideast, N Africa & C Africa • 500 kW
ITALY	
RAI INTERNATIONAL, Rome	W • Mideast • 100 kW
	W • S Europe • 100 kW
	W • N Africa • 100 kW
PAKISTAN	
RADIO PAKISTAN, Islamabad	S • Mideast • 250 kW
RUSSIA	
(con'd) †VOICE OF RUSSIA, Via Moldova	• E North Am • 1000 kW

FREQUENCY   COUNTRY, STATION, LOCATION   TARGET • NETWORK • POWER (kW)   World Time

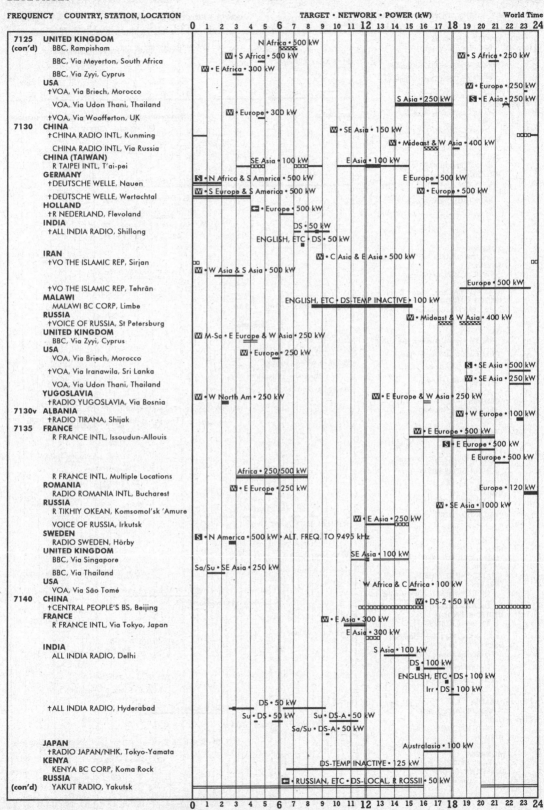

Frequency	Country, Station, Location	Target • Network • Power
7125 (con'd)	**UNITED KINGDOM** BBC, Rampisham	N Africa • 500 kW
	BBC, Via Meyerton, South Africa	W • S Africa • 500 kW / W • S Africa • 250 kW
	BBC, Via Zyyi, Cyprus	W • E Africa • 300 kW
	USA †VOA, Via Briech, Morocco	W • Europe • 250 kW
	VOA, Via Udon Thani, Thailand	S Asia • 250 kW / S • E Asia • 250 kW
	†VOA, Via Woofferton, UK	W • Europe • 300 kW
7130	**CHINA** †CHINA RADIO INTL, Kunming	W • SE Asia • 150 kW
	CHINA RADIO INTL, Via Russia	W • Mideast & W Asia • 400 kW
	CHINA (TAIWAN) R TAIPEI INTL, T'ai-pei	SE Asia • 100 kW / E Asia • 100 kW
	GERMANY †DEUTSCHE WELLE, Nauen	S • N Africa & S America • 500 kW / E Europe • 500 kW
	†DEUTSCHE WELLE, Wertachtal	W • S Europe & S America • 500 kW / W • Europe • 500 kW
	HOLLAND †R NEDERLAND, Flevoland	◄ • Europe • 500 kW
	INDIA †ALL INDIA RADIO, Shillong	DS • 50 kW / ENGLISH, ETC • DS • 50 kW
	IRAN †VO THE ISLAMIC REP, Sirjan	W • C Asia & E Asia • 500 kW / W • W Asia & S Asia • 500 kW
	†VO THE ISLAMIC REP, Tehrān	Europe • 500 kW
	MALAWI MALAWI BC CORP, Limbe	ENGLISH, ETC • DS-TEMP INACTIVE • 100 kW
	RUSSIA †VOICE OF RUSSIA, St Petersburg	W • Mideast & W Asia • 400 kW
	UNITED KINGDOM BBC, Via Zyyi, Cyprus	W M-Sa • E Europe & W Asia • 250 kW
	USA VOA, Via Briech, Morocco	W • Europe • 250 kW
	†VOA, Via Iranawila, Sri Lanka	S • SE Asia • 500 kW
	VOA, Via Udon Thani, Thailand	W • SE Asia • 250 kW
	YUGOSLAVIA †RADIO YUGOSLAVIA, Via Bosnia	W • W North Am • 250 kW / W • E Europe & W Asia • 250 kW
7130v	**ALBANIA** †RADIO TIRANA, Shijak	W • W Europe • 100 kW
7135	**FRANCE** R FRANCE INTL, Issoudun-Allouis	W • E Europe • 500 kW / S • E Europe • 500 kW / E Europe • 500 kW
	R FRANCE INTL, Multiple Locations	Africa • 250/500 kW
	ROMANIA RADIO ROMANIA INTL, Bucharest	W • E Europe • 250 kW / Europe • 120 kW
	RUSSIA R TIKHIY OKEAN, Komsomol'sk 'Amure	W • SE Asia • 1000 kW
	VOICE OF RUSSIA, Irkutsk	W • E Asia • 250 kW
	SWEDEN RADIO SWEDEN, Hörby	S • N America • 500 kW • ALT. FREQ. TO 9495 kHz
	UNITED KINGDOM BBC, Via Singapore	SE Asia • 100 kW
	BBC, Via Thailand	Sa/Su • SE Asia • 250 kW
	USA VOA, Via São Tomé	W Africa & C Africa • 100 kW
7140	**CHINA** †CENTRAL PEOPLE'S BS, Beijing	W • DS-2 • 50 kW
	FRANCE R FRANCE INTL, Via Tokyo, Japan	W • E Asia • 300 kW / E Asia • 300 kW
	INDIA ALL INDIA RADIO, Delhi	S Asia • 100 kW / DS • 100 kW / ENGLISH, ETC • DS • 100 kW / Irr • DS • 100 kW
	†ALL INDIA RADIO, Hyderabad	DS • 50 kW / Su • DS • 50 kW / Su • DS-A • 50 kW / Sa/Su • DS-A • 50 kW
	JAPAN †RADIO JAPAN/NHK, Tokyo-Yamata	Australasia • 100 kW
	KENYA KENYA BC CORP, Koma Rock	DS-TEMP INACTIVE • 125 kW
(con'd)	**RUSSIA** YAKUT RADIO, Yakutsk	◄ • RUSSIAN, ETC • DS-LOCAL, R ROSSII • 50 kW

ENGLISH ▬   ARABIC ▨   CHINESE ▭▭▭   FRENCH ▬▬   GERMAN ▬▬   RUSSIAN ══   SPANISH ▬   OTHER ▬

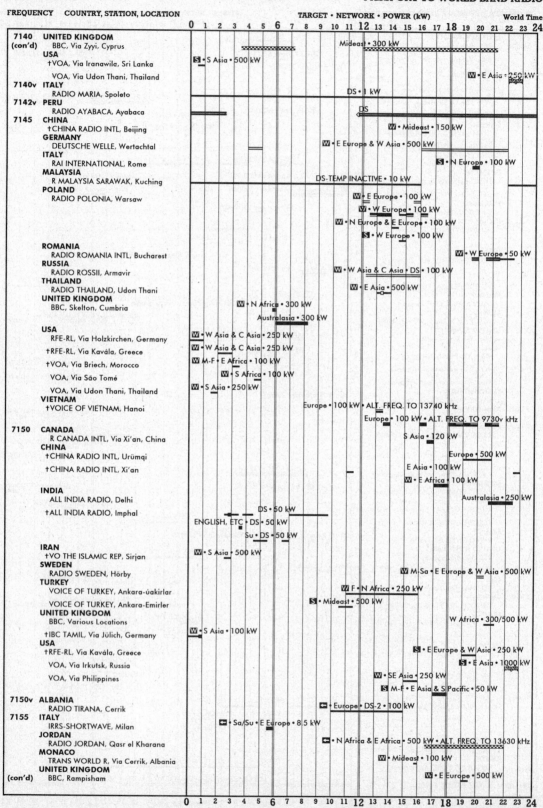

FREQUENCY	COUNTRY, STATION, LOCATION
7140	**UNITED KINGDOM**
(con'd)	BBC, Via Zyyi, Cyprus — Mideast • 300 kW
	USA
	†VOA, Via Iranawila, Sri Lanka — S • S Asia • 500 kW
	VOA, Via Udon Thani, Thailand — W • E Asia • 250 kW
7140v	**ITALY**
	RADIO MARIA, Spoleto — DS • 1 kW
7142v	**PERU**
	RADIO AYABACA, Ayabaca — DS
7145	**CHINA**
	†CHINA RADIO INTL, Beijing — W • Mideast • 150 kW
	GERMANY
	DEUTSCHE WELLE, Wertachtal — W • E Europe & W Asia • 500 kW
	ITALY
	RAI INTERNATIONAL, Rome — S • N Europe • 100 kW
	MALAYSIA
	R MALAYSIA SARAWAK, Kuching — DS-TEMP INACTIVE • 10 kW
	POLAND
	RADIO POLONIA, Warsaw — W • E Europe • 100 kW
	W • W Europe • 100 kW
	W • N Europe & E Europe • 100 kW
	S • W Europe • 100 kW
	ROMANIA
	RADIO ROMANIA INTL, Bucharest — W • W Europe • 50 kW
	RUSSIA
	RADIO ROSSII, Armavir — W • W Asia & C Asia • DS • 100 kW
	THAILAND
	RADIO THAILAND, Udon Thani — W • E Asia • 500 kW
	UNITED KINGDOM
	BBC, Skelton, Cumbria — W • N Africa • 300 kW
	Australasia • 300 kW
	USA
	RFE-RL, Via Holzkirchen, Germany — W • W Asia & C Asia • 250 kW
	†RFE-RL, Via Kavála, Greece — W • W Asia & C Asia • 250 kW
	†VOA, Via Briech, Morocco — W M-F • E Africa • 100 kW
	VOA, Via São Tomé — W • S Africa • 100 kW
	VOA, Via Udon Thani, Thailand — W • S Asia • 250 kW
	VIETNAM
	†VOICE OF VIETNAM, Hanoi — Europe • 100 kW • ALT. FREQ. TO 13740 kHz
	Europe • 100 kW • ALT. FREQ. TO 9730v kHz
7150	**CANADA**
	R CANADA INTL, Via Xi'an, China — S Asia • 120 kW
	CHINA
	†CHINA RADIO INTL, Urümqi — Europe • 500 kW
	†CHINA RADIO INTL, Xi'an — E Asia • 100 kW
	W • E Africa • 100 kW
	INDIA
	ALL INDIA RADIO, Delhi — Australasia • 250 kW
	†ALL INDIA RADIO, Imphal — DS • 50 kW
	ENGLISH, ETC • DS • 50 kW
	Su • DS • 50 kW
	IRAN
	†VO THE ISLAMIC REP, Sirjan — W • S Asia • 500 kW
	SWEDEN
	RADIO SWEDEN, Hörby — W M-Sa • E Europe & W Asia • 500 kW
	TURKEY
	VOICE OF TURKEY, Ankara-úakirlar — W F • N Africa • 250 kW
	VOICE OF TURKEY, Ankara-Emirler — S • Mideast • 500 kW
	UNITED KINGDOM
	BBC, Various Locations — W Africa • 300/500 kW
	†IBC TAMIL, Via Jülich, Germany — W • S Asia • 100 kW
	USA
	†RFE-RL, Via Kavála, Greece — S • E Europe & W Asia • 250 kW
	VOA, Via Irkutsk, Russia — S • E Asia • 1000 kW
	VOA, Via Philippines — W • SE Asia • 250 kW
	S M-F • E Asia & S Pacific • 50 kW
7150v	**ALBANIA**
	RADIO TIRANA, Cerrik — Europe • DS-2 • 100 kW
7155	**ITALY**
	IRRS-SHORTWAVE, Milan — Sa/Su • E Europe • 8.5 kW
	JORDAN
	RADIO JORDAN, Qasr el Kharana — N Africa & E Africa • 500 kW • ALT. FREQ. TO 13630 kHz
	MONACO
	TRANS WORLD R, Via Cerrik, Albania — W • Mideast • 100 kW
	UNITED KINGDOM
(con'd)	BBC, Rampisham — W • E Europe • 500 kW

FREQUENCY   COUNTRY, STATION, LOCATION   TARGET • NETWORK • POWER (kW)   World Time

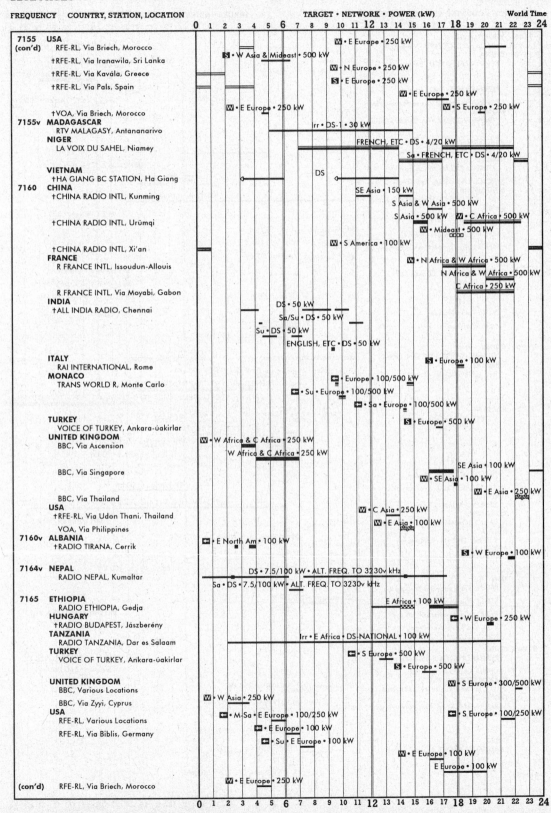

FREQUENCY	COUNTRY, STATION, LOCATION	TARGET • NETWORK • POWER (kW)
7155 (con'd)	USA	
	RFE-RL, Via Briech, Morocco	W • E Europe • 250 kW
	†RFE-RL, Via Iranawila, Sri Lanka	S • W Asia & Mideast • 500 kW
	†RFE-RL, Via Kavála, Greece	W • N Europe • 250 kW
	†RFE-RL, Via Pals, Spain	S • E Europe • 250 kW
		W • E Europe • 250 kW
	†VOA, Via Briech, Morocco	W • E Europe • 250 kW W • S Europe • 250 kW
7155v	MADAGASCAR	
	RTV MALAGASY, Antananarivo	Irr • DS-1 • 30 kW
	NIGER	
	LA VOIX DU SAHEL, Niamey	FRENCH, ETC • DS • 4/20 kW
		Sa • FRENCH, ETC • DS • 4/20 kW
	VIETNAM	
	†HA GIANG BC STATION, Ha Giang	DS
7160	CHINA	
	†CHINA RADIO INTL, Kunming	SE Asia • 150 kW
		S Asia & W Asia • 500 kW
	†CHINA RADIO INTL, Urümqi	S Asia • 500 kW W • C Africa • 500 kW
		W • Mideast • 500 kW
	†CHINA RADIO INTL, Xi'an	W • S America • 100 kW
	FRANCE	
	R FRANCE INTL, Issoudun-Allouis	W • N Africa & W Africa • 500 kW
		N Africa & W Africa • 500 kW
		C Africa • 250 kW
	R FRANCE INTL, Via Moyabi, Gabon	
	INDIA	
	†ALL INDIA RADIO, Chennai	DS • 50 kW
		Sa/Su • DS • 50 kW
		Su • DS • 50 kW
		ENGLISH, ETC • DS • 50 kW
	ITALY	
	RAI INTERNATIONAL, Rome	S • Europe • 100 kW
	MONACO	
	TRANS WORLD R, Monte Carlo	Europe • 100/500 kW
		Su • Europe • 100/500 kW
		Sa • Europe • 100/500 kW
	TURKEY	
	VOICE OF TURKEY, Ankara-úakirlar	S • Europe • 500 kW
	UNITED KINGDOM	
	BBC, Via Ascension	W • W Africa & C Africa • 250 kW
		W Africa & C Africa • 250 kW
	BBC, Via Singapore	SE Asia • 100 kW
		W • SE Asia • 100 kW
	BBC, Via Thailand	W • E Asia • 250 kW
	USA	
	†RFE-RL, Via Udon Thani, Thailand	W • C Asia • 250 kW
	VOA, Via Philippines	W • E Asia • 100 kW
7160v	ALBANIA	
	†RADIO TIRANA, Cerrik	E North Am • 100 kW
		S • W Europe • 100 kW
7164v	NEPAL	
	RADIO NEPAL, Kumaltar	DS • 7.5/100 kW • ALT. FREQ. TO 3230v kHz
		Sa • DS • 7.5/100 kW • ALT. FREQ. TO 3230v kHz
7165	ETHIOPIA	
	RADIO ETHIOPIA, Gedja	E Africa • 100 kW
	HUNGARY	
	†RADIO BUDAPEST, Jászberény	W Europe • 250 kW
	TANZANIA	
	RADIO TANZANIA, Dar es Salaam	Irr • E Africa • DS-NATIONAL • 100 kW
	TURKEY	
	VOICE OF TURKEY, Ankara-úakirlar	S Europe • 500 kW
		S • Europe • 500 kW
	UNITED KINGDOM	
	BBC, Various Locations	W • S Europe • 300/500 kW
	BBC, Via Zyyi, Cyprus	W • W Asia • 250 kW
	USA	
	RFE-RL, Various Locations	M-Sa • E Europe • 100/250 kW S • S Europe • 100/250 kW
	RFE-RL, Via Biblis, Germany	E Europe • 100 kW
		Su • E Europe • 100 kW
		W • E Europe • 100 kW
		E Europe • 100 kW
(con'd)	RFE-RL, Via Briech, Morocco	W • E Europe • 250 kW

0 1 2 3 4 5 6 7 8 9 10 11 12 13 14 15 16 17 18 19 20 21 22 23 24

ENGLISH ▬   ARABIC ⬚⬚⬚   CHINESE ▭▭▭   FRENCH ▬▬   GERMAN ▬▬   RUSSIAN ═══   SPANISH ▬▬   OTHER ──

FREQUENCY   COUNTRY, STATION, LOCATION   TARGET • NETWORK • POWER (kW)   World Time

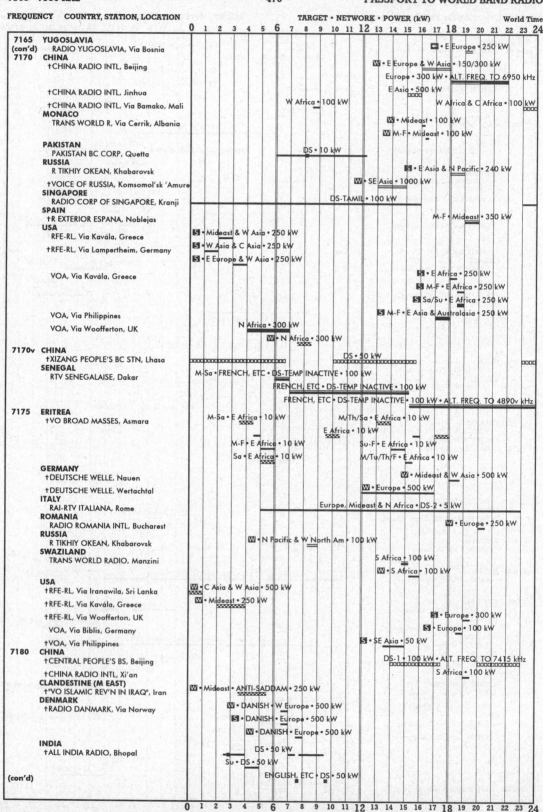

FREQUENCY	COUNTRY, STATION, LOCATION	TARGET • NETWORK • POWER (kW)
7165 (con'd)	**YUGOSLAVIA** RADIO YUGOSLAVIA, Via Bosnia	⑤ • E Europe • 250 kW
7170	**CHINA** †CHINA RADIO INTL, Beijing	ⓦ • E Europe & W Asia • 150/300 kW
		Europe • 300 kW • ALT. FREQ. TO 6950 kHz
	†CHINA RADIO INTL, Jinhua	E Asia • 500 kW
	†CHINA RADIO INTL, Via Bamako, Mali	W Africa • 100 kW W Africa & C Africa • 100 kW
	MONACO TRANS WORLD R, Via Cerrik, Albania	ⓦ • Mideast • 100 kW
		ⓦ M-F • Mideast • 100 kW
	PAKISTAN PAKISTAN BC CORP, Quetta	DS • 10 kW
	RUSSIA R TIKHIY OKEAN, Khabarovsk	⑤ • E Asia & N Pacific • 240 kW
	†VOICE OF RUSSIA, Komsomol'sk 'Amure	ⓦ • SE Asia • 1000 kW
	SINGAPORE RADIO CORP OF SINGAPORE, Kranji	DS-TAMIL • 100 kW
	SPAIN †R EXTERIOR ESPANA, Noblejas	M-F • Mideast • 350 kW
	USA RFE-RL, Via Kavála, Greece	⑤ • Mideast & W Asia • 250 kW
	†RFE-RL, Via Lampertheim, Germany	⑤ • W Asia & C Asia • 250 kW
		⑤ • E Europe & W Asia • 250 kW
	VOA, Via Kavála, Greece	⑤ • E Africa • 250 kW
		⑤ M-F • E Africa • 250 kW
		⑤ Sa/Su • E Africa • 250 kW
		⑤ M-F • E Asia & Australasia • 250 kW
	VOA, Via Philippines	N Africa • 300 kW
	VOA, Via Woofferton, UK	ⓦ • N Africa • 300 kW
7170v	**CHINA** †XIZANG PEOPLE'S BC STN, Lhasa	DS • 50 kW
	SENEGAL RTV SENEGALAISE, Dakar	M-Sa • FRENCH, ETC • DS-TEMP INACTIVE • 100 kW
		FRENCH, ETC • DS-TEMP INACTIVE • 100 kW
		FRENCH, ETC • DS-TEMP INACTIVE • 100 kW • ALT. FREQ. TO 4890v kHz
7175	**ERITREA** †VO BROAD MASSES, Asmara	M-Sa • E Africa • 10 kW M/Th/Sa • E Africa • 10 kW
		E Africa • 10 kW
		M-F • E Africa • 10 kW Su-F • E Africa • 10 kW
		Sa • E Africa • 10 kW M/Tu/Th/F • E Africa • 10 kW
	GERMANY †DEUTSCHE WELLE, Nauen	ⓦ • Mideast & W Asia • 500 kW
	†DEUTSCHE WELLE, Wertachtal	ⓦ • Europe • 500 kW
	ITALY RAI-RTV ITALIANA, Rome	Europe, Mideast & N Africa • DS-2 • 5 kW
	ROMANIA RADIO ROMANIA INTL, Bucharest	ⓦ • Europe • 250 kW
	RUSSIA R TIKHIY OKEAN, Khabarovsk	ⓦ • N Pacific & W North Am • 100 kW
	SWAZILAND TRANS WORLD RADIO, Manzini	S Africa • 100 kW
		ⓦ • S Africa • 100 kW
	USA †RFE-RL, Via Iranawila, Sri Lanka	ⓦ • C Asia & W Asia • 500 kW
	†RFE-RL, Via Kavála, Greece	ⓦ • Mideast • 250 kW
	†RFE-RL, Via Woofferton, UK	⑤ • Europe • 300 kW
	VOA, Via Biblis, Germany	⑤ • Europe • 100 kW
	†VOA, Via Philippines	⑤ • SE Asia • 50 kW
7180	**CHINA** †CENTRAL PEOPLE'S BS, Beijing	DS-1 • 100 kW • ALT. FREQ. TO 7415 kHz
	†CHINA RADIO INTL, Xi'an	S Africa • 100 kW
	CLANDESTINE (M EAST) †"VO ISLAMIC REV'N IN IRAQ", Iran	ⓦ • Mideast • ANTI-SADDAM • 250 kW
	DENMARK †RADIO DANMARK, Via Norway	ⓦ • DANISH • W Europe • 500 kW
		⑤ • DANISH • Europe • 500 kW
		ⓦ • DANISH • Europe • 500 kW
	INDIA †ALL INDIA RADIO, Bhopal	DS • 50 kW
		Su • DS • 50 kW
(con'd)		ENGLISH, ETC • DS • 50 kW

FREQUENCY   COUNTRY, STATION, LOCATION   TARGET • NETWORK • POWER (kW)   World Time

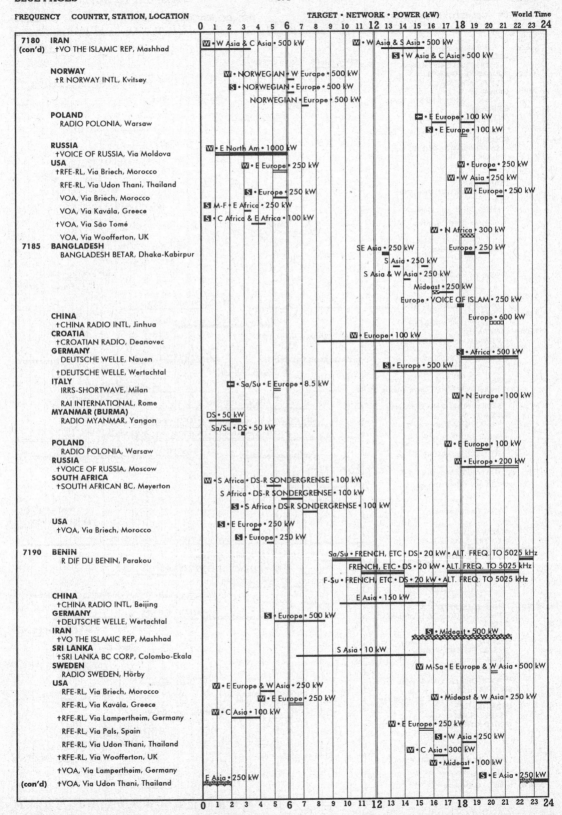

7180 (con'd)	**IRAN** †VO THE ISLAMIC REP, Mashhad	W • W Asia & C Asia • 500 kW W • W Asia & S Asia • 500 kW; S • W Asia & C Asia • 500 kW
	NORWAY †R NORWAY INTL, Kvitsøy	W • NORWEGIAN • W Europe • 500 kW; S • NORWEGIAN • Europe • 500 kW; NORWEGIAN • Europe • 500 kW
	POLAND RADIO POLONIA, Warsaw	• E Europe • 100 kW; S • E Europe • 100 kW
	RUSSIA †VOICE OF RUSSIA, Via Moldova	W • E North Am • 1000 kW
	USA †RFE-RL, Via Briech, Morocco	W • E Europe • 250 kW; W • Europe • 250 kW
	RFE-RL, Via Udon Thani, Thailand	W • W Asia • 250 kW; W • Europe • 250 kW
	VOA, Via Briech, Morocco	S • Europe • 250 kW
	VOA, Via Kavála, Greece	S M-F • E Africa • 250 kW
	†VOA, Via São Tomé	S • C Africa & E Africa • 100 kW
	VOA, Via Woofferton, UK	W • N Africa • 300 kW
7185	**BANGLADESH** BANGLADESH BETAR, Dhaka-Kabirpur	SE Asia • 250 kW Europe • 250 kW; S Asia • 250 kW; S Asia & W Asia • 250 kW; Mideast • 250 kW; Europe • VOICE OF ISLAM • 250 kW
	CHINA †CHINA RADIO INTL, Jinhua	Europe • 600 kW
	CROATIA †CROATIAN RADIO, Deanovec	W • Europe • 100 kW
	GERMANY DEUTSCHE WELLE, Nauen	S • Africa • 500 kW
	†DEUTSCHE WELLE, Wertachtal	S • Europe • 500 kW
	ITALY IRRS-SHORTWAVE, Milan	• Sa/Su • E Europe • 8.5 kW
	RAI INTERNATIONAL, Rome	W • N Europe • 100 kW
	MYANMAR (BURMA) RADIO MYANMAR, Yangon	DS • 50 kW; Sa/Su • DS • 50 kW
	POLAND RADIO POLONIA, Warsaw	W • E Europe • 100 kW
	RUSSIA †VOICE OF RUSSIA, Moscow	W • Europe • 200 kW
	SOUTH AFRICA †SOUTH AFRICAN BC, Meyerton	W • S Africa • DS-R SONDERGRENSE • 100 kW; S Africa • DS-R SONDERGRENSE • 100 kW; S • S Africa • DS-R SONDERGRENSE • 100 kW
	USA †VOA, Via Briech, Morocco	S • E Europe • 250 kW; S • Europe • 250 kW
7190	**BENIN** R DIF DU BENIN, Parakou	Sa/Su • FRENCH, ETC • DS • 20 kW • ALT. FREQ. TO 5025 kHz; FRENCH, ETC • DS • 20 kW • ALT. FREQ. TO 5025 kHz; F-Su • FRENCH, ETC • DS • 20 kW • ALT. FREQ. TO 5025 kHz
	CHINA †CHINA RADIO INTL, Beijing	E Asia • 150 kW
	GERMANY †DEUTSCHE WELLE, Wertachtal	S • Europe • 500 kW
	IRAN †VO THE ISLAMIC REP, Mashhad	S • Mideast • 500 kW
	SRI LANKA †SRI LANKA BC CORP, Colombo-Ekala	S Asia • 10 kW
	SWEDEN RADIO SWEDEN, Hörby	W M-Sa • E Europe & W Asia • 500 kW
	USA RFE-RL, Via Briech, Morocco	W • E Europe & W Asia • 250 kW; W • E Europe • 250 kW
	RFE-RL, Via Kavála, Greece	W • Mideast & W Asia • 250 kW
	†RFE-RL, Via Lampertheim, Germany	W • C Asia • 100 kW
	RFE-RL, Via Pals, Spain	W • E Europe • 250 kW
	RFE-RL, Via Udon Thani, Thailand	S • W Asia • 250 kW
	†RFE-RL, Via Woofferton, UK	W • C Asia • 300 kW
	†VOA, Via Lampertheim, Germany	W • Mideast • 100 kW
(con'd)	†VOA, Via Udon Thani, Thailand	E Asia • 250 kW; S • E Asia • 250 kW

ENGLISH ▬   ARABIC ≋   CHINESE □□□   FRENCH ━   GERMAN ═   RUSSIAN ═   SPANISH ▬   OTHER ━

FREQUENCY   COUNTRY, STATION, LOCATION   TARGET • NETWORK • POWER (kW)   World Time

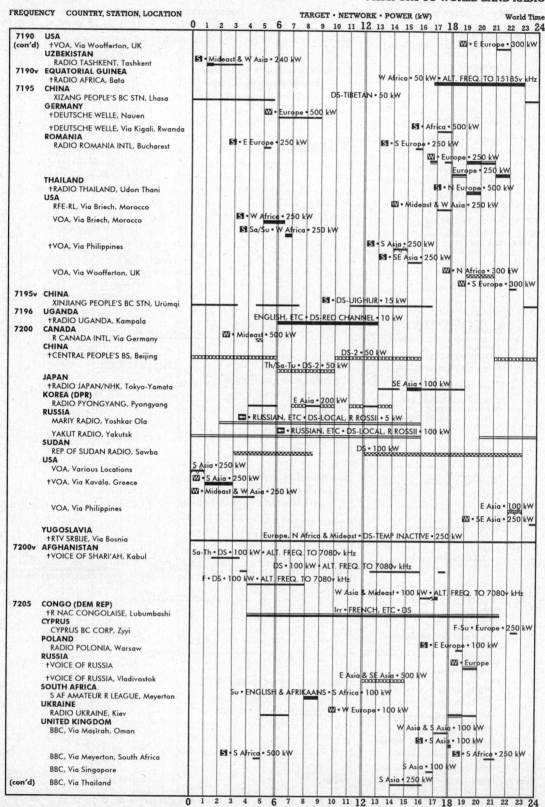

FREQUENCY	COUNTRY, STATION, LOCATION	Schedule (Target • Network • Power)
7190 (con'd)	**USA** †VOA, Via Woofferton, UK	W • E Europe • 300 kW
	UZBEKISTAN RADIO TASHKENT, Tashkent	S • Mideast & W Asia • 240 kW
7190v	**EQUATORIAL GUINEA** †RADIO AFRICA, Bata	W Africa • 50 kW • ALT. FREQ. TO 15185v kHz
7195	**CHINA** XIZANG PEOPLE'S BC STN, Lhasa	DS-TIBETAN • 50 kW
	GERMANY †DEUTSCHE WELLE, Nauen	W • Europe • 500 kW
	†DEUTSCHE WELLE, Via Kigali, Rwanda	S • Africa • 500 kW
	ROMANIA RADIO ROMANIA INTL, Bucharest	S • E Europe • 250 kW / S • S Europe • 250 kW / W • Europe • 250 kW / Europe • 250 kW
	THAILAND †RADIO THAILAND, Udon Thani	S • N Europe • 500 kW
	USA RFE-RL, Via Briech, Morocco	W • Mideast & W Asia • 250 kW
	VOA, Via Briech, Morocco	S • W Africa • 250 kW / S Sa/Su • W Africa • 250 kW
	†VOA, Via Philippines	S • S Asia • 250 kW / S • SE Asia • 250 kW
	VOA, Via Woofferton, UK	W • N Africa • 300 kW / W • S Europe • 300 kW
7195v	**CHINA** XINJIANG PEOPLE'S BC STN, Urümqi	S • DS-UIGHUR • 15 kW
7196	**UGANDA** †RADIO UGANDA, Kampala	ENGLISH, ETC • DS-RED CHANNEL • 10 kW
7200	**CANADA** R CANADA INTL, Via Germany	W • Mideast • 500 kW
	CHINA †CENTRAL PEOPLE'S BS, Beijing	DS-2 • 50 kW / Th/Sa-Tu • DS-2 • 50 kW
	JAPAN †RADIO JAPAN/NHK, Tokyo-Yamata	SE Asia • 100 kW
	KOREA (DPR) RADIO PYONGYANG, Pyongyang	E Asia • 200 kW
	RUSSIA MARIY RADIO, Yoshkar Ola	⇇ • RUSSIAN, ETC • DS-LOCAL, R ROSSII • 5 kW
	YAKUT RADIO, Yakutsk	⇇ • RUSSIAN, ETC • DS-LOCAL, R ROSSII • 100 kW
	SUDAN REP OF SUDAN RADIO, Sawba	DS • 100 kW
	USA VOA, Various Locations	S Asia • 250 kW
	†VOA, Via Kavála, Greece	W • S Asia • 250 kW / W • Mideast & W Asia • 250 kW
	VOA, Via Philippines	E Asia • 100 kW / W • SE Asia • 250 kW
	YUGOSLAVIA †RTV SRBIJE, Via Bosnia	Europe, N Africa & Mideast • DS-TEMP INACTIVE • 250 kW
7200v	**AFGHANISTAN** †VOICE OF SHARI'AH, Kabul	Sa-Th • DS • 100 kW • ALT. FREQ. TO 7080v kHz / DS • 100 kW • ALT. FREQ. TO 7080v kHz / F • DS • 100 kW • ALT. FREQ. TO 7080v kHz / W Asia & Mideast • 100 kW • ALT. FREQ. TO 7080v kHz
7205	**CONGO (DEM REP)** †R NAC CONGOLAISE, Lubumbashi	Irr • FRENCH, ETC • DS
	CYPRUS CYPRUS BC CORP, Zyyi	F-Su • Europe • 250 kW
	POLAND RADIO POLONIA, Warsaw	S • E Europe • 100 kW
	RUSSIA †VOICE OF RUSSIA	W • Europe
	†VOICE OF RUSSIA, Vladivostok	E Asia & SE Asia • 500 kW
	SOUTH AFRICA S AF AMATEUR R LEAGUE, Meyerton	Su • ENGLISH & AFRIKAANS • S Africa • 100 kW
	UKRAINE RADIO UKRAINE, Kiev	W • W Europe • 100 kW
	UNITED KINGDOM BBC, Via Maşirah, Oman	W Asia & S Asia • 100 kW / S • S Asia • 100 kW / S • S Africa • 250 kW
	BBC, Via Meyerton, South Africa	S • S Africa • 500 kW
	BBC, Via Singapore	S Asia • 100 kW
(con'd)	BBC, Via Thailand	S Asia • 250 kW

FREQUENCY   COUNTRY, STATION, LOCATION

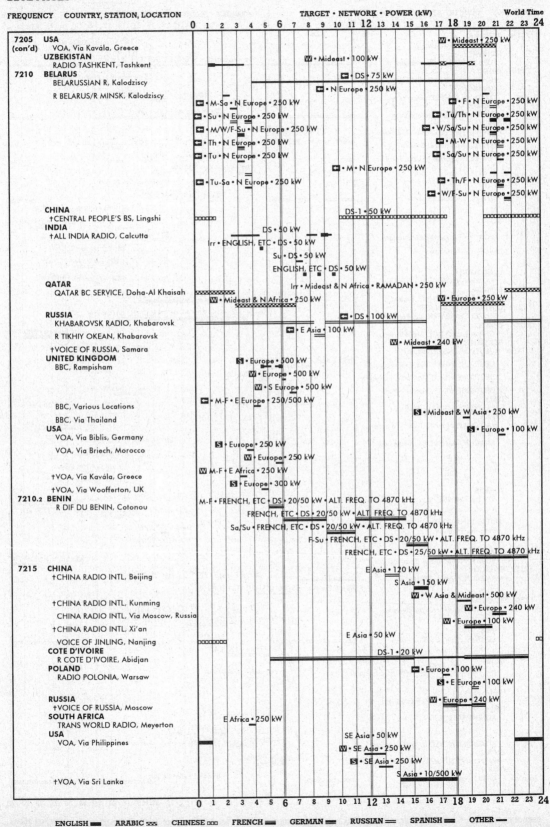

TARGET • NETWORK • POWER (kW)   World Time

7205	**USA**
(con'd)	VOA, Via Kavála, Greece
	UZBEKISTAN
	RADIO TASHKENT, Tashkent
7210	**BELARUS**
	BELARUSSIAN R, Kalodziscy
	R BELARUS/R MINSK, Kalodziscy
	CHINA
	†CENTRAL PEOPLE'S BS, Lingshi
	INDIA
	†ALL INDIA RADIO, Calcutta
	QATAR
	QATAR BC SERVICE, Doha-Al Khaisah
	RUSSIA
	KHABAROVSK RADIO, Khabarovsk
	R TIKHIY OKEAN, Khabarovsk
	†VOICE OF RUSSIA, Samara
	UNITED KINGDOM
	BBC, Rampisham
	BBC, Various Locations
	BBC, Via Thailand
	USA
	VOA, Via Biblis, Germany
	VOA, Via Briech, Morocco
	†VOA, Via Kavála, Greece
	†VOA, Via Woofferton, UK
7210.2	**BENIN**
	R DIF DU BENIN, Cotonou
7215	**CHINA**
	†CHINA RADIO INTL, Beijing
	†CHINA RADIO INTL, Kunming
	CHINA RADIO INTL, Via Moscow, Russia
	†CHINA RADIO INTL, Xi'an
	VOICE OF JINLING, Nanjing
	COTE D'IVOIRE
	R COTE D'IVOIRE, Abidjan
	POLAND
	RADIO POLONIA, Warsaw
	RUSSIA
	†VOICE OF RUSSIA, Moscow
	SOUTH AFRICA
	TRANS WORLD RADIO, Meyerton
	USA
	VOA, Via Philippines
	†VOA, Via Sri Lanka

ENGLISH ▬   ARABIC ▨   CHINESE ▯▯▯   FRENCH ═   GERMAN ▬   RUSSIAN ═   SPANISH ▬   OTHER —

FREQUENCY	COUNTRY, STATION, LOCATION	TARGET • NETWORK • POWER (kW) / World Time

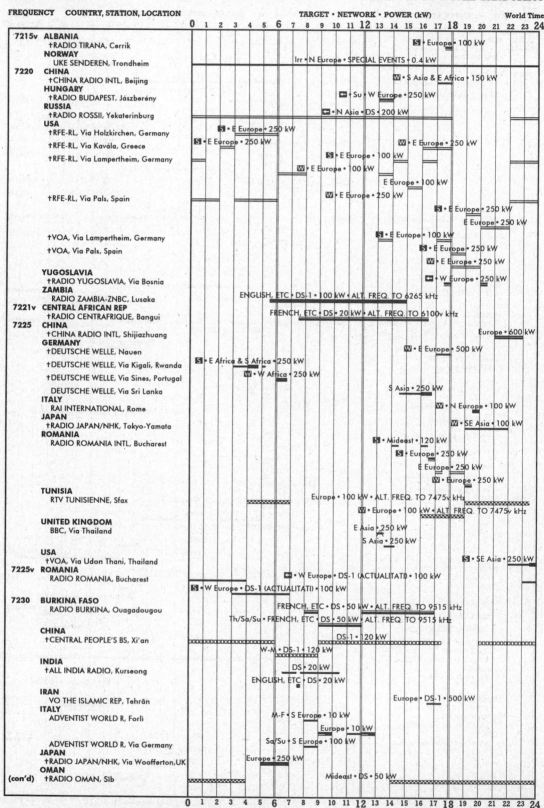

7215v ALBANIA
†RADIO TIRANA, Cerrik — S • Europe • 100 kW

NORWAY
UKE SENDEREN, Trondheim — Irr • N Europe • SPECIAL EVENTS • 0.4 kW

7220 CHINA
†CHINA RADIO INTL, Beijing — W • S Asia & E Africa • 150 kW

HUNGARY
†RADIO BUDAPEST, Jászberény — • Su • W Europe • 250 kW

RUSSIA
†RADIO ROSSII, Yekaterinburg — • N Asia • DS • 200 kW

USA
†RFE-RL, Via Holzkirchen, Germany — S • E Europe • 250 kW

†RFE-RL, Via Kavála, Greece — S • E Europe • 250 kW

†RFE-RL, Via Lampertheim, Germany — S • E Europe • 100 kW
W • E Europe • 100 kW
E Europe • 100 kW

†RFE-RL, Via Pals, Spain — W • E Europe • 250 kW
S • E Europe • 250 kW
E Europe • 250 kW

†VOA, Via Lampertheim, Germany — S • E Europe • 100 kW

†VOA, Via Pals, Spain — S • E Europe • 250 kW
W • E Europe • 250 kW

YUGOSLAVIA
†RADIO YUGOSLAVIA, Via Bosnia — • W Europe • 250 kW

ZAMBIA
RADIO ZAMBIA-ZNBC, Lusaka — ENGLISH, ETC • DS-1 • 100 kW • ALT. FREQ. TO 6265 kHz

7221v CENTRAL AFRICAN REP
†RADIO CENTRAFRIQUE, Bangui — FRENCH, ETC • DS • 20 kW • ALT. FREQ. TO 6100v kHz

7225 CHINA
†CHINA RADIO INTL, Shijiazhuang — Europe • 600 kW

GERMANY
†DEUTSCHE WELLE, Nauen — W • E Europe • 500 kW

†DEUTSCHE WELLE, Via Kigali, Rwanda — S • E Africa & S Africa • 250 kW

†DEUTSCHE WELLE, Via Sines, Portugal — W • W Africa • 250 kW

DEUTSCHE WELLE, Via Sri Lanka — S Asia • 250 kW

ITALY
RAI INTERNATIONAL, Rome — W • N Europe • 100 kW

JAPAN
†RADIO JAPAN/NHK, Tokyo-Yamata — W • SE Asia • 100 kW

ROMANIA
RADIO ROMANIA INTL, Bucharest — S • Mideast • 120 kW
S • Europe • 250 kW
E Europe • 250 kW
W • Europe • 250 kW

TUNISIA
RTV TUNISIENNE, Sfax — Europe • 100 kW • ALT. FREQ. TO 7475v kHz
W • Europe • 100 kW • ALT. FREQ. TO 7475v kHz

UNITED KINGDOM
BBC, Via Thailand — E Asia • 250 kW
S Asia • 250 kW

USA
†VOA, Via Udon Thani, Thailand — S • SE Asia • 250 kW

7225v ROMANIA
RADIO ROMANIA, Bucharest — • W Europe • DS-1 (ACTUALITATI) • 100 kW
S • W Europe • DS-1 (ACTUALITATI) • 100 kW

7230 BURKINA FASO
RADIO BURKINA, Ouagadougou — FRENCH, ETC • DS • 50 kW • ALT. FREQ. TO 9515 kHz
Th/Sa/Su • FRENCH, ETC • DS • 50 kW • ALT. FREQ. TO 9515 kHz

CHINA
†CENTRAL PEOPLE'S BS, Xi'an — DS-1 • 120 kW
W-M • DS-1 • 120 kW

INDIA
†ALL INDIA RADIO, Kurseong — DS • 20 kW
ENGLISH, ETC • DS • 20 kW

IRAN
VO THE ISLAMIC REP, Tehrān — Europe • DS-1 • 500 kW

ITALY
ADVENTIST WORLD R, Forlì — M-F • S Europe • 10 kW
Europe • 10 kW
Sa/Su • S Europe • 100 kW

ADVENTIST WORLD R, Via Germany

JAPAN
†RADIO JAPAN/NHK, Via Woofferton, UK — Europe • 250 kW

OMAN
(con'd) †RADIO OMAN, Sīb — Mideast • DS • 50 kW

SEASONAL S OR W   1-HR TIMESHIFT MIDYEAR ▣ OR ▣   JAMMING / OR ∧   EARLIEST HEARD ◁   LATEST HEARD ▷   NEW FOR 2000 †

FREQUENCY   COUNTRY, STATION, LOCATION   TARGET • NETWORK • POWER (kW)   World Time

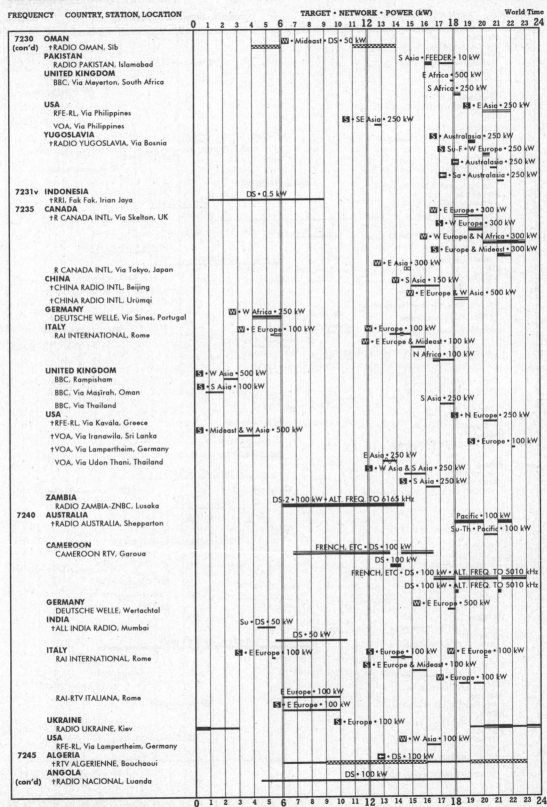

Freq	Country / Station / Location	Target • Network • Power
7230 (con'd)	**OMAN** †RADIO OMAN, Sīb	W • Mideast • DS • 50 kW
	PAKISTAN RADIO PAKISTAN, Islamabad	S Asia • FEEDER • 10 kW
	UNITED KINGDOM BBC, Via Meyerton, South Africa	E Africa • 500 kW / S Africa • 250 kW
	USA RFE-RL, Via Philippines	S • E Asia • 250 kW
	VOA, Via Philippines	S • SE Asia • 250 kW
	YUGOSLAVIA †RADIO YUGOSLAVIA, Via Bosnia	S • Australasia • 250 kW / Su-F • W Europe • 250 kW / • Australasia • 250 kW / Sa • Australasia • 250 kW
7231v	**INDONESIA** †RRI, Fak Fak, Irian Jaya	DS • 0.5 kW
7235	**CANADA** †R CANADA INTL, Via Skelton, UK	W • E Europe • 300 kW / S • W Europe • 300 kW / W • W Europe & N Africa • 300 kW / S • Europe & Mideast • 300 kW
	R CANADA INTL, Via Tokyo, Japan	W • E Asia • 300 kW
	CHINA †CHINA RADIO INTL, Beijing	W • S Asia • 150 kW
	†CHINA RADIO INTL, Urümqi	W • E Europe & W Asia • 500 kW
	GERMANY DEUTSCHE WELLE, Via Sines, Portugal	W • W Africa • 250 kW
	ITALY RAI INTERNATIONAL, Rome	W • E Europe • 100 kW / W • Europe • 100 kW / W • E Europe & Mideast • 100 kW / N Africa • 100 kW
	UNITED KINGDOM BBC, Rampisham	S • W Asia • 500 kW
	BBC, Via Maşīrah, Oman	S • S Asia • 100 kW / S Asia • 250 kW
	BBC, Via Thailand	S • N Europe • 250 kW
	USA †RFE-RL, Via Kavála, Greece	S • Europe • 100 kW
	†VOA, Via Iranawila, Sri Lanka	S • Mideast & W Asia • 500 kW
	†VOA, Via Lampertheim, Germany	E Asia • 250 kW
	VOA, Via Udon Thani, Thailand	S • W Asia & S Asia • 250 kW / S • S Asia • 250 kW
	ZAMBIA RADIO ZAMBIA-ZNBC, Lusaka	DS-2 • 100 kW • ALT. FREQ. TO 6165 kHz
7240	**AUSTRALIA** †RADIO AUSTRALIA, Shepparton	Pacific • 100 kW / Su-Th • Pacific • 100 kW
	CAMEROON CAMEROON RTV, Garoua	FRENCH, ETC • DS • 100 kW / DS • 100 kW / FRENCH, ETC • DS • 100 kW • ALT. FREQ. TO 5010 kHz / DS • 100 kW • ALT. FREQ. TO 5010 kHz
	GERMANY DEUTSCHE WELLE, Wertachtal	W • E Europe • 500 kW
	INDIA †ALL INDIA RADIO, Mumbai	Su • DS • 50 kW / DS • 50 kW
	ITALY RAI INTERNATIONAL, Rome	S • E Europe • 100 kW / S • Europe • 100 kW / W • E Europe • 100 kW / S • E Europe & Mideast • 100 kW / W • Europe • 100 kW
	RAI-RTV ITALIANA, Rome	E Europe • 100 kW / S • E Europe • 100 kW
	UKRAINE RADIO UKRAINE, Kiev	S • Europe • 100 kW
	USA RFE-RL, Via Lampertheim, Germany	W • W Asia • 100 kW
7245	**ALGERIA** †RTV ALGERIENNE, Bouchaoui	□ • DS • 100 kW
(con'd)	**ANGOLA** †RADIO NACIONAL, Luanda	DS • 100 kW

ENGLISH ▬   ARABIC ▧   CHINESE ▫▫▫   FRENCH ▭   GERMAN ▬   RUSSIAN ═   SPANISH ▭   OTHER ▬

FREQUENCY   COUNTRY, STATION, LOCATION   TARGET • NETWORK • POWER (kW)   World Time

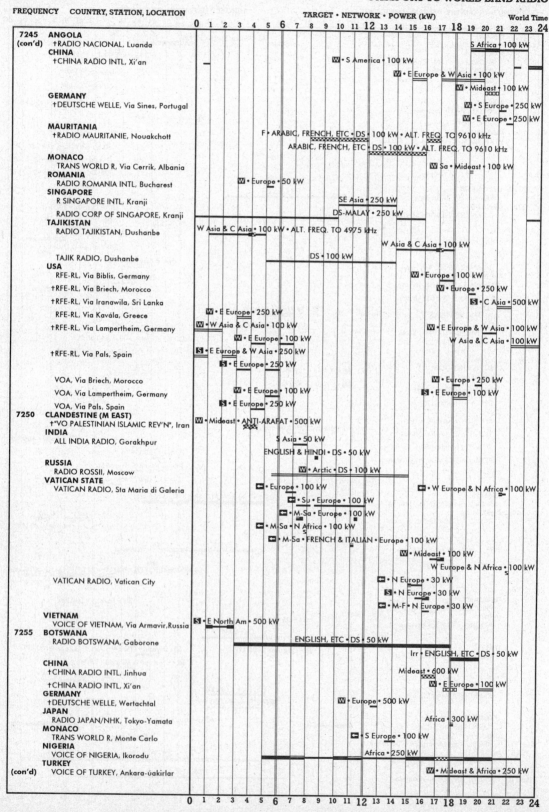

7245 ANGOLA
(con'd) †RADIO NACIONAL, Luanda — S Africa • 100 kW
CHINA
    †CHINA RADIO INTL, Xi'an — W • S America • 100 kW
        W • E Europe & W Asia • 100 kW
        W • Mideast • 100 kW
GERMANY
    †DEUTSCHE WELLE, Via Sines, Portugal — W • S Europe • 250 kW
        W • E Europe • 250 kW
MAURITANIA
    †RADIO MAURITANIE, Nouakchott — F • ARABIC, FRENCH, ETC • DS • 100 kW • ALT. FREQ. TO 9610 kHz
        ARABIC, FRENCH, ETC • DS • 100 kW • ALT. FREQ. TO 9610 kHz
MONACO
    TRANS WORLD R, Via Cerrik, Albania — W • Sa • Mideast • 100 kW
ROMANIA
    RADIO ROMANIA INTL, Bucharest — W • Europe • 50 kW
SINGAPORE
    R SINGAPORE INTL, Kranji — SE Asia • 250 kW
    RADIO CORP OF SINGAPORE, Kranji — DS-MALAY • 250 kW
TAJIKISTAN
    RADIO TAJIKISTAN, Dushanbe — W Asia & C Asia • 100 kW • ALT. FREQ. TO 4975 kHz
        W Asia & C Asia • 100 kW
    TAJIK RADIO, Dushanbe — DS • 100 kW
USA
    RFE-RL, Via Biblis, Germany — W • Europe • 100 kW
    †RFE-RL, Via Briech, Morocco — W • Europe • 250 kW
    †RFE-RL, Via Iranawila, Sri Lanka — S • C Asia • 500 kW
    RFE-RL, Via Kavála, Greece — W • E Europe • 250 kW
    †RFE-RL, Via Lampertheim, Germany — W • W Asia & C Asia • 100 kW
        W • E Europe & W Asia • 100 kW
        W • E Europe • 100 kW
        W Asia & C Asia • 100 kW
    †RFE-RL, Via Pals, Spain — S • E Europe & W Asia • 250 kW
        S • E Europe • 250 kW
    VOA, Via Briech, Morocco — W • Europe • 250 kW
    VOA, Via Lampertheim, Germany — W • E Europe • 100 kW
        S • E Europe • 100 kW
    VOA, Via Pals, Spain — S • E Europe • 250 kW
7250 CLANDESTINE (M EAST)
    †"VO PALESTINIAN ISLAMIC REV'N", Iran — W • Mideast • ANTI-ARAFAT • 500 kW
INDIA
    ALL INDIA RADIO, Gorakhpur — S Asia • 50 kW
        ENGLISH & HINDI • DS • 50 kW
RUSSIA
    RADIO ROSSII, Moscow — W • Arctic • DS • 100 kW
VATICAN STATE
    VATICAN RADIO, Sta Maria di Galeria — Europe • 100 kW
        W Europe & N Africa • 100 kW
        Su • Europe • 100 kW
        M-Sa • Europe • 100 kW
        M-Sa • N Africa • 100 kW
        M-Sa • FRENCH & ITALIAN • Europe • 100 kW
        W • Mideast • 100 kW
        W Europe & N Africa • 100 kW
    VATICAN RADIO, Vatican City — N Europe • 30 kW
        S • N Europe • 30 kW
        M-F • N Europe • 30 kW
VIETNAM
    VOICE OF VIETNAM, Via Armavir, Russia — S • E North Am • 500 kW
7255 BOTSWANA
    RADIO BOTSWANA, Gaborone — ENGLISH, ETC • DS • 50 kW
        Irr • ENGLISH, ETC • DS • 50 kW
CHINA
    †CHINA RADIO INTL, Jinhua — Mideast • 600 kW
    †CHINA RADIO INTL, Xi'an — W • E Europe • 100 kW
GERMANY
    †DEUTSCHE WELLE, Wertachtal — W • Europe • 500 kW
JAPAN
    RADIO JAPAN/NHK, Tokyo-Yamata — Africa • 300 kW
MONACO
    TRANS WORLD R, Monte Carlo — S Europe • 100 kW
NIGERIA
    VOICE OF NIGERIA, Ikorodu — Africa • 250 kW
TURKEY
(con'd) VOICE OF TURKEY, Ankara-úakirlar — W • Mideast & Africa • 250 kW

SEASONAL S OR W   1-HR TIMESHIFT MIDYEAR ⟸ OR ⟹   JAMMING / OR /\   EARLIEST HEARD ◁   LATEST HEARD ▷   NEW FOR 2000 †

FREQUENCY   COUNTRY, STATION, LOCATION   TARGET • NETWORK • POWER (kW)   World Time

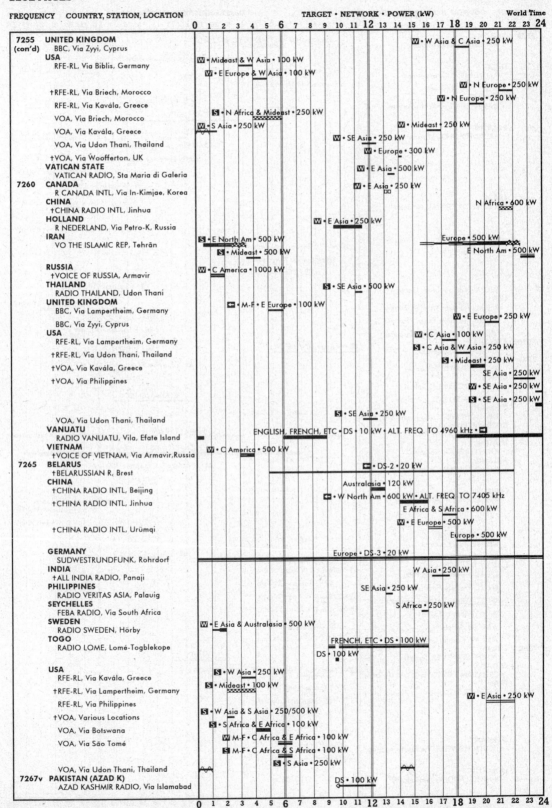

Frequency	Country, Station, Location	Target • Network • Power
7255 (con'd)	UNITED KINGDOM	
	BBC, Via Zyyi, Cyprus	W • W Asia & C Asia • 250 kW
	USA	
	RFE-RL, Via Biblis, Germany	W • Mideast & W Asia • 100 kW; W • E Europe & W Asia • 100 kW
	†RFE-RL, Via Briech, Morocco	W • N Europe • 250 kW
	RFE-RL, Via Kavála, Greece	W • N Europe • 250 kW
	VOA, Via Briech, Morocco	S • N Africa & Mideast • 250 kW
	VOA, Via Kavála, Greece	W • S Asia • 250 kW
	VOA, Via Udon Thani, Thailand	W • SE Asia • 250 kW
	†VOA, Via Woofferton, UK	W • Europe • 300 kW
	VATICAN STATE	
	VATICAN RADIO, Sta Maria di Galeria	W • E Asia • 500 kW
7260	CANADA	
	R CANADA INTL, Via In-Kimjae, Korea	W • E Asia • 250 kW
	CHINA	
	†CHINA RADIO INTL, Jinhua	N Africa • 600 kW
	HOLLAND	
	R NEDERLAND, Via Petro-K, Russia	W • E Asia • 250 kW
	IRAN	
	VO THE ISLAMIC REP, Tehrān	S • E North Am • 500 kW; Europe • 500 kW; S • Mideast • 500 kW; E North Am • 500 kW
	RUSSIA	
	†VOICE OF RUSSIA, Armavir	W • C America • 1000 kW
	THAILAND	
	RADIO THAILAND, Udon Thani	S • SE Asia • 500 kW
	UNITED KINGDOM	
	BBC, Via Lampertheim, Germany	• M-F • E Europe • 100 kW
	BBC, Via Zyyi, Cyprus	W • E Europe • 250 kW
	USA	
	RFE-RL, Via Lampertheim, Germany	W • C Asia • 100 kW
	†RFE-RL, Via Udon Thani, Thailand	S • C Asia & W Asia • 250 kW
	†VOA, Via Kavála, Greece	S • Mideast • 250 kW
	†VOA, Via Philippines	SE Asia • 250 kW; W • SE Asia • 250 kW; S • SE Asia • 250 kW
	VOA, Via Udon Thani, Thailand	S • SE Asia • 250 kW
	VANUATU	
	RADIO VANUATU, Vila, Efate Island	ENGLISH, FRENCH, ETC • DS • 10 kW • ALT. FREQ. TO 4960 kHz •
	VIETNAM	
	†VOICE OF VIETNAM, Via Armavir, Russia	W • C America • 500 kW
7265	BELARUS	
	†BELARUSSIAN R, Brest	• DS-2 • 20 kW
	CHINA	
	†CHINA RADIO INTL, Beijing	Australasia • 120 kW; • W North Am • 600 kW • ALT. FREQ TO 7405 kHz
	†CHINA RADIO INTL, Jinhua	E Africa & S Africa • 600 kW
	†CHINA RADIO INTL, Urümqi	W • E Europe • 500 kW; Europe • 500 kW
	GERMANY	
	SUDWESTRUNDFUNK, Rohrdorf	Europe • DS-3 • 20 kW
	INDIA	
	†ALL INDIA RADIO, Panaji	W Asia • 250 kW
	PHILIPPINES	
	RADIO VERITAS ASIA, Palauig	SE Asia • 250 kW
	SEYCHELLES	
	FEBA RADIO, Via South Africa	S Africa • 250 kW
	SWEDEN	
	RADIO SWEDEN, Hörby	W • E Asia & Australasia • 500 kW
	TOGO	
	RADIO LOME, Lomé-Togblekope	FRENCH, ETC • DS • 100 kW; DS • 100 kW
	USA	
	RFE-RL, Via Kavála, Greece	S • W Asia • 250 kW
	†RFE-RL, Via Lampertheim, Germany	S • Mideast • 100 kW; W • E Asia • 250 kW
	RFE-RL, Via Philippines	S • W Asia & S Asia • 250/500 kW
	†VOA, Various Locations	S • S Africa & E Africa • 100 kW
	VOA, Via Botswana	W • M-F • C Africa & E Africa • 100 kW
	VOA, Via São Tomé	S • M-F • C Africa & S Africa • 100 kW
	VOA, Via Udon Thani, Thailand	S • S Asia • 250 kW
7267v	PAKISTAN (AZAD K)	
	AZAD KASHMIR RADIO, Via Islamabad	DS • 100 kW

World Time scale: 0 1 2 3 4 5 6 7 8 9 10 11 12 13 14 15 16 17 18 19 20 21 22 23 24

ENGLISH ▬   ARABIC ﹏   CHINESE ▫▫▫   FRENCH ▭▭   GERMAN ▬▬   RUSSIAN ═   SPANISH ▬▬   OTHER ▬

FREQUENCY   COUNTRY, STATION, LOCATION   TARGET • NETWORK • POWER (kW)   World Time

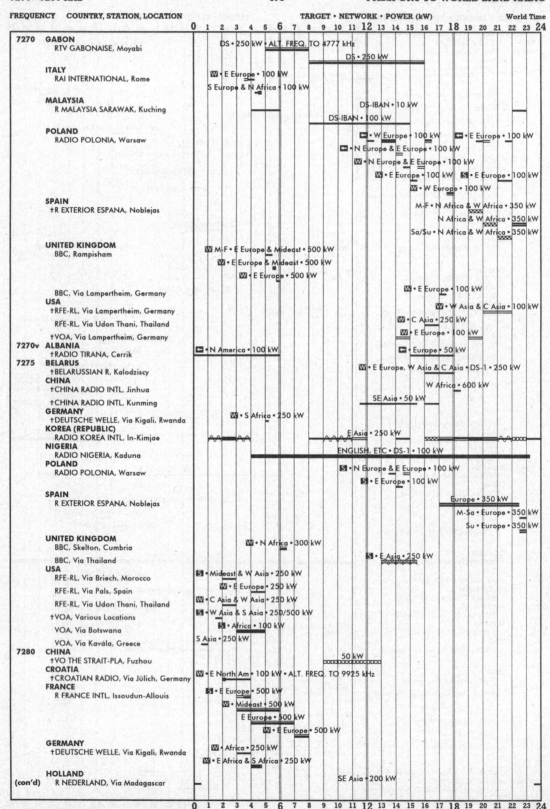

FREQUENCY	COUNTRY, STATION, LOCATION	TARGET • NETWORK • POWER (kW)
7270	**GABON** RTV GABONAISE, Moyabi	DS • 250 kW • ALT. FREQ. TO 4777 kHz / DS • 250 kW
	ITALY RAI INTERNATIONAL, Rome	W • E Europe • 100 kW / S Europe & N Africa • 100 kW
	MALAYSIA R MALAYSIA SARAWAK, Kuching	DS-IBAN • 10 kW / DS-IBAN • 100 kW
	POLAND RADIO POLONIA, Warsaw	• W Europe • 100 kW / • E Europe • 100 kW / • N Europe & E Europe • 100 kW / W • N Europe & E Europe • 100 kW / W • E Europe • 100 kW / S • E Europe • 100 kW / W • W Europe • 100 kW
	SPAIN †R EXTERIOR ESPANA, Noblejas	M-F • N Africa & W Africa • 350 kW / N Africa & W Africa • 350 kW / Sa/Su • N Africa & W Africa • 350 kW
	UNITED KINGDOM BBC, Rampisham	W • M-F • E Europe & Mideast • 500 kW / W • E Europe & Mideast • 500 kW / W • E Europe • 500 kW
	BBC, Via Lampertheim, Germany	W • E Europe • 100 kW
	USA †RFE-RL, Via Lampertheim, Germany	W • W Asia & C Asia • 100 kW
	RFE-RL, Via Udon Thani, Thailand	W • C Asia • 250 kW
	†VOA, Via Lampertheim, Germany	W • E Europe • 100 kW
7270v	**ALBANIA** †RADIO TIRANA, Cerrik	• N America • 100 kW / • Europe • 50 kW
7275	**BELARUS** †BELARUSSIAN R, Kalodziscy	W • E Europe, W Asia & C Asia • DS-1 • 250 kW
	CHINA †CHINA RADIO INTL, Jinhua	W Africa • 600 kW
	†CHINA RADIO INTL, Kunming	SE Asia • 50 kW
	GERMANY †DEUTSCHE WELLE, Via Kigali, Rwanda	W • S Africa • 250 kW
	KOREA (REPUBLIC) RADIO KOREA INTL, In-Kimjae	E Asia • 250 kW
	NIGERIA RADIO NIGERIA, Kaduna	ENGLISH, ETC • DS-1 • 100 kW
	POLAND RADIO POLONIA, Warsaw	S • N Europe & E Europe • 100 kW / S • E Europe • 100 kW
	SPAIN R EXTERIOR ESPANA, Noblejas	Europe • 350 kW / M-Sa • Europe • 350 kW / Su • Europe • 350 kW
	UNITED KINGDOM BBC, Skelton, Cumbria	W • N Africa • 300 kW
	BBC, Via Thailand	S • E Asia • 250 kW
	USA RFE-RL, Via Briech, Morocco	S • Mideast & W Asia • 250 kW
	RFE-RL, Via Pals, Spain	W • E Europe • 250 kW
	RFE-RL, Via Udon Thani, Thailand	W • C Asia & W Asia • 250 kW
	†VOA, Various Locations	S • W Asia & S Asia • 250/500 kW
	VOA, Via Botswana	S • Africa • 100 kW
	VOA, Via Kavála, Greece	S Asia • 250 kW
7280	**CHINA** †VO THE STRAIT-PLA, Fuzhou	50 kW
	CROATIA †CROATIAN RADIO, Via Jülich, Germany	W • E North Am • 100 kW • ALT. FREQ. TO 9925 kHz
	FRANCE R FRANCE INTL, Issoudun-Allouis	S • E Europe • 500 kW / W • Mideast • 500 kW / E Europe • 500 kW / W • E Europe • 500 kW
	GERMANY †DEUTSCHE WELLE, Via Kigali, Rwanda	W • Africa • 250 kW / W • E Africa & S Africa • 250 kW
(con'd)	**HOLLAND** R NEDERLAND, Via Madagascar	SE Asia • 200 kW

FREQUENCY   COUNTRY, STATION, LOCATION   TARGET • NETWORK • POWER (kW)   World Time

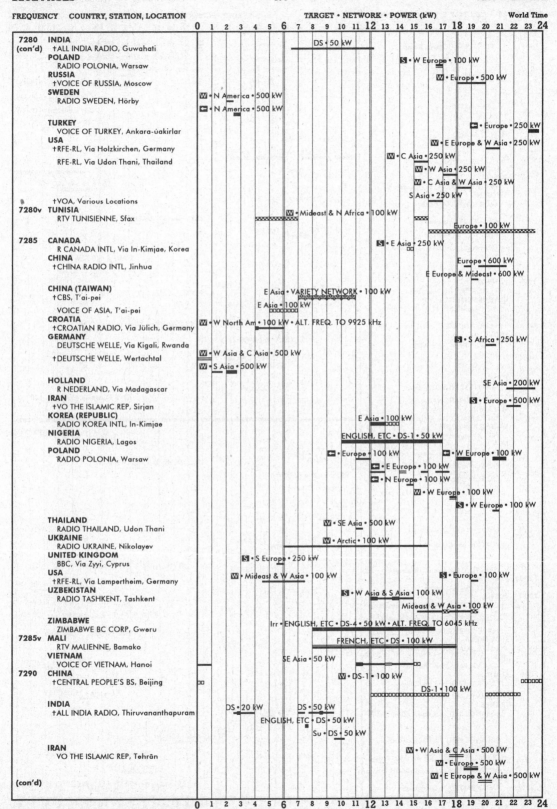

0 1 2 3 4 5 6 7 8 9 10 11 12 13 14 15 16 17 18 19 20 21 22 23 24

7280 INDIA
(con'd)   †ALL INDIA RADIO, Guwahati — DS • 50 kW
POLAND
  RADIO POLONIA, Warsaw — S • W Europe • 100 kW
RUSSIA
  †VOICE OF RUSSIA, Moscow — W • Europe • 500 kW
SWEDEN
  RADIO SWEDEN, Hörby — W • N America • 500 kW
  — N America • 500 kW
TURKEY
  VOICE OF TURKEY, Ankara-úakirlar — • Europe • 250 kW
USA
  †RFE-RL, Via Holzkirchen, Germany — W • E Europe & W Asia • 250 kW
  RFE-RL, Via Udon Thani, Thailand — W • C Asia • 250 kW
  — W • W Asia • 250 kW
  — W • C Asia & W Asia • 250 kW
  — S Asia • 250 kW
  †VOA, Various Locations
7280v TUNISIA
  RTV TUNISIENNE, Sfax — W • Mideast & N Africa • 100 kW
  — Europe • 100 kW
7285 CANADA
  R CANADA INTL, Via In-Kimjae, Korea — S • E Asia • 250 kW
CHINA
  †CHINA RADIO INTL, Jinhua — Europe • 600 kW
  — E Europe & Mideast • 600 kW
CHINA (TAIWAN)
  †CBS, T'ai-pei — E Asia • VARIETY NETWORK • 100 kW
  VOICE OF ASIA, T'ai-pei — E Asia • 100 kW
CROATIA
  †CROATIAN RADIO, Via Jülich, Germany — W • W North Am • 100 kW • ALT. FREQ. TO 9925 kHz
GERMANY
  DEUTSCHE WELLE, Via Kigali, Rwanda — S • S Africa • 250 kW
  †DEUTSCHE WELLE, Wertachtal — W • W Asia & C Asia • 500 kW
  — W • S Asia • 500 kW
HOLLAND
  R NEDERLAND, Via Madagascar — SE Asia • 200 kW
IRAN
  †VO THE ISLAMIC REP, Sirjan — S • Europe • 500 kW
KOREA (REPUBLIC)
  RADIO KOREA INTL, In-Kimjae — E Asia • 100 kW
NIGERIA
  RADIO NIGERIA, Lagos — ENGLISH, ETC • DS-1 • 50 kW
POLAND
  RADIO POLONIA, Warsaw — • Europe • 100 kW
  — • W Europe • 100 kW
  — • E Europe • 100 kW
  — • N Europe • 100 kW
  — W • W Europe • 100 kW
  — S • W Europe • 100 kW
THAILAND
  RADIO THAILAND, Udon Thani — W • SE Asia • 500 kW
UKRAINE
  RADIO UKRAINE, Nikolayev — W • Arctic • 100 kW
UNITED KINGDOM
  BBC, Via Zyyi, Cyprus — S • S Europe • 250 kW
USA
  †RFE-RL, Via Lampertheim, Germany — W • Mideast & W Asia • 100 kW
  — S • Europe • 100 kW
UZBEKISTAN
  RADIO TASHKENT, Tashkent — S • W Asia & S Asia • 100 kW
  — Mideast & W Asia • 100 kW
ZIMBABWE
  ZIMBABWE BC CORP, Gweru — Irr • ENGLISH, ETC • DS-4 • 50 kW • ALT. FREQ. TO 6045 kHz
7285v MALI
  RTV MALIENNE, Bamako — FRENCH, ETC • DS • 100 kW
VIETNAM
  VOICE OF VIETNAM, Hanoi — SE Asia • 50 kW
7290 CHINA
  †CENTRAL PEOPLE'S BS, Beijing — W • DS-1 • 100 kW
  — DS-1 • 100 kW
INDIA
  †ALL INDIA RADIO, Thiruvananthapuram — DS • 20 kW
  — DS • 50 kW
  — ENGLISH, ETC • DS • 50 kW
  — Su • DS • 50 kW
IRAN
  VO THE ISLAMIC REP, Tehrān — W • W Asia & C Asia • 500 kW
  — W • Europe • 500 kW
  — W • E Europe & W Asia • 500 kW
(con'd)

0 1 2 3 4 5 6 7 8 9 10 11 12 13 14 15 16 17 18 19 20 21 22 23 24

ENGLISH ▬   ARABIC ⧉   CHINESE ▭▭▭   FRENCH ▬   GERMAN ▬   RUSSIAN ═   SPANISH ▬   OTHER ▬

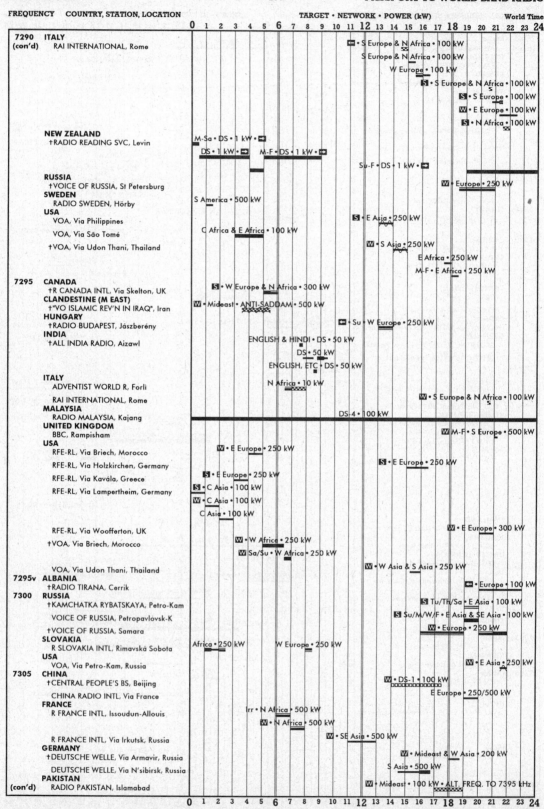

FREQUENCY	COUNTRY, STATION, LOCATION	TARGET • NETWORK • POWER (kW)	World Time

7290 ITALY
(con'd)   RAI INTERNATIONAL, Rome — S Europe & N Africa • 100 kW; S Europe & N Africa • 100 kW; W Europe • 100 kW; S Europe & N Africa • 100 kW; S Europe • 100 kW; E Europe • 100 kW; N Africa • 100 kW

NEW ZEALAND
†RADIO READING SVC, Levin — M-Sa • DS • 1 kW; DS • 1 kW; M-F • DS • 1 kW; Su-F • DS • 1 kW

RUSSIA
†VOICE OF RUSSIA, St Petersburg — W • Europe • 250 kW

SWEDEN
RADIO SWEDEN, Hörby — S America • 500 kW

USA
VOA, Via Philippines — E Asia • 250 kW

VOA, Via São Tomé — C Africa & E Africa • 100 kW

†VOA, Via Udon Thani, Thailand — W • S Asia • 250 kW; E Africa • 250 kW; M-F • E Africa • 250 kW

7295 CANADA
†R CANADA INTL, Via Skelton, UK — S • W Europe & N Africa • 300 kW

CLANDESTINE (M EAST)
†"VO ISLAMIC REV'N IN IRAQ", Iran — W • Mideast • ANTI-SADDAM • 500 kW

HUNGARY
†RADIO BUDAPEST, Jászberény — Su • W Europe • 250 kW

INDIA
†ALL INDIA RADIO, Aizawl — ENGLISH & HINDI • DS • 50 kW; DS • 50 kW; ENGLISH, ETC • DS • 50 kW

ITALY
ADVENTIST WORLD R, Forli — N Africa • 10 kW

RAI INTERNATIONAL, Rome — W • S Europe & N Africa • 100 kW

MALAYSIA
RADIO MALAYSIA, Kajang — DS-4 • 100 kW

UNITED KINGDOM
BBC, Rampisham — W M-F • S Europe • 500 kW

USA
RFE-RL, Via Briech, Morocco — W • E Europe • 250 kW

RFE-RL, Via Holzkirchen, Germany — S • E Europe • 250 kW

RFE-RL, Via Kavála, Greece — S • E Europe • 250 kW

RFE-RL, Via Lampertheim, Germany — S • C Asia • 100 kW; W • C Asia • 100 kW; C Asia • 100 kW

RFE-RL, Via Woofferton, UK — W • E Europe • 300 kW

†VOA, Via Briech, Morocco — W • W Africa • 250 kW; W Sa/Su • W Africa • 250 kW

VOA, Via Udon Thani, Thailand — W • W Asia & S Asia • 250 kW

7295v ALBANIA
†RADIO TIRANA, Cerrik — Europe • 100 kW

7300 RUSSIA
†KAMCHATKA RYBATSKAYA, Petro-Kam — S Tu/Th/Sa • E Asia • 100 kW

VOICE OF RUSSIA, Petropavlovsk-K — S Su/M/W/F • E Asia & SE Asia • 100 kW

†VOICE OF RUSSIA, Samara — W • Europe • 250 kW

SLOVAKIA
R SLOVAKIA INTL, Rimavská Sobota — Africa • 250 kW; W Europe • 250 kW

USA
VOA, Via Petro-Kam, Russia — W • E Asia • 250 kW

7305 CHINA
†CENTRAL PEOPLE'S BS, Beijing — W • DS-1 • 100 kW; E Europe • 250/500 kW

CHINA RADIO INTL, Via France

FRANCE
R FRANCE INTL, Issoudun-Allouis — Irr • N Africa • 500 kW; W • N Africa • 500 kW

R FRANCE INTL, Via Irkutsk, Russia — W • SE Asia • 500 kW

GERMANY
†DEUTSCHE WELLE, Via Armavir, Russia — W • Mideast & W Asia • 200 kW

DEUTSCHE WELLE, Via N'sibirsk, Russia — S Asia • 500 kW

PAKISTAN
(con'd)   RADIO PAKISTAN, Islamabad — W • Mideast • 100 kW • ALT. FREQ. TO 7395 kHz

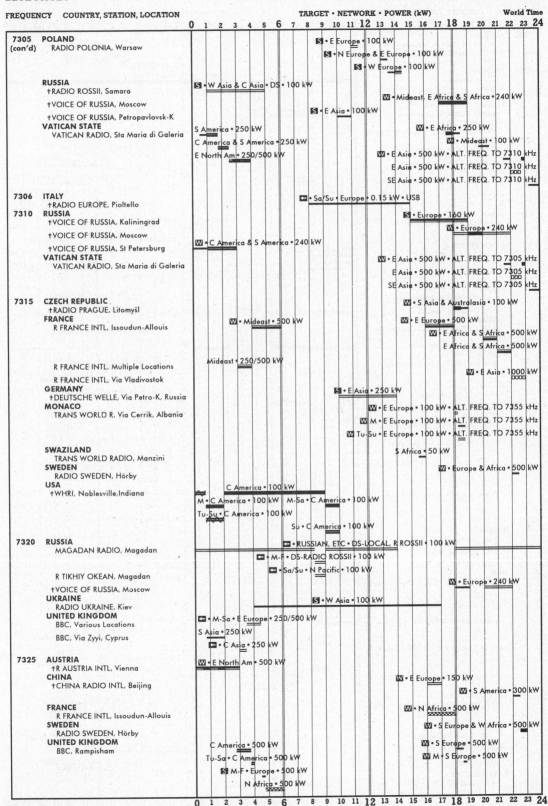

FREQUENCY	COUNTRY, STATION, LOCATION	TARGET • NETWORK • POWER (kW)	World Time

7305 POLAND
(con'd)   RADIO POLONIA, Warsaw
- S • E Europe • 100 kW
- S • N Europe & E Europe • 100 kW
- S • W Europe • 100 kW

RUSSIA
- †RADIO ROSSII, Samara — S • W Asia & C Asia • DS • 100 kW
- †VOICE OF RUSSIA, Moscow — W • Mideast, E Africa & S Africa • 240 kW
- †VOICE OF RUSSIA, Petropavlovsk-K — S • E Asia • 100 kW

VATICAN STATE
- VATICAN RADIO, Sta Maria di Galeria
  - S America • 250 kW
  - W • E Africa • 250 kW
  - C America & S America • 250 kW
  - W • Mideast • 100 kW
  - E North Am • 250/500 kW
  - W • E Asia • 500 kW • ALT. FREQ. TO 7310 kHz
  - E Asia • 500 kW • ALT. FREQ. TO 7310 kHz
  - SE Asia • 500 kW • ALT. FREQ. TO 7310 kHz

7306 ITALY
- †RADIO EUROPE, Pioltello — Sa/Su • Europe • 0.15 kW • USB

7310 RUSSIA
- †VOICE OF RUSSIA, Kaliningrad — S • Europe • 160 kW
- †VOICE OF RUSSIA, Moscow — W • Europe • 240 kW
- †VOICE OF RUSSIA, St Petersburg — W • C America & S America • 240 kW

VATICAN STATE
- VATICAN RADIO, Sta Maria di Galeria
  - W • E Asia • 500 kW • ALT. FREQ. TO 7305 kHz
  - E Asia • 500 kW • ALT. FREQ. TO 7305 kHz
  - SE Asia • 500 kW • ALT. FREQ. TO 7305 kHz

7315 CZECH REPUBLIC
- †RADIO PRAGUE, Litomyšl — W • S Asia & Australasia • 100 kW

FRANCE
- R FRANCE INTL, Issoudun-Allouis
  - W • Mideast • 500 kW
  - W • E Europe • 500 kW
  - W • E Africa & S Africa • 500 kW
  - E Africa & S Africa • 500 kW
- R FRANCE INTL, Multiple Locations — Mideast • 250/500 kW
- R FRANCE INTL, Via Vladivostok — W • E Asia • 1000 kW

GERMANY
- †DEUTSCHE WELLE, Via Petro-K, Russia — S • E Asia • 250 kW

MONACO
- TRANS WORLD R, Via Cerrik, Albania
  - W • E Europe • 100 kW • ALT. FREQ. TO 7355 kHz
  - W M • E Europe • 100 kW • ALT. FREQ. TO 7355 kHz
  - W Tu-Su • E Europe • 100 kW • ALT. FREQ. TO 7355 kHz

SWAZILAND
- TRANS WORLD RADIO, Manzini — S Africa • 50 kW

SWEDEN
- RADIO SWEDEN, Hörby — W • Europe & Africa • 500 kW

USA
- †WHRI, Noblesville, Indiana
  - C America • 100 kW
  - M • C America • 100 kW   M-Sa • C America • 100 kW
  - Tu-Su • C America • 100 kW
  - Su • C America • 100 kW

7320 RUSSIA
- MAGADAN RADIO, Magadan
  - RUSSIAN, ETC • DS-LOCAL, R ROSSII • 100 kW
  - M-F • DS-RADIO ROSSII • 100 kW
- R TIKHIY OKEAN, Magadan — Sa/Su • N Pacific • 100 kW
- †VOICE OF RUSSIA, Moscow — W • Europe • 240 kW

UKRAINE
- RADIO UKRAINE, Kiev — S • W Asia • 100 kW

UNITED KINGDOM
- BBC, Various Locations
  - M-Sa • E Europe • 250/500 kW
  - S Asia • 250 kW
- BBC, Via Zyyi, Cyprus — C Asia • 250 kW

7325 AUSTRIA
- †R AUSTRIA INTL, Vienna — W • E North Am • 500 kW

CHINA
- †CHINA RADIO INTL, Beijing
  - W • E Europe • 150 kW
  - W • S America • 300 kW

FRANCE
- R FRANCE INTL, Issoudun-Allouis — W • N Africa • 500 kW

SWEDEN
- RADIO SWEDEN, Hörby — W • S Europe & W Africa • 500 kW

UNITED KINGDOM
- BBC, Rampisham
  - C America • 500 kW
  - W • S Europe • 500 kW
  - Tu-Sa • C America • 500 kW
  - W M • S Europe • 500 kW
  - S • M-F • Europe • 500 kW
  - N Africa • 500 kW

FREQUENCY   COUNTRY, STATION, LOCATION   TARGET • NETWORK • POWER (kW)   World Time

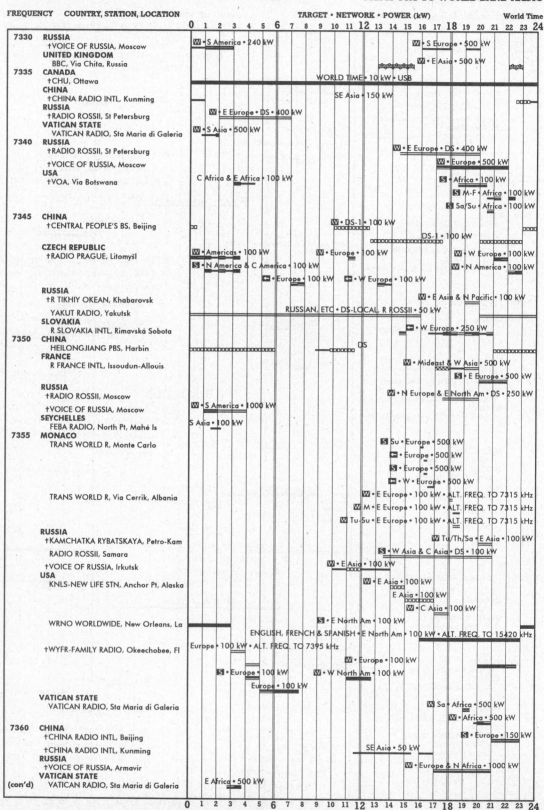

7330	**RUSSIA**
	†VOICE OF RUSSIA, Moscow
	UNITED KINGDOM
	BBC, Via Chita, Russia
7335	**CANADA**
	†CHU, Ottawa
	CHINA
	†CHINA RADIO INTL, Kunming
	RUSSIA
	†RADIO ROSSII, St Petersburg
	VATICAN STATE
	VATICAN RADIO, Sta Maria di Galeria
7340	**RUSSIA**
	†RADIO ROSSII, St Petersburg
	†VOICE OF RUSSIA, Moscow
	USA
	†VOA, Via Botswana
7345	**CHINA**
	†CENTRAL PEOPLE'S BS, Beijing
	CZECH REPUBLIC
	†RADIO PRAGUE, Litomyšl
	RUSSIA
	†R TIKHIY OKEAN, Khabarovsk
	YAKUT RADIO, Yakutsk
	SLOVAKIA
	R SLOVAKIA INTL, Rimavská Sobota
7350	**CHINA**
	HEILONGJIANG PBS, Harbin
	FRANCE
	R FRANCE INTL, Issoudun-Allouis
	RUSSIA
	†RADIO ROSSII, Moscow
	†VOICE OF RUSSIA, Moscow
	SEYCHELLES
	FEBA RADIO, North Pt, Mahé Is
7355	**MONACO**
	TRANS WORLD R, Monte Carlo
	TRANS WORLD R, Via Cerrik, Albania
	RUSSIA
	†KAMCHATKA RYBATSKAYA, Petro-Kam
	RADIO ROSSII, Samara
	†VOICE OF RUSSIA, Irkutsk
	USA
	KNLS-NEW LIFE STN, Anchor Pt, Alaska
	WRNO WORLDWIDE, New Orleans, La
	†WYFR-FAMILY RADIO, Okeechobee, Fl
	VATICAN STATE
	VATICAN RADIO, Sta Maria di Galeria
7360	**CHINA**
	†CHINA RADIO INTL, Beijing
	†CHINA RADIO INTL, Kunming
	RUSSIA
	†VOICE OF RUSSIA, Armavir
	VATICAN STATE
(con'd)	VATICAN RADIO, Sta Maria di Galeria

Schedule data (read from timeline):

- RUSSIA, VOICE OF RUSSIA, Moscow: W • S America • 240 kW; W • S Europe • 500 kW
- UNITED KINGDOM, BBC, Via Chita, Russia: W • E Asia • 500 kW
- CANADA, CHU, Ottawa: WORLD TIME • 10 kW • USB
- CHINA, CHINA RADIO INTL, Kunming: SE Asia • 150 kW
- RUSSIA, RADIO ROSSII, St Petersburg: W • E Europe • DS • 400 kW
- VATICAN STATE, VATICAN RADIO: W • S Asia • 500 kW
- RUSSIA, RADIO ROSSII, St Petersburg: W • E Europe • DS • 400 kW
- VOICE OF RUSSIA, Moscow: W • Europe • 500 kW
- USA, VOA, Via Botswana: C Africa & E Africa • 100 kW; S • Africa • 100 kW; S • M-F • Africa • 100 kW; S • Sa/Su • Africa • 100 kW
- CHINA, CENTRAL PEOPLE'S BS, Beijing: W • DS-1 • 100 kW; DS-1 • 100 kW
- CZECH REPUBLIC, RADIO PRAGUE, Litomyšl: W • Americas • 100 kW; W • Europe • 100 kW; W • W Europe • 100 kW; S • N America & C America • 100 kW; W • N America • 100 kW; ◄► • Europe • 100 kW; ◄► • W Europe • 100 kW
- RUSSIA, R TIKHIY OKEAN, Khabarovsk: W • E Asia & N Pacific • 100 kW
- YAKUT RADIO, Yakutsk: RUSSIAN, ETC • DS-LOCAL, R ROSSII • 50 kW
- SLOVAKIA, R SLOVAKIA INTL, Rimavská Sobota: ◄► • W Europe • 250 kW
- CHINA, HEILONGJIANG PBS, Harbin: DS
- FRANCE, R FRANCE INTL, Issoudun-Allouis: W • Mideast & W Asia • 500 kW; S • E Europe • 500 kW
- RUSSIA, RADIO ROSSII, Moscow: W • N Europe & E North Am • DS • 250 kW
- VOICE OF RUSSIA, Moscow: W • S America • 1000 kW
- SEYCHELLES, FEBA RADIO, North Pt, Mahé Is: S Asia • 100 kW
- MONACO, TRANS WORLD R, Monte Carlo: S • Su • Europe • 500 kW; ◄► • Europe • 500 kW; S • Europe • 500 kW; ◄► • W Europe • 500 kW
- TRANS WORLD R, Via Cerrik, Albania: W • E Europe • 100 kW • ALT. FREQ. TO 7315 kHz; W • M • E Europe • 100 kW • ALT. FREQ. TO 7315 kHz; W • Tu-Su • E Europe • 100 kW • ALT. FREQ. TO 7315 kHz
- RUSSIA, KAMCHATKA RYBATSKAYA, Petro-Kam: W • Tu/Th/Sa • E Asia • 100 kW
- RADIO ROSSII, Samara: S • W Asia & C Asia • DS • 100 kW
- VOICE OF RUSSIA, Irkutsk: W • E Asia • 100 kW
- USA, KNLS-NEW LIFE STN, Anchor Pt, Alaska: W • E Asia • 100 kW; E Asia • 100 kW; W • C Asia • 100 kW
- WRNO WORLDWIDE, New Orleans, La: S • E North Am • 100 kW; ENGLISH, FRENCH & SPANISH • E North Am • 100 kW • ALT. FREQ. TO 15420 kHz
- WYFR-FAMILY RADIO, Okeechobee, Fl: Europe • 100 kW • ALT. FREQ. TO 7395 kHz; W • Europe • 100 kW; S • Europe • 100 kW; W • W North Am • 100 kW; Europe • 100 kW
- VATICAN STATE, VATICAN RADIO: W • Sa • Africa • 500 kW; W • Africa • 500 kW
- CHINA, CHINA RADIO INTL, Beijing: S • Europe • 150 kW
- CHINA RADIO INTL, Kunming: SE Asia • 50 kW
- RUSSIA, VOICE OF RUSSIA, Armavir: W • Europe & N Africa • 1000 kW
- VATICAN STATE, VATICAN RADIO: E Africa • 500 kW

SEASONAL S OR W   1-HR TIMESHIFT MIDYEAR ◄► OR ►   JAMMING / OR ∧   EARLIEST HEARD ◄   LATEST HEARD ►   NEW FOR 2000 †

FREQUENCY   COUNTRY, STATION, LOCATION   TARGET • NETWORK • POWER (kW)   World Time

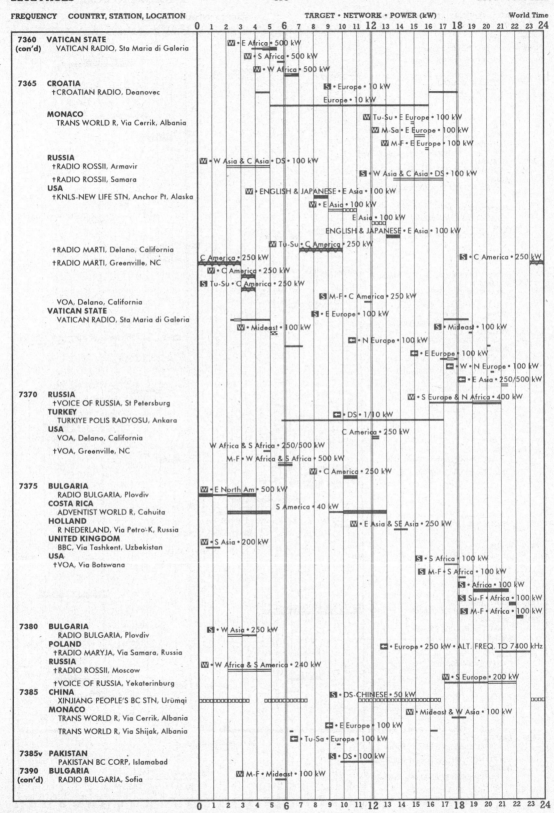

Frequency	Country, Station, Location	Target • Network • Power (kW)
7360 (con'd)	**VATICAN STATE** VATICAN RADIO, Sta Maria di Galeria	W • E Africa • 500 kW W • S Africa • 500 kW W • W Africa • 500 kW
7365	**CROATIA** †CROATIAN RADIO, Deanovec	S • Europe • 10 kW Europe • 10 kW
	MONACO TRANS WORLD R, Via Cerrik, Albania	W • Tu-Su • E Europe • 100 kW W • M-Sa • E Europe • 100 kW W • M-F • E Europe • 100 kW
	RUSSIA †RADIO ROSSII, Armavir †RADIO ROSSII, Samara	W • W Asia & C Asia • DS • 100 kW S • W Asia & C Asia • DS • 100 kW
	USA †KNLS-NEW LIFE STN, Anchor Pt, Alaska	W • ENGLISH & JAPANESE • E Asia • 100 kW W • E Asia • 100 kW E Asia • 100 kW ENGLISH & JAPANESE • E Asia • 100 kW
	†RADIO MARTI, Delano, California †RADIO MARTI, Greenville, NC	W • Tu-Su • C America • 250 kW C America • 250 kW S • C America • 250 kW W • C America • 250 kW S • Tu-Su • C America • 250 kW S • M-F • C America • 250 kW
	VOA, Delano, California **VATICAN STATE** VATICAN RADIO, Sta Maria di Galeria	S • E Europe • 100 kW W • Mideast • 100 kW S • Mideast • 100 kW • N Europe • 100 kW • E Europe • 100 kW • W • N Europe • 100 kW • E Asia • 250/500 kW
7370	**RUSSIA** †VOICE OF RUSSIA, St Petersburg **TURKEY** TURKIYE POLIS RADYOSU, Ankara **USA** VOA, Delano, California †VOA, Greenville, NC	W • S Europe & N Africa • 400 kW • DS • 1/10 kW C America • 250 kW W Africa & S Africa • 250/500 kW M-F • W Africa & S Africa • 500 kW W • C America • 250 kW
7375	**BULGARIA** RADIO BULGARIA, Plovdiv **COSTA RICA** ADVENTIST WORLD R, Cahuita **HOLLAND** R NEDERLAND, Via Petro-K, Russia **UNITED KINGDOM** BBC, Via Tashkent, Uzbekistan **USA** †VOA, Via Botswana	W • E North Am • 500 kW S America • 40 kW W • E Asia & SE Asia • 250 kW W • S Asia • 200 kW S • S Africa • 100 kW S • M-F • S Africa • 100 kW S • Africa • 100 kW S • Su-F • Africa • 100 kW S • M-F • Africa • 100 kW
7380	**BULGARIA** RADIO BULGARIA, Plovdiv **POLAND** †RADIO MARYJA, Via Samara, Russia **RUSSIA** †RADIO ROSSII, Moscow †VOICE OF RUSSIA, Yekaterinburg	S • W Asia • 250 kW • Europe • 250 kW • ALT. FREQ. TO 7400 kHz W • W Africa & S America • 240 kW W • S Europe • 200 kW
7385	**CHINA** XINJIANG PEOPLE'S BC STN, Urümqi **MONACO** TRANS WORLD R, Via Cerrik, Albania TRANS WORLD R, Via Shijak, Albania	S • DS-CHINESE • 50 kW W • Mideast & W Asia • 100 kW • E Europe • 100 kW • Tu-Sa • Europe • 100 kW
7385v	**PAKISTAN** PAKISTAN BC CORP, Islamabad	S • DS • 100 kW
7390 (con'd)	**BULGARIA** RADIO BULGARIA, Sofia	W • M-F • Mideast • 100 kW

ENGLISH ▬ ARABIC ⧨⧨⧨ CHINESE □□□ FRENCH ═══ GERMAN ▬▬ RUSSIAN ══ SPANISH ▬▬ OTHER ▬

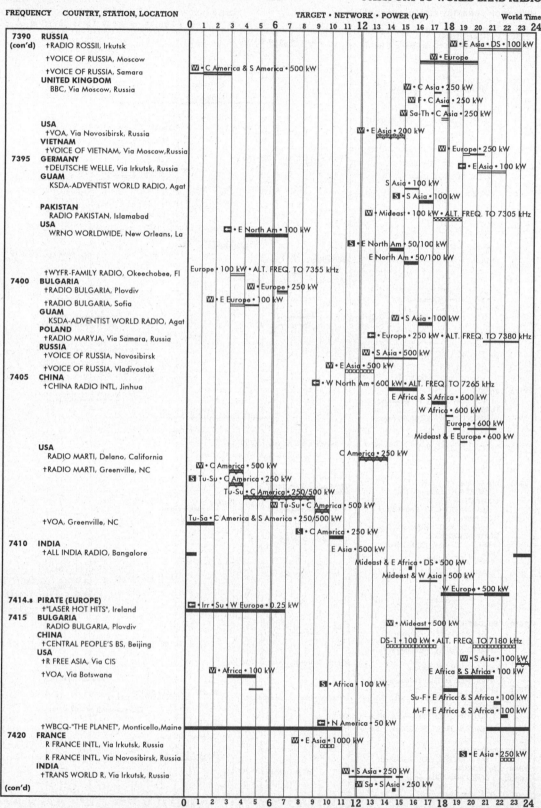

FREQUENCY   COUNTRY, STATION, LOCATION   TARGET • NETWORK • POWER (kW)   World Time

7390
(con'd) RUSSIA
  †RADIO ROSSII, Irkutsk — W • E Asia • DS • 100 kW
  †VOICE OF RUSSIA, Moscow — W • Europe
  †VOICE OF RUSSIA, Samara — W • C America & S America • 500 kW
UNITED KINGDOM
  BBC, Via Moscow, Russia — W • C Asia • 250 kW; W F • C Asia • 250 kW; W Sa-Th • C Asia • 250 kW
USA
  †VOA, Via Novosibirsk, Russia — W • E Asia • 200 kW
VIETNAM
  †VOICE OF VIETNAM, Via Moscow, Russia — W • Europe • 250 kW

7395 GERMANY
  †DEUTSCHE WELLE, Via Irkutsk, Russia — • E Asia • 100 kW
GUAM
  KSDA-ADVENTIST WORLD RADIO, Agat — S Asia • 100 kW; S • S Asia • 100 kW
PAKISTAN
  RADIO PAKISTAN, Islamabad — W • Mideast • 100 kW • ALT. FREQ. TO 7305 kHz
USA
  WRNO WORLDWIDE, New Orleans, La — • E North Am • 100 kW; S • E North Am • 50/100 kW; E North Am • 50/100 kW
  †WYFR-FAMILY RADIO, Okeechobee, Fl — Europe • 100 kW • ALT. FREQ. TO 7355 kHz

7400 BULGARIA
  †RADIO BULGARIA, Plovdiv — W • Europe • 250 kW
  †RADIO BULGARIA, Sofia — W • E Europe • 100 kW
GUAM
  KSDA-ADVENTIST WORLD RADIO, Agat — W • S Asia • 100 kW
POLAND
  †RADIO MARYJA, Via Samara, Russia — • Europe • 250 kW • ALT. FREQ. TO 7380 kHz
RUSSIA
  †VOICE OF RUSSIA, Novosibirsk — W • S Asia • 500 kW
  †VOICE OF RUSSIA, Vladivostok — W • E Asia • 500 kW

7405 CHINA
  †CHINA RADIO INTL, Jinhua — • W North Am • 600 kW • ALT. FREQ. TO 7265 kHz; E Africa & S Africa • 600 kW; W Africa • 600 kW; Europe • 600 kW; Mideast & E Europe • 600 kW
USA
  RADIO MARTI, Delano, California — C America • 250 kW
  †RADIO MARTI, Greenville, NC — W • C America • 500 kW; S Tu-Su • C America • 250 kW; Tu-Su • C America • 250/500 kW; W Tu-Su • C America • 500 kW
  †VOA, Greenville, NC — Tu-Sa • C America & S America • 250/500 kW; S • C America • 250 kW

7410 INDIA
  †ALL INDIA RADIO, Bangalore — E Asia • 500 kW; Mideast & E Africa • DS • 500 kW; Mideast & W Asia • 500 kW; W Europe • 500 kW

7414.8 PIRATE (EUROPE)
  †"LASER HOT HITS", Ireland — • Irr • Su • W Europe • 0.25 kW

7415 BULGARIA
  RADIO BULGARIA, Plovdiv — W • Mideast • 500 kW
CHINA
  †CENTRAL PEOPLE'S BS, Beijing — DS-1 • 100 kW • ALT. FREQ. TO 7180 kHz
USA
  †R FREE ASIA, Via CIS — W • S Asia • 100 kW
  †VOA, Via Botswana — W • Africa • 100 kW; E Africa & S Africa • 100 kW; S • Africa • 100 kW; Su-F • E Africa & S Africa • 100 kW; M-F • E Africa & S Africa • 100 kW
  †WBCQ-"THE PLANET", Monticello, Maine — • N America • 50 kW

7420 FRANCE
  R FRANCE INTL, Via Irkutsk, Russia — W • E Asia • 1000 kW
  R FRANCE INTL, Via Novosibirsk, Russia — S • E Asia • 250 kW
INDIA
  †TRANS WORLD R, Via Irkutsk, Russia — W • S Asia • 250 kW; W Sa • S Asia • 250 kW

(con'd)

FREQUENCY	COUNTRY, STATION, LOCATION	TARGET • NETWORK • POWER (kW)	World Time

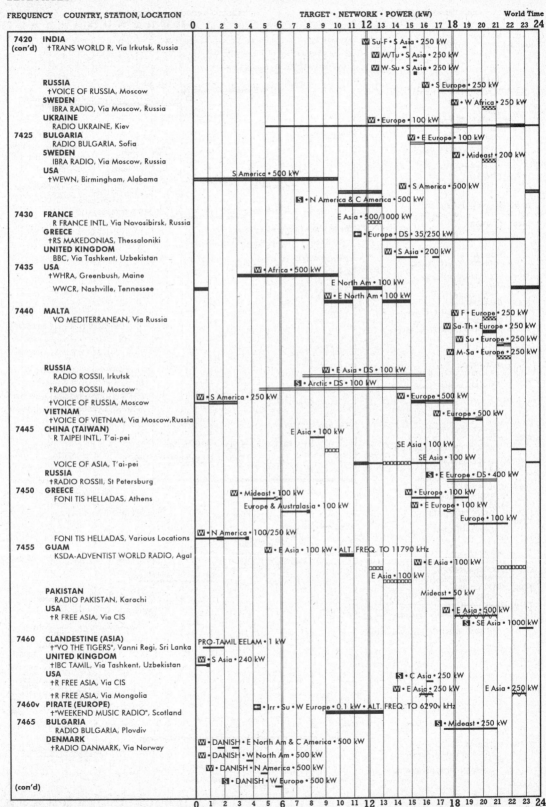

7420 (con'd)   **INDIA**   †TRANS WORLD R, Via Irkutsk, Russia   W•Su-F•S Asia•250 kW / W•M/Tu•S Asia•250 kW / W•W-Su•S Asia•250 kW

RUSSIA †VOICE OF RUSSIA, Moscow   W•S Europe•250 kW

SWEDEN IBRA RADIO, Via Moscow, Russia   W•W Africa•250 kW

UKRAINE RADIO UKRAINE, Kiev   W•Europe•100 kW

7425   **BULGARIA** RADIO BULGARIA, Sofia   W•E Europe•100 kW

SWEDEN IBRA RADIO, Via Moscow, Russia   W•Mideast•200 kW

USA †WEWN, Birmingham, Alabama   S America•500 kW / W•S America•500 kW / S•N America & C America•500 kW

7430   **FRANCE** R FRANCE INTL, Via Novosibirsk, Russia   E Asia•500/1000 kW

GREECE †RS MAKEDONIAS, Thessaloniki   •Europe•DS•35/250 kW

UNITED KINGDOM BBC, Via Tashkent, Uzbekistan   W•S Asia•200 kW

7435   **USA** †WHRA, Greenbush, Maine   W•Africa•500 kW

WWCR, Nashville, Tennessee   E North Am•100 kW / W•E North Am•100 kW

7440   **MALTA** VO MEDITERRANEAN, Via Russia   W•F•Europe•250 kW / W•Sa-Th•Europe•250 kW / W•Su•Europe•250 kW / W•M-Sa•Europe•250 kW

RUSSIA RADIO ROSSII, Irkutsk   W•E Asia•DS•100 kW

†RADIO ROSSII, Moscow   S•Arctic•DS•100 kW

†VOICE OF RUSSIA, Moscow   W•S America•250 kW / W•Europe•500 kW

VIETNAM †VOICE OF VIETNAM, Via Moscow, Russia   W•Europe•500 kW

7445   **CHINA (TAIWAN)** R TAIPEI INTL, T'ai-pei   E Asia•100 kW / SE Asia•100 kW

VOICE OF ASIA, T'ai-pei   SE Asia•100 kW

RUSSIA †RADIO ROSSII, St Petersburg   S•E Europe•DS•400 kW

7450   **GREECE** FONI TIS HELLADAS, Athens   W•Mideast•100 kW / W•Europe•100 kW / Europe & Australasia•100 kW / W•E Europe•100 kW / Europe•100 kW

FONI TIS HELLADAS, Various Locations   W•N America•100/250 kW

7455   **GUAM** KSDA-ADVENTIST WORLD RADIO, Agat   W•E Asia•100 kW•ALT. FREQ. TO 11790 kHz / W•E Asia•100 kW / E Asia•100 kW

PAKISTAN RADIO PAKISTAN, Karachi   Mideast•50 kW

USA †R FREE ASIA, Via CIS   W•E Asia•500 kW / S•SE Asia•1000 kW

7460   **CLANDESTINE (ASIA)** †"VO THE TIGERS", Vanni Regi, Sri Lanka   PRO-TAMIL EELAM•1 kW

UNITED KINGDOM †IBC TAMIL, Via Tashkent, Uzbekistan   W•S Asia•240 kW

USA †R FREE ASIA, Via CIS   S•C Asia•250 kW

†R FREE ASIA, Via Mongolia   W•E Asia•250 kW / E Asia•250 kW

7460v   **PIRATE (EUROPE)** †"WEEKEND MUSIC RADIO", Scotland   •Irr•Su•W Europe•0.1 kW•ALT. FREQ. TO 6290v kHz

7465   **BULGARIA** RADIO BULGARIA, Plovdiv   S•Mideast•250 kW

DENMARK †RADIO DANMARK, Via Norway   W•DANISH•E North Am & C America•500 kW / W•DANISH•W North Am•500 kW / W•DANISH•N America•500 kW / S•DANISH•W Europe•500 kW

(con'd)

ENGLISH ▬   ARABIC ▨   CHINESE ▫▫▫   FRENCH ═   GERMAN ▬   RUSSIAN ═   SPANISH ▬   OTHER ▬

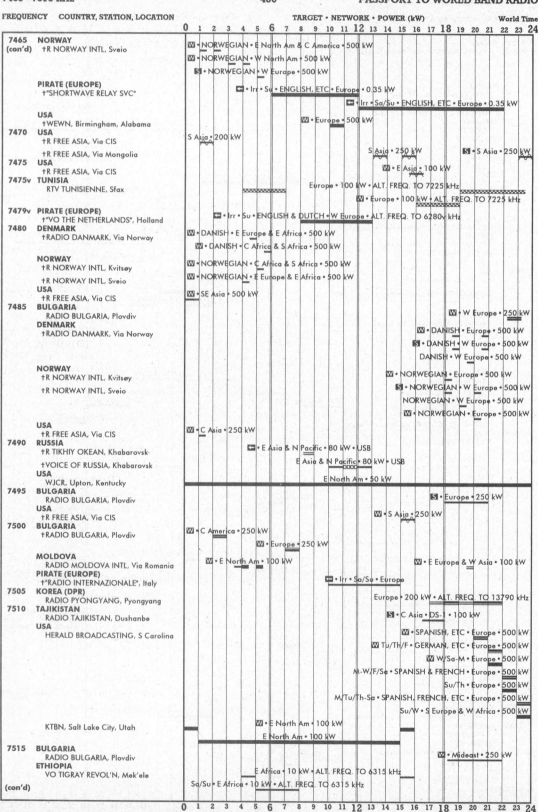

FREQUENCY	COUNTRY, STATION, LOCATION	TARGET • NETWORK • POWER (kW)

7465 **NORWAY**
(con'd)   †R NORWAY INTL, Sveio — W • NORWEGIAN • E North Am & C America • 500 kW / W • NORWEGIAN • W North Am • 500 kW / S • NORWEGIAN • W Europe • 500 kW

PIRATE (EUROPE)
†"SHORTWAVE RELAY SVC" — Irr • Su • ENGLISH, ETC • Europe • 0.35 kW / Irr • Sa/Su • ENGLISH, ETC • Europe • 0.35 kW

USA
†WEWN, Birmingham, Alabama — W • Europe • 500 kW

7470 **USA**
†R FREE ASIA, Via CIS — S Asia • 200 kW

†R FREE ASIA, Via Mongolia — S Asia • 250 kW / S • S Asia • 250 kW

7475 **USA**
†R FREE ASIA, Via CIS — W • E Asia • 100 kW

7475v **TUNISIA**
RTV TUNISIENNE, Sfax — Europe • 100 kW • ALT. FREQ. TO 7225 kHz / W • Europe • 100 kW • ALT. FREQ. TO 7225 kHz

7479v **PIRATE (EUROPE)**
†"VO THE NETHERLANDS", Holland — Irr • Su • ENGLISH & DUTCH • W Europe • ALT. FREQ. TO 6280v kHz

7480 **DENMARK**
†RADIO DANMARK, Via Norway — W • DANISH • E Europe & E Africa • 500 kW / W • DANISH • C Africa & S Africa • 500 kW

NORWAY
†R NORWAY INTL, Kvitsøy — W • NORWEGIAN • C Africa & S Africa • 500 kW

†R NORWAY INTL, Sveio — W • NORWEGIAN • E Europe & E Africa • 500 kW

USA
†R FREE ASIA, Via CIS — W • SE Asia • 500 kW

7485 **BULGARIA**
RADIO BULGARIA, Plovdiv — W • W Europe • 250 kW

DENMARK
†RADIO DANMARK, Via Norway — W • DANISH • Europe • 500 kW / S • DANISH • W Europe • 500 kW / DANISH • W Europe • 500 kW

NORWAY
†R NORWAY INTL, Kvitsøy — W • NORWEGIAN • Europe • 500 kW / S • NORWEGIAN • W Europe • 500 kW

†R NORWAY INTL, Sveio — NORWEGIAN • W Europe • 500 kW / W • NORWEGIAN • Europe • 500 kW

USA
†R FREE ASIA, Via CIS — W • C Asia • 250 kW

7490 **RUSSIA**
†R TIKHIY OKEAN, Khabarovsk — E Asia & N Pacific • 80 kW • USB

†VOICE OF RUSSIA, Khabarovsk — E Asia & N Pacific • 80 kW • USB

USA
WJCR, Upton, Kentucky — E North Am • 50 kW

7495 **BULGARIA**
RADIO BULGARIA, Plovdiv — S • Europe • 250 kW

USA
†R FREE ASIA, Via CIS — W • S Asia • 250 kW

7500 **BULGARIA**
†RADIO BULGARIA, Plovdiv — W • C America • 250 kW / W • Europe • 250 kW

MOLDOVA
RADIO MOLDOVA INTL, Via Romania — W • E North Am • 100 kW / W • E Europe & W Asia • 100 kW

PIRATE (EUROPE)
†"RADIO INTERNAZIONALE", Italy — Irr • Sa/Su • Europe

7505 **KOREA (DPR)**
RADIO PYONGYANG, Pyongyang — Europe • 200 kW • ALT. FREQ. TO 13790 kHz

7510 **TAJIKISTAN**
RADIO TAJIKISTAN, Dushanbe — S • C Asia • DS-1 • 100 kW

USA
HERALD BROADCASTING, S Carolina — W • SPANISH, ETC • Europe • 500 kW / W Tu/Th/F • GERMAN, ETC • Europe • 500 kW / W/Sa-M • Europe • 500 kW / M-W/F/Sa • SPANISH & FRENCH • Europe • 500 kW / Su/Th • Europe • 500 kW / M/Tu/Th-Sa • SPANISH, FRENCH, ETC • Europe • 500 kW / Su/W • S Europe & W Africa • 500 kW

KTBN, Salt Lake City, Utah — W • E North Am • 100 kW / E North Am • 100 kW

7515 **BULGARIA**
RADIO BULGARIA, Plovdiv — W • Mideast • 250 kW

ETHIOPIA
VO TIGRAY REVOL'N, Mek'ele — E Africa • 10 kW • ALT. FREQ. TO 6315 kHz / Sa/Su • E Africa • 10 kW • ALT. FREQ. TO 6315 kHz

(con'd)

SEASONAL **S** OR **W**   1-HR TIMESHIFT MIDYEAR ⬅ OR ➡   JAMMING / OR /\   EARLIEST HEARD ◁   LATEST HEARD ▷   NEW FOR 2000 †

FREQUENCY   COUNTRY, STATION, LOCATION   TARGET • NETWORK • POWER (kW)   World Time

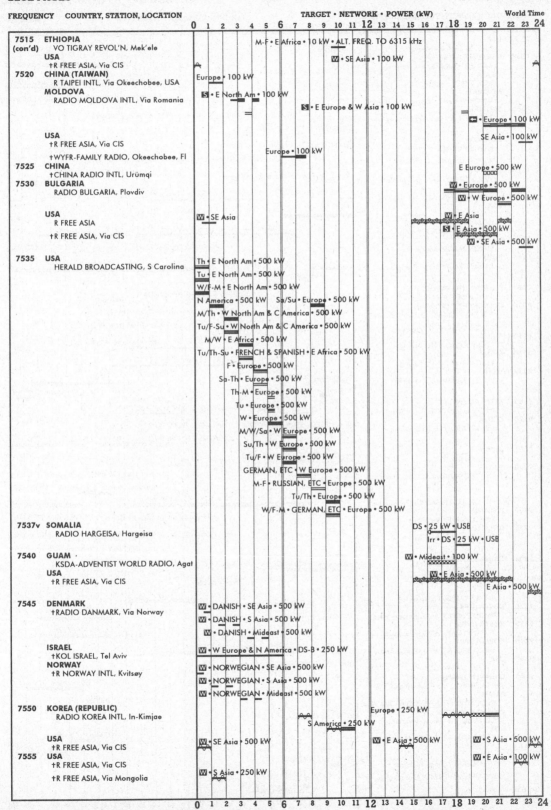

Freq	Country / Station / Location	Schedule notes
7515 (con'd)	**ETHIOPIA** — VO TIGRAY REVOL'N, Mek'ele	M-F • E Africa • 10 kW • ALT. FREQ. TO 6315 kHz
	USA — †R FREE ASIA, Via CIS	W • SE Asia • 100 kW
7520	**CHINA (TAIWAN)** — R TAIPEI INTL, Via Okeechobee, USA	Europe • 100 kW
	MOLDOVA — RADIO MOLDOVA INTL, Via Romania	S • E North Am • 100 kW ; S • E Europe & W Asia • 100 kW ; Europe • 100 kW ; SE Asia • 100 kW
	USA — †R FREE ASIA, Via CIS	
	†WYFR-FAMILY RADIO, Okeechobee, Fl	Europe • 100 kW
7525	**CHINA** — †CHINA RADIO INTL, Urümqi	E Europe • 500 kW
7530	**BULGARIA** — RADIO BULGARIA, Plovdiv	W • Europe • 500 kW ; W • W Europe • 500 kW
	USA — R FREE ASIA	W • SE Asia ; W • E Asia ; S • E Asia • 500 kW
	†R FREE ASIA, Via CIS	W • SE Asia • 500 kW
7535	**USA** — HERALD BROADCASTING, S Carolina	Th • E North Am • 500 kW ; Tu • E North Am • 500 kW ; W/F-M • E North Am • 500 kW ; N America • 500 kW Sa/Su • Europe • 500 kW ; M/Th • W North Am & C America • 500 kW ; Tu/F-Su • W North Am & C America • 500 kW ; M/W • E Africa • 500 kW ; Tu/Th-Su • FRENCH & SPANISH • E Africa • 500 kW ; F • Europe • 500 kW ; Sa-Th • Europe • 500 kW ; Th-M • Europe • 500 kW ; Tu • Europe • 500 kW ; W • Europe • 500 kW ; M/W/Sa • W Europe • 500 kW ; Su/Th • W Europe • 500 kW ; Tu/F • W Europe • 500 kW ; GERMAN, ETC • W Europe • 500 kW ; M-F • RUSSIAN, ETC • Europe • 500 kW ; Tu/Th • Europe • 500 kW ; W/F-M • GERMAN, ETC • Europe • 500 kW
7537v	**SOMALIA** — RADIO HARGEISA, Hargeisa	DS • 25 kW • USB ; Irr • DS • 25 kW • USB
7540	**GUAM** — KSDA-ADVENTIST WORLD RADIO, Agat	W • Mideast • 100 kW
	USA — †R FREE ASIA, Via CIS	W • E Asia • 500 kW ; E Asia • 500 kW
7545	**DENMARK** — †RADIO DANMARK, Via Norway	W • DANISH • SE Asia • 500 kW ; W • DANISH • S Asia • 500 kW ; W • DANISH • Mideast • 500 kW
	ISRAEL — †KOL ISRAEL, Tel Aviv	W • W Europe & N America • DS-B • 250 kW
	NORWAY — †R NORWAY INTL, Kvitsøy	W • NORWEGIAN • SE Asia • 500 kW ; W • NORWEGIAN • S Asia • 500 kW ; W • NORWEGIAN • Mideast • 500 kW
7550	**KOREA (REPUBLIC)** — RADIO KOREA INTL, In-Kimjae	Europe • 250 kW ; S America • 250 kW
	USA — †R FREE ASIA, Via CIS	W • SE Asia • 500 kW ; W • E Asia • 500 kW ; W • S Asia • 500 kW
7555	**USA** — †R FREE ASIA, Via CIS	W • E Asia • 100 kW
	†R FREE ASIA, Via Mongolia	W • S Asia • 250 kW

FREQUENCY   COUNTRY, STATION, LOCATION   TARGET • NETWORK • POWER (kW)   World Time

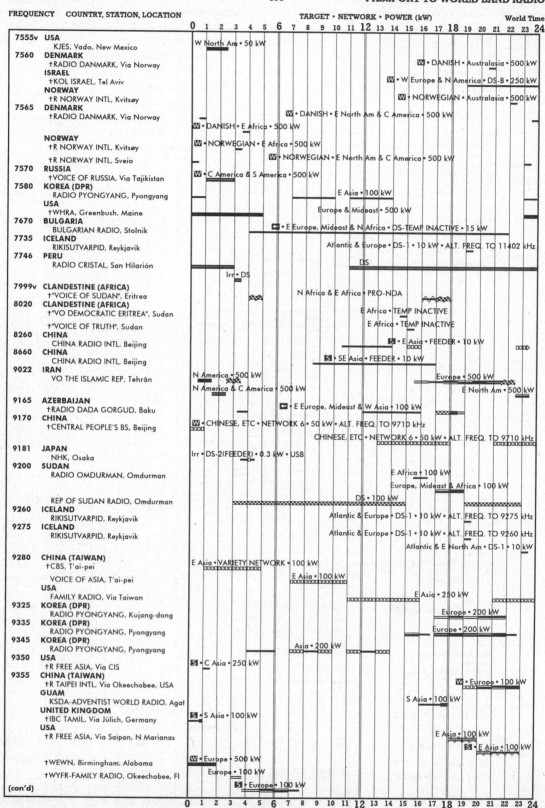

Frequency	Country, Station, Location	Target • Network • Power
7555v	USA	
	KJES, Vado, New Mexico	W North Am • 50 kW
7560	DENMARK	
	†RADIO DANMARK, Via Norway	W • DANISH • Australasia • 500 kW
	ISRAEL	
	†KOL ISRAEL, Tel Aviv	W • W Europe & N America • DS-B • 250 kW
	NORWAY	
	†R NORWAY INTL, Kvitsøy	W • NORWEGIAN • Australasia • 500 kW
7565	DENMARK	
	†RADIO DANMARK, Via Norway	W • DANISH • E North Am & C America • 500 kW
		W • DANISH • E Africa • 500 kW
	NORWAY	
	†R NORWAY INTL, Kvitsøy	W • NORWEGIAN • E Africa • 500 kW
	†R NORWAY INTL, Sveio	W • NORWEGIAN • E North Am & C America • 500 kW
7570	RUSSIA	
	†VOICE OF RUSSIA, Via Tajikistan	W • C America & S America • 500 kW
7580	KOREA (DPR)	
	RADIO PYONGYANG, Pyongyang	E Asia • 100 kW
	USA	
	†WHRA, Greenbush, Maine	Europe & Mideast • 500 kW
7670	BULGARIA	
	BULGARIAN RADIO, Stolnik	• E Europe, Mideast & N Africa • DS-TEMP INACTIVE • 15 kW
7735	ICELAND	
	RIKISUTVARPID, Reykjavik	Atlantic & Europe • DS-1 • 10 kW • ALT. FREQ. TO 11402 kHz
7746	PERU	
	RADIO CRISTAL, San Hilarión	DS
		Irr • DS
7999v	CLANDESTINE (AFRICA)	
	†"VOICE OF SUDAN", Eritrea	N Africa & E Africa • PRO-NDA
8020	CLANDESTINE (AFRICA)	
	†"VO DEMOCRATIC ERITREA", Sudan	E Africa • TEMP INACTIVE
	†"VOICE OF TRUTH", Sudan	E Africa • TEMP INACTIVE
8260	CHINA	
	CHINA RADIO INTL, Beijing	S • E Asia • FEEDER • 10 kW
8660	CHINA	
	CHINA RADIO INTL, Beijing	S • SE Asia • FEEDER • 10 kW
9022	IRAN	
	VO THE ISLAMIC REP, Tehrān	N America • 500 kW Europe • 500 kW
		N America & C America • 500 kW E North Am • 500 kW
9165	AZERBAIJAN	
	†RADIO DADA GORGUD, Baku	• E Europe, Mideast & W Asia • 100 kW
9170	CHINA	
	†CENTRAL PEOPLE'S BS, Beijing	W • CHINESE, ETC • NETWORK 6 • 50 kW • ALT. FREQ. TO 9710 kHz
		CHINESE, ETC • NETWORK 6 • 50 kW • ALT. FREQ. TO 9710 kHz
9181	JAPAN	
	NHK, Osaka	Irr • DS-2(FEEDER) • 0.3 kW • USB
9200	SUDAN	
	RADIO OMDURMAN, Omdurman	E Africa • 100 kW
		Europe, Mideast & Africa • 100 kW
	REP OF SUDAN RADIO, Omdurman	DS • 100 kW
9260	ICELAND	
	RIKISUTVARPID, Reykjavik	Atlantic & Europe • DS-1 • 10 kW • ALT. FREQ. TO 9275 kHz
9275	ICELAND	
	RIKISUTVARPID, Reykjavik	Atlantic & Europe • DS-1 • 10 kW • ALT. FREQ. TO 9260 kHz
		Atlantic & E North Am • DS-1 • 10 kW
9280	CHINA (TAIWAN)	
	†CBS, T'ai-pei	E Asia • VARIETY NETWORK • 100 kW
	VOICE OF ASIA, T'ai-pei	E Asia • 100 kW
	USA	
	FAMILY RADIO, Via Taiwan	E Asia • 250 kW
9325	KOREA (DPR)	
	RADIO PYONGYANG, Kujang-dong	Europe • 200 kW
9335	KOREA (DPR)	
	RADIO PYONGYANG, Pyongyang	Europe • 200 kW
9345	KOREA (DPR)	
	RADIO PYONGYANG, Pyongyang	Asia • 200 kW
9350	USA	
	†R FREE ASIA, Via CIS	S • C Asia • 250 kW
9355	CHINA (TAIWAN)	
	†R TAIPEI INTL, Via Okeechobee, USA	W • Europe • 100 kW
	GUAM	
	KSDA-ADVENTIST WORLD RADIO, Agat	S Asia • 100 kW
	UNITED KINGDOM	
	†IBC TAMIL, Via Jülich, Germany	S • S Asia • 100 kW
	USA	
	†R FREE ASIA, Via Saipan, N Marianas	E Asia • 100 kW
		S • E Asia • 100 kW
	†WEWN, Birmingham, Alabama	W • Europe • 500 kW
	†WYFR-FAMILY RADIO, Okeechobee, Fl	Europe • 100 kW
		S • Europe • 100 kW

(con'd)

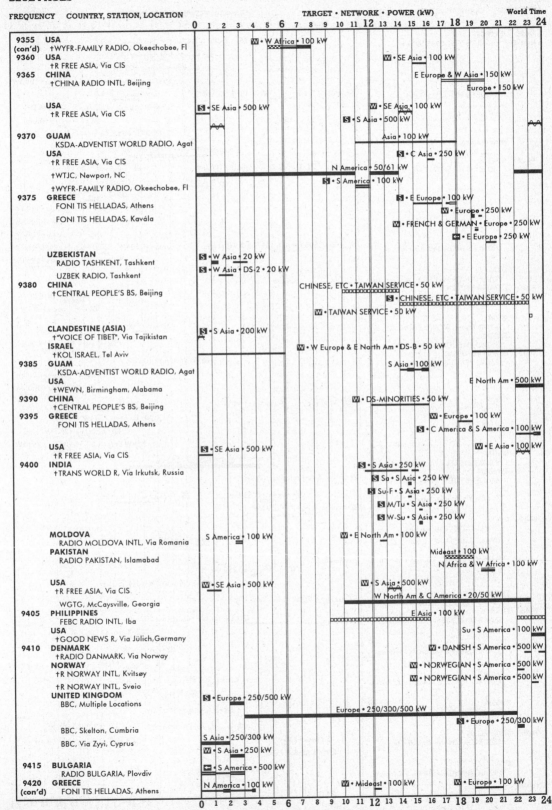

FREQUENCY   COUNTRY, STATION, LOCATION   TARGET • NETWORK • POWER (kW)   World Time

Frequency	Country, Station, Location	Target • Network • Power
9355 (con'd)	**USA** †WYFR-FAMILY RADIO, Okeechobee, Fl	W • W Africa • 100 kW
9360	**USA** †R FREE ASIA, Via CIS	W • SE Asia • 100 kW
9365	**CHINA** †CHINA RADIO INTL, Beijing	E Europe & W Asia • 150 kW — Europe • 150 kW
	USA †R FREE ASIA, Via CIS	S • SE Asia • 500 kW — W • SE Asia • 100 kW — S • S Asia • 500 kW
9370	**GUAM** KSDA-ADVENTIST WORLD RADIO, Agat	Asia • 100 kW
	USA †R FREE ASIA, Via CIS	S • C Asia • 250 kW
	†WTJC, Newport, NC	N America • 50/61 kW
	†WYFR-FAMILY RADIO, Okeechobee, Fl	S • S America • 100 kW
9375	**GREECE** FONI TIS HELLADAS, Athens	S • E Europe • 100 kW — W • Europe • 250 kW
	FONI TIS HELLADAS, Kavála	W • FRENCH & GERMAN • Europe • 250 kW — • E Europe • 250 kW
	UZBEKISTAN RADIO TASHKENT, Tashkent	S • W Asia • 20 kW
	UZBEK RADIO, Tashkent	S • W Asia • DS-2 • 20 kW
9380	**CHINA** †CENTRAL PEOPLE'S BS, Beijing	CHINESE, ETC • TAIWAN SERVICE • 50 kW — S • CHINESE, ETC • TAIWAN SERVICE • 50 kW — W • TAIWAN SERVICE • 50 kW
	CLANDESTINE (ASIA) †"VOICE OF TIBET", Via Tajikistan	S • S Asia • 200 kW
	ISRAEL †KOL ISRAEL, Tel Aviv	W • W Europe & E North Am • DS-B • 50 kW
9385	**GUAM** KSDA-ADVENTIST WORLD RADIO, Agat	S Asia • 100 kW
	USA †WEWN, Birmingham, Alabama	E North Am • 500 kW
9390	**CHINA** †CENTRAL PEOPLE'S BS, Beijing	W • DS-MINORITIES • 50 kW
9395	**GREECE** FONI TIS HELLADAS, Athens	W • Europe • 100 kW — S • C America & S America • 100 kW — W • E Asia • 100 kW
	USA †R FREE ASIA, Via CIS	S • SE Asia • 500 kW
9400	**INDIA** †TRANS WORLD R, Via Irkutsk, Russia	S • S Asia • 250 kW — S • Sa • S Asia • 250 kW — S • Su-F • S Asia • 250 kW — S • M/Tu • S Asia • 250 kW — S • W-Su • S Asia • 250 kW
	MOLDOVA RADIO MOLDOVA INTL, Via Romania	S America • 100 kW — W • E North Am • 100 kW
	PAKISTAN RADIO PAKISTAN, Islamabad	Mideast • 100 kW — N Africa & W Africa • 100 kW
	USA †R FREE ASIA, Via CIS	W • SE Asia • 500 kW — W • S Asia • 500 kW — W North Am & C America • 20/50 kW
	WGTG, McCaysville, Georgia	
9405	**PHILIPPINES** FEBC RADIO INTL, Iba	E Asia • 100 kW
	USA †GOOD NEWS R, Via Jülich, Germany	Su • S America • 100 kW
9410	**DENMARK** †RADIO DANMARK, Via Norway	W • DANISH • S America • 500 kW
	NORWAY †R NORWAY INTL, Kvitsøy	W • NORWEGIAN • S America • 500 kW
	†R NORWAY INTL, Sveio	W • NORWEGIAN • S America • 500 kW
	UNITED KINGDOM BBC, Multiple Locations	S • Europe • 250/500 kW — Europe • 250/300/500 kW — S • Europe • 250/300 kW
	BBC, Skelton, Cumbria	S Asia • 250/300 kW
	BBC, Via Zyyi, Cyprus	W • S Asia • 250 kW
9415	**BULGARIA** RADIO BULGARIA, Plovdiv	• S America • 500 kW
9420 (con'd)	**GREECE** FONI TIS HELLADAS, Athens	N America • 100 kW — W • Mideast • 100 kW — W • Europe • 100 kW

0 1 2 3 4 5 6 7 8 9 10 11 12 13 14 15 16 17 18 19 20 21 22 23 24

ENGLISH ▬   ARABIC ▨   CHINESE □□□   FRENCH ═   GERMAN ▬   RUSSIAN =   SPANISH ▭   OTHER —

FREQUENCY   COUNTRY, STATION, LOCATION   TARGET • NETWORK • POWER (kW)   World Time

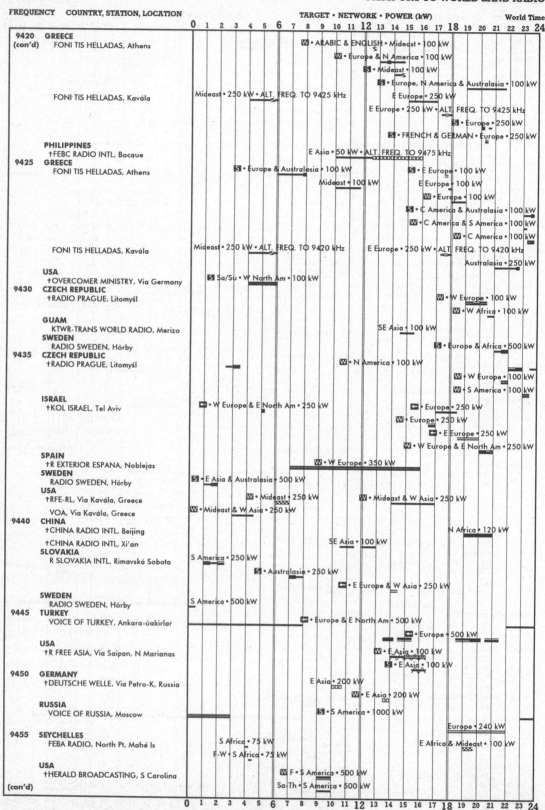

Frequency	Country, Station, Location	Target • Network • Power
9420 (con'd)	**GREECE** FONI TIS HELLADAS, Athens	W • ARABIC & ENGLISH • Mideast • 100 kW
		W • Europe & N America • 100 kW
		S • Mideast • 100 kW
		S • Europe, N America & Australasia • 100 kW
	FONI TIS HELLADAS, Kavála	Mideast • 250 kW • ALT. FREQ. TO 9425 kHz
		E Europe • 250 kW
		E Europe • 250 kW • ALT. FREQ. TO 9425 kHz
		S • Europe • 250 kW
		S • FRENCH & GERMAN • Europe • 250 kW
	PHILIPPINES †FEBC RADIO INTL, Bocaue	E Asia • 50 kW • ALT. FREQ. TO 9475 kHz
9425	**GREECE** FONI TIS HELLADAS, Athens	S • Europe & Australasia • 100 kW
		S • E Europe • 100 kW
		Mideast • 100 kW
		E Europe • 100 kW
		W • Europe • 100 kW
		S • C America & Australasia • 100 kW
		W • C America & S America • 100 kW
		W • C America • 100 kW
	FONI TIS HELLADAS, Kavála	Mideast • 250 kW • ALT. FREQ. TO 9420 kHz
		E Europe • 250 kW • ALT. FREQ. TO 9420 kHz
		Australasia • 250 kW
	USA †OVERCOMER MINISTRY, Via Germany	S Sa/Su • W North Am • 100 kW
9430	**CZECH REPUBLIC** †RADIO PRAGUE, Litomyšl	W • W Europe • 100 kW
		W • W Africa • 100 kW
	GUAM KTWR-TRANS WORLD RADIO, Merizo	SE Asia • 100 kW
	SWEDEN RADIO SWEDEN, Hörby	S • Europe & Africa • 500 kW
9435	**CZECH REPUBLIC** †RADIO PRAGUE, Litomyšl	W • N America • 100 kW
		W • W Europe • 100 kW
		W • S America • 100 kW
	ISRAEL †KOL ISRAEL, Tel Aviv	⇔ • W Europe & E North Am • 250 kW
		⇔ • Europe • 250 kW
		W • Europe • 250 kW
		⇔ • E Europe • 250 kW
		W • W Europe & E North Am • 250 kW
	SPAIN †R EXTERIOR ESPANA, Noblejas	W • W Europe • 350 kW
	SWEDEN RADIO SWEDEN, Hörby	S • E Asia & Australasia • 500 kW
	USA †RFE-RL, Via Kavála, Greece	W • Mideast • 250 kW
		W • Mideast & W Asia • 250 kW
	VOA, Via Kavála, Greece	W • Mideast & W Asia • 250 kW
9440	**CHINA** †CHINA RADIO INTL, Beijing	N Africa • 120 kW
	†CHINA RADIO INTL, Xi'an	SE Asia • 100 kW
	SLOVAKIA R SLOVAKIA INTL, Rimavská Sobota	S America • 250 kW
		S • Australasia • 250 kW
		⇔ • E Europe & W Asia • 250 kW
	SWEDEN RADIO SWEDEN, Hörby	S America • 500 kW
9445	**TURKEY** VOICE OF TURKEY, Ankara-úakirlar	⇔ • Europe & E North Am • 500 kW
		⇔ • Europe • 500 kW
	USA †R FREE ASIA, Via Saipan, N Marianas	W • E Asia • 100 kW
		S • E Asia • 100 kW
9450	**GERMANY** †DEUTSCHE WELLE, Via Petro-K, Russia	E Asia • 200 kW
		W • E Asia • 200 kW
	RUSSIA VOICE OF RUSSIA, Moscow	S • S America • 1000 kW
		Europe • 240 kW
9455	**SEYCHELLES** FEBA RADIO, North Pt, Mahé Is	S Africa • 75 kW
		E Africa & Mideast • 100 kW
		F-W • S Africa • 75 kW
	USA †HERALD BROADCASTING, S Carolina	W F • S America • 500 kW
(con'd)		Sa-Th • S America • 500 kW

FREQUENCY   COUNTRY, STATION, LOCATION   TARGET • NETWORK • POWER (kW)   World Time

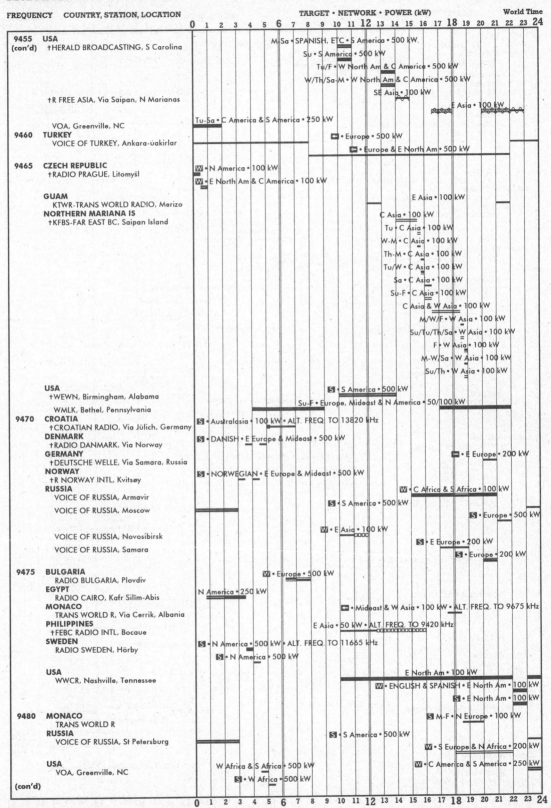

Frequency	Country, Station, Location	Target • Network • Power (kW)
9455 (con'd)	**USA** †HERALD BROADCASTING, S Carolina	M-Sa • SPANISH, ETC • S America • 500 kW.
		Su • S America • 500 kW
		Tu/F • W North Am & C America • 500 kW
		W/Th/Sa-M • W North Am & C America • 500 kW
		SE Asia • 100 kW
	†R FREE ASIA, Via Saipan, N Marianas	E Asia • 100 kW
	VOA, Greenville, NC	Tu-Sa • C America & S America • 250 kW
9460	**TURKEY** VOICE OF TURKEY, Ankara-üakirlar	• Europe • 500 kW
		• Europe & E North Am • 500 kW
9465	**CZECH REPUBLIC** †RADIO PRAGUE, Litomyšl	W • N America • 100 kW
		W • E North Am & C America • 100 kW
	GUAM KTWR-TRANS WORLD RADIO, Merizo	E Asia • 100 kW
	NORTHERN MARIANA IS †KFBS-FAR EAST BC, Saipan Island	C Asia • 100 kW
		Tu • C Asia • 100 kW
		W-M • C Asia • 100 kW
		Th-M • C Asia • 100 kW
		Tu/W • C Asia • 100 kW
		Sa • C Asia • 100 kW
		Su-F • C Asia • 100 kW
		C Asia & W Asia • 100 kW
		M/W/F • W Asia • 100 kW
		Su/Tu/Th/Sa • W Asia • 100 kW
		F • W Asia • 100 kW
		M-W/Sa • W Asia • 100 kW
		Su/Th • W Asia • 100 kW
	USA †WEWN, Birmingham, Alabama	S • S America • 500 kW
		Su-F • Europe, Mideast & N America • 50/100 kW
	WMLK, Bethel, Pennsylvania	
9470	**CROATIA** †CROATIAN RADIO, Via Jülich, Germany	S • Australasia • 100 kW • ALT. FREQ. TO 13820 kHz
	DENMARK †RADIO DANMARK, Via Norway	S • DANISH • E Europe & Mideast • 500 kW
	GERMANY †DEUTSCHE WELLE, Via Samara, Russia	• E Europe • 200 kW
	NORWAY †R NORWAY INTL, Kvitsøy	S • NORWEGIAN • E Europe & Mideast • 500 kW
	RUSSIA VOICE OF RUSSIA, Armavir	W • C Africa & S Africa • 100 kW
	VOICE OF RUSSIA, Moscow	S • S America • 500 kW
		S • Europe • 500 kW
	VOICE OF RUSSIA, Novosibirsk	W • E Asia • 100 kW
		S • E Europe • 200 kW
	VOICE OF RUSSIA, Samara	S • Europe • 200 kW
9475	**BULGARIA** RADIO BULGARIA, Plovdiv	W • Europe • 500 kW
	EGYPT RADIO CAIRO, Kafr Silīm-Abis	N America • 250 kW
	MONACO TRANS WORLD R, Via Cerrik, Albania	• Mideast & W Asia • 100 kW • ALT. FREQ. TO 9675 kHz
	PHILIPPINES †FEBC RADIO INTL, Bocaue	E Asia • 50 kW • ALT. FREQ. TO 9420 kHz
	SWEDEN RADIO SWEDEN, Hörby	S • N America • 500 kW • ALT. FREQ. TO 11665 kHz
		S • N America • 500 kW
	USA WWCR, Nashville, Tennessee	E North Am • 100 kW
		W • ENGLISH & SPANISH • E North Am • 100 kW
		S • E North Am • 100 kW
9480	**MONACO** TRANS WORLD R	S M-F • N Europe • 100 kW
	RUSSIA VOICE OF RUSSIA, St Petersburg	S • S America • 500 kW
		W • S Europe & N Africa • 200 kW
	USA VOA, Greenville, NC	W Africa & S Africa • 500 kW
		W • C America & S America • 250 kW
		S • W Africa • 500 kW
(con'd)		

ENGLISH ▬▬   ARABIC ≋≋≋   CHINESE □□□   FRENCH ══   GERMAN ▭▭   RUSSIAN ══   SPANISH ══   OTHER ▬

FREQUENCY   COUNTRY, STATION, LOCATION   TARGET • NETWORK • POWER (kW)   World Time

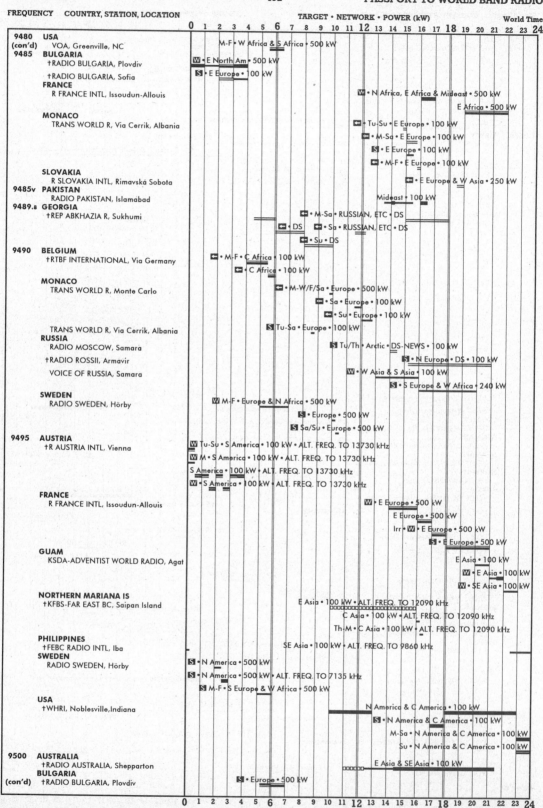

Frequency	Country / Station / Location	Schedule
9480 (con'd)	**USA** — VOA, Greenville, NC	M-F • W Africa & S Africa • 500 kW
9485	**BULGARIA** — †RADIO BULGARIA, Plovdiv	W • E North Am • 500 kW
	†RADIO BULGARIA, Sofia	S • E Europe • 100 kW
	FRANCE — R FRANCE INTL, Issoudun-Allouis	W • N Africa, E Africa & Mideast • 500 kW
		E Africa • 500 kW
	MONACO — TRANS WORLD R, Via Cerrik, Albania	Tu-Su • E Europe • 100 kW
		M-Sa • E Europe • 100 kW
		S • E Europe • 100 kW
		M-F • E Europe • 100 kW
	SLOVAKIA — R SLOVAKIA INTL, Rimavská Sobota	E Europe & W Asia • 250 kW
9485v	**PAKISTAN** — RADIO PAKISTAN, Islamabad	Mideast • 100 kW
9489.8	**GEORGIA** — †REP ABKHAZIA R, Sukhumi	M-Sa • RUSSIAN, ETC • DS
		DS Sa • RUSSIAN, ETC • DS
		Su • DS
9490	**BELGIUM** — †RTBF INTERNATIONAL, Via Germany	M-F • C Africa • 100 kW
		C Africa • 100 kW
	MONACO — TRANS WORLD R, Monte Carlo	M-W/F/Sa • Europe • 500 kW
		Sa • Europe • 100 kW
		Su • Europe • 100 kW
	TRANS WORLD R, Via Cerrik, Albania	S Tu-Sa • Europe • 100 kW
	RUSSIA — RADIO MOSCOW, Samara	Tu/Th • Arctic • DS-NEWS • 100 kW
	†RADIO ROSSII, Armavir	S • N Europe • DS • 100 kW
	VOICE OF RUSSIA, Samara	W • W Asia & S Asia • 100 kW
		S • S Europe & W Africa • 240 kW
	SWEDEN — RADIO SWEDEN, Hörby	W M-F • Europe & N Africa • 500 kW
		S • Europe • 500 kW
		S Sa/Su • Europe • 500 kW
9495	**AUSTRIA** — †R AUSTRIA INTL, Vienna	W Tu-Su • S America • 100 kW • ALT. FREQ. TO 13730 kHz
		W M • S America • 100 kW • ALT. FREQ. TO 13730 kHz
		S America • 100 kW • ALT. FREQ. TO 13730 kHz
		W • S America • 100 kW • ALT. FREQ. TO 13730 kHz
	FRANCE — R FRANCE INTL, Issoudun-Allouis	E Europe • 500 kW
		E Europe • 500 kW
		Irr • W • E Europe • 500 kW
		S • E Europe • 500 kW
	GUAM — KSDA-ADVENTIST WORLD RADIO, Agat	E Asia • 100 kW
		W • E Asia • 100 kW
		W • SE Asia • 100 kW
	NORTHERN MARIANA IS — †KFBS-FAR EAST BC, Saipan Island	E Asia • 100 kW • ALT. FREQ. TO 12090 kHz
		C Asia • 100 kW • ALT. FREQ. TO 12090 kHz
		Th-M • C Asia • 100 kW • ALT. FREQ. TO 12090 kHz
	PHILIPPINES — †FEBC RADIO INTL, Iba	SE Asia • 100 kW • ALT. FREQ. TO 9860 kHz
	SWEDEN — RADIO SWEDEN, Hörby	S • N America • 500 kW
		S • N America • 500 kW • ALT. FREQ. TO 7135 kHz
		S M-F • S Europe & W Africa • 500 kW
	USA — †WHRI, Noblesville, Indiana	N America & C America • 100 kW
		S • N America & C America • 100 kW
		M-Sa • N America & C America • 100 kW
		Su • N America & C America • 100 kW
9500	**AUSTRALIA** — †RADIO AUSTRALIA, Shepparton	E Asia & SE Asia • 100 kW
	BULGARIA (con'd) — †RADIO BULGARIA, Plovdiv	S • Europe • 500 kW

FREQUENCY   COUNTRY, STATION, LOCATION

TARGET • NETWORK • POWER (kW)   World Time

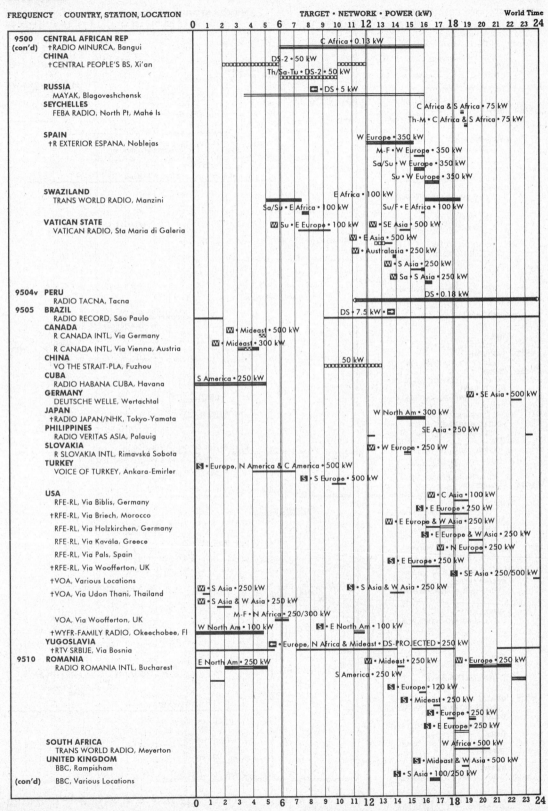

9500 **CENTRAL AFRICAN REP**
(con'd)   †RADIO MINURCA, Bangui
      CHINA
        †CENTRAL PEOPLE'S BS, Xi'an

      RUSSIA
        MAYAK, Blagoveshchensk
      SEYCHELLES
        FEBA RADIO, North Pt, Mahé Is

      SPAIN
        †R EXTERIOR ESPANA, Noblejas

      SWAZILAND
        TRANS WORLD RADIO, Manzini

      VATICAN STATE
        VATICAN RADIO, Sta Maria di Galeria

9504v **PERU**
        RADIO TACNA, Tacna
9505 **BRAZIL**
        RADIO RECORD, São Paulo
      CANADA
        R CANADA INTL, Via Germany
        R CANADA INTL, Via Vienna, Austria
      CHINA
        VO THE STRAIT-PLA, Fuzhou
      CUBA
        RADIO HABANA CUBA, Havana
      GERMANY
        DEUTSCHE WELLE, Wertachtal
      JAPAN
        †RADIO JAPAN/NHK, Tokyo-Yamata
      PHILIPPINES
        RADIO VERITAS ASIA, Palauig
      SLOVAKIA
        R SLOVAKIA INTL, Rimavská Sobota
      TURKEY
        VOICE OF TURKEY, Ankara-Emirler

      USA
        RFE-RL, Via Biblis, Germany
        †RFE-RL, Via Briech, Morocco
        RFE-RL, Via Holzkirchen, Germany
        RFE-RL, Via Kavála, Greece
        RFE-RL, Via Pals, Spain
        †RFE-RL, Via Woofferton, UK
        †VOA, Various Locations
        †VOA, Via Udon Thani, Thailand

        VOA, Via Woofferton, UK
        †WYFR-FAMILY RADIO, Okeechobee, Fl
      YUGOSLAVIA
        †RTV SRBIJE, Via Bosnia
9510 **ROMANIA**
        RADIO ROMANIA INTL, Bucharest

      SOUTH AFRICA
        TRANS WORLD RADIO, Meyerton
      UNITED KINGDOM
        BBC, Rampisham
(con'd)   BBC, Various Locations

FREQUENCY	COUNTRY, STATION, LOCATION	TARGET • NETWORK • POWER (kW)

World Time: 0 1 2 3 4 5 6 7 8 9 10 11 12 13 14 15 16 17 18 19 20 21 22 23 24

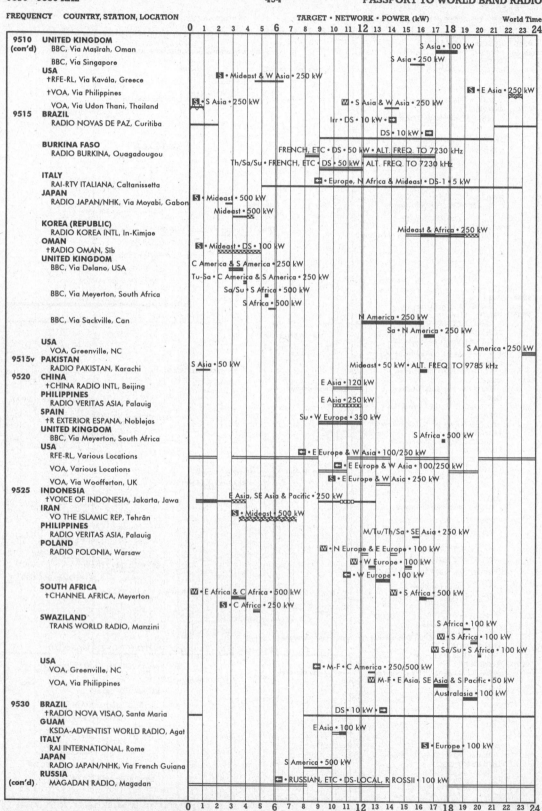

9510
(con'd)   **UNITED KINGDOM**
     BBC, Via Maṣīrah, Oman — S Asia • 100 kW
     BBC, Via Singapore — S Asia • 250 kW
     USA
     †RFE-RL, Via Kavála, Greece — S • Mideast & W Asia • 250 kW
     †VOA, Via Philippines — S • E Asia • 250 kW
     VOA, Via Udon Thani, Thailand — S • S Asia • 250 kW / W • S Asia & W Asia • 250 kW

9515   **BRAZIL**
     RADIO NOVAS DE PAZ, Curitiba — Irr • DS • 10 kW • / DS • 10 kW •
     BURKINA FASO
     RADIO BURKINA, Ouagadougou — FRENCH, ETC • DS • 50 kW • ALT. FREQ. TO 7230 kHz / Th/Sa/Su • FRENCH, ETC • DS • 50 kW • ALT. FREQ. TO 7230 kHz
     ITALY
     RAI-RTV ITALIANA, Caltanissetta — • Europe, N Africa & Mideast • DS-1 • 5 kW
     JAPAN
     RADIO JAPAN/NHK, Via Moyabi, Gabon — S • Mideast • 500 kW / Mideast • 500 kW
     KOREA (REPUBLIC)
     RADIO KOREA INTL, In-Kimjae — Mideast & Africa • 250 kW
     OMAN
     †RADIO OMAN, Sīb — S • Mideast • DS • 100 kW
     UNITED KINGDOM
     BBC, Via Delano, USA — C America & S America • 250 kW / Tu-Sa • C America & S America • 250 kW
     BBC, Via Meyerton, South Africa — Sa/Su • S Africa • 500 kW / S Africa • 500 kW
     BBC, Via Sackville, Can — N America • 250 kW / Sa • N America • 250 kW
     USA
     VOA, Greenville, NC — S America • 250 kW

9515v   **PAKISTAN**
     RADIO PAKISTAN, Karachi — S Asia • 50 kW / Mideast • 50 kW • ALT. FREQ. TO 9785 kHz

9520   **CHINA**
     †CHINA RADIO INTL, Beijing — E Asia • 120 kW
     PHILIPPINES
     RADIO VERITAS ASIA, Palauig — E Asia • 250 kW
     SPAIN
     †R EXTERIOR ESPANA, Noblejas — Su • W Europe • 350 kW
     UNITED KINGDOM
     BBC, Via Meyerton, South Africa — S Africa • 500 kW
     USA
     RFE-RL, Various Locations — • E Europe & W Asia • 100/250 kW
     VOA, Various Locations — • E Europe & W Asia • 100/250 kW
     VOA, Via Woofferton, UK — S • E Europe & W Asia • 250 kW

9525   **INDONESIA**
     †VOICE OF INDONESIA, Jakarta, Jawa — E Asia, SE Asia & Pacific • 250 kW
     IRAN
     VO THE ISLAMIC REP, Tehrān — S • Mideast • 500 kW
     PHILIPPINES
     RADIO VERITAS ASIA, Palauig — M/Tu/Th/Sa • SE Asia • 250 kW
     POLAND
     RADIO POLONIA, Warsaw — W • N Europe & E Europe • 100 kW / W • W Europe • 100 kW / • W Europe • 100 kW
     SOUTH AFRICA
     †CHANNEL AFRICA, Meyerton — W • E Africa & C Africa • 500 kW / W • S Africa • 500 kW / S • C Africa • 250 kW
     SWAZILAND
     TRANS WORLD RADIO, Manzini — S Africa • 100 kW / W • S Africa • 100 kW / W Sa/Su • S Africa • 100 kW
     USA
     VOA, Greenville, NC — • M-F • C America • 250/500 kW
     VOA, Via Philippines — W M-F • E Asia, SE Asia & S Pacific • 50 kW / Australasia • 100 kW

9530   **BRAZIL**
     †RADIO NOVA VISAO, Santa Maria — DS • 10 kW •
     GUAM
     KSDA-ADVENTIST WORLD RADIO, Agat — E Asia • 100 kW
     ITALY
     RAI INTERNATIONAL, Rome — S • Europe • 100 kW
     JAPAN
     RADIO JAPAN/NHK, Via French Guiana — S America • 500 kW
     RUSSIA
(con'd)   MAGADAN RADIO, Magadan — • RUSSIAN, ETC • DS-LOCAL, R ROSSII • 100 kW

SEASONAL S OR W   1-HR TIMESHIFT MIDYEAR ⊡ OR ⊡   JAMMING / OR ∧   EARLIEST HEARD ◁   LATEST HEARD ▷

FREQUENCY   COUNTRY, STATION, LOCATION   TARGET • NETWORK • POWER (kW)   World Time

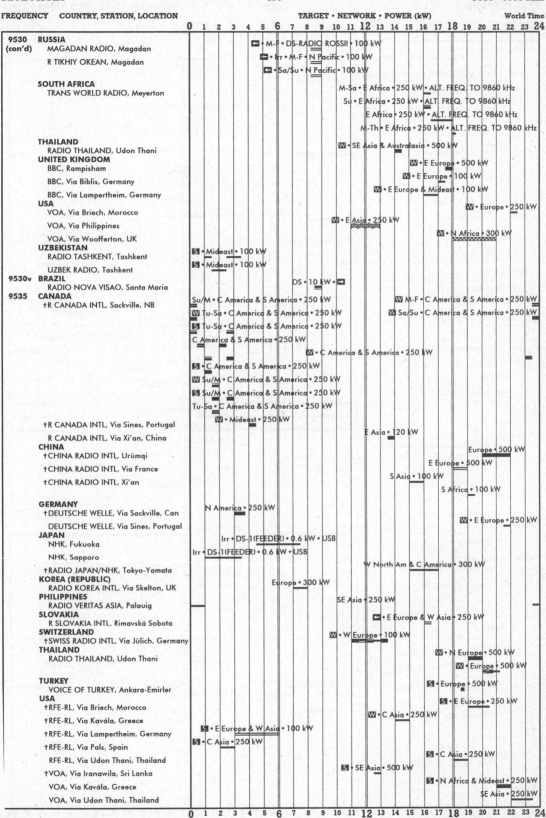

Frequency	Country, Station, Location	Target • Network • Power
9530 (con'd)	**RUSSIA**	
	MAGADAN RADIO, Magadan	M-F • DS-RADIO ROSSII • 100 kW
	R TIKHIY OKEAN, Magadan	Irr • M-F • N Pacific • 100 kW
		Sa/Su • N Pacific • 100 kW
	SOUTH AFRICA	
	TRANS WORLD RADIO, Meyerton	M-Sa • E Africa • 250 kW • ALT. FREQ. TO 9860 kHz
		Su • E Africa • 250 kW • ALT. FREQ. TO 9860 kHz
		E Africa • 250 kW • ALT. FREQ. TO 9860 kHz
		M-Th • E Africa • 250 kW • ALT. FREQ. TO 9860 kHz
	THAILAND	
	RADIO THAILAND, Udon Thani	W • SE Asia & Australasia • 500 kW
	UNITED KINGDOM	
	BBC, Rampisham	W • E Europe • 500 kW
	BBC, Via Biblis, Germany	W • E Europe • 100 kW
	BBC, Via Lampertheim, Germany	W • E Europe & Mideast • 100 kW
	USA	
	VOA, Via Briech, Morocco	W • Europe • 250 kW
	VOA, Via Philippines	W • E Asia • 250 kW
	VOA, Via Woofferton, UK	W • N Africa • 300 kW
	UZBEKISTAN	
	RADIO TASHKENT, Tashkent	S • Mideast • 100 kW
	UZBEK RADIO, Tashkent	S • Mideast • 100 kW
9530v	**BRAZIL**	
	RADIO NOVA VISAO, Santa Maria	DS • 10 kW •
9535	**CANADA**	
	†R CANADA INTL, Sackville, NB	Su/M • C America & S America • 250 kW
		W M-F • C America & S America • 250 kW
		W Tu-Sa • C America & S America • 250 kW
		W Sa/Su • C America & S America • 250 kW
		S Tu-Sa • C America & S America • 250 kW
		C America & S America • 250 kW
		W • C America & S America • 250 kW
		S • C America & S America • 250 kW
		W Su/M • C America & S America • 250 kW
		S Su/M • C America & S America • 250 kW
		Tu-Sa • C America & S America • 250 kW
	†R CANADA INTL, Via Sines, Portugal	W • Mideast • 250 kW
	R CANADA INTL, Via Xi'an, China	E Asia • 120 kW
	CHINA	
	†CHINA RADIO INTL, Urümqi	Europe • 500 kW
	†CHINA RADIO INTL, Via France	E Europe • 500 kW
	†CHINA RADIO INTL, Xi'an	S Asia • 100 kW
		S Africa • 100 kW
	GERMANY	
	†DEUTSCHE WELLE, Via Sackville, Can	N America • 250 kW
	DEUTSCHE WELLE, Via Sines, Portugal	W • E Europe • 250 kW
	JAPAN	
	NHK, Fukuoka	Irr • DS-1 (FEEDER) • 0.6 kW • USB
	NHK, Sapporo	Irr • DS-1 (FEEDER) • 0.6 kW • USB
	†RADIO JAPAN/NHK, Tokyo-Yamata	W North Am & C America • 300 kW
	KOREA (REPUBLIC)	
	RADIO KOREA INTL, Via Skelton, UK	Europe • 300 kW
	PHILIPPINES	
	RADIO VERITAS ASIA, Palauig	SE Asia • 250 kW
	SLOVAKIA	
	R SLOVAKIA INTL, Rimavská Sobota	E Europe & W Asia • 250 kW
	SWITZERLAND	
	†SWISS RADIO INTL, Via Jülich, Germany	W • W Europe • 100 kW
	THAILAND	
	RADIO THAILAND, Udon Thani	W • N Europe • 500 kW
		W • Europe • 500 kW
	TURKEY	
	VOICE OF TURKEY, Ankara-Emirler	S • Europe • 500 kW
	USA	
	†RFE-RL, Via Briech, Morocco	S • E Europe • 250 kW
	†RFE-RL, Via Kavála, Greece	W • C Asia • 250 kW
	†RFE-RL, Via Lampertheim, Germany	S • E Europe & W Asia • 100 kW
	†RFE-RL, Via Pals, Spain	S • C Asia • 250 kW
	RFE-RL, Via Udon Thani, Thailand	S • C Asia • 250 kW
	†VOA, Via Iranawila, Sri Lanka	S • SE Asia • 500 kW
	VOA, Via Kavála, Greece	S • N Africa & Mideast • 250 kW
	VOA, Via Udon Thani, Thailand	SE Asia • 250 kW

ENGLISH ▬▬ **ARABIC** ⌇⌇⌇ **CHINESE** ▭▭▭ **FRENCH** ══ **GERMAN** ▬▬ **RUSSIAN** ══ **SPANISH** ▬▬ **OTHER** ──

FREQUENCY	COUNTRY, STATION, LOCATION	TARGET • NETWORK • POWER (kW)	World Time

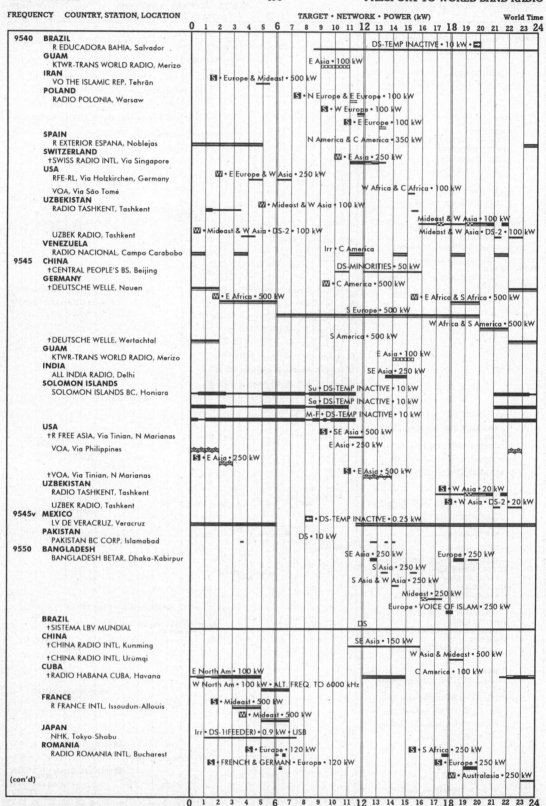

9540 BRAZIL
R EDUCADORA BAHIA, Salvador — DS-TEMP INACTIVE • 10 kW
GUAM
KTWR-TRANS WORLD RADIO, Merizo — E Asia • 100 kW
IRAN
VO THE ISLAMIC REP, Tehrān — S • Europe & Mideast • 500 kW
POLAND
RADIO POLONIA, Warsaw — S • N Europe & E Europe • 100 kW
S • W Europe • 100 kW
S • E Europe • 100 kW
SPAIN
R EXTERIOR ESPANA, Noblejas — N America & C America • 350 kW
SWITZERLAND
†SWISS RADIO INTL, Via Singapore — W • E Asia • 250 kW
USA
RFE-RL, Via Holzkirchen, Germany — W • E Europe & W Asia • 250 kW
VOA, Via São Tomé — W Africa & C Africa • 100 kW
UZBEKISTAN
RADIO TASHKENT, Tashkent — W • Mideast & W Asia • 100 kW
Mideast & W Asia • 100 kW
UZBEK RADIO, Tashkent — W • Mideast & W Asia • DS-2 • 100 kW
Mideast & W Asia • DS-2 • 100 kW
VENEZUELA
RADIO NACIONAL, Campo Carabobo — Irr • C America

9545 CHINA
†CENTRAL PEOPLE'S BS, Beijing — DS-MINORITIES • 50 kW
GERMANY
†DEUTSCHE WELLE, Nauen — W • C America • 500 kW
W • E Africa • 500 kW
W • E Africa & S Africa • 500 kW
S Europe • 500 kW
W Africa & S America • 500 kW
†DEUTSCHE WELLE, Wertachtal — S America • 500 kW
GUAM
KTWR-TRANS WORLD RADIO, Merizo — E Asia • 100 kW
INDIA
ALL INDIA RADIO, Delhi — SE Asia • 250 kW
SOLOMON ISLANDS
SOLOMON ISLANDS BC, Honiara — Su • DS-TEMP INACTIVE • 10 kW
Sa • DS-TEMP INACTIVE • 10 kW
M-F • DS-TEMP INACTIVE • 10 kW
USA
†R FREE ASIA, Via Tinian, N Marianas — S • SE Asia • 500 kW
VOA, Via Philippines — E Asia • 250 kW
S • E Asia • 250 kW
†VOA, Via Tinian, N Marianas — S • E Asia • 500 kW
UZBEKISTAN
RADIO TASHKENT, Tashkent — S • W Asia • 20 kW
UZBEK RADIO, Tashkent — S • W Asia • DS-2 • 20 kW

9545v MEXICO
LV DE VERACRUZ, Veracruz — DS-TEMP INACTIVE • 0.25 kW
PAKISTAN
PAKISTAN BC CORP, Islamabad — DS • 10 kW

9550 BANGLADESH
BANGLADESH BETAR, Dhaka-Kabirpur — SE Asia • 250 kW   Europe • 250 kW
S Asia • 250 kW
S Asia & W Asia • 250 kW
Mideast • 250 kW
Europe • VOICE OF ISLAM • 250 kW
BRAZIL
†SISTEMA LBV MUNDIAL — DS
CHINA
†CHINA RADIO INTL, Kunming — SE Asia • 150 kW
†CHINA RADIO INTL, Urümqi — W Asia & Mideast • 500 kW
CUBA
†RADIO HABANA CUBA, Havana — E North Am • 100 kW   C America • 100 kW
W North Am • 100 kW • ALT. FREQ. TO 6000 kHz
FRANCE
R FRANCE INTL, Issoudun-Allouis — S • Mideast • 500 kW
W • Mideast • 500 kW
JAPAN
NHK, Tokyo-Shobu — Irr • DS-1 (FEEDER) • 0.9 kW • USB
ROMANIA
RADIO ROMANIA INTL, Bucharest — S • Europe • 120 kW   S • S Africa • 250 kW
S • FRENCH & GERMAN • Europe • 120 kW   S • Europe • 250 kW
W • Australasia • 250 kW

(con'd)

SEASONAL S OR W   1-HR TIMESHIFT MIDYEAR ◁ OR ▷   JAMMING / OR ⋀   EARLIEST HEARD ◁   LATEST HEARD ▷

FREQUENCY   COUNTRY, STATION, LOCATION   TARGET • NETWORK • POWER (kW)   World Time

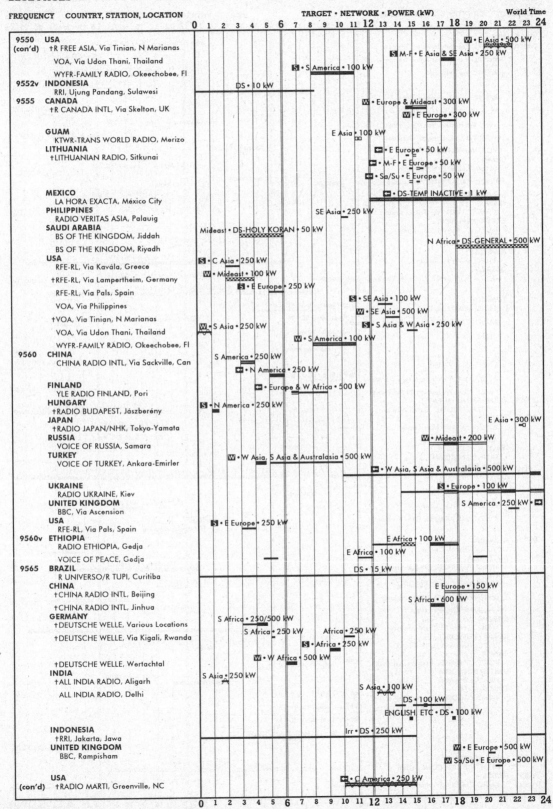

FREQUENCY	COUNTRY, STATION, LOCATION	TARGET • NETWORK • POWER (kW)
9550 (con'd)	USA	
	†R FREE ASIA, Via Tinian, N Marianas	W • E Asia • 500 kW
		M-F • E Asia & SE Asia • 250 kW
	VOA, Via Udon Thani, Thailand	
	WYFR-FAMILY RADIO, Okeechobee, Fl	S • S America • 100 kW
9552v	INDONESIA	
	RRI, Ujung Pandang, Sulawesi	DS • 10 kW
9555	CANADA	
	†R CANADA INTL, Via Skelton, UK	W • Europe & Mideast • 300 kW
		W • E Europe • 300 kW
	GUAM	
	KTWR-TRANS WORLD RADIO, Merizo	E Asia • 100 kW
	LITHUANIA	
	†LITHUANIAN RADIO, Sitkunai	• E Europe • 50 kW
		• M-F • E Europe • 50 kW
		• Sa/Su • E Europe • 50 kW
	MEXICO	
	LA HORA EXACTA, México City	• DS-TEMP INACTIVE • 1 kW
	PHILIPPINES	
	RADIO VERITAS ASIA, Palauig	SE Asia • 250 kW
	SAUDI ARABIA	
	BS OF THE KINGDOM, Jiddah	Mideast • DS-HOLY KORAN • 50 kW
	BS OF THE KINGDOM, Riyadh	N Africa • DS-GENERAL • 500 kW
	USA	
	RFE-RL, Via Kavála, Greece	S • C Asia • 250 kW
	†RFE-RL, Via Lampertheim, Germany	W • Mideast • 100 kW
	RFE-RL, Via Pals, Spain	S • E Europe • 250 kW
	VOA, Via Philippines	S • SE Asia • 100 kW
	†VOA, Via Tinian, N Marianas	W • SE Asia • 500 kW
	VOA, Via Udon Thani, Thailand	S • S Asia & W Asia • 250 kW
	WYFR-FAMILY RADIO, Okeechobee, Fl	W • S Asia • 250 kW
		W • S America • 100 kW
9560	CHINA	
	CHINA RADIO INTL, Via Sackville, Can	S America • 250 kW
		• N America • 250 kW
	FINLAND	
	YLE RADIO FINLAND, Pori	• Europe & W Africa • 500 kW
	HUNGARY	
	†RADIO BUDAPEST, Jászberény	S • N America • 250 kW
	JAPAN	
	†RADIO JAPAN/NHK, Tokyo-Yamata	E Asia • 300 kW
	RUSSIA	
	VOICE OF RUSSIA, Samara	W • Mideast • 200 kW
	TURKEY	
	VOICE OF TURKEY, Ankara-Emirler	W • W Asia, S Asia & Australasia • 500 kW
		• W Asia, S Asia & Australasia • 500 kW
	UKRAINE	
	RADIO UKRAINE, Kiev	S • Europe • 100 kW
	UNITED KINGDOM	
	BBC, Via Ascension	S America • 250 kW •
	USA	
	RFE-RL, Via Pals, Spain	S • E Europe • 250 kW
9560v	ETHIOPIA	
	RADIO ETHIOPIA, Gedja	E Africa • 100 kW
	VOICE OF PEACE, Gedja	E Africa • 100 kW
9565	BRAZIL	
	R UNIVERSO/R TUPI, Curitiba	DS • 15 kW
	CHINA	
	†CHINA RADIO INTL, Beijing	E Europe • 150 kW
	†CHINA RADIO INTL, Jinhua	S Africa • 600 kW
	GERMANY	
	†DEUTSCHE WELLE, Various Locations	S Africa • 250/500 kW
	†DEUTSCHE WELLE, Via Kigali, Rwanda	S Africa • 250 kW Africa • 250 kW
		S • Africa • 250 kW
	†DEUTSCHE WELLE, Wertachtal	W • W Africa • 500 kW
	INDIA	
	†ALL INDIA RADIO, Aligarh	S Asia • 250 kW
	ALL INDIA RADIO, Delhi	S Asia • 100 kW
		DS • 100 kW
		ENGLISH ETC • DS • 100 kW
	INDONESIA	
	†RRI, Jakarta, Jawa	Irr • DS • 250 kW
	UNITED KINGDOM	
	BBC, Rampisham	W • E Europe • 500 kW
		W • Sa/Su • E Europe • 500 kW
	USA	
(con'd)	†RADIO MARTI, Greenville, NC	• C America • 250 kW

ENGLISH ▬   ARABIC ⧖   CHINESE ▭▭▭   FRENCH ═   GERMAN ▬   RUSSIAN ═   SPANISH ▬   OTHER ▬

FREQUENCY   COUNTRY, STATION, LOCATION   TARGET • NETWORK • POWER (kW)   World Time

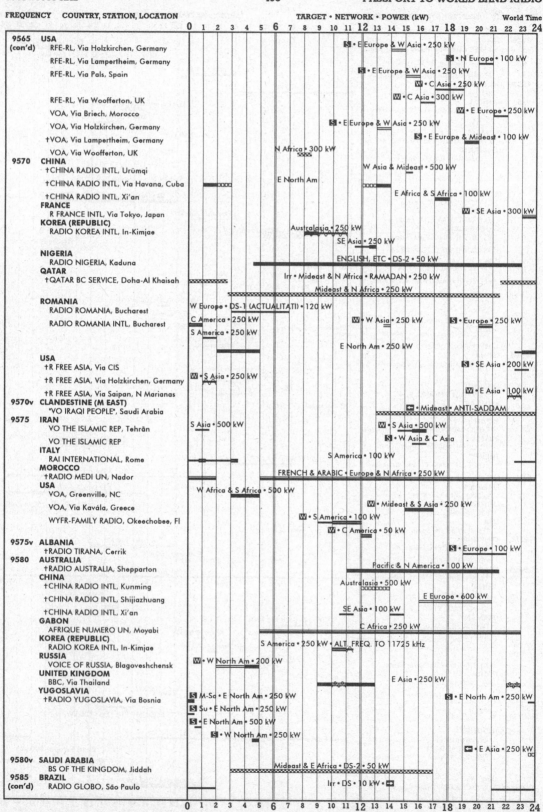

9565 (con'd) **USA**	
RFE-RL, Via Holzkirchen, Germany	S • E Europe & W Asia • 250 kW
RFE-RL, Via Lampertheim, Germany	S • N Europe • 100 kW
RFE-RL, Via Pals, Spain	S • E Europe & W Asia • 250 kW
RFE-RL, Via Woofferton, UK	W • C Asia • 250 kW
	W • C Asia • 300 kW
VOA, Via Briech, Morocco	W • E Europe • 250 kW
VOA, Via Holzkirchen, Germany	S • E Europe & W Asia • 250 kW
†VOA, Via Lampertheim, Germany	S • E Europe & Mideast • 100 kW
VOA, Via Woofferton, UK	N Africa • 300 kW
9570 CHINA	
†CHINA RADIO INTL, Urümqi	W Asia & Mideast • 500 kW
†CHINA RADIO INTL, Via Havana, Cuba	E North Am
†CHINA RADIO INTL, Xi'an	E Africa & S Africa • 100 kW
FRANCE	
R FRANCE INTL, Via Tokyo, Japan	W • SE Asia • 300 kW
KOREA (REPUBLIC)	
RADIO KOREA INTL, In-Kimjae	Australasia • 250 kW
	SE Asia • 250 kW
NIGERIA	
RADIO NIGERIA, Kaduna	ENGLISH, ETC • DS-2 • 50 kW
QATAR	
†QATAR BC SERVICE, Doha-Al Khaisah	Irr • Mideast & N Africa • RAMADAN • 250 kW
	Mideast & N Africa • 250 kW
ROMANIA	
RADIO ROMANIA, Bucharest	W Europe • DS-1 (ACTUALITATI) • 120 kW
RADIO ROMANIA INTL, Bucharest	C America • 250 kW
	W • W Asia • 250 kW
	S • Europe • 250 kW
	S America • 250 kW
	E North Am • 250 kW
USA	
†R FREE ASIA, Via CIS	S • SE Asia • 200 kW
†R FREE ASIA, Via Holzkirchen, Germany	W • S Asia • 250 kW
†R FREE ASIA, Via Saipan, N Marianas	W • E Asia • 100 kW
9570v CLANDESTINE (M EAST)	
"VO IRAQI PEOPLE", Saudi Arabia	Mideast • ANTI-SADDAM
9575 IRAN	
VO THE ISLAMIC REP, Tehrān	S Asia • 500 kW
	W • S Asia • 500 kW
VO THE ISLAMIC REP	S • W Asia & C Asia
ITALY	
RAI INTERNATIONAL, Rome	S America • 100 kW
MOROCCO	
†RADIO MEDI UN, Nador	FRENCH & ARABIC • Europe & N Africa • 250 kW
USA	
VOA, Greenville, NC	W Africa & S Africa • 500 kW
VOA, Via Kavála, Greece	W • Mideast & S Asia • 250 kW
WYFR-FAMILY RADIO, Okeechobee, Fl	W • S America • 100 kW
	W • C America • 50 kW
9575v ALBANIA	
†RADIO TIRANA, Cerrik	S • Europe • 100 kW
9580 AUSTRALIA	
†RADIO AUSTRALIA, Shepparton	Pacific & N America • 100 kW
CHINA	
†CHINA RADIO INTL, Kunming	Australasia • 500 kW
†CHINA RADIO INTL, Shijiazhuang	E Europe • 600 kW
†CHINA RADIO INTL, Xi'an	SE Asia • 100 kW
GABON	
AFRIQUE NUMERO UN, Moyabi	C Africa • 250 kW
KOREA (REPUBLIC)	
RADIO KOREA INTL, In-Kimjae	S America • 250 kW • ALT. FREQ. TO 11725 kHz
RUSSIA	
VOICE OF RUSSIA, Blagoveshchensk	W • W North Am • 200 kW
UNITED KINGDOM	
BBC, Via Thailand	E Asia • 250 kW
YUGOSLAVIA	
†RADIO YUGOSLAVIA, Via Bosnia	S M-Sa • E North Am • 250 kW
	S • E North Am • 250 kW
	S Su • E North Am • 250 kW
	S • E North Am • 500 kW
	S • W North Am • 250 kW
	E Asia • 250 kW
9580v SAUDI ARABIA	
BS OF THE KINGDOM, Jiddah	Mideast & E Africa • DS-2 • 50 kW
9585 BRAZIL (con'd)	
RADIO GLOBO, São Paulo	Irr • DS • 10 kW

FREQUENCY   COUNTRY, STATION, LOCATION

TARGET • NETWORK • POWER (kW)

World Time

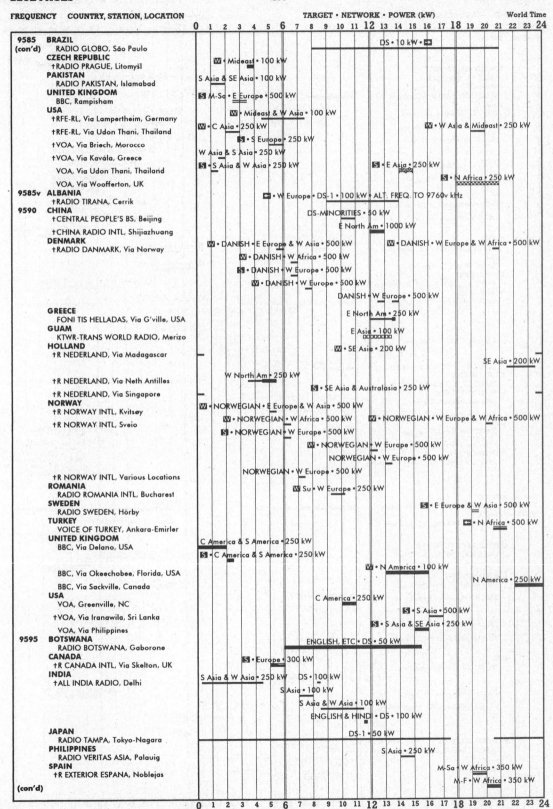

FREQUENCY	COUNTRY, STATION, LOCATION	TARGET • NETWORK • POWER (kW)
9585 (con'd)	BRAZIL	
	RADIO GLOBO, São Paulo	DS • 10 kW
	CZECH REPUBLIC	
	†RADIO PRAGUE, Litomyšl	W • Mideast • 100 kW
	PAKISTAN	
	RADIO PAKISTAN, Islamabad	S Asia & SE Asia • 100 kW
	UNITED KINGDOM	
	BBC, Rampisham	S • M-Sa • E Europe • 500 kW
	USA	
	†RFE-RL, Via Lampertheim, Germany	W • Mideast & W Asia • 100 kW
	†RFE-RL, Via Udon Thani, Thailand	W • C Asia • 250 kW / W • W Asia & Mideast • 250 kW
	†VOA, Via Briech, Morocco	S • S Europe • 250 kW
	†VOA, Via Kavála, Greece	W Asia & S Asia • 250 kW
	VOA, Via Udon Thani, Thailand	S • S Asia & W Asia • 250 kW / S • E Asia • 250 kW
	VOA, Via Woofferton, UK	S • N Africa • 250 kW
9585v	ALBANIA	
	†RADIO TIRANA, Cerrik	• W Europe • DS-1 • 100 kW • ALT. FREQ. TO 9760v kHz
9590	CHINA	
	†CENTRAL PEOPLE'S BS, Beijing	DS-MINORITIES • 50 kW
	†CHINA RADIO INTL, Shijiazhuang	E North Am • 1000 kW
	DENMARK	
	†RADIO DANMARK, Via Norway	W • DANISH • E Europe & W Asia • 500 kW / W • DANISH • W Europe & W Africa • 500 kW
		W • DANISH • W Africa • 500 kW
		S • DANISH • W Europe • 500 kW
		W • DANISH • W Europe • 500 kW
		DANISH • W Europe • 500 kW
	GREECE	
	FONI TIS HELLADAS, Via G'ville, USA	E North Am • 250 kW
	GUAM	
	KTWR-TRANS WORLD RADIO, Merizo	E Asia • 100 kW
	HOLLAND	
	†R NEDERLAND, Via Madagascar	W • SE Asia • 200 kW / SE Asia • 200 kW
	†R NEDERLAND, Via Neth Antilles	W North Am • 250 kW
	†R NEDERLAND, Via Singapore	S • SE Asia & Australasia • 250 kW
	NORWAY	
	†R NORWAY INTL, Kvitsøy	W • NORWEGIAN • E Europe & W Asia • 500 kW
	†R NORWAY INTL, Sveio	W • NORWEGIAN • W Africa • 500 kW / W • NORWEGIAN • W Europe & W Africa • 500 kW
		S • NORWEGIAN • W Europe • 500 kW
		W • NORWEGIAN • W Europe • 500 kW
		NORWEGIAN • W Europe • 500 kW
	†R NORWAY INTL, Various Locations	NORWEGIAN • W Europe • 500 kW
	ROMANIA	
	RADIO ROMANIA INTL, Bucharest	W • Su • W Europe • 250 kW
	SWEDEN	
	RADIO SWEDEN, Hörby	S • E Europe & W Asia • 500 kW
	TURKEY	
	VOICE OF TURKEY, Ankara-Emirler	• N Africa • 500 kW
	UNITED KINGDOM	
	BBC, Via Delano, USA	C America & S America • 250 kW
		S • C America & S America • 250 kW
	BBC, Via Okeechobee, Florida, USA	W • N America • 100 kW
	BBC, Via Sackville, Canada	N America • 250 kW
	USA	
	VOA, Greenville, NC	C America • 250 kW
	†VOA, Via Iranawila, Sri Lanka	S • S Asia • 500 kW
	VOA, Via Philippines	S • S Asia & SE Asia • 250 kW
9595	BOTSWANA	
	RADIO BOTSWANA, Gaborone	ENGLISH, ETC • DS • 50 kW
	CANADA	
	†R CANADA INTL, Via Skelton, UK	S • Europe • 300 kW
	INDIA	
	†ALL INDIA RADIO, Delhi	S Asia & W Asia • 250 kW / DS • 100 kW
		S Asia • 100 kW
		S Asia & W Asia • 100 kW
		ENGLISH & HINDI • DS • 100 kW
	JAPAN	
	RADIO TAMPA, Tokyo-Nagara	DS-1 • 50 kW
	PHILIPPINES	
	RADIO VERITAS ASIA, Palauig	S Asia • 250 kW
	SPAIN	
	†R EXTERIOR ESPANA, Noblejas	M-Sa • W Africa • 350 kW
		M-F • W Africa • 350 kW
(con'd)		

FREQUENCY   COUNTRY, STATION, LOCATION   TARGET • NETWORK • POWER (kW)   World Time

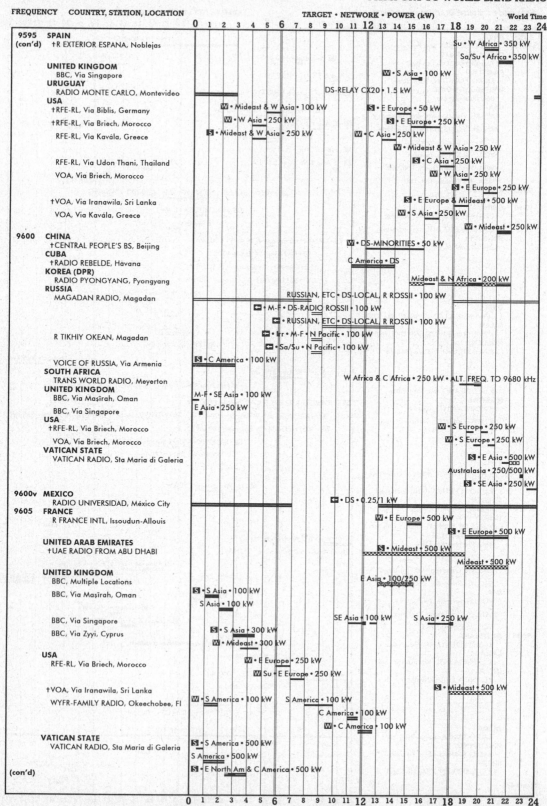

The image is a broadcast schedule chart (9595–9605 kHz) with a time grid from 0 to 24 World Time. Entries include:

9595 (con'd) SPAIN
†R EXTERIOR ESPANA, Noblejas — Su • W Africa • 350 kW; Sa/Su • Africa • 350 kW

UNITED KINGDOM
BBC, Via Singapore — W • S Asia • 100 kW

URUGUAY
RADIO MONTE CARLO, Montevideo — DS-RELAY CX20 • 1.5 kW

USA
†RFE-RL, Via Biblis, Germany — W • Mideast & W Asia • 100 kW
†RFE-RL, Via Briech, Morocco — W • W Asia • 250 kW; S • E Europe • 250 kW
RFE-RL, Via Kavála, Greece — S • Mideast & W Asia • 250 kW; W • C Asia • 250 kW; W • Mideast & W Asia • 250 kW

RFE-RL, Via Udon Thani, Thailand — S • C Asia • 250 kW
VOA, Via Briech, Morocco — W • W Asia • 250 kW; S • E Europe • 250 kW

†VOA, Via Iranawila, Sri Lanka — S • E Europe & Mideast • 500 kW
VOA, Via Kavála, Greece — W • S Asia • 250 kW

W • Mideast • 250 kW

9600 CHINA
†CENTRAL PEOPLE'S BS, Beijing — W • DS-MINORITIES • 50 kW

CUBA
†RADIO REBELDE, Havana — C America • DS

KOREA (DPR)
RADIO PYONGYANG, Pyongyang — Mideast & N Africa • 200 kW

RUSSIA
MAGADAN RADIO, Magadan — RUSSIAN, ETC • DS-LOCAL, R ROSSII • 100 kW; M-F • DS-RADIO ROSSII • 100 kW; RUSSIAN, ETC • DS-LOCAL, R ROSSII • 100 kW

R TIKHIY OKEAN, Magadan — Irr • M-F • N Pacific • 100 kW; Sa/Su • N Pacific • 100 kW

VOICE OF RUSSIA, Via Armenia — S • C America • 100 kW

SOUTH AFRICA
TRANS WORLD RADIO, Meyerton — W Africa & C Africa • 250 kW • ALT. FREQ. TO 9680 kHz

UNITED KINGDOM
BBC, Via Maşirah, Oman — M-F • SE Asia • 100 kW
BBC, Via Singapore — E Asia • 250 kW

USA
†RFE-RL, Via Briech, Morocco — W • S Europe • 250 kW
VOA, Via Briech, Morocco — W • S Europe • 250 kW

VATICAN STATE
VATICAN RADIO, Sta Maria di Galeria — S • E Asia • 500 kW; Australasia • 250/500 kW; S • SE Asia • 250 kW

9600v MEXICO
RADIO UNIVERSIDAD, México City — DS • 0.25/1 kW

9605 FRANCE
R FRANCE INTL, Issoudun-Allouis — W • E Europe • 500 kW; S • E Europe • 500 kW

UNITED ARAB EMIRATES
†UAE RADIO FROM ABU DHABI — S • Mideast • 500 kW; Mideast • 500 kW

UNITED KINGDOM
BBC, Multiple Locations — E Asia • 100/250 kW
BBC, Via Maşirah, Oman — S • S Asia • 100 kW; S Asia • 100 kW; SE Asia • 100 kW; S Asia • 250 kW
BBC, Via Singapore
BBC, Via Zyyi, Cyprus — S • S Asia • 300 kW; W • Mideast • 300 kW

USA
RFE-RL, Via Briech, Morocco — W • E Europe • 250 kW; W Su • E Europe • 250 kW
†VOA, Via Iranawila, Sri Lanka — S • Mideast • 500 kW
WYFR-FAMILY RADIO, Okeechobee, Fl — W • S America • 100 kW; S America • 100 kW; C America • 100 kW; W • C America • 100 kW

VATICAN STATE
VATICAN RADIO, Sta Maria di Galeria — S • S America • 500 kW; S America • 500 kW; S • E North Am & C America • 500 kW

(con'd)

FREQUENCY   COUNTRY, STATION, LOCATION   TARGET • NETWORK • POWER (kW)   World Time

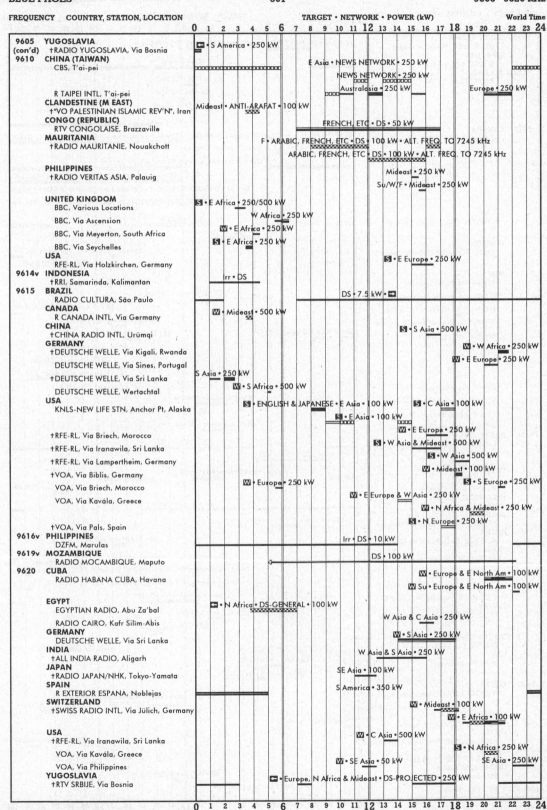

0 1 2 3 4 5 6 7 8 9 10 11 12 13 14 15 16 17 18 19 20 21 22 23 24

Frequency	Country, Station, Location	Target • Network • Power
9605 (con'd)	YUGOSLAVIA	
	†RADIO YUGOSLAVIA, Via Bosnia	S America • 250 kW
9610	CHINA (TAIWAN)	
	CBS, T'ai-pei	E Asia • NEWS NETWORK • 250 kW
		NEWS NETWORK • 250 kW
	R TAIPEI INTL, T'ai-pei	Australasia • 250 kW Europe • 250 kW
	CLANDESTINE (M EAST)	
	†"VO PALESTINIAN ISLAMIC REV'N", Iran	Mideast • ANTI-ARAFAT • 100 kW
	CONGO (REPUBLIC)	
	RTV CONGOLAISE, Brazzaville	FRENCH, ETC • DS • 50 kW
	MAURITANIA	
	†RADIO MAURITANIE, Nouakchott	F • ARABIC, FRENCH, ETC • DS • 100 kW • ALT. FREQ. TO 7245 kHz
		ARABIC, FRENCH, ETC • DS • 100 kW • ALT. FREQ. TO 7245 kHz
	PHILIPPINES	
	†RADIO VERITAS ASIA, Palauig	Mideast • 250 kW
		Su/W/F • Mideast • 250 kW
	UNITED KINGDOM	
	BBC, Various Locations	S • E Africa • 250/500 kW
	BBC, Via Ascension	W Africa • 250 kW
	BBC, Via Meyerton, South Africa	W • E Africa • 250 kW
	BBC, Via Seychelles	S • E Africa • 250 kW
	USA	
	RFE-RL, Via Holzkirchen, Germany	S • E Europe • 250 kW
9614v	INDONESIA	
	†RRI, Samarinda, Kalimantan	Irr • DS
9615	BRAZIL	
	RADIO CULTURA, São Paulo	DS • 7.5 kW •
	CANADA	
	R CANADA INTL, Via Germany	W • Mideast • 500 kW
	CHINA	
	†CHINA RADIO INTL, Urümqi	S • S Asia • 500 kW
	GERMANY	
	†DEUTSCHE WELLE, Via Kigali, Rwanda	W • W Africa • 250 kW
	DEUTSCHE WELLE, Via Sines, Portugal	W • E Europe • 250 kW
	†DEUTSCHE WELLE, Via Sri Lanka	S Asia • 250 kW
	DEUTSCHE WELLE, Wertachtal	W • S Africa • 500 kW
	USA	
	KNLS-NEW LIFE STN, Anchor Pt, Alaska	S • ENGLISH & JAPANESE • E Asia • 100 kW S • C Asia • 100 kW
		S • E Asia • 100 kW
	†RFE-RL, Via Briech, Morocco	W • E Europe • 250 kW
	†RFE-RL, Via Iranawila, Sri Lanka	S • W Asia & Mideast • 500 kW
	†RFE-RL, Via Lampertheim, Germany	S • W Asia • 500 kW
	†VOA, Via Biblis, Germany	W • Mideast • 100 kW
	VOA, Via Briech, Morocco	W • Europe • 250 kW S • S Europe • 250 kW
	VOA, Via Kavála, Greece	W • E Europe & W Asia • 250 kW
		W • N Africa & Mideast • 250 kW
	†VOA, Via Pals, Spain	S • N Europe • 250 kW
9616v	PHILIPPINES	
	DZFM, Marulas	Irr • DS • 10 kW
9619v	MOZAMBIQUE	
	RADIO MOCAMBIQUE, Maputo	DS • 100 kW
9620	CUBA	
	RADIO HABANA CUBA, Havana	W • Europe & E North Am • 100 kW
		W Su • Europe & E North Am • 100 kW
	EGYPT	
	EGYPTIAN RADIO, Abu Za'bal	N Africa • DS-GENERAL • 100 kW
	RADIO CAIRO, Kafr Silim-Abis	W Asia & C Asia • 250 kW
	GERMANY	
	DEUTSCHE WELLE, Via Sri Lanka	W • S Asia • 250 kW
	INDIA	
	†ALL INDIA RADIO, Aligarh	W Asia & S Asia • 250 kW
	JAPAN	
	†RADIO JAPAN/NHK, Tokyo-Yamata	SE Asia • 100 kW
	SPAIN	
	R EXTERIOR ESPANA, Noblejas	S America • 350 kW
	SWITZERLAND	
	†SWISS RADIO INTL, Via Jülich, Germany	W • Mideast • 100 kW
		W • E Africa • 100 kW
	USA	
	†RFE-RL, Via Iranawila, Sri Lanka	W • C Asia • 500 kW
	VOA, Via Kavála, Greece	S • N Africa • 250 kW
	VOA, Via Philippines	W • SE Asia • 50 kW SE Asia • 250 kW
	YUGOSLAVIA	
	†RTV SRBIJE, Via Bosnia	Europe, N Africa & Mideast • DS-PROJECTED • 250 kW

0 1 2 3 4 5 6 7 8 9 10 11 12 13 14 15 16 17 18 19 20 21 22 23 24

ENGLISH ▬   ARABIC ⌇⌇⌇   CHINESE ▫▫▫   FRENCH ═══   GERMAN ▬▬   RUSSIAN ══   SPANISH ▬▬   OTHER ▬

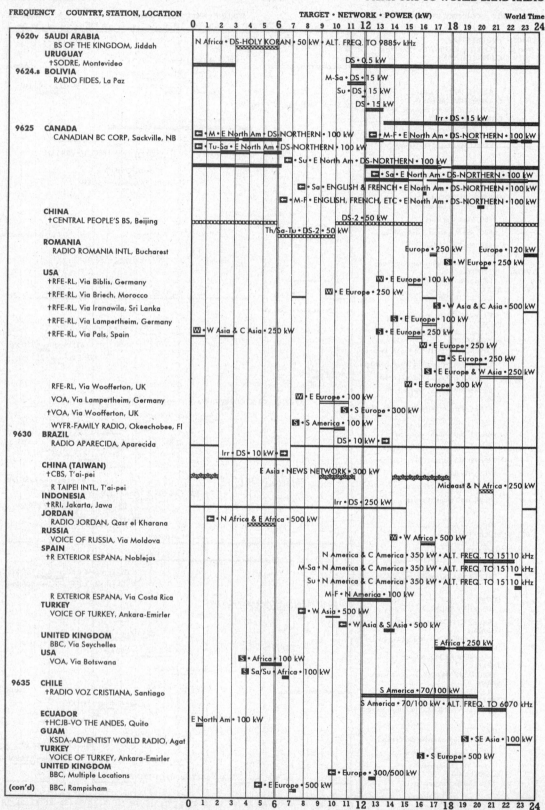

FREQUENCY   COUNTRY, STATION, LOCATION

TARGET • NETWORK • POWER (kW)   World Time

Frequency	Country, Station, Location	Details
9620v	SAUDI ARABIA	
	BS OF THE KINGDOM, Jiddah	N Africa • DS-HOLY KORAN • 50 kW • ALT. FREQ. TO 9885v kHz
	URUGUAY	
	†SODRE, Montevideo	DS • 0.5 kW
9624.8	BOLIVIA	
	RADIO FIDES, La Paz	M-Sa • DS • 15 kW
		Su • DS • 15 kW
		DS • 15 kW
		Irr • DS • 15 kW
9625	CANADA	
	CANADIAN BC CORP, Sackville, NB	M-F • E North Am • DS-NORTHERN • 100 kW / M-F • E North Am • DS-NORTHERN • 100 kW
		Tu-Sa • E North Am • DS-NORTHERN • 100 kW
		Su • E North Am • DS-NORTHERN • 100 kW
		Sa • E North Am • DS-NORTHERN • 100 kW
		Sa • ENGLISH & FRENCH • E North Am • DS-NORTHERN • 100 kW
		M-F • ENGLISH, FRENCH, ETC • E North Am • DS-NORTHERN • 100 kW
	CHINA	
	†CENTRAL PEOPLE'S BS, Beijing	DS-2 • 50 kW
		Th/Sa-Tu • DS-2 • 50 kW
	ROMANIA	
	RADIO ROMANIA INTL, Bucharest	Europe • 250 kW Europe • 120 kW
		S • W Europe • 250 kW
	USA	
	†RFE-RL, Via Biblis, Germany	W • E Europe • 100 kW
	†RFE-RL, Via Briech, Morocco	W • E Europe • 250 kW
	†RFE-RL, Via Iranawila, Sri Lanka	W • W Asia & C Asia • 500 kW
	†RFE-RL, Via Lampertheim, Germany	S • E Europe • 100 kW
	†RFE-RL, Via Pals, Spain	W • W Asia & C Asia • 250 kW / S • E Europe • 250 kW
		W • E Europe • 250 kW
		S • S Europe • 250 kW
		S • E Europe & W Asia • 250 kW
		W • E Europe • 300 kW
	RFE-RL, Via Woofferton, UK	
	VOA, Via Lampertheim, Germany	W • E Europe • 100 kW
	†VOA, Via Woofferton, UK	S • S Europe • 300 kW
	WYFR-FAMILY RADIO, Okeechobee, Fl	S • S America • 100 kW
9630	BRAZIL	
	RADIO APARECIDA, Aparecida	DS • 10 kW
		Irr • DS • 10 kW
	CHINA (TAIWAN)	
	†CBS, T'ai-pei	E Asia • NEWS NETWORK • 300 kW
	R TAIPEI INTL, T'ai-pei	Mideast & N Africa • 250 kW
	INDONESIA	
	†RRI, Jakarta, Jawa	Irr • DS • 250 kW
	JORDAN	
	RADIO JORDAN, Qasr el Kharana	N Africa & E Africa • 500 kW
	RUSSIA	
	VOICE OF RUSSIA, Via Moldova	W • W Africa • 500 kW
	SPAIN	
	†R EXTERIOR ESPANA, Noblejas	N America & C America • 350 kW • ALT. FREQ. TO 15110 kHz
		M-Sa • N America & C America • 350 kW • ALT. FREQ. TO 15110 kHz
		Su • N America & C America • 350 kW • ALT. FREQ. TO 15110 kHz
	R EXTERIOR ESPANA, Via Costa Rica	M-F • N America • 100 kW
	TURKEY	
	VOICE OF TURKEY, Ankara-Emirler	W Asia • 500 kW
		W Asia & S Asia • 500 kW
	UNITED KINGDOM	
	BBC, Via Seychelles	E Africa • 250 kW
	USA	
	VOA, Via Botswana	S • Africa • 100 kW
		S • Sa/Su • Africa • 100 kW
9635	CHILE	
	†RADIO VOZ CRISTIANA, Santiago	S America • 70/100 kW
		S America • 70/100 kW • ALT. FREQ. TO 6070 kHz
	ECUADOR	
	†HCJB-VO THE ANDES, Quito	E North Am • 100 kW
	GUAM	
	KSDA-ADVENTIST WORLD RADIO, Agat	S • SE Asia • 100 kW
	TURKEY	
	VOICE OF TURKEY, Ankara-Emirler	S • S Europe • 500 kW
	UNITED KINGDOM	
	BBC, Multiple Locations	Europe • 300/500 kW
(con'd)	BBC, Rampisham	E Europe • 500 kW

FREQUENCY   COUNTRY, STATION, LOCATION   TARGET • NETWORK • POWER (kW)   World Time

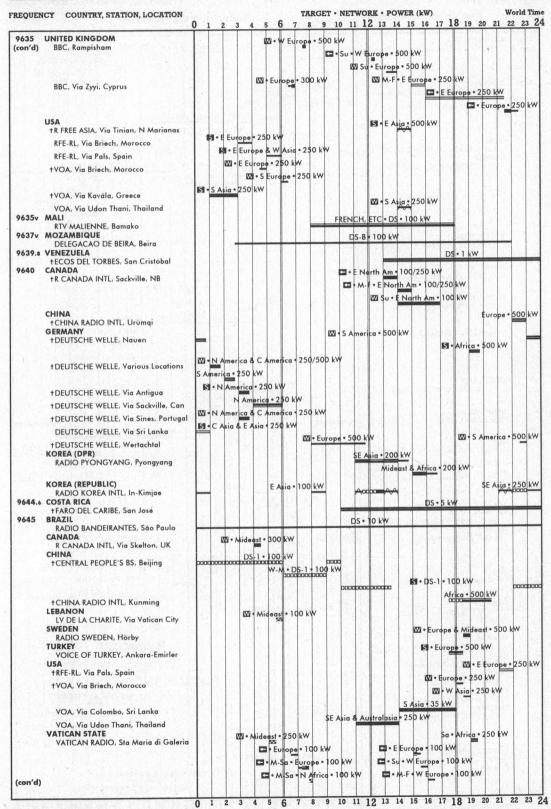

Frequency	Country, Station, Location	Target • Network • Power
9635 (con'd)	UNITED KINGDOM — BBC, Rampisham	W • W Europe • 500 kW; Su • W Europe • 500 kW; Su • Europe • 500 kW; W • Europe • 300 kW; M-F • E Europe • 250 kW
	BBC, Via Zyyi, Cyprus	E Europe • 250 kW; Europe • 250 kW
	USA	
	†R FREE ASIA, Via Tinian, N Marianas	E Asia • 500 kW
	RFE-RL, Via Briech, Morocco	E Europe • 250 kW
	RFE-RL, Via Pals, Spain	E Europe & W Asia • 250 kW
	†VOA, Via Briech, Morocco	E Europe • 250 kW; S Europe • 250 kW
	†VOA, Via Kavála, Greece	S Asia • 250 kW
	VOA, Via Udon Thani, Thailand	S Asia • 250 kW
9635v	MALI — RTV MALIENNE, Bamako	FRENCH, ETC • DS • 100 kW
9637v	MOZAMBIQUE — DELEGACAO DE BEIRA, Beira	DS-B • 100 kW
9639.8	VENEZUELA — †ECOS DEL TORBES, San Cristóbal	DS • 1 kW
9640	CANADA — †R CANADA INTL, Sackville, NB	E North Am • 100/250 kW; M-F • E North Am • 100/250 kW; Su • E North Am • 100 kW
	CHINA — †CHINA RADIO INTL, Urümqi	Europe • 500 kW
	GERMANY — †DEUTSCHE WELLE, Nauen	S America • 500 kW; Africa • 500 kW
	†DEUTSCHE WELLE, Various Locations	N America & C America • 250/500 kW; S America • 250 kW
	†DEUTSCHE WELLE, Via Antigua	N America • 250 kW; N America • 250 kW
	†DEUTSCHE WELLE, Via Sackville, Can	N America & C America • 250 kW
	†DEUTSCHE WELLE, Via Sines, Portugal	C Asia & E Asia • 250 kW
	DEUTSCHE WELLE, Via Sri Lanka	Europe • 500 kW; S America • 500 kW
	†DEUTSCHE WELLE, Wertachtal	
	KOREA (DPR) — RADIO PYONGYANG, Pyongyang	SE Asia • 200 kW; Mideast & Africa • 200 kW
	KOREA (REPUBLIC) — RADIO KOREA INTL, In-Kimjae	E Asia • 100 kW; SE Asia • 250 kW
9644.6	COSTA RICA — †FARO DEL CARIBE, San José	DS • 5 kW
9645	BRAZIL — RADIO BANDEIRANTES, São Paulo	DS • 10 kW
	CANADA — R CANADA INTL, Via Skelton, UK	Mideast • 300 kW
	CHINA — †CENTRAL PEOPLE'S BS, Beijing	DS-1 • 100 kW; W-M • DS-1 • 100 kW; DS-1 • 100 kW; Africa • 500 kW
	†CHINA RADIO INTL, Kunming	
	LEBANON — LV DE LA CHARITE, Via Vatican City	Mideast • 100 kW
	SWEDEN — RADIO SWEDEN, Hörby	Europe & Mideast • 500 kW
	TURKEY — VOICE OF TURKEY, Ankara-Emirler	Europe • 500 kW
	USA	
	†RFE-RL, Via Pals, Spain	E Europe • 250 kW
	†VOA, Via Briech, Morocco	Europe • 250 kW; W Asia • 250 kW
	VOA, Via Colombo, Sri Lanka	S Asia • 35 kW
	VOA, Via Udon Thani, Thailand	SE Asia & Australasia • 250 kW
	VATICAN STATE — VATICAN RADIO, Sta Maria di Galeria	Mideast • 250 kW; Africa • 250 kW; Europe • 100 kW; E Europe • 100 kW; M-Sa • Europe • 100 kW; Su • W Europe • 100 kW; M-Sa • N Africa • 100 kW; M-F • W Europe • 100 kW
(con'd)		

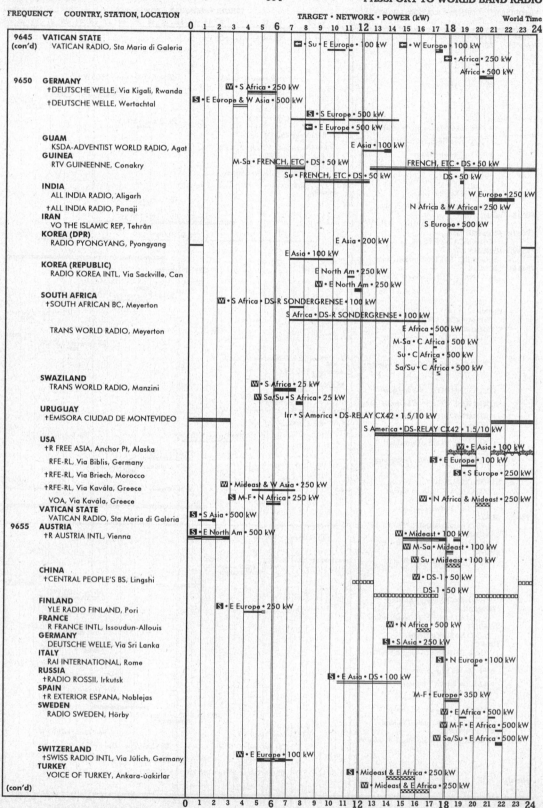

FREQUENCY   COUNTRY, STATION, LOCATION   TARGET • NETWORK • POWER (kW)   World Time

9645 **VATICAN STATE**
(con'd) VATICAN RADIO, Sta Maria di Galeria — Su • E Europe • 100 kW — W Europe • 100 kW; Africa • 250 kW; Africa • 500 kW

9650 **GERMANY**
†DEUTSCHE WELLE, Via Kigali, Rwanda — W • S Africa • 250 kW
†DEUTSCHE WELLE, Wertachtal — S • E Europe & W Asia • 500 kW; S • S Europe • 500 kW; E Europe • 500 kW

GUAM
KSDA-ADVENTIST WORLD RADIO, Agat — E Asia • 100 kW
GUINEA
RTV GUINEENNE, Conakry — M-Sa • FRENCH, ETC • DS • 50 kW; FRENCH, ETC • DS • 50 kW; Su • FRENCH, ETC • DS • 50 kW; DS • 50 kW

INDIA
ALL INDIA RADIO, Aligarh — W Europe • 250 kW
†ALL INDIA RADIO, Panaji — N Africa & W Africa • 250 kW
IRAN
VO THE ISLAMIC REP, Tehrān — S Europe • 500 kW
KOREA (DPR)
RADIO PYONGYANG, Pyongyang — E Asia • 200 kW; E Asia • 100 kW

KOREA (REPUBLIC)
RADIO KOREA INTL, Via Sackville, Can — E North Am • 250 kW; W • E North Am • 250 kW

SOUTH AFRICA
†SOUTH AFRICAN BC, Meyerton — W • S Africa • DS-R SONDERGRENSE • 100 kW; S Africa • DS-R SONDERGRENSE • 100 kW

TRANS WORLD RADIO, Meyerton — E Africa • 500 kW; M-Sa • C Africa • 500 kW; Su • C Africa • 500 kW; Sa/Su • C Africa • 500 kW

SWAZILAND
TRANS WORLD RADIO, Manzini — W • S Africa • 25 kW; W Sa/Su • S Africa • 25 kW

URUGUAY
†EMISORA CIUDAD DE MONTEVIDEO — Irr • S America • DS-RELAY CX42 • 1.5/10 kW; S America • DS-RELAY CX42 • 1.5/10 kW

USA
†R FREE ASIA, Anchor Pt, Alaska — W • E Asia • 100 kW
RFE-RL, Via Biblis, Germany — S • E Europe • 100 kW
†RFE-RL, Via Briech, Morocco — S • S Europe • 250 kW
†RFE-RL, Via Kavála, Greece — W • Mideast & W Asia • 250 kW
VOA, Via Kavála, Greece — S M-F • N Africa • 250 kW; W • N Africa & Mideast • 250 kW
VATICAN STATE
VATICAN RADIO, Sta Maria di Galeria — S • S Asia • 500 kW
9655 **AUSTRIA**
†R AUSTRIA INTL, Vienna — S • E North Am • 500 kW; W • Mideast • 100 kW; W M-Sa • Mideast • 100 kW; W Su • Mideast • 100 kW

CHINA
†CENTRAL PEOPLE'S BS, Lingshi — W • DS-1 • 50 kW; DS-1 • 50 kW

FINLAND
YLE RADIO FINLAND, Pori — S • E Europe • 250 kW
FRANCE
R FRANCE INTL, Issoudun-Allouis — W • N Africa • 500 kW
GERMANY
DEUTSCHE WELLE, Via Sri Lanka — S • S Asia • 250 kW
ITALY
RAI INTERNATIONAL, Rome — S • N Europe • 100 kW
RUSSIA
†RADIO ROSSII, Irkutsk — S • E Asia • DS • 100 kW
SPAIN
†R EXTERIOR ESPANA, Noblejas — M-F • Europe • 350 kW
SWEDEN
RADIO SWEDEN, Hörby — W • E Africa • 500 kW; W M-F • E Africa • 500 kW; W Sa/Su • E Africa • 500 kW

SWITZERLAND
†SWISS RADIO INTL, Via Jülich, Germany — W • E Europe • 100 kW
TURKEY
VOICE OF TURKEY, Ankara-úakirlar — S • Mideast & E Africa • 250 kW; W • Mideast & E Africa • 250 kW

(con'd)

World Time scale: 0 1 2 3 4 5 6 7 8 9 10 11 12 13 14 15 16 17 18 19 20 21 22 23 24

SEASONAL S OR W   1-HR TIMESHIFT MIDYEAR ⊡ OR ⊐   JAMMING / OR ∧   EARLIEST HEARD ◁   LATEST HEARD ▷   NEW FOR 2000 †

FREQUENCY   COUNTRY, STATION, LOCATION

TARGET • NETWORK • POWER (kW)   World Time

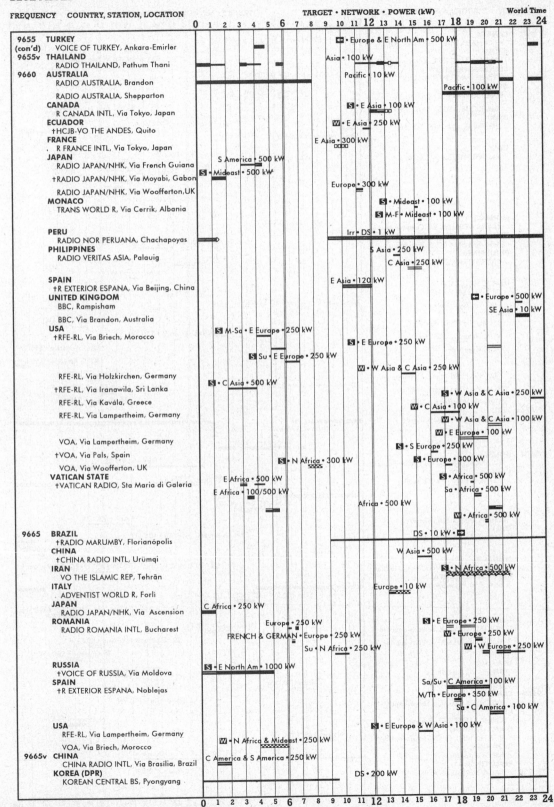

Freq	Country / Station / Location	Schedule
9655 (con'd)	**TURKEY** VOICE OF TURKEY, Ankara-Emirler	Europe & E North Am • 500 kW
9655v	**THAILAND** RADIO THAILAND, Pathum Thani	Asia • 100 kW
9660	**AUSTRALIA** RADIO AUSTRALIA, Brandon	Pacific • 10 kW
	RADIO AUSTRALIA, Shepparton	Pacific • 100 kW
	CANADA R CANADA INTL, Via Tokyo, Japan	S • E Asia • 100 kW
	ECUADOR †HCJB-VO THE ANDES, Quito	W • E Asia • 250 kW
	FRANCE R FRANCE INTL, Via Tokyo, Japan	E Asia • 300 kW
	JAPAN RADIO JAPAN/NHK, Via French Guiana	S America • 500 kW
	†RADIO JAPAN/NHK, Via Moyabi, Gabon	S • Mideast • 500 kW
	RADIO JAPAN/NHK, Via Woofferton, UK	Europe • 300 kW
	MONACO TRANS WORLD R, Via Cerrik, Albania	S • Mideast • 100 kW / S • M-F • Mideast • 100 kW
	PERU RADIO NOR PERUANA, Chachapoyas	Irr • DS • 1 kW
	PHILIPPINES RADIO VERITAS ASIA, Palauig	S Asia • 250 kW / C Asia • 250 kW
	SPAIN †R EXTERIOR ESPANA, Via Beijing, China	E Asia • 120 kW
	UNITED KINGDOM BBC, Rampisham	Europe • 500 kW
	BBC, Via Brandon, Australia	SE Asia • 10 kW
	USA †RFE-RL, Via Briech, Morocco	S • M-Sa • E Europe • 250 kW / S • E Europe • 250 kW / S • Su • E Europe • 250 kW / W • W Asia & C Asia • 250 kW
	RFE-RL, Via Holzkirchen, Germany	S • C Asia • 500 kW
	†RFE-RL, Via Iranawila, Sri Lanka	S • W Asia & C Asia • 250 kW
	RFE-RL, Via Kavála, Greece	W • C Asia • 100 kW
	RFE-RL, Via Lampertheim, Germany	W • W Asia & C Asia • 100 kW / W • E Europe • 100 kW
	VOA, Via Lampertheim, Germany	S • S Europe • 250 kW
	†VOA, Via Pals, Spain	S • Europe • 300 kW
	VOA, Via Woofferton, UK	S • N Africa • 300 kW
	VATICAN STATE †VATICAN RADIO, Sta Maria di Galeria	E Africa • 500 kW / E Africa • 100/500 kW / S • Africa • 500 kW / Sa • Africa • 500 kW / Africa • 500 kW / W • Africa • 500 kW
9665	**BRAZIL** †RADIO MARUMBY, Florianópolis	DS • 10 kW •
	CHINA †CHINA RADIO INTL, Urümqi	W Asia • 500 kW
	IRAN VO THE ISLAMIC REP, Tehrãn	S • N Africa • 500 kW
	ITALY ADVENTIST WORLD R, Forli	Europe • 10 kW
	JAPAN RADIO JAPAN/NHK, Via Ascension	C Africa • 250 kW
	ROMANIA RADIO ROMANIA INTL, Bucharest	Europe • 250 kW / S • E Europe • 250 kW / FRENCH & GERMAN • Europe • 250 kW / W • Europe • 250 kW / Su • N Africa • 250 kW / W • W Europe • 250 kW
	RUSSIA †VOICE OF RUSSIA, Via Moldova	S • E North Am • 1000 kW
	SPAIN †R EXTERIOR ESPANA, Noblejas	Sa/Su • C America • 100 kW / M/Th • Europe • 350 kW / Sa • C America • 100 kW
	USA RFE-RL, Via Lampertheim, Germany	S • E Europe & W Asia • 100 kW
	VOA, Via Briech, Morocco	W • N Africa & Mideast • 250 kW
9665v	**CHINA** CHINA RADIO INTL, Via Brasilia, Brazil	C America & S America • 250 kW
	KOREA (DPR) KOREAN CENTRAL BS, Pyongyang	DS • 200 kW

ENGLISH ▬▬   ARABIC ≈≈≈   CHINESE ▫▫▫   FRENCH ▬▬   GERMAN ▬▬   RUSSIAN ══   SPANISH ▬▬   OTHER ▬▬

FREQUENCY   COUNTRY, STATION, LOCATION   TARGET • NETWORK • POWER (kW)   World Time

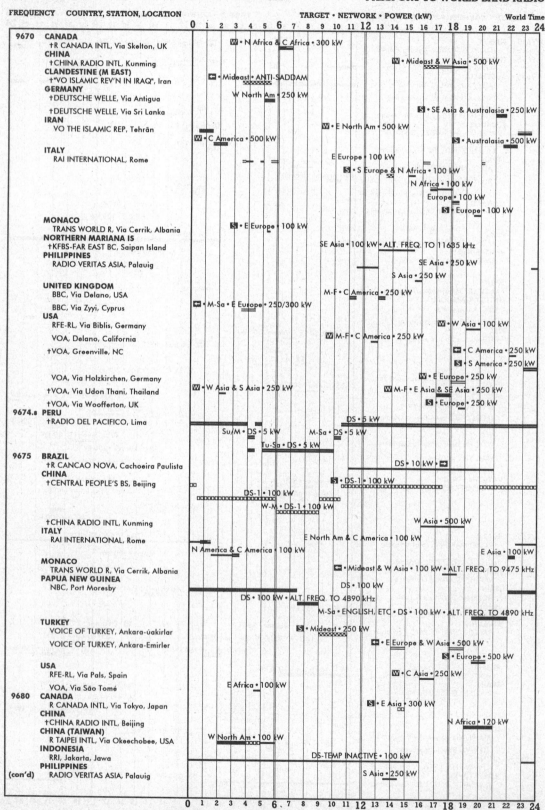

Frequency	Country, Station, Location	Target • Network • Power
9670	**CANADA**	
	†R CANADA INTL, Via Skelton, UK	W • N Africa & C Africa • 300 kW
	CHINA	
	†CHINA RADIO INTL, Kunming	W • Mideast & W Asia • 500 kW
	CLANDESTINE (M EAST)	
	†"VO ISLAMIC REV'N IN IRAQ", Iran	Mideast • ANTI-SADDAM
	GERMANY	
	†DEUTSCHE WELLE, Via Antigua	W North Am • 250 kW
	†DEUTSCHE WELLE, Via Sri Lanka	S • SE Asia & Australasia • 250 kW
	IRAN	
	VO THE ISLAMIC REP, Tehrān	W • E North Am • 500 kW
		W • C America • 500 kW
		S • Australasia • 500 kW
	ITALY	
	RAI INTERNATIONAL, Rome	E Europe • 100 kW
		S • S Europe & N Africa • 100 kW
		N Africa • 100 kW
		Europe • 100 kW
		S • Europe • 100 kW
	MONACO	
	TRANS WORLD R, Via Cerrik, Albania	S • E Europe • 100 kW
	NORTHERN MARIANA IS	
	†KFBS-FAR EAST BC, Saipan Island	SE Asia • 100 kW • ALT. FREQ. TO 11635 kHz
	PHILIPPINES	
	RADIO VERITAS ASIA, Palauig	SE Asia • 250 kW
		S Asia • 250 kW
	UNITED KINGDOM	
	BBC, Via Delano, USA	M-F • C America • 250 kW
	BBC, Via Zyyi, Cyprus	M-Sa • E Europe • 250/300 kW
	USA	
	RFE-RL, Via Biblis, Germany	W • W Asia • 100 kW
	VOA, Delano, California	W M-F • C America • 250 kW
	†VOA, Greenville, NC	C America • 250 kW
		S • S America • 250 kW
	VOA, Via Holzkirchen, Germany	W • E Europe • 250 kW
	†VOA, Via Udon Thani, Thailand	W • W Asia & S Asia • 250 kW
		W M-F • E Asia & SE Asia • 250 kW
	†VOA, Via Woofferton, UK	S • Europe • 250 kW
9674.8	**PERU**	
	†RADIO DEL PACIFICO, Lima	DS • 5 kW
		Su/M • DS • 5 kW M-Sa • DS • 5 kW
		Tu-Sa • DS • 5 kW
9675	**BRAZIL**	
	†R CANCAO NOVA, Cachoeira Paulista	DS • 10 kW
	CHINA	
	†CENTRAL PEOPLE'S BS, Beijing	S • DS-1 • 100 kW
		DS-1 • 100 kW
		W-M • DS-1 • 100 kW
	†CHINA RADIO INTL, Kunming	W Asia • 500 kW
	ITALY	
	RAI INTERNATIONAL, Rome	E North Am & C America • 100 kW
		N America & C America • 100 kW
		E Asia • 100 kW
	MONACO	
	TRANS WORLD R, Via Cerrik, Albania	Mideast & W Asia • 100 kW • ALT. FREQ. TO 9475 kHz
	PAPUA NEW GUINEA	
	NBC, Port Moresby	DS • 100 kW
		DS • 100 kW • ALT. FREQ. TO 4890 kHz
		M-Sa • ENGLISH, ETC • DS • 100 kW • ALT. FREQ. TO 4890 kHz
	TURKEY	
	VOICE OF TURKEY, Ankara-úakirlar	S • Mideast • 250 kW
	VOICE OF TURKEY, Ankara-Emirler	E Europe & W Asia • 500 kW
		S • Europe • 500 kW
	USA	
	RFE-RL, Via Pals, Spain	W • C Asia • 250 kW
	VOA, Via São Tomé	E Africa • 100 kW
9680	**CANADA**	
	R CANADA INTL, Via Tokyo, Japan	S • E Asia • 300 kW
	CHINA	
	†CHINA RADIO INTL, Beijing	N Africa • 120 kW
	CHINA (TAIWAN)	
	R TAIPEI INTL, Via Okeechobee, USA	W North Am • 100 kW
	INDONESIA	
	RRI, Jakarta, Jawa	DS-TEMP INACTIVE • 100 kW
	PHILIPPINES	
(con'd)	RADIO VERITAS ASIA, Palauig	S Asia • 250 kW

FREQUENCY   COUNTRY, STATION, LOCATION

TARGET • NETWORK • POWER (kW)   World Time

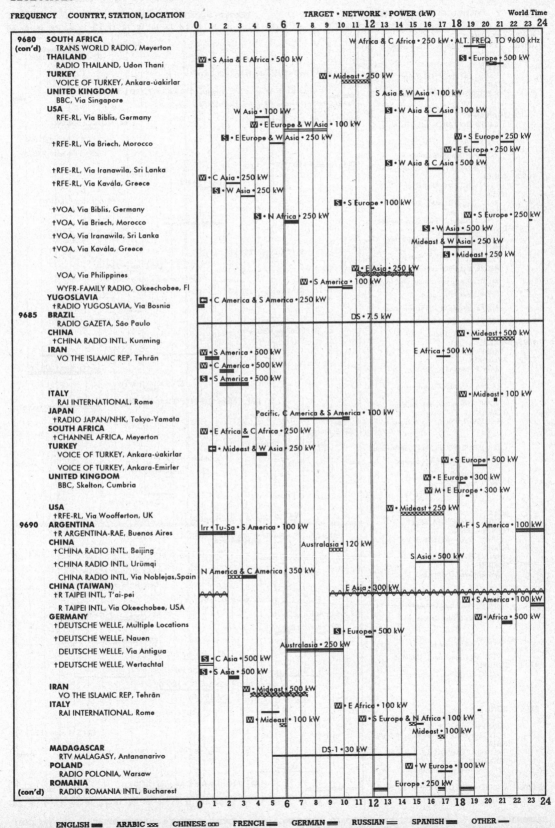

9680 (con'd) SOUTH AFRICA
  TRANS WORLD RADIO, Meyerton — W Africa & C Africa • 250 kW • ALT. FREQ. TO 9600 kHz
THAILAND
  RADIO THAILAND, Udon Thani — W • S Asia & E Africa • 500 kW / S • Europe • 500 kW
TURKEY
  VOICE OF TURKEY, Ankara-úakirlar — W • Mideast • 250 kW
UNITED KINGDOM
  BBC, Via Singapore — S Asia & W Asia • 100 kW
USA
  RFE-RL, Via Biblis, Germany — S • W Asia & C Asia • 100 kW / W • E Europe & W Asia • 100 kW
  †RFE-RL, Via Briech, Morocco — S • E Europe & W Asia • 250 kW / W • S Europe • 250 kW / W • E Europe • 250 kW
  †RFE-RL, Via Iranawila, Sri Lanka — S • W Asia & C Asia • 500 kW
  †RFE-RL, Via Kávála, Greece — W • C Asia • 250 kW / S • W Asia • 250 kW
  †VOA, Via Biblis, Germany — S • S Europe • 100 kW
  †VOA, Via Briech, Morocco — S • N Africa • 250 kW / W • S Europe • 250 kW
  †VOA, Via Iranawila, Sri Lanka — S • W Asia • 500 kW
  †VOA, Via Kávála, Greece — Mideast & W Asia • 250 kW / S • Mideast • 250 kW
  VOA, Via Philippines — W • E Asia • 250 kW
  WYFR-FAMILY RADIO, Okeechobee, Fl — W • S America • 100 kW
YUGOSLAVIA
  †RADIO YUGOSLAVIA, Via Bosnia — C America & S America • 250 kW
9685 BRAZIL
  RADIO GAZETA, São Paulo — DS • 7.5 kW
CHINA
  †CHINA RADIO INTL, Kunming — W • Mideast • 500 kW
IRAN
  VO THE ISLAMIC REP, Tehrān — W • S America • 500 kW / W • C America • 500 kW / S • S America • 500 kW / E Africa • 500 kW
ITALY
  RAI INTERNATIONAL, Rome — W • Mideast • 100 kW
JAPAN
  †RADIO JAPAN/NHK, Tokyo-Yamata — Pacific, C America & S America • 100 kW
SOUTH AFRICA
  †CHANNEL AFRICA, Meyerton — W • E Africa & C Africa • 250 kW
TURKEY
  VOICE OF TURKEY, Ankara-úakirlar — Mideast & W Asia • 250 kW
  VOICE OF TURKEY, Ankara-Emirler — W • S Europe • 500 kW
UNITED KINGDOM
  BBC, Skelton, Cumbria — W • E Europe • 300 kW / W • M • E Europe • 300 kW
USA
  †RFE-RL, Via Woofferton, UK — W • Mideast • 250 kW
9690 ARGENTINA
  †R ARGENTINA-RAE, Buenos Aires — Irr • Tu-Sa • S America • 100 kW / M-F • S America • 100 kW
CHINA
  †CHINA RADIO INTL, Beijing — Australasia • 120 kW
  †CHINA RADIO INTL, Urümqi — S Asia • 500 kW
  CHINA RADIO INTL, Via Noblejas, Spain — N America & C America • 350 kW
CHINA (TAIWAN)
  †R TAIPEI INTL, T'ai-pei — E Asia • 300 kW
  R TAIPEI INTL, Via Okeechobee, USA — W • S America • 100 kW
GERMANY
  †DEUTSCHE WELLE, Multiple Locations — W • Africa • 500 kW
  †DEUTSCHE WELLE, Nauen — S • Europe • 500 kW
  DEUTSCHE WELLE, Via Antigua — Australasia • 250 kW
  †DEUTSCHE WELLE, Wertachtal — S • C Asia • 500 kW / S • S Asia • 500 kW
IRAN
  VO THE ISLAMIC REP, Tehrān — W • Mideast • 500 kW
ITALY
  RAI INTERNATIONAL, Rome — W • E Africa • 100 kW / W • Mideast • 100 kW / W • S Europe & N Africa • 100 kW / Mideast • 100 kW
MADAGASCAR
  RTV MALAGASY, Antananarivo — DS-1 • 30 kW
POLAND
  RADIO POLONIA, Warsaw — W • W Europe • 100 kW
ROMANIA
(con'd) RADIO ROMANIA INTL, Bucharest — Europe • 250 kW

ENGLISH ▬   ARABIC ▨   CHINESE ▫▫▫   FRENCH ══   GERMAN ▬   RUSSIAN ═   SPANISH ▬   OTHER ━

FREQUENCY   COUNTRY, STATION, LOCATION   TARGET • NETWORK • POWER (kW)   World Time

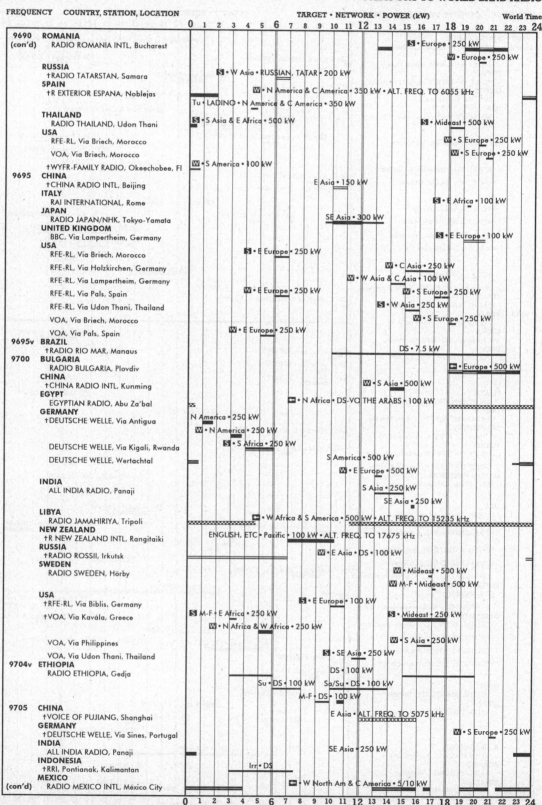

Frequency	Country, Station, Location	Details
9690 (con'd)	ROMANIA — RADIO ROMANIA INTL, Bucharest	S • Europe • 250 kW / W • Europe • 250 kW
	RUSSIA — †RADIO TATARSTAN, Samara	S • W Asia • RUSSIAN, TATAR • 200 kW
	SPAIN — †R EXTERIOR ESPANA, Noblejas	W • N America & C America • 350 kW • ALT. FREQ. TO 6055 kHz
		Tu • LADINO • N America & C America • 350 kW
	THAILAND — RADIO THAILAND, Udon Thani	S • S Asia & E Africa • 500 kW / S • Mideast • 500 kW
	USA — RFE-RL, Via Briech, Morocco	W • S Europe • 250 kW
	VOA, Via Briech, Morocco	W • S Europe • 250 kW
	†WYFR-FAMILY RADIO, Okeechobee, Fl	W • S America • 100 kW
9695	CHINA — †CHINA RADIO INTL, Beijing	E Asia • 150 kW
	ITALY — RAI INTERNATIONAL, Rome	S • E Africa • 100 kW
	JAPAN — RADIO JAPAN/NHK, Tokyo-Yamata	SE Asia • 300 kW
	UNITED KINGDOM — BBC, Via Lampertheim, Germany	S • E Europe • 100 kW
	USA — RFE-RL, Via Briech, Morocco	S • E Europe • 250 kW
	RFE-RL, Via Holzkirchen, Germany	W • C Asia • 250 kW
	RFE-RL, Via Lampertheim, Germany	W • W Asia & C Asia • 100 kW
	RFE-RL, Via Pals, Spain	W • E Europe • 250 kW / W • S Europe • 250 kW
	RFE-RL, Via Udon Thani, Thailand	S • W Asia • 250 kW
	VOA, Via Briech, Morocco	W • S Europe • 250 kW
	VOA, Via Pals, Spain	W • E Europe • 250 kW
9695v	BRAZIL — †RADIO RIO MAR, Manaus	DS • 7.5 kW
9700	BULGARIA — RADIO BULGARIA, Plovdiv	Europe • 500 kW
	CHINA — †CHINA RADIO INTL, Kunming	W • S Asia • 500 kW
	EGYPT — EGYPTIAN RADIO, Abu Za'bal	N Africa • DS-VO THE ARABS • 100 kW
	GERMANY — †DEUTSCHE WELLE, Via Antigua	N America • 250 kW
		W • N America • 250 kW
		S • S Africa • 250 kW
	DEUTSCHE WELLE, Via Kigali, Rwanda	S America • 500 kW
	DEUTSCHE WELLE, Wertachtal	W • E Europe • 500 kW
	INDIA — ALL INDIA RADIO, Panaji	S Asia • 250 kW
		SE Asia • 250 kW
	LIBYA — RADIO JAMAHIRIYA, Tripoli	W Africa & S America • 500 kW • ALT. FREQ. TO 15235 kHz
	NEW ZEALAND — †R NEW ZEALAND INTL, Rangitaiki	ENGLISH, ETC • Pacific • 100 kW • ALT. FREQ. TO 17675 kHz
	RUSSIA — †RADIO ROSSII, Irkutsk	W • E Asia • DS • 100 kW
	SWEDEN — RADIO SWEDEN, Hörby	W • Mideast • 500 kW / W M-F • Mideast • 500 kW
	USA — †RFE-RL, Via Biblis, Germany	S • E Europe • 100 kW
	†VOA, Via Kavála, Greece	S M-F • E Africa • 250 kW / S • Mideast • 250 kW
		W • N Africa & W Africa • 250 kW
	VOA, Via Philippines	W • S Asia • 250 kW
	VOA, Via Udon Thani, Thailand	S • SE Asia • 250 kW
9704v	ETHIOPIA — RADIO ETHIOPIA, Gedja	DS • 100 kW
		Su • DS • 100 kW / Sa/Su • DS • 100 kW
		M-F • DS • 100 kW
9705	CHINA — †VOICE OF PUJIANG, Shanghai	E Asia • ALT. FREQ. TO 5075 kHz
	GERMANY — †DEUTSCHE WELLE, Via Sines, Portugal	W • S Europe • 250 kW
	INDIA — ALL INDIA RADIO, Panaji	SE Asia • 250 kW
	INDONESIA — †RRI, Pontianak, Kalimantan	Irr • DS
(con'd)	MEXICO — RADIO MEXICO INTL, México City	W North Am & C America • 5/10 kW

SEASONAL S OR W   1-HR TIMESHIFT MIDYEAR ⊏▪ OR ▪⊐   JAMMING / OR ∧   EARLIEST HEARD ◁   LATEST HEARD ▷   NEW FOR 2000 †

FREQUENCY COUNTRY, STATION, LOCATION TARGET • NETWORK • POWER (kW) World Time

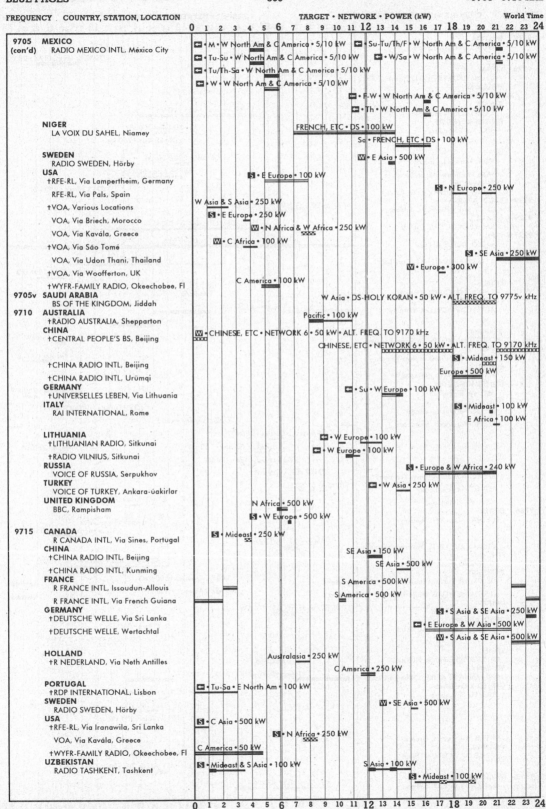

	0 1 2 3 4 5 6 7 8 9 10 11 12 13 14 15 16 17 18 19 20 21 22 23 24
9705 (con'd) **MEXICO** RADIO MEXICO INTL, México City	◨ • M • W North Am & C America • 5/10 kW ◨ • Su-Tu/Th/F • W North Am & C America • 5/10 kW
	◨ • Tu-Su • W North Am & C America • 5/10 kW ◨ • W/Sa • W North Am & C America • 5/10 kW
	◨ • Tu/Th-Sa • W North Am & C America • 5/10 kW
	◨ • W • W North Am & C America • 5/10 kW
	◨ • F-W • W North Am & C America • 5/10 kW
	◨ • Th • W North Am & C America • 5/10 kW
NIGER LA VOIX DU SAHEL, Niamey	FRENCH, ETC • DS • 100 kW
	Sa • FRENCH, ETC • DS • 100 kW
SWEDEN RADIO SWEDEN, Hörby	W • E Asia • 500 kW
USA †RFE-RL, Via Lampertheim, Germany	S • E Europe • 100 kW
RFE-RL, Via Pals, Spain	N • N Europe • 250 kW
†VOA, Various Locations	W Asia & S Asia • 250 kW
VOA, Via Briech, Morocco	S • E Europe • 250 kW
VOA, Via Kavála, Greece	W • N Africa & W Africa • 250 kW
†VOA, Via São Tomé	W • C Africa • 100 kW
VOA, Via Udon Thani, Thailand	S • SE Asia • 250 kW
†VOA, Via Woofferton, UK	W • Europe • 300 kW
†WYFR-FAMILY RADIO, Okeechobee, Fl	C America • 100 kW
9705v SAUDI ARABIA BS OF THE KINGDOM, Jiddah	W Asia • DS-HOLY KORAN • 50 kW • ALT. FREQ. TO 9775v kHz
9710 AUSTRALIA †RADIO AUSTRALIA, Shepparton	Pacific • 100 kW
CHINA †CENTRAL PEOPLE'S BS, Beijing	W • CHINESE, ETC • NETWORK 6 • 50 kW • ALT. FREQ. TO 9170 kHz
	CHINESE, ETC • NETWORK 6 • 50 kW • ALT. FREQ. TO 9170 kHz
†CHINA RADIO INTL, Beijing	S • Mideast • 150 kW
†CHINA RADIO INTL, Urümqi	Europe • 500 kW
GERMANY †UNIVERSELLES LEBEN, Via Lithuania	◨ • Su • W Europe • 100 kW
ITALY RAI INTERNATIONAL, Rome	S • Mideast • 100 kW
	E Africa • 100 kW
LITHUANIA †LITHUANIAN RADIO, Sitkunai	◨ • W Europe • 100 kW
†RADIO VILNIUS, Sitkunai	◨ • W Europe • 100 kW
RUSSIA VOICE OF RUSSIA, Serpukhov	S • Europe & W Africa • 240 kW
TURKEY VOICE OF TURKEY, Ankara-úakirlar	◨ • W Asia • 250 kW
UNITED KINGDOM BBC, Rampisham	N Africa • 500 kW
	S • W Europe • 500 kW
9715 CANADA R CANADA INTL, Via Sines, Portugal	S • Mideast • 250 kW
CHINA †CHINA RADIO INTL, Beijing	SE Asia • 150 kW
†CHINA RADIO INTL, Kunming	SE Asia • 500 kW
FRANCE R FRANCE INTL, Issoudun-Allouis	S America • 500 kW
R FRANCE INTL, Via French Guiana	S America • 500 kW
GERMANY †DEUTSCHE WELLE, Via Sri Lanka	S • S Asia & SE Asia • 250 kW
†DEUTSCHE WELLE, Wertachtal	◨ • E Europe & W Asia • 500 kW
	W • S Asia & SE Asia • 500 kW
HOLLAND †R NEDERLAND, Via Neth Antilles	Australasia • 250 kW
	C America • 250 kW
PORTUGAL †RDP INTERNATIONAL, Lisbon	◨ • Tu-Sa • E North Am • 100 kW
SWEDEN RADIO SWEDEN, Hörby	W • SE Asia • 500 kW
USA †RFE-RL, Via Iranawila, Sri Lanka	S • C Asia • 500 kW
VOA, Via Kavála, Greece	S • N Africa • 250 kW
†WYFR-FAMILY RADIO, Okeechobee, Fl	C America • 50 kW
UZBEKISTAN RADIO TASHKENT, Tashkent	S • Mideast & S Asia • 100 kW S Asia • 100 kW
	S • Mideast • 100 kW
	0 1 2 3 4 5 6 7 8 9 10 11 12 13 14 15 16 17 18 19 20 21 22 23 24

ENGLISH ▬ ARABIC ▒ CHINESE ▫▫▫ FRENCH ═ GERMAN ▬ RUSSIAN ═ SPANISH ▬ OTHER ─

FREQUENCY   COUNTRY, STATION, LOCATION

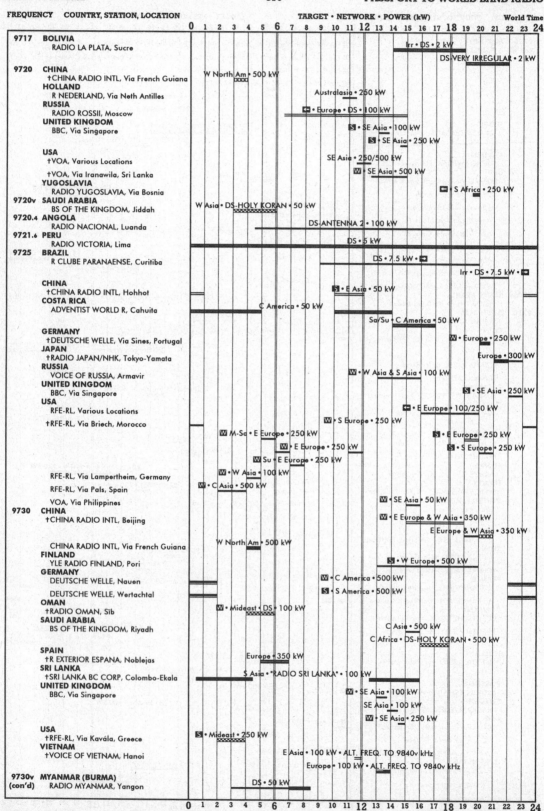

	TARGET • NETWORK • POWER (kW)				World Time
9717	**BOLIVIA**				
	RADIO LA PLATA, Sucre		Irr • DS • 2 kW		
			DS-VERY IRREGULAR • 2 kW		
9720	**CHINA**				
	†CHINA RADIO INTL, Via French Guiana	W North Am • 500 kW			
	HOLLAND				
	R NEDERLAND, Via Neth Antilles	Australasia • 250 kW			
	RUSSIA				
	RADIO ROSSII, Moscow	• Europe • DS • 100 kW			
	UNITED KINGDOM				
	BBC, Via Singapore	S • SE Asia • 100 kW			
		S • SE Asia • 250 kW			
	USA				
	†VOA, Various Locations	SE Asia • 250/500 kW			
	†VOA, Via Iranawila, Sri Lanka	W • SE Asia • 500 kW			
	YUGOSLAVIA				
	RADIO YUGOSLAVIA, Via Bosnia	S Africa • 250 kW			
9720v	**SAUDI ARABIA**				
	BS OF THE KINGDOM, Jiddah	W Asia • DS-HOLY KORAN • 50 kW			
9720.4	**ANGOLA**				
	RADIO NACIONAL, Luanda	DS-ANTENNA 2 • 100 kW			
9721.6	**PERU**				
	RADIO VICTORIA, Lima	DS • 5 kW			
9725	**BRAZIL**				
	R CLUBE PARANAENSE, Curitiba	DS • 7.5 kW •			
		Irr • DS • 7.5 kW •			
	CHINA				
	†CHINA RADIO INTL, Hohhot	S • E Asia • 50 kW			
	COSTA RICA				
	ADVENTIST WORLD R, Cahuita	C America • 50 kW			
		Sa/Su • C America • 50 kW			
	GERMANY				
	†DEUTSCHE WELLE, Via Sines, Portugal	W • Europe • 250 kW			
	JAPAN				
	†RADIO JAPAN/NHK, Tokyo-Yamata	Europe • 300 kW			
	RUSSIA				
	VOICE OF RUSSIA, Armavir	W • W Asia & S Asia • 100 kW			
	UNITED KINGDOM				
	BBC, Via Singapore	S • SE Asia • 250 kW			
	USA				
	RFE-RL, Various Locations	• E Europe • 100/250 kW			
	†RFE-RL, Via Briech, Morocco	W • S Europe • 250 kW			
		W M-Sa • E Europe • 250 kW	S • E Europe • 250 kW		
		W • E Europe • 250 kW	S • S Europe • 250 kW		
		W Su • E Europe • 250 kW			
	RFE-RL, Via Lampertheim, Germany	W • W Asia • 100 kW			
	RFE-RL, Via Pals, Spain	W • C Asia • 500 kW			
	VOA, Via Philippines	W • SE Asia • 50 kW			
9730	**CHINA**				
	†CHINA RADIO INTL, Beijing	W • E Europe & W Asia • 350 kW			
		E Europe & W Asia • 350 kW			
	CHINA RADIO INTL, Via French Guiana	W North Am • 500 kW			
	FINLAND				
	YLE RADIO FINLAND, Pori	S • W Europe • 500 kW			
	GERMANY				
	DEUTSCHE WELLE, Nauen	W • C America • 500 kW			
	DEUTSCHE WELLE, Wertachtal	S • S America • 500 kW			
	OMAN				
	†RADIO OMAN, Sib	W • Mideast • DS • 100 kW			
	SAUDI ARABIA				
	BS OF THE KINGDOM, Riyadh	C Asia • 500 kW			
		C Africa • DS-HOLY KORAN • 500 kW			
	SPAIN				
	†R EXTERIOR ESPANA, Noblejas	Europe • 350 kW			
	SRI LANKA				
	†SRI LANKA BC CORP, Colombo-Ekala	S Asia • "RADIO SRI LANKA" • 100 kW			
	UNITED KINGDOM				
	BBC, Via Singapore	W • SE Asia • 100 kW			
		SE Asia • 100 kW			
		W • SE Asia • 250 kW			
	USA				
	†RFE-RL, Via Kavála, Greece	S • Mideast • 250 kW			
	VIETNAM				
	†VOICE OF VIETNAM, Hanoi	E Asia • 100 kW • ALT. FREQ. TO 9840v kHz			
		Europe • 100 kW • ALT. FREQ. TO 9840v kHz			
9730v	**MYANMAR (BURMA)**				
(con'd)	RADIO MYANMAR, Yangon	DS • 50 kW			

SEASONAL S OR W   1-HR TIMESHIFT MIDYEAR ⊡ OR ⊡   JAMMING / OR ∧   EARLIEST HEARD ◁   LATEST HEARD ▷   NEW FOR 2000 †

FREQUENCY   COUNTRY, STATION, LOCATION   TARGET • NETWORK • POWER (kW)   World Time

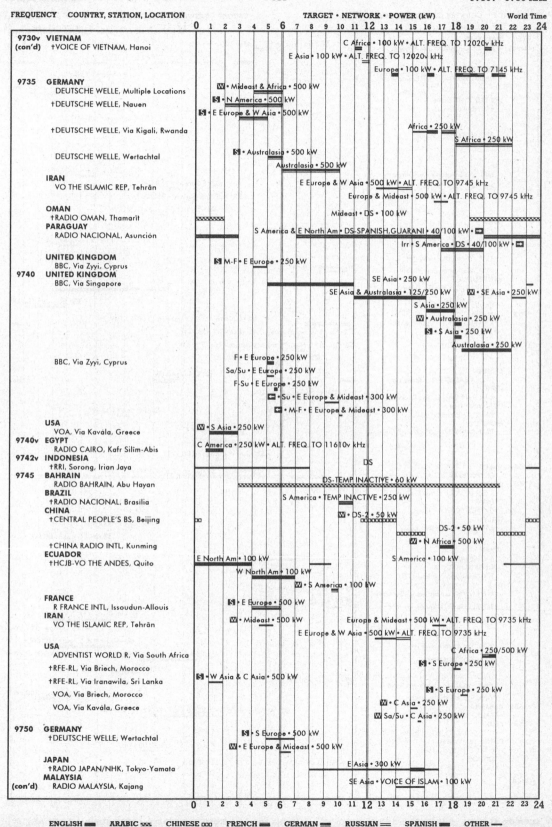

9730v VIETNAM
(con'd)   †VOICE OF VIETNAM, Hanoi

- C Africa • 100 kW • ALT. FREQ. TO 12020v kHz
- E Asia • 100 kW • ALT. FREQ. TO 12020v kHz
- Europe • 100 kW • ALT. FREQ. TO 7145 kHz

9735   GERMANY
           DEUTSCHE WELLE, Multiple Locations
           †DEUTSCHE WELLE, Nauen

- W • Mideast & Africa • 500 kW
- S • N America • 500 kW
- S • E Europe & W Asia • 500 kW

           †DEUTSCHE WELLE, Via Kigali, Rwanda

- Africa • 250 kW
- S Africa • 250 kW

           DEUTSCHE WELLE, Wertachtal

- S • Australasia • 500 kW
- Australasia • 500 kW

IRAN
           VO THE ISLAMIC REP, Tehrān

- E Europe & W Asia • 500 kW • ALT. FREQ. TO 9745 kHz
- Europe & Mideast • 500 kW • ALT. FREQ. TO 9745 kHz

OMAN
           †RADIO OMAN, Thamarīt
PARAGUAY
           RADIO NACIONAL, Asunción

- Mideast • DS • 100 kW
- S America & E North Am • DS-SPANISH,GUARANI • 40/100 kW •
- Irr • S America • DS • 40/100 kW •

UNITED KINGDOM
           BBC, Via Zyyi, Cyprus
9740   UNITED KINGDOM
           BBC, Via Singapore

- S • M-F • E Europe • 250 kW
- SE Asia • 250 kW
- SE Asia & Australasia • 125/250 kW
- W • SE Asia • 250 kW
- S Asia • 250 kW
- W • Australasia • 250 kW
- S • S Asia • 250 kW
- Australasia • 250 kW

           BBC, Via Zyyi, Cyprus

- F • E Europe • 250 kW
- Sa/Su • E Europe • 250 kW
- F-Su • E Europe • 250 kW
- Su • E Europe & Mideast • 300 kW
- M-F • E Europe & Mideast • 300 kW

USA
           VOA, Via Kaválla, Greece
9740v EGYPT
           RADIO CAIRO, Kafr Silim-Abis
9742v INDONESIA
           †RRI, Sorong, Irian Jaya
9745   BAHRAIN
           RADIO BAHRAIN, Abu Hayan
BRAZIL
           †RADIO NACIONAL, Brasilia
CHINA
           †CENTRAL PEOPLE'S BS, Beijing

- W • S Asia • 250 kW
- C America • 250 kW • ALT. FREQ. TO 11610v kHz
- DS
- DS-TEMP INACTIVE • 60 kW
- S America • TEMP INACTIVE • 250 kW
- W • DS-2 • 50 kW
- DS-2 • 50 kW

           †CHINA RADIO INTL, Kunming
ECUADOR
           †HCJB-VO THE ANDES, Quito

- W • N Africa • 500 kW
- E North Am • 100 kW
- S America • 100 kW
- W North Am • 100 kW
- W • S America • 100 kW

FRANCE
           R FRANCE INTL, Issoudun-Allouis
IRAN
           VO THE ISLAMIC REP, Tehrān

- S • E Europe • 500 kW
- W • Mideast • 500 kW
- Europe & Mideast • 500 kW • ALT. FREQ. TO 9735 kHz
- E Europe & W Asia • 500 kW • ALT. FREQ. TO 9735 kHz

USA
           ADVENTIST WORLD R, Via South Africa
           †RFE-RL, Via Briech, Morocco
           †RFE-RL, Via Iranawila, Sri Lanka
           VOA, Via Briech, Morocco
           VOA, Via Kaválla, Greece

- C Africa • 250/500 kW
- S • S Europe • 250 kW
- S • W Asia & C Asia • 500 kW
- S • S Europe • 250 kW
- W • C Asia • 250 kW
- W Sa/Su • C Asia • 250 kW

9750   GERMANY
           †DEUTSCHE WELLE, Wertachtal

- S • S Europe • 500 kW
- W • E Europe & Mideast • 500 kW

JAPAN
           †RADIO JAPAN/NHK, Tokyo-Yamata
MALAYSIA
(con'd)   RADIO MALAYSIA, Kajang

- E Asia • 300 kW
- SE Asia • VOICE OF ISLAM • 100 kW

FREQUENCY	COUNTRY, STATION, LOCATION	TARGET • NETWORK • POWER (kW)	World Time

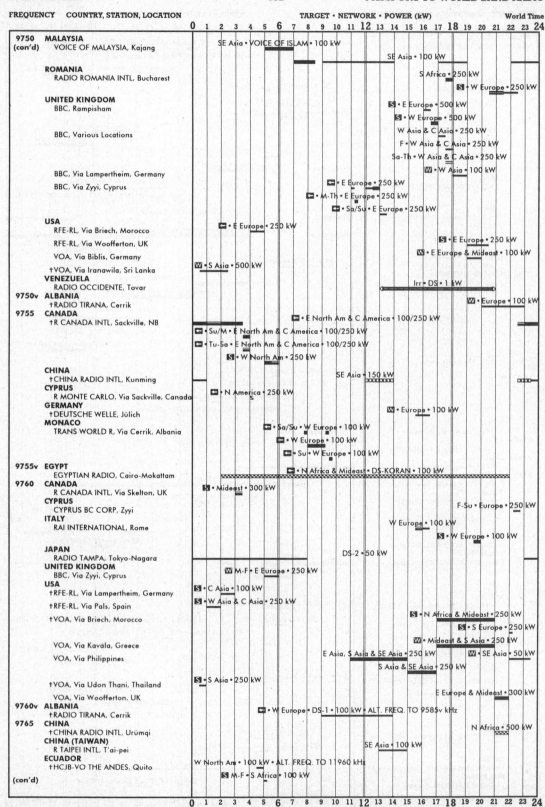

9750 **MALAYSIA**
(con'd)   VOICE OF MALAYSIA, Kajang — SE Asia • VOICE OF ISLAM • 100 kW

ROMANIA
RADIO ROMANIA INTL, Bucharest — SE Asia • 100 kW; S Africa • 250 kW; W Europe • 250 kW

UNITED KINGDOM
BBC, Rampisham — E Europe • 500 kW; W Europe • 500 kW
BBC, Various Locations — W Asia & C Asia • 250 kW; F • W Asia & C Asia • 250 kW; Sa-Th • W Asia & C Asia • 250 kW; W • W Asia • 100 kW
BBC, Via Lampertheim, Germany — E Europe • 250 kW
BBC, Via Zyyi, Cyprus — M-Th • E Europe • 250 kW; Sa/Su • E Europe • 250 kW

USA
RFE-RL, Via Briech, Morocco — E Europe • 250 kW
RFE-RL, Via Woofferton, UK — E Europe • 250 kW
VOA, Via Biblis, Germany — W • E Europe & Mideast • 100 kW
†VOA, Via Iranawila, Sri Lanka — W • S Asia • 500 kW

VENEZUELA
RADIO OCCIDENTE, Tovar — Irr • DS • 1 kW

9750v **ALBANIA**
†RADIO TIRANA, Cerrik — W • Europe • 100 kW

9755 **CANADA**
†R CANADA INTL, Sackville, NB — E North Am & C America • 100/250 kW; Su/M • E North Am & C America • 100/250 kW; Tu-Sa • E North Am & C America • 100/250 kW; S • W North Am • 250 kW

CHINA
†CHINA RADIO INTL, Kunming — SE Asia • 150 kW

CYPRUS
R MONTE CARLO, Via Sackville, Canada — N America • 250 kW

GERMANY
†DEUTSCHE WELLE, Jülich — W • Europe • 100 kW

MONACO
TRANS WORLD R, Via Cerrik, Albania — Sa/Su • W Europe • 100 kW; W Europe • 100 kW; Su • W Europe • 100 kW

9755v **EGYPT**
EGYPTIAN RADIO, Cairo-Mokattam — N Africa & Mideast • DS-KORAN • 100 kW

9760 **CANADA**
R CANADA INTL, Via Skelton, UK — S • Mideast • 300 kW

CYPRUS
CYPRUS BC CORP, Zyyi — F-Su • Europe • 250 kW

ITALY
RAI INTERNATIONAL, Rome — W Europe • 100 kW; W • Europe • 100 kW

JAPAN
RADIO TAMPA, Tokyo-Nagara — DS-2 • 50 kW

UNITED KINGDOM
BBC, Via Zyyi, Cyprus — W M-F • E Europe • 250 kW

USA
†RFE-RL, Via Lampertheim, Germany — S • C Asia • 100 kW
†RFE-RL, Via Pals, Spain — S • W Asia & C Asia • 250 kW
†VOA, Via Briech, Morocco — S • N Africa & Mideast • 250 kW; S • S Europe • 250 kW
VOA, Via Kavála, Greece — W • Mideast & S Asia • 250 kW; W • SE Asia • 50 kW
VOA, Via Philippines — E Asia, S Asia & SE Asia • 250 kW; S Asia & SE Asia • 250 kW
†VOA, Via Udon Thani, Thailand — S • S Asia • 250 kW
VOA, Via Woofferton, UK — E Europe & Mideast • 300 kW

9760v **ALBANIA**
†RADIO TIRANA, Cerrik — W Europe • DS-1 • 100 kW • ALT. FREQ. TO 9585v kHz

9765 **CHINA**
†CHINA RADIO INTL, Urümqi — N Africa • 500 kW

CHINA (TAIWAN)
R TAIPEI INTL, T'ai-pei — SE Asia • 100 kW

ECUADOR
†HCJB-VO THE ANDES, Quito — W North Am • 100 kW • ALT. FREQ. TO 11960 kHz; S M-F • S Africa • 100 kW

(con'd)

FREQUENCY   COUNTRY, STATION, LOCATION   TARGET • NETWORK • POWER (kW)   World Time

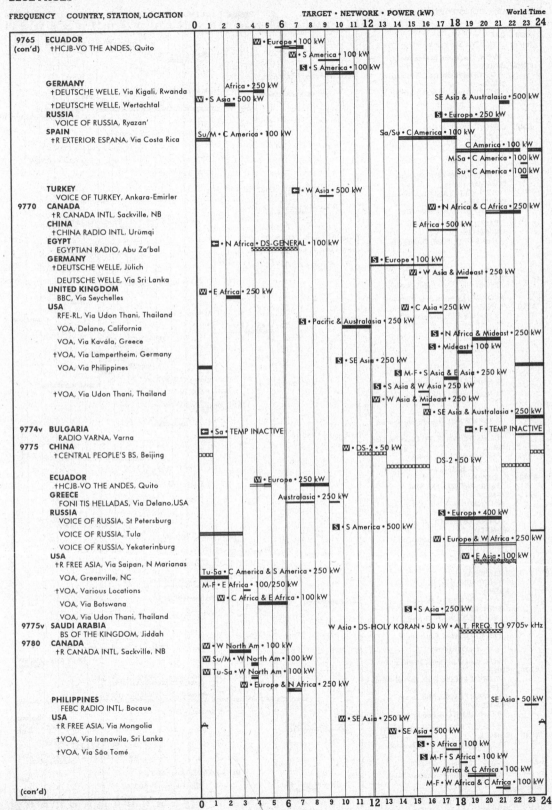

9765 ECUADOR
(con'd) †HCJB-VO THE ANDES, Quito — W • Europe • 100 kW / W • S America • 100 kW / S • S America • 100 kW

GERMANY
†DEUTSCHE WELLE, Via Kigali, Rwanda — Africa • 250 kW
†DEUTSCHE WELLE, Wertachtal — W • S Asia • 500 kW / SE Asia & Australasia • 500 kW
RUSSIA
VOICE OF RUSSIA, Ryazan' — S • Europe • 250 kW
SPAIN
†R EXTERIOR ESPANA, Via Costa Rica — Su/M • C America • 100 kW / Sa/Su • C America • 100 kW / C America • 100 kW / M-Sa • C America • 100 kW / Su • C America • 100 kW

TURKEY
VOICE OF TURKEY, Ankara-Emirler — W Asia • 500 kW

9770 CANADA
†R CANADA INTL, Sackville, NB — W • N Africa & C Africa • 250 kW
CHINA
†CHINA RADIO INTL, Ürümqi — E Africa • 500 kW
EGYPT
EGYPTIAN RADIO, Abu Za'bal — N Africa • DS-GENERAL • 100 kW
GERMANY
†DEUTSCHE WELLE, Jülich — S • Europe • 100 kW
DEUTSCHE WELLE, Via Sri Lanka — W • W Asia & Mideast • 250 kW
UNITED KINGDOM
BBC, Via Seychelles — W • E Africa • 250 kW
USA
RFE-RL, Via Udon Thani, Thailand — W • C Asia • 250 kW
VOA, Delano, California — S • Pacific & Australasia • 250 kW
VOA, Via Kavála, Greece — S • N Africa & Mideast • 250 kW
†VOA, Via Lampertheim, Germany — S • Mideast • 100 kW
VOA, Via Philippines — S • SE Asia • 250 kW / S M-F • S Asia & E Asia • 250 kW / S • S Asia & W Asia • 250 kW
†VOA, Via Udon Thani, Thailand — W • W Asia & Mideast • 250 kW / W • SE Asia & Australasia • 250 kW

9774v BULGARIA
RADIO VARNA, Varna — Sa • TEMP INACTIVE / F • TEMP INACTIVE
9775 CHINA
†CENTRAL PEOPLE'S BS, Beijing — W • DS-2 • 50 kW / DS-2 • 50 kW

ECUADOR
†HCJB-VO THE ANDES, Quito — W • Europe • 250 kW
GREECE
FONI TIS HELLADAS, Via Delano, USA — Australasia • 250 kW
RUSSIA
VOICE OF RUSSIA, St Petersburg — S • Europe • 400 kW
VOICE OF RUSSIA, Tula — S • S America • 500 kW
VOICE OF RUSSIA, Yekaterinburg — W • Europe & W Africa • 250 kW / W • E Asia • 100 kW
USA
†R FREE ASIA, Via Saipan, N Marianas — Tu-Sa • C America & S America • 250 kW
VOA, Greenville, NC — M-F • E Africa • 100/250 kW
†VOA, Various Locations — W • C Africa & E Africa • 100 kW
VOA, Via Botswana — S • S Asia • 250 kW
VOA, Via Udon Thani, Thailand
9775v SAUDI ARABIA
BS OF THE KINGDOM, Jiddah — W Asia • DS-HOLY KORAN • 50 kW • ALT. FREQ. TO 9705v kHz
9780 CANADA
†R CANADA INTL, Sackville, NB — W • W North Am • 100 kW / W Su/M • W North Am • 100 kW / W Tu-Sa • W North Am • 100 kW / W • Europe & N Africa • 250 kW

PHILIPPINES
FEBC RADIO INTL, Bocaue — SE Asia • 50 kW
USA
†R FREE ASIA, Via Mongolia — W • SE Asia • 250 kW
†VOA, Via Iranawila, Sri Lanka — W • SE Asia • 500 kW
†VOA, Via São Tomé — S • S Africa • 100 kW / S M-F • S Africa • 100 kW / W Africa & C Africa • 100 kW / M-F • W Africa & C Africa • 100 kW

(con'd)

ENGLISH ▬   ARABIC ▨   CHINESE □□□   FRENCH ═   GERMAN ▬   RUSSIAN ═   SPANISH ═   OTHER ▬

FREQUENCY   COUNTRY, STATION, LOCATION   TARGET • NETWORK • POWER (kW)   World Time

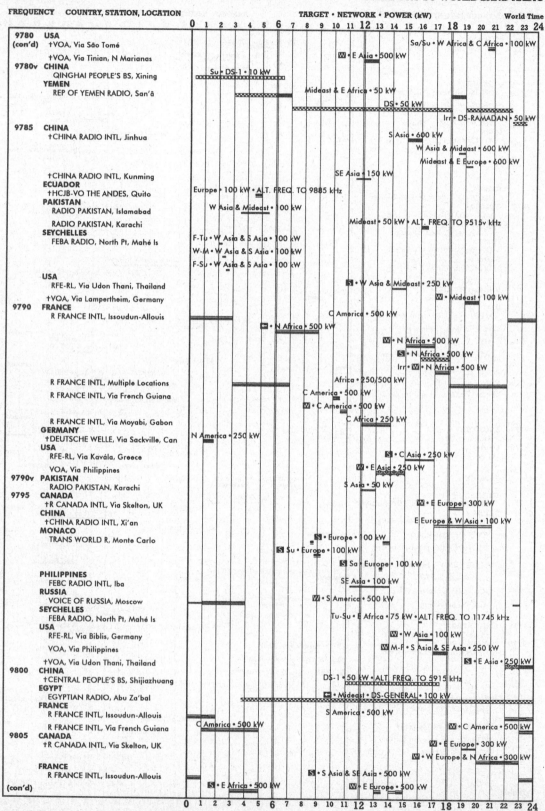

9780   **USA**
(con'd)   †VOA, Via São Tomé   Sa/Su • W Africa & C Africa • 100 kW
      †VOA, Via Tinian, N Marianas   W • E Asia • 500 kW
9780v   **CHINA**
      QINGHAI PEOPLE'S BS, Xining   Su • DS-1 • 10 kW
      YEMEN
      REP OF YEMEN RADIO, San'â   Mideast & E Africa • 50 kW
        DS • 50 kW
        Irr • DS-RAMADAN • 50 kW

9785   **CHINA**
      †CHINA RADIO INTL, Jinhua   S Asia • 600 kW
        W Asia & Mideast • 600 kW
        Mideast & E Europe • 600 kW
      †CHINA RADIO INTL, Kunming   SE Asia • 150 kW
      ECUADOR
      †HCJB-VO THE ANDES, Quito   Europe • 100 kW • ALT. FREQ. TO 9885 kHz
      PAKISTAN
      RADIO PAKISTAN, Islamabad   W Asia & Mideast • 100 kW
      RADIO PAKISTAN, Karachi   Mideast • 50 kW • ALT. FREQ. TO 9515v kHz
      SEYCHELLES
      FEBA RADIO, North Pt, Mahé Is   F-Tu • W Asia & S Asia • 100 kW
        W-M • W Asia & S Asia • 100 kW
        F-Su • W Asia & S Asia • 100 kW
      USA
      RFE-RL, Via Udon Thani, Thailand   S • W Asia & Mideast • 250 kW
      †VOA, Via Lampertheim, Germany   W • Mideast • 100 kW
9790   **FRANCE**
      R FRANCE INTL, Issoudun-Allouis   C America • 500 kW
        N Africa • 500 kW
        W • N Africa • 500 kW
        S • N Africa • 500 kW
        Irr • W • N Africa • 500 kW
      R FRANCE INTL, Multiple Locations   Africa • 250/500 kW
      R FRANCE INTL, Via French Guiana   C America • 500 kW
        W • C America • 500 kW
      R FRANCE INTL, Via Moyabi, Gabon   C Africa • 250 kW
      GERMANY
      †DEUTSCHE WELLE, Via Sackville, Can   N America • 250 kW
      USA
      RFE-RL, Via Kavála, Greece   S • C Asia • 250 kW
      VOA, Via Philippines   W • E Asia • 250 kW
9790v   **PAKISTAN**
      RADIO PAKISTAN, Karachi   S Asia • 50 kW
9795   **CANADA**
      †R CANADA INTL, Via Skelton, UK   W • E Europe • 300 kW
      CHINA
      †CHINA RADIO INTL, Xi'an   E Europe & W Asia • 100 kW
      MONACO
      TRANS WORLD R, Monte Carlo   S • Europe • 100 kW
        S Su • Europe • 100 kW
        S Sa • Europe • 100 kW
      PHILIPPINES
      FEBC RADIO INTL, Iba   SE Asia • 100 kW
      RUSSIA
      VOICE OF RUSSIA, Moscow   W • S America • 500 kW
      SEYCHELLES
      FEBA RADIO, North Pt, Mahé Is   Tu-Su • E Africa • 75 kW • ALT. FREQ. TO 11745 kHz
      USA
      RFE-RL, Via Biblis, Germany   W • W Asia • 100 kW
      VOA, Via Philippines   W • M-F • S Asia & SE Asia • 250 kW
      †VOA, Via Udon Thani, Thailand   S • E Asia • 250 kW
9800   **CHINA**
      †CENTRAL PEOPLE'S BS, Shijiazhuang   DS-1 • 50 kW • ALT. FREQ. TO 5915 kHz
      EGYPT
      EGYPTIAN RADIO, Abu Za'bal   Mideast • DS-GENERAL • 100 kW
      FRANCE
      R FRANCE INTL, Issoudun-Allouis   S America • 500 kW
      R FRANCE INTL, Via French Guiana   C America • 500 kW
        W • C America • 500 kW
9805   **CANADA**
      †R CANADA INTL, Via Skelton, UK   W • E Europe • 300 kW
        W • W Europe & N Africa • 300 kW
      FRANCE
      R FRANCE INTL, Issoudun-Allouis   S • S Asia & SE Asia • 500 kW
        S • E Africa • 500 kW
        W • E Europe • 500 kW
(con'd)

FREQUENCY   COUNTRY, STATION, LOCATION   TARGET • NETWORK • POWER (kW)   World Time

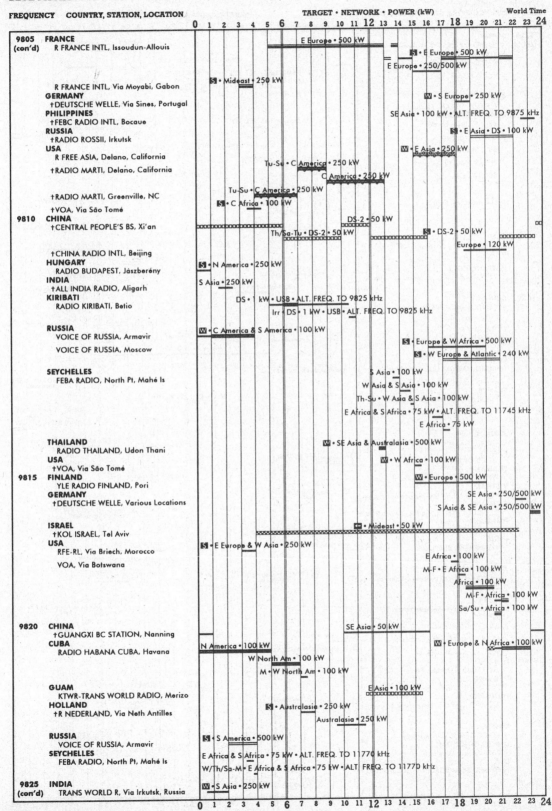

9805 (con'd) **FRANCE**
R FRANCE INTL, Issoudun-Allouis — E Europe • 500 kW; S • E Europe • 500 kW; E Europe • 250/500 kW

R FRANCE INTL, Via Moyabi, Gabon — S • Mideast • 250 kW

GERMANY
†DEUTSCHE WELLE, Via Sines, Portugal — W • S Europe • 250 kW

PHILIPPINES
†FEBC RADIO INTL, Bocaue — SE Asia • 100 kW • ALT. FREQ. TO 9875 kHz

RUSSIA
†RADIO ROSSII, Irkutsk — S • E Asia • DS • 100 kW

USA
R FREE ASIA, Delano, California — W • E Asia • 250 kW

†RADIO MARTI, Delano, California — Tu-Su • C America • 250 kW; C America • 250 kW

†RADIO MARTI, Greenville, NC — Tu-Su • C America • 250 kW

†VOA, Via São Tomé — S • C Africa • 100 kW

9810 **CHINA**
†CENTRAL PEOPLE'S BS, Xi'an — DS-2 • 50 kW; Th/Sa-Tu • DS-2 • 50 kW; S • DS-2 • 50 kW

†CHINA RADIO INTL, Beijing — Europe • 120 kW

HUNGARY
RADIO BUDAPEST, Jászberény — S • N America • 250 kW

INDIA
†ALL INDIA RADIO, Aligarh — S Asia • 250 kW

KIRIBATI
RADIO KIRIBATI, Betio — DS • 1 kW • USB • ALT. FREQ. TO 9825 kHz; Irr • DS • 1 kW • USB • ALT. FREQ. TO 9825 kHz

RUSSIA
VOICE OF RUSSIA, Armavir — W • C America & S America • 100 kW

VOICE OF RUSSIA, Moscow — S • Europe & W Africa • 500 kW; S • W Europe & Atlantic • 240 kW

SEYCHELLES
FEBA RADIO, North Pt, Mahé Is — S Asia • 100 kW; W Asia & S Asia • 100 kW; Th-Su • W Asia & S Asia • 100 kW; E Africa & S Africa • 75 kW • ALT. FREQ. TO 11745 kHz; E Africa • 75 kW

THAILAND
RADIO THAILAND, Udon Thani — W • SE Asia & Australasia • 500 kW

USA
†VOA, Via São Tomé — W • W Africa • 100 kW

9815 **FINLAND**
YLE RADIO FINLAND, Pori — W • Europe • 500 kW

GERMANY
†DEUTSCHE WELLE, Various Locations — SE Asia • 250/500 kW; S Asia & SE Asia • 250/500 kW

ISRAEL
†KOL ISRAEL, Tel Aviv — Mideast • 50 kW

USA
RFE-RL, Via Briech, Morocco — S • E Europe & W Asia • 250 kW

VOA, Via Botswana — E Africa • 100 kW; M-F • E Africa • 100 kW; Africa • 100 kW; M-F • Africa • 100 kW; Sa/Su • Africa • 100 kW

9820 **CHINA**
†GUANGXI BC STATION, Nanning — SE Asia • 50 kW

CUBA
RADIO HABANA CUBA, Havana — N America • 100 kW; W • Europe & N Africa • 100 kW; W North Am • 100 kW; M • W North Am • 100 kW

GUAM
KTWR-TRANS WORLD RADIO, Merizo — E Asia • 100 kW

HOLLAND
†R NEDERLAND, Via Neth Antilles — S • Australasia • 250 kW; Australasia • 250 kW

RUSSIA
VOICE OF RUSSIA, Armavir — S • S America • 500 kW

SEYCHELLES
FEBA RADIO, North Pt, Mahé Is — E Africa & S Africa • 75 kW • ALT. FREQ. TO 11770 kHz; W/Th/Sa-M • E Africa & S Africa • 75 kW • ALT. FREQ. TO 11770 kHz

9825 (con'd) **INDIA**
TRANS WORLD R, Via Irkutsk, Russia — W • S Asia • 250 kW

ENGLISH ▬   ARABIC ⌇⌇⌇   CHINESE ▫▫▫   FRENCH ═   GERMAN ▬   RUSSIAN ═   SPANISH ▬   OTHER —

FREQUENCY   COUNTRY, STATION, LOCATION   TARGET • NETWORK • POWER (kW)   World Time

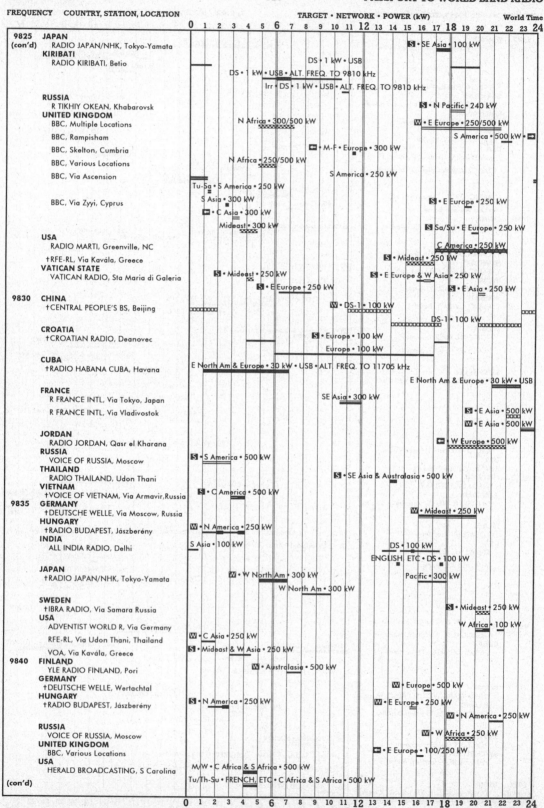

Frequency	Country, Station, Location	Target • Network • Power
9825 (con'd)	**JAPAN**	
	RADIO JAPAN/NHK, Tokyo-Yamata	S • SE Asia • 100 kW
	KIRIBATI	
	RADIO KIRIBATI, Betio	DS • 1 kW • USB
		DS • 1 kW • USB • ALT. FREQ. TO 9810 kHz
		Irr • DS • 1 kW • USB • ALT. FREQ. TO 9810 kHz
	RUSSIA	
	R TIKHIY OKEAN, Khabarovsk	S • N Pacific • 240 kW
	UNITED KINGDOM	
	BBC, Multiple Locations	N Africa • 300/500 kW W • E Europe • 250/500 kW
	BBC, Rampisham	S America • 500 kW • ⇨
	BBC, Skelton, Cumbria	⊡ • M-F • Europe • 300 kW
	BBC, Various Locations	N Africa • 250/500 kW
	BBC, Via Ascension	S America • 250 kW
		Tu-Sa • S America • 250 kW
	BBC, Via Zyyi, Cyprus	S Asia • 300 kW S • E Europe • 250 kW
		⊡ • C Asia • 300 kW
		Mideast • 300 kW S • Sa/Su • E Europe • 250 kW
	USA	
	RADIO MARTI, Greenville, NC	C America • 250 kW
	†RFE-RL, Via Kavála, Greece	S • Mideast • 250 kW
	VATICAN STATE	
	VATICAN RADIO, Sta Maria di Galeria	S • Mideast • 250 kW S • E Europe & W Asia • 250 kW
		S • E Europe • 250 kW S • E Asia • 250 kW
9830	**CHINA**	
	†CENTRAL PEOPLE'S BS, Beijing	W • DS-1 • 100 kW
		DS-1 • 100 kW
	CROATIA	
	†CROATIAN RADIO, Deanovec	S • Europe • 100 kW
		Europe • 100 kW
	CUBA	
	†RADIO HABANA CUBA, Havana	E North Am & Europe • 30 kW • USB • ALT. FREQ. TO 11705 kHz
		E North Am & Europe • 30 kW • USB
	FRANCE	
	R FRANCE INTL, Via Tokyo, Japan	SE Asia • 300 kW
	R FRANCE INTL, Via Vladivostok	S • E Asia • 500 kW
		W • E Asia • 500 kW
	JORDAN	
	RADIO JORDAN, Qasr el Kharana	⊡ • W Europe • 500 kW
	RUSSIA	
	VOICE OF RUSSIA, Moscow	S • S America • 500 kW
	THAILAND	
	RADIO THAILAND, Udon Thani	S • SE Asia & Australasia • 500 kW
	VIETNAM	
	†VOICE OF VIETNAM, Via Armavir, Russia	S • C America • 500 kW
9835	**GERMANY**	
	†DEUTSCHE WELLE, Via Moscow, Russia	W • Mideast • 250 kW
	HUNGARY	
	†RADIO BUDAPEST, Jászberény	W • N America • 250 kW
	INDIA	
	ALL INDIA RADIO, Delhi	S Asia • 100 kW DS • 100 kW
		ENGLISH ETC • DS • 100 kW
	JAPAN	
	†RADIO JAPAN/NHK, Tokyo-Yamata	W • W North Am • 300 kW Pacific • 300 kW
		W North Am • 300 kW
	SWEDEN	
	†IBRA RADIO, Via Samara Russia	S • Mideast • 250 kW
	USA	
	ADVENTIST WORLD R, Via Germany	W Africa • 100 kW
	RFE-RL, Via Udon Thani, Thailand	W • C Asia • 250 kW
	VOA, Via Kavála, Greece	S • Mideast & W Asia • 250 kW
9840	**FINLAND**	
	YLE RADIO FINLAND, Pori	W • Australasia • 500 kW
	GERMANY	
	†DEUTSCHE WELLE, Wertachtal	W • Europe • 500 kW
	HUNGARY	
	†RADIO BUDAPEST, Jászberény	S • N America • 250 kW S • E Europe • 250 kW
		W • N America • 250 kW
	RUSSIA	
	VOICE OF RUSSIA, Moscow	W • W Africa • 250 kW
	UNITED KINGDOM	
	BBC, Various Locations	⊡ • E Europe • 100/250 kW
	USA	
	HERALD BROADCASTING, S Carolina	M/W • C Africa & S Africa • 500 kW
		Tu/Th-Su • FRENCH, ETC • C Africa & S Africa • 500 kW
(con'd)		

FREQUENCY	COUNTRY, STATION, LOCATION	TARGET • NETWORK • POWER (kW) — World Time

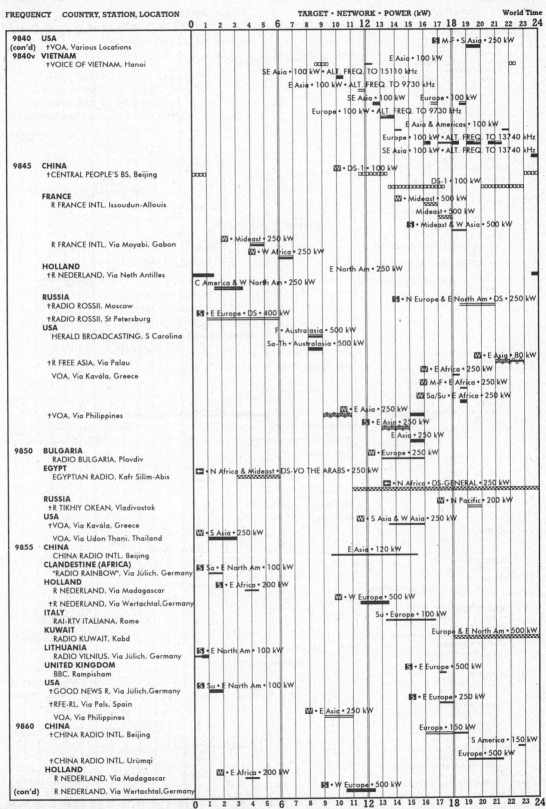

0 1 2 3 4 5 6 7 8 9 10 11 12 13 14 15 16 17 18 19 20 21 22 23 24

9840 USA
(con'd) †VOA, Various Locations — M-F • S Asia • 250 kW
9840v VIETNAM
  †VOICE OF VIETNAM, Hanoi — E Asia • 100 kW
  SE Asia • 100 kW • ALT. FREQ. TO 15110 kHz
  E Asia • 100 kW • ALT. FREQ. TO 9730 kHz
  SE Asia • 100 kW   Europe • 100 kW
  Europe • 100 kW • ALT. FREQ. TO 9730 kHz
  E Asia & Americas • 100 kW
  Europe • 100 kW • ALT. FREQ. TO 13740 kHz
  SE Asia • 100 kW • ALT. FREQ. TO 13740 kHz

9845 CHINA
  †CENTRAL PEOPLE'S BS, Beijing — DS-1 • 100 kW
  DS-1 • 100 kW

  FRANCE
  R FRANCE INTL, Issoudun-Allouis — Mideast • 500 kW
  Mideast • 500 kW
  Mideast & W Asia • 500 kW

  R FRANCE INTL, Via Moyabi, Gabon — Mideast • 250 kW
  W Africa • 250 kW

  HOLLAND
  †R NEDERLAND, Via Neth Antilles — E North Am • 250 kW
  C America & W North Am • 250 kW

  RUSSIA
  †RADIO ROSSII, Moscow — N Europe & E North Am • DS • 250 kW
  †RADIO ROSSII, St Petersburg — E Europe • DS • 400 kW
  USA
  HERALD BROADCASTING, S Carolina — F • Australasia • 500 kW
  Sa-Th • Australasia • 500 kW

  †R FREE ASIA, Via Palau — E Asia • 80 kW
  VOA, Via Kavála, Greece — E Africa • 250 kW
  M-F • E Africa • 250 kW
  Sa/Su • E Africa • 250 kW

  †VOA, Via Philippines — E Asia • 250 kW
  E Asia • 250 kW
  E Asia • 250 kW

9850 BULGARIA
  RADIO BULGARIA, Plovdiv — Europe • 250 kW
  EGYPT
  EGYPTIAN RADIO, Kafr Silim-Abis — N Africa & Mideast • DS-VO THE ARABS • 250 kW
  N Africa • DS-GENERAL • 250 kW

  RUSSIA
  †R TIKHIY OKEAN, Vladivostok — N Pacific • 200 kW
  USA
  †VOA, Via Kavála, Greece — S Asia & W Asia • 250 kW
  VOA, Via Udon Thani, Thailand — S Asia • 250 kW
9855 CHINA
  CHINA RADIO INTL, Beijing — E Asia • 120 kW
  CLANDESTINE (AFRICA)
  "RADIO RAINBOW", Via Jülich, Germany — Sa • E North Am • 100 kW
  HOLLAND
  R NEDERLAND, Via Madagascar — E Africa • 200 kW
  †R NEDERLAND, Via Wertachtal, Germany — W Europe • 500 kW
  ITALY
  RAI-RTV ITALIANA, Rome — Su • Europe • 100 kW
  KUWAIT
  RADIO KUWAIT, Kabd — Europe & E North Am • 500 kW
  LITHUANIA
  RADIO VILNIUS, Via Jülich, Germany — E North Am • 100 kW
  UNITED KINGDOM
  BBC, Rampisham — E Europe • 500 kW
  USA
  †GOOD NEWS R, Via Jülich, Germany — Su • E North Am • 100 kW
  †RFE-RL, Via Pals, Spain — E Europe • 250 kW
  VOA, Via Philippines — E Asia • 250 kW
9860 CHINA
  †CHINA RADIO INTL, Beijing — Europe • 150 kW
  S America • 150 kW
  †CHINA RADIO INTL, Urümqi — Europe • 500 kW
  HOLLAND
  R NEDERLAND, Via Madagascar — E Africa • 200 kW
(con'd) R NEDERLAND, Via Wertachtal, Germany — W Europe • 500 kW

0 1 2 3 4 5 6 7 8 9 10 11 12 13 14 15 16 17 18 19 20 21 22 23 24

ENGLISH ▬ ARABIC ⧉ CHINESE □□□ FRENCH ═ GERMAN ▬ RUSSIAN ═ SPANISH ▬ OTHER ▬

FREQUENCY   COUNTRY, STATION, LOCATION   TARGET • NETWORK • POWER (kW)   World Time

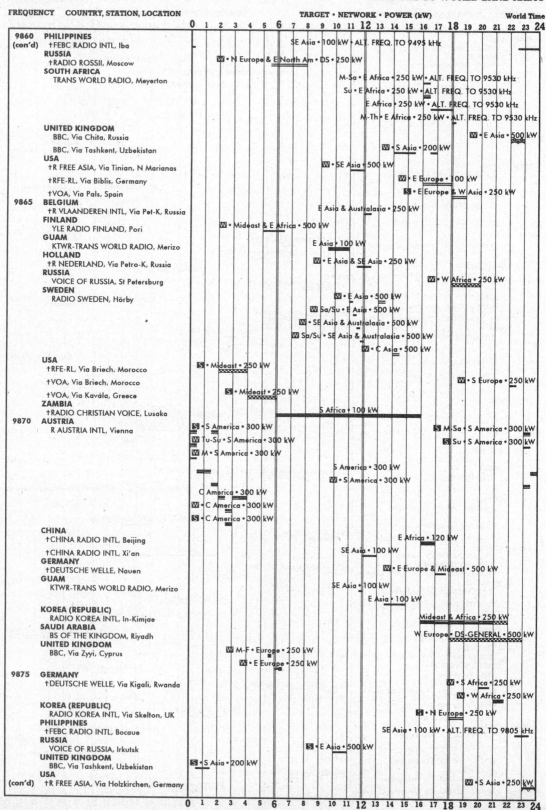

9860
(con'd)   **PHILIPPINES**
    †FEBC RADIO INTL, Iba — SE Asia • 100 kW • ALT. FREQ. TO 9495 kHz
   RUSSIA
    †RADIO ROSSII, Moscow — W • N Europe & E North Am • DS • 250 kW
   SOUTH AFRICA
    TRANS WORLD RADIO, Meyerton — M-Sa • E Africa • 250 kW • ALT. FREQ. TO 9530 kHz
     Su • E Africa • 250 kW • ALT. FREQ. TO 9530 kHz
     E Africa • 250 kW • ALT. FREQ. TO 9530 kHz
     M-Th • E Africa • 250 kW • ALT. FREQ. TO 9530 kHz

   UNITED KINGDOM
    BBC, Via Chita, Russia — W • E Asia • 500 kW
    BBC, Via Tashkent, Uzbekistan — W • S Asia • 200 kW
   USA
    †R FREE ASIA, Via Tinian, N Marianas — W • SE Asia • 500 kW
    †RFE-RL, Via Biblis, Germany — W • E Europe • 100 kW
    †VOA, Via Pals, Spain — S • E Europe & W Asia • 250 kW

9865   **BELGIUM**
    †R VLAANDEREN INTL, Via Pet-K, Russia — E Asia & Australasia • 250 kW
   FINLAND
    YLE RADIO FINLAND, Pori — W • Mideast & E Africa • 500 kW
   GUAM
    KTWR-TRANS WORLD RADIO, Merizo — E Asia • 100 kW
   HOLLAND
    †R NEDERLAND, Via Petro-K, Russia — W • E Asia & SE Asia • 250 kW
   RUSSIA
    VOICE OF RUSSIA, St Petersburg — W • W Africa • 250 kW
   SWEDEN
    RADIO SWEDEN, Hörby — W • E Asia • 500 kW
     W Sa/Su • E Asia • 500 kW
     W • SE Asia & Australasia • 500 kW
     W Sa/Su • SE Asia & Australasia • 500 kW
     W • C Asia • 500 kW

   USA
    †RFE-RL, Via Briech, Morocco — S • Mideast • 250 kW
    †VOA, Via Briech, Morocco — W • S Europe • 250 kW
    †VOA, Via Kavála, Greece — S • Mideast • 250 kW
   ZAMBIA
    †RADIO CHRISTIAN VOICE, Lusaka — S Africa • 100 kW

9870   **AUSTRIA**
    R AUSTRIA INTL, Vienna — S • S America • 300 kW   S M-Sa • S America • 300 kW
     W Tu-Su • S America • 300 kW   S Su • S America • 300 kW
     W M • S America • 300 kW
     S America • 300 kW
     W • S America • 300 kW
     C America • 300 kW
     W • C America • 300 kW
     S • C America • 300 kW

   CHINA
    †CHINA RADIO INTL, Beijing — E Africa • 120 kW
    †CHINA RADIO INTL, Xi'an — SE Asia • 100 kW
   GERMANY
    †DEUTSCHE WELLE, Nauen — W • E Europe & Mideast • 500 kW
   GUAM
    KTWR-TRANS WORLD RADIO, Merizo — SE Asia • 100 kW
     E Asia • 100 kW

   KOREA (REPUBLIC)
    RADIO KOREA INTL, In-Kimjae — Mideast & Africa • 250 kW
   SAUDI ARABIA
    BS OF THE KINGDOM, Riyadh — W Europe • DS-GENERAL • 600 kW
   UNITED KINGDOM
    BBC, Via Zyyi, Cyprus — W M-F • Europe • 250 kW
     W • E Europe • 250 kW

9875   **GERMANY**
    †DEUTSCHE WELLE, Via Kigali, Rwanda — W • S Africa • 250 kW
     W • W Africa • 250 kW
   KOREA (REPUBLIC)
    RADIO KOREA INTL, Via Skelton, UK — S • N Europe • 250 kW
   PHILIPPINES
    †FEBC RADIO INTL, Bocaue — SE Asia • 100 kW • ALT. FREQ. TO 9805 kHz
   RUSSIA
    VOICE OF RUSSIA, Irkutsk — S • E Asia • 500 kW
   UNITED KINGDOM
    BBC, Via Tashkent, Uzbekistan — S • S Asia • 200 kW
   USA
(con'd)   †R FREE ASIA, Via Holzkirchen, Germany — W • S Asia • 250 kW

FREQUENCY   COUNTRY, STATION, LOCATION   TARGET • NETWORK • POWER (kW)   World Time

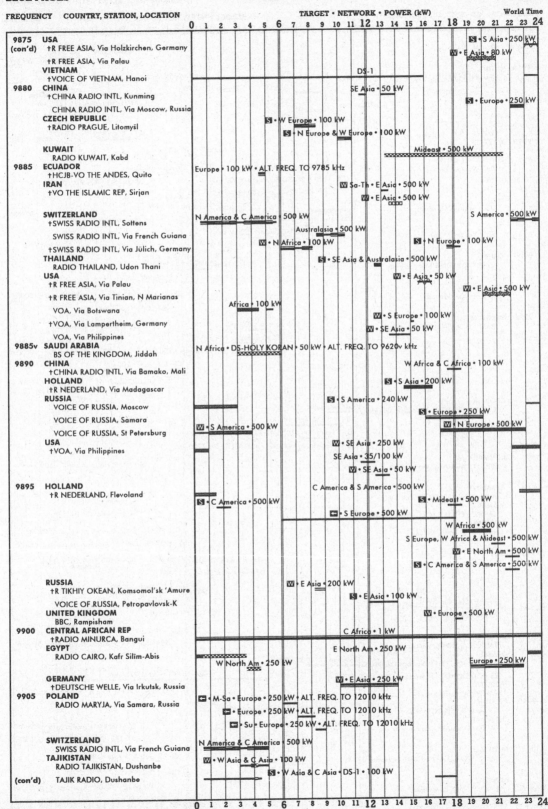

Frequency	Country, Station, Location	Target • Network • Power
9875 (con'd)	**USA**	
	†R FREE ASIA, Via Holzkirchen, Germany	S • S Asia • 250 kW
	†R FREE ASIA, Via Palau	W • E Asia • 80 kW
	VIETNAM	
	†VOICE OF VIETNAM, Hanoi	DS-1
9880	**CHINA**	
	†CHINA RADIO INTL, Kunming	SE Asia • 50 kW
	CHINA RADIO INTL, Via Moscow, Russia	S • Europe • 250 kW
	CZECH REPUBLIC	
	†RADIO PRAGUE, Litomyšl	S • W Europe • 100 kW
		S • N Europe & W Europe • 100 kW
	KUWAIT	
	RADIO KUWAIT, Kabd	Mideast • 500 kW
9885	**ECUADOR**	
	†HCJB-VO THE ANDES, Quito	Europe • 100 kW • ALT. FREQ. TO 9785 kHz
	IRAN	
	†VO THE ISLAMIC REP, Sirjan	W • Sa-Th • E Asia • 500 kW
		W • E Asia • 500 kW
	SWITZERLAND	
	†SWISS RADIO INTL, Sottens	N America & C America • 500 kW / S America • 500 kW
	SWISS RADIO INTL, Via French Guiana	Australasia • 500 kW
	†SWISS RADIO INTL, Via Jülich, Germany	W • N Africa • 100 kW / S • N Europe • 100 kW
	THAILAND	
	RADIO THAILAND, Udon Thani	S • SE Asia & Australasia • 500 kW
	USA	
	†R FREE ASIA, Via Palau	W • E Asia • 50 kW
	†R FREE ASIA, Via Tinian, N Marianas	W • E Asia • 500 kW
	VOA, Via Botswana	Africa • 100 kW
	†VOA, Via Lampertheim, Germany	W • S Europe • 100 kW
	VOA, Via Philippines	W • SE Asia • 50 kW
9885v	**SAUDI ARABIA**	
	BS OF THE KINGDOM, Jiddah	N Africa • DS-HOLY KORAN • 50 kW • ALT. FREQ. TO 9620v kHz
9890	**CHINA**	
	†CHINA RADIO INTL, Via Bamako, Mali	W Africa & C Africa • 100 kW
	HOLLAND	
	†R NEDERLAND, Via Madagascar	S • S Asia • 200 kW
	RUSSIA	
	VOICE OF RUSSIA, Moscow	S • S America • 240 kW
	VOICE OF RUSSIA, Samara	S • Europe • 250 kW
	VOICE OF RUSSIA, St Petersburg	W • S America • 500 kW / W • N Europe • 500 kW
	USA	
	†VOA, Via Philippines	W • SE Asia • 250 kW / SE Asia • 35/100 kW / W • SE Asia • 50 kW
9895	**HOLLAND**	
	†R NEDERLAND, Flevoland	C America & S America • 500 kW
		S • C America • 500 kW / S • Mideast • 500 kW
		S • S Europe • 500 kW
		W Africa • 500 kW
		S Europe, W Africa & Mideast • 500 kW
		W • E North Am • 500 kW
		S • C America & S America • 500 kW
	RUSSIA	
	†R TIKHIY OKEAN, Komsomol'sk 'Amure	W • E Asia • 200 kW
	VOICE OF RUSSIA, Petropavlovsk-K	S • E Asia • 100 kW
	UNITED KINGDOM	
	BBC, Rampisham	W • Europe • 500 kW
9900	**CENTRAL AFRICAN REP**	
	†RADIO MINURCA, Bangui	C Africa • 1 kW
	EGYPT	
	RADIO CAIRO, Kafr Silim-Abis	E North Am • 250 kW / W North Am • 250 kW / Europe • 250 kW
	GERMANY	
	†DEUTSCHE WELLE, Via Irkutsk, Russia	W • E Asia • 250 kW
9905	**POLAND**	
	RADIO MARYJA, Via Samara, Russia	M-Sa • Europe • 250 kW • ALT. FREQ. TO 12010 kHz
		S • Europe • 250 kW • ALT. FREQ. TO 12010 kHz
		Su • Europe • 250 kW • ALT. FREQ. TO 12010 kHz
	SWITZERLAND	
	SWISS RADIO INTL, Via French Guiana	N America & C America • 500 kW
	TAJIKISTAN	
	RADIO TAJIKISTAN, Dushanbe	W • W Asia & C Asia • 100 kW
		S • W Asia & C Asia • DS-1 • 100 kW
(con'd)	TAJIK RADIO, Dushanbe	

ENGLISH ▬   ARABIC ∽∽∽   CHINESE □□□   FRENCH ▬▬   GERMAN ▬▬   RUSSIAN ═══   SPANISH ▬▬   OTHER ▬

FREQUENCY   COUNTRY, STATION, LOCATION   TARGET • NETWORK • POWER (kW)   World Time

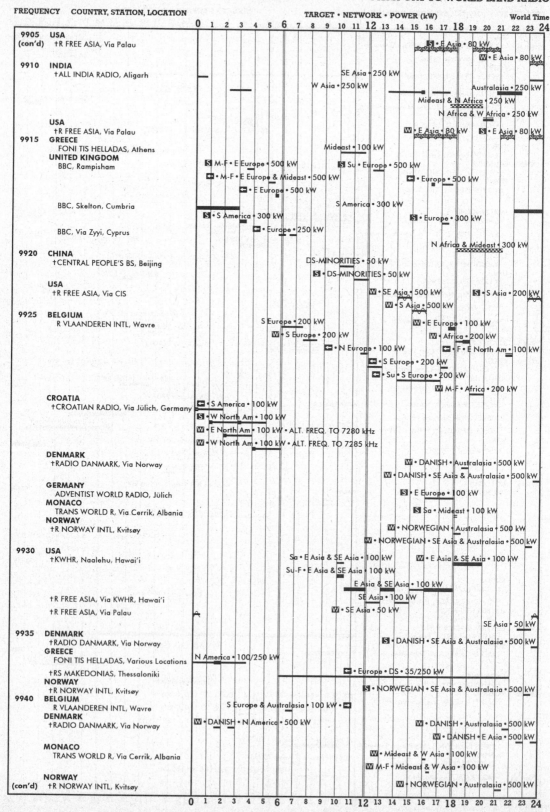

Frequency	Country, Station, Location	Target • Network • Power
9905 (con'd)	USA †R FREE ASIA, Via Palau	S • E Asia • 80 kW; W • E Asia • 80 kW
9910	INDIA †ALL INDIA RADIO, Aligarh	SE Asia • 250 kW; W Asia • 250 kW; Australasia • 250 kW; Mideast & N Africa • 250 kW; N Africa & W Africa • 250 kW
	USA †R FREE ASIA, Via Palau	W • E Asia • 80 kW; S • E Asia • 80 kW
9915	GREECE FONI TIS HELLADAS, Athens	Mideast • 100 kW
	UNITED KINGDOM BBC, Rampisham	S M-F • E Europe • 500 kW; S Su • Europe • 500 kW; M-F • E Europe & Mideast • 500 kW; Europe • 500 kW; E Europe • 500 kW
	BBC, Skelton, Cumbria	S America • 300 kW; S • S America • 300 kW; S • Europe • 300 kW
	BBC, Via Zyyi, Cyprus	Europe • 250 kW; N Africa & Mideast • 300 kW
9920	CHINA †CENTRAL PEOPLE'S BS, Beijing	DS-MINORITIES • 50 kW; S • DS-MINORITIES • 50 kW
	USA †R FREE ASIA, Via CIS	W • SE Asia • 500 kW; W • S Asia • 500 kW; S • S Asia • 200 kW
9925	BELGIUM R VLAANDEREN INTL, Wavre	S Europe • 200 kW; W • S Europe • 200 kW; N Europe • 100 kW; W • E Europe • 100 kW; W • Africa • 200 kW; F • E North Am • 100 kW; S Europe • 200 kW; Su • S Europe • 200 kW; M-F • Africa • 200 kW
	CROATIA †CROATIAN RADIO, Via Jülich, Germany	S America • 100 kW; S • W North Am • 100 kW; W • E North Am • 100 kW • ALT. FREQ. TO 7280 kHz; W • W North Am • 100 kW • ALT. FREQ. TO 7285 kHz
	DENMARK †RADIO DANMARK, Via Norway	W • DANISH • Australasia • 500 kW; W • DANISH • SE Asia & Australasia • 500 kW
	GERMANY ADVENTIST WORLD RADIO, Jülich	S • E Europe • 100 kW
	MONACO TRANS WORLD R, Via Cerrik, Albania	S Sa • Mideast • 100 kW
	NORWAY †R NORWAY INTL, Kvitsøy	W • NORWEGIAN • Australasia • 500 kW; W • NORWEGIAN • SE Asia & Australasia • 500 kW
9930	USA †KWHR, Naalehu, Hawai'i	Sa • E Asia & SE Asia • 100 kW; Su-F • E Asia & SE Asia • 100 kW; E Asia & SE Asia • 100 kW; SE Asia • 100 kW; W • E Asia & SE Asia • 100 kW
	†R FREE ASIA, Via KWHR, Hawai'i	W • SE Asia • 50 kW
	†R FREE ASIA, Via Palau	SE Asia • 50 kW
9935	DENMARK †RADIO DANMARK, Via Norway	S • DANISH • SE Asia & Australasia • 500 kW
	GREECE FONI TIS HELLADAS, Various Locations	N America • 100/250 kW; Europe • DS • 35/250 kW
	†RS MAKEDONIAS, Thessaloniki	
	NORWAY †R NORWAY INTL, Kvitsøy	S • NORWEGIAN • SE Asia & Australasia • 500 kW
9940	BELGIUM R VLAANDEREN INTL, Wavre	S Europe & Australasia • 100 kW
	DENMARK †RADIO DANMARK, Via Norway	W • DANISH • N America • 500 kW; W • DANISH • Australasia • 500 kW; W • DANISH • E Asia • 500 kW
	MONACO TRANS WORLD R, Via Cerrik, Albania	W • Mideast & W Asia • 100 kW; W M-F • Mideast & W Asia • 100 kW
	NORWAY (con'd) †R NORWAY INTL, Kvitsøy	W • NORWEGIAN • Australasia • 500 kW

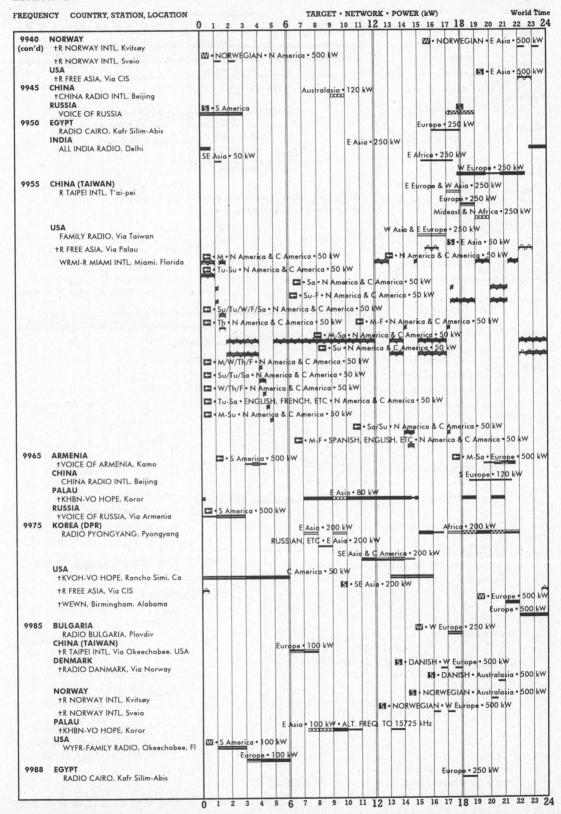

FREQUENCY	COUNTRY, STATION, LOCATION	TARGET • NETWORK • POWER (kW)	World Time

9940 (con'd)   **NORWAY**
- †R NORWAY INTL, Kvitsøy — W • NORWEGIAN • E Asia • 500 kW
- †R NORWAY INTL, Sveio — W • NORWEGIAN • N America • 500 kW

USA
- †R FREE ASIA, Via CIS — S • E Asia • 500 kW

9945   **CHINA**
- †CHINA RADIO INTL, Beijing — Australasia • 120 kW

RUSSIA
- VOICE OF RUSSIA — S • S America

9950   **EGYPT**
- RADIO CAIRO, Kafr Silim-Abis — Europe • 250 kW

INDIA
- ALL INDIA RADIO, Delhi — E Asia • 250 kW — SE Asia • 50 kW — E Africa • 250 kW — W Europe • 250 kW

9955   **CHINA (TAIWAN)**
- R TAIPEI INTL, T'ai-pei — E Europe & W Asia • 250 kW — Europe • 250 kW — Mideast & N Africa • 250 kW — W Asia & E Europe • 250 kW

USA
- FAMILY RADIO, Via Taiwan — S • E Asia • 50 kW
- †R FREE ASIA, Via Palau
- WRMI-R MIAMI INTL, Miami, Florida — M • N America & C America • 50 kW — N America & C America • 50 kW
  - Tu-Su • N America & C America • 50 kW
  - Sa • N America & C America • 50 kW
  - Su-F • N America & C America • 50 kW
  - Su/Tu/W/F/Sa • N America & C America • 50 kW
  - Th • N America & C America • 50 kW — M-F • N America & C America • 50 kW
  - M-Sa • N America & C America • 50 kW
  - Su • N America & C America • 50 kW
  - M/W/Th/F • N America & C America • 50 kW
  - Su/Tu/Sa • N America & C America • 50 kW
  - W/Th/F • N America & C America • 50 kW
  - Tu-Sa • ENGLISH, FRENCH, ETC • N America & C America • 50 kW
  - M-Su • N America & C America • 50 kW
  - Sa/Su • N America & C America • 50 kW
  - M-F • SPANISH, ENGLISH, ETC • N America & C America • 50 kW

9965   **ARMENIA**
- †VOICE OF ARMENIA, Kamo — S America • 500 kW — M-Sa • Europe • 500 kW

CHINA
- CHINA RADIO INTL, Beijing — S Europe • 120 kW

PALAU
- †KHBN-VO HOPE, Koror — E Asia • 80 kW

RUSSIA
- †VOICE OF RUSSIA, Via Armenia — S America • 500 kW

9975   **KOREA (DPR)**
- RADIO PYONGYANG, Pyongyang — E Asia • 200 kW — Africa • 200 kW
  - RUSSIAN, ETC • E Asia • 200 kW
  - SE Asia & C America • 200 kW

USA
- †KVOH-VO HOPE, Rancho Simi, Ca — C America • 50 kW
- †R FREE ASIA, Via CIS — S • SE Asia • 200 kW
- †WEWN, Birmingham, Alabama — W • Europe • 500 kW — Europe • 500 kW

9985   **BULGARIA**
- RADIO BULGARIA, Plovdiv — W • W Europe • 250 kW

CHINA (TAIWAN)
- †R TAIPEI INTL, Via Okeechobee, USA — Europe • 100 kW

DENMARK
- †RADIO DANMARK, Via Norway — S • DANISH • W Europe • 500 kW — S • DANISH • Australasia • 500 kW

NORWAY
- †R NORWAY INTL, Kvitsøy — S • NORWEGIAN • Australasia • 500 kW
- †R NORWAY INTL, Sveio — S • NORWEGIAN • W Europe • 500 kW

PALAU
- †KHBN-VO HOPE, Koror — E Asia • 100 kW • ALT. FREQ. TO 15725 kHz

USA
- WYFR-FAMILY RADIO, Okeechobee, Fl — W • S America • 100 kW — Europe • 100 kW

9988   **EGYPT**
- RADIO CAIRO, Kafr Silim-Abis — Europe • 250 kW

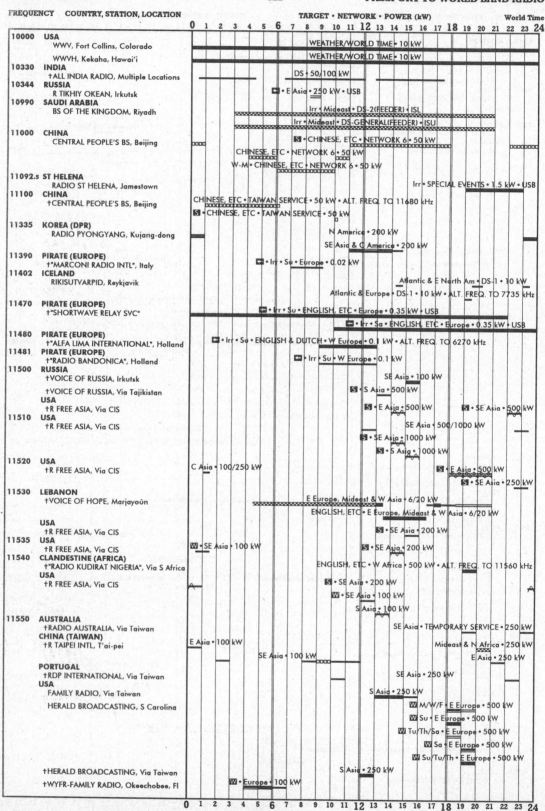

FREQUENCY   COUNTRY, STATION, LOCATION   TARGET • NETWORK • POWER (kW)   World Time

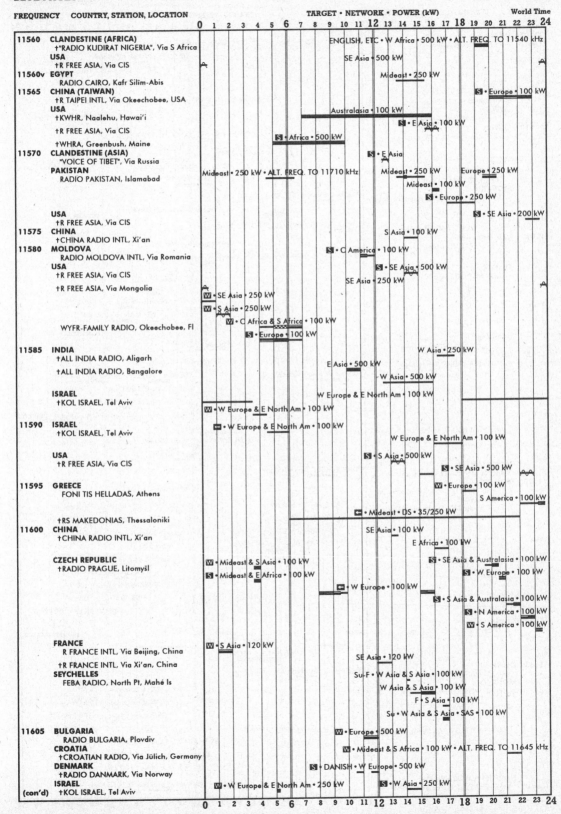

Frequency	Country, Station, Location	Target • Network • Power
11560	**CLANDESTINE (AFRICA)**	
	†"RADIO KUDIRAT NIGERIA", Via S Africa	ENGLISH, ETC • W Africa • 500 kW • ALT. FREQ. TO 11540 kHz
	USA	
	†R FREE ASIA, Via CIS	SE Asia • 500 kW
11560v	**EGYPT**	
	RADIO CAIRO, Kafr Silim-Abis	Mideast • 250 kW
11565	**CHINA (TAIWAN)**	
	†R TAIPEI INTL, Via Okeechobee, USA	S • Europe • 100 kW
	USA	
	†KWHR, Naalehu, Hawai'i	Australasia • 100 kW
	†R FREE ASIA, Via CIS	S • E Asia • 100 kW
	†WHRA, Greenbush, Maine	S • Africa • 500 kW
11570	**CLANDESTINE (ASIA)**	
	"VOICE OF TIBET", Via Russia	S • E Asia
	PAKISTAN	
	RADIO PAKISTAN, Islamabad	Mideast • 250 kW • ALT. FREQ. TO 11710 kHz Mideast • 250 kW Europe • 250 kW
		Mideast • 100 kW
		S • Europe • 250 kW
	USA	
	†R FREE ASIA, Via CIS	S • SE Asia • 200 kW
11575	**CHINA**	
	†CHINA RADIO INTL, Xi'an	S Asia • 100 kW
11580	**MOLDOVA**	
	RADIO MOLDOVA INTL, Via Romania	S • C America • 100 kW
	USA	
	†R FREE ASIA, Via CIS	S • SE Asia • 500 kW
	†R FREE ASIA, Via Mongolia	SE Asia • 250 kW
		W • SE Asia • 250 kW
		W • S Asia • 250 kW
	WYFR-FAMILY RADIO, Okeechobee, Fl	W • C Africa & S Africa • 100 kW
		S • Europe • 100 kW
11585	**INDIA**	
	†ALL INDIA RADIO, Aligarh	W Asia • 250 kW
	†ALL INDIA RADIO, Bangalore	E Asia • 500 kW
		W Asia • 500 kW
	ISRAEL	
	†KOL ISRAEL, Tel Aviv	W Europe & E North Am • 100 kW
		W • W Europe & E North Am • 100 kW
11590	**ISRAEL**	
	†KOL ISRAEL, Tel Aviv	⊡ • W Europe & E North Am • 100 kW
		W Europe & E North Am • 100 kW
	USA	
	†R FREE ASIA, Via CIS	S • S Asia • 500 kW
		S • SE Asia • 500 kW
11595	**GREECE**	
	FONI TIS HELLADAS, Athens	W • Europe • 100 kW
		S America • 100 kW
	†RS MAKEDONIAS, Thessaloniki	⊡ • Mideast • DS • 35/250 kW
11600	**CHINA**	
	†CHINA RADIO INTL, Xi'an	SE Asia • 100 kW
		E Africa • 100 kW
	CZECH REPUBLIC	
	†RADIO PRAGUE, Litomyšl	W • Mideast & S Asia • 100 kW S • SE Asia & Australasia • 100 kW
		S • Mideast & E Africa • 100 kW S • W Europe • 100 kW
		⊡ • W Europe • 100 kW
		S • S Asia & Australasia • 100 kW
		S • N America • 100 kW
		W • S America • 100 kW
	FRANCE	
	R FRANCE INTL, Via Beijing, China	W • S Asia • 120 kW
	†R FRANCE INTL, Via Xi'an, China	SE Asia • 120 kW
	SEYCHELLES	
	FEBA RADIO, North Pt, Mahé Is	Su-F • W Asia & S Asia • 100 kW
		W Asia & S Asia • 100 kW
		F • S Asia • 100 kW
		Su • W Asia & S Asia • SAS • 100 kW
11605	**BULGARIA**	
	RADIO BULGARIA, Plovdiv	W • Europe • 500 kW
	CROATIA	
	†CROATIAN RADIO, Via Jülich, Germany	W • Mideast & S Africa • 100 kW • ALT. FREQ. TO 11645 kHz
	DENMARK	
	†RADIO DANMARK, Via Norway	S • DANISH • W Europe • 500 kW
	ISRAEL	
(con'd)	†KOL ISRAEL, Tel Aviv	W • W Europe & E North Am • 250 kW S • W Asia • 250 kW

FREQUENCY   COUNTRY, STATION, LOCATION   TARGET • NETWORK • POWER (kW)   World Time

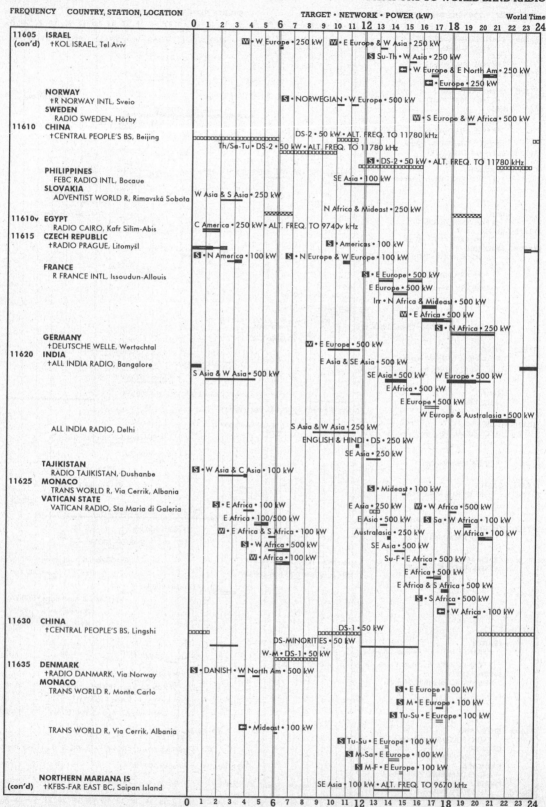

FREQUENCY	COUNTRY, STATION, LOCATION	Schedule Details
11605 (con'd)	**ISRAEL** †KOL ISRAEL, Tel Aviv	Ⓦ • W Europe • 250 kW; Ⓦ • E Europe & W Asia • 250 kW; Ⓢ Su-Th • W Asia • 250 kW; ⬌ • W Europe & E North Am • 250 kW; ⬌ • Europe • 250 kW
	NORWAY †R NORWAY INTL, Sveio	Ⓢ • NORWEGIAN • W Europe • 500 kW
	SWEDEN RADIO SWEDEN, Hörby	Ⓦ • S Europe & W Africa • 500 kW
11610	**CHINA** †CENTRAL PEOPLE'S BS, Beijing	DS-2 • 50 kW • ALT. FREQ. TO 11780 kHz; Th/Sa-Tu • DS-2 • 50 kW • ALT. FREQ. TO 11780 kHz; Ⓢ • DS-2 • 50 kW • ALT. FREQ. TO 11780 kHz
	PHILIPPINES FEBC RADIO INTL, Bocaue	SE Asia • 100 kW
	SLOVAKIA ADVENTIST WORLD R, Rimavská Sobota	W Asia & S Asia • 250 kW; N Africa & Mideast • 250 kW
11610v	**EGYPT** RADIO CAIRO, Kafr Silim-Abis	C America • 250 kW • ALT. FREQ. TO 9740v kHz
11615	**CZECH REPUBLIC** †RADIO PRAGUE, Litomyšl	Ⓢ • Americas • 100 kW; Ⓢ • N America • 100 kW; Ⓢ • N Europe & W Europe • 100 kW
	FRANCE R FRANCE INTL, Issoudun-Allouis	Ⓢ • E Europe • 500 kW; E Europe • 500 kW; Irr • N Africa & Mideast • 500 kW; Ⓦ • E Africa • 500 kW; Ⓢ • N Africa • 250 kW
	GERMANY †DEUTSCHE WELLE, Wertachtal	Ⓦ • E Europe • 500 kW
11620	**INDIA** †ALL INDIA RADIO, Bangalore	E Asia & SE Asia • 500 kW; S Asia & W Asia • 500 kW; SE Asia • 500 kW; W Europe • 500 kW; E Africa • 500 kW; E Europe • 500 kW; W Europe & Australasia • 500 kW
	ALL INDIA RADIO, Delhi	S Asia & W Asia • 250 kW; ENGLISH & HINDI • DS • 250 kW; SE Asia • 250 kW
	TAJIKISTAN RADIO TAJIKISTAN, Dushanbe	Ⓢ • W Asia & C Asia • 100 kW
11625	**MONACO** TRANS WORLD R, Via Cerrik, Albania	Ⓢ • Mideast • 100 kW
	VATICAN STATE VATICAN RADIO, Sta Maria di Galeria	Ⓢ • E Africa • 100 kW; E Africa • 100/500 kW; Ⓦ • E Africa & S Africa • 100 kW; Ⓢ • W Africa • 500 kW; Ⓦ • Africa • 100 kW; E Asia • 250 kW; E Asia • 500 kW; Ⓢ Sa • W Africa • 100 kW; Ⓦ • W Africa • 500 kW; Australasia • 250 kW; W Africa • 100 kW; SE Asia • 500 kW; Su-F • E Africa • 500 kW; E Africa • 500 kW; E Africa & S Africa • 500 kW; Ⓢ • S Africa • 500 kW; ⬌ • W Africa • 100 kW
11630	**CHINA** †CENTRAL PEOPLE'S BS, Lingshi	DS-1 • 50 kW; DS-MINORITIES • 50 kW; W-M • DS-1 • 50 kW
11635	**DENMARK** †RADIO DANMARK, Via Norway	Ⓢ • DANISH • W North Am • 500 kW
	MONACO TRANS WORLD R, Monte Carlo	Ⓢ • E Europe • 100 kW; Ⓢ M • E Europe • 100 kW; Ⓢ Tu-Su • E Europe • 100 kW
	TRANS WORLD R, Via Cerrik, Albania	⬌ • Mideast • 100 kW; Ⓢ Tu-Su • E Europe • 100 kW; Ⓢ M-Sa • E Europe • 100 kW; Ⓢ M-F • E Europe • 100 kW
(con'd)	**NORTHERN MARIANA IS** †KFBS-FAR EAST BC, Saipan Island	SE Asia • 100 kW • ALT. FREQ. TO 9670 kHz

SEASONAL Ⓢ OR Ⓦ   1-HR TIMESHIFT MIDYEAR ⬌ OR ⬌   JAMMING / OR ∧   EARLIEST HEARD ◁   LATEST HEARD ▷   NEW FOR 2000 †

FREQUENCY COUNTRY, STATION, LOCATION	TARGET • NETWORK • POWER (kW) World Time

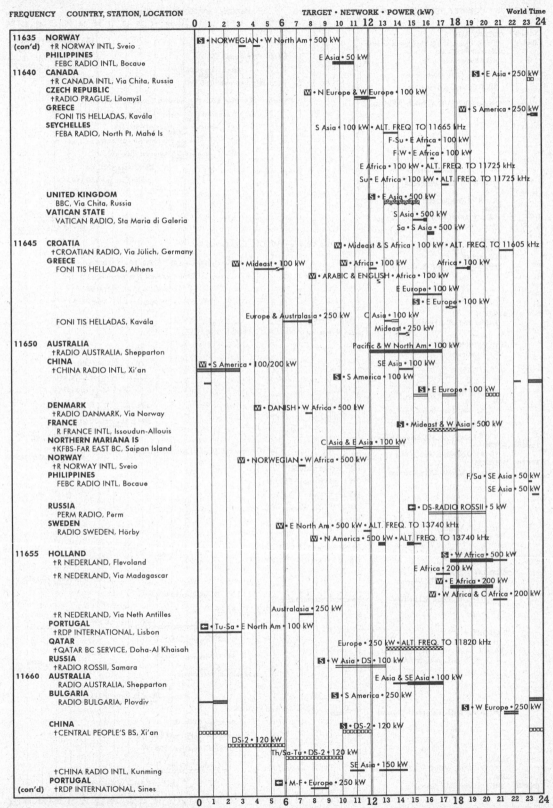

11635 NORWAY
(con'd) †R NORWAY INTL, Sveio
    S • NORWEGIAN • W North Am • 500 kW

PHILIPPINES
    FEBC RADIO INTL, Bocaue
    E Asia • 50 kW

11640 CANADA
    †R CANADA INTL, Via Chita, Russia
    S • E Asia • 250 kW

CZECH REPUBLIC
    †RADIO PRAGUE, Litomyšl
    W • N Europe & W Europe • 100 kW

GREECE
    FONI TIS HELLADAS, Kavála
    W • S America • 250 kW

SEYCHELLES
    FEBA RADIO, North Pt, Mahé Is
    S Asia • 100 kW • ALT. FREQ. TO 11665 kHz
    F-Su • E Africa • 100 kW
    F-W • E Africa • 100 kW
    E Africa • 100 kW • ALT. FREQ. TO 11725 kHz
    Su • E Africa • 100 kW • ALT. FREQ. TO 11725 kHz

UNITED KINGDOM
    BBC, Via Chita, Russia
    S • E Asia • 500 kW

VATICAN STATE
    VATICAN RADIO, Sta Maria di Galeria
    S Asia • 500 kW
    Sa • S Asia • 500 kW

11645 CROATIA
    †CROATIAN RADIO, Via Jülich, Germany
    W • Mideast & S Africa • 100 kW • ALT. FREQ. TO 11605 kHz

GREECE
    FONI TIS HELLADAS, Athens
    W • Mideast • 100 kW
    W • Africa • 100 kW
    Africa • 100 kW
    W • ARABIC & ENGLISH • Africa • 100 kW
    E Europe • 100 kW
    S • E Europe • 100 kW

    FONI TIS HELLADAS, Kavála
    Europe & Australasia • 250 kW
    C Asia • 100 kW
    Mideast • 250 kW

11650 AUSTRALIA
    †RADIO AUSTRALIA, Shepparton
    Pacific & W North Am • 100 kW

CHINA
    †CHINA RADIO INTL, Xi'an
    W • S America • 100/200 kW
    SE Asia • 100 kW
    S • S America • 100 kW
    S • E Europe • 100 kW

DENMARK
    †RADIO DANMARK, Via Norway
    W • DANISH • W Africa • 500 kW

FRANCE
    R FRANCE INTL, Issoudun-Allouis
    S • Mideast & W Asia • 500 kW

NORTHERN MARIANA IS
    †KFBS-FAR EAST BC, Saipan Island
    C Asia & E Asia • 100 kW

NORWAY
    †R NORWAY INTL, Sveio
    W • NORWEGIAN • W Africa • 500 kW

PHILIPPINES
    FEBC RADIO INTL, Bocaue
    F/Sa • SE Asia • 50 kW
    SE Asia • 50 kW

RUSSIA
    PERM RADIO, Perm
    • DS-RADIO ROSSII • 5 kW

SWEDEN
    RADIO SWEDEN, Hörby
    W • E North Am • 500 kW • ALT. FREQ. TO 13740 kHz
    W • N America • 500 kW • ALT. FREQ. TO 13740 kHz

11655 HOLLAND
    †R NEDERLAND, Flevoland
    S • W Africa • 500 kW
    †R NEDERLAND, Via Madagascar
    E Africa • 200 kW
    W • E Africa • 200 kW
    W • W Africa & C Africa • 200 kW

    †R NEDERLAND, Via Neth Antilles
    Australasia • 250 kW

PORTUGAL
    †RDP INTERNATIONAL, Lisbon
    • Tu-Sa • E North Am • 100 kW

QATAR
    †QATAR BC SERVICE, Doha-Al Khaisah
    Europe • 250 kW • ALT. FREQ. TO 11820 kHz

RUSSIA
    †RADIO ROSSII, Samara
    S • W Asia • DS • 100 kW

11660 AUSTRALIA
    RADIO AUSTRALIA, Shepparton
    E Asia & SE Asia • 100 kW

BULGARIA
    RADIO BULGARIA, Plovdiv
    S • S America • 250 kW
    S • W Europe • 250 kW

CHINA
    †CENTRAL PEOPLE'S BS, Xi'an
    S • DS-2 • 120 kW
    DS-2 • 120 kW
    Th/Sa-Tu • DS-2 • 120 kW

    †CHINA RADIO INTL, Kunming
    SE Asia • 150 kW

PORTUGAL
(con'd) †RDP INTERNATIONAL, Sines
    • M-F • Europe • 250 kW

ENGLISH ▬▬   ARABIC ⌇⌇⌇   CHINESE ▫▫▫   FRENCH ▭▭   GERMAN ▬▬   RUSSIAN ══   SPANISH ▬▬   OTHER ──

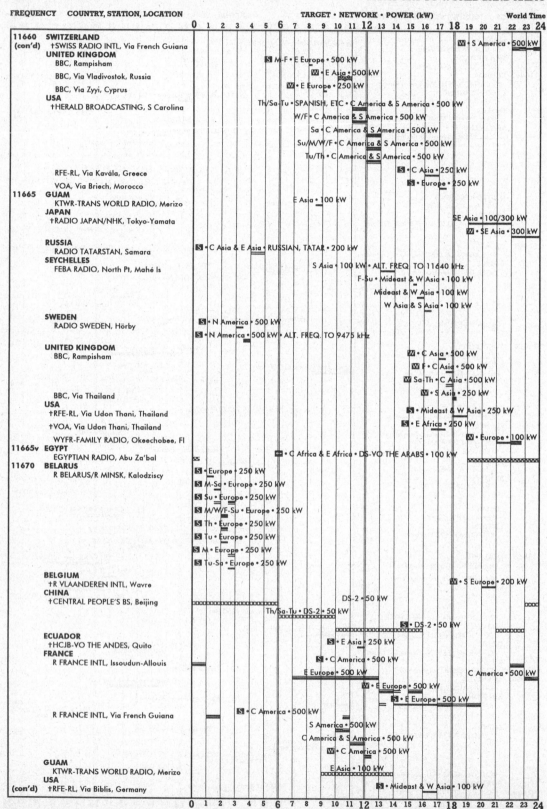

FREQUENCY	COUNTRY, STATION, LOCATION	TARGET • NETWORK • POWER (kW) — World Time
		0 1 2 3 4 5 6 7 8 9 10 11 12 13 14 15 16 17 18 19 20 21 22 23 24

11660
(con'd)   **SWITZERLAND**
    †SWISS RADIO INTL, Via French Guiana — W • S America • 500 kW
   UNITED KINGDOM
    BBC, Rampisham — S M-F • E Europe • 500 kW
    BBC, Via Vladivostok, Russia — W • E Asia • 500 kW
    BBC, Via Zyyi, Cyprus — W • E Europe • 250 kW
   USA
    †HERALD BROADCASTING, S Carolina — Th/Sa-Tu • SPANISH, ETC • C America & S America • 500 kW
    W/F • C America & S America • 500 kW
    Sa • C America & S America • 500 kW
    Su/M/W/F • C America & S America • 500 kW
    Tu/Th • C America & S • 500 kW
    RFE-RL, Via Kavála, Greece — S • C Asia • 250 kW
    VOA, Via Briech, Morocco — S • Europe • 250 kW

11665   **GUAM**
    KTWR-TRANS WORLD RADIO, Merizo — E Asia • 100 kW
   JAPAN
    †RADIO JAPAN/NHK, Tokyo-Yamata — SE Asia • 100/300 kW
    W • SE Asia • 300 kW
   RUSSIA
    RADIO TATARSTAN, Samara — S • C Asia & E Asia • RUSSIAN, TATAR • 200 kW
   SEYCHELLES
    FEBA RADIO, North Pt, Mahé Is — S Asia • 100 kW • ALT. FREQ TO 11640 kHz
    F-Su • Mideast & W Asia • 100 kW
    Mideast & W Asia • 100 kW
    W Asia & S Asia • 100 kW
   SWEDEN
    RADIO SWEDEN, Hörby — S • N America • 500 kW
    S • N America • 500 kW • ALT. FREQ. TO 9475 kHz
   UNITED KINGDOM
    BBC, Rampisham — W • C Asia • 500 kW
    W • F • C Asia • 500 kW
    W Sa-Th • C Asia • 500 kW
    W • S Asia • 250 kW
    BBC, Via Thailand
   USA
    †RFE-RL, Via Udon Thani, Thailand — S • Mideast & W Asia • 250 kW
    †VOA, Via Udon Thani, Thailand — S • E Africa • 250 kW
    WYFR-FAMILY RADIO, Okeechobee, Fl — W • Europe • 100 kW

11665v   **EGYPT**
    EGYPTIAN RADIO, Abu Za'bal — • C Africa & E Africa • DS-VO THE ARABS • 100 kW

11670   **BELARUS**
    R BELARUS/R MINSK, Kalodziscy — S • Europe • 250 kW
    S M-Sa • Europe • 250 kW
    S Su • Europe • 250 kW
    S M/W/F-Su • Europe • 250 kW
    S Th • Europe • 250 kW
    S Tu • Europe • 250 kW
    S M • Europe • 250 kW
    S Tu-Sa • Europe • 250 kW
   BELGIUM
    †R VLAANDEREN INTL, Wavre — W • S Europe • 200 kW
   CHINA
    †CENTRAL PEOPLE'S BS, Beijing — DS-2 • 50 kW
    Th/Sa-Tu • DS-2 • 50 kW
    S • DS-2 • 50 kW
   ECUADOR
    †HCJB-VO THE ANDES, Quito — S • E Asia • 250 kW
   FRANCE
    R FRANCE INTL, Issoudun-Allouis — S • C America • 500 kW
    E Europe • 500 kW
    C America • 500 kW
    W • E Europe • 500 kW
    S • E Europe • 500 kW
    R FRANCE INTL, Via French Guiana — S • C America • 500 kW
    S America • 500 kW
    C America & S America • 500 kW
    W • C America • 500 kW
   GUAM
    KTWR-TRANS WORLD RADIO, Merizo — E Asia • 100 kW
   USA
(con'd)   †RFE-RL, Via Biblis, Germany — S • Mideast & W Asia • 100 kW

| | | 0 1 2 3 4 5 6 7 8 9 10 11 12 13 14 15 16 17 18 19 20 21 22 23 24 |

SEASONAL S OR W   1-HR TIMESHIFT MIDYEAR ◨ OR ◧   JAMMING / OR /\   EARLIEST HEARD ◁   LATEST HEARD ▷   NEW FOR 2000 †

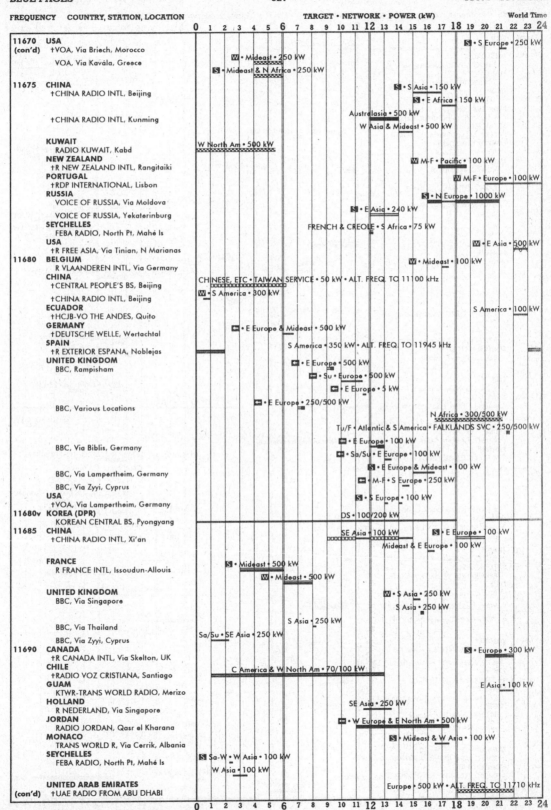

FREQUENCY	COUNTRY, STATION, LOCATION	TARGET • NETWORK • POWER (kW) / World Time
11670 (con'd)	USA	
	†VOA, Via Briech, Morocco	S Europe • 250 kW
	VOA, Via Kavála, Greece	W • Mideast • 250 kW / S • Mideast & N Africa • 250 kW
11675	CHINA	
	†CHINA RADIO INTL, Beijing	S • S Asia • 150 kW / S • E Africa • 150 kW
	†CHINA RADIO INTL, Kunming	Australasia • 500 kW / W Asia & Mideast • 500 kW
	KUWAIT	
	RADIO KUWAIT, Kabd	W North Am • 500 kW
	NEW ZEALAND	
	†R NEW ZEALAND INTL, Rangitaiki	M-F • Pacific • 100 kW
	PORTUGAL	
	†RDP INTERNATIONAL, Lisbon	M-F • Europe • 100 kW
	RUSSIA	
	VOICE OF RUSSIA, Via Moldova	N Europe • 1000 kW
	VOICE OF RUSSIA, Yekaterinburg	S • E Asia • 240 kW
	SEYCHELLES	
	FEBA RADIO, North Pt, Mahé Is	FRENCH & CREOLE • S Africa • 75 kW
	USA	
	†R FREE ASIA, Via Tinian, N Marianas	W • E Asia • 500 kW
11680	BELGIUM	
	R VLAANDEREN INTL, Via Germany	W • Mideast • 100 kW
	CHINA	
	†CENTRAL PEOPLE'S BS, Beijing	CHINESE, ETC • TAIWAN SERVICE • 50 kW • ALT. FREQ. TO 11100 kHz
	†CHINA RADIO INTL, Beijing	W • S America • 300 kW
	ECUADOR	
	†HCJB-VO THE ANDES, Quito	S America • 100 kW
	GERMANY	
	†DEUTSCHE WELLE, Wertachtal	• E Europe & Mideast • 500 kW
	SPAIN	
	†R EXTERIOR ESPANA, Noblejas	S America • 350 kW • ALT. FREQ. TO 11945 kHz
	UNITED KINGDOM	
	BBC, Rampisham	• E Europe • 500 kW / • Su • Europe • 500 kW / • E Europe • 5 kW / • E Europe • 250/500 kW
	BBC, Various Locations	N Africa • 300/500 kW / Tu/F • Atlantic & S America • FALKLANDS SVC • 250/500 kW
	BBC, Via Biblis, Germany	• E Europe • 100 kW / • Sa/Su • E Europe • 100 kW
	BBC, Via Lampertheim, Germany	S • E Europe & Mideast • 100 kW
	BBC, Via Zyyi, Cyprus	• M-F • S Europe • 250 kW
	USA	
	†VOA, Via Lampertheim, Germany	S • S Europe • 100 kW
11680v	KOREA (DPR)	
	KOREAN CENTRAL BS, Pyongyang	DS • 100/200 kW
11685	CHINA	
	†CHINA RADIO INTL, Xi'an	SE Asia • 100 kW / S • E Europe • 100 kW / Mideast & E Europe • 100 kW
	FRANCE	
	R FRANCE INTL, Issoudun-Allouis	S • Mideast • 500 kW / W • Mideast • 500 kW
	UNITED KINGDOM	
	BBC, Via Singapore	W • S Asia • 250 kW / S Asia • 250 kW
	BBC, Via Thailand	S Asia • 250 kW
	BBC, Via Zyyi, Cyprus	Sa/Su • SE Asia • 250 kW
11690	CANADA	
	†R CANADA INTL, Via Skelton, UK	S • Europe • 300 kW
	CHILE	
	†RADIO VOZ CRISTIANA, Santiago	C America & W North Am • 70/100 kW
	GUAM	
	KTWR-TRANS WORLD RADIO, Merizo	E Asia • 100 kW
	HOLLAND	
	R NEDERLAND, Via Singapore	SE Asia • 250 kW
	JORDAN	
	RADIO JORDAN, Qasr el Kharana	• W Europe & E North Am • 500 kW
	MONACO	
	TRANS WORLD R, Via Cerrik, Albania	S • Mideast & W Asia • 100 kW
	SEYCHELLES	
	FEBA RADIO, North Pt, Mahé Is	S • Sa-W • W Asia • 100 kW / W Asia • 100 kW
(con'd)	UNITED ARAB EMIRATES	
	†UAE RADIO FROM ABU DHABI	Europe • 500 kW • ALT. FREQ. TO 11710 kHz

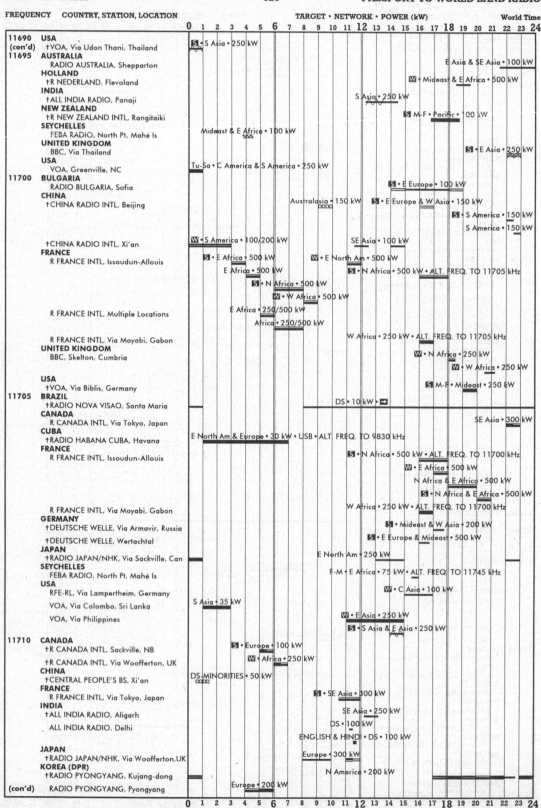

FREQUENCY	COUNTRY, STATION, LOCATION	TARGET • NETWORK • POWER (kW)	World Time

11690
(con'd)   **USA**
    †VOA, Via Udon Thani, Thailand — S • S Asia • 250 kW

11695   **AUSTRALIA**
    RADIO AUSTRALIA, Shepparton — E Asia & SE Asia • 100 kW
   HOLLAND
    †R NEDERLAND, Flevoland — W • Mideast & E Africa • 500 kW
   INDIA
    †ALL INDIA RADIO, Panaji — S Asia • 250 kW
   NEW ZEALAND
    †R NEW ZEALAND INTL, Rangitaiki — S • M-F • Pacific • 100 kW
   SEYCHELLES
    FEBA RADIO, North Pt, Mahé Is — Mideast & E Africa • 100 kW
   UNITED KINGDOM
    BBC, Via Thailand — S • E Asia • 250 kW
   USA
    VOA, Greenville, NC — Tu-Sa • C America & S America • 250 kW

11700   **BULGARIA**
    RADIO BULGARIA, Sofia — S • E Europe • 100 kW
   CHINA
    †CHINA RADIO INTL, Beijing — Australasia • 150 kW   S • E Europe & W Asia • 150 kW
       S • S America • 150 kW
       S America • 150 kW
    †CHINA RADIO INTL, Xi'an — W • S America • 100/200 kW   SE Asia • 100 kW
   FRANCE
    R FRANCE INTL, Issoudun-Allouis — S • E Africa • 500 kW   W • E North Am • 500 kW
       E Africa • 500 kW   S • N Africa • 500 kW • ALT. FREQ. TO 11705 kHz
       S • N Africa • 500 kW
       W • W Africa • 500 kW
    R FRANCE INTL, Multiple Locations — E Africa • 250/500 kW
       Africa • 250/500 kW
    R FRANCE INTL, Via Moyabi, Gabon — W Africa • 250 kW • ALT. FREQ. TO 11705 kHz
   UNITED KINGDOM
    BBC, Skelton, Cumbria — W • N Africa • 250 kW
       W • W Africa • 250 kW
   USA
    †VOA, Via Biblis, Germany — S • M-F • Mideast • 250 kW

11705   **BRAZIL**
    †RADIO NOVA VISAO, Santa Maria — DS • 10 kW •
   CANADA
    R CANADA INTL, Via Tokyo, Japan — SE Asia • 300 kW
   CUBA
    †RADIO HABANA CUBA, Havana — E North Am & Europe • 30 kW • USB • ALT. FREQ. TO 9830 kHz
   FRANCE
    R FRANCE INTL, Issoudun-Allouis — S • N Africa • 500 kW • ALT. FREQ. TO 11700 kHz
       W • E Africa • 500 kW
       N Africa & E Africa • 500 kW
       S • N Africa & E Africa • 500 kW
    R FRANCE INTL, Via Moyabi, Gabon — W Africa • 250 kW • ALT. FREQ. TO 11700 kHz
   GERMANY
    †DEUTSCHE WELLE, Via Armavir, Russia — S • Mideast & W Asia • 200 kW
    †DEUTSCHE WELLE, Wertachtal — S • E Europe & Mideast • 500 kW
   JAPAN
    †RADIO JAPAN/NHK, Via Sackville, Can — E North Am • 250 kW
   SEYCHELLES
    FEBA RADIO, North Pt, Mahé Is — F-M • E Africa • 75 kW • ALT. FREQ. TO 11745 kHz
   USA
    RFE-RL, Via Lampertheim, Germany — W • C Asia • 100 kW
    VOA, Via Colombo, Sri Lanka — S Asia • 35 kW
    VOA, Via Philippines — W • E Asia • 250 kW
       S • S Asia & E Asia • 250 kW

11710   **CANADA**
    †R CANADA INTL, Sackville, NB — S • Europe • 100 kW
    †R CANADA INTL, Via Woofferton, UK — W • Africa • 250 kW
   CHINA
    †CENTRAL PEOPLE'S BS, Xi'an — DS-MINORITIES • 50 kW
   FRANCE
    R FRANCE INTL, Via Tokyo, Japan — S • SE Asia • 300 kW
   INDIA
    †ALL INDIA RADIO, Aligarh — SE Asia • 250 kW
    ALL INDIA RADIO, Delhi — DS • 100 kW
       ENGLISH & HINDI • DS • 100 kW
   JAPAN
    †RADIO JAPAN/NHK, Via Woofferton, UK — Europe • 300 kW
   KOREA (DPR)
    †RADIO PYONGYANG, Kujang-dong — N America • 200 kW

(con'd)   RADIO PYONGYANG, Pyongyang — Europe • 200 kW

FREQUENCY   COUNTRY, STATION, LOCATION   TARGET • NETWORK • POWER (kW)   World Time

0 1 2 3 4 5 6 7 8 9 10 11 12 13 14 15 16 17 18 19 20 21 22 23 24

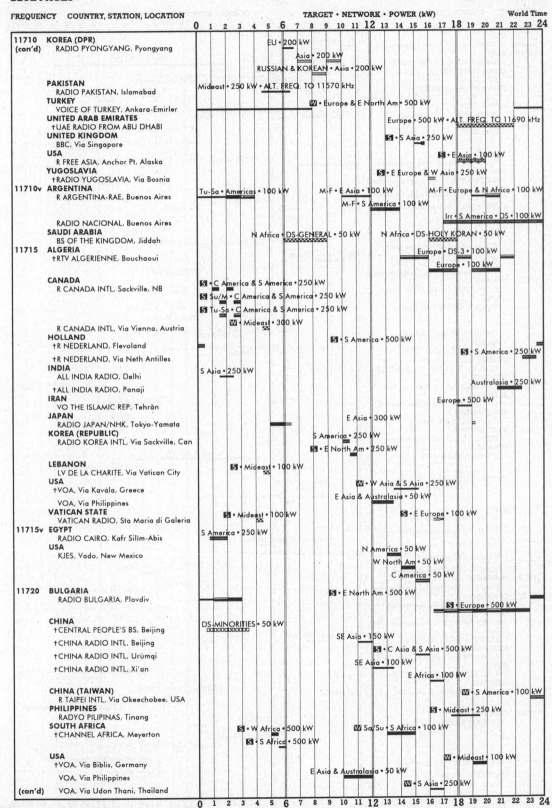

Frequency	Country, Station, Location	Target • Network • Power
11710 (con'd)	KOREA (DPR) — RADIO PYONGYANG, Pyongyang	EU • 200 kW
		Asia • 200 kW
		RUSSIAN & KOREAN • Asia • 200 kW
	PAKISTAN — RADIO PAKISTAN, Islamabad	Mideast • 250 kW • ALT. FREQ. TO 11570 kHz
	TURKEY — VOICE OF TURKEY, Ankara-Emirler	W • Europe & E North Am • 500 kW
	UNITED ARAB EMIRATES — †UAE RADIO FROM ABU DHABI	Europe • 500 kW • ALT. FREQ. TO 11690 kHz
	UNITED KINGDOM — BBC, Via Singapore	S • S Asia • 250 kW
	USA — R FREE ASIA, Anchor Pt, Alaska	S • E Asia • 100 kW
	YUGOSLAVIA — †RADIO YUGOSLAVIA, Via Bosnia	S • E Europe & W Asia • 250 kW
11710v	ARGENTINA — R ARGENTINA-RAE, Buenos Aires	Tu-Sa • Americas • 100 kW; M-F • E Asia • 100 kW; M-F • Europe & N Africa • 100 kW; M-F • S America • 100 kW
	RADIO NACIONAL, Buenos Aires	Irr • S America • DS • 100 kW
	SAUDI ARABIA — BS OF THE KINGDOM, Jiddah	N Africa • DS-GENERAL • 50 kW; N Africa • DS-HOLY KORAN • 50 kW
11715	ALGERIA — †RTV ALGERIENNE, Bouchaoui	Europe • DS-3 • 100 kW; Europe • 100 kW
	CANADA — R CANADA INTL, Sackville, NB	S • C America & S America • 250 kW; S Su/M • C America & S America • 250 kW; S Tu-Sa • C America & S America • 250 kW
	R CANADA INTL, Via Vienna, Austria	W • Mideast • 300 kW
	HOLLAND — †R NEDERLAND, Flevoland	S • S America • 500 kW
	†R NEDERLAND, Via Neth Antilles	S • S America • 250 kW
	INDIA — ALL INDIA RADIO, Delhi	S Asia • 250 kW
	†ALL INDIA RADIO, Panaji	Australasia • 250 kW
	IRAN — VO THE ISLAMIC REP, Tehrān	Europe • 500 kW
	JAPAN — RADIO JAPAN/NHK, Tokyo-Yamata	E Asia • 300 kW
	KOREA (REPUBLIC) — RADIO KOREA INTL, Via Sackville, Can	S America • 250 kW; S • E North Am • 250 kW
	LEBANON — LV DE LA CHARITE, Via Vatican City	S • Mideast • 100 kW
	USA — †VOA, Via Kavála, Greece	W • W Asia & S Asia • 250 kW
	VOA, Via Philippines	E Asia & Australasia • 50 kW
	VATICAN STATE — VATICAN RADIO, Sta Maria di Galeria	S • Mideast • 100 kW; S • E Europe • 100 kW
11715v	EGYPT — RADIO CAIRO, Kafr Silim-Abis	S America • 250 kW
	USA — KJES, Vado, New Mexico	N America • 50 kW; W North Am • 50 kW; C America • 50 kW
11720	BULGARIA — RADIO BULGARIA, Plovdiv	S • E North Am • 500 kW; S • Europe • 500 kW
	CHINA — †CENTRAL PEOPLE'S BS, Beijing	DS-MINORITIES • 50 kW
	†CHINA RADIO INTL, Beijing	SE Asia • 150 kW
	†CHINA RADIO INTL, Urümqi	S • C Asia & S Asia • 500 kW; SE Asia • 100 kW
	†CHINA RADIO INTL, Xi'an	E Africa • 100 kW
	CHINA (TAIWAN) — R TAIPEI INTL, Via Okeechobee, USA	W • S America • 100 kW
	PHILIPPINES — RADYO PILIPINAS, Tinang	S • Mideast • 250 kW
	SOUTH AFRICA — †CHANNEL AFRICA, Meyerton	S • W Africa • 500 kW; W Sa/Su • S Africa • 100 kW; S • S Africa • 500 kW
	USA — †VOA, Via Biblis, Germany	W • Mideast • 100 kW
	VOA, Via Philippines	E Asia & Australasia • 50 kW
(con'd)	VOA, Via Udon Thani, Thailand	W • S Asia • 250 kW

0 1 2 3 4 5 6 7 8 9 10 11 12 13 14 15 16 17 18 19 20 21 22 23 24

ENGLISH ▬   ARABIC ░   CHINESE ▫▫▫   FRENCH ▬▬   GERMAN ▬   RUSSIAN ═   SPANISH ▬   OTHER ▬

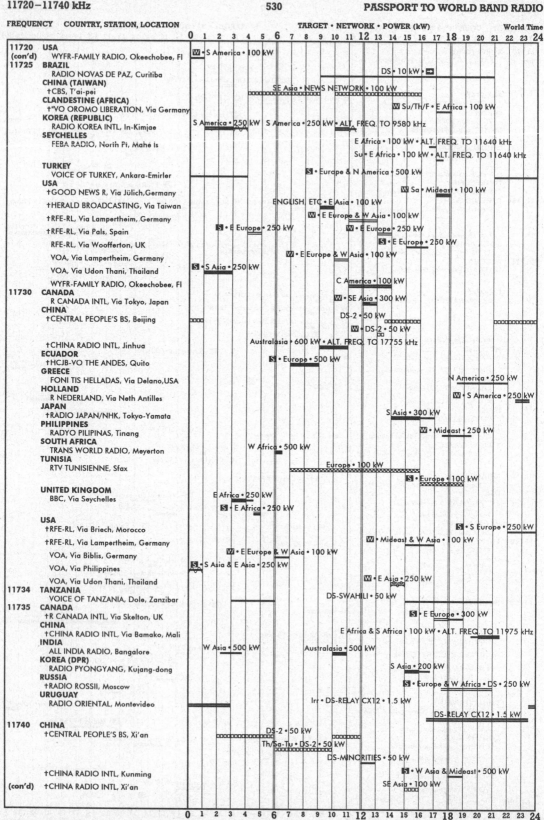

FREQUENCY	COUNTRY, STATION, LOCATION	TARGET • NETWORK • POWER (kW)	World Time

Frequency	Country, Station, Location	Details
11720 (con'd)	USA WYFR–FAMILY RADIO, Okeechobee, Fl	W • S America • 100 kW
11725	BRAZIL RADIO NOVAS DE PAZ, Curitiba	DS • 10 kW • ➡
	CHINA (TAIWAN) †CBS, T'ai-pei	SE Asia • NEWS NETWORK • 100 kW
	CLANDESTINE (AFRICA) †"VO OROMO LIBERATION, Via Germany	W Su/Th/F • E Africa • 100 kW
	KOREA (REPUBLIC) RADIO KOREA INTL, In-Kimjae	S America • 250 kW S America • 250 kW • ALT. FREQ. TO 9580 kHz
	SEYCHELLES FEBA RADIO, North Pt, Mahé Is	E Africa • 100 kW • ALT. FREQ. TO 11640 kHz
		Su • E Africa • 100 kW • ALT. FREQ. TO 11640 kHz
	TURKEY VOICE OF TURKEY, Ankara-Emirler	S • Europe & N America • 500 kW
	USA †GOOD NEWS R, Via Jülich,Germany	W Sa • Mideast • 100 kW
	†HERALD BROADCASTING, Via Taiwan	ENGLISH, ETC • E Asia • 100 kW
	†RFE-RL, Via Lampertheim, Germany	W • E Europe & W Asia • 100 kW
	†RFE-RL, Via Pals, Spain	S • E Europe • 250 kW W • E Europe • 250 kW
	RFE-RL, Via Woofferton, UK	S • E Europe • 250 kW
	VOA, Via Lampertheim, Germany	W • E Europe & W Asia • 100 kW
	VOA, Via Udon Thani, Thailand	S • S Asia • 250 kW
	WYFR–FAMILY RADIO, Okeechobee, Fl	C America • 100 kW
11730	CANADA R CANADA INTL, Via Tokyo, Japan	W • SE Asia • 300 kW
	CHINA †CENTRAL PEOPLE'S BS, Beijing	DS-2 • 50 kW
		W • DS-2 • 50 kW
	†CHINA RADIO INTL, Jinhua	Australasia • 600 kW • ALT. FREQ. TO 17755 kHz
	ECUADOR †HCJB-VO THE ANDES, Quito	S • Europe • 500 kW
	GREECE FONI TIS HELLADAS, Via Delano,USA	N America • 250 kW
	HOLLAND R NEDERLAND, Via Neth Antilles	W • S America • 250 kW
	JAPAN †RADIO JAPAN/NHK, Tokyo-Yamata	S Asia • 300 kW
	PHILIPPINES RADYO PILIPINAS, Tinang	W • Mideast • 250 kW
	SOUTH AFRICA TRANS WORLD RADIO, Meyerton	W Africa • 500 kW
	TUNISIA RTV TUNISIENNE, Sfax	Europe • 100 kW
		S • Europe • 100 kW
	UNITED KINGDOM BBC, Via Seychelles	E Africa • 250 kW
		S • E Africa • 250 kW
	USA †RFE-RL, Via Briech, Morocco	S • S Europe • 250 kW
	†RFE-RL, Via Lampertheim, Germany	W • Mideast & W Asia • 100 kW
	VOA, Via Biblis, Germany	W • E Europe & W Asia • 100 kW
	VOA, Via Philippines	S • S Asia & E Asia • 250 kW
	VOA, Via Udon Thani, Thailand	W • E Asia • 250 kW
11734	TANZANIA VOICE OF TANZANIA, Dole, Zanzibar	DS-SWAHILI • 50 kW
11735	CANADA †R CANADA INTL, Via Skelton, UK	S • E Europe • 300 kW
	CHINA †CHINA RADIO INTL, Via Bamako, Mali	E Africa & S Africa • 100 kW • ALT. FREQ. TO 11975 kHz
	INDIA ALL INDIA RADIO, Bangalore	W Asia • 500 kW Australasia • 500 kW
	KOREA (DPR) RADIO PYONGYANG, Kujang-dong	S Asia • 200 kW
	RUSSIA †RADIO ROSSII, Moscow	S • Europe & W Africa • DS • 250 kW
	URUGUAY RADIO ORIENTAL, Montevideo	Irr • DS-RELAY CX12 • 1.5 kW
		DS-RELAY CX12 • 1.5 kW
11740	CHINA †CENTRAL PEOPLE'S BS, Xi'an	DS-2 • 50 kW
		Th/Sa-Tu • DS-2 • 50 kW
		DS-MINORITIES • 50 kW
	†CHINA RADIO INTL, Kunming	S • W Asia & Mideast • 500 kW
(con'd)	†CHINA RADIO INTL, Xi'an	SE Asia • 100 kW

SEASONAL S OR W   1-HR TIMESHIFT MIDYEAR ⇦ OR ⇨   JAMMING / OR ∧   EARLIEST HEARD ◁   LATEST HEARD ▷   NEW FOR 2000 †

FREQUENCY   COUNTRY, STATION, LOCATION   TARGET • NETWORK • POWER (kW)   World Time

0 1 2 3 4 5 6 7 8 9 10 11 12 13 14 15 16 17 18 19 20 21 22 23 24

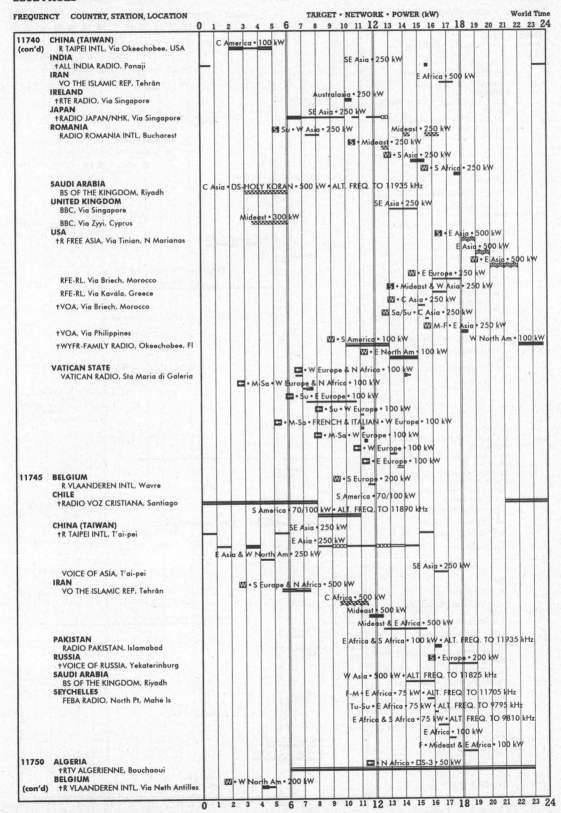

11740 (con'd)	**CHINA (TAIWAN)**
	R TAIPEI INTL, Via Okeechobee, USA — C America • 100 kW
	INDIA
	†ALL INDIA RADIO, Panaji — SE Asia • 250 kW
	IRAN
	VO THE ISLAMIC REP, Tehrān — E Africa • 500 kW
	IRELAND
	†RTE RADIO, Via Singapore — Australasia • 250 kW
	JAPAN
	†RADIO JAPAN/NHK, Via Singapore — SE Asia • 250 kW
	ROMANIA
	RADIO ROMANIA INTL, Bucharest — Su • W Asia • 250 kW / Mideast • 250 kW / Mideast • 250 kW / W • S Asia • 250 kW / W • S Africa • 250 kW
	SAUDI ARABIA
	BS OF THE KINGDOM, Riyadh — C Asia • DS-HOLY KORAN • 500 kW • ALT. FREQ. TO 11935 kHz
	UNITED KINGDOM
	BBC, Via Singapore — SE Asia • 250 kW
	BBC, Via Zyyi, Cyprus — Mideast • 300 kW
	USA
	†R FREE ASIA, Via Tinian, N Marianas — S • E Asia • 500 kW / E Asia • 500 kW / W • E Asia • 500 kW
	RFE-RL, Via Briech, Morocco — W • E Europe • 250 kW
	RFE-RL, Via Kavála, Greece — S • Mideast & W Asia • 250 kW
	†VOA, Via Briech, Morocco — W • C Asia • 250 kW / W • Sa/Su • C Asia • 250 kW
	†VOA, Via Philippines — W • M-F • E Asia • 250 kW / W North Am • 100 kW
	†WYFR-FAMILY RADIO, Okeechobee, Fl — W • S America • 100 kW / W • E North Am • 100 kW
	VATICAN STATE
	VATICAN RADIO, Sta Maria di Galeria — • W Europe & N Africa • 100 kW / • M-Sa • W Europe & N Africa • 100 kW / • Su • E Europe • 100 kW / • Su • W Europe • 100 kW / • M-Sa • FRENCH & ITALIAN • W Europe • 100 kW / • M-Sa • W Europe • 100 kW / • W Europe • 100 kW / • E Europe • 100 kW
11745	**BELGIUM**
	R VLAANDEREN INTL, Wavre — W • S Europe • 200 kW
	CHILE
	†RADIO VOZ CRISTIANA, Santiago — S America • 70/100 kW / S America • 70/100 kW • ALT. FREQ. TO 11890 kHz
	CHINA (TAIWAN)
	†R TAIPEI INTL, T'ai-pei — SE Asia • 250 kW / E Asia • 250 kW / E Asia & W North Am • 250 kW
	VOICE OF ASIA, T'ai-pei — SE Asia • 250 kW
	IRAN
	VO THE ISLAMIC REP, Tehrān — W • S Europe & N Africa • 500 kW / C Africa • 500 kW / Mideast • 500 kW / Mideast & E Africa • 500 kW
	PAKISTAN
	RADIO PAKISTAN, Islamabad — E Africa & S Africa • 100 kW • ALT. FREQ. TO 11935 kHz
	RUSSIA
	†VOICE OF RUSSIA, Yekaterinburg — S • Europe • 200 kW
	SAUDI ARABIA
	BS OF THE KINGDOM, Riyadh — W Asia • 500 kW • ALT. FREQ. TO 11825 kHz
	SEYCHELLES
	FEBA RADIO, North Pt, Mahé Is — F-M • E Africa • 75 kW • ALT. FREQ. TO 11705 kHz / Tu-Su • E Africa • 75 kW • ALT. FREQ. TO 9795 kHz / E Africa & S Africa • 75 kW • ALT. FREQ. TO 9810 kHz / E Africa • 100 kW / F • Mideast & E Africa • 100 kW
11750	**ALGERIA**
	†RTV ALGERIENNE, Bouchaoui — • N Africa • DS-3 • 50 kW
(con'd)	**BELGIUM**
	†R VLAANDEREN INTL, Via Neth Antilles — W • W North Am • 200 kW

0 1 2 3 4 5 6 7 8 9 10 11 12 13 14 15 16 17 18 19 20 21 22 23 24

ENGLISH ▬ ARABIC ▨ CHINESE ▢▢▢ FRENCH ═ GERMAN ▬ RUSSIAN ═ SPANISH ▬ OTHER ─

FREQUENCY   COUNTRY, STATION, LOCATION   TARGET • NETWORK • POWER (kW)   World Time

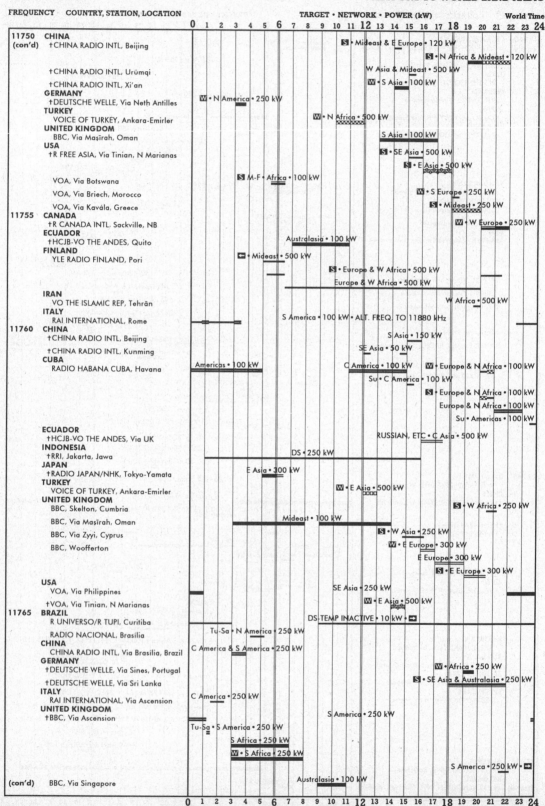

Frequency	Country, Station, Location	Target • Network • Power (kW)
11750 (con'd)	**CHINA**	
	†CHINA RADIO INTL, Beijing	S • Mideast & E Europe • 120 kW
		S • N Africa & Mideast • 120 kW
	†CHINA RADIO INTL, Urümqi	W Asia & Mideast • 500 kW
	†CHINA RADIO INTL, Xi'an	W • S Asia • 100 kW
	GERMANY	
	†DEUTSCHE WELLE, Via Neth Antilles	W • N America • 250 kW
	TURKEY	
	VOICE OF TURKEY, Ankara-Emirler	W • N Africa • 500 kW
	UNITED KINGDOM	
	BBC, Via Maşirah, Oman	S Asia • 100 kW
	USA	
	†R FREE ASIA, Via Tinian, N Marianas	S • SE Asia • 500 kW
		S • E Asia • 500 kW
	VOA, Via Botswana	S M-F • Africa • 100 kW
	VOA, Via Briech, Morocco	W • S Europe • 250 kW
	VOA, Via Kavála, Greece	W • Mideast • 250 kW
11755	**CANADA**	
	†R CANADA INTL, Sackville, NB	W • W Europe • 250 kW
	ECUADOR	
	†HCJB-VO THE ANDES, Quito	Australasia • 100 kW
	FINLAND	
	YLE RADIO FINLAND, Pori	Mideast • 500 kW
		S • Europe & W Africa • 500 kW
		Europe & W Africa • 500 kW
	IRAN	
	VO THE ISLAMIC REP, Tehrān	W Africa • 500 kW
	ITALY	
	RAI INTERNATIONAL, Rome	S America • 100 kW • ALT. FREQ. TO 11880 kHz
11760	**CHINA**	
	†CHINA RADIO INTL, Beijing	S Asia • 150 kW
	†CHINA RADIO INTL, Kunming	SE Asia • 50 kW
	CUBA	
	RADIO HABANA CUBA, Havana	Americas • 100 kW
		C America • 100 kW W • Europe & N Africa • 100 kW
		Su • C America • 100 kW
		S • Europe & N Africa • 100 kW
		Europe & N Africa • 100 kW
		Su • Americas • 100 kW
	ECUADOR	
	†HCJB-VO THE ANDES, Via UK	RUSSIAN, ETC • C Asia • 500 kW
	INDONESIA	
	†RRI, Jakarta, Jawa	DS • 250 kW
	JAPAN	
	†RADIO JAPAN/NHK, Tokyo-Yamata	E Asia • 300 kW
	TURKEY	
	VOICE OF TURKEY, Ankara-Emirler	W • E Asia • 500 kW
	UNITED KINGDOM	
	BBC, Skelton, Cumbria	S • W Africa • 250 kW
	BBC, Via Maşirah, Oman	Mideast • 100 kW
	BBC, Via Zyyi, Cyprus	S • W Asia • 250 kW
	BBC, Woofferton	W • E Europe • 300 kW
		E Europe • 300 kW
		S • E Europe • 300 kW
	USA	
	VOA, Via Philippines	SE Asia • 250 kW
	†VOA, Via Tinian, N Marianas	W • E Asia • 500 kW
11765	**BRAZIL**	
	R UNIVERSO/R TUPI, Curitiba	DS • TEMP INACTIVE • 10 kW
	RADIO NACIONAL, Brasília	Tu-Sa • N America • 250 kW
	CHINA	
	CHINA RADIO INTL, Via Brasília, Brazil	C America & S America • 250 kW
	GERMANY	
	†DEUTSCHE WELLE, Via Sines, Portugal	W • Africa • 250 kW
	†DEUTSCHE WELLE, Via Sri Lanka	S • SE Asia & Australasia • 250 kW
	ITALY	
	RAI INTERNATIONAL, Via Ascension	C America • 250 kW
	UNITED KINGDOM	
	†BBC, Via Ascension	S America • 250 kW
		Tu-Sa • S America • 250 kW
		S Africa • 250 kW
		W • S Africa • 250 kW
		S America • 250 kW
(con'd)	BBC, Via Singapore	Australasia • 100 kW

FREQUENCY COUNTRY, STATION, LOCATION   TARGET • NETWORK • POWER (kW)   World Time

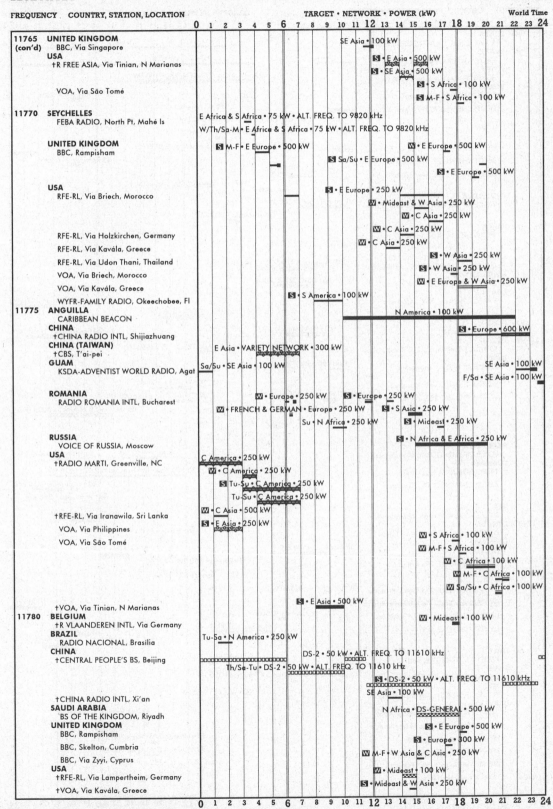

FREQUENCY	COUNTRY, STATION, LOCATION	TARGET • NETWORK • POWER (kW)
11765 (con'd)	UNITED KINGDOM BBC, Via Singapore	SE Asia • 100 kW
	USA †R FREE ASIA, Via Tinian, N Marianas	S • E Asia • 500 kW; S • SE Asia • 500 kW
	VOA, Via São Tomé	S • S Africa • 100 kW; S M-F • S Africa • 100 kW
11770	SEYCHELLES FEBA RADIO, North Pt, Mahé Is	E Africa & S Africa • 75 kW • ALT. FREQ. TO 9820 kHz; W/Th/Sa-M • E Africa & S Africa • 75 kW • ALT. FREQ. TO 9820 kHz
	UNITED KINGDOM BBC, Rampisham	S M-F • E Europe • 500 kW; W • E Europe • 500 kW; S Sa/Su • E Europe • 500 kW; S • E Europe • 500 kW
	USA RFE-RL, Via Briech, Morocco	S • E Europe • 250 kW; W • Mideast & W Asia • 250 kW; W • C Asia • 250 kW
	RFE-RL, Via Holzkirchen, Germany	W • C Asia • 250 kW
	RFE-RL, Via Kavála, Greece	W • C Asia • 250 kW
	RFE-RL, Via Udon Thani, Thailand	S • W Asia • 250 kW
	VOA, Via Briech, Morocco	S • W Asia • 250 kW
	VOA, Via Kavála, Greece	W • E Europe & W Asia • 250 kW
	WYFR-FAMILY RADIO, Okeechobee, Fl	S • S America • 100 kW
11775	ANGUILLA CARIBBEAN BEACON	N America • 100 kW
	CHINA †CHINA RADIO INTL, Shijiazhuang	S • Europe • 600 kW
	CHINA (TAIWAN) †CBS, T'ai-pei	E Asia • VARIETY NETWORK • 300 kW
	GUAM KSDA-ADVENTIST WORLD RADIO, Agat	Sa/Su • SE Asia • 100 kW; SE Asia • 100 kW; F/Sa • SE Asia • 100 kW
	ROMANIA RADIO ROMANIA INTL, Bucharest	W • Europe • 250 kW; S • Europe • 250 kW; W • FRENCH & GERMAN • Europe • 250 kW; S • S Asia • 250 kW; Su • N Africa • 250 kW; S • Mideast • 250 kW
	RUSSIA VOICE OF RUSSIA, Moscow	S • N Africa & E Africa • 250 kW
	USA †RADIO MARTI, Greenville, NC	C America • 250 kW; W • C America • 250 kW; Tu-Su • C America • 250 kW; Tu-Su • C America • 250 kW
	†RFE-RL, Via Iranawila, Sri Lanka	W • C Asia • 500 kW
	VOA, Via Philippines	S • E Asia • 250 kW
	VOA, Via São Tomé	W • S Africa • 100 kW; W M-F • S Africa • 100 kW; W • C Africa • 100 kW; W M-F • C Africa • 100 kW; W Sa/Su • C Africa • 100 kW
	†VOA, Via Tinian, N Marianas	S • E Asia • 500 kW
11780	BELGIUM †R VLAANDEREN INTL, Via Germany	W • Mideast • 100 kW
	BRAZIL RADIO NACIONAL, Brasilia	Tu-Sa • N America • 250 kW
	CHINA †CENTRAL PEOPLE'S BS, Beijing	DS-2 • 50 kW • ALT. FREQ. TO 11610 kHz; Th/Sa-Tu • DS-2 • 50 kW • ALT. FREQ. TO 11610 kHz; S • DS-2 • 50 kW • ALT. FREQ. TO 11610 kHz
	†CHINA RADIO INTL, Xi'an	SE Asia • 100 kW
	SAUDI ARABIA BS OF THE KINGDOM, Riyadh	N Africa • DS-GENERAL • 500 kW
	UNITED KINGDOM BBC, Rampisham	S • E Europe • 500 kW
	BBC, Skelton, Cumbria	S • Europe • 300 kW
	BBC, Via Zyyi, Cyprus	W M-F • W Asia & C Asia • 250 kW
	USA †RFE-RL, Via Lampertheim, Germany	W • Mideast • 100 kW
	†VOA, Via Kavála, Greece	S • Mideast & W Asia • 250 kW

ENGLISH ▬▬   ARABIC ⧢⧢   CHINESE ▫▫▫   FRENCH ▬   GERMAN ▬▬   RUSSIAN ══   SPANISH ▬▬   OTHER ──

FREQUENCY   COUNTRY, STATION, LOCATION   TARGET • NETWORK • POWER (kW)   World Time

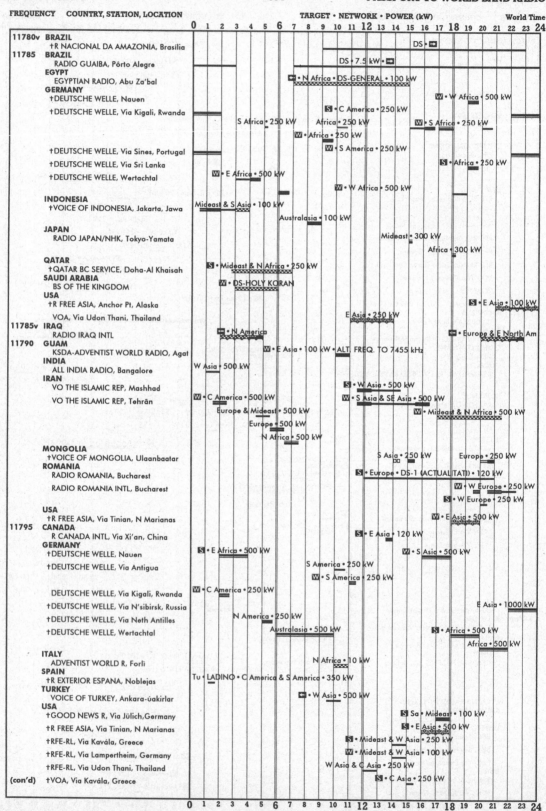

Frequency	Country, Station, Location	Target • Network • Power
11780v	**BRAZIL**	
	†R NACIONAL DA AMAZONIA, Brasília	DS
11785	**BRAZIL**	
	RADIO GUAIBA, Pôrto Alegre	DS • 7.5 kW
	EGYPT	
	EGYPTIAN RADIO, Abu Za'bal	• N Africa • DS-GENERAL • 100 kW
	GERMANY	
	†DEUTSCHE WELLE, Nauen	W • W Africa • 500 kW
	†DEUTSCHE WELLE, Via Kigali, Rwanda	S • C America • 250 kW / S Africa • 250 kW / Africa • 250 kW / W • S Africa • 250 kW / W • Africa • 250 kW
	†DEUTSCHE WELLE, Via Sines, Portugal	W • S America • 250 kW
	†DEUTSCHE WELLE, Via Sri Lanka	S • Africa • 250 kW
	†DEUTSCHE WELLE, Wertachtal	W • E Africa • 500 kW / W • W Africa • 500 kW
	INDONESIA	
	†VOICE OF INDONESIA, Jakarta, Jawa	Mideast & S Asia • 100 kW / Australasia • 100 kW
	JAPAN	
	RADIO JAPAN/NHK, Tokyo-Yamata	Mideast • 300 kW / Africa • 300 kW
	QATAR	
	†QATAR BC SERVICE, Doha-Al Khaisah	S • Mideast & N Africa • 250 kW
	SAUDI ARABIA	
	BS OF THE KINGDOM	W • DS-HOLY KORAN
	USA	
	†R FREE ASIA, Anchor Pt, Alaska	S • E Asia • 100 kW
	VOA, Via Udon Thani, Thailand	E Asia • 250 kW
11785v	**IRAQ**	
	RADIO IRAQ INTL	• N America / • Europe & E North Am
11790	**GUAM**	
	KSDA-ADVENTIST WORLD RADIO, Agat	W • E Asia • 100 kW • ALT. FREQ. TO 7455 kHz
	INDIA	
	ALL INDIA RADIO, Bangalore	W Asia • 500 kW
	IRAN	
	VO THE ISLAMIC REP, Mashhad	S • W Asia • 500 kW
	VO THE ISLAMIC REP, Tehrān	W • C America • 500 kW / W • S Asia & SE Asia • 500 kW / W • Mideast & N Africa • 500 kW / Europe & Mideast • 500 kW / Europe • 500 kW / N Africa • 500 kW
	MONGOLIA	
	†VOICE OF MONGOLIA, Ulaanbaatar	S Asia • 250 kW / Europe • 250 kW
	ROMANIA	
	RADIO ROMANIA, Bucharest	S • Europe • DS-1 (ACTUAL TATI) • 120 kW
	RADIO ROMANIA INTL, Bucharest	W • W Europe • 250 kW / W • W Europe • 250 kW
	USA	
	†R FREE ASIA, Via Tinian, N Marianas	W • E Asia • 500 kW
11795	**CANADA**	
	R CANADA INTL, Via Xi'an, China	S • E Asia • 120 kW
	GERMANY	
	†DEUTSCHE WELLE, Nauen	S • E Africa • 500 kW / W • S Asia • 500 kW
	†DEUTSCHE WELLE, Via Antigua	S America • 250 kW / W • S America • 250 kW
	DEUTSCHE WELLE, Via Kigali, Rwanda	W • C America • 250 kW
	†DEUTSCHE WELLE, Via N'sibirsk, Russia	E Asia • 1000 kW
	†DEUTSCHE WELLE, Via Neth Antilles	N America • 250 kW
	†DEUTSCHE WELLE, Wertachtal	Australasia • 500 kW / S • Africa • 500 kW / Africa • 500 kW
	ITALY	
	ADVENTIST WORLD R, Forli	N Africa • 10 kW
	SPAIN	
	†R EXTERIOR ESPANA, Noblejas	Tu • LADINO • C America & S America • 350 kW
	TURKEY	
	VOICE OF TURKEY, Ankara-úakirlar	• W Asia • 500 kW
	USA	
	†GOOD NEWS R, Via Jülich, Germany	S • Sa • Mideast • 100 kW
	†R FREE ASIA, Via Tinian, N Marianas	S • E Asia • 500 kW
	†RFE-RL, Via Kavála, Greece	S • Mideast & W Asia • 250 kW
	†RFE-RL, Via Lampertheim, Germany	W • Mideast & W Asia • 100 kW
	†RFE-RL, Via Udon Thani, Thailand	W Asia & C Asia • 250 kW
(con'd)	†VOA, Via Kavála, Greece	S • C Asia • 250 kW

FREQUENCY   COUNTRY, STATION, LOCATION

TARGET • NETWORK • POWER (kW)   World Time

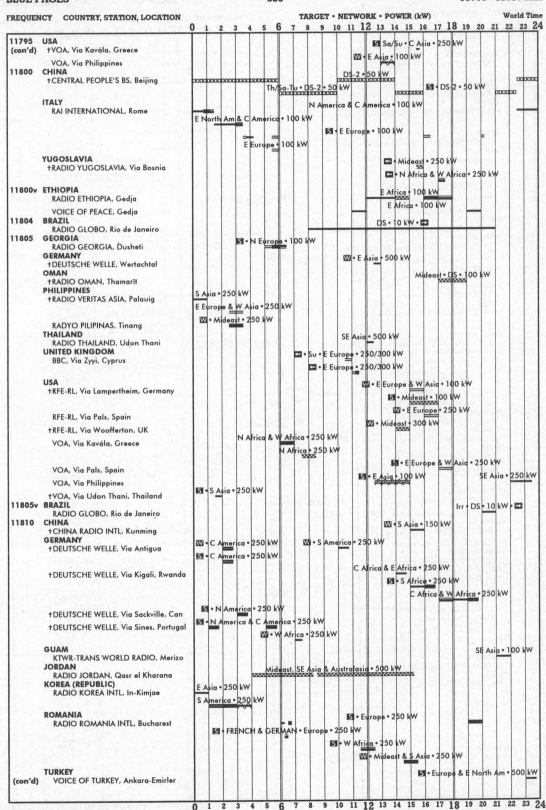

Frequency	Country, Station, Location
11795 (con'd)	**USA**
	†VOA, Via Kavála, Greece — S • Sa/Su • C Asia • 250 kW; W • E Asia • 100 kW
	VOA, Via Philippines
11800	**CHINA**
	†CENTRAL PEOPLE'S BS, Beijing — DS-2 • 50 kW; Th/Sa-Tu • DS-2 • 50 kW; S • DS-2 • 50 kW
	ITALY
	RAI INTERNATIONAL, Rome — N America & C America • 100 kW; E North Am & C America • 100 kW; S • E Europe • 100 kW; E Europe • 100 kW
	YUGOSLAVIA
	†RADIO YUGOSLAVIA, Via Bosnia — • Mideast • 250 kW; • N Africa & W Africa • 250 kW
11800v	**ETHIOPIA**
	RADIO ETHIOPIA, Gedja — E Africa • 100 kW
	VOICE OF PEACE, Gedja — E Africa • 100 kW
11804	**BRAZIL**
	RADIO GLOBO, Rio de Janeiro — DS • 10 kW •
11805	**GEORGIA**
	RADIO GEORGIA, Dusheti — S • N Europe • 100 kW
	GERMANY
	†DEUTSCHE WELLE, Wertachtal — W • E Asia • 500 kW
	OMAN
	†RADIO OMAN, Thamarīt — Mideast • DS • 100 kW
	PHILIPPINES
	†RADIO VERITAS ASIA, Palauig — S Asia • 250 kW; E Europe & W Asia • 250 kW; W • Mideast • 250 kW
	RADYO PILIPINAS, Tinang
	THAILAND
	RADIO THAILAND, Udon Thani — SE Asia • 500 kW
	UNITED KINGDOM
	BBC, Via Zyyi, Cyprus — • Su • E Europe • 250/300 kW; • E Europe • 250/300 kW
	USA
	†RFE-RL, Via Lampertheim, Germany — W • E Europe & W Asia • 100 kW; S • Mideast • 100 kW
	RFE-RL, Via Pals, Spain — W • E Europe • 250 kW
	†RFE-RL, Via Woofferton, UK — W • Mideast • 300 kW
	VOA, Via Kavála, Greece — N Africa & W Africa • 250 kW; N Africa • 250 kW
	VOA, Via Pals, Spain — • E Europe & W Asia • 250 kW
	VOA, Via Philippines — S • E Asia • 100 kW; SE Asia • 250 kW
	†VOA, Via Udon Thani, Thailand — S • S Asia • 250 kW
11805v	**BRAZIL**
	RADIO GLOBO, Rio de Janeiro — Irr • DS • 10 kW •
11810	**CHINA**
	†CHINA RADIO INTL, Kunming — W • S Asia • 150 kW
	GERMANY
	†DEUTSCHE WELLE, Via Antigua — W • C America • 250 kW; W • S America • 250 kW; S • C America • 250 kW
	†DEUTSCHE WELLE, Via Kigali, Rwanda — C Africa & E Africa • 250 kW; S • S Africa • 250 kW; C Africa & W Africa • 250 kW
	†DEUTSCHE WELLE, Via Sackville, Can — S • N America • 250 kW
	†DEUTSCHE WELLE, Via Sines, Portugal — S • N America & C America • 250 kW; W • W Africa • 250 kW
	GUAM
	KTWR-TRANS WORLD RADIO, Merizo — SE Asia • 100 kW
	JORDAN
	RADIO JORDAN, Qasr el Kharana — Mideast, SE Asia & Australasia • 500 kW
	KOREA (REPUBLIC)
	RADIO KOREA INTL, In-Kimjae — E Asia • 250 kW; S America • 250 kW
	ROMANIA
	RADIO ROMANIA INTL, Bucharest — S • Europe • 250 kW; S • FRENCH & GERMAN • Europe • 250 kW; S • W Africa • 250 kW; W • Mideast & S Asia • 250 kW
	TURKEY
(con'd)	VOICE OF TURKEY, Ankara-Emirler — S • Europe & E North Am • 500 kW

ENGLISH ▬   ARABIC ⊠⊠⊠   CHINESE □□□   FRENCH ═══   GERMAN ▬▬   RUSSIAN ═══   SPANISH ▬▬   OTHER ▬

FREQUENCY   COUNTRY, STATION, LOCATION   TARGET • NETWORK • POWER (kW)   World Time

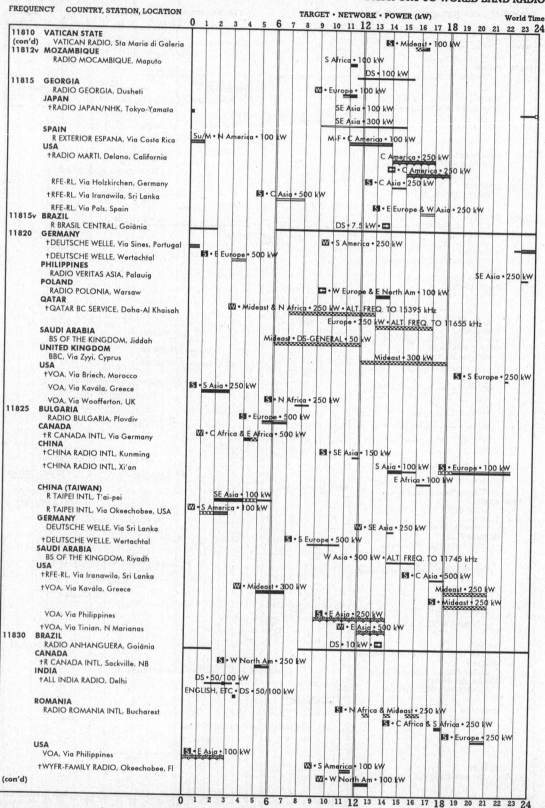

Frequency	Country, Station, Location	Target • Network • Power
11810 (con'd)	**VATICAN STATE** VATICAN RADIO, Sta Maria di Galeria	S • Mideast • 100 kW
11812v	**MOZAMBIQUE** RADIO MOCAMBIQUE, Maputo	S Africa • 100 kW / DS • 100 kW
11815	**GEORGIA** RADIO GEORGIA, Dusheti	W • Europe • 100 kW
	JAPAN †RADIO JAPAN/NHK, Tokyo-Yamata	SE Asia • 100 kW / SE Asia • 300 kW
	SPAIN R EXTERIOR ESPANA, Via Costa Rica	Su/M • N America • 100 kW / M-F • C America • 100 kW
	USA †RADIO MARTI, Delano, California	C America • 250 kW / C America • 250 kW
	RFE-RL, Via Holzkirchen, Germany	S • C Asia • 250 kW
	†RFE-RL, Via Iranawila, Sri Lanka	S • C Asia • 500 kW
	RFE-RL, Via Pals, Spain	S • E Europe & W Asia • 250 kW
11815v	**BRAZIL** R BRASIL CENTRAL, Goiânia	DS • 7.5 kW •
11820	**GERMANY** †DEUTSCHE WELLE, Via Sines, Portugal	W • S America • 250 kW
	†DEUTSCHE WELLE, Wertachtal	S • E Europe • 500 kW
	PHILIPPINES RADIO VERITAS ASIA, Palauig	SE Asia • 250 kW
	POLAND RADIO POLONIA, Warsaw	W Europe & E North Am • 100 kW
	QATAR †QATAR BC SERVICE, Doha-Al Khaisah	W • Mideast & N Africa • 250 kW • ALT. FREQ. TO 15395 kHz / Europe • 250 kW • ALT. FREQ. TO 11655 kHz
	SAUDI ARABIA BS OF THE KINGDOM, Jiddah	Mideast • DS-GENERAL • 50 kW
	UNITED KINGDOM BBC, Via Zyyi, Cyprus	Mideast • 300 kW
	USA †VOA, Via Briech, Morocco	S • S Europe • 250 kW
	VOA, Via Kavála, Greece	S • S Asia • 250 kW
	VOA, Via Woofferton, UK	S • N Africa • 250 kW
11825	**BULGARIA** RADIO BULGARIA, Plovdiv	S • Europe • 500 kW
	CANADA †R CANADA INTL, Via Germany	W • C Africa & E Africa • 500 kW
	CHINA †CHINA RADIO INTL, Kunming	S • SE Asia • 150 kW
	†CHINA RADIO INTL, Xi'an	S Asia • 100 kW / S • Europe • 100 kW / E Africa • 100 kW
	CHINA (TAIWAN) R TAIPEI INTL, T'ai-pei	SE Asia • 100 kW
	R TAIPEI INTL, Via Okeechobee, USA	W • S America • 100 kW
	GERMANY DEUTSCHE WELLE, Via Sri Lanka	W • SE Asia • 250 kW
	†DEUTSCHE WELLE, Wertachtal	S • S Europe • 500 kW
	SAUDI ARABIA BS OF THE KINGDOM, Riyadh	W Asia • 500 kW • ALT. FREQ. TO 11745 kHz
	USA †RFE-RL, Via Iranawila, Sri Lanka	S • C Asia • 500 kW
	†VOA, Via Kavála, Greece	W • Mideast • 300 kW / Mideast • 250 kW / S • Mideast • 250 kW
	VOA, Via Philippines	S • E Asia • 250 kW
	†VOA, Via Tinian, N Marianas	W • E Asia • 500 kW
11830	**BRAZIL** RADIO ANHANGUERA, Goiânia	DS • 10 kW •
	CANADA †R CANADA INTL, Sackville, NB	S • W North Am • 250 kW
	INDIA †ALL INDIA RADIO, Delhi	DS • 50/100 kW / ENGLISH, ETC • DS • 50/100 kW
	ROMANIA RADIO ROMANIA INTL, Bucharest	S • N Africa & Mideast • 250 kW / S • C Africa & S Africa • 250 kW / S • Europe • 250 kW
	USA VOA, Via Philippines	S • E Asia • 100 kW
	†WYFR-FAMILY RADIO, Okeechobee, Fl	W • S America • 100 kW / W • W North Am • 100 kW
(con'd)		

SEASONAL S OR W   1-HR TIMESHIFT MIDYEAR ⬅ OR ➡   JAMMING / OR ∧   EARLIEST HEARD ◁   LATEST HEARD ▷   NEW FOR 2000 †

FREQUENCY	COUNTRY, STATION, LOCATION	TARGET • NETWORK • POWER (kW)

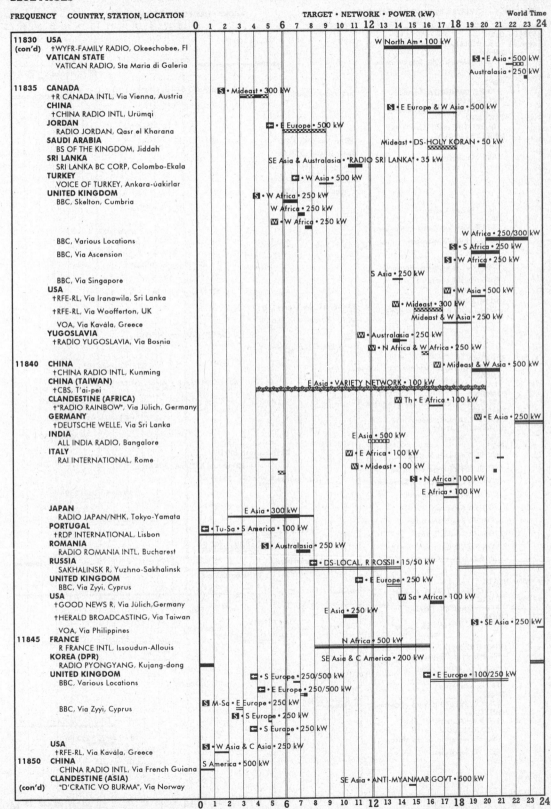

11830
(con'd)　USA
　†WYFR-FAMILY RADIO, Okeechobee, Fl — W North Am • 100 kW
VATICAN STATE
　VATICAN RADIO, Sta Maria di Galeria — S • E Asia • 500 kW; Australasia • 250 kW

11835　CANADA
　†R CANADA INTL, Via Vienna, Austria — S • Mideast • 300 kW
CHINA
　†CHINA RADIO INTL, Urümqi — S • E Europe & W Asia • 500 kW
JORDAN
　RADIO JORDAN, Qasr el Kharana — • E Europe • 500 kW
SAUDI ARABIA
　BS OF THE KINGDOM, Jiddah — Mideast • DS-HOLY KORAN • 50 kW
SRI LANKA
　SRI LANKA BC CORP, Colombo-Ekala — SE Asia & Australasia • "RADIO SRI LANKA" • 35 kW
TURKEY
　VOICE OF TURKEY, Ankara-úakirlar — • W Asia • 500 kW
UNITED KINGDOM
　BBC, Skelton, Cumbria — S • W Africa • 250 kW; W Africa • 250 kW; W • W Africa • 250 kW

　BBC, Various Locations — W Africa • 250/300 kW
　BBC, Via Ascension — S • S Africa • 250 kW; S • W Africa • 250 kW

　BBC, Via Singapore — S Asia • 250 kW
USA
　†RFE-RL, Via Iranawila, Sri Lanka — W • W Asia • 500 kW
　†RFE-RL, Via Woofferton, UK — W • Mideast • 300 kW; Mideast & W Asia • 250 kW
　VOA, Via Kavála, Greece
YUGOSLAVIA
　†RADIO YUGOSLAVIA, Via Bosnia — W • Australasia • 250 kW; W • N Africa & W Africa • 250 kW

11840　CHINA
　†CHINA RADIO INTL, Kunming — W • Mideast & W Asia • 500 kW
CHINA (TAIWAN)
　†CBS, T'ai-pei — E Asia • VARIETY NETWORK • 100 kW
CLANDESTINE (AFRICA)
　†"RADIO RAINBOW", Via Jülich, Germany — W Th • E Africa • 100 kW
GERMANY
　†DEUTSCHE WELLE, Via Sri Lanka — W • E Asia • 250 kW
INDIA
　ALL INDIA RADIO, Bangalore — E Asia • 500 kW
ITALY
　RAI INTERNATIONAL, Rome — W • E Africa • 100 kW; W • Mideast • 100 kW; S • N Africa • 100 kW; E Africa • 100 kW

JAPAN
　RADIO JAPAN/NHK, Tokyo-Yamata — E Asia • 300 kW
PORTUGAL
　†RDP INTERNATIONAL, Lisbon — • Tu-Sa • S America • 100 kW
ROMANIA
　RADIO ROMANIA INTL, Bucharest — S • Australasia • 250 kW
RUSSIA
　SAKHALINSK R, Yuzhno-Sakhalinsk — • DS-LOCAL, R ROSSII • 15/50 kW
UNITED KINGDOM
　BBC, Via Zyyi, Cyprus — • E Europe • 250 kW
USA
　†GOOD NEWS R, Via Jülich, Germany — W • Sa • Africa • 100 kW
　†HERALD BROADCASTING, Via Taiwan — E Asia • 250 kW
　VOA, Via Philippines — S • SE Asia • 250 kW

11845　FRANCE
　R FRANCE INTL, Issoudun-Allouis — N Africa • 500 kW
KOREA (DPR)
　RADIO PYONGYANG, Kujang-dong — SE Asia & C America • 200 kW
UNITED KINGDOM
　BBC, Various Locations — • S Europe • 250/500 kW; • E Europe • 250/500 kW; • E Europe • 100/250 kW
　BBC, Via Zyyi, Cyprus — S M-Sa • E Europe • 250 kW; S • S Europe • 250 kW; • S Europe • 250 kW

USA
　†RFE-RL, Via Kavála, Greece — S • W Asia & C Asia • 250 kW
11850　CHINA
　CHINA RADIO INTL, Via French Guiana — S America • 500 kW
CLANDESTINE (ASIA)
(con'd)　"D'CRATIC VO BURMA", Via Norway — SE Asia • ANTI-MYANMAR GOVT • 500 kW

FREQUENCY   COUNTRY, STATION, LOCATION   **TARGET • NETWORK • POWER (kW)**   **World Time**

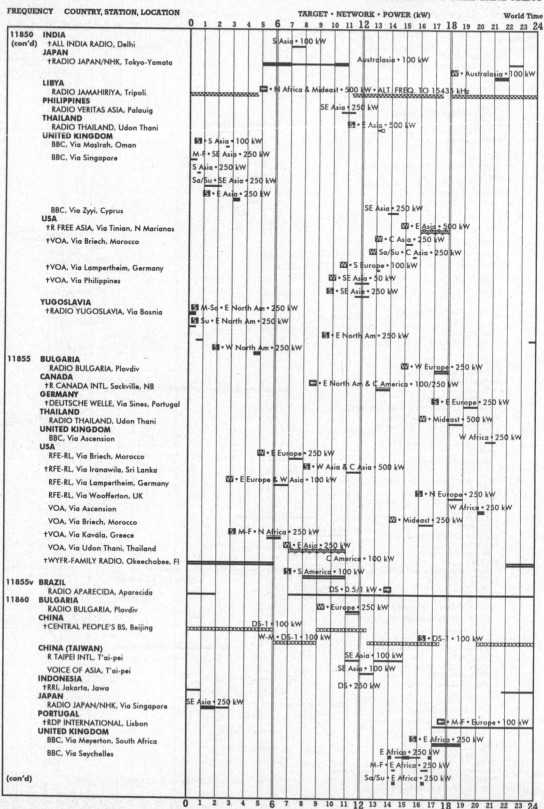

11850 **INDIA**
(con'd)   †ALL INDIA RADIO, Delhi   S Asia • 100 kW
     JAPAN
     †RADIO JAPAN/NHK, Tokyo-Yamata   Australasia • 100 kW
       W • Australasia • 100 kW
     LIBYA
     RADIO JAMAHIRIYA, Tripoli   N Africa & Mideast • 500 kW • ALT. FREQ. TO 15435 kHz
     PHILIPPINES
     RADIO VERITAS ASIA, Palauig   SE Asia • 250 kW
     THAILAND
     RADIO THAILAND, Udon Thani   S • E Asia • 500 kW
     UNITED KINGDOM
     BBC, Via Maşīrah, Oman   S • S Asia • 100 kW
     BBC, Via Singapore   M-F • SE Asia • 250 kW
       S Asia • 250 kW
       Sa/Su • SE Asia • 250 kW
       S • E Asia • 250 kW
     BBC, Via Zyyi, Cyprus   SE Asia • 250 kW
     USA
     †R FREE ASIA, Via Tinian, N Marianas   W • E Asia • 500 kW
     †VOA, Via Briech, Morocco   W • C Asia • 250 kW
       W Sa/Su • C Asia • 250 kW
     †VOA, Via Lampertheim, Germany   W • S Europe • 100 kW
     †VOA, Via Philippines   W • SE Asia • 50 kW
       S • SE Asia • 250 kW
     YUGOSLAVIA
     †RADIO YUGOSLAVIA, Via Bosnia   S M-Sa • E North Am • 250 kW
       S Su • E North Am • 250 kW
       S • E North Am • 250 kW
       S • W North Am • 250 kW

11855 **BULGARIA**
     RADIO BULGARIA, Plovdiv   W • W Europe • 250 kW
     CANADA
     †R CANADA INTL, Sackville, NB   • E North Am & C America • 100/250 kW
     GERMANY
     †DEUTSCHE WELLE, Via Sines, Portugal   S • E Europe • 250 kW
     THAILAND
     RADIO THAILAND, Udon Thani   W • Mideast • 500 kW
     UNITED KINGDOM
     BBC, Via Ascension   W Africa • 250 kW
     USA
     RFE-RL, Via Briech, Morocco   W • E Europe • 250 kW
     †RFE-RL, Via Iranawila, Sri Lanka   S • W Asia & C Asia • 500 kW
     RFE-RL, Via Lampertheim, Germany   W • E Europe & W Asia • 100 kW
     RFE-RL, Via Woofferton, UK   S • N Europe • 250 kW
     VOA, Via Ascension   W Africa • 250 kW
     VOA, Via Briech, Morocco   W • Mideast • 250 kW
     †VOA, Via Kavála, Greece   S M-F • N Africa • 250 kW
     VOA, Via Udon Thani, Thailand   W • E Asia • 250 kW
     †WYFR-FAMILY RADIO, Okeechobee, Fl   C America • 100 kW
       S • S America • 100 kW

11855v **BRAZIL**
     RADIO APARECIDA, Aparecida   DS • 0.5/1 kW •
11860 **BULGARIA**
     RADIO BULGARIA, Plovdiv   W • Europe • 250 kW
     CHINA
     †CENTRAL PEOPLE'S BS, Beijing   DS-1 • 100 kW
       W-M • DS-1 • 100 kW   S • DS-1 • 100 kW
     CHINA (TAIWAN)
     R TAIPEI INTL, T'ai-pei   SE Asia • 100 kW
     VOICE OF ASIA, T'ai-pei   SE Asia • 100 kW
     INDONESIA
     †RRI, Jakarta, Jawa   DS • 250 kW
     JAPAN
     RADIO JAPAN/NHK, Via Singapore   SE Asia • 250 kW
     PORTUGAL
     †RDP INTERNATIONAL, Lisbon   • M-F • Europe • 100 kW
     UNITED KINGDOM
     BBC, Via Meyerton, South Africa   S • E Africa • 250 kW
     BBC, Via Seychelles   E Africa • 250 kW
       M-F • E Africa • 250 kW
       Sa/Su • E Africa • 250 kW

(con'd)

FREQUENCY   COUNTRY, STATION, LOCATION   TARGET • NETWORK • POWER (kW)   World Time

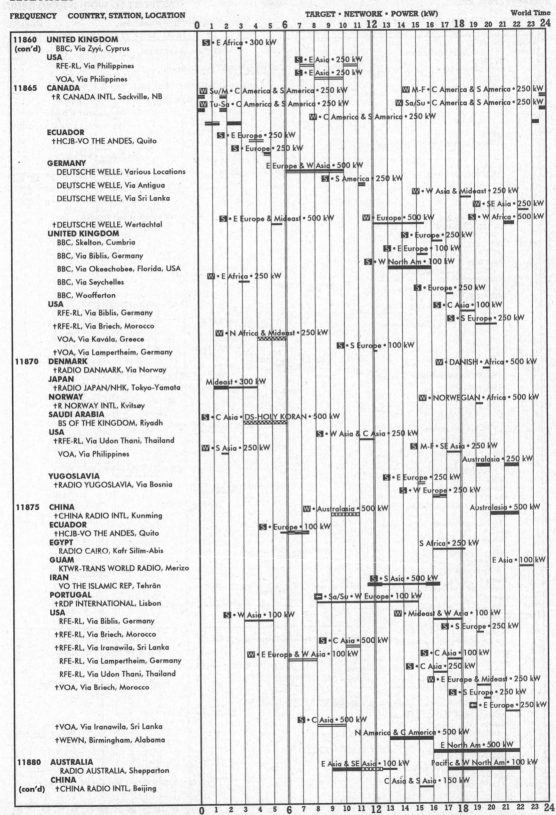

Frequency	Country, Station, Location	Target • Network • Power
11860 (con'd)	**UNITED KINGDOM** BBC, Via Zyyi, Cyprus	S • E Africa • 300 kW
	USA RFE-RL, Via Philippines	S • E Asia • 250 kW
	VOA, Via Philippines	S • E Asia • 250 kW
11865	**CANADA** †R CANADA INTL, Sackville, NB	W Su/M • C America & S America • 250 kW; W M-F • C America & S America • 250 kW; W Tu-Sa • C America & S America • 250 kW; W Sa/Su • C America & S America • 250 kW; W • C America & S America • 250 kW
	ECUADOR †HCJB-VO THE ANDES, Quito	S • E Europe • 250 kW; S • Europe • 250 kW
	GERMANY DEUTSCHE WELLE, Various Locations	E Europe & W Asia • 500 kW
	DEUTSCHE WELLE, Via Antigua	S • S America • 250 kW
	DEUTSCHE WELLE, Via Sri Lanka	W • W Asia & Mideast • 250 kW; W • SE Asia • 250 kW
	†DEUTSCHE WELLE, Wertachtal	S • E Europe & Mideast • 500 kW; W • Europe • 500 kW; S • W Africa • 500 kW
	UNITED KINGDOM BBC, Skelton, Cumbria	S • Europe • 250 kW
	BBC, Via Biblis, Germany	S • E Europe • 100 kW
	BBC, Via Okeechobee, Florida, USA	S • W North Am • 100 kW
	BBC, Via Seychelles	W • E Africa • 250 kW
	BBC, Woofferton	S • Europe • 250 kW
	USA RFE-RL, Via Biblis, Germany	S • C Asia • 100 kW
	†RFE-RL, Via Briech, Morocco	S • S Europe • 250 kW
	VOA, Via Kavála, Greece	W • N Africa & Mideast • 250 kW
	†VOA, Via Lampertheim, Germany	S • S Europe • 100 kW
11870	**DENMARK** †RADIO DANMARK, Via Norway	W • DANISH • Africa • 500 kW
	JAPAN †RADIO JAPAN/NHK, Tokyo-Yamata	Mideast • 300 kW
	NORWAY †R NORWAY INTL, Kvitsøy	W • NORWEGIAN • Africa • 500 kW
	SAUDI ARABIA BS OF THE KINGDOM, Riyadh	S • C Asia • DS-HOLY KORAN • 500 kW
	USA †RFE-RL, Via Udon Thani, Thailand	S • W Asia & C Asia • 250 kW
	VOA, Via Philippines	W • S Asia • 250 kW; S M-F • SE Asia • 250 kW; Australasia • 250 kW
	YUGOSLAVIA †RADIO YUGOSLAVIA, Via Bosnia	S • E Europe • 250 kW; S • W Europe • 250 kW
11875	**CHINA** †CHINA RADIO INTL, Kunming	W • Australasia • 500 kW; Australasia • 500 kW
	ECUADOR †HCJB-VO THE ANDES, Quito	S • Europe • 100 kW
	EGYPT RADIO CAIRO, Kafr Silīm-Abis	S Africa • 250 kW
	GUAM KTWR-TRANS WORLD RADIO, Merizo	E Asia • 100 kW
	IRAN VO THE ISLAMIC REP, Tehrān	S • S Asia • 500 kW
	PORTUGAL †RDP INTERNATIONAL, Lisbon	S • Sa/Su • W Europe • 100 kW
	USA RFE-RL, Via Biblis, Germany	S • W Asia • 100 kW; W • Mideast & W Asia • 100 kW
	†RFE-RL, Via Briech, Morocco	S • S Europe • 250 kW
	†RFE-RL, Via Iranawila, Sri Lanka	S • C Asia • 500 kW
	RFE-RL, Via Lampertheim, Germany	W • E Europe & W Asia • 100 kW; S • C Asia • 100 kW
	RFE-RL, Via Udon Thani, Thailand	S • C Asia • 250 kW
	†VOA, Via Briech, Morocco	W • E Europe & Mideast • 250 kW; S • S Europe • 250 kW; S • E Europe • 250 kW
	†VOA, Via Iranawila, Sri Lanka	S • C Asia • 500 kW
	†WEWN, Birmingham, Alabama	N America & C America • 500 kW; E North Am • 500 kW
11880	**AUSTRALIA** RADIO AUSTRALIA, Shepparton	E Asia & SE Asia • 100 kW; Pacific & W North Am • 100 kW
(con'd)	**CHINA** †CHINA RADIO INTL, Beijing	C Asia & S Asia • 150 kW

ENGLISH ▬   ARABIC ⛛⛛⛛   CHINESE ☐☐☐   FRENCH ═══   GERMAN ▭▭   RUSSIAN ═══   SPANISH ▬▬   OTHER ──

FREQUENCY   COUNTRY, STATION, LOCATION

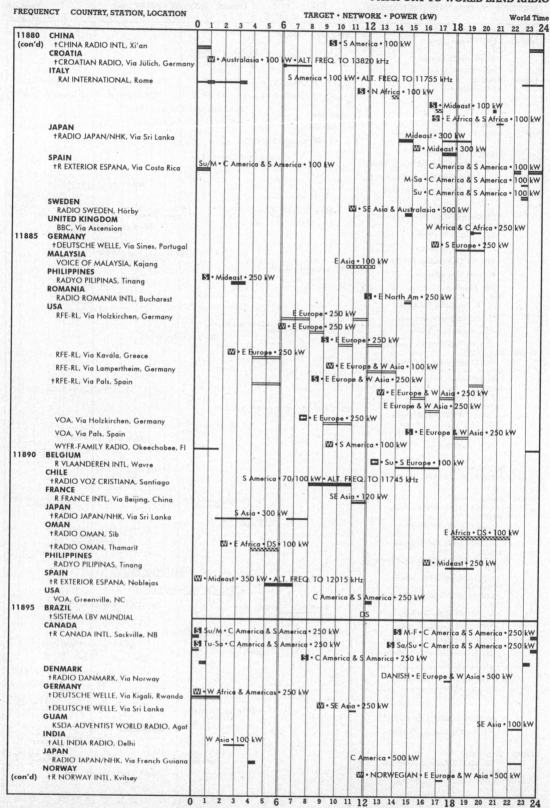

11880 **CHINA**
(con'd)   †CHINA RADIO INTL, Xi'an · S America · 100 kW
       CROATIA
          †CROATIAN RADIO, Via Jülich, Germany · Australasia · 100 kW · ALT. FREQ. TO 13820 kHz
       ITALY
          RAI INTERNATIONAL, Rome · S America · 100 kW · ALT. FREQ. TO 11755 kHz
                                                          · N Africa · 100 kW
                                                          · Mideast · 100 kW
                                                          · E Africa & S Africa · 100 kW
       JAPAN
          †RADIO JAPAN/NHK, Via Sri Lanka · Mideast · 300 kW
                                            · Mideast · 300 kW
       SPAIN
          †R EXTERIOR ESPANA, Via Costa Rica · Su/M · C America & S America · 100 kW
                                              · C America & S America · 100 kW
                                              M-Sa · C America & S America · 100 kW
                                              Su · C America & S America · 100 kW
       SWEDEN
          RADIO SWEDEN, Hörby · SE Asia & Australasia · 500 kW
       UNITED KINGDOM
          BBC, Via Ascension · W Africa & C Africa · 250 kW
11885 **GERMANY**
          †DEUTSCHE WELLE, Via Sines, Portugal · S Europe · 250 kW
       MALAYSIA
          VOICE OF MALAYSIA, Kajang · E Asia · 100 kW
       PHILIPPINES
          RADYO PILIPINAS, Tinang · Mideast · 250 kW
       ROMANIA
          RADIO ROMANIA INTL, Bucharest · E North Am · 250 kW
       USA
          RFE-RL, Via Holzkirchen, Germany · E Europe · 250 kW
                                            · E Europe · 250 kW
                                            · E Europe · 250 kW
          RFE-RL, Via Kavála, Greece · E Europe · 250 kW
          RFE-RL, Via Lampertheim, Germany · E Europe & W Asia · 100 kW
          †RFE-RL, Via Pals, Spain · E Europe & W Asia · 250 kW
                                    · E Europe & W Asia · 250 kW
                                    E Europe & W Asia · 250 kW
          VOA, Via Holzkirchen, Germany · E Europe · 250 kW
          VOA, Via Pals, Spain · E Europe & W Asia · 250 kW
          WYFR-FAMILY RADIO, Okeechobee, Fl · S America · 100 kW
11890 **BELGIUM**
          R VLAANDEREN INTL, Wavre · Su · S Europe · 100 kW
       CHILE
          †RADIO VOZ CRISTIANA, Santiago · S America · 70/100 kW · ALT. FREQ. TO 11745 kHz
       FRANCE
          R FRANCE INTL, Via Beijing, China · SE Asia · 120 kW
       JAPAN
          †RADIO JAPAN/NHK, Via Sri Lanka · S Asia · 300 kW
       OMAN
          †RADIO OMAN, Sib · E Africa · DS · 100 kW
          †RADIO OMAN, Thamarit · E Africa · DS · 100 kW
       PHILIPPINES
          RADYO PILIPINAS, Tinang · Mideast · 250 kW
       SPAIN
          †R EXTERIOR ESPANA, Noblejas · Mideast · 350 kW · ALT. FREQ. TO 12015 kHz
       USA
          VOA, Greenville, NC · C America & S America · 250 kW
11895 **BRAZIL**
          †SISTEMA LBV MUNDIAL · DS
       CANADA
          †R CANADA INTL, Sackville, NB · Su/M · C America & S America · 250 kW · M-F · C America & S America · 250 kW
                                         · Tu-Sa · C America & S America · 250 kW · Sa/Su · C America & S America · 250 kW
                                         · C America & S America · 250 kW
       DENMARK
          †RADIO DANMARK, Via Norway · DANISH · E Europe & W Asia · 500 kW
       GERMANY
          †DEUTSCHE WELLE, Via Kigali, Rwanda · W Africa & Americas · 250 kW
          †DEUTSCHE WELLE, Via Sri Lanka · SE Asia · 250 kW
       GUAM
          KSDA-ADVENTIST WORLD RADIO, Agat · SE Asia · 100 kW
       INDIA
          †ALL INDIA RADIO, Delhi · W Asia · 100 kW
       JAPAN
          RADIO JAPAN/NHK, Via French Guiana · C America · 500 kW
       NORWAY
(con'd)   †R NORWAY INTL, Kvitsøy · NORWEGIAN · E Europe & W Asia · 500 kW

FREQUENCY   COUNTRY, STATION, LOCATION   TARGET • NETWORK • POWER (kW)   World Time

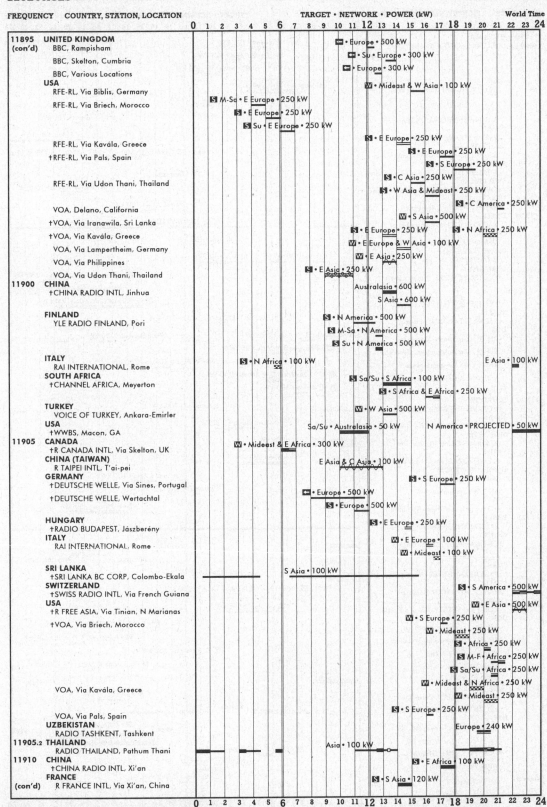

Frequency	Country, Station, Location	Target • Network • Power
11895 (con'd)	**UNITED KINGDOM**	
	BBC, Rampisham	Europe • 500 kW
	BBC, Skelton, Cumbria	Su • Europe • 300 kW
	BBC, Various Locations	Europe • 300 kW
	USA	
	RFE-RL, Via Biblis, Germany	Mideast & W Asia • 100 kW
	RFE-RL, Via Briech, Morocco	M-Sa • E Europe • 250 kW
		E Europe • 250 kW
		Su • E Europe • 250 kW
	RFE-RL, Via Kavála, Greece	E Europe • 250 kW
	†RFE-RL, Via Pals, Spain	E Europe • 250 kW
		S Europe • 250 kW
	RFE-RL, Via Udon Thani, Thailand	C Asia • 250 kW
		W Asia & Mideast • 250 kW
	VOA, Delano, California	C America • 250 kW
	†VOA, Via Iranawila, Sri Lanka	S Asia • 500 kW
	†VOA, Via Kavála, Greece	E Europe • 250 kW N Africa • 250 kW
	VOA, Via Lampertheim, Germany	E Europe & W Asia • 100 kW
	VOA, Via Philippines	E Asia • 250 kW
	VOA, Via Udon Thani, Thailand	E Asia • 250 kW
11900	**CHINA**	
	†CHINA RADIO INTL, Jinhua	Australasia • 600 kW
		S Asia • 600 kW
	FINLAND	
	YLE RADIO FINLAND, Pori	N America • 500 kW
		M-Sa • N America • 500 kW
		Su • N America • 500 kW
	ITALY	
	RAI INTERNATIONAL, Rome	N Africa • 100 kW E Asia • 100 kW
	SOUTH AFRICA	
	†CHANNEL AFRICA, Meyerton	Sa/Su • S Africa • 100 kW
		S Africa & E Africa • 250 kW
	TURKEY	
	VOICE OF TURKEY, Ankara-Emirler	W Asia • 500 kW
	USA	
	†WWBS, Macon, GA	Sa/Su • Australasia • 50 kW N America • PROJECTED • 50 kW
11905	**CANADA**	
	†R CANADA INTL, Via Skelton, UK	Mideast & E Africa • 300 kW
	CHINA (TAIWAN)	
	R TAIPEI INTL, T'ai-pei	E Asia & C Asia • 100 kW
	GERMANY	
	†DEUTSCHE WELLE, Via Sines, Portugal	S Europe • 250 kW
	†DEUTSCHE WELLE, Wertachtal	Europe • 500 kW
		Europe • 500 kW
	HUNGARY	
	†RADIO BUDAPEST, Jászberény	E Europe • 250 kW
	ITALY	
	RAI INTERNATIONAL, Rome	E Europe • 100 kW
		Mideast • 100 kW
	SRI LANKA	
	†SRI LANKA BC CORP, Colombo-Ekala	S Asia • 100 kW
	SWITZERLAND	
	†SWISS RADIO INTL, Via French Guiana	S America • 500 kW
	USA	
	†R FREE ASIA, Via Tinian, N Marianas	E Asia • 500 kW
	†VOA, Via Briech, Morocco	S Europe • 250 kW
		Mideast • 250 kW
		Africa • 250 kW
		M-F • Africa • 250 kW
		Sa/Su • Africa • 250 kW
		Mideast & N Africa • 250 kW
		Mideast • 250 kW
	VOA, Via Kavála, Greece	S Europe • 250 kW
	VOA, Via Pals, Spain	
	UZBEKISTAN	
	RADIO TASHKENT, Tashkent	Europe • 240 kW
11905.2	**THAILAND**	
	RADIO THAILAND, Pathum Thani	Asia • 100 kW
11910	**CHINA**	
	†CHINA RADIO INTL, Xi'an	E Africa • 100 kW
	FRANCE	
(con'd)	R FRANCE INTL, Via Xi'an, China	S Asia • 120 kW

World Time scale: 0 1 2 3 4 5 6 7 8 9 10 11 12 13 14 15 16 17 18 19 20 21 22 23 24

ENGLISH ▬   **ARABIC** ⁓   **CHINESE** ▭▭   **FRENCH** ▬▬   **GERMAN** ▬▬   **RUSSIAN** ═   **SPANISH** ▬▬   **OTHER** ──

FREQUENCY   COUNTRY, STATION, LOCATION   TARGET • NETWORK • POWER (kW)   World Time

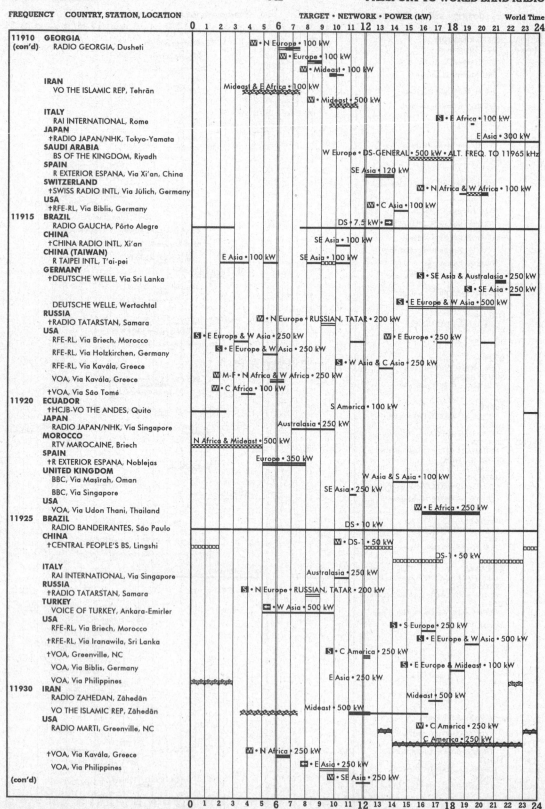

Freq	Country / Station / Location	Details
11910 (con'd)	**GEORGIA** RADIO GEORGIA, Dusheti	W • N Europe • 100 kW
		W • Europe • 100 kW
		W • Mideast • 100 kW
	IRAN VO THE ISLAMIC REP, Tehrān	Mideast & E Africa • 100 kW
		W • Mideast • 500 kW
	ITALY RAI INTERNATIONAL, Rome	S • E Africa • 100 kW
	JAPAN †RADIO JAPAN/NHK, Tokyo-Yamata	E Asia • 300 kW
	SAUDI ARABIA BS OF THE KINGDOM, Riyadh	W Europe • DS-GENERAL • 500 kW • ALT. FREQ. TO 11965 kHz
	SPAIN R EXTERIOR ESPANA, Via Xi'an, China	SE Asia • 120 kW
	SWITZERLAND †SWISS RADIO INTL, Via Jülich, Germany	W • N Africa & W Africa • 100 kW
	USA †RFE-RL, Via Biblis, Germany	W • C Asia • 100 kW
11915	**BRAZIL** RADIO GAUCHA, Pôrto Alegre	DS • 7.5 kW • ➡
	CHINA †CHINA RADIO INTL, Xi'an	SE Asia • 100 kW
	CHINA (TAIWAN) R TAIPEI INTL, T'ai-pei	E Asia • 100 kW
		SE Asia • 100 kW
	GERMANY †DEUTSCHE WELLE, Via Sri Lanka	S • SE Asia & Australasia • 250 kW
		S • SE Asia • 250 kW
	DEUTSCHE WELLE, Wertachtal	S • E Europe & W Asia • 500 kW
	RUSSIA †RADIO TATARSTAN, Samara	W • N Europe • RUSSIAN, TATAR • 200 kW
	USA RFE-RL, Via Briech, Morocco	S • E Europe & W Asia • 250 kW
		W • E Europe • 250 kW
	RFE-RL, Via Holzkirchen, Germany	S • E Europe & W Asia • 250 kW
	RFE-RL, Via Kavála, Greece	S • W Asia & C Asia • 250 kW
	VOA, Via Kavála, Greece	W • M-F • N Africa & W Africa • 250 kW
	†VOA, Via São Tomé	W • C Africa • 100 kW
11920	**ECUADOR** †HCJB-VO THE ANDES, Quito	S America • 100 kW
	JAPAN RADIO JAPAN/NHK, Via Singapore	Australasia • 250 kW
	MOROCCO RTV MAROCAINE, Briech	N Africa & Mideast • 500 kW
	SPAIN †R EXTERIOR ESPANA, Noblejas	Europe • 350 kW
	UNITED KINGDOM BBC, Via Maṣīrah, Oman	W Asia & S Asia • 100 kW
	BBC, Via Singapore	SE Asia • 250 kW
	USA VOA, Via Udon Thani, Thailand	W • E Africa • 250 kW
11925	**BRAZIL** RADIO BANDEIRANTES, São Paulo	DS • 10 kW
	CHINA †CENTRAL PEOPLE'S BS, Lingshi	W • DS-1 • 50 kW
		DS-1 • 50 kW
	ITALY RAI INTERNATIONAL, Via Singapore	Australasia • 250 kW
	RUSSIA †RADIO TATARSTAN, Samara	S • N Europe • RUSSIAN, TATAR • 200 kW
	TURKEY VOICE OF TURKEY, Ankara-Emirler	➡ • W Asia • 500 kW
	USA RFE-RL, Via Briech, Morocco	S • S Europe • 250 kW
	†RFE-RL, Via Iranawila, Sri Lanka	S • E Europe & W Asia • 500 kW
	†VOA, Greenville, NC	S • C America • 250 kW
	VOA, Via Biblis, Germany	S • E Europe & Mideast • 100 kW
	VOA, Via Philippines	E Asia • 250 kW
11930	**IRAN** RADIO ZAHEDAN, Zāhedān	Mideast • 500 kW
	VO THE ISLAMIC REP, Zāhedān	Mideast • 500 kW
	USA RADIO MARTI, Greenville, NC	W • C America • 250 kW
		C America • 250 kW
	†VOA, Via Kavála, Greece	W • N Africa • 250 kW
	VOA, Via Philippines	➡ • E Asia • 250 kW
(con'd)		W • SE Asia • 250 kW

FREQUENCY   COUNTRY, STATION, LOCATION   TARGET • NETWORK • POWER (kW)   World Time

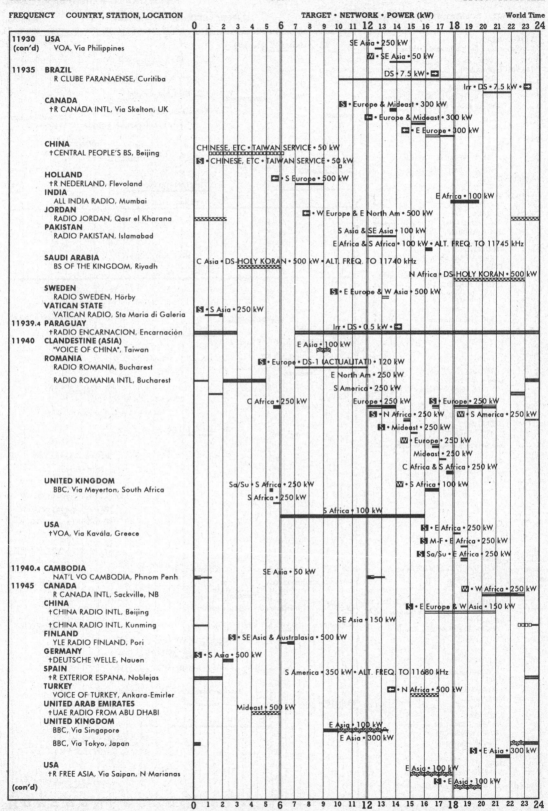

FREQUENCY	COUNTRY, STATION, LOCATION	TARGET • NETWORK • POWER (kW) / World Time
11930 (con'd)	**USA** VOA, Via Philippines	SE Asia • 250 kW / W • SE Asia • 50 kW
11935	**BRAZIL** R CLUBE PARANAENSE, Curitiba	DS • 7.5 kW • ◻ / Irr • DS • 7.5 kW • ◻
	CANADA †R CANADA INTL, Via Skelton, UK	S • Europe & Mideast • 300 kW / ◻ • Europe & Mideast • 300 kW / ◻ • E Europe • 300 kW
	CHINA †CENTRAL PEOPLE'S BS, Beijing	CHINESE, ETC • TAIWAN SERVICE • 50 kW / S • CHINESE, ETC • TAIWAN SERVICE • 50 kW
	HOLLAND †R NEDERLAND, Flevoland	◻ • S Europe • 500 kW
	INDIA ALL INDIA RADIO, Mumbai	E Africa • 100 kW
	JORDAN RADIO JORDAN, Qasr el Kharana	◻ • W Europe & E North Am • 500 kW
	PAKISTAN RADIO PAKISTAN, Islamabad	S Asia & SE Asia • 100 kW / E Africa & S Africa • 100 kW • ALT. FREQ. TO 11745 kHz
	SAUDI ARABIA BS OF THE KINGDOM, Riyadh	C Asia • DS–HOLY KORAN • 500 kW • ALT. FREQ. TO 11740 kHz / N Africa • DS–HOLY KORAN • 500 kW
	SWEDEN RADIO SWEDEN, Hörby	S • E Europe & W Asia • 500 kW
	VATICAN STATE VATICAN RADIO, Sta Maria di Galeria	S • S Asia • 250 kW
11939.4	**PARAGUAY** †RADIO ENCARNACION, Encarnación	Irr • DS • 0.5 kW • ◻
11940	**CLANDESTINE (ASIA)** "VOICE OF CHINA", Taiwan	E Asia • 100 kW
	ROMANIA RADIO ROMANIA, Bucharest	S • Europe • DS-1 (ACTUALITATI) • 120 kW
	RADIO ROMANIA INTL, Bucharest	E North Am • 250 kW / S America • 250 kW / C Africa • 250 kW / Europe • 250 kW / S • Europe • 250 kW / S • N Africa • 250 kW / W • S America • 250 kW / S • Mideast • 250 kW / W • Europe • 250 kW / Mideast • 250 kW / C Africa & S Africa • 250 kW
	UNITED KINGDOM BBC, Via Meyerton, South Africa	Sa/Su • S Africa • 250 kW / S Africa • 250 kW / W • S Africa • 100 kW / S Africa • 100 kW
	USA †VOA, Via Kavála, Greece	S • E Africa • 250 kW / S M-F • E Africa • 250 kW / S Sa/Su • E Africa • 250 kW
11940.4	**CAMBODIA** NAT'L VO CAMBODIA, Phnom Penh	SE Asia • 50 kW
11945	**CANADA** R CANADA INTL, Sackville, NB	W • W Africa • 250 kW
	CHINA †CHINA RADIO INTL, Beijing	S • E Europe & W Asia • 150 kW
	†CHINA RADIO INTL, Kunming	SE Asia • 150 kW
	FINLAND YLE RADIO FINLAND, Pori	S • SE Asia & Australasia • 500 kW
	GERMANY †DEUTSCHE WELLE, Nauen	S • S Asia • 500 kW
	SPAIN †R EXTERIOR ESPANA, Noblejas	S America • 350 kW • ALT. FREQ. TO 11680 kHz
	TURKEY VOICE OF TURKEY, Ankara-Emirler	◻ • N Africa • 500 kW
	UNITED ARAB EMIRATES †UAE RADIO FROM ABU DHABI	Mideast • 500 kW
	UNITED KINGDOM BBC, Via Singapore	E Asia • 100 kW
	BBC, Via Tokyo, Japan	E Asia • 300 kW / S • E Asia • 300 kW
	USA †R FREE ASIA, Via Saipan, N Marianas	E Asia • 100 kW / S • E Asia • 100 kW
(con'd)		

ENGLISH ▬   ARABIC ▧   CHINESE ▭▭▭   FRENCH ═   GERMAN ▬▬   RUSSIAN ══   SPANISH ▬▬   OTHER —

FREQUENCY   COUNTRY, STATION, LOCATION   TARGET • NETWORK • POWER (kW)   World Time

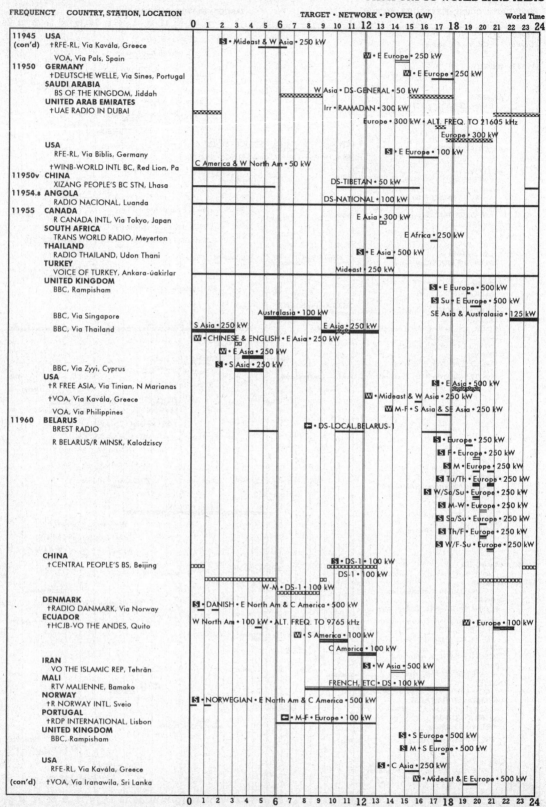

Frequency	Country, Station, Location	Target • Network • Power
11945 (con'd)	USA †RFE-RL, Via Kavála, Greece	S • Mideast & W Asia • 250 kW
	VOA, Via Pals, Spain	W • E Europe • 250 kW
11950	GERMANY †DEUTSCHE WELLE, Via Sines, Portugal	W • E Europe • 250 kW
	SAUDI ARABIA BS OF THE KINGDOM, Jiddah	W Asia • DS-GENERAL • 50 kW
	UNITED ARAB EMIRATES †UAE RADIO IN DUBAI	Irr • RAMADAN • 300 kW
		Europe • 300 kW • ALT. FREQ. TO 21605 kHz
		Europe • 300 kW
	USA RFE-RL, Via Biblis, Germany	S • E Europe • 100 kW
	†WINB-WORLD INTL BC, Red Lion, Pa	C America & W North Am • 50 kW
11950v	CHINA XIZANG PEOPLE'S BC STN, Lhasa	DS-TIBETAN • 50 kW
11954.8	ANGOLA RADIO NACIONAL, Luanda	DS-NATIONAL • 100 kW
11955	CANADA R CANADA INTL, Via Tokyo, Japan	E Asia • 300 kW
	SOUTH AFRICA TRANS WORLD RADIO, Meyerton	E Africa • 250 kW
	THAILAND RADIO THAILAND, Udon Thani	S • E Asia • 500 kW
	TURKEY VOICE OF TURKEY, Ankara-üakirlar	Mideast • 250 kW
	UNITED KINGDOM BBC, Rampisham	S • E Europe • 500 kW
		Su • E Europe • 500 kW
	BBC, Via Singapore	Australasia • 100 kW SE Asia & Australasia • 125 kW
	BBC, Via Thailand	S Asia • 250 kW E Asia • 250 kW
		W • CHINESE & ENGLISH • E Asia • 250 kW
		W • E Asia • 250 kW
	BBC, Via Zyyi, Cyprus	S • S Asia • 250 kW
	USA †R FREE ASIA, Via Tinian, N Marianas	S • E Asia • 500 kW
	†VOA, Via Kavála, Greece	W • Mideast & W Asia • 250 kW
	VOA, Via Philippines	W M-F • S Asia & SE Asia • 250 kW
11960	BELARUS BREST RADIO	S • DS-LOCAL,BELARUS-1
	R BELARUS/R MINSK, Kalodziscy	S • Europe • 250 kW
		S • F • Europe • 250 kW
		S M • Europe • 250 kW
		S Tu/Th • Europe • 250 kW
		S W/Sa/Su • Europe • 250 kW
		S M-W • Europe • 250 kW
		S Sa/Su • Europe • 250 kW
		S Th/F • Europe • 250 kW
		S W/F-Su • Europe • 250 kW
	CHINA †CENTRAL PEOPLE'S BS, Beijing	S • DS-1 • 100 kW
		DS-1 • 100 kW
		W-M • DS-1 • 100 kW
	DENMARK †RADIO DANMARK, Via Norway	S • DANISH • E North Am & C America • 500 kW
	ECUADOR †HCJB-VO THE ANDES, Quito	W North Am • 100 kW • ALT. FREQ. TO 9765 kHz W • Europe • 100 kW
		W • S America • 100 kW
		C America • 100 kW
	IRAN VO THE ISLAMIC REP, Tehrān	S • W Asia • 500 kW
	MALI RTV MALIENNE, Bamako	FRENCH, ETC • DS • 100 kW
	NORWAY †R NORWAY INTL, Svcio	S • NORWEGIAN • E North Am & C America • 500 kW
	PORTUGAL †RDP INTERNATIONAL, Lisbon	M-F • Europe • 100 kW
	UNITED KINGDOM BBC, Rampisham	S • S Europe • 500 kW
		S M • S Europe • 500 kW
	USA RFE-RL, Via Kavála, Greece	S • C Asia • 250 kW
(con'd)	†VOA, Via Iranawila, Sri Lanka	W • Mideast & E Europe • 500 kW

FREQUENCY　　COUNTRY, STATION, LOCATION

TARGET • NETWORK • POWER (kW)　　　　　World Time

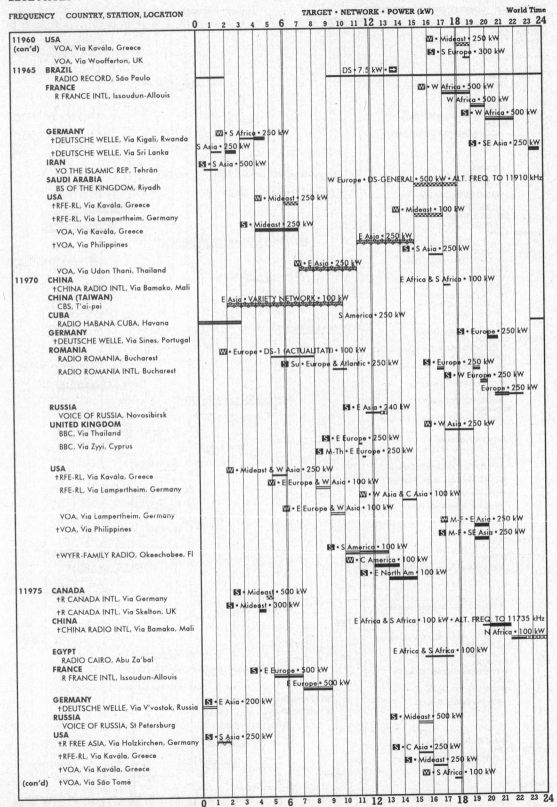

Freq	Country / Station / Location	Details
11960 (con'd)	USA	
	VOA, Via Kavála, Greece	W • Mideast • 250 kW
	VOA, Via Woofferton, UK	S • S Europe • 300 kW
11965	BRAZIL	
	RADIO RECORD, São Paulo	DS • 7.5 kW •
	FRANCE	
	R FRANCE INTL, Issoudun-Allouis	W • W Africa • 500 kW / W Africa • 500 kW / S • W Africa • 500 kW
	GERMANY	
	†DEUTSCHE WELLE, Via Kigali, Rwanda	W • S Africa • 250 kW / S • SE Asia • 250 kW
	†DEUTSCHE WELLE, Via Sri Lanka	S Asia • 250 kW
	IRAN	
	VO THE ISLAMIC REP, Tehrān	S • S Asia • 500 kW
	SAUDI ARABIA	
	BS OF THE KINGDOM, Riyadh	W Europe • DS-GENERAL • 500 kW • ALT. FREQ. TO 11910 kHz
	USA	
	†RFE-RL, Via Kavála, Greece	W • Mideast • 250 kW
	†RFE-RL, Via Lampertheim, Germany	W • Mideast • 100 kW
	VOA, Via Kavála, Greece	S • Mideast • 250 kW
	†VOA, Via Philippines	E Asia • 250 kW / S • S Asia • 250 kW
	VOA, Via Udon Thani, Thailand	W • E Asia • 250 kW / E Africa & S Africa • 100 kW
11970	CHINA	
	†CHINA RADIO INTL, Via Bamako, Mali	E Asia • VARIETY NETWORK • 100 kW
	CHINA (TAIWAN)	
	CBS, T'ai-pei	
	CUBA	
	RADIO HABANA CUBA, Havana	S America • 250 kW
	GERMANY	
	†DEUTSCHE WELLE, Via Sines, Portugal	S • Europe • 250 kW
	ROMANIA	
	RADIO ROMANIA, Bucharest	W • Europe • DS-1 (ACTUALITATI) • 100 kW
	RADIO ROMANIA INTL, Bucharest	S • Su • Europe & Atlantic • 250 kW / S • Europe • 250 kW / S • W Europe • 250 kW / Europe • 250 kW
	RUSSIA	
	VOICE OF RUSSIA, Novosibirsk	S • E Asia • 240 kW
	UNITED KINGDOM	
	BBC, Via Thailand	W • W Asia • 250 kW
	BBC, Via Zyyi, Cyprus	S • E Europe • 250 kW / S • M-Th • E Europe • 250 kW
	USA	
	†RFE-RL, Via Kavála, Greece	W • Mideast & W Asia • 250 kW
	RFE-RL, Via Lampertheim, Germany	W • E Europe & W Asia • 100 kW / W • W Asia & C Asia • 100 kW / W • E Europe & W Asia • 100 kW
	VOA, Via Lampertheim, Germany	W • M-F • E Asia • 250 kW
	†VOA, Via Philippines	S • M-F • SE Asia • 250 kW
	†WYFR-FAMILY RADIO, Okeechobee, Fl	S • S America • 100 kW / W • C America • 100 kW / S • E North Am • 100 kW
11975	CANADA	
	†R CANADA INTL, Via Germany	S • Mideast • 500 kW
	†R CANADA INTL, Via Skelton, UK	S • Mideast • 300 kW
	CHINA	
	†CHINA RADIO INTL, Via Bamako, Mali	E Africa & S Africa • 100 kW • ALT. FREQ. TO 11735 kHz / N Africa • 100 kW
	EGYPT	
	RADIO CAIRO, Abu Za'bal	E Africa & S Africa • 100 kW
	FRANCE	
	R FRANCE INTL, Issoudun-Allouis	S • E Europe • 500 kW / E Europe • 500 kW
	GERMANY	
	†DEUTSCHE WELLE, Via V'vostok, Russia	S • E Asia • 200 kW
	RUSSIA	
	VOICE OF RUSSIA, St Petersburg	S • Mideast • 500 kW
	USA	
	†R FREE ASIA, Via Holzkirchen, Germany	S • S Asia • 250 kW
	†RFE-RL, Via Kavála, Greece	S • C Asia • 250 kW
	†VOA, Via Kavála, Greece	S • Mideast • 250 kW
(con'd)	†VOA, Via São Tomé	W • S Africa • 100 kW

ENGLISH ▬　ARABIC ※※※　CHINESE □□□　FRENCH ▬▬　GERMAN ▬▬　RUSSIAN ══　SPANISH ▬▬　OTHER ▬

FREQUENCY   COUNTRY, STATION, LOCATION

TARGET • NETWORK • POWER (kW)   World Time

0 1 2 3 4 5 6 7 8 9 10 11 12 13 14 15 16 17 18 19 20 21 22 23 24

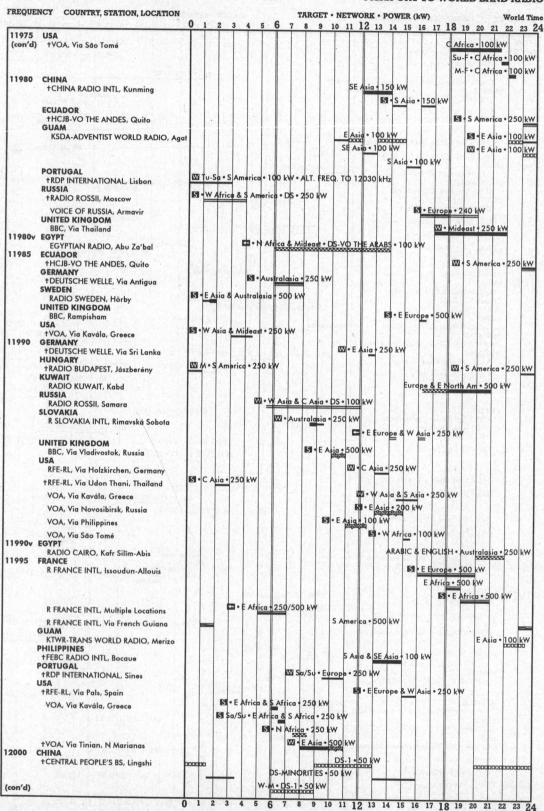

Frequency	Country / Station / Location	Schedule
11975 (con'd)	**USA** †VOA, Via São Tomé	C Africa • 100 kW; Su-F • C Africa • 100 kW; M-F • C Africa • 100 kW
11980	**CHINA** †CHINA RADIO INTL, Kunming	SE Asia • 150 kW; S • S Asia • 150 kW
	ECUADOR †HCJB-VO THE ANDES, Quito	S • S America • 250 kW
	GUAM KSDA-ADVENTIST WORLD RADIO, Agat	E Asia • 100 kW; SE Asia • 100 kW; S • E Asia • 100 kW; W • E Asia • 100 kW; S Asia • 100 kW
	PORTUGAL †RDP INTERNATIONAL, Lisbon	W Tu-Sa • S America • 100 kW • ALT. FREQ. TO 12030 kHz
	RUSSIA †RADIO ROSSII, Moscow	S • W Africa & S America • DS • 250 kW
	VOICE OF RUSSIA, Armavir	S • Europe • 240 kW
	UNITED KINGDOM BBC, Via Thailand	W • Mideast • 250 kW
11980v	**EGYPT** EGYPTIAN RADIO, Abu Za'bal	N Africa & Mideast • DS-VO THE ARABS • 100 kW
11985	**ECUADOR** †HCJB-VO THE ANDES, Quito	W • S America • 250 kW
	GERMANY †DEUTSCHE WELLE, Via Antigua	S • Australasia • 250 kW
	SWEDEN RADIO SWEDEN, Hörby	S • E Asia & Australasia • 500 kW
	UNITED KINGDOM BBC, Rampisham	S • E Europe • 500 kW
	USA †VOA, Via Kavála, Greece	S • W Asia & Mideast • 250 kW
11990	**GERMANY** †DEUTSCHE WELLE, Via Sri Lanka	W • E Asia • 250 kW
	HUNGARY †RADIO BUDAPEST, Jászberény	W M • S America • 250 kW; W • S America • 250 kW
	KUWAIT RADIO KUWAIT, Kabd	Europe & E North Am • 500 kW
	RUSSIA RADIO ROSSII, Samara	W • W Asia & C Asia • DS • 100 kW
	SLOVAKIA R SLOVAKIA INTL, Rimavská Sobota	W • Australasia • 250 kW
	UNITED KINGDOM BBC, Via Vladivostok, Russia	E Europe & W Asia • 250 kW; S • E Asia • 500 kW
	USA RFE-RL, Via Holzkirchen, Germany	W • C Asia • 250 kW
	†RFE-RL, Via Udon Thani, Thailand	S • C Asia • 250 kW
	VOA, Via Kavála, Greece	W • W Asia & S Asia • 250 kW
	VOA, Via Novosibirsk, Russia	S • E Asia • 200 kW
	VOA, Via Philippines	S • E Asia • 100 kW
	VOA, Via São Tomé	S • W Africa • 100 kW
11990v	**EGYPT** RADIO CAIRO, Kafr Silîm-Abis	ARABIC & ENGLISH • Australasia • 250 kW
11995	**FRANCE** R FRANCE INTL, Issoudun-Allouis	S • E Europe • 500 kW; E Africa • 500 kW; S • E Africa • 500 kW
	R FRANCE INTL, Multiple Locations	E Africa • 250/500 kW
	R FRANCE INTL, Via French Guiana	S America • 500 kW
	GUAM KTWR-TRANS WORLD RADIO, Merizo	E Asia • 100 kW
	PHILIPPINES †FEBC RADIO INTL, Bocaue	S Asia & SE Asia • 100 kW
	PORTUGAL †RDP INTERNATIONAL, Sines	W Sa/Su • Europe • 250 kW
	USA †RFE-RL, Via Pals, Spain	S • E Europe & W Asia • 250 kW
	VOA, Via Kavála, Greece	S • E Africa & S Africa • 250 kW; S Sa/Su • E Africa & S Africa • 250 kW; S • N Africa • 250 kW
	†VOA, Via Tinian, N Marianas	W • E Asia • 500 kW
12000	**CHINA** †CENTRAL PEOPLE'S BS, Lingshi	DS-1 • 50 kW; DS-MINORITIES • 50 kW; W-M • DS-1 • 50 kW
(con'd)		

0 1 2 3 4 5 6 7 8 9 10 11 12 13 14 15 16 17 18 19 20 21 22 23 24

FREQUENCY   COUNTRY, STATION, LOCATION

TARGET • NETWORK • POWER (kW)   World Time

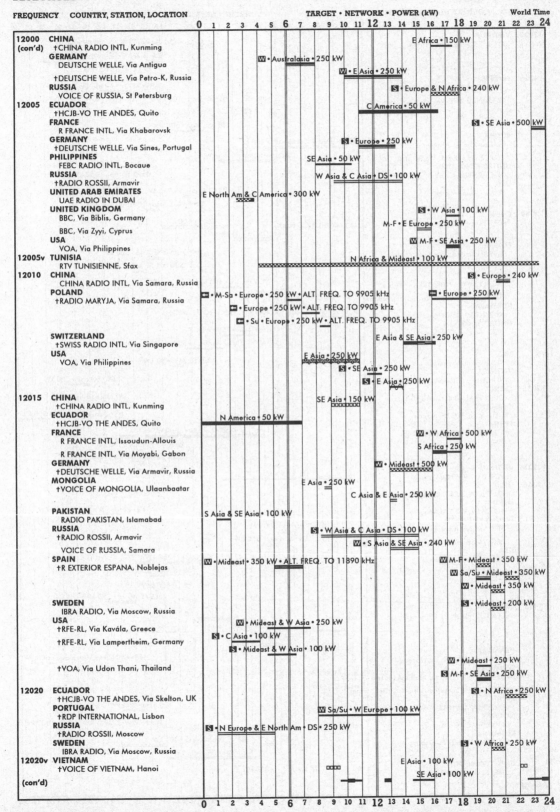

FREQUENCY	COUNTRY, STATION, LOCATION	TARGET • NETWORK • POWER (kW)	World Time
12000 (con'd)	CHINA		
	†CHINA RADIO INTL, Kunming	E Africa • 150 kW	
	GERMANY		
	DEUTSCHE WELLE, Via Antigua	W • Australasia • 250 kW	
	†DEUTSCHE WELLE, Via Petro-K, Russia	W • E Asia • 250 kW	
	RUSSIA		
	VOICE OF RUSSIA, St Petersburg	S • Europe & N Africa • 240 kW	
12005	ECUADOR		
	†HCJB-VO THE ANDES, Quito	C America • 50 kW	
	FRANCE		
	R FRANCE INTL, Via Khabarovsk	S • SE Asia • 500 kW	
	GERMANY		
	†DEUTSCHE WELLE, Via Sines, Portugal	S • Europe • 250 kW	
	PHILIPPINES		
	FEBC RADIO INTL, Bocaue	SE Asia • 50 kW	
	RUSSIA		
	†RADIO ROSSII, Armavir	W Asia & C Asia • DS • 100 kW	
	UNITED ARAB EMIRATES		
	UAE RADIO IN DUBAI	E North Am & C America • 300 kW	
	UNITED KINGDOM		
	BBC, Via Biblis, Germany	S • W Asia • 100 kW	
	BBC, Via Zyyi, Cyprus	M-F • E Europe • 250 kW	
	USA		
	VOA, Via Philippines	W M-F • SE Asia • 250 kW	
12005v	TUNISIA		
	RTV TUNISIENNE, Sfax	N Africa & Mideast • 100 kW	
12010	CHINA		
	CHINA RADIO INTL, Via Samara, Russia	S • Europe • 240 kW	
	POLAND		
	†RADIO MARYJA, Via Samara, Russia	• M-Sa • Europe • 250 kW • ALT FREQ. TO 9905 kHz • Europe • 250 kW	
		• Europe • 250 kW • ALT. FREQ. TO 9905 kHz	
		• Su • Europe • 250 kW • ALT. FREQ. TO 9905 kHz	
	SWITZERLAND		
	†SWISS RADIO INTL, Via Singapore	E Asia & SE Asia • 250 kW	
	USA		
	VOA, Via Philippines	E Asia • 250 kW	
		S • SE Asia • 250 kW	
		S • E Asia • 250 kW	
12015	CHINA		
	†CHINA RADIO INTL, Kunming	SE Asia • 150 kW	
	ECUADOR		
	†HCJB-VO THE ANDES, Quito	N America • 50 kW	
	FRANCE		
	R FRANCE INTL, Issoudun-Allouis	W • W Africa • 500 kW	
	R FRANCE INTL, Via Moyabi, Gabon	S Africa • 250 kW	
	GERMANY		
	†DEUTSCHE WELLE, Via Armavir, Russia	W • Mideast • 500 kW	
	MONGOLIA		
	†VOICE OF MONGOLIA, Ulaanbaatar	E Asia • 250 kW	
		C Asia & E Asia • 250 kW	
	PAKISTAN		
	RADIO PAKISTAN, Islamabad	S Asia & SE Asia • 100 kW	
	RUSSIA		
	†RADIO ROSSII, Armavir	S • W Asia & C Asia • DS • 100 kW	
	VOICE OF RUSSIA, Samara	W • S Asia & SE Asia • 240 kW	
	SPAIN		
	†R EXTERIOR ESPANA, Noblejas	W • Mideast • 350 kW • ALT. FREQ. TO 11890 kHz W M-F • Mideast • 350 kW	
		W Sa/Su • Mideast • 350 kW	
		W • Mideast • 350 kW	
	SWEDEN		
	IBRA RADIO, Via Moscow, Russia	S • Mideast • 200 kW	
	USA		
	†RFE-RL, Via Kavála, Greece	W • Mideast & W Asia • 250 kW	
		S • C Asia • 100 kW	
	†RFE-RL, Via Lampertheim, Germany	S • Mideast & W Asia • 100 kW	
	†VOA, Via Udon Thani, Thailand	W • Mideast • 250 kW	
		S M-F • SE Asia • 250 kW	
12020	ECUADOR		
	†HCJB-VO THE ANDES, Via Skelton, UK	S • N Africa • 250 kW	
	PORTUGAL		
	†RDP INTERNATIONAL, Lisbon	W Sa/Su • W Europe • 100 kW	
	RUSSIA		
	†RADIO ROSSII, Moscow	S • N Europe & E North Am • DS • 250 kW	
	SWEDEN		
	IBRA RADIO, Via Moscow, Russia	S • W Africa • 250 kW	
12020v	VIETNAM		
	†VOICE OF VIETNAM, Hanoi	E Asia • 100 kW	
		SE Asia • 100 kW	
(con'd)			

ENGLISH ▬   ARABIC ▨   CHINESE ▯▯▯   FRENCH ═   GERMAN ▬   RUSSIAN ═   SPANISH ▬   OTHER —

FREQUENCY   COUNTRY, STATION, LOCATION

TARGET • NETWORK • POWER (kW)   World Time

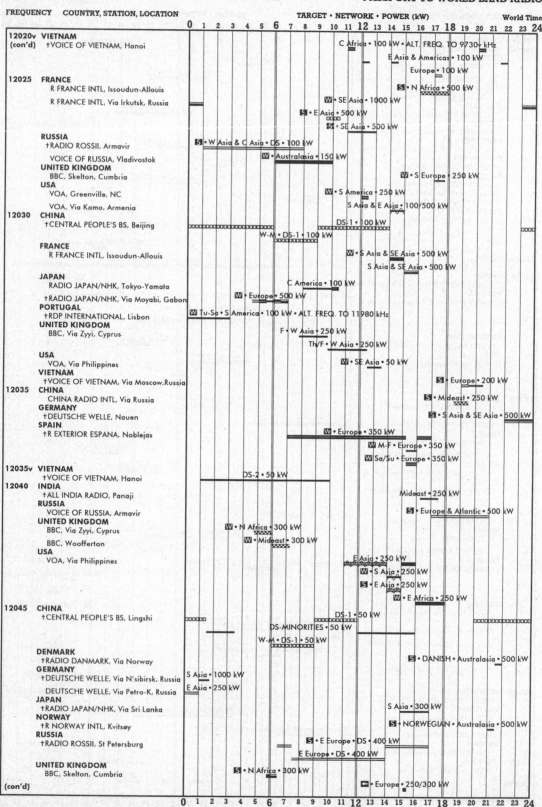

FREQUENCY	COUNTRY, STATION, LOCATION	TARGET • NETWORK • POWER (kW)
12020v (con'd)	VIETNAM †VOICE OF VIETNAM, Hanoi	C Africa • 100 kW • ALT. FREQ. TO 9730v kHz; E Asia & Americas • 100 kW; Europe • 100 kW
12025	FRANCE R FRANCE INTL, Issoudun-Allouis	S • N Africa • 500 kW
	R FRANCE INTL, Via Irkutsk, Russia	W • SE Asia • 1000 kW; S • E Asia • 500 kW; S • SE Asia • 500 kW
	RUSSIA †RADIO ROSSII, Armavir	S • W Asia & C Asia • DS • 100 kW
	VOICE OF RUSSIA, Vladivostok	W • Australasia • 150 kW
	UNITED KINGDOM BBC, Skelton, Cumbria	W • S Europe • 250 kW
	USA VOA, Greenville, NC	W • S America • 250 kW
	VOA, Via Kamo, Armenia	S Asia & E Asia • 100/500 kW
12030	CHINA †CENTRAL PEOPLE'S BS, Beijing	DS-1 • 100 kW; W-M • DS-1 • 100 kW
	FRANCE R FRANCE INTL, Issoudun-Allouis	W • S Asia & SE Asia • 500 kW; S Asia & SE Asia • 500 kW
	JAPAN RADIO JAPAN/NHK, Tokyo-Yamata	C America • 100 kW
	†RADIO JAPAN/NHK, Via Moyabi, Gabon	W • Europe • 500 kW
	PORTUGAL †RDP INTERNATIONAL, Lisbon	W Tu-Sa • S America • 100 kW • ALT. FREQ. TO 11980 kHz
	UNITED KINGDOM BBC, Via Zyyi, Cyprus	F • W Asia • 250 kW; Th/F • W Asia • 250 kW
	USA VOA, Via Philippines	W • SE Asia • 50 kW
	VIETNAM †VOICE OF VIETNAM, Via Moscow, Russia	S • Europe • 200 kW
12035	CHINA CHINA RADIO INTL, Via Russia	S • Mideast • 250 kW
	GERMANY †DEUTSCHE WELLE, Nauen	S • S Asia & SE Asia • 500 kW
	SPAIN †R EXTERIOR ESPANA, Noblejas	W • Europe • 350 kW; W M-F • Europe • 350 kW; W Sa/Su • Europe • 350 kW
12035v	VIETNAM †VOICE OF VIETNAM, Hanoi	DS-2 • 50 kW
12040	INDIA †ALL INDIA RADIO, Panaji	Mideast • 250 kW
	RUSSIA VOICE OF RUSSIA, Armavir	S • Europe & Atlantic • 500 kW
	UNITED KINGDOM BBC, Via Zyyi, Cyprus	W • N Africa • 300 kW
	BBC, Woofferton	W • Mideast • 300 kW
	USA VOA, Via Philippines	E Asia • 250 kW; W • S Asia • 250 kW; S • E Asia • 250 kW; W • E Africa • 250 kW
12045	CHINA †CENTRAL PEOPLE'S BS, Lingshi	DS-1 • 50 kW; DS-MINORITIES • 50 kW; W-M • DS-1 • 50 kW
	DENMARK †RADIO DANMARK, Via Norway	S • DANISH • Australasia • 500 kW
	GERMANY †DEUTSCHE WELLE, Via N'sibirsk, Russia	S Asia • 1000 kW
	DEUTSCHE WELLE, Via Petro-K, Russia	E Asia • 250 kW
	JAPAN †RADIO JAPAN/NHK, Via Sri Lanka	S Asia • 300 kW
	NORWAY †R NORWAY INTL, Kvitsøy	S • NORWEGIAN • Australasia • 500 kW
	RUSSIA †RADIO ROSSII, St Petersburg	S • E Europe • DS • 400 kW; E Europe • DS • 400 kW
	UNITED KINGDOM BBC, Skelton, Cumbria	S • N Africa • 300 kW; • Europe • 250/300 kW
(con'd)		

SEASONAL S OR W   1-HR TIMESHIFT MIDYEAR ⇦ OR ⇨   JAMMING / OR ∧   EARLIEST HEARD ◁   LATEST HEARD ▷   NEW FOR 2000 †

FREQUENCY   COUNTRY, STATION, LOCATION   TARGET • NETWORK • POWER (kW)   World Time

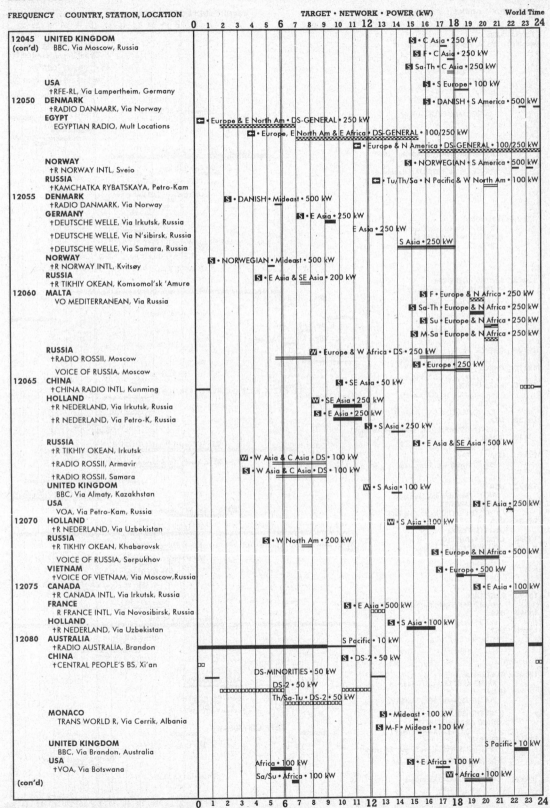

Frequency	Country, Station, Location	Target • Network • Power (kW)
12045 (con'd)	**UNITED KINGDOM** — BBC, Via Moscow, Russia	S • C Asia • 250 kW; S F • C Asia • 250 kW; S Sa-Th • C Asia • 250 kW
	USA — †RFE-RL, Via Lampertheim, Germany	S • S Europe • 100 kW
12050	**DENMARK** — †RADIO DANMARK, Via Norway	S • DANISH • S America • 500 kW
	EGYPT — EGYPTIAN RADIO, Mult Locations	• Europe & E North Am • DS-GENERAL • 250 kW; • Europe, E North Am & E Africa • DS-GENERAL • 100/250 kW; • Europe & N America • DS-GENERAL • 100/250 kW
	NORWAY — †R NORWAY INTL, Sveio	S • NORWEGIAN • S America • 500 kW
	RUSSIA — †KAMCHATKA RYBATSKAYA, Petro-Kam	• Tu/Th/Sa • N Pacific & W North Am • 100 kW
12055	**DENMARK** — †RADIO DANMARK, Via Norway	S • DANISH • Mideast • 500 kW
	GERMANY — †DEUTSCHE WELLE, Via Irkutsk, Russia	S • E Asia • 250 kW
	†DEUTSCHE WELLE, Via N'sibirsk, Russia	E Asia • 250 kW
	†DEUTSCHE WELLE, Via Samara, Russia	S Asia • 250 kW
	NORWAY — †R NORWAY INTL, Kvitsøy	S • NORWEGIAN • Mideast • 500 kW
	RUSSIA — †R TIKHIY OKEAN, Komsomol'sk 'Amure	S • E Asia & SE Asia • 200 kW
12060	**MALTA** — VO MEDITERRANEAN, Via Russia	S F • Europe & N Africa • 250 kW; S Sa-Th • Europe & N Africa • 250 kW; S Su • Europe & N Africa • 250 kW; S M-Sa • Europe & N Africa • 250 kW
	RUSSIA — †RADIO ROSSII, Moscow	W • Europe & W Africa • DS • 250 kW
	VOICE OF RUSSIA, Moscow	S • Europe • 250 kW
12065	**CHINA** — †CHINA RADIO INTL, Kunming	S • SE Asia • 50 kW
	HOLLAND — †R NEDERLAND, Via Irkutsk, Russia	W • SE Asia • 250 kW
	†R NEDERLAND, Via Petro-K, Russia	S • E Asia • 250 kW; S • S Asia • 250 kW
	RUSSIA — †R TIKHIY OKEAN, Irkutsk	S • E Asia & SE Asia • 500 kW
	†RADIO ROSSII, Armavir	W • W Asia & C Asia • DS • 100 kW
	†RADIO ROSSII, Samara	S • W Asia & C Asia • DS • 100 kW
	UNITED KINGDOM — BBC, Via Almaty, Kazakhstan	W • S Asia • 100 kW
	USA — VOA, Via Petro-Kam, Russia	S • E Asia • 250 kW
12070	**HOLLAND** — †R NEDERLAND, Via Uzbekistan	W • S Asia • 100 kW
	RUSSIA — †R TIKHIY OKEAN, Khabarovsk	S • W North Am • 200 kW
	VOICE OF RUSSIA, Serpukhov	S • Europe & N Africa • 500 kW
	VIETNAM — †VOICE OF VIETNAM, Via Moscow, Russia	S • Europe • 500 kW
12075	**CANADA** — †R CANADA INTL, Via Irkutsk, Russia	S • E Asia • 100 kW
	FRANCE — R FRANCE INTL, Via Novosibirsk, Russia	S • E Asia • 500 kW
	HOLLAND — †R NEDERLAND, Via Uzbekistan	S • S Asia • 100 kW
12080	**AUSTRALIA** — †RADIO AUSTRALIA, Brandon	S Pacific • 10 kW
	CHINA — †CENTRAL PEOPLE'S BS, Xi'an	S • DS-2 • 50 kW; DS-MINORITIES • 50 kW; DS-2 • 50 kW; Th/Sa-Tu • DS-2 • 50 kW
	MONACO — TRANS WORLD R, Via Cerrik, Albania	S • Mideast • 100 kW; S M-F • Mideast • 100 kW
	UNITED KINGDOM — BBC, Via Brandon, Australia	S Pacific • 10 kW
	USA — †VOA, Via Botswana	Africa • 100 kW; S • E Africa • 100 kW; Sa/Su • Africa • 100 kW; W • Africa • 100 kW
(con'd)		

FREQUENCY   COUNTRY, STATION, LOCATION   TARGET • NETWORK • POWER (kW)   World Time

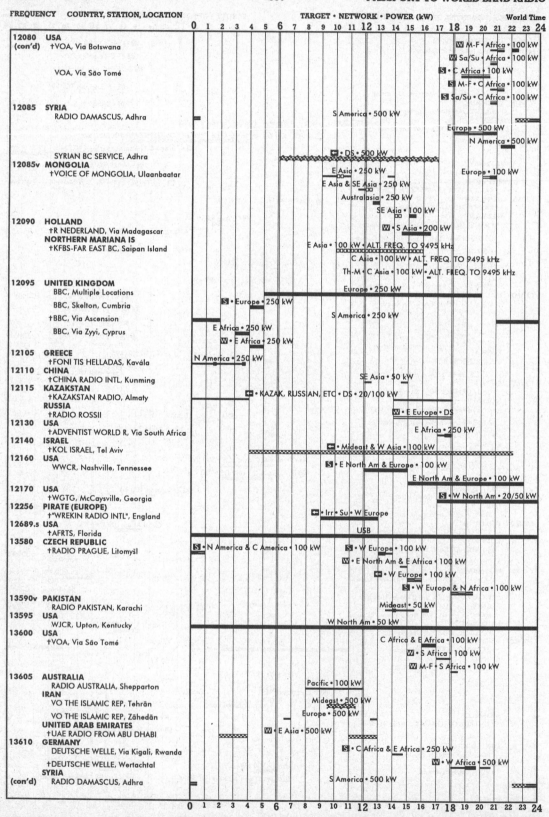

12080	USA		
(con'd)	†VOA, Via Botswana	W M-F • Africa • 100 kW	
		W Sa/Su • Africa • 100 kW	
	VOA, Via São Tomé	S • C Africa • 100 kW	
		S M-F • C Africa • 100 kW	
		S Sa/Su • C Africa • 100 kW	
12085	SYRIA		
	RADIO DAMASCUS, Adhra	S America • 500 kW	
		Europe • 500 kW	
		N America • 500 kW	
	SYRIAN BC SERVICE, Adhra	• DS • 500 kW	
12085v	MONGOLIA		
	†VOICE OF MONGOLIA, Ulaanbaatar	E Asia • 250 kW	Europe • 100 kW
		E Asia & SE Asia • 250 kW	
		Australasia • 250 kW	
		SE Asia • 100 kW	
12090	HOLLAND		
	†R NEDERLAND, Via Madagascar	W • S Asia • 200 kW	
	NORTHERN MARIANA IS		
	†KFBS-FAR EAST BC, Saipan Island	E Asia • 100 kW • ALT. FREQ. TO 9495 kHz	
		C Asia • 100 kW • ALT. FREQ. TO 9495 kHz	
		Th-M • C Asia • 100 kW • ALT. FREQ. TO 9495 kHz	
12095	UNITED KINGDOM		
	BBC, Multiple Locations	Europe • 250 kW	
	BBC, Skelton, Cumbria	S • Europe • 250 kW	
	†BBC, Via Ascension	S America • 250 kW	
	BBC, Via Zyyi, Cyprus	E Africa • 250 kW	
		W • E Africa • 250 kW	
12105	GREECE		
	†FONI TIS HELLADAS, Kavála	N America • 250 kW	
12110	CHINA		
	†CHINA RADIO INTL, Kunming	SE Asia • 50 kW	
12115	KAZAKSTAN		
	†KAZAKSTAN RADIO, Almaty	• KAZAK, RUSSIAN, ETC • DS • 20/100 kW	
	RUSSIA		
	†RADIO ROSSII	W • E Europe • DS	
12130	USA		
	†ADVENTIST WORLD R, Via South Africa	E Africa • 250 kW	
12140	ISRAEL		
	†KOL ISRAEL, Tel Aviv	• Mideast & W Asia • 100 kW	
12160	USA		
	WWCR, Nashville, Tennessee	S • E North Am & Europe • 100 kW	
		E North Am & Europe • 100 kW	
12170	USA		
	†WGTG, McCaysville, Georgia	S • W North Am • 20/50 kW	
12256	PIRATE (EUROPE)		
	†"WREKIN RADIO INTL", England	• Irr • Su • W Europe	
12689.s	USA		
	†AFRTS, Florida	USB	
13580	CZECH REPUBLIC		
	†RADIO PRAGUE, Litomyšl	S • N America & C America • 100 kW	S • W Europe • 100 kW
		W • E North Am & E Africa • 100 kW	
		• W Europe • 100 kW	
		S • W Europe & N Africa • 100 kW	
13590v	PAKISTAN		
	RADIO PAKISTAN, Karachi	Mideast • 50 kW	
13595	USA		
	WJCR, Upton, Kentucky	W North Am • 50 kW	
13600	USA		
	†VOA, Via São Tomé	C Africa & E Africa • 100 kW	
		W • S Africa • 100 kW	
		W M-F • S Africa • 100 kW	
13605	AUSTRALIA		
	RADIO AUSTRALIA, Shepparton	Pacific • 100 kW	
	IRAN		
	VO THE ISLAMIC REP, Tehrān	Mideast • 500 kW	
	VO THE ISLAMIC REP, Zāhedān	Europe • 500 kW	
	UNITED ARAB EMIRATES		
	†UAE RADIO FROM ABU DHABI	W • E Asia • 500 kW	
13610	GERMANY		
	DEUTSCHE WELLE, Via Kigali, Rwanda	S • C Africa & E Africa • 250 kW	
	†DEUTSCHE WELLE, Wertachtal	W • W Africa • 500 kW	
	SYRIA		
(con'd)	RADIO DAMASCUS, Adhra	S America • 500 kW	

FREQUENCY   COUNTRY, STATION, LOCATION   TARGET • NETWORK • POWER (kW)   World Time

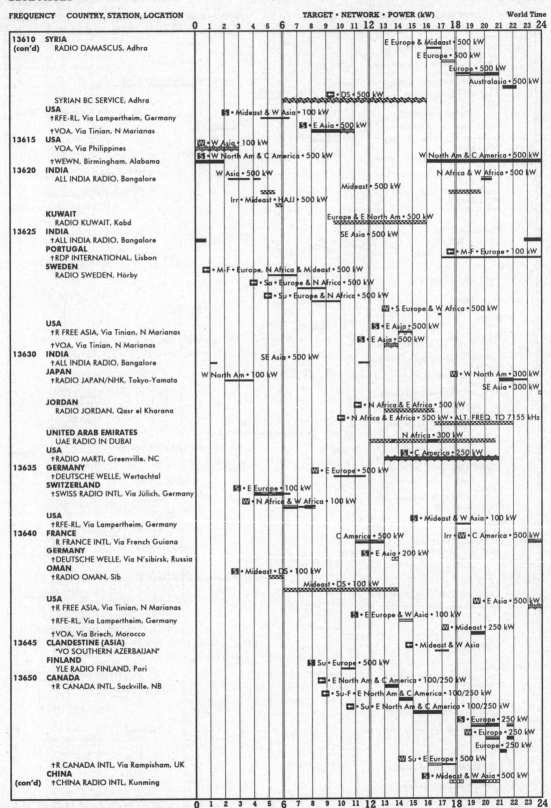

Frequency	Country, Station, Location	Target • Network • Power (kW)
13610 (con'd)	**SYRIA** RADIO DAMASCUS, Adhra	E Europe & Mideast • 500 kW; E Europe • 500 kW; Europe • 500 kW; Australasia • 500 kW
	SYRIAN BC SERVICE, Adhra	• DS • 500 kW
	USA †RFE-RL, Via Lampertheim, Germany	S • Mideast & W Asia • 100 kW
	†VOA, Via Tinian, N Marianas	S • E Asia • 500 kW
13615	**USA** VOA, Via Philippines	W • W Asia • 100 kW
	†WEWN, Birmingham, Alabama	S • W North Am & C America • 500 kW; W North Am & C America • 500 kW
13620	**INDIA** ALL INDIA RADIO, Bangalore	W Asia • 500 kW; N Africa & W Africa • 500 kW; Mideast • 500 kW; Irr • Mideast • HAJJ • 500 kW
	KUWAIT RADIO KUWAIT, Kabd	Europe & E North Am • 500 kW
13625	**INDIA** †ALL INDIA RADIO, Bangalore	SE Asia • 500 kW
	PORTUGAL †RDP INTERNATIONAL, Lisbon	• M-F • Europe • 100 kW
	SWEDEN RADIO SWEDEN, Hörby	• M-F • Europe, N Africa & Mideast • 500 kW; • Sa • Europe & N Africa • 500 kW; • Su • Europe & N Africa • 500 kW; W • S Europe & W Africa • 500 kW
	USA †R FREE ASIA, Via Tinian, N Marianas	S • E Asia • 500 kW
	†VOA, Via Tinian, N Marianas	S • E Asia • 500 kW
13630	**INDIA** †ALL INDIA RADIO, Bangalore	SE Asia • 500 kW
	JAPAN †RADIO JAPAN/NHK, Tokyo-Yamata	W North Am • 100 kW; W • W North Am • 300 kW; SE Asia • 300 kW
	JORDAN RADIO JORDAN, Qasr el Kharana	• N Africa & E Africa • 500 kW; • N Africa & E Africa • 500 kW • ALT. FREQ. TO 7155 kHz
	UNITED ARAB EMIRATES UAE RADIO IN DUBAI	N Africa • 300 kW
	USA †RADIO MARTI, Greenville, NC	S • C America • 250 kW
13635	**GERMANY** †DEUTSCHE WELLE, Wertachtal	W • E Europe • 500 kW
	SWITZERLAND †SWISS RADIO INTL, Via Jülich, Germany	S • E Europe • 100 kW; W • N Africa & W Africa • 100 kW
	USA †RFE-RL, Via Lampertheim, Germany	S • Mideast & W Asia • 100 kW
13640	**FRANCE** R FRANCE INTL, Via French Guiana	C America • 500 kW; Irr • W • C America • 500 kW
	GERMANY †DEUTSCHE WELLE, Via N'sibirsk, Russia	S • E Asia • 200 kW
	OMAN †RADIO OMAN, Sîb	S • Mideast • DS • 100 kW; Mideast • DS • 100 kW
	USA †R FREE ASIA, Via Tinian, N Marianas	W • E Asia • 500 kW
	†RFE-RL, Via Lampertheim, Germany	S • E Europe & W Asia • 100 kW
	†VOA, Via Briech, Morocco	W • Mideast • 250 kW
13645	**CLANDESTINE (ASIA)** "VO SOUTHERN AZERBAIJAN"	• Mideast & W Asia
	FINLAND YLE RADIO FINLAND, Pori	S • Su • Europe • 500 kW
13650	**CANADA** †R CANADA INTL, Sackville, NB	• E North Am & C America • 100/250 kW; • Su-F • E North Am & C America • 100/250 kW; • Su • E North Am & C America • 100/250 kW; S • Europe • 250 kW; W • Europe • 250 kW; Europe • 250 kW
	†R CANADA INTL, Via Rampisham, UK	W • Su • E Europe • 500 kW
(con'd)	**CHINA** †CHINA RADIO INTL, Kunming	S • Mideast & W Asia • 500 kW

ENGLISH ▬   ARABIC ▧▧   CHINESE ▫▫▫   FRENCH ▭▭   GERMAN ▬▬   RUSSIAN ══   SPANISH ▬▬   OTHER —

FREQUENCY   COUNTRY, STATION, LOCATION   TARGET • NETWORK • POWER (kW)   World Time

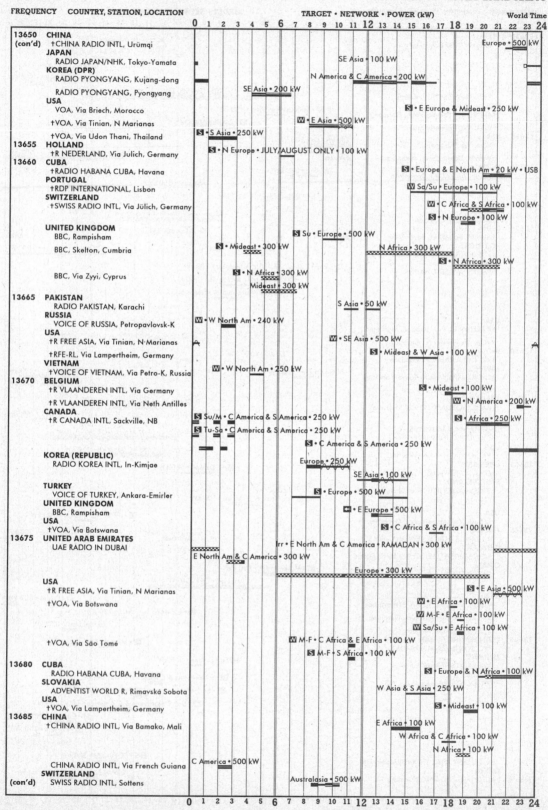

FREQUENCY	COUNTRY, STATION, LOCATION	TARGET • NETWORK • POWER (kW)
13650 (con'd)	CHINA †CHINA RADIO INTL, Urümqi	Europe • 500 kW
	JAPAN RADIO JAPAN/NHK, Tokyo-Yamata	SE Asia • 100 kW
	KOREA (DPR) RADIO PYONGYANG, Kujang-dong	N America & C America • 200 kW
	RADIO PYONGYANG, Pyongyang	SE Asia • 200 kW
	USA VOA, Via Briech, Morocco	S • E Europe & Mideast • 250 kW
	†VOA, Via Tinian, N Marianas	W • E Asia • 500 kW
	†VOA, Via Udon Thani, Thailand	S • S Asia • 250 kW
13655	HOLLAND †R NEDERLAND, Via Julich, Germany	S • N Europe • JULY/AUGUST ONLY • 100 kW
13660	CUBA †RADIO HABANA CUBA, Havana	S • Europe & E North Am • 20 kW • USB
	PORTUGAL †RDP INTERNATIONAL, Lisbon	W • Sa/Su • Europe • 100 kW
	SWITZERLAND †SWISS RADIO INTL, Via Jülich, Germany	W • C Africa & S Africa • 100 kW / S • N Europe • 100 kW
	UNITED KINGDOM BBC, Rampisham	Su • Europe • 500 kW
	BBC, Skelton, Cumbria	S • Mideast • 300 kW / N Africa • 300 kW / S • N Africa • 300 kW
	BBC, Via Zyyi, Cyprus	S • N Africa • 300 kW / Mideast • 300 kW
13665	PAKISTAN RADIO PAKISTAN, Karachi	S Asia • 50 kW
	RUSSIA VOICE OF RUSSIA, Petropavlovsk-K	W • W North Am • 240 kW
	USA †R FREE ASIA, Via Tinian, N Marianas	W • SE Asia • 500 kW
	†RFE-RL, Via Lampertheim, Germany	S • Mideast & W Asia • 100 kW
	VIETNAM †VOICE OF VIETNAM, Via Petro-K, Russia	W • W North Am • 250 kW
13670	BELGIUM †R VLAANDEREN INTL, Via Germany	S • Mideast • 100 kW
	†R VLAANDEREN INTL, Via Neth Antilles	W • N America • 200 kW
	CANADA †R CANADA INTL, Sackville, NB	Su/M • C America & S America • 250 kW / S • Africa • 250 kW / Tu-Sa • C America & S America • 250 kW / S • C America & S America • 250 kW
	KOREA (REPUBLIC) RADIO KOREA INTL, In-Kimjae	Europe • 250 kW / SE Asia • 100 kW
	TURKEY VOICE OF TURKEY, Ankara-Emirler	S • Europe • 500 kW
	UNITED KINGDOM BBC, Rampisham	E Europe • 500 kW
	USA †VOA, Via Botswana	S • C Africa & S Africa • 100 kW
13675	UNITED ARAB EMIRATES UAE RADIO IN DUBAI	Irr • E North Am & C America • RAMADAN • 300 kW / E North Am & C America • 300 kW / Europe • 300 kW
	USA †R FREE ASIA, Via Tinian, N Marianas	S • E Asia • 500 kW
	†VOA, Via Botswana	W • E Africa • 100 kW / W • M-F • E Africa • 100 kW / W • Sa/Su • E Africa • 100 kW
	†VOA, Via São Tomé	W • M-F • C Africa & E Africa • 100 kW / S • M-F • S Africa • 100 kW
13680	CUBA RADIO HABANA CUBA, Havana	S • Europe & N Africa • 100 kW
	SLOVAKIA ADVENTIST WORLD R, Rimavská Sobota	W Asia & S Asia • 250 kW
	USA †VOA, Via Lampertheim, Germany	S • Mideast • 100 kW
13685	CHINA †CHINA RADIO INTL, Via Bamako, Mali	E Africa • 100 kW / W Africa & C Africa • 100 kW / N Africa • 100 kW
	CHINA RADIO INTL, Via French Guiana	C America • 500 kW
(con'd)	SWITZERLAND SWISS RADIO INTL, Sottens	Australasia • 500 kW

FREQUENCY   COUNTRY, STATION, LOCATION   TARGET • NETWORK • POWER (kW)   World Time

0 1 2 3 4 5 6 7 8 9 10 11 12 13 14 15 16 17 18 19 20 21 22 23 24

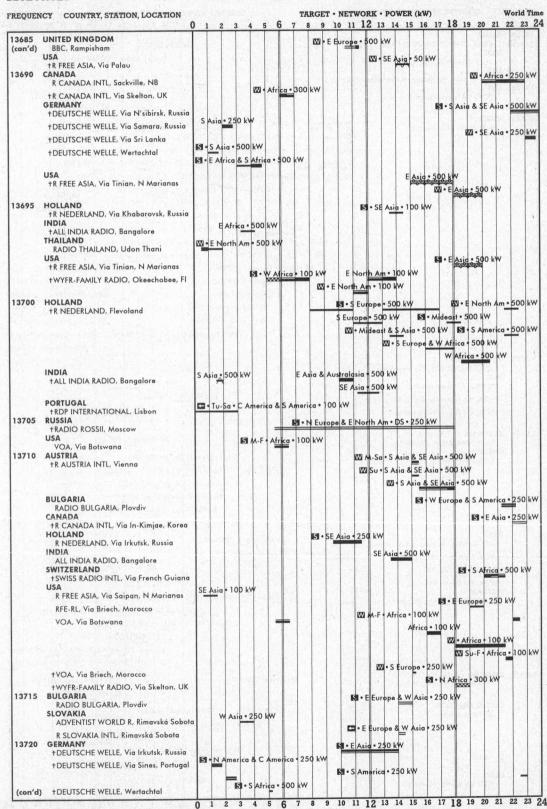

Frequency	Country / Station / Location	Schedule
13685 (con'd)	UNITED KINGDOM	
	BBC, Rampisham	W • E Europe • 500 kW
	USA	
	†R FREE ASIA, Via Palau	W • SE Asia • 50 kW
13690	CANADA	
	R CANADA INTL, Sackville, NB	W • Africa • 250 kW
	†R CANADA INTL, Via Skelton, UK	W • Africa • 300 kW
	GERMANY	
	†DEUTSCHE WELLE, Via N'sibirsk, Russia	S • S Asia & SE Asia • 500 kW
	†DEUTSCHE WELLE, Via Samara, Russia	S Asia • 250 kW
	†DEUTSCHE WELLE, Via Sri Lanka	W • SE Asia • 250 kW
	†DEUTSCHE WELLE, Wertachtal	S • S Asia • 500 kW
		S • E Africa & S Africa • 500 kW
	USA	
	†R FREE ASIA, Via Tinian, N Marianas	E Asia • 500 kW
		W • E Asia • 500 kW
13695	HOLLAND	
	†R NEDERLAND, Via Khabarovsk, Russia	S • SE Asia • 100 kW
	INDIA	
	†ALL INDIA RADIO, Bangalore	E Africa • 500 kW
	THAILAND	
	RADIO THAILAND, Udon Thani	W • E North Am • 500 kW
	USA	
	†R FREE ASIA, Via Tinian, N Marianas	S • E Asia • 500 kW
	†WYFR-FAMILY RADIO, Okeechobee, Fl	S • W Africa • 100 kW / E North Am • 100 kW
		W • E North Am • 100 kW
13700	HOLLAND	
	†R NEDERLAND, Flevoland	S • S Europe • 500 kW / W • E North Am • 500 kW
		S Europe • 500 kW / S • Mideast • 500 kW
		W • Mideast & S Asia • 500 kW / S • S America • 500 kW
		W • S Europe & W Africa • 500 kW
		W Africa • 500 kW
	INDIA	
	†ALL INDIA RADIO, Bangalore	S Asia • 500 kW / E Asia & Australasia • 500 kW
		SE Asia • 500 kW
	PORTUGAL	
	†RDP INTERNATIONAL, Lisbon	Tu-Sa • C America & S America • 100 kW
13705	RUSSIA	
	†RADIO ROSSII, Moscow	N Europe & E North Am • DS • 250 kW
	USA	
	VOA, Via Botswana	S • M-F • Africa • 100 kW
13710	AUSTRIA	
	†R AUSTRIA INTL, Vienna	W M-Sa • S Asia & SE Asia • 500 kW
		W Su • S Asia & SE Asia • 500 kW
		W • S Asia & SE Asia • 500 kW
	BULGARIA	
	RADIO BULGARIA, Plovdiv	S • W Europe & S America • 250 kW
	CANADA	
	†R CANADA INTL, Via In-Kimjae, Korea	S • E Asia • 250 kW
	HOLLAND	
	R NEDERLAND, Via Irkutsk, Russia	S • SE Asia • 250 kW
	INDIA	
	ALL INDIA RADIO, Bangalore	SE Asia • 500 kW
	SWITZERLAND	
	†SWISS RADIO INTL, Via French Guiana	S • S Africa • 500 kW
	USA	
	R FREE ASIA, Via Saipan, N Marianas	SE Asia • 100 kW
	RFE-RL, Via Briech, Morocco	S • E Europe • 250 kW
	VOA, Via Botswana	W M-F • Africa • 100 kW
		Africa • 100 kW
		W • Africa • 100 kW
		W Su-F • Africa • 100 kW
	†VOA, Via Briech, Morocco	W • S Europe • 250 kW
	†WYFR-FAMILY RADIO, Via Skelton, UK	S • N Africa • 300 kW
13715	BULGARIA	
	RADIO BULGARIA, Plovdiv	S • E Europe & W Asia • 250 kW
	SLOVAKIA	
	ADVENTIST WORLD R, Rimavská Sobota	W Asia • 250 kW
	R SLOVAKIA INTL, Rimavská Sobota	E Europe & W Asia • 250 kW
13720	GERMANY	
	†DEUTSCHE WELLE, Via Irkutsk, Russia	S • E Asia • 250 kW
	†DEUTSCHE WELLE, Via Sines, Portugal	S • N America & C America • 250 kW
		S • S America • 250 kW
(con'd)	†DEUTSCHE WELLE, Wertachtal	S • S Africa • 500 kW

0 1 2 3 4 5 6 7 8 9 10 11 12 13 14 15 16 17 18 19 20 21 22 23 24

ENGLISH ▬▬   ARABIC ⌇⌇⌇   CHINESE □□□   FRENCH ▬ ▬   GERMAN ▬▬   RUSSIAN ══   SPANISH ▬▬   OTHER ▬

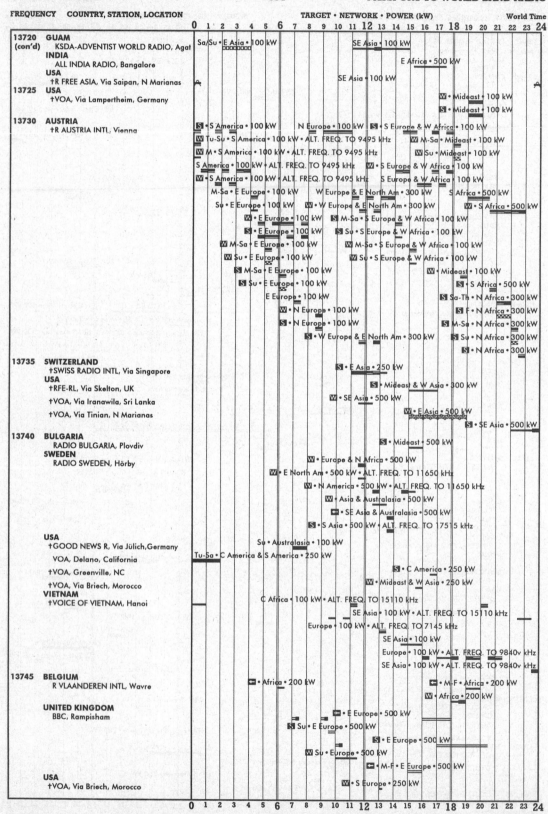

FREQUENCY   COUNTRY, STATION, LOCATION   TARGET • NETWORK • POWER (kW)   World Time

13720 GUAM
(con'd)   KSDA-ADVENTIST WORLD RADIO, Agat — Sa/Su • E Asia • 100 kW; SE Asia • 100 kW
INDIA
  ALL INDIA RADIO, Bangalore — E Africa • 500 kW
USA
  †R FREE ASIA, Via Saipan, N Marianas — SE Asia • 100 kW

13725 USA
  †VOA, Via Lampertheim, Germany — W • Mideast • 100 kW; S • Mideast • 100 kW

13730 AUSTRIA
  †R AUSTRIA INTL, Vienna
- S • S America • 100 kW
- N Europe • 100 kW
- S • S Europe & W Africa • 100 kW
- W • Tu-Su • S America • 100 kW • ALT. FREQ. TO 9495 kHz
- M-Sa • Mideast • 100 kW
- W • M • S America • 100 kW • ALT. FREQ. TO 9495 kHz
- W • Su • Mideast • 100 kW
- S America • 100 kW • ALT. FREQ. TO 9495 kHz
- W • S Europe & W Africa • 100 kW
- W • S America • 100 kW • ALT. FREQ. TO 9495 kHz
- S Europe & W Africa • 100 kW
- M-Sa • E Europe • 100 kW
- W Europe & E North Am • 300 kW
- S Africa • 500 kW
- Su • E Europe • 100 kW
- W • W Europe & E North Am • 300 kW
- W • S Africa • 500 kW
- W • E Europe • 100 kW
- S • M-Sa • S Europe & W Africa • 100 kW
- S • E Europe • 100 kW
- Su • S Europe & W Africa • 100 kW
- W • M-Sa • E Europe • 100 kW
- W • M-Sa • S Europe & W Africa • 100 kW
- W • Su • E Europe • 100 kW
- W • Su • S Europe & W Africa • 100 kW
- S • M-Sa • E Europe • 100 kW
- W • Mideast • 100 kW
- S • Su • E Europe • 100 kW
- S • S Africa • 500 kW
- E Europe • 100 kW
- S • Sa-Th • N Africa • 300 kW
- W • N Europe • 100 kW
- S • F • N Africa • 300 kW
- S • N Europe • 100 kW
- S • M-Sa • N Africa • 300 kW
- S • W Europe & E North Am • 300 kW
- S • Su • N Africa • 300 kW
- S • N Africa • 300 kW

13735 SWITZERLAND
  †SWISS RADIO INTL, Via Singapore — S • E Asia • 250 kW
USA
  †RFE-RL, Via Skelton, UK — S • Mideast & W Asia • 300 kW
  †VOA, Via Iranawila, Sri Lanka — W • SE Asia • 500 kW
  †VOA, Via Tinian, N Marianas — W • E Asia • 500 kW; S • SE Asia • 500 kW

13740 BULGARIA
  RADIO BULGARIA, Plovdiv — S • Mideast • 500 kW
SWEDEN
  RADIO SWEDEN, Hörby
- W • Europe & N Africa • 500 kW
- W • E North Am • 500 kW • ALT. FREQ. TO 11650 kHz
- W • N America • 500 kW • ALT. FREQ. TO 11650 kHz
- W • Asia & Australasia • 500 kW
- ⊟ • SE Asia & Australasia • 500 kW
- S • S Asia • 500 kW • ALT. FREQ. TO 17515 kHz

USA
  †GOOD NEWS R, Via Jülich, Germany — Su • Australasia • 100 kW
  VOA, Delano, California — Tu-Sa • C America & S America • 250 kW
  †VOA, Greenville, NC — S • C America • 250 kW
  †VOA, Via Briech, Morocco — W • Mideast & W Asia • 250 kW
VIETNAM
  †VOICE OF VIETNAM, Hanoi
- C Africa • 100 kW • ALT. FREQ. TO 15110 kHz
- SE Asia • 100 kW • ALT. FREQ. TO 15110 kHz
- Europe • 100 kW • ALT. FREQ. TO 7145 kHz
- SE Asia • 100 kW
- Europe • 100 kW • ALT. FREQ. TO 9840v kHz
- SE Asia • 100 kW • ALT. FREQ. TO 9840v kHz

13745 BELGIUM
  R VLAANDEREN INTL, Wavre
- ⊟ • Africa • 200 kW
- ⊟ • M-F • Africa • 200 kW
- W • Africa • 200 kW
UNITED KINGDOM
  BBC, Rampisham
- ⊟ • E Europe • 500 kW
- S • Su • E Europe • 500 kW
- S • E Europe • 500 kW
- W • Su • Europe • 500 kW
- ⊟ • M-F • E Europe • 500 kW
USA
  †VOA, Via Briech, Morocco — W • S Europe • 250 kW

FREQUENCY   COUNTRY, STATION, LOCATION   TARGET • NETWORK • POWER (kW)   World Time

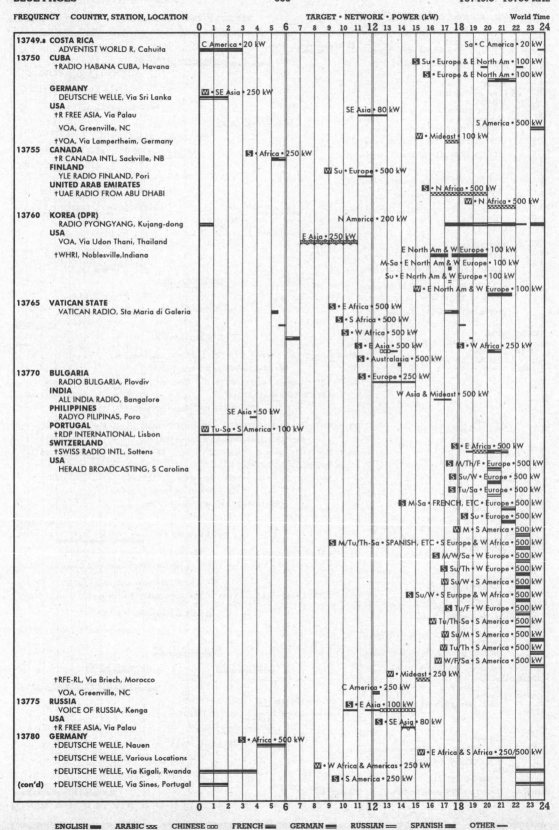

13749.a	COSTA RICA
	ADVENTIST WORLD R, Cahuita — C America • 20 kW / Sa • C America • 20 kW
13750	CUBA
	†RADIO HABANA CUBA, Havana — Su • Europe & E North Am • 100 kW / Europe & E North Am • 100 kW
	GERMANY
	DEUTSCHE WELLE, Via Sri Lanka — W • SE Asia • 250 kW
	USA
	†R FREE ASIA, Via Palau — SE Asia • 80 kW
	VOA, Greenville, NC — S America • 500 kW
	†VOA, Via Lampertheim, Germany — W • Mideast • 100 kW
13755	CANADA
	†R CANADA INTL, Sackville, NB — S • Africa • 250 kW
	FINLAND
	YLE RADIO FINLAND, Pori — W Su • Europe • 500 kW
	UNITED ARAB EMIRATES
	†UAE RADIO FROM ABU DHABI — S • N Africa • 500 kW / W • N Africa • 500 kW
13760	KOREA (DPR)
	RADIO PYONGYANG, Kujang-dong — N America • 200 kW
	USA
	VOA, Via Udon Thani, Thailand — E Asia • 250 kW
	†WHRI, Noblesville, Indiana — E North Am & W Europe • 100 kW / M-Sa • E North Am & W Europe • 100 kW / Su • E North Am & W Europe • 100 kW / W • E North Am & W Europe • 100 kW
13765	VATICAN STATE
	VATICAN RADIO, Sta Maria di Galeria — S • E Africa • 500 kW / S • S Africa • 500 kW / S • W Africa • 500 kW / S • E Asia • 500 kW / S • W Africa • 250 kW / S • Australasia • 500 kW
13770	BULGARIA
	RADIO BULGARIA, Plovdiv — S • Europe • 250 kW
	INDIA
	ALL INDIA RADIO, Bangalore — W Asia & Mideast • 500 kW
	PHILIPPINES
	RADYO PILIPINAS, Poro — SE Asia • 50 kW
	PORTUGAL
	†RDP INTERNATIONAL, Lisbon — W Tu-Sa • S America • 100 kW
	SWITZERLAND
	†SWISS RADIO INTL, Sottens — S • E Africa • 500 kW
	USA
	HERALD BROADCASTING, S Carolina — S M/Th/F • Europe • 500 kW / S Su/W • Europe • 500 kW / S Tu/Sa • Europe • 500 kW / S M-Sa • FRENCH, ETC • Europe • 500 kW / S Su • Europe • 500 kW / W M • S America • 500 kW / S M/Tu/Th-Sa • SPANISH, ETC • S Europe & W Africa • 500 kW / S M/W/Sa • W Europe • 500 kW / S Su/Th • W Europe • 500 kW / W Su/W • S America • 500 kW / S Su/W • S Europe & W Africa • 500 kW / S Tu/F • W Europe • 500 kW / W Tu/Th-Sa • S America • 500 kW / W Su/M • S America • 500 kW / W Tu/Th • S America • 500 kW / W W/F/Sa • S America • 500 kW
	†RFE-RL, Via Briech, Morocco — W • Mideast • 250 kW
	VOA, Greenville, NC — C America • 250 kW
13775	RUSSIA
	VOICE OF RUSSIA, Kenga — S • E Asia • 100 kW
	USA
	†R FREE ASIA, Via Palau — S • SE Asia • 80 kW
13780	GERMANY
	†DEUTSCHE WELLE, Nauen — S • Africa • 500 kW / W • E Africa & S Africa • 250/500 kW
	†DEUTSCHE WELLE, Various Locations — W • W Africa & Americas • 250 kW
	†DEUTSCHE WELLE, Via Kigali, Rwanda — S • S America • 250 kW
(con'd)	†DEUTSCHE WELLE, Via Sines, Portugal

0 1 2 3 4 5 6 7 8 9 10 11 12 13 14 15 16 17 18 19 20 21 22 23 24

ENGLISH ▬   ARABIC ⋙   CHINESE ⠿   FRENCH ═   GERMAN ▭   RUSSIAN ＝   SPANISH ▬   OTHER ▬

FREQUENCY   COUNTRY, STATION, LOCATION   TARGET • NETWORK • POWER (kW)   World Time

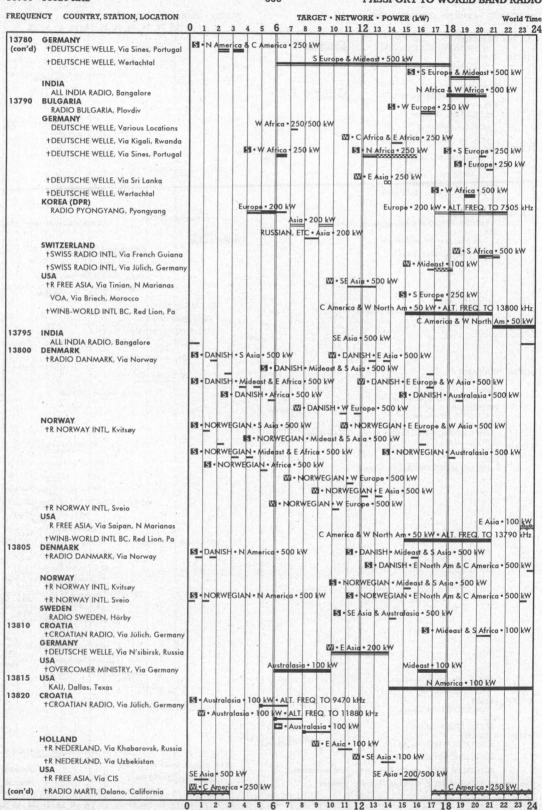

Frequency	Country, Station, Location	Target • Network • Power
13780 (con'd)	**GERMANY**	
	†DEUTSCHE WELLE, Via Sines, Portugal	S • N America & C America • 250 kW
	†DEUTSCHE WELLE, Wertachtal	S Europe & Mideast • 500 kW; S • S Europe & Mideast • 500 kW; N Africa & W Africa • 500 kW
	INDIA	
	ALL INDIA RADIO, Bangalore	
13790	**BULGARIA**	
	RADIO BULGARIA, Plovdiv	S • W Europe • 250 kW
	GERMANY	
	DEUTSCHE WELLE, Various Locations	W Africa • 250/500 kW
	†DEUTSCHE WELLE, Via Kigali, Rwanda	W • C Africa & E Africa • 250 kW
	†DEUTSCHE WELLE, Via Sines, Portugal	S • W Africa • 250 kW; S • N Africa • 250 kW; S • S Europe • 250 kW; S • Europe • 250 kW
	†DEUTSCHE WELLE, Via Sri Lanka	W • E Asia • 250 kW
	†DEUTSCHE WELLE, Wertachtal	S • W Africa • 500 kW
	KOREA (DPR)	
	RADIO PYONGYANG, Pyongyang	Europe • 200 kW; Europe • 200 kW • ALT. FREQ. TO 7505 kHz; Asia • 200 kW; RUSSIAN, ETC • Asia • 200 kW
	SWITZERLAND	
	†SWISS RADIO INTL, Via French Guiana	W • S Africa • 500 kW
	†SWISS RADIO INTL, Via Jülich, Germany	W • Mideast • 100 kW
	USA	
	†R FREE ASIA, Via Tinian, N Marianas	W • SE Asia • 500 kW
	VOA, Via Briech, Morocco	S • S Europe • 250 kW
	†WINB-WORLD INTL BC, Red Lion, Pa	C America & W North Am • 50 kW • ALT. FREQ. TO 13800 kHz; C America & W North Am • 50 kW
13795	**INDIA**	
	ALL INDIA RADIO, Bangalore	SE Asia • 500 kW
13800	**DENMARK**	
	†RADIO DANMARK, Via Norway	S • DANISH • S Asia • 500 kW; W • DANISH • E Asia • 500 kW; S • DANISH • Mideast & S Asia • 500 kW; S • DANISH • Mideast & E Africa • 500 kW; W • DANISH • E Europe & W Asia • 500 kW; S • DANISH • Africa • 500 kW; S • DANISH • Australasia • 500 kW; W • DANISH • W Europe • 500 kW
	NORWAY	
	†R NORWAY INTL, Kvitsøy	S • NORWEGIAN • S Asia • 500 kW; W • NORWEGIAN • E Europe & W Asia • 500 kW; S • NORWEGIAN • Mideast & S Asia • 500 kW; S • NORWEGIAN • Mideast & E Africa • 500 kW; S • NORWEGIAN • Australasia • 500 kW; S • NORWEGIAN • Africa • 500 kW; W • NORWEGIAN • W Europe • 500 kW; W • NORWEGIAN • E Asia • 500 kW
	†R NORWAY INTL, Sveio	W • NORWEGIAN • W Europe • 500 kW
	USA	
	R FREE ASIA, Via Saipan, N Marianas	E Asia • 100 kW
	†WINB-WORLD INTL BC, Red Lion, Pa	C America & W North Am • 50 kW • ALT. FREQ. TO 13790 kHz
13805	**DENMARK**	
	†RADIO DANMARK, Via Norway	S • DANISH • N America • 500 kW; S • DANISH • Mideast & S Asia • 500 kW; S • DANISH • E North Am & C America • 500 kW
	NORWAY	
	†R NORWAY INTL, Kvitsøy	S • NORWEGIAN • Mideast & S Asia • 500 kW
	†R NORWAY INTL, Sveio	S • NORWEGIAN • N America • 500 kW; S • NORWEGIAN • E North Am & C America • 500 kW
	SWEDEN	
	RADIO SWEDEN, Hörby	S • SE Asia & Australasia • 500 kW
13810	**CROATIA**	
	†CROATIAN RADIO, Via Jülich, Germany	S • Mideast & S Africa • 100 kW
	GERMANY	
	†DEUTSCHE WELLE, Via N'sibirsk, Russia	W • E Asia • 200 kW
	USA	
	†OVERCOMER MINISTRY, Via Germany	Australasia • 100 kW; Mideast • 100 kW
13815	**USA**	
	KAIJ, Dallas, Texas	N America • 100 kW
13820	**CROATIA**	
	†CROATIAN RADIO, Via Jülich, Germany	S • Australasia • 100 kW • ALT. FREQ. TO 9470 kHz; W • Australasia • 100 kW • ALT. FREQ. TO 11880 kHz; Australasia • 100 kW
	HOLLAND	
	†R NEDERLAND, Via Khabarovsk, Russia	W • E Asia • 100 kW
	†R NEDERLAND, Via Uzbekistan	W • SE Asia • 100 kW
	USA	
	†R FREE ASIA, Via CIS	SE Asia • 500 kW; SE Asia • 200/500 kW
(con'd)	†RADIO MARTI, Delano, California	W • C America • 250 kW; C America • 250 kW

FREQUENCY   COUNTRY, STATION, LOCATION   TARGET • NETWORK • POWER (kW)   World Time

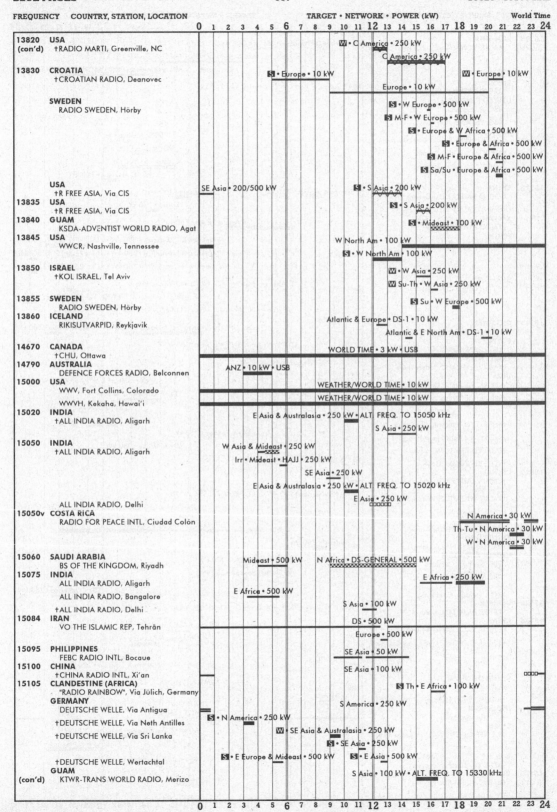

Frequency	Country / Station / Location	Target • Network • Power
13820 (con'd)	USA — †RADIO MARTI, Greenville, NC	W • C America • 250 kW; C America • 250 kW
13830	CROATIA — †CROATIAN RADIO, Deanovec	S • Europe • 10 kW; W • Europe • 10 kW; Europe • 10 kW
	SWEDEN — RADIO SWEDEN, Hörby	S • W Europe • 500 kW; M-F • W Europe • 500 kW; S • Europe & W Africa • 500 kW; S • Europe & Africa • 500 kW; M-F • Europe & Africa • 500 kW; S • Sa/Su • Europe & Africa • 500 kW
	USA — †R FREE ASIA, Via CIS	SE Asia • 200/500 kW; S • S Asia • 200 kW
13835	USA — †R FREE ASIA, Via CIS	S • S Asia • 200 kW
13840	GUAM — KSDA-ADVENTIST WORLD RADIO, Agat	S • Mideast • 100 kW
13845	USA — WWCR, Nashville, Tennessee	W North Am • 100 kW; S • W North Am • 100 kW
13850	ISRAEL — †KOL ISRAEL, Tel Aviv	W • W Asia • 250 kW; W • Su-Th • W Asia • 250 kW
13855	SWEDEN — RADIO SWEDEN, Hörby	S • Su • W Europe • 500 kW
13860	ICELAND — RIKISUTVARPID, Reykjavik	Atlantic & Europe • DS-1 • 10 kW; Atlantic & E North Am • DS-1 • 10 kW
14670	CANADA — †CHU, Ottawa	WORLD TIME • 3 kW • USB
14790	AUSTRALIA — DEFENCE FORCES RADIO, Belconnen	ANZ • 10 kW • USB
15000	USA — WWV, Fort Collins, Colorado	WEATHER/WORLD TIME • 10 kW
	WWVH, Kekaha, Hawai'i	WEATHER/WORLD TIME • 10 kW
15020	INDIA — †ALL INDIA RADIO, Aligarh	E Asia & Australasia • 250 kW • ALT. FREQ. TO 15050 kHz; S Asia • 250 kW
15050	INDIA — †ALL INDIA RADIO, Aligarh	W Asia & Mideast • 250 kW; Irr • Mideast • HAJJ • 250 kW; SE Asia • 250 kW; E Asia & Australasia • 250 kW • ALT. FREQ. TO 15020 kHz; E Asia • 250 kW
	ALL INDIA RADIO, Delhi	
15050v	COSTA RICA — RADIO FOR PEACE INTL, Ciudad Colón	N America • 30 kW; Th-Tu • N America • 30 kW; W • N America • 30 kW
15060	SAUDI ARABIA — BS OF THE KINGDOM, Riyadh	Mideast • 500 kW; N Africa • DS-GENERAL • 500 kW
15075	INDIA — ALL INDIA RADIO, Aligarh	E Africa • 250 kW
	ALL INDIA RADIO, Bangalore	E Africa • 500 kW
	†ALL INDIA RADIO, Delhi	S Asia • 100 kW
15084	IRAN — VO THE ISLAMIC REP, Tehrān	DS • 500 kW; Europe • 500 kW
15095	PHILIPPINES — FEBC RADIO INTL, Bocaue	SE Asia • 50 kW
15100	CHINA — †CHINA RADIO INTL, Xi'an	SE Asia • 100 kW
15105	CLANDESTINE (AFRICA) — "RADIO RAINBOW", Via Jülich, Germany	S • Th • E Africa • 100 kW
	GERMANY — DEUTSCHE WELLE, Via Antigua	S America • 250 kW
	†DEUTSCHE WELLE, Via Neth Antilles	S • N America • 250 kW
	†DEUTSCHE WELLE, Via Sri Lanka	W • SE Asia & Australasia • 250 kW; S • SE Asia • 250 kW
	†DEUTSCHE WELLE, Wertachtal	S • E Europe & Mideast • 500 kW; S • E Asia • 500 kW
(con'd)	GUAM — KTWR-TRANS WORLD RADIO, Merizo	S Asia • 100 kW • ALT. FREQ. TO 15330 kHz

FREQUENCY	COUNTRY, STATION, LOCATION	TARGET • NETWORK • POWER (kW)	World Time

0 1 2 3 4 5 6 7 8 9 10 11 12 13 14 15 16 17 18 19 20 21 22 23 24

15105 **ROMANIA**
(con'd)   RADIO ROMANIA, Bucharest
- W • Europe, N Africa & Mideast • DS-1 (ACTUALITATI) • 100 kW
- Europe, N Africa & Mideast • DS-1 (ACTUALITATI) • 100 kW
- S • Europe, N Africa & Mideast • DS-1 (ACTUALITATI) • 100 kW

   RUSSIA
   †RADIO TATARSTAN, Samara
- W • C Asia & E Asia • RUSSIAN, TATAR • 200 kW

   UNITED KINGDOM
   BBC, Rampisham
- N Africa • 250 kW

   BBC, Via Ascension
- W Africa • 250 kW
- W Africa & C Africa • 250 kW

   USA
   †GOOD NEWS R, Via Jülich, Germany
- S • So • Africa • 100 kW

   †RFE-RL, Via Biblis, Germany
- S • W Asia • 100 kW

   WHRI, Noblesville, Indiana
- C America • 100 kW
- W • C America • 100 kW

15110 **CHINA**
   †CHINA RADIO INTL, Beijing
- E Europe & W Asia • 150 kW
- Australasia • 150 kW

   †CHINA RADIO INTL, Urümqi
- S Asia • 500 kW

   KUWAIT
   †RADIO KUWAIT, Kabd
- S Asia & SE Asia • 500 kW

   SPAIN
   †R EXTERIOR ESPANA, Noblejas
- N America & C America • 350 kW • ALT. FREQ. TO 9630 kHz
- M-Sa • N America & C America • 350 kW • ALT. FREQ. TO 9630 kHz
- Su • N America & C America • 350 kW • ALT. FREQ. TO 9630 kHz

   VIETNAM
   †VOICE OF VIETNAM, Hanoi
- C Africa • 100 kW • ALT. FREQ. TO 13740 kHz
- SE Asia • 100 kW • ALT. FREQ. TO 13740 kHz
- SE Asia • 100 kW • ALT. FREQ. TO 9840v kHz

15115 **ECUADOR**
   †HCJB-VO THE ANDES, Quito
- N America & S America • 100 kW
- W • Europe • 100 kW

   EGYPT
   EGYPTIAN RADIO, Abu Za'bal
- W Africa • DS-GENERAL • 100 kW

   THAILAND
   †RADIO THAILAND, Udon Thani
- W • Europe • 500 kW

   USA
   †RFE-RL, Via Biblis, Germany
- S • Mideast & W Asia • 100 kW

   †RFE-RL, Via Briech, Morocco
- S • E Europe • 250 kW
- W • S Europe • 250 kW
- W • C Asia • 500 kW

   †RFE-RL, Via Iranawila, Sri Lanka

   RFE-RL, Via Pals, Spain
- S • E Europe • 250 kW
- W • S Europe • 250 kW

   †VOA, Via Briech, Morocco

   †VOA, Via Kavála, Greece
- S • W Asia & S Asia • 250 kW

15120 **CHINA**
   †CHINA RADIO INTL, Via Havana, Cuba
- S America

   HUNGARY
   †RADIO BUDAPEST, Jászberény
- M • S America • 250 kW • ALT. FREQ. TO 15550 kHz
- S America • 250 kW • ALT. FREQ. TO 15550 kHz

   NIGERIA
   VOICE OF NIGERIA, Ikorodu
- Europe & N America • 250 kW

   PHILIPPINES
   RADYO PILIPINAS, Tinang
- Mideast • 250 kW

   UNITED KINGDOM
   BBC, Skelton, Cumbria
- S • M-F • E Europe • 300 kW

   BBC, Woofferton
- S • Sa/Su • Europe • 250 kW

   USA
   †VOA, Delano, California
- S • C America • 250 kW

15120v **PAKISTAN**
   RADIO PAKISTAN, Karachi
- S Asia & SE Asia • 50 kW • ALT. FREQ. TO 15190v kHz

15125 **CHINA**
   †CHINA RADIO INTL, Beijing
- S • SE Asia • 150 kW

   †CHINA RADIO INTL, Via Bamako, Mali
- W Africa & C Africa • 100 kW
- Mideast • 100 kW
- E Africa & S Africa • 100 kW

   CHINA (TAIWAN)
   †CBS, T'ai-pei
- NEWS NETWORK

   †R TAIPEI INTL, T'ai-pei
- SE Asia

   INDONESIA
   †RRI, Jakarta, Jawa
- SE Asia • DS • 250 kW

   SPAIN
   †R EXTERIOR ESPANA, Via Costa Rica
- Sa/Su • C America & S America • 100 kW
- C America & S America • 100 kW

   USA
   VOA, Via Briech, Morocco
- W • S Europe • 250 kW

15130 **BULGARIA**
(con'd)   RADIO BULGARIA, Plovdiv
- W • Europe • 250 kW

0 1 2 3 4 5 6 7 8 9 10 11 12 13 14 15 16 17 18 19 20 21 22 23 24

FREQUENCY   COUNTRY, STATION, LOCATION   TARGET • NETWORK • POWER (kW)   World Time

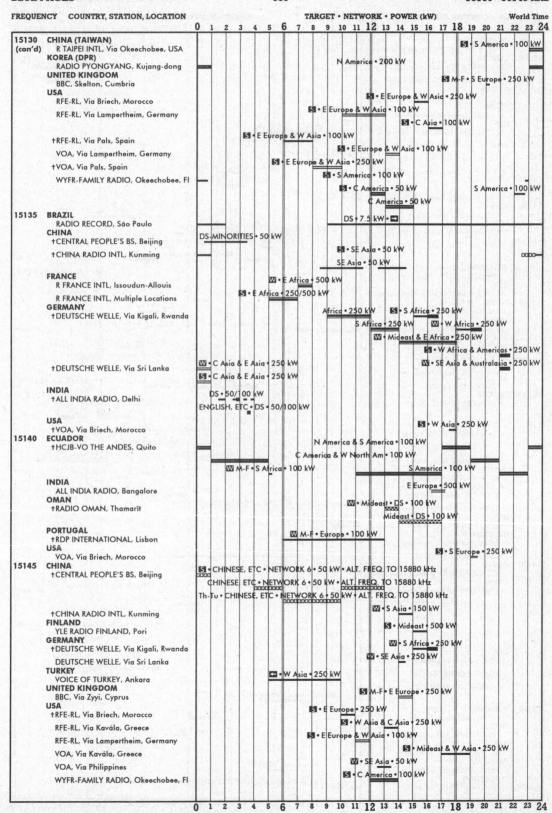

FREQUENCY	COUNTRY, STATION, LOCATION	TARGET • NETWORK • POWER (kW)
15130 (con'd)	CHINA (TAIWAN)	
	R TAIPEI INTL, Via Okeechobee, USA	S • S America • 100 kW
	KOREA (DPR)	
	RADIO PYONGYANG, Kujang-dong	N America • 200 kW
	UNITED KINGDOM	
	BBC, Skelton, Cumbria	S • M-F • S Europe • 250 kW
	USA	
	RFE-RL, Via Briech, Morocco	S • E Europe & W Asia • 250 kW
	RFE-RL, Via Lampertheim, Germany	S • E Europe & W Asia • 100 kW
		S • C Asia • 100 kW
	†RFE-RL, Via Pals, Spain	S • E Europe & W Asia • 100 kW
	VOA, Via Lampertheim, Germany	S • E Europe & W Asia • 100 kW
	†VOA, Via Pals, Spain	S • E Europe & W Asia • 250 kW
	WYFR-FAMILY RADIO, Okeechobee, Fl	S • S America • 100 kW
		S • C America • 50 kW S America • 100 kW
		C America • 50 kW
15135	BRAZIL	
	RADIO RECORD, São Paulo	DS • 7.5 kW • →
	CHINA	
	†CENTRAL PEOPLE'S BS, Beijing	DS-MINORITIES • 50 kW
	†CHINA RADIO INTL, Kunming	S • SE Asia • 50 kW
		SE Asia • 50 kW
	FRANCE	
	R FRANCE INTL, Issoudun-Allouis	W • E Africa • 500 kW
	R FRANCE INTL, Multiple Locations	S • E Africa • 250/500 kW
	GERMANY	
	†DEUTSCHE WELLE, Via Kigali, Rwanda	Africa • 250 kW S • S Africa • 250 kW
		S Africa • 250 kW W • W Africa • 250 kW
		W • Mideast & E Africa • 250 kW
		S • W Africa & Americas • 250 kW
		W • SE Asia & Australasia • 250 kW
	†DEUTSCHE WELLE, Via Sri Lanka	W • C Asia & E Asia • 250 kW
		S • C Asia & E Asia • 250 kW
	INDIA	
	†ALL INDIA RADIO, Delhi	DS • 50/100 kW
		ENGLISH, ETC • DS • 50/100 kW
	USA	
	†VOA, Via Briech, Morocco	S • W Asia • 250 kW
15140	ECUADOR	
	†HCJB-VO THE ANDES, Quito	N America & S America • 100 kW
		C America & W North Am • 100 kW
		W • M-F • S Africa • 100 kW S America • 100 kW
	INDIA	
	ALL INDIA RADIO, Bangalore	E Europe • 500 kW
	OMAN	
	†RADIO OMAN, Thamarīt	W • Mideast • DS • 100 kW
		Mideast • DS • 100 kW
	PORTUGAL	
	†RDP INTERNATIONAL, Lisbon	W • M-F • Europe • 100 kW
	USA	
	VOA, Via Briech, Morocco	S • S Europe • 250 kW
15145	CHINA	
	†CENTRAL PEOPLE'S BS, Beijing	S • CHINESE, ETC • NETWORK 6 • 50 kW • ALT. FREQ. TO 15880 kHz
		CHINESE, ETC • NETWORK 6 • 50 kW • ALT. FREQ. TO 15880 kHz
		Th-Tu • CHINESE, ETC • NETWORK 6 • 50 kW • ALT. FREQ. TO 15880 kHz
	†CHINA RADIO INTL, Kunming	W • S Asia • 150 kW
	FINLAND	
	YLE RADIO FINLAND, Pori	S • Mideast • 500 kW
	GERMANY	
	†DEUTSCHE WELLE, Via Kigali, Rwanda	W • S Africa • 250 kW
	DEUTSCHE WELLE, Via Sri Lanka	W • SE Asia • 250 kW
	TURKEY	
	VOICE OF TURKEY, Ankara	W • W Asia • 250 kW
	UNITED KINGDOM	
	BBC, Via Zyyi, Cyprus	S • M-F • E Europe • 250 kW
	USA	
	†RFE-RL, Via Briech, Morocco	S • E Europe • 250 kW
	RFE-RL, Via Kavála, Greece	S • W Asia & C Asia • 250 kW
	RFE-RL, Via Lampertheim, Germany	S • E Europe & W Asia • 100 kW
	VOA, Via Kavála, Greece	S • Mideast & W Asia • 250 kW
	VOA, Via Philippines	W • SE Asia • 50 kW
	WYFR-FAMILY RADIO, Okeechobee, Fl	S • C America • 100 kW

ENGLISH ▬▬   ARABIC ⧄⧄⧄   CHINESE ▭▭▭   FRENCH ▬▬   GERMAN ▬▬   RUSSIAN ══   SPANISH ▬▬   OTHER ──

FREQUENCY	COUNTRY, STATION, LOCATION	TARGET • NETWORK • POWER (kW)	World Time

0 1 2 3 4 5 6 7 8 9 10 11 12 13 14 15 16 17 18 19 20 21 22 23 24

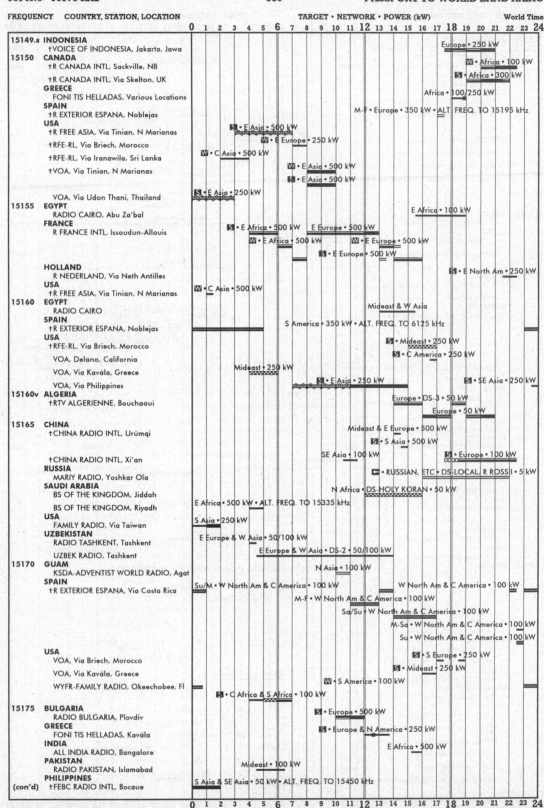

15149.8	INDONESIA
	†VOICE OF INDONESIA, Jakarta, Jawa	Europe • 250 kW
15150	CANADA
	†R CANADA INTL, Sackville, NB	W • Africa • 100 kW
	†R CANADA INTL, Via Skelton, UK	S • Africa • 300 kW
	GREECE
	FONI TIS HELLADAS, Various Locations	Africa • 100/250 kW
	SPAIN
	†R EXTERIOR ESPANA, Noblejas	M-F • Europe • 350 kW • ALT. FREQ. TO 15195 kHz
	USA
	†R FREE ASIA, Via Tinian, N Marianas	S • E Asia • 500 kW
	†RFE-RL, Via Briech, Morocco	W • E Europe • 250 kW
	†RFE-RL, Via Iranawila, Sri Lanka	W • C Asia • 500 kW
	†VOA, Via Tinian, N Marianas	W • E Asia • 500 kW / S • E Asia • 500 kW
	VOA, Via Udon Thani, Thailand	S • E Asia • 250 kW
15155	EGYPT
	RADIO CAIRO, Abu Za'bal	E Africa • 100 kW
	FRANCE
	R FRANCE INTL, Issoudun-Allouis	S • E Africa • 500 kW / E Europe • 500 kW / W • E Africa • 500 kW / W • E Europe • 500 kW / S • E Europe • 500 kW
	HOLLAND
	R NEDERLAND, Via Neth Antilles	S • E North Am • 250 kW
	USA
	†R FREE ASIA, Via Tinian, N Marianas	W • C Asia • 500 kW
15160	EGYPT
	RADIO CAIRO	Mideast & W Asia
	SPAIN
	†R EXTERIOR ESPANA, Noblejas	S America • 350 kW • ALT. FREQ. TO 6125 kHz
	USA
	†RFE-RL, Via Briech, Morocco	S • Mideast • 250 kW
	VOA, Delano, California	S • C America • 250 kW
	VOA, Via Kavála, Greece	Mideast • 250 kW
	VOA, Via Philippines	S • E Asia • 250 kW / S • SE Asia • 250 kW
15160v	ALGERIA
	†RTV ALGERIENNE, Bouchaoui	Europe • DS-3 • 50 kW / Europe • 50 kW
15165	CHINA
	†CHINA RADIO INTL, Urümqi	Mideast & E Europe • 500 kW / S • S Asia • 500 kW
	†CHINA RADIO INTL, Xi'an	SE Asia • 100 kW / S • Europe • 100 kW
	RUSSIA
	MARIY RADIO, Yoshkar Ola	• RUSSIAN, ETC • DS-LOCAL, R ROSSII • 5 kW
	SAUDI ARABIA
	BS OF THE KINGDOM, Jiddah	N Africa • DS-HOLY KORAN • 50 kW
	BS OF THE KINGDOM, Riyadh	E Africa • 500 kW • ALT. FREQ. TO 15335 kHz
	USA
	FAMILY RADIO, Via Taiwan	S Asia • 250 kW
	UZBEKISTAN
	RADIO TASHKENT, Tashkent	E Europe & W Asia • 50/100 kW
	UZBEK RADIO, Tashkent	E Europe & W Asia • DS-2 • 50/100 kW
15170	GUAM
	KSDA-ADVENTIST WORLD RADIO, Agat	N Asia • 100 kW
	SPAIN
	†R EXTERIOR ESPANA, Via Costa Rica	Su/M • W North Am & C America • 100 kW / W North Am & C America • 100 kW / M-F • W North Am & C America • 100 kW / Sa/Su • W North Am & C America • 100 kW / M-Sa • W North Am & C America • 100 kW / Su • W North Am & C America • 100 kW
	USA
	VOA, Via Briech, Morocco	S • S Europe • 250 kW
	VOA, Via Kavála, Greece	S • Mideast • 250 kW
	WYFR-FAMILY RADIO, Okeechobee, Fl	W • S America • 100 kW
		S • C Africa & S Africa • 100 kW
15175	BULGARIA
	RADIO BULGARIA, Plovdiv	S • Europe • 500 kW
	GREECE
	FONI TIS HELLADAS, Kavála	S • Europe & N America • 250 kW
	INDIA
	ALL INDIA RADIO, Bangalore	E Africa • 500 kW
	PAKISTAN
	RADIO PAKISTAN, Islamabad	Mideast • 100 kW
	PHILIPPINES
(con'd)	†FEBC RADIO INTL, Bocaue	S Asia & SE Asia • 50 kW • ALT. FREQ. TO 15450 kHz

0 1 2 3 4 5 6 7 8 9 10 11 12 13 14 15 16 17 18 19 20 21 22 23 24

SEASONAL S OR W   1-HR TIMESHIFT MIDYEAR � OR ⮕   JAMMING / OR ∧   EARLIEST HEARD ◁   LATEST HEARD ▷   NEW FOR 2000 †

FREQUENCY   COUNTRY, STATION, LOCATION   TARGET • NETWORK • POWER (kW)   World Time

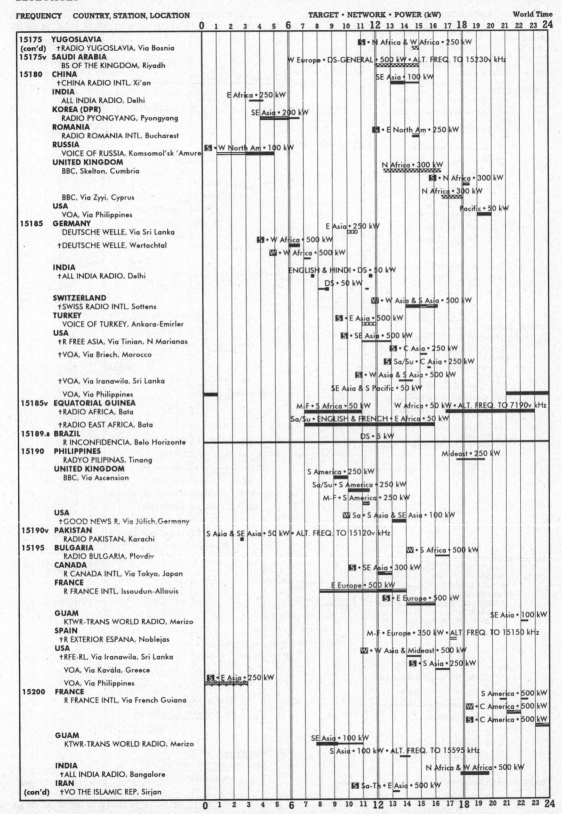

FREQUENCY	COUNTRY, STATION, LOCATION	TARGET • NETWORK • POWER (kW)
15175 (con'd)	YUGOSLAVIA †RADIO YUGOSLAVIA, Via Bosnia	N Africa & W Africa • 250 kW
15175v	SAUDI ARABIA BS OF THE KINGDOM, Riyadh	W Europe • DS-GENERAL • 500 kW • ALT. FREQ. TO 15230v kHz
15180	CHINA †CHINA RADIO INTL, Xi'an	SE Asia • 100 kW
	INDIA ALL INDIA RADIO, Delhi	E Africa • 250 kW
	KOREA (DPR) RADIO PYONGYANG, Pyongyang	SE Asia • 200 kW
	ROMANIA RADIO ROMANIA INTL, Bucharest	E North Am • 250 kW
	RUSSIA VOICE OF RUSSIA, Komsomol'sk 'Amure	W North Am • 100 kW
	UNITED KINGDOM BBC, Skelton, Cumbria	N Africa • 300 kW N Africa • 300 kW
	BBC, Via Zyyi, Cyprus	N Africa • 300 kW
	USA VOA, Via Philippines	Pacific • 50 kW
15185	GERMANY DEUTSCHE WELLE, Via Sri Lanka	E Asia • 250 kW
	†DEUTSCHE WELLE, Wertachtal	W Africa • 500 kW W Africa • 500 kW
	INDIA †ALL INDIA RADIO, Delhi	ENGLISH & HINDI • DS • 50 kW DS • 50 kW
	SWITZERLAND †SWISS RADIO INTL, Sottens	W Asia & S Asia • 500 kW
	TURKEY VOICE OF TURKEY, Ankara-Emirler	E Asia • 500 kW
	USA †R FREE ASIA, Via Tinian, N Marianas	SE Asia • 500 kW
	†VOA, Via Briech, Morocco	C Asia • 250 kW Sa/Su • C Asia • 250 kW
	†VOA, Via Iranawila, Sri Lanka	W Asia & S Asia • 500 kW
	VOA, Via Philippines	SE Asia & S Pacific • 50 kW
15185v	EQUATORIAL GUINEA †RADIO AFRICA, Bata	M-F • S Africa • 50 kW W Africa • 50 kW • ALT. FREQ. TO 7190v kHz
	†RADIO EAST AFRICA, Bata	Sa/Su • ENGLISH & FRENCH • E Africa • 50 kW
15189.8	BRAZIL R INCONFIDENCIA, Belo Horizonte	DS • 5 kW
15190	PHILIPPINES RADYO PILIPINAS, Tinang	Mideast • 250 kW
	UNITED KINGDOM BBC, Via Ascension	S America • 250 kW Sa/Su • S America • 250 kW M-F • S America • 250 kW
	USA †GOOD NEWS R, Via Jülich, Germany	Sa • S Asia & SE Asia • 100 kW
15190v	PAKISTAN RADIO PAKISTAN, Karachi	S Asia & SE Asia • 50 kW • ALT. FREQ. TO 15120v kHz
15195	BULGARIA RADIO BULGARIA, Plovdiv	S Africa • 500 kW
	CANADA R CANADA INTL, Via Tokyo, Japan	SE Asia • 300 kW
	FRANCE R FRANCE INTL, Issoudun-Allouis	E Europe • 500 kW E Europe • 500 kW
	GUAM KTWR-TRANS WORLD RADIO, Merizo	SE Asia • 100 kW
	SPAIN †R EXTERIOR ESPANA, Noblejas	M-F • Europe • 350 kW • ALT FREQ. TO 15150 kHz
	USA †RFE-RL, Via Iranawila, Sri Lanka	W Asia & Mideast • 500 kW
	VOA, Via Kavála, Greece	S Asia • 250 kW
	VOA, Via Philippines	E Asia • 250 kW
15200	FRANCE R FRANCE INTL, Via French Guiana	S America • 500 kW C America • 500 kW C America • 500 kW
	GUAM KTWR-TRANS WORLD RADIO, Merizo	SE Asia • 100 kW S Asia • 100 kW • ALT. FREQ. TO 15595 kHz
	INDIA †ALL INDIA RADIO, Bangalore	N Africa & W Africa • 500 kW
(con'd)	IRAN †VO THE ISLAMIC REP, Sirjan	Sa-Th • E Asia • 500 kW

ENGLISH ▬ ARABIC ▨ CHINESE ▢▢▢ FRENCH ▬ GERMAN ▬ RUSSIAN ═ SPANISH ▬ OTHER ─

FREQUENCY   COUNTRY, STATION, LOCATION   TARGET • NETWORK • POWER (kW)   World Time

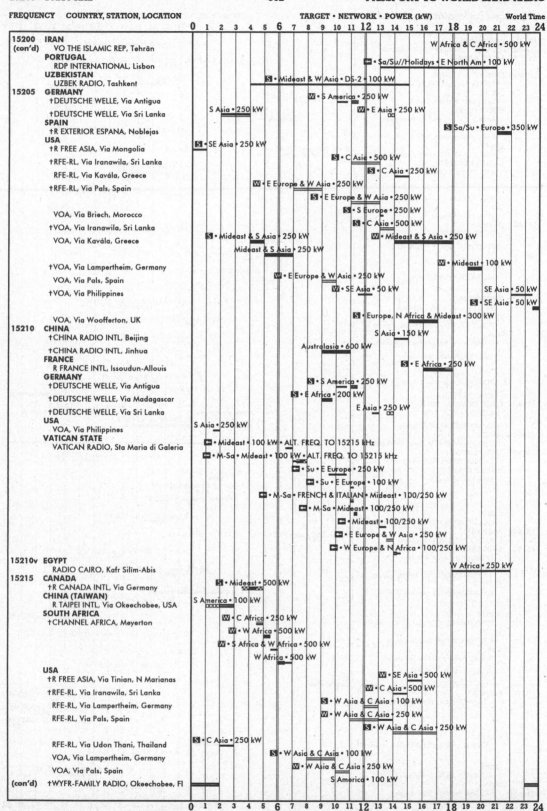

15200 IRAN
(con'd)   VO THE ISLAMIC REP, Tehrān — W Africa & C Africa • 500 kW
PORTUGAL
   RDP INTERNATIONAL, Lisbon — Sa/Su//Holidays • E North Am • 100 kW
UZBEKISTAN
   UZBEK RADIO, Tashkent — S • Mideast & W Asia • DS-2 • 100 kW
15205 GERMANY
   †DEUTSCHE WELLE, Via Antigua — W • S America • 250 kW
   †DEUTSCHE WELLE, Via Sri Lanka — S Asia • 250 kW / W • E Asia • 250 kW
SPAIN
   †R EXTERIOR ESPANA, Noblejas — S • Sa/Su • Europe • 350 kW
USA
   †R FREE ASIA, Via Mongolia — S • SE Asia • 250 kW
   †RFE-RL, Via Iranawila, Sri Lanka — S • C Asia • 500 kW
   RFE-RL, Via Kavála, Greece — S • C Asia • 250 kW
   †RFE-RL, Via Pals, Spain — W • E Europe & W Asia • 250 kW
     — S • E Europe & W Asia • 250 kW
   VOA, Via Briech, Morocco — S • S Europe • 250 kW
   †VOA, Via Iranawila, Sri Lanka — S • C Asia • 500 kW
   VOA, Via Kavála, Greece — S • Mideast & S Asia • 250 kW / W • Mideast & S Asia • 250 kW
     — Mideast & S Asia • 250 kW
   †VOA, Via Lampertheim, Germany — W • Mideast • 100 kW
   VOA, Via Pals, Spain — W • E Europe & W Asia • 250 kW
   †VOA, Via Philippines — W • SE Asia • 50 kW / SE Asia • 50 kW / S • SE Asia • 50 kW
   VOA, Via Woofferton, UK — S • Europe, N Africa & Mideast • 300 kW
15210 CHINA
   †CHINA RADIO INTL, Beijing — S Asia • 150 kW
   †CHINA RADIO INTL, Jinhua — Australasia • 600 kW
FRANCE
   R FRANCE INTL, Issoudun-Allouis — S • E Africa • 250 kW
GERMANY
   †DEUTSCHE WELLE, Via Antigua — S • S America • 250 kW
   †DEUTSCHE WELLE, Via Madagascar — S • E Africa • 200 kW
   †DEUTSCHE WELLE, Via Sri Lanka — E Asia • 250 kW
USA
   VOA, Via Philippines — S Asia • 250 kW
VATICAN STATE
   VATICAN RADIO, Sta Maria di Galeria — • Mideast • 100 kW • ALT. FREQ. TO 15215 kHz
     — • M-Sa • Mideast • 100 kW • ALT. FREQ. TO 15215 kHz
     — • Su • E Europe • 250 kW
     — • Su • E Europe • 100 kW
     — • M-Sa • FRENCH & ITALIAN • Mideast • 100/250 kW
     — • M-Sa • Mideast • 100/250 kW
     — • Mideast • 100/250 kW
     — • E Europe & W Asia • 250 kW
     — • W Europe & N Africa • 100/250 kW
15210v EGYPT
   RADIO CAIRO, Kafr Silīm-Abis — W Africa • 250 kW
15215 CANADA
   †R CANADA INTL, Via Germany — S • Mideast • 500 kW
CHINA (TAIWAN)
   R TAIPEI INTL, Via Okeechobee, USA — S America • 100 kW
SOUTH AFRICA
   †CHANNEL AFRICA, Meyerton — W • C Africa • 250 kW
     — W • W Africa • 500 kW
     — W • S Africa & W Africa • 500 kW
     — W Africa • 500 kW
USA
   †R FREE ASIA, Via Tinian, N Marianas — W • SE Asia • 500 kW
   †RFE-RL, Via Iranawila, Sri Lanka — W • C Asia • 500 kW
   RFE-RL, Via Lampertheim, Germany — S • W Asia & C Asia • 100 kW
   RFE-RL, Via Pals, Spain — W • W Asia & C Asia • 250 kW
     — S • W Asia & C Asia • 250 kW
   RFE-RL, Via Udon Thani, Thailand — S • C Asia • 250 kW
   VOA, Via Lampertheim, Germany — S • W Asia & C Asia • 100 kW
   VOA, Via Pals, Spain — W • W Asia & C Asia • 250 kW
(con'd)   †WYFR-FAMILY RADIO, Okeechobee, Fl — S America • 100 kW

FREQUENCY	COUNTRY, STATION, LOCATION	TARGET • NETWORK • POWER (kW) — World Time

15215 (con'd) USA
†WYFR-FAMILY RADIO, Okeechobee, Fl
- W • W North Am • 100 kW
- S • C Africa & S Africa • 100 kW

VATICAN STATE
VATICAN RADIO, Sta Maria di Galeria
- • Mideast • 100 kW • ALT. FREQ. TO 15210 kHz
- • M-Sa • Mideast • 100 kW • ALT. FREQ. TO 15210 kHz

15220 JAPAN
†RADIO JAPAN/NHK, Via Ascension
- W Africa • 250 kW
- S America • 250 kW
- W Africa • 250 kW • ALT. FREQ. TO 17895 kHz

SWITZERLAND
†SWISS RADIO INTL, Via Jülich, Germany
- S • Mideast • 100 kW
- S • C Africa & S Africa • 100 kW

UNITED KINGDOM
BBC, Via Antigua
- Americas • 125 kW

BBC, Via Sackville, Canada
- N America • 250 kW

USA
VOA, Via Briech, Morocco
- W • W Africa • 250 kW
- W M-F • W Africa • 250 kW
- W Sa/Su • W Africa • 250 kW

15220v EGYPT
RADIO CAIRO, Abu Za'bal
- C Africa • 100 kW

RADIO CAIRO, Kafr Silim-Abis
- C America & S America • 250 kW

15225 GUAM
KSDA-ADVENTIST WORLD RADIO, Agat
- E Asia • 100 kW
- Sa/Su • E Asia • 100 kW
- S • E Asia • 100 kW

UNITED KINGDOM
BBC, Multiple Locations
- • E Europe & W Asia • 300/500 kW

BBC, Rampisham
- • M-F • S Europe • 500 kW

BBC, Woofferton
- • M-F • E Europe & W Asia • 300/500 kW
- S • E Europe • 250 kW

USA
†R FREE ASIA, Via Tinian, N Marianas
- S • S Asia • 500 kW

VOA, Via Ascension
- S Africa • 250 kW

†VOA, Via Philippines
- S • SE Asia • 100 kW

15230 CUBA
RADIO HABANA CUBA, Havana
- S America • 100 kW

DENMARK
†RADIO DANMARK, Via Norway
- W • DANISH • E Asia & Australasia • 500 kW

ITALY
RAI INTERNATIONAL, Rome
- Africa • 100 kW

JAPAN
†RADIO JAPAN/NHK, Tokyo-Yamata
- Pacific, C America & S America • 100 kW

†RADIO JAPAN/NHK, Via Moyabi, Gabon
- W • Mideast • 500 kW

KOREA (DPR)
RADIO PYONGYANG, Kujang-dong
- Americas • 200 kW

NORWAY
†R NORWAY INTL, Kvitsøy
- W • NORWEGIAN • E Asia & Australasia • 500 kW

URUGUAY
EMISORA CIUDAD DE MONTEVIDEO
- DS (PROJECTED) • 1.5/5 kW

15230v SAUDI ARABIA
BS OF THE KINGDOM, Riyadh
- W Europe • DS-GENERAL • 500 kW • ALT. FREQ. TO 15175v kHz

15235 FINLAND
YLE RADIO FINLAND, Pori
- S • E Asia • 500 kW

HUNGARY
†RADIO BUDAPEST, Jászberény
- S • N America • 250 kW

LIBYA
RADIO JAMAHIRIYA, Tripoli
- • W Africa & S America • 500 kW • ALT. FREQ. TO 9700 kHz

RUSSIA
KHANTY-MANSIYSK R, Khanty-Mansiysk
- • DS-RADIO ROSSII • 3 kW

SWEDEN
RADIO SWEDEN, Hörby
- • N America • 500 kW • ALT. FREQ. TO 15240 kHz

UNITED KINGDOM
BBC, Via Maşīrah, Oman
- Mideast • 100 kW

USA
†VOA, Via Philippines
- S • M-F • SE Asia • 250 kW

†VOA, Via Udon Thani, Thailand
- S • SE Asia & Australasia • 250 kW

15240 AUSTRALIA
RADIO AUSTRALIA, Shepparton
- Pacific & E Asia • 100 kW
- E Asia & SE Asia • 100 kW

AUSTRIA
†R AUSTRIA INTL, Vienna
- S • Mideast • 100 kW

FINLAND
YLE RADIO FINLAND, Pori
- W • E Asia • 500 kW

ITALY
RAI INTERNATIONAL, Rome
- Mideast • 100 kW • ALT. FREQ. TO 15280 kHz

RAI-RTV ITALIANA, Rome
- E Africa • DS • 100 kW

SWEDEN
RADIO SWEDEN, Hörby
- S • Asia & Australasia • 500 kW
- S • E Asia • 500 kW

(con'd)

ENGLISH ▬   ARABIC ▨   CHINESE ▯▯▯   FRENCH ═   GERMAN ▬   RUSSIAN ═   SPANISH ▬   OTHER —

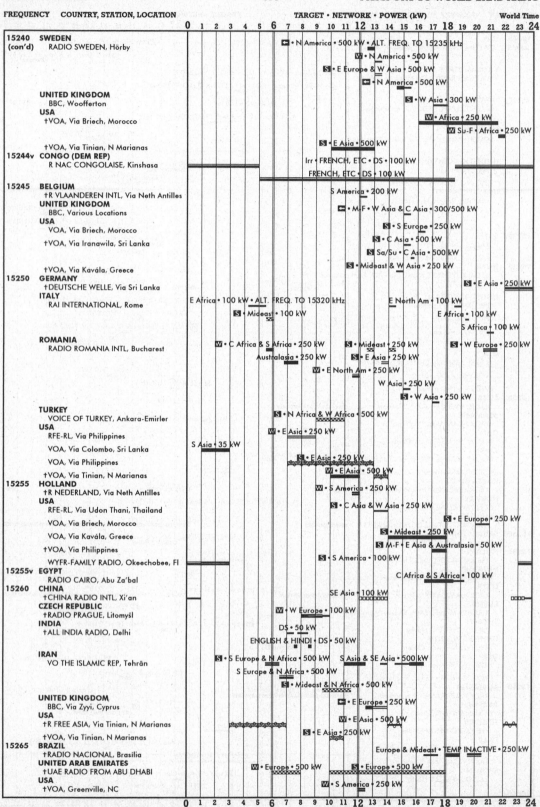

FREQUENCY   COUNTRY, STATION, LOCATION   TARGET • NETWORK • POWER (kW)   World Time

15240 **SWEDEN**
(con'd)   RADIO SWEDEN, Hörby
- ↩ • N America • 500 kW • ALT. FREQ. TO 15235 kHz
- W • N America • 500 kW
- S • E Europe & W Asia • 500 kW
- ↩ • N America • 500 kW

UNITED KINGDOM
BBC, Woofferton
- S • W Asia • 300 kW

USA
†VOA, Via Briech, Morocco
- W • Africa • 250 kW
- W • Su-F • Africa • 250 kW

†VOA, Via Tinian, N Marianas
- S • E Asia • 500 kW

15244v **CONGO (DEM REP)**
R NAC CONGOLAISE, Kinshasa
- Irr • FRENCH, ETC • DS • 100 kW
- FRENCH, ETC • DS • 100 kW

15245 **BELGIUM**
†R VLAANDEREN INTL, Via Neth Antilles
- S America • 200 kW

UNITED KINGDOM
BBC, Various Locations
- ↩ • M-F • W Asia & C Asia • 300/500 kW

USA
VOA, Via Briech, Morocco
- S • S Europe • 250 kW

†VOA, Via Iranawila, Sri Lanka
- S • C Asia • 500 kW
- S • Sa/Su • C Asia • 500 kW

†VOA, Via Kavála, Greece
- S • Mideast & W Asia • 250 kW

15250 **GERMANY**
†DEUTSCHE WELLE, Via Sri Lanka
- S • E Asia • 250 kW

ITALY
RAI INTERNATIONAL, Rome
- E Africa • 100 kW • ALT. FREQ. TO 15320 kHz
- E North Am • 100 kW
- S • Mideast • 100 kW
- E Africa • 100 kW
- S Africa • 100 kW

ROMANIA
RADIO ROMANIA INTL, Bucharest
- W • C Africa & S Africa • 250 kW
- S • Mideast • 250 kW
- S • W Europe • 250 kW
- Australasia • 250 kW
- S • E Asia • 250 kW
- W • E North Am • 250 kW
- W Asia • 250 kW
- S • W Asia • 250 kW

TURKEY
VOICE OF TURKEY, Ankara-Emirler
- S • N Africa & W Africa • 500 kW

USA
RFE-RL, Via Philippines
- W • E Asia • 250 kW

VOA, Via Colombo, Sri Lanka
- S Asia • 35 kW

VOA, Via Philippines
- S • E Asia • 250 kW

†VOA, Via Tinian, N Marianas
- W • E Asia • 500 kW

15255 **HOLLAND**
†R NEDERLAND, Via Neth Antilles
- W • S America • 250 kW

USA
RFE-RL, Via Udon Thani, Thailand
- S • C Asia & W Asia • 250 kW

VOA, Via Briech, Morocco
- S • E Europe • 250 kW

VOA, Via Kavála, Greece
- S • Mideast • 250 kW

†VOA, Via Philippines
- S • M-F • E Asia & Australasia • 50 kW

WYFR-FAMILY RADIO, Okeechobee, Fl
- S • S America • 100 kW

15255v **EGYPT**
RADIO CAIRO, Abu Za'bal
- C Africa & S Africa • 100 kW

15260 **CHINA**
†CHINA RADIO INTL, Xi'an
- SE Asia • 100 kW

CZECH REPUBLIC
†RADIO PRAGUE, Litomyšl
- W • W Europe • 100 kW

INDIA
†ALL INDIA RADIO, Delhi
- DS • 50 kW
- ENGLISH & HINDI • DS • 50 kW

IRAN
VO THE ISLAMIC REP, Tehrān
- S • S Europe & N Africa • 500 kW
- S Asia & SE Asia • 500 kW
- S Europe & N Africa • 500 kW
- S • Mideast & N Africa • 500 kW

UNITED KINGDOM
BBC, Via Zyyi, Cyprus
- ↩ • E Europe • 250 kW

USA
†R FREE ASIA, Via Tinian, N Marianas
- W • E Asia • 500 kW

†VOA, Via Tinian, N Marianas
- S • E Asia • 250 kW

15265 **BRAZIL**
RADIO NACIONAL, Brasilia
- Europe & Mideast • TEMP INACTIVE • 250 kW

UNITED ARAB EMIRATES
†UAE RADIO FROM ABU DHABI
- W • Europe • 500 kW
- S • Europe • 500 kW

USA
†VOA, Greenville, NC
- W • S America • 250 kW

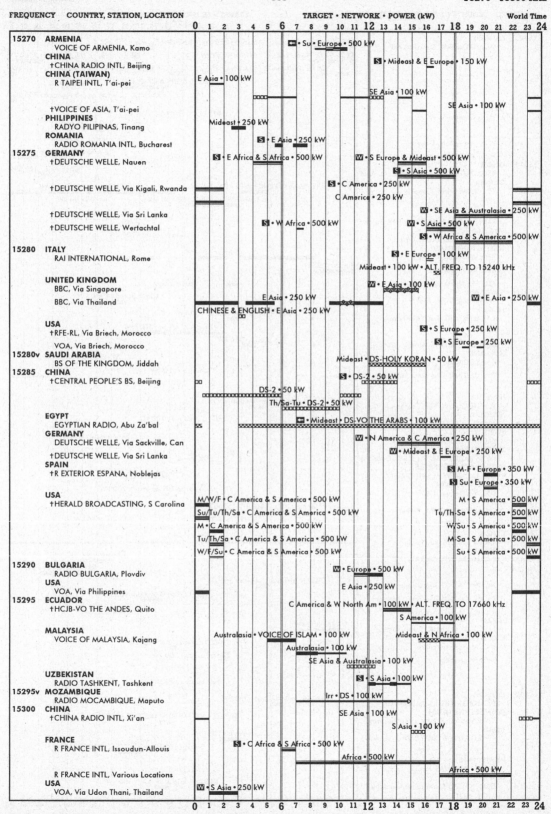

FREQUENCY   COUNTRY, STATION, LOCATION   TARGET • NETWORK • POWER (kW)   World Time

Freq	Country / Station / Location	
15270	**ARMENIA**	
	VOICE OF ARMENIA, Kamo	Su • Europe • 500 kW
	CHINA	
	†CHINA RADIO INTL, Beijing	Mideast & E Europe • 150 kW
	CHINA (TAIWAN)	
	R TAIPEI INTL, T'ai-pei	E Asia • 100 kW / SE Asia • 100 kW / SE Asia • 100 kW
	†VOICE OF ASIA, T'ai-pei	
	PHILIPPINES	
	RADYO PILIPINAS, Tinang	Mideast • 250 kW
	ROMANIA	
	RADIO ROMANIA INTL, Bucharest	E Asia • 250 kW
15275	**GERMANY**	
	†DEUTSCHE WELLE, Nauen	E Africa & S Africa • 500 kW / S Europe & Mideast • 500 kW / S Asia • 500 kW
	†DEUTSCHE WELLE, Via Kigali, Rwanda	C America • 250 kW / C America • 250 kW
	†DEUTSCHE WELLE, Via Sri Lanka	SE Asia & Australasia • 250 kW
	†DEUTSCHE WELLE, Wertachtal	W Africa • 500 kW / S Asia • 500 kW / W Africa & S America • 500 kW
15280	**ITALY**	
	RAI INTERNATIONAL, Rome	E Europe • 100 kW / Mideast • 100 kW • ALT. FREQ. TO 15240 kHz
	UNITED KINGDOM	
	BBC, Via Singapore	E Asia • 100 kW
	BBC, Via Thailand	E Asia • 250 kW / E Asia • 250 kW / CHINESE & ENGLISH • E Asia • 250 kW
	USA	
	†RFE-RL, Via Briech, Morocco	S Europe • 250 kW
	VOA, Via Briech, Morocco	S Europe • 250 kW
15280v	**SAUDI ARABIA**	
	BS OF THE KINGDOM, Jiddah	Mideast • DS-HOLY KORAN • 50 kW
15285	**CHINA**	
	†CENTRAL PEOPLE'S BS, Beijing	DS-2 • 50 kW / DS-2 • 50 kW / DS-2 • 50 kW / Th/Sa-Tu • DS-2 • 50 kW
	EGYPT	
	EGYPTIAN RADIO, Abu Za'bal	Mideast • DS-VO THE ARABS • 100 kW
	GERMANY	
	DEUTSCHE WELLE, Via Sackville, Can	N America & C America • 250 kW
	†DEUTSCHE WELLE, Via Sri Lanka	Mideast & E Europe • 250 kW
	SPAIN	
	†R EXTERIOR ESPANA, Noblejas	M-F • Europe • 350 kW / Su • Europe • 350 kW
	USA	
	†HERALD BROADCASTING, S Carolina	M/W/F • C America & S America • 500 kW / M • S America • 500 kW / Su/Tu/Th/Sa • C America & S America • 500 kW / Tu/Th-Sa • S America • 500 kW / M • C America & S America • 500 kW / W/Su • S America • 500 kW / Tu/Th/Sa • C America & S America • 500 kW / M-Sa • S America • 500 kW / W/F/Su • C America & S America • 500 kW / Su • S America • 500 kW
15290	**BULGARIA**	
	RADIO BULGARIA, Plovdiv	Europe • 500 kW
	USA	
	VOA, Via Philippines	E Asia • 250 kW
15295	**ECUADOR**	
	†HCJB-VO THE ANDES, Quito	C America & W North Am • 100 kW • ALT. FREQ. TO 17660 kHz / S America • 100 kW
	MALAYSIA	
	VOICE OF MALAYSIA, Kajang	Australasia • VOICE OF ISLAM • 100 kW / Mideast & N Africa • 100 kW / Australasia • 100 kW / SE Asia & Australasia • 100 kW
	UZBEKISTAN	
	RADIO TASHKENT, Tashkent	S Asia • 100 kW
15295v	**MOZAMBIQUE**	
	RADIO MOCAMBIQUE, Maputo	Irr • DS • 100 kW
15300	**CHINA**	
	†CHINA RADIO INTL, Xi'an	SE Asia • 100 kW / S Asia • 100 kW
	FRANCE	
	R FRANCE INTL, Issoudun-Allouis	C Africa & S Africa • 500 kW / Africa • 500 kW
	R FRANCE INTL, Various Locations	Africa • 500 kW
	USA	
	VOA, Via Udon Thani, Thailand	S Asia • 250 kW

FREQUENCY	COUNTRY, STATION, LOCATION	TARGET • NETWORK • POWER (kW)	World Time

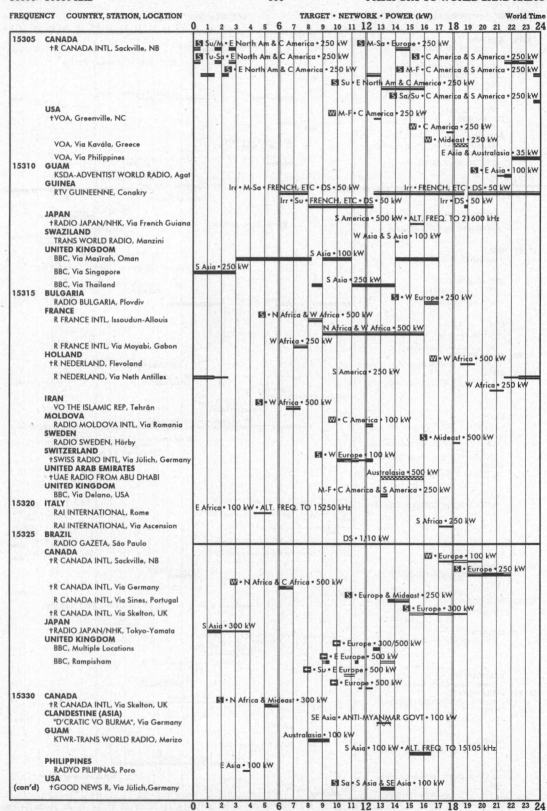

15305 CANADA
†R CANADA INTL, Sackville, NB
- S Su/M • E North Am & C America • 250 kW
- M-Sa • Europe • 250 kW
- S Tu-Sa • E North Am & C America • 250 kW
- C America & S America • 250 kW
- S • E North Am & C America • 250 kW
- M-F • C America & S America • 250 kW
- S Su • E North Am & C America • 250 kW
- Sa/Su • C America & S America • 250 kW

USA
†VOA, Greenville, NC
- W M-F • C America • 250 kW
- W • C America • 250 kW
- W • Mideast • 250 kW

VOA, Via Kavála, Greece

VOA, Via Philippines
- E Asia & Australasia • 35 kW

15310 GUAM
KSDA-ADVENTIST WORLD RADIO, Agat
- S • E Asia • 100 kW

GUINEA
RTV GUINEENNE, Conakry
- Irr • M-Sa • FRENCH, ETC • DS • 50 kW
- Irr • FRENCH, ETC • DS • 50 kW
- Irr • Su • FRENCH, ETC • DS • 50 kW
- Irr • DS • 50 kW

JAPAN
†RADIO JAPAN/NHK, Via French Guiana
- S America • 500 kW • ALT. FREQ. TO 21600 kHz

SWAZILAND
TRANS WORLD RADIO, Manzini
- W Asia & S Asia • 100 kW

UNITED KINGDOM
BBC, Via Maşīrah, Oman
- S Asia • 100 kW

BBC, Via Singapore
- S Asia • 250 kW

BBC, Via Thailand
- S Asia • 250 kW

15315 BULGARIA
RADIO BULGARIA, Plovdiv
- S • W Europe • 250 kW

FRANCE
R FRANCE INTL, Issoudun-Allouis
- S • N Africa & W Africa • 500 kW
- N Africa & W Africa • 500 kW

R FRANCE INTL, Via Moyabi, Gabon
- W Africa • 250 kW

HOLLAND
†R NEDERLAND, Flevoland
- W • W Africa • 500 kW

R NEDERLAND, Via Neth Antilles
- S America • 250 kW
- W Africa • 250 kW

IRAN
VO THE ISLAMIC REP, Tehrān
- S • W Africa • 500 kW

MOLDOVA
RADIO MOLDOVA INTL, Via Romania
- W • C America • 100 kW

SWEDEN
RADIO SWEDEN, Hörby
- S • Mideast • 500 kW

SWITZERLAND
†SWISS RADIO INTL, Via Jülich, Germany
- S • W Europe • 100 kW

UNITED ARAB EMIRATES
†UAE RADIO FROM ABU DHABI
- Australasia • 500 kW

UNITED KINGDOM
BBC, Via Delano, USA
- M-F • C America & S America • 250 kW

15320 ITALY
RAI INTERNATIONAL, Rome
- E Africa • 100 kW • ALT. FREQ. TO 15250 kHz

RAI INTERNATIONAL, Via Ascension
- S Africa • 250 kW

15325 BRAZIL
RADIO GAZETA, São Paulo
- DS • 1/10 kW

CANADA
†R CANADA INTL, Sackville, NB
- W • Europe • 100 kW
- S • Europe • 250 kW

†R CANADA INTL, Via Germany
- W • N Africa & C Africa • 500 kW

R CANADA INTL, Via Sines, Portugal
- S • Europe & Mideast • 250 kW

†R CANADA INTL, Via Skelton, UK
- S • Europe • 300 kW

JAPAN
†RADIO JAPAN/NHK, Tokyo-Yamata
- S Asia • 300 kW

UNITED KINGDOM
BBC, Multiple Locations
- • Europe • 300/500 kW

BBC, Rampisham
- • E Europe • 500 kW
- Su • E Europe • 500 kW
- • Europe • 500 kW

15330 CANADA
†R CANADA INTL, Via Skelton, UK
- S • N Africa & Mideast • 300 kW

CLANDESTINE (ASIA)
"D'CRATIC VO BURMA", Via Germany
- SE Asia • ANTI-MYANMAR GOVT • 100 kW

GUAM
KTWR-TRANS WORLD RADIO, Merizo
- Australasia • 100 kW
- S Asia • 100 kW • ALT. FREQ. TO 15105 kHz

PHILIPPINES
RADYO PILIPINAS, Poro
- E Asia • 100 kW

USA
(con'd) †GOOD NEWS R, Via Jülich, Germany
- S Sa • S Asia & SE Asia • 100 kW

SEASONAL S OR W   1-HR TIMESHIFT MIDYEAR ⊡ OR ⊟   JAMMING / OR ∧   EARLIEST HEARD ◁   LATEST HEARD ▷   NEW FOR 2000 †

FREQUENCY   COUNTRY, STATION, LOCATION   TARGET • NETWORK • POWER (kW)   World Time

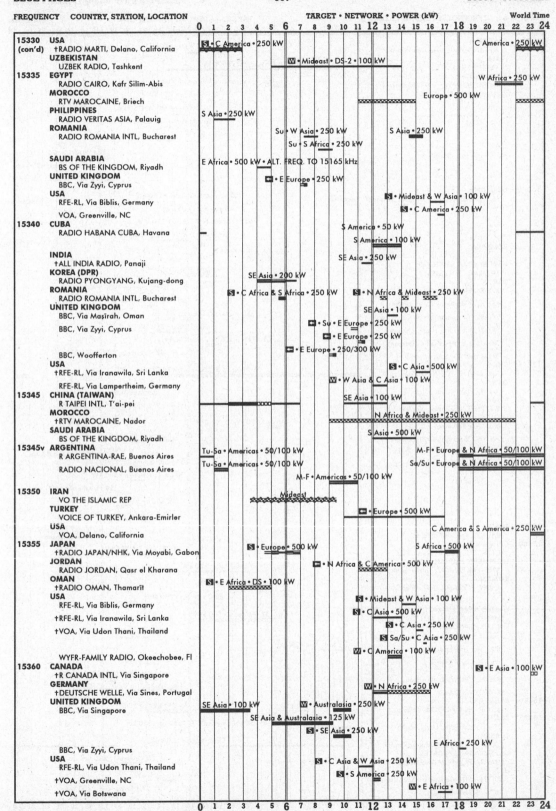

Frequency	Country, Station, Location	Target • Network • Power
15330 (con'd)	USA	
	†RADIO MARTI, Delano, California	S • C America • 250 kW / C America • 250 kW
	UZBEKISTAN	
	UZBEK RADIO, Tashkent	W • Mideast • DS-2 • 100 kW
15335	EGYPT	
	RADIO CAIRO, Kafr Silim-Abis	W Africa • 250 kW
	MOROCCO	
	RTV MAROCAINE, Briech	Europe • 500 kW
	PHILIPPINES	
	RADIO VERITAS ASIA, Palauig	S Asia • 250 kW
	ROMANIA	
	RADIO ROMANIA INTL, Bucharest	Su • W Asia • 250 kW / Su • S Africa • 250 kW
	SAUDI ARABIA	
	BS OF THE KINGDOM, Riyadh	E Africa • 500 kW • ALT. FREQ. TO 15165 kHz
	UNITED KINGDOM	
	BBC, Via Zyyi, Cyprus	• E Europe • 250 kW
	USA	
	RFE-RL, Via Biblis, Germany	S • Mideast & W Asia • 100 kW
	VOA, Greenville, NC	S • C America • 250 kW
15340	CUBA	
	RADIO HABANA CUBA, Havana	S America • 50 kW / S America • 100 kW
	INDIA	
	†ALL INDIA RADIO, Panaji	SE Asia • 250 kW
	KOREA (DPR)	
	RADIO PYONGYANG, Kujang-dong	SE Asia • 200 kW
	ROMANIA	
	RADIO ROMANIA INTL, Bucharest	S • C Africa & S Africa • 250 kW / S • N Africa & Mideast • 250 kW
	UNITED KINGDOM	
	BBC, Via Maşīrah, Oman	SE Asia • 100 kW
	BBC, Via Zyyi, Cyprus	• Su • E Europe • 250 kW / • E Europe • 250 kW
	BBC, Woofferton	• E Europe • 250/300 kW
	USA	
	†RFE-RL, Via Iranawila, Sri Lanka	S • C Asia • 500 kW
	RFE-RL, Via Lampertheim, Germany	W • W Asia & C Asia • 100 kW
15345	CHINA (TAIWAN)	
	R TAIPEI INTL, T'ai-pei	SE Asia • 100 kW
	MOROCCO	
	†RTV MAROCAINE, Nador	N Africa & Mideast • 250 kW
	SAUDI ARABIA	
	BS OF THE KINGDOM, Riyadh	S Asia • 500 kW
15345v	ARGENTINA	
	R ARGENTINA-RAE, Buenos Aires	Tu-Sa • Americas • 50/100 kW / M-F • Europe & N Africa • 50/100 kW
	RADIO NACIONAL, Buenos Aires	Tu-Sa • Americas • 50/100 kW / Sa/Su • Europe & N Africa • 50/100 kW / M-F • Americas • 50/100 kW
15350	IRAN	
	VO THE ISLAMIC REP	Mideast
	TURKEY	
	VOICE OF TURKEY, Ankara-Emirler	• Europe • 500 kW
	USA	
	VOA, Delano, California	C America & S America • 250 kW
15355	JAPAN	
	†RADIO JAPAN/NHK, Via Moyabi, Gabon	S • Europe • 500 kW / S Africa • 500 kW
	JORDAN	
	RADIO JORDAN, Qasr el Kharana	• N Africa & C America • 500 kW
	OMAN	
	†RADIO OMAN, Thamarīt	S • E Africa • DS • 100 kW
	USA	
	RFE-RL, Via Biblis, Germany	S • Mideast & W Asia • 100 kW
	†RFE-RL, Via Iranawila, Sri Lanka	S • C Asia • 500 kW
	†VOA, Via Udon Thani, Thailand	S • C Asia • 250 kW / S Sa/Su • C Asia • 250 kW
	WYFR-FAMILY RADIO, Okeechobee, Fl	W • C America • 100 kW
15360	CANADA	
	†R CANADA INTL, Via Singapore	S • E Asia • 100 kW
	GERMANY	
	†DEUTSCHE WELLE, Via Sines, Portugal	W • N Africa • 250 kW
	UNITED KINGDOM	
	BBC, Via Singapore	SE Asia • 100 kW / W • Australasia • 250 kW / SE Asia & Australasia • 125 kW / S • SE Asia • 250 kW
	BBC, Via Zyyi, Cyprus	E Africa • 250 kW
	USA	
	RFE-RL, Via Udon Thani, Thailand	S • C Asia & W Asia • 250 kW
	†VOA, Greenville, NC	S • S America • 250 kW
	†VOA, Via Botswana	W • E Africa • 100 kW

FREQUENCY   COUNTRY, STATION, LOCATION   TARGET • NETWORK • POWER (kW)   World Time

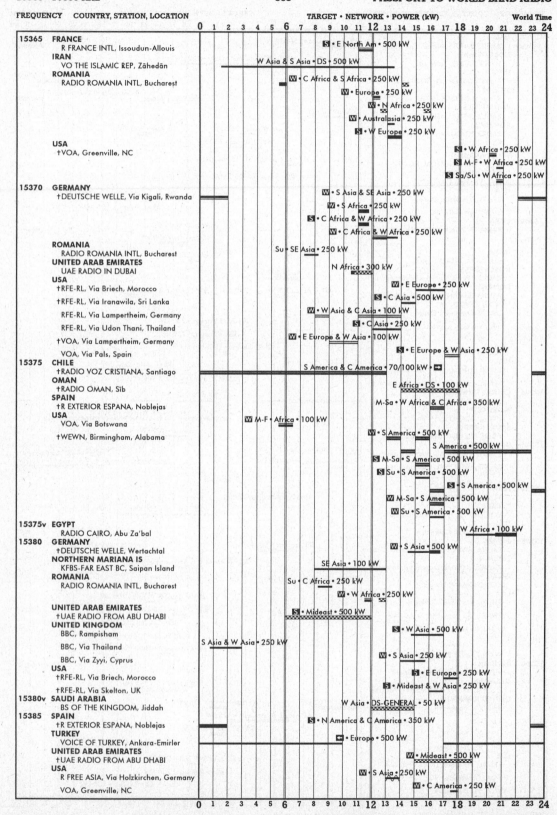

15365   **FRANCE**
    R FRANCE INTL, Issoudun-Allouis   S • E North Am • 500 kW
   IRAN
    VO THE ISLAMIC REP, Zāhedān   W Asia & S Asia • DS • 500 kW
   ROMANIA
    RADIO ROMANIA INTL, Bucharest   W • C Africa & S Africa • 250 kW
     W • Europe • 250 kW
     W • N Africa • 250 kW
     W • Australasia • 250 kW
     S • W Europe • 250 kW
   USA
    †VOA, Greenville, NC   S • W Africa • 250 kW
     S • M-F • W Africa • 250 kW
     S Sa/Su • W Africa • 250 kW

15370   **GERMANY**
    †DEUTSCHE WELLE, Via Kigali, Rwanda   W • S Asia & SE Asia • 250 kW
     W • S Africa • 250 kW
     S • C Africa & W Africa • 250 kW
     W • C Africa & W Africa • 250 kW
   ROMANIA
    RADIO ROMANIA INTL, Bucharest   Su • SE Asia • 250 kW
   UNITED ARAB EMIRATES
    UAE RADIO IN DUBAI   N Africa • 300 kW
   USA
    †RFE-RL, Via Briech, Morocco   W • E Europe • 250 kW
    †RFE-RL, Via Iranawila, Sri Lanka   S • C Asia • 500 kW
    RFE-RL, Via Lampertheim, Germany   W • W Asia & C Asia • 100 kW
    RFE-RL, Via Udon Thani, Thailand   S • C Asia • 250 kW
    †VOA, Via Lampertheim, Germany   W • E Europe & W Asia • 100 kW
    VOA, Via Pals, Spain   S • E Europe & W Asia • 250 kW

15375   **CHILE**
    †RADIO VOZ CRISTIANA, Santiago   S America & C America • 70/100 kW • ▭
   OMAN
    †RADIO OMAN, Sīb   E Africa • DS • 100 kW
   SPAIN
    †R EXTERIOR ESPANA, Noblejas   M-Sa • W Africa & C Africa • 350 kW
   USA
    VOA, Via Botswana   W • M-F • Africa • 100 kW
    †WEWN, Birmingham, Alabama   W • S America • 500 kW
     S America • 500 kW
     S M-Sa • S America • 500 kW
     S Su • S America • 500 kW
     S • S America • 500 kW
     W M-Sa • S America • 500 kW
     W Su • S America • 500 kW

15375v   **EGYPT**
    RADIO CAIRO, Abu Za'bal   W Africa • 100 kW
15380   **GERMANY**
    †DEUTSCHE WELLE, Wertachtal   W • S Asia • 500 kW
   NORTHERN MARIANA IS
    KFBS-FAR EAST BC, Saipan Island   SE Asia • 100 kW
   ROMANIA
    RADIO ROMANIA INTL, Bucharest   Su • C Africa • 250 kW
     W • W Africa • 250 kW
   UNITED ARAB EMIRATES
    †UAE RADIO FROM ABU DHABI   S • Mideast • 500 kW
   UNITED KINGDOM
    BBC, Rampisham   S • W Asia • 500 kW
    BBC, Via Thailand   S Asia & W Asia • 250 kW
    BBC, Via Zyyi, Cyprus   W • S Asia • 250 kW
   USA
    †RFE-RL, Via Briech, Morocco   S • E Europe • 250 kW
    †RFE-RL, Via Skelton, UK   S • Mideast & W Asia • 250 kW
15380v   **SAUDI ARABIA**
    BS OF THE KINGDOM, Jiddah   W Asia • DS-GENERAL • 50 kW
15385   **SPAIN**
    †R EXTERIOR ESPANA, Noblejas   S • N America & C America • 350 kW
   TURKEY
    VOICE OF TURKEY, Ankara-Emirler   ▭ • Europe • 500 kW
   UNITED ARAB EMIRATES
    †UAE RADIO FROM ABU DHABI   W • Mideast • 500 kW
   USA
    R FREE ASIA, Via Holzkirchen, Germany   W • S Asia • 250 kW
    VOA, Greenville, NC   W • C America • 250 kW

FREQUENCY   COUNTRY, STATION, LOCATION   TARGET • NETWORK • POWER (kW)   World Time

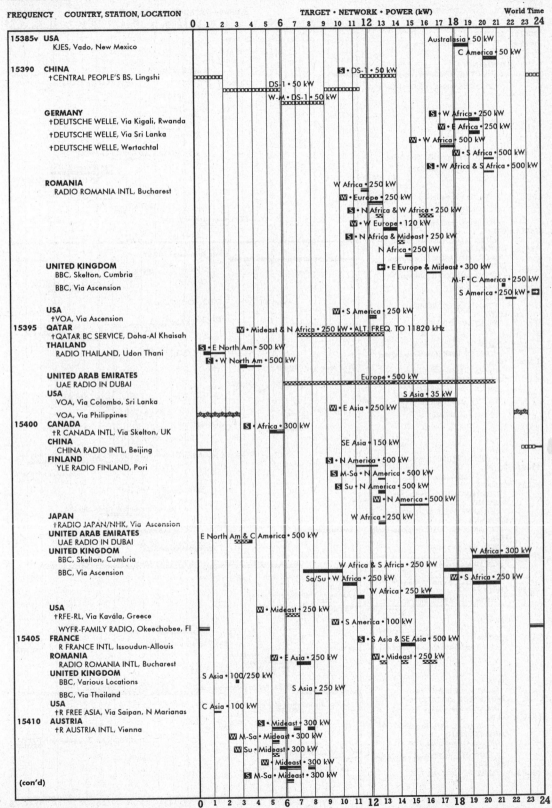

Frequency	Country, Station, Location	Schedule
15385v	**USA**	
	KJES, Vado, New Mexico	Australasia • 50 kW; C America • 50 kW
15390	**CHINA**	
	†CENTRAL PEOPLE'S BS, Lingshi	S • DS-1 • 50 kW; DS-1 • 50 kW; W-M • DS-1 • 50 kW
	GERMANY	
	†DEUTSCHE WELLE, Via Kigali, Rwanda	S • W Africa • 250 kW; W • E Africa • 250 kW
	†DEUTSCHE WELLE, Via Sri Lanka	W • W Africa • 500 kW; W • S Africa • 500 kW
	†DEUTSCHE WELLE, Wertachtal	S • W Africa & S Africa • 500 kW
	ROMANIA	
	RADIO ROMANIA INTL, Bucharest	W Africa • 250 kW; W • Europe • 250 kW; S • N Africa & W Africa • 250 kW; W • W Europe • 120 kW; S • N Africa & Mideast • 250 kW; N Africa • 250 kW
	UNITED KINGDOM	
	BBC, Skelton, Cumbria	• E Europe & Mideast • 300 kW
	BBC, Via Ascension	M-F • C America • 250 kW; S America • 250 kW •
	USA	
	†VOA, Via Ascension	W • S America • 250 kW
15395	**QATAR**	
	†QATAR BC SERVICE, Doha-Al Khaisah	W • Mideast & N Africa • 250 kW • ALT. FREQ. TO 11820 kHz
	THAILAND	
	RADIO THAILAND, Udon Thani	S • E North Am • 500 kW; S • W North Am • 500 kW
	UNITED ARAB EMIRATES	
	UAE RADIO IN DUBAI	Europe • 500 kW
	USA	
	VOA, Via Colombo, Sri Lanka	S Asia • 35 kW
	VOA, Via Philippines	W • E Asia • 250 kW
15400	**CANADA**	
	†R CANADA INTL, Via Skelton, UK	S • Africa • 300 kW
	CHINA	
	CHINA RADIO INTL, Beijing	SE Asia • 150 kW
	FINLAND	
	YLE RADIO FINLAND, Pori	S • N America • 500 kW; S • M-Sa • N America • 500 kW; S • Su • N America • 500 kW; W • N America • 500 kW
	JAPAN	
	†RADIO JAPAN/NHK, Via Ascension	W Africa • 250 kW
	UNITED ARAB EMIRATES	
	UAE RADIO IN DUBAI	E North Am & C America • 500 kW
	UNITED KINGDOM	
	BBC, Skelton, Cumbria	W Africa • 300 kW
	BBC, Via Ascension	W Africa & S Africa • 250 kW; Sa/Su • W Africa • 250 kW; W • S Africa • 250 kW; W Africa • 250 kW
	USA	
	†RFE-RL, Via Kavála, Greece	W • Mideast • 250 kW
	WYFR-FAMILY RADIO, Okeechobee, Fl	W • S America • 100 kW
15405	**FRANCE**	
	R FRANCE INTL, Issoudun-Allouis	S • S Asia & SE Asia • 500 kW
	ROMANIA	
	RADIO ROMANIA INTL, Bucharest	W • E Asia • 250 kW; W • Mideast • 250 kW
	UNITED KINGDOM	
	BBC, Various Locations	S Asia • 100/250 kW
	BBC, Via Thailand	S Asia • 250 kW
	USA	
	†R FREE ASIA, Via Saipan, N Marianas	C Asia • 100 kW
15410	**AUSTRIA**	
	†R AUSTRIA INTL, Vienna	S • Mideast • 300 kW; W • M-Sa • Mideast • 300 kW; S • Su • Mideast • 300 kW; W • Mideast • 300 kW; S • M-Sa • Mideast • 300 kW

(con'd)

World Time scale: 0 1 2 3 4 5 6 7 8 9 10 11 12 13 14 15 16 17 18 19 20 21 22 23 24

ENGLISH ▬ ARABIC ≋ CHINESE ▯▯▯ FRENCH ═ GERMAN ▬ RUSSIAN ═ SPANISH ▬ OTHER ─

FREQUENCY   COUNTRY, STATION, LOCATION   TARGET • NETWORK • POWER (kW)   World Time

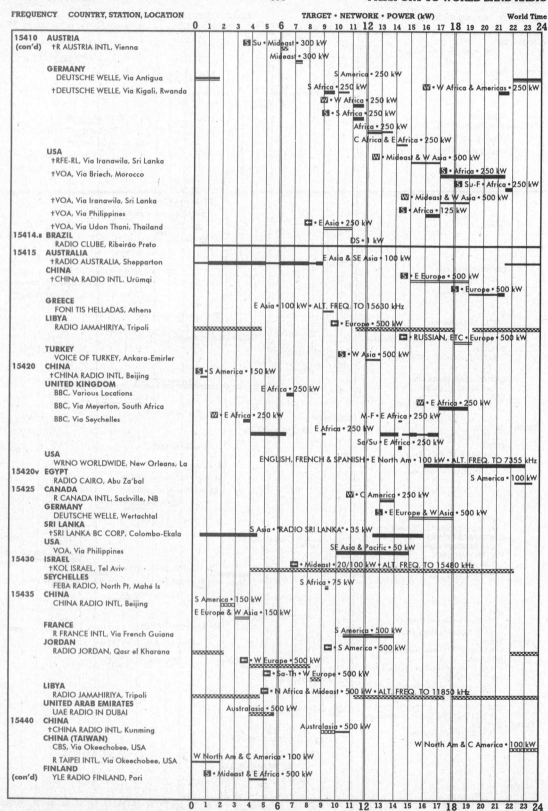

Frequency	Country / Station / Location	Details
15410 (con'd)	**AUSTRIA** †R AUSTRIA INTL, Vienna	Su • Mideast • 300 kW / Mideast • 300 kW
	GERMANY DEUTSCHE WELLE, Via Antigua	S America • 250 kW
	†DEUTSCHE WELLE, Via Kigali, Rwanda	S Africa • 250 kW / W • W Africa & Americas • 250 kW / W • W Africa • 250 kW / S • S Africa • 250 kW / Africa • 250 kW / C Africa & E Africa • 250 kW
	USA †RFE-RL, Via Iranawila, Sri Lanka	W • Mideast & W Asia • 500 kW
	†VOA, Via Briech, Morocco	S • Africa • 250 kW / Su-F • Africa • 250 kW
	†VOA, Via Iranawila, Sri Lanka	W • Mideast & W Asia • 500 kW
	†VOA, Via Philippines	S • Africa • 125 kW
	†VOA, Via Udon Thani, Thailand	E Asia • 250 kW
15414.8	**BRAZIL** RADIO CLUBE, Ribeirão Preto	DS • 1 kW
15415	**AUSTRALIA** †RADIO AUSTRALIA, Shepparton	E Asia & SE Asia • 100 kW
	CHINA †CHINA RADIO INTL, Urümqi	S • E Europe • 500 kW / S • Europe • 500 kW
	GREECE FONI TIS HELLADAS, Athens	E Asia • 100 kW • ALT. FREQ. TO 15630 kHz
	LIBYA RADIO JAMAHIRIYA, Tripoli	E • Europe • 500 kW / RUSSIAN, ETC • Europe • 500 kW
	TURKEY VOICE OF TURKEY, Ankara-Emirler	S • W Asia • 500 kW
15420	**CHINA** †CHINA RADIO INTL, Beijing	S • S America • 150 kW
	UNITED KINGDOM BBC, Various Locations	E Africa • 250 kW
	BBC, Via Meyerton, South Africa	W • E Africa • 250 kW
	BBC, Via Seychelles	W • E Africa • 250 kW / M-F • E Africa • 250 kW / E Africa • 250 kW / Sa/Su • E Africa • 250 kW
	USA WRNO WORLDWIDE, New Orleans, La	ENGLISH, FRENCH & SPANISH • E North Am • 100 kW • ALT. FREQ. TO 7355 kHz
15420v	**EGYPT** RADIO CAIRO, Abu Za'bal	S America • 100 kW
15425	**CANADA** R CANADA INTL, Sackville, NB	W • C America • 250 kW
	GERMANY DEUTSCHE WELLE, Wertachtal	S • E Europe & W Asia • 500 kW
	SRI LANKA †SRI LANKA BC CORP, Colombo-Ekala	S Asia • "RADIO SRI LANKA" • 35 kW
	USA VOA, Via Philippines	SE Asia & Pacific • 50 kW
15430	**ISRAEL** †KOL ISRAEL, Tel Aviv	E • Mideast • 20/100 kW • ALT. FREQ. TO 15480 kHz
	SEYCHELLES FEBA RADIO, North Pt, Mahé Is	S Africa • 75 kW
15435	**CHINA** CHINA RADIO INTL, Beijing	S America • 150 kW / E Europe & W Asia • 150 kW
	FRANCE R FRANCE INTL, Via French Guiana	S America • 500 kW
	JORDAN RADIO JORDAN, Qasr el Kharana	E • S America • 500 kW / E • W Europe • 500 kW / E • Sa-Th • W Europe • 500 kW
	LIBYA RADIO JAMAHIRIYA, Tripoli	E • N Africa & Mideast • 500 kW • ALT. FREQ. TO 11850 kHz
	UNITED ARAB EMIRATES UAE RADIO IN DUBAI	Australasia • 500 kW
15440	**CHINA** †CHINA RADIO INTL, Kunming	Australasia • 500 kW
	CHINA (TAIWAN) CBS, Via Okeechobee, USA	W North Am & C America • 100 kW
	R TAIPEI INTL, Via Okeechobee, USA	W North Am & C America • 100 kW
	FINLAND (con'd) YLE RADIO FINLAND, Pori	S • Mideast & E Africa • 500 kW

FREQUENCY   COUNTRY, STATION, LOCATION   TARGET • NETWORK • POWER (kW)   World Time

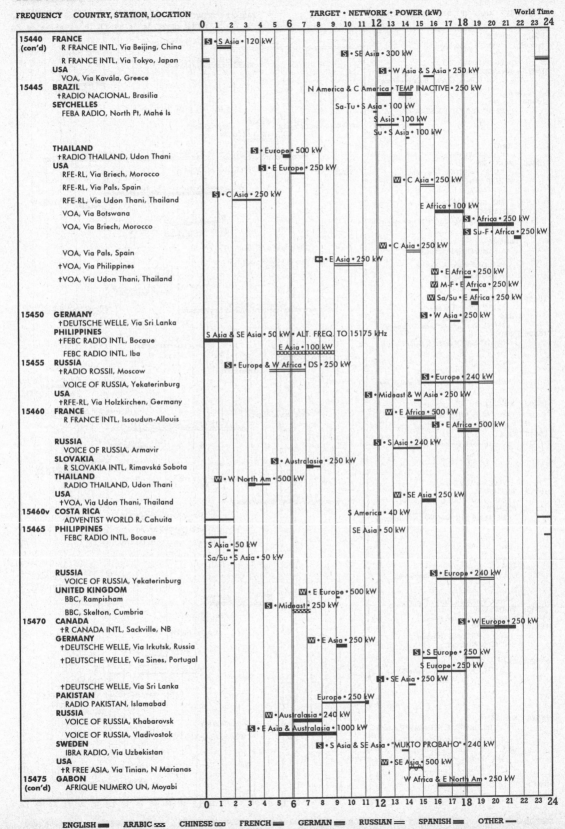

Frequency	Country, Station, Location	Target • Network • Power
15440 (con'd)	**FRANCE**	
	R FRANCE INTL, Via Beijing, China	S • S Asia • 120 kW
	R FRANCE INTL, Via Tokyo, Japan	S • SE Asia • 300 kW
	USA	
	VOA, Via Kavála, Greece	S • W Asia & S Asia • 250 kW
15445	**BRAZIL**	
	†RADIO NACIONAL, Brasilia	N America & C America • TEMP INACTIVE • 250 kW
	SEYCHELLES	
	FEBA RADIO, North Pt, Mahé Is	Sa-Tu • S Asia • 100 kW; S Asia • 100 kW; Su • S Asia • 100 kW
	THAILAND	
	†RADIO THAILAND, Udon Thani	S • Europe • 500 kW
	USA	
	RFE-RL, Via Briech, Morocco	S • E Europe • 250 kW
	RFE-RL, Via Pals, Spain	W • C Asia • 250 kW
	RFE-RL, Via Udon Thani, Thailand	S • C Asia • 250 kW
	VOA, Via Botswana	E Africa • 100 kW
	VOA, Via Briech, Morocco	S • Africa • 250 kW; Su-F • Africa • 250 kW
	VOA, Via Pals, Spain	W • C Asia • 250 kW
	†VOA, Via Philippines	☐ • E Asia • 250 kW
	†VOA, Via Udon Thani, Thailand	W • E Africa • 250 kW; W M-F • E Africa • 250 kW; W Sa/Su • E Africa • 250 kW
15450	**GERMANY**	
	†DEUTSCHE WELLE, Via Sri Lanka	S • W Asia • 250 kW
	PHILIPPINES	
	†FEBC RADIO INTL, Bocaue	S Asia & SE Asia • 50 kW • ALT. FREQ. TO 15175 kHz
	FEBC RADIO INTL, Iba	E Asia • 100 kW
15455	**RUSSIA**	
	†RADIO ROSSII, Moscow	S • Europe & W Africa • DS • 250 kW
	VOICE OF RUSSIA, Yekaterinburg	S • Europe • 240 kW
	USA	
	†RFE-RL, Via Holzkirchen, Germany	S • Mideast & W Asia • 250 kW
15460	**FRANCE**	
	R FRANCE INTL, Issoudun-Allouis	W • E Africa • 500 kW; S • E Africa • 500 kW
	RUSSIA	
	VOICE OF RUSSIA, Armavir	S • S Asia • 240 kW
	SLOVAKIA	
	R SLOVAKIA INTL, Rimavská Sobota	S • Australasia • 250 kW
	THAILAND	
	RADIO THAILAND, Udon Thani	W • W North Am • 500 kW
	USA	
	†VOA, Via Udon Thani, Thailand	W • SE Asia • 250 kW
15460v	**COSTA RICA**	
	ADVENTIST WORLD R, Cahuita	S America • 40 kW
15465	**PHILIPPINES**	
	FEBC RADIO INTL, Bocaue	SE Asia • 50 kW; S Asia • 50 kW; Sa/Su • S Asia • 50 kW
	RUSSIA	
	VOICE OF RUSSIA, Yekaterinburg	S • Europe • 240 kW
	UNITED KINGDOM	
	BBC, Rampisham	W • E Europe • 500 kW
	BBC, Skelton, Cumbria	S • Mideast • 250 kW
15470	**CANADA**	
	†R CANADA INTL, Sackville, NB	S • W Europe • 250 kW
	GERMANY	
	†DEUTSCHE WELLE, Via Irkutsk, Russia	W • E Asia • 250 kW
	†DEUTSCHE WELLE, Via Sines, Portugal	S • S Europe • 250 kW; S Europe • 250 kW
	†DEUTSCHE WELLE, Via Sri Lanka	S • SE Asia • 250 kW
	PAKISTAN	
	RADIO PAKISTAN, Islamabad	Europe • 250 kW
	RUSSIA	
	VOICE OF RUSSIA, Khabarovsk	W • Australasia • 240 kW
	VOICE OF RUSSIA, Vladivostok	S • E Asia & Australasia • 1000 kW
	SWEDEN	
	IBRA RADIO, Via Uzbekistan	S • S Asia & SE Asia • "MUKTO PROBAHO" • 240 kW
	USA	
	†R FREE ASIA, Via Tinian, N Marianas	W • SE Asia • 500 kW
15475 (con'd)	**GABON**	
	AFRIQUE NUMERO UN, Moyabi	W Africa & E North Am • 250 kW

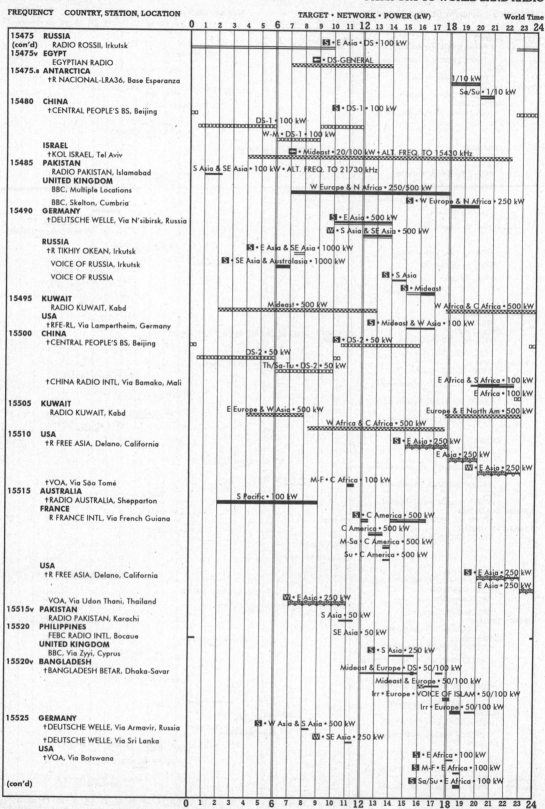

FREQUENCY   COUNTRY, STATION, LOCATION   TARGET • NETWORK • POWER (kW)   World Time

Frequency	Country, Station, Location	Target • Network • Power
15475	**RUSSIA**	
(con'd)	RADIO ROSSII, Irkutsk	S • E Asia • DS • 100 kW
15475v	**EGYPT**	
	EGYPTIAN RADIO	DS-GENERAL
15475.8	**ANTARCTICA**	
	†R NACIONAL-LRA36, Base Esperanza	1/10 kW • Sa/Su • 1/10 kW
15480	**CHINA**	
	†CENTRAL PEOPLE'S BS, Beijing	S • DS-1 • 100 kW • DS-1 • 100 kW • W-M • DS-1 • 100 kW
	ISRAEL	
	†KOL ISRAEL, Tel Aviv	Mideast • 20/100 kW • ALT. FREQ. TO 15430 kHz
15485	**PAKISTAN**	
	RADIO PAKISTAN, Islamabad	S Asia & SE Asia • 100 kW • ALT. FREQ. TO 21730 kHz
	UNITED KINGDOM	
	BBC, Multiple Locations	W Europe & N Africa • 250/500 kW
	BBC, Skelton, Cumbria	S • W Europe & N Africa • 250 kW
15490	**GERMANY**	
	†DEUTSCHE WELLE, Via N'sibirsk, Russia	S • E Asia • 500 kW • W • S Asia & SE Asia • 500 kW
	RUSSIA	
	†R TIKHIY OKEAN, Irkutsk	S • E Asia & SE Asia • 1000 kW
	VOICE OF RUSSIA, Irkutsk	S • SE Asia & Australasia • 1000 kW
	VOICE OF RUSSIA	S • S Asia • S • Mideast
15495	**KUWAIT**	
	RADIO KUWAIT, Kabd	Mideast • 500 kW • W Africa & C Africa • 500 kW
	USA	
	†RFE-RL, Via Lampertheim, Germany	S • Mideast & W Asia • 100 kW
15500	**CHINA**	
	†CENTRAL PEOPLE'S BS, Beijing	S • DS-2 • 50 kW • DS-2 • 50 kW • Th/Sa-Tu • DS-2 • 50 kW
	†CHINA RADIO INTL, Via Bamako, Mali	E Africa & S Africa • 100 kW • E Africa • 100 kW
15505	**KUWAIT**	
	RADIO KUWAIT, Kabd	E Europe & W Asia • 500 kW • Europe & E North Am • 500 kW • W Africa & C Africa • 500 kW
15510	**USA**	
	†R FREE ASIA, Delano, California	S • E Asia • 250 kW • E Asia • 250 kW • W • E Asia • 250 kW
	†VOA, Via São Tomé	M-F • C Africa • 100 kW
15515	**AUSTRALIA**	
	†RADIO AUSTRALIA, Shepparton	S Pacific • 100 kW
	FRANCE	
	R FRANCE INTL, Via French Guiana	S • C America • 500 kW • C America • 500 kW • M-Sa • C America • 500 kW • Su • C America • 500 kW
	USA	
	†R FREE ASIA, Delano, California	S • E Asia • 250 kW • E Asia • 250 kW
	VOA, Via Udon Thani, Thailand	W • E Asia • 250 kW
15515v	**PAKISTAN**	
	RADIO PAKISTAN, Karachi	S Asia • 50 kW
15520	**PHILIPPINES**	
	FEBC RADIO INTL, Bocaue	SE Asia • 50 kW
	UNITED KINGDOM	
	BBC, Via Zyyi, Cyprus	S • S Asia • 250 kW
15520v	**BANGLADESH**	
	†BANGLADESH BETAR, Dhaka-Savar	Mideast & Europe • DS • 50/100 kW • Mideast & Europe • 50/100 kW • Irr • Europe • VOICE OF ISLAM • 50/100 kW • Irr • Europe • 50/100 kW
15525	**GERMANY**	
	†DEUTSCHE WELLE, Via Armavir, Russia	S • W Asia & S Asia • 500 kW • W • SE Asia • 250 kW
	†DEUTSCHE WELLE, Via Sri Lanka	
	USA	
	†VOA, Via Botswana	S • E Africa • 100 kW • M-F • E Africa • 100 kW • S • Sa/Su • E Africa • 100 kW
(con'd)		

| FREQUENCY | COUNTRY, STATION, LOCATION | TARGET • NETWORK • POWER (kW) | World Time |

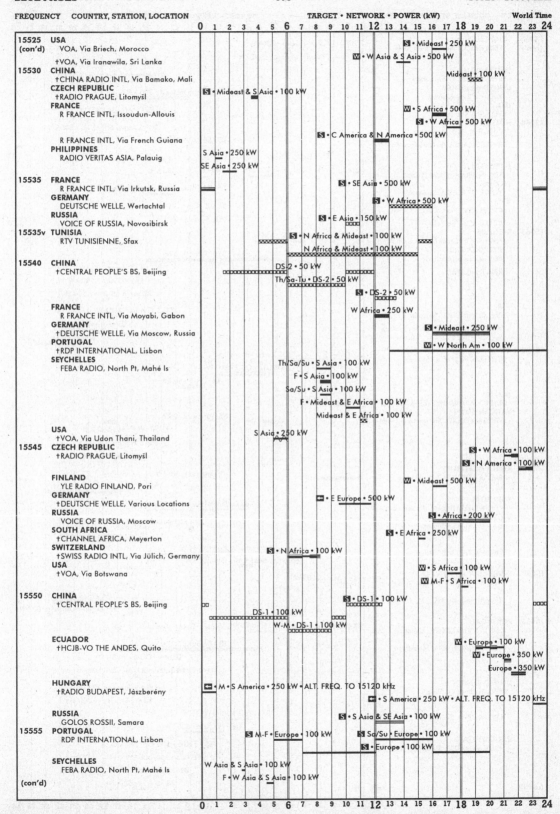

0 1 2 3 4 5 6 7 8 9 10 11 12 13 14 15 16 17 18 19 20 21 22 23 24

15525 USA
(con'd)   VOA, Via Briech, Morocco — S • Mideast • 250 kW
   †VOA, Via Iranawila, Sri Lanka — W • W Asia & S Asia • 500 kW
15530 CHINA
   †CHINA RADIO INTL, Via Bamako, Mali — Mideast • 100 kW
   CZECH REPUBLIC
   †RADIO PRAGUE, Litomyšl — S • Mideast & S Asia • 100 kW
   FRANCE
   R FRANCE INTL, Issoudun-Allouis — W • S Africa • 500 kW / S • W Africa • 500 kW / S • C America & N America • 500 kW
   R FRANCE INTL, Via French Guiana
   PHILIPPINES
   RADIO VERITAS ASIA, Palauig — S Asia • 250 kW / SE Asia • 250 kW

15535 FRANCE
   R FRANCE INTL, Via Irkutsk, Russia — S • SE Asia • 500 kW
   GERMANY
   DEUTSCHE WELLE, Wertachtal — S • W Africa • 500 kW
   RUSSIA
   VOICE OF RUSSIA, Novosibirsk — S • E Asia • 150 kW
15535v TUNISIA
   RTV TUNISIENNE, Sfax — S • N Africa & Mideast • 100 kW / N Africa & Mideast • 100 kW

15540 CHINA
   †CENTRAL PEOPLE'S BS, Beijing — DS-2 • 50 kW / Th/Sa-Tu • DS-2 • 50 kW / S • DS-2 • 50 kW
   FRANCE
   R FRANCE INTL, Via Moyabi, Gabon — W Africa • 250 kW
   GERMANY
   †DEUTSCHE WELLE, Via Moscow, Russia — S • Mideast • 250 kW
   PORTUGAL
   †RDP INTERNATIONAL, Lisbon — W • W North Am • 100 kW
   SEYCHELLES
   FEBA RADIO, North Pt, Mahé Is — Th/Sa/Su • S Asia • 100 kW / F • S Asia • 100 kW / Sa/Su • S Asia • 100 kW / F • Mideast & E Africa • 100 kW / Mideast & E Africa • 100 kW
   USA
   †VOA, Via Udon Thani, Thailand — S Asia • 250 kW
15545 CZECH REPUBLIC
   †RADIO PRAGUE, Litomyšl — S • W Africa • 100 kW / S • N America • 100 kW
   FINLAND
   YLE RADIO FINLAND, Pori — W • Mideast • 500 kW
   GERMANY
   †DEUTSCHE WELLE, Various Locations — ☜ • E Europe • 500 kW
   RUSSIA
   VOICE OF RUSSIA, Moscow — S • Africa • 200 kW
   SOUTH AFRICA
   †CHANNEL AFRICA, Meyerton — S • E Africa • 250 kW
   SWITZERLAND
   †SWISS RADIO INTL, Via Jülich, Germany — S • N Africa • 100 kW
   USA
   †VOA, Via Botswana — W • S Africa • 100 kW / W M-F • S Africa • 100 kW
15550 CHINA
   †CENTRAL PEOPLE'S BS, Beijing — S • DS-1 • 100 kW / DS-1 • 100 kW / W-M • DS-1 • 100 kW
   ECUADOR
   †HCJB-VO THE ANDES, Quito — W • Europe • 100 kW / W • Europe • 350 kW / Europe • 350 kW
   HUNGARY
   †RADIO BUDAPEST, Jászberény — ☜ • M • S America • 250 kW • ALT. FREQ. TO 15120 kHz / ☜ • S America • 250 kW • ALT. FREQ. TO 15120 kHz
   RUSSIA
   GOLOS ROSSII, Samara — S • S Asia & SE Asia • 100 kW
15555 PORTUGAL
   RDP INTERNATIONAL, Lisbon — S M-F • Europe • 100 kW / S Sa/Su • Europe • 100 kW / S • Europe • 100 kW
   SEYCHELLES
   FEBA RADIO, North Pt, Mahé Is — W Asia & S Asia • 100 kW / F • W Asia & S Asia • 100 kW
(con'd)

0 1 2 3 4 5 6 7 8 9 10 11 12 13 14 15 16 17 18 19 20 21 22 23 24

ENGLISH ▬ ARABIC ⋙ CHINESE ▢▢▢ FRENCH ▬ GERMAN ▬ RUSSIAN ▬ SPANISH ▬ OTHER ▬

FREQUENCY	COUNTRY, STATION, LOCATION	TARGET • NETWORK • POWER (kW)	World Time

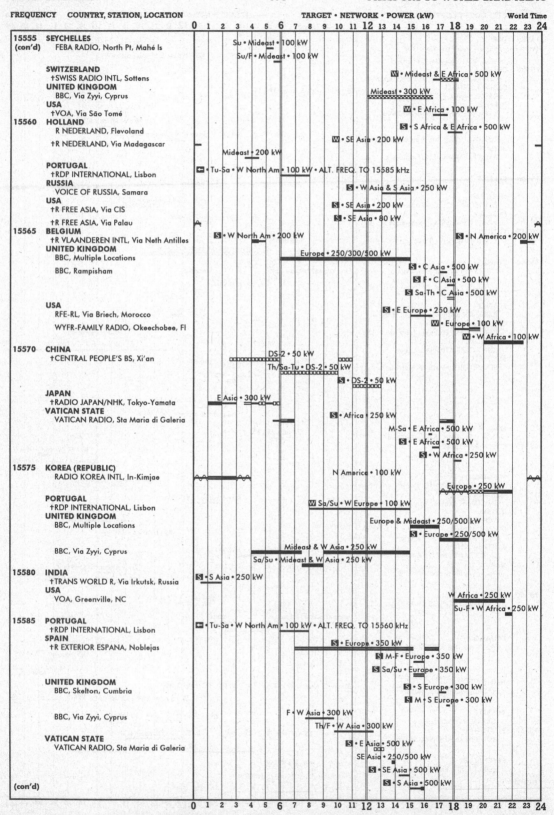

- **15555 (con'd)** SEYCHELLES
  - FEBA RADIO, North Pt, Mahé Is — Su • Mideast • 100 kW; Su/F • Mideast • 100 kW
- SWITZERLAND
  - †SWISS RADIO INTL, Sottens — W • Mideast & E Africa • 500 kW
- UNITED KINGDOM
  - BBC, Via Zyyi, Cyprus — Mideast • 300 kW
- USA
  - †VOA, Via São Tomé — W • E Africa • 100 kW
- **15560** HOLLAND
  - R NEDERLAND, Flevoland — S • S Africa & E Africa • 500 kW; W • SE Asia • 200 kW
  - †R NEDERLAND, Via Madagascar — Mideast • 200 kW
- PORTUGAL
  - †RDP INTERNATIONAL, Lisbon — Tu-Sa • W North Am • 100 kW • ALT. FREQ. TO 15585 kHz
- RUSSIA
  - VOICE OF RUSSIA, Samara — S • W Asia & S Asia • 250 kW
- USA
  - †R FREE ASIA, Via CIS — S • SE Asia • 200 kW
  - †R FREE ASIA, Via Palau — S • SE Asia • 80 kW
- **15565** BELGIUM
  - †R VLAANDEREN INTL, Via Neth Antilles — S • W North Am • 200 kW; S • N America • 200 kW
- UNITED KINGDOM
  - BBC, Multiple Locations — Europe • 250/300/500 kW
  - BBC, Rampisham — S • C Asia • 500 kW; S F • C Asia • 500 kW; S Sa-Th • C Asia • 500 kW
- USA
  - RFE-RL, Via Briech, Morocco — S • E Europe • 250 kW
  - WYFR-FAMILY RADIO, Okeechobee, Fl — W • Europe • 100 kW; W • W Africa • 100 kW
- **15570** CHINA
  - †CENTRAL PEOPLE'S BS, Xi'an — DS-2 • 50 kW; Th/Sa-Tu • DS-2 • 50 kW; S • DS-2 • 50 kW
- JAPAN
  - †RADIO JAPAN/NHK, Tokyo-Yamata — E Asia • 300 kW
- VATICAN STATE
  - VATICAN RADIO, Sta Maria di Galeria — S • Africa • 250 kW; M-Sa • E Africa • 500 kW; S • E Africa • 500 kW; S • W Africa • 250 kW
- **15575** KOREA (REPUBLIC)
  - RADIO KOREA INTL, In-Kimjae — N America • 100 kW; Europe • 250 kW
- PORTUGAL
  - †RDP INTERNATIONAL, Lisbon — W Sa/Su • W Europe • 100 kW
- UNITED KINGDOM
  - BBC, Multiple Locations — Europe & Mideast • 250/500 kW; S • Europe • 250/500 kW
  - BBC, Via Zyyi, Cyprus — Mideast & W Asia • 250 kW; Sa/Su • Mideast & W Asia • 250 kW
- **15580** INDIA
  - †TRANS WORLD R, Via Irkutsk, Russia — S • S Asia • 250 kW
- USA
  - VOA, Greenville, NC — W Africa • 250 kW; Su-F • W Africa • 250 kW
- **15585** PORTUGAL
  - †RDP INTERNATIONAL, Lisbon — Tu-Sa • W North Am • 100 kW • ALT. FREQ. TO 15560 kHz
- SPAIN
  - †R EXTERIOR ESPANA, Noblejas — S • Europe • 350 kW; S M-F • Europe • 350 kW; S Sa/Su • Europe • 350 kW
- UNITED KINGDOM
  - BBC, Skelton, Cumbria — S • S Europe • 300 kW; S M • S Europe • 300 kW
  - BBC, Via Zyyi, Cyprus — F • W Asia • 300 kW; Th/F • W Asia • 300 kW
- VATICAN STATE
  - VATICAN RADIO, Sta Maria di Galeria — S • E Asia • 500 kW; SE Asia • 250/500 kW; S • SE Asia • 500 kW; S • S Asia • 500 kW
- **(con'd)**

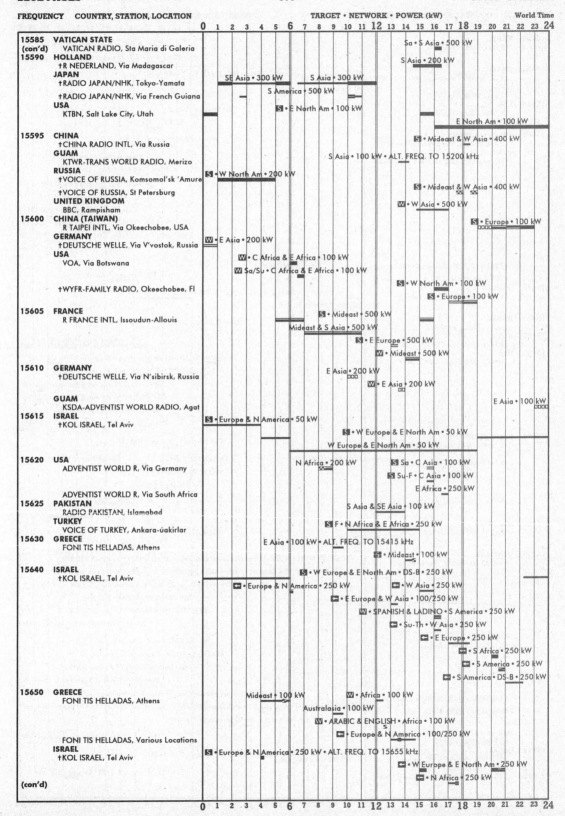

FREQUENCY	COUNTRY, STATION, LOCATION	TARGET • NETWORK • POWER (kW)
15585 (con'd)	VATICAN STATE VATICAN RADIO, Sta Maria di Galeria	Sa • S Asia • 500 kW
15590	HOLLAND †R NEDERLAND, Via Madagascar	S Asia • 200 kW
	JAPAN †RADIO JAPAN/NHK, Tokyo-Yamata	SE Asia • 300 kW S Asia • 300 kW
	†RADIO JAPAN/NHK, Via French Guiana	S America • 500 kW
	USA KTBN, Salt Lake City, Utah	S • E North Am • 100 kW E North Am • 100 kW
15595	CHINA †CHINA RADIO INTL, Via Russia	S • Mideast & W Asia • 400 kW
	GUAM KTWR-TRANS WORLD RADIO, Merizo	S Asia • 100 kW • ALT. FREQ. TO 15200 kHz
	RUSSIA †VOICE OF RUSSIA, Komsomol'sk 'Amure	S • W North Am • 200 kW
	†VOICE OF RUSSIA, St Petersburg	S • Mideast & W Asia • 400 kW
	UNITED KINGDOM BBC, Rampisham	W • W Asia • 500 kW
15600	CHINA (TAIWAN) R TAIPEI INTL, Via Okeechobee, USA	S • Europe • 100 kW
	GERMANY †DEUTSCHE WELLE, Via V'vostok, Russia	W • E Asia • 200 kW
	USA VOA, Via Botswana	W • C Africa & E Africa • 100 kW W • Sa/Su • C Africa & E Africa • 100 kW
	†WYFR-FAMILY RADIO, Okeechobee, Fl	S • W North Am • 100 kW S • Europe • 100 kW
15605	FRANCE R FRANCE INTL, Issoudun-Allouis	S • Mideast • 500 kW Mideast & S Asia • 500 kW S • E Europe • 500 kW W • Mideast • 500 kW
15610	GERMANY †DEUTSCHE WELLE, Via N'sibirsk, Russia	E Asia • 200 kW W • E Asia • 200 kW
	GUAM KSDA-ADVENTIST WORLD RADIO, Agat	E Asia • 100 kW
15615	ISRAEL †KOL ISRAEL, Tel Aviv	S • Europe & N America • 50 kW S • W Europe & E North Am • 50 kW W Europe & E North Am • 50 kW
15620	USA ADVENTIST WORLD R, Via Germany	N Africa • 200 kW S • Sa • C Asia • 100 kW S • Su-F • C Asia • 100 kW E Africa • 250 kW
	ADVENTIST WORLD R, Via South Africa	
15625	PAKISTAN RADIO PAKISTAN, Islamabad	S Asia & SE Asia • 100 kW
	TURKEY VOICE OF TURKEY, Ankara-úakirlar	S • F • N Africa & E Africa • 250 kW
15630	GREECE FONI TIS HELLADAS, Athens	E Asia • 100 kW • ALT. FREQ. TO 15415 kHz S • Mideast • 100 kW
15640	ISRAEL †KOL ISRAEL, Tel Aviv	S • W Europe & E North Am • DS-B • 250 kW • Europe & N America • 250 kW • W Asia • 250 kW • E Europe & W Asia • 100/250 kW W • SPANISH & LADINO • S America • 250 kW • Su-Th • W Asia • 250 kW • E Europe • 250 kW • S Africa • 250 kW • S America • 250 kW • S America • DS-B • 250 kW
15650	GREECE FONI TIS HELLADAS, Athens	Mideast • 100 kW W • Africa • 100 kW Australasia • 100 kW W • ARABIC & ENGLISH • Africa • 100 kW • Europe & N America • 100/250 kW
	FONI TIS HELLADAS, Various Locations	
	ISRAEL †KOL ISRAEL, Tel Aviv	S • Europe & N America • 250 kW • ALT. FREQ. TO 15655 kHz • W Europe & E North Am • 250 kW • N Africa • 250 kW
(con'd)		

ENGLISH ▬   ARABIC ⧉   CHINESE □□□   FRENCH ▭   GERMAN ▬   RUSSIAN ═   SPANISH ▬   OTHER —

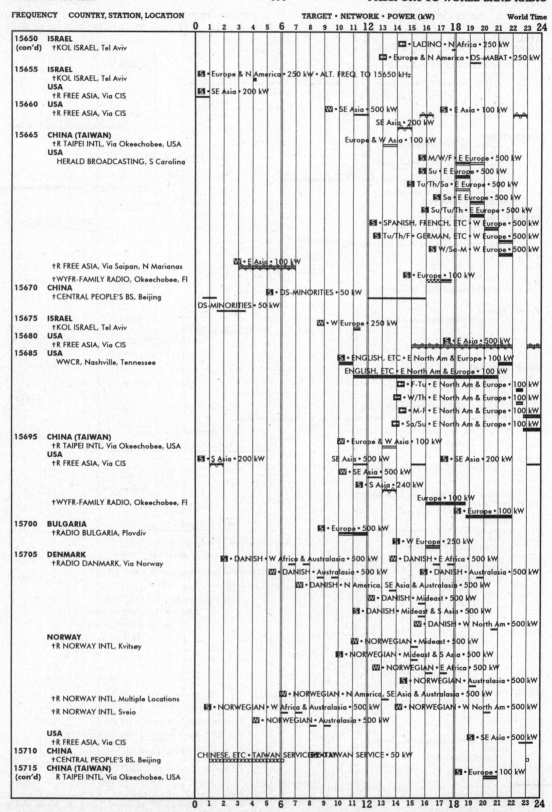

FREQUENCY   COUNTRY, STATION, LOCATION   TARGET • NETWORK • POWER (kW)   World Time

Frequency	Country, Station, Location	Target • Network • Power
15650 (con'd)	**ISRAEL** †KOL ISRAEL, Tel Aviv	• LADINO • N Africa • 250 kW
		• Europe & N America • DS-MABAT • 250 kW
15655	**ISRAEL** †KOL ISRAEL, Tel Aviv	S • Europe & N America • 250 kW • ALT. FREQ. TO 15650 kHz
	USA †R FREE ASIA, Via CIS	S • SE Asia • 200 kW
15660	**USA** †R FREE ASIA, Via CIS	W • SE Asia • 500 kW • E Asia • 100 kW
		SE Asia • 200 kW
15665	**CHINA (TAIWAN)** †R TAIPEI INTL, Via Okeechobee, USA	Europe & W Asia • 100 kW
	USA HERALD BROADCASTING, S Carolina	S • M/W/F • E Europe • 500 kW
		S • Su • E Europe • 500 kW
		S • Tu/Th/Sa • E Europe • 500 kW
		S • Sa • E Europe • 500 kW
		S • Su/Tu/Th • E Europe • 500 kW
		S • SPANISH, FRENCH, ETC • W Europe • 500 kW
		S • Tu/Th/F • GERMAN, ETC • W Europe • 500 kW
		S • W/Sa-M • W Europe • 500 kW
	†R FREE ASIA, Via Saipan, N Marianas	W • E Asia • 100 kW
	†WYFR-FAMILY RADIO, Okeechobee, Fl	S • Europe • 100 kW
15670	**CHINA** †CENTRAL PEOPLE'S BS, Beijing	S • DS-MINORITIES • 50 kW
		DS-MINORITIES • 50 kW
15675	**ISRAEL** †KOL ISRAEL, Tel Aviv	W • W Europe • 250 kW
15680	**USA** †R FREE ASIA, Via CIS	S • E Asia • 500 kW
15685	**USA** WWCR, Nashville, Tennessee	S • ENGLISH, ETC • E North Am & Europe • 100 kW
		ENGLISH, ETC • E North Am & Europe • 100 kW
		• F-Tu • E North Am & Europe • 100 kW
		• W/Th • E North Am & Europe • 100 kW
		• M-F • E North Am & Europe • 100 kW
		• Sa/Su • E North Am & Europe • 100 kW
15695	**CHINA (TAIWAN)** †R TAIPEI INTL, Via Okeechobee, USA	W • Europe & W Asia • 100 kW
	USA †R FREE ASIA, Via CIS	S • S Asia • 200 kW SE Asia • 500 kW S • SE Asia • 200 kW
		W • SE Asia • 500 kW
		S • S Asia • 240 kW
	†WYFR-FAMILY RADIO, Okeechobee, Fl	Europe • 100 kW
		S • Europe • 100 kW
15700	**BULGARIA** †RADIO BULGARIA, Plovdiv	S • Europe • 500 kW
		S • W Europe • 250 kW
15705	**DENMARK** †RADIO DANMARK, Via Norway	S • DANISH • W Africa & Australasia • 500 kW W • DANISH • E Africa • 500 kW
		W • DANISH • Australasia • 500 kW S • DANISH • Australasia • 500 kW
		W • DANISH • N America, SE Asia & Australasia • 500 kW
		W • DANISH • Mideast • 500 kW
		S • DANISH • Mideast & S Asia • 500 kW
		W • DANISH • W North Am • 500 kW
	NORWAY †R NORWAY INTL, Kvitsøy	W • NORWEGIAN • Mideast • 500 kW
		S • NORWEGIAN • Mideast & S Asia • 500 kW
		W • NORWEGIAN • E Africa • 500 kW
		S • NORWEGIAN • Australasia • 500 kW
	†R NORWAY INTL, Multiple Locations	W • NORWEGIAN • N America, SE Asia & Australasia • 500 kW
	†R NORWAY INTL, Sveio	S • NORWEGIAN • W Africa & Australasia • 500 kW W • NORWEGIAN • W North Am • 500 kW
		W • NORWEGIAN • Australasia • 500 kW
	USA †R FREE ASIA, Via CIS	S • SE Asia • 500 kW
15710	**CHINA** †CENTRAL PEOPLE'S BS, Beijing	CHINESE, ETC • TAIWAN SERVICE • 50 kW TAIWAN SERVICE • 50 kW
15715 (con'd)	**CHINA (TAIWAN)** R TAIPEI INTL, Via Okeechobee, USA	S • Europe • 100 kW

FREQUENCY   COUNTRY, STATION, LOCATION   TARGET • NETWORK • POWER (kW)   World Time

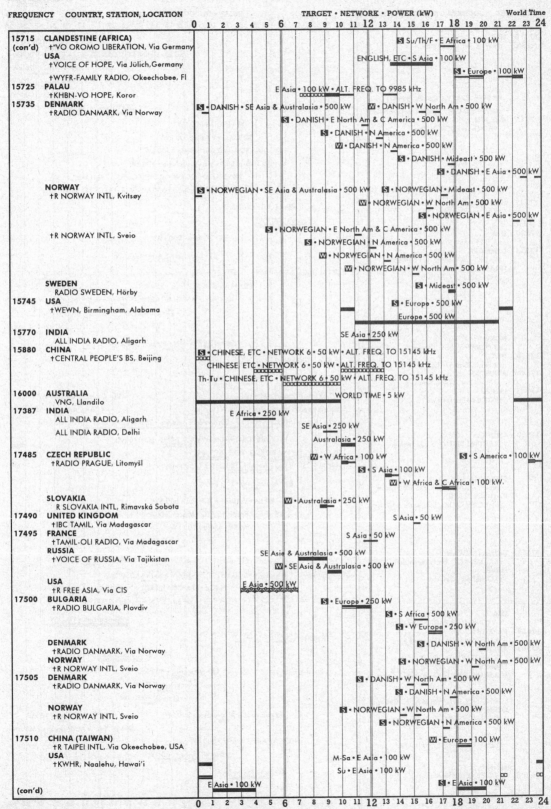

Frequency	Country, Station, Location	Target • Network • Power
15715 (con'd)	**CLANDESTINE (AFRICA)** †"VO OROMO LIBERATION, Via Germany	S • Su/TH/F • E Africa • 100 kW
	USA †VOICE OF HOPE, Via Jülich, Germany	ENGLISH, ETC • S Asia • 100 kW
	†WYFR-FAMILY RADIO, Okeechobee, Fl	S • Europe • 100 kW
15725	**PALAU** †KHBN-VO HOPE, Koror	E Asia • 100 kW • ALT. FREQ. TO 9985 kHz
15735	**DENMARK** †RADIO DANMARK, Via Norway	S • DANISH • SE Asia & Australasia • 500 kW / W • DANISH • W North Am • 500 kW
		S • DANISH • E North Am & C America • 500 kW
		S • DANISH • N America • 500 kW
		W • DANISH • N America • 500 kW
		S • DANISH • Mideast • 500 kW
		S • DANISH • E Asia • 500 kW
	NORWAY †R NORWAY INTL, Kvitsøy	S • NORWEGIAN • SE Asia & Australasia • 500 kW / S • NORWEGIAN • Mideast • 500 kW
		W • NORWEGIAN • W North Am • 500 kW
		S • NORWEGIAN • E Asia • 500 kW
	†R NORWAY INTL, Sveio	S • NORWEGIAN • E North Am & C America • 500 kW
		S • NORWEGIAN • N America • 500 kW
		W • NORWEGIAN • N America • 500 kW
		W • NORWEGIAN • W North Am • 500 kW
	SWEDEN RADIO SWEDEN, Hörby	S • Mideast • 500 kW
15745	**USA** †WEWN, Birmingham, Alabama	S • Europe • 500 kW / Europe • 500 kW
15770	**INDIA** ALL INDIA RADIO, Aligarh	SE Asia • 250 kW
15880	**CHINA** †CENTRAL PEOPLE'S BS, Beijing	S • CHINESE, ETC • NETWORK 6 • 50 kW • ALT. FREQ. TO 15145 kHz
		CHINESE, ETC • NETWORK 6 • 50 kW • ALT. FREQ. TO 15145 kHz
		Th-Tu • CHINESE, ETC • NETWORK 6 • 50 kW • ALT. FREQ. TO 15145 kHz
16000	**AUSTRALIA** VNG, Llandilo	WORLD TIME • 5 kW
17387	**INDIA** ALL INDIA RADIO, Aligarh	E Africa • 250 kW
	ALL INDIA RADIO, Delhi	SE Asia • 250 kW
		Australasia • 250 kW
17485	**CZECH REPUBLIC** †RADIO PRAGUE, Litomyšl	W • W Africa • 100 kW / S • S America • 100 kW
		S • S Asia • 100 kW
		W • W Africa & C Africa • 100 kW
	SLOVAKIA R SLOVAKIA INTL, Rimavská Sobota	W • Australasia • 250 kW
17490	**UNITED KINGDOM** †IBC TAMIL, Via Madagascar	S Asia • 50 kW
17495	**FRANCE** †TAMIL-OLI RADIO, Via Madagascar	S Asia • 50 kW
	RUSSIA †VOICE OF RUSSIA, Via Tajikistan	SE Asia & Australasia • 500 kW
		W • SE Asia & Australasia • 500 kW
	USA †R FREE ASIA, Via CIS	E Asia • 500 kW
17500	**BULGARIA** †RADIO BULGARIA, Plovdiv	S • Europe • 250 kW
		S • S Africa • 500 kW
		S • W Europe • 250 kW
	DENMARK †RADIO DANMARK, Via Norway	S • DANISH • W North Am • 500 kW
	NORWAY †R NORWAY INTL, Sveio	S • NORWEGIAN • W North Am • 500 kW
17505	**DENMARK** †RADIO DANMARK, Via Norway	S • DANISH • W North Am • 500 kW
		S • DANISH • N America • 500 kW
	NORWAY †R NORWAY INTL, Sveio	S • NORWEGIAN • W North Am • 500 kW
		S • NORWEGIAN • N America • 500 kW
17510	**CHINA (TAIWAN)** †R TAIPEI INTL, Via Okeechobee, USA	W • Europe • 100 kW
	USA †KWHR, Naalehu, Hawai'i	M-Sa • E Asia • 100 kW
		Su • E Asia • 100 kW
		S • E Asia • 100 kW
(con'd)		E Asia • 100 kW

ENGLISH ▬   ARABIC ⌇⌇⌇   CHINESE ▫▫▫   FRENCH ══   GERMAN ══   RUSSIAN ══   SPANISH ══   OTHER ▬

| FREQUENCY | COUNTRY, STATION, LOCATION | TARGET • NETWORK • POWER (kW) | World Time |

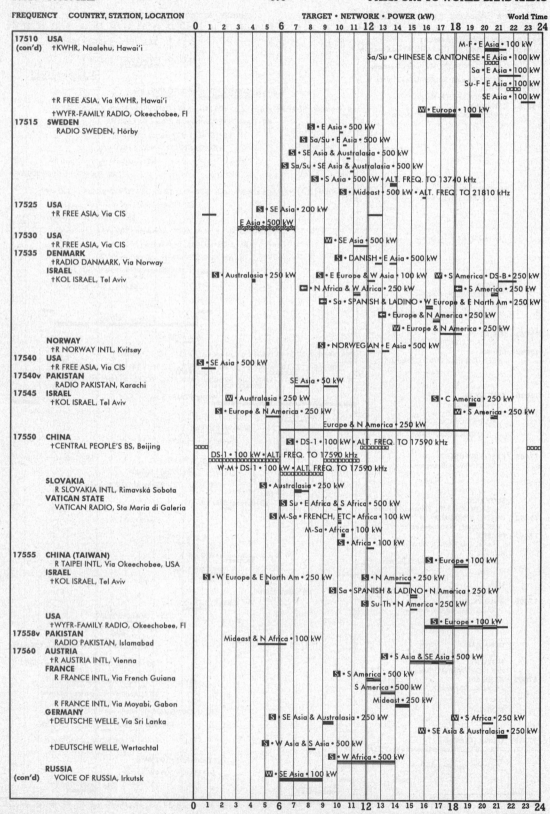

17510
(con'd)   †KWHR, Naalehu, Hawai'i — USA
- M-F • E Asia • 100 kW
- Sa/Su • CHINESE & CANTONESE • E Asia • 100 kW
- Sa • E Asia • 100 kW
- Su-F • E Asia • 100 kW
- SE Asia • 100 kW

†R FREE ASIA, Via KWHR, Hawai'i
†WYFR-FAMILY RADIO, Okeechobee, Fl
- W • Europe • 100 kW

17515 SWEDEN
RADIO SWEDEN, Hörby
- S • E Asia • 500 kW
- Sa/Su • E Asia • 500 kW
- S • SE Asia & Australasia • 500 kW
- Sa/Su • SE Asia & Australasia • 500 kW
- S • S Asia • 500 kW • ALT. FREQ. TO 13740 kHz
- S • Mideast • 500 kW • ALT. FREQ. TO 21810 kHz

17525 USA
†R FREE ASIA, Via CIS
- S • SE Asia • 200 kW
- E Asia • 500 kW

17530 USA
†R FREE ASIA, Via CIS
- W • SE Asia • 500 kW

17535 DENMARK
†RADIO DANMARK, Via Norway
- S • DANISH • E Asia • 500 kW

ISRAEL
†KOL ISRAEL, Tel Aviv
- S • Australasia • 250 kW
- S • E Europe & W Asia • 100 kW
- W • S America • DS-B • 250 kW
- N Africa & W Africa • 250 kW
- S America • 250 kW
- Sa • SPANISH & LADINO • W Europe & E North Am • 250 kW
- Europe & N America • 250 kW
- W • Europe & N America • 250 kW

NORWAY
†R NORWAY INTL, Kvitsøy
- S • NORWEGIAN • E Asia • 500 kW

17540 USA
†R FREE ASIA, Via CIS
- S • SE Asia • 500 kW

17540v PAKISTAN
RADIO PAKISTAN, Karachi
- SE Asia • 50 kW

17545 ISRAEL
†KOL ISRAEL, Tel Aviv
- W • Australasia • 250 kW
- S • C America • 250 kW
- S • Europe & N America • 250 kW
- W • S America • 250 kW
- Europe & N America • 250 kW

17550 CHINA
†CENTRAL PEOPLE'S BS, Beijing
- S • DS-1 • 100 kW • ALT. FREQ. TO 17590 kHz
- DS-1 • 100 kW • ALT. FREQ. TO 17590 kHz
- W-M • DS-1 • 100 kW • ALT. FREQ. TO 17590 kHz

SLOVAKIA
R SLOVAKIA INTL, Rimavská Sobota
- S • Australasia • 250 kW

VATICAN STATE
VATICAN RADIO, Sta Maria di Galeria
- S • Su • E Africa & S Africa • 500 kW
- S • M-Sa • FRENCH, ETC • Africa • 100 kW
- M-Sa • Africa • 100 kW
- S • Africa • 100 kW

17555 CHINA (TAIWAN)
R TAIPEI INTL, Via Okeechobee, USA
- S • Europe • 100 kW

ISRAEL
†KOL ISRAEL, Tel Aviv
- S • W Europe & E North Am • 250 kW
- S • N America • 250 kW
- S • Sa • SPANISH & LADINO • N America • 250 kW
- S • Su-Th • N America • 250 kW

USA
†WYFR-FAMILY RADIO, Okeechobee, Fl
- S • Europe • 100 kW

17558v PAKISTAN
RADIO PAKISTAN, Islamabad
- Mideast & N Africa • 100 kW

17560 AUSTRIA
†R AUSTRIA INTL, Vienna
- S • S Asia & SE Asia • 500 kW

FRANCE
R FRANCE INTL, Via French Guiana
- S • S America • 500 kW
- S America • 500 kW
- Mideast • 250 kW

R FRANCE INTL, Via Moyabi, Gabon

GERMANY
†DEUTSCHE WELLE, Via Sri Lanka
- S • SE Asia & Australasia • 250 kW
- W • S Africa • 250 kW
- W • SE Asia & Australasia • 250 kW

†DEUTSCHE WELLE, Wertachtal
- S • W Asia & S Asia • 500 kW
- S • W Africa • 500 kW

RUSSIA
(con'd)   VOICE OF RUSSIA, Irkutsk
- W • SE Asia • 100 kW

FREQUENCY   COUNTRY, STATION, LOCATION   TARGET • NETWORK • POWER (kW)   World Time

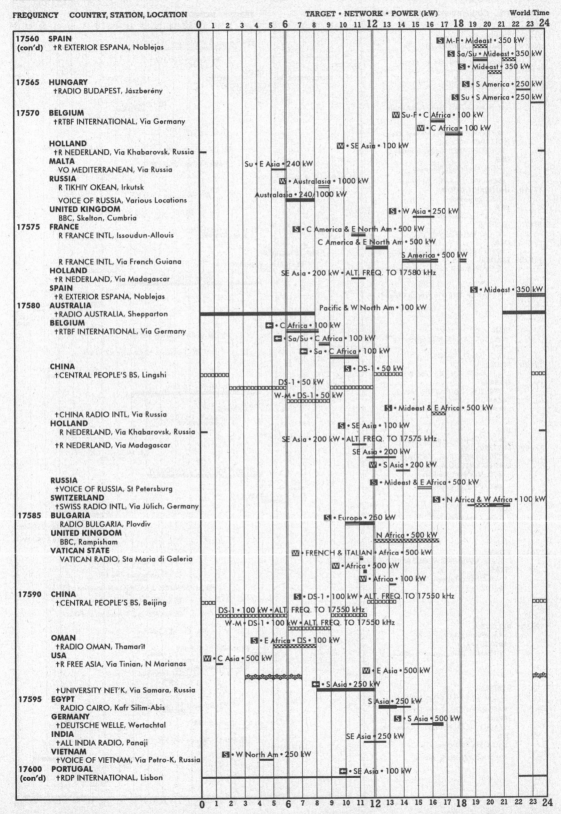

Frequency	Country, Station, Location	Target • Network • Power
17560 (con'd)	**SPAIN** †R EXTERIOR ESPANA, Noblejas	S • M-F • Mideast • 350 kW / S • Sa/Su • Mideast • 350 kW / S • Mideast • 350 kW
17565	**HUNGARY** †RADIO BUDAPEST, Jászberény	S • S America • 250 kW / S • Su • S America • 250 kW
17570	**BELGIUM** †RTBF INTERNATIONAL, Via Germany	W • Su-F • C Africa • 100 kW / W • C Africa • 100 kW
	HOLLAND †R NEDERLAND, Via Khabarovsk, Russia	W • SE Asia • 100 kW
	MALTA VO MEDITERRANEAN, Via Russia	Su • E Asia • 240 kW
	RUSSIA R TIKHIY OKEAN, Irkutsk	W • Australasia • 1000 kW
	VOICE OF RUSSIA, Various Locations	Australasia • 240/1000 kW
	UNITED KINGDOM BBC, Skelton, Cumbria	S • W Asia • 250 kW
17575	**FRANCE** R FRANCE INTL, Issoudun-Allouis	S • C America & E North Am • 500 kW / C America & E North Am • 500 kW / S America • 500 kW
	R FRANCE INTL, Via French Guiana	
	HOLLAND †R NEDERLAND, Via Madagascar	SE Asia • 200 kW • ALT. FREQ. TO 17580 kHz
	SPAIN †R EXTERIOR ESPANA, Noblejas	S • Mideast • 350 kW
17580	**AUSTRALIA** †RADIO AUSTRALIA, Shepparton	Pacific & W North Am • 100 kW
	BELGIUM †RTBF INTERNATIONAL, Via Germany	• C Africa • 100 kW / • Sa/Su • C Africa • 100 kW / • Sa • C Africa • 100 kW
	CHINA †CENTRAL PEOPLE'S BS, Lingshi	S • DS-1 • 50 kW / DS-1 • 50 kW / W-M • DS-1 • 50 kW
	†CHINA RADIO INTL, Via Russia	S • Mideast & E Africa • 500 kW
	HOLLAND R NEDERLAND, Via Khabarovsk, Russia	S • SE Asia • 100 kW / SE Asia • 200 kW • ALT. FREQ. TO 17575 kHz
	†R NEDERLAND, Via Madagascar	SE Asia • 200 kW / W • S Asia • 200 kW
	RUSSIA †VOICE OF RUSSIA, St Petersburg	S • Mideast & E Africa • 500 kW
	SWITZERLAND †SWISS RADIO INTL, Via Jülich, Germany	S • N Africa & W Africa • 100 kW
17585	**BULGARIA** RADIO BULGARIA, Plovdiv	S • Europe • 250 kW
	UNITED KINGDOM BBC, Rampisham	N Africa • 500 kW
	VATICAN STATE VATICAN RADIO, Sta Maria di Galeria	W • FRENCH & ITALIAN • Africa • 500 kW / W • Africa • 500 kW / W • Africa • 100 kW
17590	**CHINA** †CENTRAL PEOPLE'S BS, Beijing	S • DS-1 • 100 kW • ALT. FREQ. TO 17550 kHz / DS-1 • 100 kW • ALT. FREQ. TO 17550 kHz / W-M • DS-1 • 100 kW • ALT. FREQ. TO 17550 kHz
	OMAN †RADIO OMAN, Thamarīt	S • E Africa • DS • 100 kW
	USA †R FREE ASIA, Via Tinian, N Marianas	W • C Asia • 500 kW / W • E Asia • 500 kW
	†UNIVERSITY NET'K, Via Samara, Russia	• S Asia • 250 kW
17595	**EGYPT** RADIO CAIRO, Kafr Silim-Abis	S Asia • 250 kW
	GERMANY †DEUTSCHE WELLE, Wertachtal	S • S Asia • 500 kW
	INDIA †ALL INDIA RADIO, Panaji	SE Asia • 250 kW
	VIETNAM †VOICE OF VIETNAM, Via Petro-K, Russia	S • W North Am • 250 kW
17600 (con'd)	**PORTUGAL** †RDP INTERNATIONAL, Lisbon	• SE Asia • 100 kW

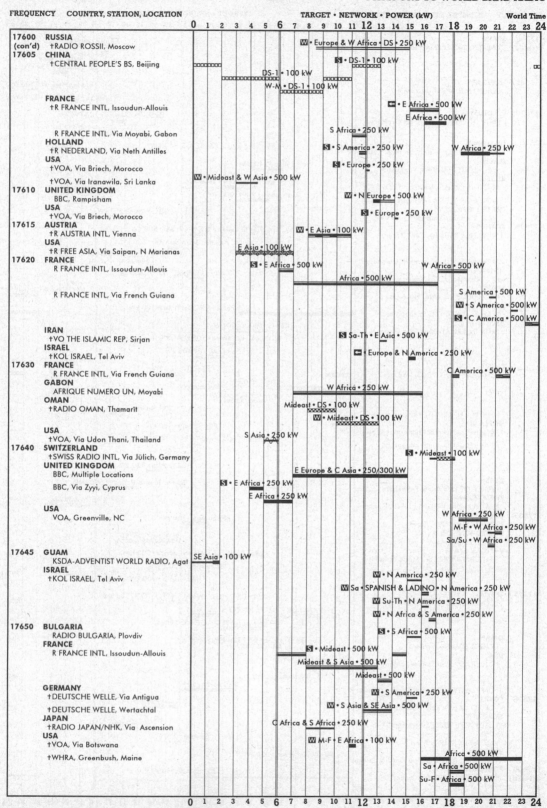

FREQUENCY   COUNTRY, STATION, LOCATION   TARGET • NETWORK • POWER (kW)   World Time

Frequency	Country, Station, Location	Target • Network • Power
17600 (con'd)	RUSSIA †RADIO ROSSII, Moscow	W • Europe & W Africa • DS • 250 kW
17605	CHINA †CENTRAL PEOPLE'S BS, Beijing	S • DS-1 • 100 kW / DS-1 • 100 kW / W-M • DS-1 • 100 kW
	FRANCE †R FRANCE INTL, Issoudun-Allouis	E Africa • 500 kW / E Africa • 500 kW
	R FRANCE INTL, Via Moyabi, Gabon	S Africa • 250 kW
	HOLLAND †R NEDERLAND, Via Neth Antilles	S • S America • 250 kW / W Africa • 250 kW
	USA †VOA, Via Briech, Morocco	S • Europe • 250 kW
	†VOA, Via Iranawila, Sri Lanka	W • Mideast & W Asia • 500 kW
17610	UNITED KINGDOM BBC, Rampisham	W • N Europe • 500 kW
	USA †VOA, Via Briech, Morocco	S • Europe • 250 kW
17615	AUSTRIA †R AUSTRIA INTL, Vienna	W • E Asia • 100 kW
	USA †R FREE ASIA, Via Saipan, N Marianas	E Asia • 100 kW
17620	FRANCE R FRANCE INTL, Issoudun-Allouis	S • E Africa • 500 kW / W Africa • 500 kW / Africa • 500 kW
	R FRANCE INTL, Via French Guiana	S America • 500 kW / W • S America • 500 kW / S • C America • 500 kW
	IRAN †VO THE ISLAMIC REP, Sirjan	S • Sa-Th • E Asia • 500 kW
	ISRAEL †KOL ISRAEL, Tel Aviv	Europe & N America • 250 kW
17630	FRANCE R FRANCE INTL, Via French Guiana	C America • 500 kW
	GABON AFRIQUE NUMERO UN, Moyabi	W Africa • 250 kW
	OMAN †RADIO OMAN, Thamarit	Mideast • DS • 100 kW / W • Mideast • DS • 100 kW
	USA †VOA, Via Udon Thani, Thailand	S Asia • 250 kW
17640	SWITZERLAND †SWISS RADIO INTL, Via Jülich, Germany	S • Mideast • 100 kW
	UNITED KINGDOM BBC, Multiple Locations	E Europe & C Asia • 250/300 kW
	BBC, Via Zyyi, Cyprus	S • E Africa • 250 kW / E Africa • 250 kW
	USA VOA, Greenville, NC	W Africa • 250 kW / M-F • W Africa • 250 kW / Sa/Su • W Africa • 250 kW
17645	GUAM KSDA-ADVENTIST WORLD RADIO, Agat	SE Asia • 100 kW
	ISRAEL †KOL ISRAEL, Tel Aviv	W • N America • 250 kW / W Sa • SPANISH & LADINO • N America • 250 kW / W Su-Th • N America • 250 kW / W • N Africa & S America • 250 kW
17650	BULGARIA RADIO BULGARIA, Plovdiv	S • S Africa • 500 kW
	FRANCE R FRANCE INTL, Issoudun-Allouis	S • Mideast • 500 kW / Mideast & S Asia • 500 kW / Mideast • 500 kW
	GERMANY †DEUTSCHE WELLE, Via Antigua	W • S America • 250 kW
	†DEUTSCHE WELLE, Wertachtal	W • S Asia & SE Asia • 500 kW
	JAPAN †RADIO JAPAN/NHK, Via Ascension	C Africa & S Africa • 250 kW
	USA †VOA, Via Botswana	W M-F • E Africa • 100 kW
	†WHRA, Greenbush, Maine	Africa • 500 kW / Sa • Africa • 500 kW / Su-F • Africa • 500 kW

SEASONAL Ⓢ OR Ⓦ   1-HR TIMESHIFT MIDYEAR ⬅ OR ➡   JAMMING / OR ∧   EARLIEST HEARD ◁   LATEST HEARD ▷   NEW FOR 2000 †

FREQUENCY	COUNTRY, STATION, LOCATION	TARGET • NETWORK • POWER (kW)	World Time

0 1 2 3 4 5 6 7 8 9 10 11 12 13 14 15 16 17 18 19 20 21 22 23 24

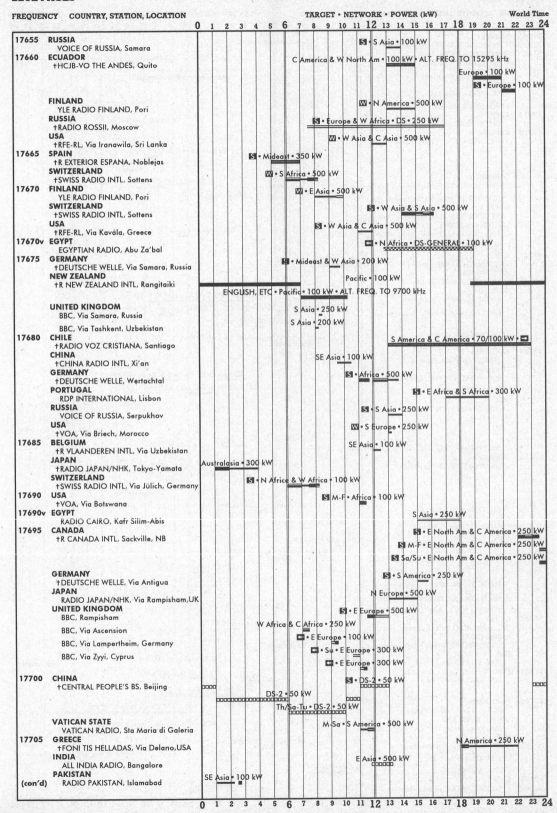

17655 RUSSIA
VOICE OF RUSSIA, Samara — S • S Asia • 100 kW

17660 ECUADOR
†HCJB-VO THE ANDES, Quito — C America & W North Am • 100 kW • ALT. FREQ. TO 15295 kHz
Europe • 100 kW
S • Europe • 100 kW

FINLAND
YLE RADIO FINLAND, Pori — W • N America • 500 kW
RUSSIA
†RADIO ROSSII, Moscow — S • Europe & W Africa • DS • 250 kW
USA
†RFE-RL, Via Iranawila, Sri Lanka — W • W Asia & C Asia • 500 kW

17665 SPAIN
†R EXTERIOR ESPANA, Noblejas — S • Mideast • 350 kW
SWITZERLAND
†SWISS RADIO INTL, Sottens — W • S Africa • 500 kW

17670 FINLAND
YLE RADIO FINLAND, Pori — W • E Asia • 500 kW
SWITZERLAND
†SWISS RADIO INTL, Sottens — S • W Asia & S Asia • 500 kW
USA
†RFE-RL, Via Kavála, Greece — S • W Asia & C Asia • 500 kW

17670v EGYPT
EGYPTIAN RADIO, Abu Za'bal — N Africa • DS-GENERAL • 100 kW

17675 GERMANY
†DEUTSCHE WELLE, Via Samara, Russia — S • Mideast & W Asia • 200 kW
NEW ZEALAND
†R NEW ZEALAND INTL, Rangitaiki — Pacific • 100 kW
ENGLISH, ETC • Pacific • 100 kW • ALT. FREQ. TO 9700 kHz

UNITED KINGDOM
BBC, Via Samara, Russia — S Asia • 250 kW
BBC, Via Tashkent, Uzbekistan — S Asia • 200 kW

17680 CHILE
†RADIO VOZ CRISTIANA, Santiago — S America & C America • 70/100 kW
CHINA
†CHINA RADIO INTL, Xi'an — SE Asia • 100 kW
GERMANY
†DEUTSCHE WELLE, Wertachtal — S • Africa • 500 kW
PORTUGAL
RDP INTERNATIONAL, Lisbon — S • E Africa & S Africa • 300 kW
RUSSIA
VOICE OF RUSSIA, Serpukhov — S • S Asia • 250 kW
USA
†VOA, Via Briech, Morocco — W • S Europe • 250 kW

17685 BELGIUM
†R VLAANDEREN INTL, Via Uzbekistan — SE Asia • 100 kW
JAPAN
†RADIO JAPAN/NHK, Tokyo-Yamata — Australasia • 300 kW
SWITZERLAND
†SWISS RADIO INTL, Via Jülich, Germany — S • N Africa & W Africa • 100 kW

17690 USA
†VOA, Via Botswana — S M-F • Africa • 100 kW

17690v EGYPT
RADIO CAIRO, Kafr Silim-Abis — S Asia • 250 kW

17695 CANADA
†R CANADA INTL, Sackville, NB — S • E North Am & C America • 250 kW
S M-F • E North Am & C America • 250 kW
S Sa/Su • E North Am & C America • 250 kW

GERMANY
†DEUTSCHE WELLE, Via Antigua — S • S America • 250 kW
JAPAN
RADIO JAPAN/NHK, Via Rampisham, UK — N Europe • 500 kW
UNITED KINGDOM
BBC, Rampisham — S • E Europe • 500 kW
BBC, Via Ascension — W Africa & C Africa • 250 kW
BBC, Via Lampertheim, Germany — E Europe • 100 kW
BBC, Via Zyyi, Cyprus — Su • E Europe • 300 kW
E Europe • 300 kW

17700 CHINA
†CENTRAL PEOPLE'S BS, Beijing — S • DS-2 • 50 kW
DS-2 • 50 kW
Th/Sa-Tu • DS-2 • 50 kW

VATICAN STATE
VATICAN RADIO, Sta Maria di Galeria — M-Sa • S America • 500 kW

17705 GREECE
†FONI TIS HELLADAS, Via Delano, USA — N America • 250 kW
INDIA
ALL INDIA RADIO, Bangalore — E Asia • 500 kW
PAKISTAN
(con'd) RADIO PAKISTAN, Islamabad — SE Asia • 100 kW

0 1 2 3 4 5 6 7 8 9 10 11 12 13 14 15 16 17 18 19 20 21 22 23 24

ENGLISH ▬ ARABIC ﹌ CHINESE ▭▭ FRENCH ▬ GERMAN ▬ RUSSIAN ═ SPANISH ▬ OTHER ▬

FREQUENCY   COUNTRY, STATION, LOCATION   TARGET • NETWORK • POWER (kW)   World Time

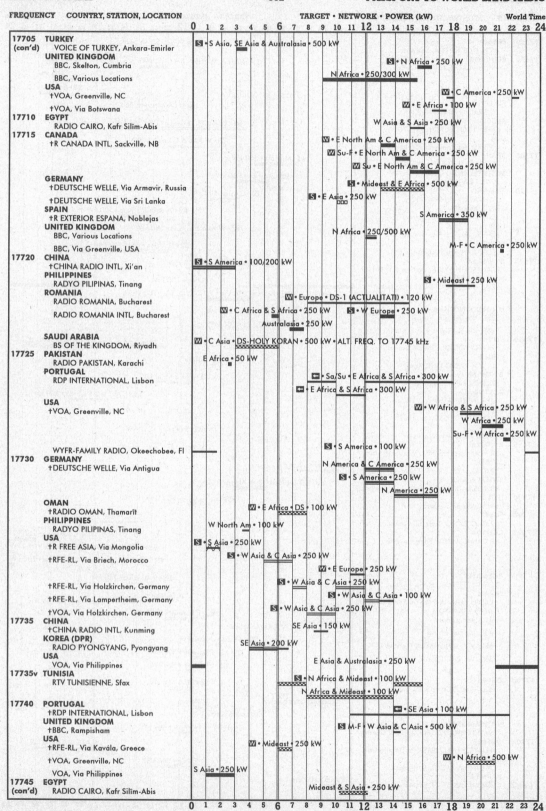

Frequency	Country, Station, Location	Target • Network • Power
17705 (con'd)	**TURKEY**	
	VOICE OF TURKEY, Ankara-Emirler	S • S Asia, SE Asia & Australasia • 500 kW
	UNITED KINGDOM	
	BBC, Skelton, Cumbria	S • N Africa • 250 kW
	BBC, Various Locations	N Africa • 250/300 kW
	USA	
	†VOA, Greenville, NC	W • C America • 250 kW
	†VOA, Via Botswana	W • E Africa • 100 kW
17710	**EGYPT**	
	RADIO CAIRO, Kafr Silim-Abis	W Asia & S Asia • 250 kW
17715	**CANADA**	
	†R CANADA INTL, Sackville, NB	W • E North Am & C America • 250 kW
		W Su-F • E North Am & C America • 250 kW
		W Su • E North Am & C America • 250 kW
	GERMANY	
	†DEUTSCHE WELLE, Via Armavir, Russia	S • Mideast & E Africa • 500 kW
	†DEUTSCHE WELLE, Via Sri Lanka	S • E Asia • 250 kW
	SPAIN	
	†R EXTERIOR ESPANA, Noblejas	S America • 350 kW
	UNITED KINGDOM	
	BBC, Various Locations	N Africa • 250/500 kW
	BBC, Via Greenville, USA	M-F • C America • 250 kW
17720	**CHINA**	
	†CHINA RADIO INTL, Xi'an	S • S America • 100/200 kW
	PHILIPPINES	
	RADYO PILIPINAS, Tinang	S • Mideast • 250 kW
	ROMANIA	
	RADIO ROMANIA, Bucharest	W • Europe • DS-1 (ACTUALITATI) • 120 kW
	RADIO ROMANIA INTL, Bucharest	W • C Africa & S Africa • 250 kW S • W Europe • 250 kW
		Australasia • 250 kW
	SAUDI ARABIA	
	BS OF THE KINGDOM, Riyadh	W • C Asia • DS-HOLY KORAN • 500 kW • ALT FREQ. TO 17745 kHz
17725	**PAKISTAN**	
	RADIO PAKISTAN, Karachi	E Africa • 50 kW
	PORTUGAL	
	RDP INTERNATIONAL, Lisbon	⇦ • Sa/Su • E Africa & S Africa • 300 kW
		⇦ • E Africa & S Africa • 300 kW
	USA	
	†VOA, Greenville, NC	W • W Africa & S Africa • 250 kW
		W Africa • 250 kW
		Su-F • W Africa • 250 kW
	WYFR-FAMILY RADIO, Okeechobee, Fl	S • S America • 100 kW
17730	**GERMANY**	
	†DEUTSCHE WELLE, Via Antigua	N America & C America • 250 kW
		S • S America • 250 kW
		N America • 250 kW
	OMAN	
	†RADIO OMAN, Thamarit	W • E Africa • DS • 100 kW
	PHILIPPINES	
	RADYO PILIPINAS, Tinang	W North Am • 100 kW
	USA	
	†R FREE ASIA, Via Mongolia	S • S Asia • 250 kW
	†RFE-RL, Via Briech, Morocco	S • W Asia & C Asia • 250 kW
		W • E Europe • 250 kW
	†RFE-RL, Via Holzkirchen, Germany	S • W Asia & C Asia • 250 kW
	†RFE-RL, Via Lampertheim, Germany	S • W Asia & C Asia • 100 kW
	†VOA, Via Holzkirchen, Germany	S • W Asia & C Asia • 250 kW
17735	**CHINA**	
	†CHINA RADIO INTL, Kunming	SE Asia • 150 kW
	KOREA (DPR)	
	RADIO PYONGYANG, Pyongyang	SE Asia • 200 kW
	USA	
	VOA, Via Philippines	E Asia & Australasia • 250 kW
17735v	**TUNISIA**	
	RTV TUNISIENNE, Sfax	S • N Africa & Mideast • 100 kW
		N Africa & Mideast • 100 kW
17740	**PORTUGAL**	
	†RDP INTERNATIONAL, Lisbon	⇦ • SE Asia • 100 kW
	UNITED KINGDOM	
	†BBC, Rampisham	S M-F • W Asia & C Asia • 500 kW
	USA	
	†RFE-RL, Via Kavála, Greece	W • Mideast • 250 kW
	†VOA, Greenville, NC	W • N Africa • 500 kW
	VOA, Via Philippines	S Asia • 250 kW
17745 (con'd)	**EGYPT**	
	RADIO CAIRO, Kafr Silim-Abis	Mideast & S Asia • 250 kW

FREQUENCY   COUNTRY, STATION, LOCATION   TARGET • NETWORK • POWER (kW)   World Time

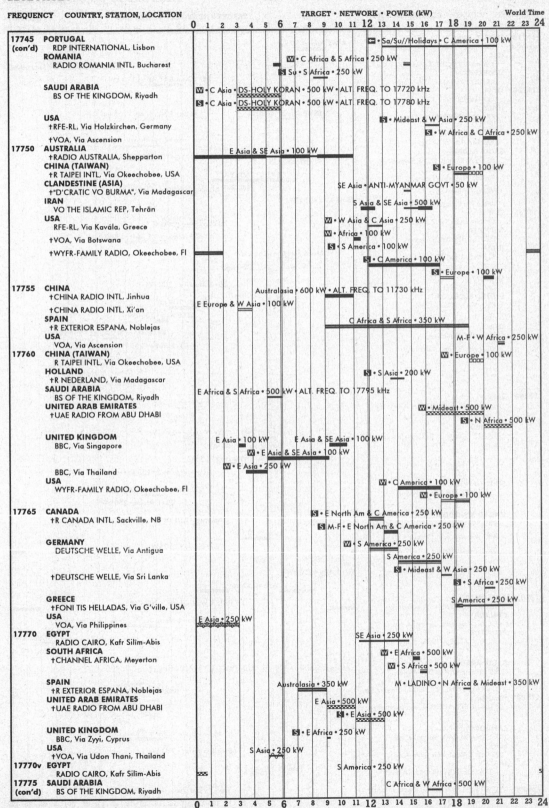

17745 PORTUGAL
(con'd)   RDP INTERNATIONAL, Lisbon — ◀▶ • Sa/Su//Holidays • C America • 100 kW
ROMANIA
   RADIO ROMANIA INTL, Bucharest — W • C Africa & S Africa • 250 kW
     S • Su • S Africa • 250 kW

SAUDI ARABIA
   BS OF THE KINGDOM, Riyadh — W • C Asia • DS-HOLY KORAN • 500 kW • ALT. FREQ. TO 17720 kHz
     S • C Asia • DS-HOLY KORAN • 500 kW • ALT. FREQ. TO 17780 kHz

USA
   †RFE-RL, Via Holzkirchen, Germany — S • Mideast & W Asia • 250 kW
   †VOA, Via Ascension — S • W Africa & C Africa • 250 kW

17750 AUSTRALIA
   †RADIO AUSTRALIA, Shepparton — E Asia & SE Asia • 100 kW
CHINA (TAIWAN)
   †R TAIPEI INTL, Via Okeechobee, USA — S • Europe • 100 kW
CLANDESTINE (ASIA)
   †"D'CRATIC VO BURMA", Via Madagascar — SE Asia • ANTI-MYANMAR GOVT • 50 kW
IRAN
   VO THE ISLAMIC REP, Tehrān — S Asia & SE Asia • 500 kW
USA
   RFE-RL, Via Kavála, Greece — W • W Asia & C Asia • 250 kW
   †VOA, Via Botswana — W • Africa • 100 kW
   †WYFR-FAMILY RADIO, Okeechobee, Fl — S • S America • 100 kW
     S • C America • 100 kW
     S • Europe • 100 kW

17755 CHINA
   †CHINA RADIO INTL, Jinhua — Australasia • 600 kW • ALT. FREQ. TO 11730 kHz
   †CHINA RADIO INTL, Xi'an — E Europe & W Asia • 100 kW
SPAIN
   †R EXTERIOR ESPANA, Noblejas — C Africa & S Africa • 350 kW
USA
   VOA, Via Ascension — M-F • W Africa • 250 kW

17760 CHINA (TAIWAN)
   R TAIPEI INTL, Via Okeechobee, USA — W • Europe • 100 kW
HOLLAND
   †R NEDERLAND, Via Madagascar — S • S Asia • 200 kW
SAUDI ARABIA
   BS OF THE KINGDOM, Riyadh — E Africa & S Africa • 500 kW • ALT. FREQ. TO 17795 kHz
UNITED ARAB EMIRATES
   †UAE RADIO FROM ABU DHABI — W • Mideast • 500 kW
     S • N Africa • 500 kW

UNITED KINGDOM
   BBC, Via Singapore — E Asia • 100 kW   E Asia & SE Asia • 100 kW
     W • E Asia & SE Asia • 100 kW
   BBC, Via Thailand — W • E Asia • 250 kW
USA
   WYFR-FAMILY RADIO, Okeechobee, Fl — W • C America • 100 kW
     W • Europe • 100 kW

17765 CANADA
   †R CANADA INTL, Sackville, NB — S • E North Am & C America • 250 kW
     S • M-F • E North Am & C America • 250 kW
GERMANY
   DEUTSCHE WELLE, Via Antigua — W • S America • 250 kW
     S America • 250 kW
   †DEUTSCHE WELLE, Via Sri Lanka — S • Mideast & W Asia • 250 kW
     S • S Africa • 250 kW
GREECE
   †FONI TIS HELLADAS, Via G'ville, USA — S America • 250 kW
USA
   VOA, Via Philippines — E Asia • 250 kW

17770 EGYPT
   RADIO CAIRO, Kafr Silim-Abis — SE Asia • 250 kW
SOUTH AFRICA
   †CHANNEL AFRICA, Meyerton — W • E Africa • 500 kW
     W • S Africa • 500 kW
SPAIN
   †R EXTERIOR ESPANA, Noblejas — Australasia • 350 kW   M • LADINO • N Africa & Mideast • 350 kW
UNITED ARAB EMIRATES
   †UAE RADIO FROM ABU DHABI — E Asia • 500 kW
     S • E Asia • 500 kW
UNITED KINGDOM
   BBC, Via Zyyi, Cyprus — S • E Africa • 250 kW
USA
   †VOA, Via Udon Thani, Thailand — S Asia • 250 kW
17770v EGYPT
   RADIO CAIRO, Kafr Silim-Abis — S America • 250 kW
17775 SAUDI ARABIA
(con'd)   BS OF THE KINGDOM, Riyadh — C Africa & W Africa • 500 kW

ENGLISH ▬   ARABIC ⌇⌇⌇   CHINESE □□□   FRENCH ═   GERMAN ▬   RUSSIAN ═   SPANISH ▬   OTHER —

FREQUENCY   COUNTRY, STATION, LOCATION   TARGET • NETWORK • POWER (kW)   World Time

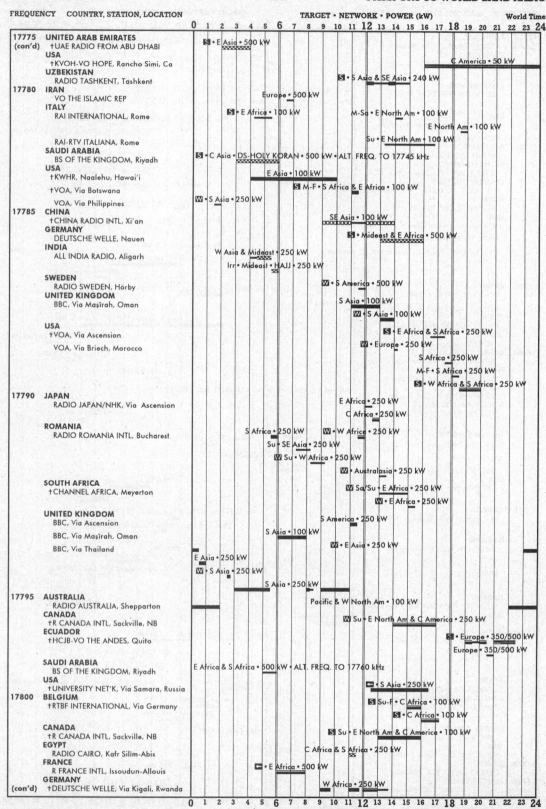

17775	**UNITED ARAB EMIRATES**
(con'd)	†UAE RADIO FROM ABU DHABI — Ⓢ • E Asia • 500 kW
	USA
	†KVOH-VO HOPE, Rancho Simi, Ca — C America • 50 kW
	UZBEKISTAN
	RADIO TASHKENT, Tashkent — Ⓢ • S Asia & SE Asia • 240 kW
17780	**IRAN**
	VO THE ISLAMIC REP — Europe • 500 kW
	ITALY
	RAI INTERNATIONAL, Rome — Ⓢ • E Africa • 100 kW / M-Sa • E North Am • 100 kW / E North Am • 100 kW
	RAI-RTV ITALIANA, Rome — Su • E North Am • 100 kW
	SAUDI ARABIA
	BS OF THE KINGDOM, Riyadh — Ⓢ • C Asia • DS-HOLY KORAN • 500 kW • ALT. FREQ. TO 17745 kHz
	USA
	†KWHR, Naalehu, Hawai'i — E Asia • 100 kW
	†VOA, Via Botswana — Ⓢ • M-F • S Africa & E Africa • 100 kW
	VOA, Via Philippines — Ⓦ • S Asia • 250 kW
17785	**CHINA**
	†CHINA RADIO INTL, Xi'an — SE Asia • 100 kW
	GERMANY
	DEUTSCHE WELLE, Nauen — Ⓢ • Mideast & E Africa • 500 kW
	INDIA
	ALL INDIA RADIO, Aligarh — W Asia & Mideast • 250 kW / Irr • Mideast • HAJJ • 250 kW
	SWEDEN
	RADIO SWEDEN, Hörby — Ⓦ • S America • 500 kW
	UNITED KINGDOM
	BBC, Via Maşīrah, Oman — S Asia • 100 kW / Ⓦ • S Asia • 100 kW
	USA
	†VOA, Via Ascension — Ⓢ • E Africa & S Africa • 250 kW
	VOA, Via Briech, Morocco — Ⓦ • Europe • 250 kW / S Africa • 250 kW / M-F • S Africa • 250 kW / Ⓢ • W Africa & S Africa • 250 kW
17790	**JAPAN**
	RADIO JAPAN/NHK, Via Ascension — E Africa • 250 kW / C Africa • 250 kW
	ROMANIA
	RADIO ROMANIA INTL, Bucharest — S Africa • 250 kW / Ⓦ • W Africa • 250 kW / Su • SE Asia • 250 kW / Ⓦ Su • W Africa • 250 kW / Ⓦ • Australasia • 250 kW
	SOUTH AFRICA
	†CHANNEL AFRICA, Meyerton — Ⓦ Sa/Su • E Africa • 250 kW / Ⓦ • E Africa • 250 kW
	UNITED KINGDOM
	BBC, Via Ascension — S America • 250 kW
	BBC, Via Maşīrah, Oman — S Asia • 100 kW
	BBC, Via Thailand — Ⓦ • E Asia • 250 kW / E Asia • 250 kW / Ⓦ • S Asia • 250 kW / S Asia • 250 kW
17795	**AUSTRALIA**
	RADIO AUSTRALIA, Shepparton — Pacific & W North Am • 100 kW
	CANADA
	†R CANADA INTL, Sackville, NB — Ⓦ Su • E North Am & C America • 250 kW
	ECUADOR
	†HCJB-VO THE ANDES, Quito — Ⓢ • Europe • 350/500 kW / Europe • 350/500 kW
	SAUDI ARABIA
	BS OF THE KINGDOM, Riyadh — E Africa & S Africa • 500 kW • ALT. FREQ. TO 17760 kHz
	USA
	†UNIVERSITY NET'K, Via Samara, Russia — ⟷ • S Asia • 250 kW
17800	**BELGIUM**
	†RTBF INTERNATIONAL, Via Germany — Ⓢ • Su-F • C Africa • 100 kW / Ⓢ • C Africa • 100 kW
	CANADA
	†R CANADA INTL, Sackville, NB — Ⓢ • Su • E North Am & C America • 100 kW
	EGYPT
	RADIO CAIRO, Kafr Silim-Abis — C Africa & S Africa • 250 kW
	FRANCE
	R FRANCE INTL, Issoudun-Allouis — ⟷ • E Africa • 500 kW
	GERMANY
(con'd)	†DEUTSCHE WELLE, Via Kigali, Rwanda — W Africa • 250 kW

FREQUENCY   COUNTRY, STATION, LOCATION

TARGET • NETWORK • POWER (kW)   World Time

0 1 2 3 4 5 6 7 8 9 10 11 12 13 14 15 16 17 18 19 20 21 22 23 24

Frequency	Country, Station, Location	Schedule
17800 (con'd)	**GERMANY** †DEUTSCHE WELLE, Wertachtal	W • E Africa & S Africa • 500 kW; W • Africa • 500 kW
	USA †VOA, Greenville, NC	S • Africa • 250 kW
17805	**CHINA (TAIWAN)** R TAIPEI INTL, Via Okeechobee, USA	S • S America • 100 kW
	ROMANIA RADIO ROMANIA INTL, Bucharest	W • Australasia • 250 kW
	USA †R FREE ASIA, Via CIS	S • SE Asia • 500 kW
	†RFE-RL, Via Holzkirchen, Germany	W • W Asia & C Asia • 250 kW
	†VOA, Via Ascension	W • E Africa & S Africa • 250 kW
	VOA, Via Pals, Spain	W • W Asia & C Asia • 250 kW
	†VOA, Via Philippines	S • S Asia • 250 kW
	WYFR-FAMILY RADIO, Okeechobee, Fl	S • S America • 100 kW
17810	**GERMANY** †DEUTSCHE WELLE, Nauen	S • Africa • 500 kW
	DEUTSCHE WELLE, Via Antigua	N America & S America • 250 kW
	†DEUTSCHE WELLE, Via Sri Lanka	Africa • 250 kW
	†DEUTSCHE WELLE, Wertachtal	W • Mideast & W Asia • 500 kW; S • W Africa & C Africa • 500 kW; W • S Asia • 500 kW
	HUNGARY †RADIO BUDAPEST, Jászberény	← Australasia • 250 kW • ALT. FREQ. TO 17830 kHz; ← • Su • Australasia • 250 kW • ALT FREQ. TO 17830 kHz
	JAPAN †RADIO JAPAN/NHK, Tokyo-Yamata	S • SE Asia • 300 kW
	UNITED KINGDOM BBC, Rampisham	S • E Europe • 500 kW
	BBC, Via Ascension	W Africa & C Africa • 250 kW
17815	**BRAZIL** RADIO CULTURA, São Paulo	DS • 1 kW • ←
	ROMANIA RADIO ROMANIA INTL, Bucharest	S • W Europe • 250 kW
17820	**CANADA** †R CANADA INTL, Sackville, NB	S • E North Am & C America • 250 kW; S • Africa • 250 kW; S • M-F • E North Am & C America • 250 kW; W • M-Sa • Africa • 250 kW; W • E Europe • 250 kW; ← • E Europe • 250 kW; W • Africa • 100 kW; Africa • 100/250 kW
	†R CANADA INTL, Via Skelton, UK	S • E Europe • 300 kW; S • Europe • 300 kW
	GERMANY †DEUTSCHE WELLE, Via Sri Lanka	E Asia • 250 kW; S • E Asia • 250 kW; W • SE Asia & Australasia • 250 kW; S • SE Asia • 250 kW
	†DEUTSCHE WELLE, Wertachtal	S • Mideast & W Asia • 500 kW; S • E Asia • 500 kW; S • SE Asia • 500 kW
	JAPAN RADIO JAPAN/NHK, Via Sri Lanka	Mideast • 300 kW; Mideast & W Asia • 300 kW
	UNITED KINGDOM BBC, Via Ascension	M-F • S America • 250 kW
	USA VOA, Via Philippines	E Asia • 100 kW; S Asia • 100 kW
17825	**GERMANY** DEUTSCHE WELLE, Wertachtal	W • W Asia & S Asia • 500 kW
	JAPAN †RADIO JAPAN/NHK, Tokyo-Yamata	S • C America • 300 kW; S • W North Am & C America • 300 kW; S • W North Am • 300 kW
	UNITED ARAB EMIRATES †UAE RADIO FROM ABU DHABI	W • Mideast • 500 kW
17830	**FINLAND** YLE RADIO FINLAND, Pori	S • SE Asia & Australasia • 500 kW
	HUNGARY †RADIO BUDAPEST, Jászberény	← • Australasia • 250 kW • ALT. FREQ. TO 17810 kHz; ← • Su • Australasia • 250 kW • ALT. FREQ. TO 17810 kHz
(con'd)		

0 1 2 3 4 5 6 7 8 9 10 11 12 13 14 15 16 17 18 19 20 21 22 23 24

ENGLISH ▬▬ ARABIC ⌇⌇⌇ CHINESE □□□ FRENCH ══ GERMAN ▬▬ RUSSIAN ══ SPANISH ▬▬ OTHER ──

FREQUENCY   COUNTRY, STATION, LOCATION   TARGET • NETWORK • POWER (kW)   World Time

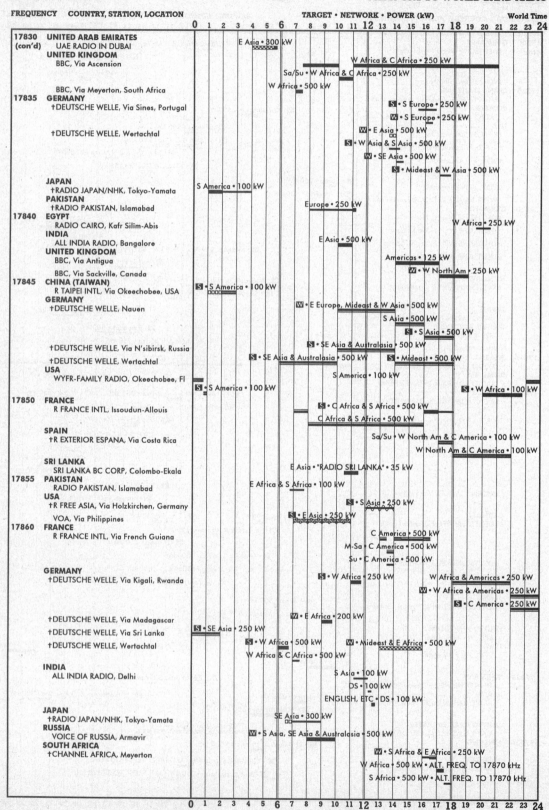

Frequency	Country, Station, Location	Target • Network • Power (kW)
17830 (con'd)	UNITED ARAB EMIRATES / UAE RADIO IN DUBAI	E Asia • 300 kW
	UNITED KINGDOM / BBC, Via Ascension	W Africa & C Africa • 250 kW / Sa/Su • W Africa & C Africa • 250 kW
	BBC, Via Meyerton, South Africa	W Africa • 500 kW
17835	GERMANY / †DEUTSCHE WELLE, Via Sines, Portugal	S • S Europe • 250 kW / W • S Europe • 250 kW
	†DEUTSCHE WELLE, Wertachtal	W • E Asia • 500 kW / S • W Asia & S Asia • 500 kW / W • SE Asia • 500 kW / S • Mideast & W Asia • 500 kW
	JAPAN / †RADIO JAPAN/NHK, Tokyo-Yamata	S America • 100 kW
	PAKISTAN / †RADIO PAKISTAN, Islamabad	Europe • 250 kW
17840	EGYPT / RADIO CAIRO, Kafr Silim-Abis	W Africa • 250 kW
	INDIA / ALL INDIA RADIO, Bangalore	E Asia • 500 kW
	UNITED KINGDOM / BBC, Via Antigua	Americas • 125 kW
	BBC, Via Sackville, Canada	W • W North Am • 250 kW
17845	CHINA (TAIWAN) / R TAIPEI INTL, Via Okeechobee, USA	S • S America • 100 kW
	GERMANY / †DEUTSCHE WELLE, Nauen	W • E Europe, Mideast & W Asia • 500 kW / S Asia • 500 kW / S • S Asia • 500 kW
	†DEUTSCHE WELLE, Via N'sibirsk, Russia	S • SE Asia & Australasia • 500 kW
	†DEUTSCHE WELLE, Wertachtal	S • SE Asia & Australasia • 500 kW / S • Mideast • 500 kW
	USA / WYFR-FAMILY RADIO, Okeechobee, Fl	S America • 100 kW / S • S America • 100 kW / S • W Africa • 100 kW
17850	FRANCE / R FRANCE INTL, Issoudun-Allouis	S • C Africa & S Africa • 500 kW / C Africa & S Africa • 500 kW
	SPAIN / †R EXTERIOR ESPANA, Via Costa Rica	Sa/Su • W North Am & C America • 100 kW / W North Am & C America • 100 kW
	SRI LANKA / SRI LANKA BC CORP, Colombo-Ekala	E Asia • "RADIO SRI LANKA" • 35 kW
17855	PAKISTAN / RADIO PAKISTAN, Islamabad	E Africa & S Africa • 100 kW
	USA / †R FREE ASIA, Via Holzkirchen, Germany	S • S Asia • 250 kW
	VOA, Via Philippines	S • E Asia • 250 kW
17860	FRANCE / R FRANCE INTL, Via French Guiana	C America • 500 kW / M-Sa • C America • 500 kW / Su • C America • 500 kW
	GERMANY / †DEUTSCHE WELLE, Via Kigali, Rwanda	S • W Africa • 250 kW / W Africa & Americas • 250 kW / W • W Africa & Americas • 250 kW / S • C America • 250 kW
	†DEUTSCHE WELLE, Via Madagascar	W • E Africa • 200 kW
	†DEUTSCHE WELLE, Via Sri Lanka	S • SE Asia • 250 kW
	†DEUTSCHE WELLE, Wertachtal	S • W Africa • 500 kW / W • Mideast & E Africa • 500 kW / W Africa & C Africa • 500 kW
	INDIA / ALL INDIA RADIO, Delhi	S Asia • 100 kW / DS • 100 kW / ENGLISH, ETC • DS • 100 kW
	JAPAN / †RADIO JAPAN/NHK, Tokyo-Yamata	SE Asia • 300 kW
	RUSSIA / VOICE OF RUSSIA, Armavir	W • S Asia, SE Asia & Australasia • 500 kW
	SOUTH AFRICA / †CHANNEL AFRICA, Meyerton	W • S Africa & E Africa • 250 kW / W Africa • 500 kW • ALT. FREQ. TO 17870 kHz / S Africa • 500 kW • ALT. FREQ. TO 17870 kHz

FREQUENCY	COUNTRY, STATION, LOCATION	TARGET • NETWORK • POWER (kW) — World Time
17870	**AUSTRIA** R AUSTRIA INTL, Vienna	S • Mideast • 300 kW
		W M-Sa • Mideast • 300 kW
		W Su • Mideast • 300 kW
		W • Mideast • 300 kW
		S M-Sa • Mideast • 300 kW
		S Su • Mideast • 300 kW
		Mideast • 300 kW
	CANADA R CANADA INTL, Sackville, NB	S • Europe & N Africa • 250 kW
	†R CANADA INTL, Via Germany	S • Mideast • 500 kW
	ITALY RAI INTERNATIONAL, Rome	E Africa • 100 kW
	JAPAN †RADIO JAPAN/NHK, Tokyo-Yamata	SE Asia • 100 kW
	SOUTH AFRICA †CHANNEL AFRICA, Meyerton	S • E Africa • 500 kW
		S • S Africa • 500 kW
		W Africa • 500 kW • ALT. FREQ. TO 17860 kHz
		S Africa • 500 kW • ALT. FREQ. TO 17860 kHz
		W Africa • 500 kW
	SWEDEN RADIO SWEDEN, Hörby	S • N America • 500 kW
	USA †VOA, Via Kavála, Greece	S • W Asia & S Asia • 250 kW
17875	**GERMANY** †DEUTSCHE WELLE, Via Sackville, Can	S • N America • 250 kW
	USA VOA, Via Ascension	S America • 250 kW
	†VOA, Via Iranawila, Sri Lanka	W • W Asia & S Asia • 500 kW
17880	**CHINA** †CHINA RADIO INTL, Via Bamako, Mali	N Africa • 100 kW
	QATAR †QATAR BC SERVICE, Doha-Al Khaisah	S • Mideast & N Africa • 250 kW
	SAUDI ARABIA BS OF THE KINGDOM, Riyadh	SE Asia • DS-HOLY KORAN • 500 kW • ALT. FREQ. TO 17895 kHz
	UNITED KINGDOM BBC, Rampisham	E Africa • 500 kW
		M-F • E Africa • 500 kW
		Sa/Su • E Africa • 500 kW
	USA †R FREE ASIA, Via Saipan, N Marianas	S • E Asia • 100 kW
17885	**IRAN** VO THE ISLAMIC REP, Tehrān	S Asia & SE Asia • 500 kW
	IRELAND †RTE RADIO, Via Ascension	S • Africa • 250 kW
	JAPAN RADIO JAPAN/NHK, Via Ascension	C Africa • 250 kW
	KUWAIT RADIO KUWAIT, Kabd	E Asia • 500 kW
	UNITED KINGDOM BBC, Various Locations	E Africa • 250 kW
	BBC, Via Ascension	W Africa • 250 kW
	BBC, Via Seychelles	W • E Africa • 250 kW
		E Africa • 250 kW
		Sa/Su • E Africa • 250 kW
	USA †VOA, Via Ascension	W • W Africa & C Africa • 250 kW
17890	**USA** †VOA, Delano, California	C America & S America • 250 kW
17895	**CANADA** R CANADA INTL, Sackville, NB	S M-Sa • Africa • 100 kW
	GERMANY †DEUTSCHE WELLE, Via Sines, Portugal	W • Europe • 250 kW
	DEUTSCHE WELLE, Via Sri Lanka	W • E Asia • 250 kW
	†DEUTSCHE WELLE, Wertachtal	W • W Asia & S Asia • 500 kW
	INDIA †ALL INDIA RADIO, Bangalore	SE Asia • 500 kW
	JAPAN †RADIO JAPAN/NHK, Via Ascension	W Africa • 250 kW • ALT. FREQ. TO 15220 kHz
	QATAR †QATAR BC SERVICE, Doha-Al Khaisah	S • Europe • 250 kW
	SAUDI ARABIA BS OF THE KINGDOM, Riyadh	SE Asia • DS-HOLY KORAN • 500 kW • ALT. FREQ. TO 17880 kHz
(con'd)	**USA** RFE-RL, Via Briech, Morocco	W • E Europe • 250 kW

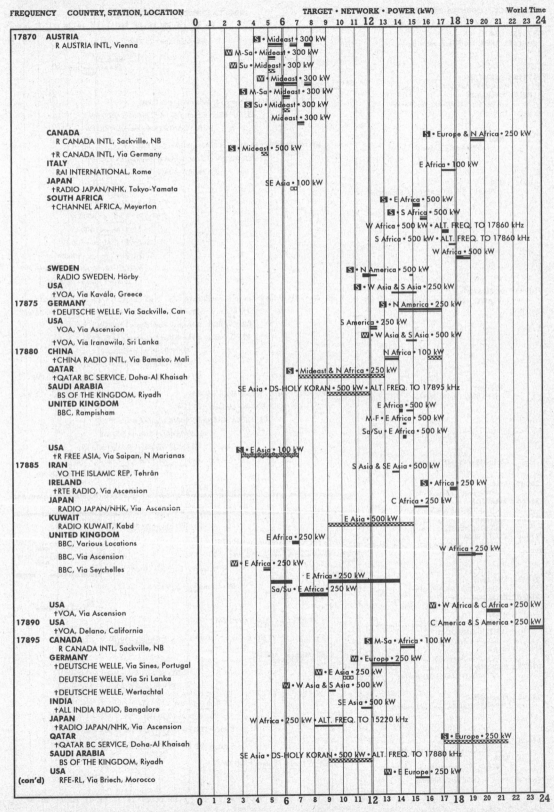

ENGLISH ▬ ARABIC ≋ CHINESE ▭▭▭ FRENCH ▬▬ GERMAN ▬▬ RUSSIAN ══ SPANISH ▬▬ OTHER ▬

FREQUENCY   COUNTRY, STATION, LOCATION   TARGET • NETWORK • POWER (kW)   World Time

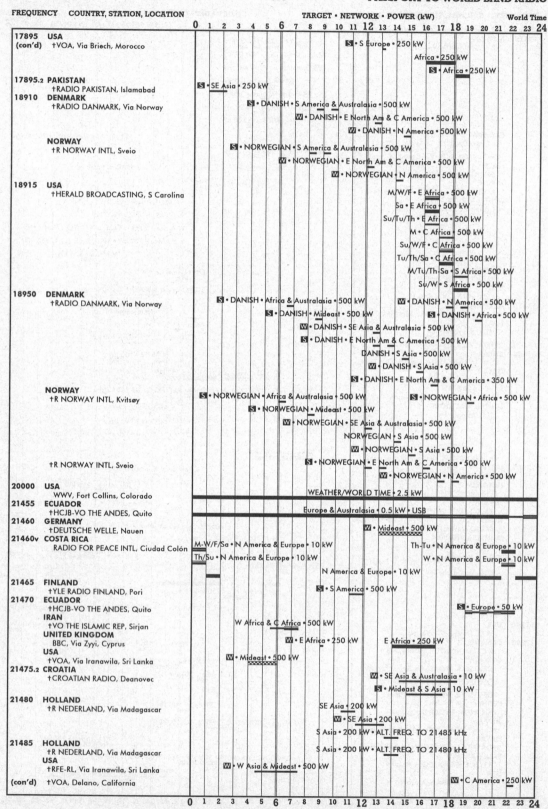

Frequency	Country, Station, Location	Schedule
17895 (con'd)	**USA** †VOA, Via Briech, Morocco	S • S Europe • 250 kW · Africa • 250 kW · S • Africa • 250 kW
17895.2	**PAKISTAN** †RADIO PAKISTAN, Islamabad	S • SE Asia • 250 kW
18910	**DENMARK** †RADIO DANMARK, Via Norway	S • DANISH • S America & Australasia • 500 kW · W • DANISH • E North Am & C America • 500 kW · W • DANISH • N America • 500 kW
	NORWAY †R NORWAY INTL, Sveio	S • NORWEGIAN • S America & Australasia • 500 kW · W • NORWEGIAN • E North Am & C America • 500 kW · W • NORWEGIAN • N America • 500 kW
18915	**USA** †HERALD BROADCASTING, S Carolina	M/W/F • E Africa • 500 kW · Sa • E Africa • 500 kW · Su/Tu/Th • E Africa • 500 kW · M • C Africa • 500 kW · Su/W/F • C Africa • 500 kW · Tu/Th/Sa • C Africa • 500 kW · M/Tu/Th/Sa • S Africa • 500 kW · Su/W • S Africa • 500 kW
18950	**DENMARK** †RADIO DANMARK, Via Norway	S • DANISH • Africa & Australasia • 500 kW · W • DANISH • N America • 500 kW · S • DANISH • Mideast • 500 kW · S • DANISH • Africa • 500 kW · W • DANISH • SE Asia & Australasia • 500 kW · S • DANISH • E North Am & C America • 500 kW · DANISH • S Asia • 500 kW · W • DANISH • S Asia • 500 kW · S • DANISH • E North Am & C America • 350 kW
	NORWAY †R NORWAY INTL, Kvitsøy	S • NORWEGIAN • Africa & Australasia • 500 kW · S • NORWEGIAN • Africa • 500 kW · S • NORWEGIAN • Mideast • 500 kW · W • NORWEGIAN • SE Asia & Australasia • 500 kW · NORWEGIAN • S Asia • 500 kW · W • NORWEGIAN • S Asia • 500 kW
	†R NORWAY INTL, Sveio	S • NORWEGIAN • E North Am & C America • 500 kW · W • NORWEGIAN • N America • 500 kW
20000	**USA** WWV, Fort Collins, Colorado	WEATHER/WORLD TIME • 2.5 kW
21455	**ECUADOR** †HCJB-VO THE ANDES, Quito	Europe & Australasia • 0.5 kW • USB
21460	**GERMANY** †DEUTSCHE WELLE, Nauen	W • Mideast • 500 kW
21460v	**COSTA RICA** RADIO FOR PEACE INTL, Ciudad Colón	M-W/F/Sa • N America & Europe • 10 kW · Th-Tu • N America & Europe • 10 kW · Th/Su • N America & Europe • 10 kW · W • N America & Europe • 10 kW · N America & Europe • 10 kW
21465	**FINLAND** †YLE RADIO FINLAND, Pori	S • S America • 500 kW
21470	**ECUADOR** †HCJB-VO THE ANDES, Quito	S • Europe • 50 kW
	IRAN †VO THE ISLAMIC REP, Sirjan	W Africa & C Africa • 500 kW
	UNITED KINGDOM BBC, Via Zyyi, Cyprus	W • E Africa • 250 kW · E Africa • 250 kW
	USA †VOA, Via Iranawila, Sri Lanka	W • Mideast • 500 kW
21475.2	**CROATIA** †CROATIAN RADIO, Deanovec	W • SE Asia & Australasia • 10 kW · S • Mideast & S Asia • 10 kW
21480	**HOLLAND** †R NEDERLAND, Via Madagascar	SE Asia • 200 kW · W • SE Asia • 200 kW · S Asia • 200 kW • ALT. FREQ. TO 21485 kHz
21485	**HOLLAND** †R NEDERLAND, Via Madagascar	S Asia • 200 kW • ALT. FREQ. TO 21480 kHz
	USA †RFE-RL, Via Iranawila, Sri Lanka	W • W Asia & Mideast • 500 kW
(con'd)	†VOA, Delano, California	W • C America • 250 kW

FREQUENCY   COUNTRY, STATION, LOCATION   TARGET • NETWORK • POWER (kW)   World Time

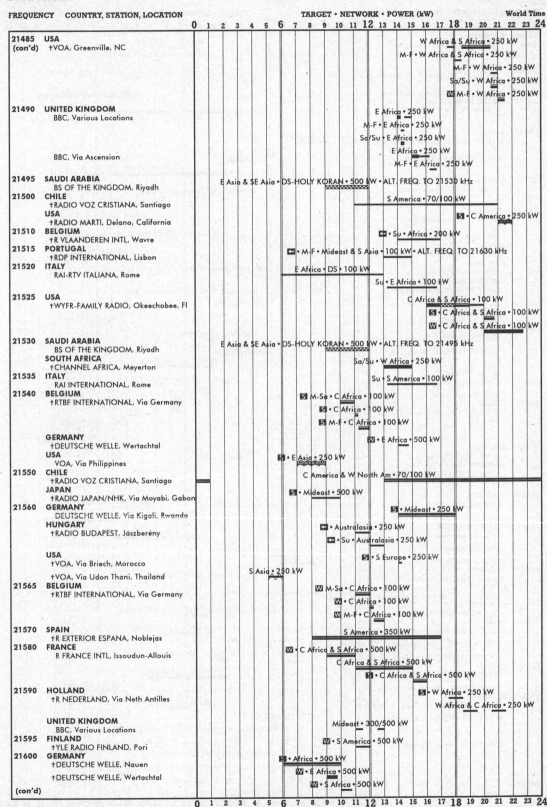

Frequency	Country, Station, Location	Target • Network • Power
21485 (con'd)	USA †VOA, Greenville, NC	W Africa & S Africa • 250 kW; M-F • W Africa & S Africa • 250 kW; M-F • W Africa • 250 kW; Sa/Su • W Africa • 250 kW; W M-F • W Africa • 250 kW
21490	UNITED KINGDOM BBC, Various Locations	E Africa • 250 kW; M-F • E Africa • 250 kW; Sa/Su • E Africa • 250 kW
	BBC, Via Ascension	E Africa • 250 kW; M-F • E Africa • 250 kW
21495	SAUDI ARABIA BS OF THE KINGDOM, Riyadh	E Asia & SE Asia • DS-HOLY KORAN • 500 kW • ALT. FREQ. TO 21530 kHz
21500	CHILE †RADIO VOZ CRISTIANA, Santiago	S America • 70/100 kW
	USA †RADIO MARTI, Delano, California	S • C America • 250 kW
21510	BELGIUM †R VLAANDEREN INTL, Wavre	Su • Africa • 200 kW
21515	PORTUGAL †RDP INTERNATIONAL, Lisbon	M-F • Mideast & S Asia • 100 kW • ALT. FREQ. TO 21630 kHz
21520	ITALY RAI-RTV ITALIANA, Rome	E Africa • DS • 100 kW; Su • E Africa • 100 kW
21525	USA †WYFR-FAMILY RADIO, Okeechobee, Fl	C Africa & S Africa • 100 kW; S • C Africa & S Africa • 100 kW; W • C Africa & S Africa • 100 kW
21530	SAUDI ARABIA BS OF THE KINGDOM, Riyadh	E Asia & SE Asia • DS-HOLY KORAN • 500 kW • ALT. FREQ. TO 21495 kHz
	SOUTH AFRICA †CHANNEL AFRICA, Meyerton	Sa/Su • W Africa • 250 kW
21535	ITALY RAI INTERNATIONAL, Rome	Su • S America • 100 kW
21540	BELGIUM †RTBF INTERNATIONAL, Via Germany	S M-Sa • C Africa • 100 kW; S • C Africa • 100 kW; S M-F • C Africa • 100 kW
	GERMANY †DEUTSCHE WELLE, Wertachtal	W • E Africa • 500 kW
	USA VOA, Via Philippines	S • E Asia • 250 kW
21550	CHILE †RADIO VOZ CRISTIANA, Santiago	C America & W North Am • 70/100 kW
	JAPAN †RADIO JAPAN/NHK, Via Moyabi, Gabon	S • Mideast • 500 kW
21560	GERMANY DEUTSCHE WELLE, Via Kigali, Rwanda	S • Mideast • 250 kW
	HUNGARY †RADIO BUDAPEST, Jászberény	Australasia • 250 kW; Su • Australasia • 250 kW
	USA †VOA, Via Briech, Morocco	S • S Europe • 250 kW
	†VOA, Via Udon Thani, Thailand	S Asia • 250 kW
21565	BELGIUM †RTBF INTERNATIONAL, Via Germany	W M-Sa • C Africa • 100 kW; W • C Africa • 100 kW; W M-F • C Africa • 100 kW
21570	SPAIN †R EXTERIOR ESPANA, Noblejas	S America • 350 kW
21580	FRANCE R FRANCE INTL, Issoudun-Allouis	W • C Africa & S Africa • 500 kW; C Africa & S Africa • 500 kW; S • C Africa & S Africa • 500 kW
21590	HOLLAND †R NEDERLAND, Via Neth Antilles	S • W Africa • 250 kW; W Africa & C Africa • 250 kW
	UNITED KINGDOM BBC, Various Locations	Mideast • 300/500 kW
21595	FINLAND †YLE RADIO FINLAND, Pori	W • S America • 500 kW
21600	GERMANY †DEUTSCHE WELLE, Nauen	S • Africa • 500 kW
	†DEUTSCHE WELLE, Wertachtal	W • E Africa • 500 kW; W • S Africa • 500 kW
(con'd)		

ENGLISH ▬   ARABIC ∾∾∾   CHINESE □□□   FRENCH ▬▬   GERMAN ▬▬   RUSSIAN ═══   SPANISH ▬▬   OTHER ▬

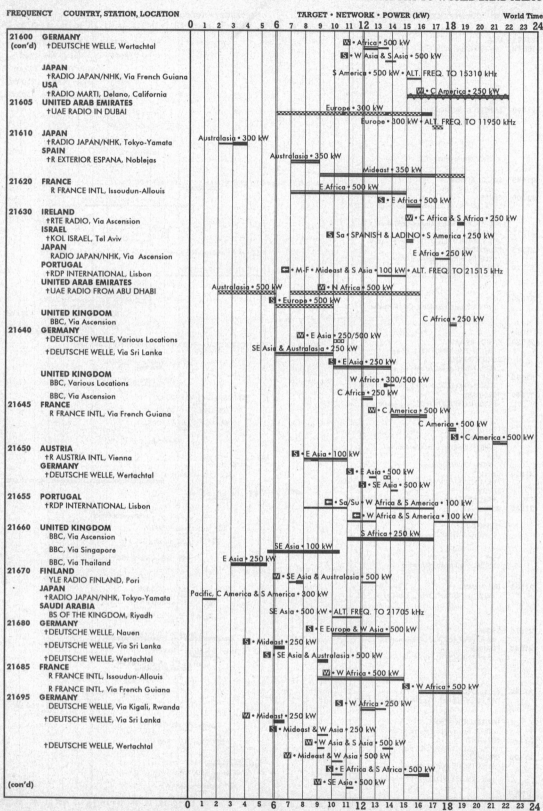

FREQUENCY   COUNTRY, STATION, LOCATION   TARGET • NETWORK • POWER (kW)   World Time

Frequency	Country, Station, Location	Target • Network • Power (kW)
21600 (con'd)	GERMANY †DEUTSCHE WELLE, Wertachtal	W • Africa • 500 kW; S • W Asia & S Asia • 500 kW
	JAPAN †RADIO JAPAN/NHK, Via French Guiana	S America • 500 kW • ALT. FREQ. TO 15310 kHz
	USA †RADIO MARTI, Delano, California	W • C America • 250 kW
21605	UNITED ARAB EMIRATES †UAE RADIO IN DUBAI	Europe • 300 kW; Europe • 300 kW • ALT. FREQ. TO 11950 kHz
21610	JAPAN †RADIO JAPAN/NHK, Tokyo-Yamata	Australasia • 300 kW
	SPAIN †R EXTERIOR ESPANA, Noblejas	Australasia • 350 kW; Mideast • 350 kW
21620	FRANCE R FRANCE INTL, Issoudun-Allouis	E Africa • 500 kW; S • E Africa • 500 kW
21630	IRELAND †RTE RADIO, Via Ascension	W • C Africa & S Africa • 250 kW
	ISRAEL †KOL ISRAEL, Tel Aviv	Sa • SPANISH & LADINO • S America • 250 kW
	JAPAN RADIO JAPAN/NHK, Via Ascension	E Africa • 250 kW
	PORTUGAL †RDP INTERNATIONAL, Lisbon	M-F • Mideast & S Asia • 100 kW • ALT. FREQ. TO 21515 kHz
	UNITED ARAB EMIRATES †UAE RADIO FROM ABU DHABI	Australasia • 500 kW; W • N Africa • 500 kW; S • Europe • 500 kW
	UNITED KINGDOM BBC, Via Ascension	C Africa • 250 kW
21640	GERMANY †DEUTSCHE WELLE, Various Locations	W • E Asia • 250/500 kW
	†DEUTSCHE WELLE, Via Sri Lanka	SE Asia & Australasia • 250 kW; S • E Asia • 250 kW
	UNITED KINGDOM BBC, Various Locations	W Africa • 300/500 kW
	BBC, Via Ascension	C Africa • 250 kW
21645	FRANCE R FRANCE INTL, Via French Guiana	W • C America • 500 kW; C America • 500 kW; S • C America • 500 kW
21650	AUSTRIA †R AUSTRIA INTL, Vienna	S • E Asia • 100 kW
	GERMANY †DEUTSCHE WELLE, Wertachtal	S • E Asia • 500 kW; S • SE Asia • 500 kW
21655	PORTUGAL †RDP INTERNATIONAL, Lisbon	Sa/Su • W Africa & S America • 100 kW; W Africa & S America • 100 kW
21660	UNITED KINGDOM BBC, Via Ascension	S Africa • 250 kW
	BBC, Via Singapore	SE Asia • 100 kW
	BBC, Via Thailand	E Asia • 250 kW
21670	FINLAND YLE RADIO FINLAND, Pori	W • SE Asia & Australasia • 500 kW
	JAPAN †RADIO JAPAN/NHK, Tokyo-Yamata	Pacific, C America & S America • 300 kW
	SAUDI ARABIA BS OF THE KINGDOM, Riyadh	SE Asia • 500 kW • ALT. FREQ. TO 21705 kHz
21680	GERMANY †DEUTSCHE WELLE, Nauen	S • E Europe & W Asia • 500 kW
	†DEUTSCHE WELLE, Via Sri Lanka	S • Mideast • 250 kW
	†DEUTSCHE WELLE, Wertachtal	S • SE Asia & Australasia • 500 kW
21685	FRANCE R FRANCE INTL, Issoudun-Allouis	W • W Africa • 500 kW
	R FRANCE INTL, Via French Guiana	S • W Africa • 500 kW
21695	GERMANY DEUTSCHE WELLE, Via Kigali, Rwanda	S • W Africa • 250 kW
	†DEUTSCHE WELLE, Via Sri Lanka	W • Mideast • 250 kW; S • Mideast & W Asia • 250 kW
	†DEUTSCHE WELLE, Wertachtal	W • W Asia & S Asia • 500 kW; W • Mideast & W Asia • 500 kW; S • E Africa & S Africa • 500 kW; W • SE Asia • 500 kW
(con'd)		

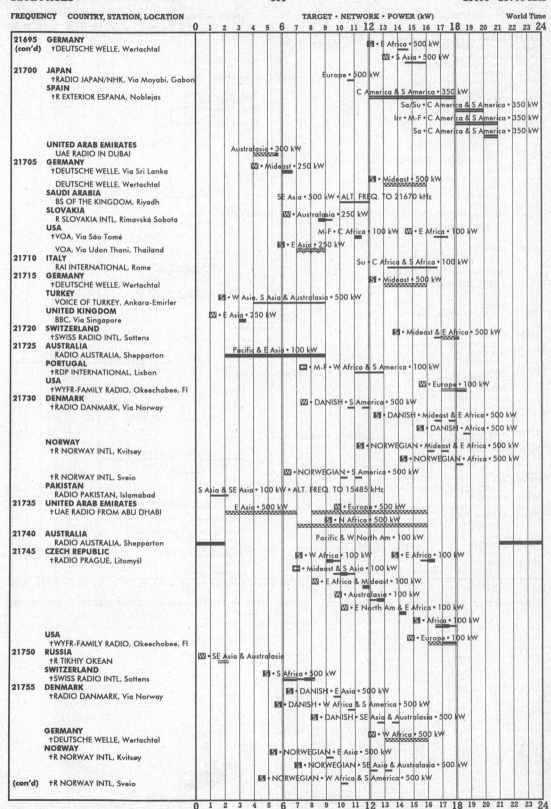

FREQUENCY   COUNTRY, STATION, LOCATION   TARGET • NETWORK • POWER (kW)   World Time

0 1 2 3 4 5 6 7 8 9 10 11 12 13 14 15 16 17 18 19 20 21 22 23 24

21695   **GERMANY**
(con'd)   †DEUTSCHE WELLE, Wertachtal
- S • E Africa • 500 kW
- W • S Asia • 500 kW

21700   **JAPAN**
     †RADIO JAPAN/NHK, Via Moyabi, Gabon
- Europe • 500 kW
     SPAIN
     †R EXTERIOR ESPANA, Noblejas
- C America & S America • 350 kW
- Sa/Su • C America & S America • 350 kW
- Irr • M-F • C America & S America • 350 kW
- Sa • C America & S America • 350 kW

     UNITED ARAB EMIRATES
     UAE RADIO IN DUBAI
- Australasia • 300 kW

21705   **GERMANY**
     †DEUTSCHE WELLE, Via Sri Lanka
- W • Mideast • 250 kW

     DEUTSCHE WELLE, Wertachtal
- S • Mideast • 500 kW
     SAUDI ARABIA
     BS OF THE KINGDOM, Riyadh
- SE Asia • 500 kW • ALT. FREQ. TO 21670 kHz
     SLOVAKIA
     R SLOVAKIA INTL, Rimavská Sobota
- W • Australasia • 250 kW
     USA
     †VOA, Via São Tomé
- M-F • C Africa • 100 kW   W • E Africa • 100 kW

     VOA, Via Udon Thani, Thailand
- S • E Asia • 250 kW

21710   **ITALY**
     RAI INTERNATIONAL, Rome
- Su • C Africa & S Africa • 100 kW

21715   **GERMANY**
     †DEUTSCHE WELLE, Wertachtal
- S • Mideast • 500 kW
     TURKEY
     VOICE OF TURKEY, Ankara-Emirler
- S • W Asia, S Asia & Australasia • 500 kW
     UNITED KINGDOM
     BBC, Via Singapore
- W • E Asia • 250 kW

21720   **SWITZERLAND**
     †SWISS RADIO INTL, Sottens
- S • Mideast & E Africa • 500 kW

21725   **AUSTRALIA**
     RADIO AUSTRALIA, Shepparton
- Pacific & E Asia • 100 kW
     PORTUGAL
     †RDP INTERNATIONAL, Lisbon
- M-F • W Africa & S America • 100 kW
     USA
     †WYFR-FAMILY RADIO, Okeechobee, Fl
- W • Europe • 100 kW

21730   **DENMARK**
     †RADIO DANMARK, Via Norway
- W • DANISH • S America • 500 kW
- S • DANISH • Mideast & E Africa • 500 kW
- S • DANISH • Africa • 500 kW

     NORWAY
     †R NORWAY INTL, Kvitsøy
- S • NORWEGIAN • Mideast & E Africa • 500 kW
- S • NORWEGIAN • Africa • 500 kW

     †R NORWAY INTL, Sveio
- W • NORWEGIAN • S America • 500 kW
     PAKISTAN
     RADIO PAKISTAN, Islamabad
- S Asia & SE Asia • 100 kW • ALT. FREQ. TO 15485 kHz

21735   **UNITED ARAB EMIRATES**
     †UAE RADIO FROM ABU DHABI
- E Asia • 500 kW
- W • Europe • 500 kW
- S • N Africa • 500 kW

21740   **AUSTRALIA**
     RADIO AUSTRALIA, Shepparton
- Pacific & W North Am • 100 kW

21745   **CZECH REPUBLIC**
     †RADIO PRAGUE, Litomyšl
- S • W Africa • 100 kW   S • E Africa • 100 kW
- Mideast & S Asia • 100 kW
- W • E Africa & Mideast • 100 kW
- W • Australasia • 100 kW
- W • E North Am & E Africa • 100 kW
- S • Africa • 100 kW
- W • Europe • 100 kW

     USA
     †WYFR-FAMILY RADIO, Okeechobee, Fl

21750   **RUSSIA**
     †R TIKHIY OKEAN
- W • SE Asia & Australasia
     SWITZERLAND
     †SWISS RADIO INTL, Sottens
- S • S Africa • 500 kW

21755   **DENMARK**
     †RADIO DANMARK, Via Norway
- S • DANISH • E Asia • 500 kW
- S • DANISH • W Africa & S America • 500 kW
- S • DANISH • SE Asia & Australasia • 500 kW

     GERMANY
     †DEUTSCHE WELLE, Wertachtal
- W • W Africa • 500 kW
     NORWAY
     †R NORWAY INTL, Kvitsøy
- S • NORWEGIAN • E Asia • 500 kW
- S • NORWEGIAN • SE Asia & Australasia • 500 kW

(con'd)   †R NORWAY INTL, Sveio
- S • NORWEGIAN • W Africa & S America • 500 kW

0 1 2 3 4 5 6 7 8 9 10 11 12 13 14 15 16 17 18 19 20 21 22 23 24

ENGLISH ▬   ARABIC ≋   CHINESE ▫▫▫   FRENCH ▭   GERMAN ▬   RUSSIAN ═   SPANISH ▭   OTHER ▬

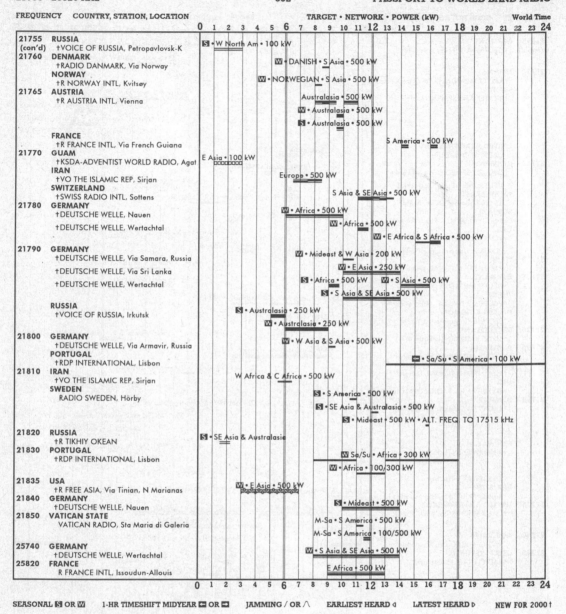